SATURN

**COUPE/SEDAN/WAGON
1991-93 REPAIR MANUAL**

CHILTON'S

President, Chilton Enterprises   David S. Loewith

Senior Vice President   Ronald A. Hoxter
Publisher & Editor-In-Chief   Kerry A. Freeman, S.A.E.
Managing Editors   Peter M. Conti, Jr., W. Calvin Settle, Jr., S.A.E.
Assistant Managing Editor   Nick D'Andrea
Senior Editors   Debra Gaffney, Ken Grabowski, A.S.E., S.A.E.
Michael L. Grady, Richard J. Rivele, S.A.E.
Richard T. Smith, Jim Taylor, Ron Webb
Project Managers   Martin J. Gunther, Jeffrey M. Hoffman
Director of Manufacturing   Mike D'Imperio
Editor   Kevin M. G. Maher

CHILTON BOOK COMPANY

ONE OF THE **DIVERSIFIED PUBLISHING COMPANIES,**
A PART OF **CAPITAL CITIES/ABC, INC.**

Manufactured in USA
© 1993 Chilton Book Company
Chilton Way, Radnor, PA 19089
ISBN 0-8019-8419-X
Library of Congress Catalog Card No. 92-054894
1234567890 2109876543

Contents

Contents

SAFETY NOTICE

Proper service and repair procedures are vital to the safe, reliable operation of all motor vehicles, as well as the personal safety of those performing repairs. This manual outlines procedures for servicing and repairing vehicles using safe, effective methods. The procedures contain many NOTES, CAUTIONS, and WARNINGS which should be followed along with standard procedures to eliminate the possibility of personal injury or improper service which could damage the vehicle or compromise its safety.

It is important to note that the repair procedures and techniques, tools and parts for servicing motor vehicles, as well as the skill and experience of the individual performing the work vary widely. It is not possible to anticipate all of the conceivable ways or conditions under which vehicles may be serviced, or to provide cautions as to all of the possible hazards that may result. Standard and accepted safety precautions and equipment should be used when handling toxic or flammable fluids, and safety goggles or other protection should be used during cutting, grinding, chiseling, prying,or any other process that can cause material removal or projectiles.

Some procedures require the use of tools specially designed for a specific purpose. Before substituting another tool or procedure, you must be completely satisfied that neither your personal safety, nor the performance of the vehicle will be endangered.

Although information in this manual is based on industry sources and is complete as possible at the time of publication, the possibility exists that some car manufacturers made later changes which could not be included here. While striving for total accuracy, Chilton Book Company cannot assume responsibility for any errors, changes or omissions that may occur in the compilation of this data.

PART NUMBERS

Part numbers listed in this reference are not recommendation by Chilton for any product by brand name. They are references that can be used with interchange manuals and aftermarket supplier catalogs to locate each brand supplier's discrete part number.

SPECIAL TOOLS

Special tools are recommended by the vehicle manufacturer to perform their specific job. Use has been kept to a minimum, but where absolutely necessary, they are referred to in the text by the part number of the tool manufacturer. These tools can be purchased, under the appropriate part number, from your Honda dealer or regional distributor, or an equivalent tool can be purchased locally from a tool supplier or parts outlet. Before substituting any tool for the one recommended, read the SAFETY NOTICE at the top of this page.

ACKNOWLEDGMENTS

The Chilton Book Company expresses appreciation to Saturn Corporation for their generous assistance.

1

GENERAL INFORMATION AND MAINTENANCE

HOW TO USE THIS BOOK

Chilton's Total Car Care Manual for the Saturn SC, SL and SW is intended to help you learn more about the inner workings of your vehicle and save you money on its upkeep and operation.

The first two sections will be the most used, since they contain maintenance and tune-up information and procedures. Studies have shown that a properly tuned and maintained car can get at least 10% better gas mileage than an out-of-tune car. The other sections deal with the more complex systems of your vehicle. Operating systems from engine through brakes are covered to the extent that the average do-it-yourselfer becomes mechanically involved. It will give you detailed instructions to help you change your own brake pads and shoes, replace spark plugs, and do many more jobs that will save you money, give you personal satisfaction, and help you avoid expensive problems.

A secondary purpose of this book is a reference for owners who want to understand their car and/or their mechanics better. In this case, no tools at all are required.

Before removing any bolts, read through the entire procedure. This will give you the overall view of what tools and supplies will be required. There is nothing more frustrating than having to walk to the bus stop on Monday morning because you were short one bolt on Sunday afternoon. So read ahead and plan ahead. Each operation should be approached logically and all procedures thoroughly understood before attempting any work.

All sections contain adjustments, maintenance, removal and installation procedures, and repair or overhaul procedures. When repair is not considered practical, we tell you how to remove the part and then how to install the new or rebuilt replacement. In this way, you at least save the labor costs.

Two basic mechanic's rules should be mentioned here. One, whenever the left side of the car or engine is referred to, it is meant to specify the driver's side of the car. Conversely, the right side of the car means the passenger's side. Secondly, most screws and bolts are removed by turning counterclockwise, and tightened by turning clockwise.

Safety is always the most important rule. Constantly be aware of the dangers involved in working on an automobile and take the proper precautions. (See the portion of this section on Servicing Your Vehicle Safely and the SAFETY NOTICE on the acknowledgment page.)

Pay attention to the instructions provided. There are 3 common mistakes in mechanical work:

1. Incorrect order of assembly, disassembly or adjustment. When taking something apart or putting it together, doing things in the wrong order usually just costs you extra time; however, it CAN break something. Read the entire procedure before beginning disassembly. Do everything in the order in which the instructions say you should do it, even if you can't immediately see a reason for it. When you're taking apart

something that is very intricate, you might want to draw a picture of how it looks when assembled at one or more points in order to assure you get everything back in its proper position. (We will supply exploded views whenever possible). When making adjustments, especially tune-up adjustments, do them in order; often, one adjustment affects another, and you cannot expect even satisfactory results unless each adjustment is made only when it cannot be changed by any other.

2. Overtorquing (or undertorquing): While it is more common for overtorquing to cause damage, undertorquing can cause a fastener to vibrate loose causing serious damage. Especially when dealing with aluminum parts, pay attention to torque specifications and utilize a torque wrench in assembly. If a torque figure is not available, remember that if you are using the right tool to do the job, you will probably not have to strain yourself to get a fastener tight enough. The pitch of most threads is so slight that the tension you put on the wrench will be multiplied many, many times in actual force on what you are tightening. A good example of how critical torque is can be seen in the case of spark plug installation, especially where you are putting the plug into an aluminum cylinder head. Too little torque can fail to crush the gasket, causing leakage of combustion gases and consequent overheating of the plug and engine parts. Too much torque can damage the threads or distort the plug, which changes the spark gap.

There are many commercial products available for ensuring the fasteners won't come loose, even if they are not torqued just right (a very common brand is Loctite®). If you're worried about getting something together tight enough to hold, but loose enough to avoid mechanical damage during assembly, one of these products might offer substantial insurance. Read the label on the package and make sure the product is compatible with the materials, fluids, etc. involved.

3. Crossthreading. This occurs when a part such as a bolt is screwed into a nut or casting at the wrong angle and forced. Cross threading is more likely to occur if access is difficult. It helps to clean and lubricate fasteners, and to start threading with the part to be installed going straight in. Then, start the bolt, spark plug, etc. with your fingers. If you encounter resistance, unscrew the part and start over again at a different angle until it can be inserted and turned several turns without much effort. Keep in mind that many parts, especially spark plugs, use tapered threads so that gentle turning will automatically bring the part you're threading to the proper angle if you don't force it or resist a change in angle. Don't put a wrench on the part until it's been turned a couple of turns by hand. If you suddenly encounter resistance, and the part has not seated fully, don't force it. Screw it back out and make sure it's clean and threading properly.

Always take your time and be patient; once you have some experience, working on your car will become an enjoyable hobby.

TOOLS AND EQUIPMENT

▶ **See Figures 1, 2 and 3**

Naturally, without the proper tools and equipment it is impossible to properly service your vehicle. It would be

impossible to catalog each tool that you would need to perform each or any operation in this book. It would also be unwise for the amateur to rush out and buy an expensive set of tools on the theory that he may need one or more of them at sometime.

The best approach is to proceed slowly, gathering together a good quality set of those tools that are used most frequently. Don't be misled by the low cost of bargain tools. It is far better to spend a little more for better quality. Forged wrenches, 6 or 12-point sockets and fine tooth ratchets are by far preferable than their less expensive counterparts. As any good mechanic can tell you, there are few worse experiences than trying to work on a car with bad tools. Your monetary savings will be far outweighed by frustration and mangled knuckles.

Begin accumulating those tools that are used most frequently; those associated with routine maintenance and tune-up.

In addition to the normal assortment of pliers and screwdrivers, you should have the following tools for routine maintenance jobs:

1. Metric and SAE wrenches, sockets and combination open end/box end wrenches in sizes from 3mm to 19mm, $\frac{1}{8}$ in. to $\frac{3}{4}$ in. and a spark plug socket ($\frac{13}{16}$ in. or $\frac{5}{8}$ in. depending on plug type). With Saturn vehicles, you will most likely find that Metric tools are usually sufficient or required for your purposes.

If possible, buy various length socket drive extensions. One break in this department is that the metric sockets available in the U.S. will all fit the ratchet handles and extensions you may already have ($\frac{1}{4}$ in., $\frac{3}{8}$ in., and $\frac{1}{2}$ in. drive).

2. Jackstands for support.
3. Oil filter wrench.
4. Oil filler spout or funnel.
5. Grease gun for lubrication.
6. Hydrometer for checking the battery.
7. A container for draining oil.
8. Many rags for wiping up the inevitable mess.

In addition to the above items there are several others that are not absolutely necessary, but handy to have around. These include oil dry, a transmission funnel and the usual supply of lubricants, antifreeze and fluids, although these can be purchased as needed. This is a basic list for routine maintenance, but only your personal needs and desire can accurately determine your list of tools.

The second list of tools is for tune-ups. While the tools involved here are slightly more sophisticated, they need not be outrageously expensive. There are several inexpensive tachometers on the market that are every bit as good for the average mechanic as a $100.00 professional model. Just be sure that the meter goes to at least 1500 rpm on the scale and that it can be used on 4, 6, or 8 cylinder engines. A basic list of tune-up equipment could include:

9. Tachometer.
10. Spark plug wrench.
11. Wire spark plug gauge/adjusting tools.

In addition to these basic tools there are several other tools and gauges you may find useful. These include:

12. A compression gauge. The screw in type is slower to use but it eliminates the possibility of a faulty reading due to escaping pressure.
13. A manifold vacuum gauge.
14. A 12 volt test light.
15. An induction meter. This is used for determining whether or not there is current in a wire. These are handy for use if a wire is broken somewhere in a wiring harness.

As a final note, you will probably find a torque wrench necessary for all but the most basic work. The beam type models are perfectly adequate although the newer click types are more precise.

Special Tools

Normally, the use of special factory tools is avoided for repair procedures, since these are not readily available for the do-it-yourself mechanic. When it is possible to perform the job with more commonly available tools, it will be pointed out, but occasionally, a special tool was designed to perform a specific function and should be used. Before substituting another tool, you should be convinced that neither your safety nor the performance of the vehicle will be compromised.

Some special tools are available commercially from major tool manufacturers. Others can be purchased from your Saturn dealer or from the OTC Division, SPX Corporation, 655 Eisenhower Drive, Owatonna, Minnesota 55060. For fast service call the toll-free order line at 1-800-533-5338 and ask for the Saturn order desk.

FROM TOP: BATTERY
TERMINAL TOOL;
FEELER GAUGES;
OIL SPOUT; FILTER
WRENCH

ALLEN WRENCHES

JACKSTAND

BEAM-TYPE TORQUE WRENCH

DWELL TACHOMETER

DWELL/TACHOMETER

VACUUM GAUGE

COMPRESSION GAUGE

TIMING LIGHT

Fig. 1 A basic collection of tools and test instruments is all you need for most maintenance on your car

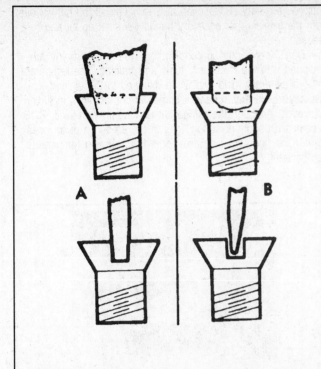

Fig. 2 Keep screwdrivers in good shape. They should fit the slot as shown in "A". If they look like those shown in "B", they need grinding or replacing

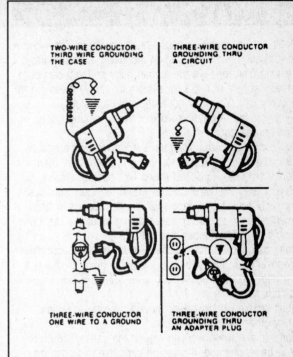

Fig. 3 When using electric tools, make sure they are properly grounded

SERVICING YOUR VEHICLE SAFELY

It is virtually impossible to anticipate all of the hazards involved with automotive maintenance and service but care and common sense will prevent most accidents.

The rules of safety for mechanics range from "don't smoke around gasoline" to 'use the proper tool for the job." The trick to avoiding injuries is to develop safe work habits and take every possible precaution.

Do's

▶ See Figure 4

• Do keep a fire extinguisher and first aid kit within easy reach.

• Do wear safety glasses or goggles when cutting, drilling, grinding or prying, even if you have 20/20 vision. If you wear glasses for the sake of vision, then they should be made of hardened glass that can serve also as safety glasses, or wear safety goggles over your regular glasses.

• Do shield your eyes whenever you work around the battery. Batteries contain sulfuric acid; in case of contact with the eyes or skin, flush the area with water or a mixture of water and baking soda and get medical attention immediately.

• Do use safety stands for any under-car service. Jacks are for raising vehicles; safety stands are for making sure the vehicle stays raised until you want it to come down. Whenever the vehicle is raised, block the wheels remaining on the ground and set the parking brake.

• Do use adequate ventilation when working with any chemicals. Like carbon monoxide, the asbestos dust resulting from brake lining wear can be poisonous in sufficient quantities.

• Do disconnect the negative battery cable when working on the electrical system. The primary ignition system can contain up to 40,000 volts.

• Do follow manufacturer's directions whenever working with potentially hazardous materials. Both brake fluid and antifreeze are poisonous if taken internally.

• Do properly maintain your tools. Loose hammerheads, mushroomed punches and chisels, frayed or poorly grounded electrical cords, excessively worn screwdrivers, spread wrenches (open end), cracked sockets, slipping ratchets, or faulty droplight sockets can cause accidents.

• Do use the proper size and type of tool for the job being done.

• Do when possible, pull on a wrench handle rather than push on it, and adjust your stance to prevent a fall.

• Do be sure that adjustable wrenches are tightly adjusted on the nut or bolt and pulled so that the face is on the side of the fixed jaw.

• Do select a wrench or socket that fits the nut or bolt. The wrench or socket should sit straight, not cocked.

• Do strike squarely with a hammer. Avoid glancing blows.

• Do set the parking brake and block the drive wheels if the work requires that the engine be running.

Don'ts

• Don't run an engine in a garage or anywhere else without proper ventilation — EVER! Carbon monoxide is poisonous; it takes a long time to leave the human body and you can build up a deadly supply of it in your system by simply breathing in a little every day. You may not realize you are slowly poisoning yourself. Always use power vents, windows, fans or open the garage door.

• Don't work around moving parts while wearing a necktie or other loose clothing. Short sleeves are much safer than long, loose sleeves. Hard-toed shoes with neoprene soles protect your toes and give a better grip on slippery surfaces. Jewelry such as watches, fancy belt buckles, beads or body adornment of any kind is not safe working around a car. Long hair should be hidden under a hat or cap.

• Don't use pockets for toolboxes. A fall or bump can drive a screwdriver deep into your body. Even a wiping cloth hanging from the back pocket can wrap around a spinning shaft or fan.

• Don't smoke when working around gasoline, cleaning solvent or other flammable material.

• Don't smoke when working around the battery. When the battery is being charged, it gives off explosive hydrogen gas.

• Don't use gasoline to wash your hands; there are excellent soaps available. Gasoline may contain lead, and lead can enter the body through a cut, accumulating in the body until you are very ill. Gasoline also removes all the natural oils from the skin so that bone dry hands will suck up oil and grease.

• Don't service the air conditioning system unless you are equipped with the necessary tools and training. The refrigerant, R-12 is extremely cold and when exposed to the air, will instantly freeze any surface it comes in contact with, including your eyes. Although the refrigerant is normally non-toxic, R-12 becomes a deadly poisonous gas in the presence of an open flame. One good whiff of the vapors from burning refrigerant can be fatal.

Fig. 4 Support the vehicle with safety stands when doing under-car service

HISTORY

With its debut in 1991, Saturn emerged as quite possibly the most innovative new American car company or division in many years. The company was developed around the concept of customer orientation and was committed to produce a line of high-quality and enjoyable vehicles, which were also inexpensive and reliable.

During the first 2 years of production (1991-1992), the company produced two basic cars, a sedan and a sport coupe. The sedan was available in 3 basic forms. The SL and SL1 were equipped with the base 1.9L Single Overhead Camshaft (SOHC) engine, while the SL2 came standard with the performance 1.9L Dual Overhead Camshaft (DOHC) engine. The sport coupe, or SC, was produced only with the performance 1.9L DOHC motor. With the exception of the most basic model, the SL, all cars could be equipped with either a 5-speed manual or 4-speed electronically controlled automatic transaxle. The transaxles themselves came in either a base or performance model depending on which engine the vehicle contained.

For the 1993 production year Saturn offered the original vehicles along with a station wagon and a base-line coupe.

The wagons, designated SW1 and SW2, shared many of the features of the like-named sedans. The SW1 was available only with the base 1.9L SOHC engine, while the SW2 enjoyed the performance of the 1.9L DOHC engine. The base-line sport coupe was introduced as the SC1 and was produced with the SOHC motor. To keep the name/engine relationship similar across the product line, the original SC was re-designated the SC2 for the 1993 model year and was still only produced with the DOHC engine.

The company's dedication to safety was evident from the beginning, when in 1991 safety features such as the Anti-lock Brake System (ABS) were available as options on all Saturns. By late 1992, a Driver's Supplemental Inflatable Restraint system (DSIR) or "AIR BAG" was also available on all vehicles. For the 1993 production year, the DSIR was made standard on all Saturns and all vehicles equipped with ABS and an automatic transaxle were also equipped with a traction control system.

MODEL IDENTIFICATION

The most evident way to distinguish models is by checking the engine. The SL, SL1, SW1 and SC1 are only equipped with the SOHC engine, while the original SC, now known as the SC2, the SL2 and the SW2 are only equipped with the DOHC engine. The performance models equipped with the DOHC engine also share a common badge on the trunk or tailgate which reads "TWIN CAM".

But without raising the hood, it is still easy to tell the base from the performance models. The SL, SL1, and SW1 are equipped with black bumper covers as opposed to the body paint matched covers on the SL2 and SW2. The SC or SC2 is the only Saturn to come equipped with hide-away headlights, while the SC1 shares it's front end with the sedan and wagon family.

SERIAL NUMBER IDENTIFICATION

Vehicle

▶ **See Figures 5 and 6**

The Vehicle Identification Number (VIN) is stamped on a metal plate that is attached to the instrument panel adjacent to the windshield. It can be seen by looking through the lower corner of the windshield on the driver's side of the vehicle. The VIN is also located on various identification stickers throughout the vehicle and on certain metal parts such as the engine or transaxle.

The VIN is a 17 digit combination of numbers and letters. The 1st digit represents the country of manufacture, this is a "1" for all Saturns and means the vehicle was built in the U.S.A. The 2nd and 3rd digits are 'G8", which represent General Motors and Saturn Corporation. The 4th and 5th digits represent the Saturn car line and the particular sales code of the vehicle. For example, the sales code for a sedan will designate if the car is an SL, SL1 or SL2. The 6th digit identifies the vehicle's body style, in other words whether it is a coupe, sedan or wagon. The 7th digit represents the safety restraint features with which that particular car was produced. This will mean either, 'passive restraint seat belts" or 'passive restraint with a DSIR". The 8th number tells with what engine the vehicle is equipped; either the SOHC or DOHC 1.9L engine. The 9th digit is a check digit for all vehicles. The 10th digit indicates the model year: M for 1991, N for 1992, or P for 1993. The 11th digit will be a 'Z" and indicates the vehicle was built in the Spring Hill, Tennessee plant. The 12th through 17th digits indicate the production sequence number.

Vehicle Certification Label

The Vehicle Certification Label is attached to the left door, below the latch striker. The upper half of the label contains the date of manufacture and vehicle weight information. The lower half of the label contains a statement that the vehicle conforms

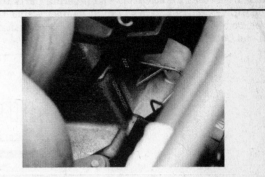

Fig. 6 The VIN is also stamped in the front of the engine block

to U.S. federal standards in effect at the time of production. The VIN is listed at the bottom of the label

The certification label is part of the Federal Vehicle Theft Prevention Standard and like the VIN label, cannot be removed or altered in any way. The label must be masked prior to painting the surrounding surface.

Fig. 5 Vehicle Identification Number (VIN) location

VEHICLE IDENTIFICATION CHART

It is important for servicing and ordering parts to be certain of the vehicle and engine identification. The VIN (vehicle identification number) is a 17 digit number visible through the windshield on the driver's side of the dash and contains the vehicle and engine identification codes. The tenth digit indicates model year and the eighth digit indicates engine code. It can be interpreted as follows:

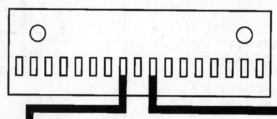

Engine Code						Model Year	
Code	Liters	Cu. In. (cc)	Cyl.	Fuel Sys.	Eng. Mfg.	Code	Year
7	1.9	116 (1901)	4	MFI	Saturn	M	1991
9	1.9	116 (1901)	4	TBI	Saturn	N	1992
						P	1993

MFI—Multi-Point Fuel Injection
TBI—Throttle Body Injection

Service Parts Identification Label

The Service Parts Identification Label is attached to the lower right inner wall of the vehicle's trunk, beneath the trunk lining fabric. The label provides information to assist in identifying vehicle parts and options so that proper replacements may be selected. The engine and transaxle 3-digit codes are located on this label along with option codes, trim combinations and paint color codes. The engine code is the 5th code located in the top row of codes. The transaxle code is the 6th code, located directly after the engine code. The VIN can be found to the upper left of the label, above the option codes.

Engine

The engine identification code is located in the VIN at the 8th digit. The VIN can be found on the Vehicle Certification Label, on the instrument panel VIN plate and also on the Service Parts Identification Label located in the vehicle's trunk. See the Engine Identification chart for engine VIN codes.

The engine block is also stamped with a 5-digit engine date stamp code on the front side of the block to indicate the day and time of manufacture. The 1st digit is a code for hour. The 2nd-4th positions indicate the Julian date. The 5th position is a code for year.

ENGINE IDENTIFICATION

Year	Model	Engine Displacement Liters (cc)	Engine Series Identification (ID/VIN)	Fuel System	No. of Cylinders	Engine Type
1991	Sedan	1.9 (1901)	7	MFI	4	DOHC
	Sedan	1.9 (1901)	9	TBI	4	SOHC
	Coupe	1.9 (1901)	7	MFI	4	DOHC
1992	Sedan	1.9 (1901)	7	MFI	4	DOHC
	Sedan	1.9 (1901)	9	TBI	4	SOHC
	Coupe	1.9 (1901)	7	MFI	4	DOHC
1993	Wagon	1.9 (1901)	7	MFI	4	DOHC
	Wagon	1.9 (1901)	9	TBI	4	SOHC
	Sedan	1.9 (1901)	7	MFI	4	DOHC
	Sedan	1.9 (1901)	9	TBI	4	SOHC
	Coupe	1.9 (1901)	9	TBI	4	SOHC
	Coupe	1.9 (1901)	7	MFI	4	DOHC

DOHC—Dual Overhead Cam
SOHC—Single Overhead Cam
MFI—Multi-Point Fuel Injection
TBI—Throttle Body Injection

Transaxle

The transaxle identification code is located on the service parts identification label. The top of the transmission case is also stamped with a date stamp code to identify the transmission model and to indicate the day and time of manufacture. The 1st digit is the last number of the year; 1=1991, 2=1992, or 3=1993. The 2nd-4th positions are the 3-digit transaxle code, which can also be found on the service identification label. The 5th position is a "1" for the Spring Hill plant. The 6th-8th digits are the Julian date, while the 9th digit is a code for hour. See the Transaxle Identification chart for 3-digit transaxle identification codes.

TRANSMISSION APPLICATION CHART

Year	Engine ID/VIN	Transmission Identification	Transmissin Type
1991	9	MP2	Base Man.
	9	MP6	Base Auto.
	7	MP3	Perf. Man.
	7	MP7	Perf. Auto.
1992-93	9	MP2	Base Man.
	9	MP6	Base Auto.
	7	MP3	Perf. Man.
	7	MP7	Perf. Auto.

Auto.—Automatic
Man.—Manual
Perf.—Performance

ROUTINE MAINTENANCE

Air Cleaner

The air cleaner is a paper element contained in a housing located on the left side of the engine compartment. The housing is in front of the engine on DOHC models and behind the engine for SOHC cars. The air filter element should be serviced according to the Maintenance Intervals Chart at the end of this section.

➡Check the air filter element more often if the vehicle is operated under severe dusty conditions and replace, as necessary

REMOVAL & INSTALLATION

SOHC Engine

▶ See Figure 7

1. Remove the thumb screws from the top of the cover, then release the 6 fastener clips
2. Lift the cover up and off of the housing.
3. Remove the air filter element and replace if dirty. If the element is only slightly dusty it can be cleaned by blowing compressed air through the element from the clean side.
   To install:
4. Wipe all dust from the inside of the housing using a clean rag or cloth.

5. Install the element into the housing, then position the cover over the element.
6. Secure the cover with the fastener clips, then tighten the thumb screws to 35 inch lbs. (4 Nm). Do not overtighten the thumb screws.

DOHC Engine

▶ See Figures 8, 9 and 10

1. Release the 2 clips located to the front of the cover.
2. Release the 2 clips located to the rear of the cover.
3. Lift the cover to expose the air filter element, remove the element and replace if dirty. If the element is only slightly dusty it can be cleaned by blowing compressed air through the element from the clean side.
   To install:
4. Wipe all dust from the inside of the housing using a clean rag or cloth. Inspect the resonator and rubber tubes for damage or cracks.
5. Install the element into the housing, then position the cover over the element.
6. Secure the cover with the fastener clips.

Fuel Filter

The fuel filter is attached to the vehicle frame in the lower left portion of the engine compartment. The filter should be serviced according to the Maintenance Intervals Chart at the end of this section.

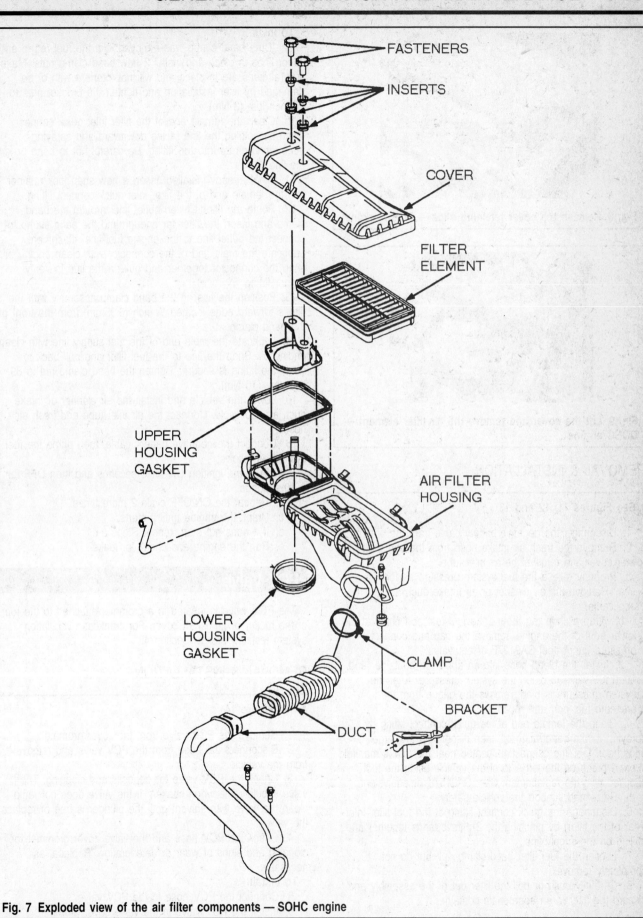

Fig. 7 Exploded view of the air filter components — SOHC engine

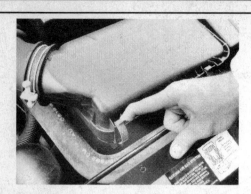

Fig. 8 Release the cover retaining clips — DOHC engine

Fig. 9 Lift the cover and remove the air filter element — DOHC engine

REMOVAL & INSTALLATION

▶ See Figures 11, 12 and 13

1. Disconnect the negative battery cable from the battery.
2. Remove the fresh air intake hose from the camshaft or rocker cover and remove the air inlet tube.
3. Properly relieve the fuel system pressure as follows:
   a. Remove the air cleaner or air intake duct, as applicable.
   b. Wrap a shop rag around the fuel test port fitting at the lower front of the engine, remove the cap and connect pressure gauge tool SA9127E or equivalent.
   c. Install the bleed hose into an approved container and open the valve to bleed the system pressure. After the system pressure is bled, remove the gauge from the pressure test port and recap it.
4. Clean the female end of the quick connect fitting by spraying it with penetrating oil, then disconnect the large underhood fuel line connection located near the intake manifold support brace on the left side of the vehicle using the tool supplied with the replacement filter, SA9157E or equivalent.
5. Raise and support the vehicle safely.
6. Disengage the quick connect fitting at the fuel filter inlet (rear of the filter) by pinching the 2 plastic tangs together and pulling on the supply line.
7. Loosen the fuel filter band clamp nut, but do not completely remove.
8. Carefully push or pull the filter out of the assembly and discard the filter in an appropriate container.

To install:
9. If the band clamp was removed, clip the fuel return and vapor lines in place and install 2 new band clamp nuts. Make sure all lines are in place and will not interfere with or be damaged by filter installation and tighten the bracket nuts to 27 inch lbs. (3 Nm).
10. Clean the female end of the filter inlet quick connect fitting by holding the line facing downward and spraying penetrating oil up into the fitting. Be careful not to bend or kink the line.
11. If not already installed, insert a new snap lock retainer into the female end of the filter inlet quick connect fitting.
12. Route the filter's nylon outlet line through the band clamp and insert the filter far enough into the band clamp to connect the outlet line to the engine fuel line attachment. Lubricate the male end of the connector with clean engine oil, snap the connector together and pull on the line to verify proper fitting.
13. Position the filter in the band clamp assembly with the filter's forward edge located 1/4 inch (6.35mm) from the front of the band clamp.
14. Lubricate the male end of the fuel supply line with clean engine oil. Snap the line to the fuel filter and pull back to verify the fitting is secure. Tighten the band clamp nut to 89 inch lbs. (10 Nm).
15. Lower the vehicle and install the air cleaner or intake duct, as applicable. Connect the air inlet tube and fresh air hose.
16. Connect the negative battery cable, then prime the fuel system as follows:
   a. Turn the ignition **ON** for 5 seconds and then **OFF** for 10 seconds.
   b. Repeat the ON/OFF cycle 2 more times.
   c. Crank the engine until it starts.
   d. If it does not start, repeat Steps a-c.
   e. Run the engine and check for leaks.

PCV Valve

The PCV valve is located in a grommet attached to the top of the rocker or camshaft cover. For crankcase ventilation system testing, refer to Section 4.

REMOVAL & INSTALLATION

▶ See Figure 14

1. Remove the PCV valve from the cover grommet.
2. Disconnect the hose from the PCV valve and remove it from the vehicle.
3. Check the PCV valve for deposits and clogging. The valve should rattle when shaken. If the valve does not rattle, clean the valve with solvent until the plunger is free or replace the valve.
4. Check the PCV hose and the valve cover grommet for clogging and signs of wear or deterioration. Replace, as necessary.
To install:
5. Connect the PCV hose to the PCV valve.
6. Install the PCV valve in the valve cover grommet.

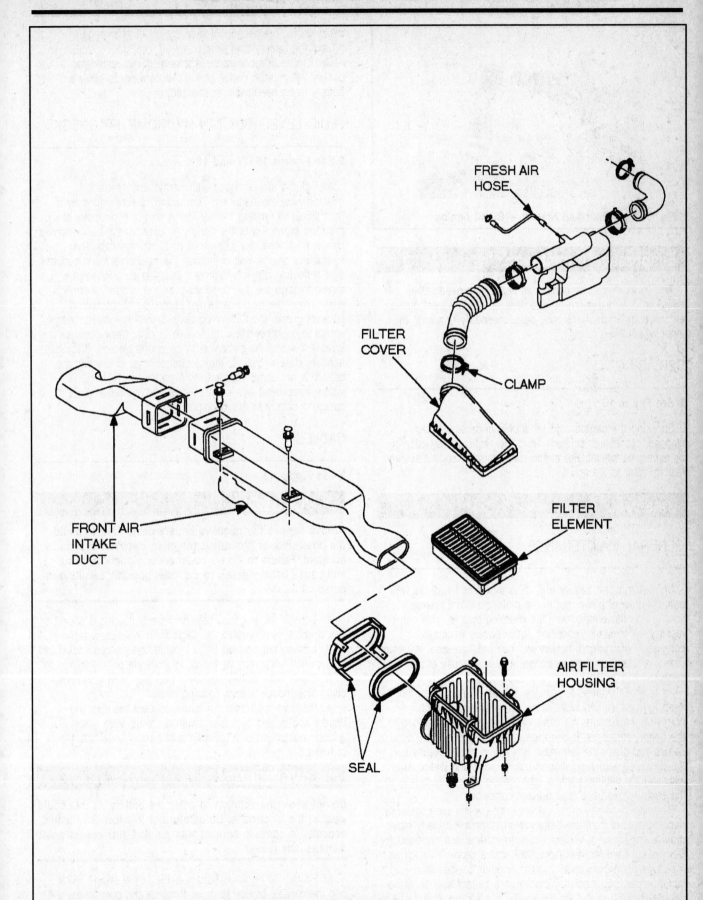

FRESH AIR HOSE

FILTER COVER

CLAMP

FRONT AIR INTAKE DUCT

FILTER ELEMENT

AIR FILTER HOUSING

SEAL

Fig. 10 Exploded view of the air filter components — DOHC engine

Fig. 11 Fuel filter and bracket — DOHC engine

Evaporative Canister

The vapor or carbon canister is part of the evaporative emission control system. It is located in the right front of the engine compartment and may be accessed by removing the inner wheel liner.

SERVICING

▶ See Figure 15

Servicing the carbon canister is only necessary if it is clogged, cracked or contains liquid fuel, indicated by odor or by excessive weight. For evaporative emission control system testing, refer to Section 4.

Battery

GENERAL MAINTENANCE

Corrosion of the battery and cable terminals interferes with both the flow of power out of the battery and the charge flowing into the battery from the charging system. This can result in a 'no start " condition. If the battery becomes completely discharged, battery life may be shortened. In some cases, a totally discharged battery may not readily accept a charge.

To reduce the need for service and to extend battery life, keep the battery and cable terminals clean and free of corrosion. Make sure the cable clamps are tightly fastened to the battery terminals. If corrosion is found, disconnect the cables and clean the terminals with a wire brush. Neutralize the corrosion with a solution of baking soda and water. After installing the cables, apply a light coating of petroleum jelly to the cable terminals to help prevent corrosion.

Parasitic loads are small current drains which are constantly drawing current from the battery. Normal parasitic loads may drain a battery on a vehicle that is in storage and not used for 6-8 weeks. Vehicles that have additional accessories such as a cellular phone, an alarm system or other devices that increase parasitic load may discharge a battery sooner. If the vehicle is to be stored for 6-8 weeks in a secure area and an alarm system, if present, is not necessary, the negative battery cable should be disconnected at the onset of storage to protect the battery charge.

Remember that constantly discharging and recharging a battery will shorten battery life. Take care not to allow a battery to be needlessly discharged.

FLUID LEVEL (BUILT-IN HYDROMETER CHECK)

▶ See Figures 16, 17 and 18

All Saturns are equipped with permanently sealed, maintenance free batteries. The battery is surrounded by a heat shield to prolong battery life. A built-in hydrometer is provided in the top of the battery to determine if the battery is charged, in need of a charge or must be replaced. The hydrometer eye is visible through the heat shield and consists of a A floating green hydrometer ball that controls what is visible through the eye depending on the current electrolyte level. When the hydrometer eye in the top of the battery appears green, the battery contains a 65% or greater charge and is in good condition. If the eye is dark, the electrolyte level is low and the battery is in need of a charge. If the eye appears clear or yellow, the electrolyte level is low and the battery is no longer chargeable. A battery with a clear or yellow hydrometer eye must be replaced, do not attempt to charge a battery in this condition.

CABLES

▶ See Figure 19

✳✳CAUTION

Always remove the negative battery cable first, to avoid the possibility of grounding the car's electrical system by accident. Failure to do so could allow a spark to occur and cause battery gases to explode, possibly resulting in personal injury.

1. Loosen the negative battery cable bolt using a socket or box wrench, then remove the cable from the battery terminal.
2. Loosen the positive battery cable bolt using a socket or box wrench, then remove the cable from the battery terminal.
3. Clean both battery terminals and the cable fasteners using side mount battery cleaning tools.
4. Remove the remaining corrosion deposits from the battery and cables by flushing with a baking soda-water solution comprised of 2 teaspoons of baking soda and 1 cup of water.

✳✳WARNING

Do not allow the solution to enter the battery as this could weaken the electrolyte. Be careful not to allow the flushed deposits to come in contact with painted surfaces as paint damage may result.

5. Follow the negative battery cable to the engine block and the chassis ground in order to check the connection. If it is loose or corroded, remove the cable and clean the cable end and contact with sandpaper, then reconnect the cable.

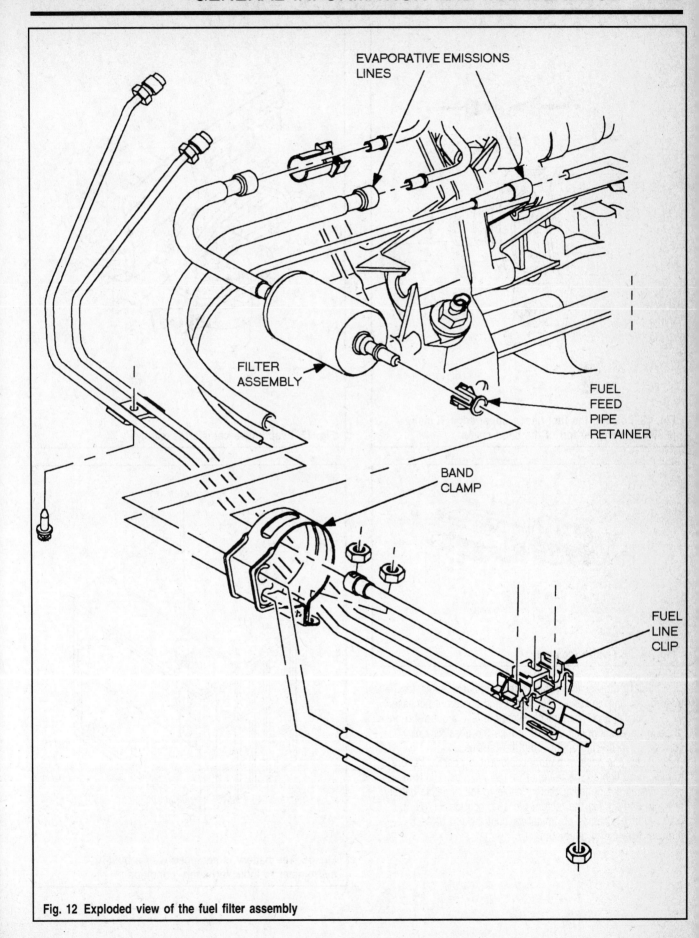

Fig. 12 Exploded view of the fuel filter assembly

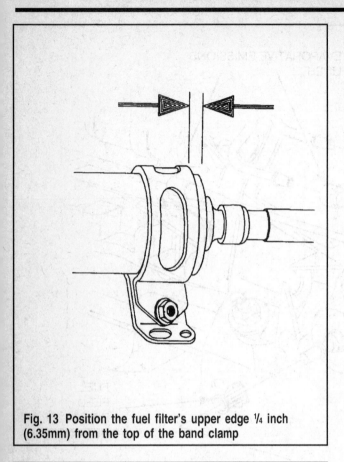

Fig. 13 Position the fuel filter's upper edge ¼ inch (6.35mm) from the top of the band clamp

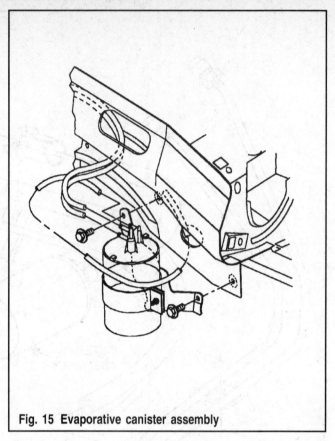

Fig. 15 Evaporative canister assembly

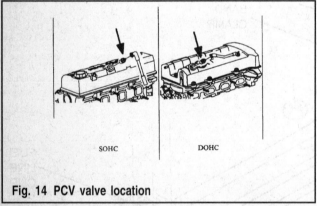

Fig. 14 PCV valve location

6. Follow the positive cable to the alternator, starter and underhood junction block, then clean and tighten, if necessary.

7. Apply a small amount of petroleum jelly around the base of each battery terminal to help reduce the possibility of corrosion. Do not thoroughly coat the terminal.

8. Install the positive battery cable to the positive battery terminal and tighten the fastener to 151 inch lbs. (17 Nm).

9. Install the negative battery cable to the negative battery terminal and tighten the fastener to 151 inch lbs. (17 Nm).

10. After the cables are installed, coat the top of each terminal lightly with petroleum jelly

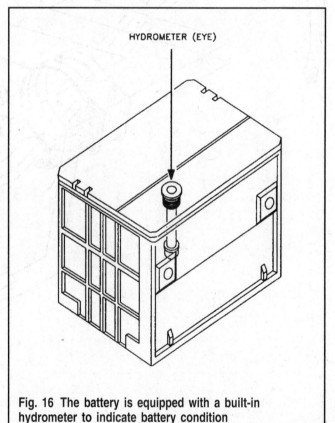

Fig. 16 The battery is equipped with a built-in hydrometer to indicate battery condition

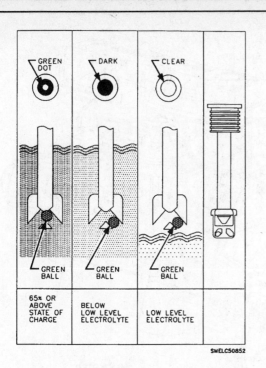

Fig. 17 A green ball in the built-in hydrometer rises or falls with the electrolyte level

Fig. 18 Battery heat shield — DOHC engine

CAPACITY TESTING

A voltmeter/battery load tester is used for this test.

1. Connect the battery tester cables to the terminal bolts or the battery terminals, according to the tester manufacturer's instructions. If the battery is installed in the vehicle, be careful not to touch any surrounding metal on the vehicle.

➡**Do not remove the surface charge from batteries which have been stored. Only remove the charge from batteries where the green dot is visible and have been recently charged from the vehicle's charging system or a battery charging device.**

2. If the battery has been charged recently, remove the surface charge from the battery by applying a 300 amp load

across the battery terminals for 15 seconds using the tester. Turn the load **OFF** for 15 seconds to allow the battery to recover.

3. Estimate the battery temperature from the battery's surrounding temperature from the past few hours proceeding the test.

4. Find the label on top of the battery that specifies the proper "Load Test " for this battery, then using the tester, apply this load across the terminals for 15 seconds. With the load still applied, observe the minimum voltage on the voltmeter, then turn the load **OFF**.

5. Compare the battery voltage to the estimated temperature to determine if the battery is good. The proper minimum readings should be as follows:

Temperature above 70°F (21°C) — minimum voltage is 9.6V

Temperature of 50-70°F (10-21°C) — minimum voltage is 9.4V

Temperature of 20-50°F (-1-10°C) — minimum voltage is 9.1V

Temperature of 15-20°F (-10--1°C) — minimum voltage is 8.8V

Temperature of 0-15°F (-18--10°C) — minimum voltage is 8.5V

Temperature below 0°F (-18°C) — minimum voltage is 8.0V

6. A battery which fails this test should be replaced.

CHARGING

✳✳CAUTION

Keep flame or sparks away from the battery. The battery emits explosive hydrogen gas, especially when being charged. Battery electrolyte contains sulfuric acid. If electrolyte accidently comes in contact with your skin or eyes, flush with plenty of clear water. If it lands in your eyes, get medical help immediately.

When the battery voltage is below 11 volts, the weakened electrolyte becomes very resistant to accepting charger current. A battery in this condition may only draw a few milliamps of current. At this rate, it may take a long time before the current flow is high enough to read on all but the most sensitive ammeters.

If after the recommended time, the current is measurable, then the battery is good and will charge normally. Be sure to charge a completely discharged battery until the green eye appears. Follow the charging procedure closely to prevent replacing a good battery.

1. Using a Digital Volt/Ohm Meter (DVOM) measure the voltage across the battery terminals. If the voltage is below 11 volts, the current draw is likely to be very slow.

2. Set the battery charger's rate at the highest applicable setting for a 12 volt battery. If the charger is equipped with a timer, set the timer for 30 minutes.

3. Check the battery every 30 minutes for a green eye indicating proper charge. Also check the battery for temperatures in excess of 125°F (52°C) and, if necessary, pause the charging procedure until the battery cools.

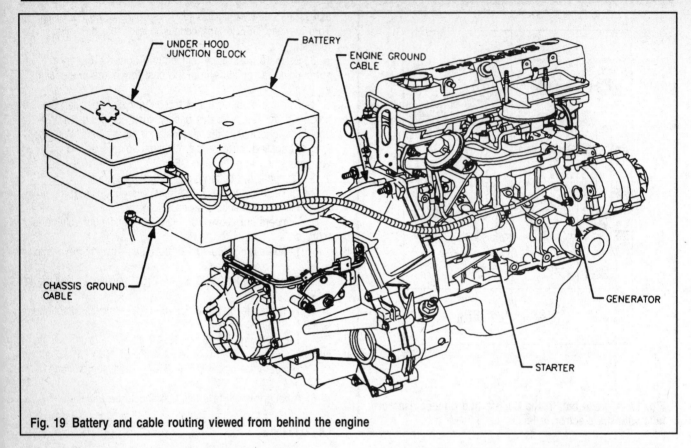

Fig. 19 Battery and cable routing viewed from behind the engine

4. Always make sure the charger is properly connected to the battery. Some chargers have a polarity protection circuit built into the charger and will prevent charging until the circuit is properly connected. A completely discharged battery may not be able to activate such a circuit, thereby appearing not to accept a charge regardless of whether the charger is properly connected or not. If this is suspected, consult the charger manufacturer's instructions on bypassing this feature so the discharged battery may be charged.

5. Because battery chargers will vary in the amount of current supplied to the battery and as stated previously, battery condition will also affect the rate of charge, the time necessary to charge a battery will also vary. The time necessary for a battery to begin accepting a charge should be approximately as follows:

High boost of 16.0 volts or more — up to 4 hours.
Medium boost of 14.0-15.9 volts — up to 8 hours
Low boost of 13.9 volts or less — up to 16 hours.

REPLACEMENT

▶ See Figure 20

1. Disconnect the negative battery cable from the battery terminal.
2. Disconnect the positive battery cable from the battery terminal.
3. Remove the hold-down retaining nut and screws, then remove the hold-down cover/heat shield assembly from the top of the battery.

4. Carefully lift the battery out of the vehicle and place in a safe location.
To install:
5. Inspect and, if necessary, clean the battery tray and the battery cables of all corrosion. Make sure the battery and terminals are free of cracks or damage and that the terminals are also free of corrosion.
6. Carefully lower the battery into position in the battery tray. Do not allow the terminals to short to any bare metal during installation.
7. Position the hold-down cover/heat shield over the battery and install the fasteners. Tighten the nut and screws to 80 inch lbs. (9 Nm).
8. Connect the positive battery cable and tighten to 151 inch lbs. (17 Nm).
9. Connect the negative battery cable and tighten to 151 inch lbs. (17 Nm).

Serpentine Drive Belt

INSPECTION

Belt Tension
▶ See Figures 21 and 22

The belt is automatically adjusted using a spring loaded tensioner. If belt slippage is suspected or unusual belt noises

GENERAL INFORMATION AND MAINTENANCE 1-19

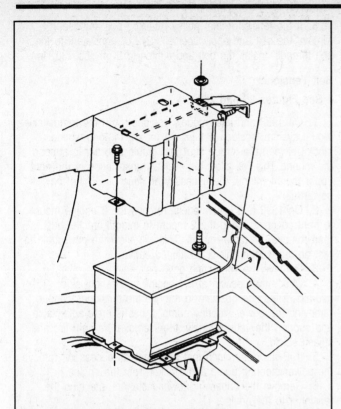

Fig. 20 Remove the battery hold-down cover/heat shield assembly to gain access to the battery

occurs, the following procedure should be used to determine if the tensioner or belt is at fault.

1. Start the engine and allow it to warm-up to normal operating temperature with all accessories (such as A/C) turned **ON**; this should take approximately 10 minutes. If the vehicle is equipped with power steering, turn the steering wheel to the left and right several times during warm-up make sure proper load is placed on the belt.

2. Turn the engine and accessories **OFF**.

3. Using a 14 mm or $^9/_{16}$ in. wrench, depress the tensioner arm until the belt becomes loosened, then slowly allow the tensioner to return to position and apply tension to the belt. Do not allow the tensioner to snap against the belt.

4. Inspect the markings located on the tensioner arm. If the marks on the arm fall outside the operating range, the drive belt must be replaced.

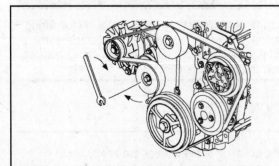

Fig. 21 Use a 14mm or $^9/_{16}$ in. wrench to depress the tensioner arm until the belt becomes loose.

5. Using tool SA9181-NE or an equivalent calibrated belt tension gauge, measure and note the tension readings at the 2 points located centrally between 2 belt pulleys as shown in the illustration. The dotted lines represent other possible paths which your belt may follow depending on the engine and accessories with which your vehicle is equipped.

6. Repeat the measurements from the previous step 2 more times, then calculate the average result for each test location. The readings should be 50-65 lbs. (22.7-29.2 kg) for new belts or a minimum of 45 lbs. (20.4 kg) for used belts. If the readings are out of this range or do not meet the minimum and the drive belt passed the test in Step 4, the drive belt tensioner must be replaced.

Belt Alignment
▶ See Figure 23

1. Measure the distance from the front machined surface of the cylinder block to the inboard edge of the belt at the location as shown.

2. The distance should be 1.102-1.220 in. (28-31mm).

3. If the distance does not fall within the specification check the following:

Check that the belt is properly located within the pulley grooves.

Check the drive belt for wear at the edges and if necessary, replace a worn belt.

Make sure the belt pulleys are not bent or damaged.

Make sure the accessory assemblies have proper shaft and bearing end-play.

Check the pulley hubs for proper installation on their shafts.

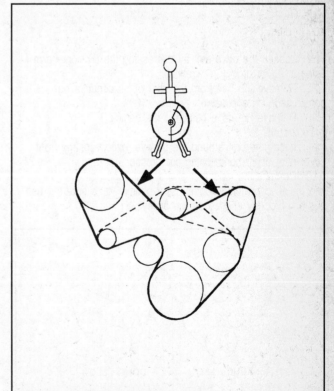

Fig. 22 Read the belt tension at 2 points centrally located between the indicated pulleys.

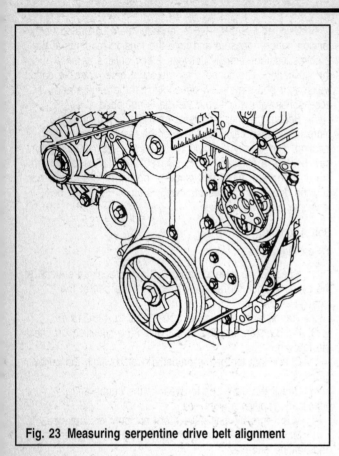

Fig. 23 Measuring serpentine drive belt alignment

REMOVAL & INSTALLATION

Belt

▶ See Figure 24

1. Loosen the drive belt by depressing the tensioner arm using a 14mm or $^9/_{16}$ in. wrench.
2. Remove the belt from the idler or air conditioning compressor, as applicable.
3. Remove the drive belt from the vehicle.

To install:

4. Install the belt around the pulleys, except for the front cover idler or air conditioning compressor.
5. Depress the tensioner arm and slip the belt over the idler or air conditioning compressor pulley. Make sure the belt ribs are properly aligned on the pulleys.

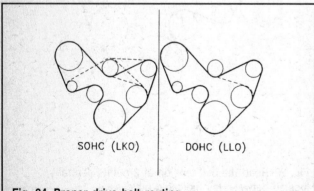

SOHC (LKO)   DOHC (LLO)

Fig. 24 Proper drive belt routing

6. If the tensioner idler pulley retaining bolt is loose, remove the bolt and apply Loctite® 242 or equivalent to the bolt threads. Install the bolt and tighten to 22 ft. lbs. (30 Nm).

Belt Tensioner

▶ See Figures 25 and 26

1. On 1992 and later models equipped with the torque axis mount system, position a 1 in. x 1 in. x 2 in. long wooden block between the torque strut and cradle in order to support the mount. This will allow removal and installation of the right upper mount without the necessity of lifting or jacking the powertrain
2. On 1992 and later models, remove the 3 engine mount to front cover nuts and the 2 mount to midrail bracket nuts, then remove the upper mount. This will allow the powertrain to rest on the wooden block positioned earlier.
3. Remove the serpentine drive belt.
4. Check the position of the engine to the right side midrails, it may be possible to remove the tensioner without removing the power steering pump. If this is preferable, raise and support the vehicle safely, then remove the right tire and splash shield.
5. If it was determined that removal was necessary, remove the power steering pump and bracket from the engine.
6. Remove the upper and lower fasteners attaching the tensioner to the engine.
7. Remove the tensioner assembly from the vehicle. If necessary, the engine may be moved slightly toward the driver's side by prying on the motor mount and frame rail. Do not pry against the aluminum engine and accessories or damage may occur.

To install:

8. Install the tensioner using the upper and lower fasteners, then tighten the fasteners to 22 ft. lbs. (30 Nm).
9. If removed, install the power steering pump assembly.
10. If removed, install the right tire and splash shield, then remove the support and lower the vehicle.
11. Install the accessory drive belt, making sure it is properly aligned on the pulleys.
12. On 1992 and later vehicles equipped with the torque axis mount system, position the upper mount and install the 3 mount to front cover nuts. Install the 2 mount to midrail bracket nuts, then tighten the 5 mount fasteners slowly and evenly to 52 ft. lbs. (70 Nm). Remove the wooden block from the engine cradle.

❋❋CAUTION

Disconnect the negative battery cable or fan motor wiring harness connector before replacing any radiator/heater hose. The fan may come ON, under certain circumstances, even though the ignition is OFF.

INSPECTION

Inspect the condition of the radiator and heater hoses periodically. Early spring and at the beginning of the fall or winter when you are performing other maintenance, are good times. Make sure the engine and cooling system is cold. Visually inspect for cracking, rotting or collapsed hoses,

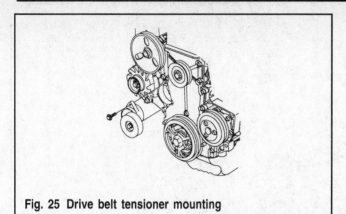

Fig. 25 Drive belt tensioner mounting

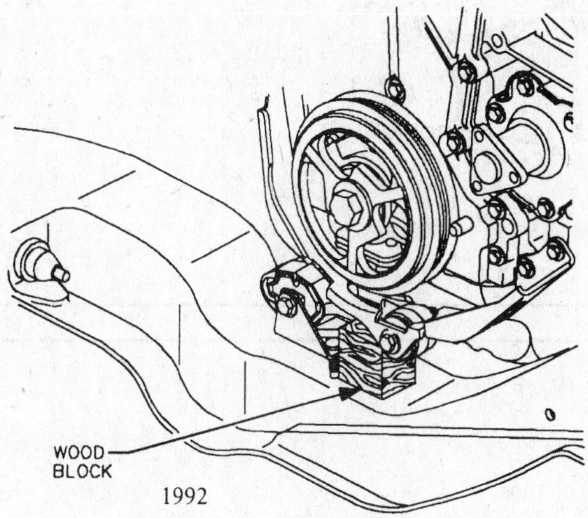

WOOD BLOCK

1992

Fig. 26 Place a wooden block between the torque strut and engine cradle to support the mount — 1992 and later models.

replace as necessary. Run your hand along the length of the hose. If a weak or swollen spot is noted when squeezing the hose wall, replace the hose.

REMOVAL & INSTALLATION

♦ See Figures 27 and 28

1. Remove the surge tank pressure cap.

✳✳CAUTION

Never remove the pressure cap while the engine is running or personal injury from scalding hot coolant or steam may result. If possible, wait until the engine has

cooled to remove the pressure cap. If this is not possible, wrap a thick cloth around the pressure cap and turn it slowly to the first stop. Step back while the pressure is released from the cooling system. When you are sure all the pressure has been released, press down on the cap, still with the cloth, and turn and remove it.

2. Position a suitable container under the radiator and block, then drain the coolant by opening radiator drain and removing the engine drain plug. The engine drain plug is a bolt which can be removed with a ratchet and socket or wrench. To open the radiator drain, grasp the plug firmly and turn counterclockwise until loosened, then use a small prybar to dislodge the plug and large rubber gasket. Make sure the plug is fully loosened before prying to prevent plug or radiator damage.

✳✳CAUTION

When draining the coolant, keep in mind that cats and dogs are attracted by the ethylene glycol antifreeze, and are quite likely to drink any that is left in an uncovered container or in puddles on the ground. This will prove fatal in sufficient quantity. Always drain the coolant into a sealable container. Coolant may be reused unless it is contaminated or several years old.

3. Loosen the hose clamps at each end of the hose requiring replacement. Pull the clamps back on the hose away from the connection.
4. Twist, pull and slide the hose off the fitting.

➡If the hose is stuck at the connection, do not try to insert a screwdriver or other sharp tool under the hose end in an effort to free it, as the connection and/or hose may become damaged. Heater connections especially are easily damaged. If the hose is not to be reused, make a slice at the end of the hose with a single edge razor blade, perpendicular to the end of the hose. Do not cut deep so as not to damage the connection. The hose can then be peeled from the connection.

5. Clean both hose mounting connections. Inspect the condition of the hose clamps and replace them, if necessary.
   To install:
6. Dip the ends of the new hose into clean engine coolant to ease installation.
7. Slide the hose clamps over the replacement hose and slide the hose ends over the connections into position.
8. Position the hose clamps. Make sure they are located beyond the raised bead of the connector, if equipped, and within 0.118 in. (3mm) of the hose end.
9. Close the radiator drainplug and fill the cooling system with the clean drained engine coolant or a suitable 50/50 mixture of water and non-phosphate coolant.
10. Start the engine and allow it to reach normal operating temperature. Check the clamped hose ends for leaks.

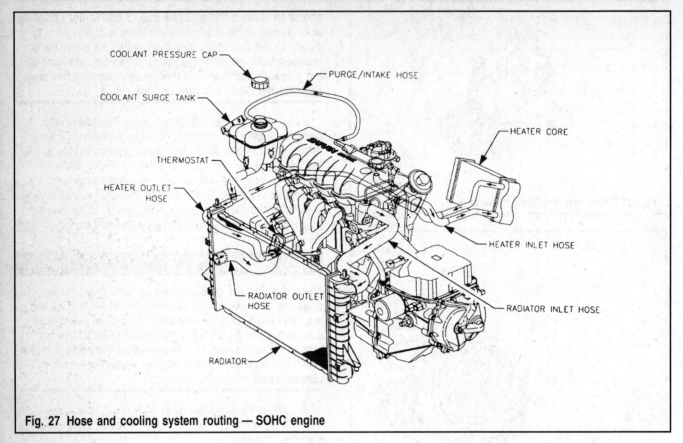

Fig. 27 Hose and cooling system routing — SOHC engine

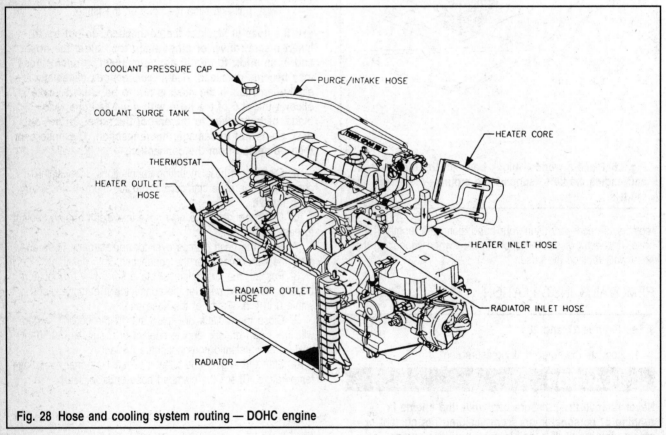

Fig. 28 Hose and cooling system routing — DOHC engine

Air Conditioning System

SAFETY WARNINGS

1. Avoid contact with a charged refrigeration system, even when working on another part of the air conditioning system or vehicle. If a heavy tool comes into contact with a section of air conditioning line, it can easily cause the relatively soft material to rupture.

2. When it is necessary to apply force to a fitting which contains refrigerant, as when checking that all system couplings are securely tightened, use a wrench on both parts of the fitting involved, if possible. This will avoid putting torque on the refrigerant tubing. (It is advisable, when possible, to use tube or line wrenches when tightening these flare nut fittings.)

3. Do not attempt to discharge the system by merely loosening a fitting, or removing the service valve caps and cracking these valves. Precise control is possible only when using the appropriate service gauges and a suitable recovery system. Wear protective gloves when connecting or disconnecting service gauge hoses.

4. Discharge the system only in a well ventilated area, as high concentrations of the gas can exclude oxygen and act as an anesthetic. When leak testing or soldering this is particularly important, as toxic gas is formed when R-12 contacts any flame.

5. Never start a system without first verifying that all service valves are properly installed and that all fittings throughout the system are snugly connected.

6. Avoid applying heat to any refrigerant line or storage vessel. Charging may be aided by using water heated to less than 125°F (51°C) to warm the refrigerant container. Never allow a refrigerant storage container to sit out in the sun or near any other source of heat, such as a radiator.

7. Always wear goggles when working on a system to protect the eyes. If refrigerant contacts the eye, it is advisable in all cases to see a physician as soon as possible.

8. Frostbite from liquid refrigerant should be treated by first gradually warming the area with cool water, and then gently applying petroleum jelly. A physician should be consulted.

9. Always keep refrigerant can fittings capped when not in use. If the container is equipped with a safety cap to protect the valve, make sure the cap is in place when the can is not being used. Avoid sudden shock to the can which might occur from dropping it, or from banging a heavy tool against it. Never carry a can in the passenger compartment of a car.

10. Always completely discharge the system into a suitable recovery unit before painting the vehicle (if the paint is to be baked on), or before welding anywhere near the refrigerant lines.

11. When servicing the system, minimize the time that any refrigerant line or fitting is open to the air to prevent moisture or dirt which can damage the internal system components. Always replace O-rings on lines or fittings which are removed. Prior to installation coat, but do not soak, replacement O-rings with a suitable compressor oil.

SYSTEM INSPECTION

The easiest and often most important check for the air conditioning system consists of a visual inspection of the system components. Visually inspect the air conditioning system for refrigerant leaks, damaged compressor clutch, compressor drive belt tension and condition, plugged evaporator drain tube, blocked condenser fins, disconnected or broken wires, blown fuses, corroded connections and poor insulation.

A refrigerant leak will usually appear as an oily residue at the leakage point in the system. The oily residue soon picks up dust or dirt particles from the surrounding air and appears greasy. Through time, this will build up and appear to be a heavy dirt impregnated grease. Most leaks are caused by damaged or missing O-ring seals at the component connections, damaged charging valve cores or missing service gauge port caps.

For a thorough visual and operational inspection, check the following:

1. Inspect the air inlet duct, lower air deflector, condenser to radiator seal and the rear hood seal for missing or damaged parts which might affect air flow.

2. Check the surface of the radiator and condenser for dirt, leaves or other material which might block air flow.

3. Check for kinks in hoses and lines. Check the system for leaks.

4. Make sure the serpentine drive belt is under the proper tension. When the air conditioning is operating, make sure the drive belt is free of noise or slippage.

5. Make sure the blower motor operates at 4 speeds, then check for equal distribution of the air from all outlets with the blower on **HIGH**. With the blower still operating at the high level, depress the recirculation button. The indicator should light and there should be an increase in both air flow and sound.

6. Make sure the air passage selection lever is operating correctly. Start the engine and warm it to normal operating temperature, then make sure the hot/cold selection lever is operating correctly.

REFRIGERANT LEVEL CHECK

1. Install a suitable manifold gauge set.

2. Install a thermometer in the passenger compartment right center air outlet, then open the vehicle doors and windows to stabilize the vehicle interior with the ambient air temperature.

3. Start the engine and allow it to idle.

4. Depress the recirculation button, set the temperature lever to full cold, select the 3rd blower speed and depress the A/C button.

5. When the engine is fully warmed, run the engine at 2000 rpm. Continue to run the engine until the system pressure and outlet temperature stabilize. This should usually take 3-5 minutes.

6. Record the pressure and temperature readings, then compare them to the following normal specifications:

   a. If the ambient air temperature is 70°F, the suction pressure gauge should read 25-30 psi, the discharge gauge should read 140-190 psi and the thermometer at the right center air duct should read 40-45°F.

b. If the ambient air temperature is 80°F, the suction pressure gauge should read 25-32 psi, the discharge gauge should read 200-250 psi and the thermometer at the right center air duct should read 45-50°F.

c. If the ambient air temperature is 90°F, the suction pressure gauge should read 25-34 psi, the discharge gauge should read 260-310 psi and the thermometer at the right center air duct should read 50-55°F.

d. If the ambient air temperature is 100°F, the suction pressure gauge should read 27-35 psi, the discharge gauge should read 320-370 psi and the thermometer at the right center air duct should read 55-60°F.

GAUGE SETS

▶ **See Figures 29, 30, 31 and 32**

Most of the service work performed in air conditioning requires the use of a set of two gauges, one for the high pressure side of the system and the other for the low pressure side of the system.

The low side gauge records both pressure and vacuum. Vacuum readings are calibrated from 0 to 30 inches Hg and the pressure graduations read from 0 to no less than 60 psi

(414kpa). The high side gauge measures pressure from 0 to at least 600 psi (4140kpa).

Both gauges are threaded into a manifold that contains two hand shut-off valves. Proper manipulation of these valves, and the use of the attached hoses allow the user to perform the following services:

1. Test high and low side pressures.
2. Remove air, moisture, and contaminated refrigerant.
3. Purge the system (of refrigerant).
4. Charge the system (with refrigerant).

The manifold valves are designed so they have no direct effect on gauge readings, but serve only to provide for, or cut off, flow of refrigerant through the manifold. During all testing and hook-up operations, the valves are kept in the closed position to avoid disturbing the refrigeration system. The valves are opened only to purge the system or to charge it.

Connect the manifold gauge set as follows:

5. Make sure that both gauges read '0", then close both valves.

6. Connect the low pressure gauge hose to the suction port located on the suction hose, then hand-tighten the hose nut.

7. Connect the high pressure gauge hose to the discharge service port located on the discharge pipe, then hand-tighten the hose nut.

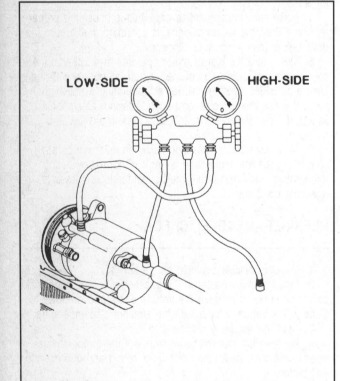

Fig. 29 Connect a suitable manifold gauge set to check the refrigerant level

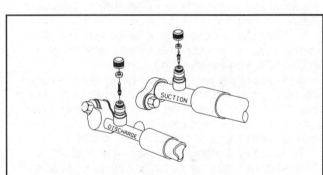

Fig. 30 Exploded view of the air conditioning service ports

Fig. 31 The air conditioning service (high pressure) discharge port — DOHC engine

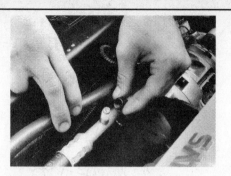

Fig. 32 The air conditioning service (low pressure) suction port — DOHC engine

DISCHARGING THE SYSTEM

➡R-12 refrigerant is a chlorofluorocarbon which, when released into the atmosphere, can contribute to the depletion of the ozone layer in the upper atmosphere. Ozone filters out harmful radiation from the sun. Consult the laws in your area before servicing the air conditioning system. In some states it is illegal to perform repairs involving refrigerant unless the work is done by a certified technician.

The use of refrigerant recovery systems and recycling stations makes possible the recovery and reuse of refrigerant after contaminants and moisture have been removed. If a recovery system or recycling station is available, the following general procedures should be observed, in addition to the operating instructions provided by the equipment manufacturer.

1. Check the system for pressure using the manifold gauge set. If a recovery system is used to draw refrigerant from a system that is already ruptured and open to the atmosphere, only air may be pulled into the tank.

2. Connect the refrigerant recycling station hose(s) to the vehicle air conditioning service ports and the recovery station inlet fitting.

➡Hoses should have shut off devices or check valves within 12 in. (305mm) of the hose end to minimize the introduction of air into the recycling station and to minimize the amount of refrigerant released when the hose(s) is disconnected.

3. Turn the power to the recycling station **ON** to start the recovery process. Allow the recycling station to pump the refrigerant from the system until the station pressure goes into a vacuum. On some stations the pump will be shut off automatically by a low pressure switch in the electrical system. On other units it may be necessary to manually turn off the pump.

4. Once the recycling station has evacuated the vehicle air conditioning system, close the station inlet valve, if equipped. Then switch **OFF** the electrical power.

5. Allow the vehicle air conditioning system to remain closed for about 2 minutes. Observe the system vacuum level as shown on the gauge. If the pressure does not rise, disconnect the recycling station hose(s).

6. If the system pressure rises, repeat Steps 3, 4 and 5 until the vacuum level remains stable for 2 minutes.

EVACUATING/CHARGING

▶ See Figure 33

Evacuating and charging the air conditioning system is a combined procedure in which the lines are purged, then refrigerant is added to the system in proper quantity. Charging is always conducted through the low pressure fitting in the pipe behind the compressor. NEVER attempt to charge the air conditioning through the high pressure side of the system.

1. Properly connect a manifold gauge set, then connect the manifold to a vacuum pump.

2. Turn the vacuum pump **ON** and slowly open the high and low side valves to the pump. Allow the system to evacuate for 20-30 minutes, then note the gauge reading.

3. Close the gauge high and low side valves, then shut the pump **OFF**.

4. Watch the low side gauge for vacuum loss. If vacuum loss is in excess of 1 in. Hg (3.38 kPa), then leak test the system, repair the leaks and return to Step 1. Before leak testing, remember to disconnect the gauge high side connector from the service port.

5. If after 1-3 minutes, the loss is less than 1 in. Hg (3.38 kPa), then proceed with the system charging.

6. Disconnect the gauge high side connection from the service port and the gauge manifold from the vacuum pump.

7. Connect the manifold connection (which was attached to the vacuum pump) to an R-12 source. If you are using a refrigerant drum instead of a charging station, place the drum on a scale to determine the amount of refrigerant being used.

8. Open the source and low side gauge valve, then monitor the weight of the drum or the rate at which the charging system is introducing R-12 into the system.

9. When 1 lb. (0.50 Kg) of R-12 has been added to the system, start the engine and turn the air conditioning system **ON**. Set the temperature lever to full cold, the blower speed on high and the selector lever to the upper outlets. Under this condition, slowly draw in the remainder of the R-12 charge.

10. When the system is charged, turn the source valves **OFF** and continue to run the engine for 30 seconds in order to clear the gauges and lines.

11. With the engine still running, carefully remove the gauge low side hose from the suction pipe service fitting. Unscrew the connection rapidly to avoid excess refrigerant loss.

❉❉CAUTION

If the hoses of the manifold gauge set disconnect from the gauge, NEVER remove a hose from the gauge while the other end of the hose is still connected to an air conditioning system service fitting. Because the service fitting check valve is depressed by the hose connection, this would cause a complete and uncontrolled discharge of the system. Serious personal injury could be caused by the escaping R-12

12. Make sure there is an O-ring seal inside each of the service fitting caps, then install and hand-tighten the caps.

13. Turn the engine **OFF**.

14. If an electronic leak tester is available, test the system for leaks.

15. If there are no leaks, perform the refrigerant level test to verify proper system charging.

LEAK TESTING

▶ See Figures 34 and 35

Whenever a refrigerant leak is suspected, begin by checking for leaks at the fittings and valves. Use of an electronic leak detector, if available is preferable. Follow the manufacturer's instructions carefully. Move the detector probe at approximately 1 in. per second in the suspected leak area. When escaping refrigerant gas is located, the ticking/beeping signal from the detector will increase in ticks/beeps per second. If the gas is relatively concentrated, the signal will be increasingly shrill.

If a tester is not available, perform a visual inspection and apply a soap solution to the questionable fitting or area. Bubbles will form to indicate a leak. Make sure to rinse the solution from the fitting before attempting repairs.

Windshield Wipers

▶ See Figure 36

For maximum effectiveness and longest element life, the windshield and wiper blades should be kept clean. Dirt, tree sap, road tar and so on will cause streaking, smearing and blade deterioration if left on the glass. It is advisable to wash the windshield carefully with a commercial glass cleaner at least once a month. Wipe off the rubber blades with the wet

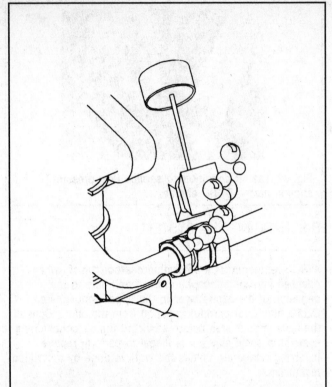

Fig. 35 A soap solution applied to a suspected leak will bubble when refrigerant is escaping

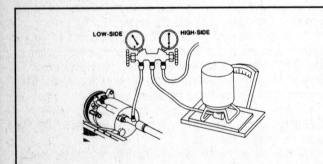

Fig. 33 Charging the air conditioning system using a refrigerant drum

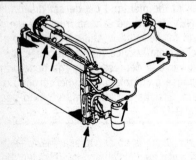

Fig. 34 When checking for refrigerant leaks, always begin at the system fittings and valves

rag afterwards. Do not attempt to move the wipers by hand; damage to the motor and drive mechanism will result.

To inspect and/or replace the wiper blades, place the wiper switch in the **LOW** speed position and the ignition switch in the **ACC** position. When the wiper blades are approximately vertical on the windshield, turn the ignition switch to **OFF**.

Examine the wiper blades. If they are found to be cracked, broken or torn, they should be replaced immediately. Replacement intervals will vary with usage, although ozone deterioration usually limits blade life to about one year. If the wiper pattern is smeared or streaked, or if the blade chatters across the glass, the elements should be replaced. It is easiest and most sensible to replace the elements in pairs.

If the original Saturn wiper blades are installed on your vehicle, it is most likely that the wiper blade insert is not serviceable and must be replaced as an assembly with the blade. On these blades, the last claw retaining the rubber insert is pinched so tightly as to make insert removal nearly impossible. To service these blades, compress the tabs located on the blade, where the arm and blade intersect. Then remove the blade assembly and replace with the same or a suitable aftermarket blade.

If your vehicle is already equipped with aftermarket blades, there are several different types of refills and your vehicle might have any kind. Aftermarket blades and arms rarely use the exact same type blade or refill as the original equipment. Here are some typical aftermarket blades, not all may be available for your car:

The Anco® type uses a release button that is pushed down to allow the refill to slide out of the yoke jaws. The new refill slides back into the frame and locks in place.

Some Trico® refills are removed by locating where the metal backing strip or the refill is wider. Insert a small screwdriver blade between the frame and metal backing strip. Press down to release the refill from the retaining tab.

Other types of Trico® refills have two metal tabs which are unlocked by squeezing them together. The rubber filler can then be withdrawn from the frame jaws. A new refill is installed by inserting the refill into the front frame jaws and sliding it rearward to engage the remaining frame jaws. There are usually four jaws; be certain when installing, that the refill is engaged in all of them. At the end of its travel, the tabs will lock into place on the front jaws of the wiper blade frame.

Another type of refill is made from polycarbonate. The refill has a simple locking device at one end which flexes downward out of the groove into which the jaws of the holder fit, allowing easy release. By sliding the new refill through all the jaws and pushing through the slight resistance when it reaches the end of its travel, the refill will lock into position.

To replace the Tridon® refill, it is necessary to remove the wiper arm or blade. This refill has a plastic backing strip with a notch about 1 in. (25mm) from the end. Hold the blade (frame) on a hard surface so the frame is tightly bowed. Grip the tip of the backing strip and pull up while twisting counterclockwise. The backing strip will snap out of the retaining tab. Do this for the remaining tabs until the refill is free of the arm. The length of these refills is molded into the end and they should be replaced with identical types.

Regardless of the type of refill used, make sure that all of the frame jaws are engaged as the refill is pushed into place and locked. If the metal blade holder and frame are allowed to touch the glass during wiper operation, the glass will be scratched.

Tires and Wheels

▶ **See Figure 37**

Inspect your tires often for signs of improper inflation and uneven wear, which may indicate a need for balancing, rotation, or wheel alignment. Check the tires frequently for cuts, stone bruises, abrasions, blisters and for objects that may have become embedded in the tread. More frequent inspections are recommended when rapid or extreme temperature changes occur or where road surfaces are rough

or occasionally littered with debris. Check the condition of the wheels and replace any that are bent, cracked, severely dented or have excessive runout.

The tires on your car have built-in wear indicators moulded into the bottom of the tread grooves. The indicators will begin to appear as the tire approaches replacement tread depth. Once the indicators are visible across 2 or more adjacent grooves and at 3 or more locations, the tires should be replaced.

Wear that occurs only on certain portions of the tire may indicate a particular problem, which when corrected or avoided, may significantly extend tire life. Wear that occurs only in the center of the tire indicates either overinflation or heavy acceleration on a drive wheel. Wear occurring at the outer edges of the tire and not at the center may indicate underinflation, excessively hard cornering or a lack of rotation. If wear occurs at only the outer edge of the tire, there may be a problem with the wheel alignment or the tire, when constructed, contained a non-uniformity defect.

TIRE ROTATION

▶ **See Figure 38**

Your tires should be rotated at the intervals recommended in the Maintenance Interval chart at the end of this section. Rotate them according to the tire rotation diagram. The spare should not be included in the rotation.

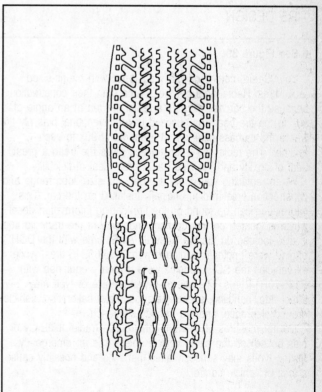

Fig. 37 Tread indicators will appear when the tire is worn out

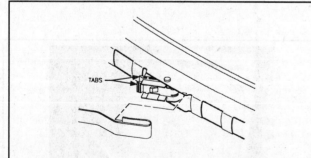

Fig. 36 Removing the original Saturn wiper blade and insert assembly

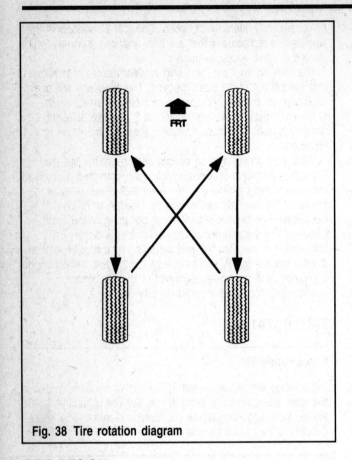

Fig. 38 Tire rotation diagram

TIRE DESIGN

▶ **See Figure 39**

Your Saturn comes originally equipped with metric-sized radial tires. Radial tires get their name from their construction, because the carcass plies on a radial tire run at an angle of 90° to the tire bead, as opposed to a conventional bias ply tire where the carcass plies run at an angle of 90° to each another. The radial tire's construction gives the tread a great deal of rigidity and the side wall a great deal of flexibility.

When replacing your tires, use only the size, load range and construction type (radial) originally installed on the car. This information can be found on the tire-loading information decal, which is located on the top right underside of the trunk lid and is also located on the tire sidewall. All Saturns with the DOHC engine were originally equipped with P195/60R15 tires, while all vehicles the SOHC engine were originally equipped with P175/70R14 tires. The use of any other size or type may affect ride, handling, speedometer/odometer calibration, vehicle ground clearance, and tire to body clearance.

Do not mix tires of different construction (radial, bias ply or bias belted) on the same vehicle unless it is an emergency. Mixing types may seriously affect handling and possibly cause a loss of vehicle control.

TIRE INFLATION

At least once a month, check the inflation pressure on all tires, including the spare. Use an accurate tire pressure gauge.

Do not trust the gauges on service station air pumps, as they are not always accurate. The inflation specifications are listed on the tire-loading information decal which is located on the top right underside of the trunk lid. Check and adjust inflation pressures only when the tires are cold, as pressures can increase as much as 4 psi (28kpa) due to heat. Tires are considered 'warmed-up'' once they are driven for more than 1 mile.

Inflation pressures that are higher than recommended can cause a hard ride, tire bruising, carcass damage and rapid tread wear at the center of the tire. Inflation pressures that are lower than recommended can cause tire squeal, hard steering, rim dents, high temperatures and rapid wear on the outer edges of the tires. Unequal tire pressures can compromise handling and cause uneven braking.

As previously stated, radial tires have a highly flexible sidewall and this accounts for the characteristic sidewall bulge that makes the tire appear underinflated. This is normal for a radial tire, so you should not attempt to reduce this bulge by overinflating the tire.

The tire valve caps are installed on the tire valve to prevent the entrance of dirt and moisture. Be sure to always replace the cap after checking or adjusting the tire pressure.

CARE OF ALUMINUM WHEELS

Aluminum wheels are standard on the DOHC engine equipped sport coupe and are optional on some other models. These wheels are coated to preserve their appearance.

To clean the aluminum wheels, use a mild soap and water solution and rinse thoroughly with clean water. If you want to use one of the commercially available wheel cleaners, make sure the label indicates that the cleaner is safe for coated wheels. Never use steel wool or any cleaner that contains an abrasive, or use strong detergents that contain high alkaline or caustic agents, as this will damage your wheels.

Fig. 39 The tire-loading information decal

FLUIDS AND LUBRICANTS

Fluid Disposal

Used fluids such as engine oil, transmission fluid, antifreeze and brake fluid are hazardous wastes and must be disposed of properly. Before draining any fluids, consult with the local authorities; in many areas, waste oil, etc. is being accepted as a part of recycling programs. A number of service stations and auto parts stores are also accepting waste fluids for recycling.

Be sure of the recycling center's policies before draining any fluids, as many will not accept different fluids that have been mixed together, such as oil and antifreeze.

Fuel and Engine Oil Recommendations

▶ See Figure 40

All Saturns are equipped with a catalytic converter, necessitating the use of unleaded gasoline. The use of leaded gasoline will damage the catalytic converter. Both the SOHC and DOHC engines are designed to use unleaded gasoline with a minimum octane rating of 87, which usually means regular unleaded.

Oil must be selected with regard to the anticipated temperatures during the period before the next oil change. Using the chart, select the oil viscosity for the lowest expected temperature and you will be assured of easy cold starting and sufficient engine protection. The oil you pour into your engine should have the designation SG marked on the container. For maximum fuel economy benefits, use an oil with the Roman Numeral II next to the words Energy Conserving in the API Service Symbol.

Engine

OIL LEVEL CHECK

▶ See Figures 41 and 42

Check the engine oil level every time you fill the gas tank. Make sure the oil level is between the **FULL** and **L** marks. The engine and oil must be warm and the vehicle parked on level ground to get an accurate reading. Always allow a few minutes after turning the engine OFF for the oil to drain back into the pan before checking, or an inaccurate reading will result. Check the engine oil level as follows:

1. Open the hood and locate the engine oil dipstick.
2. If the engine is hot, you may want to wrap a rag around the dipstick handle before removing it.
3. Remove the dipstick and wipe it with a clean, lint-free rag, then reinsert it into the dipstick tube. Make sure it is inserted all the way to avoid an inaccurate reading.
4. Pull out the dipstick and note the oil level. It should be between the marks, as stated above.
5. If the oil level is below the lower mark, replace the dipstick and add fresh oil to bring the level within the proper range. Do not overfill.
6. Recheck the oil level and close the hood.

OIL AND FILTER CHANGE

▶ See Figures 43, 44 and 45

The engine oil and oil filter should be changed together, at the recommended interval on the Maintenance Intervals chart. The oil should be changed more frequently if the vehicle is being operated in very dusty areas. Before draining the oil, make sure the engine is at operating temperature. Hot oil will hold more impurities in suspension and will flow better, allowing the removal of more oil and dirt.

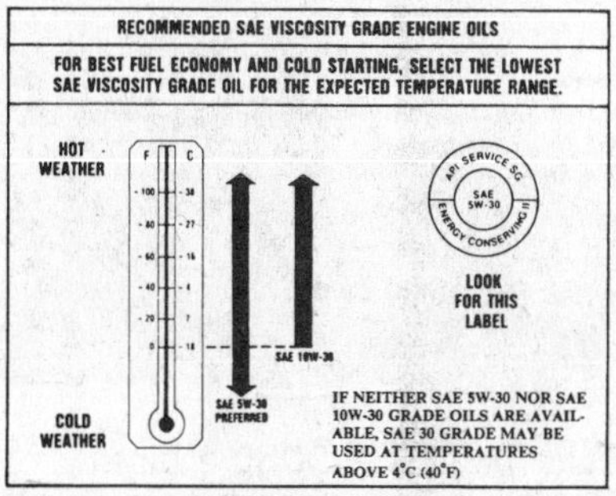

Fig. 41 Remove the engine oil dipstick from the guide tube — DOHC engine

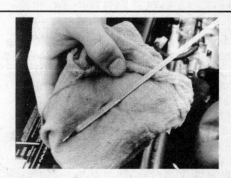

Fig. 42 Make sure the oil level is at the FULL mark — DOHC engine

---

RECOMMENDED SAE VISCOSITY GRADE ENGINE OILS

FOR BEST FUEL ECONOMY AND COLD STARTING, SELECT THE LOWEST SAE VISCOSITY GRADE OIL FOR THE EXPECTED TEMPERATURE RANGE.

HOT WEATHER

COLD WEATHER

API SERVICE SG

SAE 5W-30 ENERGY CONSERVING II

LOOK FOR THIS LABEL

SAE 5W-30 PREFERRED

SAE 10W-30

IF NEITHER SAE 5W-30 NOR SAE 10W-30 GRADE OILS ARE AVAILABLE, SAE 30 GRADE MAY BE USED AT TEMPERATURES ABOVE 4°C (40°F)

Fig. 40 Engine oil viscosity chart

As noted earlier, used oil has been classified as a hazardous waste and must be disposed of properly. Before draining any oil from the engine crankcase, make sure you are aware of the proper disposal procedures for your area.

Change the oil and filter as follows:

1. Run the engine until it reaches the normal operating temperature, then shut off the engine and remove the oil filler cap.

2. Raise and safely support the front of the car. If possible, make sure the engine drain plug is lower than the rest of the oil pan. Position a drain pan under the plug.

✷✷CAUTION

The EPA warns that prolonged contact with used engine oil may cause a number of skin disorders, including cancer! You should make every effort to minimize your exposure to used engine oil. Protective gloves should be worn when changing the oil. Wash your hands and any other exposed skin areas as soon as possible after exposure to used engine oil. Soap and water, or waterless hand cleaner should be used.

3. Wipe the drain plug and the surrounding area clean. Loosen the drain plug with a socket or box wrench, then remove it by hand using a rag to shield your fingers from the heat. Push in on the plug as you turn it out, so that no oil escapes until the plug is completely removed.

4. Allow the oil to drain into the pan. Be careful if the engine is at operating temperature, as the oil is hot enough to burn you.

5. Clean and install the drain plug, making sure that the gasket is still on the plug. Use a new drain plug gasket whenever possible, but if the gasket is damaged, a new gasket MUST be installed. Tighten the drain plug to 27 ft. lbs. (37 Nm).

6. The oil filter is on the rear right side of the block protruding towards the firewall. Slide the drain pan under the oil filter. Slip an oil filter wrench onto the filter and turn counterclockwise to loosen the filter. Wrap a rag around the filter and unscrew it the rest of the way by hand. Be careful of hot oil which may run down the side of the filter.

➡When the oil filter is removed, make sure the old filter gasket has also been removed from the engine or a proper seal will not be achieved with the new filter. More than a few people have installed the replacement filter with the old gasket still in place and have wound up with a garage floor full of clean engine oil.

7. If the filter's case separates from the base plate, a 10mm socket or wrench may be used to remove the base plate and threaded adapter from the engine. Separate the 2 parts, clean the adapter and block threads, then install the adapter and tighten to 22 ft. lbs. (30 Nm).

8. Clean the oil filter adapter on the engine with a clean rag. Wipe the oil pan drip deflector and drip rail dry prior to installing a new oil filter.

9. Coat the rubber gasket on the replacement filter with clean engine oil. Place the filter in position on the adapter

fitting and screw it on by hand until resistance is felt. Using a standard oil filter tool, tighten the filter an additional ¾-1 turn.

10. Pull the drain pan from under the vehicle, remove the supports and lower the vehicle to the ground.

11. Fill the crankcase with the proper type and quantity of engine oil right away. If the engine is started and run without oil in the crankcase, serious damage may occur almost immediately.

12. Run the engine and check for leaks. Stop the engine and check the oil level.

Fig. 43 Engine oil drain plug — DOHC engine

Fig. 44 Engine oil filter — DOHC engine

Fig. 45 Lightly coat the new filter gasket with clean engine oil

Manual Transaxle

FLUID RECOMMENDATIONS

DEXRON®IIE automatic transmission/transaxle fluid is preferred, DEXRON®II automatic transmission/transaxle fluid is acceptable.

LEVEL CHECK

▶ **See Figures 46, 47 and 48**

1. The manual transaxle fluid should be checked **COLD**, with the car parked on a level surface.
2. If necessary, move the car to a level spot and allow the powertrain to cool.
3. Reach below the brake master cylinder, located at the firewall on the left side of the engine compartment, to the top of the transaxle. Grasp the hinged dipstick lever and pull upwards to withdraw the dipstick. The dipstick hinge will automatically straighten and release the expansion plug at the bottom of the hinge so the stick may be pulled from the transaxle.
4. Note the fluid level, it should be at the **FULL** line. If necessary, add fluid to bring the amount up to the proper level. Be careful not to overfill the transaxle.
5. Insert the dipstick to the top of the transaxle case and push the hinge back to the locked position. This will expand the rubber plug below the hinge to lock and seal the transaxle.

Fig. 46 Withdraw the manual transaxle dipstick with the hinge in the upright position — DOHC engine

DRAIN AND REFILL

▶ **See Figure 49**

The manual transaxle fluid should be changed when the vehicle reaches 6,000 miles (10,000 km). No periodic changing should be necessary after the initial change.

1. Start the engine and allow it to warm to normal operating temperature, then shut the engine **OFF**.
2. If possible, raise and safely support the vehicle so that it is level. If not, support the vehicle so the drain plug is the lowest point of the transaxle case.
3. Position a drain pan under the plug.
4. Clean the area around the drain plug, then remove the plug using a socket or box wrench. Push in on the plug as you turn it out, so that no fluid escapes until the plug is completely removed. Allow the fluid to drain into the pan.
5. Clean the drain plug, then lubricate the plug using clean transaxle fluid. Wipe off the excess fluid and install the plug using a new washer. Tighten the plug to 40 ft. lbs. (55 Nm).
6. Slide the drain pan out from under the vehicle, then remove the supports and carefully lower the vehicle to the ground.
7. Withdraw the transaxle dipstick and position a suitable long necked funnel into the top of the transaxle. Fill the transaxle to the proper level using the recommended fluid.
8. Check the fluid level, then install and lock the transaxle dipstick.

Automatic Transaxle

FLUID RECOMMENDATIONS

DEXRON®IIE automatic transmission/transaxle fluid is preferred, DEXRON®II automatic transmission/transaxle fluid is acceptable.

LEVEL CHECK

▶ **See Figure 50**

1. Start the engine and operate the vehicle for 15 minutes or until the normal operating temperature is reached. An incorrect level reading will be obtained if the vehicle is operated under the following conditions immediately before checking the dipstick:

   In an ambient temperature of 90°F (32°C) or above.
   At sustained highway speeds.
   In heavy city traffic, during hot weather.
   Used as a towing vehicle.

2. Park the vehicle on a level surface and apply the parking brake.
3. Move the gear selector through all gears, then position the selector in **P**.
4. With all accessories turned **OFF**, allow the vehicle to idle for 3 minutes.
5. Withdraw the dipstick and check for proper fluid level as compared with the picture. Check the fluid color and condition; fluid should be smooth, transparent and red. If fluid is not

Fig. 47 When the dipstick is installed, position the hinge in the locked position to seal the transaxle — DOHC engine

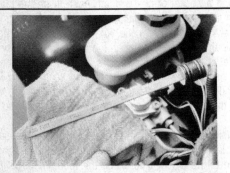

Fig. 48 Make sure the transaxle fluid level is at the FULL mark — DOHC engine

Fig. 49 Manual transaxle drain plug — DOHC engine

transparent or if it is a dark brown, the fluid is contaminated or overheated and must be replaced.

6. If necessary, change the fluid or add fluid to bring the amount to the proper level.

FLUID AND FILTER CHANGE

The automatic transaxle fluid and filter should be changed when the vehicle reaches 30,000 miles (50,000 Km). Although the manufacturer recommends changing the filter with only every other fluid change thereafter, we recommend that the fluid and filter should be changed together, at the recommended interval on the Maintenance Intervals chart. A

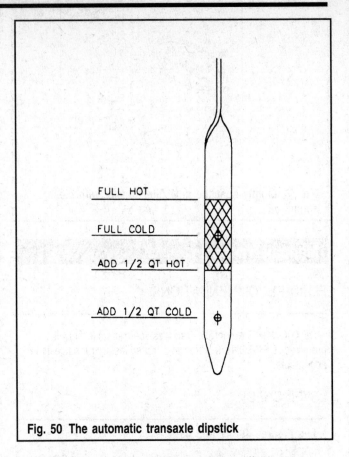

Fig. 50 The automatic transaxle dipstick

few dollars more spent on a filter today may offer an even greater protection against transaxle wear and repair in the future.

Change the fluid and filter as follows:

1. Warm the fluid to the normal operating temperature of 190-200°F (88-93°C). It should take approximately 15 miles of highway driving to reach this temperature.

2. If possible, raise and safely support the vehicle so that it is level. If not, support the vehicle so the drain plug is the lowest point of the transaxle case.

3. Position a drain pan under the plug.

4. Clean the area around the drain plug, then remove the plug using a socket or box wrench. Push in on the plug as you turn it out, so that no fluid escapes until the plug is completely removed. Allow the fluid to completely drain into the pan; it may take 5 minutes or longer.

✳✳CAUTION

The transaxle fluid was heated to operating temperature for maximum flow. Use a rag and protective gloves to make sure you are not burned by the extremely hot fluid.

5. Install the drain plug with a new washer and tighten to 40 ft. lbs. (55 Nm).

6. Position the drain pan under the fluid filter, making sure the pan will not be contacted when the vehicle is lowered. Remove the supports and lower the vehicle.

7. Remove the air inlet duct from the battery tray and reposition to allow access to the transaxle spin-on fluid pressure filter.

8. Use a nylon strap filter wrench to loosen the pressure filter, remove the filter from the transaxle. Make sure the filter seal was removed from the transaxle with the filter.

9. Lubricate the new filter seal using clean transaxle fluid, then install the filter by hand and tighten until the seal makes contact. Tighten the filter 1 additional turn by hand or, if necessary, using the nylon strap filter wrench. Do not use any tool that might scratch, dent or damage the filter. A filter that is scratched, dented or damaged must be immediately replaced.

10. Reposition the air inlet duct and tighten the fasteners to 62 inch lbs. (7 Nm).

11. Using a funnel, slowly refill the transaxle with the recommended type and quantity of fluid. Check the fluid level cold.

12. Start the engine and check for leaks, then check the level hot and add fluid as necessary to achieve the proper level.

13. For 1992 and 1993 vehicles, the Powertrain Control Module (PCM) stores a parameter called 'oil life left percent." This is used by the computer to illuminate the SERVICE ENGINE SOON light when the percent reaches a minimum level and to tell a technician that the fluid is in need of a change. If a suitable scan tool is available, connect it and reset the parameter to 100 percent. If you do not have access to a suitable scan tool as described in Chapter 4 of this manual, the vehicle should be taken to the dealer or a shop that has the appropriate tool. Simply tell them that the transmission oil has just been changed and the oil life PCM parameter needs to be reset.

Cooling System

Check the cooling system at the interval specified in the Maintenance Intervals chart at the end of this section.

If necessary, hose clamps should be checked and soft or cracked hoses replaced. Damp spots or accumulations of rust or dye near hoses, the water pump or other areas indicate areas of possible leakage. Check the surge tank cap for a worn or cracked gasket. If the cap doesn't seal properly, fluid will be lost and the engine will overheat. A worn cap should be replaced with a new one. The surge tank should be free of rust and the coolant should be free from oil. If oil is found in the coolant, the engine thermostat will not function correctly, therefore the system must be flushed and filled with fresh coolant.

Periodically clean any debris such as leaves, paper, insects, etc. from the radiator fins. Pick the large pieces off by hand. The smaller pieces can be washed away with water pressure from a hose.

Carefully straighten any bent radiator fins with a pair of needle nose pliers. Be careful — the fins are very soft. Don't wiggle the fins back and forth too much. Straighten them once and try not to move them again.

FLUID RECOMMENDATIONS

The recommended fluid is a 50/50 mixture of a non-phosphate ethylene glycol antifreeze and water for year round use. Use a good quality antifreeze with rust and other corrosion inhibitors, along with acid neutralizers.

LEVEL CHECK

▶ See Figure 51

With the engine cold, check the surge tank located against the center of the right fender in the engine compartment. The coolant should be at the Full Cold level. If it is low, check for leaks and repair as necessary. Add a suitable coolant mixture to bring the coolant to the proper level.

DRAIN AND REFILL

▶ See Figure 52

1. Make sure the engine is cool and the vehicle is parked on a level surface, then remove the surge tank pressure cap.

2. Position a large drain pan under the radiator drain plug on the right end of the radiator and engine drain plug under the right front of the block.

3. Open the radiator drain and remove the engine drain plug, then allow the coolant to drain from the system.

4. Close the radiator plug and install the engine plug to the cylinder block. Tighten the engine drain plug to 26 ft. lbs. (35 Nm).

5. Fill the system through the surge tank using a suitable solution of water and a non-phosphate ethylene glycol antifreeze.

6. Start the engine and check for leaks.

7. After the engine has run for 2 or 3 minutes, add coolant as necessary to bring the coolant level to the surge tank Full Cold line.

8. Install the surge tank pressure cap.

FLUSHING AND CLEANING THE SYSTEM

1. Prepare 2 gallons of a flushing solution consisting of 4 ounces of Calgon®, or an equivalent automatic dishwasher detergent.

2. Properly drain the engine cooling system.

3. Remove the thermostat to permit the flushing solution to circulate through the entire cooling system.

4. Fill the cooling system with the flushing solution.

Fig. 51 With the engine cold, the surge tank should be filled to the Full Cold line

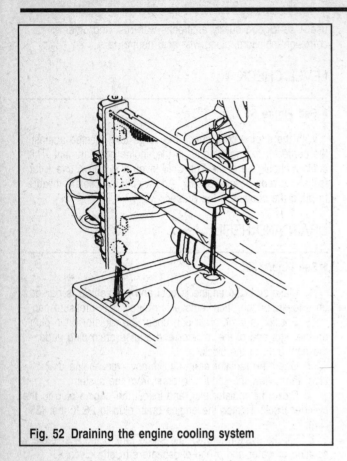

Fig. 52 Draining the engine cooling system

5. Run the engine for 5 minutes, then drain the flushing solution into a clean container.

6. Repeat Steps 4 and 5.

7. Fill the cooling system with clean water.

8. Run the engine for 5 minutes, then drain the water from the cooling system.

9. Properly fill the engine cooling system with a 50/50 mixture of water and a non-phosphate ethylene glycol antifreeze.

Master Cylinder

FLUID RECOMMENDATIONS

Both the clutch and brake fluid master cylinders require brake fluid that meets DOT 3 standards. DO NOT use DOT 5 silicone fluid or any fluid that contains a mineral or paraffin base oil or system damage could occur.

LEVEL CHECK

▶ **See Figures 53, 54, 55 and 56**

The brake master cylinder is equipped with a translucent reservoir which enables fluid level checking without removing the reservoir cap. The brake fluid level should be between the

MIN and MAX lines located on the side of the reservoir. The MAX line is at the base of the filler cap neck.

The clutch master cylinder is located beneath the brake master cylinder and slightly more toward the outside of the vehicle. The filler cap is also a dipstick and may be withdrawn to determine the fluid level.

If it is necessary to add fluid or withdraw a cap, first wipe away any accumulated dirt or grease from the reservoir and cap. Then remove the reservoir cap by twisting counterclockwise. Add fluid to the proper level. Avoid spilling brake fluid on any painted surface as it will harm the finish. Replace the reservoir cap.

Fig. 53 Brake fluid master cylinder — DOHC engine equipped with anti-lock brakes

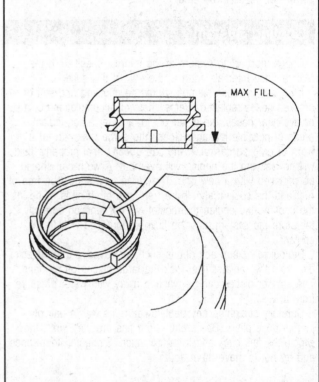

MAX FILL

Fig. 54 The brake master cylinder MAX fill line is at the base of the filler cap neck

Fig. 55 Checking the clutch master cylinder fluid level

Fig. 56 The clutch master cylinder fluid level should be between the Full and Add lines

Power Steering Pump

FLUID RECOMMENDATIONS

GM power steering fluid specification 9985010 or equivalent must be used. Failure to use a fluid which meets these specifications may cause damage and fluid leaks.

LEVEL CHECK

▶ See Figure 57

1. Raise and safely support the front of the vehicle sufficiently to just clear the front wheels from the ground. Be sure the parking brake is applied.
2. Turn the wheel from side to side several times without hitting stops. This will bleed any air which may be present from the system.
3. Check the fluid level as indicated on the side of the reservoir located at the rear of the engine compartment. If necessary, add the proper fluid to reach the FULL mark on the container. Be sure to clean the reservoir cap and surrounding area with a rag before removing the cap.
4. With the transmission in **PARK** or **NEUTRAL**, start the engine and check the fluid level. Add fluid, as necessary.
5. Return the wheels to the center or straight ahead position and lower the front of the vehicle to the ground.

6. Continue to run the engine for 2-3 minutes, then road test the vehicle. Make sure the system is free of noise and turns normally.
7. Recheck the fluid level and add as necessary. When the system has stabilized at its normal operating temperature, the fluid should be at or slightly above the FULL mark.

Chassis Greasing

The steering and suspension joints on your car are sealed at the factory and do not require any form of periodic lubrication.
At least annually, lubricate the transaxle shift linkage with GM-6031M or an equivalent chassis grease for manual transaxles and SAE 5W-30 engine oil for automatic transaxles.
Also annually, the parking brake cable guides, underbody contact points and linkage should be lubricated with GM-6031M or an equivalent chassis grease.

Body Lubrication and Maintenance

At least once a year, use a multi-purpose grease to lubricate the body door hinges, including the hood, fuel door and trunk or liftgate hinges and latches. The glovebox, console doors and folding seat hardware should also be lightly lubricated. Be careful not to stain the interior fabrics with the grease.
The door and window weather-stripping should be lubricated with silicone lubricant. Flush the underbody using plain water to remove any corrosive materials picked up from the road and used for ice, snow or dust control. Make sure you thoroughly clean areas where mud and dirt may collect. If necessary, loosen sediment packed in closed areas before flushing.
To preserve the appearance of your car, it should be washed periodically with a mild soap or detergent and water solution. A liquid dishwashing detergent that DOES NOT contain any abrasives may be useful in loosening dirt or grease from the vehicle, while not endangering the finish. Only wash the vehicle when the metal feels cool and the vehicle is in the shade. Rinse the entire vehicle with cold water, then wash and rinse one panel at a time, beginning with the roof and upper areas. After washing is complete, rinse the vehicle one final time and dry with a soft cloth or chamois. Air drying a vehicle, by driving at highway speeds for a few miles, may quickly and easily dry a vehicle without the need for excessive elbow grease.
Periodic waxing will remove harmful deposits from the vehicles surface and protect the finish. If the finish has dulled

Fig. 57 The power steering fluid reservoir — DOHC engine

due to age or neglect, polishing may be necessary to restore the original gloss.

There are many specialized products available at your local auto parts store to care for the appearance of painted metal surfaces, plastic, chrome, wheels and tires as well as the interior upholstery and carpeting. Be sure to follow the manufacturers instructions before using them.

Rear Wheel Bearings

REMOVAL & INSTALLATION

▶ **See Figure 58**

1. If equipped with ABS, disconnect the negative battery cable.
2. Raise and support the vehicle safely, then remove the rear wheel.
3. If equipped, disconnect the electrical connector from the ABS speed sensor. The connector is beneath the vertical rear strut and behind the brake assembly.
4. On disc brake equipped models, remove the 2 caliper support bolts, then support the caliper with a length of mechanic's wire or a coat hanger from the strut. Pull the rotor from the hub studs.
5. On drum brake equipped models, remove the brake drum.
6. Remove the 4 hub/bearing-to-knuckle bolts, then remove the hub and bearing assembly from the vehicle. The brake

backing plate will be freed and may come off the vehicle as the assembly is removed. The assembly is sealed and not serviceable. It should be replaced, if damaged

To install:

7. Position the brake backing plate, then install the hub/bearing assembly and retaining bolts. Tighten the bolts to 63 ft. lbs. (85 Nm).
8. Install the brake drum or the rotor and caliper. If applicable, tighten the caliper retaining bolts to 63 ft. lbs. (85 Nm).
9. If equipped, connect the ABS speed sensor connector.
10. Install the rear wheel assembly, then remove the supports and lower the vehicle.
11. If applicable, connect the negative battery cable.

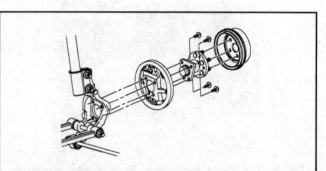

Fig. 58 Exploded view of the rear bearing/hub mounting — rear drum brake vehicles

TRAILER TOWING

All Saturn vehicles are capable of towing, if equipped with the proper equipment. It is not recommended that the trailer and load exceed a 1000 lbs. (454 Kg) capacity. The Gross Combined Weight (GCW) rating (or the combined weight of the trailer, load, vehicle and passengers) should not exceed 4,258 lbs.

If you wish to tow a trailer with your car, you will have to acquire the necessary equipment from aftermarket sources as no towing packages are currently available from Saturn.

General Recommendations

Your vehicles tires should always be properly inflated to assure the best possible traction and to minimize tire wear while towing.

Do not connect the trailer's lighting system wiring directly to your cars lighting system wiring. Obtain the proper equipment from a trailer dealer.

If you are using a rental trailer, follow the rental agency's instructions for all connections and towing procedures.

You should drive no faster than 50 mph for the first 500 miles your car tows a trailer. This will help your engine and vehicle to wear into heavier loads.

Your car should be serviced more frequently when you use it for towing.

Necessary Equipment

Only use the right equipment for the type of trailer you are towing. Never use a hitch that is designed to clamp to the bumper, as the bumper on your Saturn is not designed to bear the load. Use only a load carrying hitch, but as this type places the tongue load of the trailer on the car's rear wheels, the load must be distributed in the trailer so that only 10 percent of the trailer weight is on the tongue.

Always use safety chains. Cross them under the trailer tongue and attach them to the frame, or hook retainers, not to the bumper. Be sure to leave enough slack in the chain to be able to turn corners.

Trailer and Tongue Weight Limits

Your car can tow a trailer up to a maximum of 1000 lbs. (454 Kg) gross trailer axle weight. The trailer tongue should weigh no more than 10 percent of the total trailer weigh, therefore the maximum tongue load is 100 lbs. (45 Kg). Tongue load can often be changed simply by rearranging the trailer load.

PUSHING AND TOWING

Manual transaxle equipped cars may be started by pushing, in the event of a dead battery. But push starting IS NOT RECOMMENDED because of possible damage to the catalytic converter. If you must push start, ensure that the push car bumper doesn't override the bumper of your car. If possible, position a thick fabric such as a heavy winter jacket between the car bumpers to help prevent damage to your vehicle's bumper cover. Depress the clutch pedal. Select 2nd or 3rd gear. Switch the ignition ON. When the car reaches a speed of approximately 10 mph, release the clutch to start the engine.

If towing is required, the vehicle should be flat bedded or towed with the front wheels off of the ground on a wheel lift to prevent damage to the transaxle. DO NOT allow your vehicle to be towed by a sling type tow truck, if it is at all avoidable. If it is necessary to tow the vehicle from the rear, a wheel dolly should be placed under the front tires.

JACKING

▶ See Figure 59

The vehicle is supplied with a scissors jack for emergency road repairs. The scissors jack may be used to raise the car via the notches on either side at the front and rear of the doors. Do not attempt to use the jack in any other places. Always block the diagonally opposite wheel when using a jack.

When using floor jacks or stands, use the side members at the front or rear, the center of the rear crossmember assembly or the trailing engine cradle (shown in figure as the 2 shaded areas between the front tires). The engine cradle has been coated with a special finish to protect it. Always position a block of wood on top of the jack or stand to protect the finish when lifting or supporting the vehicle via the cradle.

Whenever you plan to work under the car, you must support it on jackstands or ramps. Never use cinder blocks or stacks of wood to support the car, even if you're only going to be under it for a few minutes. Never crawl under the car when it is supported only by the tire-changing jack or other floor jack.

Small hydraulic, screw, or scissors jacks are satisfactory for raising the car. Drive-on trestles or ramps are also a handy and safe way to both raise and support the car. Be careful though, some ramps may be too steep to drive your Saturn onto without scraping the front bottom plastic panels. Never support the car on any suspension member or underbody panel.

CAPACITIES

Year	Model	Engine ID/VIN	Engine Displacement Liters (cc)	Engine Crankcase with Filter	Transmission (pts.)			Drive Axle (pts.)	Fuel Tank (gal.)	Cooling System (qts.)
					4-Spd	5-Spd	Auto.			
1991	Sedan	7	1.9 (1901)	4.0	—	5.2	7.5	—	12.8	7.0
	Sedan	9	1.9 (1901)	4.0	—	5.2	7.5	—	12.8	7.0
	Coupe	7	1.9 (1901)	4.0	—	5.2	7.5	—	12.8	7.0
1992	Sedan	7	1.9 (1901)	4.0	—	5.2	7.5	—	12.8	7.0
	Sedan	9	1.9 (1901)	4.0	—	5.2	7.5	—	12.8	7.0
	Coupe	7	1.9 (1901)	4.0	—	5.2	7.5	—	12.8	7.0
1993	Wagon	7	1.9 (1901)	4.0	—	5.2	7.5	—	12.8	7.0
	Wagon	9	1.9 (1901)	4.0	—	5.2	7.5	—	12.8	7.0
	Sedan	7	1.9 (1901)	4.0	—	5.2	7.5	—	12.8	7.0
	Sedan	9	1.9 (1901)	4.0	—	5.2	7.5	—	12.8	7.0
	Coupe	7	1.9 (1901)	4.0	—	5.2	7.5	—	12.8	7.0
	Coupe	9	1.9 (1901)	4.0	—	5.2	7.5	—	12.8	7.0

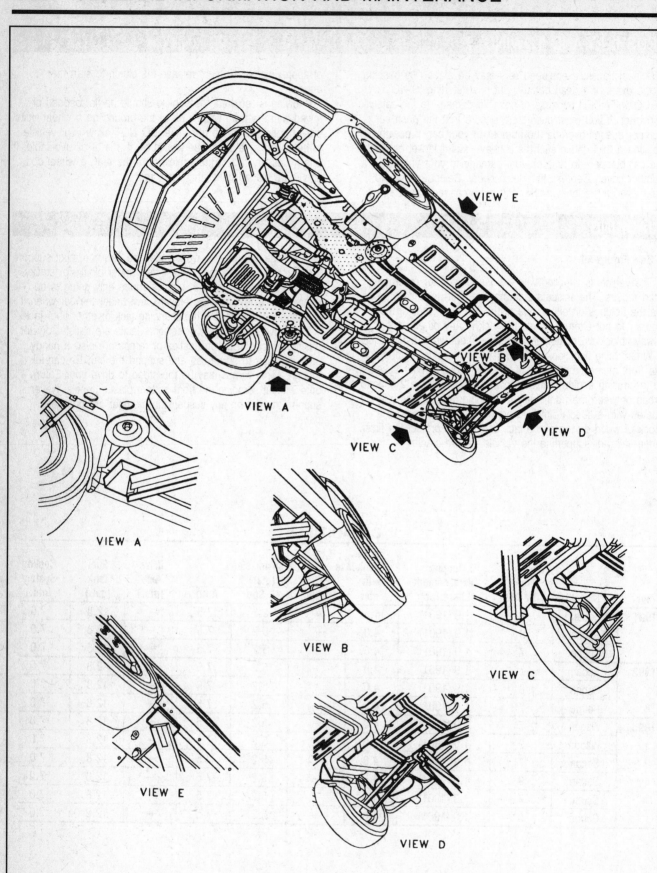

VIEW E

VIEW B

VIEW A

VIEW C

VIEW D

VIEW A

VIEW B

VIEW C

VIEW E

VIEW D

Fig. 59 Floor jacks or jackstands may be positioned at these locations

Saturn Maintenance Schedule I

Follow Schedule I if the car is usually operated under one or more of the following conditions:

- Most trips are less than 5 miles (8 km).
- It's below freezing outside, day and night.
- It's very humid outside.
- Your engine is often idling or running at low speed, as in heavy traffic.
- You're towing a trailer.
- You drive in dusty places.
- Your Saturn is used for delivery service, police, taxi or other commercial purposes.

Directions:
- Record maintenance date in top box.
- Check off service performed in corresponding box.
- Grey boxes mean that no service is needed at that mileage interval.

	Miles x 1000	3	6	9	12	15	18	21	24	27	30	33	36	39	42	45	48	51	54	57	60
	(Kilometers x 1000)	5	10	15	20	25	30	35	40	45	50	55	60	65	70	75	80	85	90	95	100
1.	Change engine oil and filter. * — Every 3 mos. or 3,000 mi (5,000 km).	X	X	X	X	X	X	X	X	X	X	X	X	X	X	X	X	X	X	X	X
2.	Inspect axle boots, suspension bushings and ball joint seals. — Every 6 mos. or 6,000 mi (10,000 km).		X		X		X		X		X		X		X		X		X		X
3.	Inspect exhaust system and shields. — Every 6 mos. or 6,000 mi (10,000 km).		X		X		X		X		X		X		X		X		X		X
4.	Inspect and rotate tires and wheels. — At 6,000 mi. (10,000 km) and then every 12,000 mi. (20,000 km).		X				X				X				X				X		
5.	Service manual transaxle, change fluid. — At 6,000 mi. (10,000 km) only.		X																		
6.	Service automatic transaxle, change fluid. — Every 30,000 mi. (50,000 km).										X										X
7.	Change automatic transaxle pressure filter. — At 30,000 mi. (50,000 km) and then every 60,000 mi. (100,000 km).										X										
8.	Replace spark plugs. * — Every 30,000 mi. (50,000 km).										X										X
9.	Inspect vacuum line/hose. * # — Every 24 mos. or 30,000 mi. (50,000 km).										X										X
10.	Inspect fuel tank, cap, and pipe/hoses. * # — Every 24 mos. or 30,000 mi. (50,000 km).										X										X
11.	Inspect engine accessory drive belt and coolant hoses. — Every 12 mos. or 18,000 mi. (30,000 km).						X						X						X		
12.	Replace engine air filter. * — Every 36 mos. or 30,000 mi. (50,000 km).										X										X
13.	Flush cooling system, change coolant and check pressure cap. * — Every 36 mos. or 36,000 mi. (60,000 km).												X								
14.	Replace fuel filter. — Every 48 mos. or 60,000 mi. (100,000 km).																				X

* An emission control service.
\# The U.S. Environmental Protection Agency has determined that the failure to perform the maintenance item will not nullify the emission warranty or limit recall liability prior to the completion of vehicle useful life. Saturn, however, urges that all recommended maintenance services be performed at the indicated intervals and the maintenance be recorded in Section C of the owner's maintenance booklet.

Saturn Maintenance Schedule II

Schedule II should only be followed if none of the conditions for Schedule I apply.

- If trips are more than 5 miles (8 km), and more than half of these miles include non-stop highway driving.

Directions:
- Record maintenance date in top box.
- Check off service performed in corresponding box.
- Grey boxes mean that no service is needed at that mileage interval.

	Miles x 1000	3	6	9	12	15	18	21	24	27	30	33	36	39	42	45	48	51	54	57	60
	(Kilometers x 1000)	5	10	15	20	25	30	35	40	45	50	55	60	65	70	75	80	85	90	95	100
1.	Change engine oil and filter. * — Every 6 mos. or 6,000 mi (10,000 km).		X		X		X		X		X		X		X		X		X		X
2.	Inspect axle boots, suspension bushings and ball joint seals. — Every 6 mos. or 6,000 mi (10,000 km).		X		X		X		X		X		X		X		X		X		X
3.	Inspect exhaust system and shields. — Every 6 mos. or 6,000 mi (10,000 km).		X		X		X		X		X		X		X		X		X		X
4.	Inspect and rotate tires and wheels. — At 6,000 mi. (10,000 km) and then every 12,000 mi. (20,000 km).		X				X				X				X				X		
5.	Service manual transaxle, change fluid. — At 6,000 mi. (10,000 km).		X																		
6.	Service automatic transaxle, change fluid. — Every 30,000 mi. (50,000 km).										X										X
7.	Change automatic transaxle pressure filter. — At 30,000 mi. (50,000 km) and then every 60,000 mi. (100,000 km).										X										
8.	Replace spark plugs. * — Every 30,000 mi. (50,000 km).										X										X
9.	Inspect vacuum line/hose. * # — Every 24 mos. or 30,000 mi. (50,000 km).										X										X
10.	Inspect fuel tank, cap, and pipe/hoses. * # — Every 24 mos. or 30,000 mi. (50,000 km).										X										X
11.	Inspect engine accessory drive belt and coolant hoses. — Every 12 mos. or 18,000 mi. (30,000 km).						X						X						X		
12.	Replace engine air filter. * — Every 36 mos. or 30,000 mi. (50,000 km).										X										X
13.	Flush cooling system, change coolant and check pressure cap. * — Every 36 mos. or 36,000 mi. (60,000 km).												X								
14.	Replace fuel filter. — Every 48 mos. or 60,000 mi. (100,000 km).																				X

* An emission control service.
\# The U.S. Environmental Protection Agency has determined that the failure to perform the maintenance item will not nullify the emission warranty or limit recall liability prior to the completion of vehicle useful life. Saturn, however, urges that all recommended maintenance services be performed at the indicated intervals and the maintenance be recorded in Section C of the owner's maintenance booklet.

TORQUE SPECIFICATIONS

Component	U.S.	Metric
Air cleaner fasteners		
SOHC engine	35 inch lbs.	4 Nm
DOHC engine	27 inch lbs.	3 Nm
Air inlet duct	62 inch lbs.	7 Nm
Battery cable	151 inch lbs.	17 Nm
Battery hold down/heat shield fasteners	80 inch lbs.	9 Nm
Belt tensioner and pulley fasteners	22 ft. lbs.	30 Nm
Engine coolant drain plug	26 ft. lbs.	35 Nm
Fuel filter bracket mounting nuts	27 inch lbs.	3 Nm
Fuel filter band clamp nut	89 inch lbs.	10 Nm
Oil filter adapter	22 ft. lbs.	30 Nm
Oil pan drain plug	27 ft. lbs.	37 Nm
Rear wheel hub/bearing assembly mounting bolts	63 ft. lbs.	85 Nm
Rear caliper bolts	63 ft. lbs.	85 Nm
Transaxle drain plug	40 ft. lbs.	55 Nm
Upper torque axis engine mount	52 ft. lbs.	70 Nm

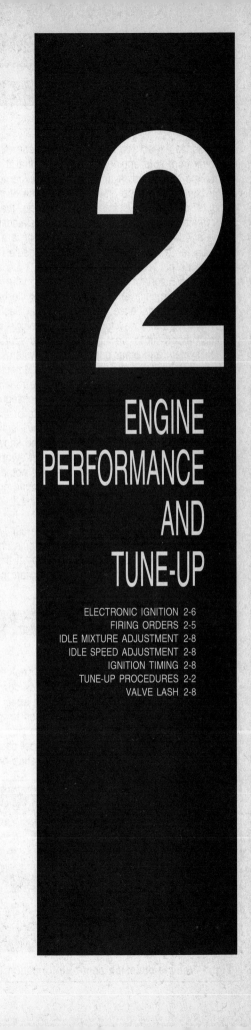

2

ENGINE PERFORMANCE AND TUNE-UP

TUNE-UP PROCEDURES

▶ See Figure 1

In order to extract the full measure of performance and economy from your engine, it is essential that it be properly maintained and tuned. A tuned engine is extremely important to the control of tailpipe emissions. Because of the many computer controlled systems on your vehicle, the annual tune-up of yesterday is gone. Today, tune-up related factors such as the air/fuel mixture, idle speed and timing are controlled and adjusted by the Powertrain Control Module (PCM) and therefore do not require periodic attention.

The most important thing you can do for your vehicle, to optimize performance and help prevent vehicle breakdown, is to follow the Maintenance Intervals Chart in Section 1. The next most important way to assure your vehicle is tuned and running properly is to thoroughly familiarize yourself with the ignition system and other engine control systems. Understanding the ignition will help you to detect subtle changes in the system which might require repair or maintenance. In other words, if you conduct regular maintenance and inspection making sure to provide your car with the proper parts and fluids, your car will stay in tune.

It is helpful to understand the system and know how it should be operating so that you can detect symptoms before problems develop. Your car's idle speed is noted in the Tune-Up Specifications chart, but can also be found on the emission information label in the engine compartment. If your Saturn is equipped with a tachometer, you can easily check for the proper idle speed whenever you are in the car.

The emission information label often reflects changes made during the model year. If the specifications on the label disagree with the Tune-Up Specifications chart in this Section, use the figures on the label.

Spark Plugs

▶ See Figure 2

A typical spark plug consists of a metal shell surrounding a ceramic insulator. A metal electrode extends downward through the center of the insulator and protrudes a small distance. Located at the end of the plug and attached to the side of the outer metal shell is the side electrode. The side electrode bends in at a 90° angle so that its tip is just past and parallel to the tip of the center electrode. The distance between these two electrodes (measured in thousandths of an inch or hundredths of a millimeter) is called the spark plug gap. The spark plug does not produce a spark but instead provides a gap across which the current can arc. The coil produces anywhere from 20,000 to 40,000 volts which travels through the wires to the spark plugs. The current passes along the center electrode and jumps the gap to the side electrode, and in doing so, ignites the fuel/air mixture in the combustion chamber.

SPARK PLUG HEAT RANGE

▶ See Figure 3

Spark plug heat range is the ability of the plug to dissipate heat. The longer the insulator (or the farther it extends into the engine), the hotter the plug will operate; the shorter the insulator (the closer the electrode is to the block's cooling passages) the cooler it will operate. A plug that absorbs little heat and remains too cool will quickly accumulate deposits of oil and carbon since it is not hot enough to burn them off. This leads to plug fouling and consequently to misfiring. A plug that absorbs too much heat will have no deposits but, due to the excessive heat, the electrodes will burn away quickly and possibly lead to preignition. Preignition takes place when plug tips get so hot that they glow sufficiently to ignite the fuel/air mixture before the actual spark occurs. This early ignition will usually cause a pinging during low speeds and heavy loads.

The general rule of thumb for choosing the correct heat range when picking a spark plug is: if most of your driving is long distance, high speed travel, use a colder plug; if most of your driving is stop and go, use a hotter plug. Original equipment plugs are generally a good compromise between the 2 styles and most people never have the need to change their plugs from the factory-recommended heat range.

REMOVAL & INSTALLATION

▶ See Figures 4, 5 and 6

Damage to the cylinder head may occur if the engine is not allowed to cool before removing the spark plugs. Remove the

Fig. 1 Vehicle emission control information label location

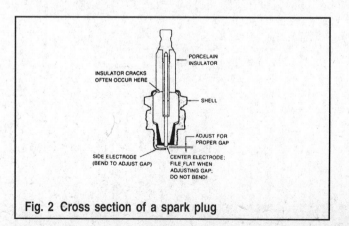

Fig. 2 Cross section of a spark plug

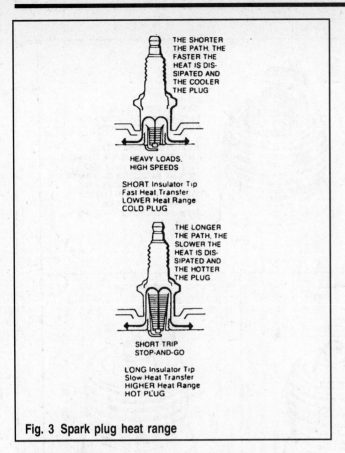

Fig. 3 Spark plug heat range

spark plugs and wires one at a time to avoid confusion and mis-wiring during installation.

1. Disconnect the negative battery cable, and if the car has been run recently, allow the engine to thoroughly cool.

2. Using compressed air, blow any water or debris from the spark plug well to assure that no harmful contaminants are allowed to enter the combustion chamber when the spark plug is removed.

3. Carefully twist the spark plug wire boot to loosen it, then pull upward and remove the boot from the plug. Be sure to pull on the boot and not on the wire, or the connector located inside the boot may become separated.

4. Using a spark plug socket that is equipped with a rubber insert to properly hold the plug, turn the spark plug counterclockwise to loosen and remove the spark plug from the bore. Be sure not to use a flexible extension on the socket. Use of a flexible extension is not necessary and could damage the spark plug insulator.

To install:

5. Inspect the spark plug boot for tears or damage. If a damaged boot is found, the spark plug wire must be replaced.

6. Using a feeler gauge, check and adjust the spark plug gap to 0.040 in. (1.02mm). When using a gauge, the proper size should pass between the electrodes with a slight drag. The next larger size should not be able to pass while the next smaller size should pass freely.

7. The replacement spark plug threads must be coated with an anti-seize compound. Saturn plugs are pre-coated, if another replacement is being used, be sure to coat the threads with a suitable compound prior to installation. Then carefully thread the plug into the bore by hand. If resistance is

felt before the plug is almost completely threaded, back the plug out and begin threading again.

✳✳WARNING

Do not use the spark plug socket to thread the plugs. Always carefully thread the plug by hand to prevent the possibility of cross-threading and damaging the cylinder head bore.

8. Using a torque wrench, tighten the spark plug to 20 ft. lbs. (27 Nm).

9. Apply a small amount of silicone dielectric compound to the end of the spark plug lead or inside the spark plug boot to prevent sticking, then install the boot to the spark plug and push until it clicks into place. The click may be felt or heard, then gently pull back on the boot to assure proper contact.

Spark Plug Wires

Visually inspect the spark plug wires for burns, cuts or breaks in the insulation. Check the spark plug boots and the coil tower connectors. Replace any damaged wiring. Using an ohmmeter, check the resistance of the wires with no spark present. Wire resistance should be below 12,000 Ohms.

When installing a new set of spark plug wires, replace the wires one at a time so there will be no mix-up. Start by replacing the longest cable first. Install the boot firmly over the spark plug. Route the wire exactly the same as the original. Connect the tower connector to the ignition coil. Repeat the process for each wire. Be sure to apply silicone dielectric

Fig. 4 Remove only 1 spark plug wire at a time to avoid confusion

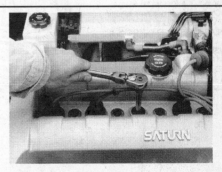

Fig. 5 Loosen and remove the plug using a spark plug socket equipped with a rubber insert

GAP BRIDGED

IDENTIFIED BY DEPOSIT BUILD—UP CLOSING GAP BETWEEN ELECTRODES.

CAUSED BY OIL OR CARBON FOULING, REPLACE PLUG, OR, IF DEPOSITS ARE NOT EXCESSIVE THE PLUG CAN BE CLEANED.

OIL FOULED

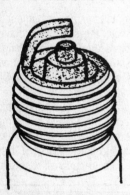

IDENTIFIED BY WET BLACK DEPOSITS ON THE INSULATOR SHELL BORE ELECTRODES.

CAUSED BY EXCESSIVE OIL ENTERING COMBUSTION CHAMBER THROUGH WORN RINGS AND PISTONS, EXCESSIVE CLEARANCE BETWEEN VALVE GUIDES AND STEMS, OR WORN OR LOOSE BEARINGS. CORRECT OIL PROBLEM. REPLACE THE PLUG.

CARBON FOULED

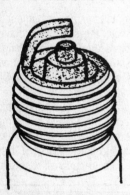

IDENTIFIED BY BLACK, DRY FLUFFY CARBON DEPOSITS ON INSULATOR TIPS, EXPOSED SHELL SURFACES AND ELECTRODES.

CAUSED BY TOO COLD A PLUG, WEAK IGNITION, DIRTY AIR CLEANER, DEFECTIVE FUEL PUMP, TOO RICH A FUEL MIXTURE, IMPROPERLY OPERATING HEAT RISER OR EXCESSIVE IDLING. CAN BE CLEANED.

NORMAL

IDENTIFIED BY LIGHT TAN OR GRAY DEPOSITS ON THE FIRING TIP.

PRE-IGNITION

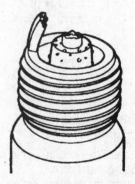

IDENTIFIED BY MELTED ELECTRODES AND POSSIBLY BLISTERED INSULATOR. METALIC DEPOSITS ON INSULATOR INDICATE ENGINE DAMAGE.

CAUSED BY WRONG TYPE OF FUEL, INCORRECT IGNITION TIMING OR ADVANCE, TOO HOT A PLUG, BURNT VALVES OR ENGINE OVERHEATING. REPLACE THE PLUG.

OVERHEATING

IDENTIFIED BY A WHITE OR LIGHT GRAY INSULATOR WITH SMALL BLACK OR GRAY BROWN SPOTS AND WITH BLUISH-BURNT APPEARANCE OF ELECTRODES.

CAUSED BY ENGINE OVER-HEATING, WRONG TYPE OF FUEL, LOOSE SPARK PLUGS, TOO HOT A PLUG, LOW FUEL PUMP PRESSURE OR INCORRECT IGNITION TIMING. REPLACE THE PLUG.

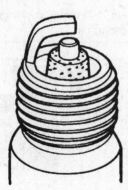

FUSED SPOT DEPOSIT

IDENTIFIED BY MELTED OR SPOTTY DEPOSITS RESEMBLING BUBBLES OR BLISTERS.

CAUSED BY SUDDEN ACCELERATION. CAN BE CLEANED IF NOT EXCESSIVE, OTHERWISE REPLACE PLUG.

Fig. 6 Inspect the spark plug to help determine engine running conditions

compound to the spark plug wire boots and tower connectors prior to installation.

If at any time all of the wires must be disconnected from the spark plugs or from the coil pack at the same time, be sure to tag the wires to assure proper reconnection. If necessary, refer to the firing order diagrams to verify proper labeling.

FIRING ORDERS

▶ See Figure 7

➡ To avoid confusion, remove and tag the wires one at a time, for replacement.

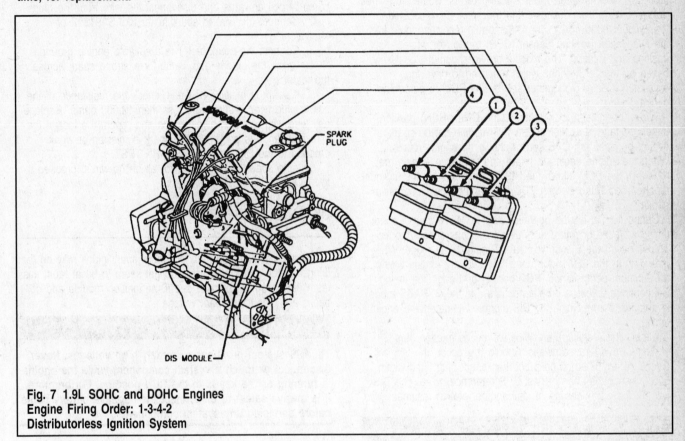

Fig. 7 1.9L SOHC and DOHC Engines
Engine Firing Order: 1-3-4-2
Distributorless Ignition System

ELECTRONIC IGNITION

Description & Operation

The Distributorless Ignition System (DIS) for both Saturn engines is an electronic system designed to provide spark for air/fuel combustion in response to timing commands from the Powertrain Control Module (PCM). System components include the PCM and the ignition module which contains 2 coil packs. Each coil pack is made up of 2 spark towers. Spark plug wires deliver voltage from the towers to the spark plugs located in the cylinder head bores. The DIS module receives inputs from the Crankshaft Position Sensor (CPS) to monitor engine position and rotation. The module provides output signals, based on the CPS signal, which are used to drive the instrument cluster tachometer and by the PCM to determine engine timing.

When the ignition is switched to the **ON**(or RUN) position, battery voltage is applied to the DIS module but no spark occurs because the CPS sensor shows no engine rotation. When the engine begins to rotate and reference signals are received, the PCM allows the DIS to fire when the first cylinder reaches Top Dead Center (TDC), the end of the compression stroke.

During normal engine operation, the PCM will control spark timing advance or retard according to various sensor inputs. This is called the Electronic Spark Timing (EST) mode. While operating in the EST mode, the PCM will vary engine timing for optimum performance. PCM control of the ignition timing will continue unless a problem occurs and the BYPASS mode is entered, during which the DIS module will determine engine timing.

If the vehicle stalls, the engine will cease rotation thus ending CPS reference pulses. Should this occur, the DIS will discharge any charged coils and halt spark plug firing within 500 milliseconds after the last CPS reference pulse. The DIS will not fire any plugs again until engine rotation resumes.

Diagnosis & Testing

Before beginning any diagnosis and testing procedures, visually inspect the components of the ignition system and check for the following:

- Discharged battery
- Damaged or loose connections
- Damaged electrical insulation
- Poor coil and spark plug connections
- Ignition module connections
- Blown fuses
- Damaged vacuum hoses
- Damaged spark plugs

Check the spark plug wires and boots for signs of poor insulation that could cause cross firing. Make sure the battery is fully charged and that all accessories are off during diagnosis and testing. Make sure the idle speed is within specification.

You will need a good quality digital volt-ohmmeter and a spark tester to check the ignition system. A spark tester resembles a spark plug without threads and the side electrode removed. Do not attempt to use a modified spark plug.

SPARK TEST

When it is suspected that a spark plug may not be firing, the simplest test consists of a visual inspection as noted above. If no loose or damaged wires can be found, each coil to plug wire should be checked for spark.

1. Twist the boot of the spark plug wire to loosen it, then carefully pull upwards and disconnect the wire from the plug.
2. Connect the wire to spark tester tool SA9199Z or equivalent.
3. Connect the spark tester to a suitable engine ground.
4. Crank the engine and watch for a strong spark across the tester gap.
5. If spark is missing or weak, check the resistance of the coil to plug wire, it should be less than 12,000 ohms. Replace any wire with too high a resistance and repeat the test. If the wire resistance is good, but the spark is missing or weak, proceed to the DIS MODULE SPARK TEST.
6. If no spark can be found for all of the wires, proceed to the NO SPARK TEST

DIS MODULE SPARK TEST

When it is suspected that 1 or more spark plugs may not be firing and the spark plug wires do not seem to be at fault, this test offers a quick check to see if the ignition module and coil packs are producing spark voltage.

✳✳CAUTION

The DIS system produces extremely high voltages. Never disconnect or touch a system component while the engine is running or the key is in the RUN position. Furthermore, it is always safest to disconnect the negative battery cable before servicing any system components.

1. Turn the ignition to the **OFF**position, then tag and disconnect all 4 spark plug wires from the ignition module towers.
2. Make sure that you are not touching the vehicle, then have a friend crank the engine for a few seconds. Sparks should appear alternately between each pair of ignition coil towers while the engine is cranking.

➡**Do not crank the engine for more than a few seconds at a time or starter damage may occur. Crank the engines for a few seconds, then release the ignition key and pause for an equal amount of time before cranking the vehicle again.**

3. If sparks appear between the 2 towers, the DIS module, Crankshaft Position Sensor (CPS) and the ignition coil packs are known to be good.
4. If a single coil pack is suspect from an initial spark test or because no sparks appeared between its 2 towers, switch the coil pack to the opposite position on the ignition module (the coil packs are interchangeable) and check to see if the problem follows it. If the problem follows, the coil pack must be replaced. If the formerly good coil pack does not produce

spark when switched with the suspect coil on the module, and the suspect coil works in the new position, then the ignition module is bad and must be replaced. Also, using an ohmmeter, check the resistance across the suspect coil's towers, it should be 7,000-10,000 ohms.

5. If no spark can be found across any tower, proceed with the NO SPARK TEST.

NO SPARK TEST

▶ **See Figure 8**

1. If no spark can be found at any spark plug or coil, you must first determine if a cranking rpm signal is present from the Crankshaft Position Sensor (CPS). This can be accomplished in various ways:

Connect a scan tool as described in Section 4 and watch for a CPS signal as the engine is cranked.

Watch the tachometer for any signs of motion as the engine is cranked.

Disconnect the 6-pin connector from the DIS ignition module and connect a voltmeter to terminal **E**(the second terminal from the end with the WHITE wire) and watch for AC voltage as the engine is cranked.

2. If it has been determined that cranking rpm is present, proceed as follows:

a. Disconnect the 6-pin connector from the DIS module, then turn the ignition key **ON**and measure the voltage to ground on terminal **A**(the ignition switch circuit). If battery voltage is not present, check for a blown fuse or an open or shorted circuit.

b. Disconnect the 5-pin connector from the DIS module, then check the resistance of terminal **E**to ground. If resistance is above 200 ohms, there is an open in the circuit. If the resistance is below 200 ohms, the problem is a loose terminal or a faulty DIS module.

3. If it has been determined that no cranking rpm is present, proceed as follows:

a. Disconnect the 5-pin connector from the DIS module, then measure the resistance between terminals **A**and **B**of the CPS. Sensor resistance should be 700-900 ohms.

b. If CPS and circuit resistance is less than specification, remove the sensor from the engine and check the resistance directly, check to see if the sensor is still magnetized and check the continuity of the sensor wiring. Replace a sensor that does not have the proper resistance and/or is demagnetized, or repair open/shorted wires.

c. If CPS resistance was within specification, set the voltmeter to the AC volt scale and connect the meter probes to terminals **A**and **B**of the DIS 5-pin connector. Crank the engine and watch for voltage. If while cranking, the sensor is putting out less than 200 millivolts, replace the CPS.

d. With the ignition key **ON**, check for voltage at terminal **A**of the DIS module 6-pin connector. If no voltage is present, check for a blown fuse or an open/short in the circuit wiring. If voltage is present, check for loose terminals or the DIS module is at fault.

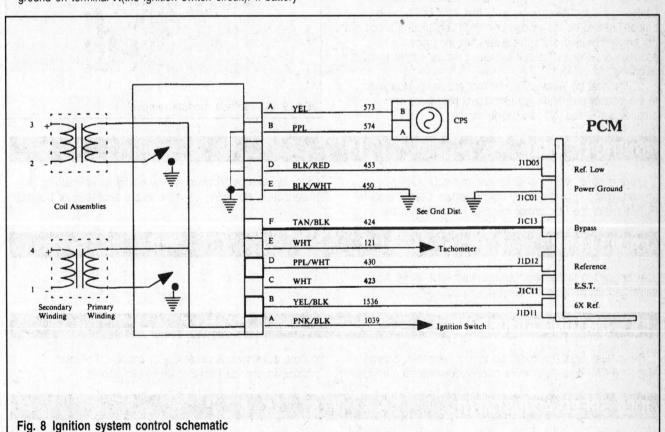

Fig. 8 Ignition system control schematic

Parts Replacement

IGNITION MODULE AND COIL PACKS

▶ See Figure 9

1. Properly disable the SIR system, if equipped, and disconnect the negative battery cable.

2. Label and disconnect the spark plug wires from the DIS ignition module located on the front side of the bell housing.

3. Disconnect the electrical connectors from the ignition module.

4. Remove the 4 retaining bolts and the DIS unit.

5. If necessary, the coils may be removed from the unit at this time by using a pair of needle-nose pliers to squeeze the retaining tabs while pulling the coils upward.

To install:

6. If removed, install the coils to the ignition module by aligning the coils with the module terminals, then carefully guiding the coils into position.

7. Run a 6x1.0mm tap through the module mounting holes on the bell housing to remove any remaining thread sealant residue and verify that the module and bell housing mating surfaces are clean and free from grit or dirt.

8. Always use new module mounting bolts. Install the ignition module/coil assembly using the new bolts equipped with factory applied thread sealant and tighten the bolts to 61 inch lbs. (7 Nm) using a torque wrench. Be careful when tightening the mounting bolts, verify that each bolt head is properly seated on the module unit when tightened. If a bolt is not properly seated when torque reaches the proper specification, remove the bolt and clean the bore threads again using the tap.

9. Connect the electrical connectors and spark plug wires to the module unit. Make sure the spark plug wires are properly connected to avoid engine damage.

10. Connect the negative battery cable and, if equipped, properly enable the SIR system.

11. Start the engine and check operation.

CRANKSHAFT POSITION SENSOR (CPS)

1. Disconnect the negative battery cable.

2. Raise and support the vehicle safely.

3. Disconnect the electrical connector from the sensor located at the lower rear of the engine block.

4. Remove the sensor retaining bolt, then remove the sensor from the engine.

To install:

5. Lubricate the sensor O-ring with clean engine oil and install the sensor into the engine block.

6. Install the sensor retaining bolt and tighten to 80 inch lbs. (9 Nm).

7. Connect the CPS electrical connection.

8. Lower the vehicle and connect the negative battery cable.

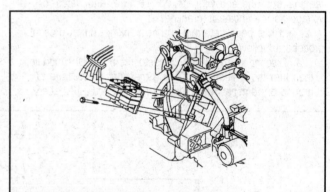

Fig. 9 DIS ignition module removal

IGNITION TIMING

There is no conventional distributor for the DIS system. Instead, timing is controlled by the Powertrain Control Module (PCM) and/or the DIS ignition module. The PCM has the ability to advance or retard ignition timing for optimal engine performance. No timing adjustments are necessary or possible.

VALVE LASH

All engines in this section use hydraulic valve lifters. No valve lash adjustments are necessary or possible.

IDLE MIXTURE ADJUSTMENT

The air/fuel mixture is controlled by the Powertrain Control Module (PCM) during all modes of operation, therefore no idle mixture adjustment is necessary or possible. For more information see the Fuel Section of this manual.

IDLE SPEED ADJUSTMENT

▶ See Figure 10

The idle stop screw controls the minimum idle speed of the engine, from which the PCM will raise idle speed as necessary for operating condition and load. The stop screw is preset at the factory and requires no periodic adjustments. Adjustments should be performed ONLY when the throttle body has been replaced and/or proper idle speed cannot be obtained. Be aware that improper adjustment of the minimum idle speed could result in false PCM trouble codes, idle instability and problems with shifting of the automatic transaxle.

The engine should be at normal operating temperature, the A/C and cooling fans should be OFF when making adjustments.

1. Because residue accumulation can affect idle speed, clean the throttle body bore before making any adjustments. Use a clean rag and a carburetor cleaner that does not contain methyl ethyl ketone. Take extreme care not to scratch or damage the throttle body bore or valve. Then check the idle speed to be sure adjustment is necessary. Proper idle speeds are as follows:

  a. SOHC with manual or automatic transaxle in N — 700-800 rpm

  b. SOHC with automatic transaxle in D — 600-700 rpm

  c. SOHC with automatic transaxle in D and A/C ON — 725-825 rpm

  d. DOHC with manual transaxle in N — 800-900 rpm

  e. DOHC with automatic transaxle in D — 700-800 rpm.

2. Block the wheels and apply the parking brake.

3. Connect IAC tester SA9195E or equivalent, to the IAC valve at the throttle body, a suitable scan tool to the diagnostic connector under the dash or the equivalent of either to the appropriate location. Use the tool to bottom the IAC pintle in the throttle. If a scan tool was used, disconnect the IAC valve electrical connector after the pintle is bottomed to make sure it remains bottomed.

4. Remove the idle stop screw plug or cover. For SOHC engines, remove the plug by piercing it with an awl and applying leverage. On DOHC engines, remove the idle stop screw cover.

5. Insert the IAC air plug in the throttle body; use tool SA9196E for TBI or tool SA9106E for MFI or an equivalent plug.

6. Connect the Saturn Portable Diagnostic Tool (PDT) or equivalent scan tool to the Assembly Line Diagnostic Link (ALDL) located under the dash, start the engine and check the minimum idle speed. Minimum idle speed should be 450-650 rpm for all engines.

7. If not within specification adjust the idle screw to obtain a minimum idle speed of 500-600 rpm.

8. Turn the ignition OFF and reconnect the IAC electrical connector.

9. Using the scan tool, check the TPS voltage. Do not replace the TPS unless setting is not between 0.35-0.70 volts.

10. Remove the IAC air plug and install the idle stop plug or cover.

11. Start the engine and check for proper idle operation.

12. Shut the engine OFF and remove the scan tool.

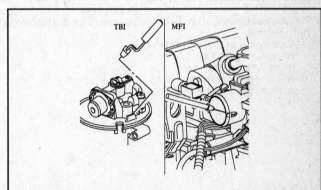

Fig. 10 Insert the IAC air plug into the throttle body

ENGINE TUNE-UP SPECIFICATIONS

Year	Engine ID/VIN	Engine Displacement Liters (cc)	Spark Plugs Gap (in.)	Ignition Timing (deg.) MT	Ignition Timing (deg.) AT	Fuel Pump (psi)	Idle Speed (rpm)② MT	Idle Speed (rpm)② AT	Valve Clearance In.	Valve Clearance Ex.
1991	7	1.9 (1901)	0.040	①	①	31–44	850	750	Hyd.	Hyd.
	9	1.9 (1901)	0.040	①	①	26–31	750	650	Hyd.	Hyd.
1992	7	1.9 (1901)	0.040	①	①	31–44	850	750	Hyd.	Hyd.
	9	1.9 (1901)	0.040	①	①	26–31	750	650	Hyd.	Hyd.
1993	7	1.9 (1901)	0.040	①	①	31–44	850	750	Hyd.	Hyd.
	9	1.9 (1901)	0.040	①	①	26–31	750	650	Hyd.	Hyd.

NOTE: The lowest cylinder pressure should be within 75% of the highest cylinder pressure reading. For example, if the highest cylinder is 134 psi, the lowest should be 101. Engine should be at normal operating temperature with throttle valve in the wide open position.

The underhood specifications sticker often reflects tune-up specification changes in production. Sticker figures must be used if they disagree with those in this chart.

Hyd.—Hydraulic

① These engines are equipped with Distributor-less Ignition System (DIS), therefore the ignition timing is not adjustable.

② Manual speed with transmission in N
Automatic speed with transmission in D

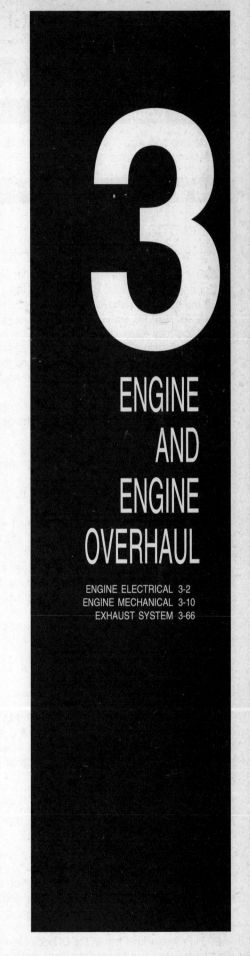

3

ENGINE AND ENGINE OVERHAUL

ENGINE ELECTRICAL

Ignition Components

For testing and repair of ignition components, see Section 2 of this manual (Electronic Ignition).

Alternator

ALTERNATOR PRECAUTIONS

Several precautions must be observed with alternator equipped vehicles to avoid damage to the unit.
- If the battery is removed for any reason, make sure it is reconnected with the correct polarity. Reversing the battery connections may result in damage to the one-way rectifiers.
- When utilizing a booster battery as a starting aid, always connect the positive to positive terminals and the negative terminal from the booster battery to a good engine ground on the vehicle being started.
- Never use a fast charger as a booster to start vehicles.
- Disconnect the battery cables when charging the battery with a fast charger.
- Never attempt to polarize the alternator.
- Do not use test lights of more than 12 volts when checking diode continuity.
- Do not short across or ground any of the alternator terminals.
- The polarity of the battery, alternator and regulator must be matched and considered before making any electrical connections within the system.
- Never separate the alternator on an open circuit. Make sure all connections within the circuit are clean and tight.
- Disconnect the battery ground terminal when performing any service on electrical components.
- Disconnect the battery if arc welding is to be done on the vehicle.

DIAGNOSIS & TESTING

Whenever troubleshooting the charging system, always check for obvious problems before proceeding, such as loose belts, bad electrical or battery connections, blown fuses, broken wires, etc. The battery must be in good condition and in the proper state of charge.

When performing the following tests, inspect the serpentine accessory drive belt to make sure it is properly tensioned. Also, make sure the ignition is **OFF** before connecting or disconnecting test equipment.

System Function Test

1. Turn the ignition key to the **OFF** position and verify that the charge lamp (which looks like a battery and is located in the left lamp grouping of the instrument cluster) is not illuminated.
2. Turn the ignition key to the **ON** position and verify that the charge lamp illuminates. If the lamp does not illuminate,

check that the battery contains the proper charge and charge if necessary, then make sure the alternator and battery connections are clean and tight.

3. Start the engine and verify that the charge lamp extinguishes and remains unlit as long as the engine is running.

ARBST Alternator Test
▶ See Figure 1

This test requires a special charging system electrical tester. If one is not available but a carbon pile load tester and voltmeter is available, perform the Carbon Pile Load Alternator Test.

✳✳CAUTION

During this test, be sure to wear safety glasses and to remove all hand jewelry such as rings, watches, etc.

1. Clean the battery terminals, then attach the red clamp of the ARBST or an equivalent charging system testing tool to the positive terminal and the black tester clamp to the negative terminal.
2. Clamp the tester probe to the negative battery terminal wire as pictured. Make sure the arrow on the probe points towards the battery. On vehicles equipped with ABS, it may be easier to clamp the probe on the wire to the far side of the master cylinder and ABS control module.
3. Press the CHARGING SYSTEM TEST button and watch the display, it should read 4 or the correct number of cylinders for the engine. If it does not, press the number 4 on the keypad.
4. Start the engine and run at 2000 rpm until the tester display flashes MAINTAIN 2000 RPM. Hold the engine speed as the counter on the display counts downward from 10 seconds, then run the engine at idle.
5. Continue to run the engine at idle until the tester display reads MAINTAIN IDLE, then continue to idle the engine for a few additional seconds until the tester reads TEST COMPLETE.
6. Turn the engine **OFF** and press the CONTINUE button to display the test results. The tester will display the system current and voltage. The tester may also give a diode pattern reading, which can generally be ignored for all Saturns. The proper current and voltage readings should be as follows:
   a. If the battery is good, voltage output should read above 13 volts.
   b. If the alternator is good, the current produced should be at least 60 amps or within 15 amps of the alternator rating.
7. If the readings are not as specified, check the following:
   a. Make sure the battery is good and that it is properly charged.
   b. Verify that the vehicle does not have any excessive electrical loads. Make sure all accessories are **OFF** and disconnect any aftermarket electrical devices, then repeat the test to check for any differences.

c. If available, replace the alternator with a known good part, then repeat the test to verify the original alternator was bad.

Carbon Pile Load Alternator Test
▶ See Figure 2

1. Make sure the battery is properly charged (a green eye is visible through the built-in hydrometer) and that all battery and alternator connections are clean and tight.

2. Install the red tester cable to the positive battery terminal and the black cable to the negative battery terminal.

3. Clamp the ammeter connection to 1 of the battery terminals.

4. Start the engine, then run at 2000 rpm and observe the voltmeter, if the voltage is uncontrolled or exceeds 16 volts, the alternator is bad.

5. If the voltage is below 16 volts, turn the carbon pile load tester **ON** and, while maintaining 2000 rpm, adjust the tester to obtain a maximum current reading on the ammeter. Do not allow the voltage to fall below 13 volts.

6. If the output current is greater than 60 amps or within 15 amps of the rated alternator voltage, the alternator is good.

REMOVAL & INSTALLATION

▶ See Figures 3, 4, 5 and 6

1. Disconnect the negative battery cable.

2. Remove the power steering pump according to the procedure in Section 8 of this manual. The pump must be removed in order to gain access to the alternator fasteners. It may be possible to remove the pump fasteners and reposition the pump sufficiently without disconnecting the pump fluid lines. If this is attempted, make sure that the lines are not stretched, kinked or otherwise damaged, otherwise the lines will have to be replaced and the extra work which was to be avoided will become necessary and more costly.

3. Remove the alternator splash shield attaching bolt and unclip the shield from the alternator.

4. Disconnect the alternator electrical connector, then remove the retaining nut and wire from the stud on the back of the alternator.

5. Remove the upper and lower alternator attaching bolts.

➡**Although the alternator fasteners can usually be removed from under the vehicle's hood, access to the lower fastener may be difficult. If necessary, raise and support the vehicle safely and attempt to remove the fastener from underneath the vehicle. If even this is too difficult, remove the passenger side tire and splash shield to access the lower alternator bolt, then remove the bolt and the alternator through the opening.**

6. Lift the alternator through the opening between the shock tower and the intake manifold and remove the alternator from the vehicle.

To install:

7. Position the alternator in the vehicle and install the lower attaching bolt.

8. Install the upper attaching bolt and the 2 wiring harness connectors.

9. Tighten the alternator attaching bolts to 27 ft. lbs. (37 Nm), then tighten the alternator positive terminal nut to 89 inch lbs. (10 Nm).

10. If removed, install the vehicle passenger's side tire and splash shield, then remove the supports and lower the vehicle.

11. Install the alternator splash shield and tighten the fastener bolt to 89 inch lbs. (10 Nm).

12. If repositioned or removed, install the power steering pump assembly.

13. Connect the negative battery cable.

14. If the power steering pump fluid lines were disconnected, it will be necessary to bleed the power steering system in order to assure proper and safe operation.

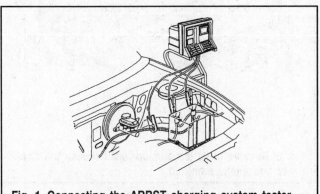

Fig. 1 Connecting the ARBST charging system tester

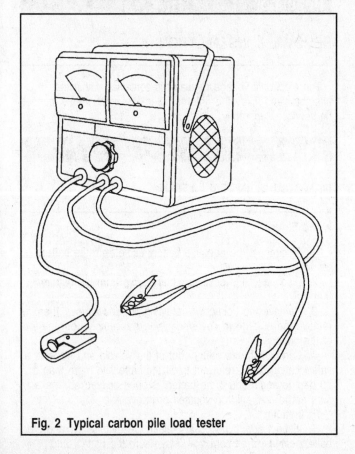

Fig. 2 Typical carbon pile load tester

Fig. 3 A view of the alternator location from underneath the vehicle — DOHC engine

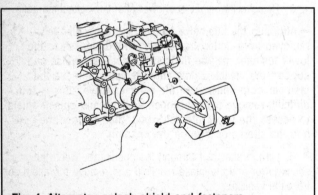

Fig. 4 Alternator splash shield and fasteners

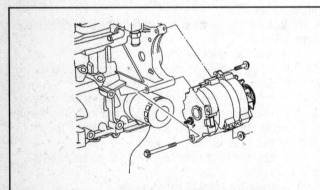

Fig. 5 Exploded view of the alternator mounting

Fig. 6 Remove the alternator upward between the shock tower and intake manifold

Regulator

REMOVAL & INSTALLATION

The electronic voltage regulator is contained within the alternator and, like other internal alternator components, cannot be serviced separately.

Battery

REMOVAL & INSTALLATION

▶ See Figure 7

1. Disconnect the negative battery cable from the battery terminal.
2. Disconnect the positive battery cable from the battery terminal.
3. Remove the hold-down retaining nut and screws, then remove the hold down cover/heat shield assembly from the top of the battery.
4. Carefully lift the battery out of the vehicle and place in a safe location. Be careful not to tilt the battery to more than a 40 degree angle and if the battery is open or cracked, make sure not to spill acid on yourself or the vehicle.
To install:
5. Inspect and, if necessary, clean the battery tray and the battery cables of all corrosion. Make sure the battery and

terminals are free of cracks or damage and that the terminals are also free of corrosion.

6. Carefully lower the battery into position in the battery tray. Do not allow the terminals to short to any bare metal during installation.

7. Position the hold down cover/heat shield over the battery and install the fasteners. Tighten the nut and screws to 80 inch lbs. (9 Nm).

8. Connect the positive battery cable and tighten to 151 inch lbs. (17 Nm).

9. Connect the negative battery cable and tighten to 151 inch lbs. (17 Nm).

Starter

DIAGNOSIS & TESTING

▶ See Figure 8

Before testing the starting system, perform a preliminary visual check. Inspect the wiring and connections for the battery cable and the starter solenoid, then check the ignition switch for proper operation. When the switch is turned **ON**, the instrument cluster lights should illuminate and accessories such as the radio may be operated. Check the instrument panel junction block for blown fuses. The ignition fuse 'IGN3" must be intact.

Clutch Start Safety Switch

On vehicles equipped with a manual transaxle, a clutch safety switch is mounted on the clutch pedal bracket to prevent starting the vehicle unless the pedal is depressed. If the switch is suspected, check it as follows:

1. Disconnect the electrical connector from the switch and position a digital volt-ohmmeter to test resistance through the switch.

2. The circuit should be open (infinite resistance) when the clutch pedal is in the clutch engaged or upper position.

3. Fully depress the clutch pedal and check resistance, if the switch is good resistance should be below 2 ohms.

Neutral Start Safety Switch

On vehicles equipped with an automatic transaxle, a neutral safety switch is mounted on the rear side of the transaxle bell housing to prevent starting the vehicle unless the shifter is in **NEUTRAL** or **PARK**. If the switch is suspected, check it as follows:

1. Disconnect the electrical connector from the neutral safety switch that contains only 2-pins. These should be terminals **A** and **B**.

2. With the transaxle in **REVERSE**, **3RD** or **2ND**, measure the resistance of the switch across terminals **A** and **B**, the circuit should be open (infinite resistance).

3. With the transaxle in **PARK** or **NEUTRAL**, the resistance across the two switch terminals should be less than 2 ohms.

ARBST Starter and Solenoid Test

1. Clean the battery terminals, then attach the red clamp of the ARBST or an equivalent starting system testing tool to the positive terminal and the black tester clamp to the negative terminal.

2. Clamp the gray tester probe to the positive battery terminal cable, making sure the arrow on the probe points towards the starter motor solenoid. On vehicles equipped with ABS, it may be easier to clamp the probe on the wire to the far side of the master cylinder and ABS control module.

3. Make sure the ignition switch is in the **OFF** position and disable the ignition system by disconnecting the electrical connector from the DIS ignition module. Use extreme caution when disconnecting the electrical connector if the negative battery cable is still connected. To be safest, disconnect the negative battery cable before disabling the module, then reconnect the cable so the test can be conducted.

4. Position the tester so that the display can be seen from the driver's seat, then press the STARTER TEST button on the ARBST tester and watch for the module to instruct you it is time for the next step.

5. When the module reads CRANK ENGINE, turn the ignition to the **START** position and hold while the tester display remains the same. The tester should read CRANK ENGINE for approximately 15 seconds.

6. When the display changes, release the ignition switch and read the tester display.

7. Proper system information should be displayed as follows:

   a. Cranking Amps (average amperage drawn by the starter motor during cranking) should be 70-130 amps depending on engine temperature.

   b. Cranking voltage (average battery voltage during cranking) should be above 9.5 volts. If lower, check the battery for proper charge and condition. Keep in mind that good cranking voltage and a slow starter speed is often caused by loose or corroded cables.

   c. GOOD/BAD STARTER. If the tester reads BAD STARTER, replace the starter only after determining that there are no flywheel binding or engine mechanical problems.

REMOVAL & INSTALLATION

▶ See Figures 9, 10, 11 and 12

1. Disconnect the negative battery cable.

2. Remove the air inlet tube and fresh air hose. For the DOHC engine, the resonator must be lifted for disengagement from the engine support bracket.

3. Remove the upper starter bolts using the access hole provided next to the intake manifold support. If necessary, remove the intake support bracket for ease of removal.

4. Raise and support the vehicle safely.

5. Remove the starter shield pin by pulling on it with pliers, then lift and release the shield from the solenoid.

6. Spray the solenoid electrical connection nuts and studs with penetrating oil and allow it to seep in for a minute to

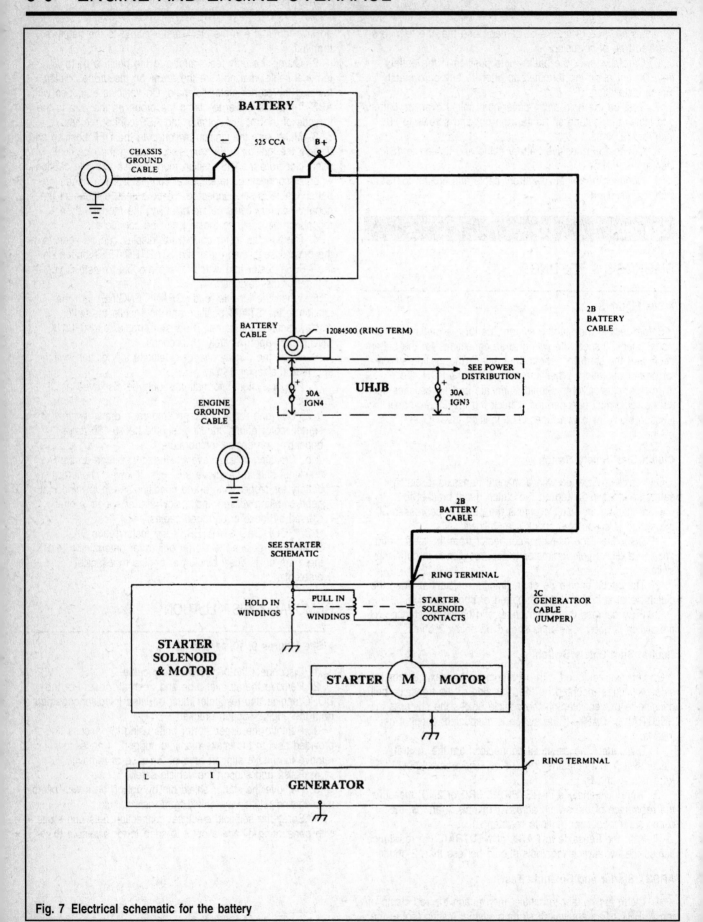

Fig. 7 Electrical schematic for the battery

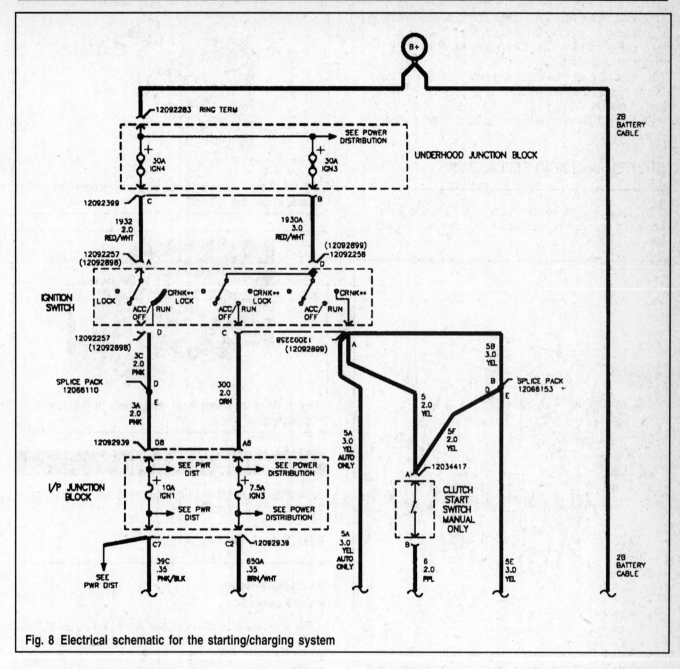

Fig. 8 Electrical schematic for the starting/charging system

loosen the connections. While the oil is soaking in, tag the solenoid electrical connectors for identification during assembly.

➡ **NOTE:It is very important that the solenoid electrical connection nuts and studs are sprayed with penetrating oil prior to removal to avoid damage to the solenoid end cap. A cracked cap will allow debris and moisture to enter and corrode the solenoid contacts.**

7. Carefully loosen the bolts and disconnect the starter electrical connectors. Position the wires to the side and out of the way.

8. Remove the lower starter bolt.

9. Remove the bolt attaching the starter rear support bracket to the vehicle.

10. Rotate the starter until the bracket misses the axle shaft support bracket. Then carefully support the starter, pulling it rearward and toward the left side of the vehicle to remove it.

To install:

11. If removed, install the rear starter support bracket to the starter. Tighten the bracket nuts to 7 ft. lbs. (9 Nm).

12. Guide the starter into the bellhousing and rotate the assembly until the lower bolt hole in the starter aligns.

13. Verify that the bracket is properly aligned and loosely install the bracket bolt, then loosely install the housing bolts. It may be necessary to raise or lower the vehicle for access to both the upper and lower bolts, but do not tighten any bolts until all of the starter and bracket bolts have been started.

14. Torque the mounting bolts to 27 ft. lbs. (37 Nm) and the bracket bolt to 22 ft. lbs. (30 Nm).

15. Reconnect the electrical connectors and install the nuts. Be careful not to overtighten the nuts and crack the solenoid end cap. Tighten the starter positive terminal to 89 inch lbs. (10 Nm) and the solenoid terminal to 44 inch lbs. (5 Nm).

16. Install the shield and push pin, being careful that the pin is positioned for possible future removal.

17. Lower the vehicle and if removed, install the intake manifold support bracket.

18. Install the air intake tube and fresh air hose. For the DOHC engine, verify the resonator is properly located in the support bracket.

19. Connect the negative battery cable and verify proper operation.

STARTER SOLENOID REPLACEMENT

The Saturn original equipment starter and solenoid are a single unit and must be replaced as an assembly if the unit fails.

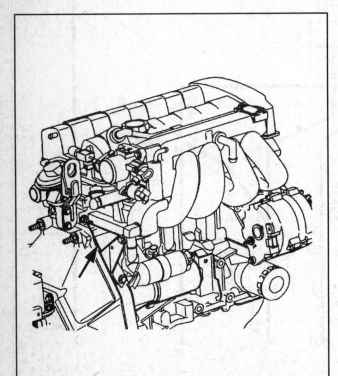

Fig. 9 Use the access hole provided in the intake manifold support bracket to reach the upper starter bolt.

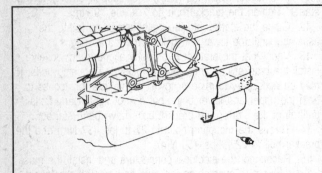

Fig. 10 Starter shield and retaining pin

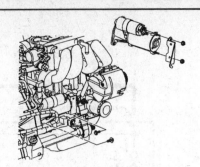

Fig. 11 If the starter is to be replaced, remove the bracket from the old part

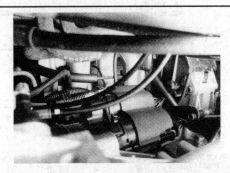

Fig. 12 View of starter from underneath the vehicle — DOHC engine

Sending Units and Sensors

For additional sensors not covered here, see Section 2 or Section 4 of this manual.

REMOVAL & INSTALLATION

Oil Pressure Sensor
▶ See Figure 13

The oil pressure sensor is located in the rear center of the block, facing the firewall. The sensor is slightly below and toward the passenger's side of the vehicle from the knock sensor.

1. Disconnect the negative battery cable.
2. Disconnect the sensor electrical connector.
3. Using a 3 inch long wobble drive extension and a 3/4 inch (19mm) crows foot, carefully loosen and remove the sensor from the engine block.

➡ NOTE:If it is too difficult to access the sensor from the engine compartment, raise and support the vehicle safely, then loosen and remove the sensor from underneath the vehicle.

To install:

4. Install the oil pressure sensor to the engine block and tighten to 26 ft. lbs. (35 Nm).
5. Connect the oil pressure sensor electrical connector.

6. If raised, remove the supports and carefully lower the vehicle.

7. Connect the negative battery cable.

Knock Sensor

▶ See Figure 14

The knock sensor is located in the rear center of the block, facing the firewall. The sensor is slightly above and toward the driver's side of the vehicle from the oil pressure sensor.

1. If equipped, properly disable the SIR system, then disconnect the negative battery cable.

2. Raise and support the vehicle safely

3. Squeeze the sides of the sensor electrical connector and carefully pull it free of the sensor. Do not remove the connector by pulling on the wires or damage may occur.

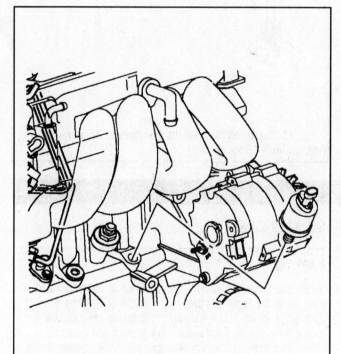

Fig. 13 The oil pressure sensor is located on the rear of the engine block between the alternator and the knock sensor

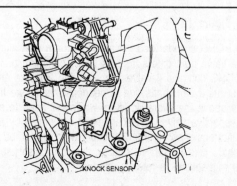

Fig. 14 Knock sensor location

4. Loosen and remove the sensor from the engine block using a suitable box wrench or socket.

To install:

5. Install the sensor to the engine block and tighten to 133 inch lbs. (15 Nm).

6. Push the electrical connector onto the sensor until a click is heard, then gently pull back to verify a firm connection.

7. Remove the supports and carefully lower the vehicle.

8. Connect the negative battery cable, and if equipped, properly arm the SIR system.

Handwheel Sensor

▶ See Figure 15

Some sport coupes are equipped with a handwheel sensor which supplies information on how fast the steering wheel is turning to help determine the proper amount of power assist the steering system should provide. On these vehicles, the sensor is located at the base of the steering column between the intermediate shaft joint and the lower column.

1. Disconnect the negative battery cable.

2. Rotate the steering wheel until the clamp bolt at the lower steering column and intermediate shaft joint is accessible. Remove the clamp bolt from the base of the steering column.

3. Slide the intermediate shaft from the lower steering column, then remove the sensor locking tabs and remove the sensor from the column support bracket.

4. Rotate the sensor 180 degrees to access the electrical connector, then disconnect the connector from the sensor and remove the sensor from the vehicle.

To install:

5. Position the sensor onto the lower steering column with the electrical terminal facing upward, then connect the sensor electrical connector.

6. Snap the sensor locking tabs into the bracket, securing the sensor to the steering column. The sensor electrical connector should remain facing upward.

7. Position the intermediate shaft onto the lower steering column and install the clamp bolt. Tighten the bolt to 35 ft. lbs. (47 Nm) using a suitable torque wrench.

8. Connect the negative battery cable.

Power Steering Pressure Switch

▶ See Figure 16

Vehicles built in 1991 may contain a power steering pressure switch. The switch is designed to monitor hydraulic system pressure and signal the PCM should is become too great. Should this occur, the PCM would increase idle and shut off the A/C compressor (if in use) to compensate for power steering pump load.

1. Disconnect the negative battery cable.

2. Raise and support the vehicle safely.

3. Disconnect the electrical connector from the pressure switch.

4. Carefully loosen and remove the switch from the power steering rack.

5. Inspect the O-ring seal on the switch, and if necessary remove and replace with a new seal.

To install:

6. Install the switch and O-ring seal to the rack, then tighten the switch to 97 inch lbs. (11 Nm).

7. Connect the switch electrical connector.

8. Remove the supports and lower the vehicle, then connect the negative battery cable.

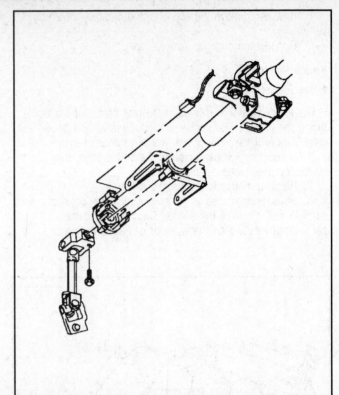

Fig. 15 Exploded view of the handwheel sensor mounting — Coupes only

ENGINE MECHANICAL

Description

ENGINE BLOCK

▶ See Figure 17

Both engines use the same lower half or block assembly, consisting of 4 cylinders situated in-line within a lost foam cast aluminum block. A cast iron crankshaft is supported in the block by 5 main bearing saddles. The cylinder bores are equipped with interference fit cast iron liners on which the piston rings seat. Aluminum alloy pistons drive the crankshaft by means of connecting rods.

Saturn is the first company to use the lost foam casting process on such a scale. In lost foam casting, an exact duplicate of the part, in this case a block, is made from polystyrene beads that resemble styrofoam. This cast can be used 1 time only as it is 'lost" or destroyed while producing the part. During the process molten metal is poured into a special case filled with sand and the polystyrene cast. The metal displaces the polystyrene cast and forms an exact duplicate. In this method, extremely complex components of the block which would otherwise necessitate machining are formed exactly during casting. If you look at the block or cylinder heads, you will notice that they look like styrofoam painted metallic gray.

SOHC ENGINE

▶ See Figure 18

Like the block, the SOHC cylinder head is aluminum and is cast using the lost foam process. It contains 2 valves per cylinder; 1 intake and 1 exhaust. The valves are actuated by rocker arms driven by the camshaft through the hydraulic lifters. The camshaft, which is supported in the cylinder head on 5 camshaft bearings, is driven off of the crankshaft by way of a steel timing chain. A ratchet mechanism is used to keep the chain tight.

DOHC ENGINE

▶ See Figure 19

The DOHC cylinder head is also lost foam cast aluminum, but the valve train differs from its single camshaft brethren. The DOHC contains 4 valves per cylinder; 2 intake and 2 exhaust. Its 2 camshafts ride in bearings that locate the shafts directly above the hydraulic lifters which are used to activate their respective valves. The camshafts are driven by a single hydraulic tensioned steel timing chain which is turned by the crankshaft. Like the SOHC engine, the chain also uses a ratchet mechanism to retain tightness.

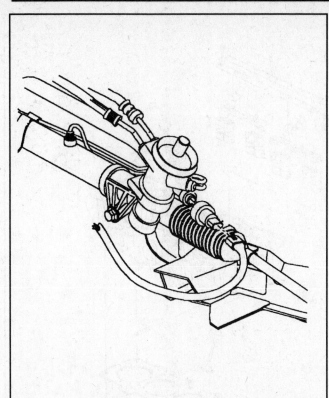

Fig. 16 Power steering pressure switch — 1991 vehicles only

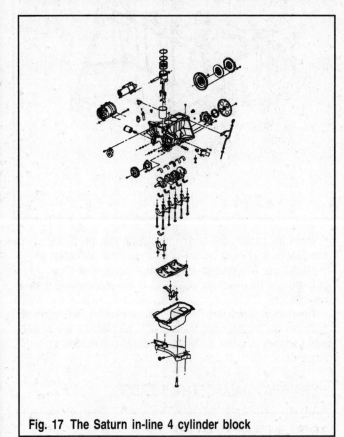

Fig. 17 The Saturn in-line 4 cylinder block

Engine Overhaul Tips

Most engine overhaul procedures are fairly standard. In addition to specific parts replacement procedures and complete specifications for your individual engine, this section also is a guide to accepted rebuilding procedures. Examples of standard rebuilding practice are shown and should be used along with specific details concerning your particular engine.

Competent and accurate machine shop services will ensure maximum performance, reliability and engine life. In most instances it is more profitable for the do-it-yourself mechanic to remove, clean and inspect the component, buy the necessary parts and deliver these to a shop for actual machine work.

On the other hand, much of the rebuilding work (crankshaft, block, bearings, piston, rods, and other components) is still within the scope of the do-it-yourself mechanic.

TOOLS

The tools required for an engine overhaul or parts replacement will depend on the depth of your involvement. With a few exceptions, they will be the tools found in a mechanic's tool kit (see Section 1). More in-depth work will require any or all of the following:
- dial indicator (reading in thousandths) mounted on a universal base.
- micrometers and telescope gauges.
- jaw and screw-type pullers.
- scraper.
- valve spring compressor.
- ring groove cleaner.
- piston ring expander and compressor.
- ridge reamer.
- cylinder hone or glaze breaker.
- Plastigage®.
- engine stand.

The use of most of these tools is illustrated in this section. Many can be rented for a one-time use from a local parts jobber or tool supply house specializing in automotive work.

Occasionally, the use of special tools is called for. See the information on Special Tools and the Safety Notice in the front of this book before substituting another tool.

INSPECTION TECHNIQUES

Procedures and specifications are given in this section for inspecting, cleaning and assessing the wear limits of most major components. Other procedures such as Magnaflux® and Zyglo® can be used to locate material flaws and stress cracks. Magnaflux® is a magnetic process applicable only to ferrous materials. The Zyglo® process coats the material with a fluorescent dye penetrant and can be used on any material. A check for suspected surface cracks can be more readily made using spot check dye. The dye is sprayed onto the suspected area, wiped off and area sprayed with a developer. Cracks will show up brightly.

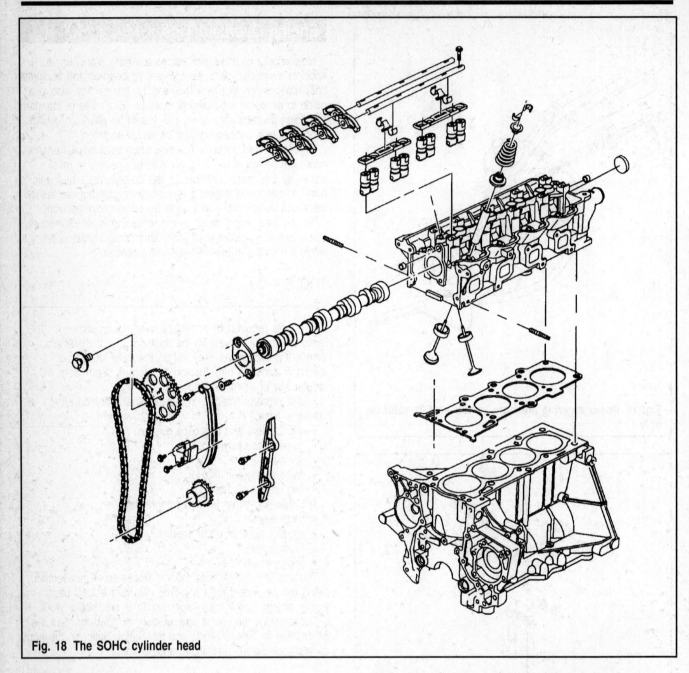

Fig. 18 The SOHC cylinder head

OVERHAUL TIPS

Aluminum has become extremely popular for use in engines, due to its low weight. Observe the following precautions when handling aluminum parts:

Never hot tank aluminum parts (the caustic hot-tank solution will eat the aluminum).

Remove all aluminum parts (identification tag, etc.) from engine parts prior to hot-tanking.

Always coat threads lightly with engine oil or anti-seize compounds before installation, to prevent seizure.

Never over-torque bolts or spark plugs, especially in aluminum threads. Stripped threads in any component can be repaired using any of several commercial repair kits (Heli-Coil®, Microdot®, Keenserts®, etc.)

When assembling the engine, any parts that will be in frictional contact must be pre-lubed to provide lubrication at initial startup. Any product specifically formulated for this purpose can be used, but engine oil is not recommended as a pre-lube.

When semi-permanent (locked, but removable) installation of bolts or nuts is desired, threads should be cleaned and coated with Loctite® or other similar, commercial non-hardening sealant.

REPAIRING DAMAGED THREADS

▶ See Figures 20, 21, 22, 23 and 24

Several methods of repairing damaged threads are available. Heli-Coil® (shown here), Keenserts® and Microdot® are among the most widely used. All involve basically the same

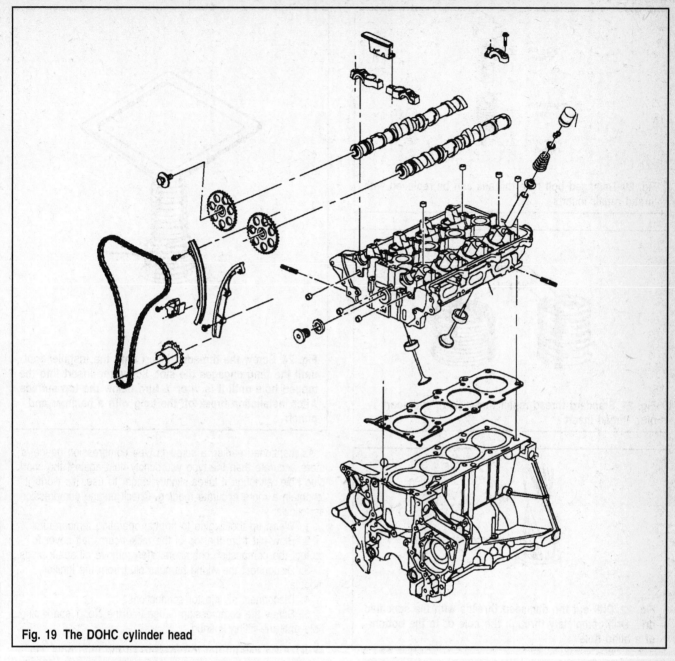

Fig. 19 The DOHC cylinder head

principle — drilling out stripped threads, tapping the hole and installing pre-wound insert — making welding, plugging and oversize fasteners unnecessary.

Two types of thread repair inserts are usually supplied: a standard type for most Inch Coarse, Inch Fine, Metric Coarse and Metric Fine thread sizes and a spark plug type to fit most spark plug port sizes. Consult the individual manufacturer's catalog to determine exact applications. Typical thread repair kits will contain a selection of pre-wound threaded inserts, a tap (corresponding to the outside diameter threads of the insert) and an installation tool. Spark plug inserts usually differ because they require a tap equipped with pilot threads and combined reamer/tap section. Most manufacturers also supply blister-packed thread repair inserts separately in addition to a master kit containing a variety of taps and inserts plus installation tools.

Before effecting a repair to a threaded hole, remove any snapped, broken or damaged bolts or studs. Penetrating oil can be used to free frozen threads; the offending item can be removed with locking pliers or with a screw or stud extractor. After the hole is clear, the thread can be repaired, as shown in the figures.

CHECKING ENGINE COMPRESSION

A noticeable lack of engine power, excessive oil consumption and/or poor fuel mileage measured over an extended period are all indicators of internal engine wear. Worn piston rings, scored or worn cylinder inserts, blown head gaskets, sticking or burnt valves and worn valve seats are all possible culprits here. A check of each cylinder's compression will help you locate the problems.

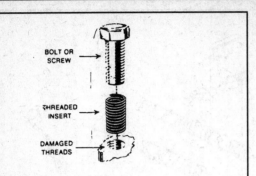

Fig. 20 Damaged bolt hole threads can be replaced with thread repair inserts

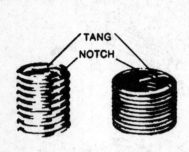

Fig. 21 Standard thread repair insert (left), and spark plug thread insert

Fig. 22 Drill out the damaged threads with the specified drill. Drill completely through the hole or to the bottom of a blind hole

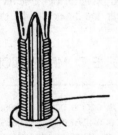

Fig. 23 With the tap supplied, tap the hole to receive the thread insert. Keep the tap well oiled and back it out frequently to avoid clogging the threads

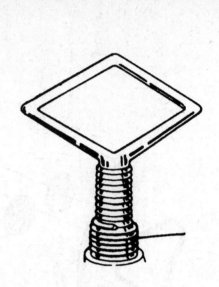

Fig. 24 Screw the threaded insert onto the installer tool until the tang engages the slot. Screw the insert into the tapped hole until it is ¼ or ½ turn below the top surface. After installation break off the tang with a hammer and punch

As mentioned earlier, a screw-in type compression gauge is more accurate than the type you simply hold against the spark plug hole, although it takes slightly longer to use. It's worth it to obtain a more accurate reading. Check engine compression as follows:

1. Warm up the engine to normal operating temperature.
2. Blow dirt from the top of the rocker/camshaft cover to protect the combustion chambers, then remove all spark plugs.
3. Disconnect the wiring harness plug from the ignition module.
4. Disconnect all injector connections.
5. Screw the compression gauge into the No. 1 spark plug hole until the fitting is snug.

➡NOTE:Be careful not to crossthread the plug hole. On aluminum cylinder heads use extra care, as the threads in these heads are easily ruined.

6. Ask an assistant to depress the accelerator pedal fully. Then, while you read the compression gauge, ask the assistant to crank the engine two or three times in short bursts using the ignition switch.
7. Read the compression gauge at the end of each series of cranks, and record the highest of these readings. Repeat this procedure for each of the engine's cylinders. Compare the highest reading to the reading in each cylinder.
8. A cylinder's compression pressure is usually acceptable if it is not less than 80% of the highest reading. For example, if the highest reading is 150 psi, the lowest should be no lower than 120 psi. No cylinder should have a reading below 100 psi.
9. If a cylinder is unusually low, pour a tablespoon of clean engine oil into the cylinder through the spark plug hole and

repeat the compression test. If the compression comes up after adding the oil, it is likely that the cylinder's piston rings and/or insert are damaged or worn. If the pressure remains low, the valves may not be seating properly (a valve job is needed), or the head gasket may be blown near that cylinder. If compression in any two adjacent cylinders is low, and if the addition of oil doesn't help the compression, there is leakage past the head gasket. Oil and coolant water in the combustion chamber can result from this problem. There may be evidence of water droplets on the engine dipstick when a head gasket has blown.

Engine

REMOVAL & INSTALLATION

▶ See Figures 25, 26, 27, 28 and 29

➡NOTE:The manufacturer recommends that the engine and transaxle be removed as a complete unit. Disconnect the cradle and lower the entire assembly instead of lifting the assembly out of the vehicle. Both the SOHC and DOHC engines are removed or installed in the same manner.

1. Properly disable the SIR system, if equipped. Disconnect the negative and then the positive battery cable.

2. Drain the engine coolant from the radiator and block drains into a suitable clean container.

✳✳CAUTION

When draining the coolant, keep in mind that cats and dogs are attracted by the ethylene glycol antifreeze, and are quite likely to drink any that is left in an uncovered container or in puddles on the ground. This will prove fatal in sufficient quantity. Always drain the coolant into a sealable container. Coolant may be reused unless it is contaminated or several years old.

3. Properly relieve the fuel system pressure as directed in Section 5 of this manual.
4. Remove the air cleaner or air intake duct, as applicable. For the DOHC engine, lift the resonator upward to disengage the button from the engine service support bracket.
5. Disconnect and label the following electrical plugs and vacuum lines, as applicable:
   a. The 2 coolant temperature sensors.
   b. Oxygen sensor and clip at the transaxle front mount bracket.
   c. Idle Air Control (IAC) valve.
   d. The 2 ignition coil module connectors.
   e. Throttle Position Sensor (TPS).
   f. Manifold Absolute Pressure (MAP) sensor.
   g. Exhaust Gas Recirculation (EGR) solenoid.
   h. Brake booster vacuum hose from the booster or intake manifold.
   i. Disconnect the 2 ground connectors from the transaxle attachment studs at the rear side of the cylinder block.

GENERAL ENGINE SPECIFICATIONS

Year	Engine ID/VIN	Engine Displacement Liters (cc)	Fuel System Type	Net Horsepower @ rpm	Net Torque @ rpm (ft. lbs.)	Bore × Stroke (in.)	Com- pression Ratio	Oil Pressure @ rpm
1991	7	1.9 (1901)	MFI	124 @ 6000	122 @ 4800	3.23 × 3.54	9.5:1	36 @ 2000
	9	1.9 (1901)	TBI	85 @ 5000	107 @ 2400	3.23 × 3.54	9.3:1	36 @ 2000
1992	7	1.9 (1901)	MFI	124 @ 5600	122 @ 4800	3.23 × 3.54	9.5:1	36 @ 2000
	9	1.9 (1901)	TBI	85 @ 5000	107 @ 2400	3.23 × 3.54	9.3:1	36 @ 2000
1993	7	1.9 (1901)	MFI	124 @ 5600	122 @ 4800	3.23 × 3.54	9.5:1	36 @ 2000
	9	1.9 (1901)	TBI	85 @ 5000	107 @ 2400	3.23 × 3.54	9.3:1	36 @ 2000

NOTE: Horsepower and torque are SAE net figures. They are measured at the rear of the transmission with all accessories installed and operating. Since the figures vary when a given engine is installed in different models, some are representative rather than exact.
MFI—Multi Point Fuel Injection
TBI—Throttle Body Injection

CAMSHAFT SPECIFICATIONS

All measurements given in inches.

Year	Engine ID/VIN	Engine Displacement Liters (cc)	Journal Diameter					Elevation		Bearing Clearance	Camshaft End Play
			1	2	3	4	5	In.	Ex.		
1991	7	1.9 (1901)	1.1398–1.1406	1.1398–1.1406	1.1398–1.1406	1.1398–1.1406	1.1398–1.1406	0.3528–0.3559	0.3409–0.3441	0.0012–0.0030	0.0020–0.0080
	9	1.9 (1901)	1.7480–1.7490	1.7480–1.7490	1.7480–1.7490	1.7480–1.7490	1.7480–1.7490	0.2531–0.2556	0.2531–0.2556	0.0020–0.0040	0.0028–0.0079
1992	7	1.9 (1901)	1.1398–1.1406	1.1398–1.1406	1.1398–1.1406	1.1398–1.1406	1.1398–1.1406	0.3528–0.3559	0.3409–0.3441	0.0012–0.0030	0.0020–0.0080
	9	1.9 (1901)	1.7480–1.7490	1.7480–1.7490	1.7480–1.7490	1.7480–1.7490	1.7480–1.7490	0.2531–0.2556	0.2531–0.2556	0.0020–0.0040	0.0028–0.0079
1993	7	1.9 (1901)	1.1398–1.1406	1.1398–1.1406	1.1398–1.1406	1.1398–1.1406	1.1398–1.1406	0.3528–0.3559	0.3409–0.3441	0.0012–0.0030	0.0020–0.0080
	9	1.9 (1901)	1.7480–1.7490	1.7480–1.7490	1.7480–1.7490	1.7480–1.7490	1.7480–1.7490	0.2531–0.2556	0.2531–0.2556	0.0020–0.0040	0.0028–0.0079

j. Fuel injector electrical connectors.

6. Disconnect the following automatic or manual transaxle electrical connectors. If access is difficult, wait until the vehicle is safely raised and supported, then unplug the connections from underneath the vehicle.:

a. The 3 neutral safety switch connectors.

b. Valve body actuator connection.

c. Turbine speed sensor.

d. Temperature sensor.

e. For manual transaxles only, the reverse light switch.

f. The 2 gear shift (PRNDL switch) connectors.

7. Disconnect the accelerator cable assembly.

8. Using service tool SA9157E or equivalent, disconnect the fuel supply and return lines at the connectors. Plug the lines to prevent fuel contamination or loss. The lines may be tied to the master cylinder lines to help prevent fuel spillage and to keep them out of the way.

9. Disconnect the upper radiator hose and the cylinder head outlet and the de-aeration hose at the engine.

10. Remove the serpentine drive belt and if equipped, remove the air conditioning compressor from its brackets and with the hoses attached. Support the compressor from the front crossbar.

➡ NOTE: It is not necessary to discharge the A/C compressor during engine removal, but be careful not to kink, damage or rupture the refrigerant lines.

11. If equipped, disconnect the automatic transaxle cooler lines at the transaxle by pinching the plastic connector tabs and carefully pulling back on the lines. Plug the openings to prevent fluid loss or contamination.

12. Disconnect the automatic transaxle shifter cable or the manual shifter cables from the transaxle.

13. If equipped with manual transaxles, remove the 2 hydraulic slave cylinder retaining nuts from the clutch housing studs, then slide the cylinder and bracket assembly from the studs. Rotate the clutch actuator 1/4 turn counterclockwise while pushing toward the housing to disengage the bayonet connector and remove it from the clutch housing. Support the clutch hydraulic system to the battery tray; being sure not to kink or pinch the hydraulic lines.

14. Using a length of an appropriate wire, tie the radiator, condenser and fan to the front crossbar. Route the wire around the 2 fan shroud supports and the crossbar.

15. Raise and support the front end of the vehicle safely.

16. Remove the front wheels and remove the fasteners connecting the side and front fender shields to the cradle.

17. Remove the brake caliper bracket attaching bolts (2 on each side) and hang the caliper assemblies from the shock tower springs using wire. Do not hang the assembly by the brake hose or damage to the brake hydraulic system may occur. The springs and shocks will remain with the body when the powertrain is lowered.

18. Disconnect the struts from the knuckles on each side of the vehicle (2 bolts per side). This will allow the knuckle and hub assembly to remain with the powertrain cradle when lowered. The stabilizer bar will remain attached to the cradle and the lower control arms.

19. Using a suitable hose clamp tool, disconnect the lower radiator and heater return hoses from the engine. Disconnect the heater inlet hose at the front of the dash or the engine.

20. Disconnect the steering shaft and pressure switch connectors at the gear, as applicable.

CRANKSHAFT AND CONNECTING ROD SPECIFICATIONS

All measurements are given in inches.

Year	Engine ID/VIN	Engine Displacement Liters (cc)	Crankshaft				Connecting Rod		
			Main Brg. Journal Dia.	Main Brg. Oil Clearance	Shaft End-play	Thrust on No.	Journal Diameter	Oil Clearance	Side Clearance
1991	7	1.9 (1901)	2.2438–2.2444	0.0002–0.0020	0.002–0.008	3	0.8500–0.8508	0.0004–0.0025	0.0065–0.1713
	9	1.9 (1901)	2.2438–2.2444	0.0002–0.0020	0.002–0.008	3	0.8500–0.8508	0.0004–0.0025	0.0065–0.1713
1992-93	7	1.9 (1901)	2.2438–2.2444	0.0002–0.0020	0.002–0.008	3	0.8500–0.8508	0.0004–0.0025	0.0065–0.1713
	9	1.9 (1901)	2.2438–2.2444	0.0002–0.0020	0.002–0.008	3	0.8500–0.8508	0.0004–0.0025	0.0065–0.1713

VALVE SPECIFICATIONS

Year	Engine ID/VIN	Engine Displacement Liters (cc)	Seat Angle (deg.)	Face Angle (deg.)	Spring Test Pressure (lbs. @ in.)	Spring Installed Height (in.)	Stem-to-Guide Clearance (in.)		Stem Diameter (in.)	
							Intake	Exhaust	Intake	Exhaust
1991	7	1.9 (1901)	44.5–45.5	45.00–45.50	163–180 @ 0.984	1.6100	0.0010–0.0025	0.0015–0.0032	0.2736–0.2740	0.2729–0.2736
	9	1.9 (1901)	44.5–45.5	44.75–45.25	202–211 @ 1.280	1.8898–1.9134	0.0010–0.0025	0.0015–0.0032	0.2736–0.2741	0.2736–0.2740
1992-93	7	1.9 (1901)	44.5–45.5	45.00–45.50	163–180 @ 0.984	1.6100	0.0010–0.0025	0.0015–0.0032	0.2736–0.2740	0.2729–0.2736
	9	1.9 (1901)	44.5–45.5	44.75–45.25	202–211 @ 1.280	1.8898–1.9134	0.0010–0.0025	0.0015–0.0032	0.2736–0.2741	0.2736–0.2740

PISTON AND RING SPECIFICATIONS

All measurements are given in inches.

Year	Engine ID/VIN	Engine Displacement Liters (cc)	Piston Clearance	Ring Gap			Ring Side Clearance		
				Top Compression	Bottom Compression	Oil Control	Top Compression	Bottom Compression	Oil Control
1991	7	1.9 (1901)	①	0.0098–0.0197	0.0098–0.0197	0.0098–0.0492	0.0016–0.0035	0.0012–0.0031	Snug
	9	1.9 (1901)	①	0.0098–0.0197	0.0098–0.0197	0.0098–0.0492	0.0016–0.0035	0.0012–0.0031	Snug
1992–93	7	1.9 (1901)	①	0.0098–0.0197	0.0098–0.0197	0.0098–0.0492	0.0016–0.0035	0.0012–0.0031	Snug
	9	1.9 (1901)	①	0.0098–0.0197	0.0098–0.0197	0.0098–0.0492	0.0016–0.0035	0.0012–0.0031	Snug

① Bore 1, 2, 3: 0.0002–0.0017
 Bore 4: 0.0006–0.0021

TORQUE SPECIFICATIONS

All readings in ft. lbs.

Year	Engine ID/VIN	Engine Displacement Liters (cc)	Cylinder Head Bolts	Main Bearing Bolts	Rod Bearing Bolts	Crankshaft Damper Bolts	Flywheel Bolts	Manifold		Spark Plugs	Lug Nut
								Intake	Exhaust		
1991	7	1.9 (1901)	②	37	33	159	59	22③	23③	20	103
	9	1.9 (1901)	①	37	33	159	59	15③	16③	20	103
1992–93	7	1.9 (1901)	②	37	33	159	59	22③	23③	20	103
	9	1.9 (1901)	①	37	33	159	59	15③	16③	20	103

① 1st step: 22 ft. lbs.
 2nd step: 33 ft. lbs.
 3rd step: 90 degrees torquing angle
② 1st step: 22 ft. lbs.
 2nd step: 37 ft. lbs.
 3rd step: 90 degrees torquing angle
③ Studs—106 inch lbs.

21. Disconnect the front exhaust pipe at the manifold, catalytic converter and powertrain stiffening bracket.

22. For 1991 vehicles, remove the powertrain stiffening bracket bolts, except the 3 bolts holding the torque resistor bracket to the transaxle.

23. Remove the flywheel cover and torque converter bolts, if equipped.

24. Remove the alternator and starter shields.

25. Label and disconnect all the remaining electrical and vacuum connectors from the following components:

    a. Unplug the connectors from the starter solenoid and the battery feed.

    b. The alternator field and battery feed connectors.

    c. Oil pressure sensor.

    d. Knock sensor.

    e. Crankshaft position sensor.

    f. If equipped, the EVO solenoid.

    g. Vehicle speed sensor.

    h. Canister purge solenoid.

    i. Powertrain Control Module (PCM) and Oxygen sensor.

    j. If equipped, the ABS wheel sensor connector grounds.

26. Unclip the brake lines from the rear side of the cradle.

27. Carefully remove the electrical harness from the engine and transaxle, then lay the electrical harness on top of the underhood junction block and battery cover.

28. For 1992-93 vehicles with a torque axis mount system, place a 1 inch **x** 1 inch **x** 2 inch long block of wood between the torque strut and cradle to ease removal and installation of the torque engine mount. Remove the 3 right side upper engine torque axis to front cover nuts and the 2 mount to midrail bracket nuts, allowing the powertrain to rest on the block of wood.

➡NOTE: **Placing a block of wood under the torque axis mount prior to removing the upper mount will allow the engine to rest on the wood, thus preventing the engine from shifting. If the engine is not to be removed from the cradle, this will allow you to install the engine and the upper mount without jacking or raising the engine.**

29. Place a powertrain support dolly under the cradle. Use two 4 inch **x** 4 inch **x** 36 inch pieces of wood to support the cradle on the dolly.

30. Remove the 2 right side front engine mount, torque strut brackets to cradle nuts.

31. Remove the 4 cradle attaching bolts and carefully lower the complete powertrain assembly from the vehicle. Verify that all necessary components are disconnected and free before complete removal.

32. Attach the 2 washers located between the cradle and body, to the cradle. They must be repositioned and installed during cradle installation.

33. Disconnect the spark plug wires at the ignition module.

34. If applicable, remove the power steering pump and bracket. Support the assembly, in an upright position, from the cradle or the steering gear.

35. Install a suitable engine lifting device to the service support brackets.

36. Remove the front mount assembly and disconnect the motion restrictor bracket, if applicable.

37. Place a ½ inch **x** 1 inch **x** 3 inch block of wood under the axle shaft and remove the starter support bracket bolt,

intake manifold support brace (on DOHC engines), and 3 axle shaft bracket support bolts. Allow the bracket to rotate rearward. Lift the engine slightly for clearance, as necessary.

38. For 1991 vehicles, remove the front engine mount assembly and disconnect the motion restrictor cable used with the DOHC engine and a manual transaxle.

39. For 1992-93 vehicles with a torque axis mount system, place a 4 inch **x** 4 inch **x** 6 inch long block of wood under the transaxle housing for support.

40. For 1992-93 vehicles, remove the engine strut bracket and torque strut from the front of the engine as an assembly. Lift the engine slightly as necessary for removal.

41. Remove the 4 transaxle attaching bolts/studs and separate the assembly. Manual transaxles will require the engine to be moved about 4 inches (100mm) forward in the cradle to disengage the input shaft.

42. Carefully lift the engine off the cradle.

To install:

43. If installing a manual transaxle, align the yellow dot on the clutch pressure plate near the mark on the flywheel. Use SA9145T or an equivalent clutch alignment tool to align the disk and input shaft, then tighten the pressure plate bolts to 19 ft. lbs. (25 Nm).

44. If installing an automatic transaxle the yellow dot on the torque converter must be in the 6 o'clock position when the first flexplate to torque converter bolt is tightened.

45. Position the engine on the cradle aligning it with the transaxle using 2 threaded 10mm **x** 6 in. guide pins in the lower attachment holes. When aligned, remove the pins and install the 4 transaxle attaching bolts along with the stiffening bracket fastener. Tighten the lower bolts to 96 ft. lbs. (130 Nm) and the upper bolts to 66 ft. lbs. (90 Nm) and the stiffening bracket to powertrain fastener to 40 ft. lbs. (54 Nm). If applicable, remove the 4 inch **x** 4 inch **x** 6 inch block of wood from under the transaxle housing.

46. Install the front engine mount assembly to the engine and tighten to 41 ft. lbs. (55 Nm). For the 1991 DOHC engine with manual transaxle, install the motion restrictor bracket and tighten to 40 ft. lbs. (54 Nm).

47. For 1991 vehicles, install the front engine mount to cradle nut and tighten to 52 ft. lbs. (70 Nm).

48. For 1992-93 vehicles, install the engine mount torque strut-to-cradle bracket and tighten the engine fasteners to 52 ft. lbs. (70 Nm). Hand-tighten the cradle fasteners, but do not torque until the upper midrail mount is installed.

49. For 1992-93 vehicles, install the 1 inch **x** 1 inch **x** 2 inch long block of wood between the torque strut and cradle to ease installation of the torque mount.

50. Attach the axle shaft and starter bracket. Tighten the axle shaft bracket fasteners to 41 ft. lbs. (55 Nm) and the starter bracket to 80 inch lbs. (9 Nm).

51. Position the powertrain and cradle assembly onto the dolly, using the 2 wooden boards to support and protect the cradle assembly.

52. Carefully lift the powertrain and cradle into position. Make sure the radiator grommets are correctly aligned and that the 2 washers are reinstalled between the cradle and body at each rear cradle attachment position. If necessary, use two /₁₆ in. **x** 18 in. long guide pins in the forward cradle holes (located next to the attaching holes) to help align the cradle. Tighten the cradle to body fasteners to 151 ft. lbs. (205 Nm).

53. Attach the brake lines to the cradle and install the steering shaft U-joint. Tighten the U-joint bolt to 35 ft. lbs. (47 Nm).

54. Position the electrical harness around the engine and connect the following components or connectors, as applicable:

    a. Starter solenoid connector and tighten to 44 inch lbs. (5 Nm).

    b. Alternator and starter battery connectors and tighten to 89 inch lbs. (10 Nm).

    c. Oil pressure sensor and tighten to 26 ft. lbs. (35 Nm).

    d. Knock sensor and tighten to 133 inch lbs. (15 Nm).

    e. Crankshaft position sensor and tighten to 80 inch lbs. (9 Nm).

    f. Canister purge valve and tighten to 22 ft. lbs. (30 Nm).

    g. Wiring harness PCM ground and tighten to 89 inch lbs. (10 Nm).

    h. Wiring harness to the transaxle case/engine block and tighten to 18 ft. lbs. (25 Nm).

    i. If equipped, the EVO solenoid.

    j. Vehicle speed sensor.

    k. Power steering pressure switch.

    l. If equipped, the ABS wheel speed sensors.

55. Install the engine stiffening bracket bolts, as applicable and tighten to 35 ft. lbs. (47 Nm).

56. Install new gaskets and the exhaust front pipe. Tighten the pipe-to-manifold fasteners to 23 ft. lbs. (31 Nm), the pipe-to-stiffener bracket fasteners to 35 ft. lbs. (47 Nm), the pipe-to-support bracket fasteners to 23 ft. lbs. (31 Nm) and the pipe-to-catalytic converter fasteners to 35 ft. lbs. (48 Nm).

57. Connect the heater, lower radiator and coolant fill hoses, then remove the radiator assembly support wires.

58. Install the cylinder block drain plug and tighten to 27 ft. lbs. (36 Nm), then close the radiator drain.

59. Install the knuckle to strut attachment bolts, tighten the bolts to 148 ft. lbs. (200 Nm).

60. Install the brake caliper assemblies and tighten the bolts to 81 ft. lbs. (110 Nm).

61. Install the shift cables using new retainers.

62. Remove the supports and carefully lower the vehicle sufficiently to gain underhood access, then reposition the supports under the vehicle.

63. If equipped with a manual transaxle, install the hydraulic clutch slave cylinder, damper and shift cables, then tighten the fasteners to 19 ft. lbs. (25 Nm).

64. If equipped, install the automatic transaxle cooler lines and/or the air conditioning compressor assembly. Tighten the compressor to front bracket bolts to 40 ft. lbs. (54 Nm) and the compressor to rear bracket bolts to 22 ft. lbs. (30 Nm).

65. Install the serpentine drive belt, making sure the belt is properly aligned in the grooves.

66. For 1992-93 vehicles equipped with a torque axis mount system, install the 2 engine mounts to midrail bracket nuts and tighten to 52 ft. lbs. (70 Nm). Next install the 3 mount to front cover nuts, tighten them uniformly to 52 ft. lbs. (70 Nm) in order to prevent front cover damage. Then remove the block of wood from under the torque strut.

67. For 1992-93 vehicles, tighten the strut bracket-to-cradle nuts to 52 ft. lbs. (70 Nm).

68. If equipped, install the automatic transaxle torque converter to flexplate bolts. Tighten the bolts to 52 ft. lbs. (70 Nm). Install the dust cover and tighten to 89 inch lbs. (10 Nm).

69. Install the tires and splash shields, tightening the lug nuts to 103 ft. lbs. (140 Nm). Remove the supports and carefully lower the vehicle to the ground.

70. Attach the following electrical and vacuum connections:

    a. Coolant temperature sensors.

    b. Oxygen sensor.

    c. IAC valve.

    d. Fuel injector connectors.

    e. The 2 ignition coil module connectors.

    f. TPS connector.

    g. MAP sensor.

    h. EGR solenoid.

    i. If equipped, the A/C compressor.

    j. The brake booster hose to the intake manifold or booster.

    k. The ground connectors to the transaxle attachment studs located at the rear side of the block, above the starter.

71. Attach the following transaxle connectors, as applicable:

    a. The 3 neutral safety switch connectors.

    b. Valve body actuator connector.

    c. Turbine speed sensor.

    d. On manual transaxles, the reverse light switch.

    e. The temperature sensor.

    f. The 2 gear shift (PRNDL switch) connectors.

72. Install the accelerator cable, then apply a drop of clean engine oil to the male ends of the fuel line connectors and attach the line quick connect fittings. Make sure the lines are not kinked or damaged.

73. Install the upper radiator and de-aeration hoses, verify proper alignment of the radiator 'L" bracket fasteners.

➡NOTE:Check the upper cooling module grommets for binding or misalignment. The module retaining pins must be centered in the grommets supported by the brackets. If the grommets are pinched, loosen the brackets and reposition them. It is extremely important that the cooling module be able to move freely.

74. Install the air induction system, PCV valve and fresh air hoses.

75. For 1991 vehicles, verify proper powertrain alignment and adjust the engine mounts as necessary.

76. Connect the battery cables and tighten to 151 inch lbs. (17 Nm).

77. If equipped, enable the SIR system.

78. Fill the engine cooling system, then check all engine and transaxle fluids, add or fill as necessary.

79. Prime the fuel system by cycling the ignition **ON** for 5 seconds and **OFF** for 10 seconds a few times without cranking the engine. Start the engine and check for leaks.

80. Perform a short road test and check the engine again for leaks. Make sure the cooling system is filled to the surge tank FULL COLD line.

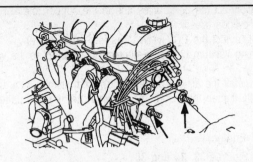

Fig. 25 Disconnect the ground connectors from the transaxle attachment studs

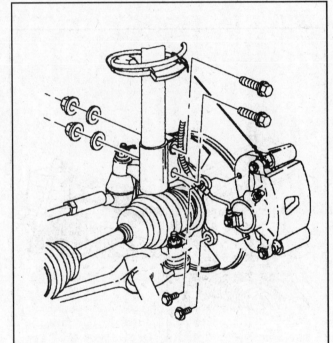

Fig. 26 Remove the 2 caliper bracket bolts and the 2 strut-to-knuckle attaching bolts in order to free the knuckle and hub assembly from the vehicle body

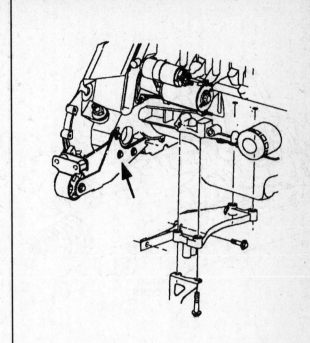

Fig. 27 For 1991 vehicles, remove the powertrain stiffening bracket, but do not remove the 3 bolts attaching the torque restrictor bracket to the transaxle

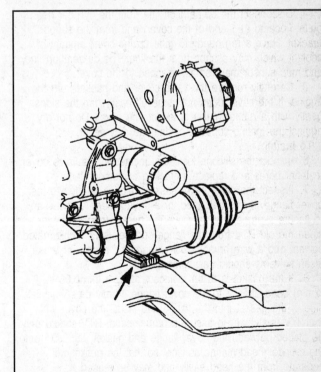

Fig. 28 Position a ½ inch x 1 inch x 3 inch block of wood under the axle shaft for support

Rocker Arm (Camshaft/Valve) Cover

REMOVAL & INSTALLATION

SOHC Engine

◗ **See Figures 30, 31 and 32**

1. Disconnect the negative battery cable.
2. Disconnect the PCV valve, fresh air hose and any remaining vacuum hoses or electrical connectors from the valve cover.
3. Remove the 2 fasteners and washers from the silicone insulators located in the top of the valve cover.

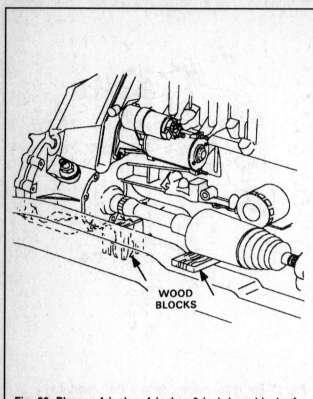

Fig. 29 Place a 4 inch x 4 inch x 6 inch long block of wood under the transaxle housing for support

4. Disconnect the de-aeration line from the cylinder head outlet (located at 1 end of the cover) and from the support bracket. Have a rag handy to wipe up the small amount of coolant which may escape from the line. The de-aeration line and map sensor may remain attached to the cover.

5. Carefully remove the valve cover and gasket from the engine. If the cover does not come off easily, tap the sides gently with a rubber mallet to loosen the cover. Do not pry against the mating surfaces or damage may occur.

To install:

6. Inspect the silicone insulators located in the valve cover fastener bores and replace if cracked or deteriorated.

7. Inspect the valve cover gasket which is bonded to the cover flange. If it is damaged, or if replacement is necessary to assure a proper seal, remove the gasket from the cover and clean the old RTV from the flange surface using a chlorinated solvent and a wire brush. Most carburetor cleaners or brake clean solvents should be appropriate.

8. If the gasket is to be replaced, apply a thin 0.08 in. (2mm) bead of RTV to the cover flange. Firmly press the flat side of the gasket into the flange and install the cover while the RTV is still wet to assure a proper bond. RTV should only be placed between the cover flange and gasket, but NOT onto the cylinder head mating surface, so that the gasket will separate from the head easily and may be reused.

9. Apply a small 0.2 in. (5mm) bead of RTV to the cylinder head T-joints where the head meets the front cover to assure a good seal. This is the only spot where RTV will be placed between the cylinder head and the cover gasket.

10. Install the valve cover and gasket, then install the washers and fasteners. Tighten the fasteners to 22 ft. lbs. (30

Nm). Connect the de-aeration line to the support bracket and to the cylinder head.

11. Connect the PCV valve, fresh air hose and any remaining vacuum hoses or electrical connectors to the valve cover.

12. Install the air cleaner assembly and air inlet duct, then carefully tighten the fasteners. Connect the negative battery cable.

DOHC Engine

▶ **See Figures 33, 34 and 35**

1. Disconnect the negative battery cable.

2. Disconnect the fresh air hose from the cover fitting and the PCV valve from the cover grommet.

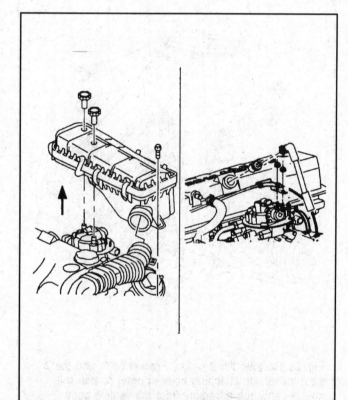

Fig. 30 Remove the air cleaner assembly along with any hoses, cables or wires that may interfere

Fig. 31 Disconnect the de-aeration hose from the cylinder head and the support bracket, but it may remain attached to the cover

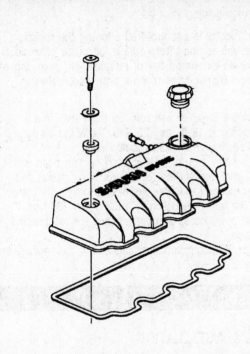

Fig. 32 Exploded view of the SOHC valve cover assembly

3. Disconnect the vacuum hose and electrical connector from the EGR solenoid located at the end of the camshaft cover, near the EGR valve and the engine lifting bracket.

→NOTE:If it is preferred or necessary, the bolt may be removed from the EGR solenoid to disconnect the solenoid from the camshaft cover.

4. The original spark plug wires are numbered, if the numbers are illegible or if the wires have been replaced with non-labeled parts, tag the wires for installation purposes. Disconnect the spark plug wires from the plugs.

5. Remove the fasteners, washers and insulators, then remove the camshaft cover and gasket from the engine. If the cover is stuck, tap the sides gently using a rubber mallet. Do not damage the aluminum cylinder head by prying the cover loose.

To install:

6. Inspect the silicone isolators through which the camshaft cover fasteners are installed and replace if cracked or deteriorated.

7. Inspect the camshaft cover gasket which is bonded to the cover flange. If it is damaged, or if replacement is necessary to assure a proper seal, remove the gasket from the cover and clean the old RTV from the flange surface using a chlorinated solvent and a wire brush. Most carburetor cleaners or brake clean solvents should be appropriate.

8. If the gasket is to be replaced, apply a thin 0.08 in. (2mm) bead of RTV to the cover flange. Firmly press the flat side of the gasket into the flange and install the cover while the RTV is still wet to assure a proper bond. RTV should only be placed between the cover flange and gasket, but NOT onto the cylinder head mating surface, so that the gasket will separate from the head easily and may be reused.

9. Apply a small 0.2 in. (5mm) bead of RTV to the cylinder head T-joints where the head meets the front cover to assure a good seal. This is the only spot where RTV will be placed between the cylinder head and the cover gasket.

10. Install the camshaft cover and gasket using the washers and fasteners. Tighten the fasteners uniformly and in the proper sequence to 89 inch lbs. (10 Nm).

11. Connect the wires to the spark plugs as labeled.

12. Connect the electrical plug and vacuum hose the EGR solenoid valve.

13. Install the PCV valve to the grommet and the fresh air hose to the fitting.

14. Connect the negative battery cable.

Rocker Arms/Shafts

The SOHC engine contains the only Saturn cylinder head that uses rocker arms in the valve train.

REMOVAL & INSTALLATION

▶ See Figures 36 and 37

1. Disconnect the negative battery cable.

2. Remove the rocker arm cover, then inspect the cover silicone isolators for cracks or deterioration and replace as necessary.

3. Uniformly remove the rocker arm assembly bolts, then carefully remove the 2 shaft and rocker arm assemblies. The

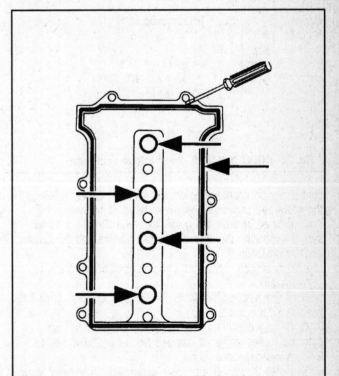

Fig. 33 If gasket replacement is necessary, carefully remove the old gasket from the camshaft cover surfaces

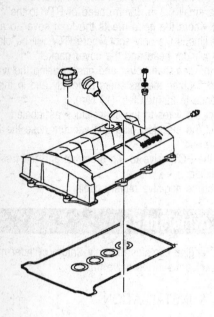

Fig. 34 Exploded view of the DOHC valve cover assembly

Intake Side

```
        6   8   9
12
     3   1   2   4
11
       5   7   10
```

Exhaust Side

Fig. 35 DOHC camshaft cover torque sequence

shafts may be unsnapped from the lifter guideplates leaving the lifters and plates in the cylinder head. If this cannot be accomplished, remove the guideplates and lifters, but make sure to reposition the lifters in the same bores and guideplates during installation.

4. If necessary, remove the rocker arms from the shafts.

To install:

5. If removed, oil the shafts and install the rocker arms into position on the shafts.

6. Snap 1 end of each lifter guide plate retaining spring onto the rocker arm shaft between No. 1-No. 2 and the No. 3-No. 4 cylinder rocker arms.

7. Install the rocker arm shaft assemblies. To prevent valve or piston damage, be sure the rocker arm tangs are squarely

seated on the lifter plungers and the retaining springs are positioned in the guide plate slots.

➡**NOTE:If difficulty is encountered aligning the rocker arms on the valves and lifters, use a flat piece of wood, cardboard or an extension bar of suitable length on top of the shafts and rocker arms to hold both assemblies in position.**

8. Tighten the 5 rocker arm bolts on each shaft in a uniform sequence to 18 ft. lbs. (25 Nm). Verify the proper position and seating of all rocker components.

9. Apply a small drop of RTV to each cylinder head and front cover T-joint. Inspect the rocker arm cover gasket and replace if necessary. Install the gasket and rocker arm cover, then tighten the fasteners uniformly to 22 ft. lbs. (30 Nm). Make sure all cover hoses and components are reconnected after installation.

10. Connect the negative battery cable, start the engine and check for leaks.

Thermostat

REMOVAL & INSTALLATION

▶ **See Figure 38**

1. Make sure the engine is cold, and position a suitable clean drainpan under the radiator and engine drains. Open the radiator drain and remove the engine drain plug located at the front right of the engine, draining the coolant into the container.

✳✳CAUTION

When draining the coolant, keep in mind that cats and dogs are attracted by the ethylene glycol antifreeze, and are quite likely to drink any that is left in an uncovered container or in puddles on the ground. This will prove fatal in sufficient quantity. Always drain the coolant into a sealable container. Coolant may be reused unless it is contaminated or several years old.

2. Disconnect the lower radiator hose from the thermostat housing.

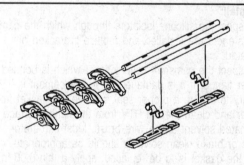

Fig. 36 Exploded view of the rocker arms, shafts and lifter guide plates

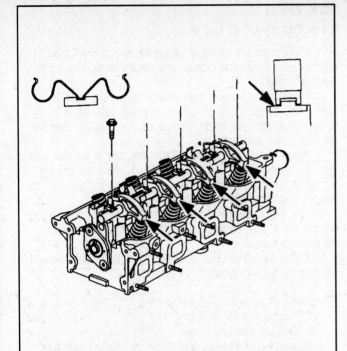

Fig. 37 The rocker arm tangs or slots must be properly positioned on the plungers and the springs must be positioned on the guide plate slots to prevent valve or piston damage

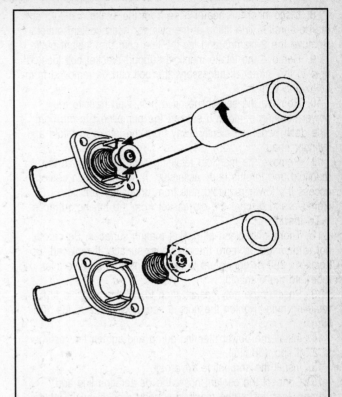

Fig. 38 Use the tool provided in the replacement kit to remove the old thermostat from the housing

3. Remove the 2 bolts from the water inlet housing, then remove the housing and thermostat assembly. Remove and discard the O-ring from the mating surface.

4. Remove the thermostat from the housing using the tool provided with the replacement thermostat element.

To install:

➡ NOTE:The thermostat will not function correctly if it has come in contact with oil. If oil is found in the cooling system at any time, both the thermostat cartridge must be replaced and the cooling system must be flushed.

5. Install the replacement thermostat using the tool provided, being careful not to damage or scratch the aluminum surface. Make sure the element's retaining tangs are properly seated in the 2 legs and the element piston is correctly positioned in the inlet housing.

6. Install a new O-ring and position the housing to the engine. Tighten the retaining bolts to 22 ft. lbs. (30 Nm).

7. Close the radiator drain plug and install the cylinder block drain plug. Tighten the block plug to 26 ft. lbs. (35 Nm).

8. Install the hose to the inlet housing.

9. Connect the negative battery cable and properly fill the engine cooling system.

10. Run the engine and check for leaks. Make sure the cooling system is filled to the proper level.

Intake Manifold

REMOVAL & INSTALLATION

SOHC Engine

▶ See Figures 39, 40 and 41

1. Disconnect the negative battery cable and drain the engine coolant from the radiator and engine block, into a suitable container.

2. Remove the air cleaner, disconnecting the fresh air tube at the valve cover. Remove the PCV tube and hose.

3. Properly relieve the fuel system pressure at the test port, then disconnect the fuel supply and return lines at the connectors using service tool SA9157E or equivalent. Plug the lines to prevent fuel contamination or loss.

4. Disconnect the throttle cable from the throttle body, then remove the throttle cable bracket attaching nuts and position the assembly aside.

5. Label and disconnect the wiring from the intake manifold, throttle body and valve cover components, as follows:

    a. The fuel injector.

    b. Idle Air Control (IAC) valve.

    c. Throttle Position Sensor (TPS).

    d. Exhaust Gas Recirculation (EGR) valve.

    e. Manifold Absolute Pressure (MAP) sensor.

6. Remove the wiring tube and lay the harness away from the manifold onto the Under Hood Junction Block (UHJB).

7. Label and disconnect all vacuum hoses from the throttle body unit. Disconnect the vacuum line from the brake booster.

8. Disconnect the heater hose from the intake manifold and the de-aeration line fitting at the cylinder head coolant outlet. Remove the 2 clamps and lay the line onto the coolant bottle.

9. Remove the intake manifold support bracket bolt located next to the starter. If necessary, the bolt can be removed from below the vehicle.

10. Remove the serpentine drive belt, then remove the power steering pump and support the pump next to the right side dash panel sufficiently away from the intake manifold and cylinder head.

11. Remove the manifold retaining nuts, then remove the manifold and throttle body assembly. It may be much easier to access the lower manifold nuts from under the vehicle. Remove and discard the old gasket from the mating surfaces.

To install:

12. Thoroughly clean all gasket mating surfaces. Be careful not to damage or score the aluminum surface. If replaced, use Loctite® 290 or equivalent to seal the new PCV valve inlet tube into the manifold.

13. Position the new gasket, then install the manifold and retaining nuts. Tighten the nuts in sequence to 22 ft. lbs. (30 Nm).

14. Install the power steering pump and tighten the fasteners to 27 ft. lbs. (38 Nm).

15. Install the serpentine drive belt.

16. Connect the coolant hose, the de-aeration line and clamps, then install the manifold support bracket bolt. Tighten the bolt to 22 ft. lbs. (30 Nm).

17. Lubricate the male ends of the fuel lines with a few drops of clean engine oil, then connect the fuel supply and return lines to the TBI and tighten the fittings to 19 ft. lbs. (25 Nm).

18. Reposition the wiring harness and connect the wiring and vacuum hoses to their original locations. The harness leads to the TPS and EGR solenoid must be routed between the intake manifold runners.

19. Inspect the air cleaner/TBI unit gasket and replace, if necessary. Install the air cleaner and fresh air tubes, then install the PCV valve hose.

20. Connect the negative battery cable, close the radiator drain and install the engine block drain plug. Tighten the block drain plug to 26 ft. lbs. (35 Nm). Fill the engine cooling system.

21. Prime the fuel system by cycling the ignition switch **ON** for 5 seconds, then **OFF** for 10 seconds and repeating 2 times. Start the engine and check for leaks.

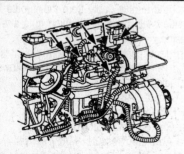

Fig. 39 Disconnect the electrical connections from these locations — SOHC

DOHC Engine

▶ See Figures 42, 43 and 44

1. Disconnect the negative battery cable and drain the engine coolant from the radiator and engine block, into a suitable container.

2. Remove the air inlet tube, disconnecting the fresh air tube at the camshaft cover. Lift the resonator upward to disengage it from the engine service support bracket. Remove the PCV valve and hose.

3. Properly relieve the fuel system pressure at the test port, then disconnect the fuel supply and return lines from the fuel rail using service tool SA9157E or equivalent. Plug the lines to prevent fuel contamination or loss.

4. Disconnect the throttle cable from the throttle body, then remove the throttle cable bracket attaching nuts and position the assembly aside.

5. Label and disconnect the wiring from the intake manifold and surrounding components, as follows:
   a. The fuel injectors.
   b. Idle Air Control (IAC) valve.
   c. Throttle Position Sensor (TPS).
   d. Manifold Absolute Pressure (MAP) sensor.

6. Disconnect the heater and de-aeration hoses from the intake manifold outlets. Disconnect the EGR solenoid vacuum hose.

7. Position the wiring harness over the brake master cylinder, then remove the intake manifold support bracket bolt attached to the manifold next to the brake master cylinder.

8. Remove the serpentine drive belt. Remove the power steering pump assembly with the support bracket, then remove the upper pump bracket attachment bolts and position the pump away from the manifold and cylinder head, near the right dash panel. Remove the lower power steering pump bracket brace.

9. Remove the 3 upper intake manifold attachment nuts, then raise and support the front of the vehicle safely.

10. Remove the lower power steering unit support bracket. Remove the intake manifold support bracket bolt located next to the alternator, then loosen the lower bracket bolt and rotate the bracket out of the way.

11. Disconnect the canister purge solenoid and brake booster vacuum hoses.

12. Remove the intake manifold attaching stud, remove the supports and lower the vehicle.

13. Remove the remaining fasteners and the intake manifold assembly, then remove and discard the old gasket.

To install:

14. Thoroughly clean the gasket mating surfaces. Be careful not to score or damage the aluminum sealing surfaces. If installing a new coolant de-aeration tube elbow into the manifold use Loctite® 290 or equivalent to achieve a proper seal.

15. Position the new gasket, then install the intake manifold and retaining nuts. Torque the nuts in sequence to 22 ft. lbs. (30 Nm).

16. Install the power steering pump and brackets. Tighten the fasteners to 28 ft. lbs. (38 Nm).

17. Install the serpentine drive belt making sure the belt is properly aligned on the pulleys.

18. Connect the heater hose and de-aeration line to the manifold.

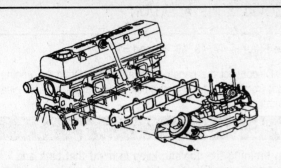

Fig. 40 Intake manifold and gasket mounting — SOHC engine

```
        Upper Side

      8   4   1   5

    7   3   2   6   9

        Lower Side
```

Fig. 41 SOHC intake manifold torque sequence

19. Position the manifold support brackets and install the bolts. Tighten the right block bolt to 41 ft. lbs. (55 Nm), then tighten the left block bolt and the support bracket to intake manifold bolts to 22 ft. lbs. (30 Nm).
20. Lubricate the male fuel supply and return connects, then install.
21. Connect the throttle cable to the throttle body and install the support bracket. Tighten the bracket retaining bolts to 19 ft. lbs. (25 Nm). Verify that the cable locking tangs are fully engaged when assembled.
22. Position the wiring harness and connect all electrical connectors and vacuum hoses in their original locations.
23. Install the PCV hose, the air inlet tube and resonator.
24. Connect the negative battery cable, close the radiator drain and install the engine block drain plug. Tighten the block

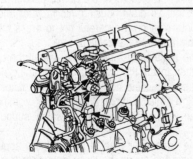

Fig. 42 Disconnect the electrical connections from these locations — DOHC engine

drain plug to 26 ft. lbs. (35 Nm). Fill the engine cooling system.
25. Prime the fuel system by cycling the ignition switch **ON** for 5 seconds, then **OFF** for 10 seconds and repeating 2 times. Start the engine and check for leaks.

Exhaust Manifold

REMOVAL & INSTALLATION

▶ See Figures 45 and 46

1. Disconnect the negative battery cable, then raise and support the vehicle safely using suitable jackstands.
2. Remove the pipe-to-manifold nuts and lower the pipe, then remove the old gasket and discard.
3. Remove the supports and lower the vehicle.
4. If equipped, remove the air conditioning compressor and bracket from the engine, then position aside. Do not disconnect the refrigerant lines.
5. Disconnect the oxygen sensor connector. If necessary, use a 19mm, 6-point, crows foot to remove the oxygen sensor from the manifold.
6. Remove the manifold retaining nuts and remove the manifold from the cylinder head. Remove and discard the old gasket from the mating surfaces.
   To install:
7. Thoroughly clean the gasket mating surfaces, being careful not to score or damage the aluminum surface.

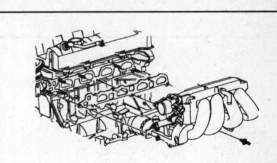

Fig. 43 Intake manifold and gasket mounting — DOHC engine

```
       Upper Side

        5   2   3

      7   4   1   6

       Lower Side
```

Fig. 44 DOHC intake manifold torque sequence

8. Install the new gasket with the smooth side facing the manifold, then install the manifold and attaching nuts. Tighten the nuts in sequence to 16 ft. lbs. (22 Nm) for the SOHC engine or to 23 ft. lbs. (31 Nm) for the DOHC engine.

9. If replacing the oxygen sensor, coat the threads with nickel based anti-seize compound and tighten to 18 ft. lbs. (25 Nm). Connect the oxygen sensor electrical connector.

10. Install the air conditioning compressor and brackets. Tighten all fasteners except the front bracket-to-compressor fasteners to 19 ft. lbs. (25 Nm). Tighten the front bracket-to-compressor fasteners to 40 ft. lbs. (54 Nm).

11. Raise and support the vehicle safely using jackstands, then install a new gasket onto the studs between the pipe and manifold.

12. Connect the pipe and manifold, then tighten the fasteners in a crosswise pattern to 23 ft. lbs. (31 Nm), then lower the vehicle.

13. Connect the negative battery cable, start the engine and check for exhaust leaks.

Radiator

The radiator drain plug is threaded into a removable drain housing. The housing may be replaced at any point after the coolant is drained from the system. To remove the housing, use a pair of pliers to pinch the tabs closed, then pull the housing straight back and out of the radiator. Squeeze the tabs of the replacement to begin inserting it into the bore, then carefully snap it into position.

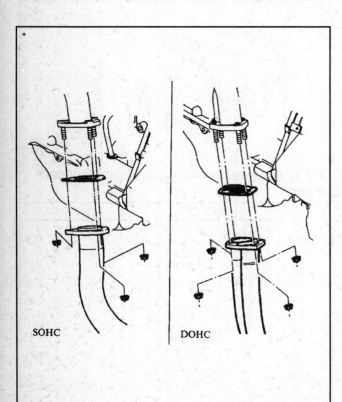

Fig. 45 Remove the pipe-to-manifold nuts in order to separate the flanges

REMOVAL & INSTALLATION

▶ See Figures 47, 48, 49, 50 and 51

1. Disconnect the negative battery cable. Drain the engine coolant from the radiator and block drains into a suitable clean container.

❊❊CAUTION

When draining the coolant, keep in mind that cats and dogs are attracted by the ethylene glycol antifreeze, and are quite likely to drink any that is left in an uncovered container or in puddles on the ground. This will prove fatal in sufficient quantity. Always drain the coolant into a sealable container. Coolant may be reused unless it is contaminated or several years old.

2. Remove the air intake ducts and disconnect the temperature sensor connector, then for the DOHC engine, remove the air cleaner housing.

3. Loosen the clamp and disconnect the upper hose from the radiator. If equipped with an automatic transaxle, disconnect the upper transaxle fluid cooler line. Plug the openings to prevent transaxle fluid contamination or loss.

4. Remove the electric cooling fan assembly.

5. Loosen the clamp and disconnect lower hose from the radiator.

6. Raise and support the front of the vehicle safely using suitable jackstands.

7. Disconnect the fasteners, the carefully lower the splash shield from the vehicle to gain access below the radiator.

8. If equipped with an automatic transaxle, disconnect and plug the lower transaxle cooler line.

9. Remove the 2 condenser bracket-to-radiator bolts from either side of the radiator. Wire the condenser to the frame assembly to keep it in place, then remove the supports and carefully lower the vehicle.

10. Remove the upper radiator nuts and brackets. On air conditioning equipped vehicles, remove the upper radiator seal.

11. Carefully lift the radiator from the vehicle. If necessary, squeeze the drain housing tabs and withdraw it from the bottom of the radiator.

To install:

12. If installing a new radiator, make sure the drain housing is in position. If the replacement did not come with a drain housing, insert the old drain housing into radiator and press until it snaps into position. Be careful not to press the housing through the hole and into the radiator tank.

13. Install the radiator into the vehicle. Install the upper seal, if applicable, then install the brackets and retaining nuts. Be sure the L-shaped brackets do not pinch the radiator locating pins and that the radiator moves freely in the grommets.

14. Raise the front of the vehicle and safely support using jackstands.

15. Install the condenser bracket bolts, then if applicable, remove the plugs and install the lower automatic transaxle cooler line.

16. Install the splash shield, remove the supports and lower the vehicle.

17. Install the lower radiator hose with the clamp tangs positioned at 1 o'clock.

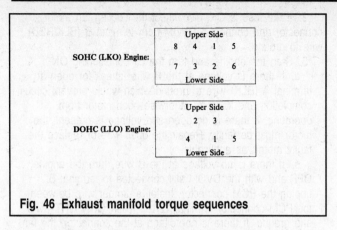

Fig. 46 Exhaust manifold torque sequences

18. Install the cooling fan assembly.
19. For 1991 vehicles with an automatic transaxle, connect the upper transaxle cooler line and tighten. For 1992-93 vehicles with an automatic transaxle, connect the upper transaxle cooler line at a 35 degree angle inward from vertical and hold while tightening.
20. Install the upper radiator hose with the clamp tangs at 12 o'clock.
21. For the DOHC engine, install the air cleaner housing.
22. Install the intake air ducts and connect the air temperature sensor plug.
23. Close the radiator drain plug and install the cylinder block drain plug. Tighten the block plug to 26 ft. lbs. (35 Nm).
24. Connect the negative battery cable and properly fill the engine cooling system.
25. Start and run the engine to check for coolant leaks.

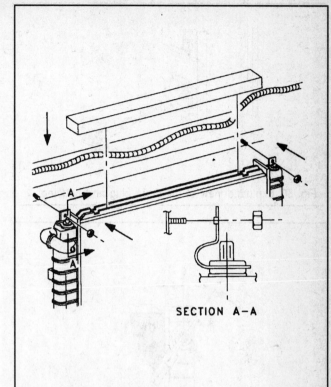

Fig. 48 Make sure the L-shaped brackets do not pinch the radiator locating pins

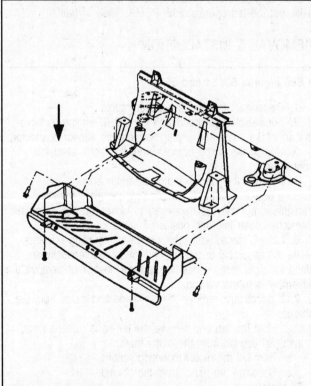

Fig. 47 Disconnect the fasteners and carefully lower the splash shield from the vehicle

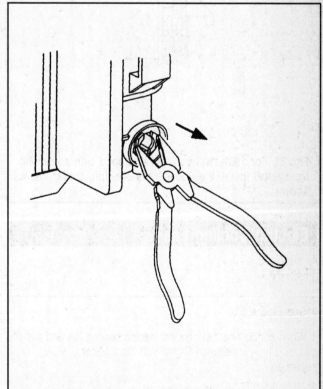

Fig. 49 Pinch the drain housing tabs closed and remove by pulling straight out

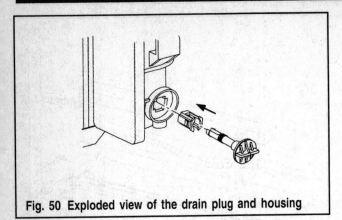

Fig. 50 Exploded view of the drain plug and housing

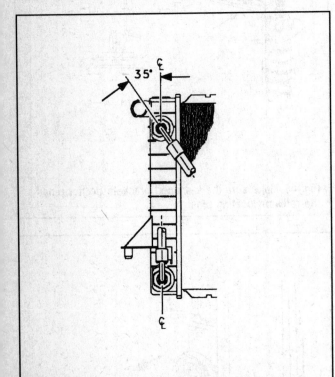

Fig. 51 For 1992-1993 vehicles equipped with automatic transaxles, install the upper transaxle fluid cooler line as shown

Electric Cooling Fan

TESTING

▶ See Figure 52

When conducting tests on the electric cooling fan and circuit, use of a high impedance Digital Volt Ohm Meter (DVOM) is necessary.

Cooling Fan Inoperative Test

1. Check the 30 amp cooling fan maxifuse (maxifuse No. 6, labeled COOL FAN) in the underhood junction block.

2. If the fuse is OK, disconnect the cooling fan motor connector and connect a DVOM from terminal B (BLK/RED) wire to ground.

3. Start the engine and turn the air conditioning **ON**:

   a. If there is voltage at the B wire, check for open at terminal A (BLK) wire to ground which would prevent circuit completion and keep an otherwise good motor from operating. If there is no open and voltage is present, the motor must be faulty. Repair the open wire or replace the faulty motor, as applicable.

   b. If there is no voltage at the B wire, turn the engine **OFF** and with the DVOM still connected to terminal B, unplug the PCM connector. Install a jumper wire between the PCM connector terminal 12A03 (DRK GRN/WHT) wire and ground. If there is no voltage at the connector, the fan relay is faulty. If there is voltage, the PCM is bad.

4. The fan motor may also be checked by jumping 12 volts to the 2 wires (A = negative, B = positive). The motor should run while voltage is applied.

Cooling Fan Constantly On Test

1. Disconnect the negative battery cable and remove the cooling fan relay from the underhood junction block. Connect the negative battery cable and inspect the motor to see if it still operates.

2. If the motor operates with the relay removed, a short to power exists in the BLK/RED wire from the underhood junction block to the fan motor.

3. If the fan does not operate with the relay removed, substitute a new relay and watch for operation. If the fan operates with a new relay, check the DRK GRN/WHT wire for a short to ground and repair, if found. If a short does not exist, yet the fan operates, the PCM is likely at fault.

REMOVAL & INSTALLATION

▶ See Figures 53, 54 and 55

1. Disconnect the negative battery cable.

2. For vehicles equipped with the DOHC engine, remove the air intake ducts and unplug temperature sensor connector.

3. Unplug the wiring harness from the motor electrical connector.

4. Remove the top fan motor assembly bolts.

5. If equipped with air conditioning and an automatic transmission, it may be necessary to loosen the top automatic transaxle cooler line and position it aside for clearance.

6. Lift the fan assembly off the lower mounting brackets. Move the assembly to the left and rotate counterclockwise lifting the right side up past the radiator hose, then remove the assembly from the vehicle.

7. If necessary, remove the fan blade and motor from the shroud:

   a. Hold the fan and remove the left-hand threaded nut, then pull the fan from the motor shaft.

   b. Remove the motor mounting screws.

   c. Separate the motor from the shroud.

To install:

8. If removed, install the motor and fan blade. Tighten the left-hand threaded fan nut to 27-44 inch lbs. (3-5 Nm).

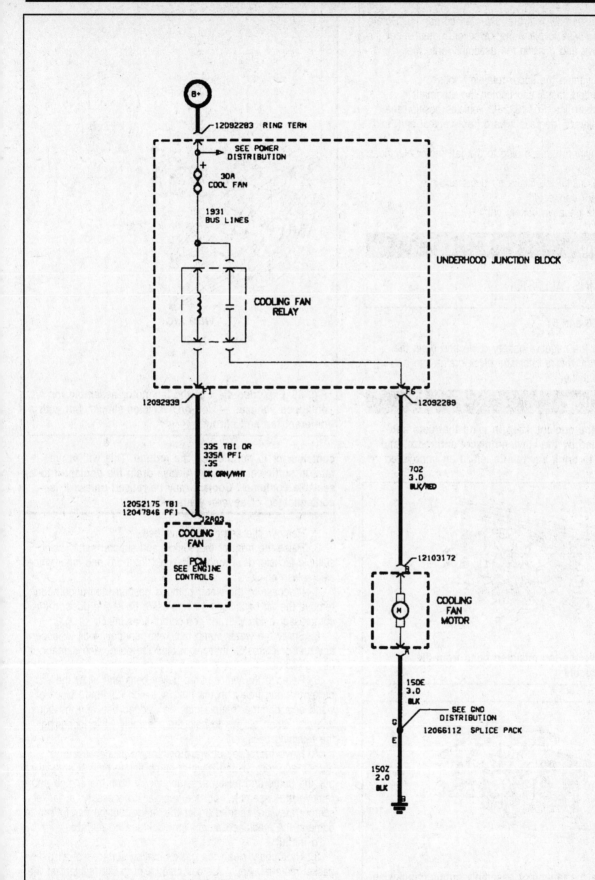

Fig. 52 Cooling fan electrical schematic

9. Install the assembly with the lower left corner 1st. Rotate the assembly clockwise to place the lower left mount under the lower radiator hose and position the assembly onto the mounting brackets.

10. Install and tighten the upper retaining bolts.

11. If disconnected, install and tighten the automatic transaxle fluid cooler line. For 1992-93 vehicles position the transaxle cooler line 35 degrees inward from vertical and hold while tightening.

12. Install the wiring harness plug to the fan motor electrical connector.

13. If removed, install the intake air ducts and the temperature sensor connector.

14. Connect the negative battery cable.

Water Pump

REMOVAL & INSTALLATION

▶ **See Figures 56 and 57**

1. Disconnect the negative battery cable and drain the engine coolant from the radiator and block drains into a suitable clean container.

✳✳CAUTION

When draining the coolant, keep in mind that cats and dogs are attracted by the ethylene glycol antifreeze, and are quite likely to drink any that is left in an uncovered

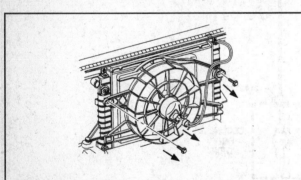

Fig. 53 Remove the top retaining bolts from the fan/motor assembly

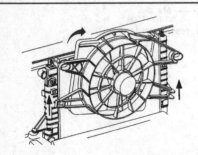

Fig. 54 Rotate the fan/motor assembly counterclockwise lifting the right side up past the radiator hose

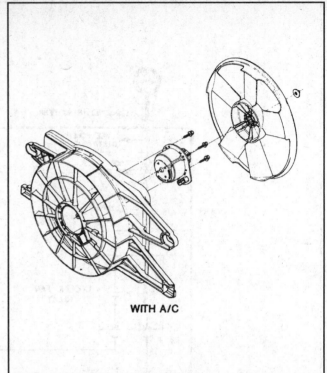

WITH A/C

Fig. 55 Exploded view of the fan/motor assembly for A/C equipped vehicles — Non-A/C vehicles similar, but with a different fan and shroud

container or in puddles on the ground. This will prove fatal in sufficient quantity. Always drain the coolant into a sealable container. Coolant may be reused unless it is contaminated or several years old.

2. Remove the serpentine drive belt.

3. Raise the front of the vehicle and support safely using suitable jackstands. Remove the right front tire and inner wheel well splash shield.

4. If access to the water pump is desired from underhood, remove the air conditioning compressor bolts and position the compressor aside with the refrigerant lines intact.

5. Spray the water pump hub with penetrating oil to loosen any rust or corrosion that might bind the pulley and damage it during removal.

6. Remove the water pump pulley bolts and allow the pulley to hang freely on the hub. A 1 inch (25.4mm) block of wood or a hammer handle may be wedged between the pump and crankshaft pulleys to hold the assembly while loosening the retaining bolts.

7. Move the pulley outward or remove as necessary for access and remove the 6 water pump flange bolts. Carefully pull the pump and pulley assembly away from the engine and remove the assembly from the vehicle. If necessary, a gasket scraper may be inserted under the flange, but be careful not to damage the machined aluminum block sealing surface.

To install:

8. Thoroughly clean the gasket mating surfaces of all old gasket material. Apply a small amount of gasket sealant at the outer edges of the bolt holes to hold the gasket in place, then install the gasket onto the water pump assembly.

9. Install the pump assembly with the small bump located next to 1 of the attaching bolts in the 11 o'clock position. Install and tighten the bolts in a criss-cross sequence as shown to 22 ft. lbs. (30 Nm).

10. Install or reposition the pump pulley, as applicable and tighten the bolts to 19 ft. lbs. (25 Nm). If the pump hub exposed through the pulley is rusty, clean it with a wire brush and apply a thin coat of primer to prevent the pulley from rusting onto the hub.

11. Install the serpentine drive belt, the right splash shield and right tire assembly.

12. If repositioned, install the air conditioning compressor.

13. Close the radiator drain plug and install the cylinder block drain plug. Tighten the block plug to 26 ft. lbs. (35 Nm).

14. Connect the negative battery cable and properly fill the engine cooling system.

15. Operate the engine and check for coolant leaks.

Cylinder Head

REMOVAL & INSTALLATION

▶ **See Figures 58, 59, 60 and 61**

✳✳WARNING

Only remove the cylinder head when the engine is cold. Warpage may result if the cylinder head is removed while the engine is hot.

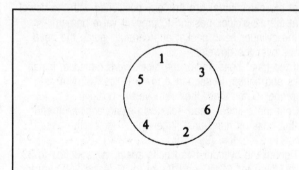

Fig. 56 Water pump bolt torque sequence

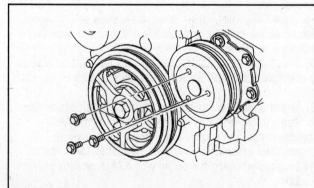

Fig. 57 Water pump pulley mounting bolts

1. Disconnect the negative battery cable and drain the engine coolant from the radiator and block drains into a suitable clean container.

✳✳CAUTION

When draining the coolant, keep in mind that cats and dogs are attracted by the ethylene glycol antifreeze, and are quite likely to drink any that is left in an uncovered container or in puddles on the ground. This will prove fatal in sufficient quantity. Always drain the coolant into a sealable container. Coolant may be reused unless it is contaminated or several years old.

2. Remove the air cleaner assembly and air inlet duct; for the DOHC engine lift the resonator upward to disengage the button from the engine service support bracket. Disconnect the PCV valve and fresh air hose from the valve/camshaft cover.

3. Disconnect the accelerator cable from the throttle body and the bracket from the intake manifold.

4. Properly relieve the fuel system pressure.

5. Label and disconnect the following electrical connectors from the cylinder head assembly and components, as applicable. Long nose pliers are necessary to disconnect the coolant temperature connectors. When disconnected, position the electrical harness over the underhood junction block.

   a. Coolant temperature and PCM connectors. These connectors are located on the rear side of the cylinder head for DOHC engines.

   b. The single injector connector (SOHC Engine) or the 4 injector connectors (DOHC Engine).

   c. Idle Air Control (IAC) valve.

   d. Manifold Air Pressure (MAP) sensor.

   e. Throttle Position Sensor (TPS).

   f. Exhaust Gas Recirculation (EGR) solenoid.

   g. Spark plug wires from the plugs.

   h. Oxygen sensor.

   i. Air conditioning compressor.

6. Label and disconnect the following vacuum hoses, as applicable, from the area around the cylinder head assembly.

   a. Canister purge valve.

   b. EGR valve.

   c. MAP sensor, for the SOHC engine only.

   d. Brake booster vacuum hose at the intake manifold or the brake booster.

   e. Throttle Body Injection (TBI) unit assembly on SOHC Engines or the throttle body for DOHC engines.

   f. Fuel regulator, for the DOHC engine only.

7. Disconnect the upper radiator hose at the cylinder head outlet, the heater hose at the intake manifold and the de-aeration hose at the connection next to the TBI assembly (SOHC Engines) or at the intake manifold (DOHC Engines).

8. Remove the bolt which retains the fuel lines to the intake manifold assembly. Disconnect the fuel feed and return lines from the fuel rail or throttle body, as applicable. For SOHC engines, remove the lower intake manifold support bracket stud. For DOHC engines, disconnect the fuel return line from the regulator, then remove the upper intake manifold support bracket bolt.

9. For 1992-93 vehicles with a torque axis mount system, unclip the lower splash shield for access. Place a 1 inch **x** 1 inch **x** 2 inch long block of wood between the torque strut and

cradle to ease removal and installation of the torque engine mount. Remove the 3 right side upper engine torque axis to front cover nuts and the 2 mount to midrail bracket nuts, allowing the powertrain to rest on the block of wood.

➡NOTE:**Placing a block of wood under the torque axis mount prior to removing the upper mount will allow the engine to rest on the wood, thus preventing the engine from shifting. This will allow you to install the mount during assembly without jacking or raising the engine.**

10. Remove the serpentine drive belt and belt tensioner. It is not necessary to remove the water pump pulley, however, for 1992-93 vehicles it will be necessary to remove the idler pulley to access the engine front cover.

11. For SOHC engines, disconnect the de-aeration line at the cylinder head water outlet and from the support bracket.

12. Remove the fasteners and the valve/camshaft cover, then inspect the cover silicone insulators for cracks or deterioration and replace as necessary. Be sure to cover the valve train area to prevent foreign debris from entering the engine.

13. Remove the power steering pump bracket attaching bolts (3 for the SOHC engine or 5 for the DOHC engine) and position the assembly next to the right side front of the dash panel away from the intake manifold and cylinder head. It is not necessary to remove the water pump pulley.

14. If equipped, remove the 3 air conditioning compressor front bracket bolts attached to the cylinder head and block, then remove the rear bracket bolts from the compressor or engine. Do not discharge the system or disconnect the refrigerant lines. Support the compressor out of the way, from the vehicle front support bar.

15. Raise and support the front of the vehicle safely using jackstands.

16. Drain the engine oil into a suitable drainpan.

17. Remove the right side tire and splash shield.

18. For DOHC engines, remove the intake manifold support brace bolt attached to the intake manifold next to the alternator.

19. Remove the crankshaft damper/pulley assembly. Use a strap wrench or a block of wood wedged between the pulley spoke and the rear lower side of the front cover to hold the assembly while removing the bolt. Then use a 3 jaw puller on the jaw slots cast into the pulley to remove the assembly.

20. Disconnect the exhaust pipe from the manifold, then remove and discard the gasket.

21. Install crankshaft gear retainer tool SA9104E or equivalent with the flat side toward the sprocket. Properly remove the engine front/timing chain cover; refer to the Timing Chain Cover procedure in this section.

✳✳WARNING

Be sure to properly install the crankshaft gear retainer tool. Failure to hold the crankshaft timing sprocket in place will cause timing chain damage.

22. Rotate the crankshaft clockwise to the position 90 degrees from Top Dead Center (TDC) so the timing mark and keyway align with the main bearing cap split line. This will make sure pistons will not contact the valves upon assembly.

23. Remove the timing chain, tensioner, guides, camshaft sprocket(s) and chain. Use a 7/8 in. (21mm) wrench to hold the camshaft when removing the sprocket bolts.

24. For the SOHC engine, remove the throttle body assembly and cover the intake manifold opening. Be sure to remove and discard the old throttle body gasket.

25. Use a 6 point socket to remove the 10 cylinder head bolts in several passes of the proper sequence. Failure to follow the proper sequence or removal of the head when hot could result in head warpage or cracking. Also, the use of a 12 point socket on the cylinder head bolts may round the bolt heads.

26. Lift the cylinder head from the dowels, if necessary use a small prybar for leverage between the cylinder head and block bosses. Be careful not to damage the sealing surfaces if prying is necessary to remove the head from the block.

27. If necessary, remove the intake manifold or the exhaust manifold by loosening the mounting nuts in the proper sequence. If any cylinder head studs back out, the threads should be cleaned, the studs carefully installed and then tightened to 106 inch lbs. (12 Nm).

To install:

28. If removed, install the intake manifold and/or the exhaust manifold and new gasket(s). Tighten to specification in the proper sequence.

29. Clean the gasket mating surfaces. Be careful not to damage the aluminum components. Make sure the block bolt holes are clean of any residual sealer, oil or foreign matter.

30. Using a dial gauge at 4 points around each cylinder, check that the cylinder liners are flush or do not deviate more than 0.0005 in. (0.013mm).

31. Make sure the crankshaft is still 90 degrees past TDC and that the camshaft(s) are properly positioned with the dowel pin(s) at the 12 o'clock position to prevent valve damage. Install the cylinder head gasket and carefully guide the head into place over the dowels.

32. If the head bolts and/or the block were replaced, install the bolts and tighten in sequence to 48 ft. lbs. (65 Nm) to insure proper clamp load, then remove the bolts.

33. Coat the cylinder head bolts with clean engine oil and thread the bolts by hand until finger-tight. Tighten the bolts in sequence to 22 ft. lbs. (30 Nm).

34. Tighten the cylinder head bolts again, in sequence to 33 ft. lbs. (45 Nm) for SOHC engines or to 37 ft. lbs. (50 Nm) for DOHC engines. Install Snap-on® tool 360, or an equivalent torque angle gauge, and calibrate the tool to zero. In sequence, tighten each cylinder head bolt an additional 90 degrees.

35. Install the timing chain, sprockets, guides and tensioner. Then install the front cover assembly. Refer to the appropriate procedures in this section.

36. Position a new gasket, then connect the exhaust pipe to the manifold. Install and tighten the fasteners to 23 ft. lbs. (31 Nm).

37. If not already done, remove the crankshaft gear retainer tool. Apply a thin film of RTV sealant to the damper/pulley assembly flange and washer only. Install the crankshaft damper/pulley assembly and tighten the bolt to 158 ft. lbs. (214 Nm) while holding the pulley with a strap wrench or block of wood.

38. For DOHC vehicles, install the intake manifold support brace bolts next to the alternator, then tighten the block bolt to

33 ft. lbs. (45 Nm) and tighten the manifold bolt to 22 ft. lbs. (30 Nm).

39. Apply a small drop of RTV across the cylinder head and front cover T-joints. Inspect the old camshaft cover gasket and replace if damaged. Install the gasket and the camshaft cover. Tighten the fasteners uniformly to 22 ft. lbs. (30 Nm) for SOHC vehicles or in proper sequence to 89 inch lbs. (10 Nm) for DOHC vehicles.

40. Install the drive belt tensioner and tighten the bolt to 22 ft. lbs. (30 Nm). For 1992-93 vehicles, install the idler pulley and tighten the fasteners to 33 ft. lbs. (45 Nm).

41. If not done during removal, drain the engine oil and change the filter, then install the drain plug and tighten to 26 ft. lbs. (35 Nm).

42. If removed, verify the gaps on all spark plugs and install. Tighten to 20 ft. lbs. (27 Nm).

43. For SOHC engines, install a new gasket and the TBI assembly. Tighten the assembly retainers to 24 ft. lbs. (33 Nm).

44. Install the power steering pump assembly to the bracket, then tighten the bolts to 22 ft. lbs. (30 Nm).

45. If equipped, install the air conditioning compressor and bolts. Tighten the rear bracket bolts to 19 ft. lbs. (25 Nm), then tighten the front bracket bolts to 40 ft. lbs. (54 Nm).

46. Install the accessory drive belt making sure the belt is properly aligned on the pulley.

47. For 1992-93 vehicles with a torque axis mounting, install the 2 mount to midrail bracket nuts and tighten to 52 ft. lbs. (70 Nm). Install the 3 upper mount to engine front cover nuts and tighten them uniformly to 52 ft. lbs. (70 Nm). Remove the support block of wood after the assembly is installed.

48. Install the splash shield, then install the tire and wheel assembly. Tighten the lug nuts to 103 ft. lbs. (140 Nm).

49. Connect the following applicable vacuum hoses disconnected during removal.
    a. Canister purge valve.
    b. EGR valve.
    c. MAP sensor, for the SOHC engine only.
    d. Brake booster vacuum hose at the intake manifold or the brake booster.
    e. Throttle Body Injection (TBI) unit assembly on SOHC Engines or the throttle body for DOHC engines.
    f. Fuel regulator, for the DOHC engine only.

50. Position the wiring harness and install the following applicable wire connectors removed during disassembly:
    a. Coolant temperature and PCM connectors. These connectors are located on the rear side of the cylinder head for DOHC engines.
    b. The single injector connector (SOHC Engine) or the 4 injector connectors (DOHC Engine).
    c. Idle Air Control (IAC) valve.
    d. Manifold Air Pressure (MAP) sensor.
    e. Throttle Position Sensor (TPS).
    f. Exhaust Gas Recirculation (EGR) solenoid.
    g. Spark plug wires from the plugs.
    h. Oxygen sensor.
    i. Air conditioning compressor.

51. Install the accelerator cable bracket and tighten the fastener to 19 ft. lbs. (25 Nm). Connect the cable, then verify that it is properly routed and not binding.

52. Connect the upper radiator hose to the cylinder head outlet, the heater hose to the intake manifold and the de-aeration hose to the connection next to the TBI assembly (SOHC Engines) or at the intake manifold (DOHC Engines).

53. Apply a few drops of clean engine oil to the male fuel line fittings. Connect any fuel line fittings and install the feed/return lines. Tighten the throttle body fittings to 19 ft. lbs. (25 Nm) or the fuel rail and pressure regulator fittings to 133 inch lbs. (15 Nm), as applicable. Install fuel bracket retaining bolts, as applicable, and tighten to 22 ft. lbs. (30 Nm).

54. Install the air cleaner and intake duct assembly.

55. Add engine oil and properly fill the engine cooling system.

56. Connect the negative battery cable.

57. Prime the fuel system by cycling the ignition a few times without cranking the engine, then start the engine and check for leaks.

58. Operate the engine at idle for 3-5 minutes and listen or unusual noises. If the lifters are noisy or the cylinders are misfiring, warm the engine to normal operating temperature running at less than 2000 rpm. Once the engine is warm and the thermostat has opened, cycle the engine between idle and 3000 rpm for 10 minutes or drive the vehicle at least 5 miles to purge air from the lifters. If air cannot be purged, the faulty lifters must be replaced.

59. Verify proper coolant level. Add coolant, if necessary, after the engine has cooled.

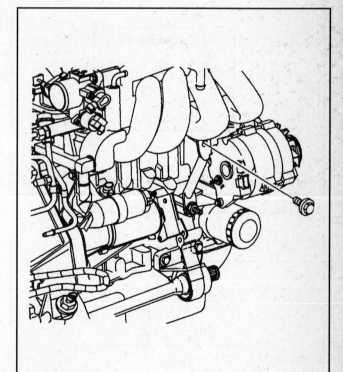

Fig. 58 Remove the intake manifold support brace bolt located next to the alternator — DOHC engine

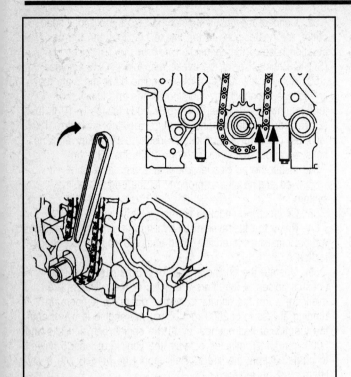

Fig. 59 Rotate the crankshaft clockwise to 90 degrees past TDC (the crankshaft sprocket timing mark will be at 3 o'clock) to prevent valve damage during assembly

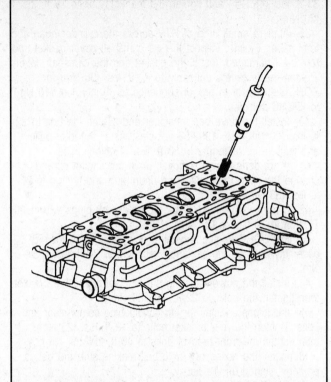

Fig. 62 Clean the combustion chamber using a drill-mounted wire brush

	Intake Side			
3	7	10	6	2
4	8	9	5	1
	Exhaust Side			

Fig. 60 Cylinder head bolt removal sequence

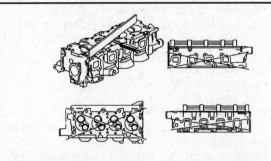

Fig. 63 Check for warpage across these planes — SOHC engine

	Intake Side			
8	4	1	5	9
7	3	2	6	10
	Exhaust Side			

Fig. 61 Cylinder head torque sequence

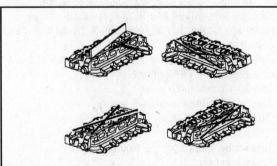

Fig. 64 Check for warpage across these planes — DOHC engine

CLEANING & INSPECTION

▶ **See Figure 62**

1. With the valves installed to protect the valve seats, remove carbon deposits from the combustion chambers and valve heads with a drill-mounted wire brush. Be careful not to damage the cylinder head gasket surface. If the head is to be disassembled, proceed to Step 3. If the head is not to be disassembled, proceed to Step 2.

2. Remove all dirt, oil and old gasket material from the cylinder head with solvent. Clean the bolt holes and the oil passage. Be careful not to get solvent on the valve seals as the solvent may damage them. If available, dry the cylinder head with compressed air. Check the head for cracks or other damage, and check the gasket surface for burrs, nicks and flatness. If you are in doubt about the head's serviceability, consult a reputable automotive machine shop.

3. Remove the valves, springs and retainers, then clean the valve guide bores with a valve guide cleaning tool. Remove all dirt, oil and old gasket material from the cylinder head with solvent. Clean the bolt holes and the oil passage.

4. Remove all deposits from the valves with a wire brush or buffing wheel.

5. Check the head for cracks using a dye penetrant in the valve seat area and ports, head surface and top. Check the gasket surface for burrs, nicks and flatness. If you are in doubt about the head's serviceability, consult a reputable automotive machine shop.

➡ **NOTE:If the cylinder head was removed due to an overheating condition and a crack is suspected, do not assume that the head is not cracked because a crack is not visually found. A crack can be so small that it cannot be seen by eye, but can pass coolant when the engine is at operating temperature. Consult an automotive machine shop that has pressure testing equipment to make sure the head is not cracked.**

RESURFACING

▶ **See Figures 63 and 64**

Whenever the cylinder head is removed, check the flatness of the cylinder head gasket surface as follows:

1. Make sure all dirt and old gasket material has been cleaned from the cylinder head. Any foreign material left on the head gasket surface can cause a false measurement.

2. Place a straightedge across the gasket surface in the positions shown in the figures. Using feeler gauges, determine the clearance at the center of the straightedge.

3. If warpage exceeds the following specifications, the cylinder head must be replaced:

    a. Transverse cylinder block side: 0.0012-0.0020 in. (0.03-0.05mm)

    b. Longitudinal cylinder block side: 0.0028-0.0040 in. (0.007-0.10mm)

    c. Longitudinal intake side: 0.004-0.006 in. (0.10-0.15mm)

    d. Longitudinal exhaust side: 0.004-0.006 in. (0.10-0.15mm)

    e. EGR flange (DOHC only): 0.004-0.006 in. (0.10-0.15mm)

Valves

REMOVAL & INSTALLATION

▶ **See Figure 65**

1. Remove the cylinder head.
2. Remove the intake and exhaust manifolds.
3. For the SOHC engine, remove the rocker arms/shafts assemblies, guide plates and lifters. Remove the camshaft from either the front or the rear of the cylinder head.

➡ **NOTE:When disassembling valve trains, parts of which are to be reused, make sure to keep all components labeled or arranged for installation in their original locations. Rocker arms and/or lifters must be installed against the same contact surfaces from which they were removed. Store lifters with the camshaft side downward to keep their oil from draining.**

4. For the DOHC engine, uniformly remove the camshaft bearing cap fasteners and caps. Remove the camshafts and the lifters. If necessary a magnet may ease lifter removal.

5. Support the head on suitable blocks with the cylinder side facing downward to facilitate valve removal.

6. Using SA9124E for DOHC engines, SA9125E for SOHC engines or an equivalent C-clamp type valve spring compressor, remove the valve spring cap retainer, valve spring and valves.

7. Place the parts from each valve in a separate container, numbered and identified for the valve and cylinder.

8. Remove and discard the valve stem oil seal with an appropriate tool, a new seal will be used at assembly time.

9. Use an electric drill and rotary wire brush to clean the intake and exhaust valve ports, combustion chamber and valve seats. In some cases, the carbon build-up will have to be chipped away. Use a blunt pointed drift for carbon chipping, being careful around valve seat areas.

10. Use a valve guide cleaning brush and safe solvent to clean the valve guides.

11. Clean the valves with a revolving wire brush. Heavy carbon deposits may be removed with a blunt drift.

➡ **NOTE:When using a wire brush to remove carbon from the cylinder head or valves, make sure the deposits are actually removed and not just burnished.**

12. Wash and clean all valve springs, retainers etc., in safe solvent. Remember to keep parts from each valve separate.

13. Check the cylinder head for cracks. Cracks usually start around the exhaust valve seat because it is the hottest part of the combustion chamber. If a crack is suspected but cannot be detected visually, have the area checked by pressure testing, with a dye penetrant or other method by an automotive machine shop.

14. Inspect the valves, guides, springs and seats and machine or replace parts, as necessary.

To install:

15. Install new valve seals using the seal removal/installation tool. Do not oil the seal's inner diameter where it contacts the guide.

16. Dip each valve in clean engine oil and install in its original location.

17. Install the valve springs, caps and retainers over the valve stems, using the removal/installation tool to compress the springs. Be careful not to depress the spring cap too far as it may cause seal and stem damage.

✳✳WARNING

Do not attempt to use a standard valve spring compressor tool when installing the valve assemblies as it may cause damage to the cylinder head hydraulic lifter surfaces and valve stems.

18. For the DOHC engine, lubricate and install the lifters, camshafts and camshaft bearing caps in their proper locations.

19. For the SOHC engine, lubricate and install the camshaft using a new rear cover plug or front thrust plate screws, as applicable. Oil and install the lifters, then install the rocker arm/shaft assemblies and guide plates, into their original locations.

20. Install the intake and exhaust manifolds to the cylinder head.

21. Install the cylinder head to the vehicle.

INSPECTION

▶ See Figures 66, 67 and 68

1. Remove the valves from the cylinder head. Clean the valves, valve guides, valve seats and related components, as explained earlier.

2. Visually check the valves for obvious wear or damage. A burnt valve will have discoloration, severe galling or pitting and even cracks on one area of the valve face. Minor pits, grooves, etc. can be removed by refacing, but a valve with a cupped head must be replaced. Check the valve stem to make sure it is not bent and check for obvious wear that is indicated by a step between the part of the stem that travels in the valve guide and the part of the stem near the keeper grooves.

3. Check the valve stem-to-guide clearance in one or more of the following manners, but do not rely on the visual inspection alone:

a. A visual inspection can give you a fairly good idea if the guide, valve stem or both are worn. Insert the valve into the guide until the valve head is slightly away from the valve seat. Wiggle the valve sideways. A small amount of wobble is normal, excessive wobble means a worn guide and/or valve stem.

b. If a dial indicator is on hand, mount the indicator so that gauge stem is 90° to the valve stem as close to the top of the valve guide as possible. Move the valve from the seat, and measure the valve guide-to-stem clearance by rocking the stem back and forth to actuate the dial indicator. Measure the valve stem using a micrometer and compare to specifications to determine whether stem or guide is causing excessive clearance.

c. If both a ball gauge and a micrometer are available, first, measure the inside diameter of the valve guide bushing at three locations using the ball gauge. The guide must not exceed 0.277 in. (7.050mm) in diameter. Second, use the micrometer to measure the stem diameter. The stem must not be smaller than 0.2736 in. (6.950mm) for intake valves or 0.373 in. (6.919mm) for exhaust valves. Finally, subtract the valve stem diameter from the corresponding valve guide inside diameter to arrive at the valve clearance. On both engines, if clearance is greater than 0.0044 in. (0.115mm) for intake valves or 0.005 in. (0.131mm) for exhaust valves, the valve and guide bushing must be replaced.

4. The valve guide, if worn, must be repaired before the valve seats can be resurfaced. A new valve guide should be installed or, in some cases, knurled. Consult the automotive machine shop.

5. If the valve guide is okay, measure the valve seat concentricity using a runout gauge. Follow the manufacturers instructions. If runout is excessive, reface or replace the valve and machine or replace the valve seat.

6. Valves and seats must always be machined together. Never use a refaced valve on a valve seat that has not been machined; never use a valve that has not been refaced on a machined valve seat.

Fig. 65 The valve spring/seal service tools may be used to remove and install their components — SOHC engine shown.

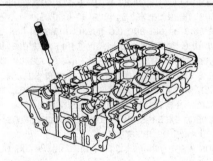

Fig. 66 Using a ball gauge, measure the inside diameter of the valve guides

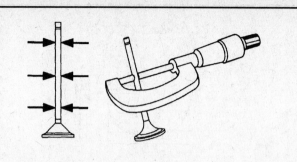

Fig. 67 Using a micrometer, measure the valve stem diameter

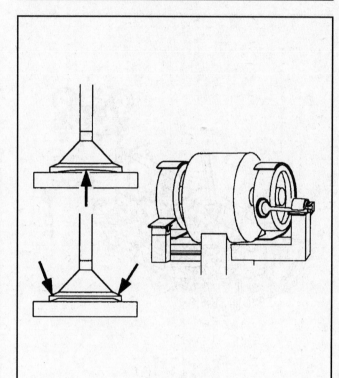

Fig. 68 Check the valve for a cupped head and replace valves found in this condition

REFACING

▶ See Figures 69, 70, 71 and 72

1. Determine if the valve is usable as explained in the Inspection procedure.

2. The correct valve grinding angle is 45.0-45.5 degrees. Make sure the valve refacer grinding wheels are properly dressed.

3. Reface the valve face only enough to remove the pits and grooves or correct any runout. If the edge or head margin thickness of the valve head is less than 0.0295 in. (0.75mm) thick after grinding, replace the valve, as the valve will run too hot in the engine.

4. Remove all grooves or score marks from the end of the valve stem, and chamfer it, as necessary. The minimum

overall valve length is 3.962 in. (100.64mm) for intake valves and 3.935 in. (99.94mm) for exhaust valves. Be sure not to grind so much from the end of the valve as to reduce it past the minimum length.

Valve Stem Seals

REPLACEMENT

Cylinder Heads Installed

▶ See Figures 73 and 74

1. Remove the spark plugs, valve/camshaft cover and the rocker arm/shaft assemblies for the SOHC engine or the bearing cap, camshaft and lifter assemblies for the DOHC engine. Refer to the procedures in this Section and Section 2, as necessary.

2. For the DOHC engine, install SA9124E, or an equivalent angle support, to the cylinder head. Use four M6 x 25mm bolts to mount the supports to the inside camshaft bearing cap holes, with the notched side of the supports toward the spark plug holes. Tighten the mounting bolts to 89 inch lbs. (10 Nm).

3. For the SOHC engine, install SA9124E, or an equivalent angle support, to the cylinder head. Use four M8 x 25mm bolts to mount the supports to the inside the end rocker arm shaft holes, with each support flange facing the center of the cylinder head. Tighten the mounting bolts to 124 inch lbs. (14 Nm).

4. Slide the rod through the supports and install the compressor lever arm assembly.

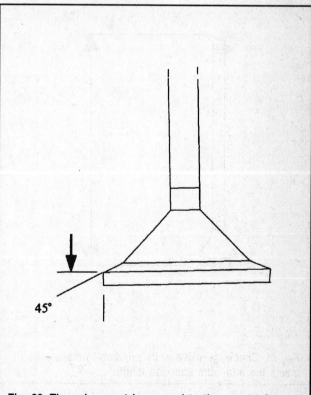

45°

Fig. 69 The valve must be ground to the correct face angle

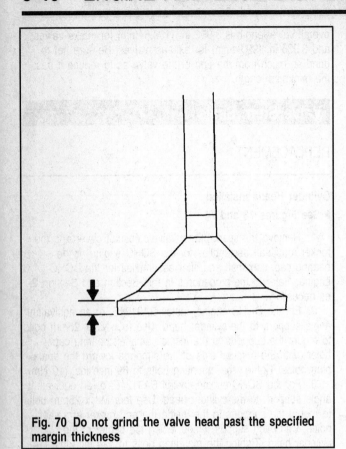

Fig. 70 Do not grind the valve head past the specified margin thickness

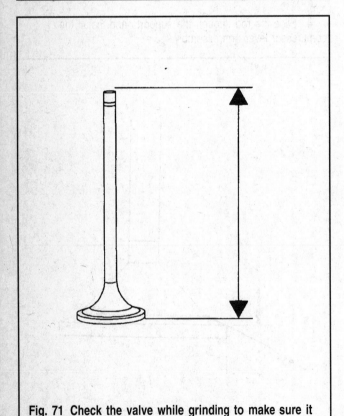

Fig. 71 Check the valve while grinding to make sure it meets the minimum specified length

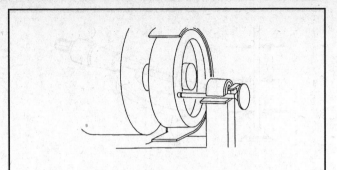

Fig. 72 Do not grind the valve stem so much as to reduce the valve past the minimum length

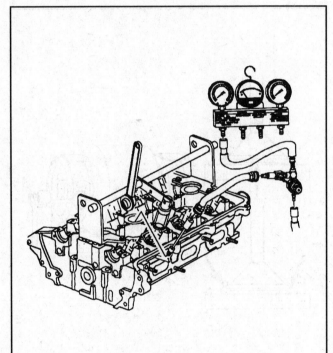

Fig. 73 Installation of the angle support, compressor lever assembly and the spark plug adapter with gauge set — DOHC engine shown

5. Turn the crankshaft so the cylinder piston corresponding to the seals to be worked on is at Top Dead Center (TDC). Install a spark plug adapter air fitting from a suitable compressed air source and gauge set to the respective spark plug hole. The hose on many screw-in compression testers will accept a quick-disconnect fitting to which an air compressor hose can be connected. Pressurize the cylinder to 100 psi (690 kpa) to hold the valve stem in the seat once the cap and spring is removed.

6. Position the lever assembly over the valve spring to be removed, then compress the spring using a ½ in. breaker bar and the compressor lever assembly. If difficulty is encountered, place a socket slightly larger than the valve stem and keepers over the valve stem and gently hit the socket with a plastic

hammer to break loose any varnish buildup. Compress the spring, remove the cap retainer and carefully release tension.

➡ NOTE:If the air pressure has forced the piston to the bottom of the cylinder, any removal of air pressure will allow the valves to fall into the cylinder. A rubber band, tape or string wrapped around the end of the valve stem will prevent this.

7. Remove the valve cap and spring, then use SA9102E, or an equivalent valve stem seal removal/installation tool, to remove the seal from the cylinder head.

To install:

8. Using the valve stem seal tool, install the new seal.

9. Install the valve spring and cap, then compress the spring and install the retainer.

10. When the valve springs are properly installed, release the air pressure from the cylinder using the gauge set, then remove the spark plug adapter.

11. Remove the compressor lever assembly, rod and supports from the cylinder head.

12. Install the rocker arm/shaft assemblies and the valve cover or the hydraulic lifters, camshafts, bearing caps and camshaft cover, as applicable.

13. Verify the proper gap and install the spark plugs.

Cylinder Heads Removed

The valve stem oil seals are replaced as a part of normal valve stem service any time the valve stems are removed from the cylinder head. Refer to the valve procedure in this Section for seal removal and installation when the cylinder head is removed from the vehicle.

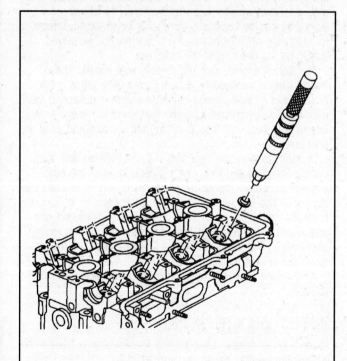

Fig. 74 Use the valve stem seal removal/installation tool to service the seals

Valve Springs

REMOVAL & INSTALLATION

1. Remove the cylinder head.
2. Remove the intake and exhaust manifolds.
3. For the SOHC engine, remove the rocker arms/shafts assemblies, guide plates and lifters. Remove the camshaft from either the front or the rear of the cylinder head.

➡NOTE:When disassembling valve trains, parts of which are to be reused, make sure to keep all components labeled or arranged for installation in their original locations. Rocker arms and/or lifters must be installed against the same contact surfaces from which they were removed. Store lifters with the camshaft side downward to keep their oil from draining.

4. For the DOHC engine, uniformly remove the camshaft bearing cap fasteners and caps. Remove the camshafts and the lifters. If necessary a magnet may ease lifter removal.

5. Support the head on suitable blocks with the cylinder side facing downward to facilitate valve removal.

6. Using SA9124E for DOHC engines, SA9125E for SOHC engines or an equivalent C-clamp type valve spring compressor, remove the valve spring cap retainer, valve spring and valves.

7. Place the parts from each valve in a separate container, numbered and identified for the valve and cylinder.

8. Inspect the valve springs for damage or wear and replace as necessary. Check the free length and/or spring pressure.

To install:

9. Install the valve springs, caps and retainers over the valve stems, using the removal/installation tool to compress the springs. Be careful not to depress the spring cap too far as it may cause seal and stem damage.

✸✸WARNING

Do not attempt to use a standard valve spring compressor tool when installing the valve assemblies as it may cause damage to the cylinder head hydraulic lifter surfaces and valve stems.

10. For the DOHC engine, lubricate and install the lifters, camshafts and camshaft bearing caps in their proper locations.

11. For the SOHC engine, lubricate and install the camshaft using a new rear cover plug or front thrust plate screws, as applicable. Oil and install the lifters, then install the rocker arm/shaft assemblies and guide plates, into their original locations.

12. Install the intake and exhaust manifolds to the cylinder head.

13. Install the cylinder head to the vehicle.

INSPECTION

▶ See Figures 75, 76 and 77

1. Check the springs for cracks or other damage.
2. Use a ruler to measure the height of each spring at 4 different locations. A bent spring must be replaced. You can also check the spring for squareness using a steel square and a flat surface. Stand the spring and square on end on a flat surface. Slide the spring up to the square, revolve the spring slowly and observe the space between the top coil of the spring and the square. If the space exceeds 0.10 in. (2.5mm), replace the spring.
3. Measure the free length of the spring using calipers or a suitable service tool. The free length should be approximately 1.61 in. (40.84mm).
4. Check the springs for proper pressure at the specified spring lengths using a valve spring tester. First completely compress the spring 3 times, then measure the tension at 2 different heights. The pressure should be 63 lbs. (280 N) @ 1.34 in. (34mm) and 157 lbs. (700 N) @ 0.984 in. (25mm). Replace springs with insufficient tension.

Valve Seats

REMOVAL & INSTALLATION

Valve seat replacement should be left to an automotive machine shop, due to the high degree of precision and special

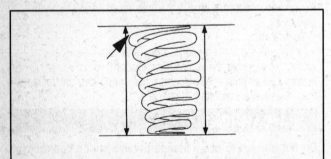

Fig. 75 One method to determine spring squareness is to measure the height at four or more points and compare the results

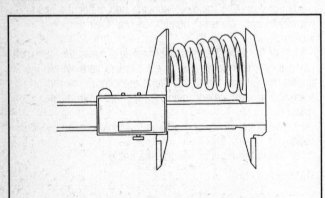

Fig. 76 Measuring the valve spring free length

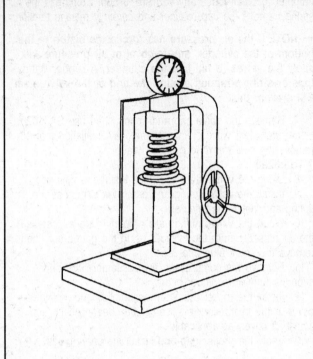

Fig. 77 Use a spring tester to determine tension at specific compression heights

equipment required. Although the seat replacement procedures are virtually the same for both engines, the specifications are unique to each cylinder head application. The following procedure can be construed as what is generally acceptable for aluminum cylinder heads; the actual method employed should be the decision of the machinist.

The Saturn engines use replaceable seat inserts. These inserts can be removed by cutting them out to within a few thousandths of their outside diameter and then collapsing the remainder. Another method sometimes used to remove seat inserts is to heat the head to a high temperature and drive the seat out.

Upon installation, the new seat may be installed with the cylinder head heated to a high temperature, then the seat, which is at room temperature or slightly chilled, is pressed into the head. The head is then allowed to cool and as it does, it contracts and grips the seat. In certain applications, the new seat may be driven in with both the head and seat at room temperature. The calculated press-fit interference will then retain the seat in the head.

After a new seat is installed, it must be inspected and refaced.

INSPECTION & REFACING

▶ See Figures 78, 79, 80, 81 and 82

When the valves are removed for service, the valve seats must be inspected to determine if they must be replaced. Saturn recommends that even their dealers send the cylinder heads to a reputable machine shop, if seat replacement is necessary.

1. Clean the valve seats and inspect for damage or cracks.

2. Use a carbide cutter or proper stone to resurface the valve seats. Use a 45 degree cutter for SOHC engines or a 44.5-45 degree cutter for DOHC engines. Remove only enough metal to clean the seats.

3. After cutting, use a micrometer to measure the seats and determine if they are within specification by comparing to the maximum service limits:
   a. SOHC intake valve seat — 0.0630 in. (1.60mm)
   b. SOHC exhaust valve seat — 0.0750 in. (1.90mm)
   c. DOHC intake valve seat — 0.0653 in. (1.66mm)
   d. DOHC exhaust valve seat — 0.0756 in. (1.92mm)

4. Check the valve seating position using a thin coat of Prussian blue or white lead on the valve face. Install the valve, apply light pressure and rotate the valve against the seat.

5. Remove the valve and check the face and seat:
   a. If the blue appears 360 degrees around the face, the valve is concentric. If not, the valve must be replaced.
   b. If blue appears 360 degrees around the valve seat, the guide and seat are concentric. If not, the seat must be ground.

6. If the valve and seat are concentric, determine if seat contact is occurring properly on the middle of the valve face. If seating is too high on the face, correct the seat width with 30 and 45 degree cutters. If seating is too low on the face, correct the seat using 60 and 45 degree cutters.

7. Using a suitable lapping tool and abrasive compound, hand lap both the valve and seat.

8. Using a suitable solvent, clean the valve and seat.

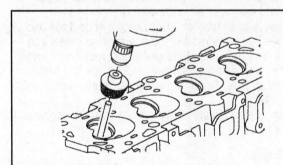

Fig. 78 Use a carbide cutter or proper stone to resurface the valve seats

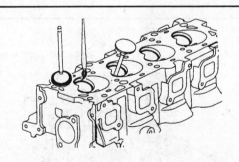

Fig. 79 Apply a thin coat of Prussian blue or white lead to the valve face

9. Finally, install the valve without the seal and use calipers to measure the tip height to make sure it is within specification. The maximum height should be 1.921 in. (48.8mm) for SOHC engines or 1.589 in. (40.35mm) for DOHC engines.

Valve Guides

▶ See Figure 83

If the valve guides are determined to be worn by discovering excessive clearance during the valve inspection procedure, they must be replaced.

➡ **NOTE: The valve seats must be refaced after guide knurling or replacement.**

REMOVAL & INSTALLATION

1. Using SA9126E or an equivalent valve guide bushing removal/installation service tool and a hammer, drive the old bushing from the cylinder head bore.

2. Using a ball gauge, measure the bore diameter. If the diameter is greater than 0.448 in. (11.368mm), the oversize reamer must be used to install the oversize replacement guide bushing. If the bore exceeds 0.457 in. (11.613mm), the cylinder head must be replaced.

To install:

3. Drive the standard or oversize bushing, as applicable, into the cylinder head bore using the service tool and a hammer. When installing, do not use any oil or thread locking material on the guide bushing or bore.

4. Drive the bushing until a height of 0.4035-0.4133 in. (10.25-10.50mm) above the valve or spring seat is achieved.

Valve Lifters

REMOVAL & INSTALLATION

SOHC Engine

▶ See Figure 84

1. Disconnect the negative battery cable.

2. Remove the rocker arm cover, then inspect the cover silicone insulators for cracks or deterioration and replace as necessary.

3. Uniformly remove the rocker arm assembly bolts, then carefully remove the 2 rocker arm/shaft assemblies, guide plates and lifters.

4. If lifters are to be reused, make sure they are arranged so that they may be installed in the same bores from which they were removed. Inspect the lifters and guide plates to see if they must be repaired or replaced.

To install:

5. Oil the lifters and install them into the bores. Before installing, rotate each lifter so that the flat sides are parallel to the intake and exhaust manifolds. If reinstalling the used lifters, make sure they are positioned in the bores from which they were removed.

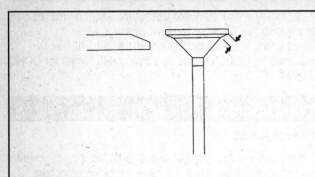

Fig. 80 Make sure contact is made on the middle of the valve face

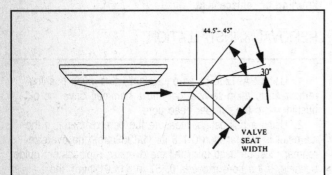

Fig. 81 If seating is too high on the face, correct the seat width with 30 and 45 degree cutters

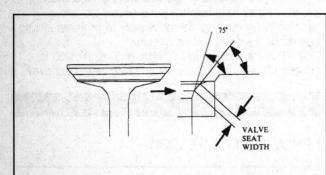

Fig. 82 If seating is too low on the face, correct the seat using 60 and 45 degree cutters

6. Install the lifter guide plates, then snap 1 end of each lifter guide plate retaining spring onto the rocker arm shaft between No. 1-No. 2 and the No. 3-No. 4 cylinder rocker arms.

7. Install the rocker arm shaft assemblies. To prevent valve or piston damage, be sure the rocker arm tangs are squarely seated on the lifter plungers and the retaining springs are positioned in the guide plate slots.

➡NOTE: If difficulty is encountered aligning the rocker arms on the valves and lifters, use a flat piece of wood, cardboard or an extension bar of suitable length on top of the shafts and rocker arms to hold both assemblies in position.

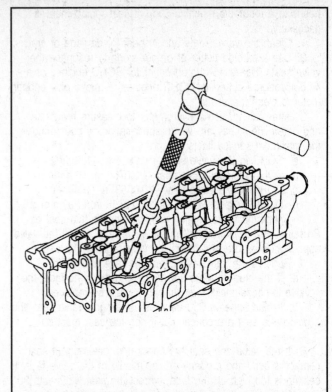

Fig. 83 Install the new valve guide bushing using the service tool and hammer — SOHC engine shown

8. Tighten the 5 rocker arm bolts on each shaft in a uniform sequence to 18 ft. lbs. (25 Nm). Verify the proper position and seating of all rocker components.

9. Apply a small drop of RTV to each cylinder head and front cover T-joint. Inspect the rocker arm cover gasket and replace if necessary. Install the gasket and rocker arm cover, then tighten the fasteners uniformly to 22 ft. lbs. (30 Nm). Make sure all cover hoses and components are reconnected after installation.

10. Connect the negative battery cable, start the engine and check for leaks.

DOHC Engine

1. Disconnect the negative battery cable.

2. Remove the camshaft cover, then inspect the cover silicone insulators for cracks or deterioration and replace as necessary.

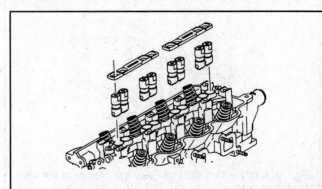

Fig. 84 Lifter and guide plate installation — SOHC engine

3. Remove the camshafts; refer to the procedure in this Section.

4. Remove the valve lifters from their bores. Be sure to place all lifters in a rack or label them to assure installation in their original locations. Store lifters with their camshaft contact face down to prevent the oil from draining.

➡ **NOTE:Do not remove the lifters from the bores using pliers or a sharp object. A magnet should easily pull the lifter from the bore without scoring or damaging the mating surfaces.**

To install:

5. Lubricate the lifters and install them in their proper locations.

6. Properly align and install the intake and exhaust camshafts.

7. Apply a small drop of RTV across the cylinder head and front cover T-joints. Inspect the old camshaft cover gasket and replace if damaged. Install the gasket and the camshaft cover. Tighten the fasteners in the proper sequence to 89 inch lbs. (10 Nm).

8. Connect the negative battery cable, start the engine and check for leaks.

INSPECTION & SERVICE

SOHC Engine

▶ **See Figures 85 and 86**

1. Remove the lifters from the cylinder head, then check the lifter roller and the cylinder head for wear.

2. Using a suitable micrometer and/or a ball gauge, as applicable, check the following dimensions. Repair or replace lifters, as necessary:

   a. Lifter body diameter — 0.8417 in. (21.380mm) minimum

   b. Lifter total roller length — 2.0531 in. (52.15mm) minimum

   c. Cylinder head bore diameter — 0.8445 in. (21.45mm) maximum

   d. Lifter body oil clearance — 0.0028 in. (0.07mm) maximum

   e. Lifter body guide flat — 0.7539 in. (19.15mm) minimum

   f. Lifter guide plate width — 0.7632 in. (19.385mm) maximum

➡**NOTE:Lifters are difficult assemblies to repair, do not attempt to disassemble and repair unless the proper testing equipment is available. Internal parts from 1 lifter should not be mixed with other assemblies.**

3. If necessary, disassemble and clean the lifters:

   a. Remove the plunger retainer.

   b. Remove the valve, disk and plunger.

   c. Clean all parts in solvent and allow to dry, then inspect the internal parts for scratches and wear.

   d. If parts are not damaged, lubricate with clean engine oil and assemble.

DOHC Engine

The lifters used in the DOHC engine are very difficult to repair and must be replaced as an assembly if worn or damaged.

1. Remove the lifters from the cylinder head, then check the lifter and the cylinder head for wear or damage. There is a

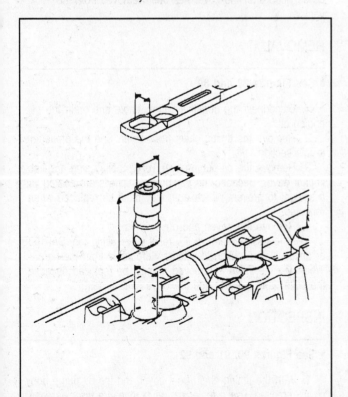

Fig. 85 Measure the lifters and guide plates for excessive wear at these points — SOHC engine

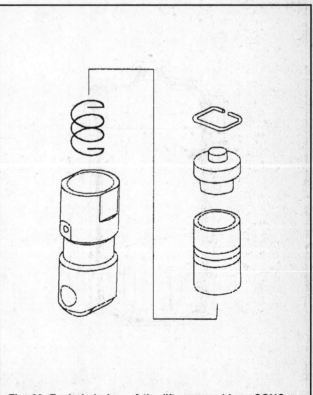

Fig. 86 Exploded view of the lifter assembly — SOHC engine

welded joint approximately 0.080 in. (2mm) from the top of the lifter (camshaft contact surface). The weld mark should not be mistaken for a crack.

2. Using a suitable micrometer and/or a ball gauge, as applicable, check the following dimensions. Replace damaged or worn lifters:

    a. Lifter diameter — 1.3 in. (32.947mm) minimum

    b. Cylinder head bore diameter — 1.3004 in. (33.03mm) maximum

    c. Oil clearance — 0.003 in. (0.083mm) maximum

Oil Pan

REMOVAL & INSTALLATION

▶ **See Figure 87**

1. Raise the front of the vehicle and support it safely using jackstands. Remove the plug and drain the engine oil from the pan and crankcase.

2. Disconnect the fasteners from the exhaust manifold flange and the pipe rear flange, then remove the front exhaust pipe and gaskets from the vehicle.

3. For 1991 vehicles, remove the engine stiffening bracket and the flywheel cover.

4. Remove the right wheel and splash shield, then loosen the 4 front motor mount bolts. Back the bolts out about ½ inch (12mm).

5. Remove all the oil pan bolts. For vehicles with a manual transaxle, an 8mm flex socket may be used to access the rear oil pan bolts located next to the flywheel.

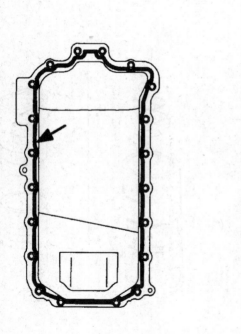

Fig. 87 Apply a 0.16 in (4mm) bead of RTV to the oil pan flange to the inner side of the bolt holes

6. Using SA9123E, or an equivalent RTV cutter tool, separate the oil pan from the engine. Drive the tool around the pan to shear the RTV seam, then tap the pan sideways with a rubber mallet to loosen.

7. Pry the engine mount away from the engine as necessary and remove the oil pan. Be careful not to damage or score component surfaces when prying.

    To install:

8. Carefully clean the gasket mating surfaces with a scraper and solvent.

9. Apply a 0.16 inch (4mm) bead of RTV sealer to the pan flange. Make sure the RTV is applied to the inner-side of the flange from the bolt holes as shown.

10. Install the oil pan within 3 minutes of RTV application and tighten the bolts to 80 inch lbs. (9 Nm).

11. Tighten the front mount bolts to 40 ft. lbs. (54 Nm).

12. Install the right splash shield and wheel.

13. For 1991 vehicles, install the engine stiffening bracket and the flywheel cover.

14. Install the exhaust pipe. Tighten the pipe to manifold nuts in a crosswise pattern to 23 ft. lbs. (31 Nm) and the pipe to converter bolts to 33 ft. lbs. (45 Nm).

15. Remove the jackstands and carefully lower the vehicle, then fill the engine crankcase with clean engine oil immediately in order to prevent an attempt to start the engine without oil.

16. Start the engine and check for leaks.

Oil Pump

The oil pump is located in a housing built into the lower portion of the timing chain/engine front cover. The pump may be serviced after the cover has been removed from the vehicle.

REMOVAL

▶ **See Figures 88 and 89**

1. Disconnect the negative battery cable and drain the engine oil.

2. Remove the timing chain front cover. See the procedure in this section.

3. Remove the oil pump cover Torx® bolts using a suitable impact driver. Because the pump cover screws are coated with a sealant to prevent oil leakage, they must be replaced when removed.

4. Remove the driven and drive rotors.

5. If necessary, remove the relief valve using tool SA9103E or an equivalent puller, to withdraw the valve from the bore. Whenever the valve is removed, it must be replaced because the puller jaws will damage the valve sealing seat.

INSPECTION

▶ **See Figures 90, 91 and 92**

1. With the timing chain front cover and the oil pump body cover removed, use a feeler gauge to measure the clearance between the driven rotor and pump body. Clearance should not exceed 0.0042 in. (0.105mm).

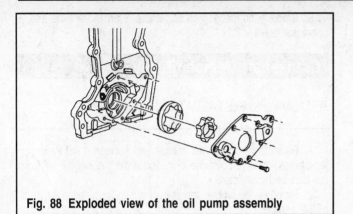

Fig. 88 Exploded view of the oil pump assembly

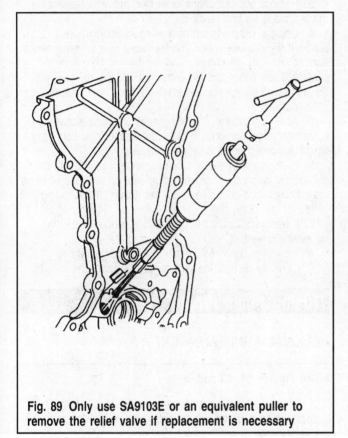

Fig. 89 Only use SA9103E or an equivalent puller to remove the relief valve if replacement is necessary

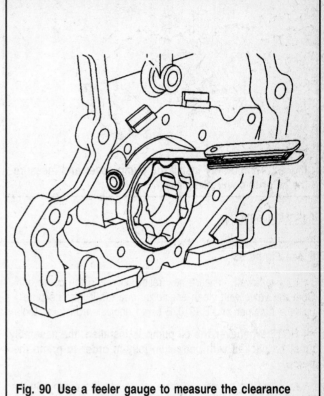

Fig. 90 Use a feeler gauge to measure the clearance between the driven rotor and pump body

2. Use a feeler gauge to measure the clearance between the both rotor tips. Clearance should not exceed 0.006 in. (0.150mm).

3. Using Plastigage® or a feeler gauge, temporarily install the pump cover and measure the rotor-to-cover clearance. Clearance should not exceed 0.005 in. (0.128mm).

4. If necessary, replace the pump components and/or the front cover assembly.

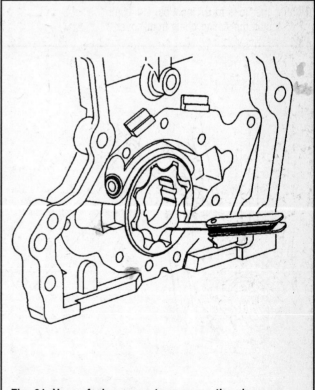

Fig. 91 Use a feeler gauge to measure the clearance between both rotor tips

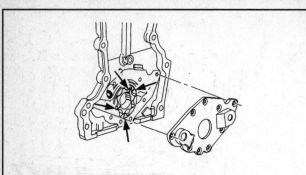

Fig. 92 Temporarily install the pump cover and measure the rotor-to-cover clearance

INSTALLATION

▶ **See Figure 93**

1. If removed, install a new relief valve into the cover bore. Coat the valve with clean engine oil and tap it into the bore using a hammer and SA9103E or an equivalent installer tool.

➡ **NOTE:Whenever the oil pump is installed, the assembly must be packed with petroleum jelly in order to prime the pump.**

2. Install the driven and drive rotors into the pump with the chamfer toward the front oil seal.

3. Install the pump body cover and secure with new bolts which are covered with a sealant to prevent oil leakage. Tighten the bolts to 97 inch lbs. (11 Nm).

4. Install the timing chain front cover.

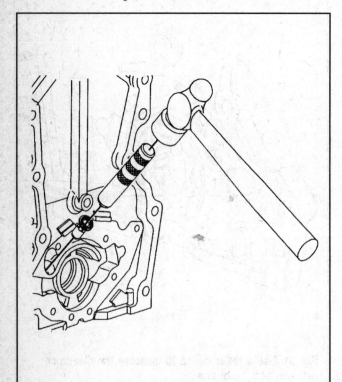

Fig. 93 Install a new pressure relief valve using a hammer and suitable installation tool

5. Properly fill the engine crankcase, start the engine and check for leaks.

Crankshaft Damper/Pulley

REMOVAL & INSTALLATION

1. Raise the front of the vehicle and support it safely using jackstands, then remove the plug and drain the engine oil from the pan and crankcase.

2. Remove the wheel and splash shield from the right front of the vehicle.

3. Remove the serpentine drive belt and, if necessary, remove the drive belt tensioner.

4. Using a strap wrench or a piece of wood wedged between the damper spoke and the lower side of the engine front cover, hold the damper and remove the bolt. With a suitable 3 jaw puller and the slots cast into the damper, pull the crankshaft damper/pulley assembly from the crankshaft.

To install:

5. Apply a thin film of RTV between the damper/pulley assembly flange and washer only, the washer and bolt head flange are designed to prevent oil leakage.

6. Position the crankshaft damper/pulley assembly to the crankshaft, then secure using a strap wrench or piece of wood (as accomplished during removal) and tighten the retaining bolt to 159 ft. lbs. (215 Nm).

7. If removed, install the drive belt tensioner. Install the serpentine drive belt.

8. Install the right front splash shield and the wheel.

9. Carefully remove the jackstands and lower the vehicle.

Timing Chain Front Cover

REMOVAL & INSTALLATION

▶ **See Figures 94, 95 and 96**

1. Disconnect the negative battery cable, then raise and support the front of the vehicle sufficiently to work both under the vehicle and under the hood. Be sure to properly position the jackstands.

2. Remove the plug from the oil pan and drain the engine oil into a suitable container. Remove the right wheel and splash shield.

3. For 1992-93 vehicles with a torque axis mount system, place a 1 inch **x** 1 inch **x** 2 inch long block of wood between the torque strut and cradle to ease removal and installation of the torque engine mount. Remove the 3 right side upper engine torque axis to front cover nuts and the 2 mount to midrail bracket nuts, allowing the powertrain to rest on the block of wood.

➡**NOTE:Placing a block of wood under the torque axis mount prior to removing the upper mount will allow the engine to rest on the wood, thus preventing the engine from shifting. This will allow you to install the mount during assembly without jacking or raising the engine.**

4. Remove the serpentine drive belt and belt tensioner. It is not necessary to remove the water pump pulley, however, for 1992-93 vehicles the idler pulley must be removed to access the engine front cover.

5. Remove the power steering pump attaching bolts and support the assembly aside with the lines attached. If equipped and if necessary for access to the front cover bolts, remove the A/C compressor from the bracket and support the assembly aside. Again, keep the compressor lines attached and do not discharge the system.

6. Remove the valve/camshaft cover. Cover the valve train assemblies to protect them from foreign debris or dirt.

7. Using a strap wrench or a piece of wood wedged between the damper spoke and the lower side of the engine front cover, hold the damper and remove the bolt. With a suitable 3 jaw puller and the slots cast into the damper, pull the crankshaft damper/pulley assembly from the crankshaft.

8. Install the special tool SA9104E or equivalent, to make sure the front crankshaft timing sprocket is held firmly in place and prevent guide damage. Install with the flat side towards the crankshaft sprocket.

9. Remove the front 4 oil pan bolts, then using a suitable RTV cutting tool, cut the front seal away from the front cover.

10. Spray the 2 dowel pin holes with penetrating oil to facilitate front cover removal from the dowel pins.

11. Remove the front cover bolts. For 1992-93 vehicles, 1 bolt is located above the serpentine drive belt pulley, under the torque axis mount flange.

12. Using a small suitable tool, carefully pry the cover away from the cylinder block at the pry location tabs which are provided. Remove the cover from under the hood or through the wheel well. Be sure to cover the front of the engine to prevent debris or dirt to enter into the oil gallery openings and the oil pan. If necessary, pry the front cover oil seal from the cover for replacement.

To install:

13. Make sure the oil galleys are clear. Carefully clean the gasket mating surfaces with a scraper or wire brush and carburetor solvent, brake clean or alcohol. Use a⁹⁄₁₆ inch drill bit and tap handle to clean the front cover holes. If removed, install a new front cover oil seal using a suitable installation tool and press or wait until the cover is installed and use the installation tool and crankshaft threads to pull the seal into position.

➡NOTE:If the engine front cover casting or assembly is replaced on 1992-93 vehicles, the 3 torque axis mount studs should also be replaced. Tighten the new studs to 19 ft. lbs. (25 Nm).

14. Apply a 0.08 inch (2mm) bead of RTV sealer along the vertical sealing surfaces of the front cover to the inside of the bolt holes and to the front of the oil pan. Extra sealer is necessary at the oil pan and cylinder head joints. For DOHC engines apply a thin bead around the 1 center cover bolt hole on 1991 vehicles or the 2 inner cover bolt holes on 1992-93 vehicles. Be sure to assemble the front cover to the engine within 3 minutes of RTV application.

15. If removed, install the crankshaft gear retaining tool to align the oil pump and crankshaft during cover installation. Position the front cover to the engine and install the bolts. Tighten the perimeter bolts starting at the center and working

outwards on both sides to 19 ft. lbs. (25 Nm) for SOHC engines or to 22 ft. lbs. (30 Nm) for DOHC engines.

16. Install and tighten the front cover center or inner bolts to 89 inch lbs. (10 Nm) except for the upper inside bolt on 1992-93 DOHC engines which should be tightened to 22 ft. lbs. (30 Nm). Install the 4 oil pan front bolts and tighten to 80 inch lbs. (9 Nm).

17. After front cover installation, spray 6-12 squirts of oil through the front oil seal drain back hole to verify that it is not plugged.

18. Apply a thin film of RTV between the damper/pulley assembly flange and washer only, the washer and bolt head flange are designed to prevent oil leakage.

19. Remove the crankshaft retaining tool and position the crankshaft damper/pulley assembly, then secure using the wood or strap wrench (as accomplished during removal) and tighten the bolt to 159 ft. lbs. (215 Nm).

20. Apply a small drop of RTV across the cylinder head and front cover T-joints. Inspect the old camshaft cover gasket and replace if damaged. Install the gasket and the camshaft cover. Tighten the fasteners uniformly to 22 ft. lbs. (30 Nm) for SOHC vehicles or in proper sequence to 89 inch lbs. (10 Nm) for DOHC vehicles.

21. Position and install the A/C compressor assembly and/or the power steering pump assembly, as applicable.

22. Install the idler pulley if removed, then install the belt tensioner and the serpentine drive belt.

23. For 1992-93 vehicles equipped with a torque axis mount system, install the 2 engine mounts to midrail bracket nuts and tighten to 52 ft. lbs. (70 Nm). Next install the 3 mount to front cover nuts, tighten them uniformly to 52 ft. lbs. (70 Nm) in order to prevent front cover damage. Then remove the block of wood from under the torque strut.

24. Install the splash shield and the wheel assembly, then remove the jackstands and carefully lower the vehicle.

25. Immediately fill the engine crankcase with clean engine oil and connect the negative battery cable.

26. Start the engine and check for leaks.

Timing Chain Cover Oil Seal

The oil seal may be replaced either with the front cover installed or with the cover out of the engine. The seal should never be installed by tapping with a hammer; in both cases, the installation tool should be used. If the cover is removed, a press may be used with the tool installed to position the seal. The safest method to prevent cover damage is probably to install the seal with the front cover on the engine, using the tool and crankshaft threads to draw the seal into position.

REPLACEMENT

With Cover Installed
▶ **See Figure 97**

1. Disconnect the negative battery cable, then raise and support the front of the vehicle sufficiently to work both under the vehicle and in the wheel well. Be sure to properly position the jackstands.

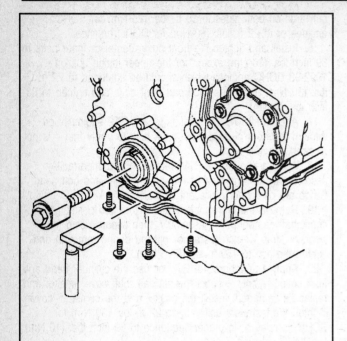

Fig. 94 Install the crankshaft sprocket retainer tool, remove the 4 front oil pan bolts and carefully cut the oil pan seal away from the front cover

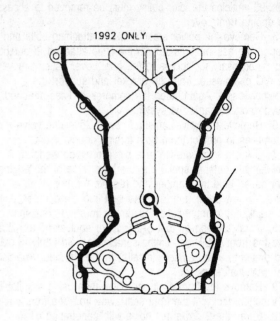

Fig. 96 Apply a thin bead of RTV sealer as shown — DOHC engine

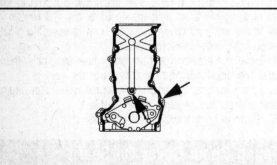

Fig. 95 Apply a thin bead of RTV sealer as shown — SOHC engine

2. Remove the plug from the oil pan and drain the engine oil into a suitable container. If the right side of the vehicle is positioned higher than the left, it may not be necessary to drain the oil from the crankcase. If this is desired, a drain pan should be positioned below the front cover to catch any oil that does leak. Remove the right wheel and splash shield.

3. For 1992-93 vehicles with a torque axis mount system, it may be necessary to remove the engine mount for access to the components. If this is determined necessary, place a 1 inch x 1 inch x 2 inch long block of wood between the torque strut and cradle to ease removal and installation of the torque engine mount. Remove the 3 right side upper engine torque

axis to front cover nuts and the 2 mount to midrail bracket nuts, allowing the powertrain to rest on the block of wood.

➡ NOTE: Placing a block of wood under the torque axis mount prior to removing the upper mount will allow the engine to rest on the wood, thus preventing the engine from shifting. This will allow you to install the mount during assembly without jacking or raising the engine.

4. Using a strap wrench or a piece of wood wedged between the damper spoke and the lower side of the engine front cover, hold the damper and remove the bolt. With a suitable 3 jaw puller and the slots cast into the damper, pull the crankshaft damper/pulley assembly from the crankshaft.

5. Use a suitable prytool to carefully pry the front oil seal from the front cover. Be careful not to damage the front cover or crankshaft.

6. Clean the seal bore and oil drain back passage.

To install:

7. Make sure the oil drain back is free of contamination. Position the oil seal and thread service seal installer tool SA9104E or equivalent onto the end of the crankshaft. Use the tool to draw the seal into position. Never tap on the seal or the seal installer with a hammer.

8. Apply a thin film of clean engine oil to the new seal lip.

9. Position the crankshaft damper/pulley assembly, then secure using the wood or strap wrench (as accomplished during removal) and tighten the bolt to 159 ft. lbs. (215 Nm).

10. If removed, install the 2 engine mounts to midrail bracket nuts and tighten to 52 ft. lbs. (70 Nm). Next install the 3 mount to front cover nuts, tighten them uniformly to 52 ft. lbs. (70 Nm) in order to prevent front cover damage. Then remove the block of wood from under the torque strut.

11. Install the splash shield and the wheel assembly, then remove the jackstands and carefully lower the vehicle.

12. Immediately fill the engine crankcase with clean engine oil and connect the negative battery cable.

13. Start the engine and check for leaks.

With Front Cover Removed

1. Note the depth to which the factory seal was installed into the front cover, then use a suitable prytool to carefully remove the oil seal from the front cover. Be careful not to score or damage the front cover or crankshaft surfaces.

2. Clean the seal bore and oil drain back passage.

3. Place the engine front cover on the base of a suitable arbor press.

4. Position the seal to the front cover and place tool SA9104E, or equivalent installation tool, over the seal.

5. Press the seal into the engine front cover approximately 0.04 inch (1mm) further into the engine front cover than the factory seal removed earlier.

6. Install the timing chain front cover to the engine.

Timing Chain and Sprockets

REMOVAL & INSTALLATION

SOHC Engine
▶ **See Figures 98, 99, 100 and 101**

1. Disconnect the negative battery cable.

2. Remove the timing chain front cover.

➡**NOTE:During timing chain and gear removal, position the crankshaft 90 degrees past Top Dead Center (TDC) to make sure the pistons will not contact the valves upon assembly.**

3. Carefully rotate the crankshaft clockwise so the timing mark on the crankshaft sprocket and keyway align with the main bearing cap split line (90 degrees past TDC).

4. Remove bolts, then remove the timing guides and tensioner.

5. Remove the camshaft sprocket bolt, using a ⅛ in. (21mm) wrench to hold the camshaft. Then remove the timing chain and camshaft sprocket. Remove the crankshaft sprocket, if necessary.

To install:

6. Inspect the chain for wear and damage. Check the inside diameter of the chain, it should be no more than 16.77 in. (426mm). Inspect the chain guides for wear or cracks and the timing gears for teeth or key wear. Replace components as necessary.

7. Verify that the crankshaft is positioned 90 degrees clockwise past TDC from the keyway (keyway at 3 o'clock).

8. Bring the camshaft up to No. 1 TDC by loosely installing the sprocket and rotating the sprocket until the timing pin can be inserted. The camshaft contains wrench flats to assist in turning the shaft. The dowel pin should be at 12 o'clock when the camshaft is at TDC and a timing pin ³⁄₁₆ inch drill bit) should then install at about the 8 o'clock position.

9. If removed, install the crankshaft sprocket, then rotate the crankshaft counterclockwise 90 degrees up to No. 1 TDC (keyway at 12 o'clock).

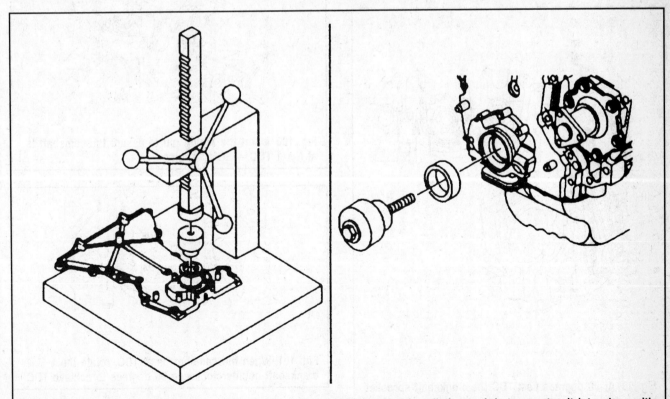

Fig. 97 Install the new front cover oil seal using a press or the threaded installation tool, but never tap it into place with a hammer

10. Position the chain under the crankshaft sprocket and over the camshaft sprocket. If necessary remove the camshaft sprocket, then slide the camshaft sprocket into position with the chain already engaged. The timing chain should be positioned so 1 silver link plate aligns with the pip mark on the camshaft sprocket and the other aligns with the downward tooth (at the 6 o'clock position) on the crankshaft sprocket. The letters FRT on the camshaft sprocket must face forward, away from the cylinder head and excess chain slack should be located on the tensioner side of the block.

11. Temporarily install the timing pin to verify proper alignment of the camshaft and sprocket, then install and tighten the sprocket bolt to 75 ft. lbs. (102 Nm). Again, use a wrench on the camshaft flats to hold the shaft in position while tightening the bolt. Do not allow the camshaft retaining bolt to torque against the timing pin or cylinder head damage will result.

12. Install the chain guides with the words FRONT facing out. Install the fixed guide first and verify the chain is snug against the guide, then install the pivot guide. Tighten the bolts to 19 ft. lbs. (26 Nm) and verify that the pivot guide moves freely.

13. Retract the tensioner plunger and pin the ratchet lever using a 1/8 in. No. 31 drill bit inserted in the alignment hole at the bottom front of the component. Install the tensioner and tighten the bolts to 14 ft. lbs. (19 Nm), then remove the drill bit.

14. Make 1 final check to verify all components are properly timed, then remove all timing pins.

15. Install the timing chain front cover.

16. Connect the negative battery cable, start the engine and check for leaks.

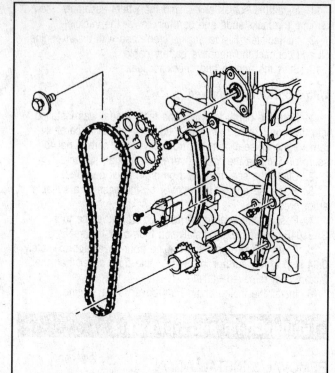

Fig. 99 Exploded view of the timing chain and sprocket assembly — SOHC engine

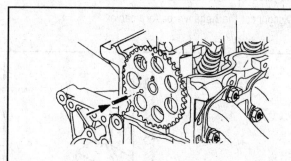

Fig. 100 Insert the timing pin to assure the camshaft is at No. 1 TDC — SOHC engine

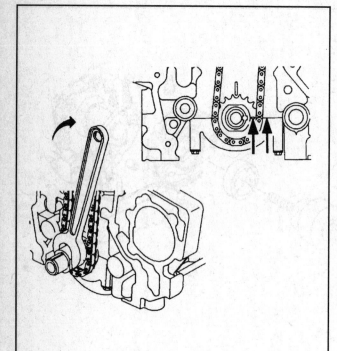

Fig. 98 At 90 degrees past TDC the crankshaft sprocket timing mark and keyway will align with the main bearing cap split line

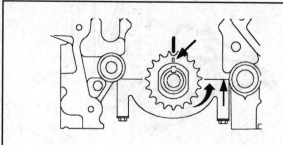

Fig. 101 When the camshaft is at TDC, rotate the crankshaft counterclockwise 90 degrees to achieve TDC

DOHC Engine

▶ **See Figures 102, 103 and 104**

1. Disconnect the negative battery cable.
2. Remove the timing chain front cover.

➡**NOTE:During timing chain and gear removal, position the crankshaft 90 degrees past Top Dead Center (TDC) to make sure the pistons will not contact the valves upon assembly.**

3. Carefully rotate the crankshaft clockwise so the timing mark on the crankshaft sprocket and keyway align with the main bearing cap split line.
4. Remove the bolts, then remove the timing guides and tensioner.
5. Remove the camshaft sprocket bolts, using a 7/8 in. (21mm) wrench to hold the camshaft. Then remove the timing chain and camshaft sprocket. Remove the crankshaft sprocket, if necessary.

To install:

6. Inspect the chain for wear and damage. Check the inside diameter of the chain, it should be no more than 23.15 in. (588mm). Inspect the chain guides for wear or cracks and the timing gears for teeth or key wear. Replace components as necessary.
7. Verify that the crankshaft is positioned 90 degrees clockwise past TDC. The crankshaft keyway should be at 3 o'clock aligned with the main bearing cap split line to prevent piston and valve damage.
8. Install the camshaft gears, retaining bolts and washers. Make sure the letters FRT on the gears face forward, away from the cylinder block. Use the wrench flats provided on the camshafts to hold the shaft and tighten the bolts to 75 ft. lbs. (102 Nm).
9. Bring the camshafts up to No. 1 TDC by rotating the camshafts and sprocket until the dowel pins are at 12 o'clock. Install a /16 in. drill bit into the hole in the sprocket about 9 o'clock.
10. If removed, install the crankshaft sprocket, then rotate the crankshaft counterclockwise 90 degree up to No. 1 TDC (keyway and sprocket timing mark at 12 o'clock, in alignment with the block timing mark).
11. Position the timing chain under the crankshaft sprocket and over the camshaft sprockets so 2 silver link plates align with the pip marks on the camshaft sprockets and another 2 plates align with the downward tooth (at 6 o'clock position) on the crankshaft sprocket. Excess chain slack should be located on the tensioner side of the cylinder block.
12. Verify that the crankshaft pip mark aligns with the cylinder block mark at 12 o'clock and that the timing pins are installed in the holes at about the 9 o'clock position. Remove the timing pins from the camshaft sprockets.
13. Install the timing chain fixed guide to the right of the block face toward the water pump. Tighten the bolts to 21 ft. lbs. (28 Nm) and verify the chain is snug against the guide.
14. Install the pivoting chain guide and check for clearance between the block and head. Tighten the bolt to 19 ft. lbs. (26 Nm) and verify the guide pivots freely.
15. Retract the tensioner plunger and pin the ratchet lever using a 1/8 in. No. 31 drill bit inserted in the alignment hole at the lower front of the component. Install the tensioner and tighten the bolts to 14 ft. lbs. (19 Nm), then remove the drill bit.
16. Install the 2 forward camshaft bearing caps and the upper timing chain guide, then tighten the retaining bolts to 124 inch lbs. (14 Nm).
17. Make 1 final check to verify all components are properly timed, then remove all timing pins.
18. Install the timing chain front cover.
19. Connect the negative battery cable, start the engine and check for leaks.

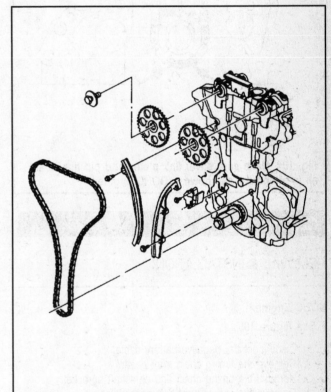

Fig. 102 Exploded view of the timing chain and sprockets assembly — DOHC engine

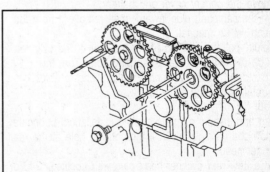

Fig. 103 Insert the timing pins to verify the camshafts are at TDC — DOHC engine

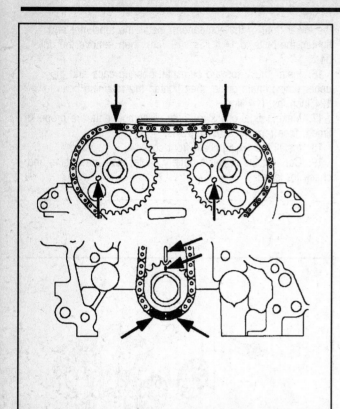

Fig. 104 Make sure silver link plates and pip marks are all in alignment as shown — DOHC engine

Camshaft

REMOVAL & INSTALLATION

SOHC Engine

▶ See Figure 105

1. Disconnect the negative battery cable.
2. Remove the timing chain front cover.
3. Remove the timing chain and camshaft sprocket.
4. Remove the rocker arm/shaft assemblies.
5. Remove the lifters and label or position them for assembly in their original locations.
6. Remove the battery cover and battery.
7. Drive the camshaft plug inward, then remove it from the cylinder head with a magnet.
8. Carefully pull the camshaft from the rear of the cylinder head through the oversized camshaft plug hole. Turn the camshaft back and forth slowly while withdrawing to help prevent journal or bearing damage.

To install:

9. Clean and inspect all parts prior to installation. Lubricate the camshaft and carefully insert it through the hole at the rear of the cylinder head.
10. Coat a new rear cylinder head plug with Loctite® 242 or equivalent and install it using a standard bushing driver.
11. Install the battery and tighten the battery hold-down nut and screw to 80 inch lbs. (9 Nm). Connect the positive battery cable only, at this time.

12. Install the valve lifters into their original bores, or if the camshaft has been replaced, install new lifters.
13. Install the rocker arm/shaft assemblies.
14. Install the timing chain and camshaft sprocket.
15. Install the timing chain front cover.
16. Connect the negative battery cable, start the engine and check for leaks.

DOHC Engine

▶ See Figures 106, 107 and 108

➡ NOTE: Be very careful when working around the camshaft sprockets and timing chain front cover during this procedure. If a bolt or washer is accidentally dropped between the front cover and engine assembly, the cover will have to be removed for retrieval

1. Disconnect the negative battery cable and remove the serpentine drive belt.
2. Disconnect the spark plug wires from the plugs, remove the EGR valve solenoid attachment screw and remove the PCV fresh air hose.
3. Remove the camshaft cover, then inspect the cover silicone insulators for cracks or deterioration and replace as necessary.
4. Turn the crankshaft clockwise until the mark on the crankshaft pulley is in alignment with the pointer on the front cover and the No. 1 cylinder is at Top Dead Center (TDC) of the compression stroke. Both camshaft dowel pins will be at the 12 o'clock position and the timing pin holes will be aligned when the No. 1 cylinder is at TDC. If necessary, the right wheel and splash shield may be removed to help observe the timing marks.

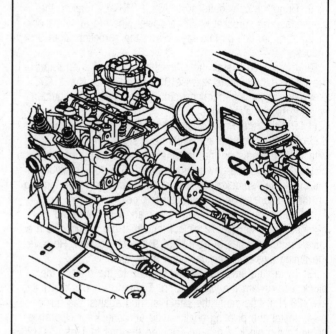

Fig. 105 Remove the camshaft through the oversize hole at the rear of the cylinder head — SOHC engine

5. Carefully remove each camshaft sprocket's retaining bolts. Use a ⅞ inch (21mm) open end wrench to hold the camshaft from turning while removing the bolts.

6. For 1992-93 vehicles, position the front angled support fixture in front of the camshaft sprockets.

7. Attach the camshaft sprocket adapters to the end of each camshaft using the pilot bolts, but do not tighten the bolts. For 1992-93 vehicles, the front angled support should come between the sprocket adapters and camshaft sprockets.

8. Remove the upper timing chain guide and both front camshaft bearing caps.

9. For 1991 vehicles, position the front support fixture.

10. Secure the support fixture using ⅞ inch bolts/blocks and align the 2 holes in each camshaft sprocket, adapter and the front support fixture. Install the 4 nuts, but do not tighten. The steel blocks should be installed against the rearward side of the camshaft sprocket. Tighten the sprocket pilot bolts to 19 ft. lbs. (25 Nm) while holding the camshafts from turning with an open end wrench.

11. Move each camshaft sprocket off the end of the camshaft by rocking the sprocket forward or by carefully prying between the end of the camshaft and the sprocket. Then tighten the 4 nuts and bolts with blocks from the side of the support fixture to 19 ft. lbs. (25 Nm).

12. Install the 2 bolts retaining the support fixture to the engine front cover and tighten the bolts to 89 inch lbs. (10 Nm). Then remove each camshaft sprocket pilot bolt while holding the camshafts with a wrench.

13. Carefully pry between the sprocket and the end of the camshaft to move the camshaft rearward. Pry only enough to remove its end from inside the sprocket pilot otherwise camshaft or lifter damage may occur.

14. Uniformly loosen and remove the remaining camshaft bearing cap bolts. To prevent bolt/cap damage, do not use power tools and make several passes. Then remove each camshaft. Position the bearing caps for installation in their original locations.

To install:

15. Clean and inspect all parts prior to installation. Oil the camshaft and install with the **IN** camshaft on the intake side and **EX** camshaft on the exhaust side.

➡**NOTE:The dowel pin in each camshaft must be located at the 12 o'clock position during installation to prevent valve and piston damage.**

16. Install all bearing caps, except for the forward pair, in their original positions, making sure the arrows on the caps are pointing forward toward the camshaft sprockets. Lightly oil each of the cap bolts, then install and uniformly tighten the bolts to 124 inch lbs. (14 Nm).

17. Install 1 camshaft sprocket pilot bolt in each camshaft and tighten to 124 inch lbs. (14 Nm) in order to pull the camshaft fully forward and align the sprocket support for installation of the sprocket onto the camshaft.

18. Remove the 4 sprocket support bolt/blocks and nuts. Then for 1991 vehicles, remove the front angled support fixture. The torque axis mount system of the 1992-93 vehicles requires the fixture to remain in place longer.

19. Verify that the camshafts are fully positioned forward and install the 2 forward bearing caps and the upper chain guide. The caps are marked **E1** or **I1** for exhaust or intake and must

be positioned with their arrows pointing towards the sprockets. Tighten the cap bolts to 124 inch lbs. (14 Nm).

20. Make sure the camshaft dowel pin aligns with the slot in each camshaft sprocket. If necessary, rotate the camshaft slightly (1-2 degrees) and move each sprocket from the adapter onto the end of the camshaft. Fully seat each sprocket on the end of each camshaft.

21. Remove the 2 sprocket pilot bolts and adapters while using a wrench on the camshaft flats to assure the camshaft cannot move.

22. For 1992-93 vehicles, remove the support angled fixture.

23. Install the camshaft sprocket retaining bolts and washers. Hold the camshafts and tighten the bolts to 76 ft. lbs. (103 Nm).

24. Verify all visible timing marks and holes are in alignment. Turn the crankshaft clockwise until the mark on the crankshaft pulley aligns with the mark on the front cover. Check timing by inserting ³⁄₁₆ inch drill bits through the camshaft sprocket alignment holes, into the cylinder head. If the alignment pins cannot be inserted, turn the crankshaft 360 degrees clockwise and repeat. If the pins cannot be inserted within 1-2 degrees of either TDC position, the camshafts are not properly timed. Do not start the engine until the camshafts are timed.

25. Apply a small drop of RTV across the cylinder head and front cover T-joints. Inspect the old camshaft cover gasket and replace if damaged. Install the gasket and the camshaft cover. Tighten the fasteners in proper sequence to 89 inch lbs. (10 Nm).

26. Install the right splash shield and wheel, if removed to observe the timing marks.

27. Install the PCV and fresh air hoses, the EGR valve solenoid attaching screw and the spark plug wires.

28. Install the serpentine drive belt and connect the negative battery cable.

29. Start the engine and check for leaks.

INSPECTION

▶ **See Figures 109, 110, 111 and 112**

1. Clean the camshaft in solvent and allow to dry.

2. Inspect the camshaft for obvious signs of wear: scores, nicks or pits on the journals or lobes. Light scuffs or nicks can be removed with an oil stone.

3. Position the camshaft in V-blocks with the front and rear journals riding on the blocks. Check if the camshaft is bent using a dial indicator on the center bearing journal. The runout limit at the center journal is 0.004 in. (0.1mm) for DOHC engines or 0.0028 in. (0.07mm) for SOHC engines. Replace the camshaft if runout is excessive.

4. Using a micrometer, measure the camshaft lobes across their maximum and minimum lobe height dimensions. Subtract the lobe width from the lobe height to arrive at lobe rise. Replace a SOHC camshaft if any lobes have a rise of less than 0.252 in. (6.4mm). Replace a DOHC camshaft if any intake rise is less than 0.351 in. (8.91mm) or any exhaust rise is less than 0.339 in. (8.61mm).

5. Using a micrometer, measure the diameter of the journals and replace any camshaft containing a journal that is less than the minimum. For SOHC engines, journal diameter should be greater than 1.747 in. (44.375mm). DOHC engine

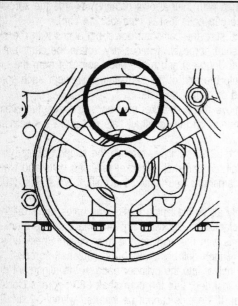

Fig. 106 To assure proper engine timing during assembly, turn the crankshaft clockwise until the mark on the damper/pulley is in alignment with the cover pointer

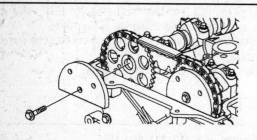

Fig. 107 For 1991 vehicles without the torque axis mount system, position the adapters directly to the sprockets — DOHC engine

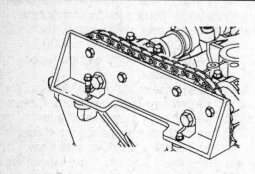

Fig. 108 The front angled support fixture — DOHC engine

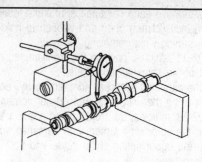

Fig. 109 Use a dial indicator to measure camshaft runout at the center journal — DOHC camshaft shown

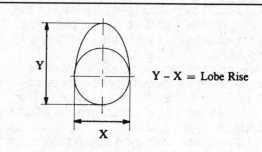

Fig. 110 Subtract the lobe width from the height to determine lobe rise

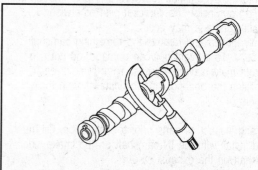

Fig. 111 Measure camshaft journal diameter using a micrometer

should have a minimum camshaft journal diameter of 1.139 in. (28.925mm).

6. Measure the diameter of the camshaft bearings. For the DOHC engine, temporarily install the bearing caps to the cylinder head in order to take the measurement. Bore diameter must be less than 1.753 in. (44.513mm) for SOHC engines or 1.144 in. (29.05mm) for DOHC engines or the cylinder head must be replaced.

7. Subtract the journal diameter measurements from their respective bore diameter measurements to calculate oil clearance. Replace the camshaft and/or cylinder head if clearance is more than 0.0054 in. (0.138mm) for SOHC engines or 0.005 in. (0.125mm) for DOHC engines.

8. Position a precision straightedge across the bottom of the cylinder head camshaft contact surfaces. Use a feeler

gauge to inspect for warpage and replace a cylinder head with warpage of more than 0.0025 in. (0.064mm) for SOHC engines or 0.003 in. (0.075mm) for DOHC engines.

Pistons and Connecting Rods

REMOVAL

▶ **See Figures 113 and 114**

1. Remove the engine from the vehicle and mount it on a suitable workstand.
2. Remove the cylinder head and the oil pan.
3. Check the connecting rod side clearance vertically along the side of the rod using a feeler gauge while moving the rod back and forth. The maximum allowable clearance is 0.185 in. (0.470mm). Replace the connecting rod assembly or the crankshaft to correct extreme clearance(s).
4. The position of each piston, connecting rod and connecting rod cap should be noted before any are removed, to assure that they can be reinstalled in the same location. Connecting rods and caps are color coded during assembly to prevent interchanging of parts. Prior to disconnecting the rods from the crankshaft, use a punch or numbering stamp to place match marks on the rod and cap to ensure correct reassembly.
5. Loosen and remove the connecting rod cap nuts, then tap the connecting rod bolts with a plastic-faced hammer to loosen the bearing cap. Remove the bearing cap from the connecting rod.

➡ **NOTE: At no time during disassembly should the piston be pulled down past its normal travel within the cylinder lining. If this is done, the oil control rings may dislodge between the liner and machined step. A dislodged oil control ring will act as a snaring preventing piston removal until the liner is removed.**

6. Clean the rod journal and bearing. Inspect the crank pin and bearing for pitting and scratches to determine if rod journals must be ground, or if the bearings and/or crankshaft must be replaced.
7. Lay a strip of Plastigage® across the rod journal, then install the rod cap and tighten the retainers to 31 ft. lbs. (45 Nm). Remove the retainers and the rod cap, then determine oil clearance by comparing the widest point of the Plastigage® to

the chart as per the manufacturers instructions. The maximum allowable clearance is 0.0025 in. (0.063mm). Completely remove the Plastigage® after the measurement has been taken.

8. Cover the connecting rod bolts with a short piece of ¼ in. (6.34mm) inner diameter rubber hose to protect the crankshaft from scoring or damage. The connecting rod should not be removed until measurements are taken and the cylinder ridge, if present, has been removed.
9. Check the top of the cylinder liner for a ridge. If a ridge can be felt, it must be removed before the piston is can be withdrawn from the bore. Install a ridge reamer and remove the ridge from the bore per the reamer manufacturer's instructions. See the procedure in this Section for more information regarding ridge reaming.
10. Using a hammer handle or piece of wood or plastic, tap the rod and piston upward in the bore until the piston rings clear the cylinder block. Remove the piston and connecting rod assembly from the top of the cylinder bore.

CLEANING AND INSPECTION

▶ **See Figures 115 and 116**

1. Remove the piston rings using a piston ring expander. Refer to the Piston Ring Replacement procedure.
2. Clean the ring grooves with a ring groove cleaner or a broken piston ring, being careful not to cut into the piston metal. Heavy carbon deposits can be cleaned from the top of the piston with a wire brush, however, do not use a wire

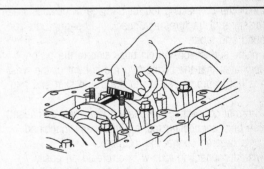

Fig. 113 Measure the connecting rod oil clearance using Plastigage® or equivalent

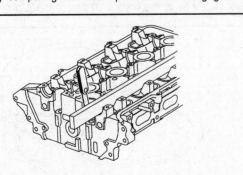

Fig. 112 Measuring camshaft contact surface warpage — DOHC engine shown

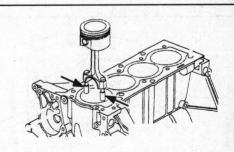

Fig. 114 Remove the piston from the top of the cylinder bore

wheel on the ring grooves or lands. Clean the oil drain holes in the ring grooves. Clean all remaining dirt, carbon and varnish from the piston with a suitable solvent and a brush; do not use a caustic solution.

3. After cleaning, inspect the piston for scuffing, scoring, cracks, pitting or excessive ring groove wear. Replace any piston that is obviously worn.

4. If the piston appears okay, measure the piston diameter using a micrometer. Measure the piston diameter at a right angle to the piston pin hole center line and about 0.2 in. (5mm) from the bottom of the piston. The piston should be 3.2270-3.2277 in. (81.966-81.984mm).

5. Measure the cylinder bore diameter using a bore gauge, or with a telescope gauge and micrometer. Make 2 measurements longitudinal and transverse at a depth of 2.5 in. (63.5mm) below the top of the block, then average the 2 results.

6. Subtract the piston diameter measurement made in Step 4 from the cylinder bore measurement made in Step 5 to determine the piston-to-bore clearance. The maximum allowable clearance is 0.0028 in. (0.07mm). If the clearance is within specification, light finish honing is all that is necessary. If the clearance is excessive, the cylinder must be bored and the piston replaced. Consult an automotive machine shop. If the pistons are replaced, the piston rings must also be replaced.

7. If the piston-to-bore clearance is okay, check the ring groove clearance. Insert the ring that will be used in the ring groove and check the clearance with a feeler gauge, as shown in the figure. Compare your measurement with specification. Replace the piston if the ring groove clearance is not within specification.

8. Check the connecting rod for damage or obvious wear. Check for signs of fractures and check the bearing bore for out-of-round and taper.

9. A shiny surface on the pin boss side of the piston usually indicates that the connecting rod is bent or the wrist pin hole is not in proper relation to the piston skirt and ring grooves.

10. Abnormal connecting rod bearing wear can be caused by either a bent connecting rod, an improperly machined journal, or a tapered connecting rod bore.

11. Twisted connecting rods will not create an easily identifiable wear pattern, but badly twisted rods will disturb the action of the entire piston, rings, and connecting rod assembly and may be the cause of excessive oil consumption.

12. If a connecting rod problem is suspected, consult an automotive machine shop to have the rod checked.

RIDGE REMOVAL AND HONING

▶ See Figures 117 and 118

1. Before the piston is removed from the cylinder, check for a ridge at the top of the cylinder bore. This ridge occurs because the piston ring does not travel all the way to the top of the bore, thereby leaving an unused portion of cylinder bore.

2. Clean away any carbon buildup at the top of the cylinder with sand paper, in order to see the extent of the ridge more clearly. If the ridge is slight, it will be safe to remove the pistons without damaging the rings or piston ring lands. If the ridge is severe, and easily catches your fingernail, it will have to be removed using a ridge reamer.

➡NOTE:A severe ridge is an indication of excessive bore wear. Before removing the piston, check the cylinder bore diameter with a bore gauge, as explained in the piston and connecting rod cleaning and inspection procedure. Compare your measurement with specification. If the bore is excessively worn, the cylinder will have to bored oversize and the piston and rings replaced.

3. Install the ridge removal tool in the top of the cylinder bore. Carefully follow the manufacturers instructions for operation. Only remove the amount of material necessary to remove the ridge.

✳✳WARNING

Be very careful if you are unfamiliar with operating a ridge reamer. It is very easy to remove more cylinder bore material than you want, possibly requiring a cylinder overbore and piston replacement that may not have been necessary.

4. After the piston and connecting rod assembly have been removed, check the clearances as explained in the piston and connecting rod cleaning and inspection procedure, to determine whether boring and honing or just light honing are required. If boring is necessary, consult an automotive machine shop. If light honing is all that is necessary, proceed to Step 5.

5. Honing is best done with the crankshaft removed, to prevent damage to the crankshaft and to make post-honing

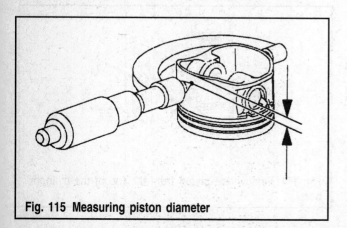

Fig. 115 Measuring piston diameter

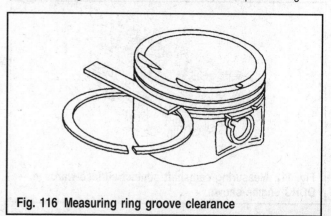

Fig. 116 Measuring ring groove clearance

cleaning easier, as the honing process will scatter metal particles. However, if you do not want to remove the crankshaft, position the connecting rod journal for the cylinder being honed as far away from the bottom of the cylinder bore as possible, and wrap a shop cloth around the journal.

6. Honing can be done either with a flexible glaze breaker type hone or with a rigid hone that has honing stones and guide shoes. The flexible hone removes the least amount of metal, and is especially recommended if your piston-to-cylinder bore clearance is on the loose side. The flexible hone is useful to provide a finish on which the new piston rings will seat. A rigid hone will remove more material than the flexible hone and requires more operator skill.

7. Regardless of which type of hone you use, carefully follow the manufacturers instructions for operation.

8. The hone should be moved up and down the bore at sufficient speed to obtain a uniform finish. A rigid hone will provide a definite cross-hatch finish; operate the rigid hone at a speed to obtain a 45° included angle in the cross-hatch. The finish marks should be clean but not sharp, free from embedded particles and torn or folded metal.

9. Periodically during the honing procedure, perform a thorough cleaning of the cylinder bore and check the piston-to-bore clearance with the piston for that cylinder.

10. After honing is completed, thoroughly wash the cylinder bores and the rest of the engine with hot water and detergent. Scrub the bores well with a stiff bristle brush and rinse thoroughly with hot water. Thorough cleaning is essential, for if any abrasive material is left in the cylinder bore, it will rapidly wear the new rings and the cylinder bore. If any abrasive material is left in the rest of the engine, it will be picked up by the oil and carried throughout the engine, damaging bearings and other parts.

11. After the bores are cleaned, wipe them down with a clean cloth coated with light engine oil, to keep them from rusting.

PISTON PIN REPLACEMENT

▶ **See Figures 119 and 120**

1. With the pistons removed from the block, check the fit between the piston and pin. Grasp the piston and try to move it back and forth on the pin. If movement is felt, check the piston pin to piston and to connecting rod clearances. The maximum allowable clearances are 0.0004 in. (0.011mm) for the pin to piston and 0.0009 in. (0.024mm) for the pin to connecting rod.

2. If necessary, disassemble the piston components:
   a. Use a small suitable tool to remove the snaprings from the side of the piston.
   b. Inspect the piston bore for burrs and remove, if found, using a sharp blade. This will prevent piston pin scoring during removal.
   c. Use a plastic faced hammer and service tool SA9101E, or equivalent, to tap the pin from the piston, then remove the connecting rod.

3. Inspect the piston assembly for the following dimensions:
   a. A minimum piston pin diameter of 0.7676 in. (19.496mm).
   b. A maximum piston pin bore diameter of 0.768 in. (19.507mm).
   c. A maximum pin oil clearance of 0.0004 in. (0.011mm).

4. Position the piston so the mark located on top will align with the front of the engine. Using this as a reference point, position the connecting rod so the bearing tang slots are directed toward the exhaust manifold side of the engine.

5. Coat the piston pin with clean engine oil, then use the service tool and a plastic hammer to install the pin into the bore.

6. Make sure the piston and connecting rod move smoothly back and forth on the pin.

7. Prepare for snapring to piston assembly by installing the service tool cone with the ring's open ends directed away from the tools slotted opening. Set the cone on it's base and push the snapring down through the cone until it is seated with the driver.

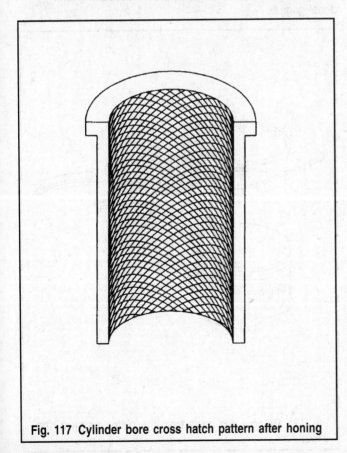

Fig. 117 Cylinder bore cross hatch pattern after honing

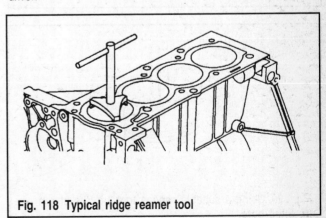

Fig. 118 Typical ridge reamer tool

8. Position the piston sideways on a clean block of wood, then position the cone, snapring and driver tool over the piston pin hole. The cones slotted opening should face toward the top of the piston. Push the driver downward firmly until the retainer is seated in the snapring groove.

PISTON RING REPLACEMENT

▶ See Figures 121, 122 and 123

1. Remove the piston rings from the piston using a piston ring expander.
2. Clean the piston ring grooves, check the piston-to-cylinder bore clearance and check the ring groove clearance as explained in the piston and connecting rod cleaning and inspection procedure.
3. After the cylinder bores have been finish honed and cleaned, check the piston ring end gap. Compress the piston rings to be used in the cylinder, one at a time, into that cylinder. Using an inverted piston, push the ring down into the cylinder bore area where normal ring wear is not encountered, about 3.94 in. (100mm) below the top of the cylinder sleeve.
4. Measure the ring end gap with a feeler gauge and compare to specification. A gap that is too tight is more harmful than one that is too loose (If ring end gap is excessively loose, the cylinder bore is probably worn beyond specification).
5. If the ring end gap is too tight, carefully remove the ring and file the ends squarely with a fine file or replace the ring to obtain the proper clearance.

6. Install the rings on the piston, lowest rings first. The lowest (oil) ring expander and 2 side rails are installed by hand; the top 2 (compression) rings must be installed using a piston ring expander. There is a high risk of breaking or distorting the compression rings if they are installed by hand.
7. Position each ring with it's gap 90-120 degrees from the next.
8. Compression rings must be installed with the pip marks facing upwards. On the SOHC engine, only the top compression ring contains a pip mark.

➡NOTE:If the instructions on the ring packaging differ from this information regarding ring gap positioning, follow the ring manufacturers instructions.

ROD BEARING REPLACEMENT

1. Inspect the rod bearings for scoring, chipping or other wear.
2. Inspect the crankshaft rod bearing journal for wear. Measure the journal diameter in several locations around the journal and compare to specification. If the crankshaft journal is scored or has deep ridges, or its diameter is below specification, the crankshaft must be removed from the engine and reground. Consult an automotive machine shop.
3. If the crankshaft journal appears usable, clean it and the rod bearing shells until they are completely free of oil. Blow any oil from the oil hole in the crankshaft.

➡NOTE:The journal surfaces and bearing shells must be completely free of oil to get an accurate reading with Plastigage®.

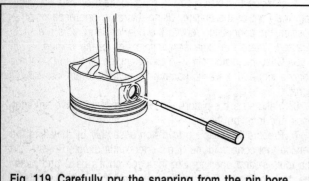

Fig. 119 Carefully pry the snapring from the pin bore using a small tool

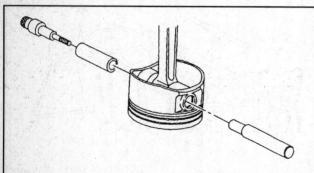

Fig. 120 Using a suitable service tool, tap the piston pin from the bore

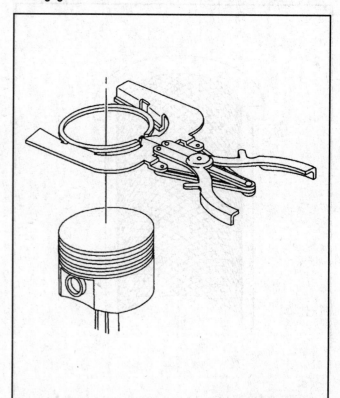

Fig. 121 Remove the rings from the piston using a ring expander

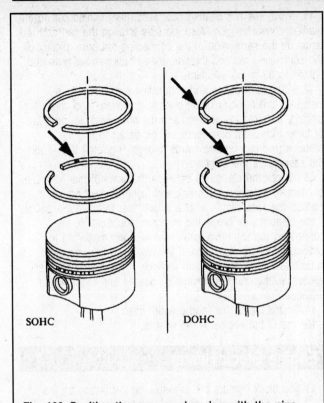

SOHC

DOHC

Fig. 122 Position the compression ring with the pips facing upward

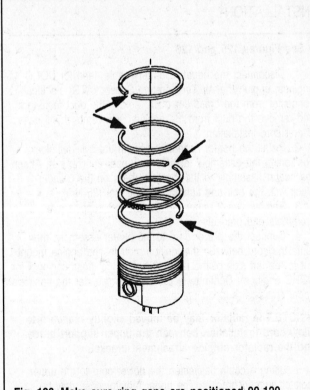

Fig. 123 Make sure ring gaps are positioned 90-120 degrees from each other

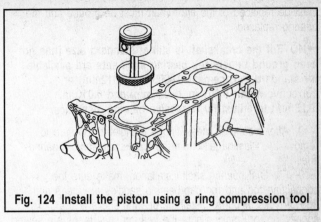

Fig. 124 Install the piston using a ring compression tool

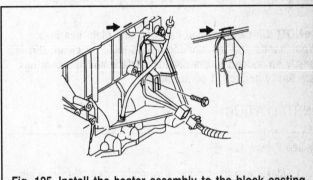

Fig. 125 Install the heater assembly to the block casting slot

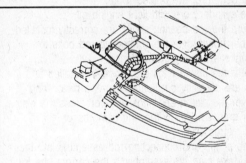

Fig. 126 Use a tie to hold the coiled power cord to the facia bracket

4. Place a strip of Plastigage® lengthwise along the bottom center of the lower bearing shell, then install the cap with the shell and torque the connecting rod nuts to specification. Do not turn the crankshaft with the Plastigage® installed in the bearing.

5. Remove the bearing cap with the shell. The flattened Plastigage® will either be sticking to the bearing shell or the crankshaft journal.

6. Using the printed scale on the Plastigage® package, measure the flattened Plastigage® at its widest point. The number on the scale that most closely corresponds to the width of the Plastigage® indicates the bearing clearance in thousandths of an inch or hundredths of a millimeter.

7. Compare your findings with the bearing clearance specification. If the bearing clearance is excessive, the bearing

must be replaced or the crankshaft must be ground and the bearing replaced.

➡NOTE:**If the crankshaft is still at standard size (has not been ground undersize), bearing shell sets are available for standard replacement 0.0005 in. (0.012mm) or corrective repair 0.001 in. (0.025mm) and 0.010 in. (0.25mm) to adjust for excessive bearing clearance.**

8. After clearance measuring is completed, be sure to remove the Plastigage® from the crankshaft and/or bearing shell.

9. For final bearing shell installation, make sure the connecting rod and rod cap bearing saddles are clean and free of nicks or burrs. Install the bearing shells in the connecting rod, making sure the bearing shell tangs are seated in the notches.

➡NOTE:**Be careful when handling any plain bearings. Your hands and the working area should be clean. Dirt is easily embedded in the bearing surface and the bearings are easily scratched or damaged.**

INSTALLATION

▶ **See Figure 124**

1. Make sure the cylinder bore and crankshaft journal are clean.
2. Position the crankshaft journal at its furthest position away from the bottom of the cylinder bore.
3. Coat the cylinder bore with light engine oil.
4. Make sure the rod bearing shells are correctly installed. Install the rubber hoses over the connecting rod bolts to protect the crankshaft during installation.
5. Make sure the piston rings are properly installed and the ring end gaps are correctly positioned. Install a piston ring compressor over the piston and rings and compress the piston rings into their grooves. Follow the ring compressor manufacturers instructions.
6. Place the piston and connecting rod assembly into the cylinder bore. Make sure the assembly is the correct one for that bore and that the piston and connecting rod are facing in the proper direction. Most pistons have an arrow or notch on the top of the piston to indicate this side should face the front of the engine.
7. Make sure the ring compressor is seated squarely on the block deck surface. If the compressor is not seated squarely, a ring could pop out from beneath the compressor and hang up on the deck surface, as the piston is tapped into the bore, possibly breaking the ring.
8. Make sure that the connecting rod is not hung up on the crankshaft counterweights and is in position to come straight on to the crankshaft.
9. Tap the piston slowly into the bore, making sure the compressor remains squarely against the block deck. When the piston is completely in the bore, remove the ring compressor.
10. Coat the crankshaft journal and the bearing shells with engine assembly lube or clean engine oil. Pull the connecting rod onto the crankshaft journal. After the rod is seated, remove the rubber hoses from the rod bolts.

11. Install the rod bearing cap. Match the marked cap to the marked connecting rod. Also, be sure to align the cap and rod tangs on the same side of the connecting rod bore. Lightly oil the connecting rod bolt threads, then install the cap nuts and tighten to 33 ft. lbs. (45 Nm).
12. After each piston and connecting rod assembly is installed, turn the crankshaft over several times and check for binding. If there is a problem and the crankshaft will not turn, or turns with great difficulty, it will be easier to find the problem (rod cap on backwards, broken ring, etc.) than if all the assemblies are installed.
13. Check the clearance between the sides of the connecting rods and the crankshaft using a feeler gauge. Spread the rods slightly with a screwdriver to insert the gauge. If the clearance is below the minimum specification, the connecting rod will have to be removed and machined to provide adequate clearance. If the clearance is excessive, substitute an unworn rod and recheck. If the clearance is still excessive, the crankshaft must be welded and reground, or replaced.
14. Install the oil pan and cylinder head.
15. Install the engine in the vehicle.

Engine Block Heater

Engine block heaters are available for installation on the front face of the cylinder block, behind the engine oil dipstick. Allow the engine to thoroughly cool before attempting installation.

INSTALLATION

▶ **See Figures 125 and 126**

1. Disconnect the negative battery cable, then for DOHC engines, unplug the Air Temperature Sensor (ATS) electrical connector from the cross car duct, remove the duct fasteners and remove the duct from the engine. Duct removal will ease heater cord installation.
2. Install the heater assembly against the cylinder block, positioning the assembly tab into the upper casting slot. Attach the heater assembly to the threaded boss on the cylinder block with the bolt and tighten to 19 ft. lbs. (25 Nm).
3. Remove the 2 upper radiator bracket support nuts, grommets and brackets.
4. Connect the power cord to the heater assembly, then route the cord between the ignition module and engine mount out to the left side of the radiator (under the cross car duct for DOHC engines). Continue to route the cord under the vehicle's upper cross-car support brace.

➡NOTE:**The radiator may be moved slightly rearward to allow cord installation between the upper support brace and the radiator outside attachment bracket.**

5. Using a cable tie, fasten the power cord to the upper radiator support bracket. The upper radiator hose may be moved slightly upward to ease tie installation.
6. Coil the cord and position it behind the driver's side facia support bracket, in front of the radiator and next to the headlamp assembly bracket. Make sure the plug protective cap

is positioned to protect it from road debris, then install a tie to hold the coiled cord in position.

7. Install the upper radiator support brackets, grommets and nuts. Tighten the nuts to 89 inch lbs. (10 Nm).

8. For the DOHC engine, install the cross car duct and connect the ATS electrical plug.

9. Connect the negative battery cable.

Rear Main Seal

REMOVAL & INSTALLATION

▶ See Figures 127 and 128

Both engines use a 1-piece round seal mounted in a seal carrier. The seal may be replaced with the carrier installed or removed from the engine. To replace the seal with the carrier installed:

1. Disconnect the negative battery cable.

2. Remove the transaxle assembly from the vehicle. Refer to Section 7 of this manual.

3. As applicable, remove the clutch and flywheel assembly or the flexplate.

4. Use the prying tangs provided in the carrier to remove the seal with a small suitable prybar and hammer. Be careful not to damage the crankshaft oil seal lip contact surface.

To install:

5. Clean the carrier and crankshaft with solvent and a rag to prevent seal lip damage during installation. Check for scores or damage to the sealing surfaces.

6. Apply a light coat of clean engine oil to the seal lip and the carrier inner diameter. Install using SA9121E or an equivalent seal installer. The tool is designed to prevent seal lip from rolling during installation and will seat the seal 0.04 inch (1mm) lower than the factory seal. Never tap on the seal or seal installer with a hammer.

7. Install the flywheel or flexplate assembly.

8. Install the transaxle assembly into the vehicle.

9. Connect the negative battery cable, start the engine and check for leaks.

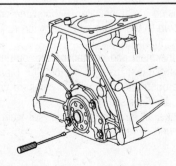

Fig. 127 Use the pry tangs provided in the carrier to remove the rear seal

Crankshaft and Main Bearings

REMOVAL & INSTALLATION

▶ See Figures 129, 130, 131 and 132

1. Remove the engine assembly from the vehicle and install on a suitable workstand.

2. Remove the cylinder head, oil pan and baffle (DOHC engine), oil pump pickup assembly and the flywheel.

3. Remove the 4 retaining bolts, then carefully pry the rear main seal carrier away from the block and remove the carrier from the engine.

4. Remove the piston and connecting rod assemblies. Refer to the procedure in this Section.

5. Position a dial indicator at the end of the crankshaft assembly to measure thrust clearance. Carefully pry the crankshaft assembly back and forth with a small prybar and measure the clearance. If the measurement is greater than 0.0098 in. (0.25mm), the thrust bearing must be replaced during assembly.

6. Make sure the main bearing caps are numbered so they can be reinstalled in their original positions. Uniformly loosen and remove the bolts, then remove the bearing caps. If necessary loosen the caps with light blows from a plastic hammer.

7. Lift the crankshaft from the cylinder block. Inspect the crankshaft and bearings and repair and/or replace as necessary.

To install:

8. After cleaning, inspecting and measuring the crankshaft and checking the main bearing clearance, install the crankshaft. Apply engine assembly lube or clean engine oil to the upper bearing shells prior to installation.

9. Apply engine assembly lube or clean engine oil to the lower bearing shells, then install the main bearing caps in their original positions. Make sure the arrow on the caps is pointing towards the front of the engine. Tighten the bolts in several passes of the proper torque sequence to 37 ft. lbs. (50 Nm).

10. After each cap is tightened, check to see and feel that the crankshaft can be rotated by hand. If not, remove the bearing cap and check for the source of the interference.

11. When the caps are all installed, recheck thrust clearance and replace the thrust bearing, if clearance is greater than maximum.

12. Install the piston and connecting rod assemblies.

13. Thoroughly clean the mating surfaces of old RTV, then apply a fresh 0.08 in. (2mm) bead of RTV to the seal carrier. Install the carrier while the RTV is still wet and tighten the retaining bolts to 97 inch lbs. (11 Nm). If available, use a rear seal installer as a pilot to prevent seal damage during carrier installation.

14. Install the oil baffle plate and the pickup assembly (using a new O-ring), then tighten the retainers. Tighten the tube to block bolt to 133 inch lbs. (15 Nm), the baffle plate (DOHC engine) to block bolts to 42 ft. lbs. (55 Nm), the oil pipe bracket to block bolt (SOHC engine) to 42 ft. lbs. (55 Nm) and the oil pipe bracket to baffle plate bolt (DOHC engine) to 133 inch lbs. (15 Nm).

15. Install the flywheel, oil pan and the cylinder head.

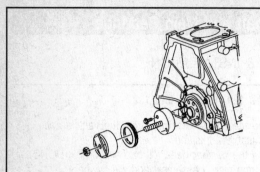

Fig. 128 The seal installation tool will draw the seal to the proper depth in the carrier

16. Install the engine assembly in the vehicle.

CLEANING AND INSPECTION

▶ See Figures 133, 134 and 135

1. Clean the crankshaft with solvent and a brush. Clean the oil passages with a suitable brush, then blow them out with compressed air.

2. Inspect the crankshaft for obvious damage or wear. Check the main and connecting rod journals for cracks, scratches, grooves or scores. Inspect the crankshaft oil seal

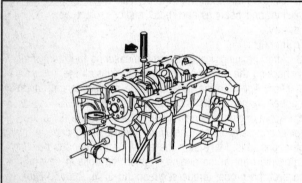

Fig. 129 Checking crankshaft thrust clearance

Intake Side				
8	4	1	5	9
7	3	2	6	10
Exhaust Side				

Fig. 130 Main bearing cap bolt torque sequence

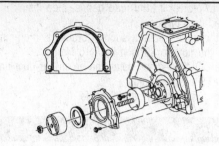

Fig. 131 Apply a bead of RTV to the rear carrier, then assemble to the engine using a seal installer to protect the carrier seal.

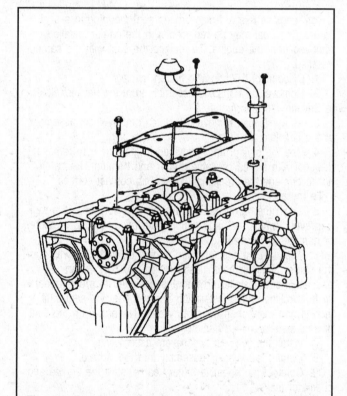

Fig. 132 Install the oil baffle and pickup tube — DOHC engines

surface for nicks, sharp edges or burrs that could damage the oil seal or cause premature seal wear.

3. If the crankshaft passes a visual inspection, check journal runout using a dial indicator. Support the crankshaft in V-blocks as shown in the figure and check the runout as shown. Compare to specifications.

4. measure the main and connecting rod journals for wear, out-of-roundness or taper, using a micrometer. Measure in at least 4 places around each journal and compare your findings with the journal diameter specifications.

5. If the crankshaft fails any inspection for wear or damage, it must be reground or replaced.

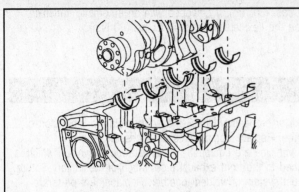

Fig. 133 Crankshaft and main bearings

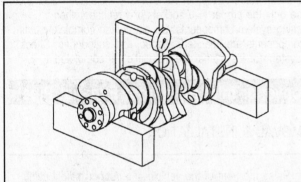

Fig. 134 Checking crankshaft runout using a dial gauge

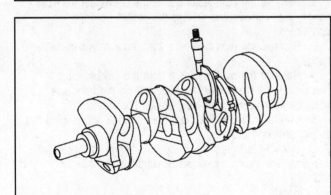

Fig. 135 Using a micrometer to check journal diameter

BEARING REPLACEMENT

▶ See Figure 136

1. Inspect the bearings for scoring, chipping or other wear.
2. Inspect the crankshaft journals as detailed in the Cleaning and Inspection procedure.
3. If the crankshaft journals appear usable, clean them and the bearing shells until they are completely free of oil. Blow any oil from the oil hole in the crankshaft.

➡NOTE:The journal surfaces and bearing shells must be completely free of oil to get an accurate reading with Plastigage®.

4. Place a strip of Plastigage® lengthwise along the bottom center of the lower bearing shell, then install the cap with the shell and torque the connecting rod nuts or main cap bolts to specification. Do not turn the crankshaft with the Plastigage® installed in the bearing.
5. Remove the bearing cap with the shell. The flattened Plastigage® will either be sticking to the bearing shell or the crankshaft journal.
6. Using the printed scale on the Plastigage® package, measure the flattened Plastigage® at its widest point. The number on the scale that most closely corresponds to the width of the Plastigage® indicates the bearing clearance in thousandths of an inch or hundredths of a millimeter.
7. Compare your findings with the bearing clearance specification. If the bearing clearance is excessive, the bearing must be replaced or the crankshaft must be ground and the bearing replaced.

➡NOTE:Bearing shell sets over standard size are available to correct excessive bearing clearance.

8. After clearance measuring is completed, be sure to remove the Plastigage® from the crankshaft and/or bearing shell.
9. For final bearing shell installation, make sure the connecting rod and rod cap and/or cylinder block and main cap bearing saddles are clean and free of nicks or burrs. Install the bearing shells in the bearing saddles, making sure the bearing shell tangs are seated in the notches.

➡NOTE:Be careful when handling any plain bearings. Your hands and the working area should be clean. Dirt is easily embedded in the bearing surface and the bearings are easily scratched or damaged.

Flywheel/Flexplate

REMOVAL & INSTALLATION

1. Disconnect the negative battery cable.
2. Raise and safely support the vehicle.
3. Remove the transaxle assembly. Refer to Section 7.
4. If equipped with a manual transaxle, remove the clutch assembly. Refer to Section 7.
5. If equipped with manual transaxle, remove the flywheel-to-crankshaft bolts and the flywheel. If equipped with automatic

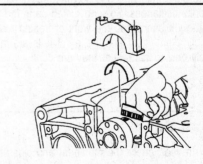

Fig. 136 Checking main bearing clearance using Plastigage®

transaxle, remove the flexplate-to-crankshaft bolts and the flexplate. Remove the flexplate shims, if equipped.

6. Installation is the reverse of the removal procedure. If equipped with a manual transaxle, tighten the flywheel bolts to 59 ft. lbs. (80 Nm). If equipped with an automatic transaxle, tighten the flexplate bolts to 44 ft. lbs. (60 Nm).

EXHAUST SYSTEM

Safety Precautions

Exhaust system work can be the most dangerous type of work you can do on your car. Always observe the following precautions:

• Support the car extra securely. Not only will you often be working directly under it, but you'll frequently be using a lot of force, say, heavy hammer blows, to dislodge rusted parts. This can cause a car that's improperly supported to shift and possibly fall.

• Wear goggles. Exhaust system parts are usually rusty. Metal chips can be dislodged, even when you're only turning rusted bolts. Attempting to pry pipes apart with a chisel makes the chips fly even more frequently.

• If you're using a cutting torch, keep it a great distance from either the fuel tank or lines. Stop what you're doing and feel the temperature of the fuel bearing pipes on the tank frequently. Even slight heat can expand and/or vaporize fuel, resulting in accumulated vapor, or even a liquid leak, near your torch.

• Watch where your hammer blows fall and make sure you hit squarely. You could easily tap a brake or fuel line when you hit an exhaust system part with a glancing blow. Inspect all lines and hoses in the area where you've been working.

✳✳CAUTION

Be very careful when working on or near the catalytic converter! External temperatures can reach 1,500°F (816°C) and more, causing severe burns. Removal or installation should be performed only on a cold exhaust system.

Special Tools

A number of special exhaust system tools can be rented from auto supply houses or local stores that rent special equipment. A common one is a tail pipe expander, designed to enable you to join pipes of identical diameter.

It may also be quite helpful to use solvents designed to loosen rusted bolts or flanges. Soaking rusted parts the night before you do the job can speed the work of freeing rusted parts considerably. Remember that these solvents are often flammable. Apply only to parts after they are cool!

INSPECTION

▶ **See Figures 137 and 138**

Once or twice a year, check the muffler(s) and pipes for signs of corrosion and damage. Check the hangers for wear, cracks or hardening. Check the heat shields for corrosion or damage. Replace components as necessary.

All vehicles are equipped with a catalytic converter, which is attached to the front exhaust pipe. Much of the factory Saturn exhaust system is welded together. Replacement parts are usually the same as or similar to the original system, with the exception of some mufflers. Splash shield removal will be required, in some cases, for removal and installation clearance.

Use only the proper size sockets or wrenches when unbolting system components. Do not tighten completely until all components are attached, aligned, and suspended. Check the system for leaks after the installation is completed.

Converter Inlet Pipe(Front Exhaust Pipe)

REMOVAL & INSTALLATION

1. Raise the front of the vehicle and support safely using jackstands.
2. Remove the pipe fasteners from the exhaust manifold flange, then remove and discard the gasket from the connection.
3. Remove the pipe fasteners from the catalytic converter flange.
4. Remove the pipe fasteners from the pipe support bracket. On 1991 vehicles, the nuts are on the front side, while on later vehicles the nuts are on the rear side.
5. Carefully remove the pipe, then remove and discard the converter flange gasket.
6. Inspect the front pipe to manifold flange for excessive warpage. The maximum allowable warpage is 0.028 in. (0.7mm).

To install:

7. Position a new gasket on the exhaust manifold studs and position the pipe, then install the fasteners and tighten to 23 ft. lbs. (31 Nm).
8. Make sure the exhaust pipe bracket is positioned on the rearward side of the bracket bolted to the powertrain. Install the 2 pipe support bracket fasteners and tighten to 23 ft. lbs. (31 Nm).
9. Install the front pipe to the catalytic converter flange using a new gasket, and if necessary, using a stud/nut thread repair kit instead of the original fasteners. Tighten the new or original fasteners to 33 ft. lbs. (45 Nm).
10. Start the engine briefly and inspect for leaks.
11. Shut the engine **OFF**, remove the supports and carefully lower the vehicle.

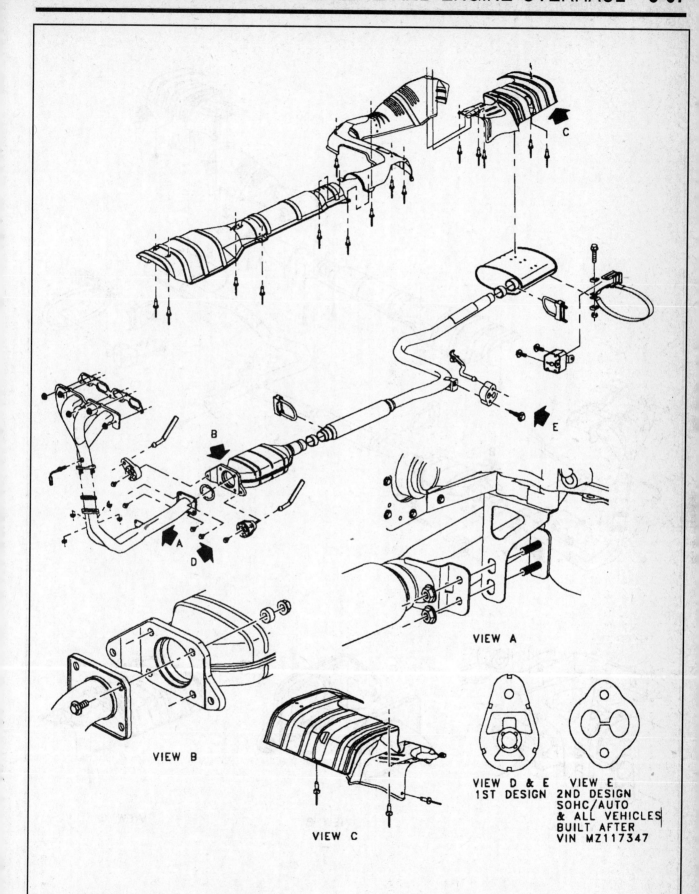

VIEW A

VIEW B

VIEW C

VIEW D & E
1ST DESIGN

VIEW E
2ND DESIGN
SOHC/AUTO
& ALL VEHICLES
BUILT AFTER
VIN MZ117347

Fig. 137 Exhaust system — for 1991 vehicles

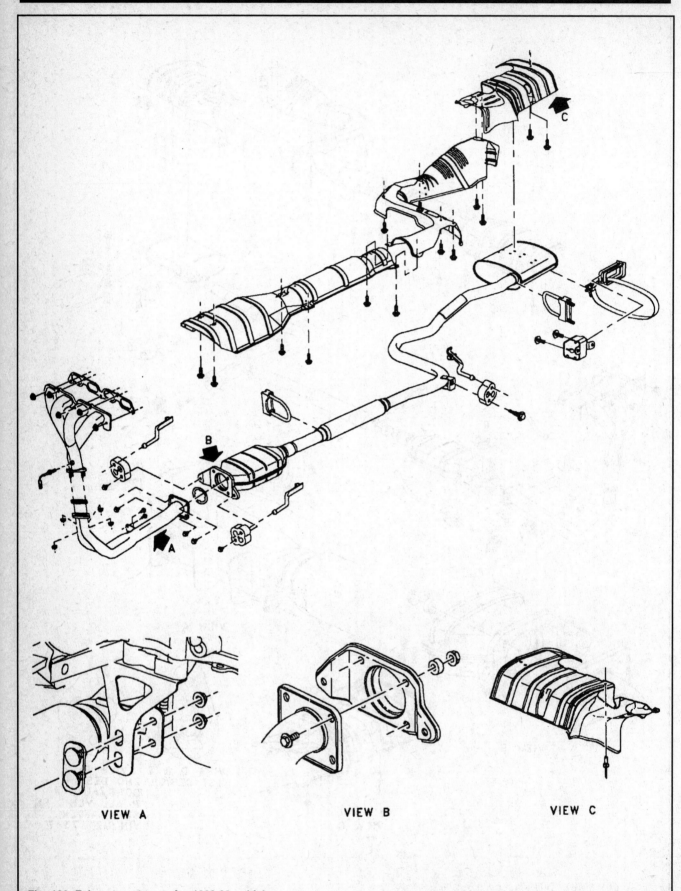

Fig. 138 Exhaust system — for 1992-93 vehicles

Catalytic Converter

REMOVAL & INSTALLATION

▶ **See Figures 139, 140 and 141**

1. Raise and support the vehicle safely.

2. Using SA9168-NE or an equivalent chain cutter, separate the converter from the outlet pipe. Make the cut 1 in. (25.4mm) from the weld, which should leave approximately 2 in. (50.8mm) of intermediate pipe.

➡**NOTE:When cutting stainless steel exhaust pipes, always use a chain cutter. A torch will leave a rough edge and will warp the pipe ends, making a proper seal difficult or impossible to obtain.**

3. Remove the 4 self-tapping bolts from the from the front of the converter, then separate the converter from the front exhaust pipe. Save the self-tapping bolts for installation purposes.

4. Remove the 2 converter isolator fasteners, then remove and discard the converter and gasket.

To install:

5. Remove any burrs from the intermediate pipe using a file.

6. Install the service clamp assembly to the intermediate pipe.

7. Clean the front converter and exhaust pipe flange surfaces.

8. Install a new gasket on the front exhaust pipe.

9. Position the service converter below the vehicle, making sure the drain holes are pointed downward.

10. Slide the converter outlet into the intermediate pipe inlet.

11. Verify that the converter gasket is in position, then install the 4 front exhaust pipe fasteners and tighten to 33 ft. lbs. (45 Nm). If the converter threads are damaged or stripped, a catalytic converter fastener repair kit, 21010753, is available to attach the front exhaust pipe.

12. Install the 2 isolator fasteners and tighten to 33 ft. lbs. (45 Nm).

13. Inspect the system for proper alignment.

14. Position the slip joint clamp ¾ in. (19mm) from the cut off end of the pipe, then turn the clamp to prevent shield contact and tighten to 44 ft. lbs. (60 Nm).

15. Lower the vehicle as necessary and check the entire system for exhaust leaks.

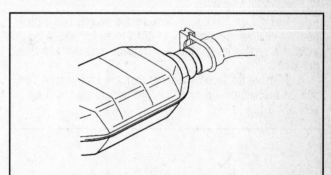

Fig. 140 Position the service clamp assembly over the sleeve connecting the converter and intermediate pipe

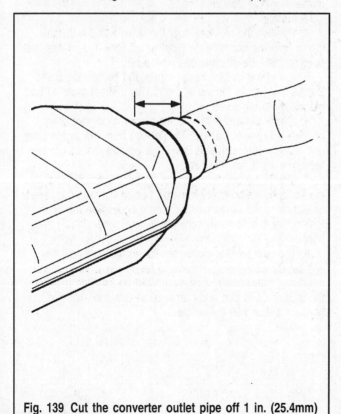

Fig. 139 Cut the converter outlet pipe off 1 in. (25.4mm) from the weld

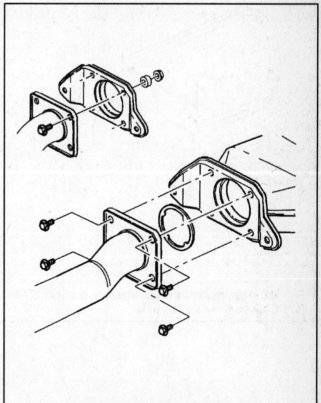

Fig. 141 Front exhaust pipe to converter flange

Intermediate Pipe

REMOVAL & INSTALLATION

▶ **See Figure 142**

1. Raise and support the vehicle safely using jackstands.
2. Using SA9168-NE or an equivalent chain cutter, separate the converter from the outlet pipe. Make the cut 1 in. (25.4mm) from the weld, which should leave approximately 2 in. (50.8mm) of intermediate pipe.

➡ NOTE: **When cutting stainless steel exhaust pipes, always use a chain cutter. A torch will leave a rough edge and will warp the pipe ends, making a proper seal difficult or impossible to obtain.**

3. Using the chain cutter, separate the intermediate pipe from the muffler inlet pipe 2$^7/_{16}$ in. (61.91mm) forward of the weld. If a service muffler has already been installed, separate the joint.
4. Remove the isolator fastener from the intermediate pipe support bracket, then remove the intermediate pipe from the vehicle.

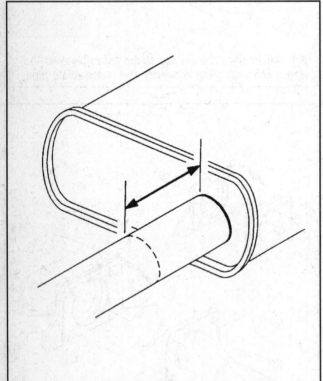

Fig. 142 When replacing the intermediate pipe cut 2 $^7/_{16}$ in. (61.91mm) from the muffler weld

To install:

5. Position the service intermediate pipe under the vehicle.
6. Install the sleeves and clamps onto the pipes, then insert the intermediate pipe outlet into the muffler inlet. The pipe must extend a minimum of 1$^1/_3$ in. (31.75mm) into the muffler inlet.
7. Slide the intermediate inlet pipe over the converter outlet, then verify proper pipe alignment and install the isolator fasteners. Tighten the isolator fasteners to 18 ft. lbs. (25 Nm).
8. Check the entire exhaust system for proper alignment, then position the converter and muffler slips joint clamps, both $^3/_4$ in. (19mm) from inlet ends. Tighten the converter clamp and then the muffler clamp to 44 ft. lbs. (60 Nm).
9. Lower the vehicle and check the entire system for leaks.

Muffler

REMOVAL & INSTALLATION

▶ **See Figures 143 and 144**

1. Raise and support the vehicle safely using jackstands.
2. Using the chain cutter, separate the intermediate pipe from the muffler inlet pipe directly next to the weld.

➡ NOTE: **When cutting stainless steel exhaust pipes, always use a chain cutter. A torch will leave a rough edge and will warp the pipe ends, making a proper seal difficult or impossible to obtain.**

3. Remove the muffler strap fasteners, then lower the muffler from the vehicle.
To install:
4. Position the muffler under the vehicle and a suitable clamp onto the intermediate pipe outlet. Slide the muffler inlet opening over the intermediate pipe outlet.
5. Install the muffler hanger strap and tighten the clamp. Bumps have been formed in the muffler's sheet metal to hold it squarely in the strap.
6. Check the entire system for proper alignment, then position a slip joint clamp $^3/_4$ in. (19mm) from the muffler inlet end. Position the clamp so it will not contact the shield, then tighten to 23 ft. lbs. (31 Nm).
7. Check the system again for proper alignment. The muffler body clamp blade must be free to move in the hanger or vibrations will be transmitted to the body. See the figure; the muffler should move vertically $^1/_{16}$ in. (dimension A) and horizontally $^1/_8$ in. (dimension B) within the isolator block.
8. If proper muffler movement cannot be obtained, the entire exhaust system will have to be carefully lowered and adjusted. If necessary, washers should be installed between the muffler block bolt and frame rail in order to align the hanger parallel with the muffler.

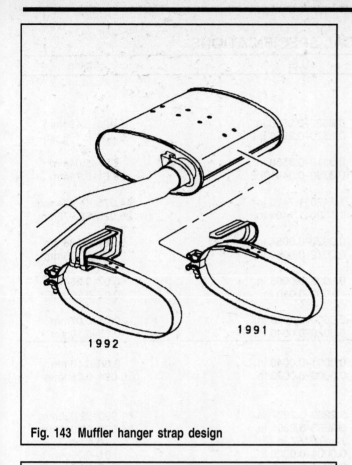

Fig. 143 Muffler hanger strap design

1992

1991

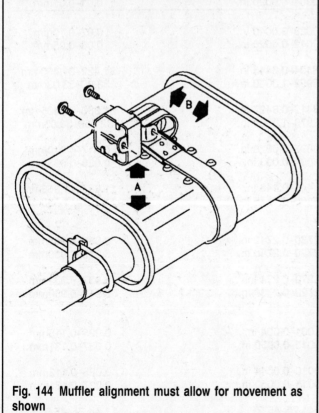

Fig. 144 Muffler alignment must allow for movement as shown

ENGINE MECHANICAL SPECIFICATIONS

Component	U.S.	Metric
Camshaft		
Lobe height		
SOHC engine		
Intake	0.2520–0.2556 in.	6.400–6.493mm
Exhaust	0.2520–0.2556 in.	6.400–6.493mm
DOHC engine		
Intake	0.3510–0.3559 in.	8.91–9.04mm
Exhaust	0.3390–0.3441 in.	8.61–8.74mm
Journal diameter		
SOHC engine	1.7470–1.7490 in.	44.375–44.424mm
DOHC engine	1.1390–1.1406 in.	28.925–28.970mm
Journal-to-bearing clearance		
SOHC engine	0.0020–0.0054 in.	0.051–0.138mm
DOHC engine	0.0012–0.0050 in.	0.076–0.125mm
Endplay		
SOHC engine	0.0028–0.0098 in.	0.07–0.25mm
DOHC engine	0.002–0.010 in.	0.05–0.25mm
Camshaft runout		
SOHC engine	0.0020–0.0028 in.	0.05–0.07mm
DOHC engine	0.0020–0.0040 in.	0.05–0.10mm
Cylinder block		
Longitudinal deck warpage	0.0031–0.0040 in.	0.08–0.10mm
Transverse deck warpage	0.0009–0.0020 in.	0.024–0.050mm
Cylinder bore		
Diameter		
No. 1, 2 and 3	3.2280–3.2297 in.	81.990–82.035mm
No. 4	3.2283–3.2301 in.	82.000–82.045mm
Re-boring limit	0.0157 in.	0.4mm
Out-of-round limit	0.0004–0.0020 in.	0.01–0.05mm
Taper limit	0.0004–0.0020 in.	0.01–0.05mm
Cylinder head		
Longitudinal deck warpage	0.0028–0.0040 in.	0.07–0.10mm
Transverse deck warpage	0.0012–0.0020 in.	0.03–0.05mm
Lifter bore diameter		
SOHC engine	0.8434–0.8445 in.	21.422–21.450mm
DOHC engine	1.2992–1.3000 in.	33.00–33.03mm
Lifter diameter		
SOHC engine	0.8417–0.8427 in.	21.380–21.405mm
DOHC engine	1.2976–1.3000 in.	32.959–33.03mm
Lifter-to-bore clearance		
SOHC engine	0.0007–0.0028 in.	0.017–0.070mm
DOHC engine	0.001–0.003 in.	0.025–0.083mm
Valve guide bore diameter		
SOHC engine	0.446–0.448 in.	11.337–11.368mm
DOHC engine	0.4460–0.4475 in.	11.337–11.368mm
Valve stem diameter		
SOHC engine		
Intake	0.2730–0.2741 in.	6.935–6.962mm
Exhaust	0.2720–0.2740 in.	6.915–6.950mm
DOHC engine		
Intake	0.273–0.274 in.	6.937–6.962mm
Exhaust	0.2720–0.2736 in.	6.919–6.950mm
Valve stem-to-guide clearance		
SOHC engine		
Intake	0.001–0.004 in.	0.025–0.115mm
Exhaust	0.0015–0.0050 in.	0.037–0.131mm
DOHC engine		
Intake	0.0010–0.0044 in.	0.025–0.113mm
Exhaust	0.0015–0.0050 in.	0.037–0.131mm
Valve face angle		
SOHC engine	44.75–45.5°	44.75–45.5°
DOHC engine	44.5–45.5°	44.5–45.5°
Valve seat angle	44.5–45.5°	44.5–45.5°

ENGINE MECHANICAL SPECIFICATIONS

Component	U.S.	Metric
	1990 1.5L	
Valve seat width		
SOHC engine		
Intake	0.0310–0.0653 in.	0.79–1.66mm
Exhaust	0.0410–0.0756 in.	1.05–1.92mm
DOHC engine		
Intake	0.0394–0.0630 in.	1.0–1.6mm
Exhaust	0.0512–0.0750 in.	1.3–1.9mm
Valve spring pressure		
SOHC engine		
Minimum	196 lbs. @ 1.28 in.	870N @ 30mm
Maximum	211 lbs. @ 1.28 in.	983N @ 30mm
DOHC engine		
Minimum	157 lbs. @ 0.984 in.	700N @ 25mm
Maximum	180 lbs. @ 0.984 in.	802N @ 25mm
Valve spring free length		
SOHC engine	1.8898–1.9134 in.	48.001–48.600mm
DOHC engine	1.61 in.	40.84mm
Rocker arm shaft diameter		
SOHC engine	0.620–0.625 in.	15.860–15.875mm
Piston and connecting rod		
Piston diameter	3.2266–3.2277 in.	81.956–81.984mm
Piston-to-bore clearance		
No. 1, 2 and 3	0.0002–0.0028 in.	0.006–0.070mm
No. 4	0.0006–0.0028 in.	0.016–0.070mm
Piston pin diameter	0.7676–0.7677 in.	19.496–19.500mm
Piston pin-to-piston clearance	0.0001–0.0004 in.	0.002–0.011mm
Ring groove clearance		
Top ring	0.0016–0.0035 in.	0.040–0.090mm
Second ring	0.0012–0.0031 in.	0.030–0.080mm
Ring end gap		
Top and second	0.0098–0.0236 in.	0.25–0.60mm
Oil control	0.0098–0.0551 in.	0.25–1.40mm
Connecting rod alignment		
Twist	0.0110 in. per 3.94 in.	0.28mm per 100mm
Bend	0.0126 in. per 3.94 in.	0.032mm per 100mm
Connecting rod side play on crankshaft	0.0065–0.1850 in.	0.165–0.470mm
Crankshaft		
Main journal diameter	2.2437–2.2444 in.	56.990–57.007mm
Main journal out-of-round limit	0.0004 in.	0.01mm
Main bearing-to-crankshaft oil clearance	0.0002–0.0024 in.	0.006–0.060mm
Connecting rod journal diameter	1.8500–1.8508 in.	46.99–47.01mm
Connecting rod journal out-of-round		
Limit	0.0004 in.	0.01mm
Connecting rod bearing oil clearance	0.00039–0.00290 in.	0.010–0.073mm
Crankshaft runout	0.0020 in.	0.05mm
Crankshaft endplay	0.0020–0.0098 in.	0.05–0.25mm
Oil Pump		
Tip clearance	0.006 in. Max.	0.15mm Max.
End-to-end clearance	0.0011–0.0049 in.	0.280–0.125mm
Body-to-side clearance	0.0042–0.0110 in.	0.105–0.277mm

TORQUE SPECIFICATIONS

Component	U.S.	Metric
A/C compressor front bracket-to-block	40 ft. lbs.	54 Nm
A/C compressor front bracket-to-head	22 ft. lbs.	30 Nm
A/C compressor rear bracket	22 ft. lbs.	30 Nm
A/C compressor-to-front bracket	40 ft. lbs.	54 Nm
A/C compressor-to-rear bracket	22 ft. lbs.	30 Nm
Accelerator control cable stud (SOHC)	62 inch lbs.	7 Nm
Accelerator control cable bracket	19 ft. lbs.	25 Nm
Air cleaner/resonator attachment bolts	89 inch lbs.	10 Nm
Air cleaner/resonator clamps	18 inch lbs.	2 Nm
Axle shaft intermediate bracket-to-block	41 ft. lbs.	55 Nm
Battery cable-to-battery	151 inch lbs.	17 Nm
Battery cable-to-alternator	89 inch lbs.	10 Nm
Battery case bracket stud and nut	80 inch lbs.	9 Nm
Belt idler pulley-to-front cover	33 ft. lbs.	45 Nm
Belt tensioner-to-block	22 ft. lbs.	30 Nm
Belt tensioner pulley	22 ft. lbs.	30 Nm
Block oil gallery plug	22 ft. lbs.	30 Nm
Camshaft bearing cap (DOHC)	124 inch lbs.	14 Nm
Camshaft cover-to-head (DOHC)	89 inch lbs.	10 Nm
Camshaft sprocket-to-camshaft	75 ft. lbs.	102 Nm
Camshaft thrust bearing (SOHC)	19 ft. lbs.	25 Nm
Canister assembly band clamp	31 inch lbs.	3.5 Nm
Canister purge solenoid-to-block	22 ft. lbs.	30 Nm
Catalytic converter-to-isolator	19 ft. lbs.	25 Nm
Clamp, air cleaner ducts	15 inch lbs.	1.7 Nm
Clutch pressure plate-to-flywheel	19 ft. lbs.	25 Nm
Connecting rod cap-to-rod	33 ft. lbs.	45 Nm
Coolant/cylinder block heater	19 ft. lbs.	25 Nm
Coolant drain-to-plug/block	26 ft. lbs.	35 Nm
Cradle-to-body	151 ft. lbs.	205 Nm
Crankshaft bearing cap-to-block	37 ft. lbs.	50 Nm
Crankshaft damper/pulley	159 ft. lbs.	215 Nm
Crankshaft rear oil seal carrier-to-block	97 inch lbs.	8 Nm
Cylinder head torque angle procedure		
SOHC engine		
Step 1	33 ft. lbs.	45 Nm
Step 2	+90 degrees	+90 degrees
DOHC engine		
Step 1	37 ft. lbs.	50 Nm
Step 2	+90 degrees	+90 degrees
Cylinder head water jacket plug (DOHC)	55 ft. lbs.	75 Nm
De-aeration line fitting (SOHC)	53 inch lbs.	6 Nm
De-aeration line nut (SOHC)	151 inch lbs.	17 Nm
De-aeration line clamp (SOHC)	80 inch lbs.	9 Nm
De-aeration line fitting-to-cylinder head	97 inch lbs.	11 Nm
Engine lift bracket-to-head (no A/C)	22 ft. lbs.	30 Nm
Engine lift bracket-to-block (no A/C)	40 ft. lbs.	54 Nm
EGR solenoid bracket		
SOHC engine	19 ft. lbs.	25 Nm
DOHC engine	89 inch lbs.	10 Nm
EGR valve-to-head/intake manifold nut	21 ft. lbs.	28 Nm
EGR valve stud-to-head/intake manifold	62 inch lbs.	7 Nm

TORQUE SPECIFICATIONS

Component	U.S.	Metric
Engine lift bracket-to-head	22 ft. lbs.	30 Nm
Engine lift bracket-to-block	40 ft. lbs.	54 Nm
Exhaust manifold-to-exhaust pipe	115 inch lbs.	13 Nm
Exhaust manifold studs-to-head	106 inch lbs.	12 Nm
Exhaust manifold-to-head		
SOHC engine	16 ft. lbs.	22 Nm
DOHC engine	23 ft. lbs.	31 Nm
Exhaust pipe-to-converter	33 ft. lbs.	45 Nm
Exhaust pipe center hanger-to-vehicle	160 inch lbs.	18 Nm
Exhaust pipe-to-isolator	19 ft. lbs.	25 Nm
Exhaust pipe (front)-to-manifold	23 ft. lbs.	31 Nm
Exhaust pipe service clamps	44 ft. lbs.	60 Nm
Exhaust pipe support bracket-to-block	35 ft. lbs.	47 Nm
Exhaust pipe-to-support bracket	23 ft. lbs.	31 Nm
Flexplate-to-crankshaft	44 ft. lbs.	60 Nm
Flexplate-to-converter	41 ft. lbs.	55 Nm
Flywheel/flexplate cover-to-case	89 inch lbs.	10 Nm
Flywheel-to-crankshaft	59 ft. lbs.	80 Nm
Front cover-to-block (lower center bolt)	89 inch lbs.	10 Nm
Front cover-to-head/block		
Perimeter fasteners	22 ft. lbs.	30 Nm
Top studs (torque axis mount system)	19 ft. lbs.	25 Nm
1992–93 DOHC top center	22 ft. lbs.	30 Nm
Fuel canister bracket-to-frame rail	22 ft. lbs.	30 Nm
Fuel feed/return pipes		
SOHC engine	19 ft. lbs.	25 Nm
DOHC engine	133 inch lbs.	15 Nm
Fuel line support bracket	22 ft. lbs.	30 Nm
Fuel line support clip-to-bracket	106 inch lbs.	12 Nm
Fuel rail-to-intake manifold	22 ft. lbs.	30 Nm
Fuel tank fill pipe-to-pocket	18 inch lbs.	2 Nm
Fuel tank fill pipe bracket-to-rail	53 inch lbs.	6 Nm
Fuel tank fill hose-to-clamp	27 inch lbs.	3 Nm
Fuel tank straps-to-body	25 ft. lbs.	34 Nm
Fuel/vapor lines-to-body	27 inch lbs.	3 Nm
Alternator-to-block (upper/lower bolt)	27 ft. lbs.	37 Nm
Heater return nipple-to-block	37 ft. lbs.	50 Nm
Intake manifold heater outlet	26 ft. lbs.	19 Nm
Ignition module-to-transaxle case	35 inch lbs.	4 Nm
Fuel line clamp stud (SOHC)	62 inch lbs.	7 Nm
Intake manifold studs		
Studs-to-head	106 inch lbs.	12 Nm
P/S bracket studs-to-head (DOHC)	22 ft. lbs.	30 Nm
Intake manifold bolts-to-head		
SOHC engine	188 inch lbs.	20 Nm
DOHC engine	22 ft. lbs.	30 Nm
Intake manifold support bracket-to-block		
Left hand	22 ft. lbs.	30 Nm
Right hand (DOHC)	41 ft. lbs.	55 Nm
Intake support bracket-to-manifold		
Nut (SOHC)	21 ft. lbs.	28 Nm
Fastener (DOHC)	22 ft. lbs.	30 Nm
Motion restrictor bracket-to-cradle	40 ft. lbs.	54 Nm

TORQUE SPECIFICATIONS

Component	U.S.	Metric
Motion restrictor bracket-to-front of block	40 ft. lbs.	54 Nm
Motion restrictor bracket-to-side of block	22 ft. lbs.	30 Nm
Motor mount, front-to-block	52 ft. lbs.	70 Nm
Motor mount, rear-to-block	35 ft. lbs.	48 Nm
Muffler isolator block-to-body	160 inch lbs.	18 Nm
Muffler strap (around muffler)	23 ft. lbs.	31 Nm
Oil filter fitting-to-block	22 ft. lbs.	30 Nm
Oil gallery plug-to-block	22 ft. lbs.	30 Nm
Oil level indicator tube-to-block	22 ft. lbs.	30 Nm
Oil pan-to-block	80 inch lbs.	9 Nm
Oil pan drain plug-to-pan	27 ft. lbs.	37 Nm
Oil pick-up tube-to-block	133 inch lbs.	15 Nm
Oil pipe bracket-to-block/baffle plate		
SOHC engine	41 ft. lbs.	55 Nm
DOHC engine	133 inch lbs.	15 Nm
Oil pump cover-to-front cover	97 inch lbs.	11 Nm
Oil baffle plate-to-block (DOHC)	41 ft. lbs.	55 Nm
Power steering hoses-to-gear and pump	41 ft. lbs.	55 Nm
Power steering pump		
Bracket-to-manifold	22 ft. lbs.	30 Nm
Except bracket-to-manifold	28 ft. lbs.	38 Nm
Power steering hose clamp	89 inch lbs.	10 Nm
Radiator support brackets	89 inch lbs.	10 Nm
Rocker arm cover-to-head (SOHC)	22 ft. lbs.	30 Nm
Rocker arm shaft-to-head (SOHC)	19 ft. lbs.	25 Nm
ESC knock sensor-to-block	133 inch lbs.	15 Nm
Idle air control valve	28 inch lbs.	3.2 Nm
MAP sensor		
SOHC engine (rocker cover)	53 inch lbs.	6 Nm
DOHC engine (intake manifold)	44 inch lbs.	5 Nm
Oil pressure sensor-to-block	26 ft. lbs.	35 Nm
Throttle position sensor	18 inch lbs.	2 Nm
Coolant temperature sensors-to-head	71 inch lbs.	8 Nm
Crankshaft position sensor-to-block	80 inch lbs.	9 Nm
Oxygen sensor-to-exhaust manifold	19 ft. lbs.	25 Nm
Intake air sensor-to-intake tube	44 inch lbs.	5 Nm
Spark plug-to-head	20 ft. lbs.	27 Nm
Starter		
Motor-to-block	27 ft. lbs.	37 Nm
Support bracket-to-axle shaft bracket	22 ft. lbs.	30 Nm
Support bracket-to-starter motor	80 inch lbs.	9 Nm
Steering joint-to-gear	35 ft. lbs.	47 Nm
Stiffening bracket	40 ft. lbs.	54 Nm
Strut-to-knuckle	148 ft. lbs.	200 Nm
TBI assembly-to-air intake manifold	24 ft. lbs.	33 Nm
TBI assembly fuel line (inlet/return)	19 ft. lbs.	25 Nm
Thermostat housing-to-block	22 ft. lbs.	30 Nm
Throttle body-to-intake manifold (DOHC)	23 ft. lbs.	31 Nm
Wiring harness PCM ground-to-block	89 inch lbs.	10 Nm
Wiring harness-to-alternator or starter		
Positive terminal	89 inch lbs.	10 Nm
Starter solenoid terminal	44 inch lbs.	5 Nm
Wiring harness-to-transaxle/engine	19 ft. lbs.	25 Nm

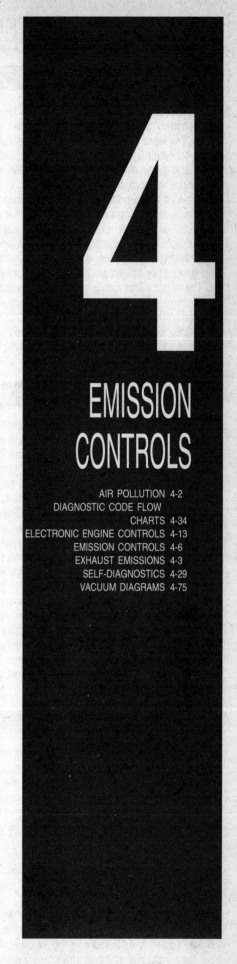

4

EMISSION
CONTROLS

AIR POLLUTION

The earth's atmosphere, at or near sea level, consists approximately of 78% nitrogen, 21% oxygen and 1% other gases. If it were possible to remain in this state, 100% clean air would result. However, many varied causes allow other gases and particulates to mix with the clean air, causing the air to become unclean or polluted.

Certain of these pollutants are visible while others are invisible, with each having the capability of causing distress to the eyes, ears, throat, skin and respiratory system. Should these pollutants become concentrated in a specific area and under the right conditions, death could result due to the displacement or chemical change of the oxygen content in the air. These pollutants can also cause great damage to the environment and to the many man made objects that are exposed to the elements.

To better understand the causes of air pollution, the pollutants can be categorized into 3 separate types, natural, industrial and automotive.

Natural Pollutants

Natural pollution has been present on earth since before man appeared and continues to be a factor when discussing air pollution, although it causes only a small percentage of the overall pollution problem existing in our country today. It is the direct result of decaying organic matter, wind born smoke and particulates from such natural events as plain and forest fires (ignited by heat or lightning), volcanic ash, sand and dust which can spread over a large area of the countryside.

Such a phenomenon of natural pollution has been recent volcanic eruptions, with the resulting plume of smoke, steam and volcanic ash blotting out the sun's rays as it spreads and rises higher into the atmosphere, where the upper air currents catch and carry the smoke and ash, while condensing the steam back into water vapor. As the water vapor, smoke and ash traveled on their journey, the smoke dissipates into the atmosphere while the ash and moisture settle back to earth in a trail hundred of miles long. In some cases, lives are lost and millions of dollars of property damage result. Ironically, man can only stand by and watch it happen.

Industrial Pollution

Industrial pollution is caused primarily by industrial processes, the burning of coal, oil and natural gas, which in turn produce smoke and fumes. Because the burning fuels contain large amounts of sulfur, the principal ingredients of smoke and fumes are sulfur dioxide (SO_2) and particulate matter. This type of pollutant occurs most severely during still, damp and cool weather, such as at night. Even in its less severe form, this pollutant is not confined to just cities. Because of air movements, the pollutants move for miles over the surrounding countryside, leaving in its path a barren and unhealthy environment for all living things.

Working with Federal, State and Local mandated rules, regulations and by carefully monitoring the emissions, industries have greatly reduced the amount of pollutant emitted from their industrial sources, striving to obtain an acceptable

level. Because of the mandated industrial emission clean up, many land areas and streams in and around the cities that were formerly barren of vegetation and life, have now begun to move back in the direction of nature's intended balance.

Automotive Pollutants

The third major source of air pollution is automotive emissions. The emissions from the internal combustion engine were not an appreciable problem years ago because of the small number of registered vehicles and the nation's small highway system. However, during the early 1950's, the trend of the American people was to move from the cities to the surrounding suburbs. This caused an immediate problem in transportation because the majority of suburbs were not afforded mass transit conveniences. This lack of transportation created an attractive market for the automobile manufacturers, which resulted in a dramatic increase in the number of vehicles produced and sold, along with a marked increase in highway construction between cities and the suburbs. Multi-vehicle families emerged with a growing emphasis placed on an individual vehicle per family member. As the increase in vehicle ownership and usage occurred, so did pollutant levels in and around the cities, as suburbanites drove daily to their busin esses and employment, returning at the end of the day to their homes in the suburbs.

It was noted that a fog and smoke type haze was being formed and at times, remained in suspension over the cities, taking time to dissipate. At first this "smog", derived from the words "smoke" and "fog", was thought to result from industrial pollution but it was determined that the automobile emissions were also to blame. It was discovered that when normal automobile emissions were exposed to sunlight for a period of time, complex chemical reactions would take place.

It is now known that smog is a photo chemical layer which develops when certain oxides of nitrogen (NOx) and unburned hydrocarbons (HC) from automobile emissions are exposed to sunlight. Polution was more severe when smog would reamain stagnant over an area in which a warm layer of air settled over the top of the cooler air mass, trapping and holding the cooler mass at ground level. The trapped cooler air would keep the emissions from being dispersed and diluted through normal air flows. This type of air stagnation was given the name "Temperature Inversion".

Temperature Inversion

In normal weather situations, the surface air is warmed by heat radiating from the earth's surface and the sun's rays and will rise upward, into the atmosphere. Upon rising it will cool through a convection type heat exchange with the cooler upper air. As warm air rises, the surface pollutants are carried upward and dissipated into the atmosphere.

When a temperature inversion occurs, we find the higher air is no longer cooler but warmer than the surface air, causing the cooler surface air to become trapped. This warm air blanket can extend from above ground level to a few hundred or even a few thousand feet into the air. As the surface air is trapped, so are the pollutants, causing a severe smog condition. Should this stagnant air mass extend to a few thousand feet high, enough air movement with the inversion takes place to allow the smog layer to rise above ground level but the pollutants still cannot dissipate. This inversion can remain for days over an area, with the smog level only rising or lowering from ground level to a few hundred feet high. Meanwhile, the pollutant levels increase, causing eye irritation, respiratory problems, reduced visibility, plant damage and in some cases, disease.

This inversion phenomenon was first noted in the Los Angeles, California area. The city lies terrain resembling a basin and with certain weather conditions, a cold air mass is held in the basin while a warmer air mass covers it like a lid.

Because this type of condition was first documented as prevalent in the Los Angeles area, this type of trapped polution was named Los Angeles Smog, although it occurs in other areas where a large concentration of automobiles are used and the air remains stagnant for any length of time.

Internal Combustion Engine Pollutants

Consider the internal combustion engine as a machine in which raw materials must be placed so a finished product comes out. As in any machine operation, a certain amount of wasted material is formed. When we relate this to the internal combustion engine, we find that through the input of air and fuel, we obtain power during the combustion process to drive the vehicle. The by-product or waste of this power is, in part, heat and exhaust gases with which we must dispose.

EXHAUST EMISSIONS

Composition Of The Exhaust Gases

The exhaust gases emitted into the atmosphere are a combination of burned and unburned fuel. To understand the exhaust emission and its composition, we must review some basic chemistry.

When the air/fuel mixture is introduced into the engine, we are mixing air, composed of nitrogen (78%), oxygen (21%) and other gases (1%) with the fuel, which is 100% hydrocarbons (HC), in a semi-controlled ratio. As the combustion process is accomplished, power is produced to move the vehicle while the heat of combustion is transferred to the cooling system. The exhaust gases are then composed of nitrogen, a diatomic gas (N_2), the same as was introduced in the engine, carbon dioxide (CO2), the same gas that is used in beverage carbonation and water vapor (H_2O). The nitrogen (N_2), for the most part passes through the engine unchanged, while the oxygen (O_2) reacts (burns) with the hydrocarbons (HC) and produces the carbon dioxide (CO_2) and the water vapors (H_2O). If this chemical process would be the only process to take place, the exhaust emissions would be harmless. However, during the combustion process, other compounds are formed which are considered dangerous. These pollutants are carbon monoxide (CO), hydrocarbons (HC), oxides of nitrogen (NOx) oxides of sulfur (SOx) and engine particulates.

HEAT TRANSFER

The heat from the combustion process can rise to over 4000°F (2204°C). The dissipation of this heat is controlled by a ram air effect, the use of cooling fans to cause air flow and having a liquid coolant solution surrounding the combustion area to transfer the heat of combustion through the cylinder walls and into the coolant. The coolant is then directed to a thin-finned, multi-tubed radiator, from which the excess heat is transferred to the atmosphereby 1 of the 3 heat transfer methods, conduction, convection or radiation.

The cooling of the combustion area is an important part in the control of exhaust emissions. To understand the behavior of the combustion and transfer of its heat, consider the air/fuel charge. It is ignited and the flame front burns progressively across the combustion chamber until the burning charge reaches the cylinder walls. Some of the fuel in contact with the walls is not hot enough to burn, thereby snuffing out or quenching the combustion process. This leaves unburned fuel in the combustion chamber. This unburned fuel is then forced out of the cylinder and into the exhaust system, along with the exhaust gases.

Many attempts have been made to minimize the amount of unburned fuel in the combustion chambers due to the snuffing out or quenching, by increasing the coolant temperature and lessening the contact area of the coolant around the combustion area. Design limitations within the combustion chambers prevent the complete burning of the air/fuel charge, so a certain amount of the unburned fuel is still expelled into the exhaust system, regardless of modifications to the engine.

HYDROCARBONS

Hydrocarbons (HC) are essentially fuel which was not burned during the combustion process or which has escaped into the atmosphere through fuel evaporation. The main sources of incomplete combustion are rich air/fuel mixtures, low engine temperatures and improper spark timing. The main sources of hydrocarbon emission through fuel evaporation used to be the vehicle's fuel tank and carburetor bowl.

To reduce combustion hydrocarbon emission, engine modifications were made to minimize dead space and surface area in the combustion chamber. In addition the air/fuel mixture was made more lean through the improved control which fuel injection offers and by the addition of external controls to aid in further combustion of the hydrocarbons outside the engine. Two such methods were the addition of an air injection system, to inject fresh air into the exhaust manifolds and the installation of a catalytic converter, a unit that is able to burn traces of hydrocarbons without affecting the internal combustion process or fuel economy. Saturn vehicles use only the second of these methods, the catalytic converter.

To control hydrocarbon emissions through fuel evaporation, modifications were made to the fuel tank to allow storage of the fuel vapors during periods of engine shut-down. Modifications were also made to the air intake system so that

4-4 EMISSION CONTROLS

at specific times during engine operation, these vapors may be purged and burned by blending them with the air/fuel mixture.

CARBON MONOXIDE

Carbon monoxide is formed when not enough oxygen is present during the combustion process to convert carbon (C) to carbon dioxide (CO_2). An increase in the carbon monoxide (CO) emission is normally accompanied by an increase in the hydrocarbon (HC) emission because of the lack of oxygen to completely burn all of the fuel mixture.

Carbon monoxide (CO) also increases the rate at which the photo chemical smog is formed by speeding up the conversion of nitric oxide (NO) to nitrogen dioxide (NO_2). To accomplish this, carbon monoxide (CO) combines with oxygen (O_2) and nitrogen dioxide (NO_2) to produce carbon dioxide (CO_2) and nitrogen dioxide (NO_2). ($CO + O_2 + NO = CO_2 + NO_2$).

The dangers of carbon monoxide, which is an odorless, colorless, toxic gas are many. When carbon monoxide is inhaled into the lungs and passed into the blood stream, oxygen is replaced by the carbon monoxide in the red blood cells, causing a reduction in the amount of oxygen being supplied to the many parts of the body. This lack of oxygen causes headaches, lack of coordination, reduced mental alertness and should the carbon monoxide concentration be high enough, death.

NITROGEN

Normally, nitrogen is an inert gas. When heated to approximately 2500°F (1371°C) through the combustion process, this gas becomes active and causes an increase in the nitric oxide (NOx) emission.

Oxides of nitrogen (NOx) are composed of approximately 97-98% nitric oxide (NO2). Nitric oxide is a colorless gas but when it is passed into the atmosphere, it combines with oxygen and forms nitrogen dioxide (NO2). The nitrogen dioxide then combines with chemically active hydrocarbons (HC) and when in the presence of sunlight, causes the formation of photo chemical smog.

OZONE

To further complicate matters, some of the nitrogen dioxide (NO_2) is broken apart by the sunlight to form nitric oxide and oxygen. (NO_2 + sunlight = NO + O). This single atom of oxygen then combines with diatomic (meaning 2 atoms) oxygen (O_2) to form ozone (O_3). Ozone is 1 of the smells associated with smog. It has a pungent and offensive odor, irritates the eyes and lung tissues, affects the growth of plant life and causes rapid deterioration of rubber products. Ozone can be formed by sunlight as well as electrical discharge into the air.

The most common discharge area on the automobile engine is the secondary ignition electrical system, especially when inferior quality spark plug cables are used. As the surge of high voltage is routed through the secondary cable, the circuit builds up an electrical field around the wire, acting upon the oxygen in the surrounding air to form the ozone. The faint glow along the cable with the engine running that may be visible on a dark night, is called the "corona discharge." It is the result of the electrical field passing from a high along the cable, to a low in the surrounding air, which forms the ozone gas. The combination of corona and ozone has been a major cause of cable deterioration. Recently, different and better quality insulating materials have lengthened the life of the electrical cables.

Although ozone at ground level can be harmful, ozone is beneficial to the earth's inhabitants. By having a concentrated ozone layer called the 'ozonosphere', between 10 and 20 miles (16-32km) up in the atmosphere much of the ultra violet radiation from the sun's rays are absorbed and screened. If this ozone layer were not present, much of the earth's surface would be burned, dried and unfit for human life.

There is much discussion concerning the ozone layer and its density. A feeling exists that this protective layer of ozone is slowly diminishing and corrective action must be directed to this problem. Much experimentation is presently being conducted to determine if a problem exists and if so, the short and long term effects of the problem and how it can be remedied.

OXIDES OF SULFUR

Oxides of sulfur (SOx) were initially ignored in the exhaust system emissions, since the sulfur content of gasoline as a fuel is less than $\frac{1}{10}$ of 1%. Because of this small amount, it was felt that it contributed very little to the overall pollution problem. However, because of the difficulty in solving the sulfur emissions in industrial pollutions and the introduction of catalytic converter to the automobile exhaust systems, a change was mandated. The automobile exhaust system, when equipped with a catalytic converter, changes the sulfur dioxide (SO_2) into the sulfur trioxide (SO_3).

When this combines with water vapors (H_2O), a sulfuric acid mist (H_2SO_4) is formed and is a very difficult pollutant to handle since it is extremely corrosive. This sulfuric acid mist that is formed, is the same mist that rises from the vents of an automobile storage battery when an active chemical reaction takes place within the battery cells.

When a large concentration of vehicles equipped with catalytic converters are operating in an area, this acid mist will rise and be distributed over a large ground area causing land, plant, crop, paints and building damage.

PARTICULATE MATTER

A certain amount of particulate matter is present in the burning of any fuel, with carbon constituting the largest percentage of the particulates. In gasoline, the remaining particulates are the burned remains of the various other compounds used in its manufacture. When a gasoline engine is in good internal condition, the particulate emissions are low but as the engine wears internally, the particulate emissions increase. By visually inspecting the tail pipe emissions, a determination can be made as to where an engine defect may exist. An engine with light gray smoke emitting from the tail pipe normally indicates an increase in the oil consumption through burning due to internal engine wear. Black smoke would indicate a defective fuel delivery system, causing the engine to operate in a rich mode. Regardless of the color of the smoke, the internal part of the engine or the fuel delivery system should be repaired to a "like new" condition to prevent excess particulate emissions.

Diesel and turbine engines emit a darkened plume of smoke from the exhaust system because of the type of fuel used. Emission control regulations are mandated for this type of emission and more stringent measures are being used to prevent excess emission of the particulate matter. Electronic components are being introduced to control the injection of the fuel at precisely the proper time of piston travel, to achieve the optimum in fuel ignition and fuel usage. Other particulate after-burning components are being tested to achieve a cleaner emission.

Good grades of engine lubricating oils should be used, which meet the manufacturers specification. 'Cut-rate' oils can contribute to the particulate emission problem because of their low "flash" or ignition temperature point. Such oils burn prematurely during the combustion process causing emissions of particulate matter.

The cooling system is an important factor in the reduction of particulate matter. With the cooling system operating at a temperature specified by the manufacturer, the optimum of combustion will occur. The cooling system must be maintained in the same manner as the engine oiling system, as each system is required to perform properly in order for the engine to operate efficiently for a long time.

Other Automobile Emission Sources

Before emission controls were mandated on the internal combustion engines, other sources of engine pollutants were discovered, along with the exhaust emission. It was determined the engine combustion exhaust produced 60% of the total emission pollutants, fuel evaporation from the fuel tank and carburetor vents produced 20%, with the another 20% being produced through the crankcase as a by-product of the combustion process.

CRANKCASE EMISSIONS

Crankcase emissions are made up of water, acids, unburned fuel, oil fumes and particulates. The emissions are classified as hydrocarbons (HC) and are formed by the small amount of unburned, compressed air/fuel mixture entering the crankcase from the combustion area during the compression and power strokes, between the cylinder walls and piston rings. The head of the compression and combustion help to form the remaining crankcase emissions.

Since the first engines, crankcase emissions were allowed into the atmosphere through a road draft tube, mounted on the lower side of the engine block. Fresh air came in through an open oil filler cap or breather. The air passed through the crankcase mixing with blow-by gases. The motion of the vehicle and the air blowing past the open end of the road draft tube caused a low pressure area at the end of the tube.

Crankcase emissions were simply drawn out of the road draft tube into the air.

To control the crankcase emission, the road draft tube was deleted. A hose and/or tubing was routed from the crankcase to the intake manifold so the blow-by emission could be burned with the air/fuel mixture. However, it was found that intake manifold vacuum, used to draw the crankcase emissions into the manifold, would vary in strength at the wrong time and not allow the proper emission flow. A regulating type valve was needed to control the flow of air through the crankcase.

Testing, showed the removal of the blow-by gases from the crankcase as quickly as possible, was most important to the longevity of the engine. Should large accumulations of blow-by gases remain and condense, dilution of the engine oil would occur to form water, soots, resins, acids and lead salts, resulting in the formation of sludge and varnishes. This condensation of the blow-by gases occur more frequently on vehicles used in numerous starting and stopping conditions, excessive idling and when the engine is not allowed to attain normal operating temperature through short runs.

FUEL EVAPORATIVE EMISSIONS

Gasoline fuel is a major source of pollution, before and after it is burned in the automobile engine. From the time the fuel is refined, stored, pumped and transported, again stored until it is pumped into the fuel tank of the vehicle, the gasoline gives off unburned hydrocarbons (HC) into the atmosphere. Through redesigning of the storage areas and venting systems, the pollution factor was diminished, but not eliminated, from the refinery standpoint. However, the automobile still remained the primary source of vaporized, unburned hydrocarbon (HC) emissions.

Fuel pumped from an underground storage tank is cool but when exposed to a warner ambient temperature, will expand. Before controls were mandated, an owner would fill the fuel tank with fuel from an underground storage tank and park the vehicle for some time in warm area, such as a parking lot. As the fuel would warm, it would expand and should no provisions or area be provided for the expansion, the fuel would spill out the filler neck and onto the ground, causing hydrocarbon (HC) pollution and creating a severe fire hazard. To correct this condition, the vehicle manufacturers added overflow plumbing and/or gasoline tanks with built in expansion areas or domes.

However, this did not control the fuel vapor emission from the fuel tank. It was determined that most of the fuel evaporation occurred when the vehicle was stationary and the engine not operating. Most vehicles carry 5-25 gallons (19-95 liters) of gasoline. Should a large concentration of vehicles be parked in one area, such as a large parking lot, excessive fuel vapor emissions would take place, increasing as the temperature increases.

To prevent the vapor emission from escaping into the atmosphere, the fuel system is designed to trap the fuel vapors while the vehicle is stationary, by sealing the fuel system from the atmosphere. A storage system is used to collect and hold the fuel vapors from the carburetor and the fuel tank when the engine is not operating. When the engine is started, the storage system is then purged of the fuel vapors, which are drawn into the engine and burned with the air/fuel mixture.

EMISSION CONTROLS

The emission control system begins at the air intake and ends at the tailpipe. The emission control system includes various sub-systems such as the positive crankcase ventilation system, evaporative emission control system, the exhaust gas recirculation system and exhaust catalyst, as well as the electronic controls that govern the fuel and ignition system. These components are combined to control engine operation for maximum engine efficiency and minimal exhaust emissions.

Positive Crankcase Ventilation System

OPERATION

▶ **See Figures 1 and 2**

The system consists of a tube from the air filter housing to the rocker/camsahft cover and a second tube from the rocker/camshaft cover to the intake manifold. Under normal operating conditions, clean air flows from the air filter into the rocker/camshaft cover where it mixes with crankcase oil vapors. These vapors are drawn through the PCV valve and into the intake manifold to be burned with the air/fuel mixture. The flow to the intake manifold is metered by the PCV valve.

When manifold vacuum is high, the valve is pulled closed and flow is restricted to maintain a smooth idle. If crankcase pressure is very high, vapors can flow directly into the air filter housing.

A plugged PCV system will cause oil leaks or a build up of sludge in the engine. An air filter coated with engine oil indicates excessive crankcase pressure. A leaking valve or hose might cause rough or high idle, engine stalling and/or Powertrain Control Module (PCM) trouble codes.

SERVICE

1. Visually inspect the PCV valve hose and the fresh air supply hose and their attaching nipples or grommets for splits, cuts, damage, clogging, or restrictions. Repair or replace, as necessary.
2. If the hoses pass inspection, start the engine and allow it to warm until normal operating temperature is reached.
3. Remove the PCV valve from the rocker arm cover, but leave it connected to the hose. With the engine at idle, feel the end of the valve for manifold vacuum. If there is no vacuum, check for a plugged or leaking hose, PCV valve or manifold port. Replace a plugged or damaged hose.
4. Stop the engine and remove the PCV valve. It should rattle when shaken. If the valve does not rattle or it is plugged, replace the valve.

REMOVAL & INSTALLATION

▶ **See Figure 3**

1. Remove the PCV valve from the mounting grommet in the rocker/camshaft cover.
2. Disconnect the valve from the PCV hose and remove the valve from the vehicle.
3. Installation is the reverse of the removal procedure.

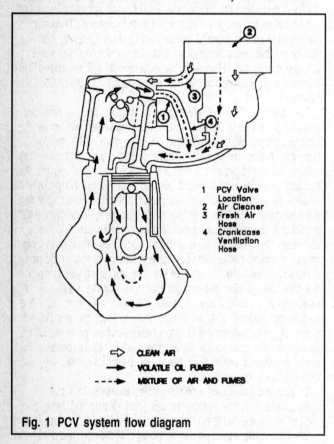

1 PCV Valve Location
2 Air Cleaner
3 Fresh Air Hose
4 Crankcase Ventilation Hose

⇨ CLEAN AIR
➡ VOLATILE OIL FUMES
- - -▶ MIXTURE OF AIR AND FUMES

Fig. 1 PCV system flow diagram

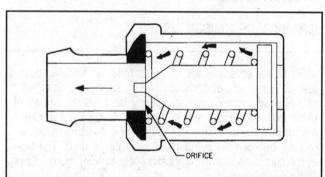

ORIFICE

Fig. 2 Cut-away view of the PCV valve allowing the flow of the mixed air into the intake manifold

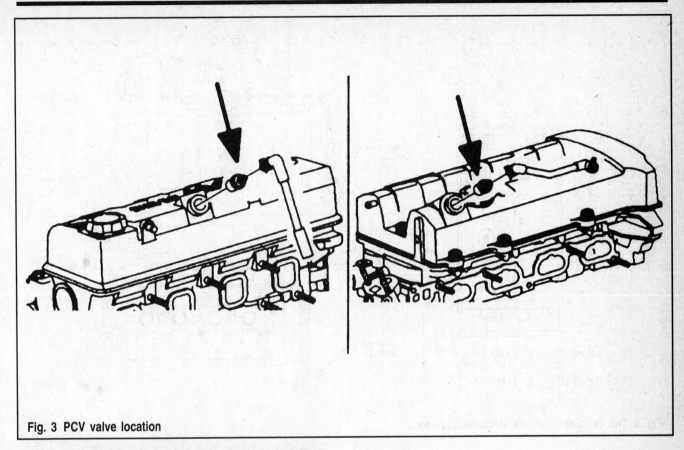

Fig. 3 PCV valve location

Fuel Evaporative Emission Control System

OPERATION

▶ See Figure 4

The Evaporative Emission Control System (EECS) limits the amount of fuel vapors allowed to escape into the air. When the engine is not running, fuel vapors from the sealed fuel tank flow through the single vapor line to the charcoal canister mounted against the inner wheel well, in the right front of the engine compartment. The charcoal absorbs the fuel vapors and retains them until they are purged with fresh air.

Any time the ignition switch is **ON**, the canister purge solenoid valve is supplied with 12 volts. Under the appropriate engine operating conditions, the PCM completes the circuit to ground, opening the valve. With the valve open, intake manifold vacuum is applied to the canister drawing in fresh air and purging the vapors. The purged vapors are then drawn into the engine and burned efficiently during the normal combustion process.

The purge valve is opened when the coolant temperature is above 158°F (70°C), vehicle speed is more than 1 mph and throttle position is more than 4 percent open.

SERVICE

Carefully check for cracks or leaks in the vacuum lines or in the canister itself. The lines and fittings can be reached without removing the canister. Cracks or leaks in the system may cause poor idle, stalling, poor driveability, fuel loss or a fuel vapor odor.

Vapor odor and fuel loss may also be caused by; fuel leaking from the lines, tank or injectors, loose, disconnected or kinked lines or an improperly seated air cleaner and gasket.

If the system passes the visual inspection and a problem is still suspected, proceed as follows:

1. With the ignition switch in the **OFF** position, unplug the electrical connector from the canister purge solenoid. Use an ohmmeter to check the solenoid coil resistance, it should be 22-42 ohms.

2. Turn the ignition switch **ON** then, disconnect the vacuum line from the intake manifold and connect a hand vacuum pump to the valve.

3. Apply a vacuum of about 10 in. Hg (34 kPa) to the hose and solenoid, then observe if the valve holds the vacuum. If the valve does not hold, apply vacuum directly to the solenoid to determine if the solenoid or hose is at fault, then replace the component which allowed vacuum to release.

4. If the vacuum holds in the initial test, jumper the test terminals on the ALDL (terminals A and B are the test terminals and are the two most upper right terminals of the ALDL connector) and observe if the valve activates, releasing the vacuum. If the valve does not activate and release the vacuum, replace the solenoid.

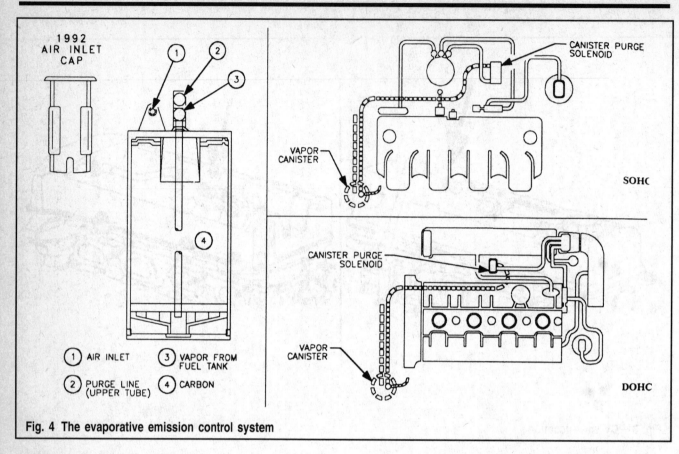

Fig. 4 The evaporative emission control system

REMOVAL & INSTALLATION

Canister Purge Solenoid Valve

▶ See Figure 5

The purge solenoid valve is mounted on the engine, towards the rear and below the intake manifold.

1. If equipped, properly disable the SIR system as follows:

a. Align the steering wheel so the tires are in the straight-ahead position, then turn the ignition **OFF**.

b. Remove the 10 amp SIR fuse from the top left of the Instrument Panel Junction Block (IPJB).

c. Remove the Connector Position Assurance (CPA), then disconnect the yellow 2-way SIR connector at the base of the steering column.

2. Disconnect the negative battery cable.

3. Remove the air cleaner assembly for SOHC engines or the air intake tube and resonator for DOHC engines.

➡ **For DOHC engines, the solenoid may be reached through the access hole located next to the intake manifold support bracket.**

4. Unplug the solenoid vacuum hoses and electrical connector.

5. Remove the attaching bolt, then remove the canister purge solenoid.

To install:

6. Install the solenoid and tighten the retaining bolt to 19 ft. lbs. (25 Nm).

7. Connect the vacuum lines to the solenoid, then install and push in the electrical connector until it clicks firmly into place.

8. Install the air cleaner assembly or the air intake tube and resonator.

9. Connect the negative battery cable.

10. If equipped, enable the SIR system as follows:

a. Verify the ignition switch is **OFF**, then connect the SIR electrical connector at the base of the steering column. Install the CPA device to the connector.

b. Install the SIR fuse to the IPJB and install the junction block cover.

c. Turn the ignition **ON** and verify that the AIR BAG indicator lamp flashes 7-9 times, then goes out. If the light does not flash as indicated, inspect the system for a malfunction.

Charcoal Canister

▶ See Figure 6

1. Raise the front of vehicle sufficiently for underhood and undervehicle service, then support safely using jackstands.

2. Remove the right front tire from the vehicle.

3. Remove the right inner fender well. The fasteners at the front corner should be carefully pried free using a small prybar.

4. Disconnect the vacuum hoses from the canister.

5. Remove the bracket assembly fasteners or the band clamp fasteners, as necessary, then remove the canister from the vehicle.

Fig. 5 The canister purge solenoid is mounted below the intake manifold

To install:

6. Install the canister into the bracket assembly with the ports correctly positioned, but do not tighten the bracket fasteners until the vapor lines are installed.

7. Connect the vacuum hoses to the top of the canister, making sure that no lines are kinked or damaged. Tighten the canister/bracket assembly fasteners to 22 ft. lbs. (30 Nm). The canister air inlet is routed into the vehicle frame rail on 1991 vehicles while 1992-93 vehicles are equipped with a special air inlet cap.

➡Be careful not to overtighten the assembly fasteners or the charcoal canister may be damaged.

8. Install the inner fender well and the right front tire.
9. Remove the jackstands and carefully lower the vehicle.

Exhaust Gas Recirculation System

OPERATION

The Exhaust Gas Recirculation (EGR) valve is used to allow a controlled amount of exhaust gas to be recirculated into the intake system. This limits peak flame temperature in the combustion chamber so the engine produces less NOx (oxides of nitrogen).

A negative backpressure EGR valve is used to control the amount of exhaust gas which is recirculated. Intake manifold vacuum is supplied directly to the top of the diaphragm to pull open the normally closed valve. Exhaust backpressure pushing against the valve keeps the diaphragm pushed against the bleed hole. When the rpm is high but the throttle is closed, exhaust backpressure becomes negative and the diaphragm is pulled down just enough to uncover the bleed hole. The vacuum on top of the diaphragm leaks off and the valve slowly closes.

The EGR vacuum is controlled by the PCM through a solenoid valve. The PCM energizes or de-energizes the solenoid by providing or withholding ground at the appropriate times. When the solenoid is energized, it prevents vacuum from reaching the EGR valve by venting it to the atmosphere. Once the proper conditions have been met, the PCM removes the ground thus de-energizing the solenoid and allowing vacuum to open the EGR valve. The valve is open only when the throttle is open more than 4 percent and coolant temperature is above 104°F (40°C) on the DOHC engine with automatic transaxle or 122°F (50°C) on all others.

SERVICE

▶ **See Figures 7 and 8**

If fault Code 32 is present along with Code 26, trouble shoot Code 26 first and then clear the code memory. Drive the vehicle to see if Code 32 sets again, then proceed to trouble shoot the EGR system. A complete listing of trouble codes may be found later in this section.

If code 32 resets, or a problem is still suspected with the EGR system, test the EGR valve and solenoid:

1. Make sure the ignition is **OFF** so that the solenoid is not energized.

2. Disconnect the EGR valve vacuum hose from the solenoid and attach a hand vacuum pump. Apply vacuum and observe the EGR valve for movement. The valve should easily open and vacuum should be held for a minimum of 20 seconds. If the valve does not open check for damaged, plugged or kinked lines or for restrictions in the valve vacuum port which would prevent vacuum from opening the valve. Clean restrictions and/or replace the lines or valve, as necessary to correct the condition.

3. If the valve opened and vacuum held, disconnect the vacuum hose from the EGR valve port and attach the hand vacuum pump directly to the EGR valve. Apply vacuum and observe the valve opening again. While you watch the valve and the vacuum gauge, have a friend start the engine. The valve should close and vacuum should drop immediately as the engine is started. If the this does not occur, remove the valve and either clean the plugged passages or replace the faulty valve.

4. If the valve is working, but system trouble is still suspected, test the solenoid. Turn the ignition **OFF** and reconnect the vacuum lines to the valve and solenoid.

5. Disconnect the solenoid vacuum line from the throttle body and attach the vacuum pump to the line. Apply vacuum to the lines and observe to see if it holds for at least 20 seconds. If the vacuum does not hold, replace the leaking lines or the bad solenoid, whichever was at fault. Remember, the non-energized solenoid should allow the EGR valve to open.

6. A suspected bad solenoid can also be checked using an ohm meter. Resistance across the solenoid's terminals should be 22-42 ohms.

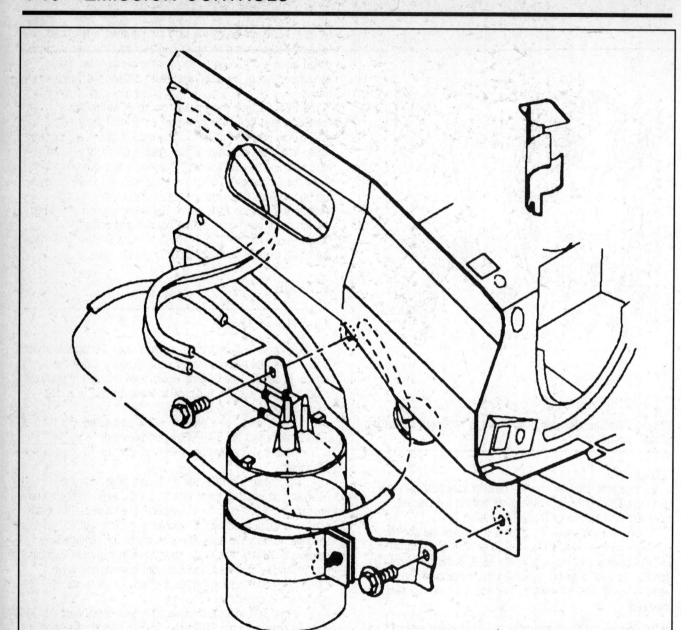

Fig. 6 Installation and vapor hose routing for the charcoal canister

REMOVAL & INSTALLATION

EGR Solenoid

▶ **See Figures 9 and 10**

1. If equipped, properly disable the SIR system as follows:
   a. Align the steering wheel so the tires are in the straight-ahead position, then turn the ignition **OFF**.
   b. Remove the 10 amp SIR fuse from the top left of the Instrument Panel Junction Block (IPJB).
   c. Remove the Connector Position Assurance (CPA), then disconnect the yellow 2-way SIR connector at the base of the steering column.
2. Disconnect the negative battery cable.
3. Remove the air cleaner assembly for SOHC engines or the air intake tube and resonator for DOHC engine.

4. Unplug the solenoid electrical connector and vacuum line.
5. Remove the solenoid attaching bolt, then remove the solenoid from the engine.
   To install:
6. Install the solenoid and tighten the bolt to 89 inch lbs. (10 Nm) for DOHC engines or to 18 ft. lbs. (25 Nm) for SOHC engines.
7. Connect the vacuum lines, then install the electrical connector and push until it clicks firmly into place.
8. Install the air cleaner assembly or the intake tube and resonator, as applicable.
9. Connect the negative battery cable.
10. If equipped, enable the SIR system as follows:
    a. Verify the ignition switch is **OFF**, then connect the SIR electrical connector at the base of the steering column. Install the CPA device to the connector.

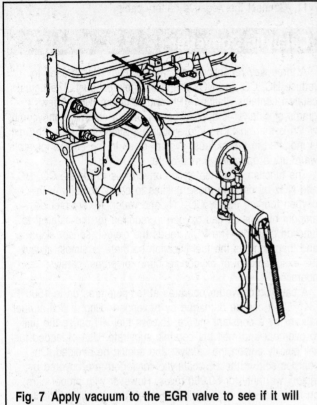

Fig. 7 Apply vacuum to the EGR valve to see if it will open properly

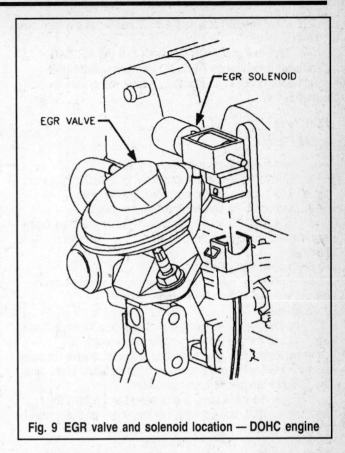

Fig. 9 EGR valve and solenoid location — DOHC engine

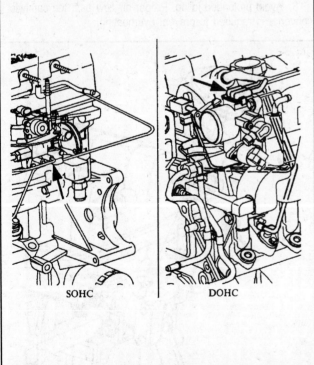

SOHC   DOHC

Fig. 8 Apply vacuum to the throttle body vacuum line to see if the solenoid is causing a problem with the EGR system

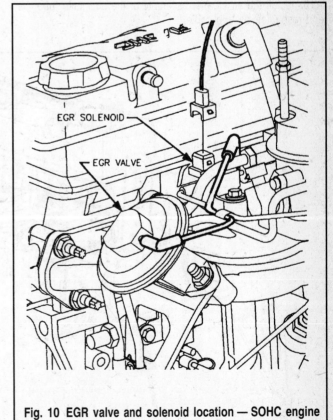

Fig. 10 EGR valve and solenoid location — SOHC engine

b. Install the SIR fuse to the IPJB and install the fuse box cover.

c. Turn the ignition **ON** and verify that the AIR BAG indicator lamp flashes 7-9 times, then extinguishes. If the light does not flash as indicated, inspect the system for malfunction.

EGR Valve

▶ See Figure 11

1. Disconnect the negative battery cable.
2. Remove the air cleaner assembly for SOHC engines or the air intake tube and resonator for DOHC engines.
3. Disconnect the vacuum line from the valve.
4. For the SOHC engine, remove the intake manifold brace and the fuel line clips in order to access the EGR valve fasteners.
5. Remove the valve fasteners.
6. Remove the valve from the vehicle, then remove and discard the gasket from the mating surfaces.

To install:

7. Inspect the EGR passages on the engine for excessive deposits and remove using a screwdriver or length of odometer cable. Use a wire brush or wheel to remove deposits from the EGR valve and engine mounting surfaces. Make sure the surfaces are free of scores or cracks.
8. Install the valve using a new gasket and tighten the fasteners to 19 ft. lbs. (25 Nm). For the SOHC engine, install the intake manifold brace and the fuel line clips.
9. Connect the vacuum hose to the valve.
10. Install the air cleaner assembly or the air intake tube and resonator, as applicable.

11. Connect the negative battery cable.

Catalytic Converter

A three-way reduction type catalytic converter is used to reduce HC, CO and NOx in the engine's exhaust. The actual catalyst contains Platinum (Pt) and Rhodium (Rh). A few grams of catalyst is applied evenly onto a ceramic honeycomb, which is then installed into a stainless-steel enclosure. The unit is mounted in the exhaust system close to the engine for rapid warm-up to operating temperature.

The function of the catalytic converter is to reduce CO, HC, and NOx by causing these gasses to easily combine with oxygen forming mostly CO_2, N_2 and water. A very precise amount of exhaust gas oxygen is required for the catalyst to function properly. The PCM reads the oxygen sensor signal and then controls the fuel injection so there is almost always the exact amount of oxygen required for proper catalyst operation.

A catalytic converter operates at temperatures up to 1500°F (815°C). It can be damaged by prolonged idling, a rich air/fuel ratio or by a constant misfire. Excess fuel will cause the unit to overheat and melt the ceramic substrate. Use of leaded fuel will quickly poison the catalyst and should be avoided. On vehicles sold in the US, catalytic converters are covered by factory warranty for 50,000 miles. However with proper care, on most vehicles a catalytic converter should still be effective for more than 100,000 miles.

1. Keep the engine in proper running condition at all times.
2. Use only unleaded fuel.
3. Avoid prolonged idling. Proper air flow past the catalytic converter is required to prevent overheating.

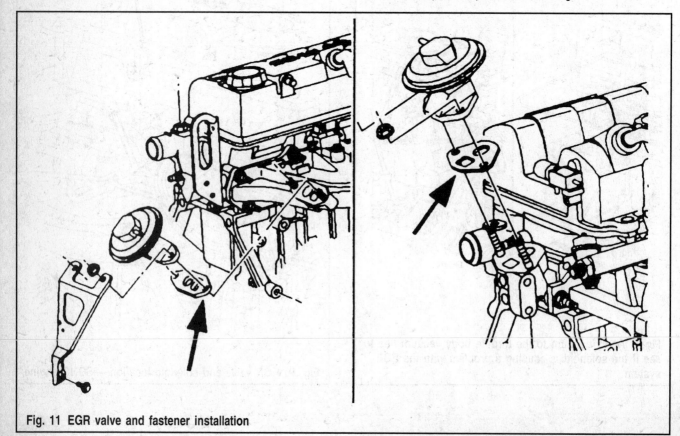

Fig. 11 EGR valve and fastener installation

4. Do not disconnect any of the spark plug wires while the engine is running.

5. Make engine compression checks as quickly as possible to minimize the fuel pumped into the exhaust system.

If replacement of the catalytic converter or exhaust pipe components is necessary, refer to Section 3 of this manual for the relevant procedures.

ELECTRONIC ENGINE CONTROLS

Operation

▶ **See Figures 12 and 13**

The fuel injection system, described in detail in Section No. 5 of this manual, is operated along with the ignition system to obtain optimum performance and fuel economy along with a minimum of exhaust emissions. The various sensors described below are used by the Powertrain Control Module (PCM) for feedback to determine proper engine operating conditions.

➡**Although many of the following tests may be conducted using a Digital Volt/Ohm Meter (DVOM), certain steps or procedures may require use of the Saturn Portable Diagnostic Tool (PDT), a specialized tester or an equivalent scan/testing tool. If these testers are not available, the vehicle should be taken to a reputable service station which has the appropriate equipment.**

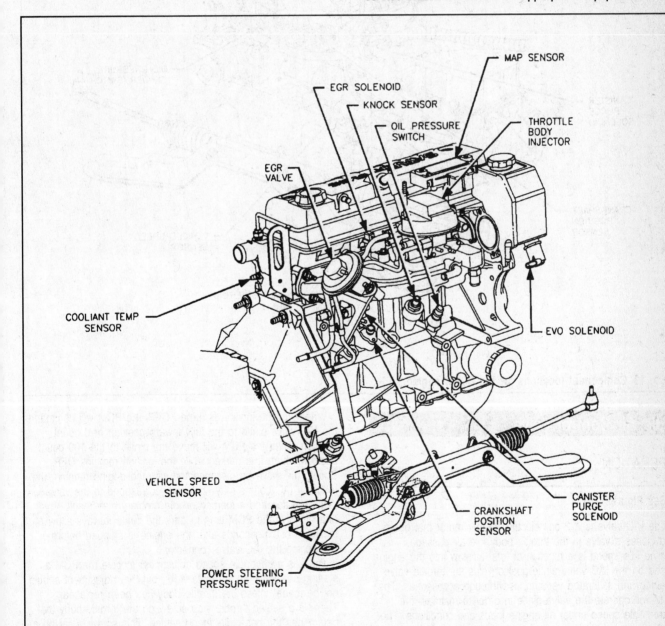

Fig. 12 Component locations for the SOHC engine

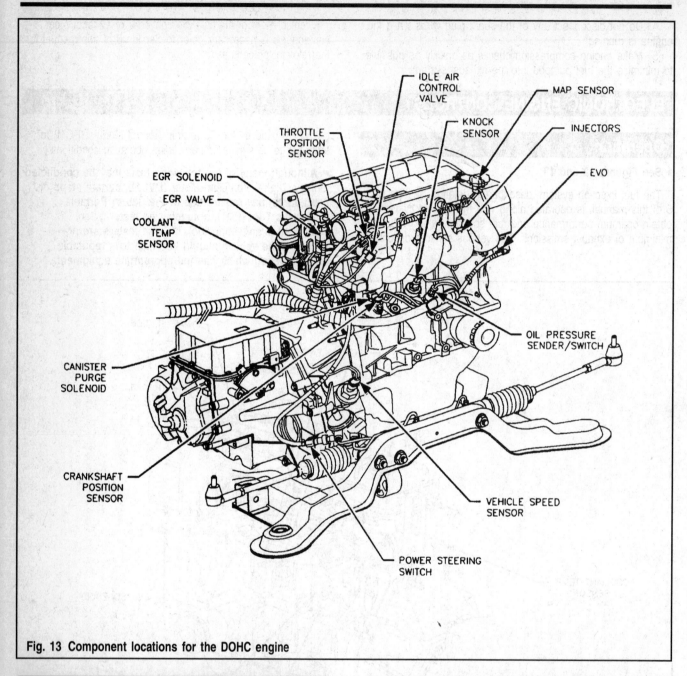

THROTTLE POSITION SENSOR

EGR SOLENOID

EGR VALVE

COOLANT TEMP SENSOR

IDLE AIR CONTROL VALVE

KNOCK SENSOR

MAP SENSOR

INJECTORS

EVO

OIL PRESSURE SENDER/SWITCH

CANISTER PURGE SOLENOID

CRANKSHAFT POSITION SENSOR

VEHICLE SPEED SENSOR

POWER STEERING SWITCH

Fig. 13 Component locations for the DOHC engine

Idle Air Control Valve

OPERATION

▶ See Figures

The IAC valve is a 2 coil electric stepper motor that opens and closes a valve in the throttle body idle air passage. Engine idle speed is a function of total air flow into the engine based on the IAC valve pintle position plus the throttle valve opening and calibrated vacuum loss through accessories. The PCM will operate the valve pintle in order to maintain the correct idle speed under all engine loads and conditions. The pintle is moved inward or outward based on a number of steps or counts sent from the PCM in the form of voltage pulses.

Whenever the ignition is turned **OFF**, the PCM will command the IAC valve pintle to the fully inward position or 0 count position. Then the PCM will move the pintle to the 100 count position where it is parked while the ignition remains **OFF**. Should the valve be disconnected with the engine running, the resulting IAC counts may no longer correspond to the valve pintle position and a starting or idle problem may result. In order to give the PCM time to park the pintle, always allow a minimum of 10 seconds after the engine is stopped before unplugging the IAC valve connector.

There is a base idle speed adjustment to give the PCM a starting position from which to work, but that adjustment should not be made unless the throttle body has been replaced. There is a sealed throttle stop screw on the throttle body that determines the base idle speed setting. This screw is set on a flow bench at the factory. If idle speed is incorrect, Code 35 will be set, indicating that the PCM is unable to properly control idle speed using the IAC valve.

TESTING

▶ **See Figure 15**

1. To check minimum idle speed adjustment, start and warm the engine to its normal operating temperature. Use a suitable scan tool to bottom the IAC pintle, then locate and plug the IAC valve inlet in the throttle body. To plug the inlet use special tool SA9196E for SOHC systems, SA9106E for DOHC systems or use an equivalent air plug.

2. With the engine at operating temperature, the transaxle in **N** or **P** and all accessories and fans **OFF**, base idle speed

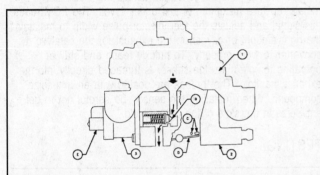

Fig. 14 Cross sectional view of the IAC valve — SOHC engine

should be 450-650 rpm. If not, check for a vacuum leak, a bad electrical connection, a clogged air or PCV passage, or misadjustment of the cruise control or throttle cables.

3. To check power to the IAC valve, turn the ignition switch **OFF** and wait at least 10 seconds for the PCM to park the pintle, then unplug the IAC valve connector. With the ignition switch **ON** but the engine not running, connect a voltmeter to terminals **A** and **B**. Voltage should fluctuate from 0-10.75 volts. Connect the voltmeter to terminals **C** and **D** and look for the same results.

4. If there is no voltage to the IAC valve, turn the ignition **OFF** and use the PCM pin-out chart in this section to check the wiring between the PCM and the valve for short or open circuits.

5. If power is reaching the IAC valve, check the resistance across all possible combinations terminals of the valve. There should be at least 200 ohms between the terminals.

REMOVAL & INSTALLATION

▶ **See Figures 16 and 17**

1. If equipped, properly disable the SIR system as follows:
   a. Align the steering wheel so the tires are in the straight-ahead position, then turn the ignition **OFF**.
   b. Remove the 10 amp SIR fuse from the top left of the Instrument Panel Junction Block (IPJB).
   c. Remove the Connector Position Assurance (CPA), then disconnect the yellow 2-way SIR connector at the base of the steering column.

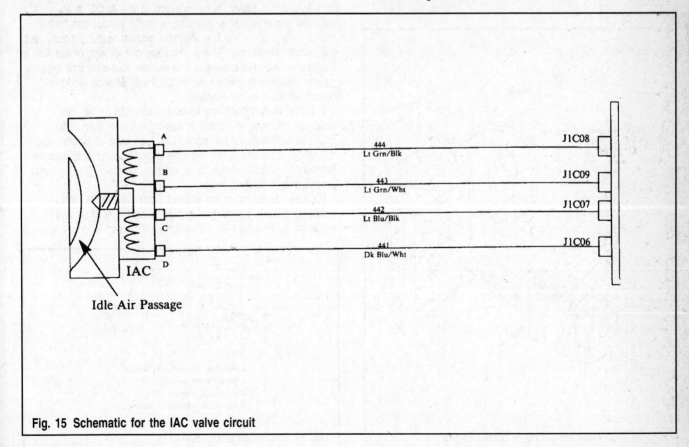

Fig. 15 Schematic for the IAC valve circuit

2. Disconnect the negative battery cable, then remove the air cleaner assembly for SOHC engines or the air intake tube and resonator for DOHC engine.

3. Disconnect the IAC valve electrical connector.

4. Remove the mounting screws, then remove the IAC valve from the throttle body. Remove and discard the valve O-ring.

To install:

5. Carefully clean the IAC valve mounting surface to assure proper O-ring seal.

➡When replacing the IAC valve, make sure only to use an identical part. The pintle shape and diameter are essential to proper valve operation and may vary from application to application.

6. Retract the pintle of a new IAC valve using a suitable scan tool, then lubricate the new O-ring with clean engine oil and install on the IAC valve.

7. Install the valve to the throttle body. Coat the mounting screws with Loctite ® 242 or an equivalent threadlock, then install the screws and tighten to 27 inch lbs. (3 Nm).

8. Connect the IAC valve electrical connector.

9. Install the air cleaner assembly or the air intake tube and resonator, as applicable.

10. Connect the negative battery cable.

11. If equipped, enable the SIR system as follows:

a. Verify the ignition switch is **OFF**, then connect the SIR electrical connector at the base of the steering column. Install the CPA device to the connector.

b. Install the SIR fuse to the IPJB and install the fuse box cover.

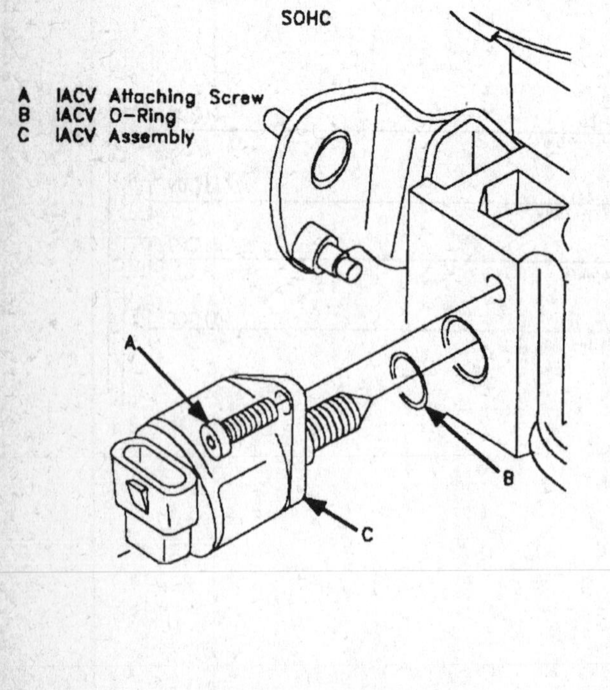

c. Turn the ignition **ON** and verify that the AIR BAG indicator lamp flashes 7-9 times, then goes out. If the light does not flash as indicated, inspect the system for malfunction.

Oxygen Sensor

OPERATION

This sensor is used to report the concentration of oxygen in the exhaust. It consists of an arrangement of platinum and zirconia plates, all protected with a slotted outer shield. At about 600°F (318°C), the presence of oxygen in the exhaust will cause voltage to be generated across the dissimilar metals, up to a maximum of just under 1 volt. The PCM reads this signal and adjusts the fuel injector pulse width to maintain the right amount of oxygen in the exhaust for the catalytic converter to work properly. To quickly reach and stay at operating temperature, the sensor is threaded directly into the exhaust manifold. The threads are coated with an anti-seize compound. When replacing the sensor, be careful not to get anti-seize in the slots of the outer shield.

TESTING

▶ **See Figure 18**

The only way to properly test just the oxygen sensor and circuit is with a Scan Tool connected to the ALDL. If an exhaust gas analyzer is available, a faulty sensor can be found if the rest of the fuel injection system works properly, yet the sensor sends the PCM a message of too lean or too rich. Information about the sensor and engine operation can also be gained by running the engine in the Field Service Mode described later in this manual.

If Code 44 has been set without Codes 33 or 34, this indicates the oxygen sensor is putting out less than 300 millivolts continuously for more than 3 minutes of closed loop operation. It means either the engine really is running lean or the sensor is faulty. Look for a vacuum leak, low fuel system pressure or a faulty injector.

If Code 45 has been set without Codes 33 or 34, this indicates the oxygen sensor is putting out more than 750 millivolts continuously for 30 seconds of closed loop operation,

SOHC

A IACV Attaching Screw
B IACV O-Ring
C IACV Assembly

Fig. 16 IAC valve mounting — SOHC engine

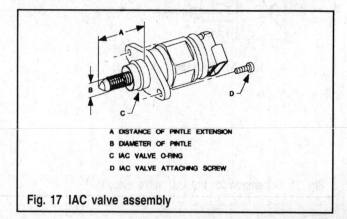

A DISTANCE OF PINTLE EXTENSION
B DIAMETER OF PINTLE
C IAC VALVE O-RING
D IAC VALVE ATTACHING SCREW

Fig. 17 IAC valve assembly

with the TPS in the 2-20 percent range. It means sensor is contaminated or there is no oxygen in the exhaust. This could be caused by an open canister purge valve, open EGR valve, leaking or stuck open injector, burning oil or high fuel system pressure.

1. If Code 13 has been set, first check PCM ground connections and check continuity of the wire between the sensor and PCM. If the vehicle stalls or runs out of fuel while in motion, the Code will be set and it should be erased. If Codes 21 or 22 are set, trouble shoot the TPS first.

2. Using an ohm meter, check the resistance of the oxygen sensor circuit to ground. Disconnect the connector for the purple wire from the oxygen sensor and read the wire resistance to ground, it should be at least 200 ohms.

3. With a Scan tool connected, run the engine to normal operating temperature and use the follow the tool menu to read oxygen sensor voltage. Sensor output should vary from approximately 350-550 millivolts.

4. Stop the engine and disconnect the sensor wire. With the wire from the PCM grounded and the ignition switch **ON**, the Scan tool should show less than 100 millivolts. If not, the wiring or the PCM is faulty.

5. To test with an exhaust gas analyzer:

    a. No other faults can exist.

    b. Run the engine at normal operating temperature for more than 1 minute.

    c. The TPS must read more than 6.5 percent throttle opening.

6. When the above conditions are met and all other engine systems work properly, the exhaust analyzer will change when the sensor wire is disconnected to simulate Open Loop Mode.

REMOVAL & INSTALLATION

▶ **See Figure 19**

➡**The oxygen sensor uses a permanently attached pigtail and connector, removal of which may affect the proper operation of the sensor.**

1. If equipped, properly disable the SIR system as follows:

    a. Align the steering wheel so the tires are in the straight-ahead position, then turn the ignition **OFF**.

    b. Remove the 10 amp SIR fuse from the top left of the Instrument Panel Junction Block (IPJB).

    c. Remove the Connector Position Assurance (CPA), then disconnect the yellow 2-way SIR connector at the base of the steering column.

2. Disconnect the negative battery cable.

3. Unplug the sensor electrical connector.

4. Using a 19mm, 6-point crows foot, loosen and remove the oxygen sensor from the exhaust manifold.

    To install:

➡**Be careful not to drop or damage the oxygen sensor when handling. The pigtail, connector and louvered end should be kept free of dirt or contaminants, but avoid using a solvent to clean the sensor.**

5. Coat the oxygen sensor threads with a nickel based anti-seize compound that does not contain silicone.

6. Install the oxygen sensor into the exhaust manifold and tighten to 18 ft. lbs. (25 Nm).

7. Install the sensor electrical connector and install the Connector Position Assurance (CPA).

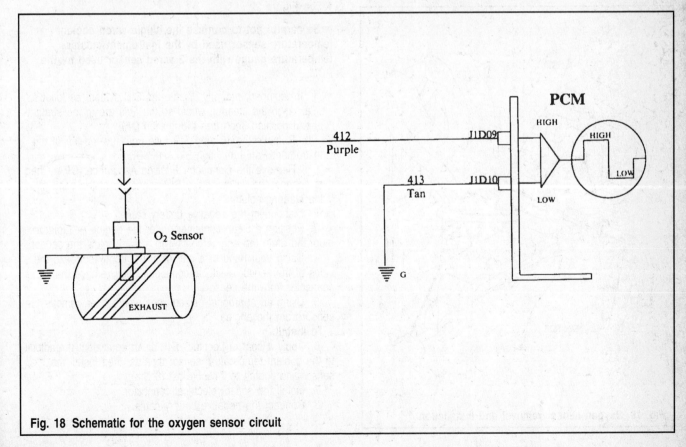

Fig. 18 Schematic for the oxygen sensor circuit

8. Connect the negative battery cable.

9. If equipped, enable the SIR system as follows:

a. Verify the ignition switch is **OFF** then connect the SIR electrical connector at the base of the steering column. Install the CPA device to the connector.

b. Install the SIR fuse to the IPJB and install the fuse box cover.

c. Turn the ignition **ON** and verify that the AIR BAG indicator lamp flashes 7-9 times, then goes out. If the light does not flash as indicated, inspect the system for malfunction.

Coolant Temperature Sensor (CTS)

OPERATION

This sensor is a thermistor type, meaning as the temperature increases, the sensor resistance decreases. It is the same sensor as the ATS. The PCM sends a 5 volt reference signal to the sensor (pin B) and a sensor reference ground to the sensor (pin A). The PCM calculates coolant temperature depending on the return signal.

TESTING

▶ See Figures 20 and 21

If Code 14 is set, the PCM will turn the coolant fan **ON** at all times. The thermostat opens at 190°F (88°C) and coolant

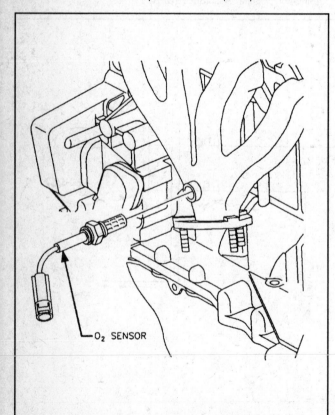

Fig. 19 Oxygen sensor removal and installation

temperature should stabilize there at idle. The sensor is threaded into the coolant passage in the back of the cylinder head.

1. If Code 17 has been set, the fault is in the PCM and cannot be repaired. Code 14 indicates the CTS signal is above sensor range, Code 15 indicates the signal is below sensor range. Test the sensor first.

2. Unplug the connector from the sensor and use the chart to check the sensor resistance with an ohmmeter.

3. With the ignition switch **ON**, there should be some voltage across the connector terminals. If not, check the wiring between the sensor and the PCM.

4. If using a Scan tool, the reading should be the same as the actual coolant temperature with the ignition switch **ON**.

a. If the reading is less than -32°F (-35°C), unplug the sensor connector and jumper the PCM circuit terminals together. If the reading goes to above 266°F (130°C), the problem is in the PCM connector, ground or in the sensor. If the reading does not change or go high enough, the problem is in the wiring or the PCM.

b. If the reading is more than 284°F (140°C), unplug the sensor connector. If the reading goes below -32°F (-35°C), the problem is in the sensor. If it does not change or does not go low enough, the problem is in the wiring or the PCM.

5. If a scan tool is available, allow the engine too cool to the ambient temperature overnight, then compare the CTS and the ATS readings. Temperatures should be within 4 degrees of each other with the ignition **ON** and the engine not running.

REMOVAL & INSTALLATION

▶ See Figure 22

➡Be careful not to confuse the single wired coolant temperature sensor used by the instrument cluster temperature gauge with the 2 wired sensor used by the PCM.

1. If equipped, properly disable the SIR system as follows:

a. Align the steering wheel so the tires are in the straight-ahead position, then turn the ignition **OFF**.

b. Remove the 10 amp SIR fuse from the top left of the Instrument Panel Junction Block (IPJB).

c. Remove the Connector Position Assurance (CPA), then disconnect the yellow 2-way SIR connector at the base of the steering column.

2. Disconnect the negative battery cable.

3. Position a clean container under the engine or radiator plug and drain the engine coolant to a level below the sensor.

4. Using your hand or a pair of pliers, gently squeeze the sides of the sensor electrical connector, then remove the connector from the sensor.

5. Using an appropriate sized deep well socket, remove the sensor from the engine.

To install:

6. Apply a coat of Loctite® 242 or an equivalent threadlock to the coolant temperature sensor threads, then install the sensor and tighten to 71 inch lbs. (8 Nm).

7. Install the sensor electrical connector.

8. Connect the negative battery cable.

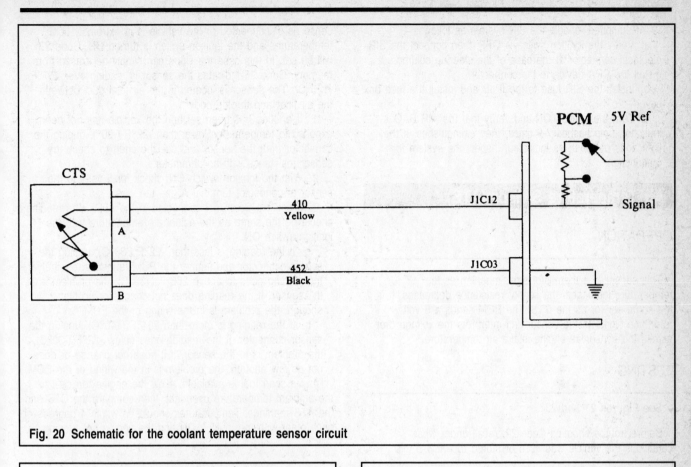

Fig. 20 Schematic for the coolant temperature sensor circuit

DEGREES (°C)	DEGREES (°F)	SENSOR RESISTANCE (OHMS)
−40	−40	77k – 109k
−29	−20	39k – 53k
−18	0	21k – 27k
−7	20	11k – 15k
4	40	6.6k – 8.4k
16	60	3.9k – 4.5k
27	80	2.4k – 2.7k
38	100	1.5k – 1.7k
49	120	.98k – 1.1k
60	140	650 – 730
72	160	430 – 480
83	180	302 – 334
94	200	215 – 235
105	220	159 – 172
120	248	104 – 113
140	284	63 – 68

Fig. 21 Sensor resistance chart for the CTS and ATS

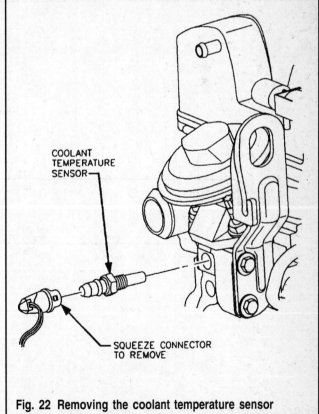

Fig. 22 Removing the coolant temperature sensor

9. If equipped, enable the SIR system as follows:

a. Verify the ignition switch is **OFF**, then connect the SIR electrical connector at the base of the steering column. Install the CPA device to the connector.

b. Install the SIR fuse to the IPJB and install the fuse box cover.

c. Turn the ignition **ON** and verify that the AIR BAG indicator lamp flashes 7-9 times, then extinguishes. If the light does not flash as indicated, inspect the system for malfunction.

Air Temperature Sensor (ATS)

OPERATION

This sensor is a thermistor type, meaning as the temperature increases, the sensor resistance decreases. It is the same sensor as the CTS. The PCM sends a 5 volt reference signal to the sensor and interprets the voltage drop across the sensor as engine intake air temperature.

TESTING

▶ **See Figures 21 and 23**

Before trouble shooting Code 23, recall under what conditions the vehicle was used or stored recently. If this sensor is disconnected or the vehicle is in extremely cold temperatures and the ignition switch is turned **ON**, Code 23 will be set. In this case the Code can simply be erased from memory. Code 25 indicates the sensor is reading over 257°F (125°C). The sensor is located in the air inlet duct between the air filter and throttle body.

1. If a Code has been set and the vehicle has not been exposed to temperatures lower than -22°F (-30°), unplug the connector from the sensor and use the chart to check the sensor resistance with an ohmmeter.

2. With the ignition switch **ON**, check for 5 volts to the sensor at connector terminal **A**, the tan wire.

3. If using a Scan tool connected to the ALDL, the reading should be the same as the actual air temperature with the ignition switch **ON**.

a. If the reading is less than -22°F (-30°C), unplug the sensor connector and jumper the PCM terminals together. If the reading goes to above 266°F (130°C), the problem is in the sensor. If the reading does not change or go high enough, the problem is in the wiring or the PCM.

b. If the reading is more than 284°F (140°C), unplug the sensor connector. If the reading goes below -22°F (-30°C), the problem is in the sensor. If it does not change or does not go low enough, the problem is in the wiring or the PCM.

4. f a scan tool is available, allow the engine too cool to the ambient temperature overnight, then compare the CTS and the ATS readings. Temperatures should be within 4 degrees of each other with the ignition **ON** and the engine not running.

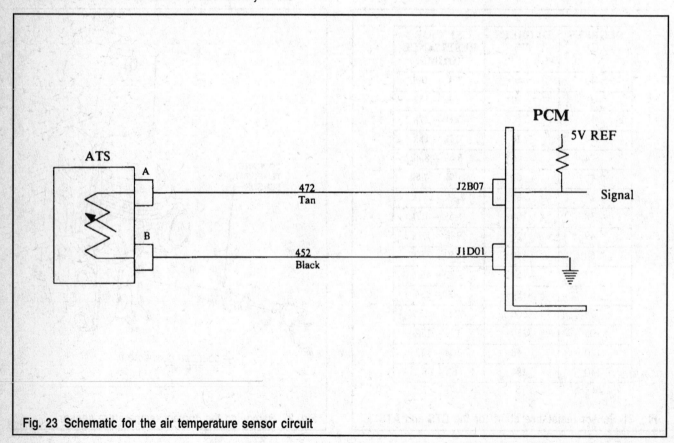

Fig. 23 Schematic for the air temperature sensor circuit

REMOVAL & INSTALLATION

▶ **See Figures 24 and 25**

1. If equipped, properly disable the SIR system as follows:

a. Align the steering wheel so the tires are in the straight-ahead position, then turn the ignition **OFF**.

b. Remove the 10 amp SIR fuse from the top left of the Instrument Panel Junction Block (IPJB).

c. Remove the Connector Position Assurance (CPA), then disconnect the yellow 2-way SIR connector at the base of the steering column.

2. Disconnect the negative battery cable.

3. Remove the air inlet tube fasteners, then rotate the tube to access the sensor.

4. Using your hand or a pair of pliers, gently squeeze the sides of the sensor electrical connector, then remove the connector from the sensor.

5. Using a 13mm deep well socket, loosen and remove the sensor from the inlet duct.

To install:

6. Install the sensor and tighten to 44 inch lbs. (5 Nm).

7. Connect the sensor electrical connector.

8. Install the air inlet tube using the fasteners.

9. Connect the negative battery cable.

10. If equipped, enable the SIR system as follows:

a. Verify the ignition switch is **OFF**, then connect the SIR electrical connector at the base of the steering column. Install the CPA device to the connector.

b. Install the SIR fuse to the IPJB and install the fuse box cover.

c. Turn the ignition **ON** and verify that the AIR BAG indicator lamp flashes 7-9 times, then extinguishes. If the light does not flash as indicated, inspect the system for malfunction.

Vehicle Speed Sensor (VSS)

OPERATION

The PCM uses the vehicle speed signal to calculate air/fuel delivery and ignition functions. Through a different circuit in the PCM, the same sensor is used to drive the speedometer. The sensor is a permanent magnet variable reluctance sensor mounted in the differential housing of the transaxle. It detects the rotation of the differential assembly and when vehicle speed reaches 3 mph (5 kph), transmits 16 pulses per revolution to the PCM.

TESTING

▶ **See Figure 26**

Code 24 will be set if engine speed is above idle, the vehicle is in gear, the MAP sensor output is less than 0.5 volts and the VSS signal is less than 1 mph (1.6 kph).

1. If the speedometer is faulty but there is no Code 24, the problem is most likely in the instrument cluster.

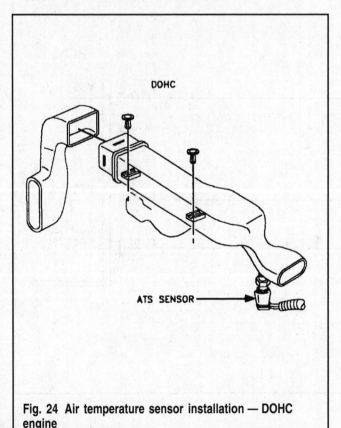

Fig. 24 Air temperature sensor installation — DOHC engine

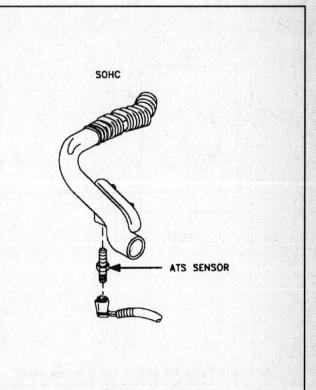

Fig. 25 Air temperature sensor installation — SOHC engine

2. If Code 24 is set, unplug the VSS connector and connect an ohmmeter to the sensor terminals. The sensor resistance should be 700-900 ohms.

3. Check the continuity of the wiring between the sensor and the PCM.

REMOVAL & INSTALLATION

▶ **See Figure 27**

1. If equipped, properly disable the SIR system as follows:
   a. Align the steering wheel so the tires are in the straight-ahead position, then turn the ignition **OFF**.
   b. Remove the 10 amp SIR fuse from the top left of the Instrument Panel Junction Block (IPJB).
   c. Remove the Connector Position Assurance (CPA), then disconnect the yellow 2-way SIR connector at the base of the steering column.

2. Disconnect the negative battery cable.

3. Raise the front of the vehicle and support safely using jackstands.

4. Unplug the electrical connector from the sensor.

5. Remove the sensor from the transaxle housing.

To install:

6. Install the VSS to the transaxle.

7. Connect the sensor electrical connector.

8. Lower the vehicle and connect the negative battery cable.

9. If equipped, enable the SIR system as follows:
   a. Verify the ignition switch is **OFF**, then connect the SIR electrical connector at the base of the steering column. Install the CPA device to the connector.
   b. Install the SIR fuse to the IPJB and install the fuse box cover.
   c. Turn the ignition **ON** and verify that the AIR BAG indicator lamp flashes 7-9 times, then extinguishes. If the light does not flash as indicated, inspect the system for malfunction.

Quad Driver Module (QDM)

OPERATION

The PCM operates its output devices, such as solenoid valves, relays or indicator lights, by commanding a driver module. A driver module is an electronic switch that turns ON to complete the ground circuit and operate the 12 volt device. A Quad Driver Module operates 4 electronic switches for 4 output devices. There are 2 QDMs in the PCM. Each has a feedback circuit that detects an open or short circuit on an output device that it controls.

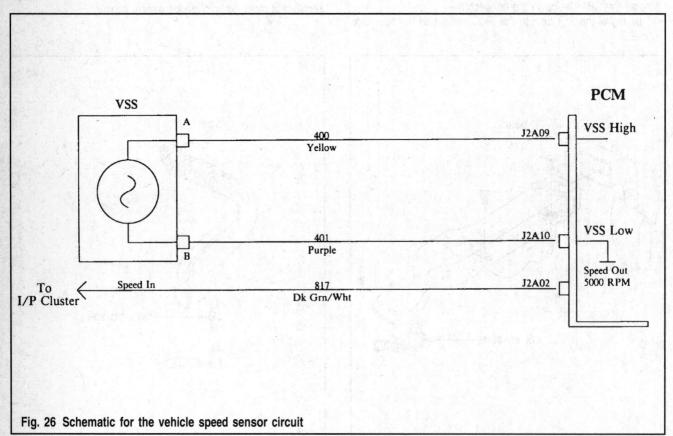

Fig. 26 Schematic for the vehicle speed sensor circuit

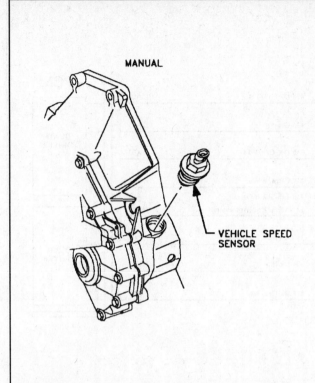

Fig. 27 Vehicle speed sensor installation — manual transaxle

TESTING

▶ **See Figure 28**

A Code 26 indicates an open or short in the wire between the QDM and the output device or an internal fault in the output device. If an output device is faulty, the PCM will shut down only that circuit and not the whole QDM.

1. If Code 26 appears with any other Code, trouble shoot the QDM circuits first. Check for continuity of the ground wire between the output device and the PCM connector.

2. Check all fuses, relays and light bulbs on the power side of the circuit. Failure of any of these can set a Code 26.

3. All relays should have 70-90 ohms resistance. All solenoids should have 22-42 ohms resistance.

4. Turn the ignition switch **ON** and watch the lights on the instrument panel. The SERVICE ENGINE SOON and coolant temperature lights should turn **ON**, then the coolant temperature light should go out. If not, check the fuses, bulbs and ground circuits.

5. Jumper terminals **A** and **B** on the ALDL. The cooling fan on the radiator should run.

6. Remove the jumper wire, start the engine and operate the vehicle as required to test the remaining components.

Manifold Air Pressure (MAP) Sensor

OPERATION

This sensor is used to read the air pressure in the intake manifold, which is always positive (but less than atmospheric pressure) when the engine is running. The PCM sends a reference voltage to the sensor, then a pressure sensitive resistor in the sensor reduces the voltage returning to the PCM. The portion of the voltage returned to the PCM is interpreted as engine load. The return signal is low (low load) when engine vacuum is high (throttle closed). As the throttle is opened and engine vacuum decreases (increased manifold air pressure), the return signal increases. While the engine is running, this type of load sensing automatically accounts for changes in altitude, so no separate altitude sensor is needed. A high pressure (14-15 psi) will allow 4-5 volts to return to the PCM while a low pressure (5-7 psi) will allow 0.5-0.9 volts. On the SOHC engine, the MAP sensor is mounted on the valve cover. On the DOHC engine, the sensor is mounted directly to the end of the intake manifold.

TESTING

▶ **See Figures 29 and 30**

Code 33 means the sensor reading is too high. This code will be set under the following conditions:
- MAP voltage greater than 4.2 is returned to the PCM
- TPS signal is less than 5 percent
- Codes 21 and 22 are not present

Code 34 means the sensor reading is too low. This code will be set if conditions A or B apply:
- RPM is less than 1200, MAP signal is less than 0.2 volts and Codes 21 and 22 are not present
- RPM is more than 1200, MAP signal is less than 0.2 volts, TPS signal is more than 15.2 percent and Codes 21 and 22 are not present

1. If Code 33 or 34 is set, unplug the MAP sensor connector and turn the ignition switch **ON**. Check for about 4.5-5 volts between connector terminal **C** (gray wire) and ground.

2. Check for the same voltage between terminals **C** and **A** (black wire). This is a ground through the PCM.

3. Reconnect the wiring and install a Saturn diagnostic probe on the green wire and connect a voltmeter probe or connect a Scan tool to the ALDL. Connect a vacuum gauge to the intake manifold.

4. With the ignition switch **ON** and the engine not running, the return signal voltage should be close to the supply voltage in Step 1 below 1000 ft. (305 meters) altitude. If above this altitude, see the chart for the correct voltage.

5. With the engine at idle, there should be at least 16 in. Hg (54 kPa) of manifold vacuum and 1-1.5 volts on the signal return wire. When the throttle is opened suddenly, the signal voltage should increase. It may only change momentarily.

6. If the voltage at idle is the same as in Step 1 or if the voltage does not change when the throttle is moved suddenly, the sensor is faulty and must be replaced.

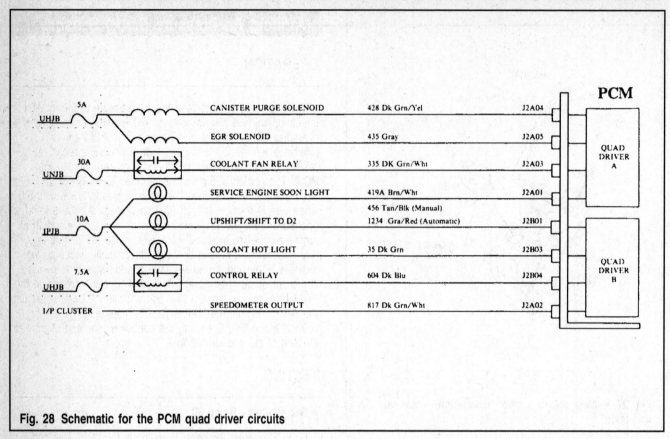

Fig. 28 Schematic for the PCM quad driver circuits

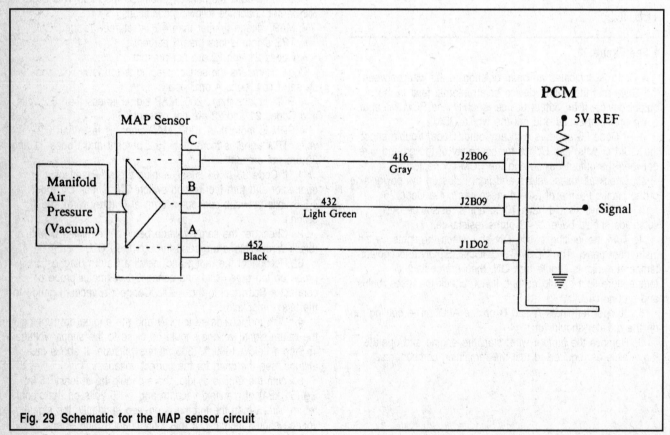

Fig. 29 Schematic for the MAP sensor circuit

ALTITUDE		VOLTAGE RANGE
Meters	Feet	
Below 305	Below 1,000	3.8 – 5.5V
305 – 610	1,000 – 2,000	3.6 – 5.3V
610 – 914	2,000 – 3,000	3.5 – 5.1V
914 – 1219	3,000 – 4,000	3.3 – 5.0V
1219 – 1524	4,000 – 5,000	3.2 – 4.8V
1524 – 1829	5,000 – 6,000	3.0 – 4.6V
1829 – 2133	6,000 – 7,000	2.9 – 4.5V
2133 – 2438	7,000 – 8,000	2.8 – 4.3V
2438 – 2743	8,000 – 9,000	2.6 – 4.2V
2743 – 3948	9,000 – 10,000	2.5 – 4.0V

LOW ALTITUDE = HIGH PRESSURE = HIGH VOLTAGE

Fig. 30 MAP sensor return voltage altitude compensation chart with the ignition ON and the engine not running

REMOVAL & INSTALLATION

▶ **See Figures 31 and 32**

1. If equipped, properly disable the SIR system as follows:
   a. Align the steering wheel so the tires are in the straight-ahead position, then turn the ignition **OFF**.
   b. Remove the 10 amp SIR fuse from the top left of the Instrument Panel Junction Block (IPJB).
   c. Remove the Connector Position Assurance (CPA), then disconnect the yellow 2-way SIR connector at the base of the steering column.
2. Disconnect the negative battery cable.
3. For SOHC engines, remove the sensor attaching nuts and pull the sensor from the engine, then disconnect the sensor vacuum hose.

4. For DOHC engines, remove the attaching bolts and pull the sensor from the engine. If the port seal remained in the intake manifold, remove the sensor.
5. Unplug the sensor electrical connector and remove the sensor from the vehicle.

To install:

6. On SOHC engines, connect the vacuum hose to the sensor.
7. On DOHC engines, install the port seal in the intake manifold. To assure proper seating, the seal must be installed directly into the manifold, not onto the sensor and then with into the manifold as an assembly.
8. Install the electrical connector to the MAP sensor.
9. Position the sensor to the engine and install the fasteners. Tighten the retaining nuts to 53 inch lbs. (6 Nm) or the retaining bolts to 44 inch lbs. (5 Nm).
10. Connect the negative battery cable.
11. If equipped, enable the SIR system as follows:
    a. Verify the ignition switch is **OFF** then connect the SIR electrical connector at the base of the steering column. Install the CPA device to the connector.
    b. Install the SIR fuse to the IPJB and install the fuse box cover.
    c. Turn the ignition **ON** and verify that the AIR BAG indicator lamp flashes 7-9 times, then extinguishes. If the light does not flash as indicated, inspect the system for malfunction.

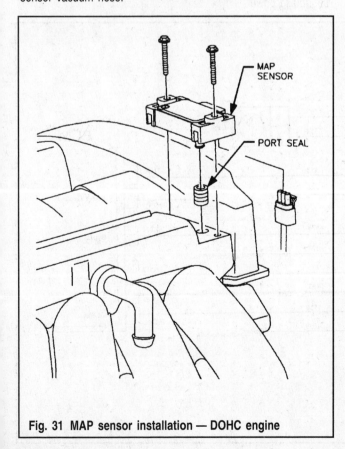

Fig. 31 MAP sensor installation — DOHC engine

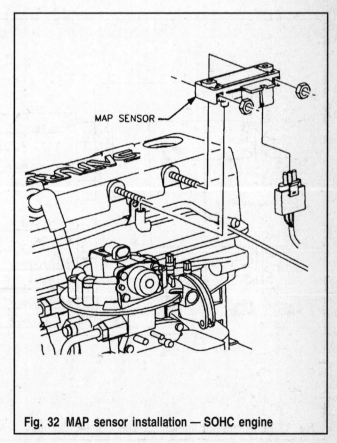

Fig. 32 MAP sensor installation — SOHC engine

EST Circuit

TESTING

▶ **See Figure 33**

If Codes 41 and 42 are both set together, go to the EST/Bypass circuit tests. If only Code 41 is set, this indicates that the PCM is not sending timing commands to the DIS module because the circuit is open or shorted to ground or voltage. The fault could be either the EST circuit or the Reference circuit that sends rpm pulses to the PCM.

1. Clear the Codes and run the engine for at least 10 seconds above 2500 rpm. If the Code does not set again, the problem is most likely faulty connections or a bad ground.

2. If the Code appears again, stop the engine and unplug the 6-pin DIS module connector. With the ignition switch **ON**, check for voltage at terminal **C** of the connector. If there is more than about 1 volt, check for a short to voltage in that wire.

3. With the ignition switch **OFF**, use an ohmmeter to make sure the same wire is not shorted to ground at terminal **C** on the connector. Make sure the circuit is not open.

4. Install a diagnostic connector or a Saturn diagnostic probe on the white EST wire to connect a voltmeter probe. With the engine at operating temperature and running at idle, check for 1-4 volts on the EST circuit. If voltage is present, the problem lies within the DIS module, if missing, the problem is with the PCM.

Bypass Circuit

TESTING

▶ **See Figure 33**

When the ignition switch is **ON**, a 5 volt signal is sent from the DIS module to the PCM on the Bypass circuit, but the signal is not yet accepted. Once the engine is running, the PCM activates an internal solid state switch to accept the Bypass signal and the PCM then takes over ignition timing control.

If Codes 41 and 42 are both set together, go to the EST/Bypass circuit tests. If only Code 42 is set, a fault in the Bypass circuit is indicated. When only the Bypass circuit is open or shorted, Code 42 will be set and ignition timing control will remain with the DIS module.

1. If only Code 42 is set, clear the Codes and turn the ignition switch **OFF** for at least 10 seconds. Start the engine. If the Code does not return, the problem is intermittent and probably in a connector or PCM ground.

2. If the Code returns, turn the ignition switch **OFF** and unplug the 6-pin DIS connector. Use an ohmmeter to measure the resistance between terminal **F** and ground. If resistance is less than 200 ohms, the wire is shorted to ground. If it is above 50,000 ohms, the circuit is open.

3. Switch the volt/ohm meter to DC volts. Turn the ignition switch **ON** (engine not running) and measure the voltage at the same terminal. If there is more than 0.5 volts, the circuit is shorted to power.

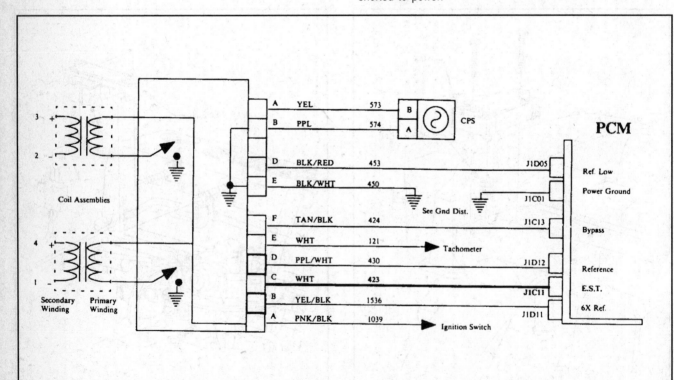

Fig. 33 Schematic for the ignition/spark timing circuits

4. Turn the ignition **OFF** and connect the wiring to the DIS module. Install a diagnostic connector or a Saturn diagnostic probe on the tan/black Bypass wire to connect a voltmeter probe. With the engine running at idle, there should be at least 4 volts on the Bypass circuit after 4 seconds. Missing voltage indicates a connector or PCM problem. If the voltage is present, the DIS module is at fault.

EST/Bypass Code 41 and 42

TESTING

▶ **See Figure 33**

1. If both Codes are set together, most likely the wiring or a connector is faulty. With the ignition switch **OFF**, unplug the 6-pin connector from the DIS module and check for a short to ground at terminal **C**. Resistance should be more than 200 ohms.

2. Move the ohmmeter probe to the Bypass circuit, terminal **F** on the connector. With the ignition switch **ON**, the resistance to ground should be 200-50,000 ohms. This is the solid state switch in the PCM that turns **ON** to accept the Bypass signal. At this point it should be **OFF** but resistance should not be infinite.

3. If the wiring and terminal connections are good but both codes are set again, check all the ignition system components before deciding the PCM or DIS is faulty.

Electronic Spark Circuit (ESC)

TESTING

▶ **See Figure 34**

This circuit is connected to the knock sensor mounted on the block below the intake manifold. The PCM sends a constant reference voltage to the sensor, which then completes the ground circuit. Under no-knock conditions, the sensor resistance causes the reference voltage to drop to 2.5 volts. When engine knock occurs, the sensor resistance changes and an AC signal is produced. The PCM will retard ignition timing as required to stop engine knock. If the reference voltage goes above 3.5 volts or below 1.5 volts for at least 10 seconds, a Code 43 will be set.

1. Disconnect the sensor at the PCM and measure the resistance between the sensor and ground. It should be 3300-4500 ohms. Sensor installation torque is 11 ft. lbs. (15 Nm). Torque and position are critical to correct operation.

2. Reconnect the wiring. With the ignition switch **ON**, there should be 1.5-3.5 volts going to the sensor.

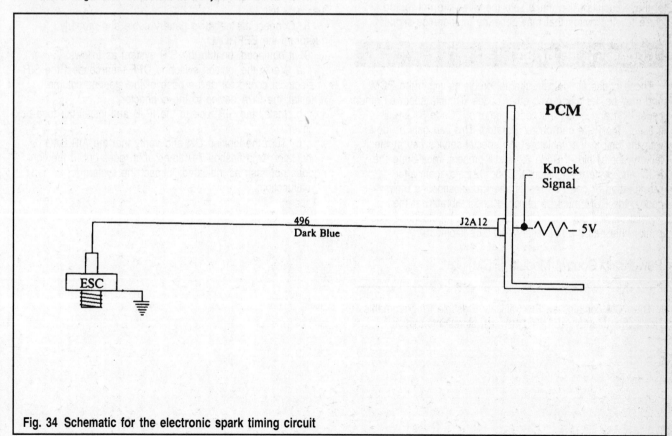

Fig. 34 Schematic for the electronic spark timing circuit

Crankshaft Position Sensor (CPS)

TESTING

This sensor is mounted in the engine block below the intake manifold. It is a simple pulse generator that signals the DIS module when specific crankshaft position markers move past it. If there is no rpm signal or no ignition output, unplug the sensor and connect an ohmmeter across the terminals. Resistance should be 700-900 ohms. The sensor and its circuit have a polarity, meaning if the sensor wiring is reversed the PCM sees an open circuit. Reversing the CPS wires will result in a no-start condition.

➡**For more information regarding the crankshaft position sensor and the ignition system, refer to Section 2 of this manual.**

Reference LineReference Low Line6X Reference

TESTING

These circuits transmit crankshaft position and rpm signals to the PCM. If there is no ignition or rpm signal, check continuity of these circuits. Also make sure the wires are not routed close to other wires that may generate interference signals.

Codes 51, 55 or 82

These codes all indicate internal problems within the PCM and may be set along with other codes. Trouble shoot all other codes first and erase the code memory. If Code 51 is still present, the PCM can be recalibrated. This can only be done with the unit in the vehicle at the special service bay at the factory dealership. If Code 82 is still present, recalibrate the PCM and cycle the ignition. If Code 82 sets again after recalibration or code 55 resets after troubleshooting other codes, the PCM must be replaced and calibrated at the special service bay. Refer to a dealer or a reputable service station that has the necessary service equipment.

Powertrain Control Module (PCM)

The PCM contains an Electronicaly Erasable Programmable Read Only Memory (EEPROM) which stores information

necessary for proper vehicle operation. Any time the PCM is replaced, this memory must be reprogrammed in order for the vehicle to operate. The vehicle may not even start if this is not done. Only a dealer/serivce station equipped with the Saturn Service Stall System, or an equivalent EEPROM reprogramming computer will be able to properly calibrate the PCM.

REMOVAL & INSTALLATION
▶ **See Figure 35**

1. If equipped, properly disable the SIR system as follows:
   a. Align the steering wheel so the tires are in the straight-ahead position, then turn the ignition **OFF**.
   b. Remove the 10 amp SIR fuse from the top left of the Instrument Panel Junction Block (IPJB).
   c. Remove the Connector Position Assurance (CPA), then disconnect the yellow 2-way SIR connector at the base of the steering column.
2. Disconnect the negative battery cable.
3. Remove the driver's side kick panel and/or the knee bolster for access to the PCM.
4. Rotate the retaining screw ¼ turn counterclockwise and remove the PCM from the carrier.
5. Unplug the electrical connectors from the PCM and remove the unit from the vehicle.

To install:

6. Install the wiring harness connectors to the PCM, then position the unit into the carrier.
7. Push the unit upward in the carrier until 2 clicks are heard or felt.
8. Connect the negative battery cable and properly reproram the EEPROM.
9. If equipped, enable the SIR system as follows:
   a. Verify the ignition switch is **OFF** then connect the SIR electrical connector at the base of the steering column. Install the CPA device to the connector.
   b. Install the SIR fuse to the IPJB and install the fuse box cover.
   c. Turn the ignition **ON** and verify that the AIR BAG indicator lamp flashes 7-9 times, then goes out. If the light does not flash as indicated, inspect the system for malfunction.

Fig. 35 Powertrain control module mounting

SELF-DIAGNOSTICS

General Information

▶ See Figures 36, 37 and 38

The Powertrain Control Module (PCM) performs a continual self-diagnosis on many circuits of the engine control system and, if equipped, on the automatic transaxle control system. If a problem or irregularity is detected, the PCM will set either a Code or a Flag. A Code indicates a suspected failure that currently exists or that has existed in an engine system. A currently present code will illuminate the SERVICE ENGINE SOON light. A Flag is a diagnostic aid that indicates an intermittent problem or irregularity, but is does not necessarily indicate a failure. A flag will not normally illuminate the indicator light.

There are 2 levels of PCM memory, "General Information" and "Malfunction History." Codes are stored in both places, while flags are only stored in malfunction history. Any Code stored in General Information can be read by observing the flashing SERVICE ENGINE SOON lamp while the system is in diagnostic mode. Flags and codes that are stored in Malfunction History can only be retrieved with a suitable scan tool. Most tools will be menu driven and although their use is not specifically covered in this section, most described tests are useful for interpreting scan tool test results. Unlike flags for the engine control system, flags which are designated for the automatic transaxle will flash on the SHIFT TO D2 lamp along with any stored transaxle codes.

Assembly Line Diagnostic Link (ALDL)

▶ See Figure 39

There are many Saturn test procedures that require the connection of a scan tool or connecting a jumper wire to terminals A and B of the ALDL (the main diagnostic tool connector). The ALDL is used during vehicle assembly to test the engine before it leaves the assembly plant and after the factory to communicate with the PCM. The ALDL is located under the left side of the dashboard, near the hood release handle. Terminal A is an internal ground and is the top right terminal in the connector. Terminal B, directly adjacent and to the left of Terminal A, is the main diagnostic terminal. When these terminals are jumpered together and the ignition switch turned ON, the SERVICE ENGINE SOON light will flash Code 12. This indicates that the internal diagnostic system is operating and that specific output device signals are being generated.

Saturn Diagnostic Probe

▶ See Figure 40

This is a service tool that provides an easy way of checking circuits for power without disconnecting any wires. The connector clamps around the wire and pierces the insulation, providing a "T" connection through which you can insert a

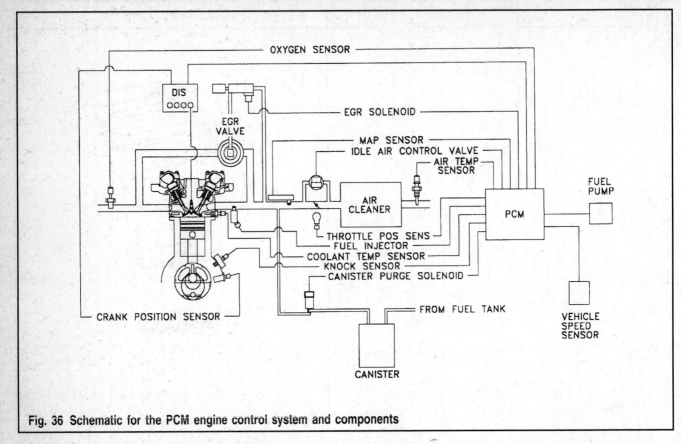

Fig. 36 Schematic for the PCM engine control system and components

voltmeter probe or jumper wire without disrupting an operating circuit. They are available for a variety of wire sizes: 22, 20 and 18 gauge (0.35, 0.5 and 0.8 sq. mm). Once this tool is installed, is must be left on the wire. It contains a sealant that will protect the broken insulation from corrosion.

Entering Self-Diagnosis

‣ See Figure 41

To enter the diagnostics, either connect a scan tool to the ALDL or use a jumper wire to connect terminals A and B of the ALDL. Turn the ignition switch **ON**, then the PCM will enter the diagnostic program and report trouble codes on the scan tool or by flashing the SERVICE ENGINE SOON light.

All codes are 2 digits between 11 and 99. Codes are displayed on the SERVICE ENGINE SOON light by flashing the light with short and long pauses to distinguish digits of 1 code from digits of another. The short pause is used between digits of the same code, long pauses are between codes. For Code 12, the sequence will be: flash, pause, flash-flash, long pause.

1. When the diagnostic mode is entered, Code 12 is displayed 3 times. This indicates that the internal diagnostic system is operating. If Code 12 is not displayed, the self-diagnostic program is not functioning properly. If only Code 12 is displayed, no system malfunctions have been stored.

2. Any existing system fault codes are displayed in order from low to high, except for Code 11. Each code is displayed 3 times, followed by the next code, if any.

3. On vehicles with an automatic transaxle and on which exist stored transaxle codes, Code 11 will be displayed last,

then the SHIFT TO D2 light will begin flashing transaxle codes or flags.

4. When all engine and transaxle codes have been displayed, Code 12 will flash again. At this point all output devices are driven, except the fuel pump, so these circuits can be checked.

5. This procedure can be repeated as required by cycling the ignition switch **OFF**, then **ON** again with the ALDL terminals jumpered together. The Code display will begin again as in Step 1.

Field Service Mode

If the diagnostic terminal is grounded and the engine is started, the system will enter the Field Service Mode. In this mode the SERVICE ENGINE SOON light can be used to determine open or closed loop operation and to monitor whether the fuel/air mixture is running rich or lean.

When the engine is in open loop operation, the light will flash 2½ times per second. Once the engine enters closed loop operation and the PCM begins to regulate fuel/air mixture using feedback from the oxygen sensor, the light will only flash 1 time per second. If the lamp remains OFF most of the time, then engine is running lean. If the lamp remains ON most of the time, the engine is running rich.

Clearing Codes

Removing power from the PCM will clear Codes from the General Information portion of the PCM memory. Flags and Codes stored in Malfunction History however, will remain in the

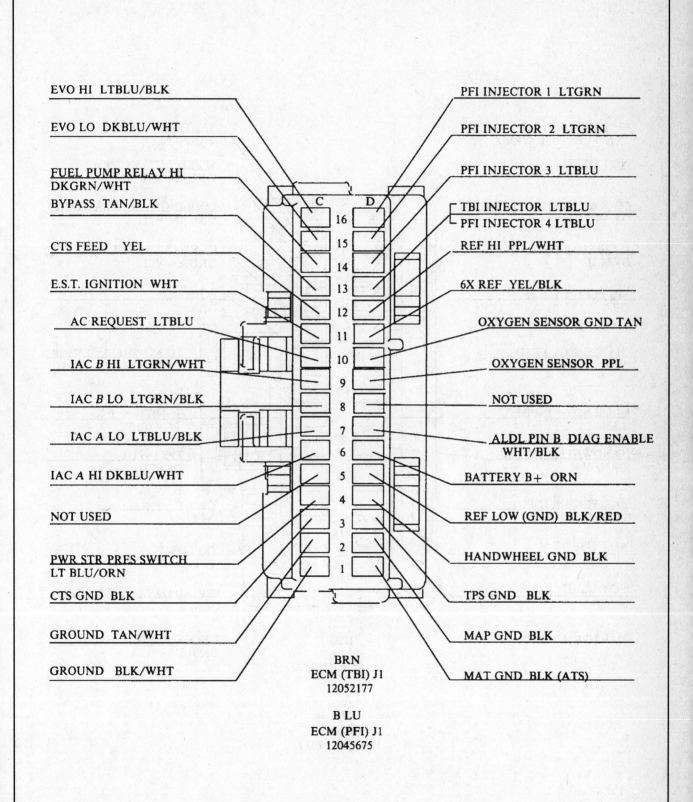

EVO HI LTBLU/BLK

EVO LO DKBLU/WHT

FUEL PUMP RELAY HI
DKGRN/WHT
BYPASS TAN/BLK

CTS FEED   YEL

E.S.T. IGNITION WHT

AC REQUEST LTBLU

IAC *B* HI LTGRN/WHT

IAC *B* LO LTGRN/BLK

IAC *A* LO LTBLU/BLK

IAC *A* HI DKBLU/WHT

NOT USED

PWR STR PRES SWITCH
LT BLU/ORN

CTS GND BLK

GROUND TAN/WHT

GROUND BLK/WHT

PFI INJECTOR 1 LTGRN

PFI INJECTOR 2 LTGRN

PFI INJECTOR 3 LTBLU

TBI INJECTOR LTBLU
PFI INJECTOR 4 LTBLU

REF HI PPL/WHT

6X REF YEL/BLK

OXYGEN SENSOR GND TAN

OXYGEN SENSOR PPL

NOT USED

ALDL PIN B DIAG ENABLE
WHT/BLK

BATTERY B+ ORN

REF LOW (GND) BLK/RED

HANDWHEEL GND BLK

TPS GND BLK

MAP GND BLK

MAT GND BLK (ATS)

C   D

16
15
14
13
12
11
10
9
8
7
6
5
4
3
2
1

BRN
ECM (TBI) J1
12052177

B LU
ECM (PFI) J1
12045675

Fig. 37 PCM connector J1 pin-outs

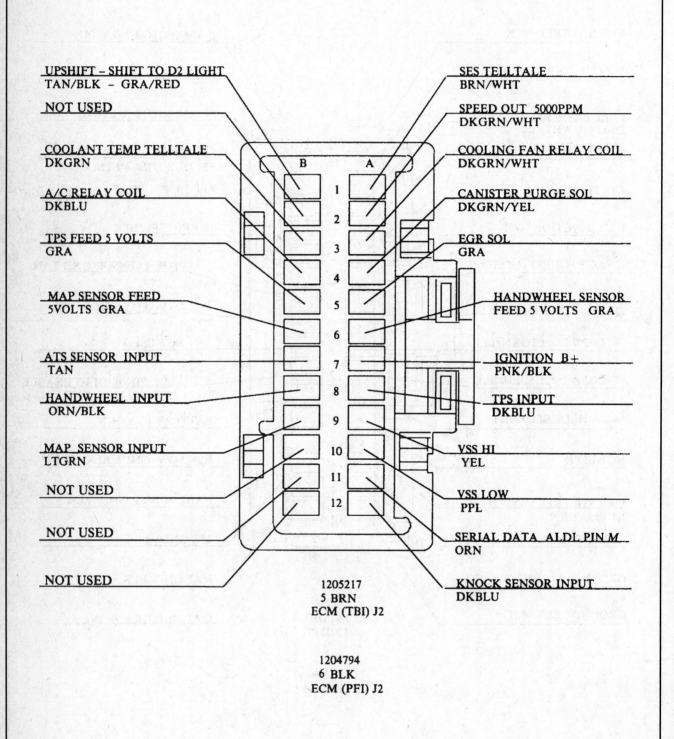

UPSHIFT – SHIFT TO D2 LIGHT
TAN/BLK – GRA/RED

NOT USED

COOLANT TEMP TELLTALE
DKGRN

A/C RELAY COIL
DKBLU

TPS FEED 5 VOLTS
GRA

MAP SENSOR FEED
5VOLTS GRA

ATS SENSOR INPUT
TAN

HANDWHEEL INPUT
ORN/BLK

MAP SENSOR INPUT
LTGRN

NOT USED

NOT USED

NOT USED

SES TELLTALE
BRN/WHT

SPEED OUT 5000PPM
DKGRN/WHT

COOLING FAN RELAY COIL
DKGRN/WHT

CANISTER PURGE SOL
DKGRN/YEL

EGR SOL
GRA

HANDWHEEL SENSOR
FEED 5 VOLTS GRA

IGNITION B+
PNK/BLK

TPS INPUT
DKBLU

VSS HI
YEL

VSS LOW
PPL

SERIAL DATA ALDL PIN *M*
ORN

KNOCK SENSOR INPUT
DKBLU

B   A

1
2
3
4
5
6
7
8
9
10
11
12

1205217
5 BRN
ECM (TBI) J2

1204794
6 BLK
ECM (PFI) J2

Fig. 38 PCM connector J2 pin-outs

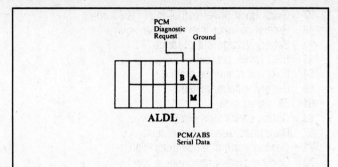

Fig. 39 Jumper terminals A and B of the ALDL to access self-diagnostic codes

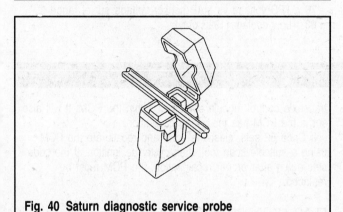

Fig. 40 Saturn diagnostic service probe

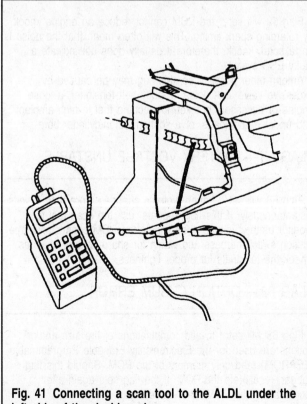

Fig. 41 Connecting a scan tool to the ALDL under the left side of the dashboard

PCM memory even if power is disconnected. Data in Malfunction History can only be read or cleared using a scan tool.

To clear General Information without cutting PCM power, therefore preserving other on-board data such as radio presets or the PCM learning ability, a scan tool may be used. If no scan tool is available proceed as follows:

1. Turn the ignition switch **ON**, then jumper terminals A and B of the ALDL together 3 times within 5 seconds. The SERVICE ENGINE SOON light should stop flashing and any Codes should be cleared.

2. Enter diagnostic mode to be certain that all codes have been erased. If necessary, repeat Step 1 to assure all codes are removed from General Information memory.

3. If all faults have been repaired, cycling the ignition switch 50 times will automatically clear General Information of fault Codes.

PCM Learning Ability

The PCM module contains a built-in learning ability that allows it to maximize driveability by correcting for minor variations in the fuel system. Any time the PCM is replaced or the power is removed from the PCM, the module must go through a relearning process. Maximum performance may not return until after this is accomplished. To enable the PCM to relearn the fuel system:

1. Start the vehicle and warm it to normal operating temperature.

2. Drive the vehicle at part throttle, with moderate acceleration and idle conditions, until normal performance returns.

3. Park the vehicle and engage the parking brake.

4. For automatic transaxles, shift into **D**. For manual transaxles, shift into **N**.

5. Allow the engine idle at normal operating temperature for about 2 minutes, until the engine stabilizes.

Diagnostic Codes

11	Transaxle Codes present
12	Diagnostic System Check
13	Oxygen sensor, circuit open or not ready
14	CTS circuit, out of range high
15	CTS circuit, out of range low
17	PCM fault, pullup resistor
19	6X signal fault, no 6X signal between reference pulses
21	TPS circuit, out of range high
22	TPS circuit, out of range low
23	ATS circuit, out of range low
24	VSS circuit, no signal
25	ATS circuit, out of range high
26	Quad Driver output fault
32	EGR system fault
33	MAP sensor circuit, out of range high
34	MAP sensor circuit, out of range low
35	IAC valve, rpm out of range
41A	EST circuit open
41B	EST circuit shorted
42A	Bypass circuit grounded
42B	Bypass circuit open

42C	Bypass circuit shorted
41	EST bypass, open or shorted
42	EST bypass, open or shorted
43	ESC (knock sensor) circuit open or shorted
44	Oxygen sensor indicates system lean
45	Oxygen sensor indicates system rich
46	Power steering pressure switch circuit, open
49	Idle rpm out of limit high (vacuum leak)
51	PCM memory error
55	A/D converter error in PCM
81	ABS message fault (1993 vehicles with TCS)
82	PCM internal communication fault

27	Quick quad driver output fault (1993 only)
48	Reference input intermittent or noisy
52	Battery voltage out of range
53	ESC knock present
54	Five volt reference ground
58	Battery voltage unstable
61	6X signal fault
63	Option check sum error
67	Handwheel sensor circuit fault
71	Cooling system temperature high
72	Cooling system temperature low
73	CTS sensor unstable
74	CTS/transaxle temperature sensor ratio error
75	ATS sensor unstable
76	TPS voltage vs MAP sensor voltage out of range
83	Low coolant (1993 only)

DIAGNOSTIC FLAGS

21EVO fault in power steering system

DIAGNOSTIC CODE FLOW CHARTS

The following flow charts may be used to diagnose the causes of various engine trouble codes which may be recorded by the PCM. The charts are expanded versions of the specific tests given earlier in this section for components of the electronic engine control system

CODE 17 — PCM FAULT

Code 17 will set if the pullup resistor inside the PCM switches and there is no change in the coolant temperature signal. Because Code 17 is an internal PCM fault, there is no repair procedure. The PCM must be replaced.

CODE 51 — PCM FAULT

Code 51 will set if the PCM memory is malfunctioning. Because Code 51 indicates an internal PCM malfunction, there is no repair procedure. The PCM must be replaced.

CODE 55 — PCM FAULT

Code 55 will set if the analog to digital conversion takes too long. In this case the low voltage of a square wave is greater than 0.1 volt and/or the high voltage is less than 4.88 volts. Because Code 55 indicates an internal PCM malfunction, there is no repair procedure. The PCM must be replaced.

CODE 82 — PCM INTERNAL COMMUNICATION FAULT

Code 82 will set if a certain number of incorrect messages have been sent between the engine control module and the

transaxle control module contained within the PCM. It will also set is the PCM has the wrong calibration.

If Code 82 sets, clear the code and recalibrate the PCM using a suitable scan tool, then cycle the ignition. If the code sets again after proper recalibration, the PCM must be replaced.

FLAG 53 — ESC KNOCK PRESENT

Flag 53 will set if the PCM cannot reduce an engine knock by retarding spark timing. This will often mean that the noise is not a spark knock, therefore it usually does not indicate a faulty ESC system.

Among other possibilities, this flag may be caused by excessive valve lifter noise, a faulty belt tensioner, a loose engine or accessory bracket, low octane fuel in high ambient and under heavy loads, or a scuffed piston/cylinder bore.

FLAG 58 — BATTERY VOLTAGE UNSTABLE

Flag 58 will set if battery voltage changes more than 3 volts instantaneously. If this flag appears, use the scan tool to monitor battery voltage, then wiggle the PCM connector or the ignition switch harness and watch for sharp voltage changes. Check the terminals for proper tightness.

FLAG 63 — OPTION CKSUM ERROR

Flag 63 will set if invalid combinations of tire size and/or options are used for the Electronically Erasable Programmable (EEPROM) read only memory of the PCM. Should this flag appear, recalibrate the PCM. If the flag sets again after recalibration, the PCM must be replaced.

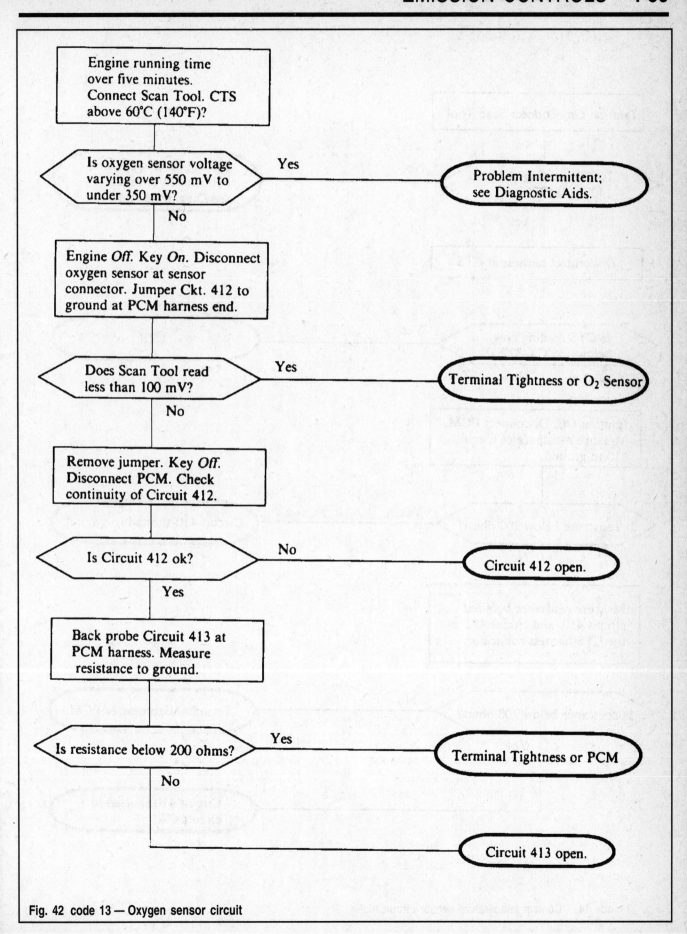

Fig. 42 code 13 — Oxygen sensor circuit

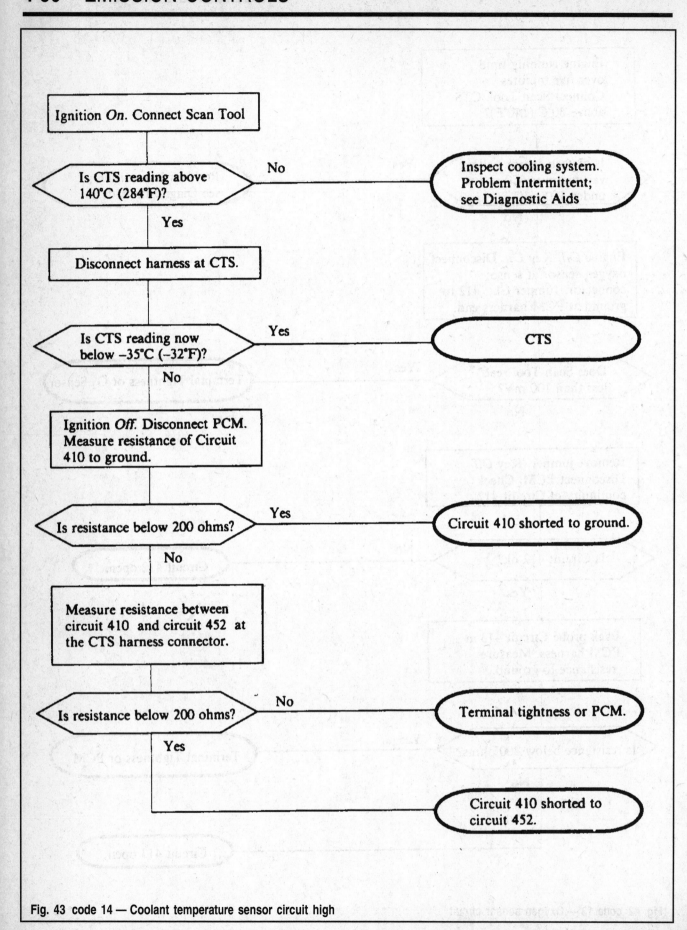

Fig. 43 code 14 — Coolant temperature sensor circuit high

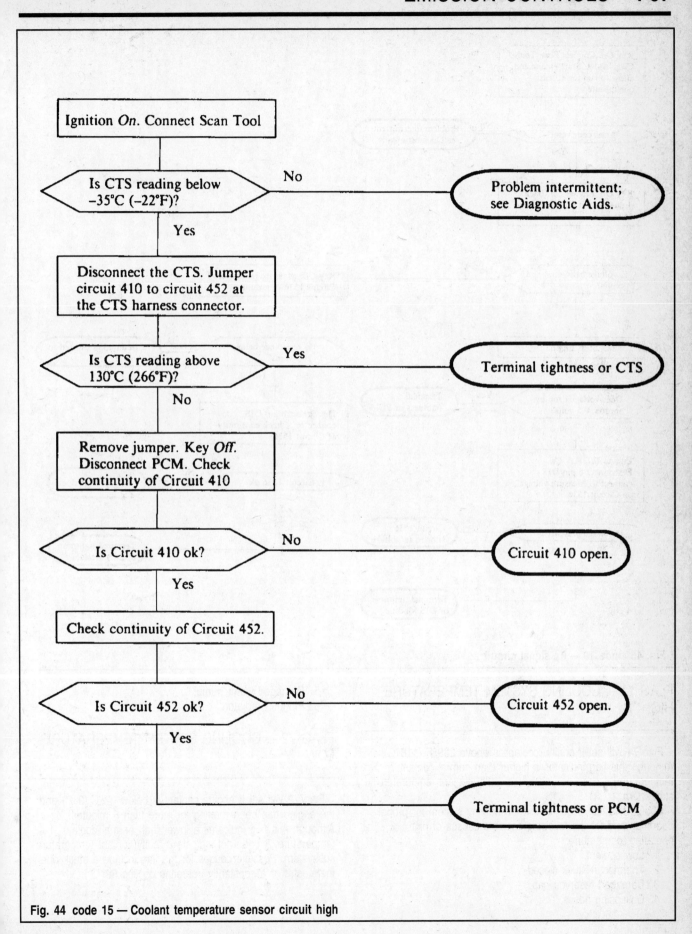

Fig. 44 code 15 — Coolant temperature sensor circuit high

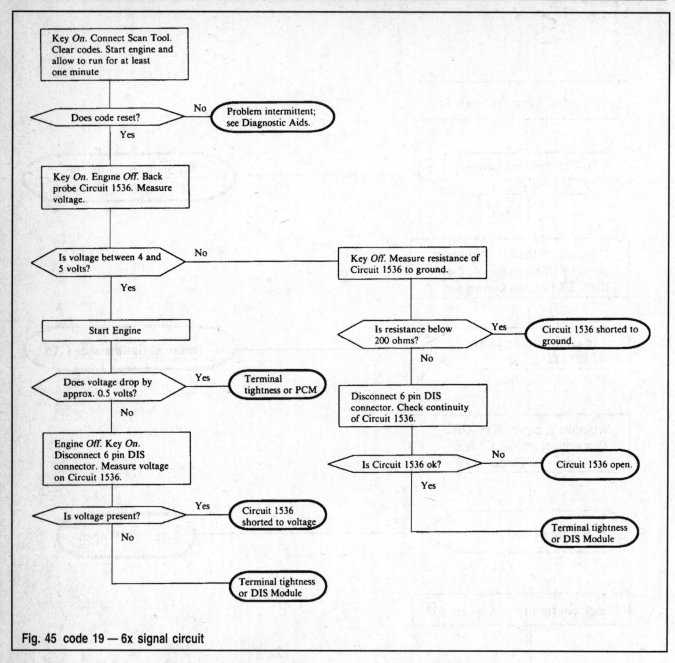

Fig. 45 code 19 — 6x signal circuit

FLAG 71 — COOLING SYSTEM TEMPERATURE HIGH

Flag 71 will set if engine coolant is above 239°F (118°C). Although this flag indicates a higher than normal coolant temperature, it does not indicate a faulty coolant temperature subsystem.

Should this flag occur, check the cooling system for proper operation and for the following possible causes of high operating temperature.

1. Low coolant.
2. Thermostat stuck closed.
3. Damaged reservoir cap.
4. Collapsing hoses.
5. Damaged water pump.
6. Plugged radiator.

FLAG 72 — COOLING SYSTEM TEMPERATURE LOW

Flag 72 will set if engine coolant is below 32°F (0°C) and the engine has been running for more than 5 minutes. Although this flag indicates a lower than normal coolant temperature, it does not indicate a faulty coolant temperature subsystem. Possible causes for the flag include a stuck open thermostat or a constantly operating cooling fan.

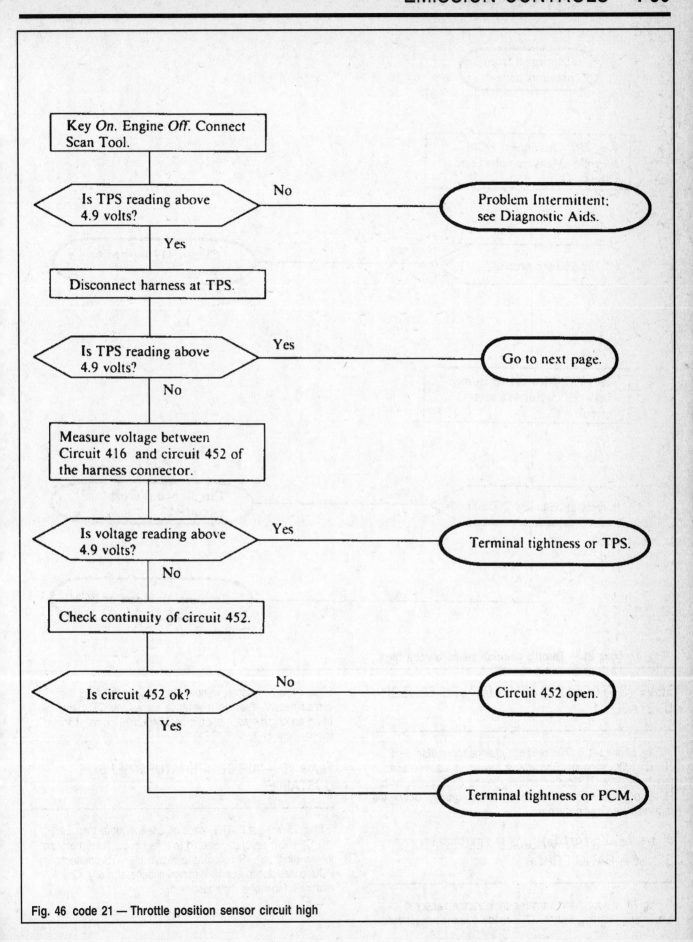

Fig. 46 code 21 — Throttle position sensor circuit high

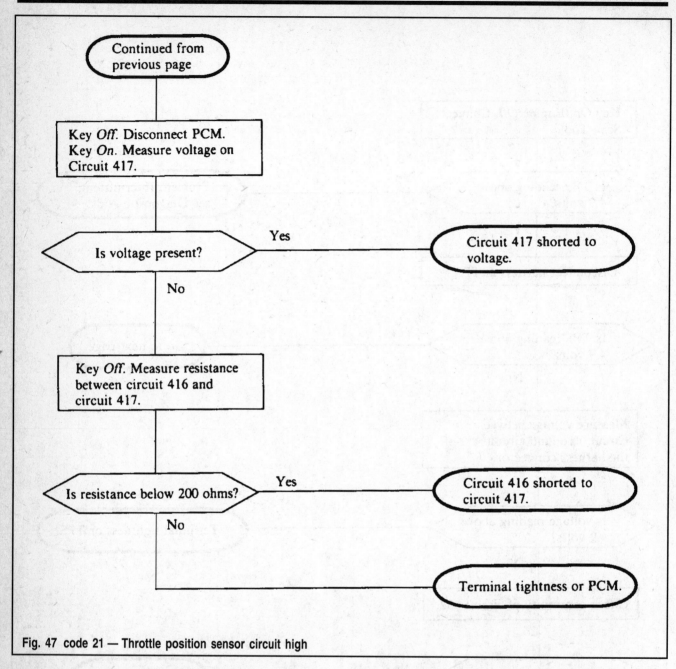

Fig. 47 code 21 — Throttle position sensor circuit high

FLAG 73 — COOLING TEMPERATURE SENSOR UNSTABLE

Flag 73 will set if CTS readings change more than 59°F (15°C) 100m seconds. Should this flag occur, use the scan tool to monitor CTS output and wiggle the CTS connector or PCM connector to see if readings change abruptly. Check the terminals for proper tightness.

FLAG 74 — CTS/TRANSAXLE TEMPERATURE SENSOR RATIO ERROR

Flag 74 will set if the transaxle temperature sensor is functioning properly, but the CTS reads a lower temperature.

Should this flag occur, remove and inspect the CTS for contamination. Measure resistance across the CTS terminals using an ohmmeter, it should be 2746-2826 ohms at room temperature of 77°F (25°C).

FLAG 75 — AIR TEMPERATURE SENSOR UNSTABLE

Flag 75 will set if ATS readings change more than 59°F (15°C) 100m seconds. Should this flag occur, use the scan tool to monitor ATS output and wiggle the ATS connector or PCM connector to see if readings change abruptly. Check the terminals for proper tightness.

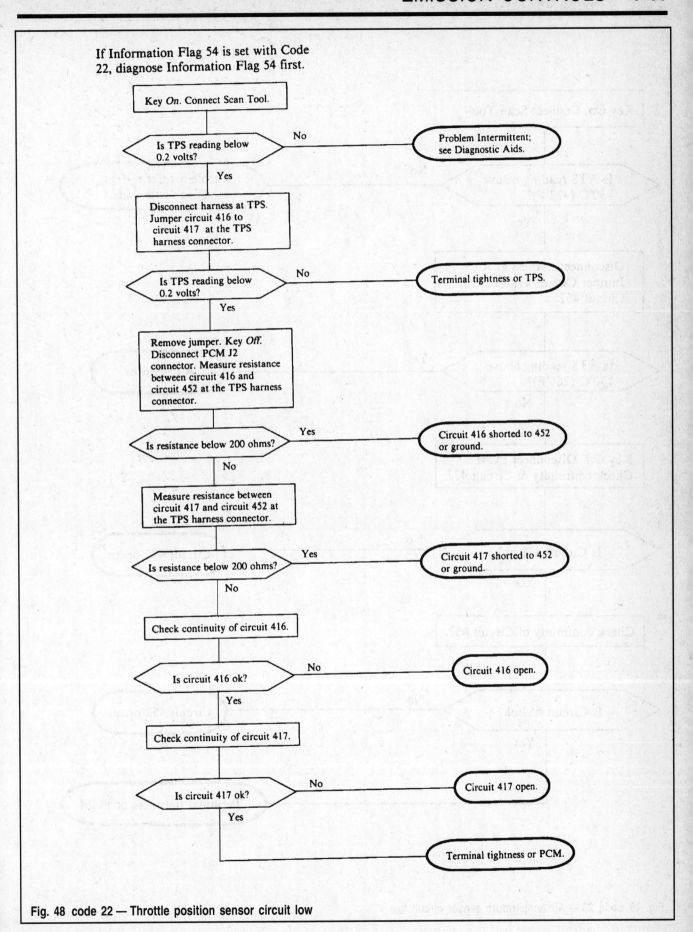

If Information Flag 54 is set with Code 22, diagnose Information Flag 54 first.

Key *On*. Connect Scan Tool.

Is TPS reading below 0.2 volts? — No → Problem Intermittent; see Diagnostic Aids.

Yes ↓

Disconnect harness at TPS. Jumper circuit 416 to circuit 417 at the TPS harness connector.

Is TPS reading below 0.2 volts? — No → Terminal tightness or TPS.

Yes ↓

Remove jumper. Key *Off*. Disconnect PCM J2 connector. Measure resistance between circuit 416 and circuit 452 at the TPS harness connector.

Is resistance below 200 ohms? — Yes → Circuit 416 shorted to 452 or ground.

No ↓

Measure resistance between circuit 417 and circuit 452 at the TPS harness connector.

Is resistance below 200 ohms? — Yes → Circuit 417 shorted to 452 or ground.

No ↓

Check continuity of circuit 416.

Is circuit 416 ok? — No → Circuit 416 open.

Yes ↓

Check continuity of circuit 417.

Is circuit 417 ok? — No → Circuit 417 open.

Yes ↓

Terminal tightness or PCM.

Fig. 48 code 22 — Throttle position sensor circuit low

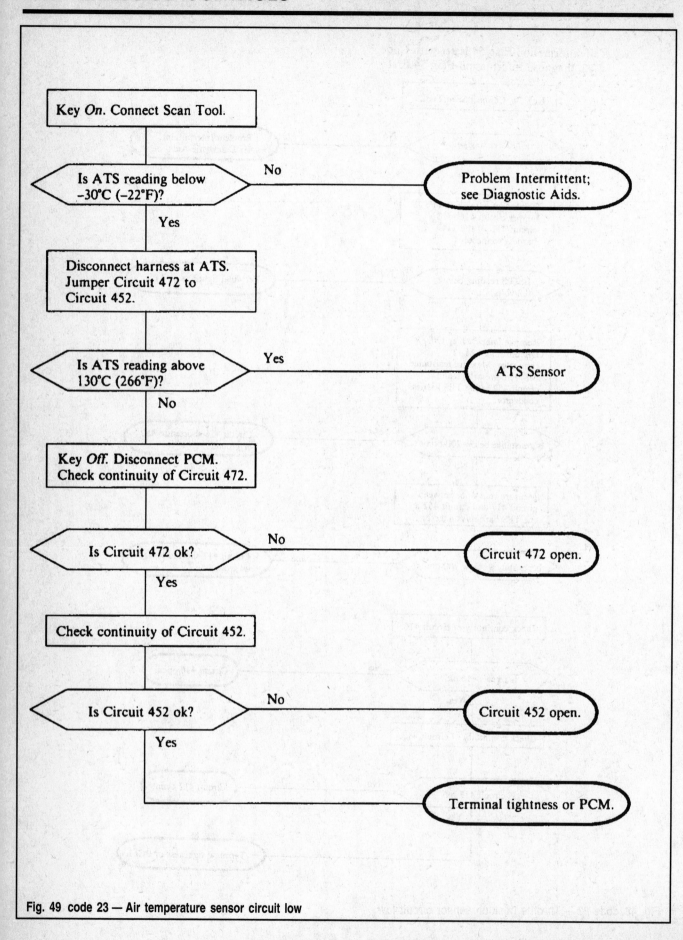

Fig. 49 code 23 — Air temperature sensor circuit low

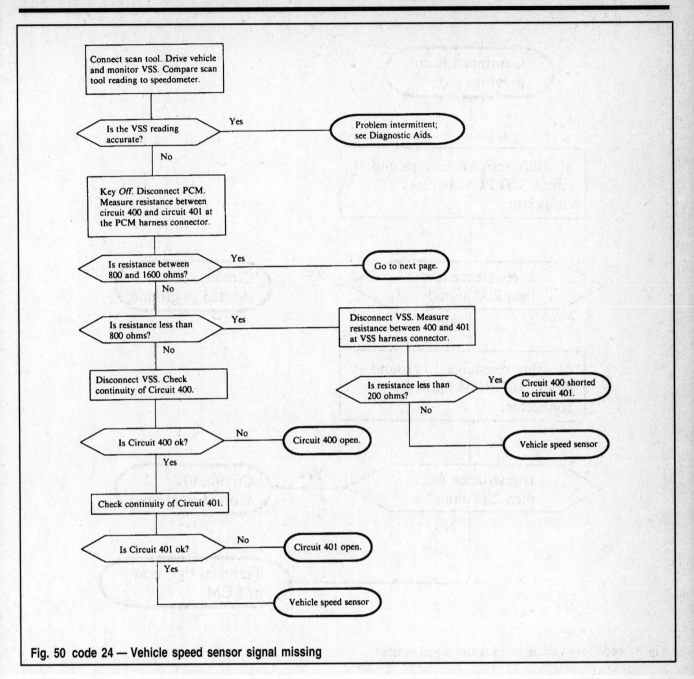

Fig. 50 code 24 — Vehicle speed sensor signal missing

FLAG 76 — TPS vs MAP VOLTAGE OUT OF RANGE

Flag 76 will set if the TPS and MAP signals are inconsistent with normal engine operation. Should this flag occur, check the sensor and PCM connectors for corrosion. Attach the scan tool and operate the throttle watching for voltage readings. At closed throttle TPS output should be about 0.4 volts and as the throttle is opened, the voltage should raise smoothly to 4.9 volts.

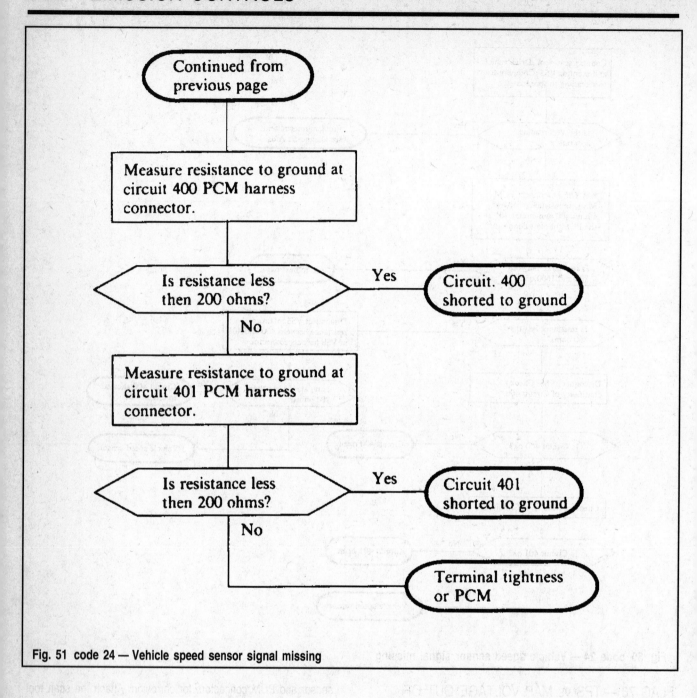

Fig. 51 code 24 — Vehicle speed sensor signal missing

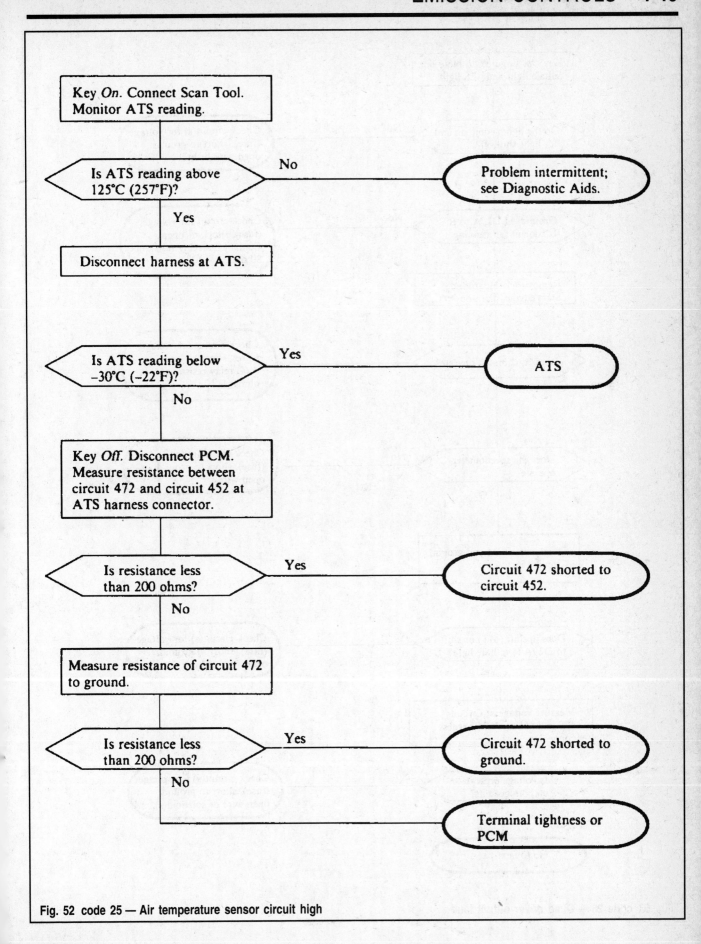

Fig. 52 code 25 — Air temperature sensor circuit high

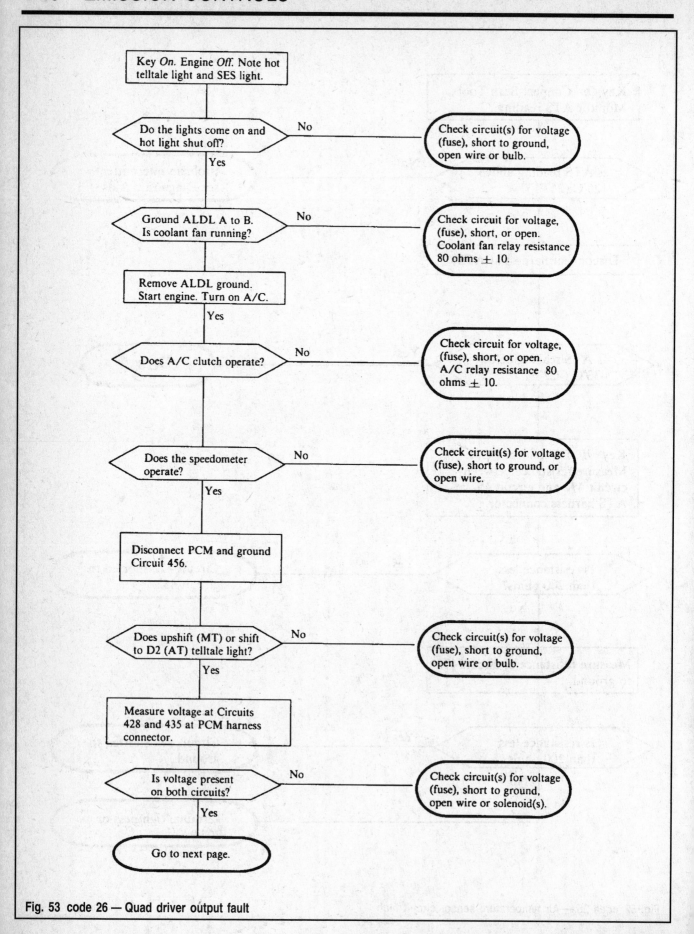

Key *On*. Engine *Off*. Note hot telltale light and SES light.

Do the lights come on and hot light shut off? — No → Check circuit(s) for voltage (fuse), short to ground, open wire or bulb.

Yes

Ground ALDL A to B. Is coolant fan running? — No → Check circuit for voltage, (fuse), short, or open. Coolant fan relay resistance 80 ohms ± 10.

Remove ALDL ground. Start engine. Turn on A/C.

Yes

Does A/C clutch operate? — No → Check circuit for voltage, (fuse), short, or open. A/C relay resistance 80 ohms ± 10.

Does the speedometer operate? — No → Check circuit(s) for voltage (fuse), short to ground, or open wire.

Yes

Disconnect PCM and ground Circuit 456.

Does upshift (MT) or shift to D2 (AT) telltale light? — No → Check circuit(s) for voltage (fuse), short to ground, open wire or bulb.

Yes

Measure voltage at Circuits 428 and 435 at PCM harness connector.

Is voltage present on both circuits? — No → Check circuit(s) for voltage (fuse), short to ground, open wire or solenoid(s).

Yes

Go to next page.

Fig. 53 code 26 — Quad driver output fault

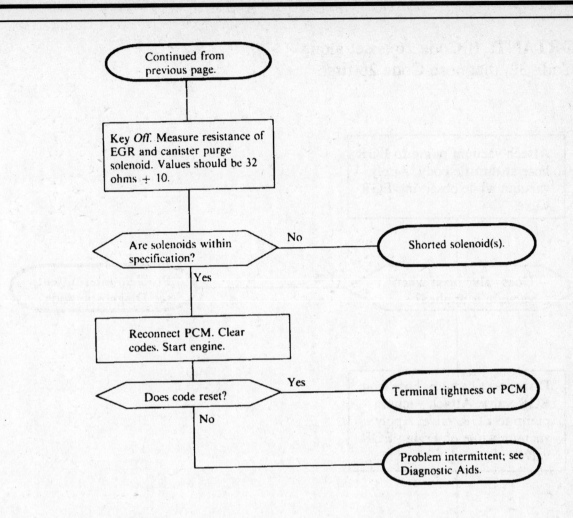

COMPONENT	PCM PIN	COLOR
SERVICE ENGINE SOON	J2D01	BRN / WHT
Cooling Fan Relay	J2A03	DK GRN/WHT
A/C Clutch	J2B04	DK BLU
CCP Solenoid	J2A04	DK GRN/YEL
EGR Solenoid	J2A05	GRAY
Coolant Hot Light	J2B03	DK GRN
Upshift/Shift to D2	J2B01	TAN / BLK
Speedo Cutout	J2A02	DK GRN/WHT

Fig. 54 code 26 — Quad driver output fault

IMPORTANT: If Code 26 is set along with Code 32, diagnose Code 26 first.

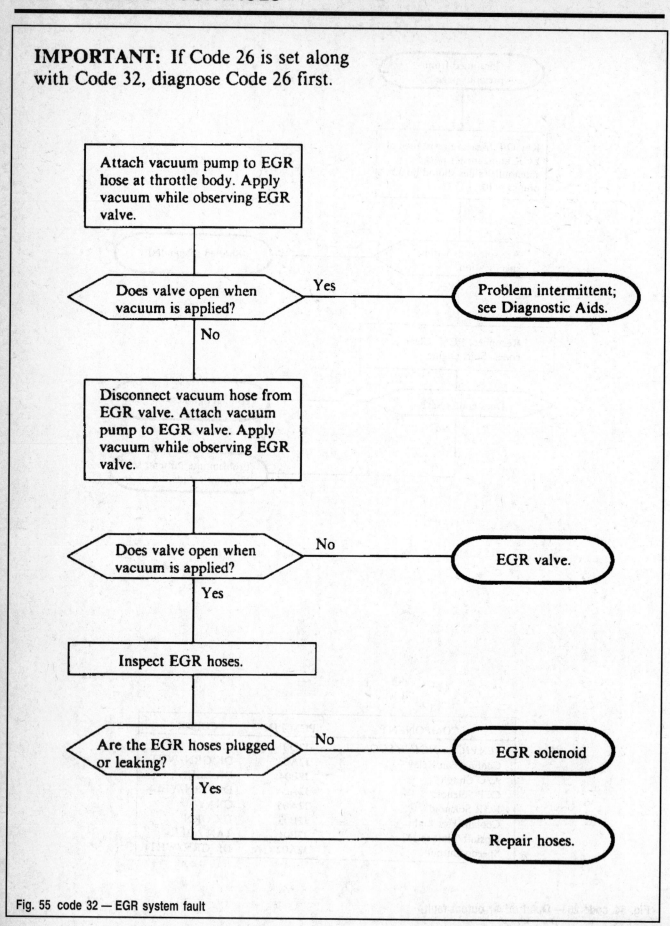

Fig. 55 code 32 — EGR system fault

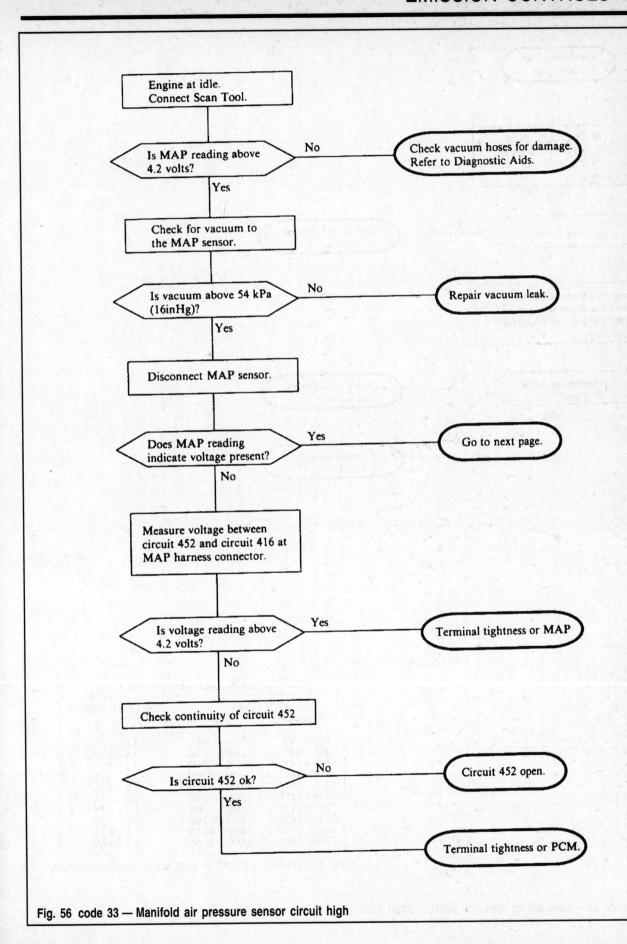

Fig. 56 code 33 — Manifold air pressure sensor circuit high

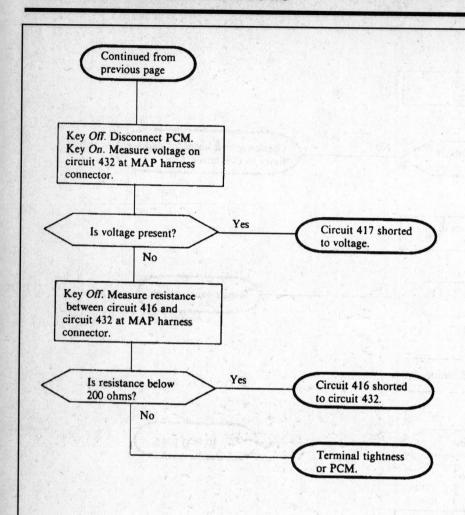

Continued from previous page

Key *Off.* Disconnect PCM. Key *On.* Measure voltage on circuit 432 at MAP harness connector.

Is voltage present? — Yes → Circuit 417 shorted to voltage.

No

Key *Off.* Measure resistance between circuit 416 and circuit 432 at MAP harness connector.

Is resistance below 200 ohms? — Yes → Circuit 416 shorted to circuit 432.

No

Terminal tightness or PCM.

IGNITION *ON* ENGINE *OFF* VOLTAGE

ALTITUDE		VOLTAGE RANGE
Meters	Feet	
Below 305	Below 1,000	3.8 – 5.5V
305 – 610	1,000 – 2,000	3.6 – 5.3V
610 – 914	2,000 – 3,000	3.5 – 5.1V
914 – 1219	3,000 – 4,000	3.3 – 5.0V
1219 – 1524	4,000 – 5,000	3.2 – 4.8V
1524 – 1829	5,000 – 6,000	3.0 – 4.6V
1829 – 2133	6,000 – 7,000	2.9 – 4.5V
2133 – 2438	7,000 – 8,000	2.8 – 4.3V
2438 – 2743	8,000 – 9,000	2.6 – 4.2V
2743 – 3948	9,000 – 10,000	2.5 – 4.0V

LOW ALTITUDE = HIGH PRESSURE = HIGH VOLTAGE

Fig. 57 code 33 — Manifold air pressure sensor circuit high

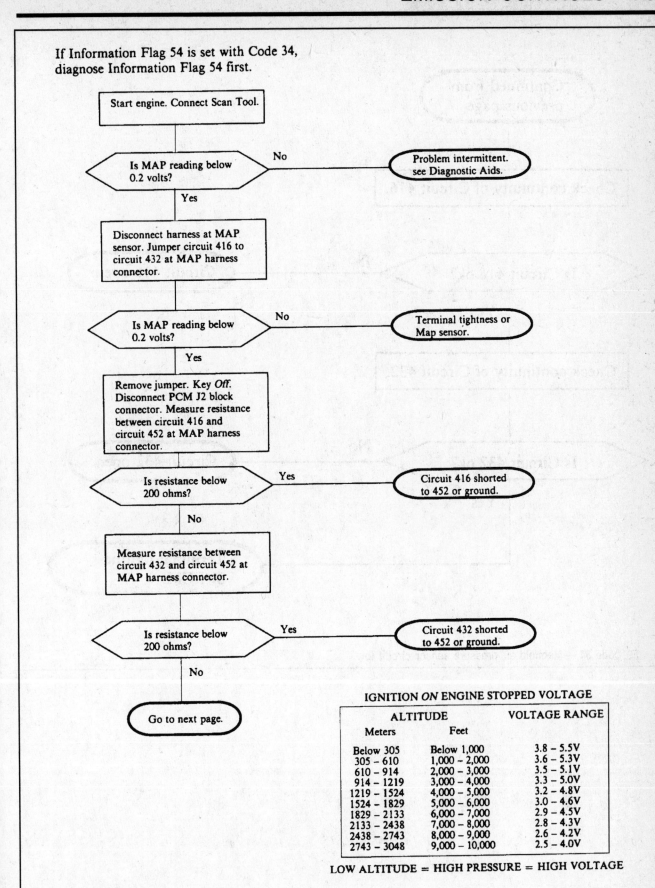

If Information Flag 54 is set with Code 34, diagnose Information Flag 54 first.

Start engine. Connect Scan Tool.

Is MAP reading below 0.2 volts? — No → Problem intermittent. see Diagnostic Aids.

Yes

Disconnect harness at MAP sensor. Jumper circuit 416 to circuit 432 at MAP harness connector.

Is MAP reading below 0.2 volts? — No → Terminal tightness or Map sensor.

Yes

Remove jumper. Key *Off*. Disconnect PCM J2 block connector. Measure resistance between circuit 416 and circuit 452 at MAP harness connector.

Is resistance below 200 ohms? — Yes → Circuit 416 shorted to 452 or ground.

No

Measure resistance between circuit 432 and circuit 452 at MAP harness connector.

Is resistance below 200 ohms? — Yes → Circuit 432 shorted to 452 or ground.

No

Go to next page.

IGNITION *ON* ENGINE STOPPED VOLTAGE

ALTITUDE		VOLTAGE RANGE
Meters	Feet	
Below 305	Below 1,000	3.8 – 5.5V
305 – 610	1,000 – 2,000	3.6 – 5.3V
610 – 914	2,000 – 3,000	3.5 – 5.1V
914 – 1219	3,000 – 4,000	3.3 – 5.0V
1219 – 1524	4,000 – 5,000	3.2 – 4.8V
1524 – 1829	5,000 – 6,000	3.0 – 4.6V
1829 – 2133	6,000 – 7,000	2.9 – 4.5V
2133 – 2438	7,000 – 8,000	2.8 – 4.3V
2438 – 2743	8,000 – 9,000	2.6 – 4.2V
2743 – 3048	9,000 – 10,000	2.5 – 4.0V

LOW ALTITUDE = HIGH PRESSURE = HIGH VOLTAGE

Fig. 58 code 34 — Manifold air pressure sensor circuit low

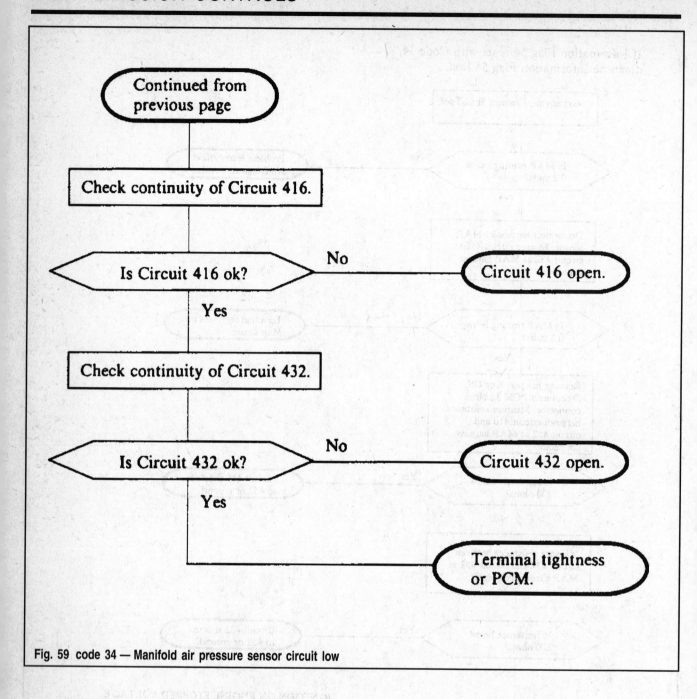

Fig. 59 code 34 — Manifold air pressure sensor circuit low

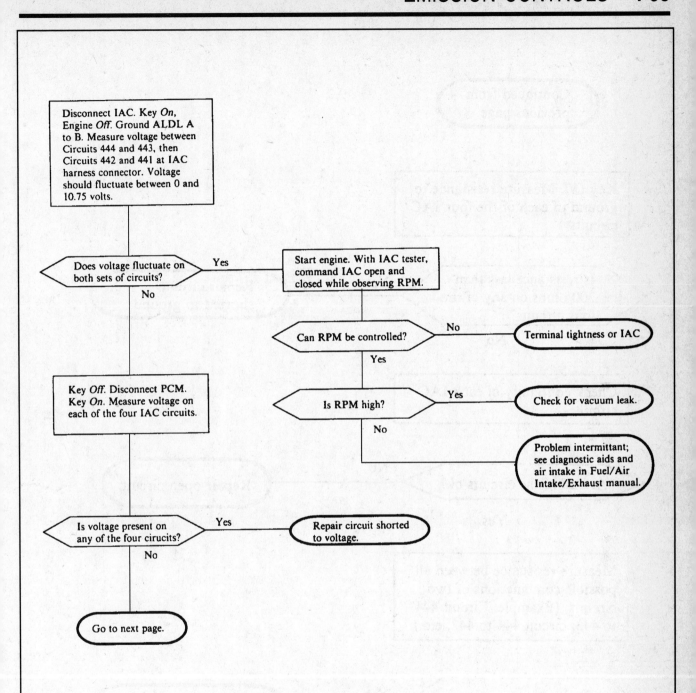

Disconnect IAC. Key *On*, Engine *Off*. Ground ALDL A to B. Measure voltage between Circuits 444 and 443, then Circuits 442 and 441 at IAC harness connector. Voltage should fluctuate between 0 and 10.75 volts.

Does voltage fluctuate on both sets of circuits?

Yes → Start engine. With IAC tester, command IAC open and closed while observing RPM.

No

Can RPM be controlled?

No → Terminal tightness or IAC

Yes

Is RPM high?

Yes → Check for vacuum leak.

No → Problem intermittant; see diagnostic aids and air intake in Fuel/Air Intake/Exhaust manual.

Key *Off*. Disconnect PCM. Key *On*. Measure voltage on each of the four IAC circuits.

Is voltage present on any of the four cirucits?

Yes → Repair circuit shorted to voltage.

No

Go to next page.

Circuit #	Color	Gage	PCM Pin	IAC Pin
444	Lt Grn/Blk	22	J1C08	A
443	Lt Grn/Wht	22	J1C09	B
442	Lt Blu/Blk	22	J1C07	C
441	Dk Blu/Wht	22	J1C06	D

Fig. 60 code 35 — Idle air control, rpm out of range

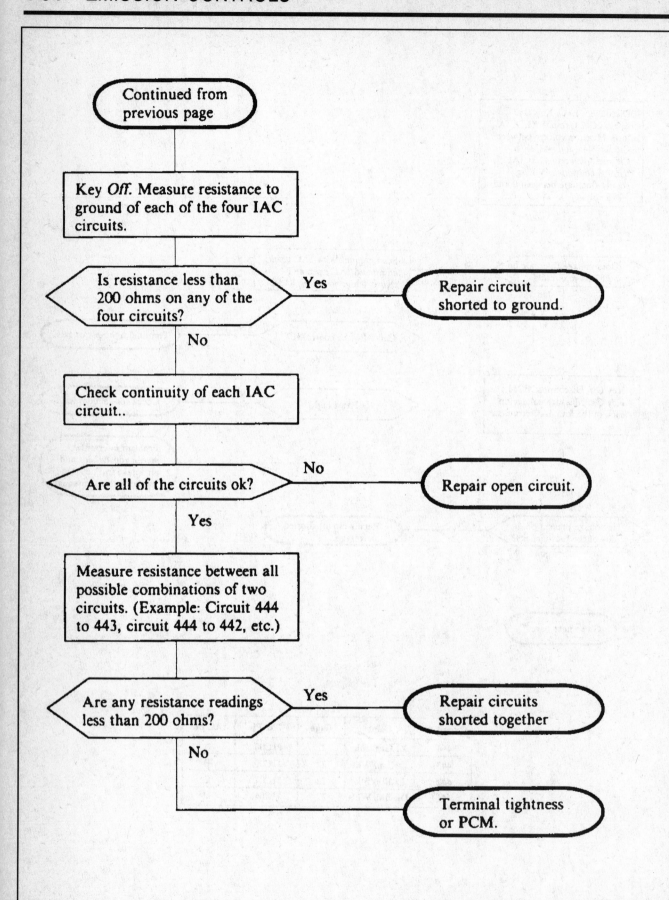

Continued from previous page

Key *Off.* Measure resistance to ground of each of the four IAC circuits.

Is resistance less than 200 ohms on any of the four circuits? — Yes → Repair circuit shorted to ground.

No

Check continuity of each IAC circuit..

Are all of the circuits ok? — No → Repair open circuit.

Yes

Measure resistance between all possible combinations of two circuits. (Example: Circuit 444 to 443, circuit 444 to 442, etc.)

Are any resistance readings less than 200 ohms? — Yes → Repair circuits shorted together

No

Terminal tightness or PCM.

Fig. 61 code 35 — Idle air control, rpm out of range

41A EST Open
41B EST shorted to voltage or ground.

IMPORTANT: If Code 41 is set along with Code 42, refer to Chart Codes 41–42.

Key *On.* Connect Scan Tool. Clear codes. Start Engine and accelerate over 2500 RPM for at least 10 seconds.

Does Code 41 only reset? — No → Problem intermittent. see Diagnostic Aids. If 41 and 42 set, refer to 41–42 chart.

Yes

Key *On.* Engine *Off.* Disconnect 6 pin connector at DIS module. Measure voltage on Circuit 423 at 6 pin harness connector.

Is voltage below 1 volt? — No → Circuit 423 shorted to voltage.

Yes

Key *Off.* Measure resistance to ground of Circuit 423 at 6 pin harness connector.

Is resistance below 200 ohms? — Yes → Circuit 423 shorted to ground.

No

Disconnect PCM. Check continuity of Circuit 423.

Is Circuit 423 ok? — No → Circuit 423 open.

Yes

Reconnect 6 pin connector to DIS. Install a Diagnostic Service Probe #12092782 to Circuit 423. Measure voltage to ground. Start engine.

• See Diagnostic Service Probe at beginning of PCM Code section.

Is voltage between 1 and 4 volts? — Yes → DIS module

No

PCM.

Fig. 62 code 41 — Electronic spark timing circuit open/short

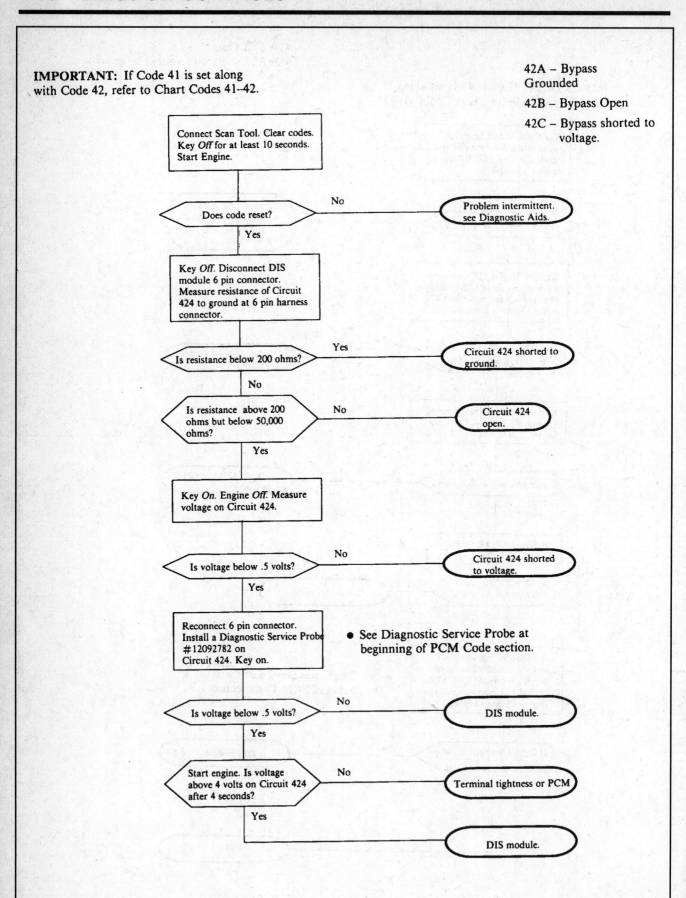

IMPORTANT: If Code 41 is set along with Code 42, refer to Chart Codes 41–42.

42A – Bypass Grounded

42B – Bypass Open

42C – Bypass shorted to voltage.

Connect Scan Tool. Clear codes. Key *Off* for at least 10 seconds. Start Engine.

Does code reset? — No → Problem intermittent. see Diagnostic Aids.

Yes

Key *Off.* Disconnect DIS module 6 pin connector. Measure resistance of Circuit 424 to ground at 6 pin harness connector.

Is resistance below 200 ohms? — Yes → Circuit 424 shorted to ground.

No

Is resistance above 200 ohms but below 50,000 ohms? — No → Circuit 424 open.

Yes

Key *On.* Engine *Off.* Measure voltage on Circuit 424.

Is voltage below .5 volts? — No → Circuit 424 shorted to voltage.

Yes

Reconnect 6 pin connector. Install a Diagnostic Service Probe #12092782 on Circuit 424. Key on.

● See Diagnostic Service Probe at beginning of PCM Code section.

Is voltage below .5 volts? — No → DIS module.

Yes

Start engine. Is voltage above 4 volts on Circuit 424 after 4 seconds? — No → Terminal tightness or PCM

Yes

DIS module.

Fig. 63 code 42 — Bypass circuit open/short

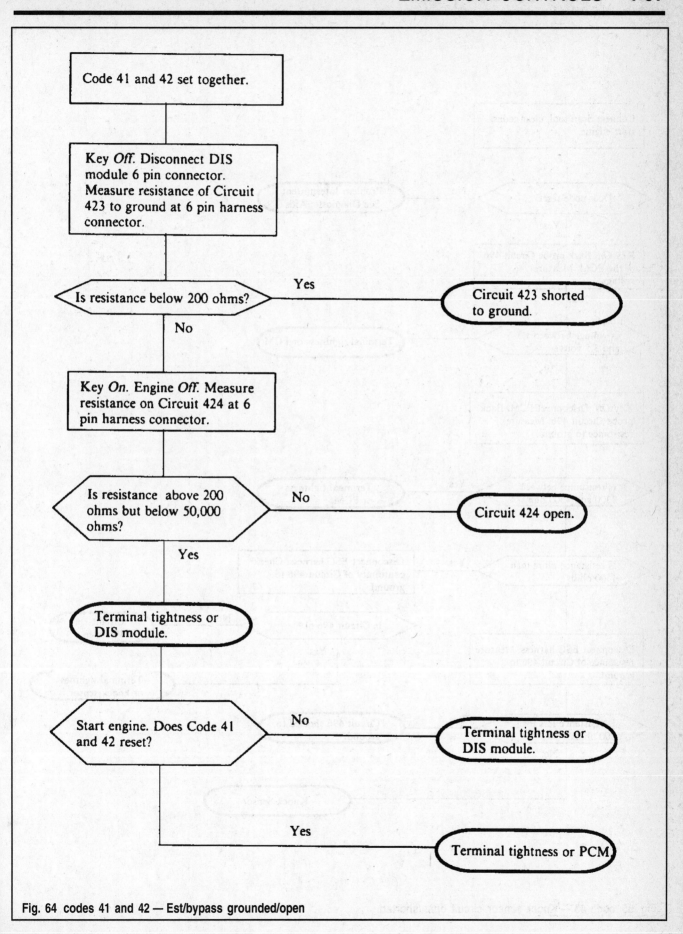

Fig. 64 codes 41 and 42 — Est/bypass grounded/open

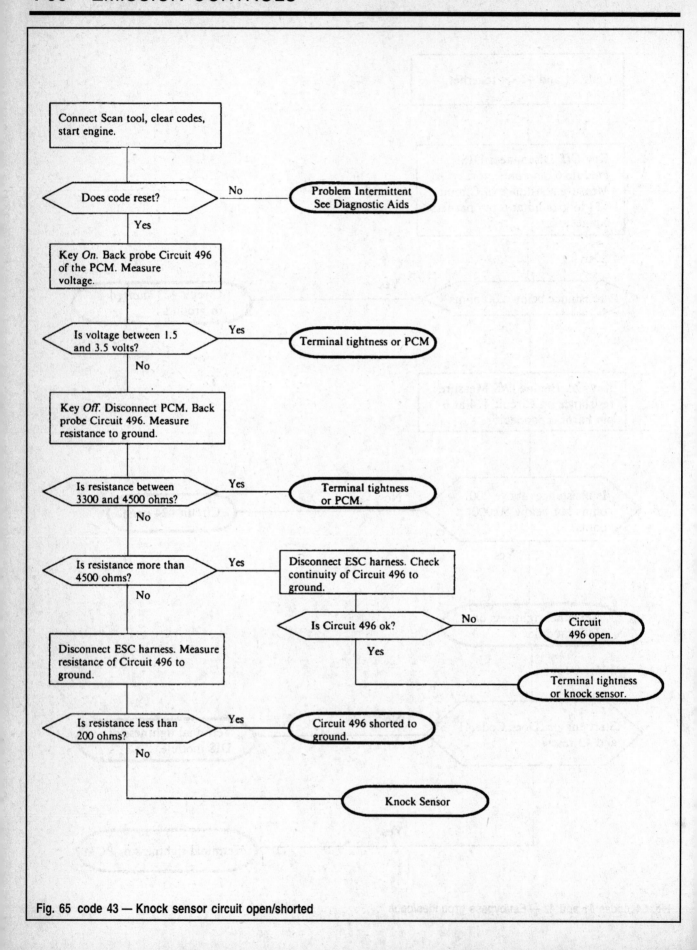

Fig. 65 code 43 — Knock sensor circuit open/shorted

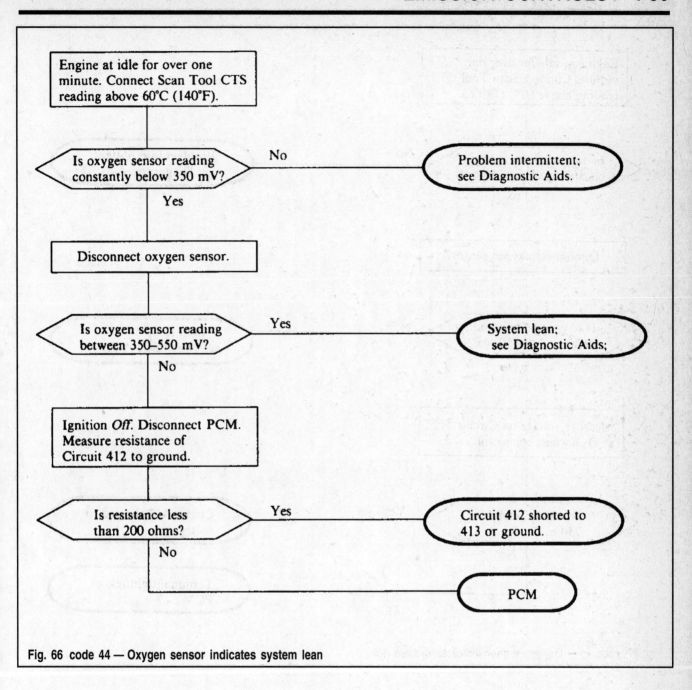

Fig. 66 code 44 — Oxygen sensor indicates system lean

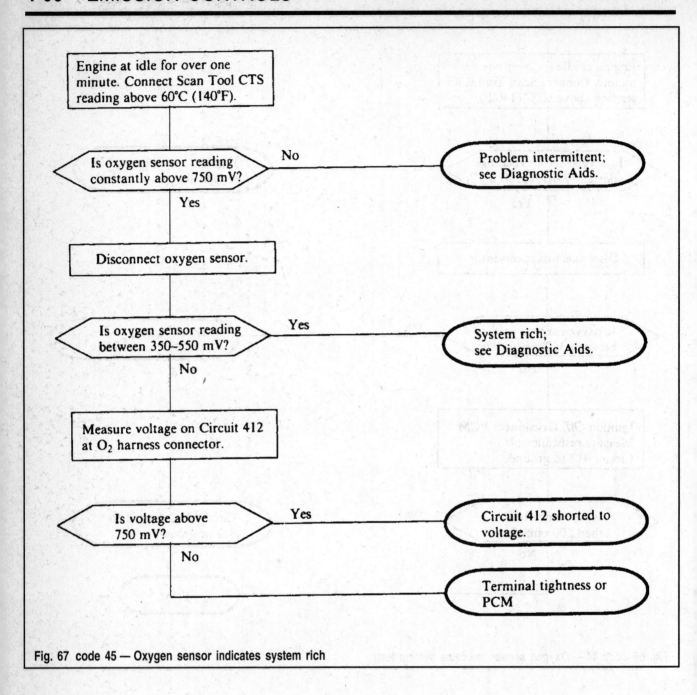

Fig. 67 code 45 — Oxygen sensor indicates system rich

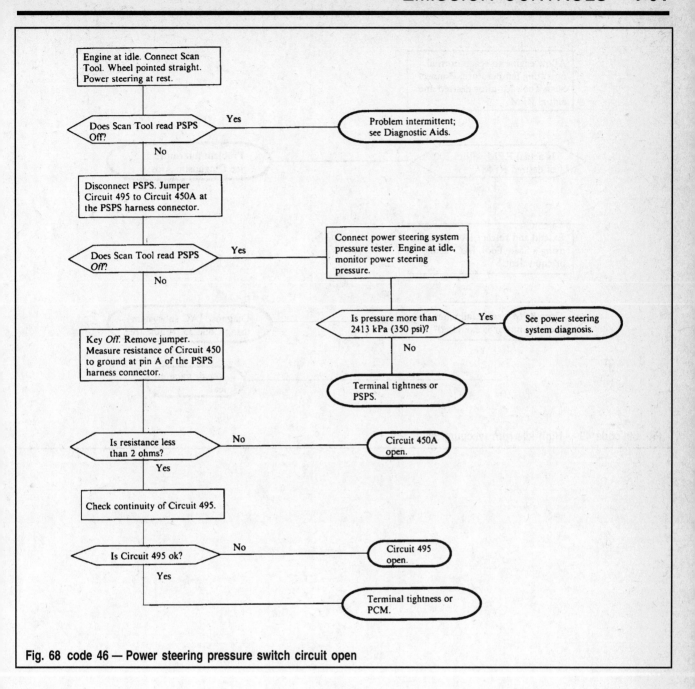

Fig. 68 code 46 — Power steering pressure switch circuit open

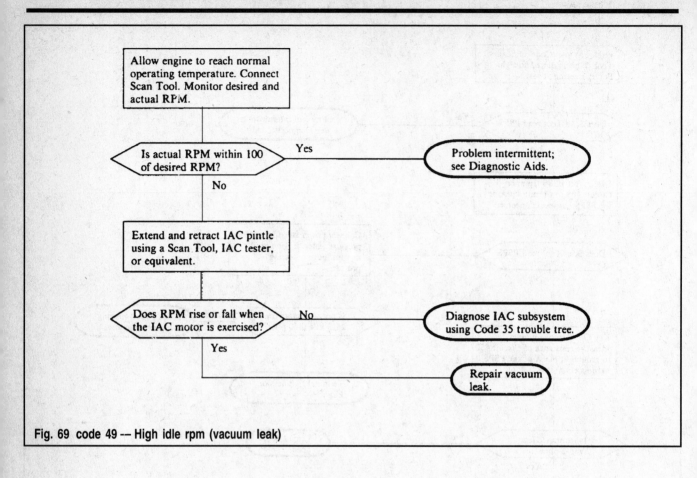

Allow engine to reach normal operating temperature. Connect Scan Tool. Monitor desired and actual RPM.

Is actual RPM within 100 of desired RPM?

Yes → Problem intermittent; see Diagnostic Aids.

No

Extend and retract IAC pintle using a Scan Tool, IAC tester, or equivalent.

Does RPM rise or fall when the IAC motor is exercised?

No → Diagnose IAC subsystem using Code 35 trouble tree.

Yes → Repair vacuum leak.

Fig. 69 code 49 -- High idle rpm (vacuum leak)

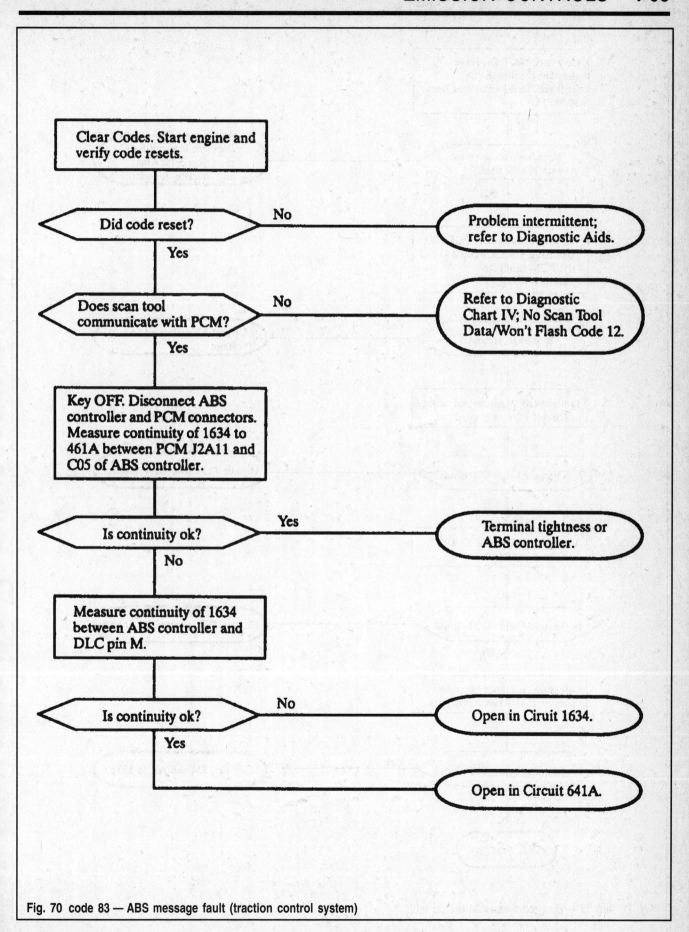

Clear Codes. Start engine and verify code resets.

Did code reset? — No → Problem intermittent; refer to Diagnostic Aids.

Yes

Does scan tool communicate with PCM? — No → Refer to Diagnostic Chart IV; No Scan Tool Data/Won't Flash Code 12.

Yes

Key OFF. Disconnect ABS controller and PCM connectors. Measure continuity of 1634 to 461A between PCM J2A11 and C05 of ABS controller.

Is continuity ok? — Yes → Terminal tightness or ABS controller.

No

Measure continuity of 1634 between ABS controller and DLC pin M.

Is continuity ok? — No → Open in Ciruit 1634.

Yes

Open in Circuit 641A.

Fig. 70 code 83 — ABS message fault (traction control system)

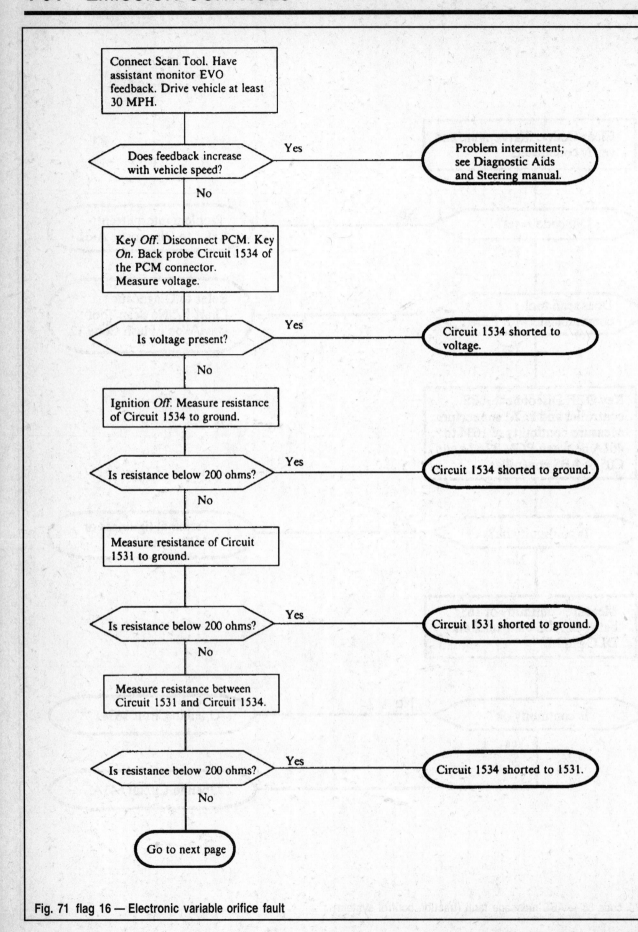

Fig. 71 flag 16 — Electronic variable orifice fault

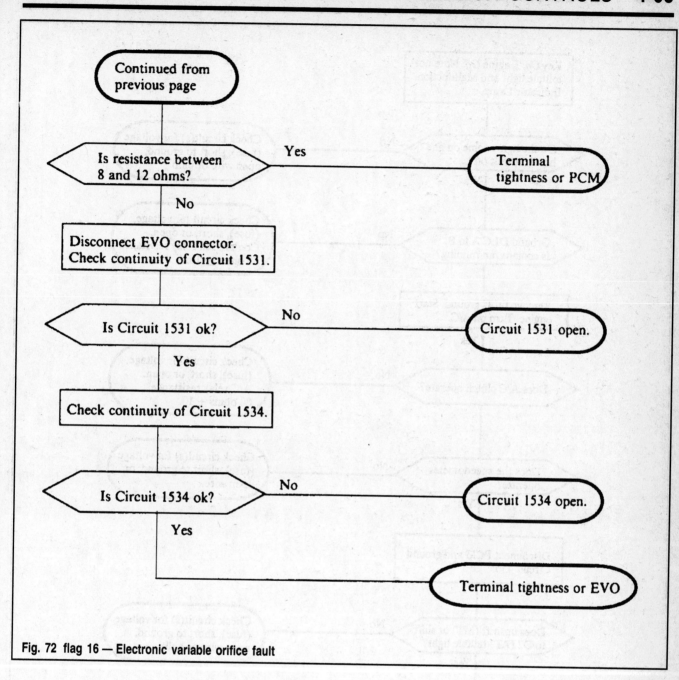

Fig. 72 flag 16 — Electronic variable orifice fault

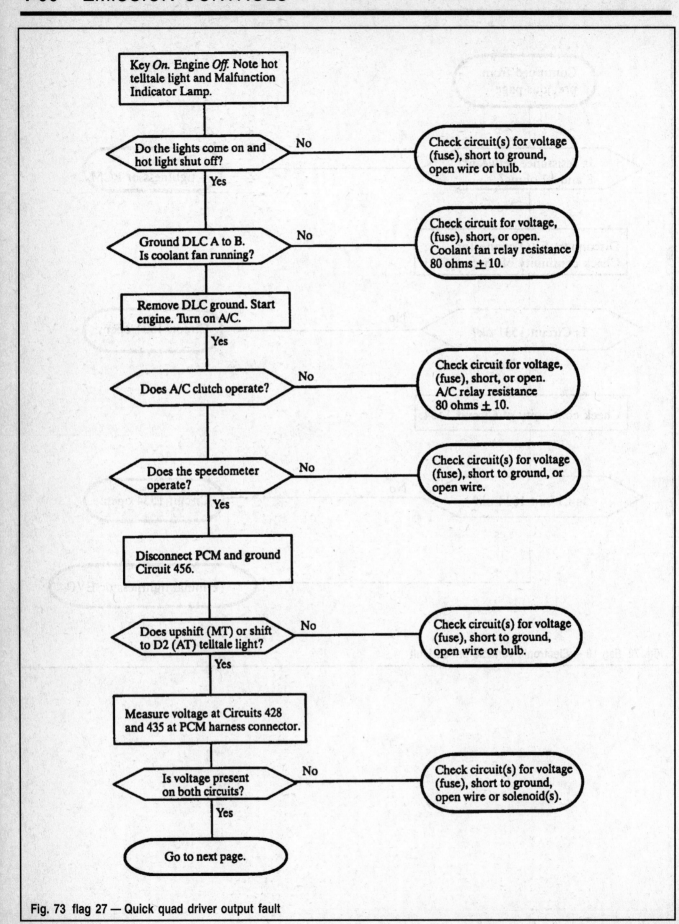

Fig. 73 flag 27 — Quick quad driver output fault

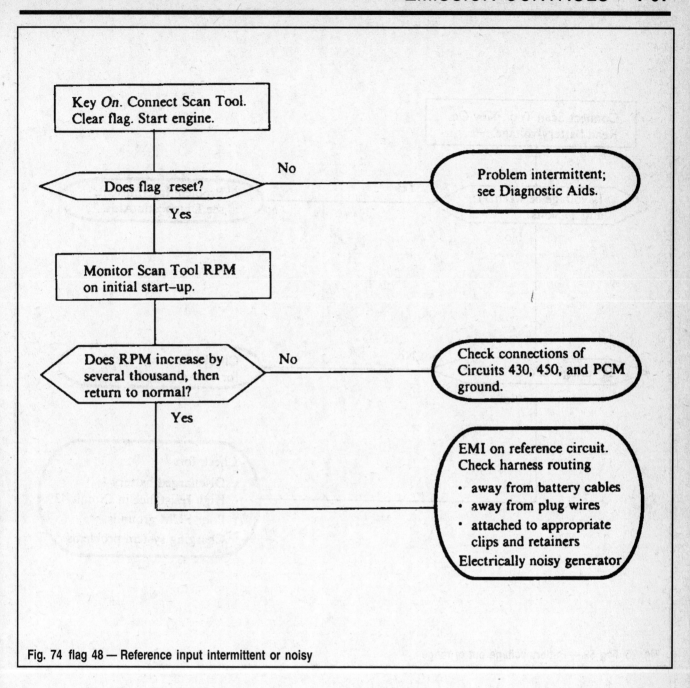

Fig. 74 flag 48 — Reference input intermittent or noisy

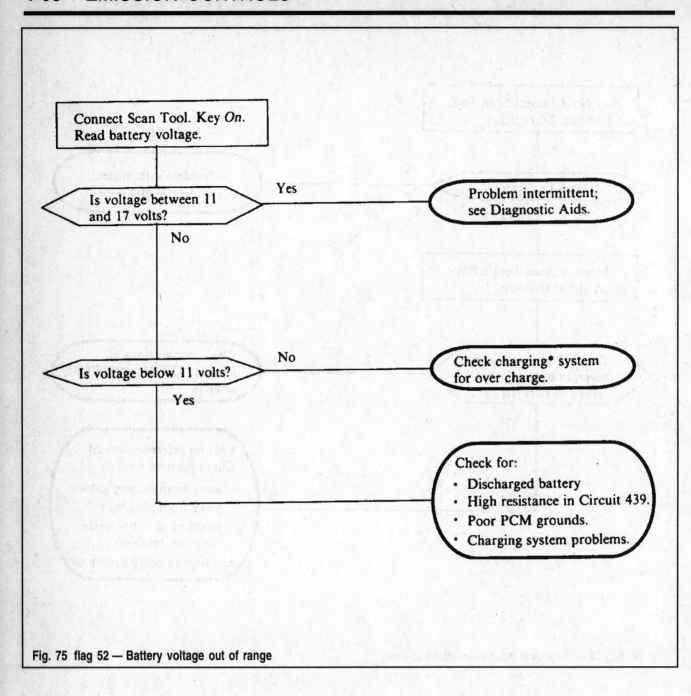

Fig. 75 flag 52 — Battery voltage out of range

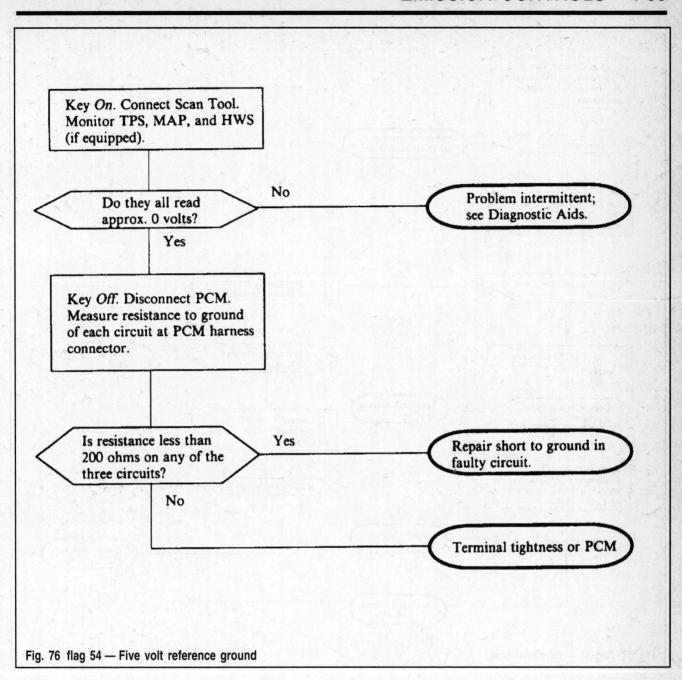

Fig. 76 flag 54 — Five volt reference ground

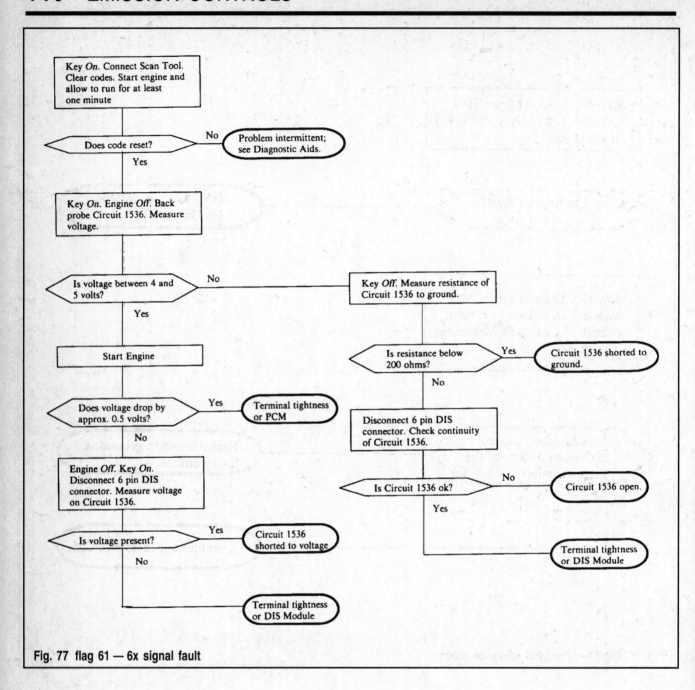

Fig. 77 flag 61 — 6x signal fault

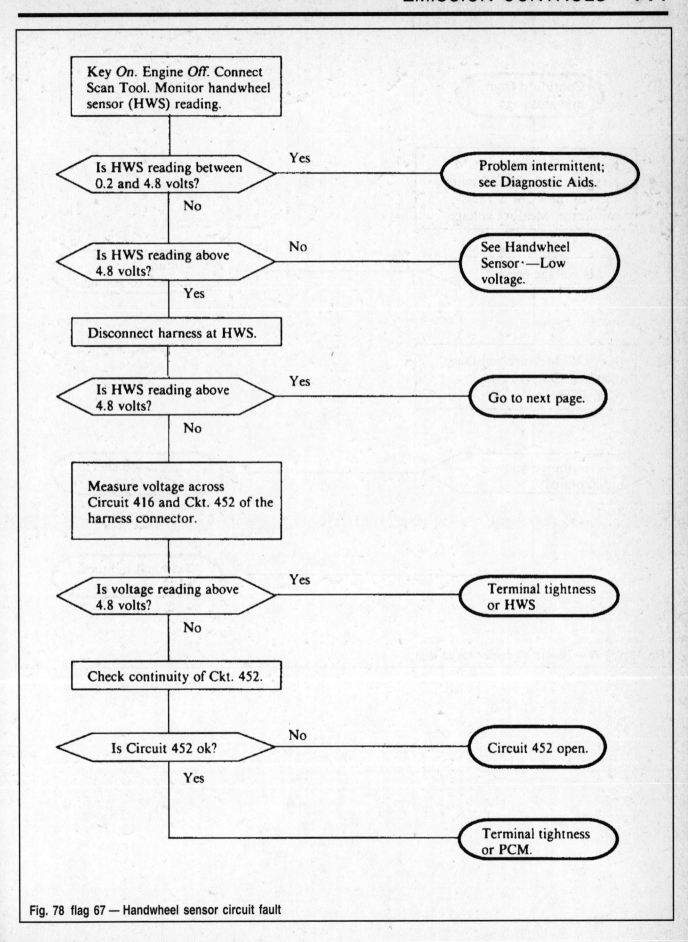

Key *On*. Engine *Off*. Connect Scan Tool. Monitor handwheel sensor (HWS) reading.

Is HWS reading between 0.2 and 4.8 volts?
Yes → Problem intermittent; see Diagnostic Aids.
No

Is HWS reading above 4.8 volts?
No → See Handwheel Sensor·—Low voltage.
Yes

Disconnect harness at HWS.

Is HWS reading above 4.8 volts?
Yes → Go to next page.
No

Measure voltage across Circuit 416 and Ckt. 452 of the harness connector.

Is voltage reading above 4.8 volts?
Yes → Terminal tightness or HWS
No

Check continuity of Ckt. 452.

Is Circuit 452 ok?
No → Circuit 452 open.
Yes

Terminal tightness or PCM.

Fig. 78 flag 67 — Handwheel sensor circuit fault

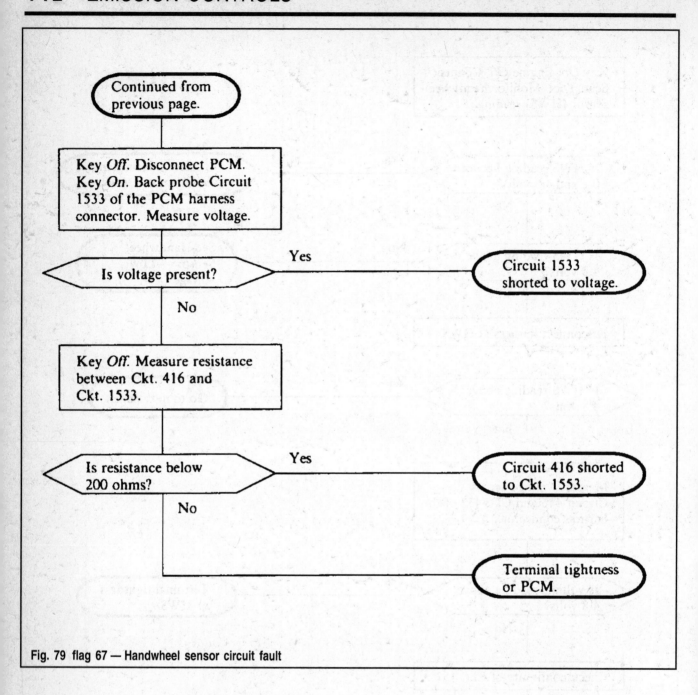

Fig. 79 flag 67 — Handwheel sensor circuit fault

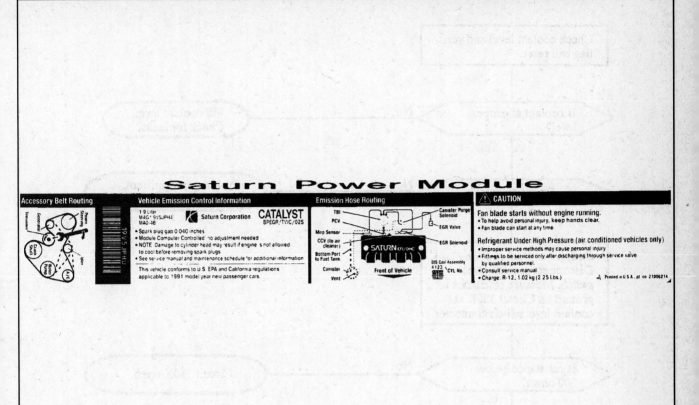

Fig. 80 flag 67 — Handwheel sensor circuit fault

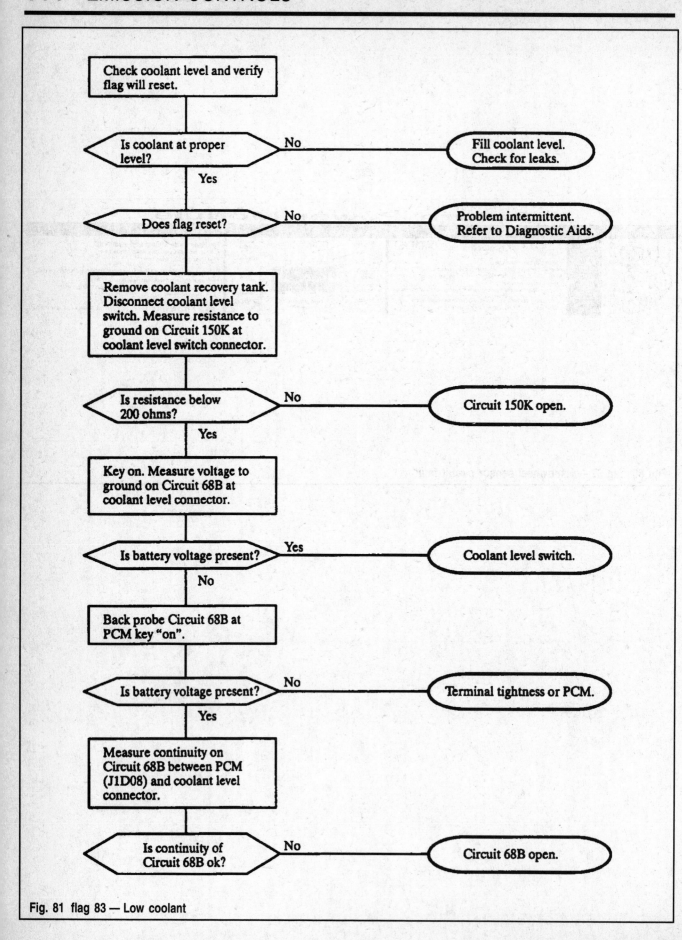

Fig. 81 flag 83 — Low coolant

VACUUM DIAGRAMS

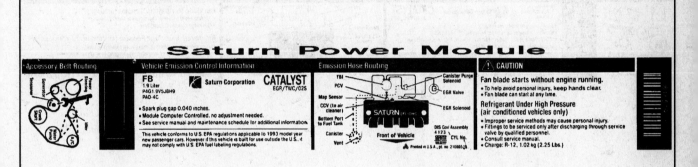

Fig. 82 Vehicle emission label — 1991 SOHC engine

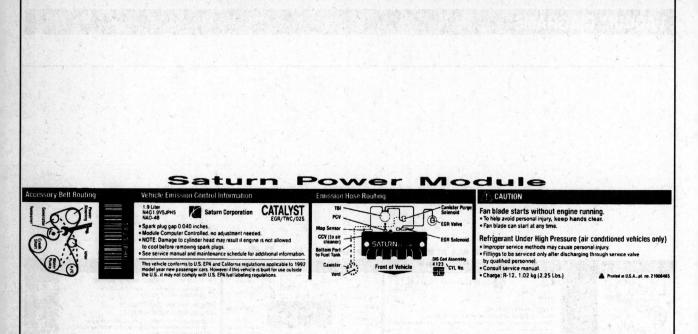

Fig. 83 Vehicle emission label — 1992 SOHC engine

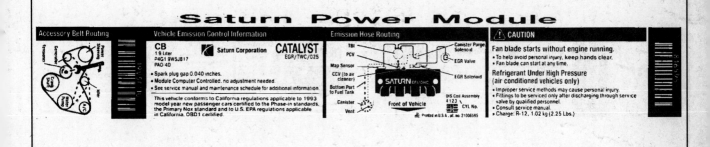

Saturn Power Module

Accessory Belt Routing

Vehicle Emission Control Information

CB
1.9 Liter
P4G1 9W5JB17
PAO-4D

Saturn Corporation

CATALYST
EGR/TWC/O2S

- Spark plug gap 0.040 inches.
- Module Computer Controlled, no adjustment needed.
- See service manual and maintenance schedule for additional information.

This vehicle conforms to California regulations applicable to 1993 model year new passenger cars certified to the Phase-in standards, the Primary Nox standard and to U.S. EPA regulations applicable in California. OBD1 certified.

Emission Hose Routing

TBI
PCV
Map Sensor
CCV (to air cleaner)
Bottom Port to Fuel Tank
Canister
Vent

Canister Purge Solenoid
EGR Valve
EGR Solenoid

SATURN EFI/OHC

Front of Vehicle

DIS Coil Assembly
4 1 2 3
CYL No.

Printed in U.S.A., pt. no. 21006595

⚠ CAUTION

Fan blade starts without engine running.
- To help avoid personal injury, keep hands clear.
- Fan blade can start at any time.

Refrigerant Under High Pressure (air conditioned vehicles only)
- Improper service methods may cause personal injury.
- Fittings to be serviced only after discharging through service valve by qualified personnel.
- Consult service manual.
- Charge: R-12, 1.02 kg (2.25 Lbs.)

Fig. 84 Vehicle emission label — 1993 SOHC engine (Federal)

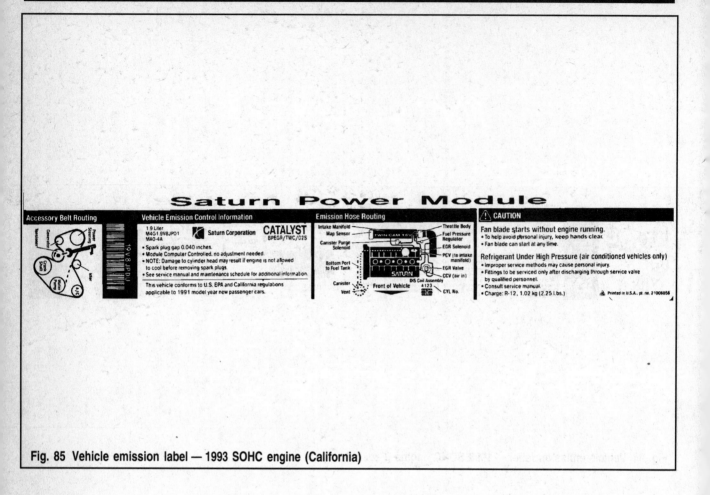

Fig. 85 Vehicle emission label — 1993 SOHC engine (California)

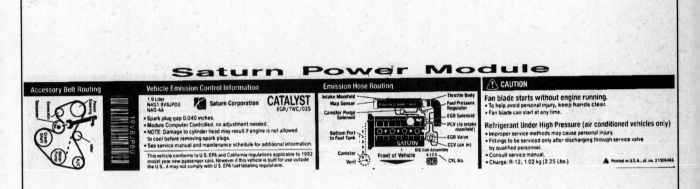

Fig. 86 Vehicle emission label — 1991 DOHC engine

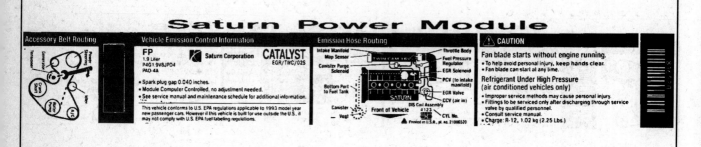

Fig. 87 Vehicle emission label — 1993 DOHC engine (Federal)

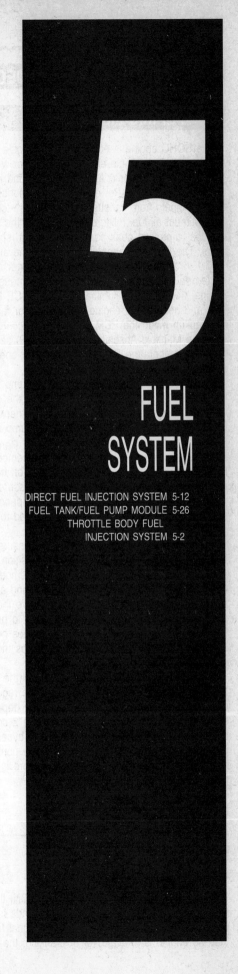

5

FUEL
SYSTEM

THROTTLE BODY FUEL INJECTION SYSTEM

General Information

The SOHC engine is equipped with Throttle Body Injection (TBI) and uses a single electric fuel injector which is mounted in the throttle body unit. All fuel injection and ignition functions are controlled by the Powertrain Control Module (PCM). It accepts inputs from various sensors and switches, calculates the optimum air/fuel mixture and operates the various output devices to provide peak performance within specific emissions limits. The PCM will attempt to maintain the air/fuel mixture of 14.7:1 in order to optimize catalytic converter operation. If a system failure occurs that is not serious enough to stop the engine, the PCM will illuminate the SERVICE ENGINE SOON light and operate the engine in a backup or fail-safe mode. In the backup mode the PCM delivers fuel according to inputs from the Manifold Absolute Pressure (MAP) sensor and the Coolant Temperature Sensor (CTS). Other operating modes in the PCM program are described later.

Fuel is supplied to the engine from a pump mounted in the fuel tank. The fuel pump module includes the gauge/sending unit, which can be replaced separately. Otherwise, the module must be replaced as an assembly. The pump is operated through a relay mounted in the Instrument Panel Junction Block (IPJB), which is located under the center of the instrument panel on the passenger's side of the vehicle. A check valve in the tank unit maintains pressure in the system for a period of time after the engine is stopped in order to aid hot starting. The fuel tank must be removed to remove the pump module.

Other system components include a pressure regulator, an Idle Air Control (IAC) valve, a Throttle Position Sensor (TPS), Air Temperature Sensor (ATS), Coolant Temperature Sensor (CTS), a power steering pressure switch and an oxygen sensor. The fuel injector is a solenoid valve that the PCM pulses on and off many times per second to promote proper fuel atomization. The pulse width determines how long the injector is ON each cycle and this regulates the amount of fuel supplied to the engine.

The system pressure regulator is part of the throttle body. Intake manifold pressure is supplied to the regulator diaphragm, making system pressure partly dependent on engine load. The idle air control valve is a 2 coil stepper motor that controls the amount of air allowed to bypass the throttle plate. With this valve the PCM can closely control idle speed even when the engine is cold or when there is a high engine load at idle.

OPERATING MODES

▶ See Figure 1

Starting Mode

When the ignition switch is first turned **ON**, the fuel pump relay is energized by the PCM for 2 seconds to build system pressure. When the crankshaft position signal tells the PCM that the engine is turning over or cranking, the pump will run continuously. In the start mode, the PCM checks the MAP sensor, TPS and CTS to determine the best air/fuel ratio for starting. Ratios could range from 1.5:1 at -33°F (-36°C), to 14.6:1 at 201°F (94°C).

Clear Flood Mode

If the engine becomes flooded, it can be cleared by opening the accelerator to the full throttle position. When the throttle is open all the way and engine rpm is less than 400, the PCM will close the fuel injector while the engine is turning over in order to clear the engine of excess fuel. If throttle position is reduced below about 75 percent, the PCM will return to the start mode.

Open Loop Mode

When the engine first starts and engine speed rises above 400 rpm, the PCM operates in the Open Loop mode until specific parameters are met. Fuel requirements are calculated based on information from the MAP sensor and CTS.

Closed Loop Mode

When the correct parameters are met, the PCM will use O_2 sensor output and adjust the air/fuel mixture in order to maintain a narrow band of exhaust gas oxygen concentration. When the PCM is correcting and adjusting fuel mixture based on the oxygen sensor signal along with the other sensors, this is known as feedback air/fuel ratio control. The PCM will shift into Closed Loop mode when:

• Oxygen sensor output voltage is varies, indicating that the sensor has warmed up to operating temperature, minimum 600°F (318°C)
• Coolant temperature is above 68°F (20°C)
• The PCM has received an rpm signal greater than 400 for more than 1 minute
• On 1992-93 vehicles, a change in throttle position is detected

Acceleration Mode

If the throttle position and manifold pressure are quickly increased, the PCM will provide extra fuel for smooth acceleration.

Deceleration Mode

As the throttle closes and the manifold pressure decreases, fuel flow is reduced by the PCM. If both conditions remain for a specific number of engine revolutions, the PCM decides fuel flow is not needed and stops the flow by shutting off the injector.

Fuel Cut-Off Mode

When the PCM is receiving a Vehicle Speed Sensor (VSS) signal and rpm goes above 6750, the injectors are shut off to prevent engine overspeed. The PCM will also shut off the injectors if the VSS signal is 0 and engine speed reaches 4000 rpm.

Battery Low Mode

If the PCM detects a low battery, it will increase injector pulse width to compensate for the low voltage and provide proper fuel delivery. It will also increase idle speed to increase alternator output.

Field Service Mode

When terminals A and B of the ALDL are jumpered with the engine running, the PCM will enter the Field Service Mode. If the engine is running in Open Loop Mode, the SERVICE ENGINE SOON light will flash quickly, about 2½ times per second. When the engine is in Closed Loop Mode, the light will flash only about once per second. If the light stays OFF most of the time in Close Loop, the engine is running lean. If the light is ON most of the time, the engine is running rich.

Relieving Fuel System Pressure

▶ See Figure 2

1. Unless battery voltage is necessary for testing, disconnect the negative battery cable. This will prevent the fuel pump from running and causing a fuel spill through the disconnected components if the ignition key is accidentally turned on.
2. Remove the air cleaner assembly.
3. Wrap a shop rag around the fuel test port fitting, located at the lower front of the engine, then remove the cap and connect the fuel pressure gauge tool SA9127E or equivalent.

4. Install the bleed hose from the pressure gauge into an approved container and open the valve to bleed the system pressure.
5. After the pressure is bleed, remove the gauge from the test port and recap it.
6. Install the air cleaner assembly
7. After repairs, connect the negative battery cable and prime the fuel system as follows:

   a. Turn the ignition ON for 5 seconds, then OFF for 10 seconds.
   b. Repeat the ON/OFF cycle 2 more times.
   c. Crank the engine until it starts.
   d. If the engine does not readily start, repeat Steps A-C.
   e. Run the engine and check for leaks.

Electric Fuel Pump

REMOVAL & INSTALLATION

Fuel pump replacement or service requires the removal of the fuel tank. Refer to the fuel tank procedure found later in this section for the proper pump replacement techniques.

TESTING

Pump Pressure Test

A trouble Code 44 or 45 could indicate pressure regulator or system pressure problems. The pump pressure test may be

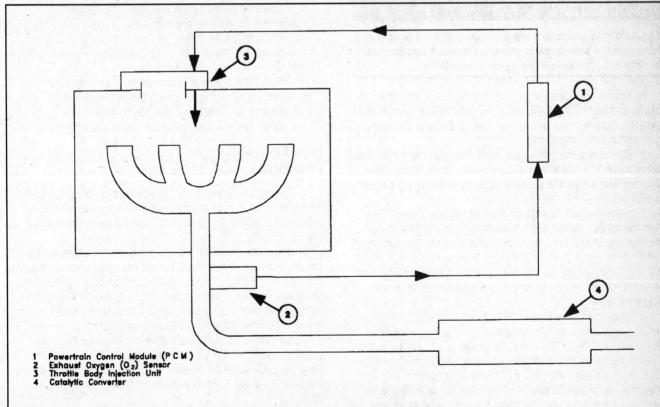

1 Powertrain Control Module (P C M)
2 Exhaust Oxygen (O₂) Sensor
3 Throttle Body Injection Unit
4 Catalytic Converter

Fig. 1 Data flow schematic for closed loop fuel injection control — SOHC engine

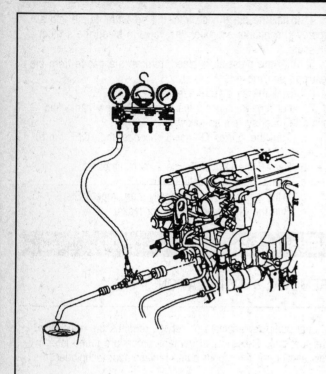

Fig. 2 Connecting a gauge with bleeder to the test port on the fuel supply line

used to determine if the fuel pump is delivering fuel at the proper pressure or if the pump must be replaced.

✳✳CAUTION

The following procedure will produce a small fuel spill and fumes. Make sure there is proper ventilation and be sure to take the appropriate fire safety precautions.

1. Locate the pressure test port on the fuel supply line, below and behind the EGR valve. Properly relieve any residual system pressure, then remove the fuel gauge from the test port and install the port cap.

2. Disconnect the fuel supply hose from the metal line, then connect the fuel gauge to the supply hose using a suitable adapter. Make sure the gauge is capable of reading 0-100 psi (0-690 kPa).

3. Verify that the fuel gauge shut-off valve is closed, then turn the ignition switch **ON** without starting the engine to run the fuel pump and build pressure in the system. The pump will only run for about 2 seconds without the engine running. Bleed the air out of the gauge line and cycle the fuel pump again as required to fully bleed the gauge and establish an accurate pressure reading.

4. Once maximum pressure has been achieved, allow the reading to stabilize for 30 seconds. Normal pump pressure is 58-94 psi (400-650 kPa). Allow the gauge to sit undisturbed for five minutes after the pump stops running, pressure should leak down no more than 6-8 psi (41-55 kPa) from the maximum stabilized reading. This is a fuel pump pressure test only and the results will differ from the system pressure test.

5. Bleed off the fuel system pressure and repeat the test a minimum of 2 additional times to be certain of accurate results.

6. Install the bleed hose into an approved container, then bleed the fuel system pressure and remove the gauge from the line. Lubricate the male end of the fitting with clean engine oil and reconnect the fuel line.

System Pressure Test

✳✳CAUTION

The following procedure will produce a small fuel spill and fumes. Make sure there is proper ventilation and be sure to take the appropriate fire safety precautions.

1. Remove the air cleaner or air intake tube assembly for access, then connect fuel pressure gauge SA9127E or an equivalent gauge capable of 0-100 psi (0-690 kPa) to the fuel system test port.

2. Close the fuel gauge shut-off valve. Turn the ignition switch **ON** to run the fuel pump and build pressure in the system, then turn the ignition **OFF** again. The pump will only run for about 2 seconds without the engine running. Bleed the air out of the gauge line and cycle the fuel pump again as required to fully bleed the gauge.

3. Start and run the engine to normal operating temperature, then check the gauge for proper operating pressure. At both idle and 3000 rpm, system pressure should be 26-31 psi (179 — 214 kPa) for the throttle body injection system.

4. Shut the ignition **OFF** and allow the system to leak down. After about 5 minutes with the pump not running, pressure should leak down no more than 6-8 psi (41-55 kPa).

5. If pressure readings are low check the following:
   a. Check for bent or pinched lines.
   b. Replace the fuel filter.
   c. Check for proper fuel pump pressure.
   d. Check the fuel pump for flow.
   e. Substitute a known good fuel pressure regulator.

6. If pressure readings are high check the following:
   a. Inspect for a restricted fuel return lines.
   b. Substitute a known good fuel pressure regulator.

Pump Electrical Test
▶ See Figures 3, 4, 5, 27 and 28

1. On the Instrument Panel Junction Block (IPJB), located inside the vehicle beneath the center of the instrument panel, check the condition of fuse No. 12, the 10 Amp fuel pump fuse.

2. Locate and remove the fuel pump relay located to the top left of relays in the IPJB. To test the relay, another relay from the same block may be substituted, as they are identical. Using a voltmeter or test light, check for power to the fuel pump relay. With the ignition switch **ON** or **OFF**, there should be 12 volts between terminal 30 and ground.

3. Connect a voltmeter or test light to terminal **85** and a suitable ground. When the ignition switch is first turned **ON**, there will be voltage for about 2 seconds. This is power for the relay coil from the PCM. If there is no voltage, the PCM may be faulty.

4. Locate the fuel pump wiring harness connector in the trunk. When terminals **87** and **30** are jumpered together in the

relay socket, there should be 12 volts at terminal **A** on the connector. The other terminals are for the fuel gauge. The pump ground wire connects directly from the pump to chassis ground.

Throttle Body Unit

▶ See Figure 6

The throttle body injection unit is made up of 2 major casting assemblies. The top piece, or fuel meter body, contains the fuel injector and the pressure regulator. The bottom piece, or throttle body, contains the throttle valve, IAC valve, TPS, and the vacuum manifold or tubes which supply manifold vacuum to various engine control solenoids.

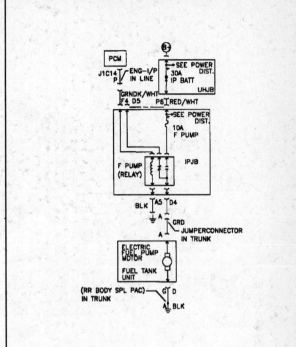

Fig. 5 Schematic of the fuel pump power supply — all Saturn vehicles

REMOVAL & INSTALLATION

▶ See Figures 7, 8 and 9

1. Disconnect the negative battery cable and remove the air cleaner assembly.

2. Properly relieve the fuel system pressure. Refer to the procedure in this Section.

3. Unplug the electrical connectors from the following components:

   a. Idle Air Control (IAC) valve
   b. Throttle Position Sensor (TPS)
   c. Fuel injector

4. Remove the grommet (with the wires) from the throttle body.

5. Disconnect the throttle cable from the accelerator lever on the throttle body.

6. Label and disconnect the vacuum lines from the throttle body fittings.

7. Using a backup wrench to prevent stress and damage to the fittings, remove the fuel supply and return lines. Remove the O-rings from the line nuts and discard.

8. Remove the throttle body unit attaching bolts, then carefully remove the throttle body from the intake manifold.

9. Remove and discard the old gasket from the mating surface, being careful not to score the intake manifold surface. Place and clean rag or cloth over the opening to prevent debris from entering the intake manifold.

   To install:

10. Thoroughly clean any remaining gasket material from the intake manifold and remove any old threadlock from the throttle body attaching bolt threads. Inspect the intake manifold

Fig. 3 Remove the access panel from the base of the dashboard center console in order to examine the fuel pump fuse and relay

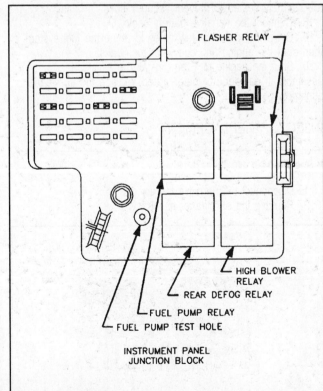

Fig. 4 The fuel pump relay is to the top left of the relays located in the IPJB — all Saturn vehicles

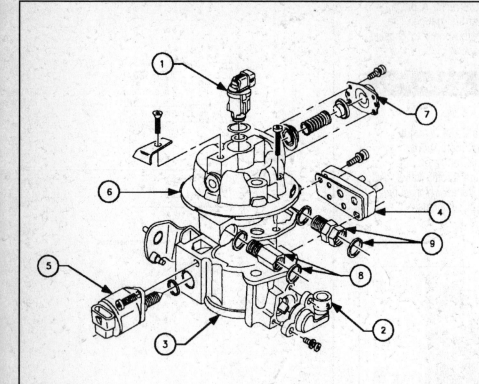

1	Fuel Injector Assembly
2	Throttle Position Sensor (TPS)
3	Throttle Body Assembly
4	Tube Module Assembly
5	Idle Air Control (IAC) Valve
6	Fuel Meter Assembly
7	Pressure Regulator Cover Assembly
8	Fuel Inlet
9	Fuel Return

Fig. 6 Exploded view of the throttle body injection unit — SOHC engine

opening for any loose parts or debris and make sure the sealing surfaces are not scored or damaged.

11. Position a new throttle body unit gasket onto the manifold flange, then install the unit. Apply a coat of Loctite® 242 or an equivalent threadlock to the attaching bolts, then install the bolts and tighten to 24 ft. lbs. (33 Nm).

12. If removed, install the fuel meter body attaching screws.

13. Even if they were not removed, torque the fuel meter body attaching screws to 35 inch lbs. (4 Nm).

14. Install new O-rings to the fuel supply and return lines, then install the lines and tighten to 19 ft. lbs. (25 Nm) using a backup wrench.

15. Connect the throttle cable to the accelerator lever on the throttle body. Make sure the cable does not hold the lever open when the accelerator pedal is in the released position.

16. Install the electrical connectors to the TPS, IAC valve and the fuel injector.

17. Connect the vacuum hoses from the EGR solenoid, canister purge solenoid and the MAP sensor to the TBI unit vacuum ports, as labeled during removal. Make sure the hoses are securely seated to prevent vacuum leaks.

18. Connect the negative battery cable.

19. Cycle the ignition a few times to prime the fuel system, then start the engine and check for fuel leaks.

20. Shut the engine **OFF** and install the air cleaner assembly. If damaged or deteriorated, replace the air cleaner assembly gasket.

INJECTOR REPLACEMENT

▶ **See Figures 10, 11 and 12**

1. Disconnect the negative battery cable.
2. Remove the air cleaner assembly.

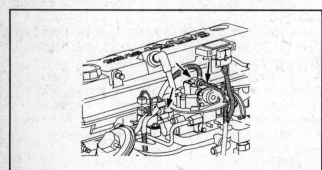

Fig. 7 Unplug the electrical connectors at these locations — SOHC engine

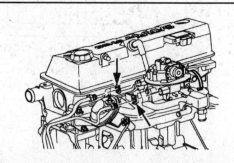

Fig. 8 Remove and discard the O-rings from fuel line nuts — SOHC engine

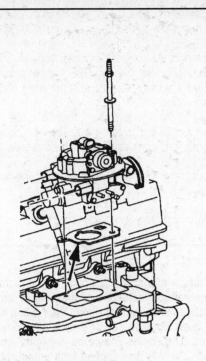

Fig. 9 Removing the throttle body assembly from the intake manifold — SOHC engine

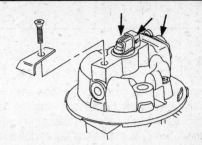

Fig. 12 Before installing the injector retaining bracket and screw, make sure the electrical connector is pointing toward the pressure regulator — SOHC engine

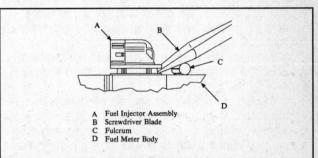

A   Fuel Injector Assembly
B   Screwdriver Blade
C   Fulcrum
D   Fuel Meter Body

Fig. 10 Using a smooth fulcrum and a small prybar, remove the fuel injector from the throttle body assembly — SOHC engine

3. Properly relieve the fuel system pressure. Refer to the procedure in this Section.

4. Unplug the injector electrical connector.

5. Remove the injector retaining screw and bracket.

6. Using a smooth fulcrum and a suitable prybar, carefully pry the injector out of the throttle body. Make sure the electrical connector and nozzle are protected from damage during removal.

7. Remove and discard the upper and lower injector O-rings, then inspect the injector for dirt or contamination. The injector may be cleaned using safety glasses and compressed air, but the screen may not be removed from the injector. If the injector replacement is necessary, be sure to use an identical part.

To install:

8. Install the new O-rings and lubricate with clean engine oil. Be sure the upper O-ring is in the injector groove and the lower ring is properly installed in the fuel meter body cavity.

9. Install the injector, pushing it straight into the injector cavity with the electrical connector facing toward the fuel pressure regulator.

10. Install the retaining bracket. Coat the screw with Loctite® 242, or equivalent threadlock, then install and tighten the screw to 35 inch lbs. (3 Nm).

11. Install the injector wiring harness, then connect and the negative battery cable.

12. Prime the fuel system by cycling the ignition switch, then start the engine and check for leaks.

13. Shut the engine **OFF** and install the air cleaner assembly.

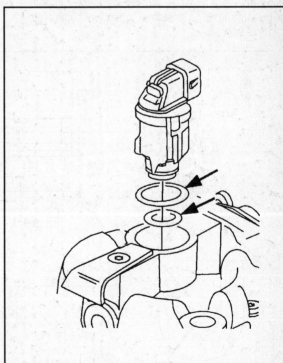

Fig. 11 Replace the upper and lower injector O-rings any time the injector is removed — SOHC engine

INJECTOR TESTING

◆ **See Figure 13**

Electrical Test

1. Unplug the injector connector and use an ohmmeter to check the resistance of the injector coil. It should be 1-2 ohms.

2. Connect a Noid light (or an equivalent low voltage injector harness tester) to the injector connector terminal. Position the harness so the light can be seen from the driver's seat. Then operate the starter and observe the Noid light.

3. If the Noid does not illuminate at all, check for power to the injector(s). The injectors receive power through the pink/black wire from the 7.5 Amp "INJ" fuse in the underhood junction box, any time the ignition switch is on. The PCM operates the injectors by completing the ground circuit through the light blue wire.

4. If the test light stays on steadily, check for a short to ground of the wire between the injector connector and the PCM.

5. A pulsing Noid light does not necessarily indicate enough voltage to properly operate the fuel injector. If it is still questionable whether or not an injector is pulsing, connect a known good injector to the circuit and tightly grip the injector while a friend cranks the engine. If injector pulses are felt, the circuit is good.

Pressure Test

1. Connect the test gauge and run the fuel pump and system pressure tests as described in the fuel pump tests earlier in this section.

2. Disconnect the fuel return hose from the metal line and cap the line carefully, as full fuel pressure may go as high as 94 psi (650 kPa).

3. Disconnect the pressure regulator vacuum line.

4. Cycle the ignition **ON** and **OFF**, without starting the engine, to build system pressure to a minimum of 58 psi (400 kPa) on the gauge.

5. Look into the throttle body. If there is a leak, there will be drops of fuel on the throttle plate. The leak could from be the injector O-ring, the injector tip or the pressure regulator diaphragm.

6. If necessary, remove and examine the injector, a leak will be obvious.

BASE IDLE SPEED ADJUSTMENT

◆ **See Figures 14, 15 and 16**

➡**The minimum idle speed is preset at the factory and requires no periodic adjustment, checking or other service. Adjustments should be performed ONLY when the throttle body has been replaced and/or proper idle speed can not be obtained. The engine should be at normal operating temperature, the A/C and cooling fans should be OFF when making adjustments.**

1. Before making any adjustments, clean the throttle body bore with a clean rag and carburetor cleaner that does not contain methyl ethyl ketone. Then check the idle speed to be sure adjustment is necessary. Proper idle speeds are as follows:

 a. SOHC engine with manual transaxle in **N** 700-800 rpm.

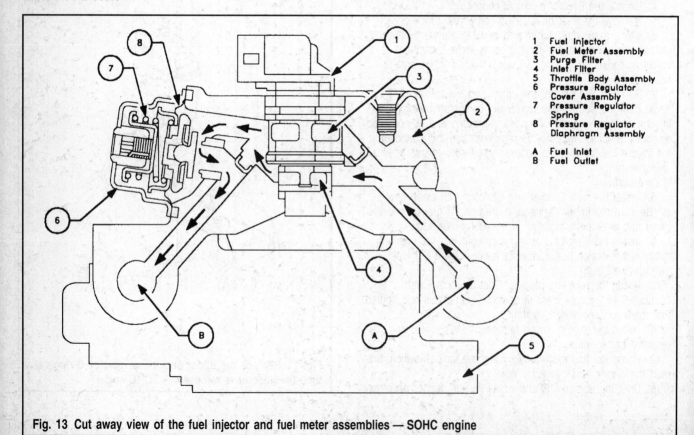

```
1  Fuel Injector
2  Fuel Meter Assembly
3  Purge Filter
4  Inlet Filter
5  Throttle Body Assembly
6  Pressure Regulator
   Cover Assembly
7  Pressure Regulator
   Spring
8  Pressure Regulator
   Diaphragm Assembly

A  Fuel Inlet
B  Fuel Outlet
```

Fig. 13 Cut away view of the fuel injector and fuel meter assemblies — SOHC engine

b. SOHC engine with automatic transaxle in **D** 600-700 rpm

c. SOHC engine with automatic transaxle in **D** and A/C **ON** 725-825 rpm.

2. If adjustment is necessary, block the wheels and apply the parking brake.

3. The IAC pintle must be properly seated in the throttle body. Connect the IAC tester SA9195E or equivalent, to the IAC valve at the throttle body. The Saturn PDT or an equivalent scan tool may attached to the ALDL and used instead of the IAC tester.

4. Remove the idle stop screw plug by piercing it with an awl and applying leverage.

5. Insert the IAC air plug, SA9196E or equivalent, into the throttle body.

6. Connect the Saturn Portable Diagnostic Tool (PDT) or equivalent to the Assembly Line Diagnostic Link (ALDL) in order monitor engine RPM. Start the engine and check the minimum idle speed. Engine idle should be 450-650 rpm.

7. If not within specification adjust the idle screw to obtain an minimum idle speed of 500-600 rpm.

8. Turn the ignition **OFF** and reconnect the IAC electrical connector.

9. Using the Saturn PDT or equivalent scan tool, check the TPS voltage. Do not replace the TPS unless setting is not between 0.35-0.70 volts.

10. Remove the IAC air plug and install the idle stop plug.

11. Start the engine and check for proper idle operation.

12. Shut the engine OFF and remove the PDT or scan tool.

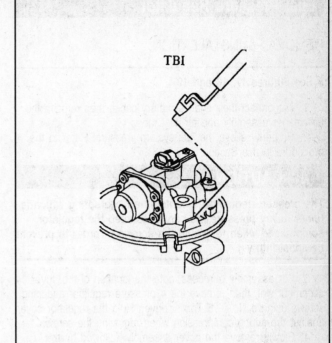

Fig. 16 Install the IAC air plug into the throttle body — SOHC engine

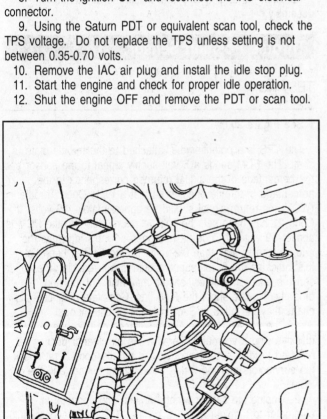

Fig. 14 Connect the IAC valve tester to the valve terminal

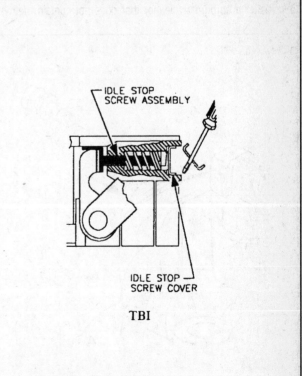

Fig. 15 Pierce the idle stop screw plug with an awl and remove — SOHC engine

Fuel Pressure Regulator

REMOVAL & INSTALLATION

▶ **See Figures 17, 18 and 19**

1. Disconnect the negative battery cable, then remove the air cleaner assembly and air inlet tubes.
2. Properly relieve the fuel system pressure. Refer to the procedure in this Section.

✳✳CAUTION

The pressure regulator is contains a large spring which is under heavy pressure. Be careful to keep the regulator compressed when removing the screws in order to prevent personal injury

3. For assembly purposes, note the location of the cover alignment slot, then remove the 4 pressure regulator attaching screws using a No. T15 Torx® driver. Hold the regulator cover against the spring compression when removing the screws.
4. Slowly remove the cover assembly, followed by the regulator spring. Keep both parts aside to be used with the new diaphragm assembly.
5. Remove the pressure regulator diaphragm assembly, inspect for debris and then discard.

To install:

6. Thoroughly clean the pressure regulator bore and valve seat using a carburetor cleaner that does not contain methyl

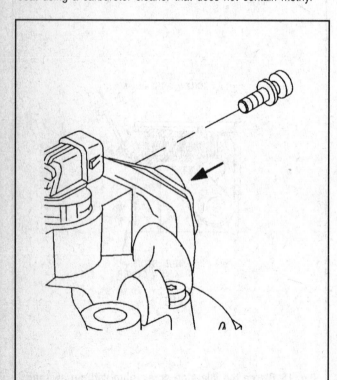

Fig. 17 Remove the regulator cover screws while holding the cover against the spring compression — SOHC engine

ethyl ketone, then allow to air dry for a few minutes before regulator reinstalled

7. Inspect the regulator valve seat which is pressed into the fuel meter body cavity. If necessary use a mirror and a magnifying glass to inspect for small particles in the throttle body bore and seat. If cracks, nicks, debris or pitting are found, the fuel meter body must be replaced.
8. Install the pressure regulator diaphragm assembly, making sure that it is properly seated in the fuel meter body groove.
9. Install the regulator spring seat into the cover, then install the cover over the spring and diaphragm assembly. Align the mounting holes and mounting pins, then align the cover as noted prior to removal.

➡**Use care to properly align the regulator cover. Fuel leaks may be caused by cover misalignment.**

10. Maintain pressure on the regulator, then install the 4 retaining screws. Tighten the screws to 22 inch lbs. (2.5 Nm).
11. Cycle the ignition a few times in order to prime the fuel system, then start the engine and check for leaks.
12. Shut the engine **OFF** and install the air cleaner assembly.

Throttle Position Sensor

TESTING

▶ **See Figure 20**

The TPS is a potentiometer attached to the throttle plate shaft. The PCM sends a 5 volt supply signal to the sensor and the percentage of the signal returned corresponds to the percentage of throttle opening so that a Wide Open Throttle (WOT) the return signal should be approximately 4.9 volts. If Code 21 has been set, the voltage return signal to the PCM is above 4.9 volts. If Code 22 has been set, this indicates the return signal is less than 0.2 volts. If Flag 54 has been set, this indicates the 5 volt supply signal is not reaching the sensors and some other sensors may also not function properly. Trouble shoot the Flag first. Complete diagnostic flow charts may be found in Section No. 4 of this manual.

1. The sensor and the signal voltages can be checked quickly using a voltmeter. Remove the air cleaner ducting as required to locate the sensor on the throttle body. First check the connectors and the wiring between the sensor and the PCM.
2. Unplug the sensor wiring harness and connect an ohmmeter to terminal A and C on the TPS. Resistance should be above 200 ohms and should change smoothly as the throttle is moved.
3. Connect a voltmeter between connector terminal A and ground. With the ignition switch **ON** but the engine not running, there should be 5 volts, which is the supply signal directly from the PCM.
4. Turn the ignition switch **OFF** and check for continuity to ground at terminal B on the connector.
5. Reconnect the wiring and install a diagnostic connector or a Saturn diagnostic probe and a voltmeter on the blue wire to terminal C. With the ignition switch **ON** but the engine not

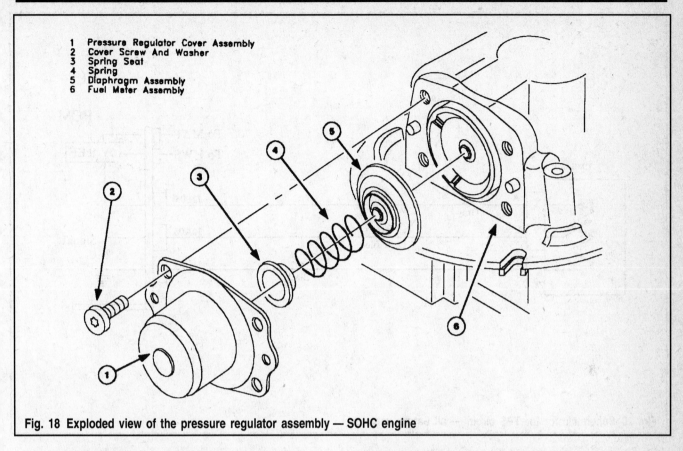

1 Pressure Regulator Cover Assembly
2 Cover Screw And Washer
3 Spring Seat
4 Spring
5 Diaphragm Assembly
6 Fuel Meter Assembly

Fig. 18 Exploded view of the pressure regulator assembly — SOHC engine

running, the voltage should change smoothly from about 0.4-4.7 volts as the throttle is moved from idle to full throttle. A

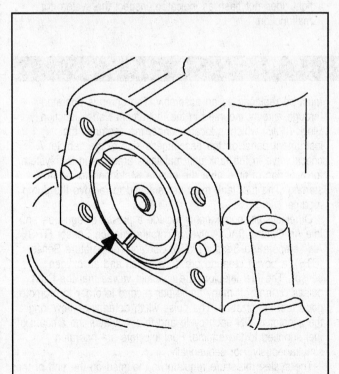

Fig. 19 Inspect the regulator valve seat which is pressed into the fuel meter body cavity. If any damage is found, the fuel meter body must be replaced — SOHC engine

suitable scan tool such as the Saturn PDT may be connected to the ALDL and used to monitor TPS output, instead of attaching a probe to the wire.

REMOVAL & INSTALLATION

▶ See Figure 21

1. If equipped, properly disable the SIR system as follows:
   a. Align the steering wheel so the tires are in the straight-ahead position, then turn the ignition **OFF**.
   b. Remove the 10 amp SIR fuse from the top left of the Instrument Panel Junction Block (IPJB).
   c. Remove the Connector Position Assurance (CPA), then disconnect the yellow 2-way SIR connector at the base of the steering column.
2. Disconnect the negative battery cable and remove the air cleaner assembly.
3. Unplug the electrical connector from the TPS.
4. Remove the TPS retaining bolts, then remove the sensor from the throttle body.

To install:

5. Make sure the throttle valve is closed, then install the TPS to the throttle shaft.
6. Rotate the sensor counterclockwise to align the mounting holes, then install the retaining bolts and tighten to 18 inch lbs. (2 Nm).
7. Connect the wiring harness to the sensor.
8. Install the air cleaner assembly and connect the negative battery cable.
9. If equipped, enable the SIR system as follows:
   a. Verify the ignition switch is **OFF**.

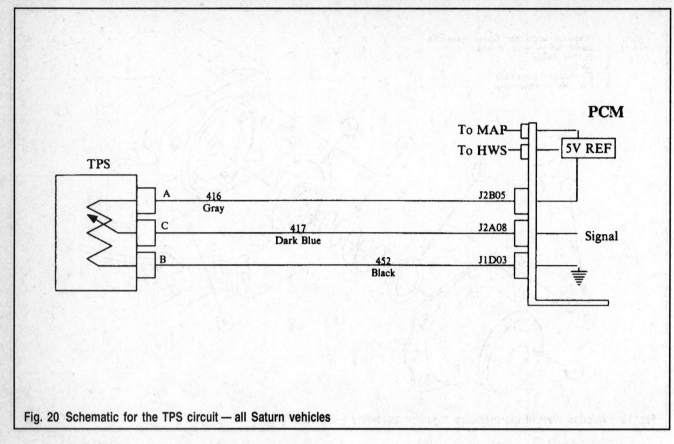

Fig. 20 Schematic for the TPS circuit — all Saturn vehicles

b. Reconnect the SIR electrical connector at the base of the steering column.

c. Install the CPA device to the connector.

d. Install the SIR fuse to the IPJB and install the fuse box cover.

e. Turn the ignition **ON** and verify that the AIR BAG indicator lamp flashes 7-9 times, then extinguishes. If the light does not flash as indicated, inspect the system for malfunction.

DIRECT FUEL INJECTION SYSTEM

General Information

▶ See Figures 22 and 23

The DOHC engine is equipped with Multi-port Fuel Injection (MFI) and is equipped with Multi-port Fuel Injection (MFI) that uses 1 injector for each cylinder. All fuel injection and ignition functions are controlled by the Powertrain Control Module (PCM). It accepts inputs from various sensors and switches, calculates the optimum air/fuel mixture and operates the various output devices to provide peak performance within specific emissions limits. The PCM will attempt to maintain the air/fuel mixture of 14.6:1 in order to optimize catalytic converter operation. If a system failure occurs that is not serious enough to stop the engine, the PCM will illuminate the SERVICE ENGINE SOON light and operate the engine in a backup or fail-safe mode. In the backup mode the PCM delivers fuel according to inputs from the Manifold Absolute Pressure (MAP) sensor and the Coolant Temperature Sensor (CTS). Other operating modes are in the PCM program and described later.

Fuel is supplied to the engine from a pump mounted in the fuel tank. The fuel pump module includes the gauge/sending unit, which can be replaced separately. Otherwise, the module must be replaced as an assembly. The pump is operated through a relay mounted in the Instrument Panel Junction Block (IPJB) which is located under the center of the instrument panel on the passenger's side of the vehicle. A check valve in the tank unit maintains pressure in the system for a period of time after the engine is stopped to aid hot starting. The fuel tank must be removed to remove the pump module.

Other system components include a pressure regulator, an Idle Air Control (IAC) valve, a Throttle Position Sensor (TPS), Air Temperature Sensor (ATS), Coolant Temperature Sensor (CTS), a power steering pressure switch and an oxygen sensor. The fuel injectors are solenoid valves that the PCM pulses on and off many times per second in order to promote good fuel atomization. The pulse width determines how long the injector is ON each cycle and this regulates the amount of fuel supplied to the engine. Fuel injectors are operated simultaneously, not sequentially.

The system pressure regulator is mounted on the end of the fuel rail that feeds the injectors. Intake manifold pressure is supplied to the regulator diaphragm, making system pressure partly dependent on engine load. The idle air control valve is a 2 coil stepper motor that controls the amount of air allowed to

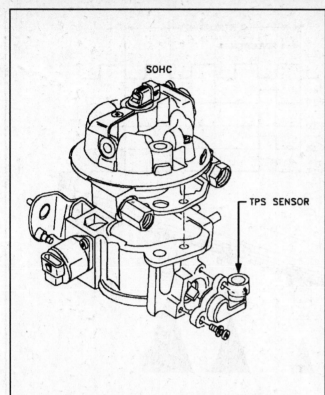

Fig. 21 Throttle position sensor mounting — SOHC engine

bypass the throttle plate. With this valve the PCM can closely control idle speed even when the engine is cold or when there is a high engine load at idle.

OPERATING MODES

▶ See Figure 24

Starting Mode

When the ignition switch is first turned **ON**, the fuel pump relay is energized by the PCM for 2 seconds to build system pressure. When the crankshaft position signal tells the PCM that the engine is turning over or cranking, the pump will run continuously. In the start mode, the PCM checks the TPS and CTS to determine the best air/fuel ratio for starting. Ratios could range from 0.8:1 at -40°F (-40°C), to 14.6:1 at 220°F (104°C).

Clear Flood Mode

If the engine becomes flooded, it can be cleared by opening the accelerator to the full throttle position. When the throttle is open all the way and engine rpm is less than 400, the PCM will close the fuel injectors while the engine is turning over in order to clear the engine of excess fuel. If throttle position is reduced below about 75 percent, the PCM will return to the start mode.

Open Loop Mode

When the engine first starts and engine speed rises above 400 rpm, the PCM operates in the Open Loop mode until

specific parameters are met. Fuel requirements are calculated based on information from the MAP sensor and CTS.

Closed Loop Mode

When the correct parameters are met, the PCM will use O_2 sensor output and adjust the air/fuel mixture in order to maintain a narrow band of exhaust gas oxygen concentration. When the PCM is correcting and adjusting fuel mixture based on the oxygen sensor signal along with the other sensors, this is known as feedback air/fuel ratio control.

The PCM will shift into Closed Loop mode when:
Oxygen sensor output voltage is varies, indicating that the sensor has warmed up to operating temperature, minimum 600°F (318°C)

Coolant temperature is above 68°F (20°C)

The PCM has received an rpm signal greater than 400 for more than 1 minute

1992 and later vehicles, also require a change in throttle position.

Acceleration Mode

If the throttle position and manifold pressure are quickly increased, the PCM will provide extra fuel for smooth acceleration.

Deceleration Mode

As the throttle closes and the manifold pressure decreases, fuel flow is reduced by the PCM. If both conditions remain for a specific number of engine revolutions, the PCM decides fuel flow is not needed and stops the flow by shutting off the injectors.

Fuel Cut-Off Mode

When the PCM is receiving a Vehicle Speed Sensor (VSS) signal and rpm goes above 6750, the injectors are shut off to prevent engine overspeed. The PCM will also shut off the injectors if the VSS signal is 0 and engine speed reaches 4000 rpm.

Battery Low Mode

If the PCM detects a low battery, it will increase injector pulse width to compensate for the low voltage and provide proper fuel delivery. It will also increase idle speed to increase alternator output.

Field Service Mode

When terminals A and B of the ALDL are jumpered with the engine running, the PCM will enter the Field Service Mode. If the engine is running in Open Loop Mode, the SERVICE ENGINE SOON light will flash quickly, about 2½ times per second. When the engine is in Closed Loop Mode, the light will flash only about once per second. If the light stays OFF most of the time in Close Loop, the engine is running lean. If the light is ON most of the time, the engine is running rich.

Relieving Fuel System Pressure
▶ See Figure 25

1. Unless battery voltage is necessary for testing, disconnect the negative battery cable. This will prevent the fuel pump from running and causing a fuel spill through the

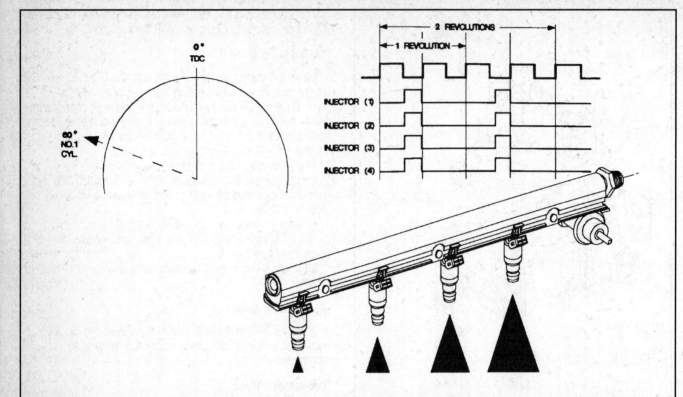

Fig. 22 All fuel injectors are pulsed once per revolution, each time the No. 1 cylinder is 60 degrees before TDC — DOHC engine

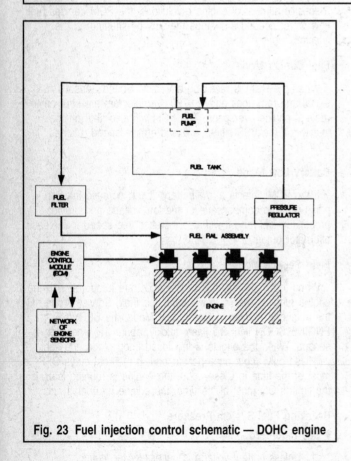

Fig. 23 Fuel injection control schematic — DOHC engine

disconnected components if the ignition key is accidentally turned **ON**.

2. Remove the air intake tube and resonator.

3. Wrap a shop rag around the fuel test port fitting, located at the lower front of the engine, then remove the cap and connect the fuel pressure gauge tool SA9127E or equivalent.

4. Install the bleed hose from the pressure gauge into an approved container and open the valve to bleed the system pressure.

5. After the pressure is bleed, remove the gauge from the test port and recap it.

6. Install the air intake duct and resonator tube.

7. After repairs, connect the negative battery cable and prime the fuel system as follows:

    a. Turn the ignition ON for 5 seconds, then OFF for 10 seconds.

    b. Repeat the ON/OFF cycle 2 more times.

    c. Crank the engine until it starts. If the engine does not readily start, repeat Steps A through C.

    d. Run the engine and check for leaks.

Electric Fuel Pump

REMOVAL & INSTALLATION

Fuel pump replacement or service requires the removal of the fuel tank. Refer to the fuel tank procedure found later in this section for the proper pump replacement techniques.

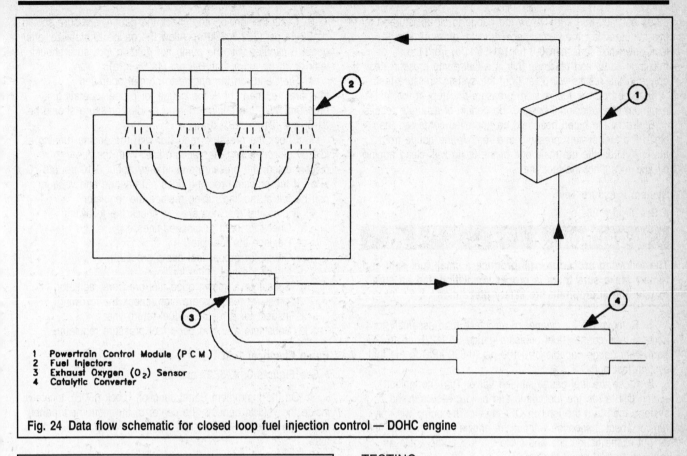

Fig. 24 Data flow schematic for closed loop fuel injection control — DOHC engine

1 Powertrain Control Module (P C M)
2 Fuel Injectors
3 Exhaust Oxygen (O_2) Sensor
4 Catalytic Converter

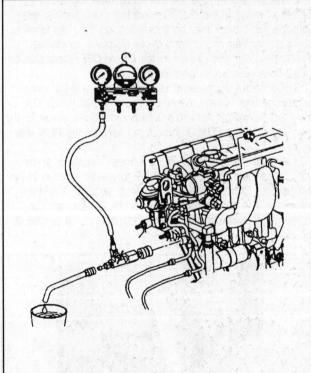

Fig. 25 Connecting a gauge with bleeder to the test port on the fuel supply line

TESTING

Fuel Pump Pressure Test

A trouble Code 44 or 45 could indicate pressure regulator or system pressure problems. The pump pressure test may be used to determine if the fuel pump is delivering fuel at the proper pressure or if the pump must be replaced.

⁕⁕CAUTION

The following procedure will produce a small fuel spill and fumes. Make sure there is proper ventilation and be sure to take the appropriate fire safety precautions.

1. Locate the pressure test port on the fuel supply line, below and behind the EGR valve. Properly relieve any residual system pressure, then remove the fuel gauge from the test port and install the port cap.

2. Disconnect the fuel supply hose from the metal line, then connect the fuel gauge to the supply hose using a suitable adapter. Make sure the gauge is capable of reading 0-100 psi (0-690 kPa).

3. Verify that the fuel gauge shut-off valve is closed, then turn the ignition switch **ON** without starting the engine to run the fuel pump and build pressure in the system. The pump will only run for about 2 seconds without the engine running. Bleed the air out of the gauge line and cycle the fuel pump again as required to fully bleed the gauge and establish an accurate pressure reading.

4. Once maximum pressure has been achieved, allow the reading to stabilize for 30 seconds. Normal pump pressure is

58-94 psi (400-650 kPa). Allow the gauge to sit undisturbed for five minutes after the pump stops running, pressure should leak down no more than 6-8 psi (41-55 kPa) from the maximum stabilized reading. This is a fuel pump pressure test only and the results will differ from the system pressure test.

5. Bleed off the fuel system pressure and repeat the test a minimum of 2 additional times to be certain of accurate results.

6. Install the bleed hose into an approved container, then bleed the fuel system pressure and remove the gauge from the line. Lubricate the male end of the fitting with clean engine oil and reconnect the fuel line.

System Pressure Test

▶ See Figure 26

✳✳CAUTION

The following procedure will produce a small fuel spill and fumes. Make sure there is proper ventilation and be sure to take the appropriate fire safety precautions.

1. Remove the air cleaner or air intake tube assembly for access, then connect fuel pressure gauge SA9127E or an equivalent gauge capable of 0-100 psi (0-690 kPa) to the fuel system test port.

2. Close the fuel gauge shut-off valve. Turn the ignition switch **ON** to run the fuel pump and build pressure in the system, then turn the ignition **OFF** again. The pump will only run for about 2 seconds without the engine running. Bleed the air out of the gauge line and cycle the fuel pump again as required to fully bleed the gauge.

Fig. 26 For the DOHC engine, disconnect the vacuum supply from the fuel pressure regulator — if the regulator is good, fuel pressure will vary

3. Cycle the ignition and check the gauge, pressure should be 38-44 psi (262-306 kPa). Allow the gauge to stabilize; after about 5 minutes with the pump not running, pressure should leak down no more than 6-8 psi (41-55 kPa).

4. Start and run the engine to normal operating temperature, then check the gauge for proper operating pressure. With the engine running at idle, pressure should be 31-36 psi (214 — 281 kPa).

5. Check the pressure regulator with the engine running at idle by disconnecting the vacuum line. With the line disconnected, the pressure should vary about 6-10 psi (40-70 kPa). If the pressure reading does not change and vacuum can be felt at the line's inlet, replace the regulator.

6. If pressure readings are low check the following:
   a. Check for bent or pinched lines.
   b. Replace the fuel filter.
   c. Check for proper fuel pump pressure.
   d. Check the fuel pump for flow.
   e. Substitute a known good fuel pressure regulator.

7. If pressure readings are high, check the following:
   a. Inspect for a restricted fuel return line.
   b. Substitute a known good fuel pressure regulator.

Pump Electrical Test

▶ See Figures 3, 4, 5, 27 and 28

1. On the Instrument Panel Junction Block (IPJB), located inside the vehicle beneath the center of the instrument panel, check the condition of fuse No. 12, the 10 Amp fuel pump fuse.

2. Locate and remove the fuel pump relay located to the top left of relays in the IPJB. To test the relay, another relay from the same block may be substituted, as they are identical. Using a voltmeter or test light, check for power to the fuel pump relay. With the ignition switch **ON** or **OFF**, there should be 12 volts between terminal 30 and ground.

3. Connect a voltmeter or test light to terminal 85 and a suitable ground. When the ignition switch is first turned **ON**, there will be voltage for about 2 seconds. This is power for the relay coil from the PCM. If there is no voltage, the PCM may be faulty.

4. Locate the fuel pump wiring harness connector in the trunk. When terminals 87 and 30 are jumpered together in the relay socket, there should be 12 volts at terminal A on the connector. The other terminals are for the fuel gauge. The pump ground wire connects directly from the pump to chassis ground.

Fig. 27 The fuel pump relay is located in the Instrument Panel Junction Block (IPJB)

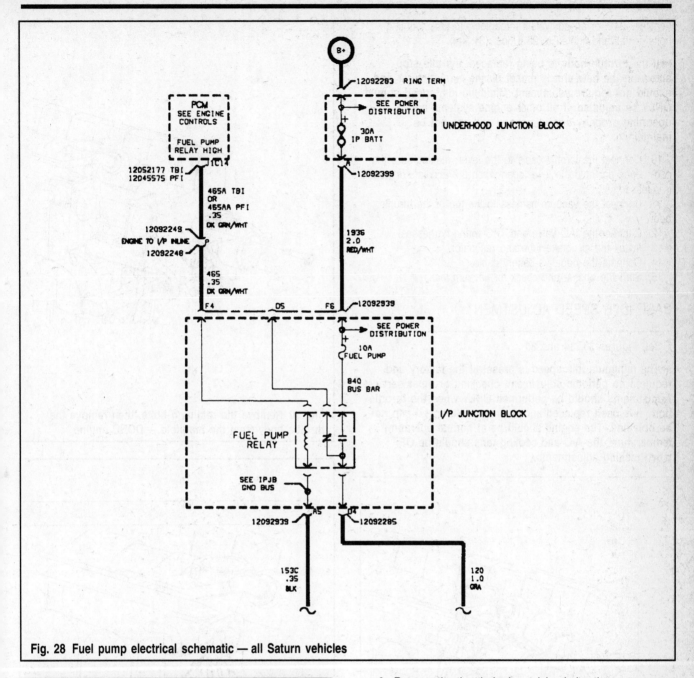

Fig. 28 Fuel pump electrical schematic — all Saturn vehicles

Throttle Body

REMOVAL & INSTALLATION

▶ **See Figures 29, 30, 31 and 32**

1. Disconnect the negative battery cable.
2. Remove the air intake tube and resonator.
3. Unplug the electrical connectors from the Idle Air Control (IAC) valve and the Throttle Position Sensor (TPS).
4. Disconnect the vacuum harness from the top of the throttle body.
5. Disconnect the throttle cable.

6. Remove the throttle body retaining bolts, then remove the throttle body assembly from the side of the intake manifold. Block the intake manifold entry with a clean cloth to prevent dirt or debris from entering and damaging the engine.

To install:

7. Remove the old gasket and discard, then thoroughly clean the gasket mating surfaces. Clean the old Loctite® threadlock from the throttle body mounting bolt threads.
8. Remove the cloth from the intake manifold opening, then inspect the opening for any foreign debris or pieces of gasket material.
9. Position a new flange gasket, then install the throttle body assembly to the intake manifold. Apply a coat of

Loctite® 242, or an equivalent threadlock, to the mounting bolts, install and tighten to 23 ft. lbs. (31 Nm).

➡If the throttle body is being replaced, the idle stop screw on the new unit is preset by the manufacturer and should not require adjustment. Minimum idle speed should ONLY be adjusted, if all other engine systems are operating properly and idle speed still can not be maintained.

10. Connect the throttle cable to the lever, making sure the cable does not hold the lever open when the accelerator pedal is released.
11. Connect the vacuum harness to the top of the throttle body.
12. Connect the IAC valve and TPS wiring harnesses.
13. Install the air intake tube and resonator.
14. Connect the negative battery cable.
15. Start the engine and check for vacuum leaks.

BASE IDLE SPEED ADJUSTMENT

▶ See Figures 33, 34 and 35

➡The minimum idle speed is preset at the factory and requires no periodic adjustment, checking or other service. Adjustments should be performed ONLY when the throttle body has been replaced and/or proper idle speed can not be obtained. The engine should be at normal operating temperature, the A/C and cooling fans should be OFF when making adjustments.

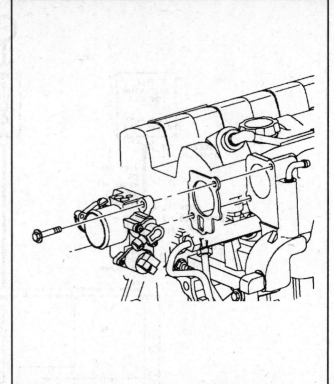

Fig. 30 Remove the retaining bolts, then remove the throttle body from the manifold — DOHC engine

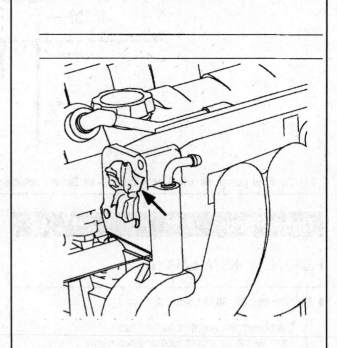

Fig. 31 Cover the intake manifold with a clean cloth to protect the internal engine parts from debris — DOHC engine

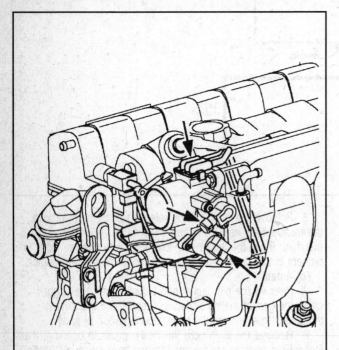

Fig. 29 Unplug the electrical connectors and disconnect the vacuum harness from the throttle body assembly — DOHC engine

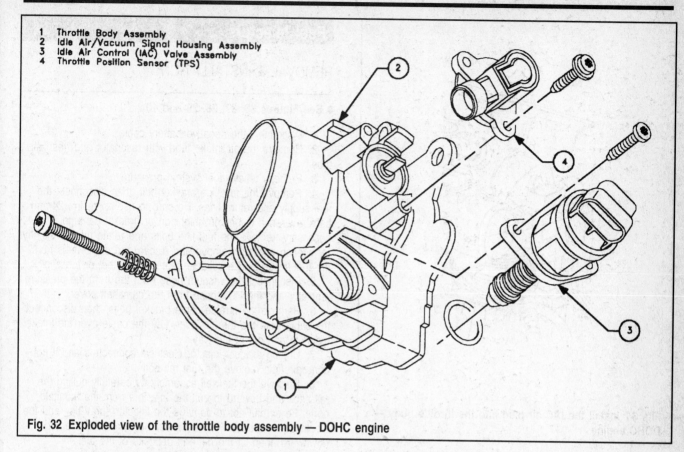

1 Throttle Body Assembly
2 Idle Air/Vacuum Signal Housing Assembly
3 Idle Air Control (IAC) Valve Assembly
4 Throttle Position Sensor (TPS)

Fig. 32 Exploded view of the throttle body assembly — DOHC engine

1. Before making any adjustments, clean the throttle body bore with a shop towel and carburetor cleaner that does not

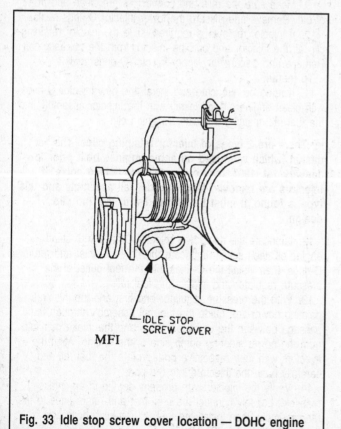

IDLE STOP
SCREW COVER

MFI

Fig. 33 Idle stop screw cover location — DOHC engine

contain methyl ethyl ketone. Then check the idle speed to be sure adjustment is necessary. Proper idle speeds are as follows:

    a. DOHC with manual transaxle in **N** 800-900 rpm.
    b. DOHC with automatic transaxle in **D** 700-800 rpm.

2. If adjustment is necessary, block the wheels and apply the parking brake.

3. The IAC pintle must be properly seated in the throttle body. Connect the IAC tester SA9195E or equivalent, to the IAC valve at the throttle body. The Saturn PDT or an equivalent scan tool may attached to the ALDL and used instead of the IAC tester.

4. Remove the idle stop screw cover.

5. Insert the IAC air plug, SA9106E or equivalent, into the throttle body.

6. Connect the Saturn Portable Diagnostic Tool (PDT) or equivalent to the Assembly Line Diagnostic Link (ALDL) in order monitor engine RPM. Start the engine and check the minimum idle speed. Engine idle should be 450-650 rpm.

7. If not within specification adjust the idle screw to obtain an minimum idle speed of 500-600 rpm.

8. Turn the ignition **OFF** and reconnect the IAC electrical connector.

9. Using the Saturn PDT or equivalent scan tool, check the TPS voltage. Do not replace the TPS unless setting is not between 0.35-0.70 volts.

10. Remove the IAC air plug and install the idle stop cover.

11. Start the engine and check for proper idle operation.

12. Shut the engine **OFF** and remove the PDT or scan tool.

MFI

Fig. 34 Install the IAC air plug into the throttle body — DOHC engine

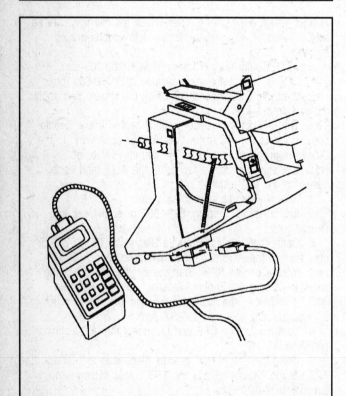

Fig. 35 Connecting the Saturn PDT or an equivalent scan tool to the ALDL

Fuel Injectors

REMOVAL & INSTALLATION

▶ **See Figures 36, 37, 38, 39 and 40**

1. Disconnect the negative battery cable.
2. Remove the air intake tube with resonator and fresh air tube.
3. Properly relieve fuel system pressure.
4. Remove the fuel line bracket bolt, then disconnect the fuel supply and return lines. Be sure to use a $^{15}/_{16}$ in. (24mm) backup wrench to prevent inlet port or bracket damage. If necessary, remove the fuel line bolts and rotate the rail slightly for wrench access. Remove and discard the old O-rings from the fuel lines using a suitable seal removal tool or brass pick.
5. Disconnect the vacuum hose from the from the pressure regulator and the PCV hose from the camshaft cover.
6. Remove the throttle cable bracket bolts, then disconnect the cable from the throttle lever. Lay the cable over the intake manifold and out of the way.
7. Unplug the fuel injector electrical connectors and if not done already, remove the fuel rail bolts.
8. Remove the fuel rail assembly by carefully pulling the rail back and upward to pull the injectors from the manifold ports. Be careful not to damage the injector spray tips and the electrical connectors. Rotate the rail so the injectors point downward, then lift the rail end opposite of the fuel connections to remove the rail from between the camshaft cover and intake manifold.
9. Make sure the rails and connectors are clean and free of dirt. Remove and discard the lower injector O-rings seals.
10. If injector removal is required, slide the injector retaining clip off the injector and pull the injector from the rail assembly. Remove and discard the Upper injector O-rings seals.
   To install:
11. If removed, lubricate and install the new injector O-rings with clean engine oil and install with the injector assembly into the fuel rail. Install the injector retaining clip.

➡ **There are 2 types of injector retaining clips. The 1st design, which was used on some engines built prior to January 1st, 1991, may cause injector ticking noise. If injectors are removed from the fuel rail assembly and this type is found, it must be replaced with the 2nd clip design.**

12. Lubricate the new lower injector O-rings with clean engine oil, then install. Lubricate the new fuel inlet and return O-rings, then install the O-rings into the fuel outlet of the pressure regulator and inlet of the fuel rail.
13. With the pressure regulator end first and the injectors pointing downward, guide the fuel rail assembly through the passage between the camshaft cover and the intake manifold from the power steering pump side of the engine. Align the injectors with their respective ports, rotate the fuel rail and carefully push the injectors into the port.
14. Verify the injectors are properly seated in the intake manifold. Loosely connect the fuel inlet and return lines to the rail assembly, then install the fuel rail retaining bolts and tighten to 22 ft. lbs. (30 Nm).

15. Connect the fuel injector wiring harnesses.

16. Connect the PCV valve hose to the camshaft cover, and the vacuum line to the pressure regulator, making sure they are properly seated.

17. Install the throttle cable bracket bolts and tighten to 19 ft. lbs. (25 Nm), then connect the throttle cable.

18. Using a backup wrench, tighten the fuel inlet and return line fittings to 133 inch lbs. (15 Nm). Install the fuel line bracket bolt and tighten to 106 inch lbs. (12 Nm).

19. Connect the negative battery cable, then prime the fuel system by cycling the ignition key **ON** and **OFF**.

20. Start the engine and check for leaks.

21. Shut the engine , then install the air intake tube and resonator assembly.

TESTING

Electrical Check
▶ **See Figures 41 and 42**

1. Unplug the injector connector and use an ohmmeter to check the resistance of the injector coil. It should be 1-2 ohms.

➡**A single MFI injector may short internally causing a no start condition, yet not blow the fuse or damage the PCM. If a multimeter is not available to test the injectors, disconnect the injector electrical connectors, 1 at a time, and attempt to start the engine. If the engine starts with 1 injector disconnected, the faulty injector has been found.**

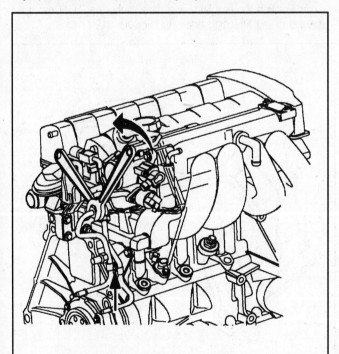

Fig. 36 Disconnect the fuel supply and return lines, using a backup wrench to prevent fitting stress or damage

2. Make sure all injector harnesses are unplugged, then connect a Noid light to the injector connector terminal so the light can be seen from the driver's seat. Operate the starter and observe the Noid light.

   a. If the Noid does not illuminate at all, check for power to the injector(s). The injectors receive power through the pink/black wire from the 7.5 Amp "INJ" fuse in the underhood junction box, any time the ignition switch is **ON**. The PCM operates the injectors by completing the ground circuit through the dark green or dark blue wires.

   b. If the test light stays on steadily, check for a short to ground of the wire between the injector connector and the PCM.

   c. A pulsing Noid light does not necessarily indicate enough voltage to properly operate the fuel injector. If it is still questionable whether or not an injector is pulsing, connect a known good injector to the circuit and tightly grip the injector while a friend cranks the engine. If injector pulses are felt, the circuit is good.

Injector Pressure Check
▶ **See Figure 43**

❊❊CAUTION

The following procedure will produce a small fuel spill and fumes. Make sure there is proper ventilation and take the appropriate fire safety precautions.

1. Connect the test gauge and run the fuel pump and system pressure tests as described in the fuel pump tests.

2. Disconnect the fuel return hose from the metal line and cap the line carefully as full fuel pressure may go as high as 94 psi (650 kPa).

3. Disconnect the pressure regulator vacuum line.

4. Disconnect the fuel line bracket retaining bolt, but leave the lines attached to the rail assembly and connectors.

5. Remove the bolts holding the fuel rail and pull the rail and injectors straight out so the tips are visible yet still in the ports. It may be necessary to rotate the throttle. Use wire to hold the assembly back against the intake manifold.

6. Wipe the injector tips free of fuel or debris and place a clean cloth under them, just contacting the injector tips to spot leaking fuel.

7. Cycle the ignition **ON** and **OFF** , without starting the engine, to build system pressure to a minimum of 58 psi (400 kPa) on the gauge.

8. Allow the pressure to hold for five minutes, then check the cloth for fuel leakage. If a portion of the towel becomes wet with fuel, the faulty injector(s) must be replaced.

9. Bleed off the system pressure, cycle the ignition to rebuild fuel pressure, then allow the system to sit for five minutes. Check the cloth again for signs of leakage and if any is found, replace the faulty injector(s).

10. Remember to lubricate the injector O-rings with clean engine oil upon installation of the fuel rail/injector assembly.

Fig. 37 When the injectors clear the manifold ports, rotate the fuel rail so the injectors point downward and carefully remove the rail. Enough space for removal exists between the throttle body and the pressure regulator

Pressure Regulator

REMOVAL & INSTALLATION

▶ See Figures 44, 45 and 46

1. Remove the air intake tube and resonator assembly.
2. Properly relieve the fuel system pressure. Refer to the procedure in this Section.
3. Remove the bolts from the fuel line clip.
4. Using a $^{15}/_{16}$ (24mm) backup wrench to prevent damage to the inlet port and bracket, disconnect the fuel inlet and return lines from the pressure regulator/fuel rail assembly.

➡If difficulty is encountered accessing the fuel return line nut, loosen and/or remove the fuel supply and rail attachment fasteners.

5. Remove the regulator assembly attaching screw, then remove the regulator assembly. Plug the regulator port in the fuel rail with a clean rag to prevent system contamination.
6. Do not remove the O-ring from the retaining in the pressure regulator fuel outlet unless it is damaged and requires replacing. Always remove and discard the O-ring from the fuel inlet.

To install:

7. Lubricate the new fuel inlet O-ring and if necessary the new outlet O-ring with clean engine oil, then install the O-ring(s) in the pressure regulator assembly.
8. Position the regulator assembly to the fuel rail. Coat the threads of the attaching bolt with Loctite® 242 or an

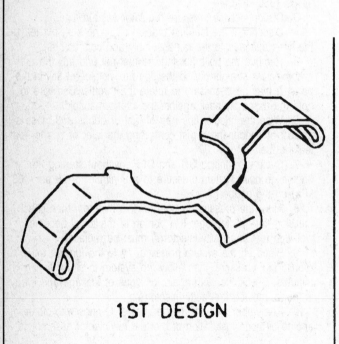

1ST DESIGN

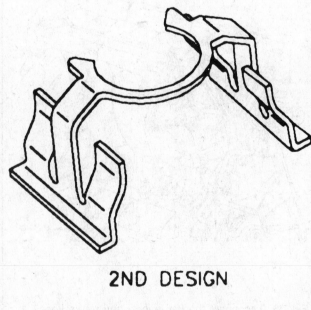

2ND DESIGN

Fig. 38 Injector clips of the 1st design should be replaced with the 2nd and improved retainer clip design

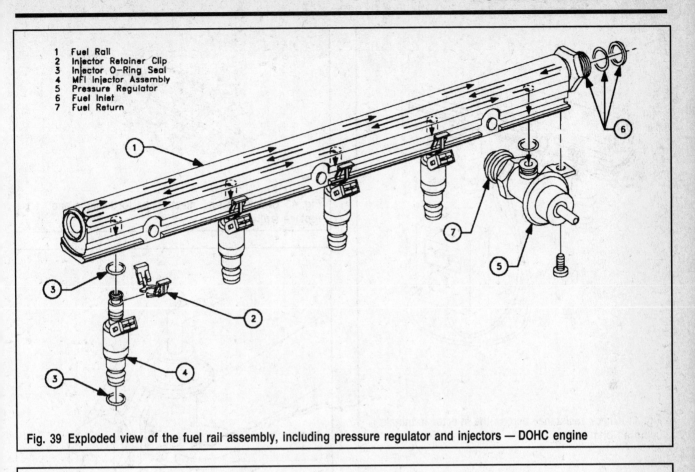

1   Fuel Rail
2   Injector Retainer Clip
3   Injector O—Ring Seal
4   MFI Injector Assembly
5   Pressure Regulator
6   Fuel Inlet
7   Fuel Return

Fig. 39 Exploded view of the fuel rail assembly, including pressure regulator and injectors — DOHC engine

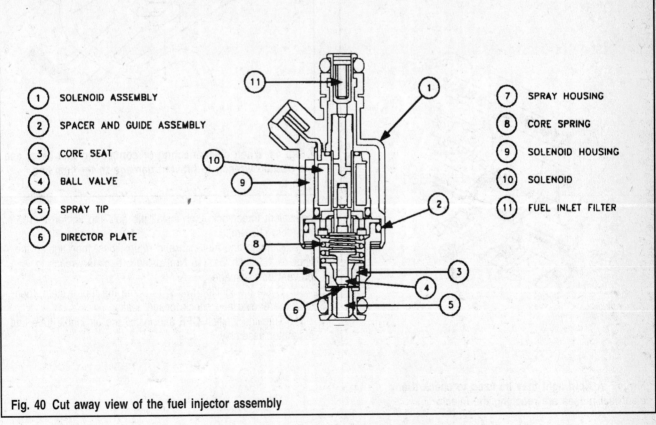

1 SOLENOID ASSEMBLY	7 SPRAY HOUSING
2 SPACER AND GUIDE ASSEMBLY	8 CORE SPRING
3 CORE SEAT	9 SOLENOID HOUSING
4 BALL VALVE	10 SOLENOID
5 SPRAY TIP	11 FUEL INLET FILTER
6 DIRECTOR PLATE	

Fig. 40 Cut away view of the fuel injector assembly

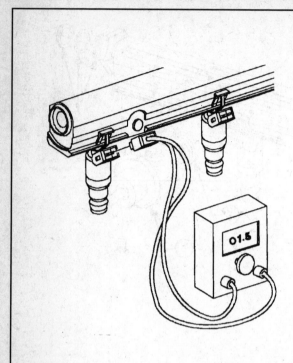

Fig. 41 Check resistance across the injector terminals using an ohm meter

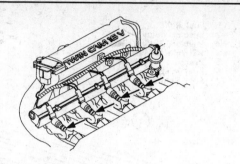

Fig. 43 Check the fuel injector tips for leakage and replace faulty injectors

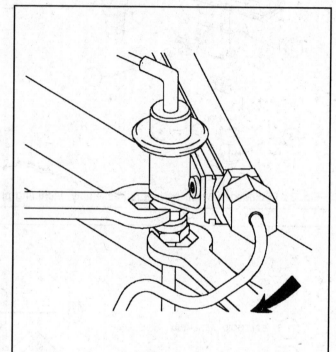

Fig. 44 When disconnecting or connecting fuel lines, use a backup wrench to prevent damage to the fuel line ports

equivalent threadlock, then install the bolt and tighten to 106 inch lbs. (12 Nm).

9. Connect the fuel inlet and return lines, then tighten the lines to 133 inch lbs. (15 Nm) using a backup wrench to prevent port damage.

10. Cycle the ignition switch to prime the fuel system, then start the engine and check for fuel leaks.

11. Turn the ignition **OFF** and install the air intake tube and resonator assembly.

Fig. 42 A Noid light may be used to check if any electrical pulses are reaching the injector

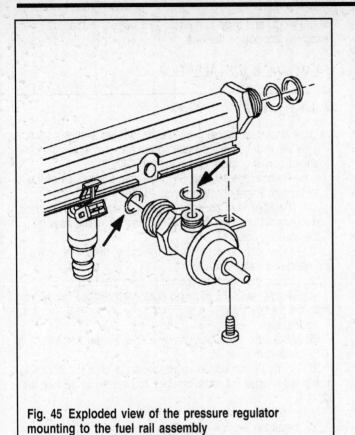

Fig. 45 Exploded view of the pressure regulator mounting to the fuel rail assembly

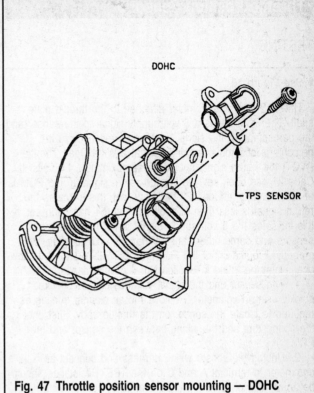

Fig. 47 Throttle position sensor mounting — DOHC engine

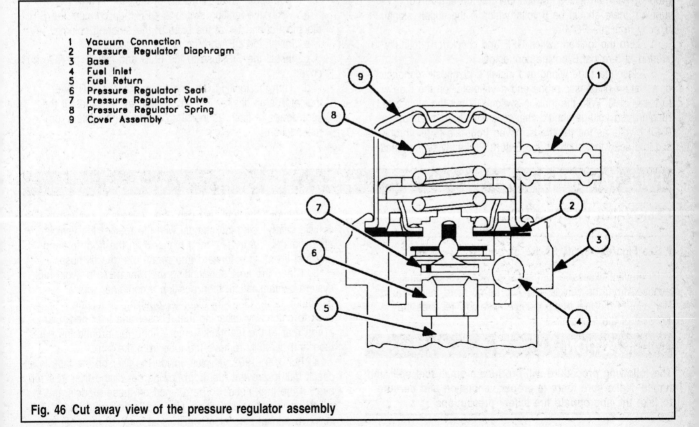

1 Vacuum Connection
2 Pressure Regulator Diaphragm
3 Base
4 Fuel Inlet
5 Fuel Return
6 Pressure Regulator Seat
7 Pressure Regulator Valve
8 Pressure Regulator Spring
9 Cover Assembly

Fig. 46 Cut away view of the pressure regulator assembly

Throttle Position Sensor

TESTING

▶ See Figure 20

The TPS is a potentiometer attached to the throttle plate shaft. The PCM sends a 5 volt supply signal to the sensor and the percentage of the signal returned corresponds to the percentage of throttle opening so that a Wide Open Throttle (WOT) the return signal should be approximately 4.9 volts. If Code 21 has been set, the voltage return signal to the PCM is above 4.9 volts. If Code 22 has been set, this indicates the return signal is less than 0.2 volts. If Flag 54 has been set, this indicates the 5 volt supply signal is not reaching the sensors and some other sensors may also not function properly. Trouble shoot the Flag first. Complete diagnostic flow charts may be found in Section No. 4 of this manual.

1. The sensor and the signal voltages can be checked quickly using a voltmeter. Remove the air cleaner ducting as required to locate the sensor on the throttle body. First check the connectors and the wiring between the sensor and the PCM.

2. Unplug the sensor wiring harness and connect an ohmmeter to terminal A and C on the TPS. Resistance should be above 200 ohms and should change smoothly as the throttle is moved.

3. Connect a voltmeter between connector terminal A and ground. With the ignition switch ON but the engine not running, there should be 5 volts, which is the supply signal directly from the PCM.

4. Turn the ignition switch OFF and check for continuity to ground at terminal B on the connector.

5. Reconnect the wiring and install a diagnostic connector or a Saturn diagnostic probe and a voltmeter on the blue wire to terminal C. With the ignition switch ON but the engine not running, the voltage should change smoothly from about 0.4-4.7 volts as the throttle is moved from idle to full throttle. A suitable scan tool such as the Saturn PDT may be connected to the ALDL and used to monitor TPS output, instead of attaching a probe to the wire.

REMOVAL & INSTALLATION

▶ See Figure 47

1. If equipped, properly disable the SIR system as follows:
    a. Align the steering wheel so the tires are in the straight-ahead position, then turn the ignition OFF.
    b. Remove the 10 amp SIR fuse from the top left of the Instrument Panel Junction Block (IPJB).
    c. Remove the Connector Position Assurance (CPA), then disconnect the yellow 2-way SIR connector at the base of the steering column.
2. Disconnect the negative battery cable, then remove the air intake tube and resonator
3. Unplug the electrical connector from the TPS.
4. Remove the TPS retaining bolts, then remove the sensor from the throttle body.
    To install:
5. Make sure the throttle valve is closed, then install the TPS to the throttle shaft.
6. Rotate the sensor counterclockwise to align the mounting holes, then install the retaining bolts and tighten to 18 inch lbs. (2 Nm).
7. Install wiring harness to the sensor.
8. Install the air intake tube and resonator.
9. Connect the negative battery cable.
10. If equipped, enable the SIR system as follows:
    a. Verify the ignition switch is OFF then connect the SIR electrical connector at the base of the steering column.
    b. Install the CPA device to the connector.
    c. Install the SIR fuse to the IPJB and install the fuse box cover.
    d. Turn the ignition ON and verify that the AIR BAG indicator lamp flashes 7-9 times, then extinguishes. If the light does not flash as indicated, inspect the system for malfunction.

FUEL TANK/FUEL PUMP MODULE

REMOVAL & INSTALLATION

▶ See Figures 48, 50, 51, 52, 53 and 54

To prevent excessive fuel spillage, whenever the tank is removed from the vehicle it should be no more than ¾ full. Removal of the fuel pump module assembly requires the removal of the fuel tank.

✳✳CAUTION

The following procedure will produce a small fuel spill and fumes. Make sure there is proper ventilation and be sure to take the appropriate fire safety precautions.

1. Disconnect the negative battery cable, then properly relieve the fuel system pressure. Refer to the procedure in this Section.

2. Remove the fuel filler cap, then raise and support the vehicle safely using jackstands, with the rear of the vehicle approximately 28 in. (711mm) higher than the front to keep any fuel in the tank forward and away from the fill hose.

3. Clean the area surrounding the filler neck to avoid fuel system contamination, then position a container with a minimum 12 in. (300mm) diameter opening under the filler neck to catch any escaping fuel. Loosen the filler neck clamp at the rear of the fuel tank, wrap a shop rag around the neck tube and carefully remove the tube from the tank.

4. For 1991-1992 vehicles, inside the filler on the tank is a check ball to prevent fuel from flowing out of the filler in a roll-over. If the tank needs to be drained on these models, the check ball must be dislodged. Use the large round end of a ½ in. drive ratchet extension (which is at least 18 in. long) to push the check ball into the fuel tank. For 1993, the fuel check ball was relocated to the filler pipe so that the pipe may simply be removed to allow siphoning. These pipes may be installed

to 1991-1992 vehicles, but the check ball must be removed from the tank first.

➡**Once the check ball has been knocked into the fuel tank on 1991-1992, the tank must be removed from the vehicle and the pump module must be removed from the tank in order to reinstall the check ball.**

5. If the check ball was dislodged (1991-1992) or the fuel neck removed (1993) for siphoning, use a clean length of hose and/or an appropriate hand pump to siphon or pump the fuel from the tank and into an approved gas can.

6. Remove the filler neck bracket fastener at the left side of the rear frame rail, then loosen the fuel vent hose retaining clamp at the tank.

➡ **It is easier to remove hoses from the tank than to pull them from the steel vent and fill tubes.**

7. Disconnect the fuel pressure and return line quick connects by pinching the 2 plastic tangs together, then grasp both ends of 1 fuel line connection and twist ¼ turn in each direction while pulling them apart. Disconnect the fuel vent hose by holding the line and by pushing on the rubber connector with a small open end wrench.

➡ **Do not allow the fuel tank retaining straps to become bent during tank removal or strap damage may occur. Always use an assistant when removing the fuel tank to prevent damage.**

8. With the aid of an assistant, remove the 2 support strap fasteners at the rear of the tank, then lower the tank and support panel approximately 8 in. (203mm). Reach upward and unplug the electrical connector from the top of the tank, then remove the tank and support panel from the vehicle.

9. If the check ball was removed or fuel pump module replacement/service is necessary:

a. Clean the area surrounding the fuel pump module and spray the cam lockring tangs with a suitable penetrating oil to loosen the fitting.

b. Using SA9156E, or an equivalent fuel module lockring removal tool, and a ½ inch breaker bar of approximately 18 in. (457mm) in length, remove the pump unit locking ring from the tank. Attempting to use a 12 in. or shorter breaker bar may cause lockring damage.

c. Lift and tilt the unit out at a 45 degree angle, being careful not to bend the sending unit float arm. Remove and discard the unit to tank O-ring.

10. The sending unit is the only portion of the module that may be serviced. The filter may be cleaned with mineral spirits, but must be replaced as an assembly with the module if damaged. If necessary, remove the sending unit from the module as follows:

a. Unplug the 2 electrical connections using needle-nose pliers or by pressing down the locking tab and pulling the connectors from the terminal.

b. Using a small suitable tool, push in on the sender assembly attaching tang, then lift upward and remove the sender.

c. Late 1992 and all 1993 vehicles use a brass float instead of plastic. Brass floats may be serviced. Use a ¼ in. flat-tipped screwdriver to carefully pry the float from the wire loop. Do not bend the float arm or deform the wire loop.

To install

11. If removed, pinch a brass float onto the float arm wire loop and/or install the sending unit to the pump module by positioning the tang in the locator slot and snapping the unit into place. Connect the 2 sending unit electrical connectors to their terminals.

12. If removed for service or access to the check ball, install the fuel pump assembly:

a. Before installing the pump module, remove the filler check ball and examine it for cracks or damage. Reach into the tank through the pump unit hole and carefully push the check ball into the filler tube opening from the inside. If necessary, carefully spread the plastic ball supports to ease installation.

b. Install a new O-ring to the opening in the top of the fuel tank, then carefully insert the pump module into the tank at a 45 degree angle to prevent sending unit and float damage. The filter and flow arm must be directed toward the front of the tank.

c. Align the pump locator tabs with the fuel tank slots, then install the cam lockring using the ring service tool.

13. With the aid of an assistant, position the tank and support panel so the wires can be connected to the module, install the module electrical connector, then secure the tank in place using the retaining straps. Tighten the strap bolts to 35 ft. lbs. (47 Nm).

14. Loosely install the filler tube, vent lines and clamps. Align the fill neck and tank so the fender will not be deflected or pushed outward by the hose. When everything is properly positioned, install the fill neck tube and bracket fastener. Vent lines should be installed into the rubber boot until the tube white marks align with the side of the boot.

15. Tighten the clamps to 18 inch lbs. (2 Nm) and tighten the fill neck bracket fastener to 53 inch lbs. (6 Nm). If the clamps must be replaced, original equipment or equivalent parts must be used, because the original parts are designed to prevent hose damage.

16. Lubricate the male ends of the fuel supply and return quick connect fittings with a few drops of clean engine oil. Push the connectors together until the retaining tabs snap into place, then pull on opposite ends of each connection to verify the connection is secure.

17. Remove the jackstands and carefully lower the vehicle, then install the fuel filler cap and connect the negative battery cable.

18. Prime the fuel system and check for leaks:

a. Turn the ignition for 5 seconds, then OFF for 10 seconds.

b. Repeat the ON/OFF cycle 2 more times.

c. Crank the engine until it starts.

d. If the engine does not readily start, repeat Steps a-thru e.

e. Run the engine and check for leaks.

TORQUE SPECIFICATIONS

Component	U.S.	Metric
Injector retaining bracket bolt (1)	35 inch lbs.	3 Nm
Fuel meter body screws (SOHC engine)	35 inch lbs.	4 Nm
Fuel inlet and return lines		
SOHC engine	19 ft. lbs.	25 Nm
DOHC engine	133 inch lbs.	15 Nm
Fuel line bracket bolt (DOHC engine)	106 inch lbs.	12 Nm
Fuel pressure regulator cover screws		
SOHC engine	22 inch lbs.	2.5 Nm
Fuel rail retaining bolts (DOHC engine)	22 ft. lbs.	30 Nm
Fuel tank neck/vent clamps	18 inch lbs.	2 Nm
Fuel tank fill neck bracket fastener	53 inch lbs.	6 Nm
Fuel tank retaining strap bolts	35 ft. lbs.	47 Nm
Regulator assembly attaching bolt (1)		
DOHC engine	106 inch lbs.	12 Nm
Throttle body attaching bolts (1)		
SOHC engine	24 ft. lbs.	33 Nm
DOHC engine	23 ft. lbs.	31 Nm
Throttle cable bracket bolts		
DOHC engine	19 ft. lbs.	25 Nm
Throttle position sensor mounting bolts	18 inch lbs.	2 Nm

(1)-Apply a coat of Loctite® 242 or an equivalent threadlock

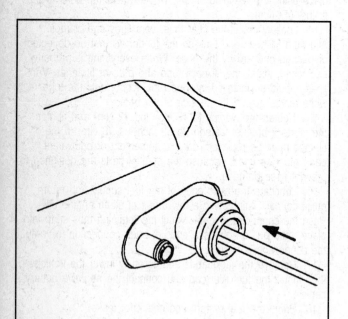

Fig. 48 For 1991-1992 vehicles with the check ball installed in the fuel tank, use an 18 in. or longer ratchet extension to dislodge the fuel filler check ball knocking it into the tank. If this is done the tank must be removed in order to retrieve the ball for installation

Fig. 49   View of the fuel filler neck — 1992 SC

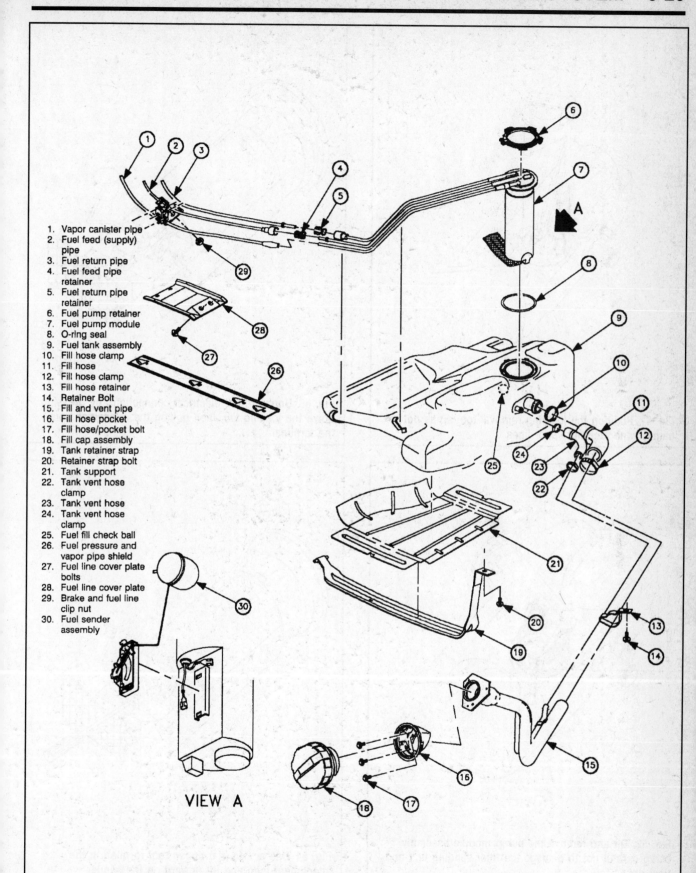

1. Vapor canister pipe
2. Fuel feed (supply) pipe
3. Fuel return pipe
4. Fuel feed pipe retainer
5. Fuel return pipe retainer
6. Fuel pump retainer
7. Fuel pump module
8. O-ring seal
9. Fuel tank assembly
10. Fill hose clamp
11. Fill hose
12. Fill hose clamp
13. Fill hose retainer
14. Retainer Bolt
15. Fill and vent pipe
16. Fill hose pocket
17. Fill hose/pocket bolt
18. Fill cap assembly
19. Tank retainer strap
20. Retainer strap bolt
21. Tank support
22. Tank vent hose clamp
23. Tank vent hose
24. Tank vent hose clamp
25. Fuel fill check ball
26. Fuel pressure and vapor pipe shield
27. Fuel line cover plate bolts
28. Fuel line cover plate
29. Brake and fuel line clip nut
30. Fuel sender assembly

VIEW A

Fig. 50 Exploded view of the fuel tank/pump module and hose assembly

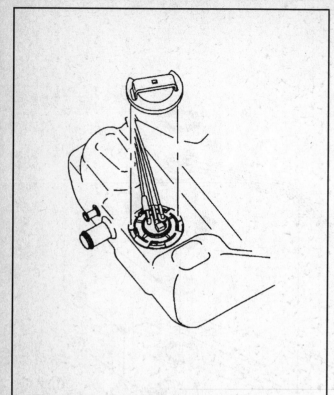

Fig. 51 Position the lockring removal tool so as not to damage the fuel and vapor lines

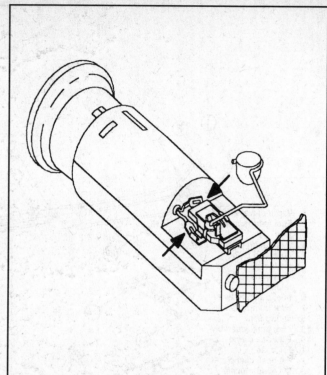

Fig. 53 Unplug the 2 electrical connections by pressing down the locking tab, then pulling the connector from the terminal

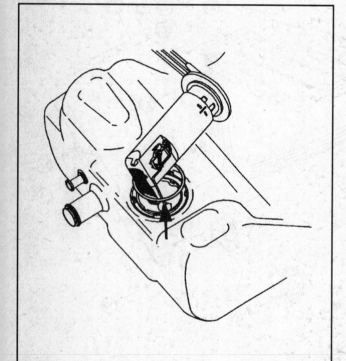

Fig. 52 Tilt and remove the pump module assembly, being careful not to damage the filter sending unit and float arm

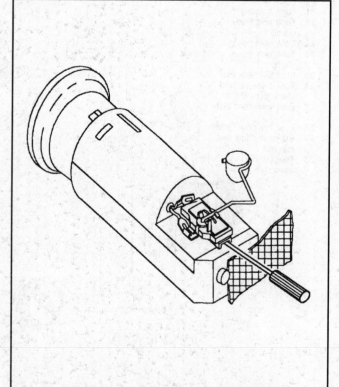

Fig. 54 Use a ¼ in. flat tipped tool to push in the attachment tang and lift upward on the sender

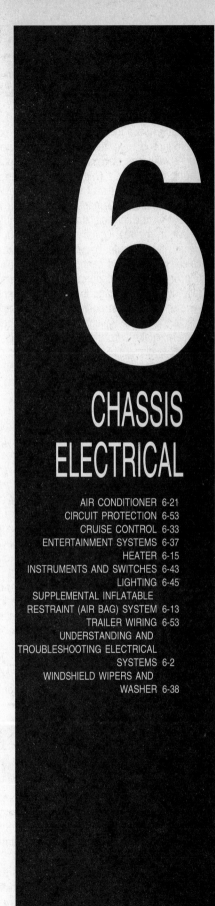

6
CHASSIS ELECTRICAL

UNDERSTANDING AND TROUBLESHOOTING ELECTRICAL SYSTEMS

With the rate at which both import and domestic manufacturers are incorporating electronic control systems into their production lines, today almost every new vehicle is equipped with one or more on-board computer. These electronic components (with no moving parts) should theoretically last the life of the vehicle, provided nothing external happens to damage the circuits or memory chips.

While it is true that electronic components should never wear out, in the real world malfunctions do occur. It is also true that any computer-based system is extremely sensitive to electrical voltages and cannot tolerate careless or haphazard testing or service procedures. An inexperienced individual can literally do major damage looking for a minor problem by using the wrong kind of test equipment or connecting test leads or connectors with the ignition switch ON. When selecting test equipment, make sure the manufacturers instructions state that the tester is compatible with whatever type of electronic control system is being serviced. Read all instructions carefully and double check all test points before installing probes or making any test connections.

The following section outlines basic diagnosis techniques for dealing with computerized automotive control systems. Along with a general explanation of the various types of test equipment available to aid in servicing modern electronic automotive systems, basic repair techniques for wiring harnesses and connectors is given. Read the basic information before attempting repairs or testing on any computerized system. This information will provide the background of information necessary to avoid the most common and obvious mistakes that can cost both time and money. Although the replacement and testing procedures are simple in themselves, the systems are not, and unless one has a thorough understanding of all components and their function within a particular computerized control system, the logical test sequence, which these systems demand, cannot be followed. Minor malfunctions can make a big difference, so it is important to know how each component affects the operation of the overall electronic system to find the ultimate cause of a problem without unnecessarily replacing good components. It is not enough to use the correct test equipment; the test equipment must be used correctly.

Safety Precautions

✳✳CAUTION

Whenever working on or around any computer based microprocessor control system, always observe these general precautions to prevent the possibility of personal injury or damage to electronic components.

• Never install or remove battery cables with the ignition key **ON** or the engine running. Jumper cables should be connected with the key ignition key **OFF** to avoid power surges that could damage electronic control units. Engines equipped with computer controlled systems should avoid both giving and getting jump starts due to the possibility of serious damage to components from arcing in the engine compartment when connections are made with the ignition **ON**.

• Always remove the battery cables before charging the battery. Never use a high output charger on an installed battery or attempt to use any type of 'hot shot" (24 volt) starting aid.

• Exercise care when inserting test probes into wiring harnesses to insure good contact without damaging the connector or spreading the pins. Always probe connectors from the rear (wire) side, NOT the pin side, to avoid accidental shorting of terminals during test procedures.

• Never remove or attach wiring harness connectors with the ignition switch **ON**　especially to an electronic control unit.

• Do not drop any components during service procedures and never apply 12 volts directly to any component (like a solenoid or relay) unless instructed specifically to do so. Some component electrical windings are designed to safely handle only 4 or 5 volts and can be destroyed in seconds if 12 volts are applied directly to the connector.

• Remove the electronic control unit if the vehicle is to be placed in an environment where temperatures exceed approximately 176°F (80°C), such as a paint spray booth or when arc or gas welding near the control unit location in the car.

ORGANIZED TROUBLESHOOTING

When diagnosing a specific problem, organized troubleshooting is a must. The complexity of a modern automobile demands that you approach any problem in a logical, organized manner. There are certain troubleshooting techniques that are standard:

1. Establish when the problem occurs. Does the problem appear only under certain conditions? Were there any noises, odors, or other unusual symptoms?

2. Isolate the problem area. To do this, make some simple tests and observations; then eliminate the systems that are working properly. Check for obvious problems such as broken wires, dirty connections or split or disconnected vacuum hoses. Always check the obvious before assuming something complicated is the cause.

3. Test for problems systematically to determine the cause once the problem area is isolated. Are all the components functioning properly? Is there power going to electrical switches and motors? If there is no power to a component, is there also no power to related components on the same circuit or system. Is there vacuum at vacuum switches and/or actuators? Is there a mechanical problem such as bent linkage or loose mounting screws? Doing careful, systematic checks will often turn up most causes on the first inspection without wasting time checking components that have little or no relationship to the problem.

4. Test all repairs after the work is done to make sure that the problem is fixed. Some causes can be traced to more than one component, so a careful verification of repair work is important to pick up additional malfunctions that may cause a problem to reappear or a different problem to arise. A blown fuse, for example, is a simple problem that may require more

than another fuse to repair. If you don't look for a problem that caused a fuse to blow, for example, a shorted wire or other problem may go undetected.

Experience has shown that most problems tend to be the result of a fairly simple and obvious cause, such as loose or corroded connectors or air leaks in the intake system; making careful inspection of components during testing essential to quick and accurate troubleshooting. Special, hand held computerized testers designed specifically for diagnosing the Saturn electronic control systems are available from a variety of aftermarket sources, as well as from the vehicle manufacturer, but care should be taken that any test equipment being used is designed to diagnose that particular computer controlled system accurately without damaging the Electronic Control Module (ECM) or components being tested.

➡**Pinpointing the exact cause of trouble in an electrical system can sometimes only be accomplished by the use of special test equipment. The following describes commonly used test equipment and explains how to put it to best use in diagnosis. In addition to the information covered below, the equipment manufacturer's instruction booklet, provided with the tester, should be read and clearly understood before attempting any test procedures.**

TEST EQUIPMENT

Jumper Wires
▶ See Figure 1

Jumper wires are simple, yet extremely valuable testing tools, that are used to bypass sections of a circuit. The simplest type of jumper wire is merely a length of multi strand wire with an alligator clip at each end. Jumper wires are usually fabricated from lengths of standard automotive wire and whatever type of connector (alligator clip, spade connector or pin connector) that is required for the particular vehicle being tested. The well equipped tool box will have several different styles of jumper wires in several different lengths. Some jumper wires are made with three or more terminals coming from a common splice for special purpose testing. In cramped, hard-to-reach areas, it is advisable to have insulated boots over the jumper wire terminals in order to prevent accidental grounding, sparks, and possible fire, especially when testing fuel system components.

Jumper wires are used primarily to locate open electrical circuits, on either the ground (-) side of the circuit or on the hot (+) side. If an electrical component fails to operate, connect the jumper wire between the proper component terminal and a good ground. If the component operates only with the jumper installed, the ground circuit is open. If the ground circuit is good, but the component does not operate, the circuit between the power feed and component is open. You can sometimes connect the jumper wire directly from the battery to the hot terminal of the component, but first make sure the component uses 12 volts in operation. Some electrical components, such as fuel injectors, are designed to operate on about 4 volts and running 12 volts directly to the injector terminals can burn out the wiring. By inserting an in-line fuseholder between a set of test leads, a fused jumper wire can be used for bypassing open circuits. Use a 5 amp fuse to

provide protection against voltage spikes. When in doubt, use a voltmeter to check the voltage input to the component and measure how much voltage is being applied normally. By moving the jumper wire successively back from a component toward the power source, you can isolate the area of the circuit where the open is located. When the component stops functioning, or the power is cut off, the open is in the segment of wire between the jumper and the point previously tested.

Jumper wires may also be constructed to test connector terminals. Insertion of a meter probe into a connector may spread the contacts, thus damaging the connector and preventing a proper circuit completion. Male and female terminals taken from a scrap wiring harness or service part cut lead kits may be used along with a short length wire to provide a jumper probe. Plug the connector into the terminal to be tested, then probe the end of the jumper wire using the meter lead.

✳✳CAUTION

Never use jumpers made from wire that is of lighter gauge than used in the circuit under test. If the jumper wire is of too small gauge, it may overheat and possibly melt. Never use jumpers to bypass high resistance loads (such as motors) in a circuit. Bypassing resistances, in effect, creates a short circuit which may, in turn, cause damage and fire. Never use a jumper for anything other than temporary bypassing of components in a circuit.

Test Lights

Due to the complexity of the circuitry and the use of electronic components, a multimeter is required to safely test

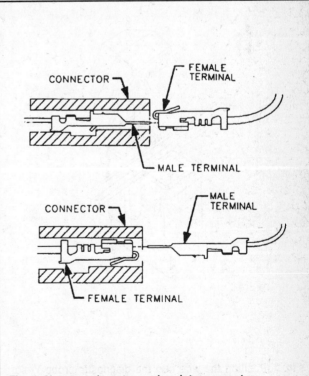

Fig. 1 Never push meter probes into connector terminals, instead construct jumper probes using an old male or female connector

the electrical circuits of a Saturn vehicle. The manufacturer warns that a test light should not be used to troubleshoot electrical circuits on your Saturn.

A test light provides a low-resistance load on an electrical circuit. Because most Saturn electronics are designed to be used with high-resistance circuits, the use of a low-resistance test light could damage an electronic module.

Saturn Diagnostic Probe
▶ See Figures 2, 3 and 4

Saturn recommends that circuits should not be tested by piercing wire installation with meter probes. Piercing insulation will give a path for electricity to arc, will render insulation useless (allowing wire corrosion) and may break wire strands (damaging the circuit continuity).

If testing must be done on an unbroken circuit, Saturn provides a solution in the form of a diagnostic probe. The probe may be permanently installed on a wire of the appropriate gauge in order to provide a 'Tee' fitting through which the unbroken circuit may be checked. When the probe is installed, it pierces the wire insulation, while a gel material inside the probe will seal the wire to prevent corrosion. The diagnostic probe can then be used multiple times to insert the lead from a meter.

To install the Saturn diagnostic probe:

1. Select an appropriate probe for the wire gauge, then position the wire into the V-slot of the probe terminal.

2. Press the cable, by hand, into the slot and partially close the probe cover.

3. Snap the cover fully into place using a pair of pliers. A snap will be heard of felt when the cover locks.

4. Insert the meter test lead through the probe housing and gel material in order to contact the terminal.

Voltmeter

A voltmeter is used to measure voltage at any point in a circuit, or to measure the voltage drop across any part of a circuit. It can also be used to check continuity in a wire or circuit by indicating current flow from one end to the other. Voltmeters usually have various scales on the meter dial and a selector switch to allow the selection of different voltages. The voltmeter has a positive and a negative lead. To avoid damage to the meter, always connect the negative lead to the negative (-) side of circuit (to ground or nearest the ground side of the circuit) and connect the positive lead to the positive (+) side of the circuit (to the power source or the nearest power source). Note that the negative voltmeter lead will always be black and that the positive voltmeter will always be some color other than black (usually red). Depending on how the voltmeter is connected into the circuit, it has several uses.

A voltmeter can be connected either in parallel or in series with a circuit and it has a very high resistance to current flow. When connected in parallel, only a small amount of current will flow through the voltmeter current path; the rest will flow through the normal circuit current path and the circuit will work normally. When the voltmeter is connected in series with a circuit, only a small amount of current can flow through the

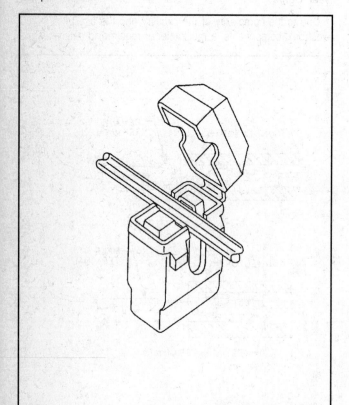

Fig. 2 Position the wire into the diagnostic probe V-slot

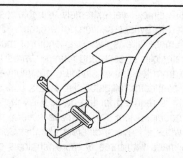

Fig. 3 Snap the cover into place over the wire using a pair of pliers

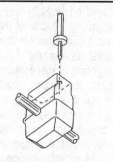

Fig. 4 Insert a meter test lead through the housing to test the circuit

circuit. The circuit will not work properly, but the voltmeter reading will show if the circuit is complete or not.

✳✳CAUTION

Do not use a multimeter to probe electronic ignition spark plug or coil wires. Small pin holes in secondary ignition wires will allow high voltage to arc from the wire to a metal part, external to the secondary ignition circuit. This arcing may cause misfiring, leading to a driveability complaint.

Available Voltage Measurement

Set the voltmeter selector switch to the 20V position and connect the meter negative lead to the negative post of the battery. Connect the positive meter lead to the positive post of the battery and turn the ignition switch **ON** to provide a load. Read the voltage on the meter or digital display. A well charged battery should register over 12 volts. If the meter reads below 11.5 volts, the battery power may be insufficient to operate the electrical system properly. This test determines voltage available from the battery and should be the first step in any electrical trouble diagnosis procedure. Many electrical problems, especially on computer controlled systems, can be caused by a low state of charge in the battery. Excessive corrosion at the battery cable terminals can cause a poor contact that will prevent proper charging and full battery current flow.

Normal battery voltage is 12 volts when fully charged. When the battery is supplying current to one or more circuits it is said to be 'under load". When everything is off the electrical system is under a 'no-load" condition. A fully charged battery may show about 12.5 volts at no load; will drop to 12 volts under medium load; and will drop even lower under heavy load. If the battery is partially discharged the voltage decrease under heavy load may be excessive, even though the battery shows 12 volts or more at no load. When allowed to discharge further, the battery's available voltage under load will decrease more severely. For this reason, it is important that the battery be fully charged during all testing procedures to avoid errors in diagnosis and incorrect test results.

Voltage Drop

When current flows through a resistance, the voltage beyond the resistance is reduced (the larger the current, the greater the reduction in voltage). When no current is flowing, there is no voltage drop because there is no current flow. All points in the circuit which are connected to the power source are at the same voltage as the power source. The total voltage drop always equals the total source voltage. In a long circuit with many connectors, a series of small, unwanted voltage drops due to corrosion at the connectors can add up to a total loss of voltage which impairs the operation of the normal loads in the circuit.

INDIRECT COMPUTATION OF VOLTAGE DROPS

1. Set the voltmeter selector switch to the 20 volt position.
2. Connect the meter negative lead to a good ground.
3. Probe all resistances in the circuit with the positive meter lead.

4. Operate the circuit in all modes and observe the voltage readings.

DIRECT MEASUREMENT OF VOLTAGE DROPS

1. Set the voltmeter switch to the 20 volt position.
2. Connect the voltmeter negative lead to the ground side of the resistance load to be measured.
3. Connect the positive lead to the positive side of the resistance or load to be measured.
4. Read the voltage drop directly on the 20 volt scale.

Too high a voltage indicates too high a resistance. If, for example, a blower motor runs too slowly, you can determine if there is too high a resistance in the resistor pack. By taking voltage drop readings in all parts of the circuit, you can isolate the problem. Too low a voltage drop indicates too low a resistance. If, for example, a blower motor runs too fast in the MED and/or LOW position, the problem can be isolated in the resistor pack by taking voltage drop readings in all parts of the circuit to locate a possibly shorted resistor. The maximum allowable voltage drop under load is critical, especially if there is more than one high resistance problem in a circuit because all voltage drops are cumulative. A small drop is normal due to the resistance of the conductors.

HIGH RESISTANCE TESTING

1. Set the voltmeter selector switch to the 4 volt position.
2. Connect the voltmeter positive lead to the positive post of the battery.
3. Turn on the headlights and heater blower to provide a load.
4. Probe various points in the circuit with the negative voltmeter lead.
5. Read the voltage drop on the 4 volt scale. Some average maximum allowable voltage drops are:

   FUSE PANEL — 7 volts
   IGNITION SWITCH — 5 volts
   HEADLIGHT SWITCH — 7 volts
   IGNITION COIL (+) — 5 volts
   ANY OTHER LOAD — 1.3 volts

➡**Voltage drops are all measured while a load is operating; without current flow, there will be no voltage drop.**

Ohmmeter

The ohmmeter is designed to read resistance (ohms) in a circuit or component. Although there are several different styles of ohmmeters, all will usually have a selector switch which permits the measurement of different ranges of resistance (usually the selector switch allows the multiplication of the meter reading by 10, 100, 1000, and 10,000). A calibration knob allows the meter to be set at zero for accurate measurement. Since all ohmmeters are powered by an internal battery (usually 9 volts), the ohmmeter can be used as a self-powered tester. When the ohmmeter is connected, current from the ohmmeter flows through the circuit or component being tested. Since the ohmmeter's internal resistance and voltage are known values, the amount of current flow through the meter depends on the resistance of the circuit or component being tested.

The ohmmeter can be used to perform continuity test for opens or shorts (either by observation of the meter needle or as a self-powered tester), and to read actual resistance in a circuit. It should be noted that the ohmmeter is used to check the resistance of a component or wire while there is no voltage applied to the circuit. Current flow from an outside voltage source (such as the vehicle battery) can damage the ohmmeter, so the circuit or component should be isolated from the vehicle electrical system before any testing is done. Since the ohmmeter uses its own voltage source, either lead can be connected to any test point.

➡ When checking diodes or other solid state components, the ohmmeter leads can only be connected one way in order to measure current flow in a single direction. Make sure the positive (+) and negative (-) terminal connections are correctly positioned to verify the one-way diode operation.

In using the meter for making continuity checks, do not be concerned with the actual resistance readings. Zero resistance, or any resistance readings, indicate continuity in the circuit. Infinite resistance indicates an open in the circuit. A high resistance reading where there should be none indicates a problem in the circuit. Checks for short circuits are made in the same manner as checks for open circuits except that the circuit must be isolated from both power and normal ground. Infinite resistance indicates no continuity to ground, while zero resistance indicates a dead short to ground.

RESISTANCE MEASUREMENT

The batteries in an ohmmeter will weaken with age and temperature, so the ohmmeter must be calibrated or 'zeroed" before taking measurements. To zero the meter, place the selector switch in its lowest range and touch the two ohmmeter leads together. Turn the calibration knob until the meter needle is exactly on zero.

➡ All analog (needle) type ohmmeters must be zeroed before use, but some digital ohmmeter models are automatically calibrated when the switch is turned on. Self-calibrating digital ohmmeters do not have an adjusting knob, but its a good idea to check for a zero readout before use by touching the leads together. All computer controlled systems require the use of a digital ohmmeter with at least 10 megohms impedance for testing. Before any test procedures are attempted, make sure the ohmmeter used is compatible with the electrical system or damage to the on-board computer could result.

To measure resistance, first isolate the circuit from the vehicle power source by disconnecting the battery cables or the harness connector. Make sure the key is **OFF** when disconnecting any components or the battery. Where necessary, also isolate at least one side of the circuit to be checked to avoid reading parallel resistances. Parallel circuit resistances will always give a lower reading than the actual resistance of either of the branches. When measuring the resistance of parallel circuits, the total resistance will always be lower than the smallest resistance in the circuit. Connect the meter leads to both sides of the circuit (wire or component) and read the actual measured ohms on the meter scale. Make sure the selector switch is set to the proper ohm scale for the

circuit being tested to avoid misreading the ohmmeter test value.

✲✲CAUTION

Never use an ohmmeter with power applied to the circuit. The ohmmeter is designed to operate on its own power supply. The normal 12 volt automotive electrical system current could damage the meter.

Ammeters

An ammeter measures the amount of current flowing through a circuit in units called amperes or amps. Amperes are units of electron flow which indicate the speed at which electrons are flowing through the circuit. Since Ohms Law dictates that current flow in a circuit is equal to the circuit voltage divided by the total circuit resistance, increasing voltage also increases the current level (amps). Likewise, any decrease in resistance will increase the amount of amps in a circuit. At normal operating voltage, most circuits have a characteristic amount of amperes, called 'current draw" which can be measured using an ammeter. By referring to a specified current draw rating, measuring the amperes, and comparing the two values, one can determine what is happening within the circuit to aid in diagnosis. An open circuit, for example, will not allow any current to flow so the ammeter reading will be zero. More current flows through a heavily loaded circuit or when the charging system is operating.

An ammeter is always connected in series with the circuit being tested. All of the current that normally flows through the circuit must also flow through the ammeter; if there is any other path for the current to follow, the ammeter reading will not be accurate. The ammeter itself has very little resistance to current flow and therefore will not affect the circuit, but it will measure current draw only when the circuit is closed and electricity is flowing. Excessive current draw can blow fuses and drain the battery, while a reduced current draw can cause motors to run slowly, lights to dim and other components to not operate properly. The ammeter can help diagnose these conditions by locating the cause of the high or low reading.

Multimeters
▶ See Figure 5

Different combinations of test meters can be built into a single unit designed for specific tests. Some of the more common combination test devices are known as Volt/Amp testers, Tach/Dwell meters, or Digital Multimeters. The Volt/Amp tester is used for charging system, starting system or battery tests and consists of a voltmeter, an ammeter and a variable resistance carbon pile. The voltmeter will usually have at least two ranges for use with 6, 12 and 24 volt systems. The ammeter also has more than one range for testing various levels of battery loads and starter current draw and the carbon pile can be adjusted to offer different amounts of resistance. The Volt/Amp tester has heavy leads to carry large amounts of current and many later models have an inductive ammeter pickup that clamps around the wire to simplify test connections. On some models, the ammeter also has a zero-center scale to allow testing of charging and starting systems without switching leads or polarity. A digital multimeter i s a voltmeter, ammeter and ohmmeter combined in an instrument which gives a digital readout. These are often used when testing solid state circuits because of their high input impedance (usually 10 megohms or more).

The tach/dwell meter combines a tachometer and a dwell (cam angle) meter and is a specialized kind of voltmeter. The tachometer scale is marked to show engine speed in rpm and the dwell scale is marked to show degrees of distributor shaft rotation. In most electronic ignition systems, dwell is determined by the control unit, but the dwell meter can also be used to check the duty cycle (operation) of some electronic engine control systems. Some tach/dwell meters are powered by an internal battery, while others take their power from the car battery in use. The battery powered testers usually require calibration much like an ohmmeter before testing.

Special Test Equipment

A variety of diagnostic tools are available to help troubleshoot and repair computerized engine control systems. The most sophisticated of these devices are the console type engine analyzers that usually occupy a garage service bay, but there are several types of aftermarket electronic testers available that will allow quick circuit tests of the engine control system by plugging directly into a special connector located in the engine compartment or under the dashboard. Several tool and equipment manufacturers offer simple, hand held testers or scan tools that measure various circuit voltage levels on command to check all system components for proper operation. Although these testers usually cost about $300-$500, consider that the average computer control unit (or ECM) can cost just as much and the money saved by not replacing perfectly good sensors or components in an attempt

to correct a problem could justify the purchase price of a special diagnostic tester the first time it's used.

These computerized scan tools can allow quick and easy test measurements while the engine is operating or while the car is being driven. In addition, the on-board computer memory can be read to access any stored trouble codes; in effect allowing the computer to tell you where it hurts and aid trouble diagnosis by pinpointing exactly which circuit or component is malfunctioning. In the same manner, repairs can be tested to make sure the problem has been corrected. The biggest advantage these special testers have is their relatively easy hookups that minimize or eliminate the chances of making the wrong connections and getting false voltage readings or damaging the computer accidentally.

➡️**It should be remembered that these testers check voltage levels in circuits; they don't detect mechanical problems or failed components if the circuit voltage falls within the preprogrammed limits stored in the tester PROM unit. Also, most of the hand held tests are designed to work only on one or two systems made by a specific manufacturer.**

A variety of aftermarket testers are available to help diagnose different computerized control systems. Owatonna Tool Company (OTC), for example, markets a device called the OTC Monitor which plugs directly into the assembly line diagnostic link (ALDL). The OTC tester makes diagnosis a simple matter of pressing the correct buttons and, by changing the internal PROM or inserting a different diagnosis cartridge, it will work on any model from full size to subcompact, over a wide range of years. An adapter is supplied with the tester to allow connection to all types of ALDL links, regardless of the number of pin terminals used. By inserting an updated PROM into the OTC tester, it can be easily updated to diagnose any new modifications of computerized control systems. Always check with the tool manufacturer before purchase to make sure the tool is compatible with your Saturn vehicle.

Wiring Harnesses

The average automobile contains about ½ mile of wiring, with hundreds of individual connections. To protect the many wires from damage and to keep them from becoming a confusing tangle, they are organized into bundles, enclosed in plastic or taped together and called wire harnesses. Different wiring harnesses serve different parts of the vehicle. Individual wires are color coded to help trace them through a harness where sections are hidden from view.

A loose or corroded connection or a replacement wire that is too small for the circuit will add extra resistance and an additional voltage drop to the circuit. A ten percent voltage drop can result in slow or erratic motor operation, for example, even though the circuit is complete. Automotive wiring or circuit conductors can be in any one of three forms:

1. Single strand wire
2. Multi strand wire
3. Printed circuitry

Single strand wire has a solid metal core and is usually used inside such components as alternators, motors, relays and other devices. Multi strand wire has a core made of many small strands of wire twisted together into a single conductor.

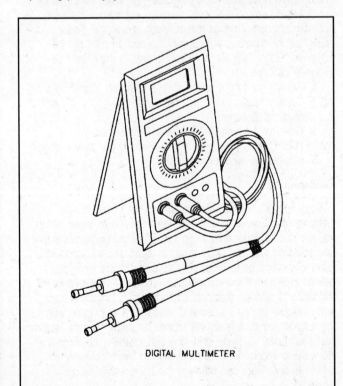

DIGITAL MULTIMETER

Fig. 5 A digital multimeter with an input impedance of 10 megohms is recommended for troubleshooting Saturn vehicles

Most of the wiring in an automotive electrical system is made up of multi strand wire, either as a single conductor or grouped together in a harness. All wiring is color coded on the insulator, either as a solid color or as a colored wire with an identification stripe. A printed circuit is a thin film of copper or other conductor that is printed on an insulator backing. Occasionally, a printed circuit is sandwiched between two sheets of plastic for more protection and flexibility. A complete printed circuit, consisting of conductors, insulating material and connectors for lamps or other components is called a printed circuit board. Printed circuitry is used in place of individual wires or harnesses in places where space is limited, such as behind instrument panels.

Wire Gauge

Since computer controlled automotive electrical systems are very sensitive to changes in resistance, the selection of properly sized wires is critical when systems are repaired. The wire gauge number is an expression of the cross section area of the conductor. The most common system for expressing wire size is the American Wire Gauge (AWG) system.

Wire cross section area is measured in circular mils. A mil is $1/1000$ in. (0.001 in.); a circular mil is the area of a circle one mil in diameter. For example, a conductor $1/4$ in. diameter is 0.250 in. or 250 mils. The circular mil cross section area of the wire is 250 squared (250^2) or 62,500 circular mils. Imported car models usually use metric wire gauge designations, which is simply the cross section area of the conductor in square millimeters (mm^2).

Gauge numbers are assigned to conductors of various cross section areas. As gauge number increases, area decreases and the conductor becomes smaller. A 5 gauge conductor is smaller than a 1 gauge conductor and a 10 gauge is smaller than a 5 gauge. As the cross section area of a conductor decreases, resistance increases and so does the gauge number. A conductor with a higher gauge number will carry less current than a conductor with a lower gauge number.

➡ **Gauge wire size refers to the size of the conductor, not the size of the complete wire. It is possible to have two wires of the same gauge with different diameters because one may have thicker insulation than the other.**

12 volt automotive electrical systems generally use 10, 12, 14, 16 and 18 gauge wire. Main power distribution circuits and larger accessories usually use 10 and 12 gauge wire. Battery cables are usually 4 or 6 gauge, although 1 and 2 gauge wires are occasionally used. Wire length must also be considered when making repairs to a circuit. As conductor length increases, so does resistance. An 18 gauge wire, for example, can carry a 10 amp load for 10 feet without excessive voltage drop; however if a 15 foot wire is required for the same 10 amp load, it must be a 16 gauge wire.

Wiring Diagrams
▶ **See Figures 6 and 7**

An electrical schematic shows the electrical current paths when a circuit is operating properly. It is essential to understand how a circuit works before trying to figure out why it doesn't. Schematics break the entire electrical system down into individual circuits and show only one particular circuit. In a schematic, no attempt is made to represent wiring and components as they physically appear on the vehicle (except for wiring colors); switches and other components are shown as simply as possible. Face views of harness connectors show the cavity or terminal locations in all multi-pin connectors to help locate test points.

If you need to backprobe a connector while it is on the component, the order of the terminals must be mentally reversed. The wire color code can help in this situation, as well as a keyway, lock tab or other reference mark.

WIRING REPAIR

There are 2 types of wiring repair which may be used on vehicles. Wire splicing using special sleeves is the method of repair which is recommended by Saturn for your vehicle's low current and voltage wires. Wire soldering, is also an effective method of wire repair, and is appropriate on some systems, when properly conducted.

Splicing
▶ **See Figures 8 and 9**

Saturn recommends the use of Packard Electric Crimp and Seal Splice Sleeves or equivalent splice sets to repair wires.
1. Remove about ⅜ in. (9.53mm) of insulation from both ends of the wire section which is to be repaired. Caution must be used to avoid cutting wire strands. Make sure the splice is a minimum of 1.5 in. (40mm) from an outlet or other splice.
2. Select the proper sleeve for the wire gauge, the position the stripped ends into the sleeve until the wires hit the stop.
3. Hand crimp the sleeve using an appropriate crimping tool. Do not use pliers or a tool which is not specifically designed for crimping or a proper connection may not be obtained. Gently tug on the wires to assure they have be properly secured.
4. Apply heat to the splice sleeve using an Ultratorch® or an equivalent heating device. The heater must NOT consist of a match or open flame.
5. Continue heating the sleeve to approximately 295°F(175°C) and glue becomes evident at the sleeve edges.
6. Inspect the wire for continuity.

Soldering

Soldering is a quick, efficient method of joining metals permanently. Everyone who has the occasion to make wiring repairs should know how to solder. Electrical connections that are soldered are less likely to come apart and will conduct electricity much better than connections that are only 'pig-tailed" together. The most popular (and preferred) method of soldering is with an electrical soldering gun. Soldering irons are available in many sizes and wattage ratings. Irons with higher wattage ratings deliver higher temperatures and recover lost heat faster. A small soldering iron rated for no more than 50 watts is recommended, especially on electrical systems where excess heat can damage the components being soldered.

There are three ingredients necessary for successful soldering; proper flux, good solder and sufficient heat. A soldering flux is necessary to clean the metal of tarnish, prepare it for soldering and to enable the solder to spread into

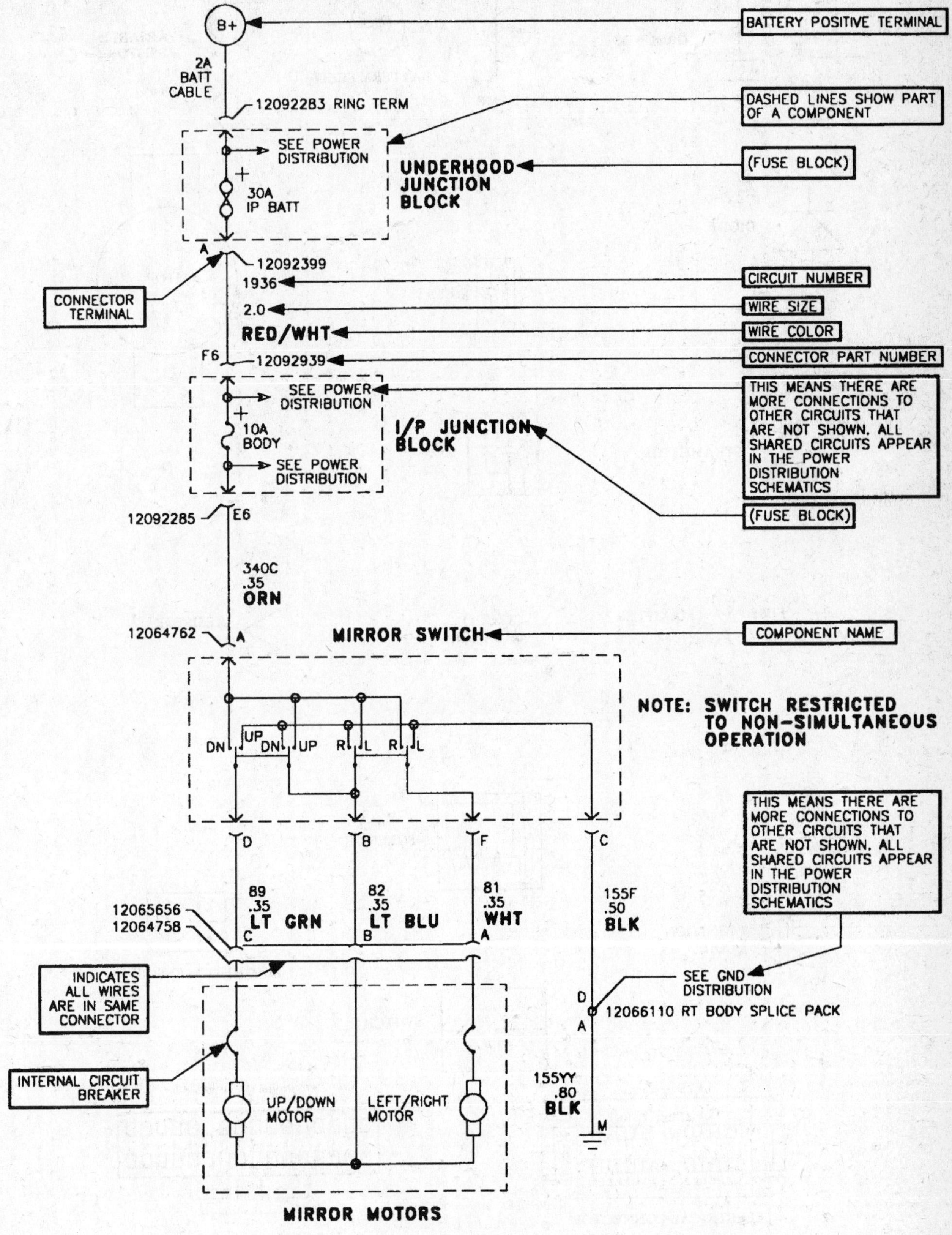

B+ BATTERY POSITIVE TERMINAL

2A BATT CABLE

12092283 RING TERM

DASHED LINES SHOW PART OF A COMPONENT

SEE POWER DISTRIBUTION

UNDERHOOD JUNCTION BLOCK

(FUSE BLOCK)

30A IP BATT

A

CONNECTOR TERMINAL

12092399

1936 — CIRCUIT NUMBER

2.0 — WIRE SIZE

RED/WHT — WIRE COLOR

F6 — 12092939 — CONNECTOR PART NUMBER

SEE POWER DISTRIBUTION

I/P JUNCTION BLOCK

10A BODY

SEE POWER DISTRIBUTION

THIS MEANS THERE ARE MORE CONNECTIONS TO OTHER CIRCUITS THAT ARE NOT SHOWN. ALL SHARED CIRCUITS APPEAR IN THE POWER DISTRIBUTION SCHEMATICS

(FUSE BLOCK)

12092285 — E6

340C .35 ORN

12064762 — A MIRROR SWITCH — COMPONENT NAME

NOTE: SWITCH RESTRICTED TO NON-SIMULTANEOUS OPERATION

DN UP DN UP R L R L

THIS MEANS THERE ARE MORE CONNECTIONS TO OTHER CIRCUITS THAT ARE NOT SHOWN. ALL SHARED CIRCUITS APPEAR IN THE POWER DISTRIBUTION SCHEMATICS

D B F C

89 .35 LT GRN

82 .35 LT BLU

81 .35 WHT

155F .50 BLK

12065656
12064758

C B A

INDICATES ALL WIRES ARE IN SAME CONNECTOR

INTERNAL CIRCUIT BREAKER

SEE GND DISTRIBUTION

D
A 12066110 RT BODY SPLICE PACK

UP/DOWN MOTOR

LEFT/RIGHT MOTOR

155YY .80 BLK

M

MIRROR MOTORS

Fig. 6 How to read electrical schematics — power mirror schematic example

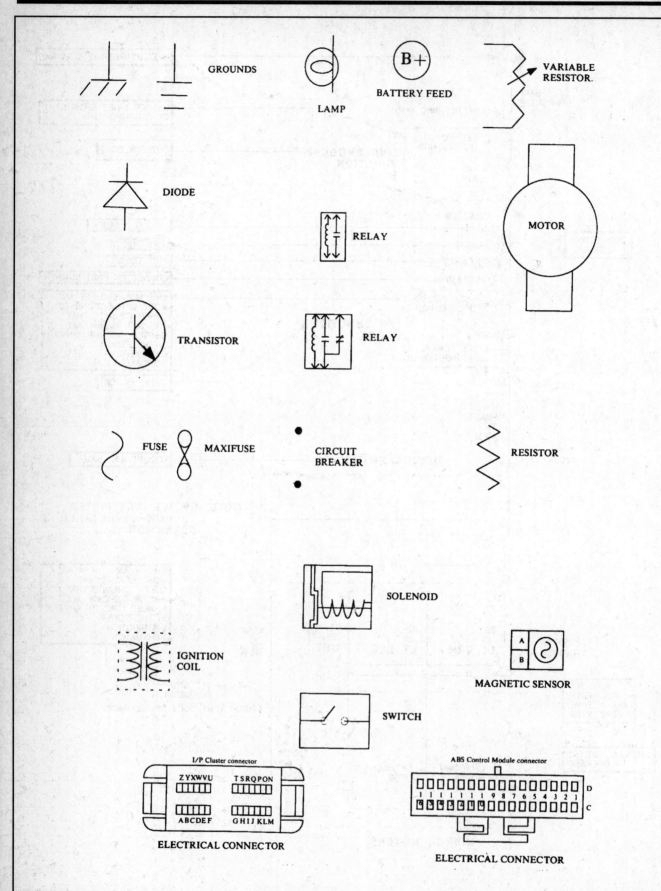

Fig. 7 Various electrical symbols used in electrical schematics

once the job is finished. Other types of flux (acid core) will leave a residue that will attract moisture and cause the wires to corrode. Tin is a unique metal with a low melting point. In a molten state, it dissolves and alloys easily with many metals. Solder is made by mixing tin with lead. The most common proportions are 40/60, 50/50 and 60/40, with the percentage of tin listed first. Low priced solders usually contain less tin, making them very difficult for a beginner to use because more heat is required to melt the solder. A common solder is 40/60 which is well suited for all-around general use, but 60/40 melts easier, has more tin f or a better joint and is preferred for electrical work.

Soldering Techniques

Successful soldering requires that the metals to be joined be heated to a temperature that will melt the solder — usually 360-460°F (182-238°C). Contrary to popular belief, the purpose of the soldering iron is not to melt the solder itself, but to heat the parts being soldered to a temperature high enough to melt the solder when it is touched to the work. Melting flux-cored solder on the soldering iron will usually destroy the effectiveness of the flux.

➡**Soldering tips are made of copper for good heat conductivity, but must be 'tinned" regularly for quick transference of heat to the project and to prevent the solder from sticking to the iron. To 'tin" the iron, simply heat it and touch the flux-cored solder to the tip; the solder will flow over the hot tip. Wipe the excess off with a clean rag, but be careful as the iron will be hot.**

After some use, the tip may become pitted. If so, simply dress the tip smooth with a smooth file and 'tin" the tip again. An old saying holds that 'metals well cleaned are half soldered." Flux-cored solder will remove oxides but rust, bits of insulation and oil or grease must be removed with a wire brush or emery cloth. For maximum strength in soldered parts, the joint must start off clean and tight. Weak joints will result in gaps too wide for the solder to bridge.

If a separate soldering flux is used, it should be brushed or swabbed on only those areas that are to be soldered. Most solders contain a core of flux and separate fluxing is unnecessary. Hold the work to be soldered firmly. It is best to solder on a wooden board, because a metal vise will only rob the piece to be soldered of heat and make it difficult to melt the solder. Hold the soldering tip with the broadest face against the work to be soldered. Apply solder under the tip close to the work, using enough solder to give a heavy film between the iron and the piece being soldered, while moving slowly and making sure the solder melts properly. Keep the work level or the solder will run to the lowest part and favor the thicker parts, because these require more heat to melt the solder. If the soldering tip overheats (the solder coating on the face of the tip burns up), it should be retinned. Once the soldering is completed, let the soldered joint stand until cool. Tape and seal all soldered wire splices after the repair has cooled.

Wire Harness and Connectors

The on-board computer (ECM) wire harness electrically connects the control unit to the various solenoids, switches and sensors used by the control system. Most connectors in

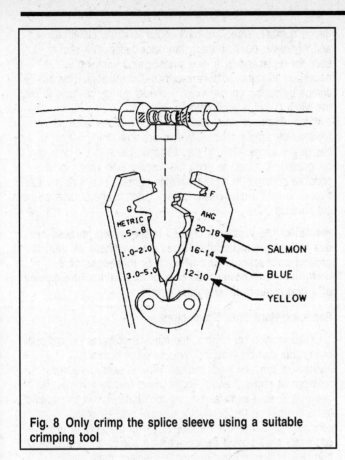

Fig. 8 Only crimp the splice sleeve using a suitable crimping tool

tiny crevices. When soldering, always use a resin flux or resin core solder which is non-corrosive and will not attract moisture

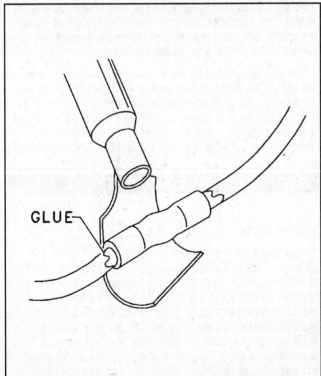

Fig. 9 Apply heat to the splice using a suitable (non-flame) heat source, until glue appears at the edges of the sleeve

the engine compartment or otherwise exposed to the elements are protected against moisture and dirt which could create oxidation and deposits on the terminals. This protection is important because of the very low voltage and current levels used by the computer and sensors. Most connectors have a lock which secures the male and female terminals together, with a secondary lock holding the seal and terminal into the connector. All terminal locks must be released when disconnecting ECM connectors.

These special connectors are weather-proof and all repairs require the use of a special terminal and the tool required to service it. This tool is used to remove the pin and sleeve terminals. If removal is attempted with an ordinary pick, there is a good chance that the terminal will be bent or deformed. Unlike standard blade type terminals, these terminals cannot be straightened once they are bent. Make certain that the connectors are properly seated and all of the sealing rings in place when connecting leads. On some models, a hinge-type flap provides a backup or secondary locking feature for the terminals. Most secondary locks are used to improve the connector reliability by retaining the terminals if the small terminal lock tangs are not positioned properly.

Molded-on connectors require complete replacement of the connection. This means splicing a new connector assembly into the harness. Use care when probing the connections or replacing terminals in them as it is possible to short between opposite terminals. If this happens to the wrong terminal pair, it is possible to damage certain components. Always use jumper wires between connectors for circuit checking and never probe through weatherproof seals, unless installing a Saturn diagnostic probe.

Open circuits are often difficult to locate by sight because corrosion or terminal misalignment are hidden by the connectors. Merely wiggling a connector on a sensor or in the wiring harness may correct the open circuit condition. This should always be considered when an open circuit or a failed sensor is indicated. Intermittent problems may also be caused by oxidized or loose connections. When using a circuit tester for diagnosis, always probe connections from the wire side. Be careful not to damage sealed connectors with test probes.

All wiring harnesses should be replaced with identical parts, using the same gauge wire and connectors. When signal wires are spliced into a harness, use wire with high temperature insulation only. With the low voltage and current levels found in the system, it is important that the best possible connection at all wire splices be made by soldering the splices together. It is seldom necessary to replace a complete harness. If replacement is necessary, pay close attention to insure proper harness routing. Secure the harness with suitable plastic wire clamps to prevent vibrations from causing the harness to wear in spots or contact any hot components.

➡**Weatherproof connectors cannot be replaced with standard connectors. Instructions are provided with replacement connector and terminal packages. Some wire harnesses have mounting indicators (usually pieces of colored tape) to mark where the harness is to be secured.**

In making wiring repairs, it's important that you always replace damaged wires with wires that are the same gauge as the wire being replaced. The heavier the wire, the smaller the gauge number. Wires are color-coded to aid in identification and whenever possible the same color coded wire should be used for replacement. A wire stripping and crimping tool is necessary to install solderless terminal connectors. Test all crimps by pulling on the wires; it should not be possible to pull the wires out of a good crimp.

Wires which are open, exposed or otherwise damaged are repaired by simple splicing. Where possible, if the wiring harness is accessible and the damaged place in the wire can be located, it is best to open the harness and check for all possible damage. In an inaccessible harness, the wire must be bypassed with a new insert, usually taped to the outside of the old harness.

➡**Most of the problems caused in the wiring harness are due to bad ground connections. Always check all vehicle ground connections for corrosion or looseness before performing any power feed checks to eliminate the chance of a bad ground affecting the circuit.**

Repairing Hard Shell Connectors

Unlike molded connectors, the terminal contacts in hard shell connectors can be replaced. Weatherproof hard-shell connectors with the leads molded into the shell have non-replaceable terminal ends. Replacement usually involves the use of a special terminal removal tool that depress the locking tangs (barbs) on the connector terminal and allow the connector to be removed from the rear of the shell. The connector shell should be replaced if it shows any evidence of burning, melting, cracks, or breaks. Replace individual terminals that are burnt, corroded, distorted or loose.

➡**The insulation crimp must be tight to prevent the insulation from sliding back on the wire when the wire is pulled. The insulation must be visibly compressed under the crimp tabs, and the ends of the crimp should be turned in for a firm grip on the insulation.**

The wire crimp must be made with all wire strands inside the crimp. The terminal must be fully compressed on the wire strands with the ends of the crimp tabs turned in to make a firm grip on the wire. Check all connections with an ohmmeter to insure a good contact. There should be no measurable resistance between the wire and the terminal when connected.

Mechanical Test Equipment

Vacuum Gauge

Most gauges are graduated in inches of mercury (in. Hg), although a device called a manometer reads vacuum in inches of water (in. H_2O). The normal vacuum reading usually varies between 18 and 22 in. Hg at sea level. To test engine vacuum, the vacuum gauge must be connected to a source of manifold vacuum. Connect the vacuum gauge to a fitting, if available, using a suitable rubber hose or, if no manifold fitting is available, connect the vacuum gauge to any device using manifold vacuum, such as EGR valves, etc. The vacuum gauge can be used to determine if enough vacuum is reaching a component to allow its actuation.

Hand Vacuum Pump

Small, hand-held vacuum pumps come in a variety of designs. Most have a built-in vacuum gauge and allow the component to be tested without removing it from the vehicle. Operate the pump lever or plunger to apply the correct amount of vacuum required for the test specified in the diagnosis routines. The level of vacuum in inches of Mercury (in. Hg) is indicated on the pump gauge. For some testing, an additional vacuum gauge may be necessary.

Intake manifold vacuum is used to operate various systems and devices on late model vehicles. To correctly diagnose and solve problems in vacuum control systems, a vacuum source is necessary for testing. In some cases, vacuum can be taken from the intake manifold when the engine is running, but vacuum is normally provided by a hand vacuum pump. These hand vacuum pumps have a built-in vacuum gauge that allow testing while the device is still attached to the component. For some tests, an additional vacuum gauge may be necessary.

SUPPLEMENTAL INFLATABLE RESTRAINT (AIR BAG) SYSTEM

General Information

SYSTEM OPERATION

▶ See Figure 10

The Supplemental Inflatable Restraint (SIR) system was available on Saturn vehicles produced very late in 1992 and was standard on all vehicles built for 1993. The SIR or Air Bag system is designed to supplement the normal restraint of the driver's seat belt in the event of a frontal collision. Should an accident occur within certain specifications of force and direction, an air bag will be deployed from the center of the steering wheel. A knee bolster is also provided to help prevent the driver from sliding downward or forward in the seat during impact.

The very name of the SIR system includes the word SUPPLEMENTAL, which indicates that the system is secondary in the protection of a driver in case of an accident. The system may not be effective at all if not used in conjunction with the lap and shoulder belts.

SYSTEM COMPONENTS

▶ See Figure 11

There are 2 main portions of the SIR system; the deployment loop and the Diagnostic Energy Reserve Module

(DERM). The deployment loop supplies current to the inflator module located in the steering wheel in order to inflate the bag in case of a frontal impact with certain minimum amount of force. The deployment loop is made up of the arming sensor, inflator coil assembly, inflator module and the crash discriminating sensors. The DERM unit is a computer control module that is designed to supply power to the deployment loop if the ignition feed to the arming sensor is lost during a collision. The DERM also is used to monitor the electrical function of the system whenever the ignition is switched **ON** in order to alert the driver of a condition which might prevent deployment of the air bag in a crash. If such a condition does occur, the DERM will store a diagnostic code and illuminate the AIR BAG lamp on the instrument panel.

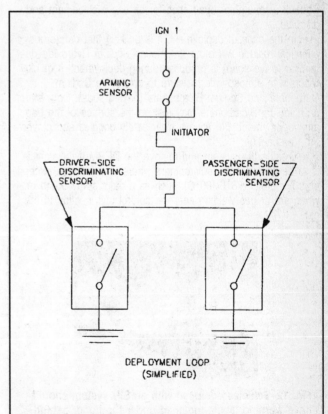

Fig. 11 Simplified schematic of the deployment loop

Fig. 10 The air bag works along with the driver's seat belts and knee bolster to protect the driver from a frontal collision

SERVICE PRECAUTIONS

▶ **See Figure 12**

✳✳CAUTION

Whenever working on or around SIR components, always observe these general precautions to prevent the possibility of personal injury or damage to the SIR system through unwanted detonation or accidental disabling of the system.

- The DERM unit contains can maintain sufficient voltage to deploy the air bag up to 10 minutes after the ignition is turned **OFF**. Always temporarily disable the SIR system before performing ANY work around system wiring or components.
- The SIR discriminating sensors are located in the front of the vehicle, under the hood. They are specifically calibrated and are keyed to the mounting brackets and SIR wiring harness. Never disturb the sensors or modify the keying of the sensors to the structure through the differently sized mounting holes.
- Never strike or jar a sensor, under certain circumstances, this could cause air bag deployment or improper SIR system operation.
- In the unlikely event that the SIR module is deployed while servicing the vehicle, do not touch metal surrounding the system for at least 10 minutes to allow the metal to cool. Consult a reputable repair shop for air bag replacement and disposal.
- In the case of deployment, it is unlikely that dangerous chemical residue will remain. Although Sodium Hydroxide dust (similar to lye soap) is produced during deployment, it quickly reacts with atmospheric moisture to convert to Sodium Carbonate and Sodium Bicarbonate (baking soda). Corn starch and Sodium Bicarbonate may rest on the surface of the bag after deployment. But always wear safety goggles and gloves as a precaution.
- Disable the system and remove the DERM if the vehicle is to be placed in an environment where temperatures exceed approximately 176°F (80°C), such as a paint spray booth or when arc or gas welding near the control unit location in the car.

DISABLING THE SYSTEM

▶ **See Figure 13**

Before working on or near any component of the SIR system, always disable the system to prevent unwanted deployment. Replacement of inflator modules can cost in excess of $1000.00 plus installation and disposal of the old module.

1. Align the steering wheel so the tires are in the straight-ahead position, then turn the ignition **OFF**.
2. Remove the 10 amp SIR fuse from the top left of the Instrument Panel Junction Block (IPJB).
3. Remove the Connector Position Assurance (CPA) device, then disconnect the yellow 2-way SIR connector at the base of the steering column.

ENABLING THE SYSTEM

After completing work on or near components of the SIR system, always properly enable the system and check for proper operation by watching the AIR BAG light in the instrument cluster.

1. Verify the ignition switch is **OFF**, then connect the SIR electrical connector at the base of the steering column. Install the CPA device to the connector.
2. Install the SIR fuse to the IPJB and install the fuse box cover.
3. Turn the ignition **ON** and verify that the AIR BAG indicator lamp flashes 7-9 times, then extinguishes. If the light does not flash as indicated, recheck the fuse and connector. If the light still does not function properly, consult a reputable repair shop.

Fig. 12 Vehicles equipped with an SIR system should have warning labels mounted under the hood, behind both headlights and near the hood latch

Fig. 13 Remove the 10 amp AIR BAG fuse from the upper left of the Instrument Panel Junction Block (IPJB)

HEATER

Blower Motor

REMOVAL & INSTALLATION

▶ **See Figures 14, 15 and 16**

1. Disconnect the negative battery cable.
2. Unplug the blower motor electrical connector under the glove compartment.
3. Remove the blower motor mounting screws, the carefully lower the motor assembly from the Heating Ventilation Air Conditioning (HVAC) module.
4. Install the motor in the reverse order and check operation.

Heater Core

REMOVAL & INSTALLATION

▶ **See Figures 17, 18, 19, 20, 21 and 22**

The Saturn Heating Ventilation Air Conditioning (HVAC) module is the same basic unit on all models, regardless of whether or not they are equipped with air conditioning. The module contains the blower motor, heater core, A/C evaporator (if equipped) and various valve/seal assemblies which route

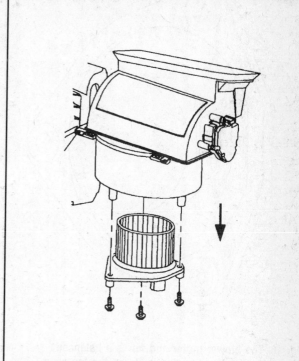

Fig. 15 Remove the blower mounting screws, then carefully lower the blower from the HVAC module

fresh or passenger compartment air by the A/C evaporator and/or the heater core.

1. Disconnect the negative battery cable, the drain the engine cooling system in a suitable container.
2. Raise the front of the vehicle and support safely using jackstands.
3. While squeezing the retaining tabs, move the heater core clamps up the hoses and off the fittings, then remove the jackstands and carefully lower the vehicle.
4. For the DOHC engine, remove the air cleaner housing cover and disconnect the air induction hose at the intake manifold. For the SOHC engine, remove the air cleaner housing assembly.
5. Carefully remove the hoses from the heater core. Never pry hoses against the heater core pipes or the core may be damaged. Using compressed air or a length of clean hose, blow the remaining coolant out of the heater core to prevent spilling it on the vehicle's interior.
6. Remove the left and right lower trim lower trim panel extensions by disconnecting the velcro at the bottom of the panels and pulling them out of the upper retaining clips.
7. Remove the retaining screws and lower the heater duct straight downward. Carefully slide the duct to the side and remove it from the vehicle. Make sure the heater duct-to-rear floor duct seal is not damaged during removal.
8. Push down on the cable and lift the plastic tab to release the temperature cable hold down clip, then disconnect the temperature cable by squeezing the valve pin and pulling

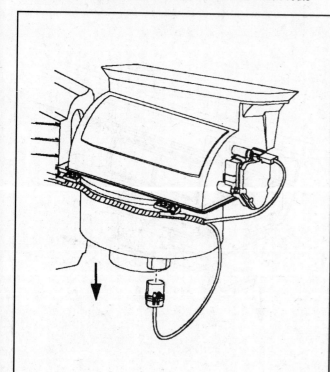

Fig. 14 Unplug the electrical connector from the blower motor

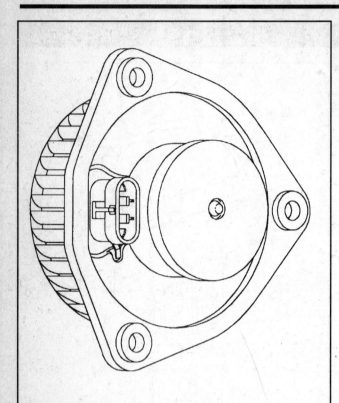

Fig. 16 The blower motor and fan is a balanced assembly. Weights may be visible on the fan cage

the cable straight off the Heating Ventilation Air Conditioning (HVAC) module.

9. Locate the heater core side cover, on the driver's side of the HVAC module, then remove the retaining screws and the side cover.

10. Remove the screws and the lower heater core cover. Remove the screw from the heater core pipe clamp.

11. Remove the screw and the lower core retainer, then carefully remove the heater core from the vehicle.

To install:

12. Install the heater core being careful not to damage the pipe seal. Use a coating of petroleum jelly to ease installation of the pipes through the cowl.

13. Install the lower heater core retainer and the pipe clamp using the retaining screws. Install the lower and side covers.

14. Push the temperature cable over the pin and snap the cable hold down clip over the cable holder.

15. Slide the heater duct in sideways and raise it into position being careful not to damage the rear floor heater seal. Install the duct screws.

16. Install the left and right trim panel extensions.

17. Raise the front of the vehicle and support safely using jackstands.

18. Install the heater hoses, positioning the left hose clamp tangs to the 7-8 o'clock position and the right hose to the 6 o'clock position.

19. If not done already, install the radiator drain plug, then install the cylinder block drain plug and tighten the block plug to 26 ft. lbs. (35 Nm).

20. Remove the jackstands and carefully lower the vehicle, then install the air cleaner housing components, as applicable.

21. Connect the negative battery cable and properly fill the engine cooling system.

Fig. 17 Slide the retaining clamps upward on the heater core hoses so they no longer compress the hoses on the fittings

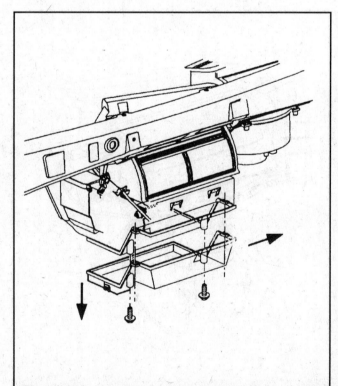

Fig. 18 After removing the lower duct fasteners, carefully drop the duct downward and slide it sideways, removing the duct from the vehicle

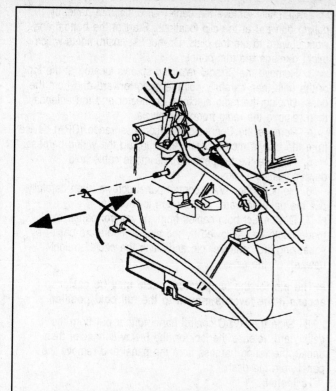

Fig. 19 Remove the temperature cable from the HVAC module

22. Pressure test the cooling system or start the engine and check for leaks.

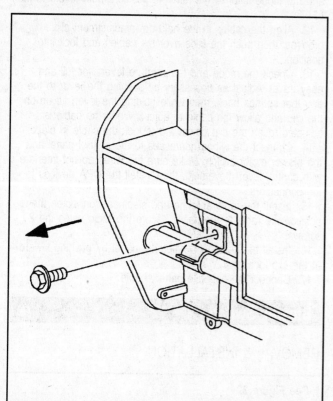

Fig. 20 Remove the screw from the heater core pipe clamp

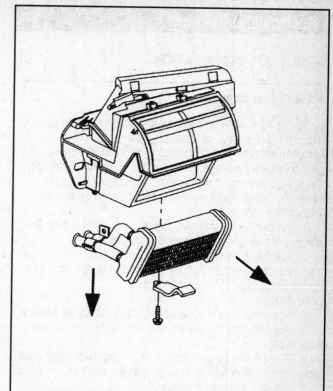

Fig. 21 Remove the lower heater core retainer, then carefully remove the heater core from the HVAC module

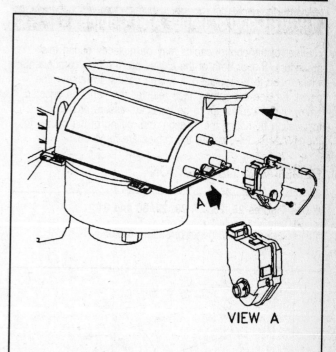

VIEW A

Fig. 22 The same basic HVAC module is used on all Saturn vehicles regardless of whether they are equipped with A/C. On vehicles not equipped with A/C, the evaporator is absent

Recirculation Motor

REMOVAL & INSTALLATION

▶ **See Figures 23 and 24**

The HVAC module contains a recirculation motor which is used to rotate a valve between the fresh or passenger compartment air. When the motor is activated it rotates to a position where passenger compartment air is drawn through the system and mixed with a small amount of outside air. When the button is not activated, only fresh air is drawn through the vent.

1. Disconnect the negative battery cable, then unplug the electrical connector from the recirculation motor.
2. Remove the motor mounting screws.
3. Pull the motor straight off of the recirculation door shaft and from the side of the HVAC module.

To install:
4. Position the recirculation door to the outside air position.
5. Align the flats on the motor shaft and the recirculation door shaft.
6. Push the motor straight onto the recirculation door shaft while rotating back and forth to engage the shaft on the motor.
7. Install the mounting screws.
8. Install the motor electrical connector.
9. Connect the negative battery cable.

HVAC Control Panel And Cables

Either of the control cables may be replaced during this procedure. If 1 or both of the cables are the only components which need to be replaced, it will be easiest to remove the panel, replace the cables, then reinstall the panel as directed below. If the cables are to be replaced, assure proper installation by noting the location and routing of the cables to the HVAC module, before the cables are removed.

REMOVAL & INSTALLATION

▶ **See Figures 25, 26, 27, 28, 29, 30 and 31**

1. Disconnect the negative battery cable.

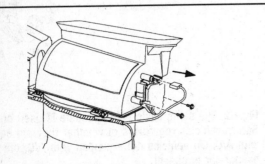

Fig. 23 Unplug the electrical connector and remove the mounting screws

2. Carefully remove the center air outlet/trim panel by pulling outward at the clip locations. Start at the bottom and work upward to the top clips. Do not use instruments which might damage the trim panel.
3. Remove the 2 radio retaining screws located at the top of the unit, then carefully pull the radio forward and from the dash. Unplug the radio electrical connector and the antenna, then remove the radio from the vehicle.
4. Remove the Connector Position Assurance (CPA) device from the blower motor switch, then unplug the wiring harness.
5. Release the temperature and mode cable hold down/adjustment clips.
6. Remove the HVAC control panel screws, then carefully pull the panel forward, just enough for access.
7. Disconnect both cables from the control panel (black mode cable first, followed by the blue temperature cable) by squeezing the controller pin and lifting the cable straight upward, off the pin.

➡ **The pin for the temperature cable may be easier to access if the lever is moved to the full cold position.**

8. Slide the HVAC control panel further out from the dashboard, release the lock on the 6-way connector then unplug the wiring harness from the panel and remove the panel from the dash.

To install:
9. Position the HVAC control panel to the dash and install the retaining screws.
10. Install the blue temperature and the black mode cables over the pins.
11. Position the temperature lever to the full cold position and the mode lever to the full vent position (both levers to the LEFT).
12. Align the cables in the hold down/adjustment clip grooves, then push the clips over the cables and lock into position.
13. Check the mode and temperature levers for full and easy travel. Adjust as necessary by pushing the lever to the end that springs back, then while holding the lever, lift up on the clip and allow the cable to adjust. When the cable is adjusted, push the clip downward to lock the cable in place.
14. Connect the wiring harnesses to the control panel and the blower motor switch. Make sure the wires do not interfere with control lever movement, then install the CPA devices to the connectors.
15. Install the radio antenna and electrical connector, then position the radio to the dash. Secure the radio using the 2 screws.
16. Install the center air outlet/trim panel by pushing inward at the clip locations.
17. Connect the negative battery cable.

Blower Switch

REMOVAL & INSTALLATION

▶ **See Figure 32**

1. Remove the HVAC control panel as described earlier in this Section. It may be possible to remove the switch screws

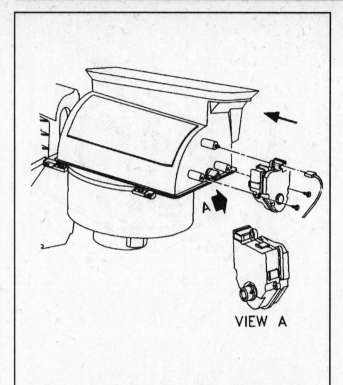

Fig. 24 Align the motor and door flats, then push the motor straight onto the door shaft while rotating the motor back and forth to align the 2 components

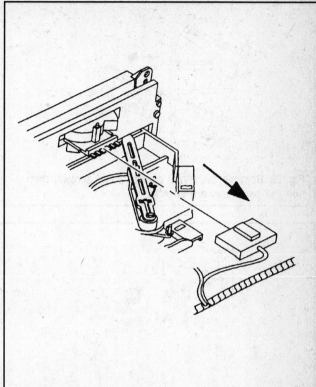

Fig. 26 Remove the CPA, then unplug the wiring harness connector from the blower motor switch

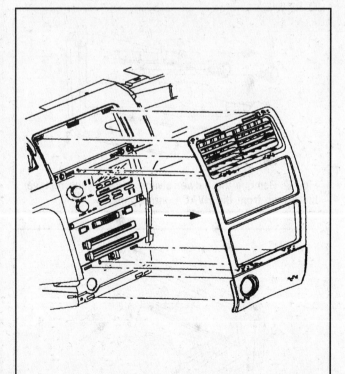

Fig. 25 Pull outward at the clip locations to remove the center console air outlet/trim panel from the dash — 1992-93 vehicles shown

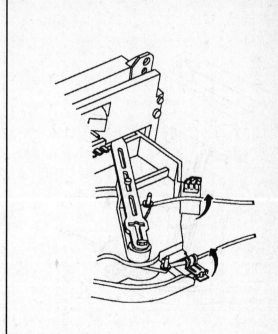

Fig. 27 Release the temperature and mode cable hold down/adjustment clips

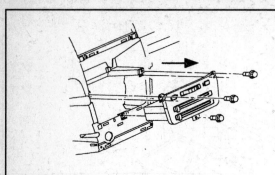

Fig. 28 Remove the HVAC control panel screws, then pull the panel forward slightly

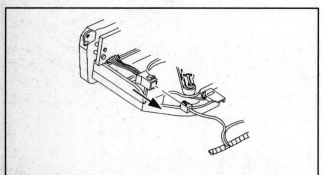

Fig. 29 Release the lock on the 6-way connector, then unplug the wiring harness from the control panel

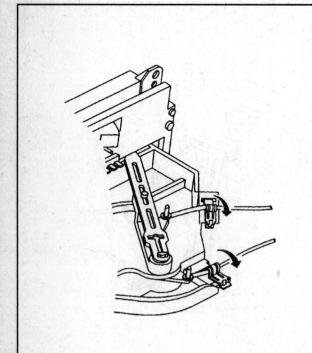

Fig. 30 Align the cables in the clip grooves, then push the clips downward to lock the cables in position

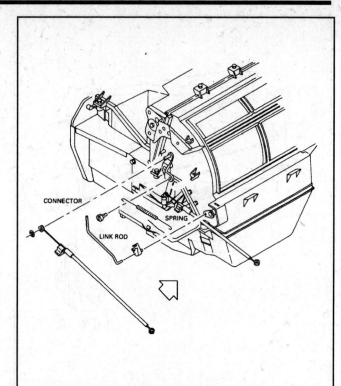

CONNECTOR

SPRING

LINK ROD

Fig. 31 If the control cables are to be replaced, note their positions on and routing to the HVAC module prior to removal

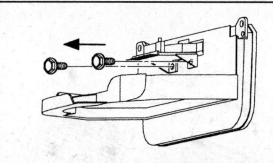

Fig. 32 Remove the blower switch screws, then remove the switch from the HVAC control panel

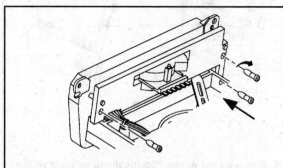

Fig. 33 Insert the bulb into the HVAC control panel, then rotate clockwise to engage it with the circuit board

and switch without disconnecting the control cables, if so, they will not need to be adjusted upon installation.

2. Remove the blower motor switch screws from the rear of the panel.

3. Remove the switch from the panel.

4. To install, position the switch to the panel and secure using the mounting screws.

5. Install the HVAC control panel and, if necessary, adjust the cables.

HVAC Control Panel Bulb

REMOVAL & INSTALLATION

▶ See Figure 33

1. Remove the HVAC control panel as described earlier in this Section. It may be possible to remove the faulty bulb without disconnecting the control cables, if so, they will not need to be adjusted upon installation.

2. Rotate the bulb counterclockwise and pull straight backwards to remove it from the control panel assembly.

3. To install the bulb, insert it into the panel and turn clockwise to engage it with the circuit board.

4. Install the HVAC control panel and, if necessary, adjust the cables.

AIR CONDITIONER

➡**Refer to SECTION 1 for discharging, charging, etc. of the air conditioning system.**

Compressor

REMOVAL & INSTALLATION

▶ See Figures 34, 35, 36 and 37

Whenever servicing the compressor, make sure to keep all dirt and foreign material from entering the compressor or system. Always clean the area around fittings before they are disconnected. Before assembly, all parts should be cleaned with a non-petroleum based solvent and dried with air. Do not allow solvent to enter into the fittings.

1. Disconnect the negative battery cable.

2. Discharge the refrigerant into a suitable recovery system. Measure and note the amount of oil lost from the system during recovery for assembly purposes.

3. For the DOHC engine, remove the air intake ducts.

4. Remove the serpentine drive belt from the compressor clutch by rotating the belt tensioner clockwise to release the tension.

5. Remove the Connector Position Assurance (CPA) device, then unplug the electrical connector from the compressor.

✳✳CAUTION

Never disconnect refrigerant hoses unless the system has been fully discharged.

6. Disconnect the low and high side hoses at the compressor. Install plastic bags over the open ends of the hoses to prevent system contamination.

7. Remove the rear compressor bracket bolts.

8. Support the compressor and remove the front bracket bolts. Remove the compressor, but be sure to keep the unit level to prevent spilling oil from the low or high side ports.

9. Install SA9149AC-6 and SA9149AC-5, or equivalent low and high side oil drain adapters, to the compressor ports.

Drain the old oil into a clean measuring cup or container. Begin draining from the high side first, making sure all the oil possible has been removed. Invert the compressor and drain oil from the low side, rotating the drive plate in both directions to assure oil has been removed from the compressor chambers. Finally, invert the compressor 1 last time to assure all oil has been drained from the high side. Stop draining when oil only appears in drops. Measure and record the amount of oil which was drained.

To install:

10. Inspect the oil which was removed for the compressor for signals of color change from clear to dark brown or black and/or for the presence of metal filings or other foreign substances. If either of these conditions are found, the receiver/drier must be replaced to prevent new compressor damage.

11. If installing a new compressor, position the unit with the low and high side ports in an upright position, then slowly remove the high side cap retaining bolt to release the nitrogen charge from the compressor. Remove the low and high side caps, and install the drain adapters. Carefully drain the compressor as described in Step 9. Make sure the oil is drained into a clean measuring container, as it will be reused. New compressors are charged with 200cc of oil at the factory, there at least 150cc of oil can be drained from the new part.

12. To determine the amount of oil which is needed by the A/C system, add the amount lost during recover (Step 2) and the amount drained from the old compressor (Step 9). This is the total amount of clean fluid which must be added to the compressor prior to installation.

13. Add the appropriate amount of oil, then remove the drain caps.

14. Keeping the compressor level so as to prevent oil spill, position the compressor to the front bracket and install the bolts finger-tight.

15. Install the rear compressor bracket bolts, finger-tight. Using a torque wrench, tighten the front bolts to 36 ft. lbs. (49 Nm), then tighten the rear bolts to 19 ft. lbs. (25 Nm).

16. Remove the plugs or plastic bags from the low and high side hoses, then lubricate using compressor oil and install new O-rings.

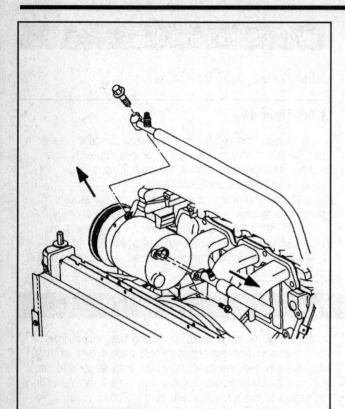

Fig. 34 Disconnect the low and high side hoses from the compressor

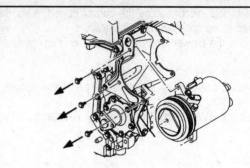

Fig. 36 Remove the front bracket bolts, then carefully remove the compressor

Fig. 37 Drain compressor oil starting from the high side, then from the low side while rotating the drive plate

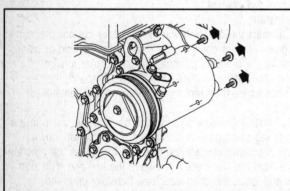

Fig. 35 Remove the rear compressor bracket bolts

17. Install the hoses to the compressor ports, then tighten the bolts to 19 ft. lbs. (25 Nm).
18. Install the compressor electrical connector, then install the CPA device.
19. Install the serpentine drive belt and, for the DOHC engine, install the air intake ducts.
20. Connect the negative battery cable, then properly charge and test the A/C system.

Condenser

REMOVAL & INSTALLATION

▶ See Figures 38, 39, 40, 41, 42 and 43

1. Discharge the refrigerant into a suitable recovery system.
2. For the DOHC engine, remove the air cleaner housing and the air induction hose at the intake manifold. For SOHC engines, remove the air intake ducts.
3. Disconnect the compressor discharge hose from the condenser inlet.
4. Raise and support the front of the vehicle safely using jackstands.
5. Remove the lower the splash shield from the front underside of the vehicle.
6. Disconnect the receiver/drier hose from the condenser outlet.
7. Remove the condenser bracket bolts from the radiator.
8. From the front of the vehicle, pull the condenser back slightly in order to release it from the mounting pads, then carefully slide it straight downward until it can be rotated.
9. Rotate the left end of the condenser downward so the inlet pipe is straight up, then rotate the bottom of the condenser rearward to unhook the inlet pipe from the lower radiator mount. Carefully remove the condenser from the vehicle.

To install:

10. Check the part to make sure it is the proper condenser for the engine application. The DOHC engine uses a serpentine condenser while the SOHC engine utilizes a tube and fin unit. For the 1993 model year, Saturn used a new header type high efficiency aluminum condenser. This slightly smaller unit will lower the system charge level to 2 $\frac{1}{8}$ lbs. (34 oz) and is recommended by the manufacturer for use in all model year vehicles.

11. Position the condenser under the vehicle at a right angle to the radiator and the inlet pointing upward. Hook the inlet over the lower radiator hose, then carefully rotate the condenser to a position parallel to the radiator.

12. Slide the condenser upward and engage it to the mounting pads. Be careful not to damage the radiator or the condenser during installation.

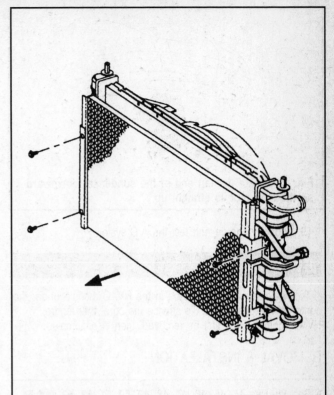

Fig. 40 Remove the condenser bracket bolts from the radiator

13. Install the bracket-to-radiator bolts.

14. Lubricate using compressor oil and install a new O-ring on the receiver/drier hose, then install the hose to the condenser outlet. After tightening the fitting, the hose must be parallel to the condenser in order to provide sufficient clearance between the hose and the vehicle and therefore prevent hose damage.

15. Install the lower splash shield.

16. Remove the jackstands and carefully lower the vehicle to the ground.

17. Lubricate and install new O-rings on the compressor discharge hose, then install the hose to the condenser inlet. After tightening the fitting, make sure the hose is horizontal to prevent the hose from contacting the suction hose and/or transaxle oil cooler lines.

18. Install the air cleaner and/or the air intake ducts, as applicable.

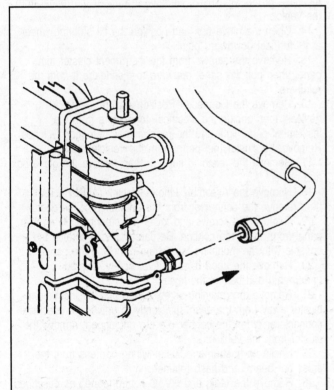

Fig. 38 Disconnect the compressor discharge hose from the condenser inlet

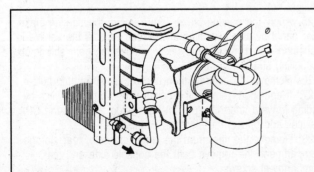

Fig. 39 Disconnect the receiver/drier hose from the condenser outlet

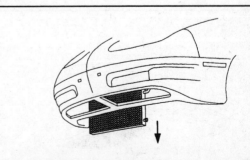

Fig. 41 Release the condenser from the mounting pads, then carefully slide it straight downward sufficiently to allow rotation

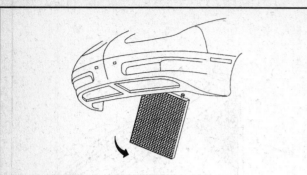

Fig. 42 Rotate the left end of the condenser downward so the inlet pipe is straight up

19. Properly charge and test the A/C system.

Evaporator Core

To evaporator core is located in the HVAC module under the center of the dashboard. To service the core, then entire HVAC module must first be removed, then disassembled.

REMOVAL & INSTALLATION

▶ **See Figures 44, 45, 46, 47, 48, 49, 50, 51, 52, 53 and 54**

1. Disconnect the negative battery cable and drain the engine cooling system into a clean container.
2. Discharge the refrigerant into a suitable recovery system.
3. For the DOHC engine, remove the air cleaner housing and the air induction hose at the intake manifold. For SOHC engines, remove the cleaner housing.
4. Remove the suction hose and liquid line from the thermal expansion valve located on the vehicle's firewall, next to the brake booster assembly.
5. Remove the thermal expansion valve from the evaporator, then plug all A/C opening to prevent system contamination.
6. Raise and support the front of the vehicle safely using jackstands.
7. Move the hose clamps up the hoses and away from the heater core inlet and outlet.
8. Remove the supports, then lower the vehicle.

9. Disconnect the hoses from the heater core. Using a length of clean hose, blow the remaining coolant from the heater core in order to avoid spilling it on the vehicle's interior.
10. Remove the left and right lower trim lower trim panel extensions by disconnecting the velcro at the bottom of the panels and pulling them out of the upper retaining clips.
11. Remove the cigar lighter trim bezel (1991 vehicles), then carefully remove the center air outlet/trim panel by pulling outward at the clip locations. Begin at the bottom of the panel and work towards the upper clips, being careful not to score or damage the panel.
12. Remove the 2 dashboard upper trim panel screw caps (located near the windshield at either end of the dash) by carefully prying with a small flathead tool. Remove the upper trim panel screws.
13. Lift the upper trim panel to disengage the clips at the rear edge, the pull the panel rearward and out of the clips at the base of the windshield. Remove the upper trim panel from the vehicle.
14. Open the glove box and position the tilt steering wheel at its furthest downward point.
15. Remove the screws from the instrument cluster trim panel, then pull the panel rearward to disengage it from the retainers.
16. Remove the Connector Position Assurance (CPA) devices, then unplug the electrical connectors from the instrument panel light and the rear window defogger switches. Remove the cluster trim panel from the vehicle.
17. Remove the retaining screws, then remove the glove box and striker.
18. Remove the Assembly Line Data Link (ALDL) screws, then remove the connector from the underside of the dash.
19. Remove the screws and lower the steering column filler panel from under the column. Be careful not to scratch the console with the mounting tabs when removing the panel.
20. Remove the hood release lever screw, located underneath and behind the lever.
21. Remove the retaining screws, then pull the instrument cluster away from the dash sufficiently to unplug the electrical connectors. When the connectors are unplugged, remove the cluster from the vehicle.
22. Unclip the instrument cluster wiring harness from the cross car beam, and dash retainer.
23. Remove the radio and HVAC control panel, as described in this section.
24. Unplug the cigarette lighter connector, then remove the lighter bulb holder by rotating counterclockwise and pulling straight out.
25. Apply the parking brake, then remove the parking brake filler panel by carefully lifting at the rear edge. If the vehicle is equipped with a manual transaxle, remove the gear shift knob by pulling straight upward.
26. Remove the ashtray, then unclip the astray bulb holder.
27. If equipped, remove the power window/mirror switch by sliding forward, then lifting at the rear edge. Remove the CPA devices and unplug the electrical connectors.
28. Remove the liner from the center console, rear storage compartment, the remove both the console side and rear compartment screws.
29. Lift the back of the console sufficiently to reach underneath and push out the seat belt bezels. Feed the seat belts though the cutouts and remove the console.

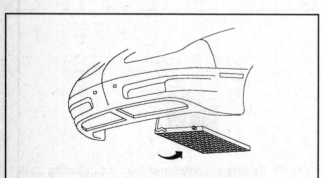

Fig. 43 Rotate the bottom of the condenser rearward to unhook the inlet pipe from the lower radiator mount

30. Remove the retaining screws, then carefully pull the Instrument Panel Junction Block (IPJB) away from the dash reinforcement. Disconnect the ground wire from the reinforcement.

31. Remove the screw and electrical connector from the rear of the IPJB. If equipped with an automatic transaxle, remove the CPA devices, then disconnect the 2-way instrument panel-to-body harness connector.

32. Unclip the IPJB from the dash retainer.

33. Remove the wiring harness and antenna hold down clips from the dash reinforcement.

34. Loosen the floor shifter assembly. Remove the nuts and bolts, then lift the lower reinforcement bracket off of the studs and slide the bracket rearward.

35. Remove the screws and nuts from the dash retainer and the reinforcement bracket.

36. Remove the bolts, then carefully lower steering column assembly onto the driver's seat.

37. Carefully remove the instrument panel/dash assembly from the vehicle.

38. Remove the lower heater duct, then lift the rear floor heater duct from the mounting bolt and remove. Be careful not to damage the seal.

39. Remove the screws, then remove the center air outlet duct.

40. Remove the screws, then unsnap the windshield defroster nozzle from the mode valve assembly.

41. Remove the defroster nozzle by rotating the front of the nozzle upward and away from the windshield.

42. Remove the CPA devices, then disconnect the blower motor resistor connector. Remove the wire harness and hold down clips from the HVAC module.

43. Unplug the blower motor and recirculation motor electrical connectors. Remove the wiring harness and hold down clips from the HVAC module.

44. In the engine compartment, remove the fuel vapor line and clips from the HVAC module stud in order to gain access to the nut

45. Remove the 3 screws and 2 nuts which retain the HVAC module to the cowl. The bolts may be found to the upper right side of the Thermal Expansion Valve (TXV), below the heater core outlet pipe and just above the HVAC module case drain. The nuts are to the upper left of the heater core outlet pipe (below the TXV) and on the left side of the cowl.

46. Remove the HVAC module from inside the vehicle.

47. Disassemble the HVAC module:

a. Remove and discard the front dash seals.

b. Remove the mode valve assembly screws, then lift the assembly straight upward and from the HVAC module.

c. Remove the upper air inlet case screws and spring clips, then lift the air inlet straight up and from the lower HVAC case assembly.

d. Remove the screw and the evaporator pipe clamp.

e. Lift the evaporator straight upward and remove from the lower HVAC case assembly.

To install:

48. Assemble the HVAC module:

a. Position the water filter, retainers, evaporator seal and spacer pad to the new evaporator. Add 1.5 ounces of new refrigerant oil and replace the evaporator pipe cover. Some replacement parts may come with the filter and pad already installed.

b. Lower the evaporator into the lower HVAC case assembly.

c. Install the evaporator pipe clamp and screw.

d. Position the upper air inlet case to the lower case assembly. To avoid case damage, make sure that all tongue and groove parts fit properly before tightening screws, then install the screws and spring clips.

e. Install the mode valve assembly, making sure that tongue and groove parts are properly fitted, then install and tighten the screws.

49. Install new front dash seals to the heater core pipes, case drain and evaporator block.

50. Install the HVAC module through the cowl, then install the bolts and nuts.

51. Install the fuel vapor line and clip to the stud located below the TXV.

52. Install the blower motor and recirculation motor electrical connectors, then position the wiring harness hold down clips on the HVAC module.

53. Install the blower motor resistor electrical connector and the CPA devices, then position the wiring harness hold down clips on the HVAC module.

54. Rotate the windshield defroster nozzle onto the mode valve assembly, make sure the duct is snapped onto both sides of the HVAC module, then install the screws.

55. Install the center air outlet duct and screws. Make sure the plastic mounting tabs are located between the knee beam and mounting bracket.

56. Install the rear heater duct onto the mounting stud, then install the lower heater duct.

57. Install the instrument panel assembly. When positioning the panel, feed the fuse block and wiring harness through the lower reinforcement and into position. Install and tighten the screws and nuts on the dash retainer and reinforcement bracket.

58. Carefully raise the steering column assembly into position, then install the retaining bolts and tighten to 33 ft. lbs. (45 Nm).

59. Install the lower reinforcement bracket and nuts, then tighten the floor shifter assembly.

60. Install the wiring harness and antenna hold down clips onto the dash reinforcement.

61. Install the electrical connector to the rear of the IPJB, then tighten the screw. If equipped with an automatic transaxle, connect the panel-to-body harness connector and install the lock pin. Install the IPJB to the dash reinforcement using the retaining screws, then install the ground wire to the reinforcement.

62. Install the console while feeding the seat belts and wire harness through the console cut outs. Snap the seat belt bezels into position.

63. Secure the console using the side screws at the front and the compartment screws at the top of the rear. Position the liner into the rear storage compartment and over the screws.

64. If equipped, connect the power window/mirror electrical wiring harnesses and install the CPA devices, then install the switch by inserting the front edge first and snapping the rear of the switch into the console.

65. Install the ash tray bulb holder, then install the ash tray to the console.

66. If equipped with a manual transaxle, push the shift knob onto the shifter.

67. Install the parking brake filler panel by pressing down at the clip locations.

68. Install the cigarette lighter bulb by inserting into position and rotating counterclockwise to lock it in, then install the lighter electrical connector.

69. Install the HVAC control panel and adjust the cables accordingly.

70. Install the radio assembly.

71. Connect the instrument cluster wiring harnesses, then position the cluster. Make sure the cluster lighting and rear window defogger harnesses are in position then install and tighten the cluster retaining screws.

72. Install the hood release lever and screw.

73. Install the steering column filler panel and screws.

74. Install the ALDL connector and screws.

75. Install the glove box, striker and screws. Adjust the striker, as necessary for proper glove box operation.

76. Position the instrument cluster trim panel and connect the wiring harness to the instrument light and rear window defogger switches. Install the CPA devices into the electrical connectors, then install the cluster trim panel into the retainers and secure using the screws.

77. Install the upper trim panel by inserting into the clips at the windshield, then snapping the rear of the panel into place. Install the upper trim panel screws, then snap the screw covers into position.

78. Install the center air outlet/trim panel, then install the lower left and right trim panel extensions. For 1991 vehicles, install the cigarette lighter trim bezel.

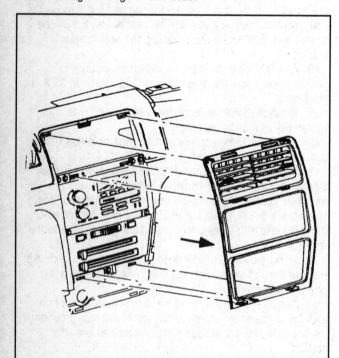

Fig. 44 Pull outward at the clip locations to remove the center console air outlet/trim panel from the dash — 1991 vehicles shown

79. Raise and support the front of the vehicle safely using jackstands, then install the heater core hoses. Make sure the left clamp (core outlet) is positioned at the 7-8 o'clock position and the right hose clamp (core inlet) is at the 6 o'clock position.

80. Remove the supports and carefully lower the vehicle.

81. Remove the protective covers from the A/C fittings, then lubricate using compressor oil and install new O-rings on the evaporator pipes. Install the TXV onto the evaporator and tighten the retaining bolts to 89 inch lbs. (10 Nm).

82. Lubricate and install new O-rings onto the suction hose and liquid line, then install the lines to the TXV. Tighten the fittings to 19 ft. lbs. (25 Nm).

83. Install the air intake ducts and/or the air cleaner housing, as applicable.

84. Connect the negative battery cable, then properly fill the engine cooling system and check for leaks.

85. Properly charge and test the A/C system.

Thermal Expansion Valve (TXV)

REMOVAL & INSTALLATION

▶ See Figures 55 and 56

1. Discharge the refrigerant into a suitable recovery system.

2. For the DOHC engine, remove the air cleaner cover and the air induction hose at the intake manifold. For SOHC engines, remove the air cleaner housing.

3. Remove the retaining bolts, then disconnect the suction hose and liquid lines from the TXV. Remove and discard the line O-rings.

4. Remove the fasteners, then remove the valve from the evaporator. Remove and discard the old evaporator pipe O-rings.

To install:

5. Lubricate using compressor oil and install new O-rings on the evaporator pipes

6. Install the TXV valve to the evaporator and tighten the fasteners to 89 inch lbs. (10 Nm).

7. Lubricate and install new O-rings on the suction hose and liquid line, then install the lines and tighten the retaining bolts to 19 ft. lbs.

8. Install the air cleaner housing, cover and/or ducts, as applicable.

9. Properly charge and test the A/C system.

Receiver/Drier

REMOVAL & INSTALLATION

▶ See Figures 57, 58, 59 and 60

1. Discharge the refrigerant into a suitable recovery system.

2. Raise and support the front of the vehicle safely using jackstands.

3. Remove the push nut and pull back the receiver/drier splash shield.

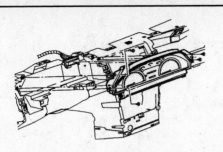

Fig. 45 Remove the retainers and pull the instrument cluster out sufficiently to unplug the electrical connectors.

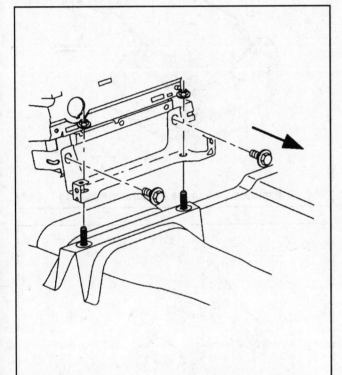

Fig. 46 Remove the nuts and bolts, then lift the lower reinforcement bracket off of the studs and slide the bracket rearward.

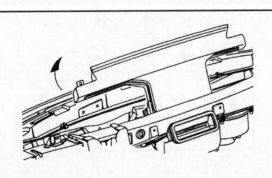

Fig. 47 Remove the defroster nozzle by rotating the front of the nozzle upward and away from the windshield

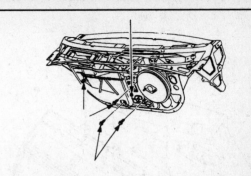

Fig. 48 Remove the 3 screws and 2 nuts which retain the HVAC module to the cowl

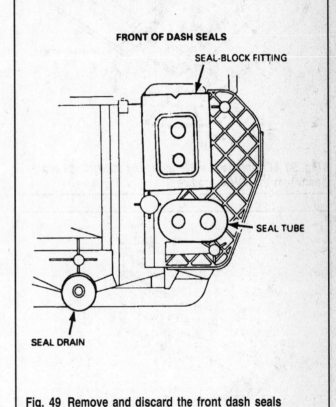

FRONT OF DASH SEALS

SEAL-BLOCK FITTING

SEAL TUBE

SEAL DRAIN

Fig. 49 Remove and discard the front dash seals

4. Disconnect the receiver/drier hose from the condenser outlet and the liquid line from the receiver/drier. Remove and discard the O-rings from the fittings.

5. Remove the retaining nut, then rotate the receiver/drier assembly off the stud. Pull the assembly rearward to disengage it from the retaining slot and remove it from the vehicle.

To install:

6. Position the receiver/drier assembly near the vehicle frame, then feed the hose up over the frame and down to the condenser outlet.

7. Install the assembly into the retaining slot, then rotate onto the stud. When properly positioned, the retaining tab will be fully forward and at the bottom of the slot. Make sure the pipe does not touch the frame rail.

8. Install and tighten the retaining nut.

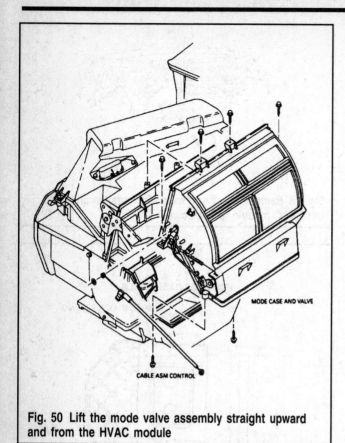

Fig. 50 Lift the mode valve assembly straight upward and from the HVAC module

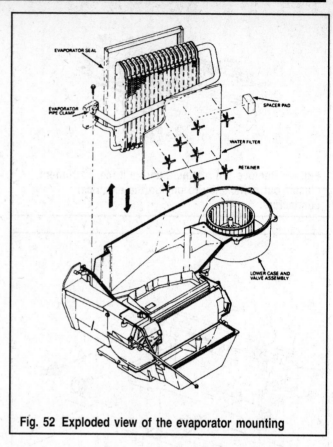

Fig. 52 Exploded view of the evaporator mounting

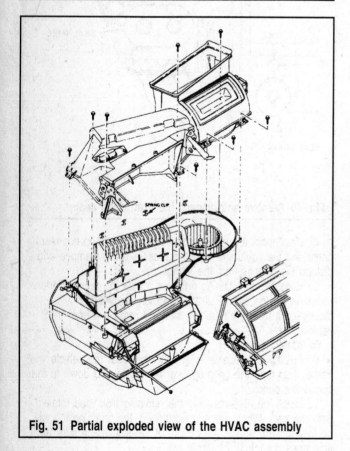

Fig. 51 Partial exploded view of the HVAC assembly

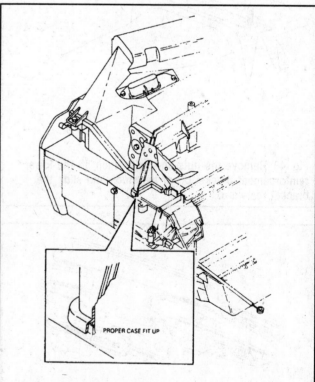

Fig. 53 Make sure that all tongue and groove parts fit properly before tightening screws

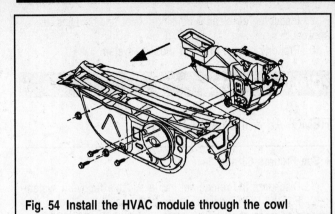

Fig. 54 Install the HVAC module through the cowl

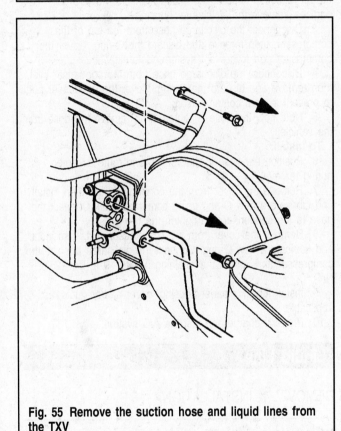

Fig. 55 Remove the suction hose and liquid lines from the TXV

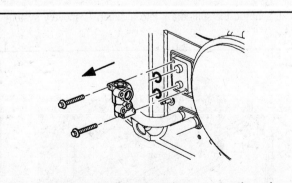

Fig. 56 Remove the fasteners, then remove the valve from the evaporator

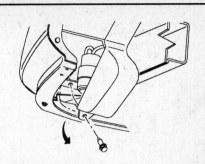

Fig. 57 Remove the push nut and pull back the receiver/drier splash shield

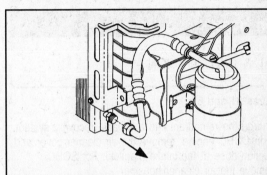

Fig. 58 Disconnect the receiver/drier hose from the condenser outlet

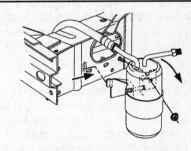

Fig. 59 Rotate the receiver/drier off the stud, then pull the assembly rearward to disengage it from the retaining slot

9. Lubricate using compressor oil and install a new O-ring, then connect the receiver/drier hose to the condenser outlet. The hose should be parallel with the condenser after tightening; this will provide proper clearance and prevent hose damage.

10. Lubricate and install a new O-ring, then connect the liquid line to the receiver/drier. To prevent hose damage, make sure the line is not touching the sheet metal body cut out after tightening.

11. Rotate the receiver/drier splash shield into position, then install the push nut.

12. Remove the jackstands and carefully lower the vehicle.

13. Properly charge and test the A/C system.

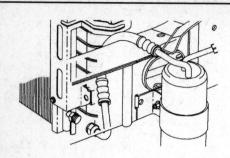

Fig. 60 When installing the receiver/drier, feed the hose over the vehicle frame and down to the condenser outlet

Suction Hose

REMOVAL & INSTALLATION

▶ See Figures 61 and 62

1. Discharge the refrigerant into a suitable recovery system.
2. For the DOHC engine, remove the air cleaner cover and the air induction hose at the intake manifold. For SOHC engines, remove the air cleaner housing.
3. Disconnect the suction hose from the top of thermal expansion valve, then remove and discard the O-ring. Cover the valve port to prevent system contamination.
4. Disconnect the suction hose from the rear of the rear of the compressor, then remove and discard the O-ring. Cover the compressor port to prevent system contamination.
5. Note how the hose is routed, then remove the hose from the vehicle.

To install:

6. Position the hose in the vehicle and route as noted during removal. The hose should route outside the transaxle dip stick tube (automatic transaxles), under the edge of the battery tray and under the negative battery cable.
7. Remove the cover from the compressor port, then install and lubricate a new O-ring using compressor oil. Connect the suction hose to the compressor and tighten the retaining bolt to 19 ft. lbs. (25 Nm).
8. Remove the cover from the TXV port, then install and lubricate a new O-ring. Connect the hose to the TXV port and tighten the retaining bolt to 19 ft. lbs. (25 Nm).

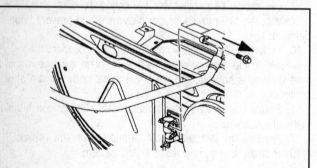

Fig. 61 Disconnect the suction hose from the top of the TXV

9. Install the air cleaner housing, cover and/or ducts, as applicable.
10. Properly charge and test the A/C system.

Discharge Hose

REMOVAL & INSTALLATION

▶ See Figures 63 and 64

1. Discharge the refrigerant into a suitable recovery system.
2. For the DOHC engine, remove the air cleaner cover and the air induction hose at the intake manifold. For SOHC engines, remove the air cleaner housing.
3. Disconnect the discharge hose from the top of the compressor, then remove and discard the O-ring. Cover the compressor port to prevent system contamination.
4. Disconnect the discharge hose from the condenser inlet, then remove and discard the O-ring. Cover the condenser port to prevent system contamination.
5. Note how the hose is routed, then remove the hose from the vehicle.

To install:

6. Position the hose in the vehicle and route as noted during removal.
7. Remove the cover from the condenser port, then install and lubricate a new O-ring using compressor oil. Connect the hose to the condenser and tighten the fitting.
8. Remove the cover from the compressor port, then install and lubricate a new O-ring. Connect the discharge hose to the compressor and tighten the retaining bolt to 19 ft. lbs. (25 Nm).
9. Install the air cleaner housing, cover and/or ducts, as applicable.
10. Properly charge and test the A/C system.

Liquid Line

REMOVAL & INSTALLATION

▶ See Figures 65, 66, 67 and 68

1. Discharge the refrigerant into a suitable recovery system.

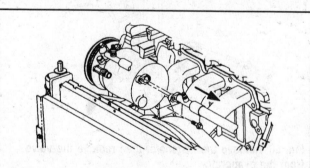

Fig. 62 Disconnect the suction hose from the rear of the compressor

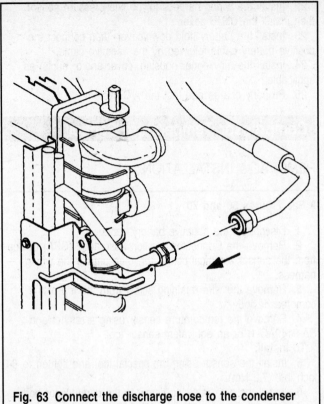

Fig. 63 Connect the discharge hose to the condenser inlet

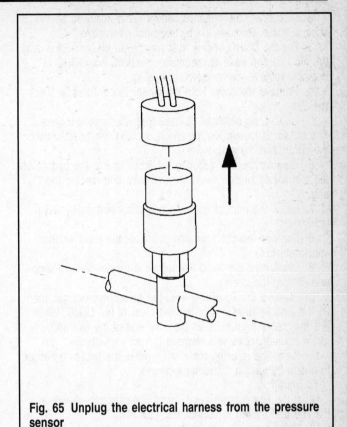

Fig. 65 Unplug the electrical harness from the pressure sensor

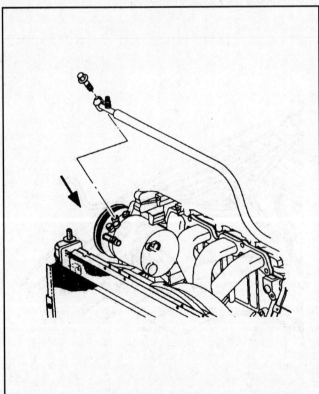

Fig. 64 Connect the discharge hose to the compressor outlet

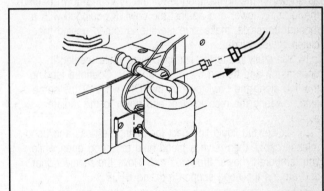

Fig. 66 Disconnect the liquid line from the receiver/drier

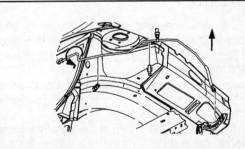

Fig. 67 When the liquid line clears the UHJB, lift the TXV end of the line and rotate counterclockwise to remove it from the vehicle

2. Disconnect the negative battery cable, followed by the positive cable. Remove the battery hold down/cover.

3. For the DOHC engine, remove the air cleaner cover and the air induction hose at the intake manifold. For SOHC engines, remove the air cleaner housing.

4. Remove the cover from the Under Hood Junction Block (UHJB).

5. Unplug the electrical harness from the pressure sensor. The sensor is located on the line, along the fender (between the UHJB and the strut tower).

6. Remove the bolt securing the liquid line to the bottom of the thermal expansion valve, then remove and discard the O-ring.

7. Raise the front of the vehicle and support safely using jackstands.

8. Remove the push nut and pull back the receiver/drier splash shield.

9. Disconnect the liquid line from the receiver/drier. Remove and discard the O-ring.

10. Remove the liquid line from the hold down clamps, then lift the receiver/drier end of the line clear of the UHJB. When the line clears the UHJB, lift the TXV end of the line and rotate counterclockwise to remove it from the vehicle.

11. If the line is being replaced, remove the pressure sensor from line by turning it counterclockwise.

To install:

12. If the line was replaced, install the pressure sensor to the line and tighten to 49 inch lbs. (5.5 Nm).

13. Using the pressure sensor as a reference, hold the line as shown in the figure, then lower the TXV end down behind the left strut tower and against the cowl. If equipped with a manual transaxle, make sure the line is routed behind the clutch slave cylinder.

14. Carefully rotate the line clockwise while feeding it underneath and behind the brake booster. Continue feeding the line along the cowl towards the TXV while at the same time, lowering the receiver/drier end down to the radiator support.

15. Lower the liquid line past the wiring harness and hood release cable, then have a friend hold the hood open while you temporarily lower the hood rod. Move the receiver/drier end around the hood support rod and UHJB.

➡**Do not bend the liquid line around the hood support rod. After lowering the rod, gently flex the line around the radiator core support.**

16. Insert the receiver/drier end of the line through the body cut out and install the line in the front clamp which is located just behind the pressure switch (along the fender wall between the UHJB and the strut tower).

17. Lubricate using compressor oil and install a new O-ring, then install the line to the bottom TXV port. Install the retaining bolt and tighten to 19 ft. lbs. (25 Nm).

18. Install the line to the rear clamp at the top of the frame rail and snap the clamp shut.

19. Raise the front of the vehicle and support safely using jackstands.

20. Lubricate and install a new O-ring, then connect the line to the receiver/drier and tighten the fitting. Rotate the splash shield into position, then install the push nut.

21. Remove the supports and carefully lower the vehicle.

22. Install the wiring harness to the line pressure sensor, then install the UHJB cover.

23. Install the battery hold down/cover, then connect the positive battery cable followed by the negative cable.

24. Install the air cleaner housing, cover and/or ducts, as applicable.

25. Properly charge and test the A/C system.

Compressor Temperature Sensor

REMOVAL & INSTALLATION

▶ **See Figures 69 and 70**

1. Disconnect the negative battery cable.

2. Remove the Connector Position Assurance (CPA) device from the sensor electrical connector, then unplug the wiring harness.

3. Remove the wire retaining screw from the top of the compressor body.

4. Remove the temperature sensor using a ratchet and SA-9149AC-1, or an equivalent sensor tool.

To install:

5. Install the sensor using the special tool and tighten to 64 inch lbs. (7.2 Nm).

6. Install the wire retaining screw to the compressor body.

7. Connect the wiring harness to the sensor, then install the CPA device.

8. Connect the negative battery cable.

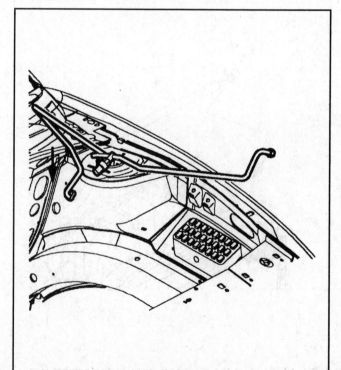

Fig. 68 Using the pressure sensor as a reference, hold the line as shown, then lower the TXV end down behind the left strut tower and against the cowl

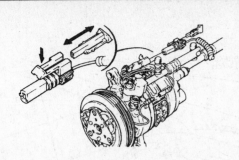

Fig. 69 Remove the CPA device, then unplug the sensor electrical connector

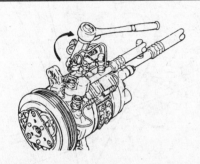

Fig. 70 Install the sensor using the temperature sensor removal/installation tool

Compressor Pressure Relief Valve

REMOVAL & INSTALLATION

▶ See Figure 71

1. Discharge the refrigerant into a suitable recovery system.

CRUISE CONTROL

Control Module

The control module for the cruise control system monitors input from the PCM, the control pad or stalk and the various switches which comprise the system. Through these inputs the module will regulate the cable and adjuster assembly to keep the vehicle running at the desired speed. The system is nearly identical on all vehicles, with one exception. Vehicles equipped with a Supplemental Inflatable Restraint (SIR) system or 'AIR BAG" have the control switches relocated from the control pad at the center of the steering wheel to a control stalk on the column.

REMOVAL & INSTALLATION

▶ See Figures 72 and 73

1. Disconnect the negative battery cable.

2. Remove the retaining bolt from the compressor high side hose (located on top of the compressor), then remove the hose.

3. Remove the pressure relief valve, which was located underneath the high side hose port, using a wrench.

4. Remove and discard the valve and the high side hose O-rings.

To install:

5. Lubricate the new valve O-ring using compressor oil, then install the valve and O-ring to the top of the compressor. Tighten the valve to 63 inch lbs. (7.2 Nm).

6. Lubricate and install a new O-ring on the high side hose, then install the hose and secure using the bolt. Tighten the retaining bolt to 19 ft. lbs. (25 Nm).

7. Properly charge and test the A/C system.

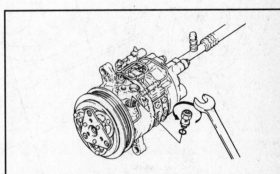

Fig. 71 Remove the compressor pressure relief valve using a wrench

2. Remove the Connector Position Assurance (CPA) device from the wiring harness, then disconnect the module electrical connector.

3. Disconnect the control cable from the accelerator pedal.

4. Remove the 3 attaching nuts from the module and steering column, then remove the module from the vehicle.

To install:

5. The modules differ slightly for the DOHC or SOHC engines, make sure the correct part has been obtained.

6. Install the cruise control module to the steering column, then tighten the attaching nuts to 44 inch lbs. (5 Nm).

7. Connect the cruise control cable to the accelerator cable. Check and, if necessary adjust the control cable.

8. Connect the negative battery cable and verify proper system operation.

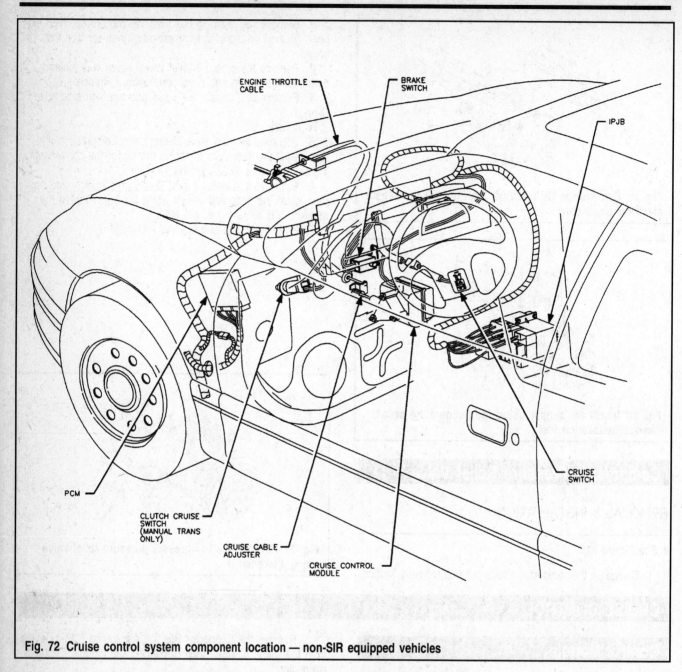

Fig. 72 Cruise control system component location — non-SIR equipped vehicles

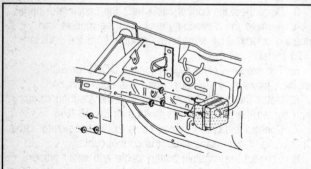

Fig. 73 Exploded view of the control module mounting at the base of the steering column

CABLE ADJUSTMENT

▶ See Figure 74

1. Remove the air intake tube from the throttle body.
2. Observe the position of the throttle plate.
3. Gently pull the cruise cable adjuster out and turn the assembly to lengthen or shorten the cable. The cable is properly adjusted when the throttle plate is closed, then the adjuster is loosened ½ turn to allow approximately 0.040-0.079 in. (1-2mm) slack in the cable.

➡️Improper cable adjustment may result in driveability problems.

4. When the cable is properly adjusted, install the air intake tube.

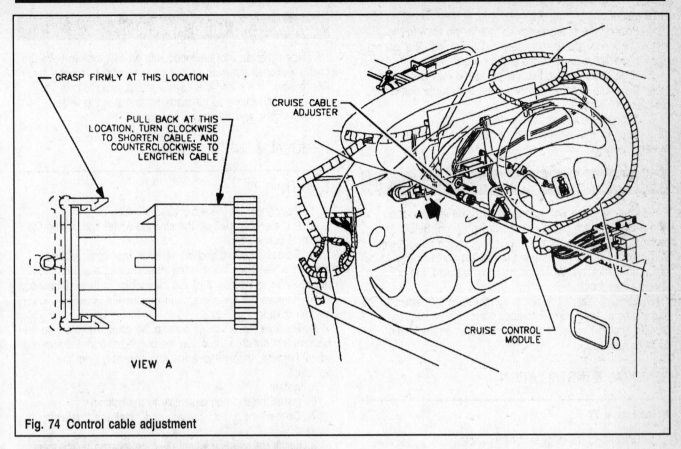

Fig. 74 Control cable adjustment

Control Switch Assembly

Most Saturn vehicles built in 1991 and 1992 were not equipped with an SIR system, therefore there was room for the control switch assembly on the steering wheel. Once SIR systems were added to the Saturn line (in late 1992), then switch assembly was relocated to a stalk on the steering column. See the combination switch procedure in Section 8 of this manual for access to steering column stalks.

REMOVAL & INSTALLATION

▶ **See Figure 75**

1. Disconnect the negative battery cable.

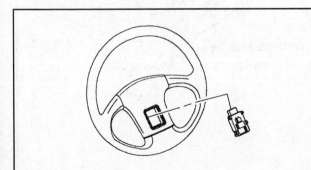

Fig. 75 Control switch assembly mounting — non-SIR equipped vehicles

2. Carefully pry the bottom of the switch away from the horn.
3. Pull the switch out sufficiently to unplug the electrical connector, then remove the switch from the vehicle.
4. Position the switch and install the connector.
5. Press the switch assembly into the horn pad.
6. Connect the negative battery cable and verify proper system operation.

Brake Switch Assembly

Before replacing the brake switch, always check switch adjustment. With the brake pedal depressed the switch contacts should be open (no continuity). When the brake is released, the contacts should close (continuity).

If necessary, adjust the switch by loosening the retaining bolt and sliding it away from or towards the brake pedal. The plunger should always be fully depressed when the brake pedal is released.

REMOVAL & INSTALLATION

▶ **See Figure 76**

1. Disconnect the negative battery cable.
2. Unplug the electrical connector from the switch assembly.
3. Remove the bolt, then remove the switch from the vehicle.

To install:

4. Position the brake switch so that its tab fits into the slotted hole provided, then loosely install the bolt. The tab will keep the switch parallel to the brake pedal.

5. Slide the switch so that the plunger is fully depressed when the brake pedal is released, then tighten the bolt to 89 inch lbs. (10 Nm).

6. Connect the wiring harness to the switch.

7. Connect the negative battery cable, then verify proper system operation.

Clutch Switch Assembly

Vehicles equipped with a manual transaxle are equipped with a clutch switch along with the brake switch. Before replacing the brake switch, always check switch adjustment. With the clutch pedal depressed the switch contacts should be open (no continuity). When the brake is released, the contacts should close (continuity).

If necessary, adjust the switch by loosening the retaining bolt and sliding it away from or towards the clutch pedal. The plunger should always be fully depressed when the clutch pedal is released.

REMOVAL & INSTALLATION

▶ **See Figure 77**

1. Disconnect the negative battery cable.
2. Unplug the electrical connector from the switch assembly.
3. Remove the bolt, then remove the switch from the vehicle.

To install:

4. Position the clutch switch so that its tab fits into the slotted hole provided, then loosely install the bolt. The tab will keep the switch parallel to the clutch pedal.

5. Slide the switch so that the plunger is fully depressed when the clutch pedal is released, then tighten the bolt to 89 inch lbs. (10 Nm).

6. Connect the wiring harness to the switch.

7. Connect the negative battery cable, then verify proper system operation.

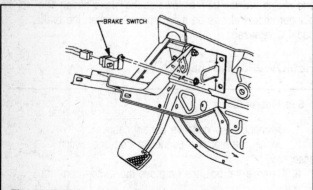

Fig. 76 Brake switch assembly mounting

Column Slip Ring Assembly

Vehicles that are not equipped with an SIR system have the control switches mounted on the steering wheel. In order for this to work, a slip ring device is installed which allows the electrical connections to be made without steering wheel motion twisting and damaging the wires.

REMOVAL & INSTALLATION

▶ **See Figure 78**

1. Disconnect the negative battery cable.
2. Pull the horn pad off the steering wheel and unplug the electrical connectors.
3. Remove the clip and the retainer, then remove the steering wheel from the steering column using a suitable puller. Refer to Section 8 of this manual for further information.
4. Remove the fasteners, then remove the upper and lower column covers.
5. Remove the 3 screws holding the column slip ring to the combination switch and unplug the connector from the steering wheel harness, then remove the ring assembly from the vehicle.

To install:

6. Install the slip ring assembly to the column.
7. Connect the wiring harness and install the 3 retaining screws.
8. Install the steering wheel over the locating notch, then install the retainer and the retainer clip.

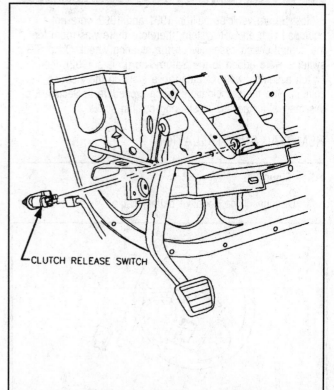

Fig. 77 Clutch switch assembly mounting — manual transaxle vehicles only

9. Connect the wiring harnesses, then install the horn pad to the steering wheel.

10. Connect the negative battery cable, then verify proper system operation.

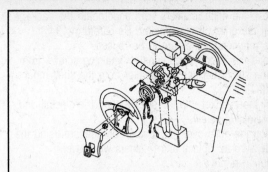

Fig. 78 Column slip ring mounting and access — non-SIR equipped vehicles

ENTERTAINMENT SYSTEMS

Radio Receiver/Amplifier, Tape Player and Compact Disc Player

REMOVAL & INSTALLATION

▶ **See Figure 79**

1. Disconnect the negative battery cable.

2. Carefully remove the center air outlet/trim panel by pulling outward at the clip locations. Start at the bottom and work upward to the top clips. Do not use instruments which might damage the trim panel.

3. Remove the 2 radio retaining screws located at the top of the unit, then carefully pull the radio forward and from the dash sufficiently to reach behind the unit.

4. Unplug the radio electrical connector and the antenna, then remove the radio from the vehicle.

To install:

5. Position the radio in from the center outlet, then install the wiring harness and antenna connector.

6. Slide the radio into position and secure using the 2 retaining screws.

7. Install the center air outlet/trim panel by pushing inward at the clip locations.

8. Connect the negative battery cable.

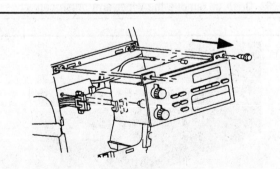

Fig. 79 Pull the radio forward sufficiently to reach the antenna and electrical connections

Front Speaker

REMOVAL & INSTALLATION

1. Disconnect the negative battery cable.

2. Remove the speaker grille by carefully lifting 1 corner of the grille and releasing the tabs located all around the edge of the grille. A small screwdriver may be used to initially lift a corner of the grille, but be very careful not to force any components and score or damage the plastic.

3. Remove the Torx® head screws from the speaker, then carefully pull the speaker from the mounting sufficiently to unplug the electrical connector.

4. Unplug the connector, then remove the speaker from the vehicle.

To install:

5. Install the electrical connector to the speaker, then position the speaker into the mounting plate. Be careful not to damage the foam insulators to the top and sides of the speaker.

6. Install the speaker retaining screws.

7. Position the cover, then carefully push down at the tab locations to snap the cover into place.

8. Connect the negative battery cable and enjoy the tunes.

Rear Speaker

REMOVAL & INSTALLATION

▶ **See Figure 80**

1. Disconnect the negative battery cable.

2. Access the speaker grille fasteners and speaker electrical connector located in the trunk. This may be accomplished from either outside the vehicle, by opening the trunk or from inside the vehicle, by folding down the rear seat.

3. Unplug the speaker electrical connector.

4. Remove the grille retainers from underneath the package shelf, the lift the grille off the speaker. Be careful not to damage the retainers, if they are to be reused.

5. Remove the Torx® head speaker retaining screws from the top of the shelf, then lift the speaker from the shelf mount.

To install:

6. Lower the speaker into the shelf mount, then install and tighten the retaining screws.

7. Position the grille over the speaker and secure using the retainers. Be sure to replace and retainers which were damaged during removal.

8. Connect the wiring harness to the speaker.

9. Connect the negative battery cable and enjoy the tunes.

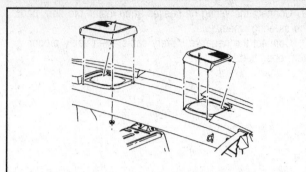

Fig. 80 Remove the clips and lift the speaker grille from the package shelf

WINDSHIELD WIPERS AND WASHER

Windshield Wiper Blade and Arm

REMOVAL & INSTALLATION

▶ **See Figures 81, 82 and 83**

1. Open or remove the wiper arm finish cap, then loosen the retaining nut using a wrench.

2. Lift the wiper blade away from the windshield and remove the blade/arm assembly.

3. If replacements are available, remove the wiper blade from the arm.

To install:

4. If used, install the replacement blade onto the wiper arm.

5. Position the arm onto the pivot shaft, the install the retaining nut and tighten to 21 ft. lbs. (28 Nm).

6. Install or position the finish cap over the retaining nut.

Rear Liftgate Wiper Blade and Arm

Unlike the front wiper blade assemblies, whose stock blades are not replaceable separately, the factory rear wiper blades may be replaced without removing the wiper arm.

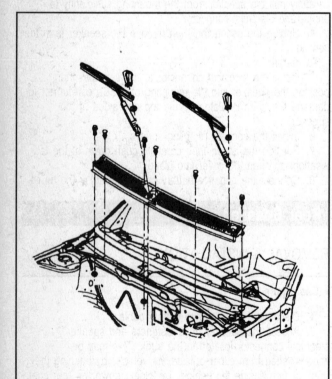

Fig. 81 Exploded view of the windshield wiper arm assembly

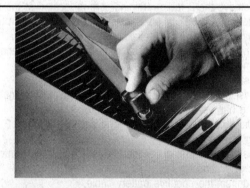

Fig. 82 Open or remove the wiper arm finish cap

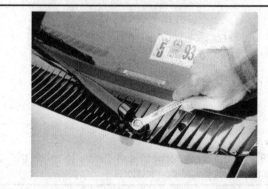

Fig. 83 Loosen the retaining nut using a wrench

REMOVAL & INSTALLATION

▶ **See Figures 84 and 85**

1. Remove the rear wiper arm finish cap, then loosen the retaining nut using a wrench.
2. Lift the wiper blade away from the liftgate window and remove the blade/arm assembly.
3. Pinch the wiper blade attachment clip together and slide the blade from the arm.

To install:

4. Position the blade clip into the wiper arm hook, then slide the blade into the hook until it clicks into position.
5. Position the arm onto the pivot shaft with the blade horizontal to the liftgate glass lower edge, then install the retaining nut and tighten to 159 inch lbs. (18 Nm).
6. Install the finish cap over the retaining nut.

Windshield Wiper Motor Module

REMOVAL & INSTALLATION

▶ **See Figures 86, 87, 88 and 89**

1. Make sure that the wipers are in the **PARK** position, then disconnect the negative battery cable.
2. Close the hood, then remove the wiper arm finish cap and wiper arm fastening nut. Lift the blade away from the windshield and remove. Repeat for the other blade.

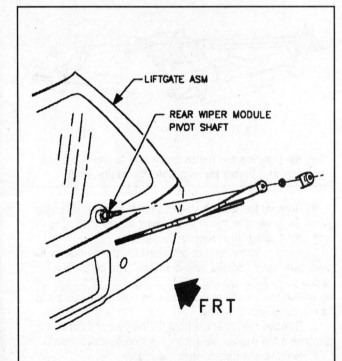

Fig. 84 Exploded view of the rear wiper arm assembly mounting — SW1 and SW2 vehicles only

3. Remove the cowl trim fasteners at the windshield edge of the panel, then open the hood and remove the remaining fasteners. Carefully remove the cowl trim panel.
4. Remove the screw caps from the instrument panel top cover, then remove the retaining screws. Carefully remove the cover by lifting at the rear edge to disengage the retaining clips and sliding the panel out of the windshield clips.
5. Disconnect the defroster duct from the HVAC module and reposition it towards the glove box to expose the wiper module rear fasteners.
6. Remove the wiper module fasteners and reposition the module slightly to disconnect the wiring from the motor and module frame. Carefully remove the wiper module and motor assembly from the top of the instrument panel.

➡ **Be very careful when removing the wiper module/motor assembly to avoid contacting or damaging the windshield.**

7. Remove the crank arm nut and disconnect the arm from the motor shaft, then remove the wiper motor attaching screws and remove the motor from the module.

To install:

8. Verify that the motor is in the **PARK** position. If necessary, temporarily connect the motor wiring and the negative battery cable, turn the wiper control **ON** then **OFF** and the motor will move to the correct position.
9. Install the motor to the module. Position the motor crank arm to the 9 o'clock position and install the arm onto the motor shaft. Install a new retaining nut and tighten to 21 ft. lbs. (28 Nm).
10. Position the wiper module assembly into the vehicle and connect the wiring to the wiper motor and to the module frame.

➡ **Whenever possible during the remaining steps, the vehicle manufacturer recommends using new fasteners, as the torque retention of the old fasteners may be insufficient.**

11. Install the module retaining bolts and tighten to 89 inch lbs. (10 Nm).
12. Install the cowl trim panel.
13. Install the wiper arm assemblies and tighten the nuts to 21 ft. lbs. (28 Nm).
14. Position the defroster duct to the HVAC module.
15. Install the instrument panel top cover and screws, then insert the panel cover screw caps.
16. Connect the negative battery cable and verify proper system operation.

Rear Liftgate Wiper Motor Module

REMOVAL & INSTALLATION

▶ **See Figures 90, 91 and 92**

1. Make sure that the wiper is in the **PARK** position, then disconnect the negative battery cable.
2. Remove the wiper arm/blade assembly from the liftgate.
3. Raise the liftgate, then remove the wedge blocks from either end of the liftgate assembly.

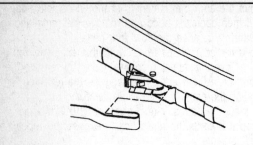

Fig. 85 Position the blade clip into the wiper arm hook, then slide the blade into the hook until it clicks into position.

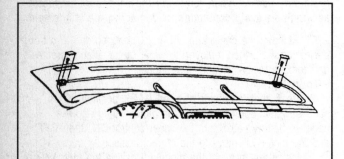

Fig. 86 Remove the screw caps from the instrument panel top cover, then remove the retaining screws

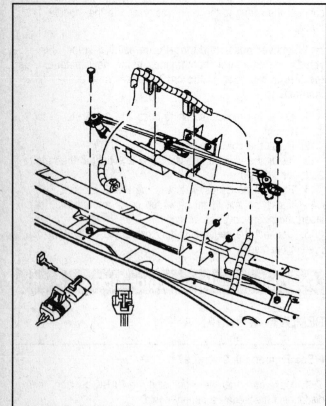

Fig. 87 Exploded view of the wiper module mounting

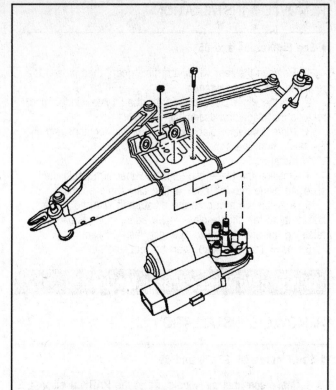

Fig. 88 Remove the fasteners, then separate the wiper motor from the module

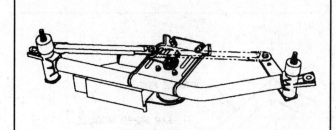

Fig. 89 Position the motor crank arm to the 9 o'clock position and install the arm onto the motor shaft

4. Remove the lower fasteners from the liftgate lower trim panel, by pushing in the of each center pin approximately 1/8 inch until it clicks, then remove the fastener.

5. Insert a screwdriver or small prybar into the hole in the lower trim panel (located near the wiper pivot on the pivot hump) so that the tool sits on top of the pivot as shown. Lift up on the tool handle to disengage the trim panel upper clips, then remove the trim panel.

6. Remove the fasteners from the rear wiper module, then disconnect the washer hose from the module check valve.

7. Remove the module from the liftgate.

To install:

8. Position the wiper module to the liftgate and connect the washer hose to the check valve.

9. Install the module fasteners and tighten to 89 inch lbs. (10 Nm).

10. Install the grommet, washer and nut on the wiper module pivot shaft, then tighten the nut to 119 inch lbs. (14 Nm).

11. Align the upper clips on the lower trim panel to the liftgate slots, then install the panel by pushing at the clip locations.

12. Reset the trim panel push-in fasteners by spreading the center pin tabs and moving the pin so that it sits approximately ¼ in. out of the fastener. Insert the fasteners into the bottom of the trim panel and push the center pin until flush.

13. Install the liftgate wedge blocks.
14. Install the rear wiper pivot bushing.
15. Install the rear wiper arm/blade assembly.
16. Connect the negative battery cable and verify proper system operation.

Windshield Wiper Washer Bottle/Pump Motor

REMOVAL & INSTALLATION

▶ **See Figures 93, 94 and 95**

1. Disconnect the negative battery cable.
2. Disconnect the wiring harness from the pump motor.
3. Remove the fastener attaching the washer bottle to the vehicle.
4. Lift the assembly and release the lower attachment tab on the bottle.

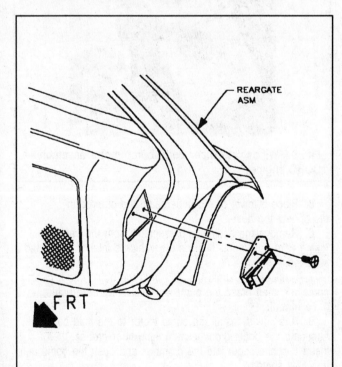

Fig. 90 Remove the wedge blocks from either end of the liftgate assembly

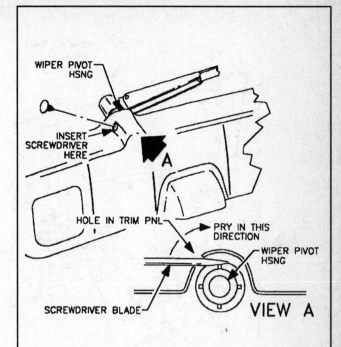

Fig. 91 Insert a screwdriver or small prybar into the hole in the lower trim panel so that the tool sits on top of the pivot

5. Carefully remove the fluid hose from the pump. Be sure to avoid spilling fluid on painted surfaces.
6. Remove the washer assembly from the vehicle.
7. If necessary, drain the fluid into a clean container and remove the pump from the fluid bottle.

To install:

8. If removed, install the pump motor to the fluid bottle.
9. Connect the fluid hose to the pump.
10. Position the fluid bottle into the vehicle and fasten the engagement tab.
11. Install and tighten the bottle assembly fastener.
12. Connect the wiring harness to the pump.
13. If necessary, fill the bottle with washer solvent.
14. Connect the negative battery cable and verify proper system operation.

Rear Liftgate Wiper Washer Bottle/Pump Motor

REMOVAL & INSTALLATION

▶ **See Figures 96 and 97**

1. Disconnect the negative battery cable.
2. Remove the passenger side, rear quarter inner trim panel for access to the assembly.
3. Remove the bottle fasteners.
4. Pull the bottle away from the body sufficiently to reach the wiring harness, then disconnect the harness from the pump motor.

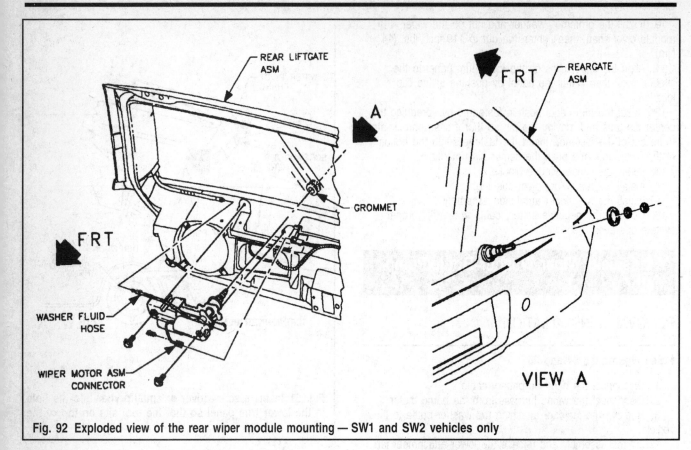

Fig. 92 Exploded view of the rear wiper module mounting — SW1 and SW2 vehicles only

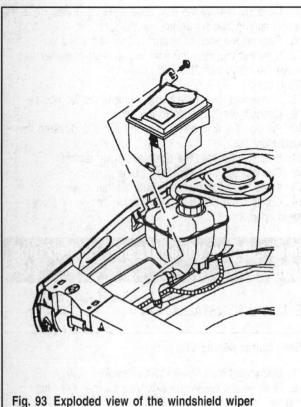

Fig. 93 Exploded view of the windshield wiper bottle/pump motor assembly

Fig. 94 Windshield wiper bottle/pump motor assembly — DOHC engine

5. Place a towel or rag underneath the pump and disconnect the hose.

6. Remove the bottle/pump assembly from the vehicle, taking care not to spill fluid on the vehicle's interior or painted surfaces.

7. If necessary, drain the fluid from the bottle into a clean container, then grasp the pump and pull it from the bottle.

To install:

8. If removed, install the pump motor to the fluid bottle. Lubricate the bottle grommet with light oil or grease, then insert the inlet spout into the grommet and push the bottle until it is fully seated.

9. Connect the fluid hose and the wiring harness to the pump.

10. Position the fluid bottle onto the studs in the rear body and install the fasteners.

11. If necessary, fill the bottle with washer solvent.

12. Install the rear quarter inner trim panel.

13. Connect the negative battery cable and verify proper system operation.

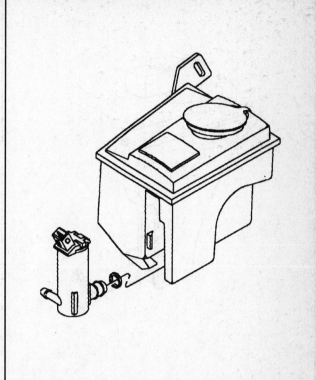

Fig. 95 Pump motor mounting to the windshield wiper bottle

INSTRUMENTS AND SWITCHES

➡ This sections covers the removal and installation of various switches and gauges in and around the instrument cluster. Procedures for their related components may be found in Section No. 3 or 4 of this manual.

Instrument Cluster Assembly

The gauges located in the instrument cluster (speedometer, tachometer, fuel gauge, voltmeter and coolant temperature gauge) are not serviceable. The entire cluster must be replaced as an assembly.

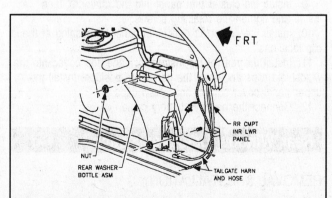

Fig. 96 Rear wiper bottle/pump motor mounting

REMOVAL & INSTALLATION

▶ See Figures 98 and 99

1. Disconnect the negative battery cable.

2. Remove the 2 instrument panel top cover screw caps and screws. Carefully remove the cover by lifting at the rear edge to disengage the retaining clips and by sliding the panel out of the windshield clips.

3. Carefully remove the center air outlet/trim panel by pulling outward at the clip locations. Start at the bottom and move upward. Do not use tools that might damage the trim panel.

4. Open the glove box, then remove the 4 cluster trim panel attaching screws.

5. Carefully pull the cluster trim panel rearward to disengage it from the retainers, then remove the CPA device and unplug the electrical connectors from the instrument panel lighting and rear window defogger switches. Remove the panel from the vehicle.

6. Remove the instrument cluster retaining screws, pull the cluster out sufficiently to unplug the electrical connectors. Unplug the connectors by depressing the retainer legs and remove the assembly.

To install:

7. Connect the wiring harnesses to the instrument cluster assembly.

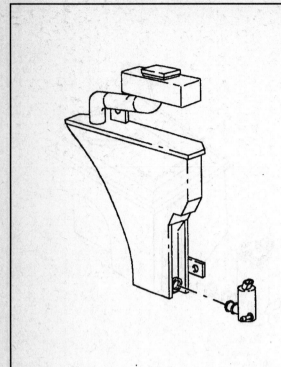

Fig. 97 Rear wiper washer pump motor is mounted to the lower portion of the bottle assembly

8. Verify that the connectors for the cluster trim panel lighting and rear window defogger switches are properly positioned, then install the instrument cluster assembly and retaining screws.

9. Position the cluster trim panel and connect the electrical connectors to the panel lighting and the rear defogger switches, then install the CPA devices.

10. Install the cluster trim panel into the retainers, then secure using the retaining screws.

11. Install the center air outlet/trim panel by pushing at the clip locations.

12. Install the rear of the instrument panel top cover into the windshield clips and snap the panel into position. Install the upper panel screws and screw caps.

13. Connect the negative battery cable.

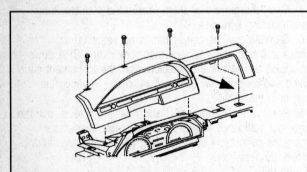

Fig. 98 Remove the attaching screws, then pull the cluster trim panel by rearward to disengage the retainers

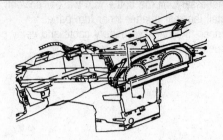

Fig. 99 Remove the cluster retaining screws, then pull the cluster out sufficiently to unplug the wiring harnesses

Dimmer Switch (Instrument Cluster Lighting Rheostat)

REMOVAL & INSTALLATION

1. Disconnect the negative battery cable.

2. Remove the 2 instrument panel top cover screw caps and screws. Carefully remove the cover by lifting at the rear edge to disengage the retaining clips and by sliding the panel out of the windshield clips.

3. Carefully remove the center air outlet/trim panel by pulling outward at the clip locations. Start at the bottom and move upward. Do not use tools that might damage the trim panel.

4. Open the glove box, then remove the 4 cluster trim panel attaching screws.

5. Carefully pull the cluster trim panel rearward to disengage it from the retainers, then remove the CPA device and unplug the electrical connector from the instrument panel dimmer switch.

6. Remove the fastener, then remove the dimmer switch from the cluster trim panel.

To install:

7. Install the dimmer switch to the cluster trim panel and secure using the fastener.

8. Connect the wiring harness to the dimmer switch and install the CPA device.

9. Install the cluster trim panel into the retainers, then install and tighten the retaining screws.

10. Install the center air outlet/trim panel by pushing at the clip locations.

11. Install the rear of the instrument panel top cover into the windshield clips and snap the panel into position. Install the upper panel cover screws and screw caps.

12. Connect the negative battery cable.

Rear Window Defogger Switch

REMOVAL & INSTALLATION

1. Disconnect the negative battery cable.

2. Remove the 2 instrument panel top cover screw caps and screws. Carefully remove the cover by lifting at the rear edge to disengage the retaining clips and by sliding the panel out of the windshield clips.

3. Carefully remove the center air outlet/trim panel by pulling outward at the clip locations. Start at the bottom and move upward. Do not use tools that might damage the trim panel.

4. Open the glove box, then remove the 4 cluster trim panel attaching screws.

5. Carefully pull the cluster trim panel rearward to disengage it from the retainers, then remove the CPA device and unplug the electrical connector from the rear defogger switch.

6. Remove the fastener, then remove the defogger switch from the cluster trim panel.

To install:

7. Install the defogger switch to the cluster trim panel and secure using the fastener.

8. Connect the wiring harness to the defogger switch and install the CPA device.

9. Install the cluster trim panel into the retainers, then install and tighten the retaining screws.

10. Install the center air outlet/trim panel by pushing at the clip locations.

11. Install the rear of the instrument panel top cover into the windshield clips and snap the panel into position. Install the upper panel cover screws and screw caps.

12. Connect the negative battery cable.

LIGHTING

Headlights

REMOVAL & INSTALLATION

Except SC or SC2
▶ **See Figure 100**

1. Disconnect the negative battery cable and make sure the headlamp is has cooled if it was operated in the past few minutes.

2. Disconnect the headlamp bulb socket from the from the rear of the lens by rotating the socket 1/4 turn, then pulling the socket rearward until the bulb clears the housing. Lift the socket/harness for access.

3. Remove the bulb from the socket/harness.

4. Installation is the reverse of removal. Adjustment of the headlamp on these vehicles should not be necessary unless the housing assembly is removed or loosened. Nonetheless, headlight aim should always be checked and, if necessary adjusted for safety.

SC or SC2
▶ **See Figures 101, 102, 103 and 104**

The SC2, originally known as the SC, is the only Saturn vehicle equipped with concealed headlights. The headlight doors can be opened automatically by turning the headlight switch to the headlamps **ON** position. Turning the switch back 1 click to the parking lights **ON** only position or 2 clicks to the lights **OFF** position will leave the doors open. To close the headlight doors turn the switch a total of 3 clicks back to the headlight closed position.

A manual headlight control knob is located next to each headlight door and may be used to open the doors without the aid of the electric motor. To manually open the door, raise the vehicle's hood and turn the control knob until the door is fully opened. Although the knob is knurled, the top also contains a socket into which a hex key may be inserted to speed up manual headlight door operation.

1. Prior to disrupting a properly aimed headlamp, check the headlight aiming procedure for suggestions to ease adjustment. Open the headlight doors and disconnect the negative battery cable. Make sure the headlamp is has cooled if it was operated in the past few minutes.

2. Remove the headlamp trim bezel screws from the sides of the lamp housing, then manually rotate the lamp down sufficiently to provide clearance between the bezel at the lower inside corner of the lamp.

3. Manually rotate the lamp door back upward and remove the trim bezel.

4. Disconnect the spring and disengage the adjusters from the retainer, then carefully pull the lamp from the housing and disconnect the electrical harness.

Fig. 100 The headlamp housing assembly does not need to be removed in order the replace the headlamp bulb — except SC or SC2

5. Pull the headlamp assembly from the housing. Remove the screws, then remove the retaining ring and backing from the headlamp.

To install:

6. Insert the headlamp in the backing, then position the retaining ring or the assembly and secure using the screws.

7. Connect the wiring harness to the back of the lamp assembly, then position the assembly into the housing. Engage the retaining ring adjusters and install the spring.

8. Install the trim bezel to the lamp housing and secure using the screws. Raise or lower the housing door using the manual knob, as necessary to provide clearance for bezel installation.

9. Connect the negative battery cable, then check and adjust the headlight aiming, as necessary for safety.

AIMING

▶ **See Figure 105**

Headlights adjustment may be temporarily made on a wall, as described below, or on the rear of another vehicle. When adjusted, the lights should not glare in oncoming cars windshields, nor should they illuminate the passenger compartment of cars driving in front of you. These adjustments are rough and should always be fine-tuned by a repair shop which is equipped with a headlight aiming tools. Improper adjustments may be both dangerous and illegal.

Headlights are adjusted on most Saturn vehicles by turning the adjusting wheel on the outer side of the headlight assembly for horizontal adjustment or the adjusting screw on

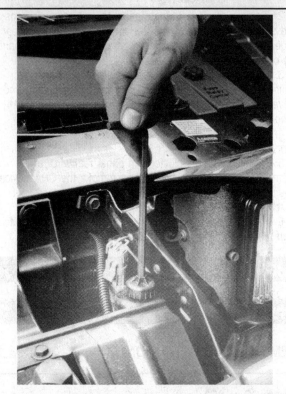

Fig. 102 The headlight knob may also be turned using an hex key — SC or SC2

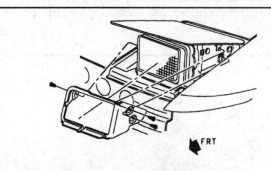

Fig. 103 Remove the screws, then remove the trim bezel from the headlamp housing

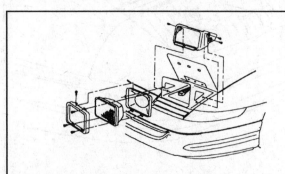

Fig. 104 Exploded view of the headlamp assembly — SC or SC2

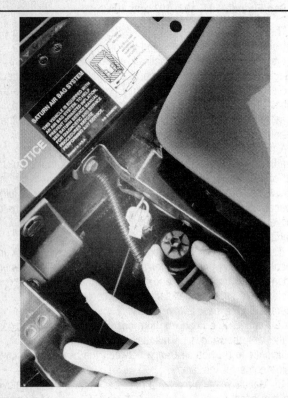

Fig. 101 Turn the headlight knob in order to manually operate the lamp door — SC or SC2

the top center of the assembly for vertical adjustment. On the SC or SC2, which are equipped with concealed headlights, the beams are adjusted horizontally by the screw on the side center and vertically by the screw at the bottom center of the assembly.

Before removing the headlight from the lamp on SC or SC2 vehicles, or before disturbing the headlamp housing assembly for all Saturn vehicles, note the current settings in order to make adjusting the headlights upon reassembly easier. If the high or low beam setting of the old lamp still works, this can be done using the wall of a garage or a building as follows:

1. Park the car on a level surface, with the fuel tank no more than ½ full and with the vehicle empty of all extra cargo. The vehicle should be facing a wall which is no less the 6 feet high and 12 feet wide. The front of the vehicle should be about 25 feet from the wall.

2. If this is be performed outdoors, it is advisable to wait until dusk in order to properly see the headlight beams on the wall. If done in a garage, darken the area around the wall as much as possible by closing shades or hanging cloth over the windows.

3. Turn the headlights **ON** and mark the wall at the center of each light's low beam, then switch on the brights and mark the center of each light's high beam. A short length of masking tape which is visible from the front of the car may be used. Although marking all 4 positions is advisable, marking 1 position from each light should be sufficient.

4. If neither beam on 1 side of the vehicle is working, park another like-sized car in the exact spot where the Saturn was and mark the beams using the same side light on that car. Then switch the cars so the Saturn is back in the original spot. The Saturn must be parked no closer or farther away from the wall than the second vehicle.

5. Perform the necessary repairs, but make sure the car in not moved or is returned to the exact spot from which the lights were marked. Turn the headlights **ON** and adjust the beams to match the marks on the wall.

6. Have the headlight adjustment checked as soon as possible by a reputable repair shop.

Signal and Marker Lights

REMOVAL & INSTALLATION

Front Turn Signal and Parking Lights

TURN SIGNALS: EXCEPT SC OR SC2

1. Disconnect the negative battery cable and make sure the headlamp is has cooled if it was operated in the past few minutes.

2. Disconnect the headlamp bulb socket from the from the rear of the lens by rotating the socket ¼ turn, then pulling the socket rearward until the bulb clears the housing. Lift the socket/harness for access.

3. Remove the bulb from the socket/harness.

4. Installation is the reverse of removal.

TURN SIGNALS AND PARKING LIGHTS: SC OR SC2

▶ See Figure 106

1. Disconnect the negative battery cable.

2. Lower the front ½ of the wheelhouse liner by removing the front retaining screws and the plastic pushpin fasteners.

3. Remove the nuts and the reinforcement plate from the horizontal fender-to-facia joint and the lower rear of the facia.

4. Remove the turn signal/parking lamp by disconnecting the lamp sockets. Replace the bulbs, as necessary.

5. Installation is the reverse of removal.

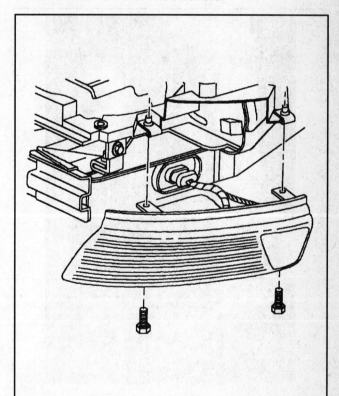

Fig. 106 Removing the front turn signal/parking lamp — SC or SC2

Fig. 105 Adjusting the horizontal aim of the headlamp assembly — SC or SC2

Side Marker Lights: Except SC or SC2

▶ **See Figure 107**

1. Disconnect the negative battery cable.
2. Remove the retaining screw, then carefully pull the lamp out of the front facia.
3. Disconnect the lamp socket from the lamp, then remove the bulb.
4. Installation is the reverse of removal.

Side Marker Lights: SC or SC2

The side marker lights for the SC or SC2 are part of the turn signal and parking light assembly. Refer to the procedure in this section for lamp removal and bulb replacement.

Rear Turn Signal, Brake and Parking Lights

EXCEPT WAGON

▶ **See Figures 108, 109, 110, 111 and 112**

1. Disconnect the negative battery cable.
2. Remove the trim panel fasteners, then carefully remove the trim panel.
3. Remove the 2 retaining screws from the side of the lamp assembly, then pull the lamp assembly straight back and out of the opening.
4. Tilt the assembly downward for access to the sockets, then twist and remove the socket from the lamp assembly. Replace the bulbs, as necessary.
5. Installation is the reverse of removal.

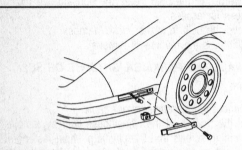

Fig. 107 Marker lights are mounted to the side of the front facia and are separate from the turn signals — except SC or SC2

Fig. 109 Carefully remove the trim panel — except wagon

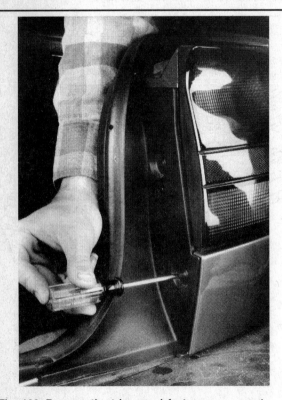

Fig. 108 Remove the trim panel fasteners — except wagon

Fig. 110 Pull the lamp assembly straight back and out of the opening — except wagon

Fig. 111 Tilt the assembly downward for access to the sockets — except wagon

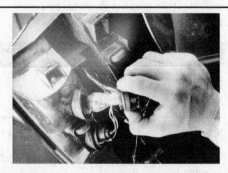

Fig. 112 Twist and remove the socket with bulb from the lamp assembly — except wagon

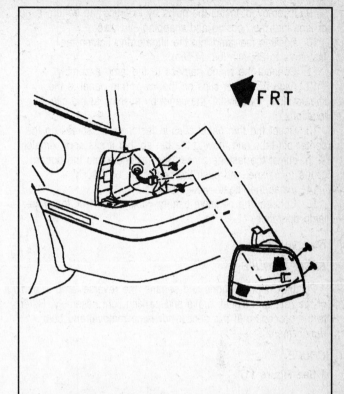

Fig. 113 Exploded view of the taillamp assembly — wagon

WAGON

▶ See Figure 113

1. Disconnect the negative battery cable.
2. Remove the retaining screws from the side of the lamp assembly, then pull the lamp assembly straight back and out of the opening.
3. Tilt the assembly for access to the sockets, then twist and remove the socket from the lamp assembly. Replace the bulbs, as necessary.
4. Installation is the reverse of removal.

High-Mount Brake Light

EXCEPT WAGON

▶ See Figure 114

1. Disconnect the negative battery cable.
2. Open the trunk for access to the lamps.
3. Locate the bulbs at the top of the underside of the rear trunk lid. Remove bulbs by twisting, then pulling straight out.
4. Installation is the reverse of the removal.

WAGON

▶ See Figures 115 and 116

1. Disconnect the negative battery cable.
2. Raise the liftgate, then remove the wedge blocks from either end of the liftgate assembly.
3. Remove the lower fasteners from the liftgate lower trim panel, by pushing in the of each center pin approximately 1/8 inch until it clicks, then remove the fastener.

Fig. 114 Remove the high-mount brake lamp bulbs by twisting, then pulling — except wagon

4. Insert a screwdriver or small prybar into the hole in the lower trim panel (located near the wiper pivot on the pivot hump) so that the tool sits on top of the pivot as shown. Lift up on the tool handle to disengage the trim panel upper clips, then remove the lower trim panel from the vehicle.
5. Unplug the high-mount brake light wiring harness.
6. Remove the brake light fasteners, then remove the lamp assembly from the liftgate.
7. To remove the bulbs, push slightly on the top edge of the lens and rotate outboard of housing. Remove the bulbs from the housing.
To install:
8. In order to prevent the possibility of water leaks into the liftgate, inspect the lamp gasket for damage and replace, if necessary.

9. If removed, install the bulbs by inserting the bottom edge of lens into the housing and snapping into place.

10. Position the lamp into the liftgate and tighten the fasteners to 35 inch lbs. (4 Nm).

11. Connect the wiring harness to the lamp assembly.

12. Align the upper clips on the lower trim panel to the liftgate slots, then instal' the panel by pushing at the clip locations.

13. Reset the trim panel push-in fasteners by spreading the center pin tabs and moving the pin so that it sits approximately ¼ in. out of the fastener. Insert the fasteners into the bottom of the trim panel and push the center pin until flush.

14. Install the liftgate wedge blocks.

15. Connect the negative battery cable and check for proper lamp operation.

Reverse Light

EXCEPT COUPE

For the Saturn wagons and sedans, the reverse lamp is part of the rear turn signal, brake and parking light assembly. Refer to the procedure in this section for lamp removal and bulb replacement.

COUPE

▶ See Figure 117

1. Disconnect the negative battery cable.
2. Reach behind the bumper bar and disconnect the harness and socket from the reverse lamp. Remove the bulb from the socket.

3. If necessary, remove the retaining nuts and remove the lamp from the bar.
4. Installation is the reverse of the removal.

Dome Light

1. Disconnect the negative battery cable.
2. Grasp the front and back of the light cover and remove by squeezing slightly while pulling downward and tilting toward the driver's side of the vehicle.
3. Remove the bulb from between the connectors.
4. Installation is the reverse of removal.

Trunk/Cargo Light

1. Disconnect the negative battery cable.
2. Remove the bulb from the electrical connector.
3. Installation is the reverse of removal.

Fog Lights

REMOVAL & INSTALLATION

▶ See Figure 118

For 1993, the Saturn sedan and wagon were offered with optional fog lights.

1. Disconnect the negative battery cable.
2. Remove the fasteners on the front of the bezel, then unplug the wiring connectors from the lamp.
3. Remove the lens from the housing.

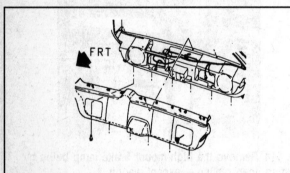

Fig. 115 Removing the liftgate lower trim panel assembly — wagon

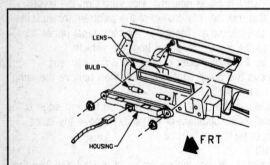

Fig. 116 Exploded view of the high-mount brake light bulb and lens assembly — wagon

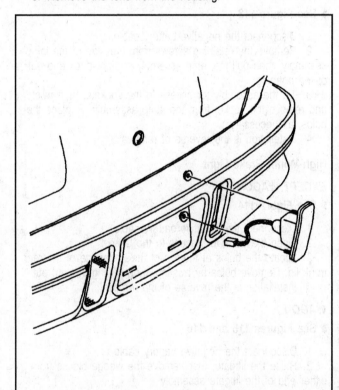

Fig. 117 Exploded view of the reverse lamp mounting — coupe

4. Remove the retainer clip, then remove the bulb from the housing.

5. Installation is the reverse of removal.

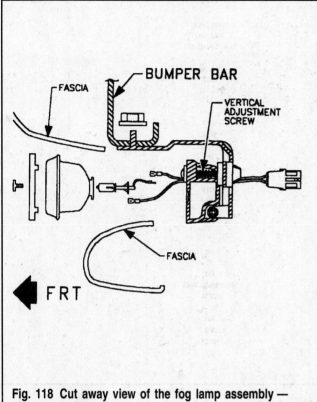

Fig. 118 Cut away view of the fog lamp assembly — sedan or wagon

AIMING

▶ **See Figures 119, 120**

To assure safety and proper operation, the fog lights should be aimed whenever the housing has been disturbed. Vertical adjustment is possible on all fog lamp equipped Saturn vehicles, but horizontal adjustment is not always possible. If your vehicle contains fog lamps which are horizontally adjustable, make sure the beams are located so they cross at the straight ahead positions of the centerline of each fog lamp before adjusting the vertical aim.

1. Park the car on a level surface, with the fuel tank no more than ½ full and with the vehicle empty of all extra cargo. The vehicle should be facing a wall which is no less the 6 feet high and 12 feet wide. The front of the vehicle should be about 25 feet from the wall.

2. If this is be performed outdoors, it is advisable to wait until dusk in order to properly see the fog lamp beams on the wall. If done in a garage, darken the area around the wall as much as possible by closing shades or hanging cloth over the windows.

3. Measure the distance from the floor to the center of each fog lamp. The numbers should be the same unless the floor is not level. Measure the same distance from the floor, up the aiming wall and mark a wide horizontal line using masking tape. The line should be about 6 feet long.

4. Turn the fog lamps **ON** and compare the beams to the horizontal marking line. The center of the high intensity zone should be no more than 4 in. (102mm) above or below the centerline. Adjust the beams, as necessary.

BULBS, FUSES AND RELAYS

REPLACEMENT BULBS

EXTERIOR LAMPS

	TYPE
Headlamps	
HI Beam (4–Door Sedan)	9005 HB3
LO Beam (4–Door Sedan)	9006 HB4
HI/LO Beam (2+2 Coupe)	Sealed Beam 2E1
Front Park/Turn Lamps	
4–Door Sedan	3057NA
2+2 Coupe	2057
Front Side Marker Lamps	
4–Door Sedan	24
2+2 Coupe	194
Stop/Tail Lamps	2057
Rear Turn Lamps	1156
Rear Side Marker Lamps	
4–Door Sedan	194
2+2 Coupe	168
Back–Up Lamps	
4–Door Sedan	2057
2+2 Coupe	1156
License Lamps	24
Center High–Mounted Stop Lamps	175

INTERIOR LAMPS

Ashtray Lamp	161
Cigar lamper Ring Lamp	73
Dome Lamp	562
Heater & A/C Control Lamps	NEO Wedge Bulb
Instrument Panel Warning Lamps	GE74
Instrument Cluster Illumination Lamps	GE73
Luggage Compartment Lamp	906
MAP Lamp	562
Panel Dimmer Lamp	GE73
PRND32 Shift Indicator Lamp	161

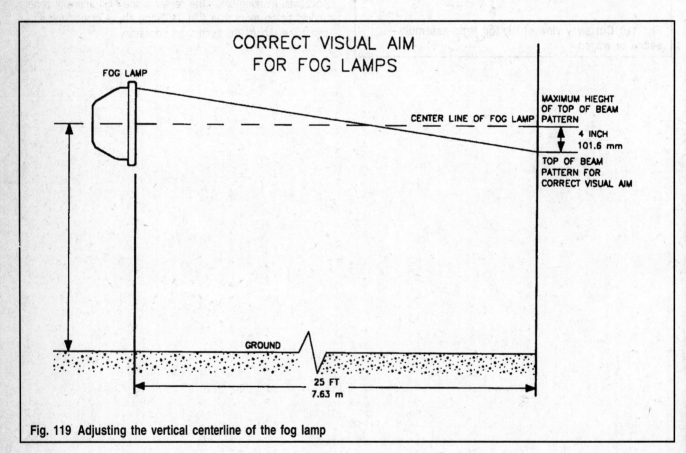

Fig. 119 Adjusting the vertical centerline of the fog lamp

TRAILER WIRING

Wiring the car for towing is fairly easy. There are a number of good wiring kits available and these should be used, rather than trying to design your own. All trailers will need brake lights and turn signals as well as tail lights and side marker lights. Most states require extra marker lights for overly wide trailers. Also, most states have recently required back-up lights for trailers. Most trailer manufacturers have been building trailers with back-up lights for several years.

Additionally, some Class I, most Class II and just about all Class III trailers will have electric brakes.

Add to this number an accessories wire, to operate trailer internal equipment or to charge the trailer's battery, and you can have as many as seven wires in the harness.

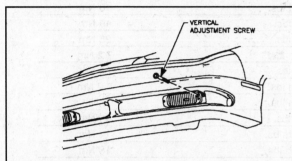

Fig. 120 Fog lamp vertical aiming is accomplished with the adjustment screw

Determine the equipment on your trailer and buy the wiring kit necessary. The kit will contain all the wires needed, plus a plug adapter set which includes the female plug, mounted on the bumper or hitch, and the male plug, wired into, or plugged into the trailer harness.

When installing the kit, follow the manufacturer's instructions. The color coding of the wires is standard throughout the industry.

One point to note, most vehicles today have separate turn signals. On older domestic vehicles, the brake lights and rear turn signals operate with the same bulb. For those vehicles with separate turn signals, you can purchase an isolation unit so that the brake lights won't blink whenever the turn signals are operated, or, you can go to your local electronics supply house and buy four diodes to wire in series with the brake and turn signal bulbs. Diodes will isolate the brake and turn signals. The choice is yours. The isolation units are simple and quick to install, but far more expensive than the diodes. The diodes, however, require more work to install properly, since they require the cutting of each bulb's wire and soldering in place of the diode.

One final point, the best kits are those with a spring loaded cover on the vehicle mounted socket. This cover prevents dirt and moisture from corroding the terminals. Never let the vehicle socket hang loosely. Always mount it securely to the bumper or hitch.

CIRCUIT PROTECTION

Fuses And Relays

There are 2 fuse or junction blocks in your Saturn vehicle. Both contain minifuses (small fuses with ratings from 5-30 amps), maxifuses (large fuses with ratings from 20-60 amps) and/or relays. The Under Hood Junction Block (UHJB) is located on the driver's side of the vehicle, near the battery. The Instrument Panel Junction Block (IPJB) is located at the base of the instrument panel center console, behind a trim piece on the passengers side.

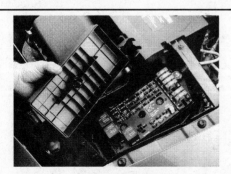

Fig. 121 Loosen the retaining screw, then remove the UHJB cover

REPLACEMENT

Under Hood Junction Block

▶ **See Figure 121**

1. Disconnect the negative battery cable.
2. Loosen the retaining screw, then remove the UHJB cover.
3. Pull the fuse or relay from it's terminals. A small plastic puller is provided to help secure a firm grip on the fuses.
4. Installation is the reverse of the removal procedure.

Instrument Panel Junction Block

1. Remove the lower right trim panel from the instrument panel center column. Separate the velcro fastener at the bottom of the trim panel and carefully unsnap the top corners of the panel from the fasteners.
2. Remove the fuse or relay from the IPJB according to the identification label located on the back of the trim panel. A plastic puller is also located on the trim panel to ease fuse removal.
3. Installation is the reverse of removal.

Circuit Breaker

Saturn vehicles use circuit breakers to protect devices which are subject to intermittent overloads such as the window motor. These breakers will automatically reset once the overload condition is removed (for example, the window switch is released).

Flasher

The turn signal flasher is located in the IPJB. Check the label on the back of the trim panel for the exact location on your vehicle.

TORQUE SPECIFICATIONS

Component	U.S.	Metric
A/C inline pressure sensor	49 inch lbs.	5.5 Nm
A/C lines	19 ft. lbs.	25 Nm
Brake switch assembly	89 inch lbs.	10 Nm
Clutch switch assembly	89 inch lbs.	10 Nm
Compressor front bolts	36 ft. lbs.	49 Nm
Compressor hose retaining bolts	19 ft. lbs.	25 Nm
Compressor pressure relief valve	63 inch lbs.	7.2 Nm
Compressor rear bolts	19 ft. lbs.	25 Nm
Compressor temperature sensor	64 inch lbs.	7.2 Nm
Cruise control module attaching nuts	44 inch lbs.	5 Nm
Cylinder block drain plug	26 ft. lbs.	35 Nm
Liftgate wiper pivot shaft nut	119 inch lbs.	14 Nm
Liftgate wiper arm nut	159 inch lbs.	18 Nm
Liftgate wiper module retaining bolts	89 inch lbs.	10 Nm
Steering column assembly retaining bolts	33 ft. lbs.	45 Nm
Thermal expansion valve retaining bolts	89 inch lbs.	10 Nm
Windshield wiper arm nut	21 ft. lbs.	28 Nm
Windshield wiper module retaining bolts	89 inch lbs.	10 Nm
Windshield wiper motor crank arm nut	21 ft. lbs.	28 Nm

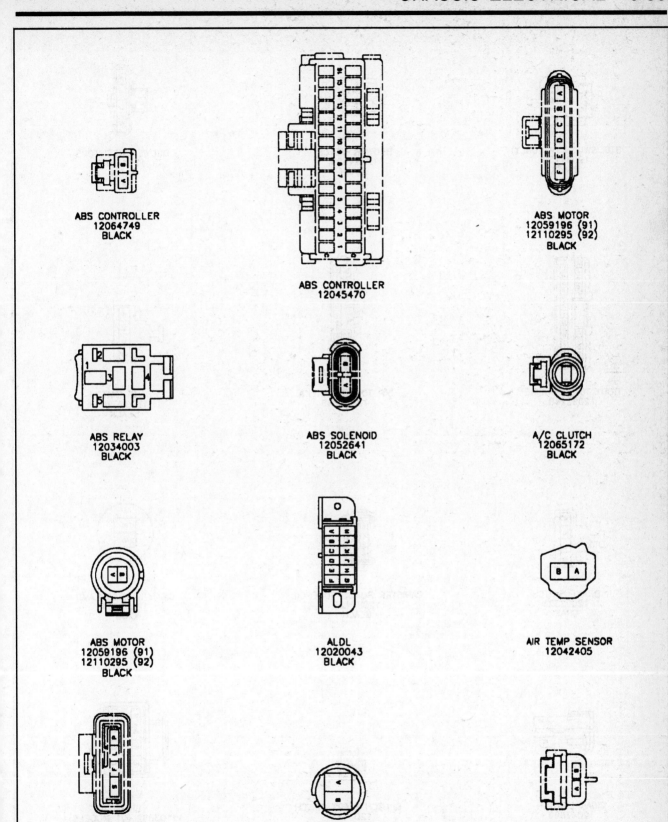

Fig. 122 Saturn electrical connector terminal identifications

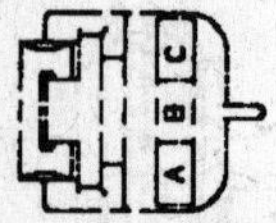

BTSI SWITCH (91 ONLY)
12064758
BLACK

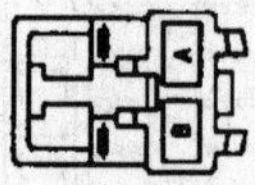

BLOWER MOTOR
12064829
BLACK

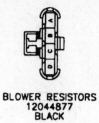

BLOWER RESISTORS
12044877
BLACK

BODY TO I/P INLINE
12092248

I/P TO BODY INLINE
12092249

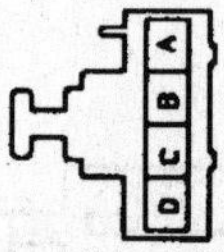

BRAKE.SWITCH
12092370
BLACK

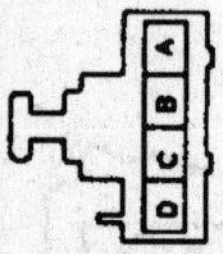

BRAKE.SWITCH
12092371
GRAY

CANISTER PURGE SOLENOID
12084126
BLACK

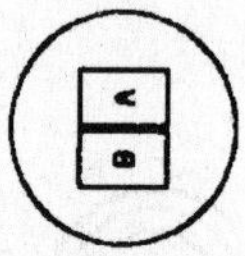

CIGAR LIGHTER LAMP
12092411
GRAY

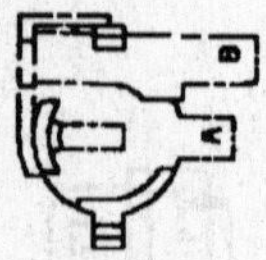

CIGAR LIRHTER
12047699
GRAY

CLUTCH START SWITCH
12034417
BLACK

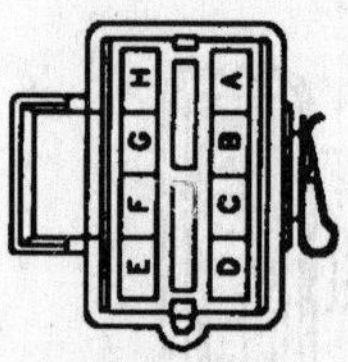

CHMSL
12103382 (91 MODELS)
12089451 (92 MODELS)
BLACK

Fig. 123 Saturn electrical connector terminal identifications

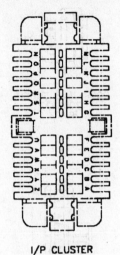

I/P CLUSTER
12089908
BLACK

COOLING FAN
12103172
BLACK

COOLANT LEVEL SWITCH
12052641
BLACK

COOLANT TEMP SENSOR
12052642

CRANK POSITION SENSOR
12052642
BLACK

CRIUSE CLUTCH SWITCH
12052832
BLACK

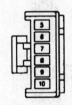

CRUISE CONTROL MODULE
12064993
BLACK

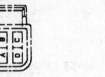

CRUISE CONTROL SWITCHES
12064761
BLACK

DECKLID INLINE (F) SEDAN
12064998 (91 MODELS)
12064766 (92 MODELS)
BLACK

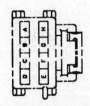

DECKLID INLINE (M) SEDAN
12103955 (91 MODELS)
12064767 (92 MODELS)
BLACK

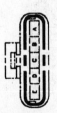

DISTRIBUTOR SYSTEM
12084416
BLACK

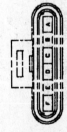

DISTRIBUTOR SYSTEM
12084420
BLACK

Fig. 124 Saturn electrical connector terminal identifications

DIMMER, SWITCH
12052832
BLACK

DOME LAMP, MAP LIGHTS
12047781
BLACK

DOOR JAMB SWITCH
12052832
BLACK

DOOR LOCK ACTUATOR
12077900
BLACK

DOOR LOCK, KEY SWITCH
12052843
BLACK

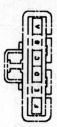

DOOR LOCK RELAY
12059561
BLACK

DOOR LOCK SWITCH
12064758
BLACK

DRIVER LATCH PROXIMITY SWITCH
12052832
BLACK

EGR SOLENOID
12084126(TBI)
12052644(PFI)
BLACK

I/P TO ENGINE INLINE
12092248

ENGINE TO.I/P INLINE
12092249

ENGINE TEMPERATURE
SENSOR (GAGE)
12092511

Fig. 125 Saturn electrical connector terminal identifications

EVO SOLENOID
12052643
RED

FUEL TANK. INLINE (M)
12020397
BLACK

FUEL TANK. INLINE (F)
12020398
BLACK

FUEL TANK UNIT
12078082
BLACK

FWD LAMP TO I/P INLINE
12052641
BLACK

I/P TO FWD .LAMP INLINE
12052647
BLACK

HANDWHEEL SENSOR
12064758
BLACK

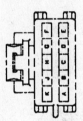

HEADLAMP SWITCH
12064769
NATURAL

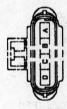

HEADLAMP DOOR CONTROL
12059199
GRAY

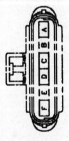

HEADLAMP DOOR CONTROL
12059196
GRAY

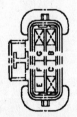

HEADLAMP HI/LO BEAM
& MOTOR (COUPE)
12052600
GRAY

HIGH BEAM HEADLAMP
(SEDAN)
12059183
BLACK

Fig. 126 Saturn electrical connector terminal identifications

HORN
12052644
GRAY

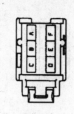

HVAC MODULE CONTROL HEAD
12064754
BLACK

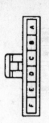

HVAC MODULE FAN SWITCH
12092374
BLACK

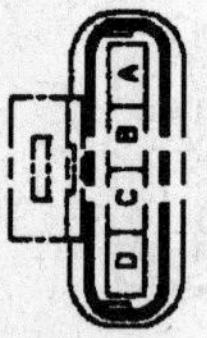

IDLE AIR CONTROL
12078082
BLACK

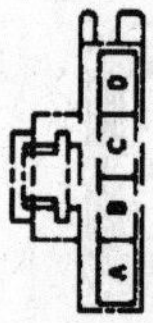

IGNITION SWITCH
12092257
GRAY

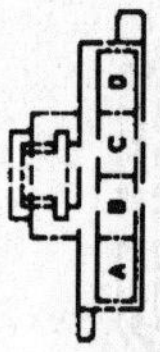

IGNITION SWITCH
12092258
BLUE

INJECTORS (PFI)
12084126
BLACK

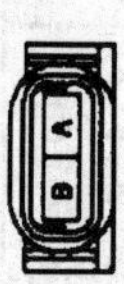

INJECTORS (TBI)
12084422
BLACK

I/P JUNCTION BLOCK HVAC
12064749
BLACK

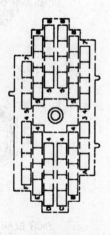

I/P JUNCTION BLOCK
12092939
BROWN

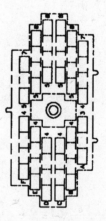

I/P JUNCTION BLOCK
12092285
BLACK

Fig. 127 Saturn electrical connector terminal identifications

I/P JUNCTION BLOCK HVAC
12064752
BLACK

I/P JUNCTION BLOCK
12064998
BLACK

KNOCK SENSOR
12015375
BLACK

LOW BEAM HEADLIGHTS
12059181
GRAY

LICENCE LAMPS (SEDAN)
12065157
CREAM

LICENCE LAMPS (COUPE)
12052644
GRAY

LOW BRAKE FLUID SWITCH
12078084
BLACK

M.A.P. SENSOR
12020403
GREEN

MAP LIGHTS
12047781
BLACK

MIRROR SWITCH
12064762
GRAY

MIRROR MOTOR
12065656
BLACK

NUETRAL START SWITCH
12084420

Fig. 128 Saturn electrical connector terminal identifications

NEUTRAL START SWITCH

OXYGEN SENSOR

OIL PRESSURE SENDER

PARK BRAKE SWITCH
12064758
BLACK

PARK/TURN/DRL

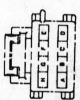

PASSIVE RESTRAINT CONTROL MODULE
12064998
BLACK

PASSIVE RESTRAINT MODULE
12064762
GRAY

PASSIVE RESTRAINT MODULE
12064266
BLUE

PASSIVE RESTRAINT MOTOR
12064752

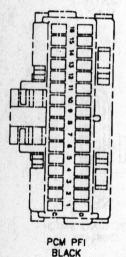

PCM PFI
BLACK

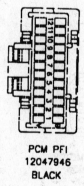

PCM PFI
12047946
BLACK

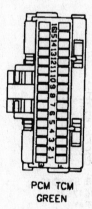

PCM TCM
GREEN

Fig. 129 Saturn electrical connector terminal identifications

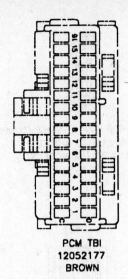

PCM TBI
12052177
BROWN

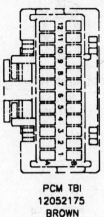

PCM TBI
12052175
BROWN

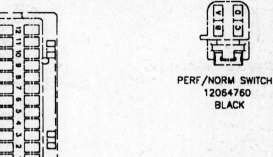

PERF/NORM SWITCH
12064760
BLACK

PRNDL LAMP
12059952
NATURAL

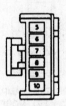

POWER STEERING
PRESSURE SWITCH
(91 MODELS)
12020599
BLACK

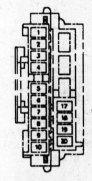

RADIO MODULE
(2 CONNECTORS LOCKED TOGHTER)
(12047531 10W—BLACK)
(12047530 4W—BLUE)

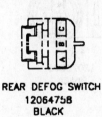

REAR DEFOG SWITCH
12064758
BLACK

RECIRC MOTOR
12064993
BLACK

REVERSE LAMP SWITCH
12015792
BLACK

REAR BACK-UP LAMP (COUPE)
12052641
BLACK

SEAT BELT BUCKLE SWITCH
12052832
BLACK

FRONT SPEAKERS (91 MODELS)
FRONT & REAR
SPEAKERS (92 MODELS)
12077887
BLACK

Fig. 130 Saturn electrical connector terminal identifications

REAR SPEAKERS (91 MODELS)
12092428
BLACK

REAR SPEAKERS (91 MODELS)
12092428
CREAM

SIDE MARKER/PARK/TURN/ (COUPE)
12052843 (91 MODELS)
12110293 (92 MODELS)
BLACK

SUNROOF MODULE
12064750 (91 MODELS)
12052833 (92 MODELS)
BLACK

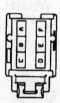

SUNROOF TO BODY INLINE
12064752 (91 MODELS)
12064760 (92 MODELS)
(NOTE: 4-WAY 92 MODELS)
BLACK

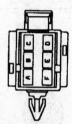

SUNROOF INLINE (SEDAN)
12065653 (91 MODELS)
12064761 (92 MODELS)
(NOTE: 4-WAY 92 MODELS)
BLACK

SUNROOF INLINE (COUPE)
12064754 (91 MODELS)
12064761 (92 MODELS)
(NOTE: 4-WAY 92 MODELS)
BLACK

STOP/TAIL LAMP
12064754 (91 MODELS)
12064763 (92 MODELS)
12064761 (92 COUPES)
(NOTE: 4-WAY 92 COUPES)
BLACK

T.P.S.
12078090
BLACK

TRANS TEMP SENSOR
12092512

TRANS ACTUATORS
12092172
BLACK

TRUNK LAMP & SWITCH
12052832
BLACK

Fig. 131 Saturn electrical connector terminal identifications

TURBINE SPEED SENSOR
12052644
GRAY

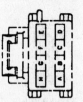

TURN HAZARD SWITCH
12064766
BLUE

TURN HAZARD SWITCH
12064760
BLACK

UNDERHOOD JUNCTION BLOCK
12092400
GRAY

UNDERHOOD JUNCTION BLOCK
12092399
BLACK

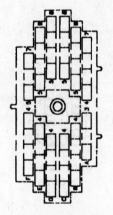

UNDERHOOD JUNCTION BLOCK
12092285
BLACK

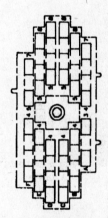

UNDERHOOD JUNCTION BLOCK
12092939
BROWN

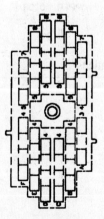

UNDERHOOD JUNCTION BLOCK
12092289
GRAY

Fig. 132 Saturn electrical connector terminal identifications

VEHICLE SPEED SENSOR/WHEEL SENSORS
12052644
GRAY

WASHER PUMP
12084126

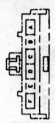

WINDOW MASTER SWITCH
12084795

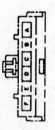

WINDOW MASTER SWITCH
12084796

WINDOW MOTOR
12064749
BLACK

WINDOW SWITCHES
12066571
BLACK

WINDOW SWITCHES
12064749
BLACK

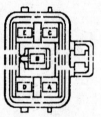

WIPER MOTOR
12052813
BLACK

WIPER SWITCH
12064758
BLACK

Fig. 133 Saturn electrical connector terminal identifications

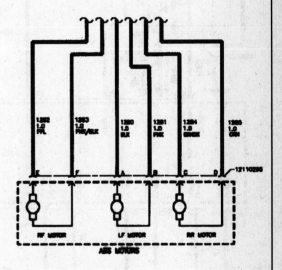

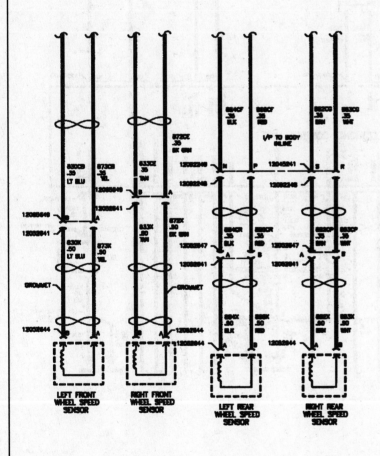

Fig. 134 Anti-lock brake system schematics — 1993

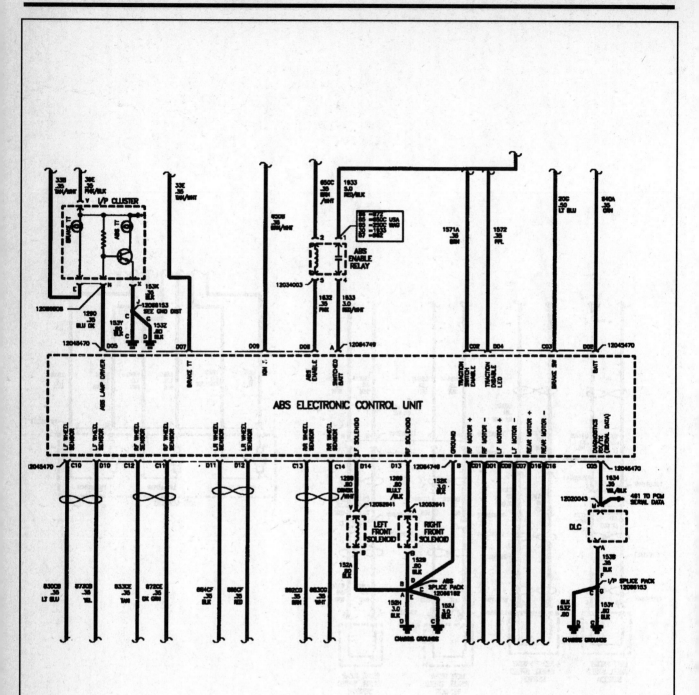

Fig. 135 Anti-lock brake system schematics — 1993

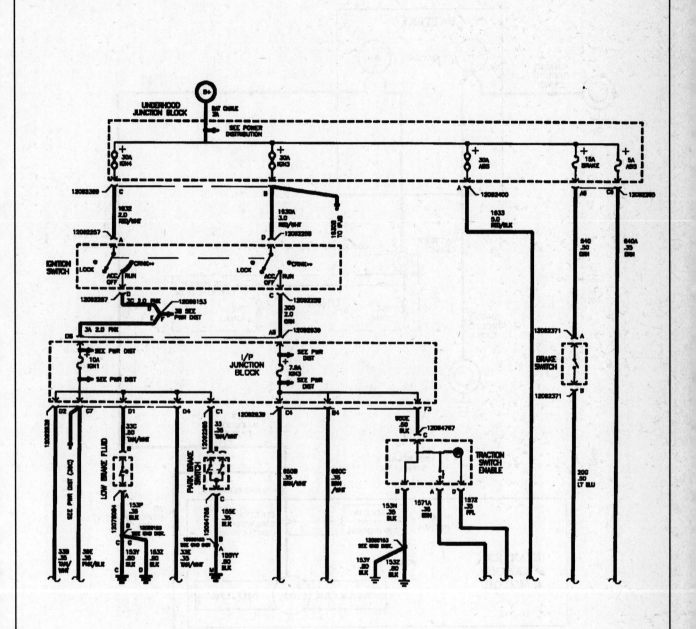

Fig. 136 Anti-lock brake system schematics — 1993

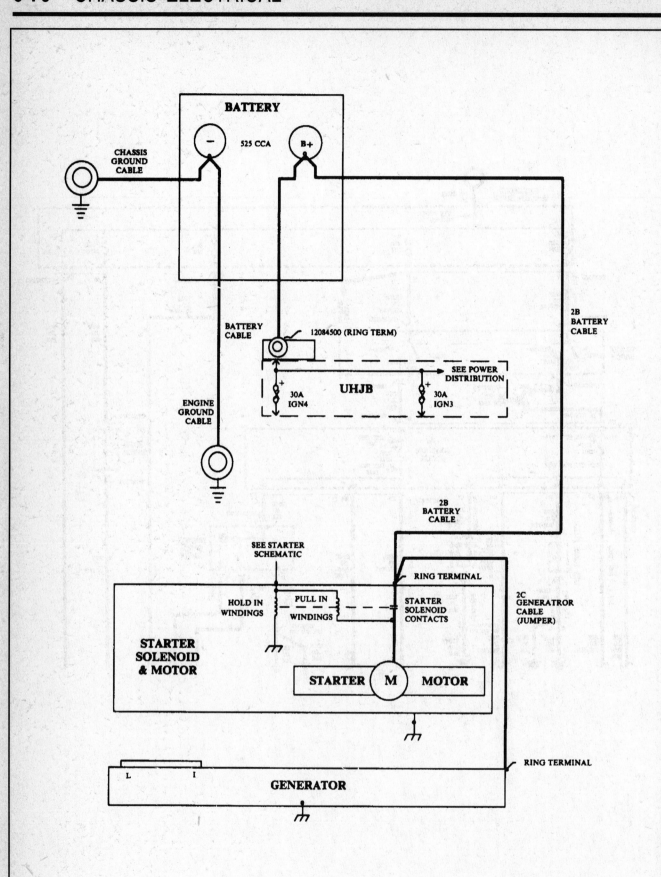

Fig. 137 Battery schematics

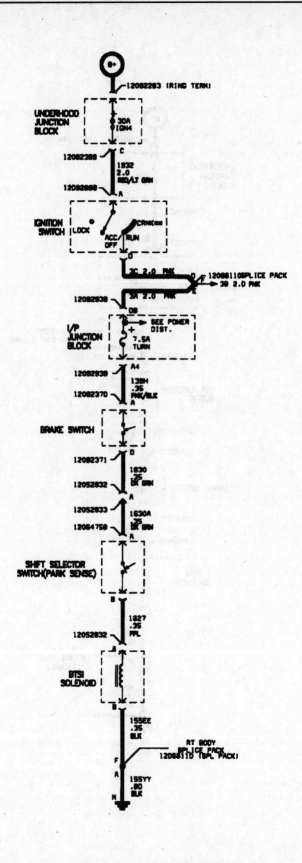

Fig. 138 Brake transaxle safety interlock schematics — 1991 automatic transaxle

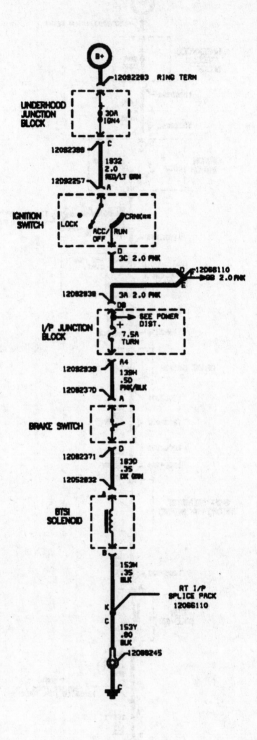

Fig. 139 Brake transaxle safety interlock schematics — 1992 automatic transaxle

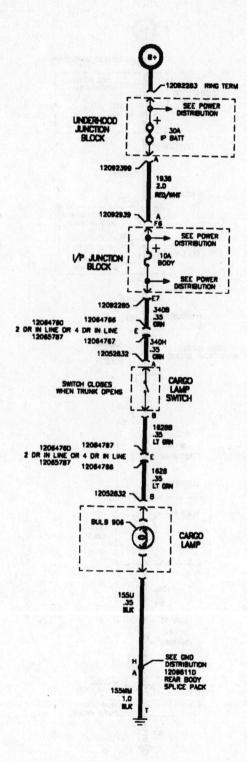

Fig. 140 Cargo lamp schematics — 1991

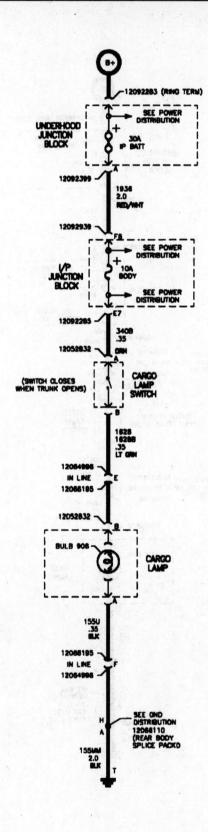

Fig. 141 Cargo lamp schematics — 1991

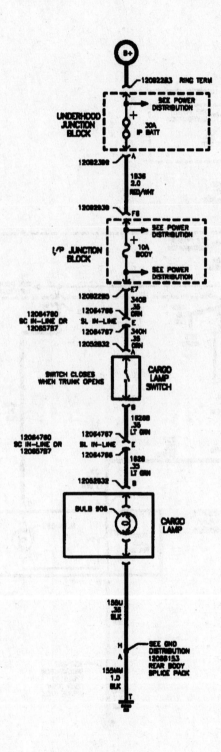

Fig. 142 Cargo lamp schematics — 1993 sedan and coupe

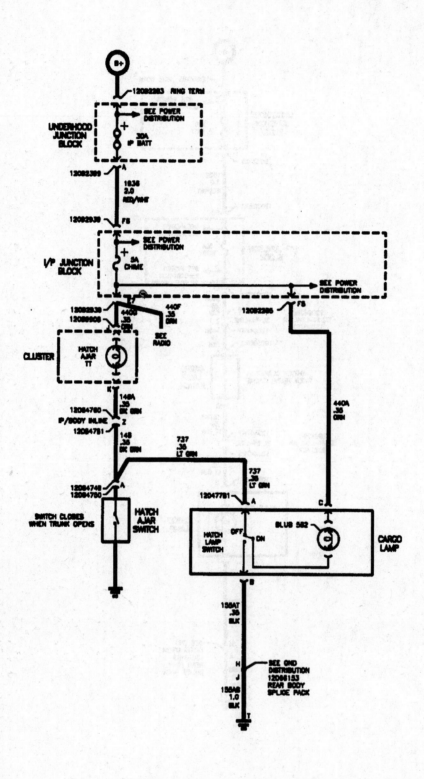

Fig. 143 Cargo lamp schematics — 1993 wagon

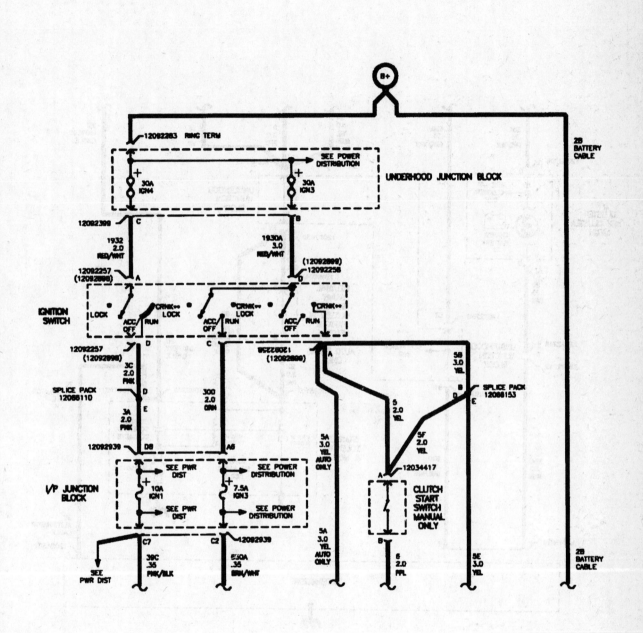

Fig. 144 Charging/starting system schematics

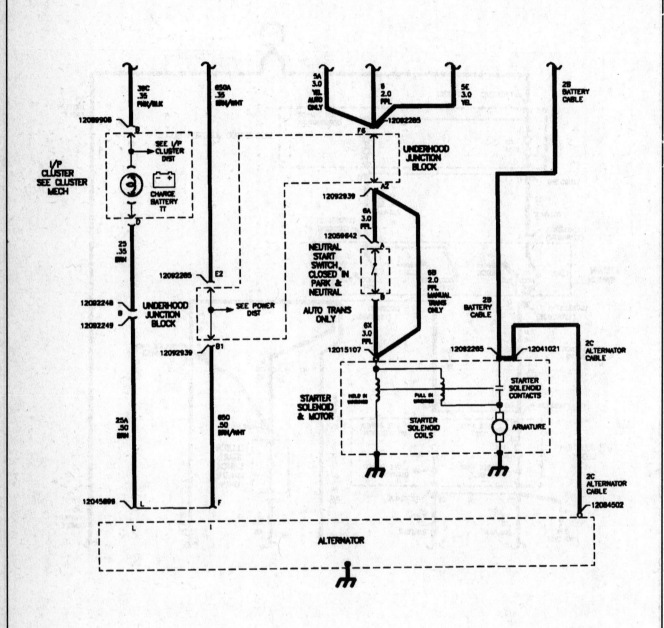

Fig. 145 Charging/starting system schematics

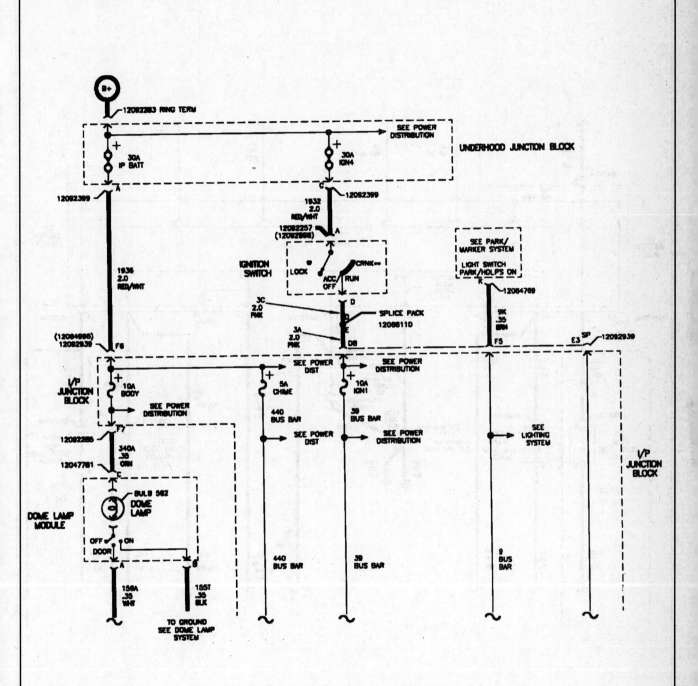

Fig. 146 Chime delay/dome lamp schematics

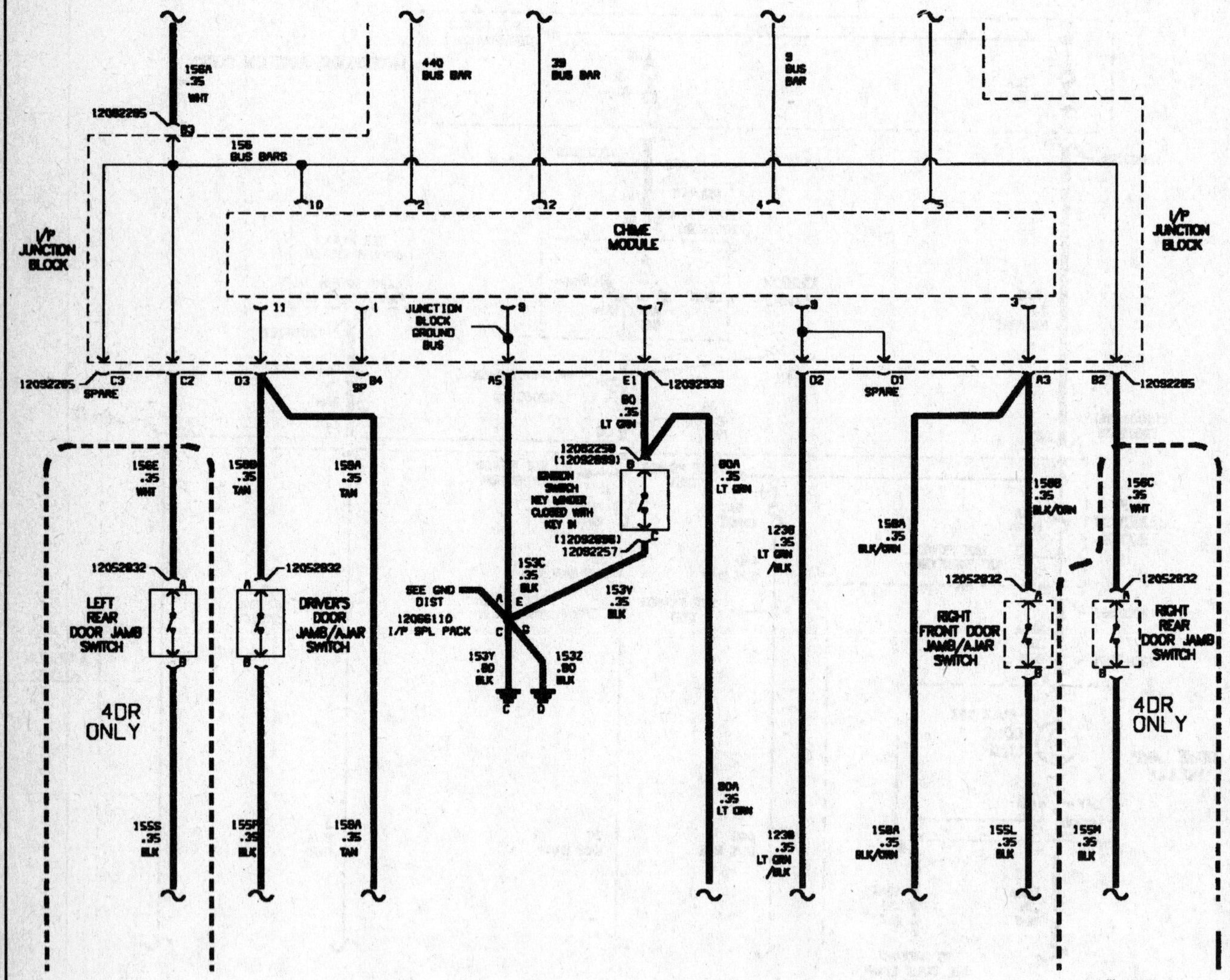

Fig. 147 Chime delay/dome lamp schematics

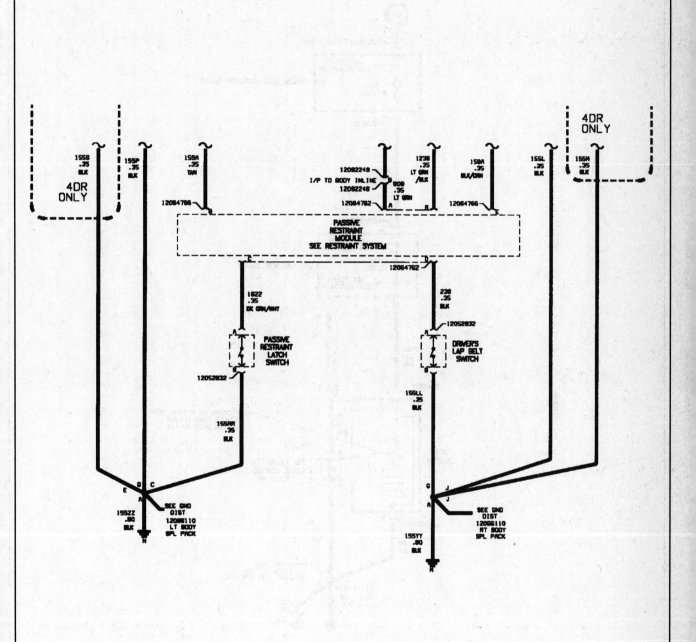

Fig. 148 Chime delay/dome lamp schematics

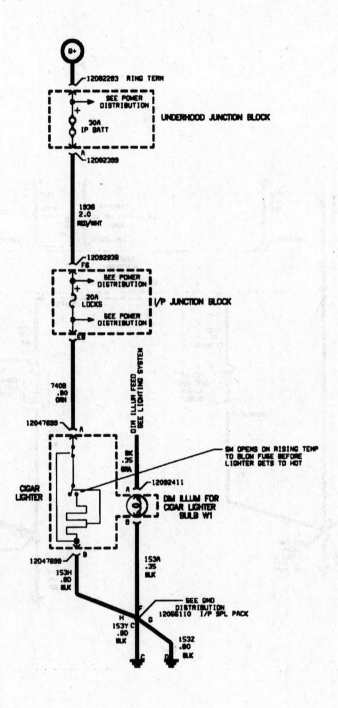

Fig. 149 Cigar lighter schematics

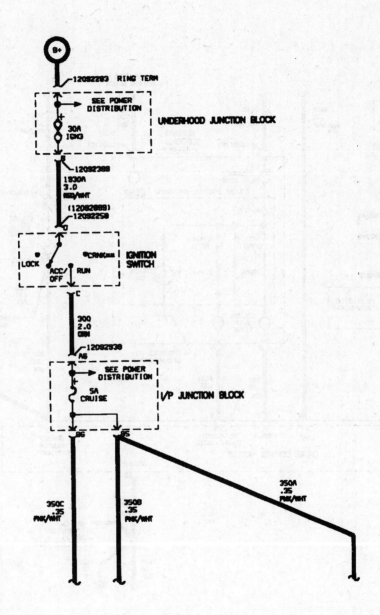

Fig. 150 Cruise control system schematics

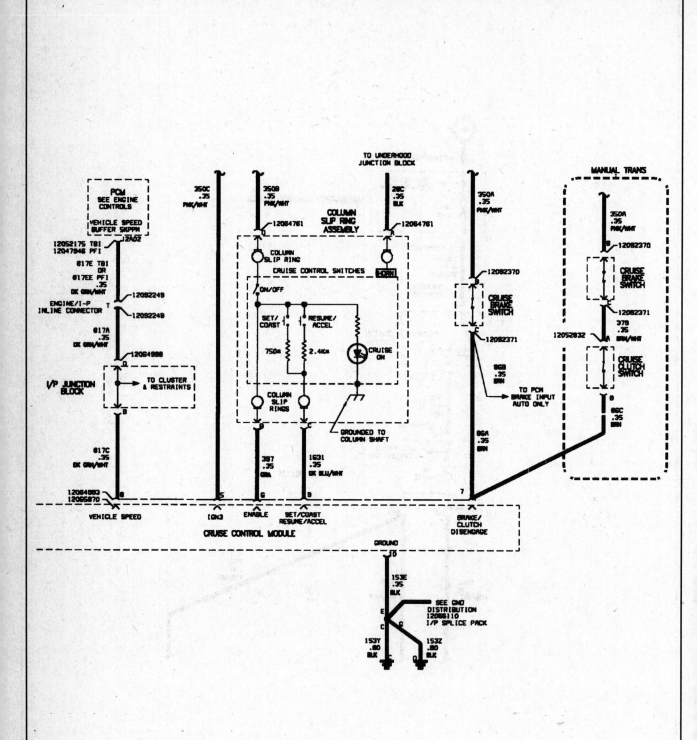

Fig. 151 Cruise control system schematics

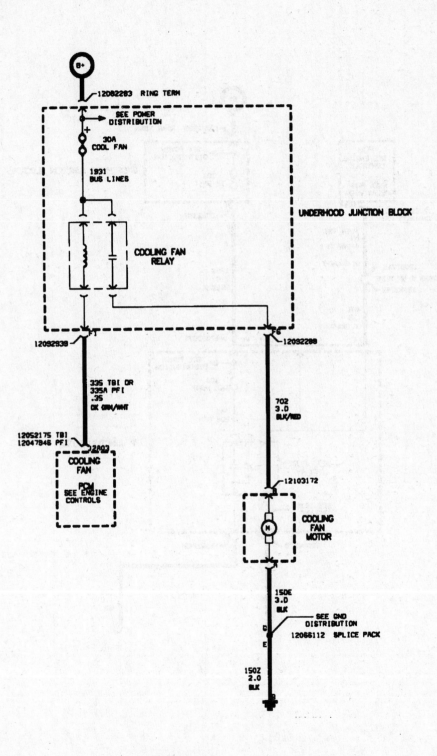

Fig. 152 Cooling fan schematics — engine

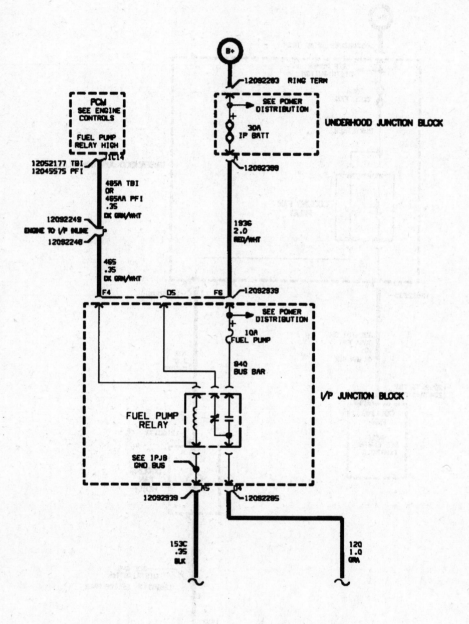

Fig. 153 Fuel system schematics — 1991 and 1992

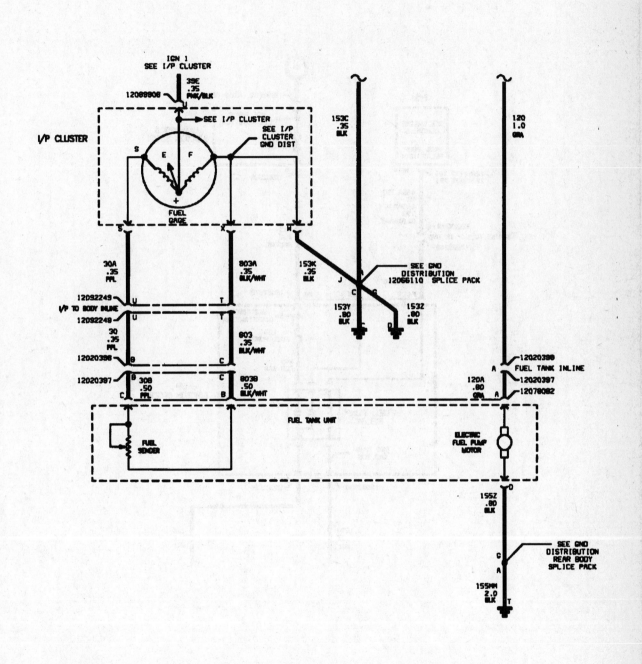

Fig. 154 Fuel system schematics — 1991 and 1992

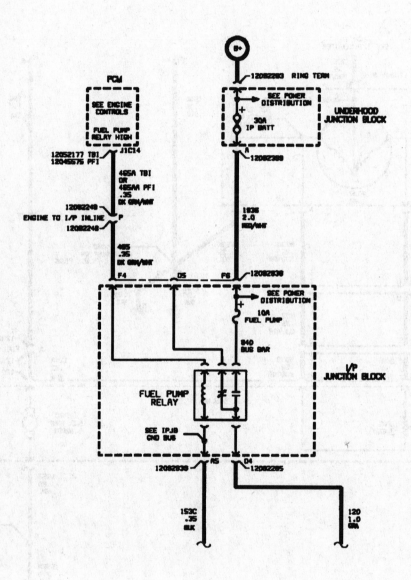

Fig. 155 Fuel system schematics — 1993

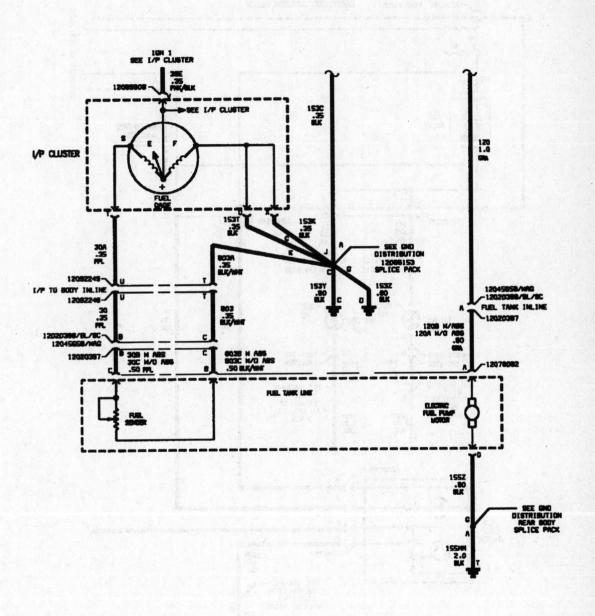

Fig. 156 Fuel system schematics — 1993

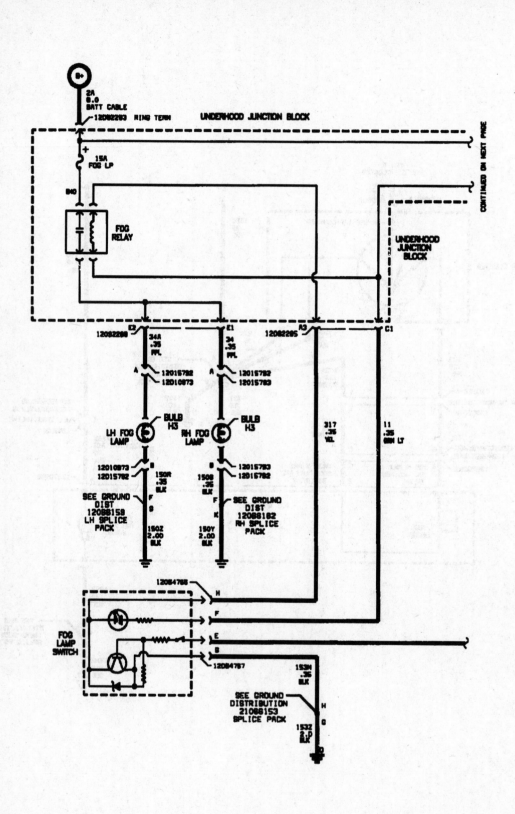

Fig. 157 Fog lamp schematics

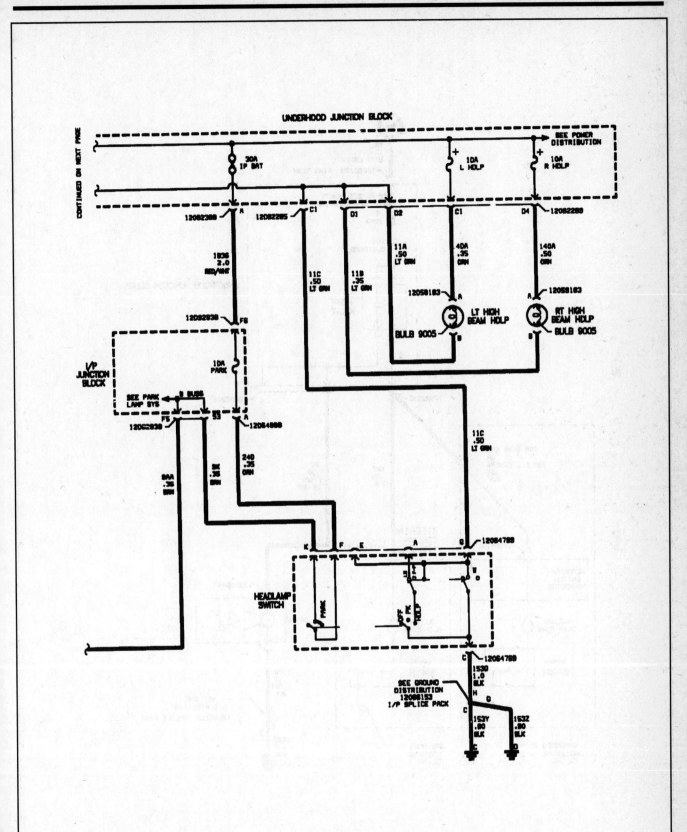

Fig. 158 Fog lamp schematics

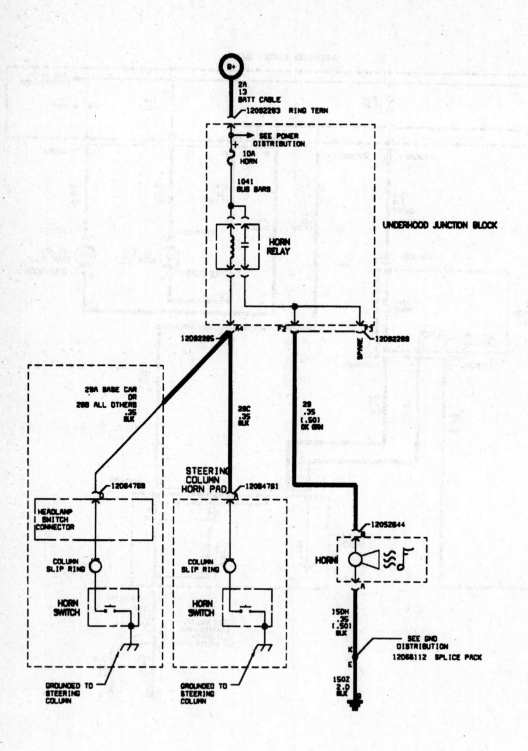

Fig. 159 Horn schematics

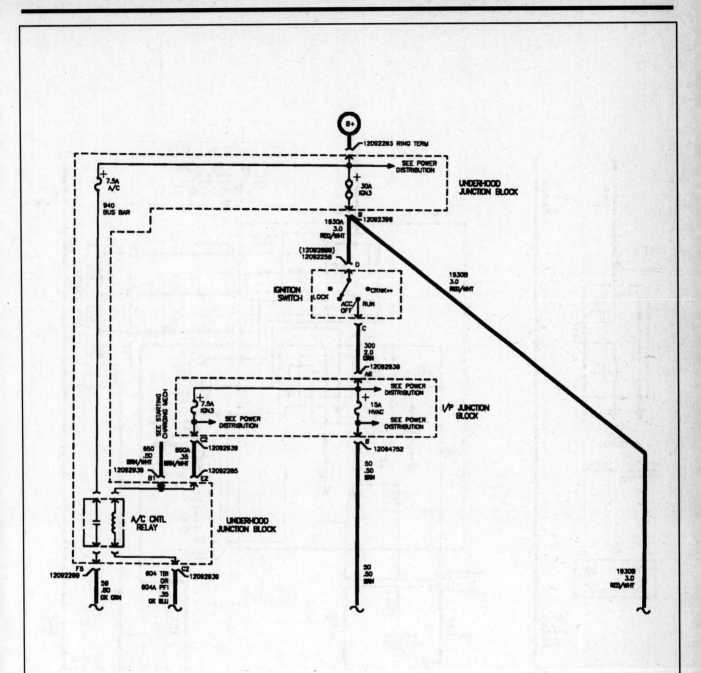

Fig. 160 HVAC system schematics — 1991 and 1992

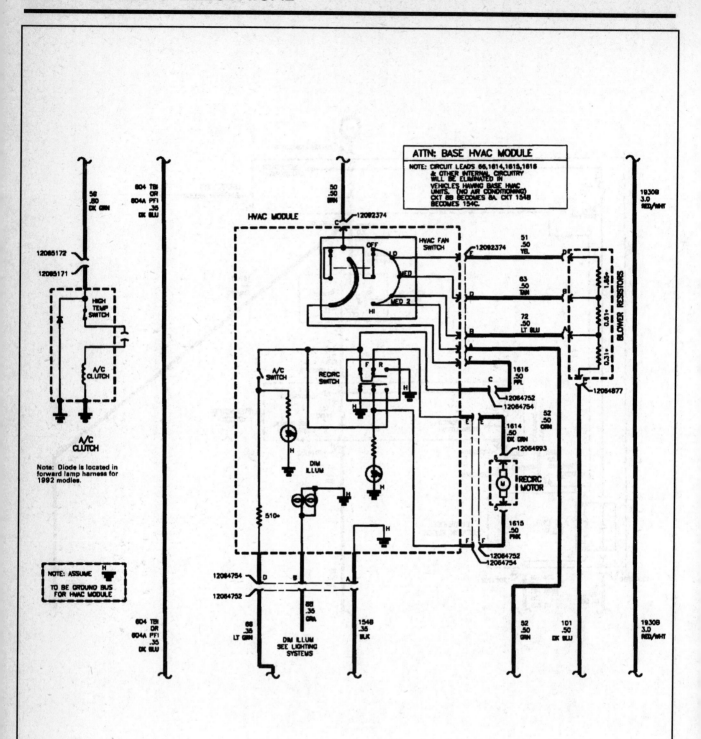

Fig. 161 HVAC system schematics — 1991 and 1992

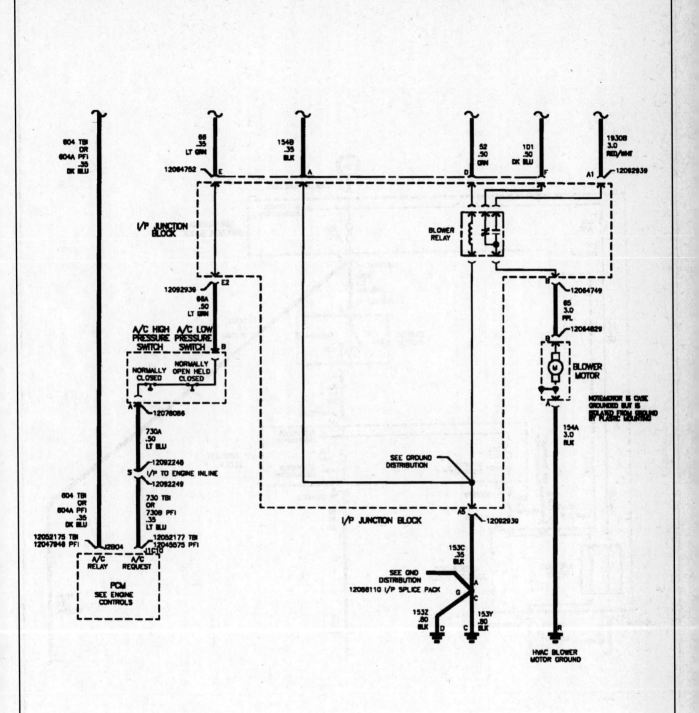

Fig. 162 HVAC system schematics — 1991 and 1992

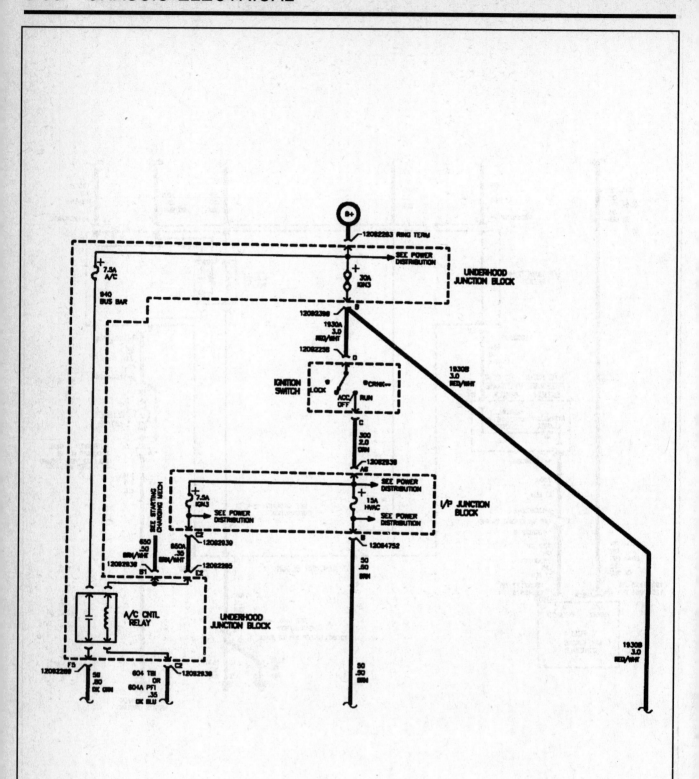

Fig. 163 HVAC system schematics — 1993

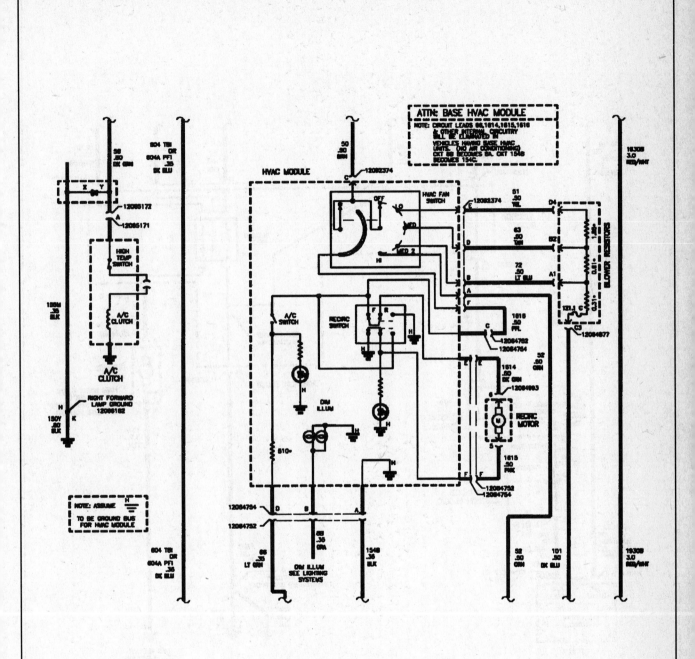

Fig. 164 HVAC system schematics — 1993

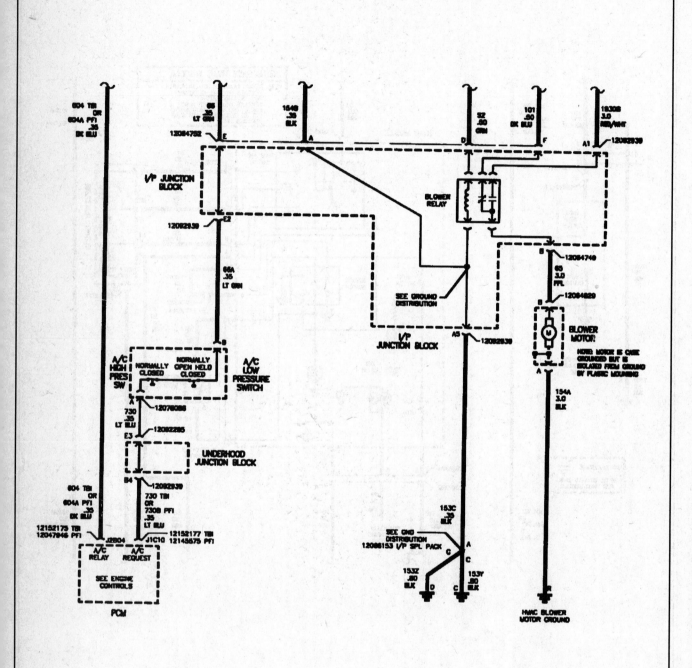

Fig. 165 HVAC system schematics — 1993

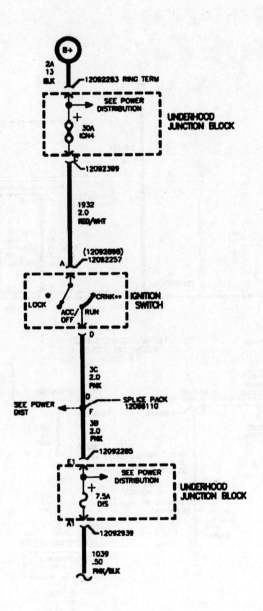

Fig. 166 Ignition system schematics

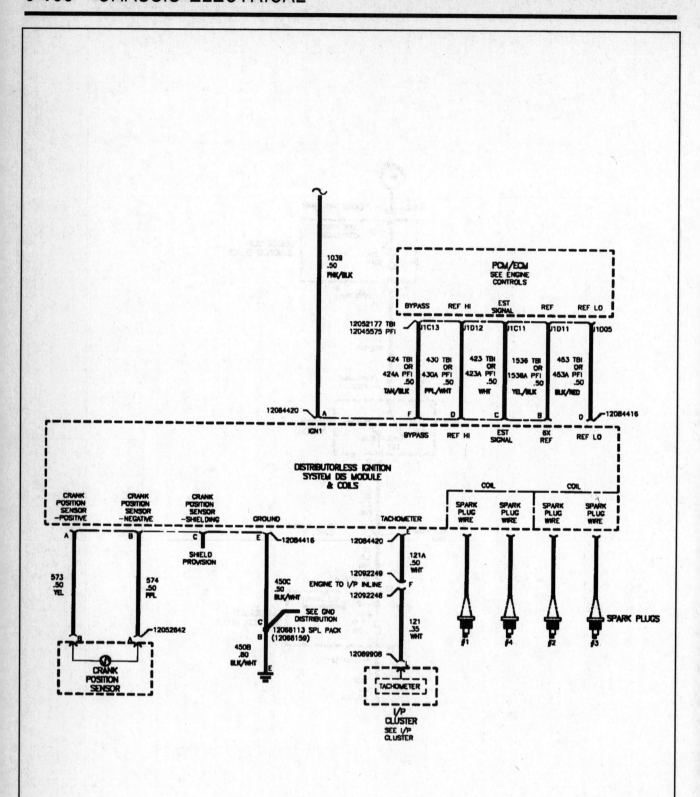

Fig. 167 Ignition system schematics

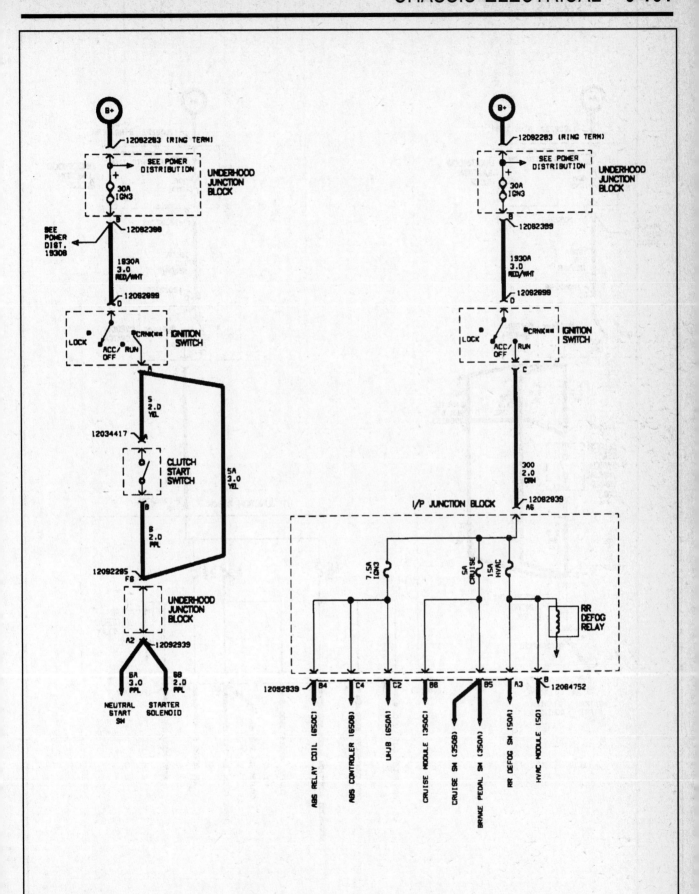

Fig. 168 Ignition switch schematics — 1991

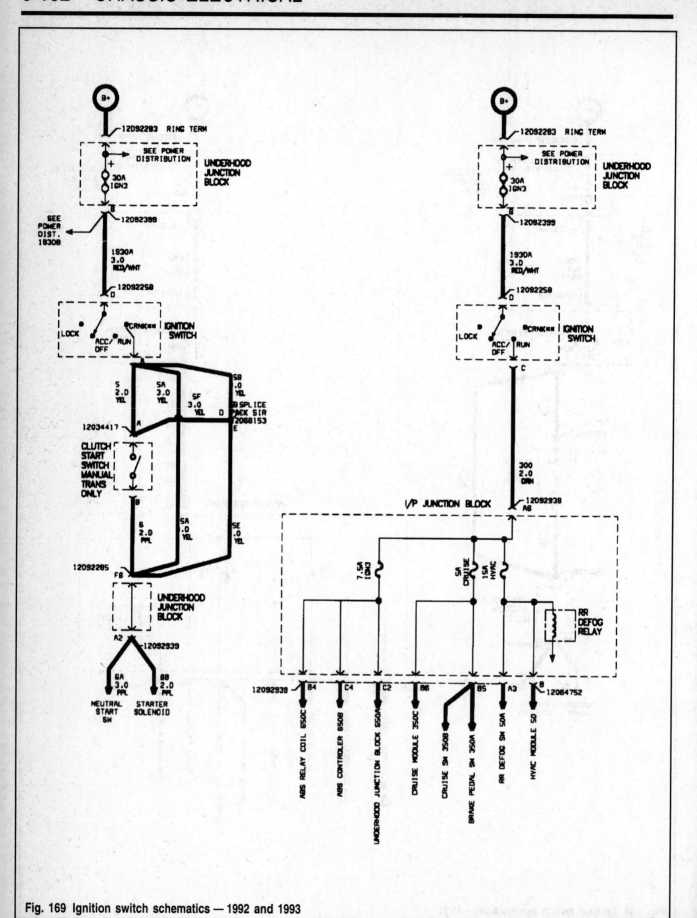

Fig. 169 Ignition switch schematics — 1992 and 1993

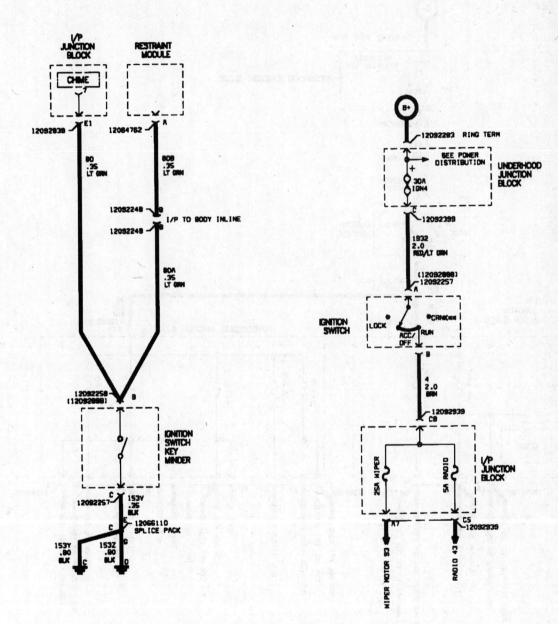

Fig. 170 Ignition switch schematics

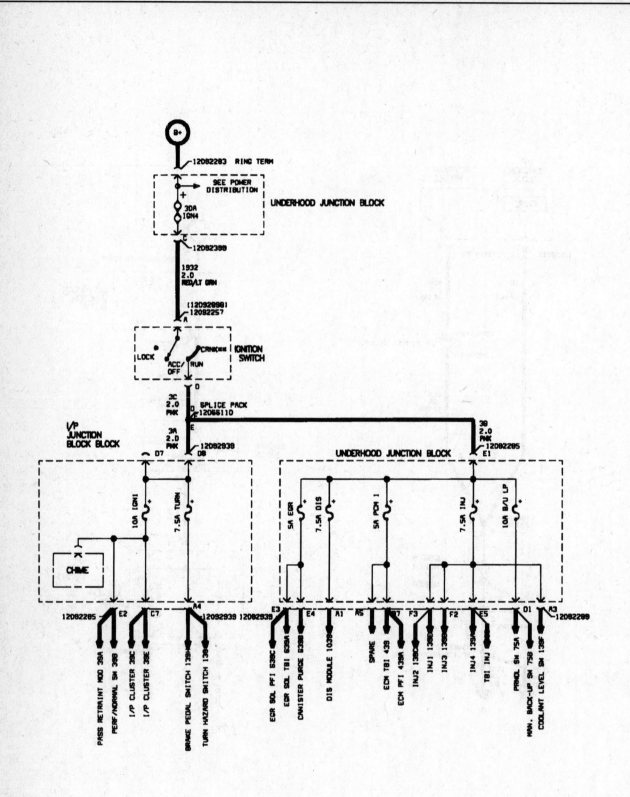

Fig. 171 Ignition switch schematics

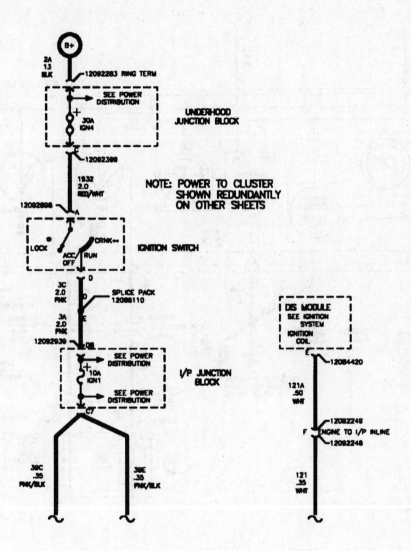

Fig. 172 Instrument panel cluster schematics — 1991 and 1992

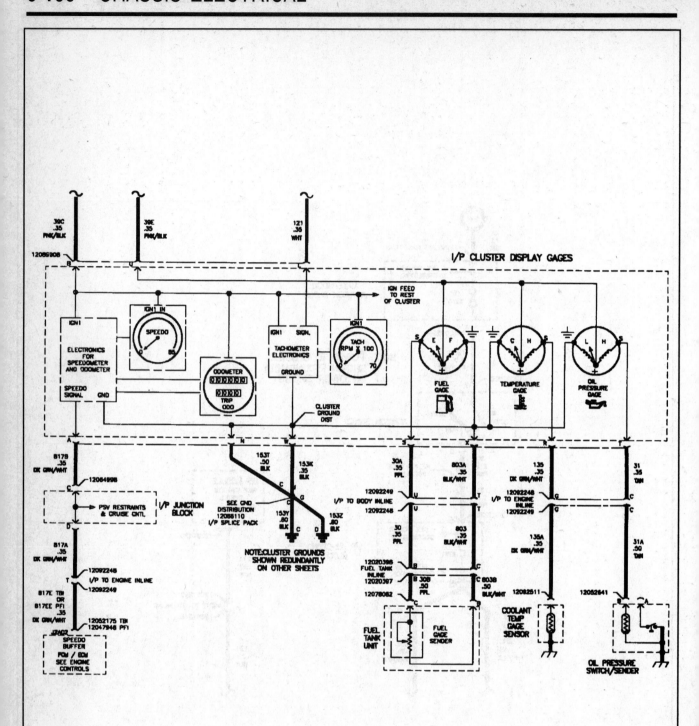

Fig. 173 Instrument panel cluster schematics — 1991 and 1992

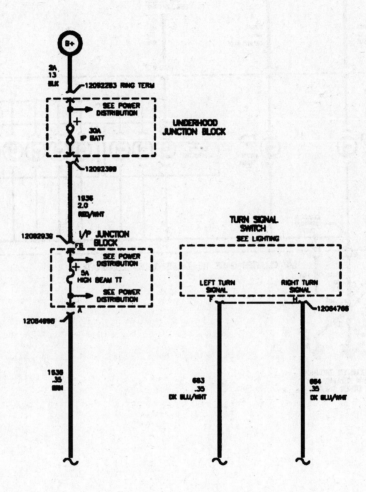

Fig. 174 Instrument panel cluster schematics — gage telltales and dim illumination (1991 and 1992)

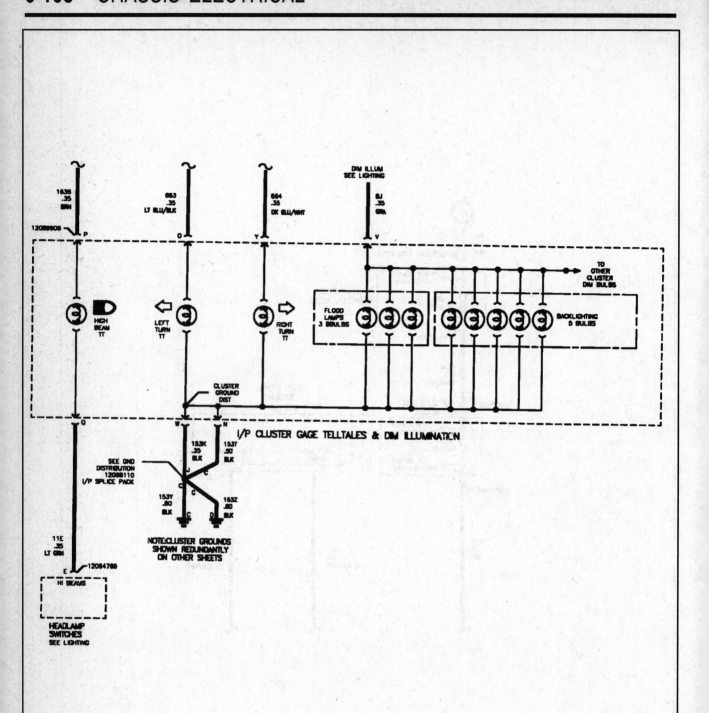

Fig. 175 Instrument panel cluster schematics — gage telltales and dim illumination (1991 and 1992)

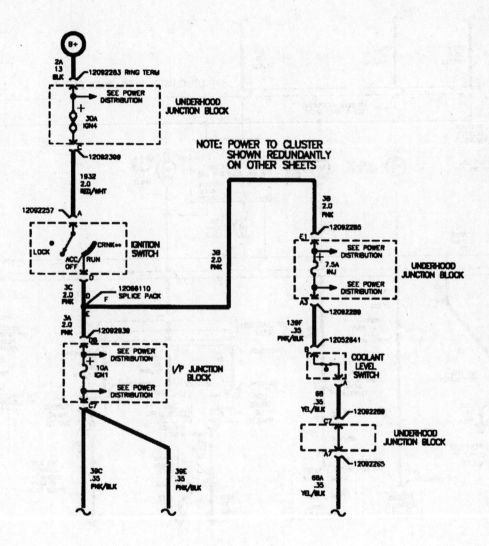

Fig. 176 Instrument panel cluster telltale schematics — 1991 and 1992

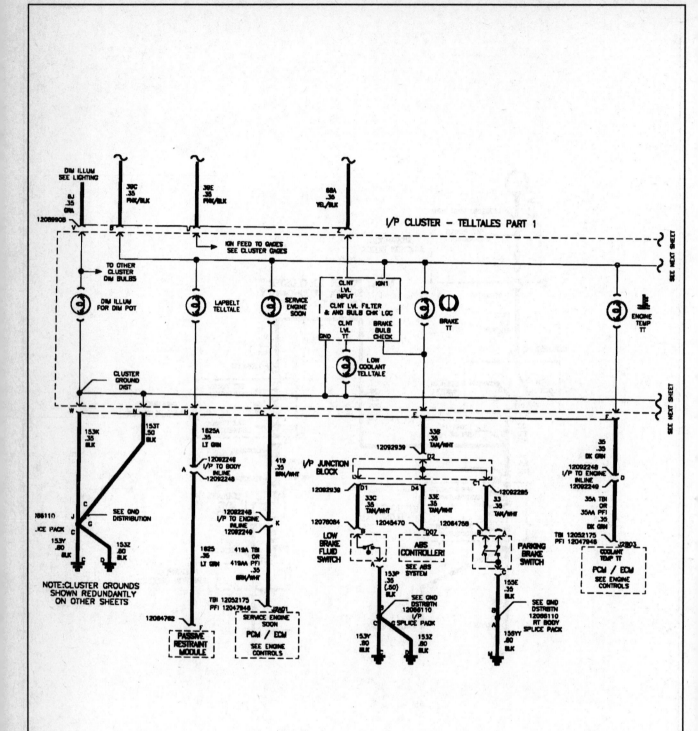

Fig. 177 Instrument panel cluster telltale schematics — 1991 and 1992

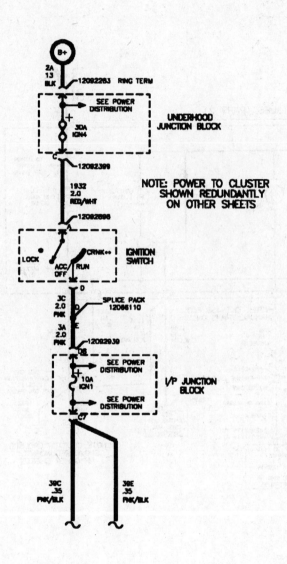

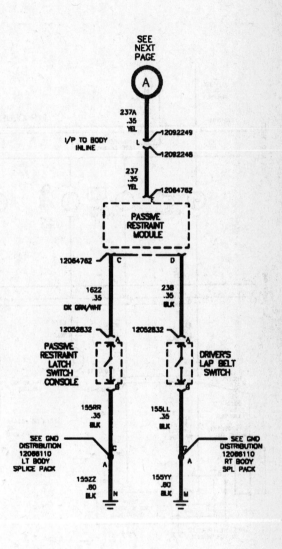

Fig. 178 Instrument panel cluster telltale schematics — 1991 and 1992

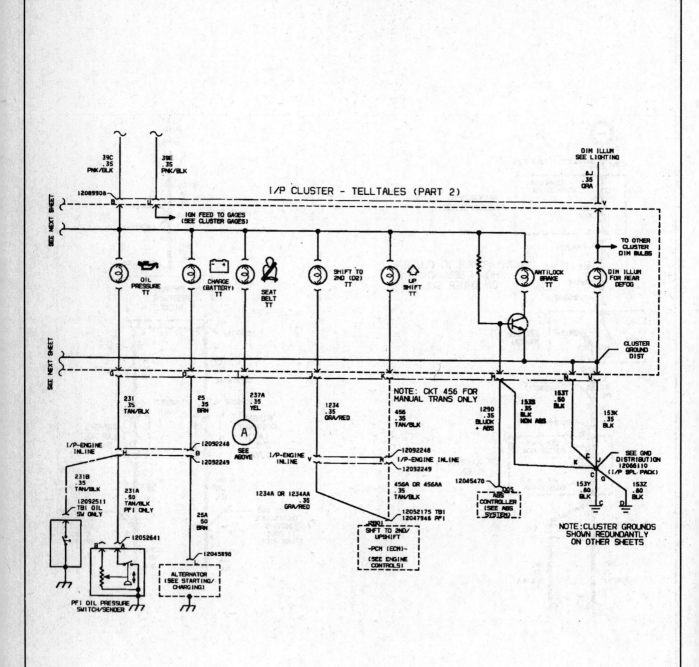

Fig. 179 Instrument panel cluster telltale schematics — 1991

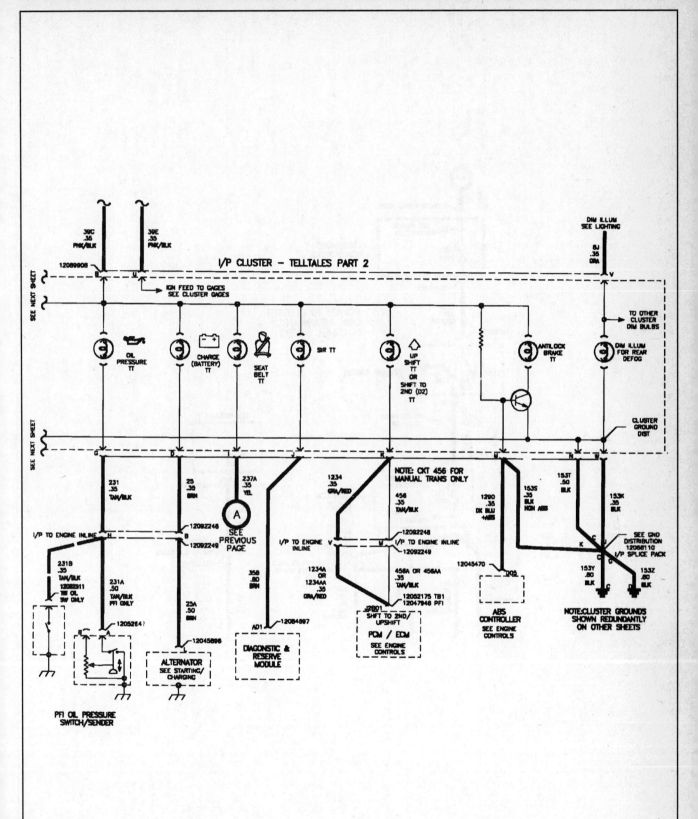

Fig. 180 Instrument panel cluster telltale schematics — 1992

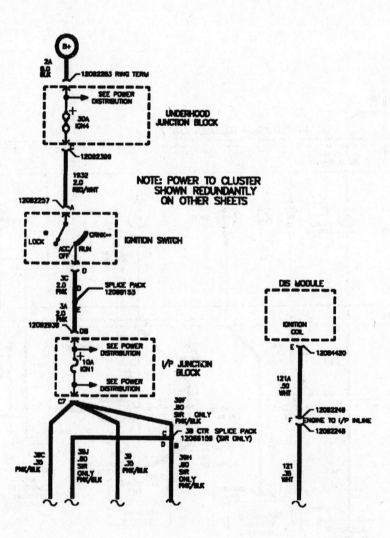

Fig. 181 Instrument panel cluster display gages schematics — 1993

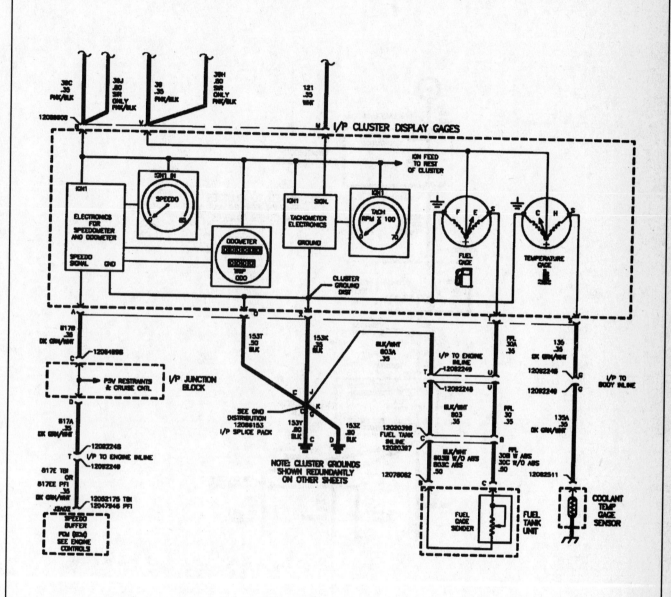

Fig. 182 Instrument panel cluster display gages schematics — 1993

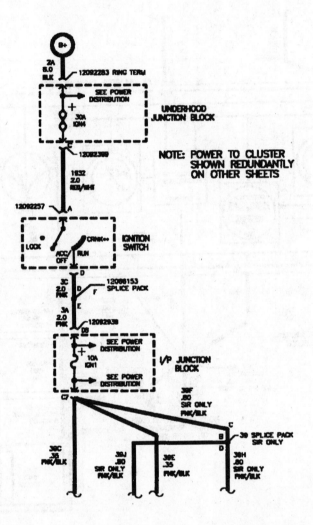

Fig. 183 Instrument panel cluster telltale schematics — 1993

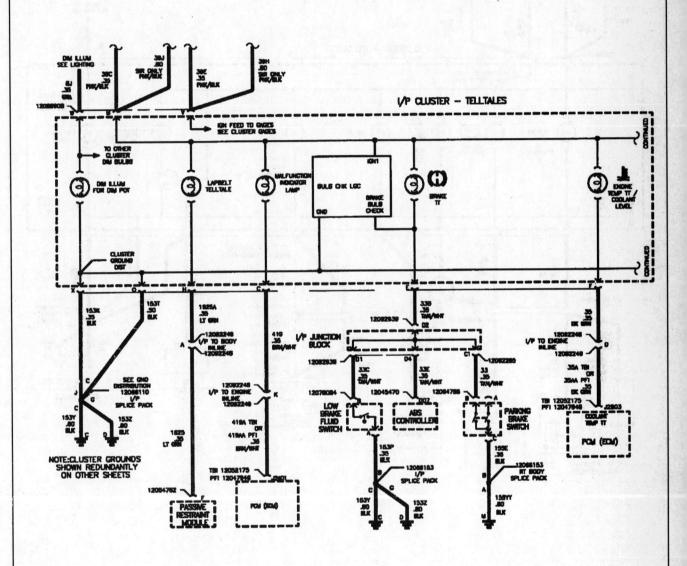

Fig. 184 Instrument panel cluster telltale schematics — 1993

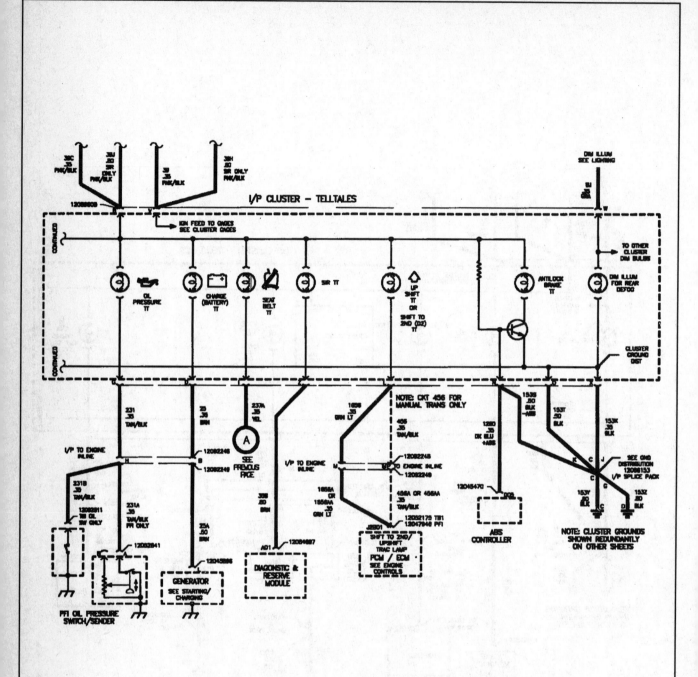

Fig. 185 Instrument panel cluster telltale schematics — 1993

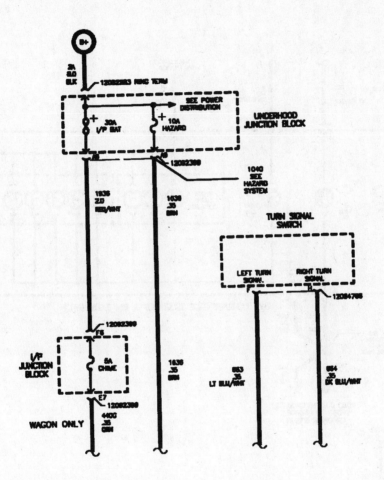

Fig. 186 Instrument panel cluster turn indicators, hi beam telltale and gages dim illumination schematics — 1993

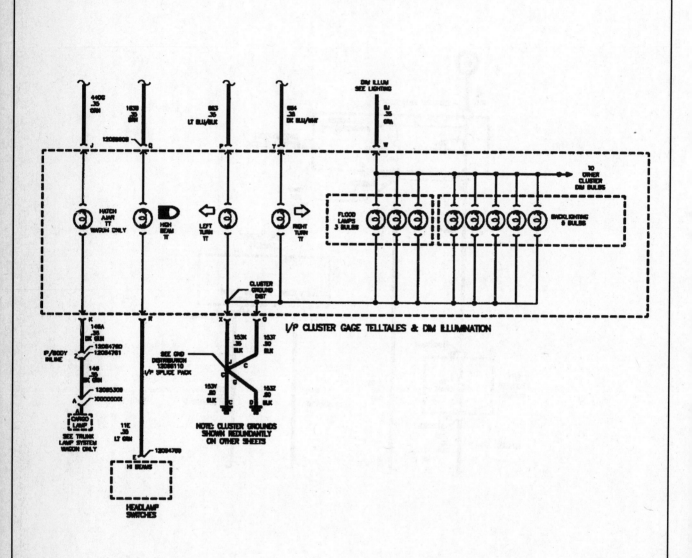

Fig. 187 Instrument panel cluster turn indicators, hi beam telltale and gages dim illumination schematics — 1993

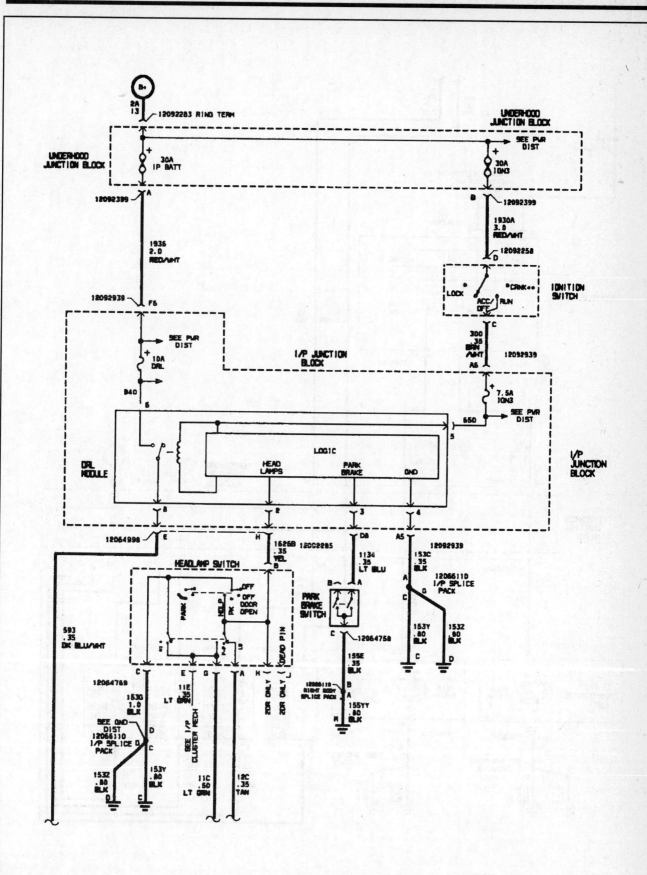

Fig. 188 Daytime running light schematics — Canada sedan

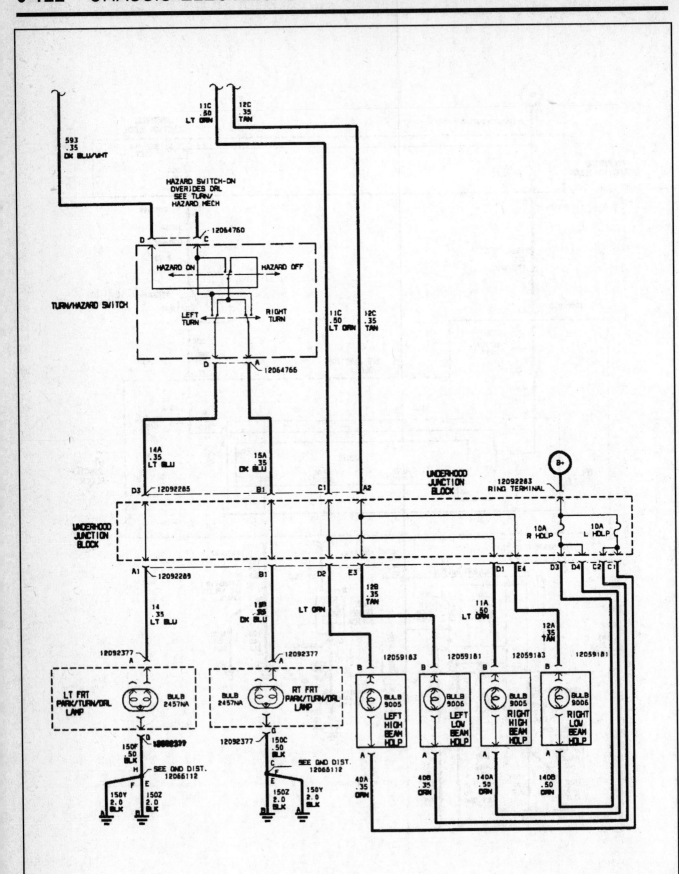

Fig. 189 Daytime running light echematics — Canada sedan

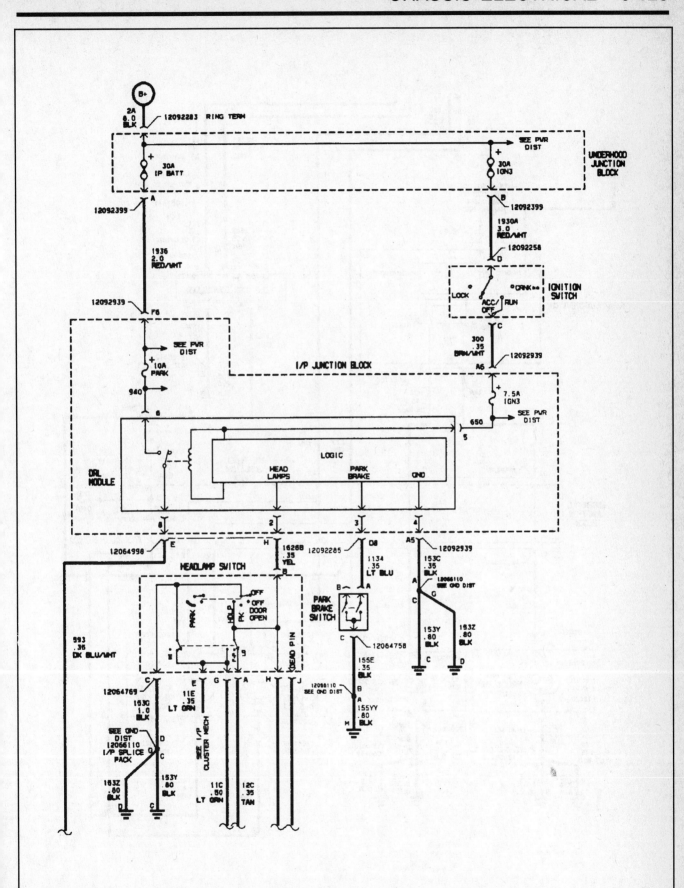

Fig. 190 Daytime running light schematics — Canada coupe

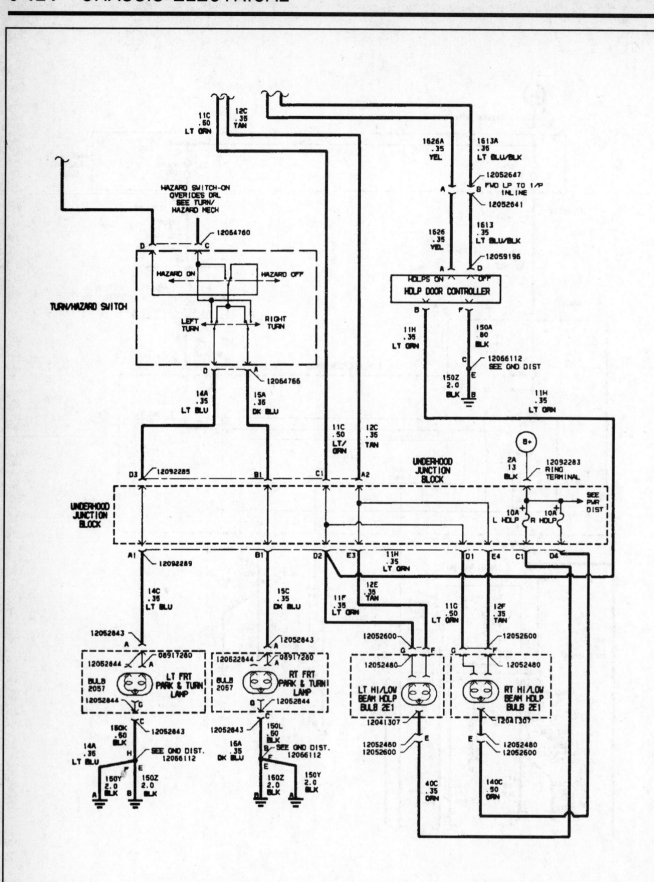

Fig. 191 Daytime running light schematics — Canada coupe

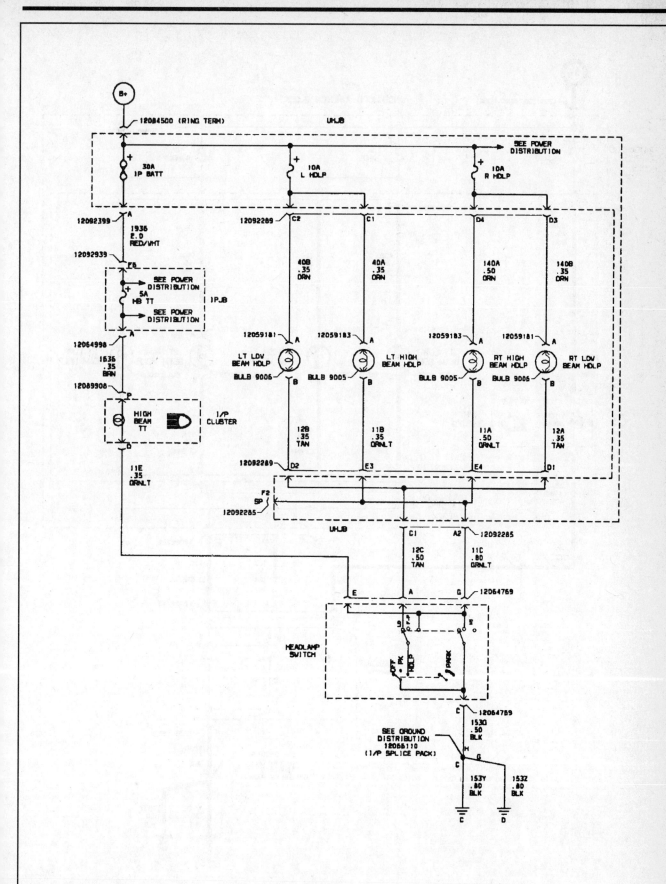

Fig. 192 High/low beam headlamp schematics — 1991 sedan

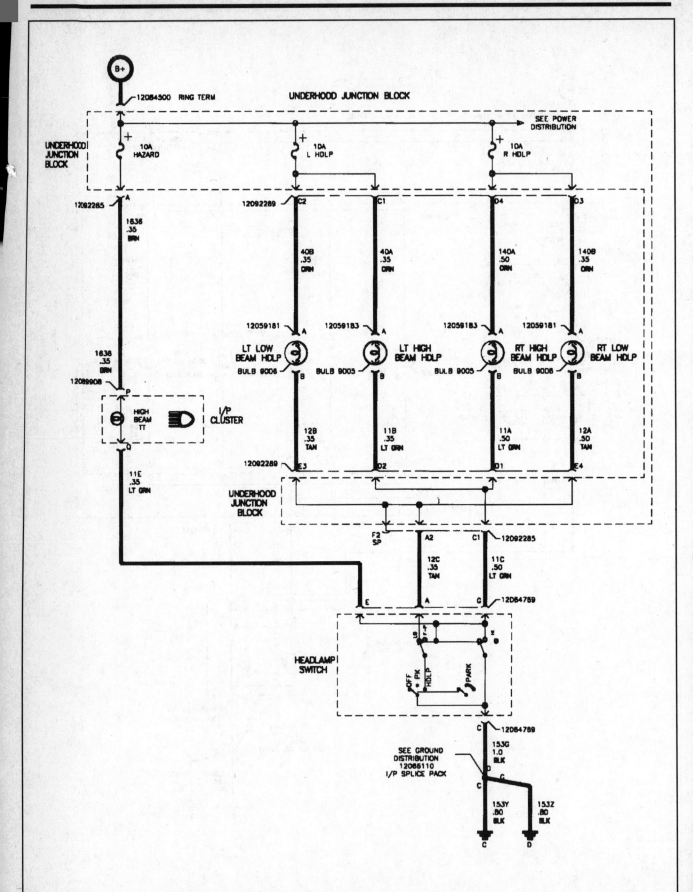

Fig. 193 High/low beam headlamp schematics — 1991 and 1992 sedan

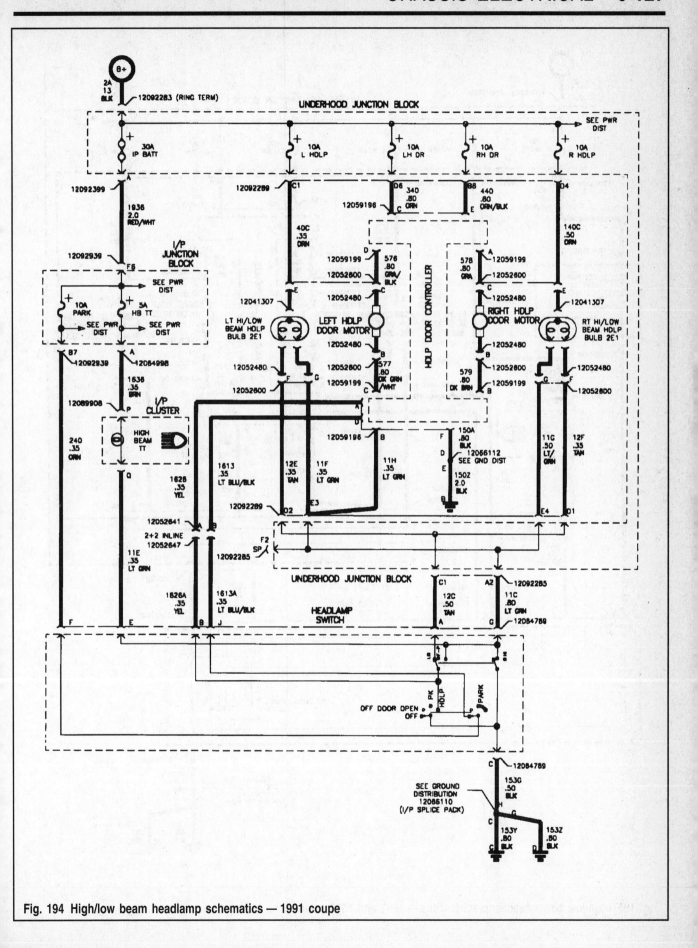

Fig. 194 High/low beam headlamp schematics — 1991 coupe

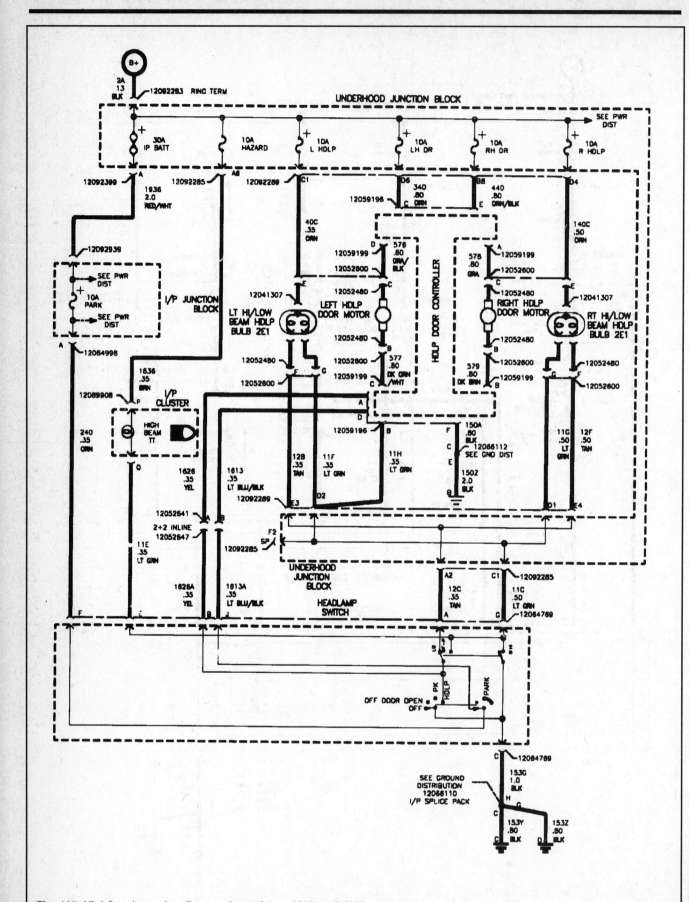

Fig. 195 High/low beam headlamp schematics — 1992 and 1993 coupe

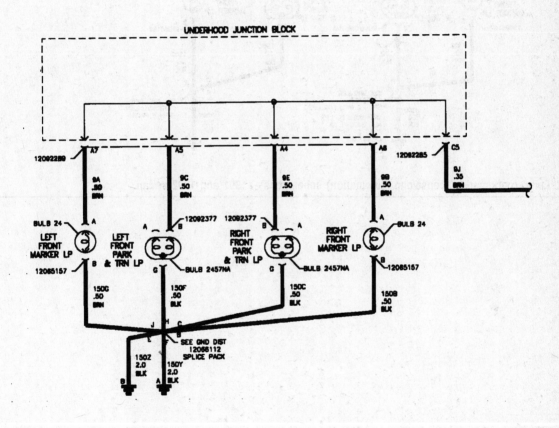

Fig. 196 Lamp (park/marker/license/dim illumination) schematics — 1991 and 1992 sedan

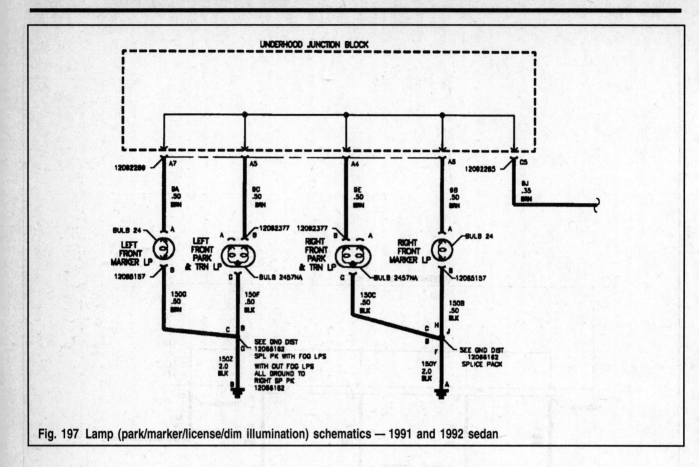

Fig. 197 Lamp (park/marker/license/dim illumination) schematics — 1991 and 1992 sedan

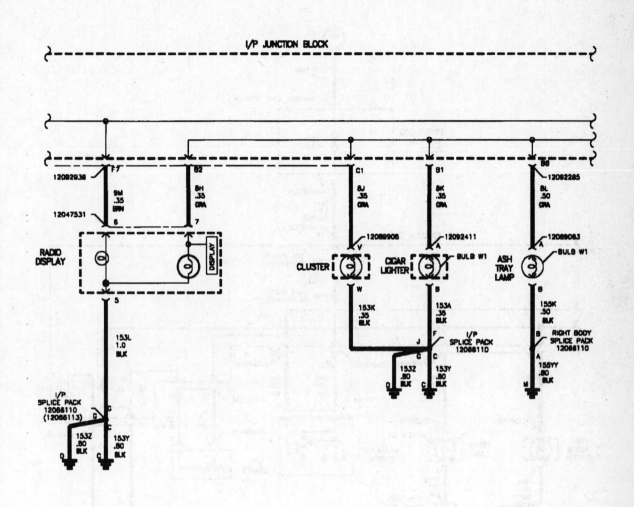

Fig. 198 Lamp (park/marker/license/dim illumination) schematics — 1991 and 1992 sedan

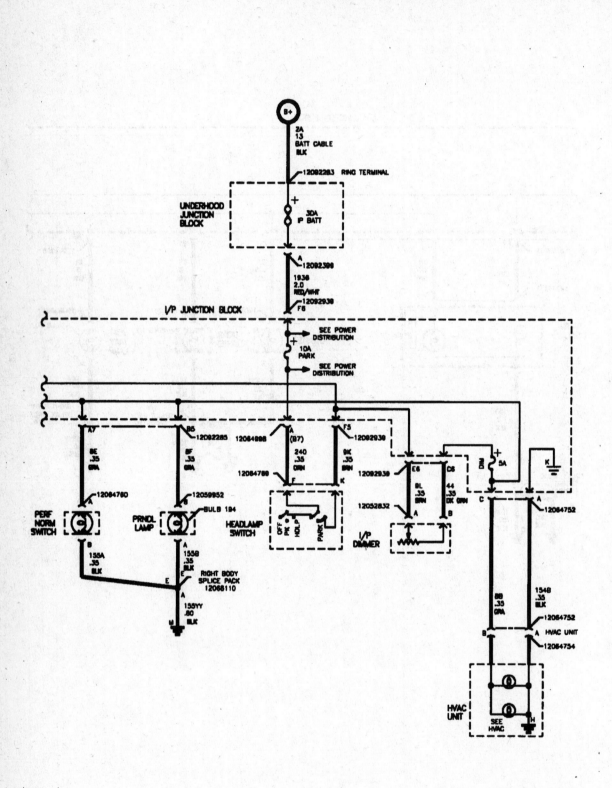

Fig. 199 Lamp (park/marker/license/dim illumination) schematics — 1991 and 1992 sedan

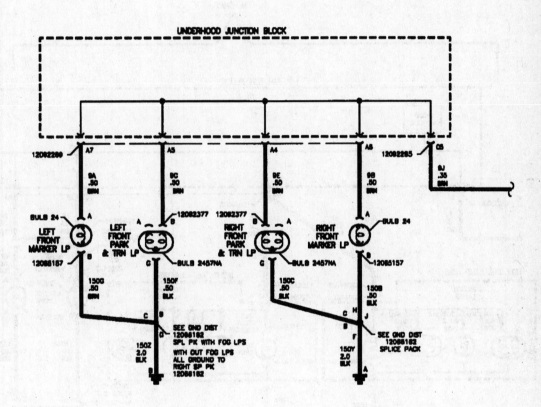

Fig. 200 Lamp (park/marker/license/dim illumination) schematics — 1993 sedan and wagon

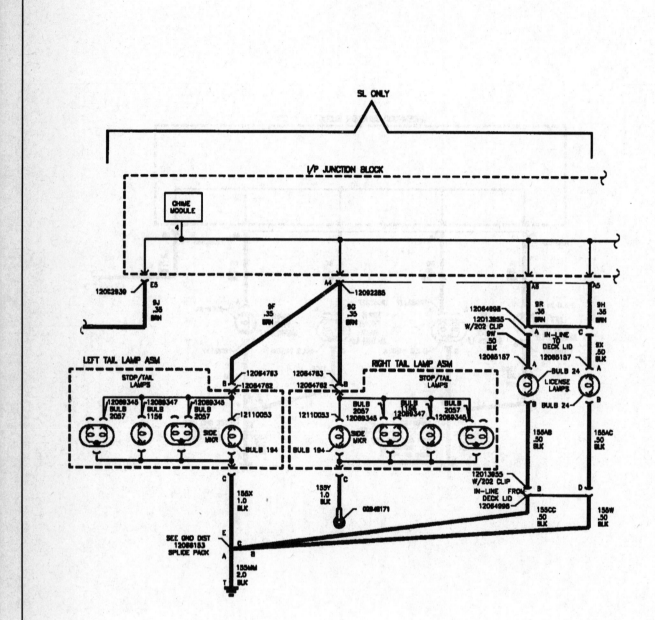

Fig. 201 Lamp (park/marker/license/dim illumination) schematics — 1993 sedan and wagon

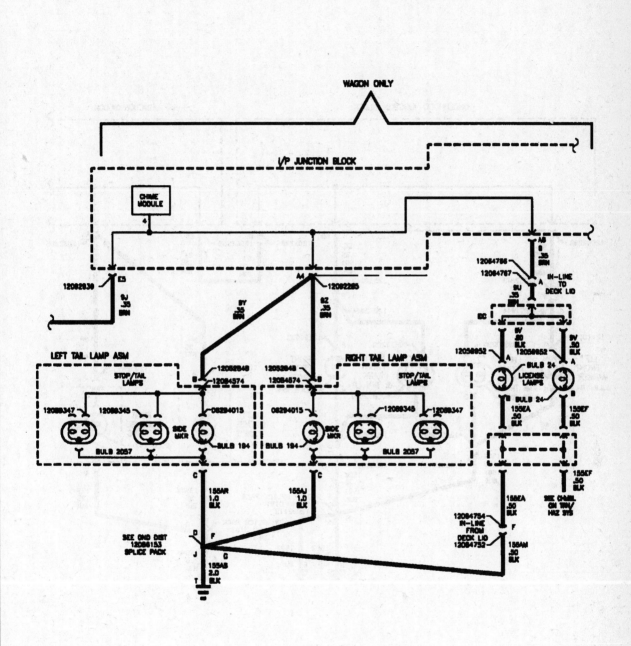

Fig. 202 Lamp (park/marker/license/dim illumination) schematics — 1993 sedan and wagon

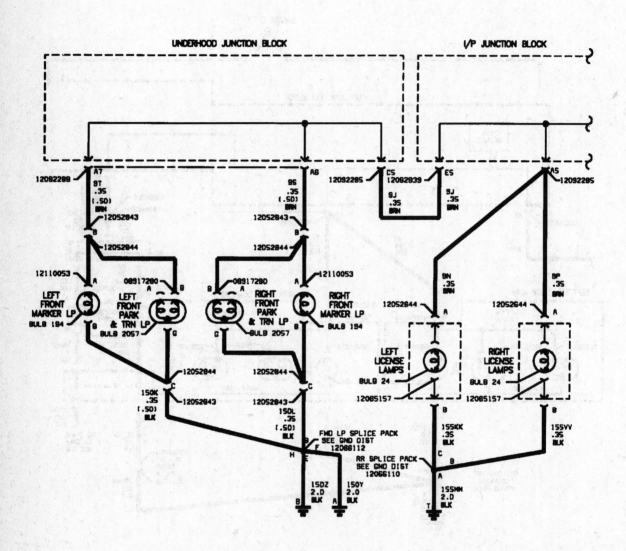

Fig. 203 Lamp (park/marker/license/dim illumination) schematics — 1992 and 1993 coupe

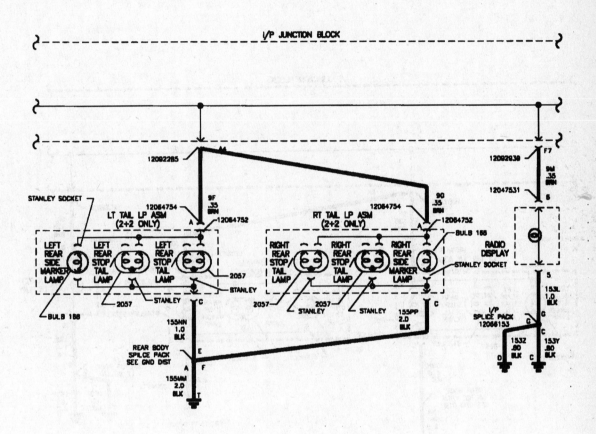

Fig. 204 Lamp (park/marker/license/dim illumination) schematics — 1991 coupe

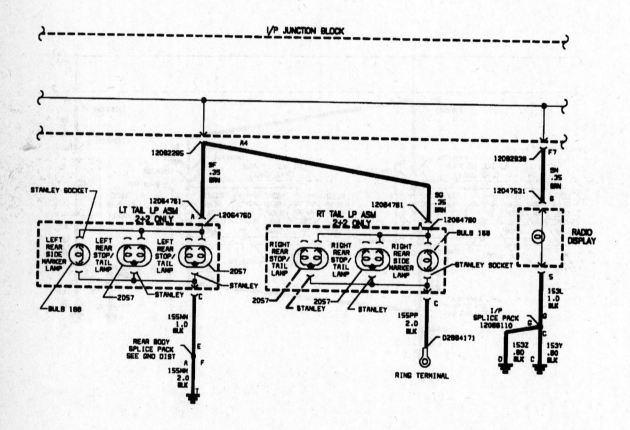

Fig. 205 Lamp (park/marker/license/dim illumination) schematics — 1992 and 1993 coupe

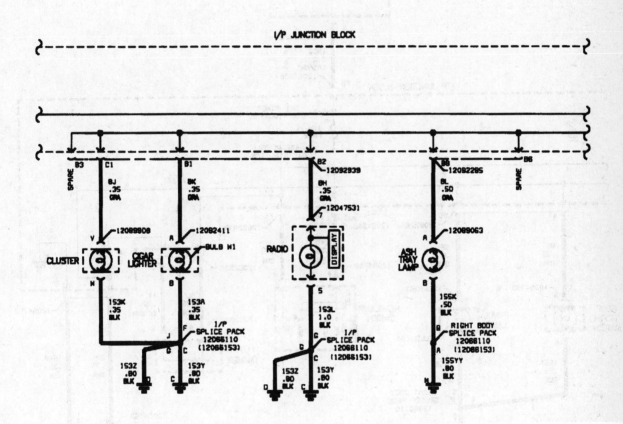

Fig. 206 Lamp (park/marker/license/dim illumination) schematics — coupe

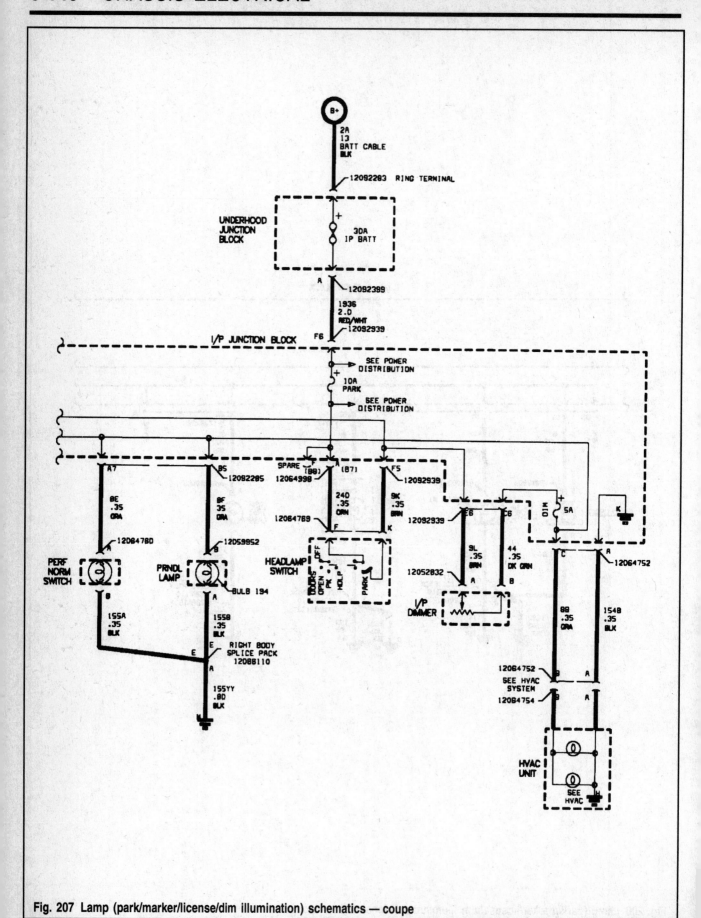

Fig. 207 Lamp (park/marker/license/dim illumination) schematics — coupe

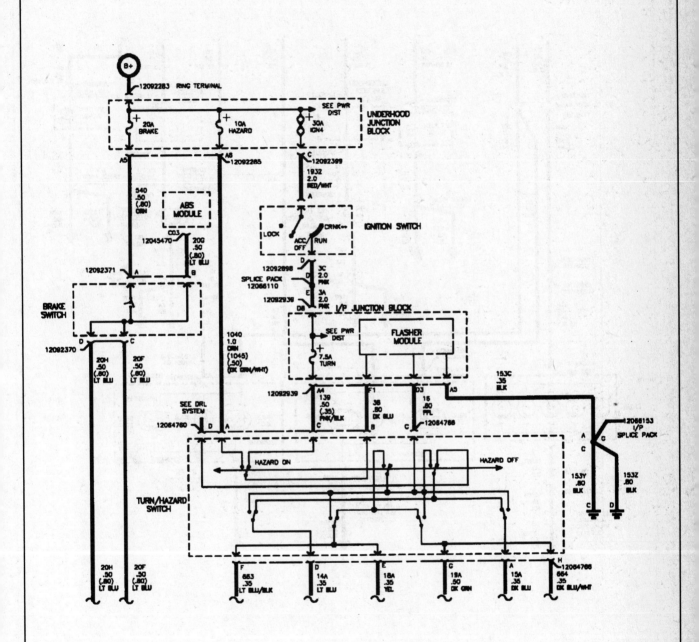

Fig. 208 Lamp (turn/hazard/stop) schematics — 1991 and 1992 sedan

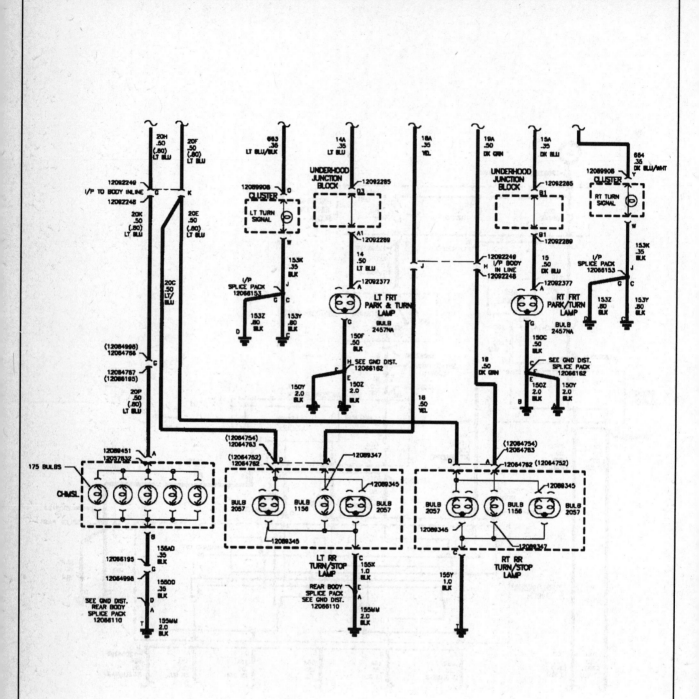

Fig. 209 Lamp (turn/hazard/stop) schematics — 1991 and 1992 sedan

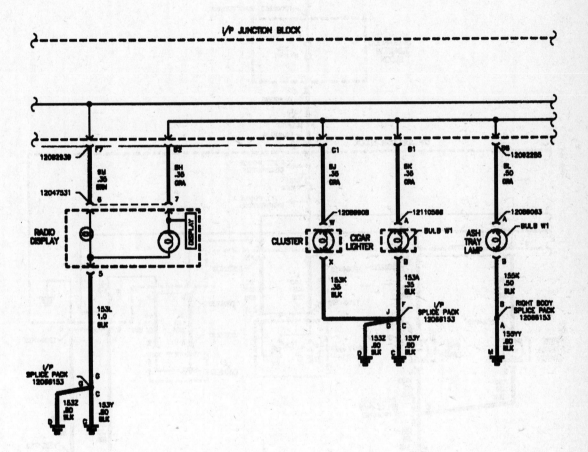

Fig. 210 Lamp (turn/hazard/stop) schematics — 1993 sedan

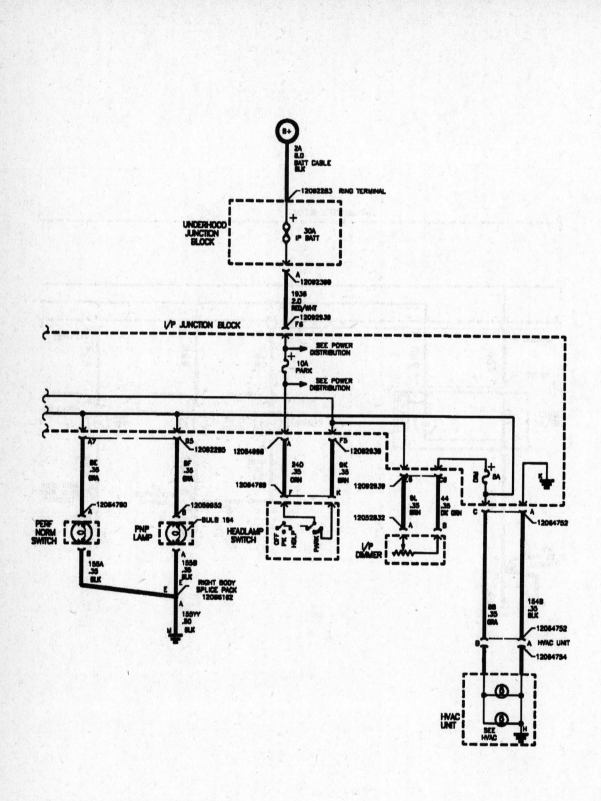

Fig. 211 Lamp (turn/hazard/stop) schematics — 1993 sedan

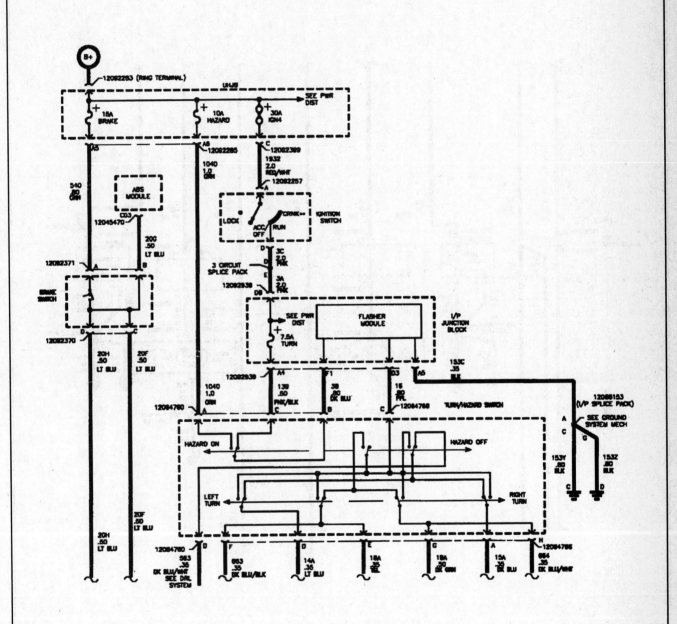

Fig. 212 Lamp (turn/hazard/stop) schematics — wagon

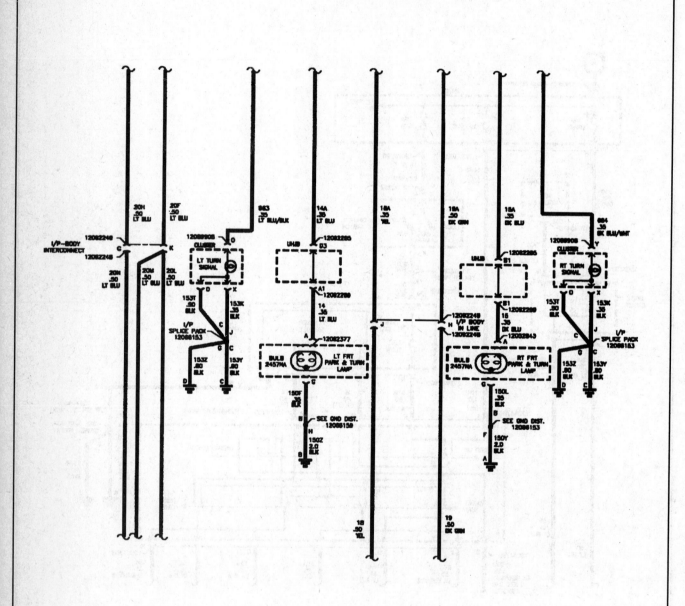

Fig. 213 Lamp (turn/hazard/stop) schematics — wagon

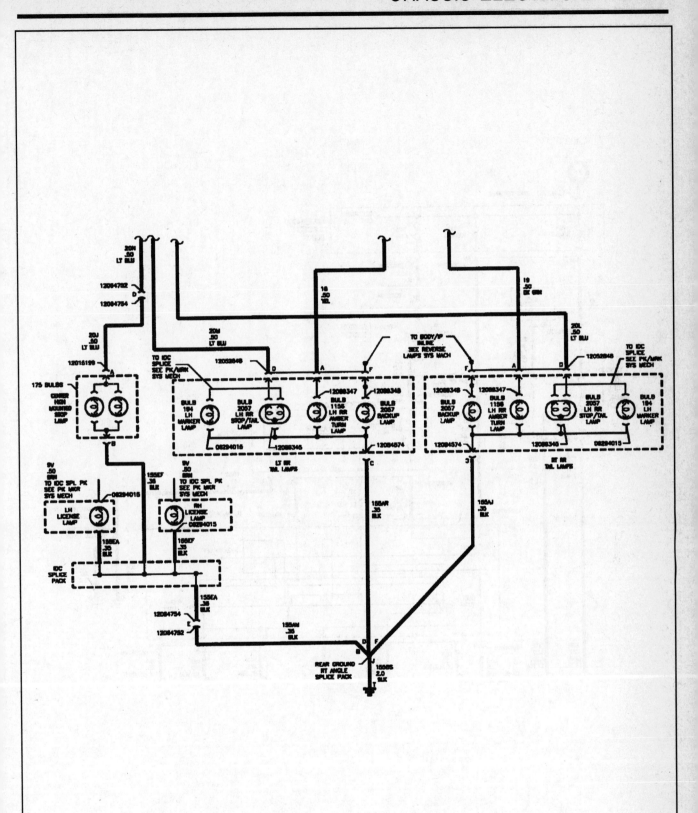

Fig. 214 Lamp (turn/hazard/stop) schematics — wagon

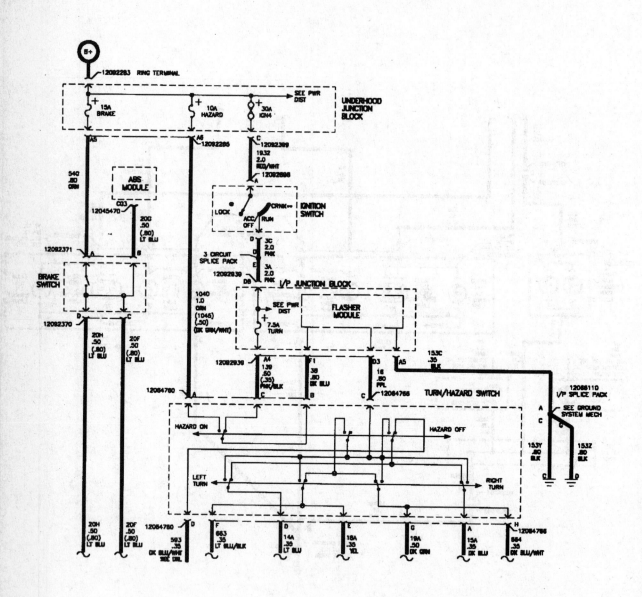

Fig. 215 Lamp (turn/hazard/stop) schematics — coupe

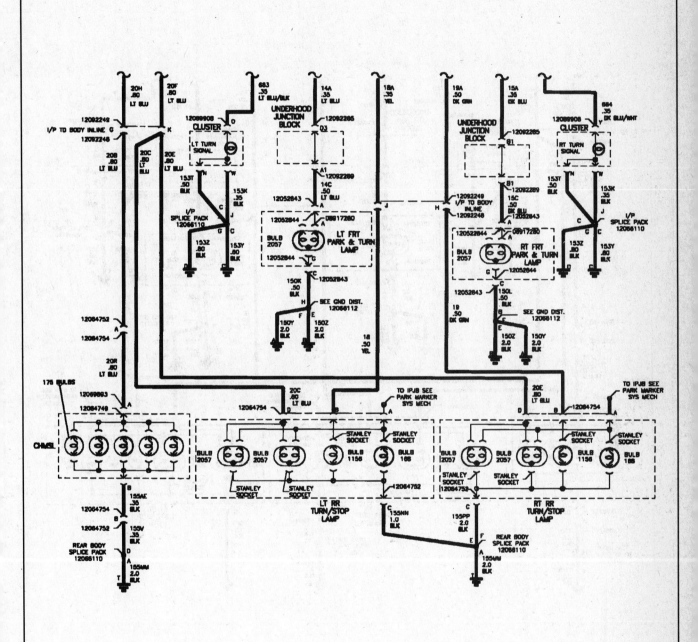

Fig. 216 Lamp (turn/hazard/stop) schematics — 1991 coupe

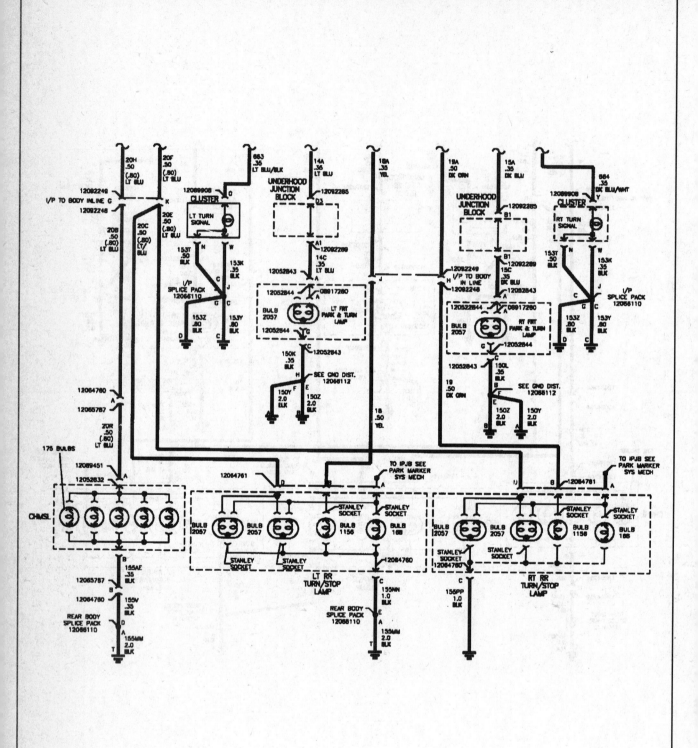

Fig. 217 Lamp (turn/hazard/stop) schematics — 1992 and 1993 coupe

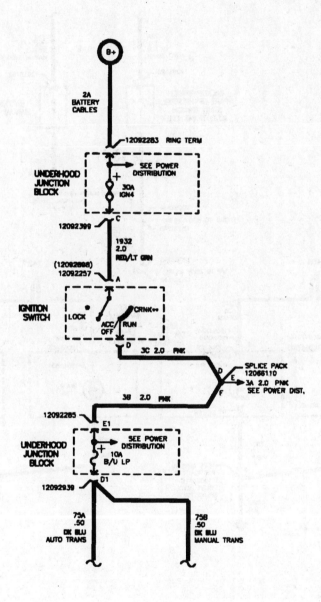

Fig. 218 Lamp (back-up) schematics — 1991 and 1992

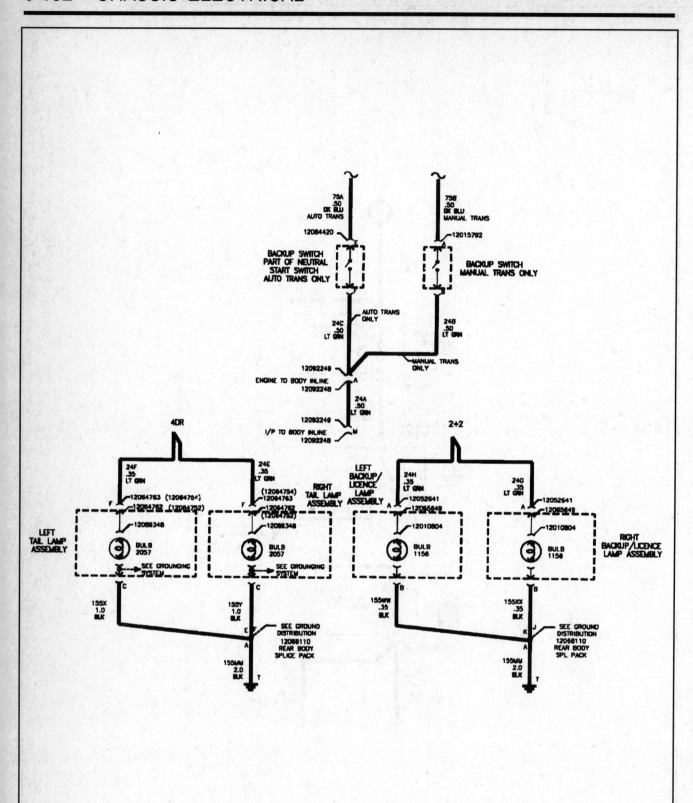

Fig. 219 Lamp (back-up) schematics — 1991 and 1992

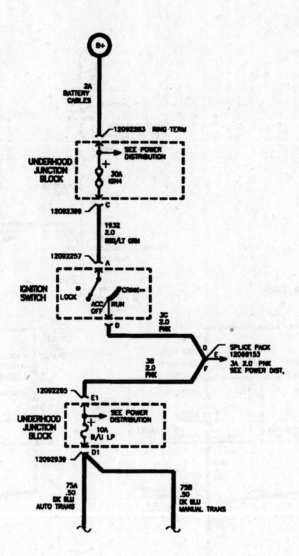

Fig. 220 Lamp (back-up) schematics — 1993

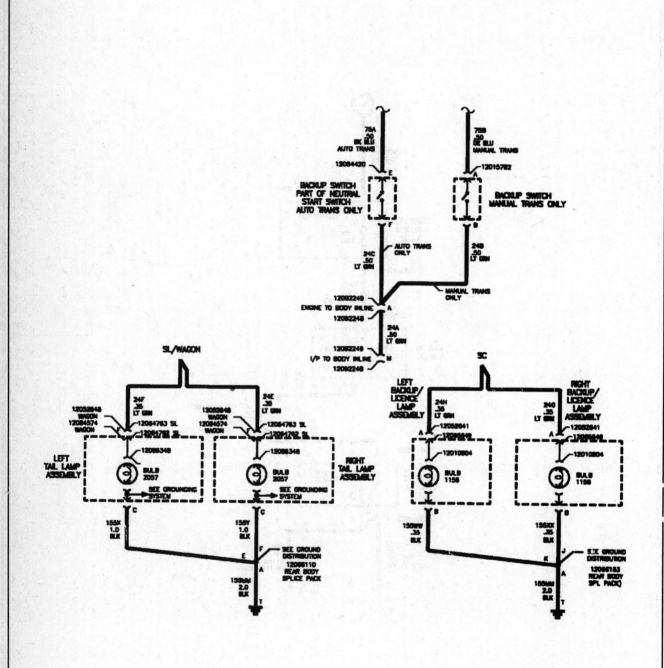

Fig. 221 Lamp (back-up) schematics — 1993

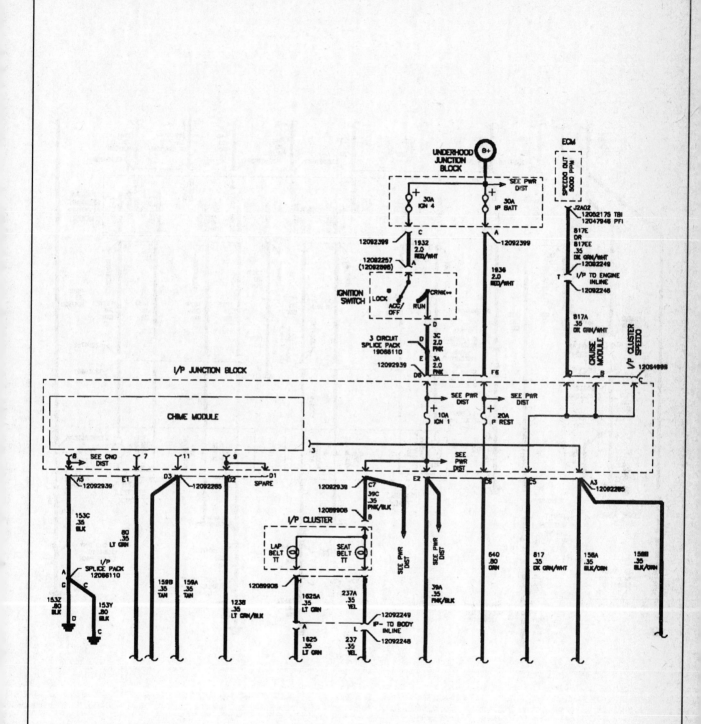

Fig. 222 Passive restrain system schematics

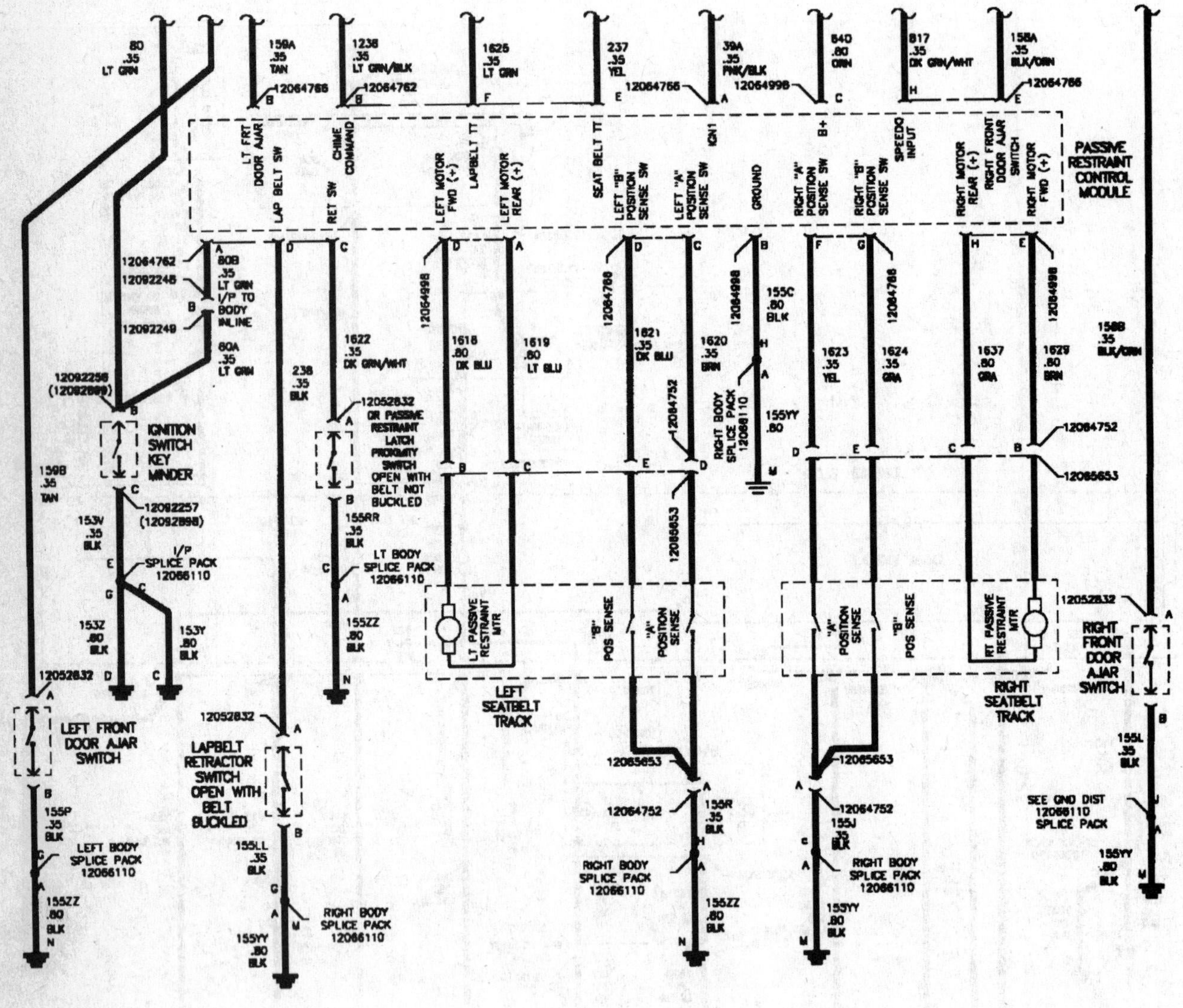

Fig. 223 Passive restrain system schematics

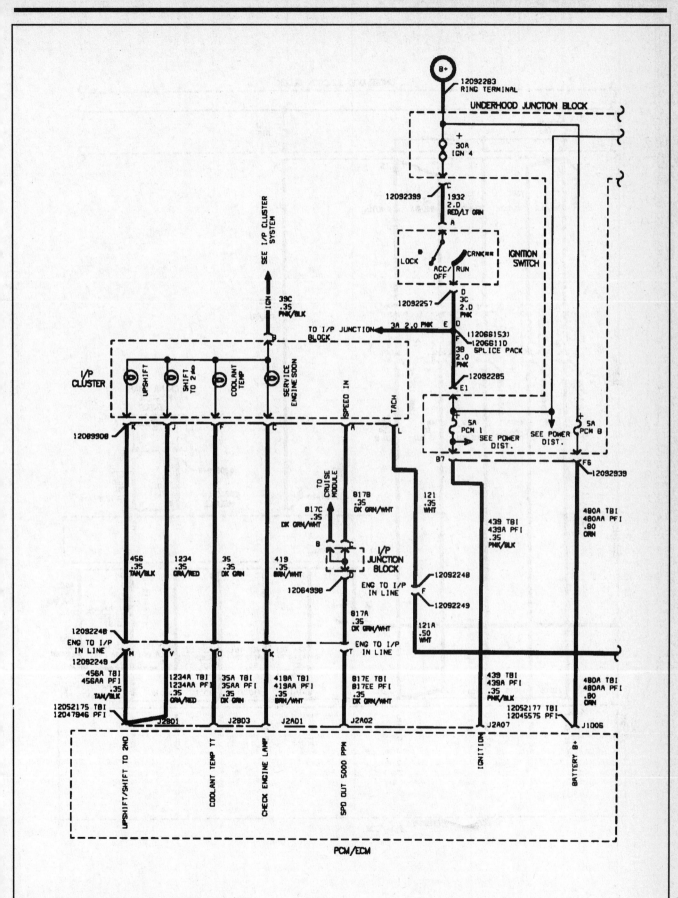

Fig. 224 PCM schematics — 1991 and 1992

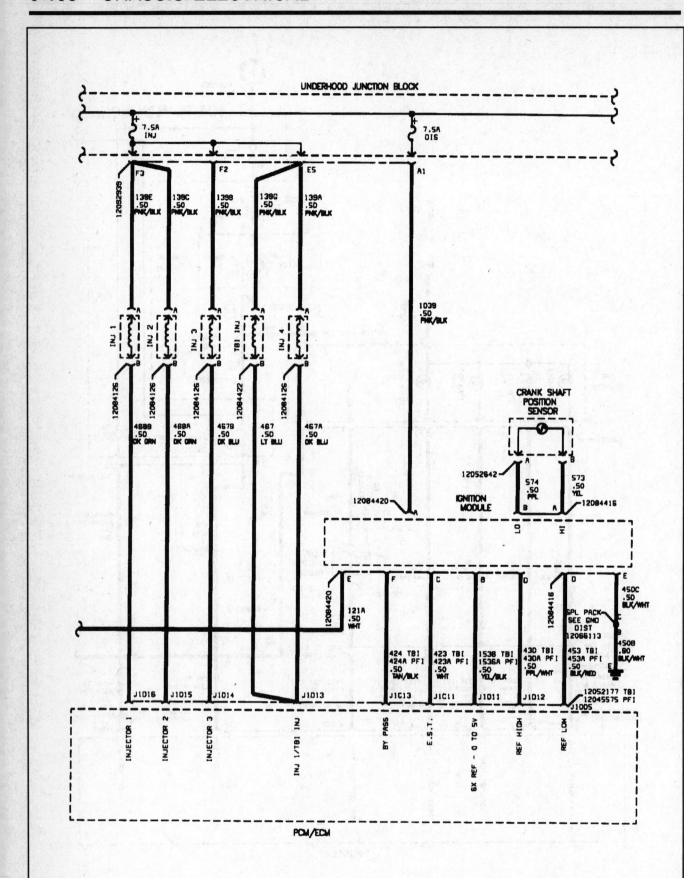

Fig. 225 PCM schematics — 1991 and 1992

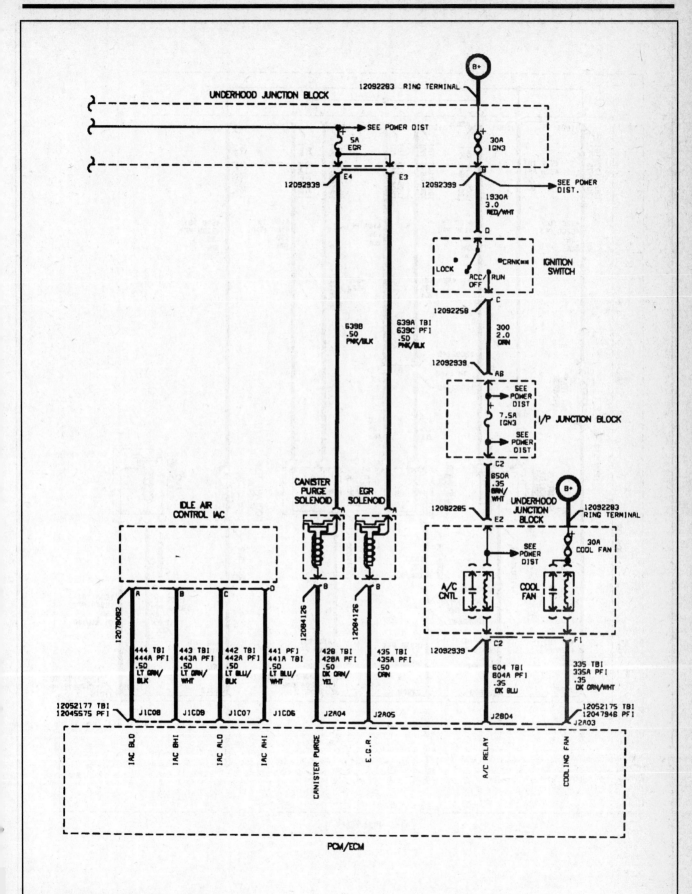

Fig. 226 PCM schematics — 1991 and 1992

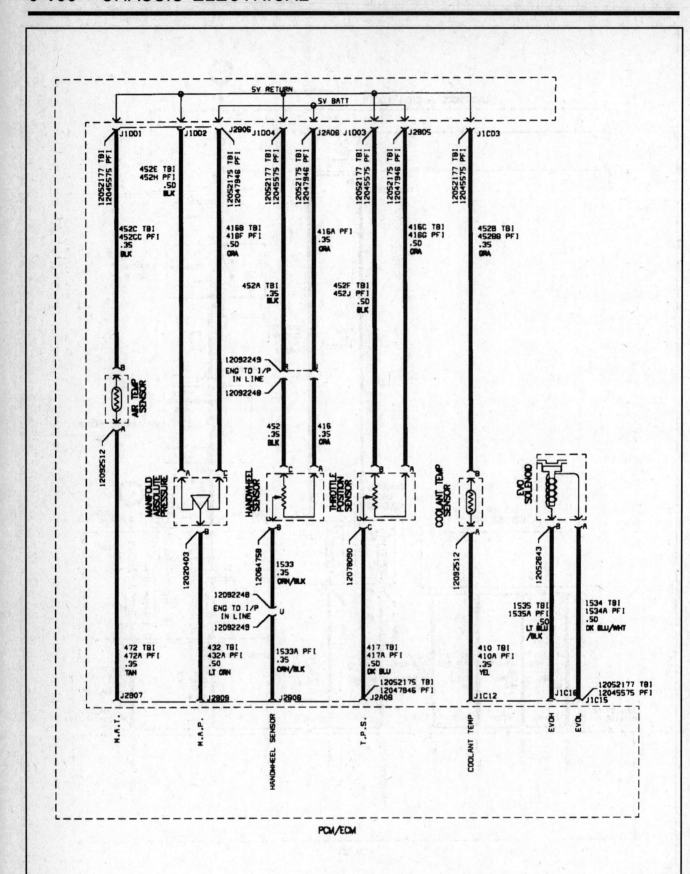

Fig. 227 PCM schematics — 1991 and 1992

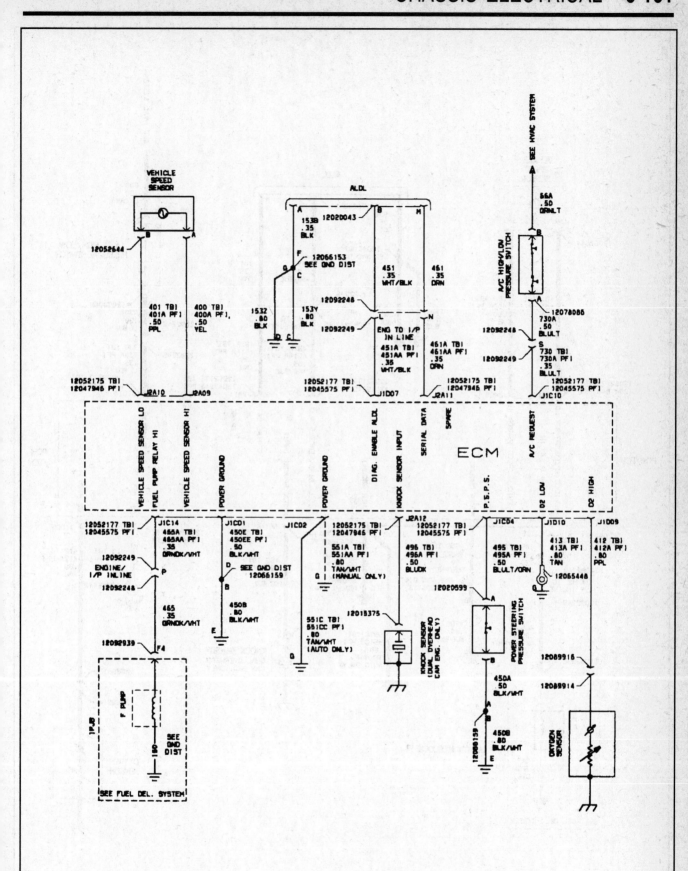

Fig. 228 PCM schematics — 1991

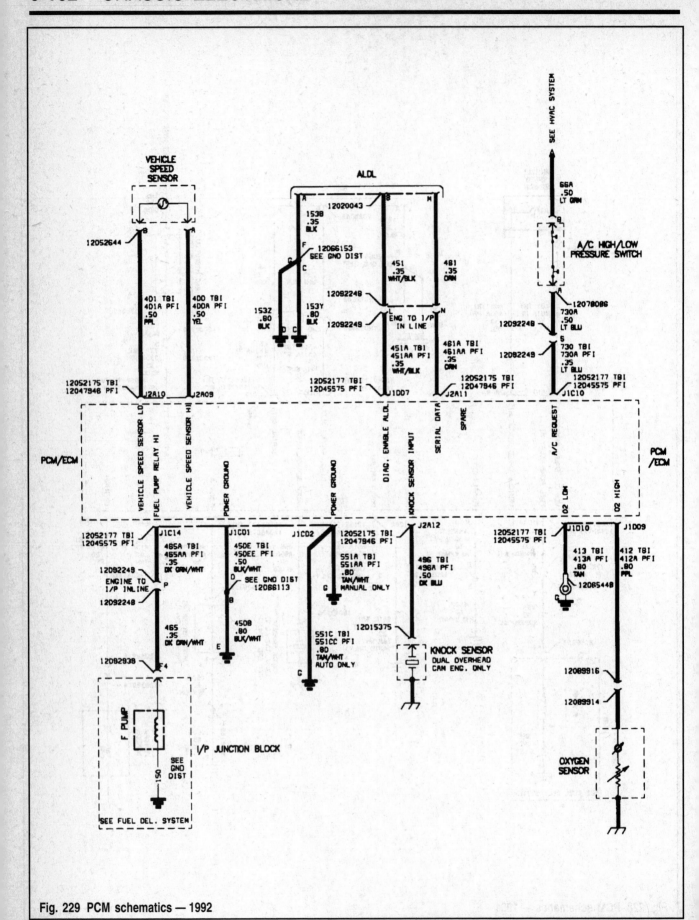

Fig. 229 PCM schematics — 1992

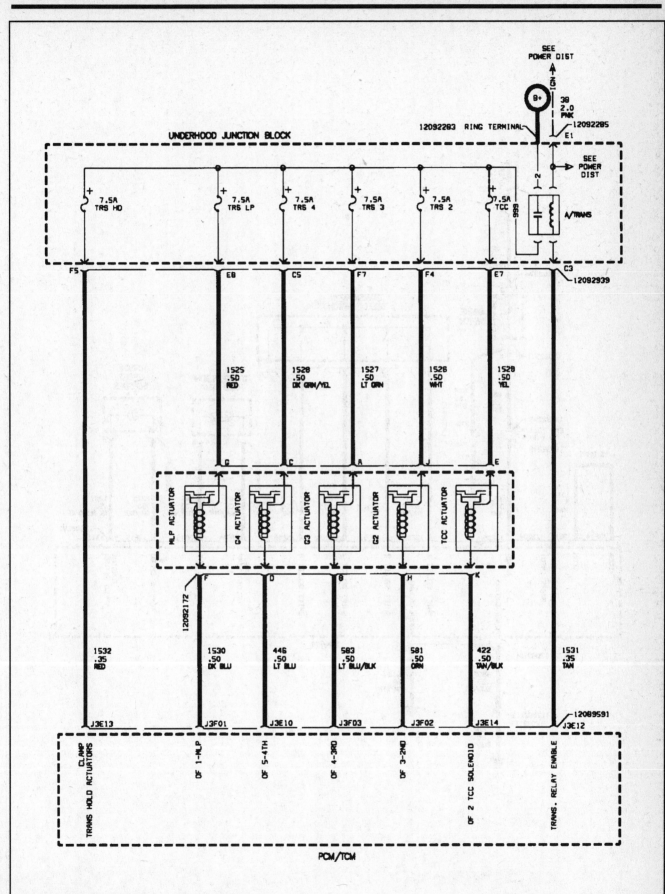

Fig. 230 PCM schematics — 1991 and 1992

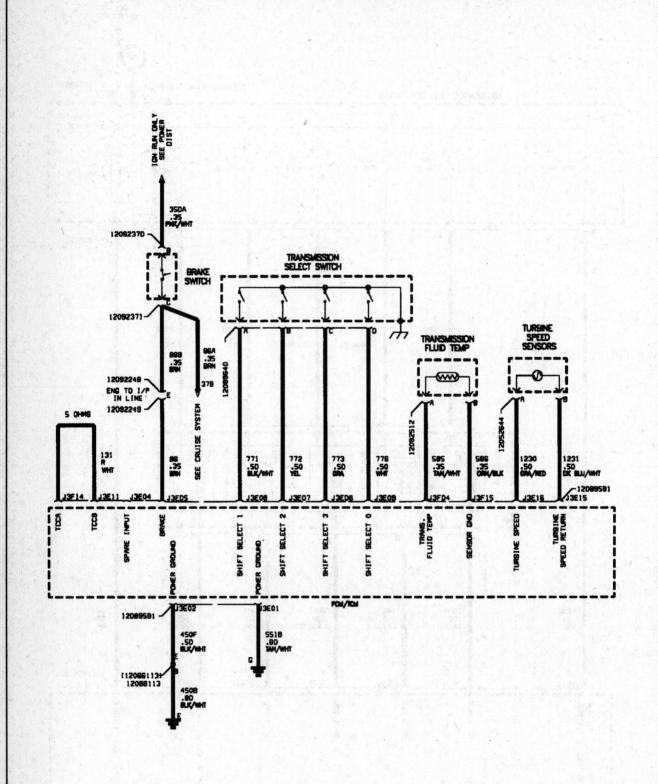

Fig. 231 PCM schematics — 1991 and 1992

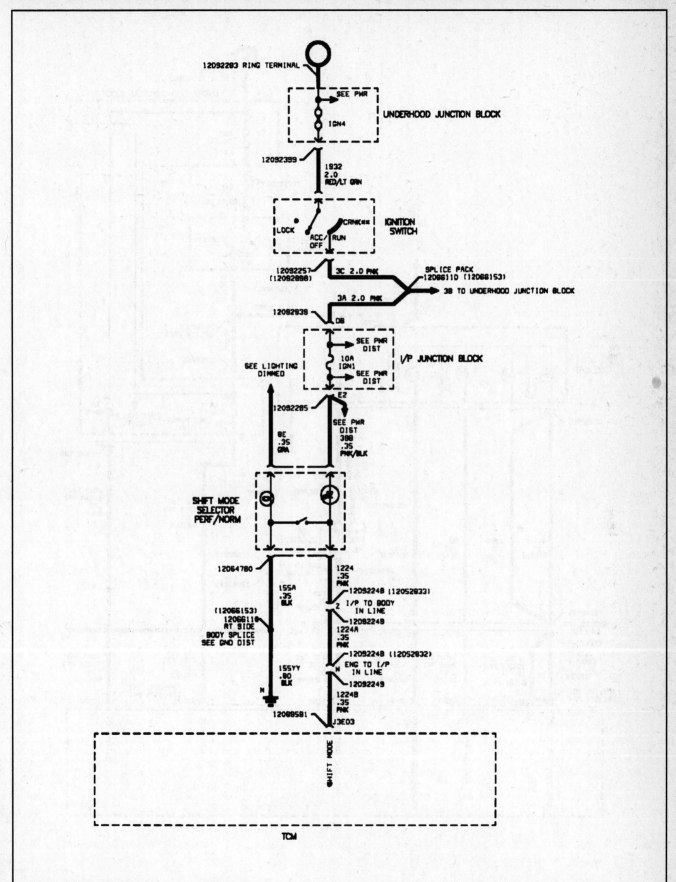

Fig. 232 PCM schematics — 1991 and 1992

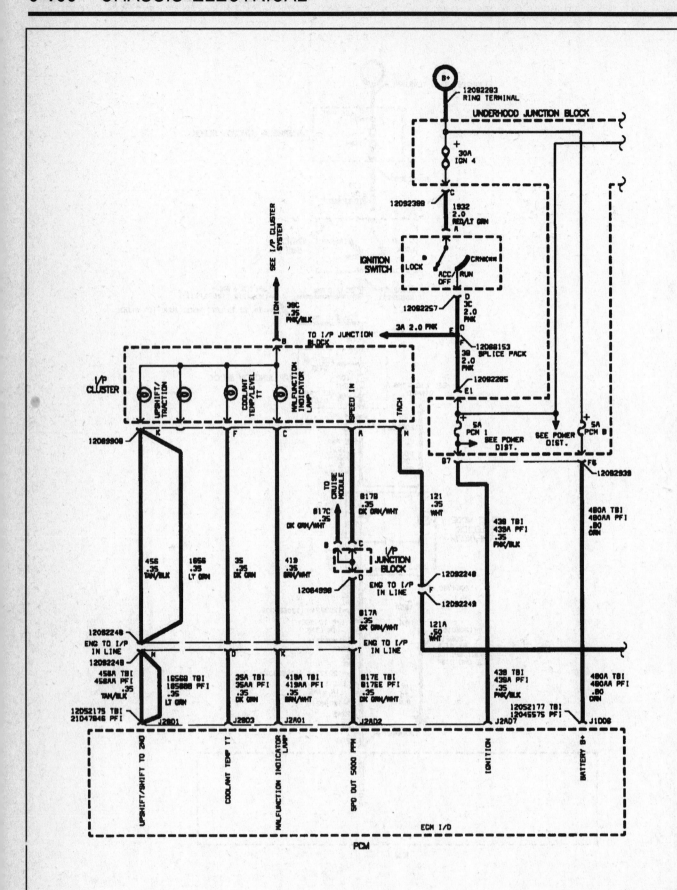

Fig. 233 PCM schematics — 1993

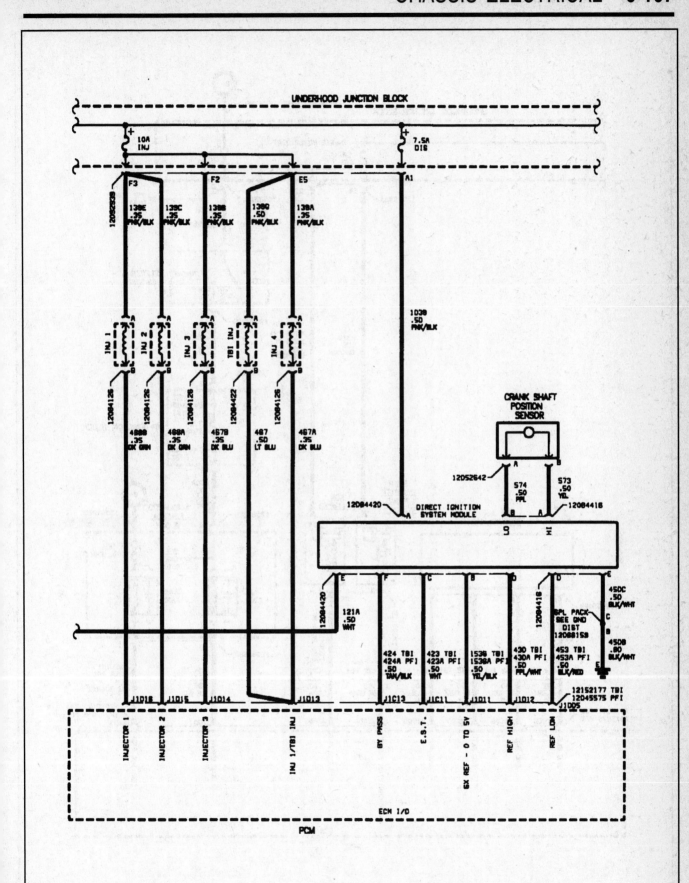

Fig. 234 PCM schematics — 1993

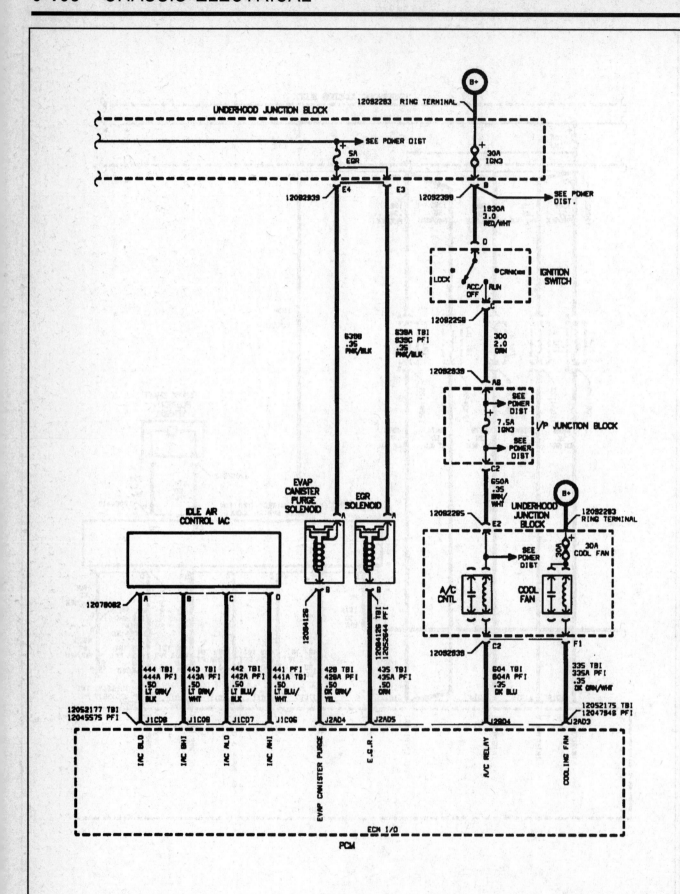

Fig. 235 PCM schematics — 1993

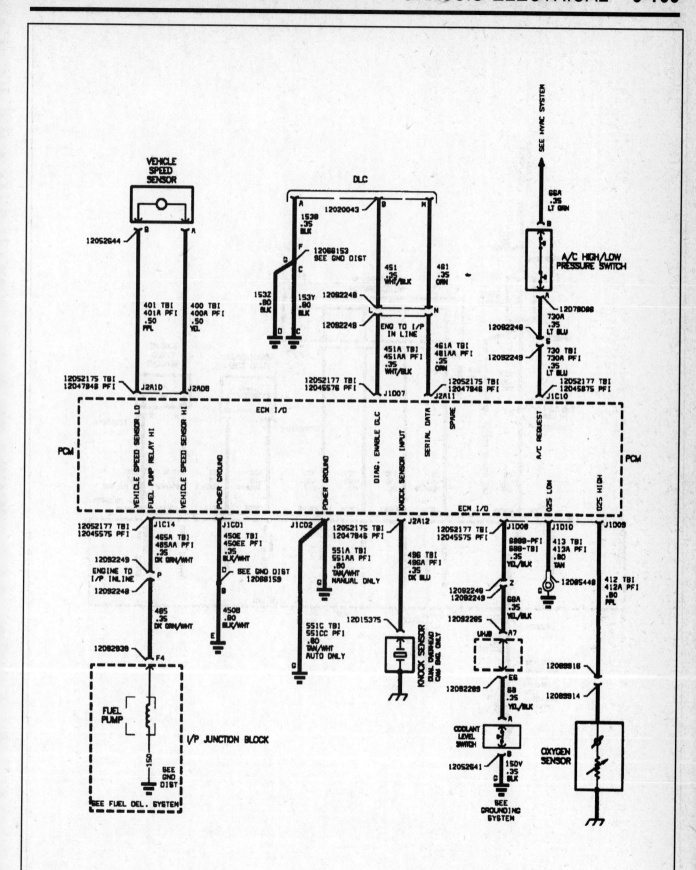

Fig. 236 PCM schematics — 1993

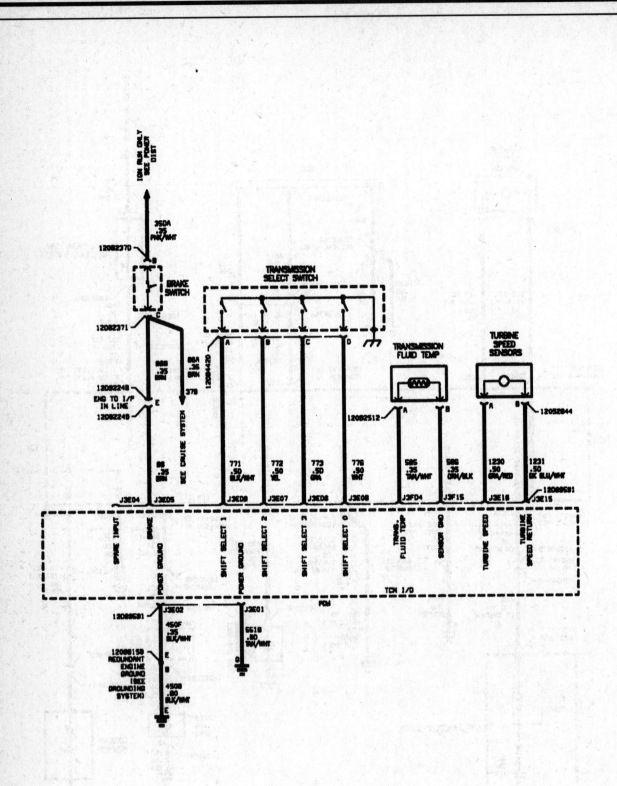

Fig. 237 PCM schematics — 1993

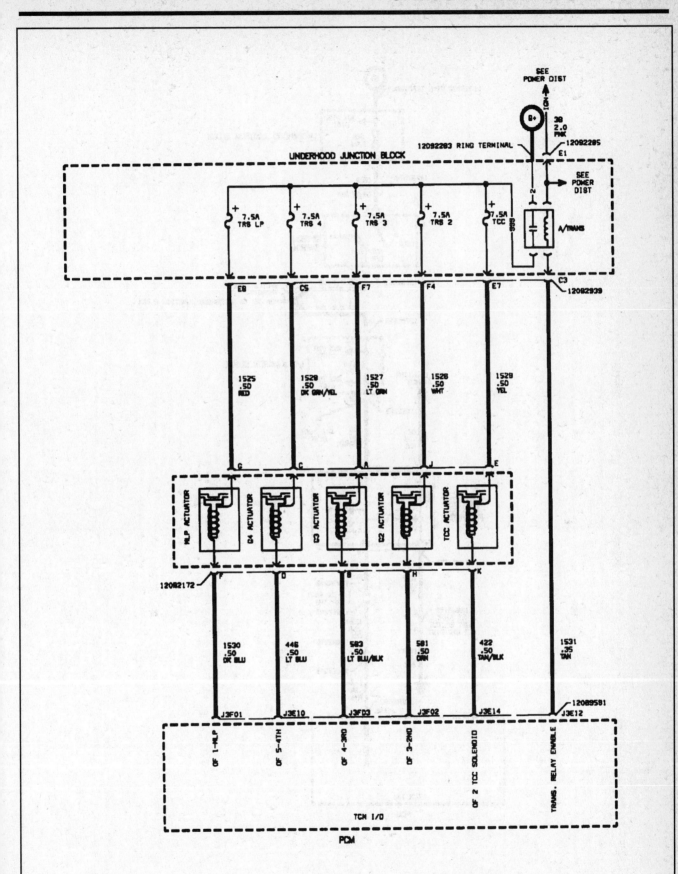

Fig. 238 PCM schematics — 1993

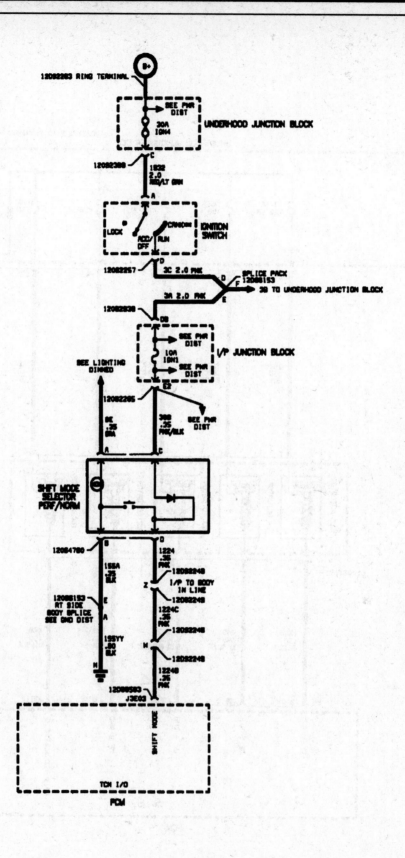

Fig. 239 PCM schematics — 1993

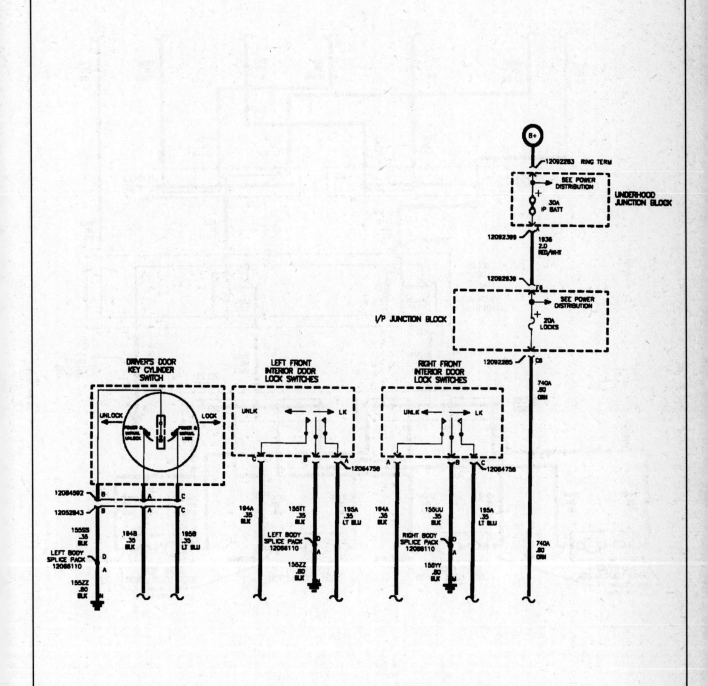

Fig. 240 Power door lock schematics — sedan

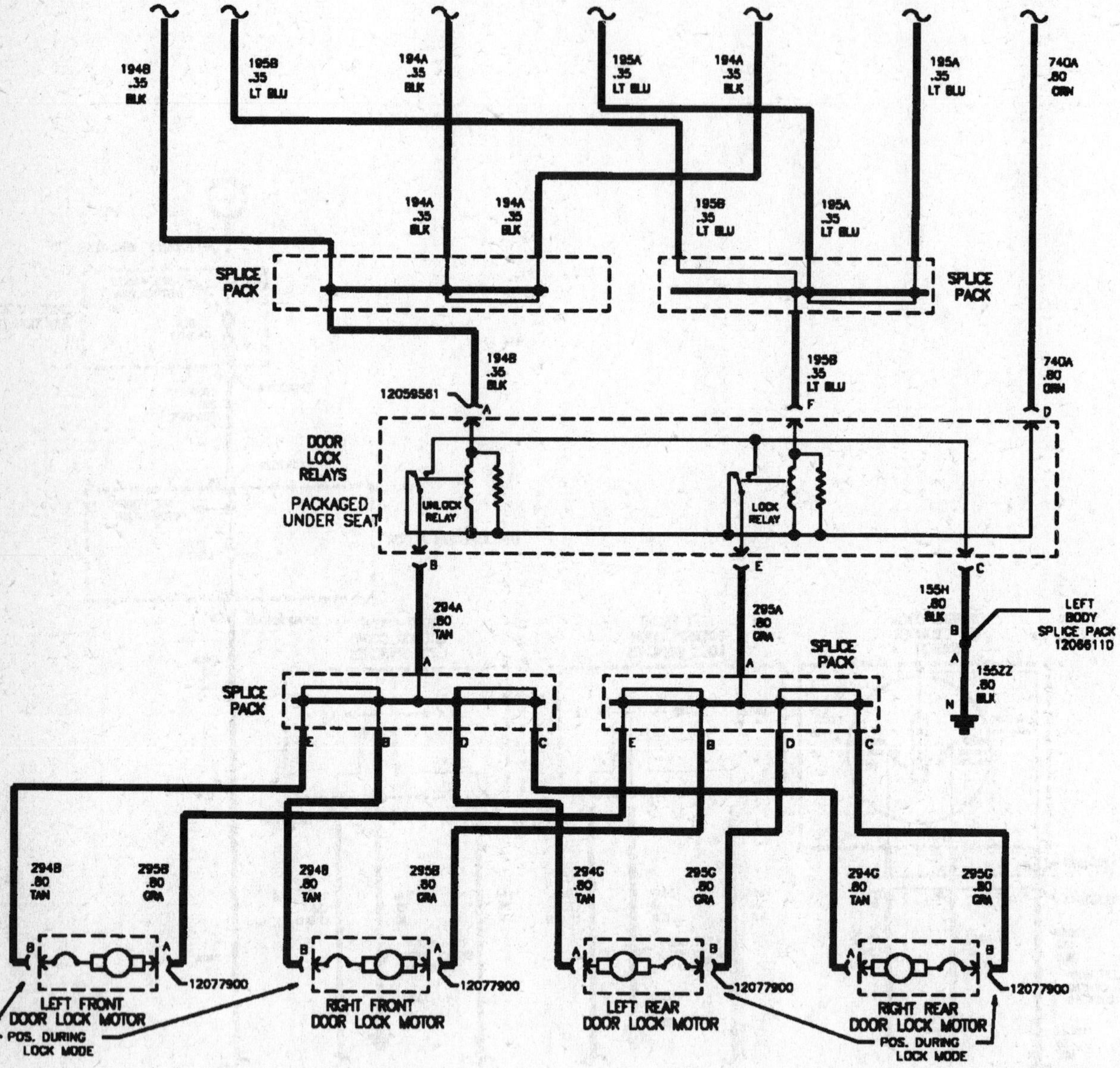

Fig. 241 Power door lock schematics — sedan

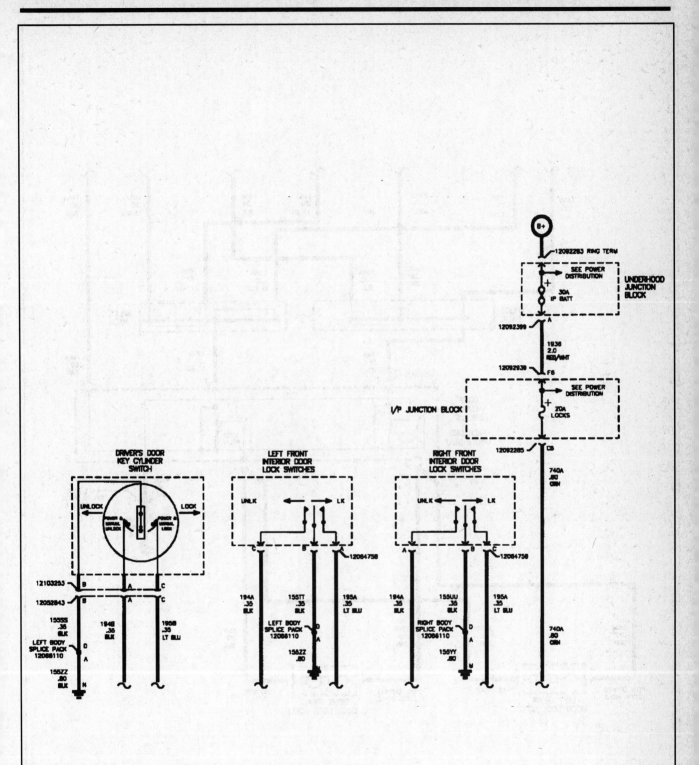

Fig. 242 Power door lock schematics — coupe

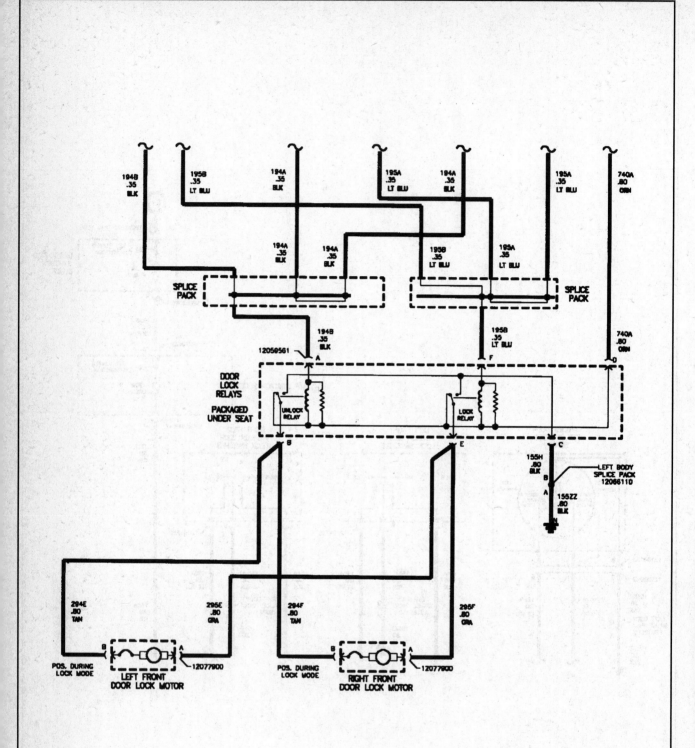

Fig. 243 Power door lock schematics — coupe

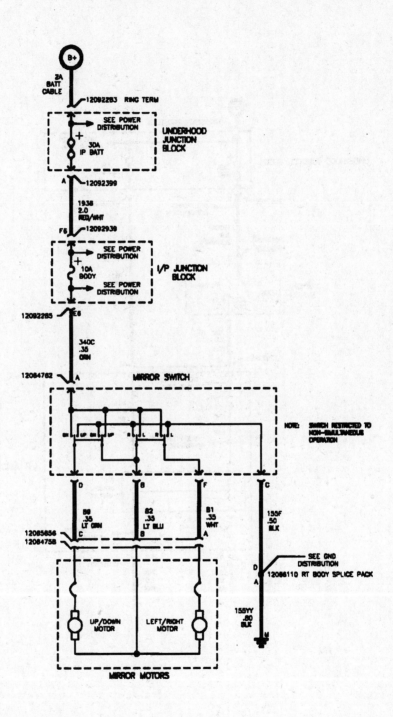

Fig. 244 Power mirror system schematics

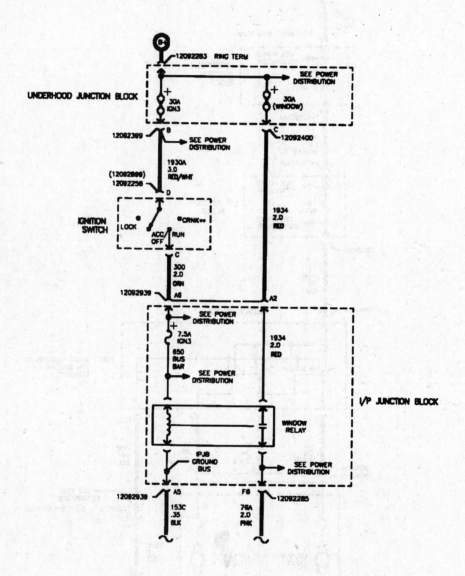

Fig. 245 Power window schematics — sedan

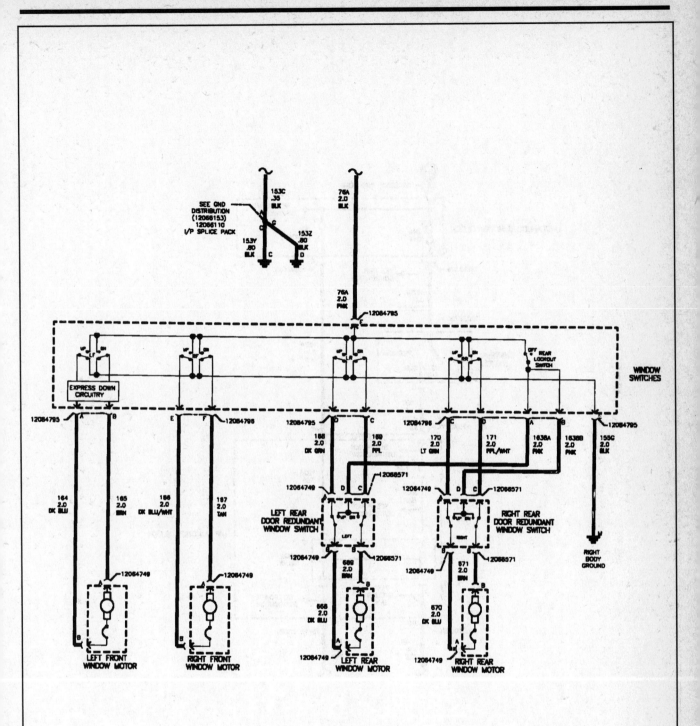

Fig. 246 Power window schematics — sedan

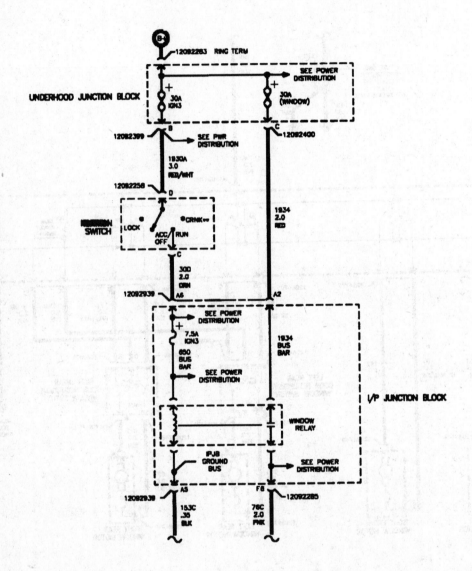

Fig. 247 Power window schematics — coupe

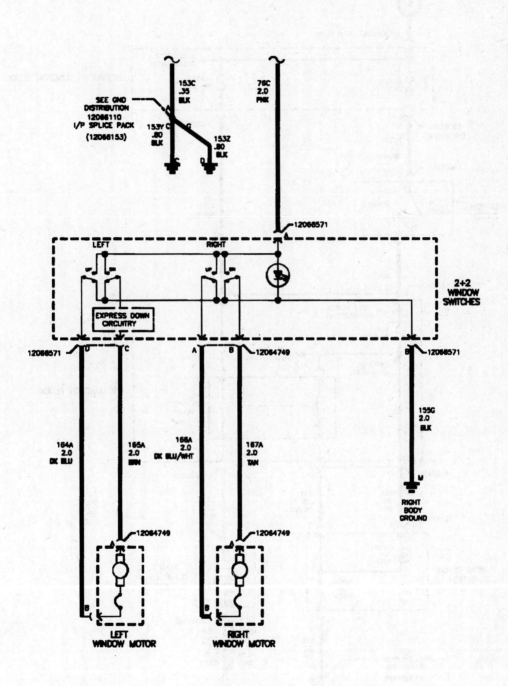

Fig. 248 Power window schematics — coupe

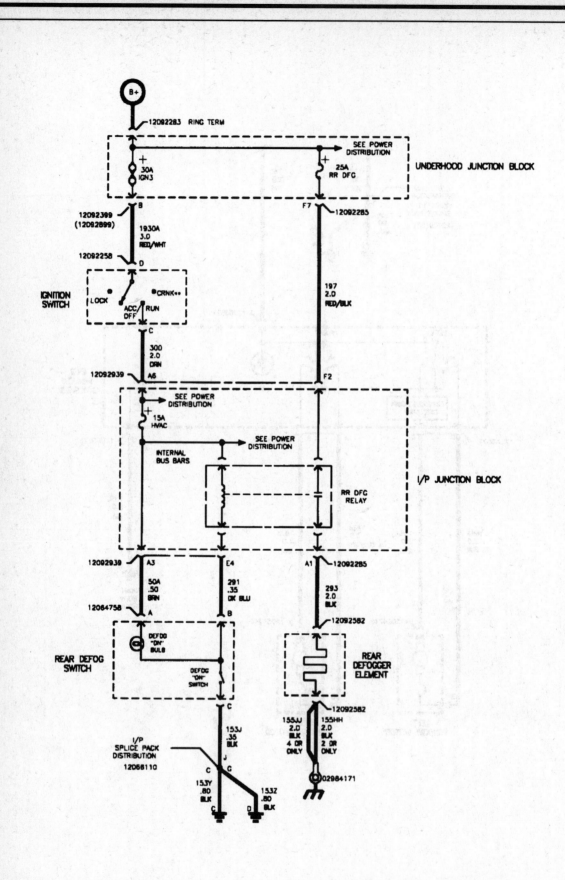

Fig. 249 Rear defogger schematics — 1991 and 1992

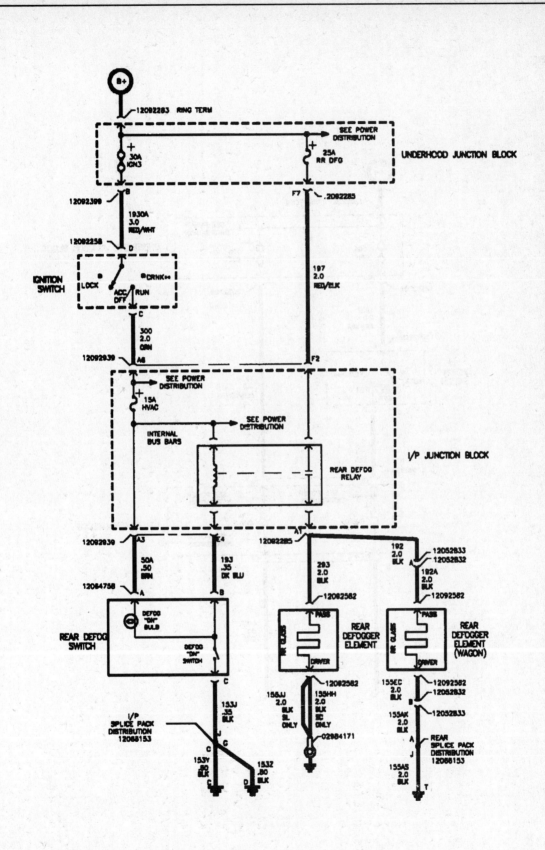

Fig. 250 Rear defogger schematics — 1993

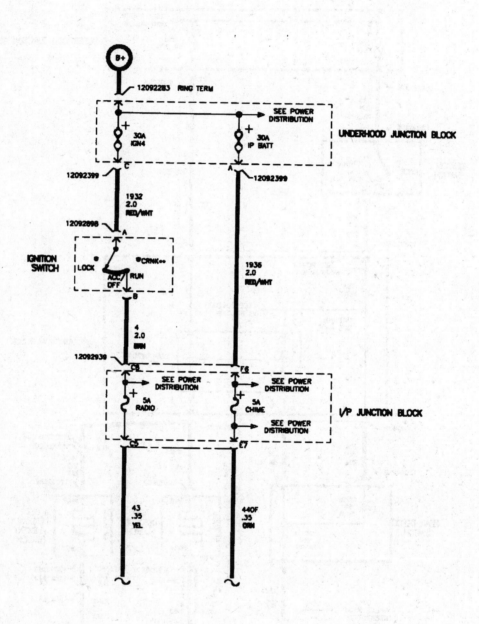

Fig. 251 Radio (audio) system schematics

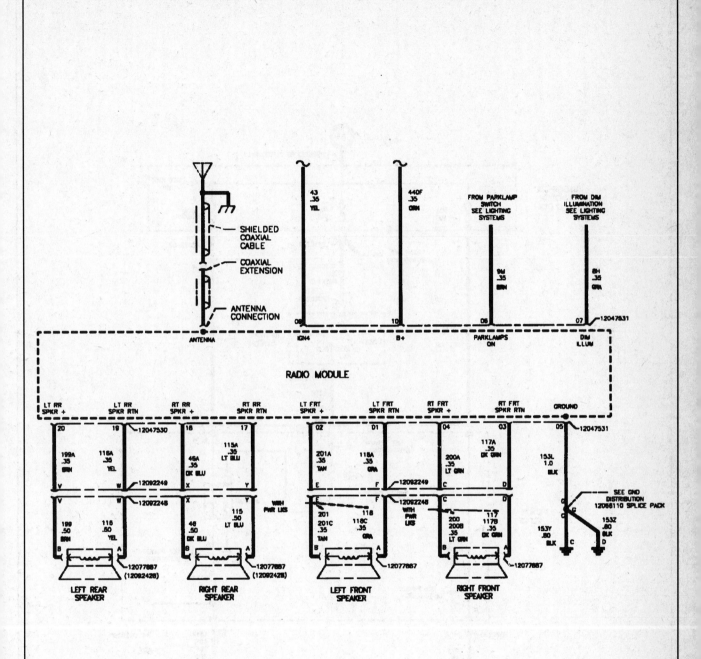

Fig. 252 Radio (audio) system schematics

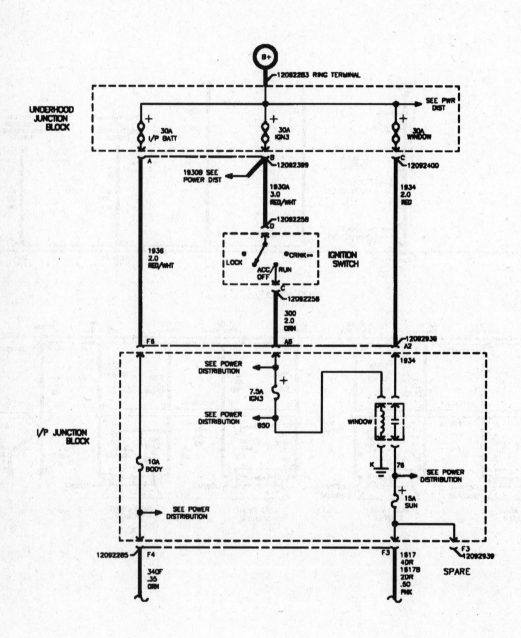

Fig. 253 Power sunroof map light schematics

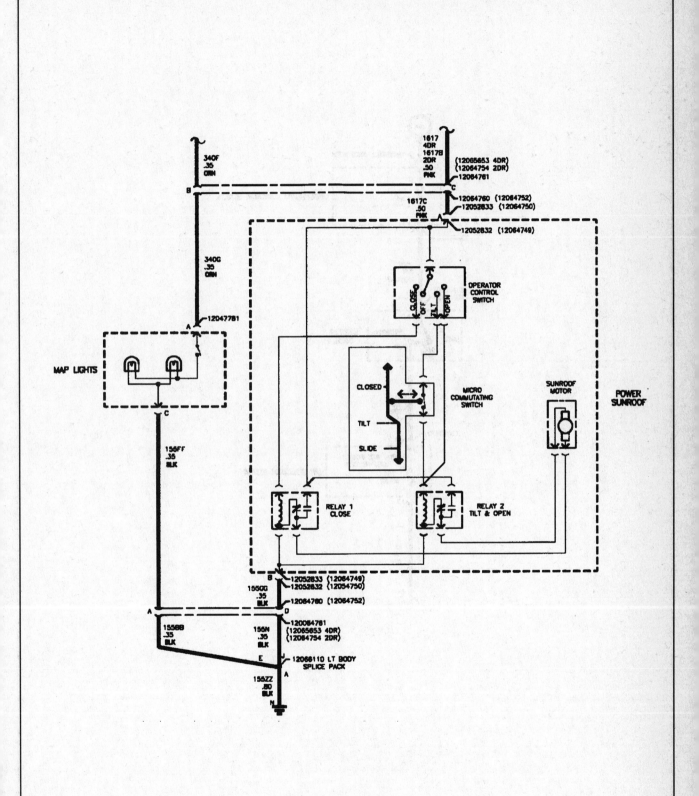

Fig. 254 Power sunroof map light schematics

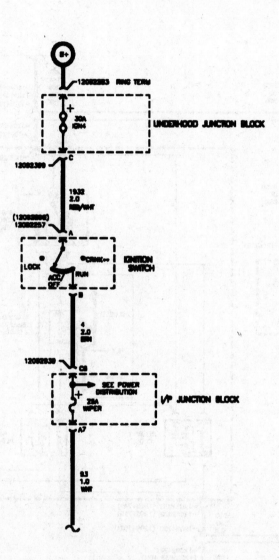

Fig. 255 Windshield wiper system schematics

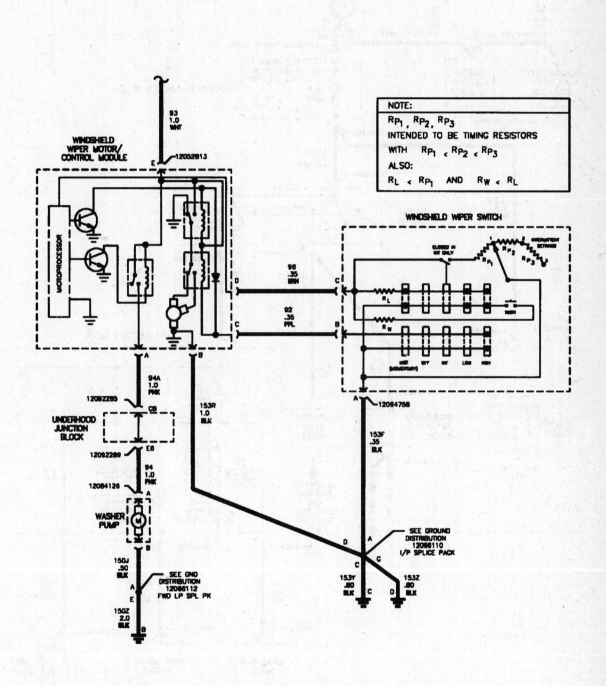

Fig. 256 Windshield wiper system schematics

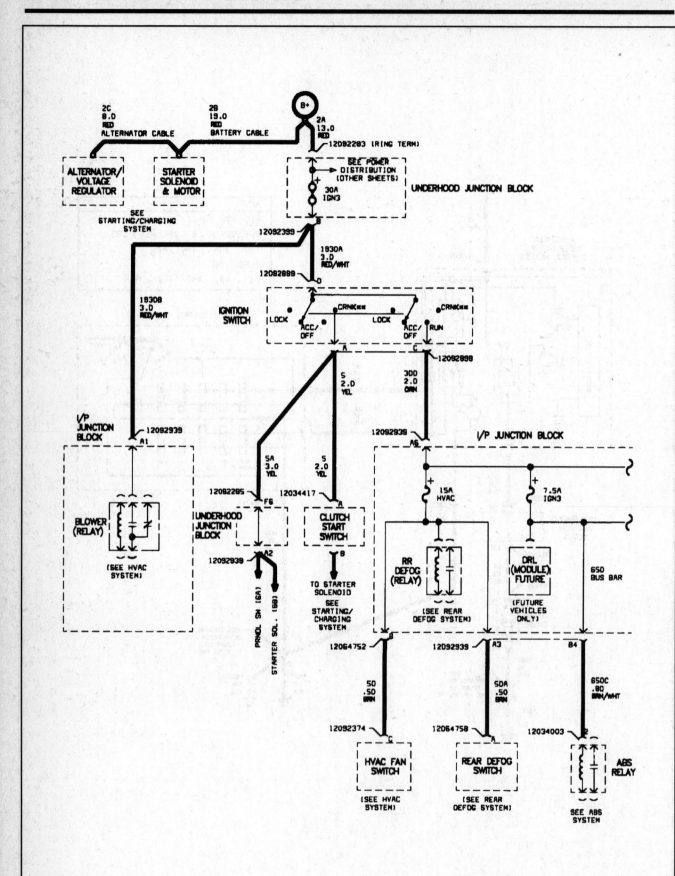

Fig. 257 Power distribution schematics — 1991

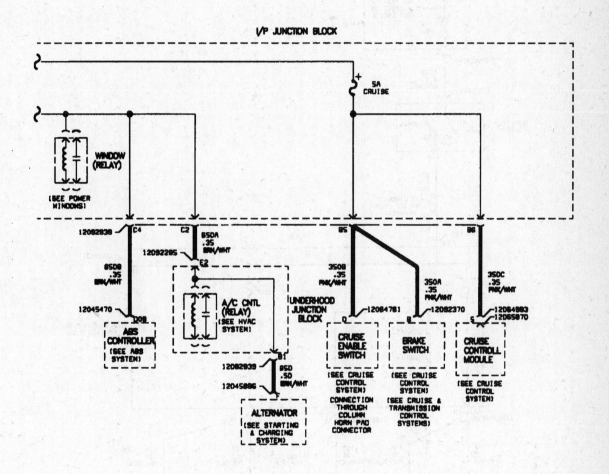

Fig. 258 Power distribution schematics — 1991

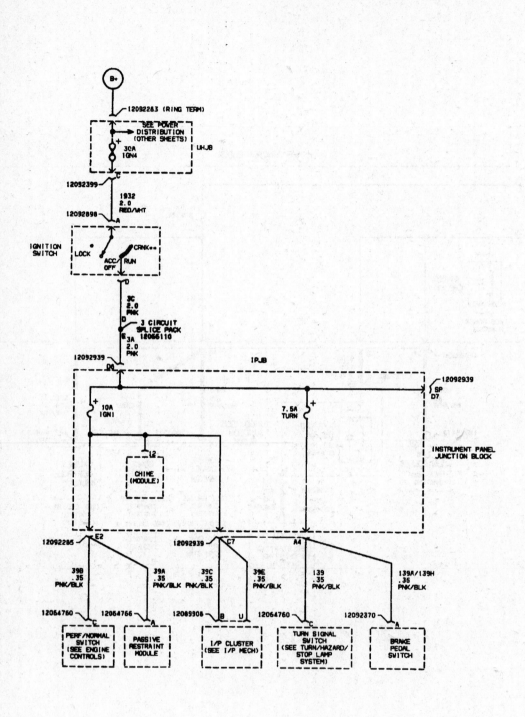

Fig. 259 Power distribution schematics — 1991

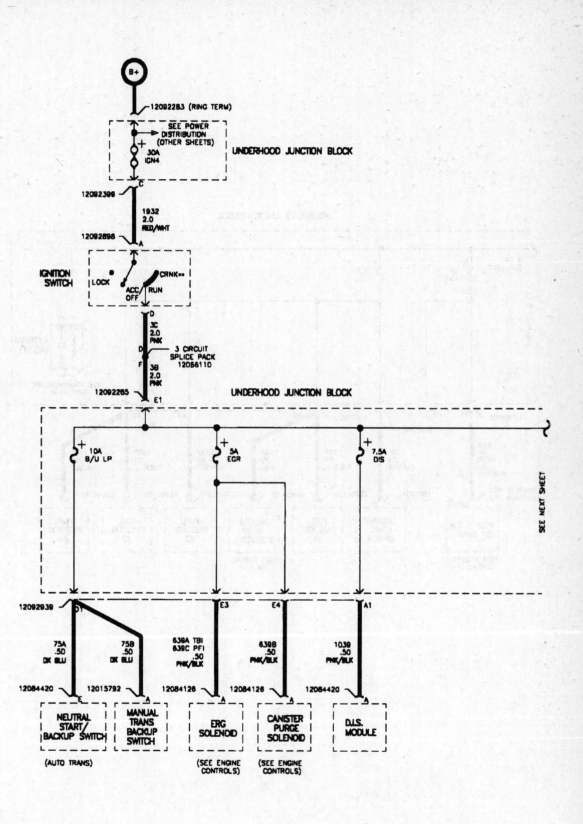

Fig. 260 Power distribution schematics — 1991

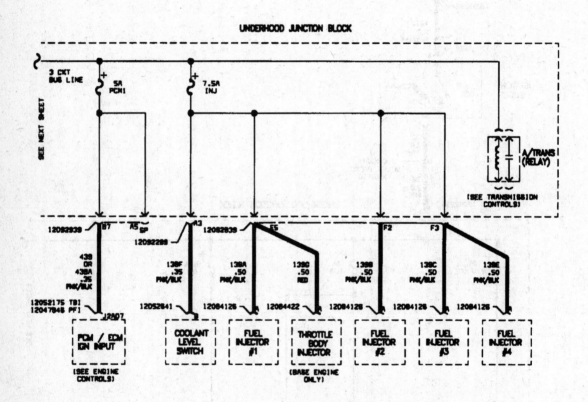

Fig. 261 Power distribution schematics — 1991

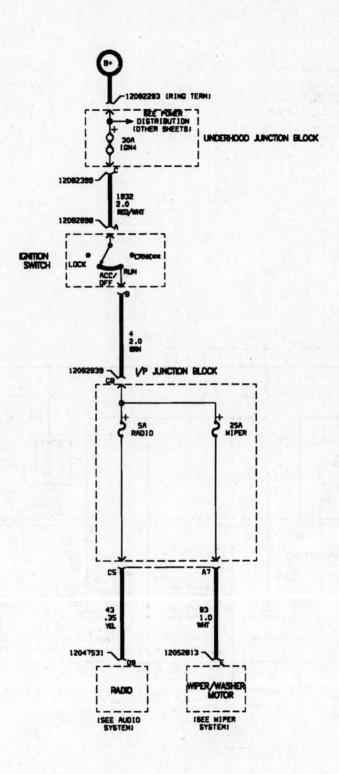

Fig. 262 Power distribution schematics — 1991

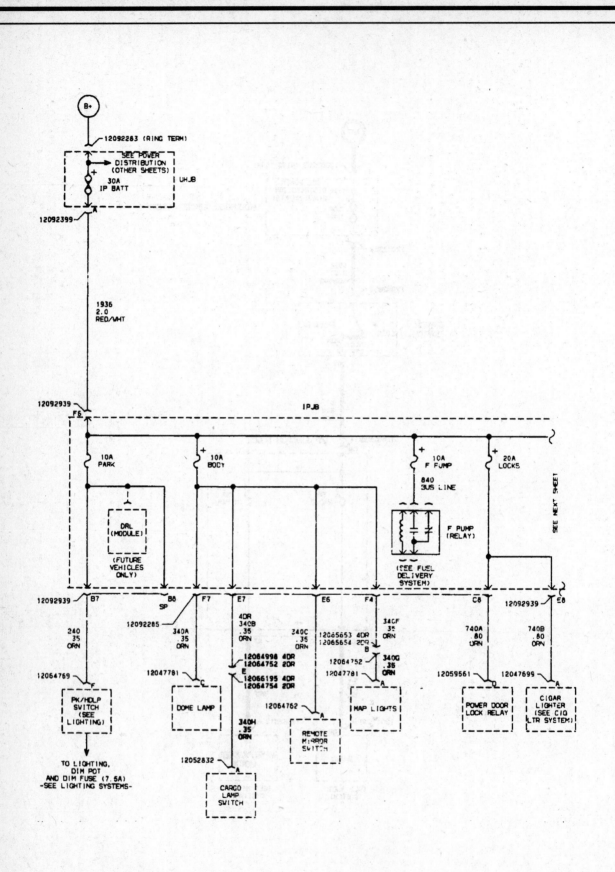

Fig. 263 Power distribution schematics — 1991

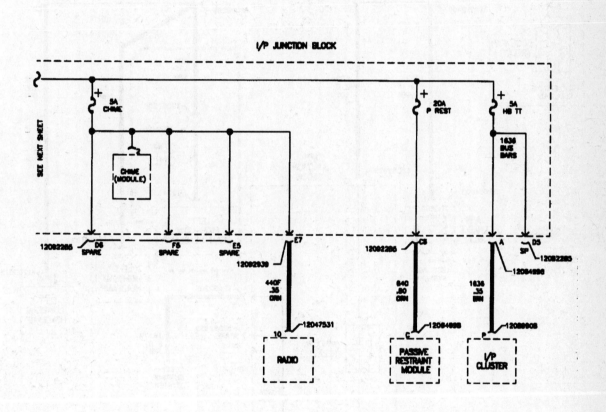

Fig. 264 Power distribution schematics — 1991

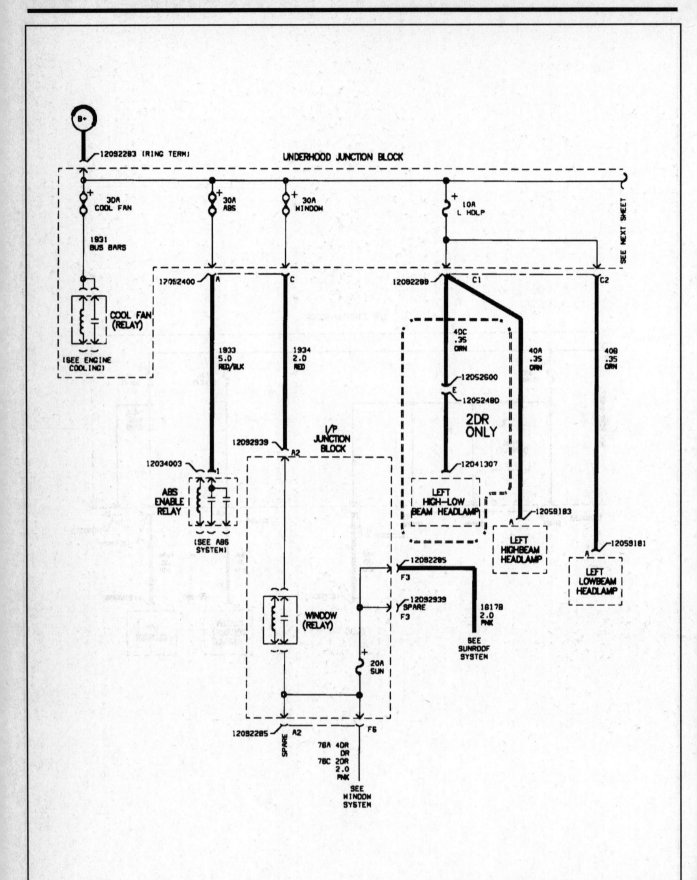

Fig. 265 Power distribution schematics — 1991

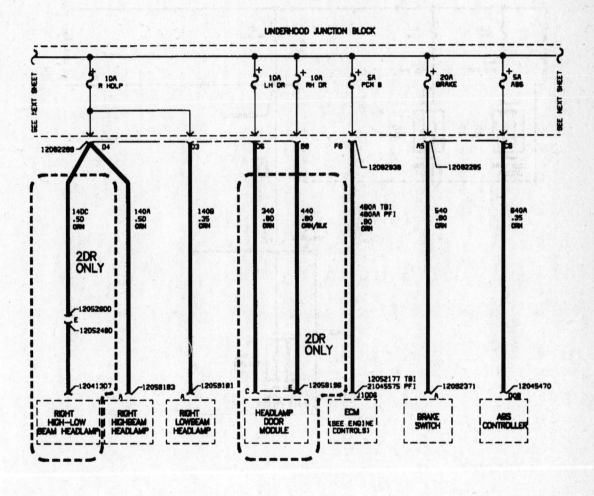

Fig. 266 Power distribution schematics — 1991

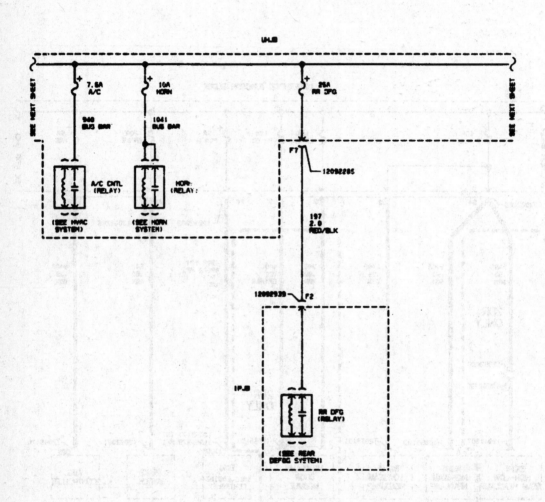

Fig. 267 Power distribution schematics — 1991

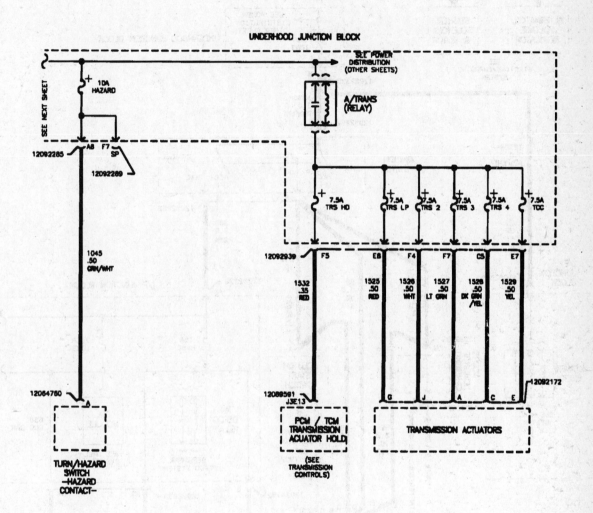

UNDERHOOD JUNCTION BLOCK

SEE POWER
DISTRIBUTION
(OTHER SHEETS)

A/TRANS
(RELAY)

1DA
HAZARD

SEE NEXT SHEET

12092285   A8 F7
                 SP

12092289

7.5A   7.5A   7.5A   7.5A   7.5A   7.5A
TRS HD   TRS LP   TRS 2   TRS 3   TRS 4   TCC

1045
.50
GRN/WHT

12092939   F5   E8   F4   F7   C5   E7

1532   1525   1526   1527   1528   1529
.35   .50   .50   .50   .50   .50
RED   RED   WHT   LT GRN   DK GRN   YEL
                                                /YEL

12064760   12092172

12088591
J3E13   G   J   A   C   E

TURN/HAZARD
SWITCH   PCM/TCM   TRANSMISSION ACTUATORS
—HAZARD   TRANSMISSION
CONTACT—   ACUATOR HOLD

            (SEE
            TRANSMISSION
            CONTROLS)

Fig. 268 Power distribution schematics — 1991

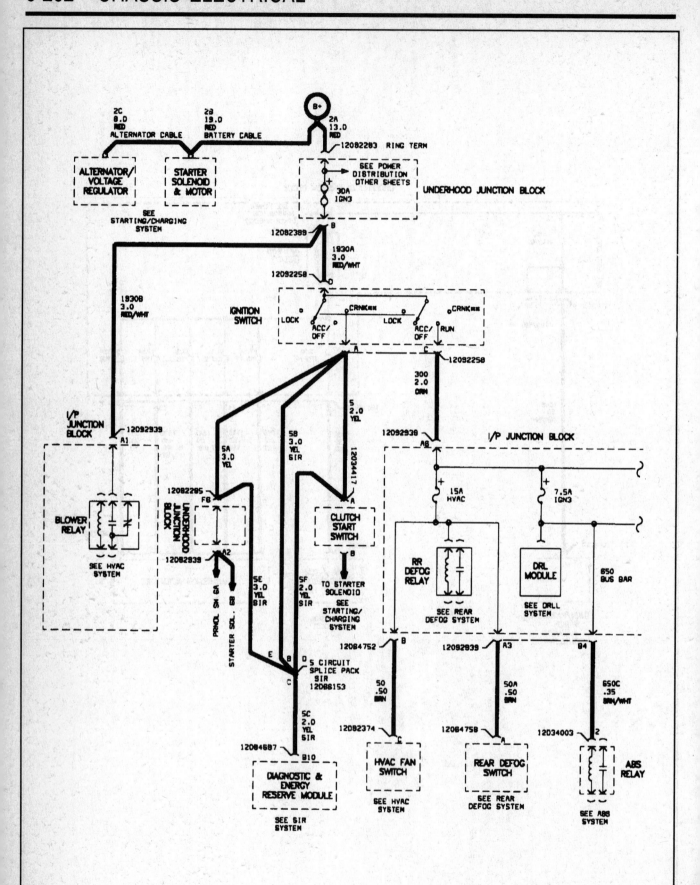

Fig. 269 Power distribution schematics — 1992

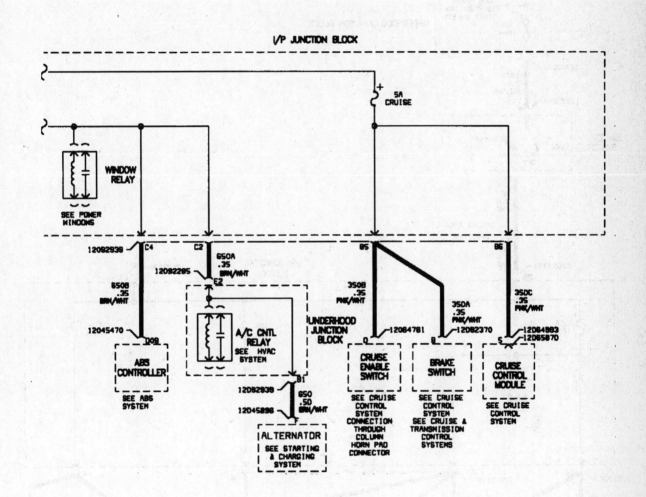

Fig. 270 Power distribution schematics — 1992

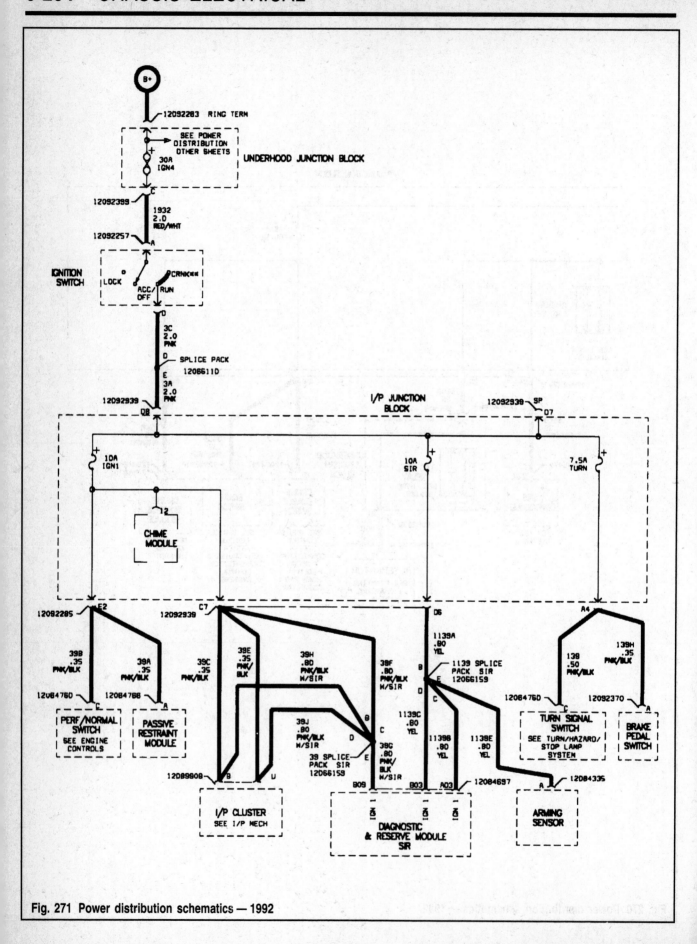

Fig. 271 Power distribution schematics — 1992

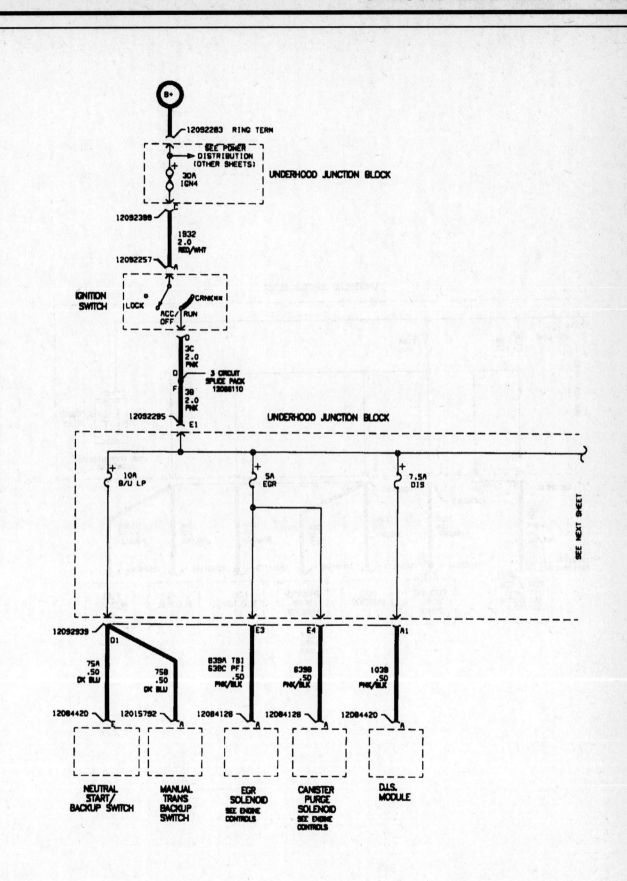

Fig. 272 Power distribution schematics — 1992

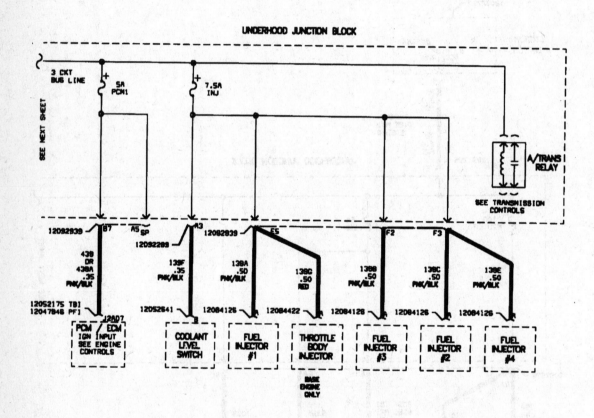

Fig. 273 Power distribution schematics — 1992

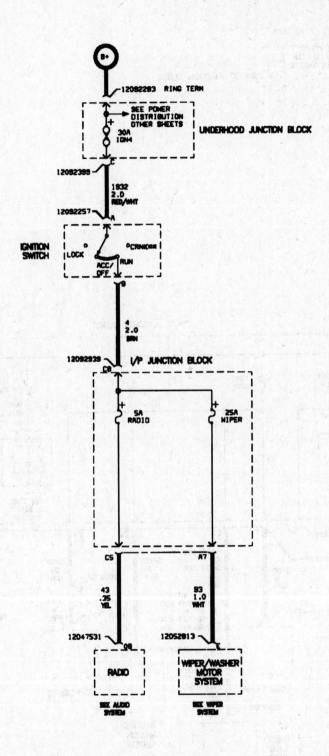

Fig. 274 Power distribution schematics — 1992

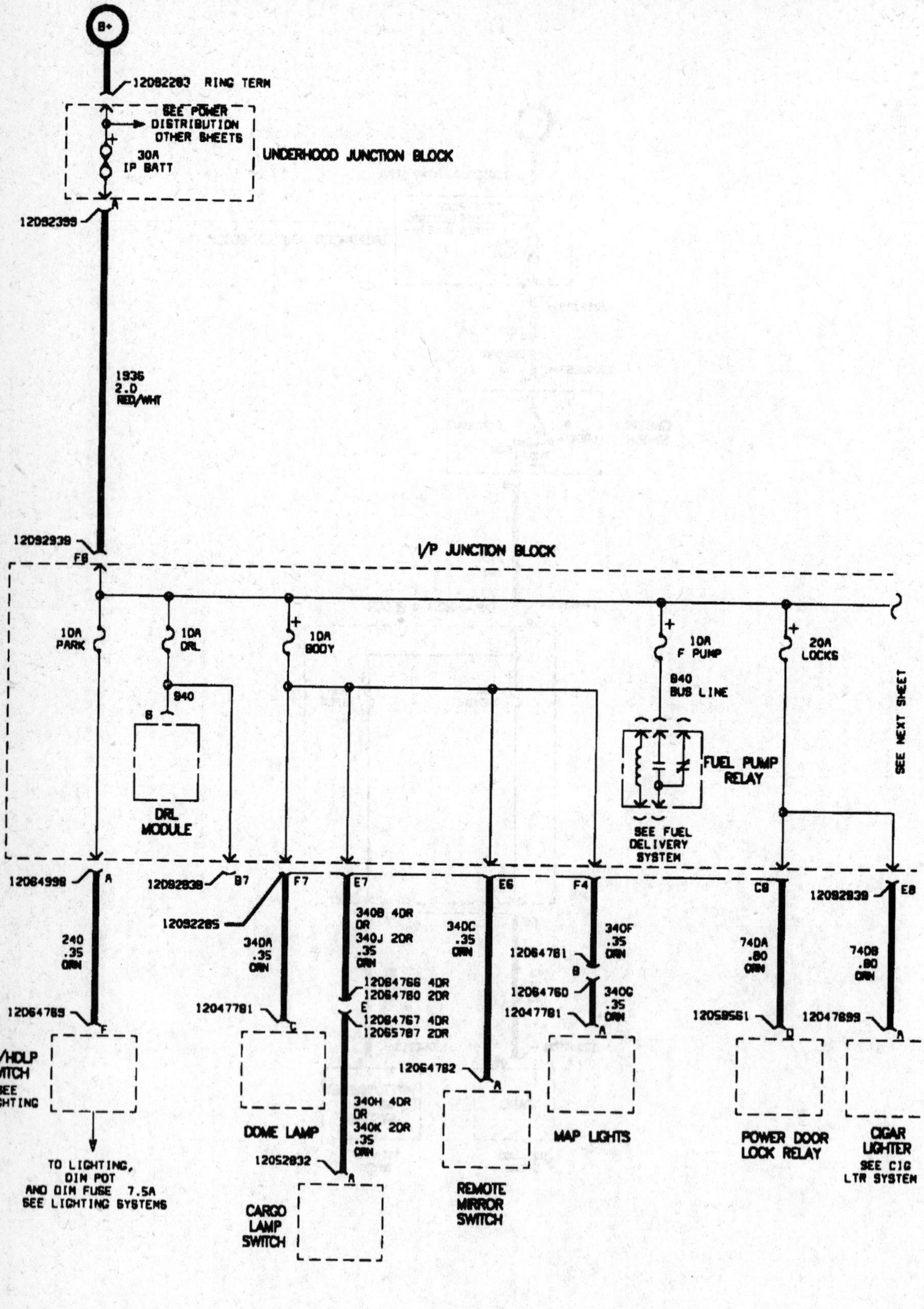

B+

12082283 RING TERM

SEE POWER
DISTRIBUTION
OTHER SHEETS

30A
IP BATT

UNDERHOOD JUNCTION BLOCK

12082399

A

1936
2.0
RED/WHT

12092939

F8

I/P JUNCTION BLOCK

10A
PARK

10A
DRL

10A
BODY

10A
F PUMP

20A
LOCKS

SEE NEXT SHEET

940

DRL
MODULE

940
BUS LINE

FUEL PUMP
RELAY

SEE FUEL
DELIVERY
SYSTEM

12084998

A

12082838

B7

F7

E7

E6

F4

C8

12082839

E8

12092285

240
.35
ORN

340A
.35
ORN

3408 4DR
OR
340J 2DR
.35
ORN

340C
.35
ORN

340F
.35
ORN

740A
.80
ORN

740B
.80
ORN

12064789

F

12047781

12064766 4DR
12064780 2DR

E

12064782

340G
.35
ORN

12064760

12047781

12059561

12047899

A

PK/HDLP
SWITCH
SEE
LIGHTING

DOME LAMP

12064767 4DR
12065787 2DR

340H 4DR
OR
340K 2DR
.35
ORN

A

REMOTE
MIRROR
SWITCH

MAP LIGHTS

POWER DOOR
LOCK RELAY

CIGAR
LIGHTER
SEE CIG
LTR SYSTEM

TO LIGHTING,
DIM POT
AND DIM FUSE 7.5A
SEE LIGHTING SYSTEMS

12052832

CARGO
LAMP
SWITCH

Fig. 275 Power distribution schematics — 1992

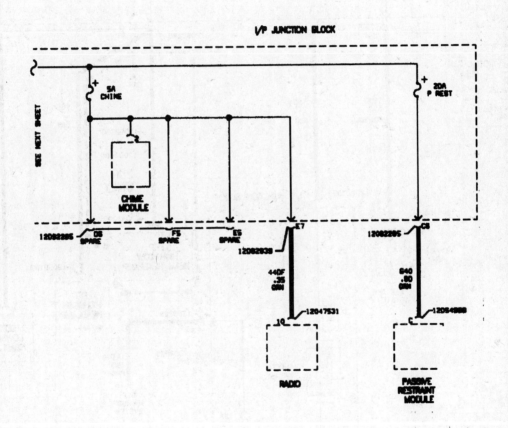

Fig. 276 Power distribution schematics — 1992

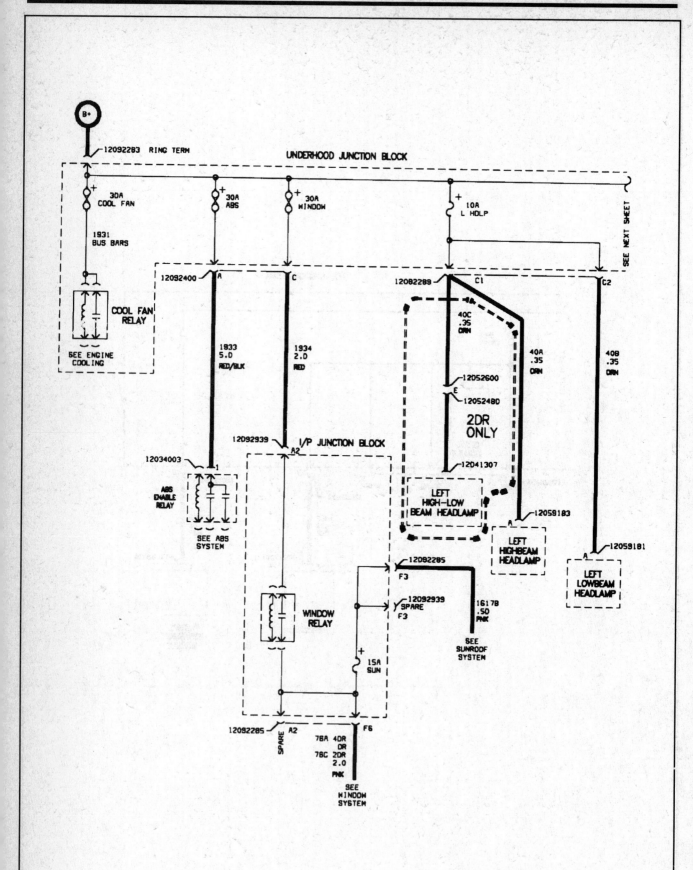

Fig. 277 Power distribution schematics — 1992

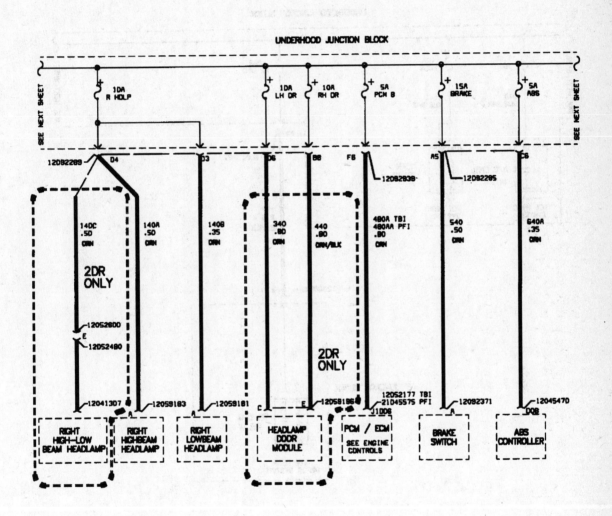

Fig. 278 Power distribution schematics — 1992

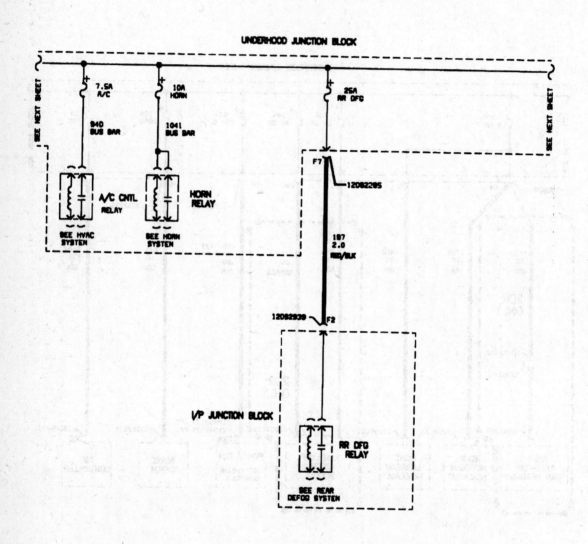

Fig. 279 Power distribution schematics—1992

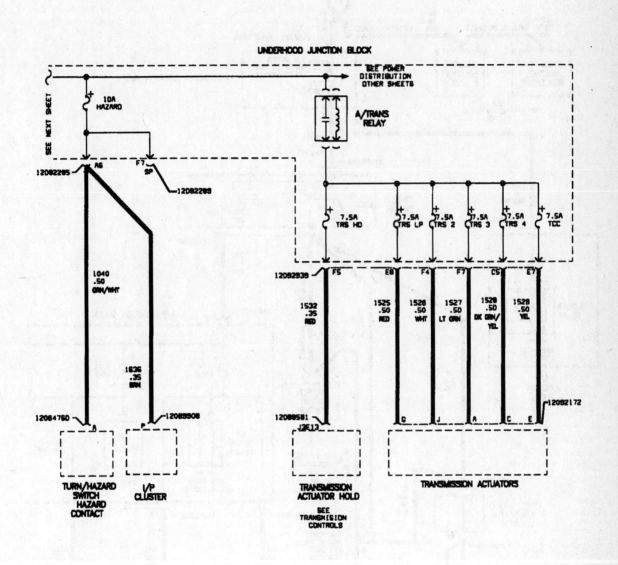

Fig. 280 Power distribution schematics — 1992

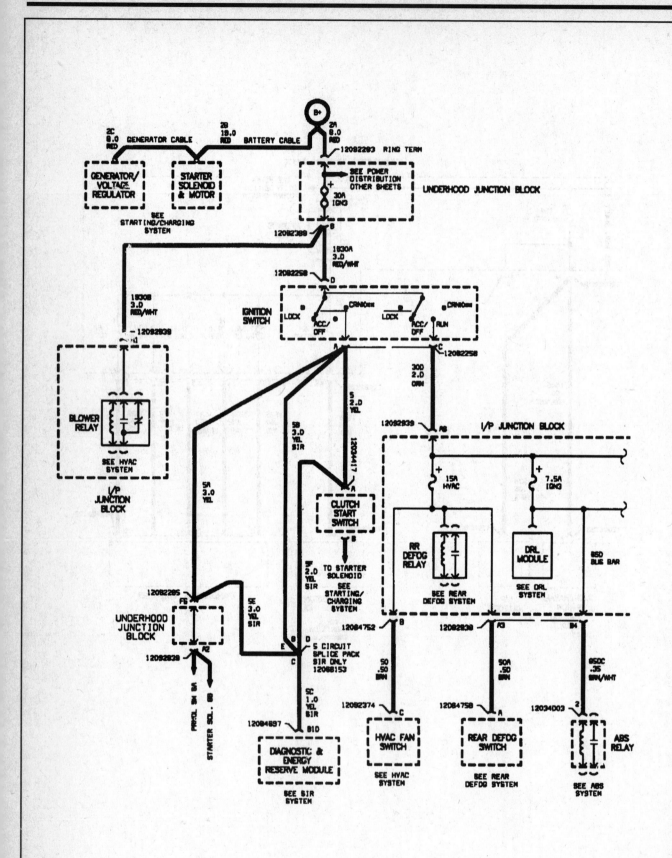

Fig. 281 Power distribution schematics — 1993

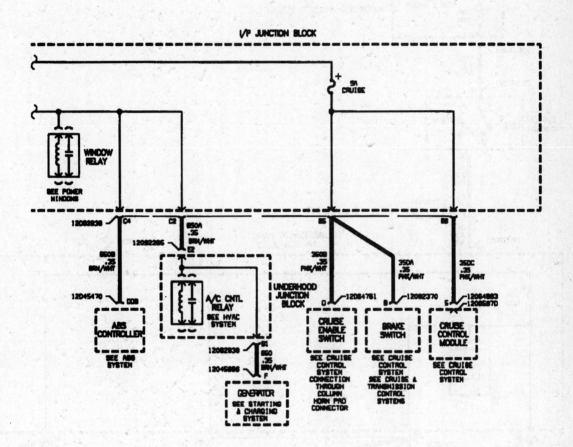

Fig. 282 Power distribution schematics — 1993

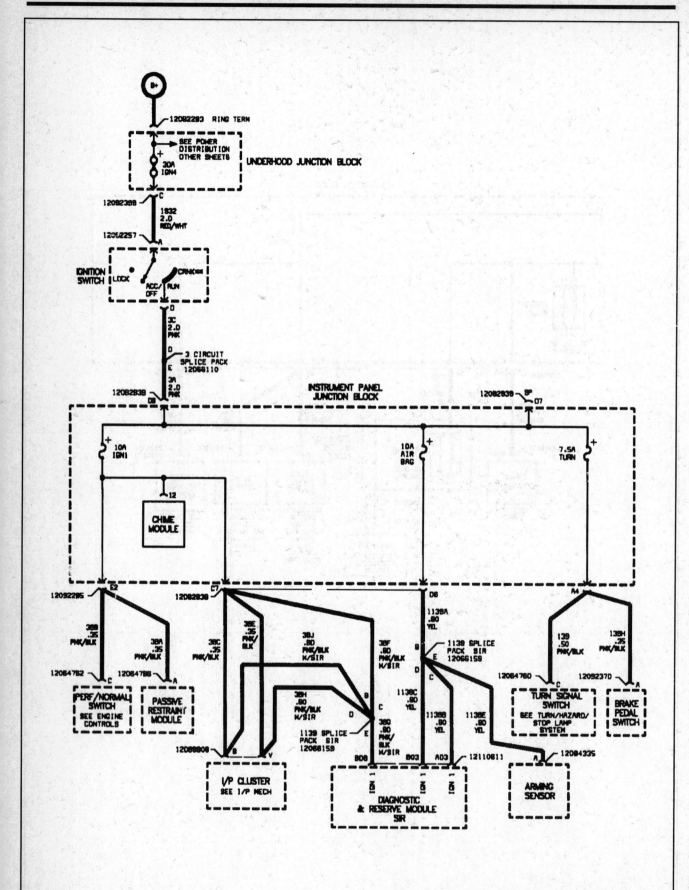

Fig. 283 Power distribution schematics — 1993

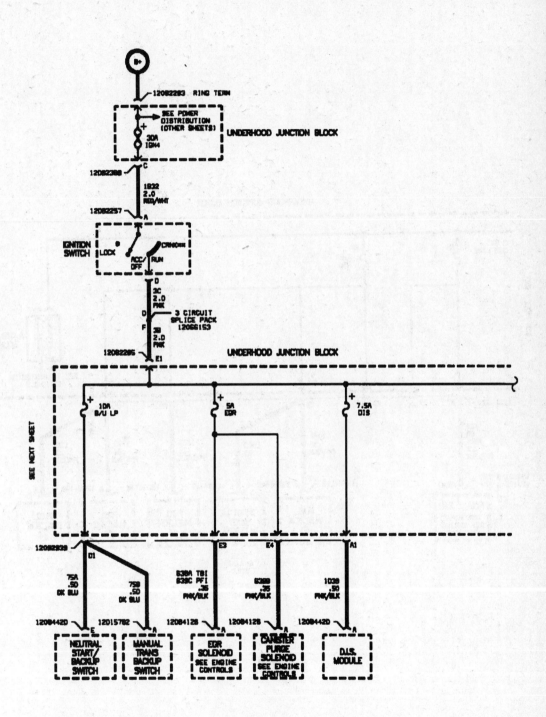

Fig. 284 Power distribution schematics — 1993

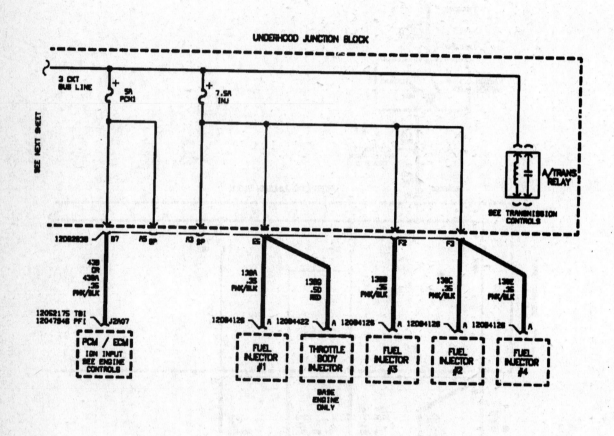

Fig. 285 Power distribution schematics — 1993

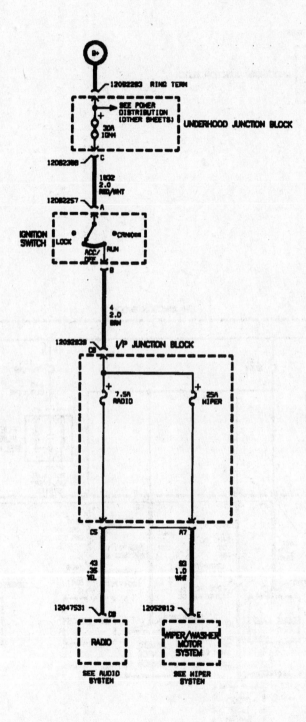

Fig. 286 Power distribution schematics — 1993

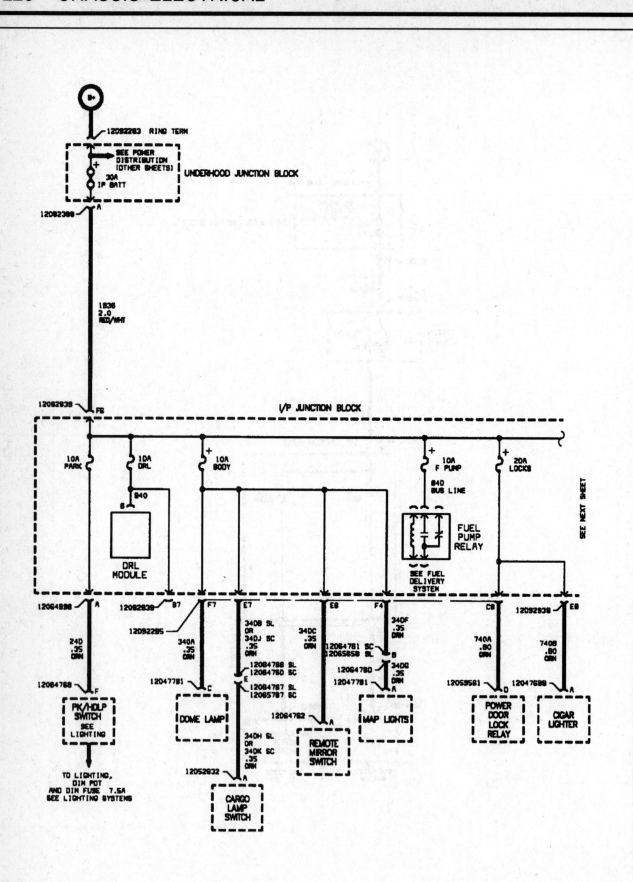

Fig. 287 Power distribution schematics — 1993

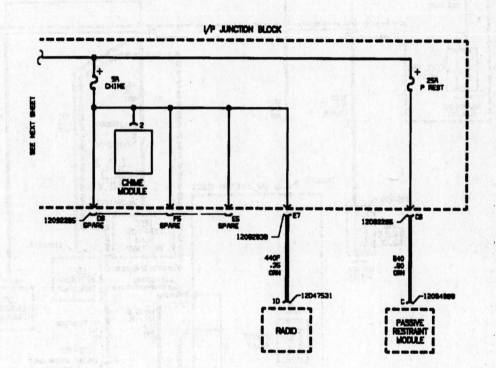

Fig. 288 Power distribution schematics — 1993

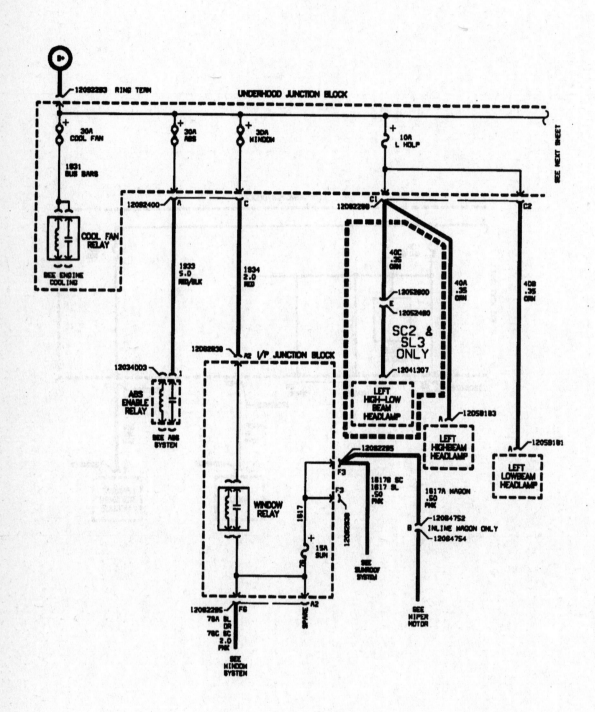

Fig. 289 Power distribution schematics — 1993

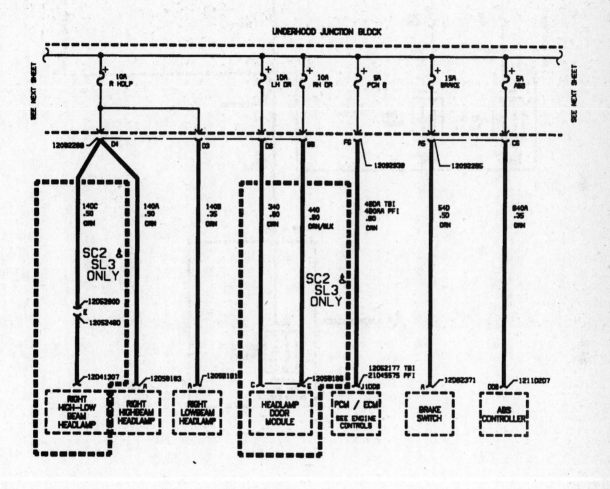

Fig. 290 Power distribution schematics — 1993

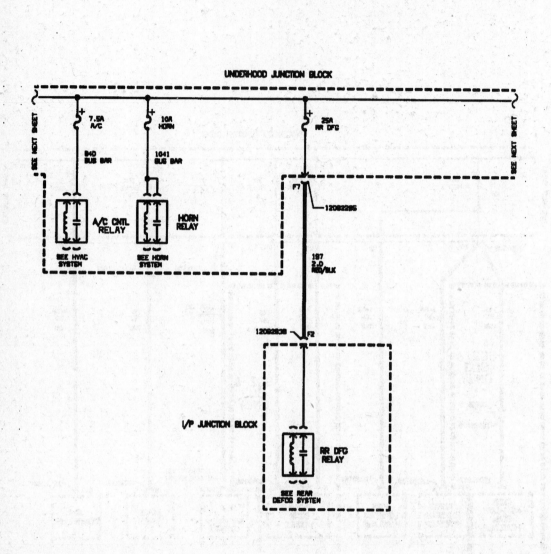

Fig. 291 Power distribution schematics — 1993

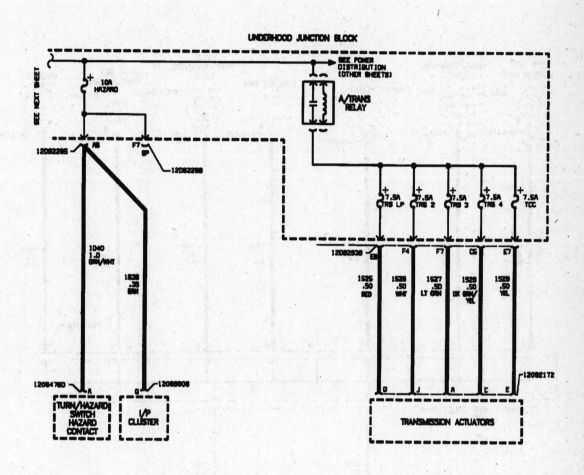

UNDERHOOD JUNCTION BLOCK

Fig. 292 Power distribution schematics — 1993

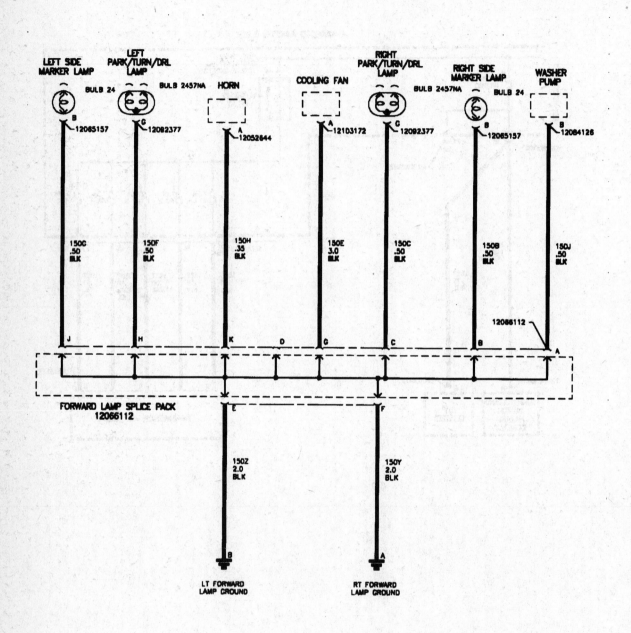

Fig. 293 Forward lamp harness ground schematics — 1991 sedan

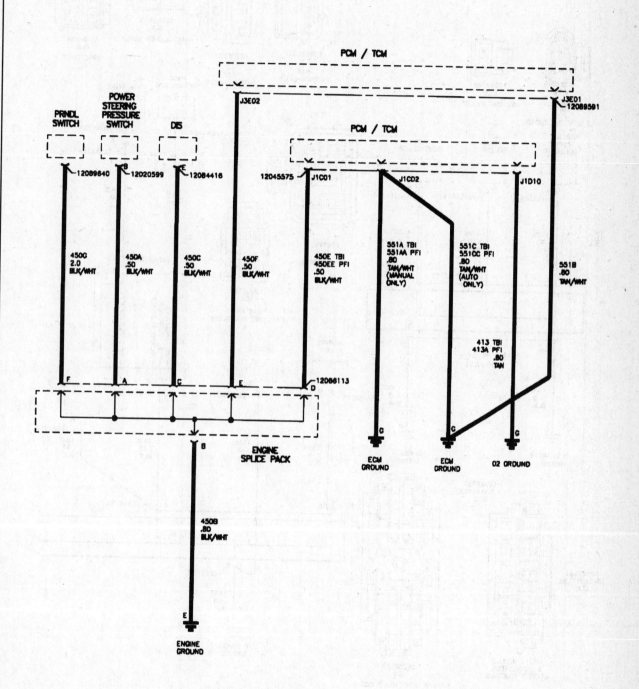

Fig. 294 Engine harness ground schematics — 1991 sedan

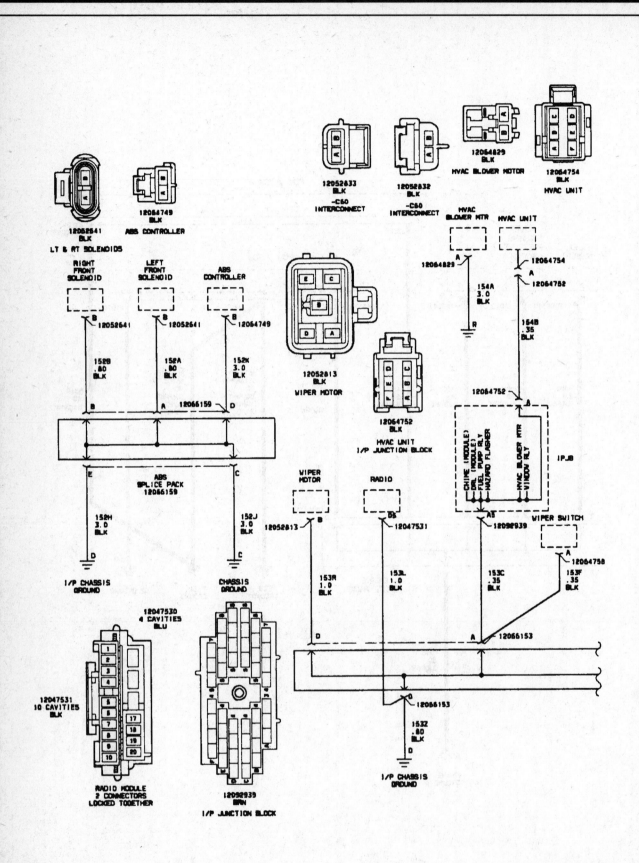

Fig. 295 HVAC/ABS/wiper and underhood ground schematics — 1991 sedan

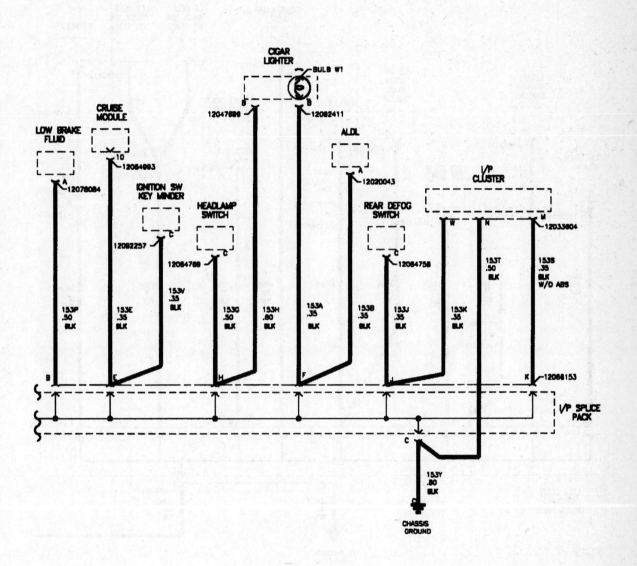

Fig. 296 Instrument panel splice pack ground schematics — 1991 sedan

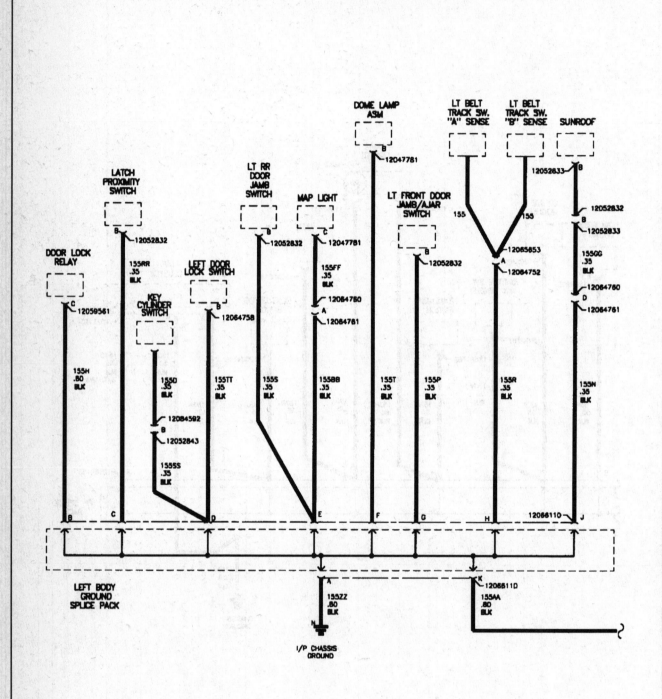

Fig. 297 Left body splice pack ground schematics — 1991 sedan

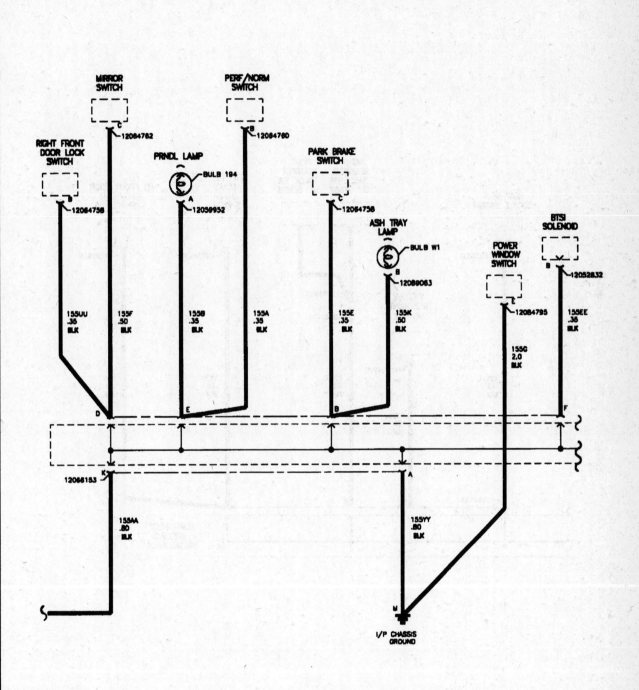

Fig. 298 Right body splice pack ground schematics — 1991 sedan

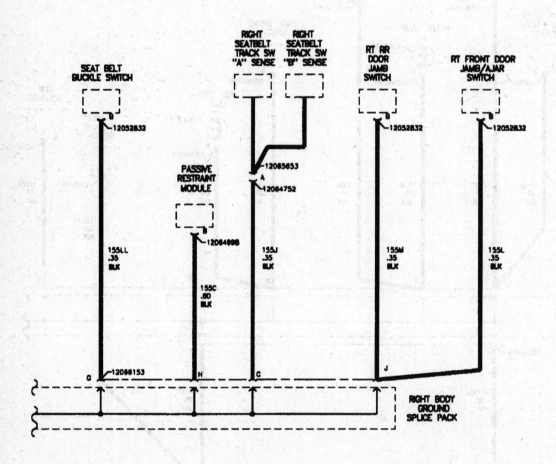

Fig. 299 Right body splice pack ground schematics — 1991 sedan

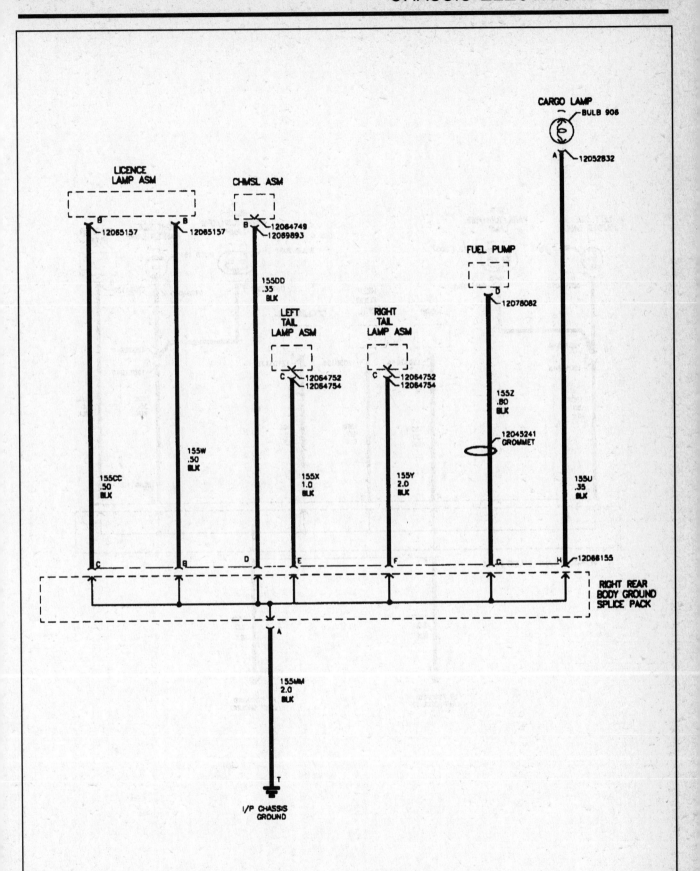

Fig. 300 Right rear splice pack ground schematics — 1991 sedan

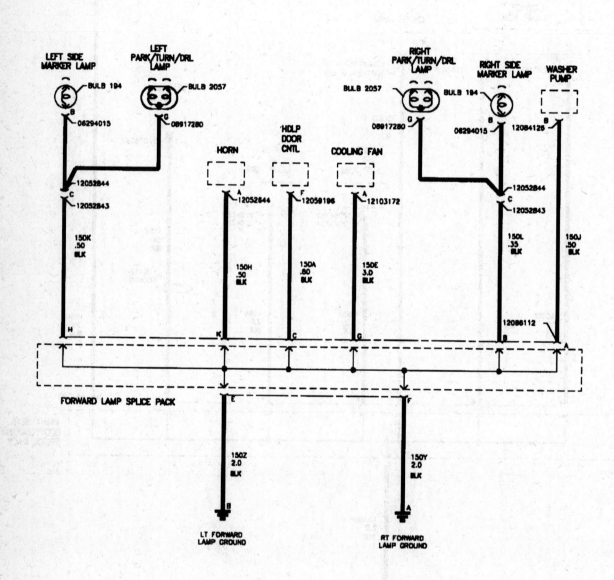

Fig. 301 Forward lamp harness ground schematics — 1991 coupe

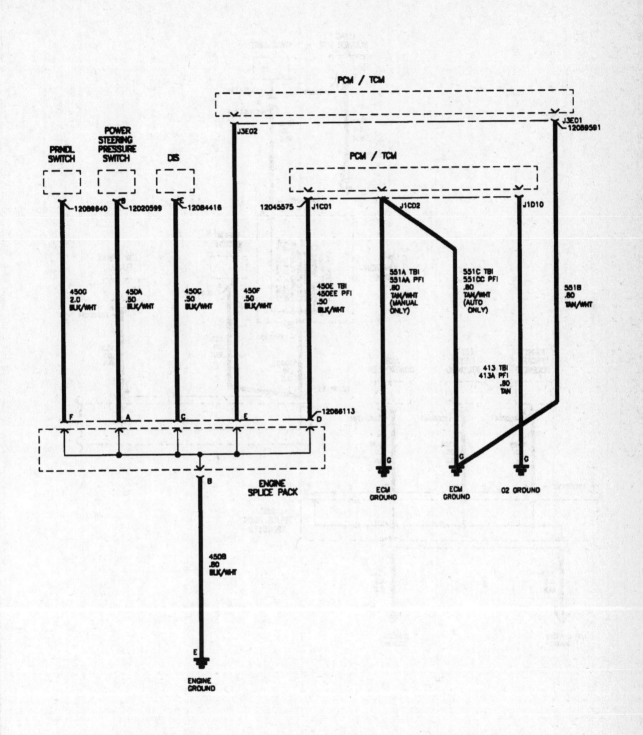

Fig. 302 Engine harness ground schematics — 1991 coupe

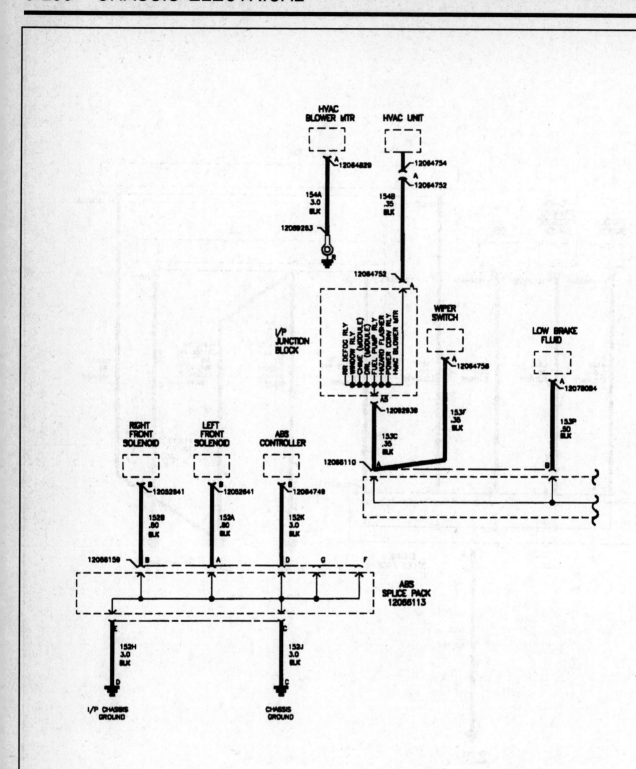

Fig. 303 HVAC/ABS/wiper and underhood ground schematics — 1991 coupe

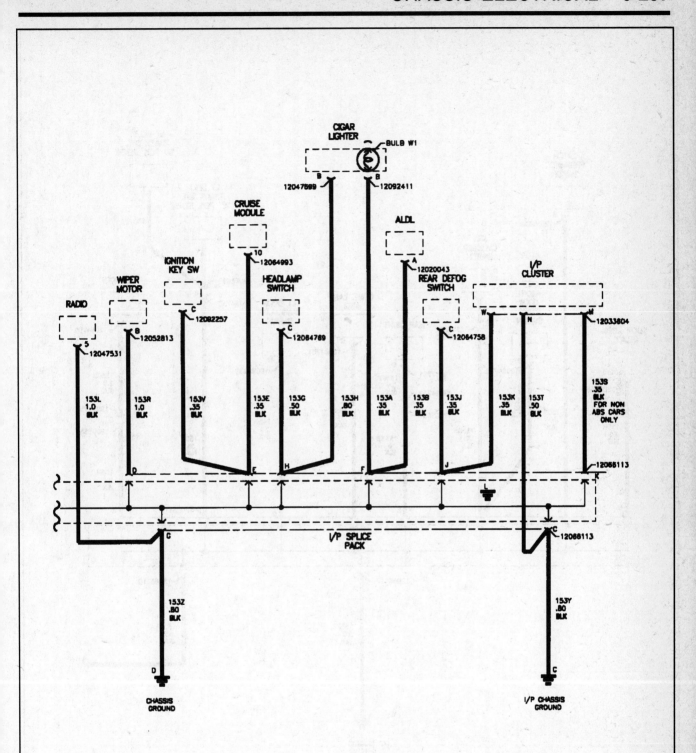

Fig. 304 Instrument panel splice pack ground schematics — 1991 coupe

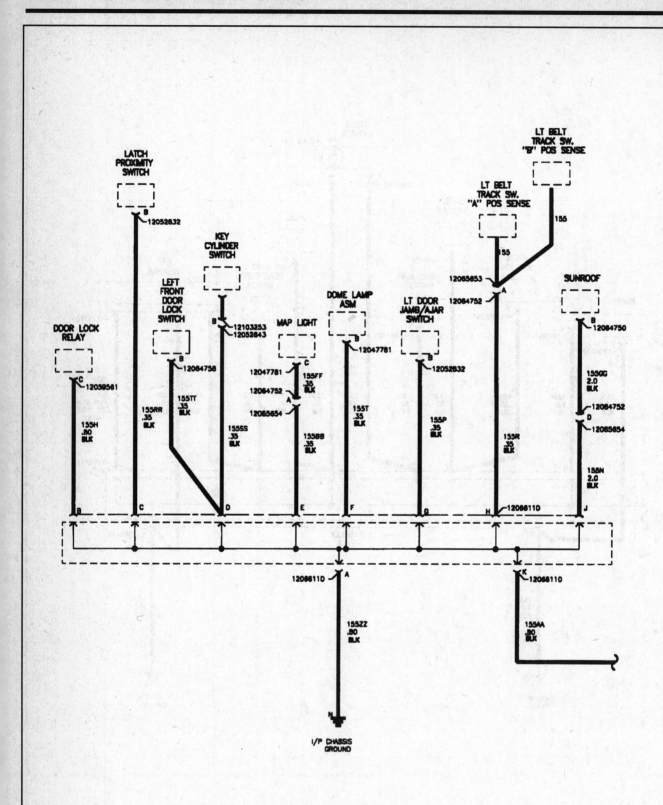

Fig. 305 Left body splice pack ground schematics — 1991 coupe

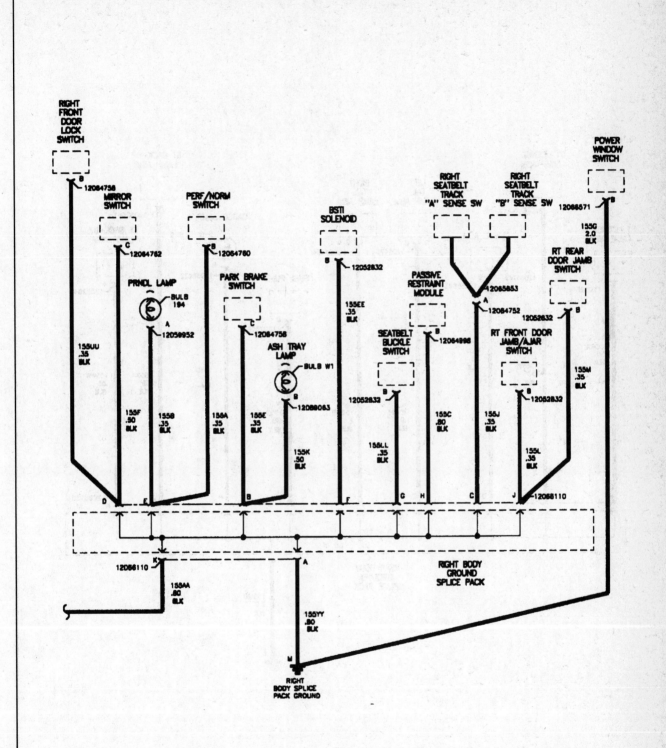

Fig. 306 Right body splice pack ground schematics — 1991 coupe

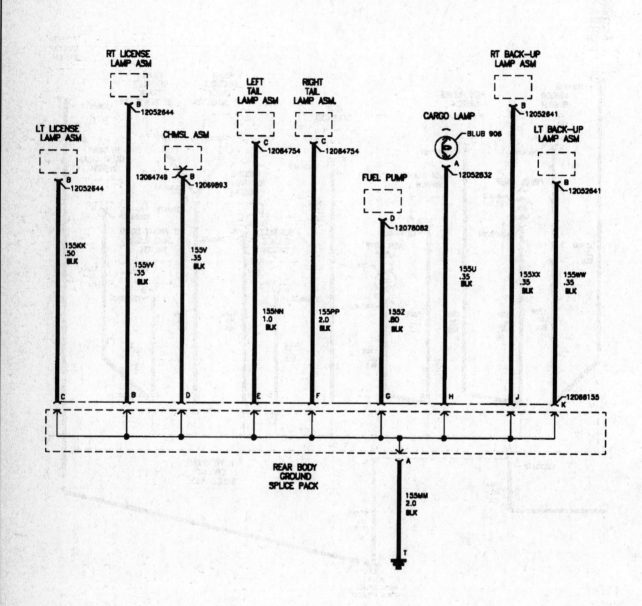

Fig. 307 Rear body splice pack ground schematics — 1991 coupe

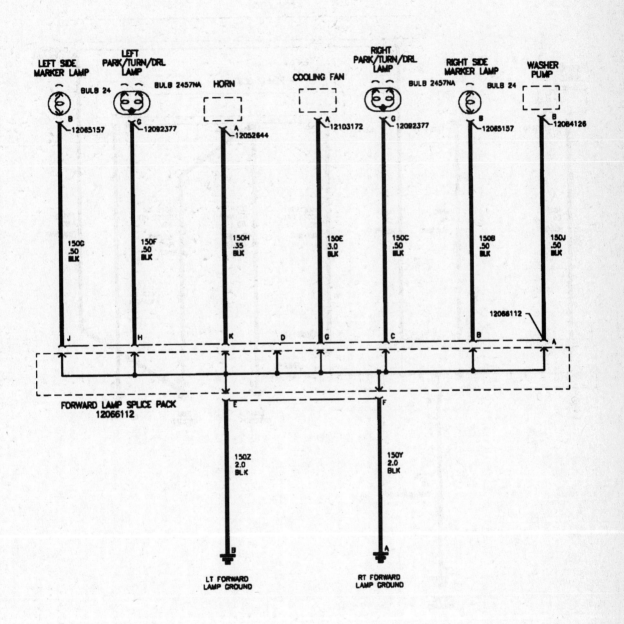

Fig. 308 Forward lamp harness ground schematics — 1992 sedan

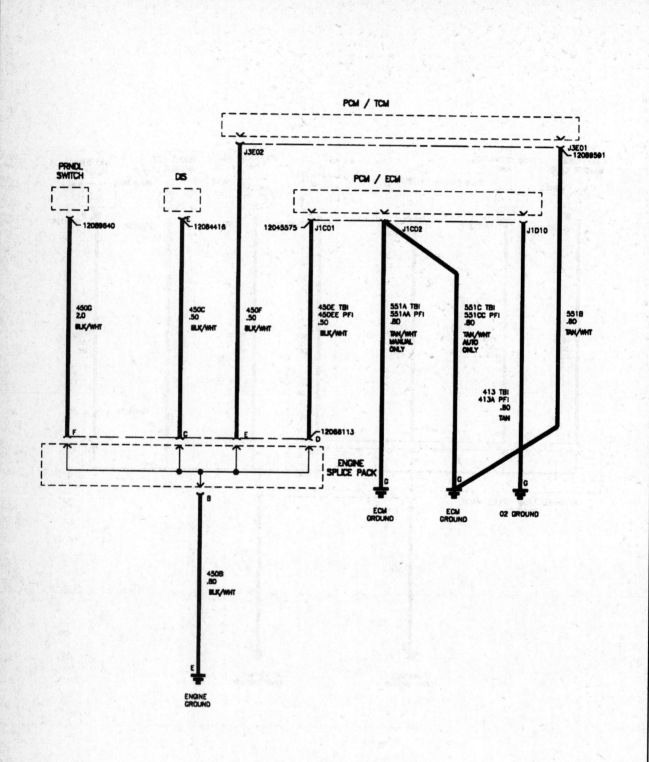

Fig. 309 Engine harness ground schematics — 1992 sedan

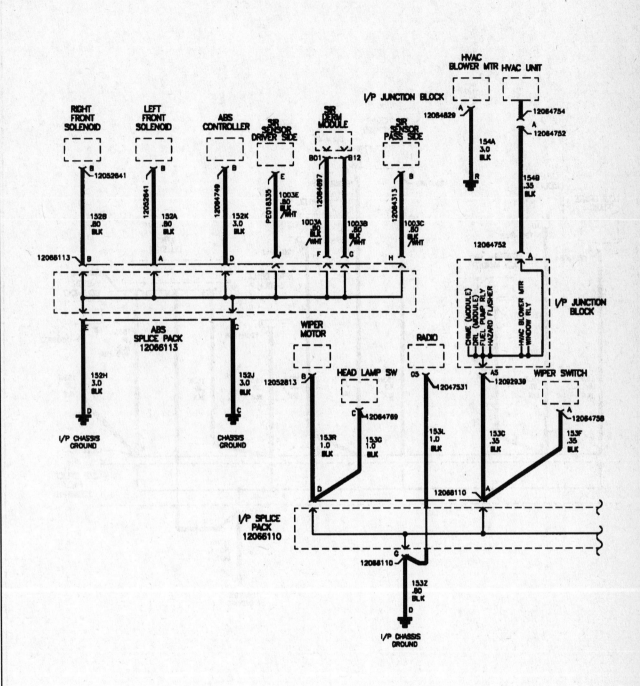

Fig. 310 HVAC/ABS/wiper and underhood ground schematics — 1992 sedan

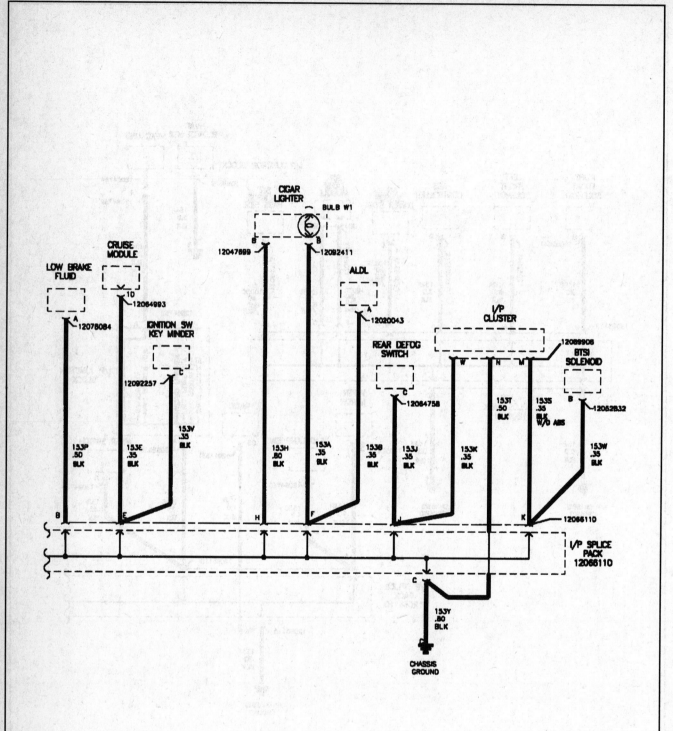

Fig. 311 Instrument panel splice pack ground schematics — 1992 sedan

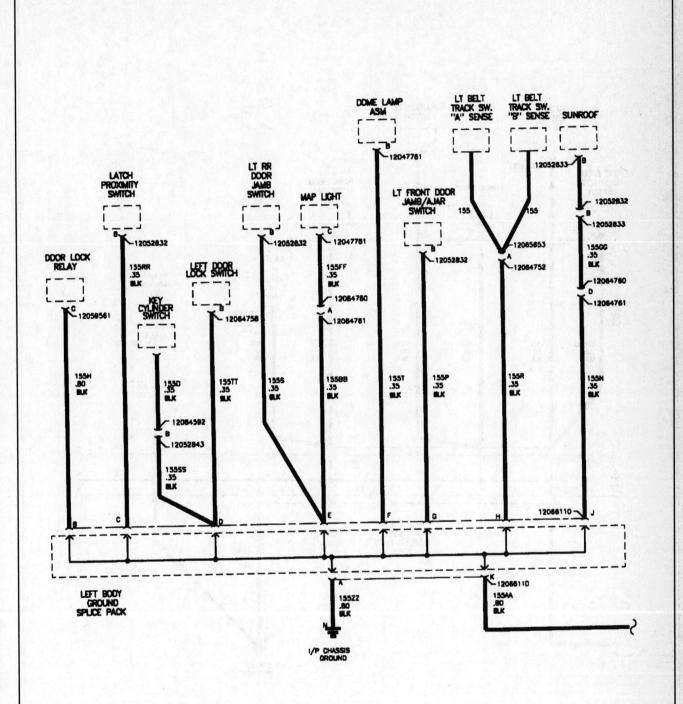

Fig. 312 Left body splice pack ground schematics — 1992 sedan

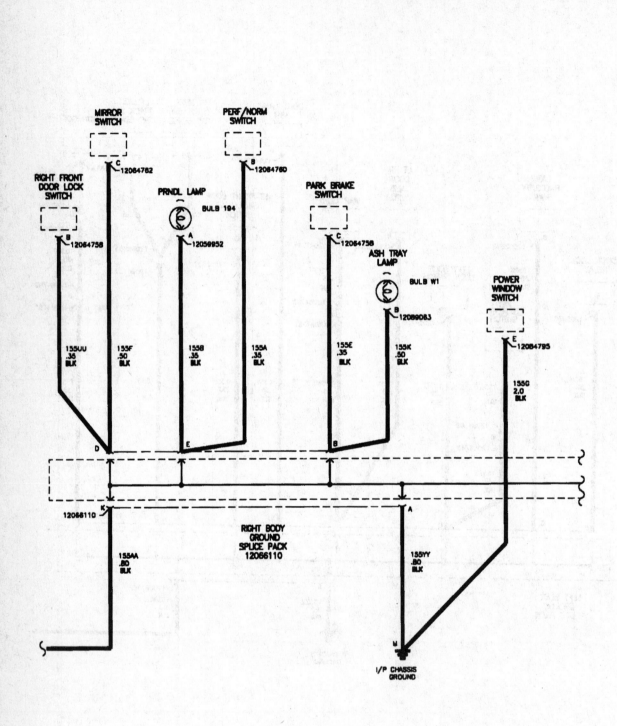

Fig. 313 Right body splice pack ground schematics — 1992 sedan

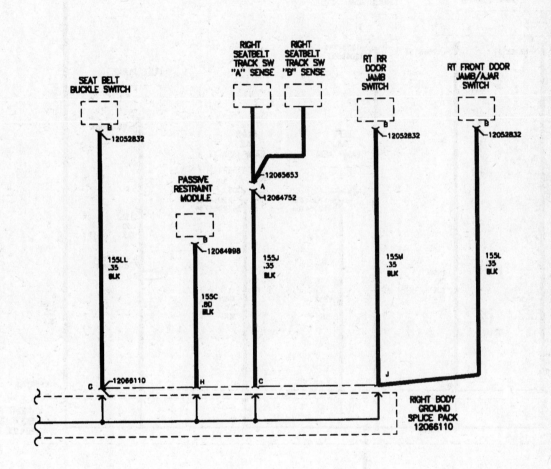

Fig. 314 Right body splice pack ground schematics — 1992 sedan

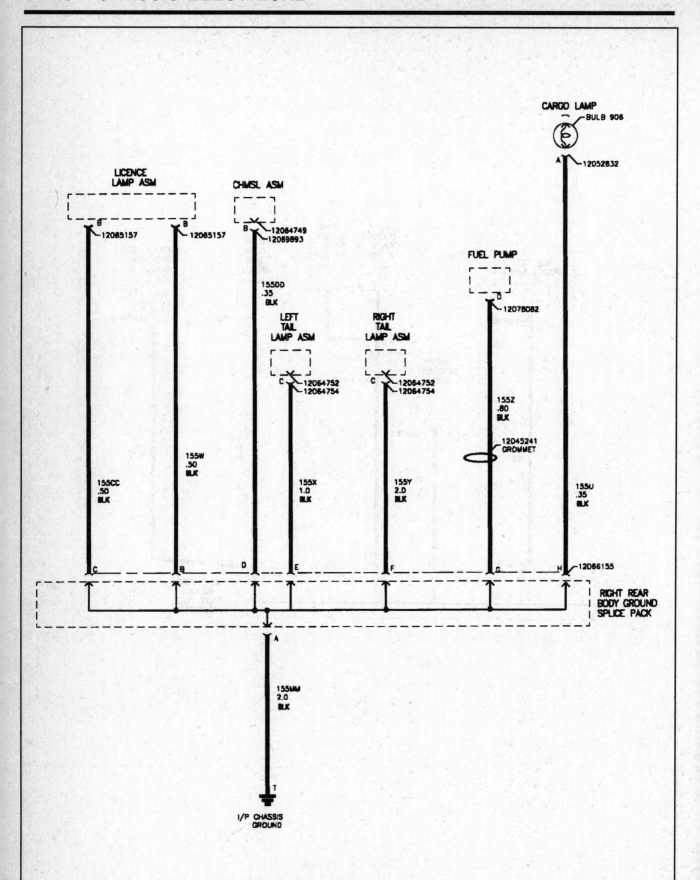

Fig. 315 Right rear splice pack ground schematics — 1992 sedan

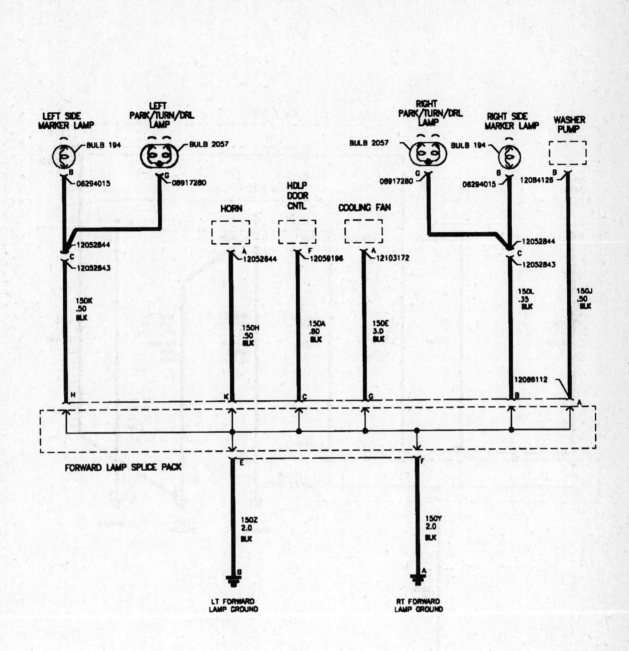

Fig. 316 Forward lamp harness ground schematics — 1992 coupe

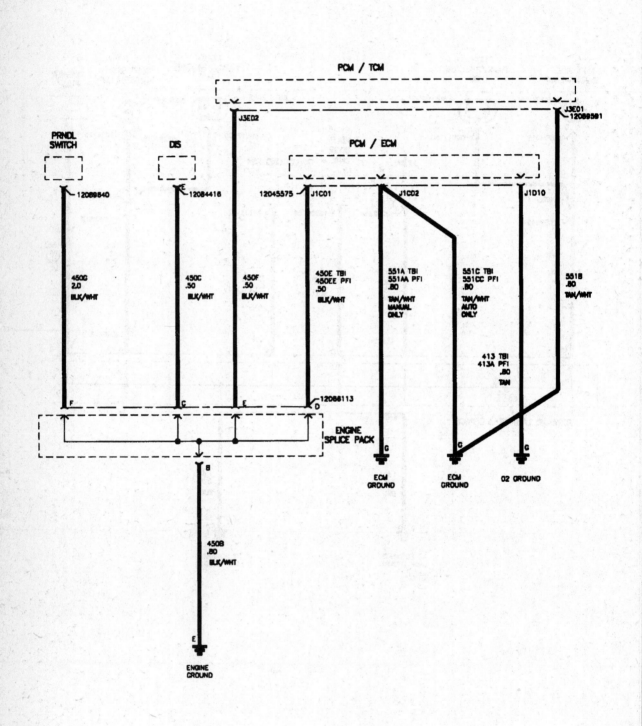

Fig. 317 Engine harness ground schematics — 1992 coupe

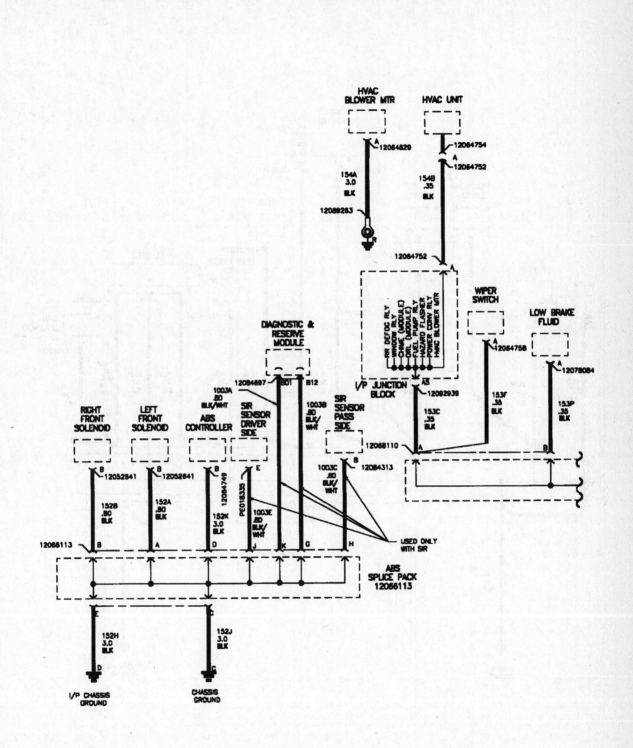

Fig. 318 HVAC/ABS/wiper and underhood ground schematics — 1992 coupe

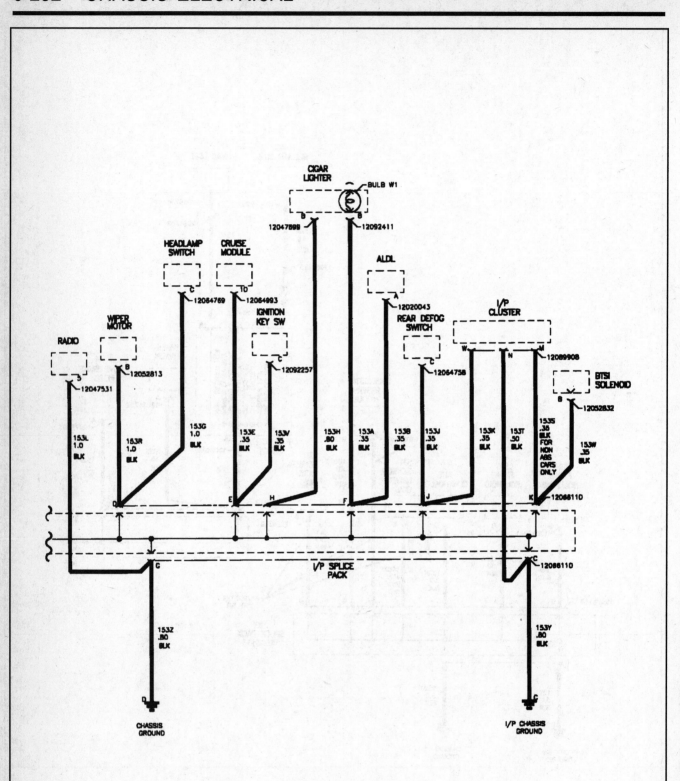

Fig. 319 Instrument panel splice pack ground schematics — 1992 coupe

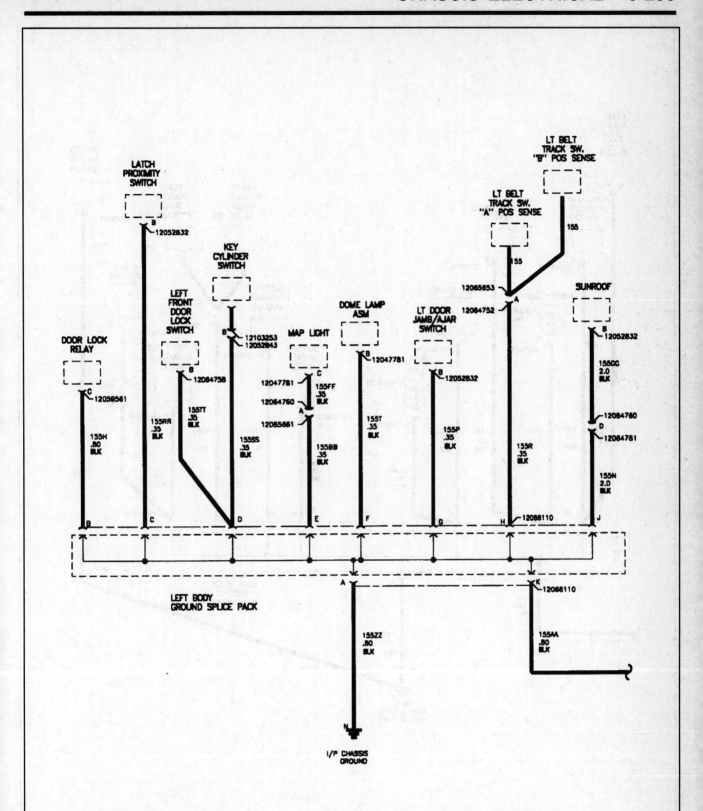

Fig. 320 Left body splice pack ground schematics — 1992 coupe

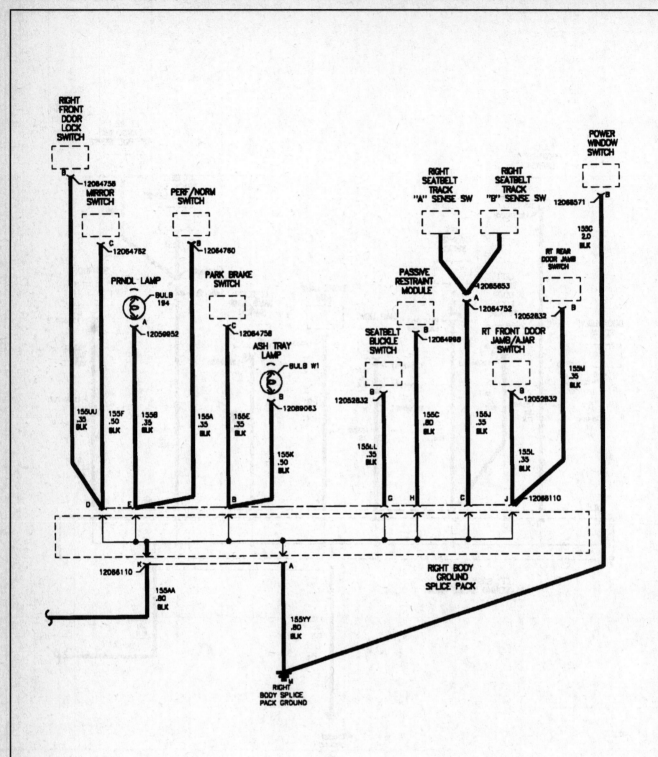

Fig. 321 Right body splice pack ground schematics — 1992 coupe

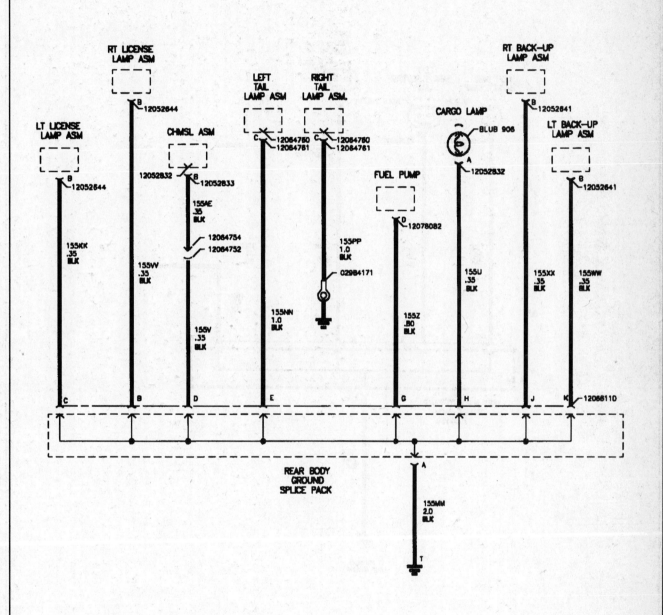

Fig. 322 Rear body splice pack ground schematics — 1992 coupe

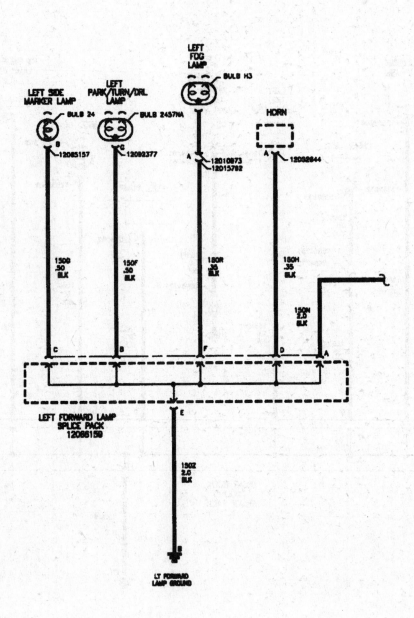

Fig. 323 Forward lamp harness ground schematics — 1993 sedan and wagon

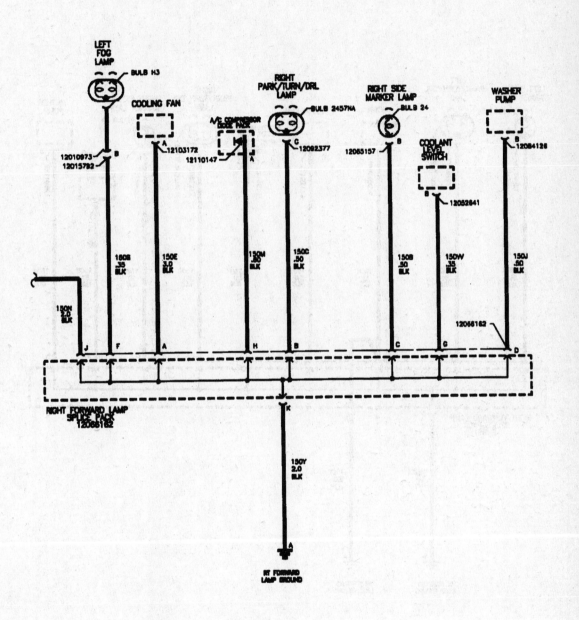

Fig. 324 Forward lamp harness ground schematics — 1993 sedan and wagon

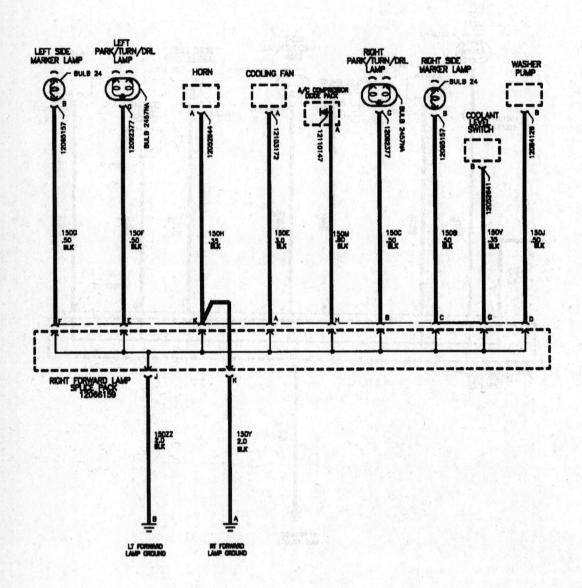

Fig. 325 Forward lamp harness ground schematics — 1993 sedan and wagon without fog lamps

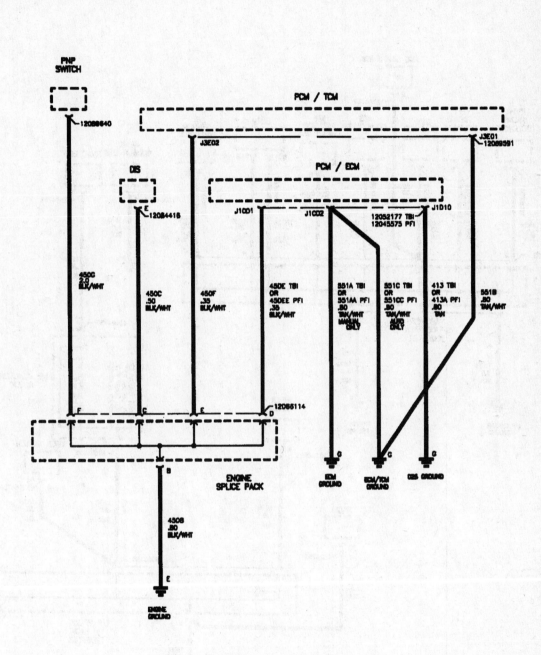

Fig. 326 Engine harness ground schematics — 1993 sedan and wagon

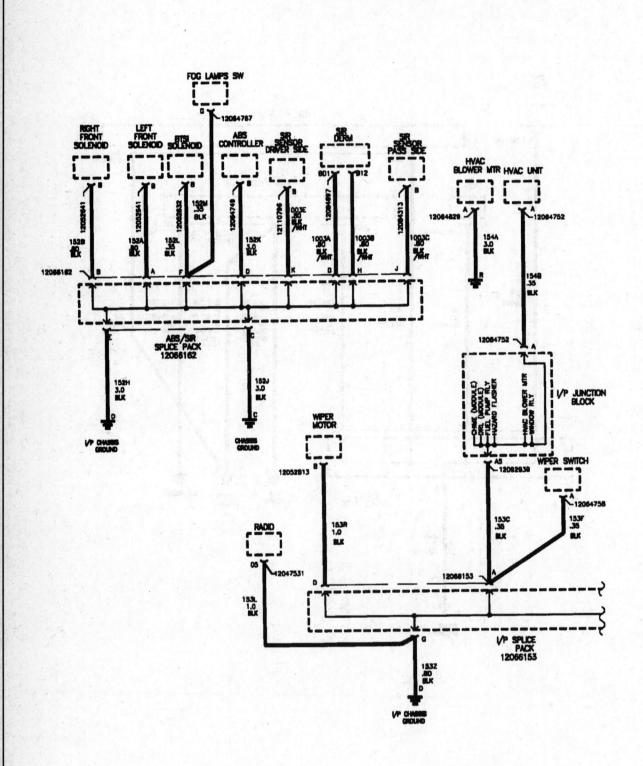

Fig. 327 ABS/SIR and instrument panel splice pack ground schematics — 1993 sedan and wagon

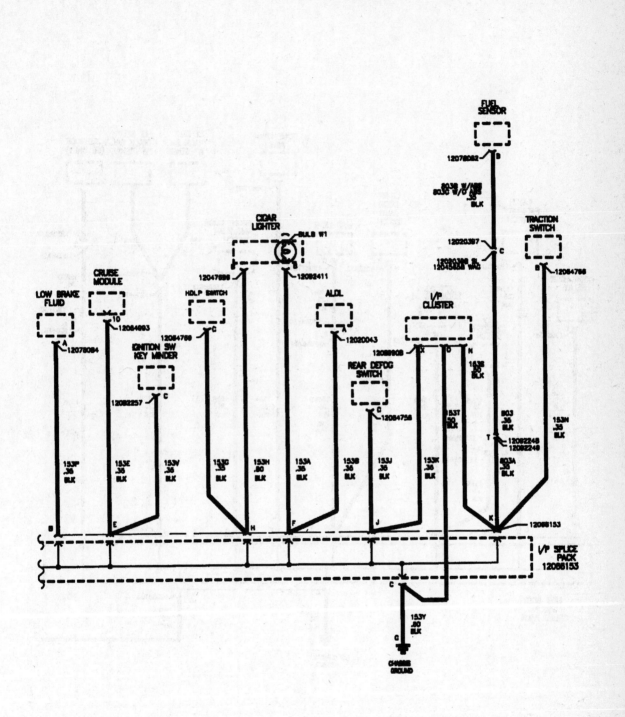

Fig. 328 Instrument panel splice pack ground schematics — 1993 sedan and wagon

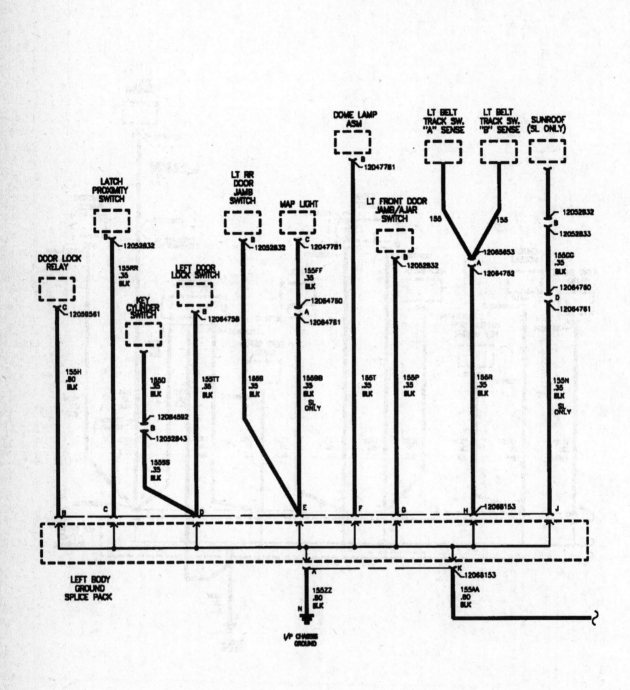

Fig. 329 Left body splice pack schematics — 1993 sedan and wagon

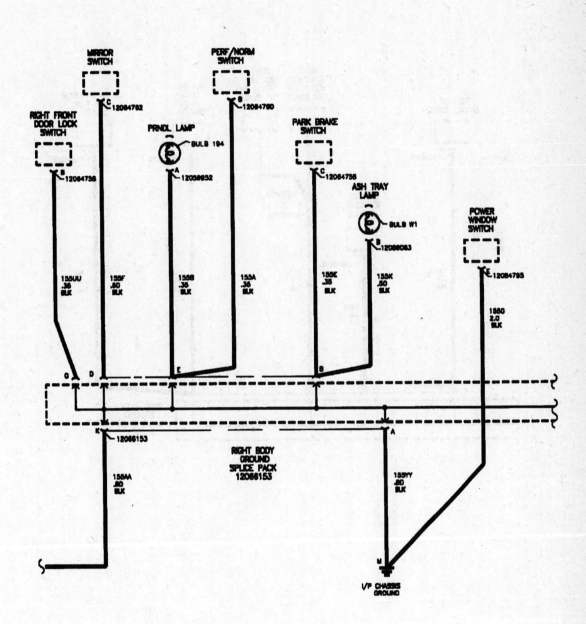

Fig. 330 Right body splice pack schematics — 1993 sedan and wagon

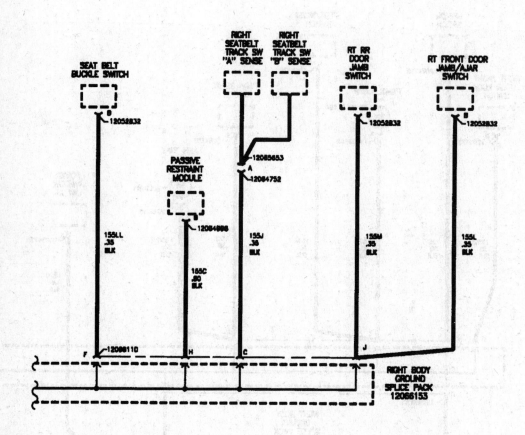

Fig. 331 Right body splice pack elchematics — 1993 sedan and wagon

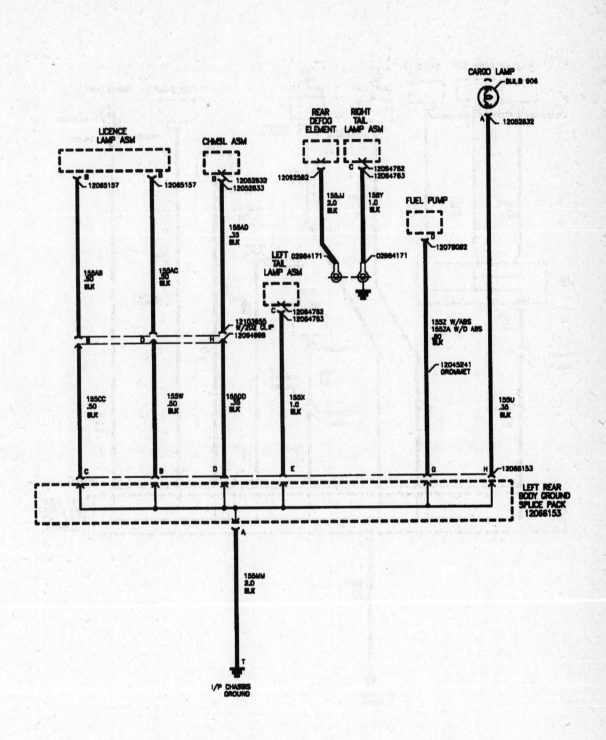

Fig. 332 Rear body splice pack schematics — 1993 sedan

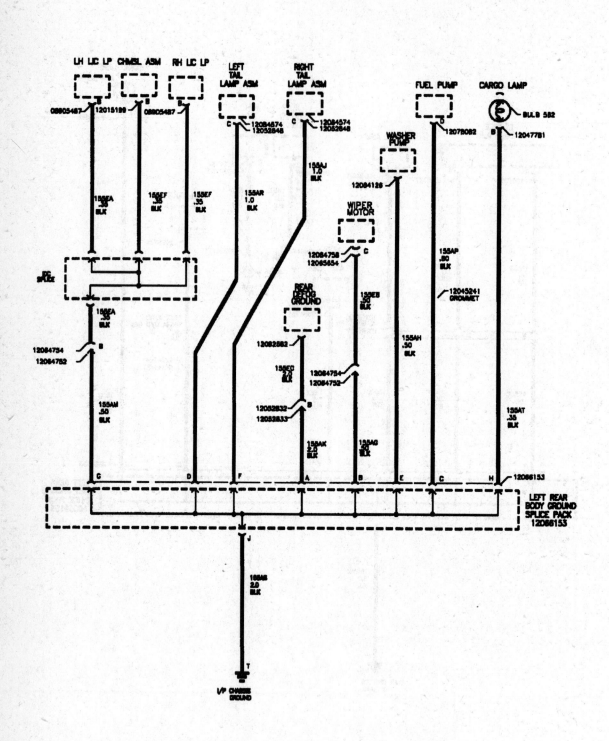

Fig. 333 Rear body splice pack schematics — 1993 wagon

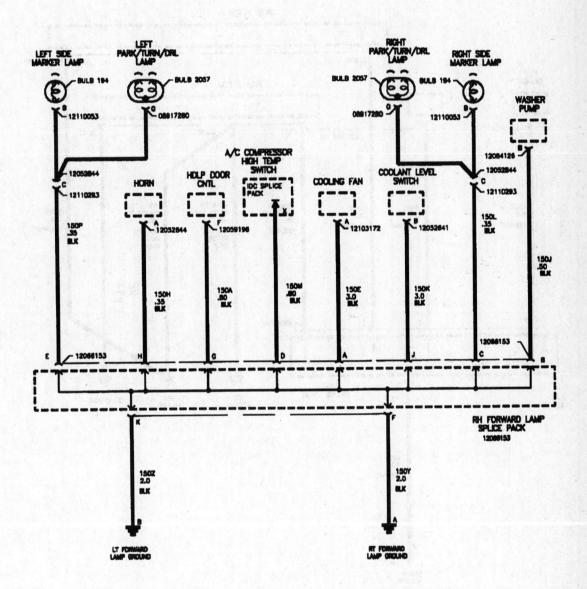

Fig. 334 Forward lamp harness ground schematics — 1993 coupe

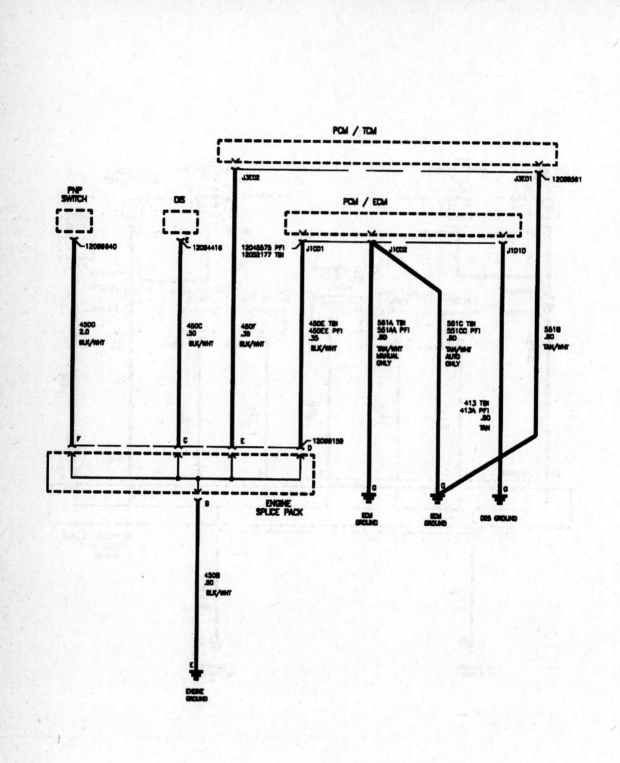

Fig. 335 Engine harness ground schematics — 1993 coupe

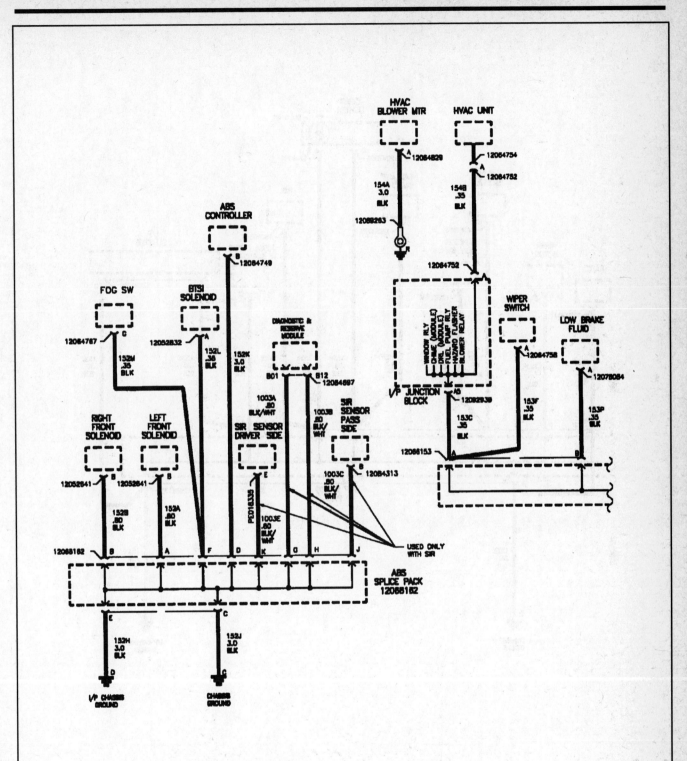

Fig. 336 ABS/SIR and instrument panel splice pack ground schematics — 1993 coupe

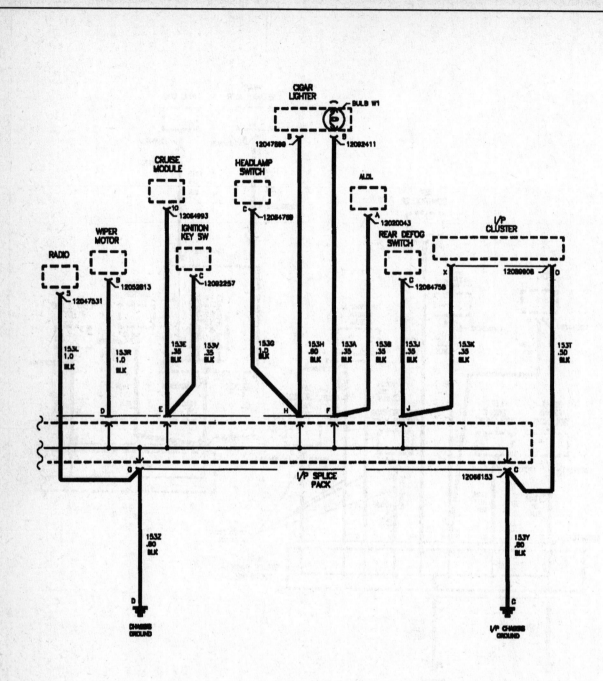

Fig. 337 Instrument panel splice pack ground schematics — 1993 coupe

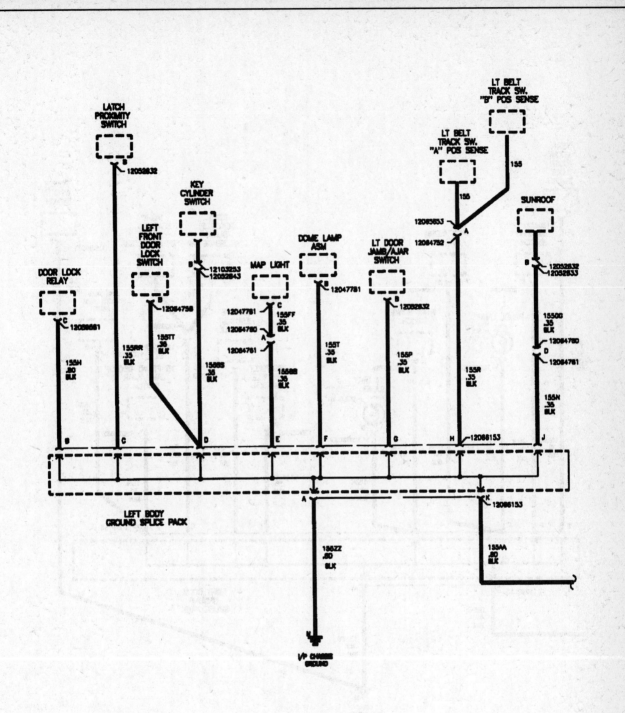

Fig. 338 Left body splice pack schematics — 1993 coupe

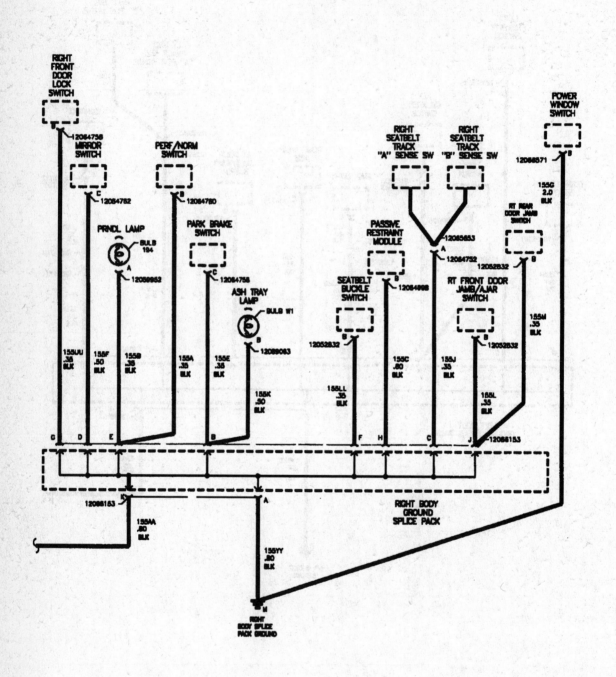

Fig. 339 Right body splice pack schematics — 1993 coupe

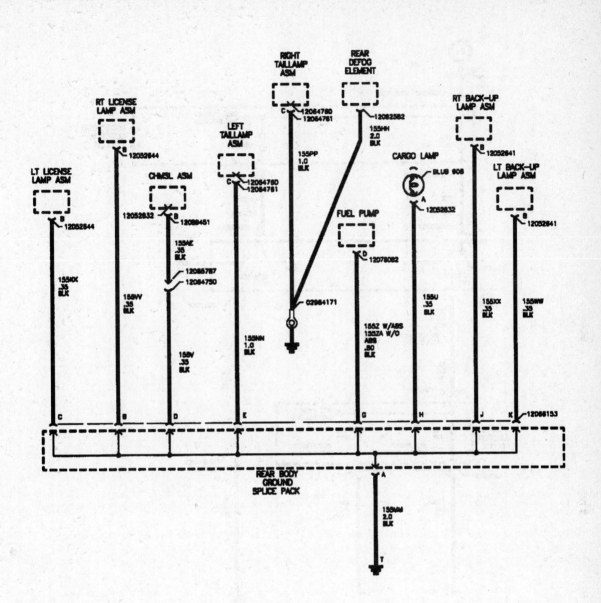

Fig. 340 Rear body splice pack schematics — 1993 coupe

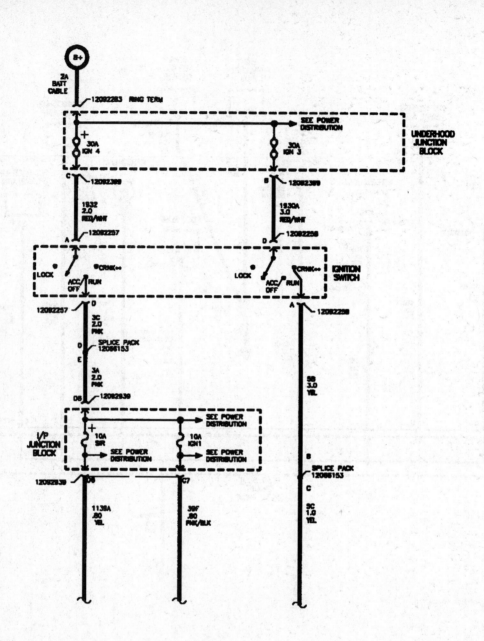

Fig. 341 Supplemental inflatable restraint system schematics

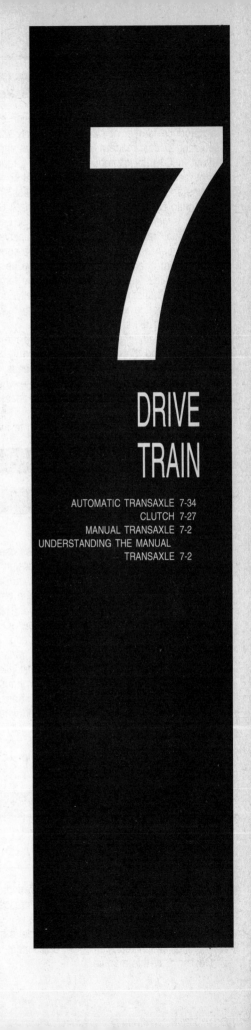

7

DRIVE
TRAIN

UNDERSTANDING THE MANUAL TRANSAXLE

Because of the way an internal combustion engine breathes, it can produce torque, or twisting force, only within a narrow speed range. Most modern, overhead valve engines must turn at about 2,500 rpm to produce their peak torque. By 4,500 rpm they are producing so little torque that continued increases in engine speed produce no power increases. The torque peak on overhead camshaft engines, with which all Saturns are equipped, is generally much higher, but much narrower.

The manual transaxle and clutch are employed to vary the relationship between engine speed and the speed of the wheels so that adequate engine power can be produced under all circumstances. The clutch allows engine torque to be applied to the transaxle input shaft gradually, due to mechanical slippage. Consequently, the car may be started smoothly from a full stop.

The transaxle changes the ratio between the rotating speeds of the engine and the wheels by the use of gears. All Saturn manual transaxles are equipped with 5-speeds. The gear ratios allow full engine power to be applied to the wheels during acceleration at low speeds and at highway/passing speeds.

The transaxle contains an input shaft which passes all the way through the transaxle, from the clutch to the fifth or overdrive gear located in the rear housing. On rear wheel drive transmissions, this shaft is separated at one point, so that front and rear portions can turn at different speeds. The rear portion would then be called the mainshaft, which normally be turned by a countershaft. The countershaft, located beneath the main and input shafts, is driven by the input shaft drive gear.

In a front wheel drive transaxle, power is transmitted from the input shaft to a mainshaft or output shaft located slightly beneath and to the side of the input shaft. The gears of the mainshaft mesh with gears on the input shaft, allowing power to be carried from one to the other. All forward gears are in constant mesh by are free from rotating with the shaft unless the synchronizer and clutch is engaged. Shifting from one gear to the next causes one of the gears to be freed from rotating with the shaft and locks another to it. Gears are locked and unlocked by internal dog clutches which slide between the center of the gear and the shaft. The forward gears employ synchronizers; friction members which smoothly bring gear and shaft to the same speed before the toothed dog clutches are engaged.

MANUAL TRANSAXLE

Identification

▶ See Figures 1 and 2

There are two 5-speed manual transaxles used in all Saturn vehicles. They are virtually the same by design and differ internally almost only by gear ratio. The 2 transaxles are equipped with different ratio/toothed gears in order to best utilize the engines to which they are mated. The MP2 transaxle is found only on vehicles with the SOHC engine, while the MP3 came only with the DOHC engine.

If there is a question as to whether the transaxle in your vehicle is the original component, an identification code is stamped on the top of the transaxle clutch housing. The code includes information such as model year, transaxle type (MP2 or MP3), where the transaxle was built and when the unit was built. Once disassembled, there is another way to identify the transaxle. All gears from the MP3 have an identification groove on the outer diameter of the gear teeth. No such groove will appear on the gears of the MP2.

Adjustments

CLUTCH SWITCH

A safety switch is installed on the clutch pedal to prevent starting the engine unless the clutch is depressed. This will assure that the vehicle will not lurch if the key is accidentally turned to the start position while the vehicle is in gear.

For proper switch replacement or adjustment procedures, see Section 6 of this manual.

Back-up Light Switch

REMOVAL & INSTALLATION

▶ See Figure 3

1. Disconnect the negative battery cable.
2. Unplug the switch electrical connector.
3. If necessary for access on ABS equipped vehicles, remove the air intake tube.
4. Loosen the switch and remove it from the transaxle shift housing.
5. Installation is the reverse of removal. Tighten the switch to 17 ft. lbs. (23 Nm).

Shift/Selector Cables

REMOVAL & INSTALLATION

▶ See Figures 4, 5, 6, 7 and 8

1. Disconnect the negative battery cable.
2. Remove the air intake tube. For the DOHC engine, lift the resonator upward to release it from the engine support bracket.
3. Note the position of the cables on the shifter arms. If necessary tag the cables for installation purposes. Remove the small retainers from the cable ends and the cable ends from the shift arms, then remove the large cable clutch housing retaining clips.

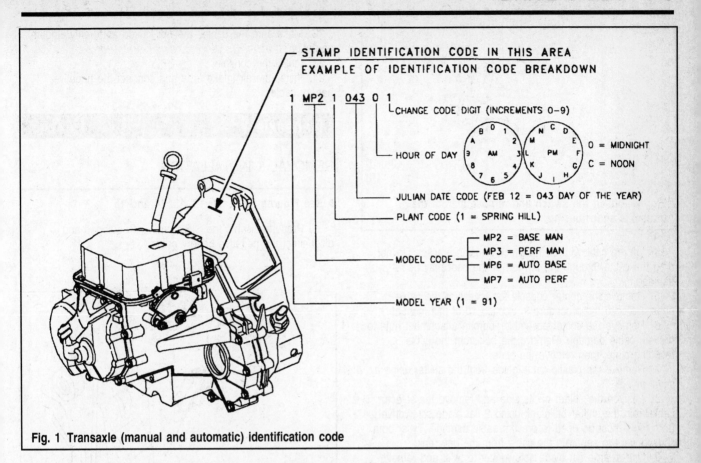

Fig. 1 Transaxle (manual and automatic) identification code

	MP2 (Base) Transaxle Teeth	MP3 (Performance) Transaxle Teeth			MP2 (Base) Transaxle Ratios	MP3 (Performance) Transaxle Ratios
			1st Gear:		3.077	3.250
1st Drive:	13	12	2nd Gear:		1.810	2.056
1st Driven:	40	39	3rd Gear:		1.207	1.423
2nd Drive:	21	18	4th Gear:		0.861	1.033
2nd Driven:	38	37	5th Gear:		0.643	0.730
3rd Drive:	29	26	Reverse Gear:		2.923	2.923
3rd Driven:	35	37	Final Drive Ratio:		4.063	4.063
4th Drive:	36	31				
4th Driven:	31	32				
5th Drive:	42	37				
5th Driven:	27	27				
Reverse Drive:	13	13				
Reverse Idler:	31	31				
Reverse Driven:	38	38				

Fig. 2 Manual transaxle gear identification

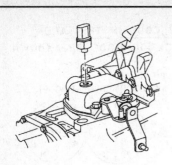

Fig. 3 Loosen the switch and remove it from the transaxle shift housing

4. Lift the cable out of the clutch housing bracket. Do not drag the cable through the bracket or the boot may be damaged.

5. Remove the center console for access to the cable ends. Refer to the procedure in Section 10 of this manual.

6. Remove the shifter assembly floorpan attachment nuts to prevent cable damage. Remove the bolt from the cable retaining plate, then remove the plate.

7. Remove the plastic cable guide from the shifter using a small prybar.

8. Position the shifter on its side and remove the selector cable from the shifter bellcrank using 2 flat blade screwdrivers. Both tools must be used to prevent cable damage. Twist both screwdrivers to separate the cable from the bellcrank.

9. Use a large flat blade screwdriver to twist and remove the shift cable end as shown.

10. Separate the sound deadening material from the front of the dash. For cable removal, it is necessary to make a 3 in. cut in the sound deadener in order to allow it to roll back enough to remove the cable grommet.

11. Lift the front of the vehicle and support safely using jackstands.

12. Remove the 2 retaining nuts, then remove the cable grommet from the front of the dash by pushing the grommet and retaining plate into the vehicle.

13. Remove the cables from the vehicle.

To install:

14. Separate and fold back the sound deadener from the front of the dash, then place the cables and the retaining plate through the dash, align the grommet pilot with the dash and push the grommet into the opening. Installation material should not become trapped between the grommet and the dash.

15. Position the retaining plate over the studs, then install the retaining nuts and tighten to 62 inch lbs. (7 Nm).

16. Remove the jackstands and carefully lower the vehicle.

17. Insert the cables onto the housing, making sure that they are not crossed or kinked. With the knurls facing upward, connect the cables to the shift arms and install the retainers.

18. Connect the cables to the shifter assembly using a pair of channel lock pliers to snap the cable end socket into the ball. Be careful not to bend the push rods or the shifter assembly will not function properly.

19. Position the shifter assembly to the floorpan, then install the retaining nuts and tighten to 18 ft. lbs. (25 Nm).

20. Install the cable retainer bracket and tighten the retaining bolt to 89 inch lbs. (10 Nm).

21. Install the plastic cable guide to the shifter.

22. Make sure the cables are not kinked and verify smooth operation.

23. Install the console.

24. Install the air intake tube and connect the negative battery cable.

Transaxle

REMOVAL & INSTALLATION

▶ **See Figures 9, 10, 11, 12, 13, 14 and 15**

1. Properly disable the SIR system, if equipped and disconnect the negative battery cable.

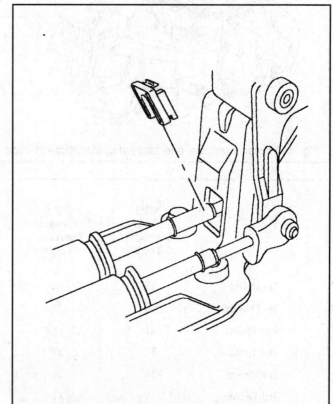

Fig. 4 Remove the plastic cable guide from the shifter

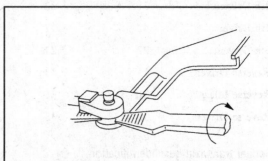

Fig. 5 Use 2 flat blade screwdrivers to separate the selector cable from the bellcrank

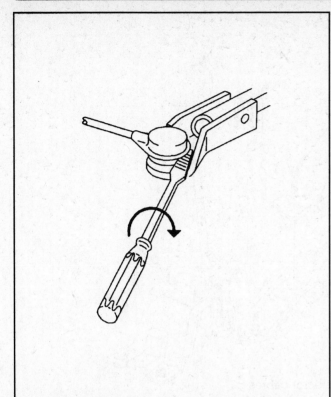

Fig. 6 Use a large flat blade screwdriver to twist and remove the shift cable

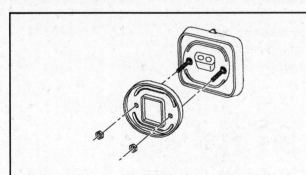

Fig. 7 Remove the cable grommet from the front of the dash

2. Remove the 2 air inlet duct fasteners, disconnect the air temperature sensor connector and remove the air inlet duct. For the DOHC engine, loosen the flex tube to air box clamp, remove the 3 air box fasteners and remove the air box.

3. For 1992-93 vehicles, remove the transaxle strut-to-cradle bracket through bolt located on the radiator side of the transaxle.

4. Disconnect the back-up light switch and vehicle speed sensor electrical connectors from the transaxle. Remove the vent tube retaining clip and discard if damaged.

5. Remove the 2 ground terminals from the top 2 clutch housing studs, then unclip the oxygen sensor wire from the clutch housing.

6. For DOHC engines, remove the nut from the cradle to front engine cable bracket at the front right corner of the cradle, below the water pump.

7. Remove the top 2 clutch housing studs.

8. Remove the 4 DIS coil to clutch housing bolts, then wire the coil to the cylinder head coolant outlet in order to keep it out of the way. Discard the old coil retaining bolts and replace with new bolts upon installation.

9. For 1991 vehicles, loosen the 2 front transaxle mount-to-transaxle bolts.

10. Remove the shifter cables from the shift arms and clutch housing taking care not to damage the cable bolt.

11. Rotate the clutch slave cylinder ¼ turn counterclockwise while pushing into the clutch housing, then remove the cylinder from the housing. Remove the 2 clutch hydraulic damper-to-clutch housing bolts, then wire the hydraulic assembly to the battery tray.

12. Wire the radiator to the upper radiator support to hold the assembly in place when the cradle is removed.

13. Install SA9105E or an equivalent engine support bar assembly. Make sure the support feet are positioned on the outer edge of the shock tower, the bar hooks are connected to the engine bracket and the stabilizer foot is on the engine blots.

14. Raise the front of the vehicle sufficiently to lower the transaxle and the engine cradle. Support the vehicle safely using jackstands. Make sure the jackstands are not positioned under the engine cradle. Remove the drain plug from the lower center of the housing and drain the transaxle fluid into a clean container.

15. Remove the front wheels and the left, right and center splash shields from the vehicle. For coupes, remove the left and right lower facia braces.

16. For 1992-93 vehicles, remove the front engine strut cradle bracket to cradle nuts from below the cradle.

17. Remove the transaxle mount to cradle nut from under the cradle.

18. Remove the front exhaust pipe nuts at the manifold, then disconnect the pipe from the support bracket.

19. Remove the front pipe-to-catalytic converter bolts and lower the pipe from the vehicle.

20. Remove the engine-to-transaxle stiffening bracket bolts and remove the bracket. For 1991 vehicles, remove the rear transaxle mount bracket to transaxle bolt, then loosen the mount bolt and allow the bracket to hang out of the way.

21. Remove the clutch housing dust cover. Remove the steering rack to cradle bolts and wire the gear for support when cradle is removed. Remove the brake line and retainer from the cradle.

22. Remove and discard the cotter pin from the lower ball joints. Back the ball joint nut until the top of the nut is even with the top of the threads.

23. Use tool SA9132S to separate the ball joint from the lower control arm, then remove the nut. Do not use a wedge tool or seal damage may occur.

✳✳WARNING

The outer CV-joint for vehicles equipped with ABS contains a speed sensor ring. Use of an incorrect tool to separate the control arm from the knuckle may result in damage to and loss of the ABS system.

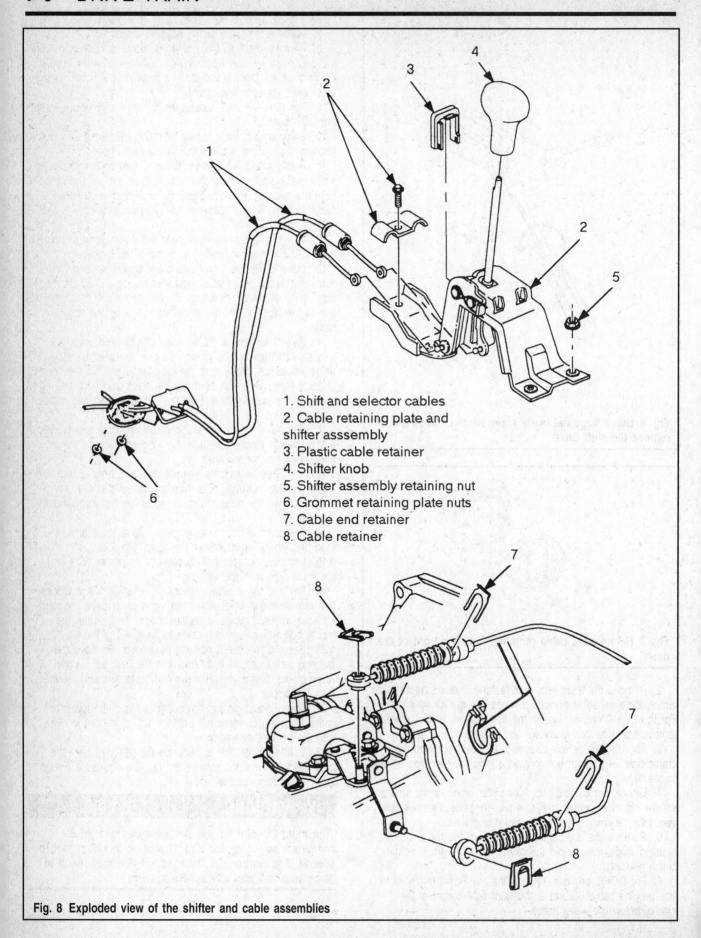

1. Shift and selector cables
2. Cable retaining plate and shifter asssembly
3. Plastic cable retainer
4. Shifter knob
5. Shifter assembly retaining nut
6. Grommet retaining plate nuts
7. Cable end retainer
8. Cable retainer

Fig. 8 Exploded view of the shifter and cable assemblies

24. For 1991 vehicles, remove the front transaxle mount-to-cradle nuts and the engine lower mount-to-cradle nuts. Nuts are all located under the front or side cradle members.

25. Position two 4 in. **x** 4 in. **x** 36 in. pieces of wood onto a powertrain support dolly, then position the dolly under the vehicle and against the cradle.

26. Remove the 4 cradle to body bolts and carefully lower the cradle from the vehicle with the support dolly. Tape or wire the 2 large washers from the rear cradle-to-body attachments in position to prevent loss.

27. Support the transaxle securely with a suitable jack.

28. Use an appropriate prybar to separate the left side axle from the transaxle. Remove the axle sufficiently to install SA91112T or an equivalent seal protector around the axle and into the seal to prevent the seal from being cut by the shaft spline.

29. Remove the 2 bottom clutch housing-to-engine bolts and install a guide bolt into the bottom rear clutch housing bolt hole from the side of the engine block.

30. Carefully separate the transaxle from the engine enough to clear the intermediate shaft and lower the transaxle from the vehicle.

To install:

31. Place the transaxle assembly securely onto the jack and position under the vehicle.

32. Install axle seal protectors into seals on both sides, then place the transaxle in any gear.

33. Raise the transaxle into the vehicle guiding the unit onto the intermediate shaft. While guiding the transaxle onto the shaft, rotate the shaft back and forth to align the splines. When aligned, continue to rotate the intermediate shaft until the input shaft splines are aligned with the clutch.

34. Verify that the intermediate shaft splines line up with the differential side gear spline, then install the 2 lower clutch housing-to-engine bolts and tighten to 96 ft. lbs. (130 Nm). The bolts should not be used to draw the transaxle to the engine.

35. Install the left side axle into the transaxle and remove the seal protectors. Lower the transaxle jack.

36. Clean and lubricate the ball joint threads, then raise the cradle up on the support dolly and place the ball joints into the knuckles.

37. Verify the correct positioning of the lower control arm bar studs to the knuckles, the cooling module support bushings, the engine strut bracket and the transaxle mount.

38. Insert 1/16 in. round steel rods into the cradle-to-body alignment holes near the front cradle-to-body fastener holes. Guide the cradle into position making sure all mount studs are properly guided into their holes.

39. Make sure the washers are in place and install the 2 rear cradle to body bolts. Verify proper cradle positioning and install the 2 front cradle bolts. Tighten the 4 cradle bolts to 151 ft. lbs. (205 Nm).

40. Remove the support dolly and, if necessary, lower the vehicle sufficiently for underhood access. Remove the engine support bar assembly.

41. For 1992-93 vehicles, install the transaxle strut-to-cradle bracket through bolt and nut, then tighten the fasteners to 52 ft. lbs. (70 Nm).

42. Remove the radiator assembly support wire.

43. Use a 6 **x** 1.0mm tap to clean the sealant from the ignition module mounting holes in the transaxle. Install the

ignition module and the new bolts coated with yellow sealant. Use extreme caution to assure proper bolt installation. Tighten the bolts to 61 inch lbs. (7 Nm) and verify that the bolt heads are properly seated on the ignition module.

44. Install the 2 top clutch housing-to-engine studs and tighten to 74 ft. lbs. (100 Nm). Connect the 2 ground terminals to the studs and tighten to 18 ft. lbs. (25 Nm).

45. Connect the vehicle speed sensor and back-up light switch electrical connectors to the transaxle.

46. Install the vent hose clip and the oxygen sensor wire clip to the housing.

47. Connect the shift control cables to the shift arms and the clutch housing, then install the cable retainers.

48. Remove the support wire from the battery tray, position the damper, then install the 2 slave damper-to-clutch housing nuts and tighten to 18 ft. lbs. (25 Nm). Push the actuator into the clutch housing and rotate 1/4 turn clockwise, then install the retaining clip. Check that the master cylinder at front of dash connection is locked in place.

49. For 1991 vehicles, check and, if necessary, align the engine mounts.

50. For DOHC vehicles, install the air box and tighten the fasteners to 89 inch lbs. (10 Nm). Connect the flex tube to the air box, align the arrows and tighten the clamp.

51. Install the air inlet duct and fasteners, then connect the air temperature sensor electrical connector.

52. If lowered, raise and support the vehicle safely using jackstands.

53. For 1992-93 vehicles, install the transaxle mount-to-cradle nut and the 2 engine strut cradle bracket-to-cradle nuts from under the cradle, then tighten the nuts to 52 ft. lbs. (70 Nm).

54. For 1991 vehicles, tighten the front transaxle mount-to-transaxle bolts and install the front transaxle mount cradle nuts. Tighten the fasteners to 35 ft. lbs. (48 Nm). Then install the right side mount-to-cradle nuts and tighten to 40 ft. lbs. (54 Nm).

55. Remove the steering gear support wire and position the gear to the cradle. Install the gear bolts and nuts, then tighten the fasteners to 40 ft. lbs. (54 Nm). Connect the brake line and retainer to the cradle.

56. Install the clutch housing dust cover and tighten the fasteners to 89 inch lbs. (10 Nm).

57. For 1991 vehicles, install the rear pitch restrictor-to-transaxle bolts and tighten to 40 ft. lbs. (55 Nm). Then install the powertrain stiffening bracket and tighten the bracket-to-powertrain bolts to 35 ft. lbs. (47 Nm).

58. Position the exhaust manifold front pipe and gasket into the vehicle, then install the manifold retaining nuts. Tighten the nuts in a crosswise pattern to 23 ft. lbs. (31 Nm). Install the front pipe-to-the catalytic converter and tighten the bolts to 33 ft. lbs. (45 Nm). Finally, install the front pipe -to-transaxle support bracket and tighten the fasteners to 23 ft. lbs. (31 Nm).

➡ **If the converter flange threads are damaged use the Saturn 21010753 converter fastener kit in place of the self tapping screws to provide proper clamp load and prevent exhaust leaks.**

59. Install the nuts onto the ball joint studs and tighten to 55 ft. lbs. (75 Nm). Continue to tighten the nuts as necessary and install new cotter pi

60. Install the center and both wheel splash shields.

61. For coupes, install the right left lower facia braces, J-nuts and fasteners. Tighten the fasteners to 89 inch lbs. (10 Nm).

62. Install the tire and wheel assemblies, then lower the vehicle.

63. Connect the negative battery cable and fill the transaxle with Dexron®IIE (preferred), Dexron®II or equivalent fluid.

64. Properly enable the SIR system, if equipped.

65. Check the vehicle alignment and adjust as necessary.

OVERHAUL

Before Disassembly: When servicing the unit, it is recommended that as each part is disassembled, it is cleaned in solvent and dried with compressed air. Disassembly and reassembly of this unit and its parts must be done on a clean work bench. Also, before installing bolts into aluminum parts, always dip the threads into clean transmission oil. Anti-seize compound can also be used to prevent bolts from galling the aluminum and seizing. Always use a torque wrench to keep from stripping the threads. Take care with the seals when installing them, especially the smaller O-rings. The slightest damage can cause leaks: Aluminum parts are very susceptible to damage so great care should be exercised when handling them. The internal snaprings should be expanded and the external snaprings compressed if they are to be reused. This will help insure proper seating when installed. Be sure to replace any O-ring, gasket, or seal that is removed.

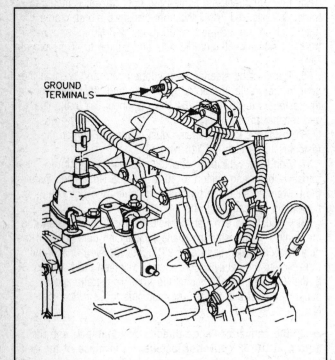

Fig. 9 Remove the electrical wiring from the transaxle assembly

Disassembly

TRANSAXLE HOUSING

▶ See Figures 16, 17, 18, 19, 20, 21, 22, 23 and 24

1. Mount the transaxle on a bench mounting fixture or equivalent. The unit may be bolted to a wooden bench through the top 2 transaxle-to-engine bolt holes.

2. Remove the clutch fork and bearing assembly.

3. Remove the shift housing bolts, then remove the shift housing from the top of the transaxle. Remove and discard the old gasket from the mating surface.

4. Remove the rear cover bolts and rear cover from the transaxle. Remove and discard the gasket from mating surface.

5. Remove the vehicle speed sensor from the transaxle housing.

6. Move the 2 shift forks in order to lock the transaxle in 2 gears and prevent shaft turning.

7. Loosen and remove the nut from the rear of the input shaft.

8. Loosen and remove the nut from the rear of the output shaft.

9. Remove the reverse cone, thrust washer and the reverse blocker assembly.

➡ **For 1993, the reverse cone bearing of the 5th/reverse synchronizer assembly was eliminated. Service parts may come with or without the reverse brake cone bearing installed. All 1991-1993 vehicles can use a 5th/reverse synchronizer assembly with or without the cone bearing**

10. Remove the 5th/reverse shift fork; it may contain 2 retaining rings or a 1 piece retainer.

11. Remove the synchronizer sleeve, blocker assembly and the 5th drive gear. Be sure to keep the synchronizer hub and sleeve together as a matched set. Note the spline alignment mark on the hub and sleeve.

12. Remove the 5th driven gear. If necessary, release the bearing, race, snapring and thrust washer to provide access and use a puller to remove the gear from the rear of the output shaft.

13. Remove the case-to-clutch housing bolts. Use snapring pliers to open the output and input shaft bearing snaprings and allow the ring grooves to drop below the snapring.

14. Use the provided pry slots to separate the case and clutch housing, then remove the case.

15. Remove the 5th/reverse actuator retainer, then remove the shift fork shaft.

16. Remove the 1st/2nd, 3rd/4th and 5th/reverse actuator.

17. Remove the flow tube, then remove the shifter lever bolts and the idler gear shift lever assembly.

18. Remove the idler gear thrust washer and the reverse idler gear. Remove the idler gear shaft.

19. Lift the input and output shafts out of the clutch housing together. Be careful not to damage the output shaft machined surface during removal.

20. Lift the differential from the clutch housing, then remove the transaxle magnet.

DIFFERENTIAL

▶ See Figures 25, 26 and 27

1. Drive the roll pin out of the differential housing and remove the pinion shaft.

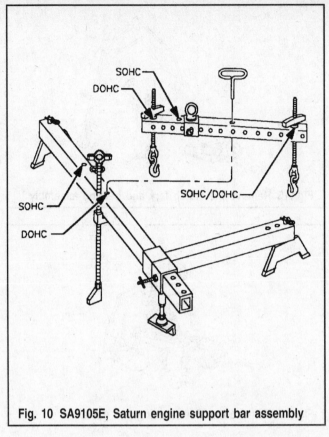

Fig. 10 SA9105E, Saturn engine support bar assembly

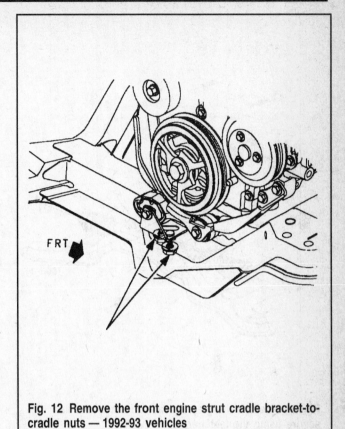

Fig. 12 Remove the front engine strut cradle bracket-to-cradle nuts — 1992-93 vehicles

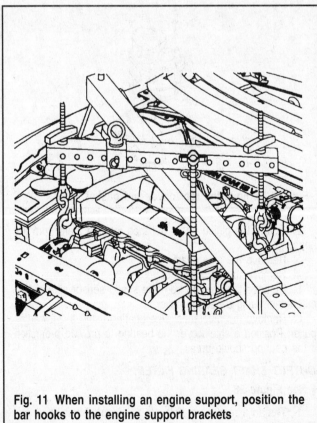

Fig. 11 When installing an engine support, position the bar hooks to the engine support brackets

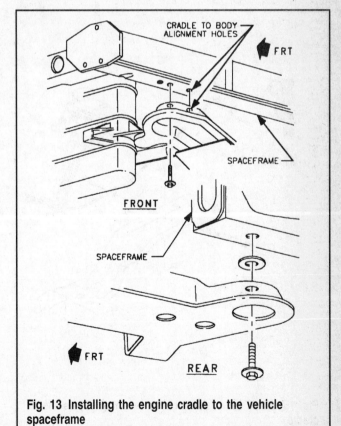

Fig. 13 Installing the engine cradle to the vehicle spaceframe

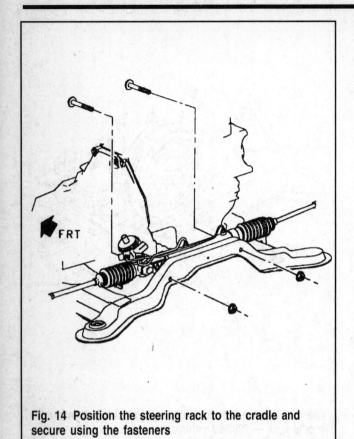

Fig. 14 Position the steering rack to the cradle and secure using the fasteners

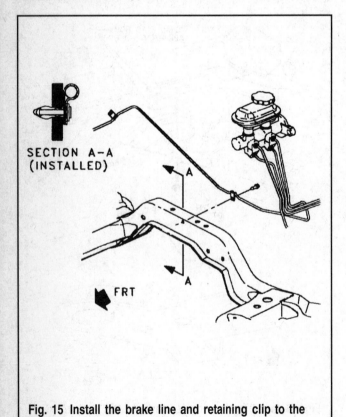

Fig. 15 Install the brake line and retaining clip to the cradle

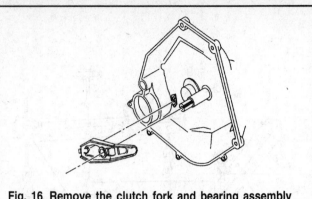

Fig. 16 Remove the clutch fork and bearing assembly

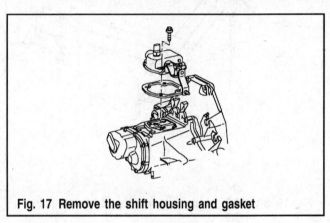

Fig. 17 Remove the shift housing and gasket

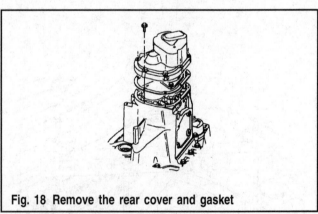

Fig. 18 Remove the rear cover and gasket

2. Rotate the pinion gears out then remove them from the housing.

3. Remove the side gears.

4. Remove the housing liner.

5. Remove the bearing from the speed sensor side of the differential using a bearing puller.

6. Remove the differential side bearing using a 2-jawed puller. Position a shield over the bearing to provide protection if the bearing should break.

OUTPUT SHAFT BEARING FILTER

▶ See Figure 28

1. Thread a rear cover bolt into the output shaft bearing filter.

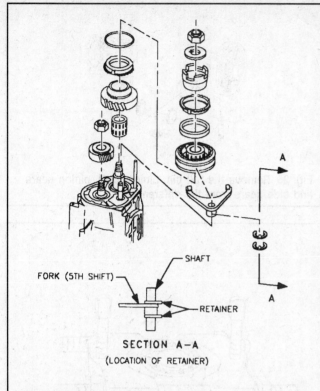

FORK (5TH SHIFT) — SHAFT — RETAINER

SECTION A—A
(LOCATION OF RETAINER)

Fig. 19 Exploded view of the components located under the transaxle rear cover

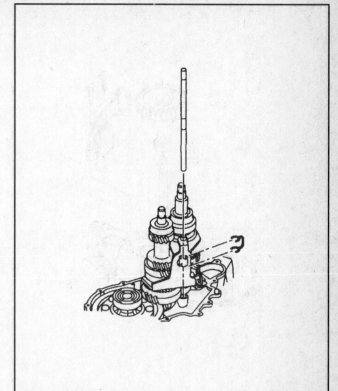

Fig. 21 Remove the 5th/reverse actuator retainer, then remove the shift fork shaft

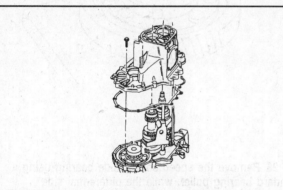

Fig. 20 Remove the case from the clutch housing

2. Pull the filter from the clutch housing assembly using the rear cover bolt for leverage.

3. Remove stake, if necessary.

OUTPUT SHAFT ROLLER BEARING

▶ See Figure 29

1. Remove the bearing retaining ring.

2. Install SA9191T, or an equivalent bearing removal tool, and tighten it securely to the bearing.

3. Install SA9173G, or an equivalent slide hammer, to the bearing puller.

4. Place the housing with the bearing side down in a press with wooden blocks positioned to protect the sealing surface. Use the slide hammer to remove the bearing.

5. Remove the oil baffle plate.

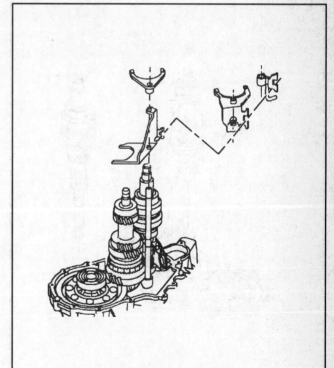

Fig. 22 Remove the 1st/2nd, 3rd/4th and 5th/reverse actuator

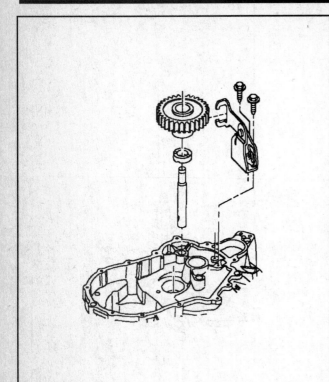

Fig. 23 Remove the reverse idler shift lever and gear assemblies

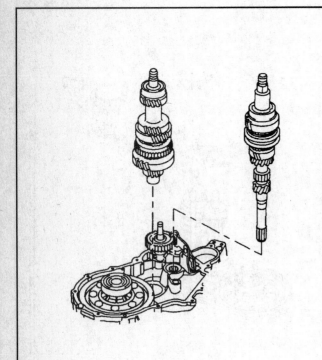

Fig. 24 Lift both the input and output shafts from the housing together

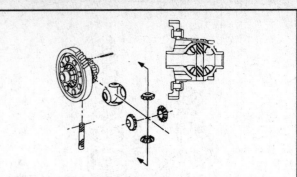

Fig. 25 Remove the roll pin, pinion shaft, pinion gears and side gears from the differential

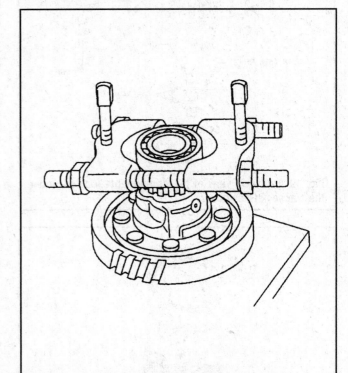

Fig. 26 Remove the speed sensor side bearing using a standard bearing puller, while the differential side bearing should be removed using a jawed puller

INPUT SHAFT ROLLER BEARING

▶ See Figure 30

1. Install SA9129T, or an equivalent support fixture, to the clutch housing. After the fixture is bolted to the case, snug the large center screw.
2. Position the clutch housing and support fixture into a press.
3. Using SA9128T, or an equivalent bearing remover, press the bearing from the clutch housing bore.

OUTPUT SHAFT

▶ See Figures 31 and 32

1. Position the output shaft into a press so that it is supported at the bottom by the sides of the 1st driven gear.

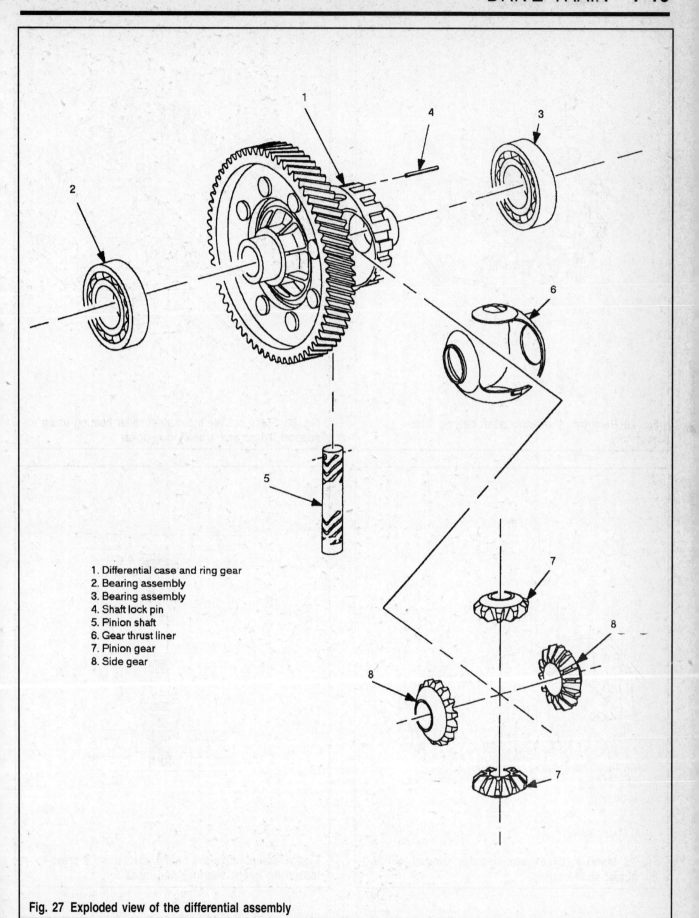

1. Differential case and ring gear
2. Bearing assembly
3. Bearing assembly
4. Shaft lock pin
5. Pinion shaft
6. Gear thrust liner
7. Pinion gear
8. Side gear

Fig. 27 Exploded view of the differential assembly

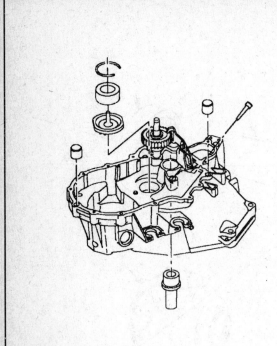

Fig. 28 Removing the output shaft bearing filter assembly

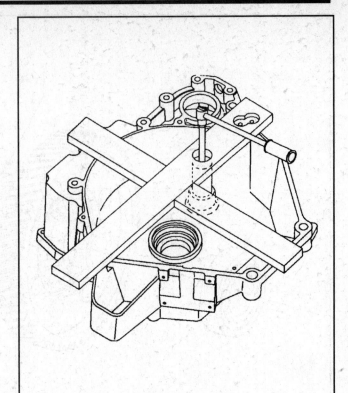

Fig. 30 Press out the input shaft roller bearing using a support fixture and a bearing remover

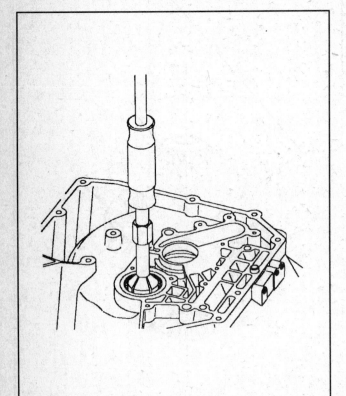

Fig. 29 Install a suitable bearing puller removal tool to the output shaft bearing

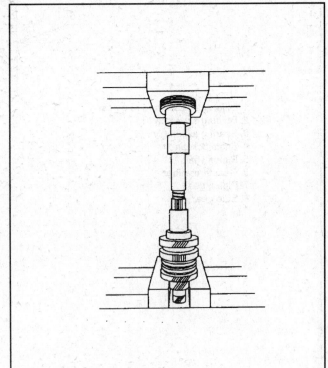

Fig. 31 Disassemble the output shaft using a press to loosen the gears, bearings and races

2. Using the press, loosen and remove the gears from the shaft.

➡Synchronizer hubs and sleeves must always be kept together and treated as a matched set. Do not use sleeves from 1 synchronizer with the hub from another.

3. Remove the output shaft ball bearing.
4. Remove the 3rd/4th driven gear.
5. Remove the 2nd driven gear.
6. Remove the 2nd driven gear bearing.
7. Remove the 2nd driven gear bearing race.
8. Remove the 2nd driven gear blocker ring and 1st/2nd synchronizer sleeve.
9. Remove the 1st/2nd synchronizer hub.
10. Remove the 1st gear blocker ring.
11. Remove the 1st driven gear.
12. Remove the 1st driven gear bearing.
13. Remove the 1st driven gear thrust bearing.

INPUT SHAFT

▶ See Figure 33

1. Position the input shaft into a press so that it is supported at the bottom by the sides of the 3rd drive gear.
2. Using the press, loosen and remove the gears from the shaft.

➡Synchronizer hubs and sleeves must always be kept together and treated as a matched set. Do not use sleeves from 1 synchronizer with the hub from another.

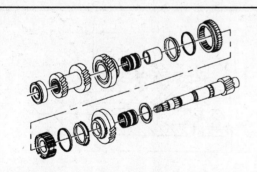

Fig. 32 Keep each component in the order it was removed from the output shaft to ease assembly

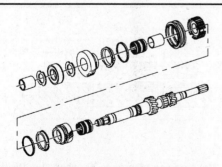

Fig. 33 Remove each component from the input shaft and store in the order of removal for assembly purposes

3. Remove the 5th gear bearing, inner race and thrust washer.
4. Remove the input shaft bearing.
5. Remove the 4th drive gear thrust washer.
6. Remove the 4th drive gear.
7. Remove the 4th gear blocker ring and spring.
8. Remove the 4th gear bearing.
9. Remove the 4th gear race.
10. Remove the 3rd/4th synchronizer sleeve.
11. Remove the 3rd/4th synchronizer hub.
12. Remove the 3rd gear blocker ring and spring.
13. Remove the 3rd drive gear and bearing.

Inspection

All parts of the transaxle should be thoroughly cleaned and inspected prior to disassembly. Any part of questionable condition should be replaced to avoid the danger of early part failure, possible leading to another costly and time consuming transaxle tear down.

GEAR SYNCHRONIZER BLOCKER RING

▶ See Figures 34, 35 and 36

1. Inspect the fiber liner of the synchronizer blocker ring for wear or damage. Make sure the liner surface is not glazed, burned or missing.
2. Inspect the ring teeth for wear.
3. Inspect the gear thrust surface for wear or scoring.
4. Inspect the gear teeth for uneven wear, scoring, galling or cracks.
5. Install the synchronizer blocker ring to the matching gear and rotate until it stops, then measure the clearance between the blocker ring and the gear in four evenly spaced positions. The minimum allowable clearance is 0.02 in. (0.4mm).

➡New blocker rings should be soaked in Dexron®II or an equivalent automatic transaxle fluid for 15 minutes prior to measuring clearances.

6. Replace synchronizer assemblies which are damaged or worn.

INPUT/OUTPUT SHAFT ASSEMBLIES

Inspect the shafts and gears for signs of wear or damage. Gears with chipped teeth or shafts which have been cracked or bent must not be reused. The shafts and gears must be assembled in order to measure clearances and fully determine

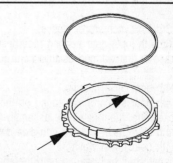

Fig. 34 Inspect the fiber liner and the ring teeth for wear or damage

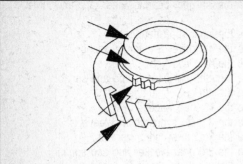

Fig. 35 Make sure the gear thrust surface, gear cone surface and gear teeth are all free from damage

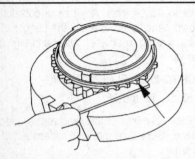

Fig. 36 Measure the clearance between the blocker ring and the gear in four evenly spaced positions

if all parts are good. Clearance inspection is part of the assembly procedures.

Assembly

INPUT SHAFT

▶ See Figures 37, 38 and 39

During shaft assembly, all rotating parts should be generously lubricated with Dexron®II or an equivalent automatic transaxle fluid. New blocker rings should be soaked in the fluid for at least 15 minutes prior to installation.

1. Install the 3rd drive gear bearing onto the shaft.
2. Install the 3rd drive gear.
3. Install the 3rd gear synchronizer spring on the 3rd blocker.
4. Press the 3rd/4th gear synchronizer hub onto the blocker, making sure the blocker ring tangs are aligned with the hub slots.
5. Install the 3rd/4th synchronizer sleeve.
6. Install the 3rd/4th input gear bearing race. Installation will be eased if the race is first warmed using a heat gun or hair drier.
7. Install the 4th gear drive bearing.
8. Install the 4th gear synchronizer spring on the 4th gear synchronizer blocker ring, then install the assembly.
9. Install the 4th drive gear with the hub side down.
10. Install the 4th gear thrust washer.
11. Press the input shaft ball bearing onto the shaft with the snapring groove facing downward toward 4th gear.
12. In order to measure input shaft clearance, temporarily install the 5th gear bearing, 5th gear, 5th/reverse synchronizer

assembly, reverse cone and washer. Retain the components using the old nut and tighten to 110 ft. lbs. (150 Nm).

13. Measure the clearance between the 5th drive gear and 5th gear thrust washer. Clearance should be 0.008-0.014 in. (0.20-0.35mm).

14. Measure the clearance between the 4th drive gear and 4th gear thrust washer. Clearance should be 0.008-0.014 in. (0.20-0.35mm).

15. Measure the clearance between the 3rd drive gear and the input shaft. Clearance should be 0.008-0.014 in. (0.20-0.35mm).

16. Remove the nut and the temporarily installed components.

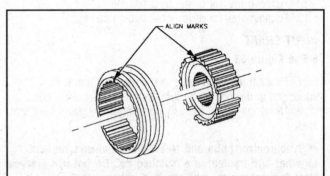

Fig. 37 Certain input and output shaft components are marked for proper alignment

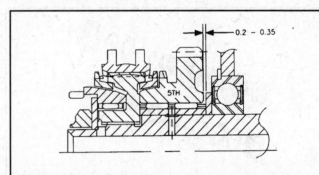

Fig. 38 Measure the clearance between the 5th drive gear and 5th gear thrust washer — input shaft assembly

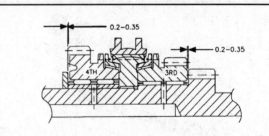

Fig. 39 Measure the clearance between the 4th drive gear and 4th gear thrust washer, then measure the clearance between the 3rd drive gear and the input shaft

OUTPUT SHAFT

▶ See Figures 40 and 41

During shaft assembly, all rotating parts should be generously lubricated with Dexron®II or an equivalent automatic transaxle fluid. New blocker rings should be soaked in the fluid for at least 15 minutes prior to installation.

1. Install the 1st driven gear thrust bearing with the black side downward.
2. Install the 1st driven gear bearing.
3. Install the 1st driven gear.
4. Install the 1st gear synchronizer blocker ring and the synchronizer spring.
5. Press the 1st/2nd synchronizer hub onto the shaft, making sure to align the blocker ring tangs with the hub slots.
6. Install the 1st/2nd synchronizer sleeve with the gear side downward and making sure to properly position the hub/sleeve alignment marks. Check to make sure there is free movement between 1st and 2nd gears.
7. Install the 2nd gear synchronizer spring on the 2nd gear synchronizer blocker ring, then install the assembly.
8. Install the 2nd gear bearing race. Installation will be eased if the race is first warmed using a heat gun or hair drier.
9. Install the 2nd gear bearing.
10. Install the 2nd driven gear.
11. Install the 3rd/4th driven gear, with the larger gear (3rd) positioned towards the bottom.
12. Press the output shaft ball bearing onto the shaft with the snapring groove facing upward away from the gears.
13. Temporarily install the remaining output shaft components in order to measure output shaft clearances. Secure using the old nut and tighten to 110 ft. lbs. (150 Nm).
14. Measure the clearance between the 3rd/4th driven gear and the 2nd driven gear. Clearance should be 0.008-0.014 in. (0.20-0.35mm).
15. Measure the clearance between the 1st driven gear and the thrust bearing. Clearance should be 0.008-0.014 in. (0.20-0.35mm).
16. Loosen the nut and remove the temporarily installed components.

DIFFERENTIAL

1. Using SA9120T, or an equivalent installation tool, press the ball bearings onto the differential case. Make sure the bearings are properly seated.

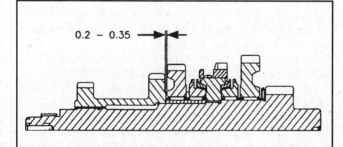

Fig. 40 Measure the clearance between the 3rd/4th driven gear and the 2nd driven gear — output shaft assembly

2. Roll up the differential thrust liner and insert it into the case. Position the liner to the inside of the case so that side gear section and alignment ring sets into the pocket on the ring gear side of the case.
3. Position and hold the side gears in the housing, then install the pinion on the tabbed side of the thrust liner. Pull the thrust liner partially over the pinion gear to hold it in place.
4. Position the 2nd pinion, directly opposite the 1st, and pull the liner out until the pinion shaft hole in the cover and pinions line up.
5. Rotate the pinions and the thrust liner into the housing together until they line up with the pinion shaft bore in the housing.
6. Verify that the side gears are positioned properly, then install the pinion shaft and roll pin. Be sure to drive the roll pin flush with the case in order to prevent interference in the speed sensor signal.

TRANSAXLE AND CLUTCH HOUSING

▶ See Figures 42, 43, 44, 45 and 46

1. Using SA9118T, or an equivalent installation tool, press the input shaft quill bearing into the clutch housing bore.
2. Install SA9129T, or an equivalent press fixture tool, and align the tool with the housing. Install the filter and use a small punch to stake the filter in place.
3. Install the oil baffle plate, making sure that it positioned flat in the bore.
4. Press the output shaft roller bearing into the housing bore. The marked bearing surface should be facing towards the top.
5. Install the roller bearing retaining ring.
6. Install the 2 case-to-housing dowel pins into the clutch housing. If necessary, a bolt may be used to pull the dowels into the housing.
7. Tap the reverse idler gear shaft roll pin into the reverse idler gear shaft, then them to the housing.
8. Install the reverse idler thrust washer and the idler gear assembly onto the shaft.
9. Install the reverse shift lever assembly with the idler gear positioned in the fork part of the lever.
10. Clean the bolt holes and threads, then apply a coat of Loctite® 242, or an equivalent threadlock to the shift lever retaining bolts. Install the bolts and tighten to 124 inch lbs. (14 Nm).
11. Install the transaxle magnet, then lube the outer bearing race and lower the differential assembly into the housing. If the bearing cocks in the bore, work the differential back and forth in order to seat the bearing.
12. Lift the input and output shaft and mesh their gears, then lower the shaft into the housing while rotating back and forth to align them with the differential ring gear and start the output shaft into its bearing.
13. Install the oil flow tube into the pocket of the clutch housing, next to the reverse shift lever.
14. Position the 1st/2nd shift and 3rd/4th shift forks into there respective synchronizer sleeves.
15. Install the 5th/reverse actuator rod into the slot on the reverse shift lever.
16. Align the shift fork shaft hole in the shift forks and the 5th/reverse actuator, then install the shift fork shaft through the forks with the retaining ring groove upward.

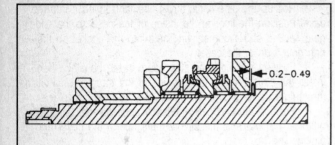

Fig. 41 Measure the clearance between the 1st driven gear and the thrust bearing — output shaft assembly

17. Verify that the actuator rod is still in the reverse shift lever, then hold the 5th/reverse actuator in position to expose the snapring groove on each end of the actuator. Install the 5th/reverse actuator retainer.

✳✳WARNING

Carefully align the retainer to grooves in the shift shaft. If the retainer is not properly aligned during installation, it will be bent and must be replaced with a new retainer.

18. Make sure the clutch housing and transaxle case mating surfaces are clean and dry. Apply a thin bead of Loctite® 518, or an equivalent sealant down the center of the mating flange on the clutch housing. Make sure the bead stays inside the bolt holes as shown.

➡ **Although 1991 and 1992 vehicles used a gasket between the clutch housing and transaxle case from the factory, only the sealant should be used upon reassembly for all vehicles.**

19. Lubricate the differential and shaft ball bearings, the shift fork shaft and the reverse idler shaft, then lower the transaxle case over the clutch housing. Spread the input and output shaft bearing snaprings to allow the rings to slide over the bearings.

20. Seat the case to the clutch housing, then lubricate the fasteners with Dexron®II or an equivalent fluid and wipe off excessive fluid. Install the fasteners and tighten to 21 ft. lbs. (28 Nm) using the sequence shown in the figure.

21. Install a used shaft nut on the input shaft, then use a small prybar to pry the shaft upward and seat the snaprings. Remove the nut and repeat the procedure for the output shaft.

22. Using SA9112T, or an equivalent differential end-play feeler gauge tool, measure the end-play on the case side of the differential bearing. The end-play should be set to 0 using the largest gauge that will fit between the bearing and the case. A snapring of the same thickness should then be installed into the housing, on top of the differential ball bearing and into the groove.

23. Apply a light coat of Loctite® 518, or an equivalent sealant, to the area of the seal that presses into the case. Install the left (transaxle case) side axle seal using SA9113T, or an equivalent seal installer.

24. If a groove is present on the case, install a retaining snapring.

25. Install the 5th driven gear, then move the forks to lock the transaxle in 2 gears at the same time.

26. Make sure the shaft threads are clean, then install a new output shaft nut and tighten to 110 ft. lbs. (150 Nm).

27. Unlock the shaft by lining the shift forks to the neutral gate.

28. Install the 5th gear thrust washer.

29. Install the 5th gear bearing race.

30. Install the 5th drive gear bearing.

31. Install the 5th drive gear.

32. Install the 5th gear synchronizer blocker ring to 5th gear.

33. Install the 5th gear synchronizer spring to the 5th synchronizer.

34. Slide the 5th/reverse fork over the 5th/reverse synchronizer sleeve, then install the sleeve to the hub and the fork to the shift shaft at the same time.

35. Install the new 5th/reverse fork retaining ring(s). The retainer may be 1 piece or 2, but most service kits will contain the 2 piece version.

36. Install the synchronizer spring to the reverse blocker, then install the assembly to the 5th/reverse sleeve.

37. Install the reverse cone and the thrust washer.

38. Move 2 shift forks to lock the transaxle in 2 gears at the same time, make sure the input shaft threads are clean, then install a new input shaft nut. Tighten the nut to 110 ft. lbs. (150 Nm).

39. Unlock the shafts by lining the shift forks to the neutral gate.

40. Turn the reverse cone so one of the slots is facing the top of the transaxle in order to align the cone to the rear cover.

41. Install the rear cover using a new gasket. Lubricate the fasteners with Dexron®II or an equivalent fluid and wiper off excess, then install the fasteners and tighten to 106 inch lbs. (12 Nm) in a crisscross sequence.

42. Install the shift housing using a new gasket. Lubricate the fasteners with Dexron®II or an equivalent fluid and wipe off excess, then install the fasteners and tighten to 21 ft. lbs. (21 Nm) in a crisscross sequence.

✳✳WARNING

To prevent damage to the transaxle case and the shift housing cover, do not tighten bolts unless the cover is properly aligned to the case.

43. Install and tighten the speed sensor to 20 ft. lbs. (26 Nm).

44. Lubricate the transaxle oil drain plug with Dexron®II or an equivalent fluid and wipe off excess, then install the plug and tighten to 40 ft. lbs. (55 Nm).

45. Apply a light coat of Loctite® 518, or an equivalent sealant, to the area of the seal that presses into the case. Install the right (clutch housing) side axle seal using SA9113T, or an equivalent seal installer.

46. Install the clutch fork stabilizer and ball stud in the clutch housing. the hole for the ball stud is located to the lower left of the input shaft. Lubricate the fastener with Dexron®II or an equivalent fluid and wiper off excess, then install the fastener and tighten to 18 ft. lbs. (24 Nm).

47. Install the clutch fork retainer to the clutch fork.

48. Install the clutch release bearing into the clutch fork. Do not grease the clutch release bearing or the bearing quill.

49. Lube the pivot fork with high temperature grease and install the fork and bearing assembly. snap the fork over the ball stud.

50. Coat the input shaft spline with a light film of high temperature grease.

Halfshafts

REMOVAL & INSTALLATION

▶ **See Figures 47, 48, 49, 50, 51, 52, 53, 54 and 55**

1. Remove the wheel cover or the center cap for access to the halfshaft nut. Have a friend depress the brake pedal and loosen the front halfshaft nut. If no one is available, pump the brakes a few times to so the calipers grab and hold the brake pads, then loosen the nut.

2. Raise the front of the vehicle and support safely using jackstands, then remove the corresponding wheel and splash shield.

3. If removing the left side axle or intermediate shaft, loosen the plug and drain the transaxle fluid into a clean container.

4. Remove the halfshaft nut and washer.

5. Remove and discard the cotter pin from the lower control arm ball joints. Back the ball joint nut until the top of the nut is even with the top of the threads.

6. Use tool SA9132S, or equivalent, to loosen the lower control arm ball joint in the steering knuckle, then remove the

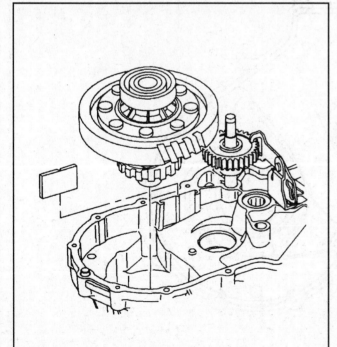

Fig. 42 Lube the outer bearing race and lower the differential assembly into the housing

nut. Do not use a wedge tool or seal damage may occur. The ball joint will be completely removed from the knuckle after the tie rod ball joint is separated.

✳✳WARNING

The outer CV-joint for vehicles equipped with ABS contains a speed sensor ring. Use of an incorrect tool to separate the control arm from the knuckle may result in damage and loss of the ABS system.

7. Remove the tie rod cotter pin and loosen the castle nut, then separate the tie rod end from the knuckle using a tie rod separator SA91100C or equivalent. Once loosened sufficiently, remove the castle nut and separate the components completely. Do not use a wedge-type tool or the seal may be damaged.

8. Place a cloth over the sway bar to protect the surface, then position a prybar over the cloth with which to leverage to the knuckle and separate the lower control arm ball joint. Position a cloth at the prybar contact point with the cradle, then push down on the bar and separate the ball joint from the knuckle. Make sure the knuckle does not contact and damage the ball stud se

9. While pulling the knuckle/strut assembly away from the halfshaft, pull the end of the halfshaft from the wheel hub. If difficulty is encountered, tap on the end of the halfshaft using a block of wood and a hammer. Support the halfshaft assembly using a length of mechanic's wire or with a jack stand.

10. If removing the right halfshaft, disconnect the halfshaft from the intermediate shaft by tapping the inner joint with a hammer and a block of wood. Remove the halfshaft from the vehicle.

11. If removing the left halfshaft, disconnect the halfshaft by inserting a large prybar into the space between the inner joint and transaxle. Pry the halfshaft from the transaxle being careful not to contact and damage the transaxle oil seal. Remove the halfshaft from the vehicle.

To install:

12. If installing the left side halfshaft, install SA91112T or equivalent transaxle seal protector. Install the halfshaft into the transaxle, after the splines have safely passed the transaxle oil seal, remove the seal protector and fully seat the halfshaft.

13. If installing the right side halfshaft, insert the shaft onto the intermediate shaft and push firmly to engage the circlip.

14. Insert the outer end of the halfshaft into the wheel hub. Be careful not to damage the CV-joint boot.

15. Thoroughly clean and lubricate the ball joint stud threads of the lower control arm and tie rod end.

16. Install the lower control arm ball stud to the steering knuckle, then install the nut, but do not tighten at this time.

17. Install the tie rod end to the steering knuckle, then install the nut. Tighten the nut to 33 ft. lbs. (45 Nm) and install a new cotter pin. If necessary, tighten the nut additionally, do not back off to insert the cotter pin.

18. Tighten the lower control arm ball stud nut to 55 ft. lbs. (75 Nm), tighten additionally if necessary and install a new cotter pin.

19. Install the washer and a new halfshaft nut, then tighten the nut to 145 ft. lbs. (200 Nm).

20. Install the inner splash shield and wheel.

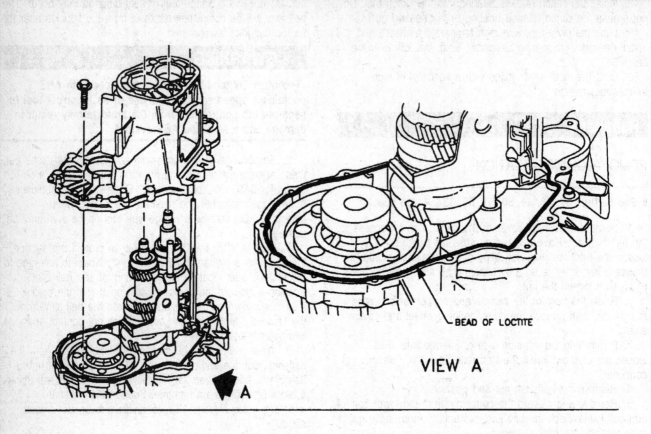

BEAD OF LOCTITE

VIEW A

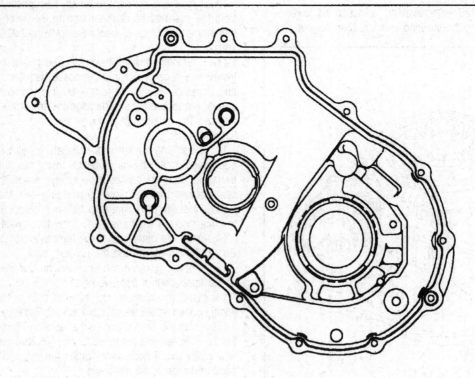

Fig. 43 No gasket is used when rejoining the clutch housing and transaxle case assemblies, instead a thin bead of sealant is run around the mating surface on the clutch housing

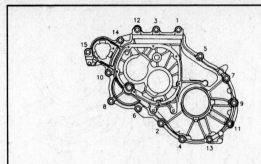

Fig. 44 Transaxle case-to-clutch housing fastener torque sequence

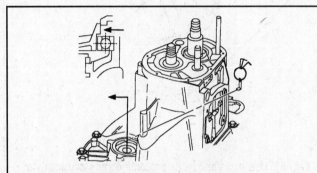

Fig. 45 Measure the differential end-play using a feeler gauge

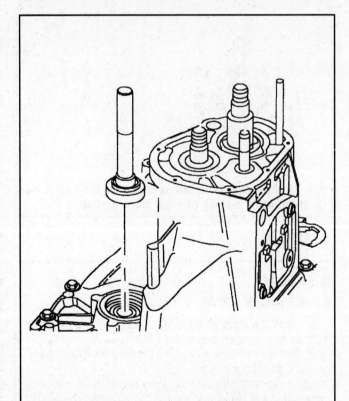

Fig. 46 Drive the side axle seal into position using a suitable seal installation tool

Fig. 47 If removing the left halfshaft or the intermediate shaft, drain the transaxle fluid

21. Lower the vehicle and properly fill the transaxle.
22. Check and adjust the alignment as necessary.

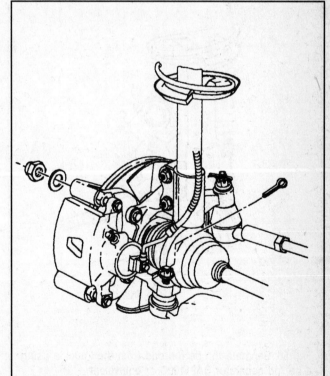

Fig. 48 Remove and discard the cotter pin from the lower control arm ball joint so the nut may be removed

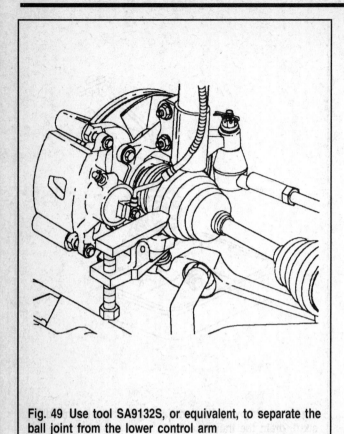

Fig. 49 Use tool SA9132S, or equivalent, to separate the ball joint from the lower control arm

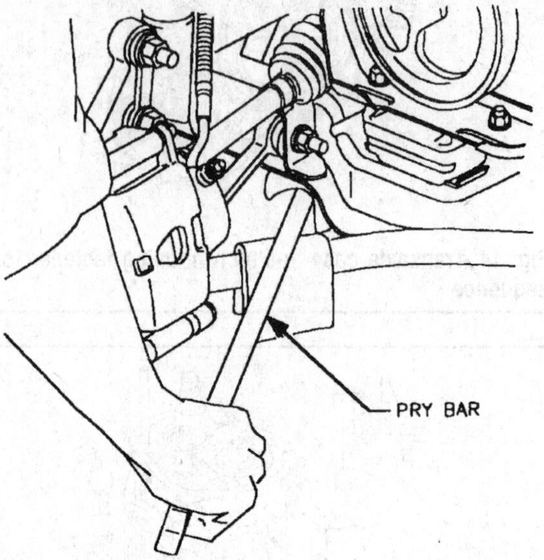

Fig. 51 Use a prybar (with protective rags or cloth) to apply leverage and separate the control arm ball joint from the steering knuckle.

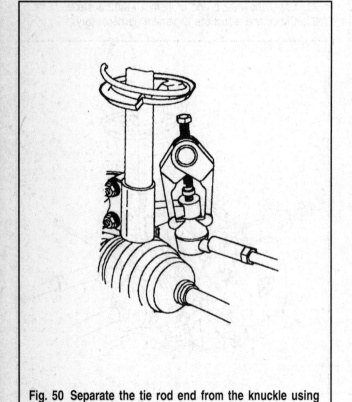

Fig. 50 Separate the tie rod end from the knuckle using a tie rod separator SA91100C or equivalent

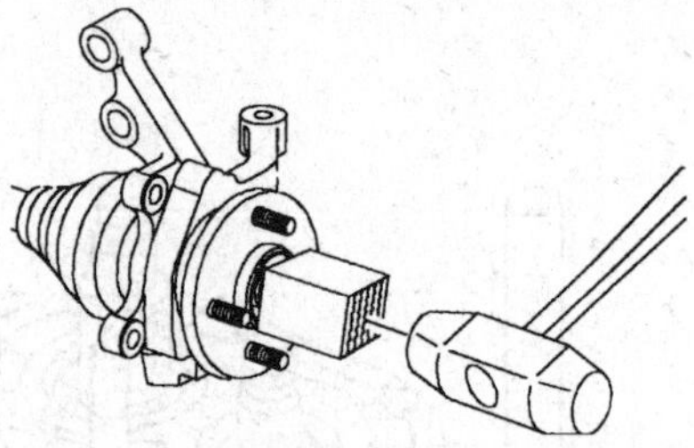

Fig. 52 If difficulty is encountered, tap on the end of the halfshaft using a block of wood and a hammer

OVERHAUL

Disassembly

▶ **See Figures 56, 57, 58, 59, 60 and 61**

1. Using soft metal or wood to protect the shaft, clamp the halfshaft to a workbench in a vise.

2. Remove and service the CV-joint from the end of the halfshaft, as follows:

    a. If the halfshaft has a damaged deflector ring, use a brass drift and hammer to remove the damaged component from the CV outer race.

    b. Either cut the outer seal retaining clamps using a side cutter or use a flat bladed screwdriver to disengage the

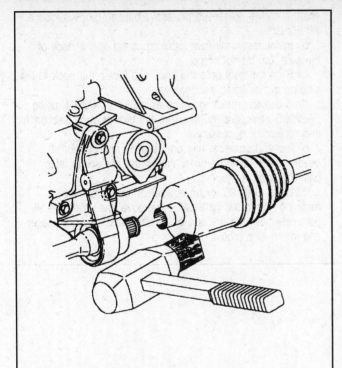

Fig. 53 Use a block of wood to protect the right side halfshaft from hammer blows

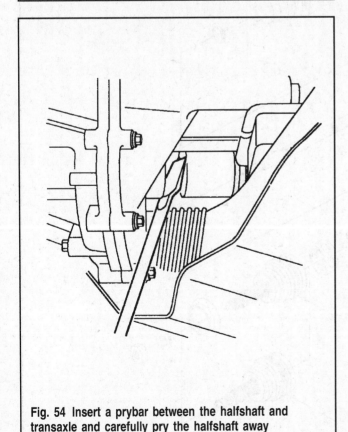

Fig. 54 Insert a prybar between the halfshaft and transaxle and carefully pry the halfshaft away

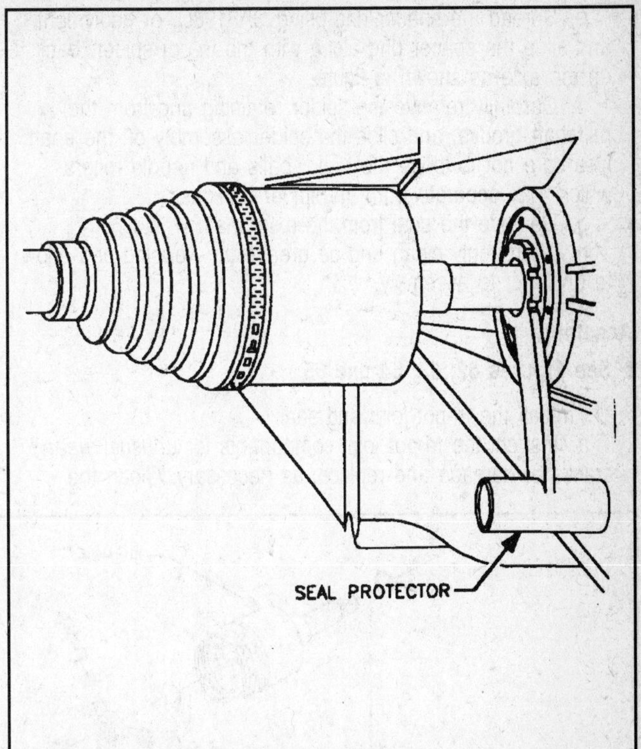

Fig. 55 Failure to use a seal protector may allow the halfshaft splines to damage the transaxle seal, causing a need for replacement

SEAL PROTECTOR

outer band from the inner band at the retaining peg, then discard the clamp.

c. Separate the joint seal from the CV-joint race at the large diameter, then slide the seal away from the joint, along the halfshaft. Wipe any excess grease from the CV inner race.

d. Use a suitable pair of snapring pliers to spread the ears of the inner race retaining ring, then remove the CV-joint assembly from the shaft.

e. Remove the seal from the halfshaft.

f. Use a brass drift and gently tap on the cage until it is cocked and the first ball may be removed. Repeat this to remove the remaining balls.

g. When the balls are removed, pivot the cage and inner race at a 90 degree angle to the center line of outer race. Cage windows should align with the lands of the outer race, then lift the cage and inner race.

h. Rotate the inner race up and out of the cage.

i. Thoroughly clean and de grease all CV-joint parts and allow to dry before assembly.

3. Remove and service the tri-pot joint and joint seal from the halfshaft's other end, as follows:

a. Cut the eared seal retaining clamp on the tri-pot seal using a side cutter, then discard the clamp.

b. Remove and discard the earless clamp using a small flat blade screwdriver.

c. Separate the seal from the tri-pot housing at the large diameter, then slide the seal away from the joint along the halfshaft. Wipe away excess grease from the face of the tri-pot spider and the inside of the housing.

d. Remove the tri-pot housing from the spider and shaft.

e. Spread the spacer ring using SA9198C, or equivalent, and slide the spacer ring along with the tri-pot spider, back on the axle as shown in figure.

f. Carefully remove the spider retaining ring from the halfshaft groove, and slide the spider assembly off the shaft. Use care not to loose the tri-pot balls and needle rollers which may separate from the spider trunions.

g. Remove the seal from the axle shaft.

h. Thoroughly clean and de grease the housing and allow to dry prior to assembly.

Assembly

▶ **See Figures 62, 63, 64 and 65**

1. Install the tri-pot joint and seal:

a. Inspect the tri-pot joint components for unusual wear, cracks or damage and replace, as necessary. Clean the shaft; if rust is present in the seal mounting grooves, use a wire brush.

b. Install the small seal retaining clamp on the neck of the seal, but do not crimp.

c. Slide the seal onto the shaft and locate the neck of the seal on the halfshaft seal groove

d. Crimp the retaining clamp as shown in Fig. 64, using SA9203C or equivalent. Measure the dimension or section A and recrimp, if necessary.

e. Install the spacer ring on the shaft and position it beyond the retaining groove, then install the spider, also past the retaining groove.

f. Using SA9198, or an equivalent tool, install the retaining ring to the halfshaft ring groove, then slide the tri-pot spider towards the end of the shaft and seat the spacer ring in the axle groove.

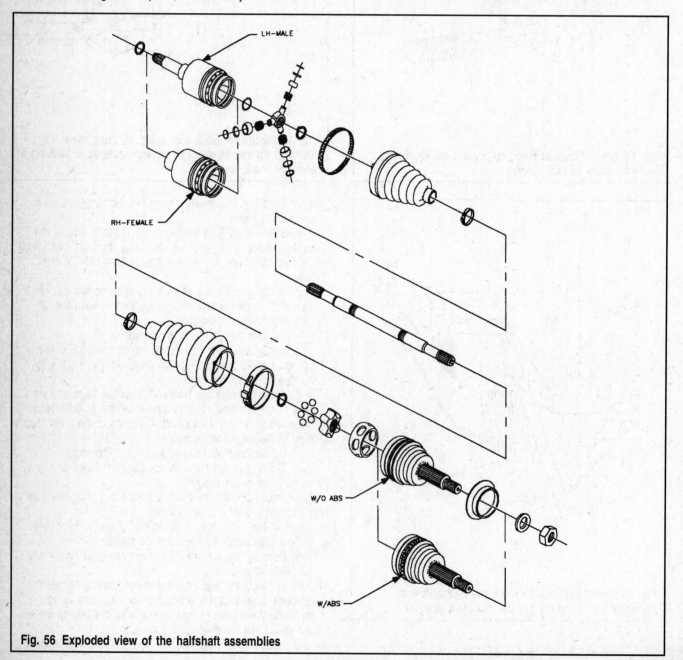

Fig. 56 Exploded view of the halfshaft assemblies

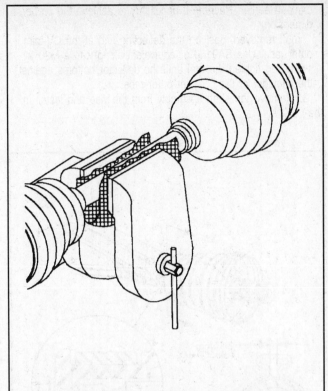

Fig. 57 Use soft metal or wood to protect the halfshaft from the vise

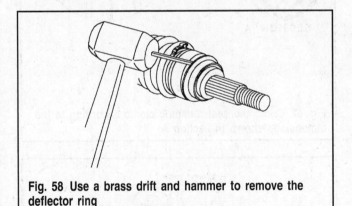

Fig. 58 Use a brass drift and hammer to remove the deflector ring

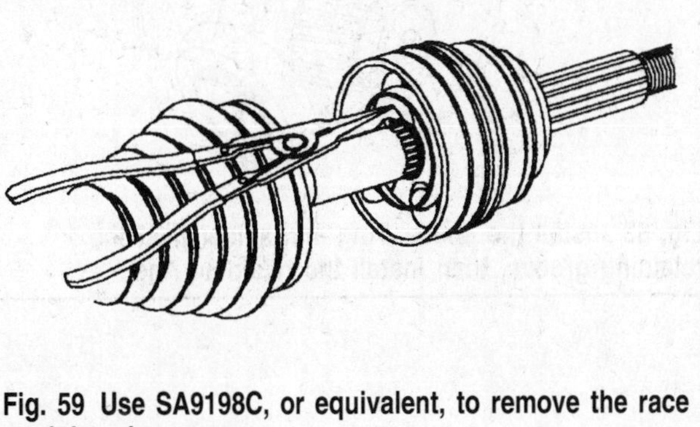

Fig. 59 Use SA9198C, or equivalent, to remove the race retaining ring

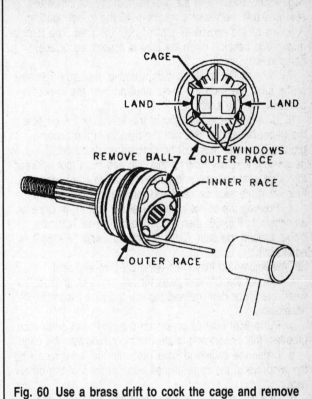

Fig. 60 Use a brass drift to cock the cage and remove the balls from the CV-joint

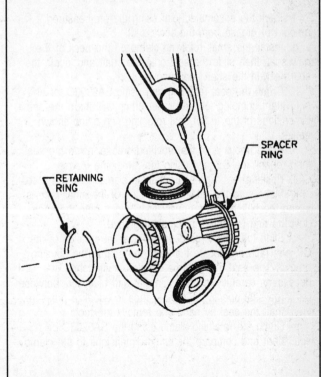

Fig. 61 Slide the spacer ring and spider back along the halfshaft, then remove the retaining ring

g. Place about ½ of the grease from the kit inside the seal and use the remainder to re-pack the tri-pot housing.

h. Install the convolute retainer over the seal. The retainer must be in position when the joint is assembled or seal damage may result.

i. Position the retaining clamp around the large diameter of the seal, the slide the tri-pot housing over the tri-pot assembly on the shaft.

j. Slide the large diameter of the seal over the outside of the tri-pot housing and locate the seal lip in the housing groove. The seal must not be dimpled or stretched. If necessary, carefully insert a thin, flat and blunt tool between the large seal opening and outer race to equalize pressure, then shaft the seal by hand and remove the tool.

k. Position the tri-pot assembly at the proper dimensions, as shown in Fig. 66, then install the large seal retaining clamp around the seal. Close the clamp using SA9161C or equivalent.

2. Assemble and install the outer CV-joint and seal:

a. Inspect the CV-joint parts for any signs of unusual wear, cracks or damage and replace the joint assembly, if necessary.

b. Put a light coat of grease on the inner and outer race grooves, then insert and rotate the inner race into the cage.

c. Install the cage and inner race into the outer race with the windows of the cage aligned with the lines of the outer race.

d. Use a brass drift to gently cock the cage/race and install the balls.

e. If removed, install the race retaining ring into the inner race.

f. Pack the assembled joint using the premeasured amount of grease from the service kit.

g. Install the small retaining clamp on the neck of the new seal, then slide the seal onto the shaft and locate the seal neck in the shaft seal groove.

h. Crimp the seal retaining ring using SA9203C, or an equivalent crimping tool. A proper crimp will share the same dimensions of the tri-pot seal retaining ring crimp shown earlier.

i. Place about ½ of the provided grease inside the seal, then repack the CV-joint using the remaining grease.

j. Position the large seal retaining clamp around the seal.

k. Make sure the retaining ring side of the inner race is facing the halfshaft, then push the CV-joint onto the shaft until the ring is seated in the shaft groove.

l. Slide the seal large diameter over the outside of the CV-joint race and locate the lip of the seal in the housing groove. The seal must not be dimpled or stretched. If necessary, carefully insert a thin, flat and blunt tool between the large seal opening and outer race to equalize pressure, then shaft the seal by hand and remove the tool.

m. Crimp the retaining clamp using the SA9203C or equivalent and compare the crimp dimensions to the clamp

crimped earlier. Recrimp if necessary to achieve the proper dimension.

n. If removed, position the deflecting ring at the CV-joint outer race. Use SA9160 or equivalent along with a M20 x 1.0 nut to tighten the tool until the deflector bottoms against the shoulder of the CV-joint outer race.

3. Remove the shaft assembly from the vise and install in the vehicle.

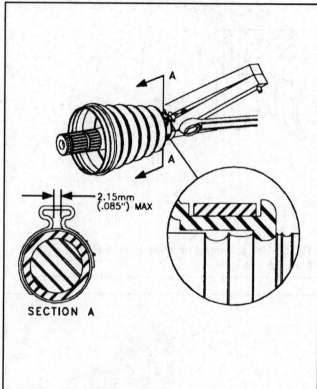

Fig. 62 Crimp the seal retaining clamp according to the dimensions shown in section A

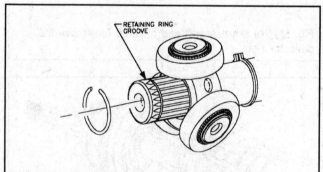

Fig. 63 Install the spacer ring and spider past the retaining groove, then install the retaining ring

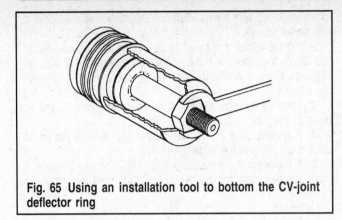

Fig. 65 Using an installation tool to bottom the CV-joint deflector ring

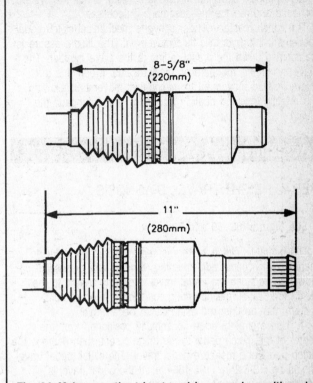

Fig. 64 Make sure the tri-pot seal is properly positioned before installing the large seal retaining clamp

CLUTCH

▶ See Figures 66 and 67

✳✳CAUTION

The clutch driven disc contains asbestos, which has been determined to be a cancer causing agent. Never clean clutch surfaces with compressed air! Avoid inhaling any dust from any clutch surface! When cleaning clutch surfaces, use a commercially available brake cleaning fluid.

The purpose of the clutch is to disconnect and connect engine power at the transmission. A car at rest requires a lot of engine torque to get all that weight moving. An internal combustion engine does not develop a high starting torque (unlike steam engines), so it must be allowed to operate without any load until it builds up enough torque to move the car. Torque increases with engine rpm. The clutch allows the engine to build up torque by physically disconnecting the engine from the transmission, relieving the engine of any load or resistance. The transfer of engine power to the transmission (the load) must be smooth and gradual; if it weren't, drive line components would wear out or break quickly. This gradual power transfer is made possible by gradually releasing the clutch pedal. The clutch disc and pressure plate are the connecting link between the engine and transmission. When the clutch pedal is released, the disc and plate contact each other (clutch engagement), physically joining the engine and

transmission. When the pedal is pushed in, the disc and plate separate (the clutch is disengaged), disconnecting the engine from the transmission.

The Saturn clutch is a single plate, dry friction disc with a diaphragm-style spring pressure plate. The clutch disc has a splined hub which attaches the disc to the input shaft. The disc has friction material where it contacts the flywheel and pressure plate. Torsion springs on the disc help absorb engine torque pulses. The pressure plate applies pressure to the clutch disc, holding it tight against the surface of the flywheel. The clutch operating mechanism consists of a release bearing, fork and cylinder assembly. The release fork and slave cylinder transfer pedal motion to the release bearing. In the engaged position (pedal released), the diaphragm spring holds the pressure plate against the clutch disc, so engine torque is transmitted to the input shaft. When the clutch pedal is depressed, the release bearing pushes the diaphragm spring center toward the flywheel. The diaphragm spring pivots the fulcrum, relieving the load on the pressure plate. Steel spring straps riveted to the clutch cover lift the pressure plate from the clutch disc, disengaging the engine drive from the transaxle and enabling the gears to be changed.

The clutch hydraulic control system consists of a fluid reservoir, master cylinder, slave cylinder and pressure line. The clutch master cylinder and reservoir are mounted on the firewall (bulkhead). Fluid level is checked at the reservoir. The hydraulic unit is self-adjusting, no adjustments are necessary or possible. Also, the system is a sealed unit which should not require periodic checking. If fluid is missing, check the system for leaks and replace the assembly, if necessary.

The clutch master cylinder converts mechanical clutch pedal movement into hydraulic fluid movement. The fluid pressure is transmitted down the pressure line to the slave cylinder. The slave cylinder is mounted on the transaxle. It converts the hydraulic fluid movement to mechanical movement, allowing the release fork and bearing to engage and disengage the clutch.

Adjustments

PEDAL HEIGHT/TRAVEL DIAGNOSIS

▶ See Figures 68, 69 and 70

The hydraulic clutch system is self-adjusting, therefore no manual clutch pedal adjustments are necessary or possible. However, because the pedal travel is directly related to the clutch fork travel, the operating condition of the hydraulic system may be checked using clutch pedal travel.

1. Use a straight edge horizontally positioned from the center of the clutch pedal to the driver's seat, then depress the clutch pedal and measure pedal travel. The clutch pedal travel should be 5.3-6.2 in. (135-156mm). If the pedal travel is insufficient, look for an obvious cause such as carpet or floor mat blocking the pedal or a faulty/damaged pedal.

2. Through the access hole on the side of the transaxle (immediately to the right of the slave cylinder), use a caliper or depth gauge to measure travel of the clutch fork with the pedal in the full up and full down positions. Subtract the full down measurement from the full up to arrive at fork travel

➡If no caliper or depth gauge is available, use a round wire rod in the access hole and mark the pedal up/down positions. Then measure the distance between the 2 marks to arrive at fork travel.

3. Compare the fork and pedal travel measurements using the chart in Fig. 72.

4. If fork travel is less than the minimum allowable, check the following. Conditions A and B require replacement of the master/slave cylinder assembly:
   a. Fluid leaks in the hydraulic system.
   b. Air in the system.
   c. Damaged master or slave cylinder
   d. Damage to the front of the dash.

5. If fork travel is acceptable and the hydraulics are working properly, check for a bent fork or damaged pressure plate which may cause the improper pedal travel.

Clutch Pedal

REMOVAL & INSTALLATION

▶ See Figures 71 and 72

1. Remove the 2 dashboard upper trim panel screw caps (located near the windshield at either end of the dash) by

carefully prying with a small flathead tool. Remove the upper trim panel screws.

2. Lift the upper trim panel to disengage the clips at the rear edge, then pull the panel rearward and out of the clips at the base of the windshield. Remove the upper trim panel from the vehicle.

3. Remove the clutch pushrod retainer, then remove the pushrod from the clutch pedal.

4. If replacing the clutch pedal assembly, remove the pedal pivot shaft nut and the pedal assembly.

5. If replacing the pivot bushings, remove the pedal pivot shaft retainer,, then remove the clutch pedal and the pedal bushings.

To install:

6. If replacing the pivot bushings, install the new bushings and lubricate the bushing inner diameters. Install the clutch pedal onto the pivot and install the retainer.

7. If replacing the pedal assembly, install the assembly and tighten the retaining nut to 151 inch lbs. (17 Nm).

8. Install the pushrod retainer.

9. Install the upper trim panel by inserting into the clips at the windshield, then snapping the rear of the panel into place. Install the upper trim panel screws, then snap the screw covers into position.

Clutch Disc and Plate Assembly

REMOVAL & INSTALLATION

▶ See Figures 73, 74, 75, 76, 77 and 78

1. Properly disable the SIR system, if equipped, and disconnect the negative battery cable.

2. Remove the transaxle from the vehicle.

3. Unsnap the release fork from the ball stud, then remove the fork and bearing from the vehicle. Slide the bearing from the fork. The bearing should be checked for excessive play and for minimal bearing drag. It should be replaced if no/little drag or excessive play is found.

➡The release bearing is packed with grease and should not be washed with solvent.

4. Using a feeler gauge, measure the distance between the pressure plate and flywheel surfaces in order to determine clutch face thickness. Replace the clutch disc if it is not within specification; 0.205-0.287 in. (5.2-7.3mm).

5. Remove the pressure plate-to-flywheel bolts in a progressive crisscross pattern to prevent warping the cover, then remove the pressure plate and clutch disc.

6. Inspect the pressure plate:
   a. Check for excessive wear, chatter marks, cracks or overheating (indicated by a blue discoloration). Black random spots on the friction surface of the pressure plate is normal.
   b. Then check the plate for warpage using a straight edge and a feeler gauge; the maximum allowable warpage is 0.276 in. (0.7mm).
   c. Replace the plate, if necessary.

7. Inspect the clutch disc:
   a. Check the disc face for oil or burnt spots.
   b. Check the disc for loose damper springs, hub or rivets.

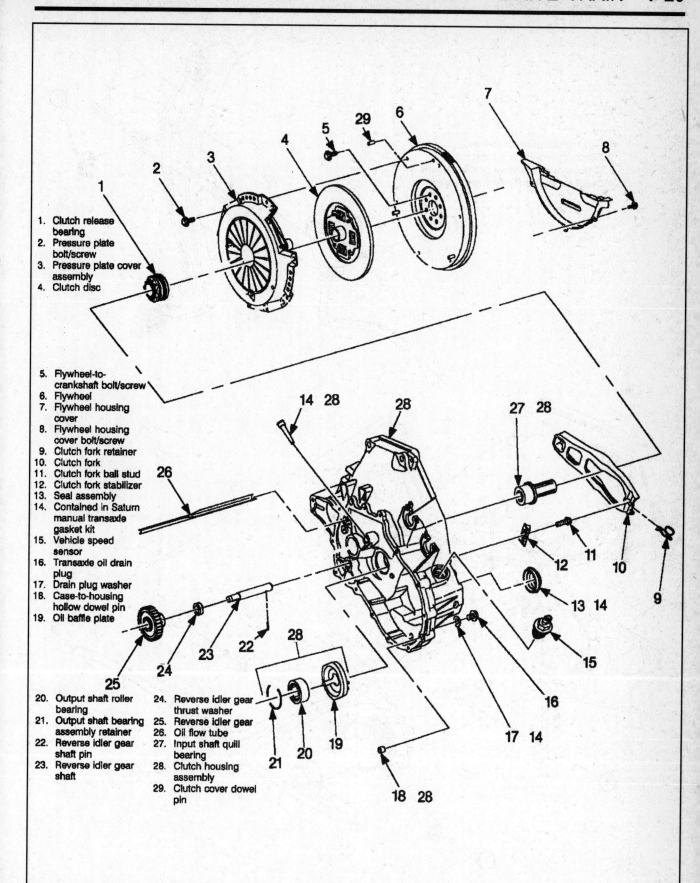

1. Clutch release bearing
2. Pressure plate bolt/screw
3. Pressure plate cover assembly
4. Clutch disc
5. Flywheel-to-crankshaft bolt/screw
6. Flywheel
7. Flywheel housing cover
8. Flywheel housing cover bolt/screw
9. Clutch fork retainer
10. Clutch fork
11. Clutch fork ball stud
12. Clutch fork stabilizer
13. Seal assembly
14. Contained in Saturn manual transaxle gasket kit
15. Vehicle speed sensor
16. Transaxle oil drain plug
17. Drain plug washer
18. Case-to-housing hollow dowel pin
19. Oil baffle plate

20. Output shaft roller bearing
21. Output shaft bearing assembly retainer
22. Reverse idler gear shaft pin
23. Reverse idler gear shaft
24. Reverse idler gear thrust washer
25. Reverse idler gear
26. Oil flow tube
27. Input shaft quill bearing
28. Clutch housing assembly
29. Clutch cover dowel pin

Fig. 66 Exploded view of the clutch assembly

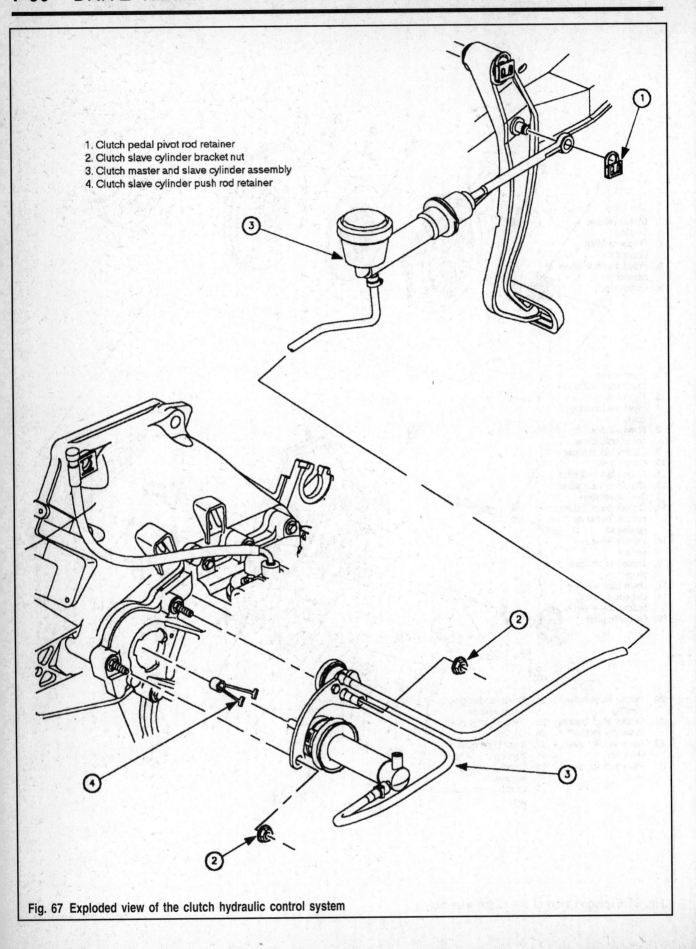

1. Clutch pedal pivot rod retainer
2. Clutch slave cylinder bracket nut
3. Clutch master and slave cylinder assembly
4. Clutch slave cylinder push rod retainer

Fig. 67 Exploded view of the clutch hydraulic control system

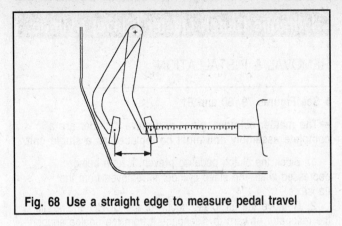

Fig. 68 Use a straight edge to measure pedal travel

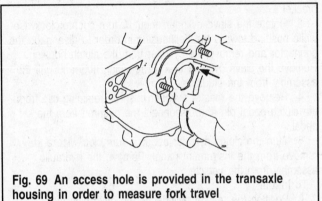

Fig. 69 An access hole is provided in the transaxle housing in order to measure fork travel

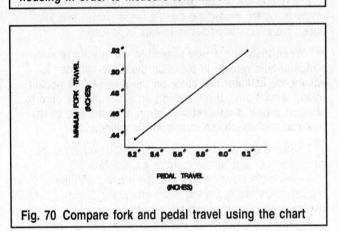

Fig. 70 Compare fork and pedal travel using the chart

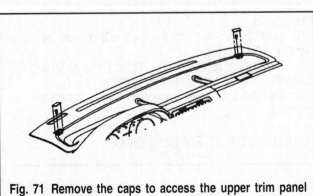

Fig. 71 Remove the caps to access the upper trim panel retaining screws

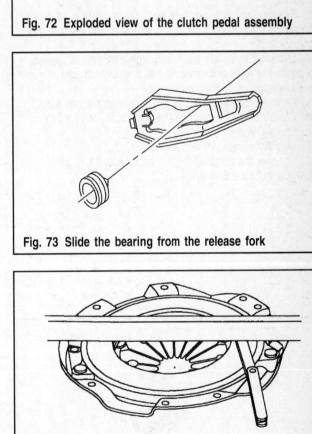

Fig. 72 Exploded view of the clutch pedal assembly

Fig. 73 Slide the bearing from the release fork

Fig. 74 Check the pressure plate for warpage

c. Replace the disc, if necessary.

8. Check the flywheel:

a. Check the ring gear for wear or damage.

b. Check the friction surface for excessive wear, chatter marks, cracks or overheating (indicated by a blue discoloration). Black random spots on the friction surface of the pressure plate is normal.

c. Check flywheel thickness; the minimum allowable is 1.102 in. (28mm).

d. Measure flywheel runout using a dial indicator, positioned for at least 2 flywheel revolutions. Push the crankshaft forward to take up thrust bearing clearance. Maximum flywheel runout is 0.006 in. (0.15mm).

e. Replace the flywheel, if necessary.

9. If necessary, remove the flywheel retaining bolts and remove the flywheel from the crankshaft.

To install:

10. If removed, install the flywheel and tighten the bolts in a criss-cross sequence to 59 ft. lbs. (80 Nm).

11. Install the clutch disc and pressure plate with the yellow dot on the pressure plate aligned as close as possible to the mark on the flywheel. The clutch disc is labeled FLYWHEEL SIDE in order to help correctly position the disc. Start the pressure plate bolts.

12. Install clutch alignment tool SA9145T or equivalent, in the clutch disc and push in until it bottoms out in the crankshaft.

13. Tighten the pressure plate bolts using multiple passes of a crisscross sequence to 18 ft. lbs. (25 Nm) and remove the alignment tool.

14. Lube the fork pivot point with high temperature grease and install the release bearing to the fork. Do not lube the release bearing or bearing quill.

15. Snap the release bearing and fork onto the ball stud.

16. Lube the splines of the input shaft lightly with a high temperature grease.

17. Install the transaxle assembly.

18. Connect the negative battery cable and if equipped, properly enable the SIR system.

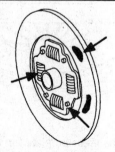

Fig. 75 Check the clutch disc for oil or burnt spots and check for loose springs, hub or rivets

Hydraulic Clutch Master (Slave) Cylinder

REMOVAL & INSTALLATION

▶ **See Figures 79, 80 and 81**

➡**The master cylinder, pipes and slave cylinder are a complete assembly and must be replaced as a single unit.**

1. Block the clutch pedal to prevent it from being depressed while the slave cylinder is removed from the transaxle.

2. Remove the air intake duct. For the DOHC engine, lift the resonator upward to disengage it from the engine support bracket.

3. Rotate the slave cylinder about ¼ turn counterclockwise while pushing toward the bellhousing in order to disengage the connector and remove the cylinder from the clutch housing. Remove the slave cylinder bracket retaining nuts and pull the assembly from the studs.

4. Remove the master cylinder pushrod retaining clip from the clutch pedal pin and disconnect the pushrod from the pedal.

5. Turn the clutch cylinder about ⅛ turn clockwise and remove from the instrument panel. Remove the hydraulic assembly from the vehicle.

To install:

6. Position the master cylinder to the dash with the reservoir leaning toward the driver's fender. Install and turn about ⅛ turn counterclockwise to lock in position.

➡ **When installing a new assembly, the plastic retainer straps should remain in place on the slave cylinder to ensure the actuator rod seats on the release fork pocket upon installation. If reinstalling an assembly, be sure to position a new plastic retainer strap onto the end of the pushrod and attach the straps to the cylinder.**

7. Slide the slave cylinder onto the clutch housing studs, install the nuts and tighten to 18 ft. lbs. (25 Nm).

8. Insert the slave cylinder into the housing with the bleeder screw facing forward and rotate about ¼ turn clockwise while pushing into the housing.

9. Lube the clutch pedal pin with silicone grease, then connect the pushrod to the clutch pedal and install the retaining clip.

10. Install the air inlet duct assembly and connect the negative battery cable.

11. Remove the block from behind the clutch pedal and if equipped, properly enable the SIR system.

12. Start the engine and check the pedal for proper operation.

HYDRAULIC SYSTEM BLEEDING

The clutch hydraulic assembly is serviced as a complete unit which has been filled with fluid and bled of air at the factory. The unit does not require periodic checking. The system is full when the reservoir is half full.

Only DOT 3 brake fluid should be added to the system. If fluid levels drop, inspect the system, including the slave

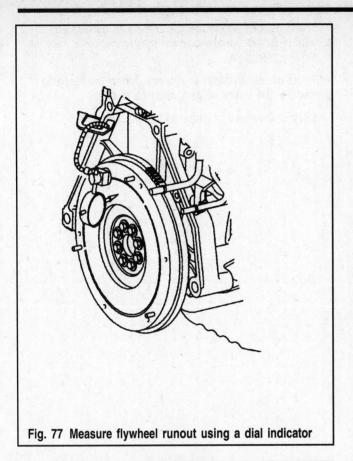

Fig. 77 Measure flywheel runout using a dial indicator

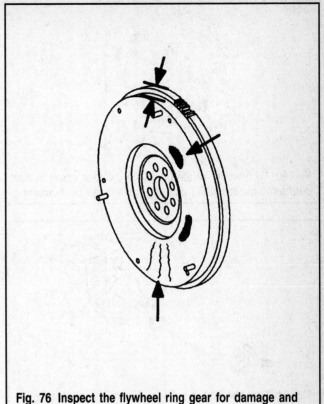

Fig. 76 Inspect the flywheel ring gear for damage and the contact surface for wear

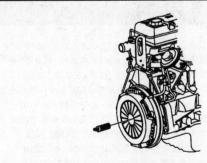

Fig. 78 Install a proper clutch alignment tool before tightening the pressure plate retaining bolts

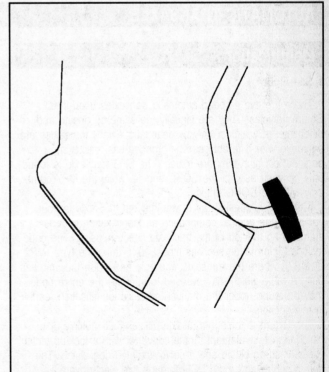

Fig. 79 Block the clutch pedal to prevent the slave cylinder from damage should the pedal be depressed while the cylinder is removed from the transaxle

cylinder, for leakage. A slight wetting of the slave cylinder surface is normal. Should an assembly have air in the system and not require replacement, bleed the assembly as follows:

1. Fill the clutch master cylinder reservoir with brake fluid. Be careful not to spill brake fluid on the painted surface of the vehicle.

2. Fit a vinyl bleeder tube over the bleeder screw at the front of the slave cylinder and place the other end in a clean jar half filled with brake fluid.

3. Have an assistant depress the clutch pedal several times. Loosen the bleeder screw and allow the fluid to flow into the jar.

4. Tighten the screw and have the assistant release the clutch pedal.

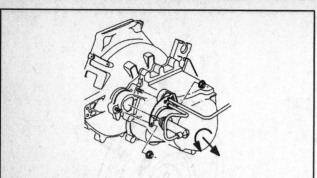

Fig. 80 To remove, rotate the slave cylinder about ¼ turn counterclockwise while pushing toward the bellhousing

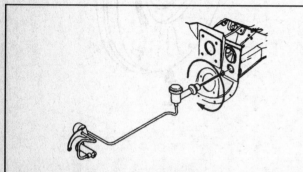

Fig. 81 Turn the clutch cylinder about ⅛ turn clockwise and remove from the instrument panel

5. Repeat bleeding procedure until no air bubbles are present in the fluid. Make sure the master cylinder is kept full during the procedure.

➡ **If the master cylinder is run dry during the bleeding procedure, the entire system must be re-bled.**

6. Refill the master cylinder to the specified level.

AUTOMATIC TRANSAXLE

Identification

▶ **See Figure 1**

There are two 4-speed automatic transaxles used in all Saturn vehicles. They are virtually the same by design and differ internally almost only by gear ratio. The 2 transaxles are equipped with different gears in order to best utilize the engines to which they are mated. The MP6 transaxle is found only on vehicles with the SOHC engine, while the MP7 came only with the DOHC engine.

If there is a question as to whether the transaxle in your vehicle is the original component, an identification code is stamped on the top of the transaxle clutch housing. The code includes information such as model year, transaxle type (MP2 or MP3), where the transaxle was built and when the unit was built. A table which may be used to interpret the entire code may be found under the manual transaxle identification, earlier in this section.

The Saturn automatic transaxle utilizes four multiple disc clutches, a four element torque converter with a lock-up clutch, 1st gear sprag clutch and a servo actuated dog clutch. The unit is controlled by the PCM through five electrohydraulic actuators in order to provide shift timing, shift feel and on-board diagnosis. A POWER/NORMAL button in the center console can be used to communicate with the PCM to alter shift points for performance/economy.

The PCM is capable of performing self-diagnostic functions on the various electronic transaxle control circuits. The SHIFT TO D2 light will illuminate and remain on if certain trouble codes are present in memory. Codes and flags are extracted using the ALDL, as described in Section 4 of this manual.

For the 1993 model year no significant change was made in the transaxle itself, but the PCM transaxle controller was changed in order to produce smoother and more efficient shifts. This new controller also contained additional trouble codes and flags.

Fluid and Filter

The Saturn automatic transaxles utilize a spin-on type fluid filter for ease of maintenance. Refer to Section 1, of this manual for fluid and filter replacement procedures.

Neutral Safety/Selector/Reverse Light Switch

REMOVAL & INSTALLATION

▶ **See Figure 82**

1. Disconnect the negative battery cable.

2. Remove the air induction tube. For the DOHC engine, remove the air filter box. Lift the resonator upward to disengage it from the support bracket.

3. Unplug the electrical connectors from the switch and disconnect the shifter cable from the control lever.

4. For assembly purposes, note the position of the control lever shaft and manual lever, then remove the retaining nut from the control lever shaft and remove the manual lever.

5. Remove the 2 switch retaining bolts, then remove the switch from the transaxle.

To install:

6. Install the switch to the transaxle and loosely install the retaining bolts.

7. Position the manual lever as noted during removal and install the nut. Tighten the nut to 97 inch lbs. (11 Nm).

8. Adjust the switch and tighten the retaining bolts.

9. Install the cable to the control lever and adjust as necessary. Refer to the procedure found later in this section.

10. Connect the switch electrical connectors and install the air induction tube.

11. Connect the negative battery cable and verify proper switch operation.

ADJUSTMENT

▶ **See Figure 83**

1. Place the transaxle selector in **D**. Use an ohmmeter or continuity tester to check for continuity across the switch terminals.

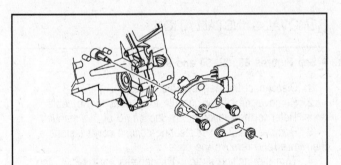

Fig. 82 Exploded view of the neutral safety/selector/reverse light switch mounting

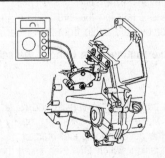

Fig. 83 Use an ohmmeter to properly adjust the neutral safety switch

2. If no continuity exists, loosen the bolts and rotate the switch to achieve continuity.

3. Tighten the switch bolts to 142 inch lbs. (16 Nm) and recheck continuity.

Shift/Selector Cables

REMOVAL & INSTALLATION

▶ **See Figures 84, 85 and 86**

Before beginning this procedure, place the transaxle in **P** and note the position of the transaxle shift lever for installation purposes.

1. Disconnect the negative battery cable and block the drive wheels.

2. Remove the center console for access to the cable ends. Refer to the procedure in Section 10 of this manual.

3. Position the shifter in 2nd gear, then disconnect the cable end from the shift lever. Reposition the shifter in **P**.

4. Depress the 2 tabs on the cable housing, then remove the cable from the shifter assembly.

5. Remove the air induction tube. For the DOHC engine, remove the air filter box. Lift the resonator upward to disengage it from the support bracket.

6. Disconnect the cable from the transaxle shift lever.

7. Carefully press the 2 retaining tabs and remove the cable from the converter housing.

8. Lift the front of the vehicle and support safely using jackstands.

9. Remove the 2 retaining nuts, then remove the cable grommet from the front of the dash by pushing the grommet and retaining plate into the vehicle.

10. Remove the cables from the vehicle.

To install:

11. Feed the cable and the retainer plate through the front of the dash, then install retainer plate to the grommet and tighten the retaining nuts to 62 inch lbs. (7 Nm).

12. Remove the jackstands and carefully lower the vehicle.

13. Connect the cable end to the console shifter lever.

14. Install the cable housing to the shifter assembly.

15. Install the center console.

16. Install the cable into the converter housing and position the transaxle shift lever in the **P** position.

17. Adjust the cable by releasing the lock tab using a screwdriver to pry the tab upward, then lifting the tab by hand. Connect the shift cable to the transaxle lever and install the retainer, then move the cable back and forth in the adjuster to not end-play. Center the cable in the middle of the end-play, press in the lock tab and verify proper operation.

18. Install the air intake tube, remove the wheel blocks and connect the negative battery cable.

ADJUSTMENT

▶ **See Figure 87**

This procedure begins with the shift cable disconnected from the transaxle.

1. Place the transaxle in the **P** position.

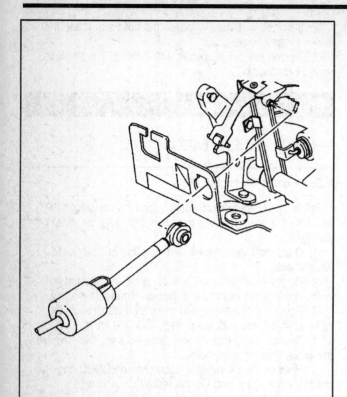

Fig. 84 Disconnect the cable end from the console shifter

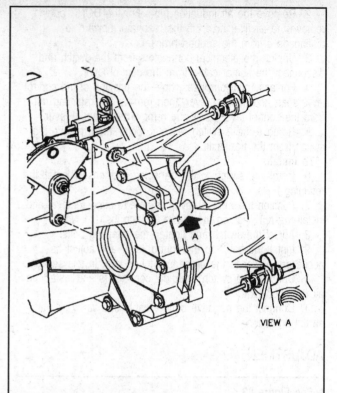

Fig. 85 Disconnect the cable from the transaxle shift lever and converter housing

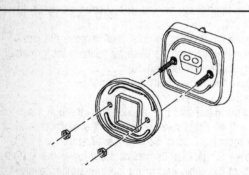

Fig. 86 Remove the 2 nuts and the grommet from the front of the dash

2. Place the transaxle shift lever in the **P** position.
3. Release the cable adjustment lock tab using a screwdriver to pry the tab upward, then lift the tab by hand.
4. Connect the cable to the shift transaxle lever and install the retainer.
5. Move the cable housing back and forth in the adjuster to note end-play.
6. Center the cable housing in the middle of the end-play.
7. Press in the lock tab and check operation.

Park Lock Cable

REMOVAL & INSTALLATION

◗ See Figures 88, 89, 90 and 91

1. Disconnect the negative battery cable.
2. Remove the center console for access to the cable ends. Refer to the procedure in Section 10 of this manual.
3. Remove the 3 lower steering column cover fasteners, then lower and remove the cover.
4. Turn the ignition switch **ON**, depress the retaining tab and remove the cable from the retaining module.
5. For 1992-1993 vehicles, unplug the Brake Transaxle Shift Interlock (BTSI) electrical connector.
6. Unsnap the end terminal of the park lock cable from the plastic lock-out lever on the shift
7. Depress the 2 tabs on the end fitting of the cable housing, then remove the cable from the shifter assemble.

➡Note the cable routing, then remove the cable from the vehicle.

To install:

8. Install the cable into the vehicle and route as noted during removal. Make sure the cable is properly routed through the retainer on the accelerator pedal bracket.
9. Turn the ignition switch **ON**, then insert the cassette end of the cable into the ignition module and turn the ignition **OFF**.
10. Install and fully seat the cable fitting end to the shifter assembly.

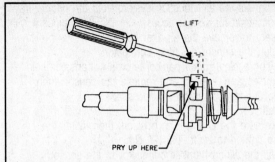

Fig. 87 To release the selector cable lock tab, lift upward using a screwdriver or small prybar

11. Lift the lock tab on the cable end fitting to allow the housing to move freely in the end fitting.

12. Attach the end terminal to the plastic lock-out lever on the shifter.

13. For 1992-1993 vehicles, connect the BTSI wiring harness.

14. Properly adjust the cable, connect the negative battery cable and verify proper cable operation.

15. Install the lower column cover and the center console.

ADJUSTMENT

▶ **See Figure 92**

1. Remove the console assembly. Refer to the procedure in Section 10 of this manual.

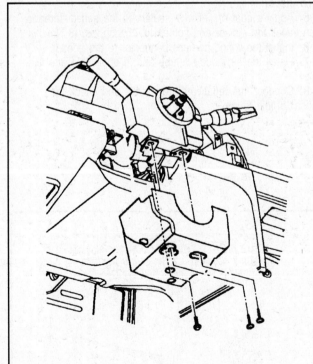

Fig. 88 Remove the lower steering column cover for access to the cable end

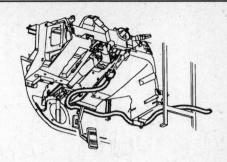

Fig. 90 Note the cable routing before removing the park lock cable from the vehicle

2. For 1991 vehicles, turn the ignition switch **OFF**. For 1992-93 vehicles, turn the ignition switch to **ON**.

3. Place the shifter in **P** and make sure the brake pedal is released, then depress the lock on the cable end fitting and remove the adjustment clip from the end terminal on a new cable.

4. If adjusting a cable which does not have an adjustment clip, secure the end of the cable to provide a 0.05 inch (1.25mm) gap between the cable end and the park lock connector.

5. Verify proper adjustment:

   a. With the ignition **OFF** the lever should not shift out of **P**.

   b. Turn the ignition to the **ON** position and the lever should shift.

   c. With the lever out of **P** and the ignition **OFF**, the key cannot be removed from the ignition.

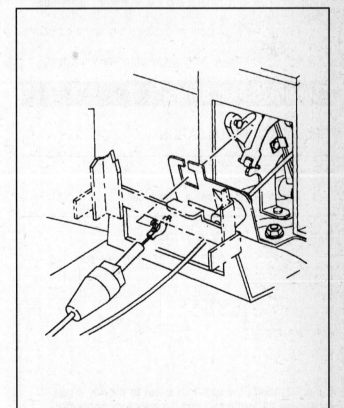

Fig. 89 Remove the cable from the shifter assembly

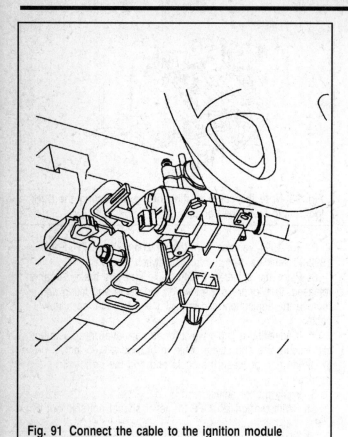

Fig. 91 Connect the cable to the ignition module

d. With the lever out of **P** and the ignition **OFF**, the lever should not shift.

e. With the ignition **OFF** and the lever in **P**, remove the key.

6. Repeat the adjustment procedure if any of the conditions were incorrect.

7. Install the console assembly when properly adjusted.

Turbine Speed Sensor

REMOVAL & INSTALLATION

▶ See Figure 93

1. Disconnect the negative battery cable.

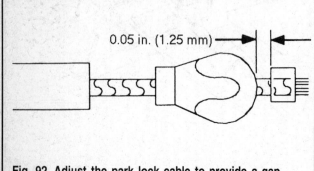

Fig. 92 Adjust the park lock cable to provide a gap between the cable end and the park lock connector

2. Disconnect the air induction system from the battery tray and position aside for sensor access. On DOHC engines it will be necessary to remove the air filter box.

3. Unplug the sensor electrical connector.

4. Position a clean drain pan to catch any transaxle fluid which might escape. Loosen and remove the sensor, then inspect the O-ring and replace, if necessary.

To install:

5. Make sure the O-ring is in position, then install the sensor and tighten to 20 ft. lbs. (26 Nm).

6. Install the wiring harness connector to the sensor.

7. Install the air induction tube and, if applicable, the filter box.

8. Connect the negative battery cable and check the transaxle fluid level.

Transaxle Temperature Sensor

REMOVAL & INSTALLATION

▶ See Figure 94

1. Disconnect the negative battery cable.

2. Disconnect the air induction system from the battery tray and position aside for sensor access. On DOHC engines it will be necessary to remove the air filter box.

3. Using a pair of pliers to squeeze the connector, unplug the wiring harness from the sensor.

4. Position a clean drain pan to catch any transaxle fluid which might escape., then remove the sensor from the transaxle.

To install:

5. Apply a coat of Teflon® sealant to the sensor threads, then install the sensor and tighten to 71 inch lbs. (8 Nm).

6. Install the wiring harness connector to the sensor.

7. Install the air induction tube and, if applicable, the filter box.

8. Connect the negative battery cable and check the transaxle fluid level.

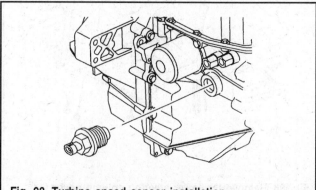

Fig. 93 Turbine speed sensor installation

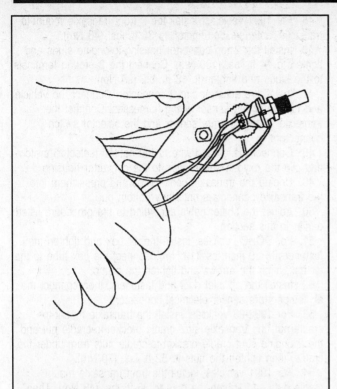

Fig. 94 Unplug the wiring harness from the transaxle temperature sensor connector by squeezing with a pair of pliers and pulling the connector from the sensor

Transaxle

REMOVAL & INSTALLATION

▶ See Figures 95, 96, 97, 98, 99, 100, 101, 101, 102, 103, 104, 105 and 106

1. Properly disable the SIR system, if equipped and disconnect the negative battery cable.

2. Remove the 2 air inlet duct fasteners, unplug the air temperature sensor connector and remove the air inlet duct. For the DOHC engine, loosen the flex tube to air box clamp, remove the 3 air box fasteners and remove the air box.

3. For 1992-93 vehicles, remove the transaxle strut-to-cradle bracket through bolt located on the radiator side of the transaxle.

4. Unplug the vehicle and turbine speed sensor, transaxle temperature sensor, selector switch and actuator connectors from the transaxle.

5. Remove the 2 ground terminals from the top 2 converter housing studs.

6. Remove the ground wire from the neutral (selector) switch and unclip the oxygen sensor wire retainer from the converter housing.

7. Remove the top 2 converter housing studs.

8. Remove the 4 DIS coil to converter housing bolts, then wire the coil to the cylinder head coolant outlet. Discard the old coil retaining bolts and replace with new bolts upon installation.

9. For 1991 vehicles, loosen the 2 front transaxle mount-to-transaxle fasteners.

10. Wire the radiator to the upper radiator support in order to hold the assembly in place when the cradle is removed.

11. Install SA9105E or an equivalent engine support bar assembly. Make sure the support feet are positioned on the outer edge of the shock tower, the bar hooks are connected to the engine bracket and the stabilizer foot is on the engine block (to the right of the oil dipstick).

12. Raise the front of the vehicle sufficiently to lower the transaxle and the engine cradle. Support the vehicle safely using jackstands. Make sure the jackstands are not positioned under the engine cradle.

13. Remove the drain plug from the transaxle housing and drain the transaxle fluid. The drain plug is on the lower cowl side of the housing and is inserted from the engine side of the vehicle.

14. Remove the front wheels and engine splash shields from the vehicle. For coupes, remove the left and right lower facia braces.

15. For 1992-93 vehicles, remove the front engine strut cradle bracket-to-cradle nuts from below the cradle.

16. Remove the transaxle mount-to-cradle nut from under the cradle.

17. Remove and discard the cotter pin from the lower ball joints. Back the ball joint nut until the top of the nut is even with the top of the threads.

18. Use tool SA9132S to separate the ball joint from the lower control arm, then remove the nut. Do not use a wedge tool or seal damage may occur.

❊❊WARNING

The outer CV-joint for vehicles equipped with ABS contains a speed sensor ring. Use of an incorrect tool to separate the control arm from the knuckle may result in damage to and loss of the ABS system.

19. Remove the front exhaust pipe nuts at the manifold, then disconnect the pipe from the support bracket.

20. Remove the front pipe to catalytic converter bolts and lower the pipe from the vehicle.

21. Remove the engine-to-transaxle stiffening bracket bolts and remove the bracket. For 1991 vehicles, remove the rear transaxle mount bracket-to-transaxle bolts, then loosen the mount bolt and allow the bracket to hang out of the w

22. Remove the steering rack to cradle bolts and wire the gear for support when the cradle is removed. Remove the brake line and retainer from the cradle.

23. Remove the clutch housing dust cover, then remove the torque converter to flywheel bolts.

24. For 1991 vehicles, remove the front transaxle mount-to-cradle nuts and the engine lower mount-to-cradle nuts. Nuts are all located under the front or side cradle member.

25. Position two 4 inch x 4 inch x 36 inch pieces of wood onto a powertrain support dolly and position the dolly under the vehicle.

26. Remove the 4 cradle-to-body bolts and carefully lower the cradle from the vehicle with the support dolly. Tape or wire the 2 large washers from the rear cradle to body attachments in position to prevent lo

27. Squeeze the plastic tabs at the transaxle cooler line connectors and pull the lines out of the connectors. The plastic retainer should remain on the lines. Connect 1 end of a $^5/_8$ inch rubber hose over each cooler line to prevent fluid contamination or lo

28. If necessary for the transaxle to clear the body, lower the transaxle side of the assembly until the valve body cover clears the frame.

29. Support the transaxle securely with a suitable jack.

30. Use an appropriate pry bar to separate the left side axle from the transaxle. Only remove the axle sufficiently to install SA91112T or an equivalent seal protector around the axle and into the seal to prevent the seal from being cut by the shaft spline.

31. Remove the 2 bottom converter housing to engine bolts and lower the transaxle sufficiently to reach the shifter cable. Separate the axle from the right side, also using a seal protect

32. Disconnect the transaxle shifter cable and remove the cable from the converter housing.

33. Carefully lower the transaxle from the vehicle. Use SA9165T or an equivalent transaxle cooler cleaning tool to clean the cooler and lines.

To install:

34. Place the transaxle assembly securely onto the jack and position under the vehicle. Install axle seal protectors into seals on both sides.

35. Raise the transaxle sufficiently and connect the shifter cable to the gear selector lever and to the converter housing.

36. Raise the transaxle into the vehicle and verify that the intermediate shaft splines line up with the differential side gear spline, then install the 2 lower clutch housing to engine bolts and tighten to 96 ft. lbs. (130 Nm). The bolts should not be used to draw the transaxle to the engine.

37. Install the axle into the transaxle. After the splines clear the seal, but before the axle snaps into place remove the seal protectors. Push the axle all of the way into the transaxle and install the snapring. Remove the transaxle jack.

38. Clean and lubricate the ball joint threads, then raise the cradle up on the support dolly and place the ball joints into the knuckles. Verify the correct positioning of the lower control arm ball studs to the knuckles, the cooling module support bushings, the engine strut bracket and the transaxle mount.

39. Insert $^9/_{16}$ inch round steel rods into the cradle-to-body alignment holes near the front cradle-to-body fastener holes. Guide the cradle into position making sure all mount studs are properly guided into their holes.

40. Make sure the washers are in place and install the 2 rear cradle-to- body bolts. Verify proper cradle positioning and install the 2 front cradle bolts. Tighten the 4 cradle bolts to 151 ft. lbs. (205 Nm).

41. Remove the support dolly, then remove the engine support bar assembly.

42. For 1992-93 vehicles, install the transaxle strut to cradle bracket through bolt and nut, then tighten the fasteners to 52 ft. lbs. (70 Nm).

43. Remove the radiator assembly support wire.

44. Use a 6 **x** 1.0mm tap to clean the sealant from the ignition module mounting holes in the transaxle. Install the ignition module, then secure using the new bolts with sealant. Use extreme caution to assure proper bolt installation. Tighten the bolts to 61 inch lbs. (7 Nm) and verify that the bolt heads are properly seated on the ignition module.

45. For 1991 vehicles, install the 2 front transaxle mount-to-transaxle fasteners and tighten to 35 ft. lbs. (48 Nm).

46. Install the 2 top converter housing-to-engine studs and tighten to 74 ft. lbs. (100 Nm). Connect the 2 ground terminals to the studs and tighten to 18 ft. lbs. (25 Nm).

47. Install the actuator circuit connector. Connect the vehicle and turbine speed sensor wiring harnesses. Connect the transaxle oil temperature sensor and the selector switch connectors.

48. Connect the ground wire to the neutral (selector) switch and clip the oxygen sensor wire to the converter housing.

49. Unplug the transaxle cooler lines and press them into the transaxle connectors until they bottom out.

50. Adjust the shifter cable according to the procedure listed earlier in this section.

51. For DOHC vehicles, install the air box and tighten the fasteners to 89 inch lbs. (10 Nm). Connect the flex tube to the air box, align the arrows and tighten the clamp.

52. Install the air inlet duct and fasteners, then connect the air temperature sensor electrical connector.

53. For 1992-93 vehicles, install the transaxle mount-to-cradle nut, the transaxle strut cradle bracket-to-cradle nut and the 2 engine strut cradle bracket-to-cradle nuts from under the cradle, then tighten the nuts to 52 ft. lbs. (70 Nm).

54. For 1991 vehicles, install the front transaxle mount cradle nuts and tighten the nuts to 35 ft. lbs. (48 Nm). Then install the right side mount-to-cradle nuts and tighten to 40 ft. lbs. (54 Nm).

55. Remove the steering gear support wire and position the gear to the cradle. Install the gear bolts and nuts, then tighten the fasteners to 40 ft. lbs. (54 Nm). Connect the brake line and retainer to the cradle.

56. Install the torque converter-to-flexplate bolts and tighten to 52 ft. lbs. (70 Nm). Install the converter housing dust cover and tighten the bolts to 89 inch lbs. (10 Nm).

57. For 1991 vehicles, install the rear pitch restrictor-to-transaxle bolts and tighten to 40 ft. lbs. (55 Nm). Then install the powertrain stiffening bracket and tighten the bracket-to-powertrain bolts to 35 ft. lbs. (47 Nm).

58. Position the exhaust manifold front pipe into the vehicle and install the manifold retaining nuts. Tighten the nuts in a crosswise pattern to 23 ft. lbs. (31 Nm). Install the front pipe to the catalytic converter and tighten the bolts to 33 ft. lbs. (45 Nm). Finally, install the front pipe to the transaxle support bracket and tighten the fasteners to 23 ft. lbs. (31 Nm).

➡ **If the converter flange threads are damaged use the Saturn 21010753 converter fastener kit in place of the self tapping screws to provide proper clamp load and prevent exhaust leaks.**

59. Install the nuts onto the ball joint studs and tighten to 55 ft. lbs. (75 Nm). Continue to tighten the nuts as necessary and install new cotter pi

60. Install the center and both wheel splash shields.

61. For coupes, install the right left lower facia braces, J-nuts and fasteners. Tighten the fasteners to 89 inch lbs. (10 Nm).

62. Install the tire and wheel assemblies, then remove the jackstands and lower the vehicle.

63. Connect the negative battery cable and fill the transaxle with Dexron®II or equivalent fluid.

64. Properly enable the SIR system, if equipped.

65. Warm the engine and check the transaxle fluid. Check and adjust vehicle alignment, as necessary.

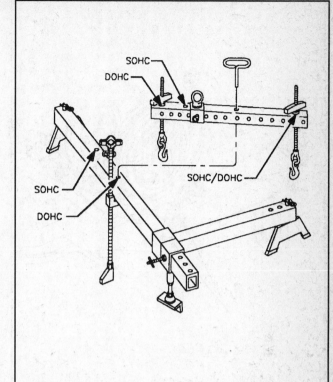

Fig. 97 The Saturn engine support bar assembly — SA9105E

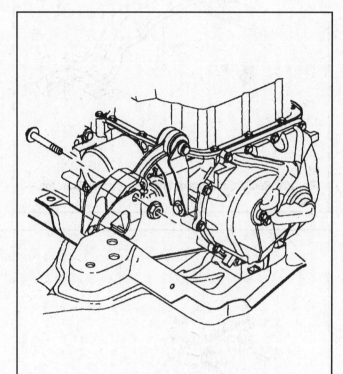

Fig. 95 Remove the transaxle strut-to-cradle bracket through bolt — 1992-1993 vehicles

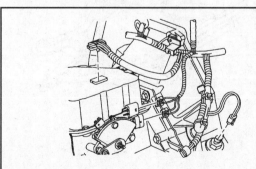

Fig. 96 Unplug the electrical connectors from these transaxle points

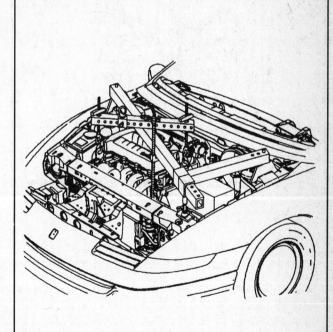

Fig. 98 Properly install SA9105E, or an equivalent engine support bar, to retain the engine when the cradle is removed

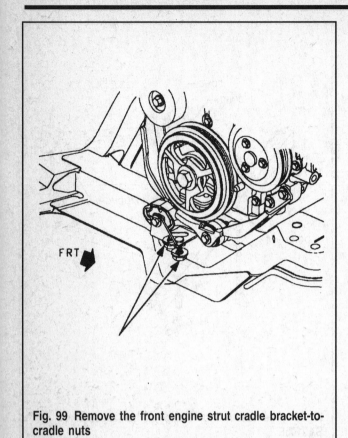

Fig. 99 Remove the front engine strut cradle bracket-to-cradle nuts

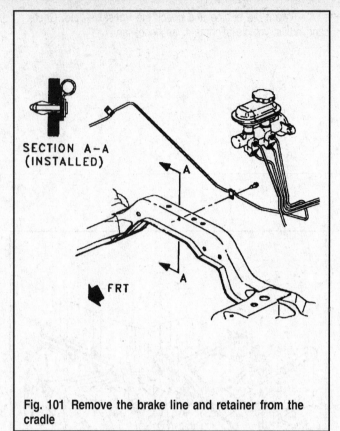

Fig. 101 Remove the brake line and retainer from the cradle

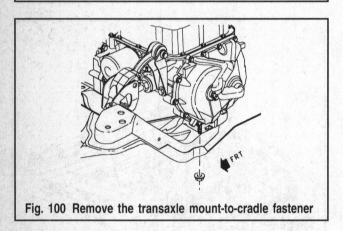

Fig. 100 Remove the transaxle mount-to-cradle fastener

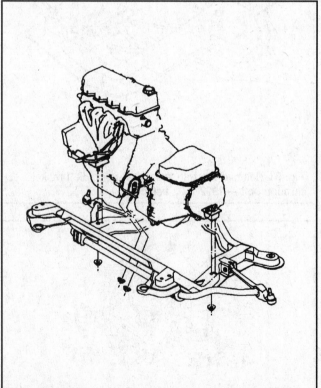

Fig. 102 Front transaxle and engine lower mount nuts — 1991 vehicles

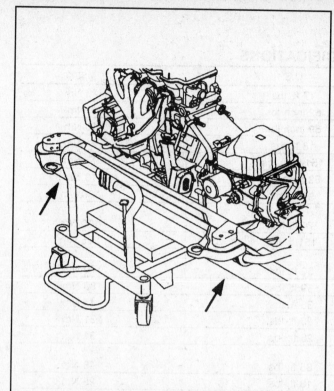

Fig. 103 Position wood on a powertrain support dolly to protect the cradle

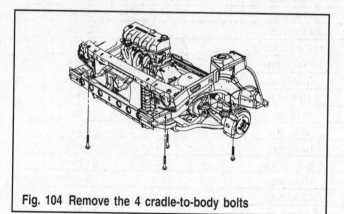

Fig. 104 Remove the 4 cradle-to-body bolts

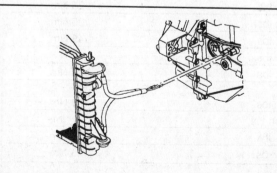

Fig. 105 Remove the transaxle cooler lines from the connectors

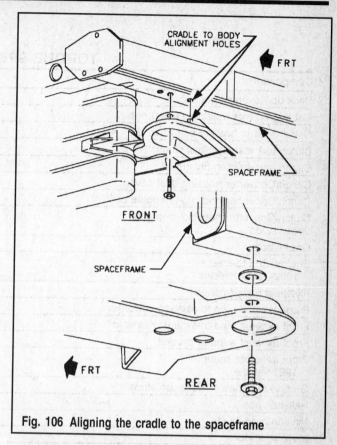

Fig. 106 Aligning the cradle to the spaceframe

Halfshafts

The halfshaft removal, installation and overhaul procedures for the automatic transaxle are identical to those for the manual transaxle. Refer to the halfshaft procedures under the manual transaxle portion of this section.

TORQUE SPECIFICATIONS

Component	U.S.	Metric
Back-up/Reverse light switch	17 ft. lbs.	23 Nm
Cable grommet (retaining plate) nuts	62 inch lbs.	7 Nm
Cable retainer bracket bolt (manual)	89 inch lbs.	10 Nm
Clutch fork stabilizer ball stud	18 ft. lbs.	24 Nm
Clutch pedal assembly nut	151 inch lbs.	17 Nm
Clutch/Converter housing dust cover	89 inch lbs.	10 Nm
Clutch/Converter housing-to-engine bolts	96 ft. lbs.	130 Nm
Clutch/Converter housing-to-engine upper studs	74 ft. lbs.	100 Nm
Cradle bolts	151 ft. lbs.	205 Nm
Engine strut-to-cradle 1992–1993 vehicles	52 ft. lbs.	70 Nm
Flywheel bolts (manual)	59 ft. lbs.	80 Nm
Front exhaust pipe-to-catalytic converter	33 ft. lbs.	45 Nm
Front exhaust pipe-to-exhaust manifold	23 ft. lbs.	31 Nm
Front exhaust support bracket	23 ft. lbs.	31 Nm
Front transaxle mount 1991 vehicle	35 ft. lbs.	48 Nm
Ground terminals-to-transaxle studs	18 ft. lbs.	25 Nm
Halfshaft nut	145 ft. lbs.	200 Nm
Ignition module (1)	61 inch lbs.	7 Nm
Input shaft nut	110 ft. lbs.	150 Nm
Lower ball joint stud nuts	55 ft. lbs.	75 Nm
Lower facia braces and J-nuts (Coupe)	89 inch lbs.	10 Nm
Neutral safety switch bolts	142 inch lbs.	16 Nm
Neutral safety switch lever nut	97 inch lbs.	11 Nm
Oil drain plug	40 ft. lbs.	55 Nm
Output shaft nut	110 ft. lbs.	150 Nm
Power steering gear	40 ft. lbs.	54 Nm
Powertrain stiffening bracket (1991)	35 ft. lbs.	47 Nm
Pressure plate bolts	18 ft. lbs.	25 Nm
Rear cover (manual)	106 inch lbs.	21 Nm
Rear pitch restrictor-to-transaxle (1991)	40 ft. lbs.	55 Nm
Right side mount-to-cradle (1991)	40 ft. lbs.	54 Nm
Shift lever bolts (2)(manual)	124 inch lbs.	14 Nm
Shifter assembly retaining nuts (manual)	18 ft. lbs.	25 Nm
Slave damper-to-clutch housing nuts	18 ft. lbs.	25 Nm
Tie rod end-to-steering knuckle nut	33 ft. lbs.	45 Nm
Torque converter-to-flexplate bolts	52 ft. lbs.	70 Nm
Transaxle case-to-clutch housing	21 ft. lbs.	28 Nm
Transaxle strut-to-cradle 1992–1993 vehicles	52 ft. lbs.	70 Nm
Transaxle temperature sensor	71 inch lbs.	8 Nm
Turbine speed sensor	20 ft. lbs.	26 Nm
Vehicle speed sensor	20 ft. lbs.	26 Nm

(1)- New bolts come coated with yellow sealant
(2)- Coat threads with Loctite® 242 or equivalent

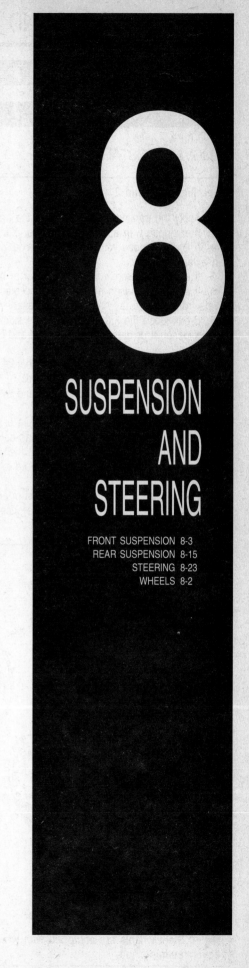

8

SUSPENSION AND STEERING

WHEELS

Wheels

REMOVAL & INSTALLATION

▶ See Figures 1 and 2

1. Apply the parking brake and block the opposite wheel.
2. If equipped with automatic transaxle, place the selector lever in **P**. If equipped with manual transaxle, place the transaxle in reverse.
3. If equipped, remove the wheel cover or hub cap.
4. If equipped, loosen and unscrew the black plastic lug nut covers from the nuts by hand, or if necessary, using a socket.
5. Break loose the lug nuts. If a nut is stuck, never use heat to loosen it or damage to the wheel and bearings may occur.
6. Raise the vehicle until the tire is clear of the ground. Support the vehicle safely using jackstands.
7. Remove the lug nuts and the tire and wheel assembly.

To install:

8. Make sure the wheel and brake drum or hub mating surfaces and the wheel lug studs are clean and free of all foreign material. Always remove rust from the wheel mounting surfaces and the brake rotors/drums. Failure to do so may cause the lug nuts to loosen in service.
9. Position the wheel on the hub or drum and hand-tighten the lug nuts. Tighten all the lug nuts, in a criss-cross pattern, until they are snug.

10. Remove the supports, if any, and lower the vehicle. Tighten the lug nuts, in a criss-cross pattern, to 130 ft. lbs. (140 Nm). Always use a torque wrench to achieve the proper lug nut torque and to prevent stretching the wheel studs.
11. Repeat the torque pattern to assure proper wheel tightening.
12. If your Saturn is equipped with steel wheels, install the wheel cover on the wheel, then hand tighten the 4 wheel cover cap nuts with a socket. Once tightened, use the ratchet to tighten the nuts an additional 1/4 turn.
13. If equipped with aluminum wheels, the black plastic nut covers and hand tighten, then use a socket to tighten the caps an additional 1/2 turn.

INSPECTION

▶ See Figures 3 and 4

Check the wheels for any damage. They must be replaced if they are bent, dented, heavily rusted, have elongated bolt holes, or have excessive lateral or radial runout. Wheels with excessive runout may cause a high-speed vehicle vibration.

Replacement wheels must be of the same load capacity, diameter, width, offset and mounting configuration as the original wheels. Using the wrong wheels may affect wheel bearing life, ground and tire clearance, or speedometer and odometer calibrations.

The factory installed Saturn wheels have identification information in the wheel castings. This information includes size and in the case of aluminum wheels, the part number.

Wheel Lug Studs

REPLACEMENT

▶ See Figure 5

1. Raise the front of the vehicle and support using jackstands, then remove the wheel assembly.
2. Remove the brake drum or caliper, as applicable.

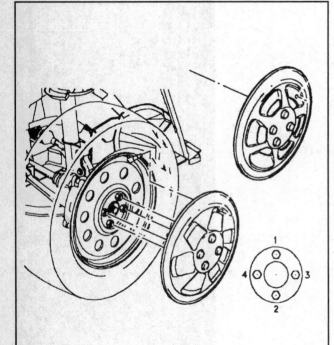

Fig. 1 Steel wheels are equipped with wheel covers and cover retaining nuts

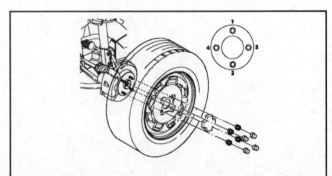

Fig. 2 Aluminum wheels have a center cap and black plastic lug nut covers

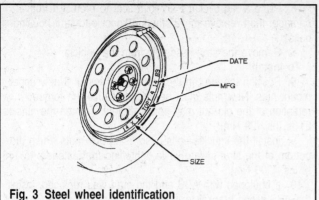

Fig. 3 Steel wheel identification

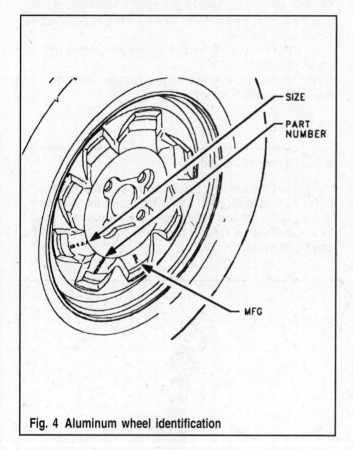

Fig. 4 Aluminum wheel identification

loose in the hub, rotate the hub to a position where the least amount of interference occurs, mark the location on the knuckle and remove ONLY enough material to allow stud removal.

4. Start the new wheel stud into the hub, then place 4 washers over the stud.
5. Install the wheel mounting nut with the flat side toward the washer, then tighten using an open end wrench until the stud is seated.
6. Install the brake drum or caliper.
7. Install the wheel, remove the supports and lower the vehicle.

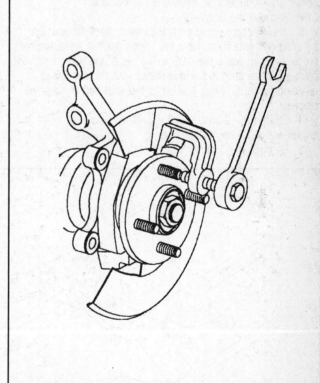

Fig. 5 Pressing the old stud from the wheel hub — front wheel shown

3. Install SA91107NE or an equivalent wheel stud remover to the hub and press out the stud.

➡When replacing front wheel hub studs, it may be necessary to remove a small amount of material from the knuckle in order to provide clearance. Once the stud is

FRONT SUSPENSION

▶ See Figure 6

The front suspension consists of 4 major components; the MacPherson struts, the lower control arm, the steering knuckle assembly and the stabilizer or sway bar. Strut towers located in the wheel wells locate the upper ends of the MacPherson struts. The lower end of the strut is attached to the steering knuckle and the control arm. The control arm provides side-to-side stability, while body lean on turns is controlled by a sway bar that connects to both lower control arms. The strut assembly, which consists of a coil spring and a strut provides both functions that a spring and a shock absorber would.

The front suspension components are lubricated for life and require no routine greasing or lubrication. However, they should be periodically checked for damage or wear.

MacPherson Struts

REMOVAL & INSTALLATION

▶ See Figures 7, 8, 9 and 10

✳✳CAUTION

The MacPherson strut is under extreme spring pressure. Do not remove the strut shaft center support nut at the top without using an approved spring compressor. Personal injury may result if this caution is not followed.

1. If equipped with ABS, disconnect the negative battery cable and then raise the front of the vehicle. Support the vehicle safely using jackstands. Make sure the vehicle is at a height where underhood access is still possible.
2. Remove the front wheel.
3. If equipped, unplug and disconnect the ABS wire from the strut wiring bracket. Note the wiring position for assembly purposes, then place the ABS wiring out of the way to prevent damage. If the strut is being replaced, drill the rivet head retaining the ABS wiring bracket to the strut and remove the bracket.
4. Loosen the 2 steering knuckle-to-strut housing bolts, but do not remove them at this time.
5. Remove the 3 upper strut-to-body nuts.

6. Place a rag over the CV-joint seal to protect it from damage, then remove the 2 steering knuckle-to-strut housing bolts.
7. Remove the strut assembly from the vehicle.
To install:
8. Position the strut in the vehicle and install 3 new upper mount nuts. New nuts must be used because the torque retention of the old nut may be insufficient. Tighten the nuts to 21 ft. lbs. (29 Nm).
9. Install the knuckle bolts, also using new nuts. Push the bottom of the strut inward while tightening the fasteners to 148 ft. lbs. (200 Nm).
10. If equipped with ABS and the strut was replaced, install the ABS wiring bracket to the strut using a new rivet. Connect the ABS wiring to the bracket and install the wiring to the speed sensor connector. Make sure the wiring is positioned as noted during removal.
11. Install the wheel assembly, remove the supports and lower the vehicle.
12. Connect the negative battery cable, then check and adjust the alignment as necessary.

OVERHAUL

▶ See Figures 12, 13 and 14

1. Mount the strut in a suitable spring compressor/holding fixture such as SA9155S or equivalent. Fasten the strut using a strut/knuckle bolt and nut through the lower mounting hole.
2. Compress the spring sufficiently to completely unload the upper strut mount.

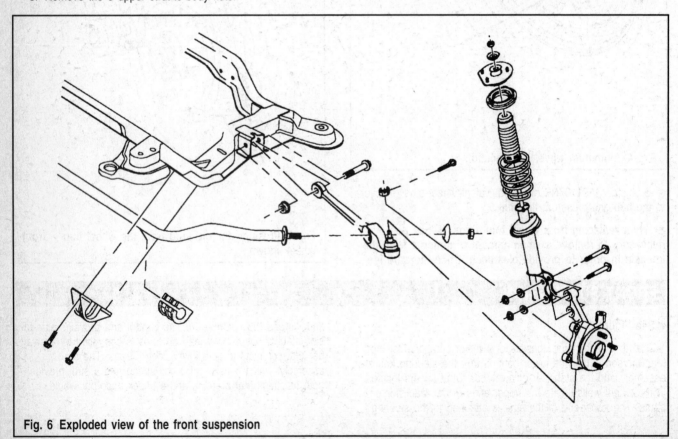

Fig. 6 Exploded view of the front suspension

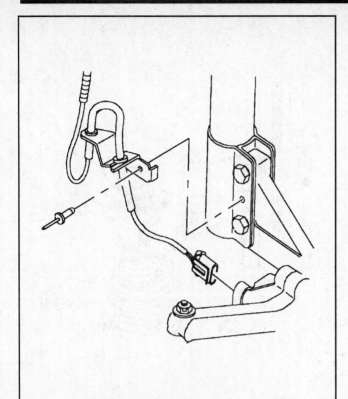

Fig. 7 Exploded view of the ABS wiring connector, bracket and attaching rivet

Fig. 9 Remove the 3 strut top fasteners from the shock tower

Fig. 8 View of the ABS wiring bracket and the strut-to-knuckle bolts

3. Remove the strut shaft nut while holding the strut stationary with a Torx® head socket wrench.

4. Carefully release the spring compressor and tilt the strut assembly outward in the fixture.

5. Remove the upper mount assembly and inspect the rubber for cracks or deterioration. Rotate the support bearing by hand and check for smooth operation.

6. Remove the spring from the strut and inspect the spring for damage.

7. Remove the dust shield assembly and inspect for cracks or deterioration.

8. Remove the strut from the compressor, then extend and retract the strut shaft, checking for smooth, even resistance.

To assemble:

9. Position the strut into the mounting and secure using the knuckle fastener in the lower mounting hole.

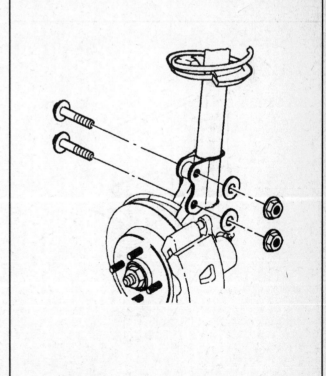

Fig. 10 Remove the 2 strut lower fasteners from the strut and knuckle

10. Tilt the strut outward slightly and extend it to the limit of its travel.

11. Install the dust shield assembly onto the strut, then install the spring.

12. Install the spring isolator and the strut mount to the top of the assembly.

13. Tilt the assembly back into the fixture and compress the spring while guiding the shaft through the upper strut mount assembly. Compress until the washer and shaft nut can be installed to the end of the shaft, but do not over compress and damage the spring.

14. Tighten the shaft to the nut using a Torx® head socket wrench and a torque wrench, while holding the nut steady with an open end wrench. Tighten the fastener to 37 ft. lbs. (50 Nm).

15. Release the spring compressor tool and remove the strut from the fixture.

Lower Ball Joints

INSPECTION

Raise and safely support the vehicle until the front wheel is clear of the floor. Try to rock the wheel up and down. If any play is felt, have an friend rock the wheel while observing the lower ball joint. If any movement is seen between the steering knuckle and control arm, the ball joint is bad. If not, any wheel play indicates wheel bearing wear.

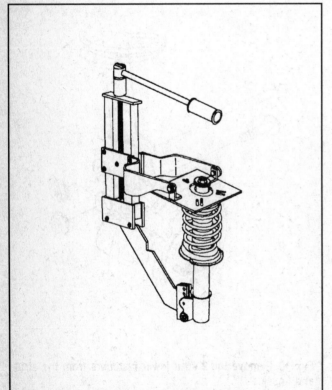

Fig. 11 Mount the strut in a suitable spring compressor/holding fixture

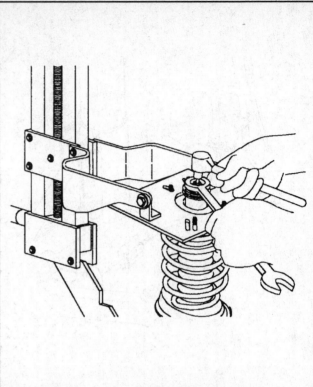

Fig. 12 Remove the strut shaft nut while holding the strut stationary with a Torx® head socket wrench

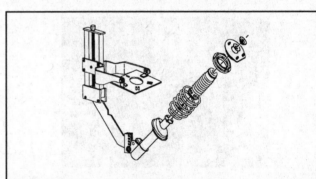

Fig. 13 Tilt the strut assembly outward in the fixture and remove the strut components

REMOVAL & INSTALLATION

The lower ball joint is an integral part of the lower control arm. If the ball joint needs replacement, the entire lower arm must be replaced as an assembly.

Stabilizer Bar (Sway Bar)

REMOVAL & INSTALLATION

▶ See Figures 14, 15, 16, 17, 18 and 19

1. Place the steering in the unlocked position, then raise the front of the vehicle and support safely using jackstands.

2. Remove the left wheel and splash shield.

3. Remove and discard the cotter pin from the left lower control arm ball joint stud. Back the ball joint nut until the top of the nut is even with the top of the threads.

4. Use tool SA9132S or equivalent, to separate the ball joint from the lower control arm, then remove the nut. Do not use a wedge tool or seal damage may occur.

✳✳WARNING

The outer CV-joint for vehicles equipped with ABS contains a speed sensor ring. Use of an incorrect tool to separate the control arm from the knuckle may result in damage to and a loss of the ABS system.

5. Remove the left lower control arm-to-cradle fastener.

6. Turn the steering wheel to the left to access and remove the right stabilizer bar nut and washer.

7. Remove both stabilizer bar-to-cradle mounting brackets. If a cradle nut is damaged, cross-threaded or broken loose from the cradle, replace the nut as follows:

   a. If the nut is damaged but not broken loose and the bolt can be removed, distort the bolt threads sufficiently to lock the bolt into the nut. Insert the bolt and tighten with an air impact wrench. Continue to turn the bolt until the nut breaks free of the cradle.

   b. If the nut was already broken loose and the bolt could not be extracted or if the bolt was used to break the nut loose, cut the bolt head off.

   c. Retrieve the bolt shank and nut from the cradle cavity.

   d. Install a new bolt Saturn Part No. 21010823 and nut No. 21006321 or equivalents.

8. Remove the stabilizer bar with the left control arm from the vehicle. If necessary, remove the nut and the left control arm from the bar.

To install:

9. If removed, position the left control arm to the bar, but do not tighten the fastener at this time.

10. Install the mounting bushings onto the bar with the installation slits facing the front of the vehicle.

11. Position the right end of the bar into the right control arm (still on the vehicle), then position the left control arm into the cradle. Do not install fasteners at this time.

12. Using new bolts or a suitable threadlock such as Loctite® 242, install the mounting brackets and tighten the bolts to 103 ft. lbs. (140 Nm). Then tighten the fasteners a second time to 103 ft. lbs. (140 Nm).

13. Temporarily install the left wheel assembly onto the vehicle and have a friend push the bottom of the left wheel into the vehicle to allow lower control arm-to-cradle bolt installation.

14. Tighten the lower control arm cradle bolt to 92 ft. lbs. (125 Nm), then tighten the nut to 74 ft. lbs. (100 Nm). Remove the wheel assembly from the vehicle.

15. Install new nuts onto the right and left stabilizer bar to control arm studs and tighten the right nut, then left nut to 106 ft. lbs. (144 Nm). New nuts must be used because the torque retention of the old nuts may be insufficient.

16. Thoroughly clean and lubricate the left ball joint stud threads, then install the left lower control arm ball stud into the left steering knuckle. Install the nut and tighten the stud nut to

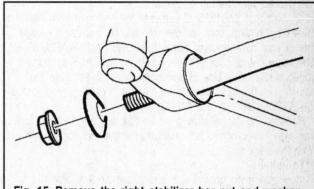

Fig. 15 Remove the right stabilizer bar nut and washer

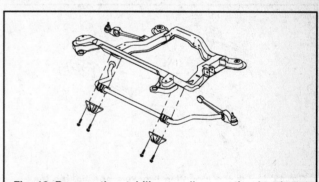

Fig. 16 Remove the stabilizer cradle mounting brackets to free the bar from the cradle

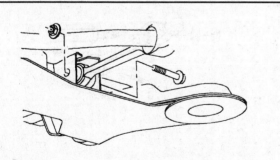

Fig. 14 Remove the left lower control arm-to-cradle fastener

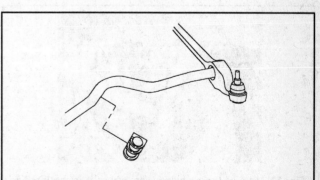

Fig. 17 Position the cradle mounting bushings with the installation slits facing the front of the vehicle

55 ft. lbs. (75 Nm), tighten additionally if necessary and install a new cotter pin.

17. Install the splash shield, then install the wheel assembly.

18. Remove the supports and lower the vehicle. Check and adjust the alignment as necessary.

Lower Control Arm

REMOVAL & INSTALLATION

▶ See Figures 20 and 21

1. Raise the front of the vehicle and support safely using jackstands. Remove the wheel and splash shield.

2. Remove and discard the cotter pin from the lower control arm ball joint stud. Back the ball joint nut until the top of the nut is even with the top of the threads.

3. Use tool SA9132S to separate the ball joint from the lower control arm, then remove the nut. Do not use a wedge tool or seal damage may occur. {243}uf96 {242} WARNING: The outer CV-joint for vehicles equipped with ABS contains a speed sensor ring. Use of an incorrect tool to separate the control arm from the knuckle may result in damage and loss of the ABS system. {243}uf69 {242}4.

Remove the control arm-to-cradle bolt and nut, then remove the sway bar-to-control arm nut and remove the control arm from the vehicle.

To install:

4. Position the control arm and install the arm onto the sway bar without the fastener, then place the end of the arm

into the cradle. Install the cradle nut and bolt. Tighten the cradle bolt to 92 ft. lbs. (125 Nm), then tighten the cradle nut to 74 ft. lbs. (100 Nm).

5. Install the sway bar nut and tighten to 106 ft. lbs. (144 Nm).

6. Thoroughly clean and lubricate the ball joint stud threads, then install the lower control arm ball stud into the steering knuckle. Install the nut and tighten the lower control arm ball stud nut to 55 ft. lbs. (75 Nm), tighten additionally if necessary and install a new cotter pin.

7. Install the splash shield and the wheel assembly.

8. Remove the supports and lower the vehicle. Check and adjust the alignment, as necessary.

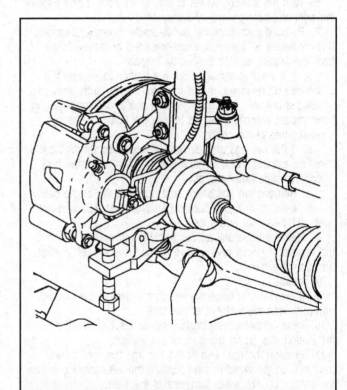

Fig. 20 Use only SA9132S or an equivalent separator tool whenever the lower control arm ball joint is separated from the knuckle

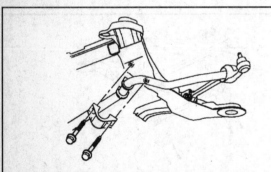

Fig. 18 Install the mounting brackets and tighten the bolts 2 times to ensure proper torque

Fig. 19 View of the stabilizer bar, where it is mounted to the lower control arm

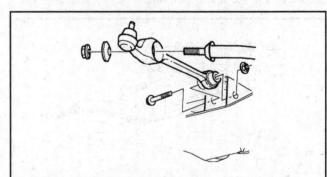

Fig. 21 Position the lower control arm and install the fasteners

Steering Knuckle Assembly

REMOVAL & INSTALLATION

▶ **See Figures 22, 23 and 24**

1. If equipped with ABS, disconnect the negative battery cable.

2. Have a friend assistant depress the brake pedal and loosen the front halfshaft nut, then raise the front of the vehicle and support safely using jackstands.

3. Remove the wheel assembly.

4. Remove the brake caliper mounting bracket bolts and suspend the assembly from the strut spring with mechanic's wire or a coat hanger. Make sure the brake line is positioned so that it is not under stress and is not damaged.

5. Loosen the strut-to-knuckle bolts, but do not remove at this time.

6. Remove the rotor; if difficulty is encountered use two M8 **x** 1.25 self tapping bolts in the provided holes to drive the rotor from the hub. Remove the axle nut and washer.

7. Remove and discard the cotter pin from the lower control arm ball joint stud. Back the ball joint nut until the top of the nut is even with the top of the threads.

8. Use tool SA9132S to separate the ball joint from the lower control arm, then remove the nut. Do not use a wedge tool or seal damage may occur.

✳✳WARNING

The outer CV-joint for vehicles equipped with ABS contains a speed sensor ring. Use of an incorrect tool to separate the control arm from the knuckle may result in damage and loss of the ABS system.

9. Remove the tie rod cotter pin and castle nut, then separate the tie rod end from the knuckle using a tie rod separator SA91100C or equivalent. Do not use a wedge-type tool.

10. If equipped, unplug the ABS wheel speed sensor electrical connector.

11. Suspend the halfshaft from the body with wire, then remove the knuckle/hub fasteners and remove the knuckle/hub assembly from the vehicle.

12. If difficulty is encountered removing the knuckle, position a block of wood on the end of the halfshaft and tap on the wood with a hammer to free the hub assembly.

To install:

13. Thoroughly clean and lubricate the ball joint stud threads of the lower control arm and tie rod end.

14. Install the knuckle/hub assembly onto the axle shaft. Then install the washer with a new nut, but do not tighten the nut at this time. A new nut must be used because the torque retention of the old nut may not be sufficient.

15. Install the lower control arm ball stud and install the nut, but do not tighten at this time.

16. Install the steering knuckle-to-strut fasteners, but do not tighten at this time.

17. Install the tie rod end and nut. Tighten the nut to 33 ft. lbs. (45 Nm) and install a new cotter pin. If necessary, tighten the nut additionally, but do not back off to insert the cotter pin.

18. Push inward on the bottom of the strut and tighten the knuckle fasteners to 148 ft. lbs. (200 Nm).

19. Tighten the lower control arm ball stud nut to 55 ft. lbs. (75 Nm), tighten additionally only as necessary to install a new cotter pin.

20. Install the rotor onto the hub and the caliper mount bracket onto the knuckle. Tighten the mount bracket assembly bolts to 81 ft. lbs. (110 Nm).

21. If equipped, engage the ABS electrical connector to the wheel speed sensor.

22. Have an assistant depress the brake pedal and tighten the halfshaft nut to 148 ft. lbs. (200 Nm).

23. Install the wheel assembly, remove the supports and lower the vehicle.

24. Connect the negative battery cable, check and adjust the alignment, as necessary.

Wheel Bearing and Hub Assembly

Any time the hub or bearing is removed from the knuckle, a new bearing must be used during assembly.

BEARING REPLACEMENT

▶ **See Figures 25, 26, 27, 28, 29, 30 and 31**

1. Remove the knuckle assembly from the vehicle as described earlier in this section.

2. For 1991 vehicles, remove the 3 dust shield fasteners and separate the shield from the assembly.

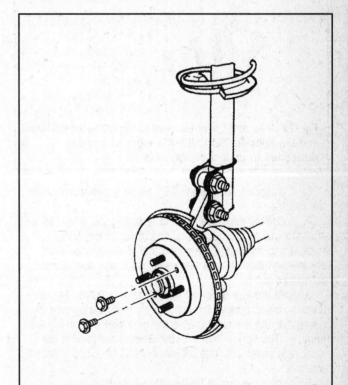

Fig. 22 Two holes are provided to insert self tapping bolts and drive the rotor from the hub

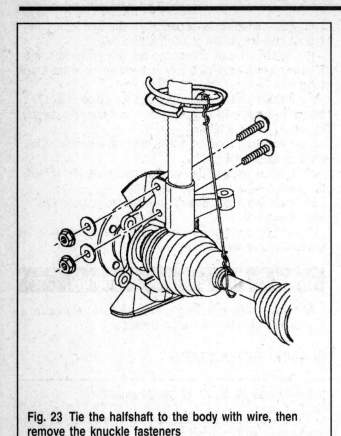

Fig. 23 Tie the halfshaft to the body with wire, then remove the knuckle fasteners

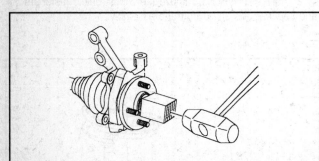

Fig. 24 A hammer may be used to separate the halfshaft and the knuckle, but ONLY if a block of wood is positioned to protect components

3. If equipped, remove the ABS wheel speed sensor from the knuckle.

4. Assemble the wheel bearing removing tool SA9159S or equivalent using the hub driver, hub driver screw, bridge retainer and the bridge. Install the tool to the knuckle and secure the assembly in a vise using the bridge as the vise contact point.

5. Hold the hub driver with a wrench and tighten the hub driver screw to remove the hub. If the inner bearing race is pulled out with the hub, remove the race with a bearing race remover. The service tool may be used by assembling the inner race puller, 2 bridge retainer bolts, 2 bolts and 2 flat washers.

6. Inspect the hub at the bearing location for pitting, scoring or wear and replace, if necessary.

7. Remove the assembly from the vice and remove the wheel hub removal tools.

8. Remove the bearing retainer snapring.

9. Position the knuckle in a shop press on the service tool knuckle support tube and press the bearing from the knuckle with a small driver.

10. Inspect the knuckle bore for pitting, scoring, wear or corrosion. If damage cannot be easily cleaned with light sanding, the knuckle must be replaced.

To install:

11. Use the large driver from the service tool kit and position the knuckle into the press in the inverted position from bearing removal. Using the driver press in the new bearing until seated.

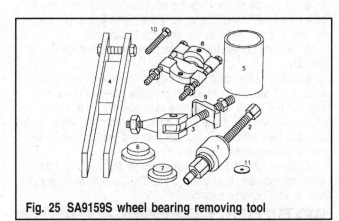

Fig. 25 SA9159S wheel bearing removing tool

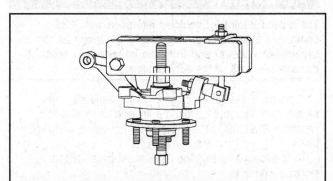

Fig. 26 Assemble the removal tool and install to the knuckle as shown

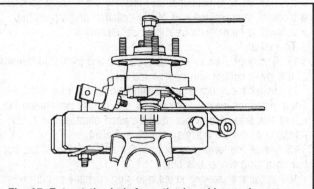

Fig. 27 Extract the hub from the knuckle as shown

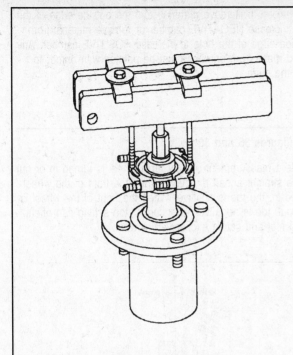

Fig. 28 If the race is pulled from the knuckle with the hub, the removal tool may be used to draw the race from the hub

12. Use the small driver and the knuckle support tube to press in the hub assembly. The small driver must be used to support the bearing inner race with its small (pilot) side facing toward the press and away from the bearing.

13. Install the bearing retainer snapring.

14. If equipped, install the ABS wheel speed sensor into the knuckle and tighten the fastener to 6 ft. lbs. (8 Nm).

15. For 1991 vehicles, install the brake dust shield and tighten the fasteners to 18 ft. lbs. (25 Nm).

16. Install the knuckle assembly to the vehicle.

Front End Alignment

➡Rear wheel alignment must always be checked and adjusted before a front end alignment is attempted. The proper order of adjustment is rear camber, rear toe, front camber, front caster and front toe.

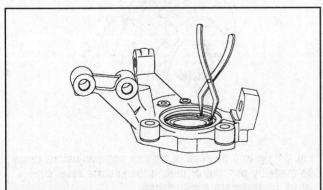

Fig. 29 Remove the bearing retaining snapring

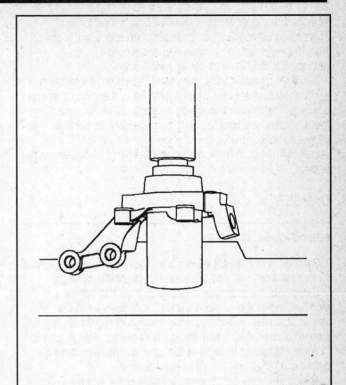

Fig. 30 Position the knuckle in a press using the support tube and the small driver

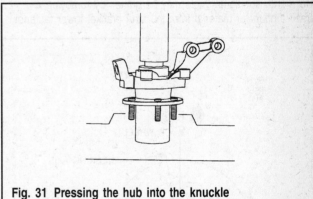

Fig. 31 Pressing the hub into the knuckle

CASTER

▶ See Figure 32

Caster is a measure of the angle between the steering axis and vertical, as viewed from the side of the vehicle when the wheels are in the straight ahead position. It is measured by the location of the lower control arm ball joint and the center of the strut-to-body attachment. A line drawn through the center of these 2 points represents the steering axis. When the center of the strut attachment is rearward of the ball joint, caster is positive. When the strut attachment is forward of the ball joint, caster is negative.

The front wheel caster setting is fixed by body geometry and the fixed lengths of the suspension components. Therefore, front caster should not vary unless components are worn or damaged. If caster is not to specification, check for bent suspension components or body structure and worn bushings. Also, be very certain of measuring techniques before determining the caster is out of specification.

If in light of these facts, the caster is determined to be in need of adjustment, the wheels must be in the straight ahead position. The top strut mounting nuts should be loosened and the assembly slid back or forth, as necessary to achieve proper specification. Moving the top of the strut 0.157 in. (4mm) will result in an approximate change of ½ degree caster angle.

CAMBER

▶ See Figures 33 and 34

Camber is usually set before any other adjustments. Camber can cause both pull and tire wear if it is not set correctly.

Camber is the measure of wheel tilt from the vertical direction, when the wheel is viewed from the rear of the vehicle. Camber is negative when the top of the wheel is inboard and positive when the top is outboard. Always check for bent, damaged or worn suspension components before determining that adjustment is necessary.

Adjustment may be achieved by locking the wheels in the straight ahead position, loosening the 2 knuckle fasteners and pushing or pulling the knuckle in the desired direction. Up to 3 degrees of camber angle may be adjusted with this method. If this adjustment is not sufficient, and no damaged components are found, additional angle may be gained by removing a small amount of material from the strut bracket lower fastener

hole to widen it. Remove material from the outside edge of the hole to increase NEGATIVE camber or remove material from the inside edge of the hole to increase POSITIVE camber. Any exposed metal from grinding must be painted with primer to protect the surface.

TOE

▶ See Figures 35 and 36

Toe is a measurement of how far a wheel is turned in or out from the straight ahead direction. When the front of the wheel is turned in, the toe is positive. When the front of the wheel is turned out, toe is negative. An incorrect toe setting can affect steering feel and cause excessive tire wear.

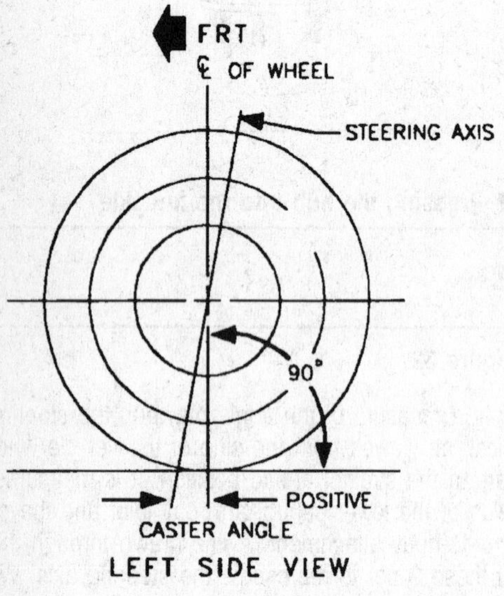

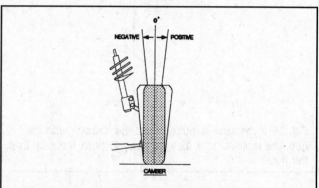

Fig. 33 Measuring camber of the right wheel

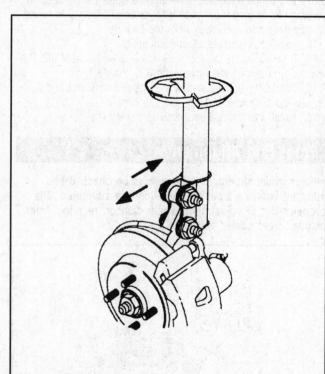

Fig. 34 Up to 3 degrees of camber angle adjustment may be made by pushing or pulling the knuckle assembly when the fasteners are loosened

Fig. 32 Measuring caster of the left wheel

Before adjusting toe, lock the steering wheel in the straight ahead position. The toe setting is adjusted by loosening the outer tie rod locknut or jamnuts and turning the rod (using the flats) until the toe is within specification. The tie rods must be turned in or out an equal amount on each side to keep the steering wheel centered.

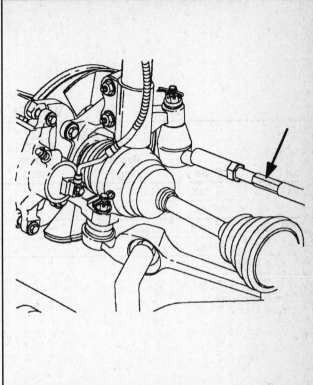

Fig. 36 Adjust the toe by loosening the outer tie rod lock nuts and turning the inner tie rods

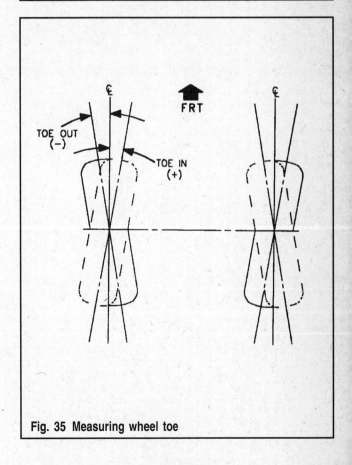

Fig. 35 Measuring wheel toe

WHEEL ALIGNMENT

Year	Model	Caster Range (deg.)	Caster Preferred Setting (deg.)	Camber Range (deg.)	Camber Preferred Setting (deg.)	Toe-in ① (in.)	Steering Axis Inclination (deg.)
1991	All front	1.00P–2.10P	1.50P	1.00N–0.65P	0.00	0.20P	NA
	All rear	—	—	1.25N–0.00	0.60N	0.20P	NA
1992–93	All front	1.00P–2.10P	1.50P	1.00N–0.65P	0.00	0.20P	NA
	All rear	—	—	1.25N–0.00	0.60N	0.20P	NA

NA—Not available
N—Negative
P—Positive
① Specification is total toe
   Toe per wheel: 0.10P

REAR SUSPENSION

▶ **See Figure 37**

The major components of the rear suspension are; the MacPherson struts, rear crossmember, knuckle, stabilizer bar (sway bar), lateral links and trailing arm. The upper ends of the MacPherson struts are attached to the body by fasteners. The lower end of the strut is attached to the crossmember through the knuckle, lateral links and the trailing arm. The lateral links provide side-to-side stability, while the trailing arm provides front-to-rear stability. The strut assembly, which consists of a coil spring and a strut provides both functions that a spring and a shock absorber would.

The rear suspension components are lubricated for life and require no routine greasing or lubrication. However, they should be periodically checked for damage or wear.

MacPherson Strut

REMOVAL & INSTALLATION

▶ **See Figures 38, 39, 40 and 41**

✳✳CAUTION

The MacPherson strut is under extreme spring pressure. Do not remove the strut shaft support nut at the top center of the assembly without using an approved spring compressor. Personal injury may result if this caution is not followed.

1. On coupes, remove the rear seat cushion bottom, left or right rocker panel interior moldings and the left or right rear sail interior panels.
2. On sedans, remove the left or right C-pillar interior molding.
3. Fold down the rear seat backs and remove the rear seat side bolsters from the vehicle.
4. On coupes, remove the rear deck package shelf screws that attach the shelf to the side of the cargo area.
5. Remove the speaker grill fasteners and grills from the shelf, then remove the seatbelt bezel and separate the seat belts from the shelf. Remove the rear package shelf carpeting.

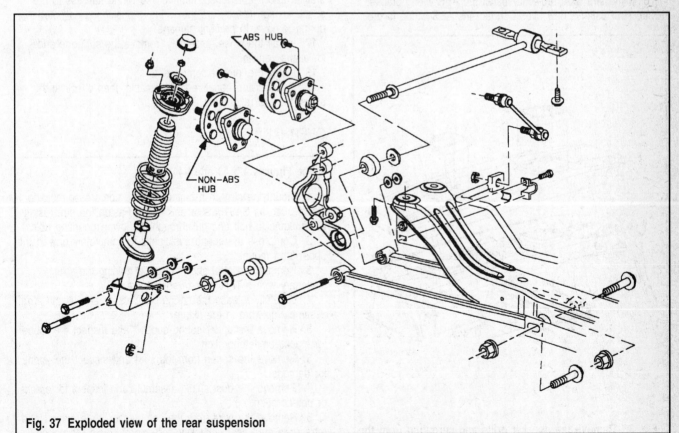

Fig. 37 Exploded view of the rear suspension

6. If equipped with ABS, disconnect the negative battery cable.

7. Raise the rear of the vehicle and support safely using jackstands, then remove the appropriate rear wheel.

8. If equipped, disconnect the ABS wiring from the strut wring bracket. If the strut is being replaced, drill the rivet head retaining the ABS wiring bracket to the strut and remove the bracket. In either case, note the position of the wiring and move the wiring to prevent damage. If necessary, unplug the wheel speed sensor connecter.

9. Loosen the 2 strut-to-knuckle bolts; but do not remove at this time.

10. Position a floor jack under the rear knuckle, then raise the jack only enough to support the knuckle. If a 2nd floor jack is not available, position a jackstand under the knuckle to support the strut.

11. Remove the 3 upper strut-to-body nut.

12. Slowly raise the vehicle using another jack, lowering the strut from the body. If another jack is not available, lower the jack holding the strut, but do so very slowly and carefully as the spring unload.

13. Remove the strut-to-knuckle bolts and remove the strut assembly from the vehicle.

To install:

14. Install 3 new strut to upper mount nuts and tighten the nuts to 21 ft. lbs. (29 Nm). New nuts must be used because the torque retention of the old fasteners may not be sufficient.

15. Install the knuckle bolts with new nuts, then push the bottom of the strut inward and tighten the fasteners to 148 ft. lbs. (200 Nm).

16. If the strut was replaced, install the ABS wiring bracket to the strut using a new rivet. Connect the ABS wiring to the

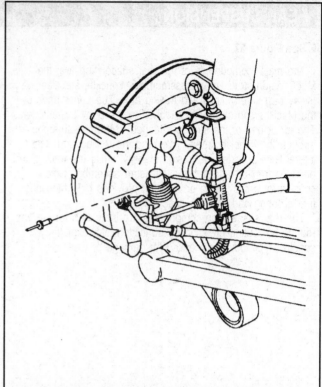

Fig. 39 If replacing the strut, drill of the ABS bracket rivet head and remove the bracket from the strut

bracket and if unplugged, connect the wiring harness to the speed sensor. Make sure the wiring is positioned as noted during removal to prevent damage.

17. Install the wheel assembly, remove the supports and lower the vehicle.

18. Install the interior components.

19. Connect the negative battery cable, then check and adjust the rear alignment as necessary.

OVERHAUL

▶ **See Figures 42, 43 and 44**

1. Mount the strut in a suitable spring compressor/holding fixture such as SA9155S or equivalent. Fasten the strut using a strut/knuckle bolt and nut through the lower mounting hole.

2. Compress the spring sufficiently to completely unload the upper strut mount.

3. Remove the strut shaft nut while holding the strut stationary with a Torx® head socket wrench.

4. Carefully release the spring compressor and tilt the strut assembly outward in the fixture.

5. Remove the upper spring support and inspect the rubber for cracks or deterioration.

6. Remove the spring from the strut and inspect the spring for damage.

7. Remove the dust shield assembly and inspect for cracks or deterioration.

8. Remove the strut from the compressor, then extend and retract the strut shaft, checking for smooth, even resistance.

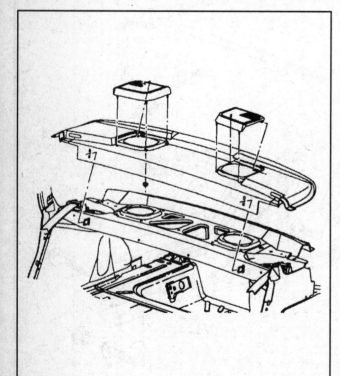

Fig. 38 Remove the speaker grills and carpeting from the rear deck package shelf

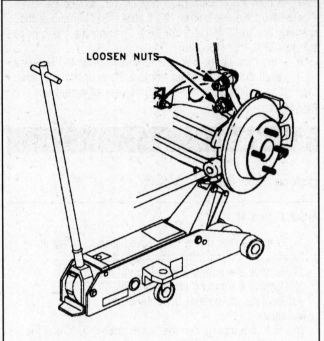

Fig. 40 Loosen the knuckle-to-strut fasteners and position a floor jack to support the strut when the upper fasteners are removed

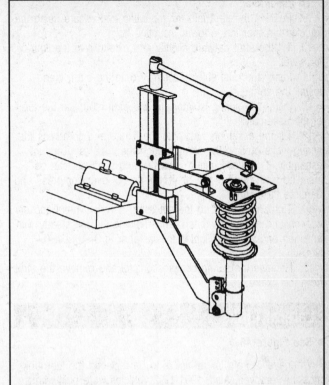

Fig. 42 The spring compressor fixture should be mounted to a work bench

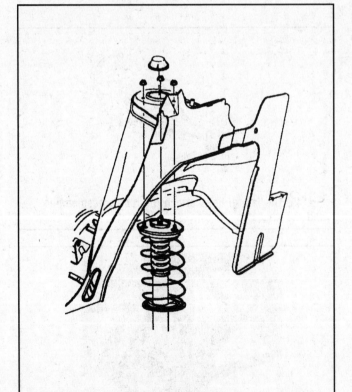

Fig. 41 Remove the upper fasteners, raise the vehicle and remove the strut

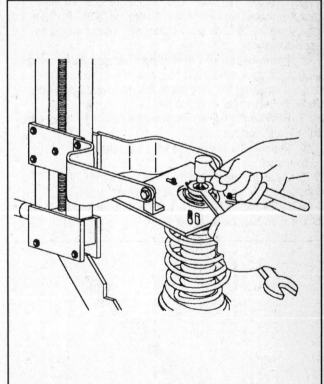

Fig. 43 Use an open end wrench and a Torx® head socket wrench to install or remove the strut shaft nut

To assemble:

9. Position the strut into the mounting and secure using the knuckle fastener in the lower mounting hole.

10. Tilt the strut outward slightly and extend it to the limit of its travel.

11. Install the dust shield assembly onto the strut, then install the spring.

12. Install the spring isolator and the strut mount to the top of the assembly.

13. Tilt the assembly back into the fixture and compress the spring while guiding the shaft through the upper strut mount assembly. Compress until the washer and shaft nut can be installed to the end of the shaft, but do not over compress and damage the spring.

14. Tighten the shaft to the nut using a Torx® head socket wrench and a torque wrench, while holding the nut steady with an open end wrench. Tighten the fastener to 37 ft. lbs. (50 Nm).

15. Release the spring compressor tool and remove the strut from the fixture.

Lateral Links

▶ **See Figure 45**

Whenever a front lateral link is to be replaced the fuel tank must be removed. Also, 1991-1992 vehicles were built with a rear assembly which contained a special washer at the lateral link-to-crossmember attachment locations. For 1993, this washer was omitted which necessitated the use of a special truss head bolt. The truss head bolt can be used on any model year, but the hex head bolt from the 1991-1992 vehicles should not be used on rear suspensions without the built-in special washer.

1. Raise the rear of the vehicle and support safely using jackstands, then remove the rear wheels.

2. If removing the front lateral link, remove the fuel tank. Refer to Section No. 5 of this manual.

3. Remove the lateral link-to-knuckle bolt, then remove the link-to-crossmember bolt(s).

4. Remove the link or links from the vehicle.

To install:

5. Install the link(s) into the crossmember with the fastener(s), but do not tighten at this time.

6. Install the link(s) to the knuckle with the knuckle-to-link bolt, but do not tighten at this time.

7. Tighten the crossmember bolt or bolts as applicable. Tighten the front link bolt to 126 ft. lbs. (170 Nm) and/or the rear link bolt to 89 ft. lbs. (120 Nm). Then tighten the knuckle bolt to 122 ft. lbs. (165 Nm).

8. If the front lateral link was removed, install the fuel tank.

9. Install the rear wheel(s), remove the supports and lower the vehicle, then check and adjust the rear alignment as necessary.

Trailing Arm

REMOVAL & INSTALLATION

▶ **See Figure 46**

1. Raise the rear of the vehicle and support safely using jackstands, then remove the rear wheel(s).

2. Remove the trailing arm-to-knuckle nut.

3. Remove the trailing arm body bolts.

4. Slide the trailing arm from the knuckle.

To install:

5. Install the trailing arm into the knuckle and torque the nut to 106 ft. lbs. (144 Nm).

6. Position the arm to the body, install and tighten the body bolts to 89 ft. lbs. (120 Nm).

7. Install the rear wheel(s).

8. Remove the supports and lower the vehicle

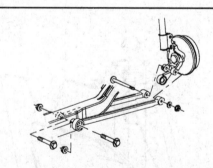

Fig. 45 The lateral links attach the rear crossmember and the knuckles

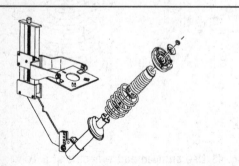

Fig. 44 With the spring compression released, tilt the strut outward to remove or install components

Fig. 46 A view of the trailing arm and the 2 lateral links mounted to the knuckle of an ABS equipped vehicle

Stabilizer Bar (Sway Bar) and Links

REMOVAL & INSTALLATION

▶ **See Figures 47, 48 and 49**

1. Raise the rear of the vehicle and support safely using jackstands, then remove the right rear wheel.

2. Position a drainpan under the left rear brake line, at the brake line hose junction and disconnect the line from the hose. Plug the brake line and hose to prevent excessive fluid loss and to avoid the possibility of contamination.

3. Remove the right and left stabilizer bar link-to-bracket fasteners.

4. Remove the stabilizer bar-to-crossmember fasteners.

5. Loosen, but do not remove, the left lateral link-to-knuckle fastener.

6. Remove the left trailing arm-to-knuckle nut, then remove the body fasteners. Slide the arm from the knuckle and remove it from the vehicle.

7. Remove the left lateral link fastener and pivot the links downward, away from the knuckle.

8. Note the position of the brake line to the crossmember, then unfasten the crossbody brake line by unsnapping the fasteners from the crossmember.

✳✳WARNING

Attempting to remove the stabilizer bar from the crossmember without first loosening the brake lines, may result in a bent/damaged line which must be replaced.

9. Remove the stabilizer bar from the crossmember and the vehicle.

To install:

10. Install the stabilizer bar to the crossmember and secure using the bracket fasteners. Tighten the retaining bolts to 41 ft. lbs. (55 Nm).

11. Pivot the lateral links into the knuckle and loosely install the fastener, but do not tighten at this time.

12. Slide the trailing arm into the knuckle and loosely install the fastener grommets, washer and nut. Install the arm-to-body fasteners and tighten to 89 ft. lbs. (120 Nm), then tighten the nut at the knuckle to 106 ft. lbs. (144 Nm).

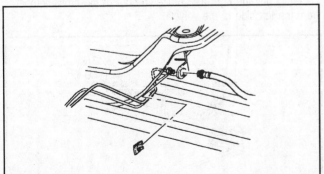

Fig. 47 Disconnect the left brake line from the brake hose

13. Tighten the lateral link-to-knuckle fastener to 122 ft. lbs. (165 Nm).

14. Remove the plugs from the brake line and hose, then connect the fitting and tighten to 14 ft. lbs. (19 Nm).

15. Install the crossbody brake line to the crossmember by snapping the fasteners into the member. Make sure the line is positioned as noted during removal.

16. Properly bleed the brake system. Refer to the procedure in Section No. 9 of this manual.

17. Install the wheel.

18. Remove the supports and lower the vehicle.

Fig. 48 View of the stabilizer bar end and the stabilizer link. Note the rear disc indicates the vehicle is equipped with ABS

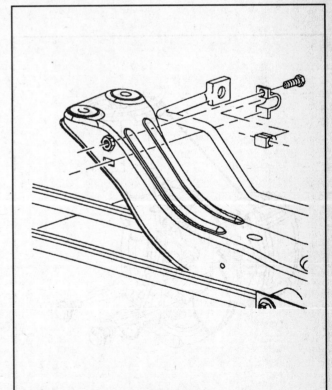

Fig. 49 Secure the stabilizer bar to the crossmember using the bracket fasteners

Knuckle

REMOVAL & INSTALLATION

▶ See Figures 50, 51 and 52

1. Raise the rear of the vehicle and support safely using jackstands.
2. Remove the wheel from the vehicle.
3. For ABS equipped vehicles, disconnect the negative battery cable and unplug the electrical connector from the speed sensor. Remove the 2 caliper-to-knuckle mounting bolts from the rear of the knuckle, use a length of wire to suspend the caliper from the strut and clear of the knuckle. Remove the rotor from the hub and bearing assembly.
4. For vehicles not equipped with ABS, remove the brake drum.
5. Remove the 4 mounting bolts, then remove the hub and bearing assembly from the knuckle. For ABS equipped vehicles, remove the brake backing plate from the vehicle.
6. If equipped with rear drum brakes, suspend the brake assembly from the strut and clear of the knuckle using wire.
7. Loosen the lateral link-to-knuckle bolts, but do not remove at this time.
8. Remove the trailing arm knuckle nut and body bolts.
9. Slide the trailing arm out of the knuckle.
10. Remove the lateral link and remove the strut-to-knuckle bolts, then remove the knuckle from the vehicle.

To install:
11. Place the knuckle in the strut and install the bolts, but do not tighten at this time.
12. Loosely install the lateral links and trailing arm with bushings.
13. Tighten the trailing arm-to-body bolts to 89 ft. lbs. (120 Nm), trailing arm-to-knuckle nut to 106 ft. lbs. (144 Nm) and the lateral link-to-knuckle bolts to 122 ft. lbs. (165 Nm). Push inward on the bottom of the strut and tighten the strut-to-knuckle bolts to 148 ft. lbs. (200 Nm).
14. Position the brake backing plate (ABS equipped vehicles) or the brake assembly (non-ABS equipped vehicles), then install the hub and bearing assembly using the 4 mounting bolts. Tighten the bolts to 63 ft. lbs. (85 Nm).
15. Install the rotor or the brake drum, as applicable.
16. For ABS equipped vehicles, install the caliper and tighten the mounting bolts to 63 ft. lbs. (85 Nm). Connect the wiring harness to the ABS wheel speed sensor, then connect the negative battery cable.
17. Remove the supports and carefully lower the vehicle.
18. Check and adjust the alignment, as necessary.

Rear Crossmember Assembly

REMOVAL & INSTALLATION

▶ See Figures 53, 54, 55 and 56

1. Raise the rear of the vehicle and support safely using jackstands, then remove both rear wheels.
2. Remove the left and right trailing arms starting with the knuckle fasteners, then with the body retainers.
3. Remove the left and right lateral link bolts and disconnect the links from the knuckles.
4. Unsnap the brake line fasteners and disconnect the crossbody brake line from the crossmember.
5. If equipped, remove the left and right stabilizer bar-to-link fasteners.
6. Note the position and routing of all rear brake lines to assure proper assembly, then disconnect the left and right lines from their junction brackets. Plug the lines to prevent fluid contamination or loss.
7. Remove the left and right brake hose to crossmember securing clips. Remove the brake line longitudinal fastener. Carefully pull the right rear brake line out of the crossmember from the left side of the vehicle.

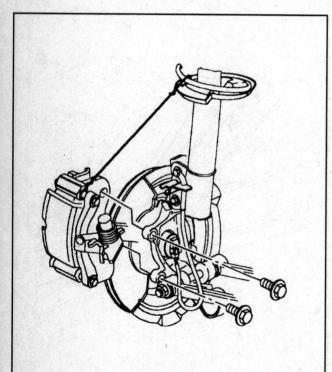

Fig. 50 Remove the caliper mounting bolts from the rear of the knuckle and suspend the caliper from the strut — ABS equipped vehicles

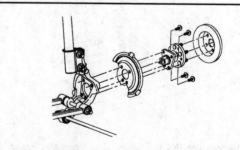

Fig. 51 Exploded view of the rotor, hub and bearing assembly and brake backing plate mounting — ABS equipped vehicles

9. Place a floor jack and additional supports under the rear crossmember to prevent the member from falling or cocking when the retaining bolts are removed.

10. Note the size and location of all crossmember bolts, then remove the 4 crossmember-to-body attaching bolts. Remove the additional supports and carefully lower the crossmember from the vehicle. If necessary, remove the lateral links from the crossmember.

To install:

11. If removed, install the lateral links to the crossmember, then position the crossmember into the vehicle. Align the member to the body using $3/8$ inch rods at the alignment holes near the crossmember-to-body fastener holes and slots.

12. Install the crossmember to the body using 4 new bolts of the proper size and specification, then tighten the bolts to 89 ft. lbs. (120 Nm). New bolts must be used because the torque retention of the old bolts may not be sufficient.

13. Position the trailing arms with bushings into the knuckles and install the nuts, but do not tighten at this time.

14. Install the trailing arms to the body and tighten the bolts to 89 ft. lbs. (120 Nm).

15. Install the lateral links to the knuckles with the link bolts, but do not tighten at this time.

16. Tighten the trailing arm fastener nuts to 106 ft. lbs. (144 Nm), then tighten the lateral link knuckle fasteners to 122 ft. lbs. (165 Nm).

17. If equipped, install the stabilizer bar to the links with fasteners and tighten to 30 ft. lbs. (40 Nm).

18. Position all brake lines as noted earlier, then attach the left and right brake lines to the crossmember with the securing clips. Install the left and right brake lines into their respective junction brackets. Install the brake line longitudinal fastener.

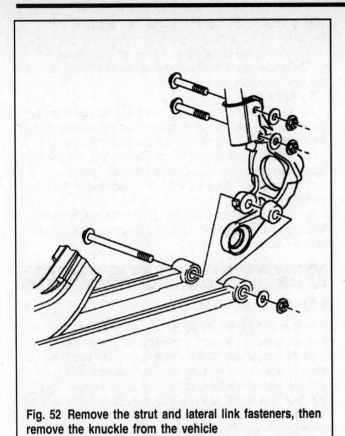

Fig. 52 Remove the strut and lateral link fasteners, then remove the knuckle from the vehicle

8. If equipped with ABS, remove the left and right ABS speed sensor harness-to-crossmember fasteners.

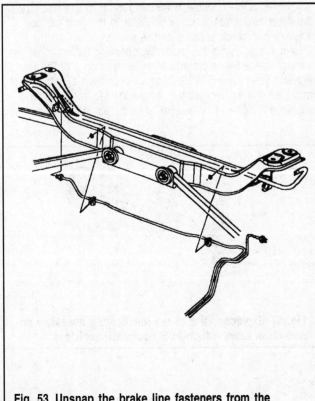

Fig. 53 Unsnap the brake line fasteners from the crossmember

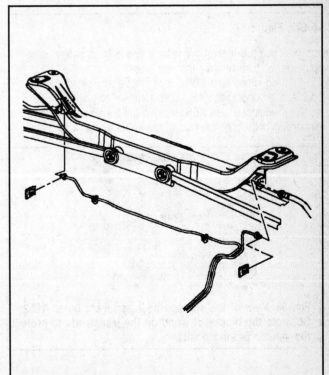

Fig. 54 Disconnect the left and right lines from their junction brackets, then remove the securing clips from the crossmember

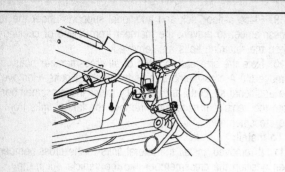

Fig. 55 Remove the speed sensor harness fastener — ABS equipped vehicles

19. If equipped with ABS, install the speed sensor harness-to-crossmember fasteners and tighten the fasteners to 53 inch lbs. (6 Nm).

20. Properly bleed the hydraulic brake system. Refer to the procedure in Section No. 9 of this manual.

21. Install the rear wheel assemblies, then remove the supports and carefully lower the vehicle.

22. Check and adjust the rear alignment as necessary.

Rear Wheel Hub/Bearing Assembly

The rear hub/bearing assembly is a sealed assembly, requiring no periodic maintenance and which cannot be serviced. If the hub/bearing assembly becomes worn or damaged, the entire unit must be replaced.

REMOVAL & INSTALLATION

▶ See Figure 57

1. Raise the rear of the vehicle and support safely using jackstands, then remove the rear wheel.

2. If equipped with ABS, disconnect the negative battery cable, then unplug the ABS speed sensor connector.

3. If equipped with ABS, remove the 2 caliper-to-knuckle mounting bolts from the rear of the knuckle, use a length of

Fig. 56 View of the crossmember assembly on an 1992 SC, note the blocks of wood on the jackstands to protect the vehicle jacking points

wire to suspend the caliper from the strut and clear of the knuckle.

4. Remove the brake drum or rotor, as applicable.

5. Remove the 4 hub/bearing-to-knuckle bolts and remove the assembly from the vehicle.

To install:

6. Position the brake backing plate and the hub/bearing assembly, then secure the components to the knuckle using the retaining bolts. Tighten the bolts to 63 ft. lbs. (85 Nm).

7. Install the brake drum or rotor and caliper. If applicable, tighten the caliper retaining bolts to 63 ft. lbs. (85 Nm).

8. If equipped, install the ABS wiring harness to the speed sensor.

9. Install the wheel assembly, remove the supports and carefully lower the vehicle. If applicable, connect the negative battery cable.

Rear End Alignment

▶ See Figures 58 and 59

Rear end alignment should be checked whenever the front end is aligned. If the rear camber and toe are not set correctly, accelerated tire wear may occur. The thrust line of the rear wheels may also be affected. The thrust line is the path the rear wheels take as they roll down the road. Ideally, the thrust line should align perfectly with the center line of the vehicle. If the thrust line is not correct, the vehicle will slightly understeer in one direction and oversteer in the other. It will also affect wheel centering.

Rear camber may be adjusted by loosening the 2 strut-to-knuckle fasteners, then pushing or pulling on the knuckle in the necessary direction of change. Up to 3 degrees of adjustment angle is possible without having to alter the size of the lower strut bracket bolt hole. Refer to the front camber adjustment procedure earlier in this section.

Rear toe adjustment is made by loosening the rearmost inboard lateral link-to-crossmember fastener on 1 of the rear wheels. Then using SA9158C, or an equivalent alignment tool, move the link as necessary to adjust the toe angle. After adjustment, tighten the fastener to 89 ft. lbs. (120 Nm).

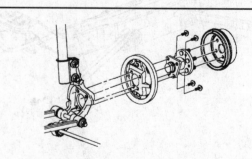

Fig. 57 Exploded view of the hub/bearing assembly on rear drum brake (non-ABS equipped) vehicles

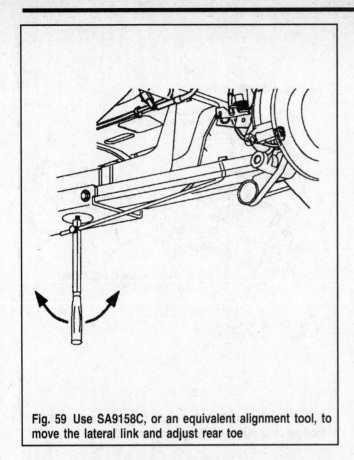

Fig. 59 Use SA9158C, or an equivalent alignment tool, to move the lateral link and adjust rear toe

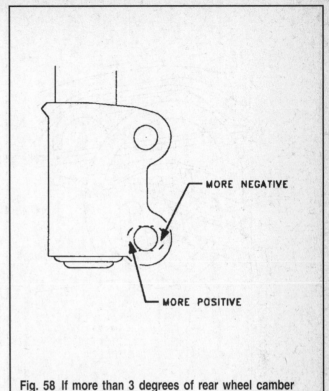

Fig. 58 If more than 3 degrees of rear wheel camber adjustment is necessary, material must be removed from the strut bracket

STEERING

Steering Wheel

REMOVAL & INSTALLATION

Without Air Bag
▶ **See Figures 60 and 61**

1. Disconnect the negative battery cable.
2. Lift the horn pad from the steering wheel by pulling on the edge of the pad firmly, then disconnect the wires and remove the horn pad from the vehicle.
3. Remove the clip on the end of the steering column shaft and remove the retaining nut.
4. Note the position of the steering wheel locating notch for reassembly purposes.
5. Install a suitable steering wheel puller and remove the steering wheel from the steering column.

To install:
6. Route the wires through the wheel and position the steering wheel making sure to properly align the locating notch. If the locating notch is not properly positioned, any attempt to install the steering wheel will damage the wheel and column beyond repair.
7. Install a new steering wheel nut. Tighten the nut to 30 ft. lbs. (40 Nm) and install a new clip on the end of the column.

8. Connect the wires to the horn pad and press the pad firmly into position on the wheel.
9. Connect the negative battery cable.

With Air Bag
▶ **See Figure 62**

✲✲CAUTION

If your vehicle is equipped with a Supplemental Inflatable Restraint (SIR) system, follow the recommended disarming procedures before performing any work on or around the system. Failure to do so may result in possible deployment of the air bag and/or personal injury.

1. If equipped, properly disable the SIR system as follows:
    a. Align the steering wheel so the tires are in the straight-ahead position, then turn the ignition **OFF**.
    b. Remove the 10 amp SIR fuse from the top left of the Instrument Panel Junction Block (IPJB).
    c. Remove the Connector Position Assurance (CPA) device, then disconnect the yellow 2-way SIR connector at the base of the steering column.
2. Disconnect the negative battery cable.
3. Loosen the 4 fasteners from the back of the steering wheel and lift the inflator module from the steering wheel.

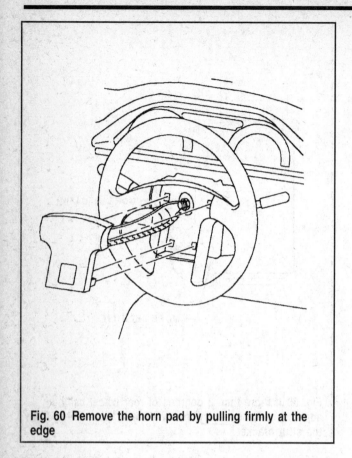

Fig. 60 Remove the horn pad by pulling firmly at the edge

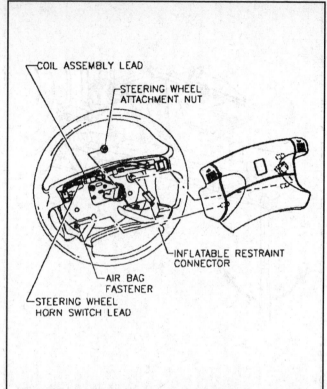

Fig. 62 Exploded view of the steering wheel and inflator module assembly — SIR equipped vehicles

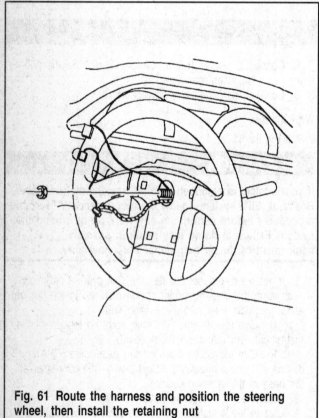

Fig. 61 Route the harness and position the steering wheel, then install the retaining nut

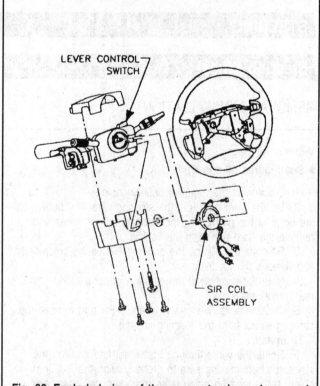

Fig. 63 Exploded view of the upper steering column and combination switch — SIR equipped vehicles

4. Remove the CPA device and unplug the wiring harness from the module, then remove the inflator module from the steering wheel.

✳✳CAUTION

When carrying a live inflator module, ensure the bag and trim cover are pointed away from the body. Never carry the inflator module by the wires or connector on the underside of the module. This will minimize the chance of injury should the module accidentally deploy.   When placing a live inflator module on a bench or other surface, always place the bag and trim cover up, away from the surface. This is necessary so a free space is provided to allow for air bag expansion in the unlikely event of accidental deployment.

5. Unplug the horn connector and, if equipped, unplug the cruise control switch connector.
6. Remove the clip on the end of the steering column shaft and remove the retaining nut.
7. Note the position of the steering wheel locating notch for reassembly purposes.
8. Install a suitable steering wheel puller and remove the steering wheel from the steering column.
9. Install a yellow retaining tab into the SIR coil assembly to keep it from rotating. If a retaining tab is not available, tape the coil in position to prevent coil damage.

To install:
10. Route the SIR wire and other electrical connections through the wheel, then position the steering wheel making sure to properly align the locating notch. If the locating notch is not properly positioned, any attempt to install the steering wheel will damage the wheel and column beyond repair.
11. Install a new steering wheel nut. Tighten the nut to 30 ft. lbs. (40 Nm) and install a new clip on the end of the column.
12. Remove the yellow retaining tap or the tape from the SIR coil assembly.
13. Connect the wiring harness to the horn and, if equipped, to the cruise control switch.
14. Position the inflator module and connect the SIR wiring harness, then seat the module on the steering wheel.
15. Secure the module using NEW fasteners, then tighten the new fasteners to 106 inch lbs. (12 Nm).
16. Connect the negative battery cable.
17. If equipped, enable the SIR system as follows:
    a. Verify the ignition switch is **OFF**, then connect the SIR electrical connector at the base of the steering column. Install the CPA device to the connector.
    b. Install the SIR fuse to the IPJB and install the junction block cover.
    c. Turn the ignition ON and verify that the AIR BAG indicator lamp flashes 7-9 times, then extinguishes. If the light does not flash as indicated, inspect the system for malfunction.

Turn Signal (Combination) Switch

REMOVAL & INSTALLATION

▶ See Figures 63 and 64

1. If equipped, properly disable the SIR system as follows:
    a. Align the steering wheel so the tires are in the straight-ahead position, then turn the ignition **OFF**.
    b. Remove the 10 amp SIR fuse from the top left of the Instrument Panel Junction Block (IPJB).
    c. Remove the Connector Position Assurance (CPA) device, then disconnect the yellow 2-way SIR connector at the base of the steering column.
2. Disconnect the negative battery cable.
3. Remove the steering wheel. Refer to the procedure earlier in this section.
4. Remove the 2 retaining screws and the upper steering column cover from the steering column.
5. Remove the ignition lock bezel, then remove the 2 retaining screws and the lower steering column cover.
6. If equipped with an SIR system, remove the coil from the combination meter.
7. Remove the CPA device and disconnect the wires from the lever control (combination) switch.
8. Remove the retaining bolts and remove the combination switch assembly from the steering column. It may be necessary to remove the instrument panel trim covers and center console trim in order to access the switch fasteners; if this is necessary refer to the procedures in Section 10 or the steering column removal procedure later in this section.

To install:
9. Install the combination switch and retaining bolts. Tighten the lower mounting bolt first to assure proper location and seating, then connect the switch electrical connectors and insert the CPA device.
10. If applicable, install the SIR coil to the combination switch assembly.
11. If removed, install the instrument panel and center console trim panels.
12. Install the steering column covers and the ignition bezel.
13. Install the steering wheel.
14. Connect the negative battery cable.
15. If equipped, enable the SIR system as follows:
    a. Verify the ignition switch is **OFF**, then connect the SIR electrical connector at the base of the steering column. Install the CPA device to the connector.
    b. Install the SIR fuse to the IPJB and install the junction block cover.
    c. Turn the ignition ON and verify that the AIR BAG indicator lamp flashes 7-9 times, then extinguishes. If the light does not flash as indicated, inspect the system for malfunction.

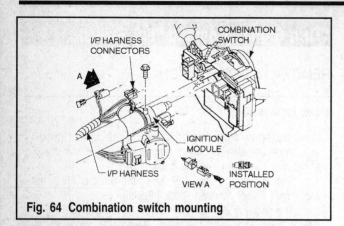

Fig. 64 Combination switch mounting

Ignition Switch

REMOVAL & INSTALLATION

▶ See Figure 65

1. If equipped, properly disable the SIR system as follows:
   a. Align the steering wheel so the tires are in the straight-ahead position, then turn the ignition **OFF**.
   b. Remove the 10 amp SIR fuse from the top left of the Instrument Panel Junction Block (IPJB).
   c. Remove the Connector Position Assurance (CPA) device, then disconnect the yellow 2-way SIR connector at the base of the steering column.
2. Disconnect the negative battery cable.
3. Remove the steering wheel. Refer to the procedure earlier in this section.
4. Remove the combination switch. Refer to the procedure earlier in this section.
5. Unplug the ignition switch electrical connector and remove the 2 retaining screws, then disconnect the switch from the ignition module and remove the switch from the vehicle.

To install:
6. Install the combination switch and retaining bolts. Tighten the lower mounting bolt first to assure proper location and seating.
7. Connect the wiring harness to the ignition switch.
8. Install the ignition switch and retaining bolts to the ignition module.
9. If applicable, install the SIR coil to the combination switch assembly.
10. If removed, install the instrument cluster and center console trim panels.
11. Install the steering column covers and the ignition bezel.
12. Install the steering wheel.
13. Connect the negative battery cable.
14. If equipped, enable the SIR system as follows:
   a. Verify the ignition switch is **OFF**, then connect the SIR electrical connector at the base of the steering column. Install the CPA device to the connector.
   b. Install the SIR fuse to the IPJB and install the junction block cover.
   c. Turn the ignition ON and verify that the AIR BAG indicator lamp flashes 7-9 times, then extinguishes. If the

light does not flash as indicated, inspect the system for malfunction.

Ignition Lock Assembly

REMOVAL & INSTALLATION

▶ See Figures 66 and 67

1. If equipped, properly disable the SIR system as follows:
   a. Align the steering wheel so the tires are in the straight-ahead position, then turn the ignition **OFF**.
   b. Remove the 10 amp SIR fuse from the top left of the Instrument Panel Junction Block (IPJB).
   c. Remove the Connector Position Assurance (CPA) device, then disconnect the yellow 2-way SIR connector at the base of the steering column.
2. Disconnect the negative battery cable.
3. Remove the steering wheel. Refer to the procedure earlier in this section.
4. Remove the steering column. Refer to the procedure earlier in this section.
5. Position the steering column in a vise at the upper bracket.

➡ **Always wear the proper eye protection when using drills, chisels and punches.**

6. Using a center punch, mark the center of the shear bolts on the ignition lock assembly.
7. Drill a small ⅛ in. hole in the shear bolts at the center mark. Remove the shear bolts with a screw extractor and remove the ignition lock assembly and clamp from the steering column.

To install:
8. Using new shear bolts, install the ignition lock assembly to the steering column. Torque the bolts until the heads break off.
9. Install the steering column.
10. Install the steering wheel.
11. Connect the negative battery cable.
12. If equipped, enable the SIR system as follows:
   a. Verify the ignition switch is **OFF**, then connect the SIR electrical connector at the base of the steering column. Install the CPA device to the connector.

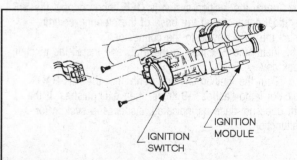

Fig. 65 The ignition switch is mounted to the ignition module/lock cylinder on the underside of the steering column

b. Install the SIR fuse to the IPJB and install the junction block cover.

c. Turn the ignition ON and verify that the AIR BAG indicator lamp flashes 7-9 times, then extinguishes. If the light does not flash as indicated, inspect the system for malfunction.

Steering Column

REMOVAL & INSTALLATION

▶ **See Figures 68, 69, 70, 71 and 72**

1. If equipped, properly disable the SIR system as follows:
   a. Align the steering wheel so the tires are in the straight-ahead position, then turn the ignition **OFF**.
   b. Remove the 10 amp SIR fuse from the top left of the Instrument Panel Junction Block (IPJB).
   c. Remove the Connector Position Assurance (CPA) device, then disconnect the yellow 2-way SIR connector at the base of the steering column.
2. Disconnect the negative battery cable.
3. Remove the steering wheel. Refer to the procedure earlier in this section.
4. Remove the 2 retaining screws and the upper steering column cover from the steering column.
5. Remove the ignition lock bezel, then remove the 2 retaining screws and the lower steering column cover.
6. Disconnect the velcro fasteners, then remove the left and right lower center console trim panel extensions by pulling

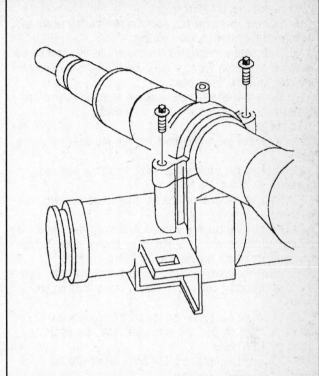

Fig. 67 Install the ignition lock module using new shear bolts, then tighten until the heads break off

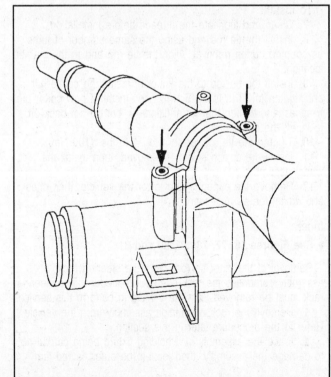

Fig. 66 Center punch the ignition lock module retaining bolts, then drill the bolts and remove with a screw extractor

them out of the 2 upper fasteners on the top corners of each panel.

7. Carefully remove the center air outlet/radio trim panel by pulling outward at the clip locations. Start at the bottom and move upward. Do not use tools that might damage the trim panel.

8. If necessary, remove the trim panel extension strip by pulling out at the fastener location.

9. Remove the 2 instrument panel top cover screw caps and screws. Carefully remove the cover by lifting at the rear edge to disengage the retaining clips and by sliding the panel out of the windshield clips.

10. Remove the 4 cluster trim panel attaching screws. Carefully pull the cluster trim panel upward to disengage it from the retainers.

11. Remove the CPA device and unplug the electrical connectors from the instrument panel lighting and rear window defogger switches. Remove the cluster trim panel from the vehicle.

12. Remove the 6 screws attaching the steering column opening filler assembly, then carefully remove the assembly. Protect the console from the damage when removing the assembly.

13. If equipped, remove the coil assembly from the combination switch.

14. Remove the CPA device and disconnect the wires from the lever control switch.

15. Remove the 2 retaining bolts and remove the combination switch assembly from the steering column.

16. Remove the 2 retaining screws, disconnect the ignition switch from the ignition module and remove the switch from the vehicle.

17. Remove the 2 upper steering column bolts and carefully lower the column onto the seat.

18. Remove the upper bolt from the intermediate shaft and disconnect the shaft from the column.

19. If necessary, disconnect the coupe's hand wheel sensor electrical connector. Remove the 2 lower bolts and disconnect the column at the hinge point.

20. Verify that all wires are removed from the column and carefully remove the column from the vehicle.

To install:

21. Install the steering column into the vehicle at the hinge point.

22. Connect the intermediate shaft, install the bolt and tighten to 33 ft. lbs. (45 Nm).

23. If applicable, connect the hand wheel sensor electrical connector.

24. Position the column wires as necessary, then raise the column into place and install the upper column bolts. Tighten the steering column fasteners to 26 ft. lbs. (35 Nm).

25. Install the combination switch and retaining bolts. Tighten the lower mounting bolt first to assure proper location and seating.

26. Install the bolts retaining the combination switch connector, then connect the switch electrical connectors and insert the CPA device.

27. If applicable, install the SIR coil assembly to the combination switch assembly

28. Install the ignition switch and retaining bolts to the ignition module.

29. Install the steering column opening filler and attaching screws.

30. Position the instrument cluster trim panel and connect the wiring harnesses to the panel lighting and the rear defogger switches, then install the CPA device.

31. Install the cluster trim panel into the retainers, then install and tighten the retaining screws

32. Install the rear of the instrument panel top cover into the windshield clips and snap the panel into position. If necessary, replace the 6 rearward clips. Install the upper panel cover screws and screw caps.

33. Install the trim panel extension strip if removed, then push the center air outlet/radio panel into the clip locations.

34. Install the lower left and right center console trim panel extensions.

35. Install the steering column covers and the ignition bezel.

36. Install the steering wheel.

37. Connect the negative battery cable.

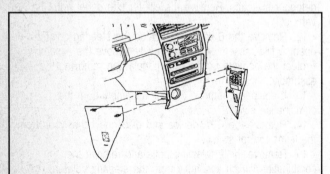

Fig. 68 Remove the center console lower trim panel extensions

38. If equipped, enable the SIR system as follows:

a. Verify the ignition switch is **OFF**, then connect the SIR electrical connector at the base of the steering column. Install the CPA device to the connector.

b. Install the SIR fuse to the IPJB and install the junction block cover.

c. Turn the ignition ON and verify that the AIR BAG indicator lamp flashes 7-9 times, then extinguishes. If the light does not flash as indicated, inspect the system for malfunction.

Tie Rod Ends

REMOVAL & INSTALLATION

Outer

▶ See Figures 73, 74 and 75

1. Raise the front of the vehicle and support safely using jackstands.

2. Remove the front wheel and if necessary for access, remove the splash shield.

3. Remove the cotter pin and nut from the tie rod end.

4. Separate the tie rod end from the knuckle with separator tool SA91100C or equivalent. Do not use a wedge-type tool or the seal may be damaged.

5. Mark the threaded portion of the steering arm for installation purposes.

6. Loosen the tie rod jam nut and thread the tie rod end off the steering shaft. Count the number of turns necessary to remove.

To install:

7. Clean and lubricate the threads before installation.

8. Install the tie rod end using the same number of turns as counted during removal. Align the tie rod end to the marked location.

9. Install the tie rod to the knuckle. Install the castle nut and tighten to 33 ft. lbs. (45 Nm), then install a new cotter pin. If necessary, tighten the nut additionally, but do not back off, to insert the cotter pin.

10. Tighten the tie rod jam nut to 74 ft. lbs. (100 Nm).

11. Install the splash shield, if removed, then install the wheel assembly.

12. Remove the supports and lower the vehicle, then check and adjust toe as necessary.

Inner

▶ See Figures 76, 77, 78, 79, 80 and 81

Removal of the inner tie rods from the steering rack assembly comprises the rack overhaul procedure. The steering rack must be removed from the vehicle to perform this service.

1. Remove the rack and pinion assembly from the vehicle. Refer to the procedure later in this section.

2. Place the assembly in a holding fixture being careful not to damage the assembly, then loosen the outer tie rod jam nut.

3. Unthread the outer tie rod from the inner tie rod. Count the number of turns necessary or mark for realignment.

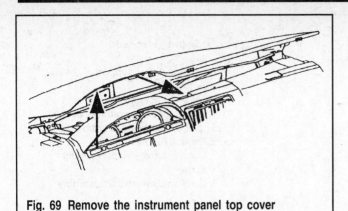

Fig. 69 Remove the instrument panel top cover

4. Remove the outer tie rod jam nut, then remove the steering gear boot. The boot is retained by 2 clamps, the tie rod end may be loosened, but the steering gear clamp should be cut and discarded.

5. Slide the shock damper toward the steering gear and off the inner tie rod.

6. Remove the inner tie rod assembly from the steering gear. To prevent damage, place a shop cloth over the gear teeth and hold the teeth with a suitable open end wrench. If removing the right inner tie rod, the left side boot must be removed to access the teeth.

To install:

7. Remove the old Loctite® from the rack and inner tie rod threads. Then, apply an even coat of Loctite® 262, or an equivalent threadlock, to the inner tie rod threads.

8. Slide the shock damper onto the steering gear.

9. Hold the gear teeth with a wrench and a protective cloth, then install the inner tie rod assembly onto the steering gear. Tighten the inner rod to 70 ft. lbs. (95 Nm).

10. Slide the shock damper up against the inner tie rod assembly and apply to the locations shown in the illustration.

11. Position a new boot clamp on the steering gear end of the boot, then slide the boot onto the rod assembly until the large end of the boot is seated in the gear housing groove. Make sure the boot is turned so the pad is toward the front of the vehicle and that it is not twisted or puckered.

12. Crimp the clamp on the boot housing end, then install the tie rod end clamp.

13. Thread the outer tie rod jam nut onto the inner tie rod, then install the outer tie rod to the assembly. Use the same number or turns or align the marks made earlier and tighten the jam nut to 74 ft. lbs. (100 Nm).

14. Install the rack and pinion assembly to the vehicle.

15. Check and adjust the alignment and bleed the power steering, as necessary.

Manual Rack and Pinion

BEARING PRELOAD ADJUSTMENT

▶ See Figure 82

1. Center the steering wheel, then raise the front of the vehicle and support safely using jackstands.

2. Loosen the locknut on the steering gear adjuster plug, then turn the adjuster plug clockwise until it bottoms in the gear housing.

3. Tighten the plug to 106 inch lbs. (12 Nm).

4. Back off the adjuster plug 50-70 degrees (about 1 flat of the nut).

5. While holding the plug steady, tighten the locknut with a crows foot wrench to 52 ft. lbs. (70 Nm).

6. Check the steering for returnability, binding or difficulty in turning.

REMOVAL & INSTALLATION

▶ See Figures 83 and 84

1. Disconnect the negative battery cable, then raise the front of the vehicle and support safely using jackstands.

2. Remove the front wheels and the left inner splash shield.

3. Remove and discard the tie rod cotter pins, then remove the castle nuts. Disconnect the tie rod ends using SA91100C or an equivalent separator tool. Do not use a wedge-type tool or seal damage may occur.

4. Loosen the intermediate shaft cover from the steering gear and move it up enough to access the pinch bolt. Remove the pinch bolt.

5. Remove the steering gear fasteners and remove the gear through the left fenderwell.

To install:

6. Install the steering gear and tighten the steering gear-to-cradle bolts to 52 ft. lbs. (70 Nm).

7. Install the intermediate steering shaft to the gear and tighten the pinch bolt to 35 ft. lbs. (47 Nm). Position the shaft cover.

8. Thoroughly clean and lubricate the threads of the tie rod ends, then install the ends into the steering knuckles. Install the castle nuts and tighten to 33 ft. lbs. (45 Nm). Install new cotter pins. If necessary, tighten the nut additionally to install the pin, but do not back off the specified torque.

9. Install the left inner splash shield and install the front wheels.

10. Remove the supports and carefully lower the vehicle, then connect the negative battery cable.

11. Check alignment and adjust vehicle toe, as necessary.

OVERHAUL

The gear must be removed from the vehicle for overhaul, which consists of removing the inner tie rod boots and ends from the gear. This service is the same for either manual or power rack and pinion assemblies. Refer to the inner tie rod end procedure earlier in this section.

Power Rack and Pinion

BEARING PRELOAD ADJUSTMENT

Bearing preload adjustment is the same for either the manual or power rack and pinion assemblies. Refer to the

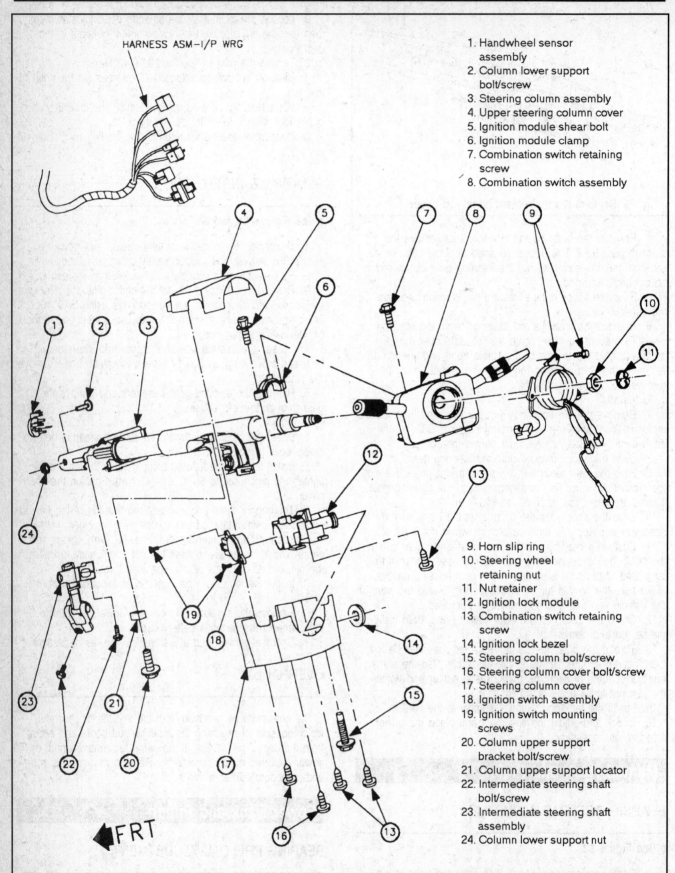

HARNESS ASM—I/P WRG

1. Handwheel sensor assembly
2. Column lower support bolt/screw
3. Steering column assembly
4. Upper steering column cover
5. Ignition module shear bolt
6. Ignition module clamp
7. Combination switch retaining screw
8. Combination switch assembly
9. Horn slip ring
10. Steering wheel retaining nut
11. Nut retainer
12. Ignition lock module
13. Combination switch retaining screw
14. Ignition lock bezel
15. Steering column bolt/screw
16. Steering column cover bolt/screw
17. Steering column cover
18. Ignition switch assembly
19. Ignition switch mounting screws
20. Column upper support bracket bolt/screw
21. Column upper support locator
22. Intermediate steering shaft bolt/screw
23. Intermediate steering shaft assembly
24. Column lower support nut

FRT

Fig. 70 Exploded view of the steering column assembly for non-SIR vehicles, SIR vehicles have a SIR coil assembly instead of the horn slip ring

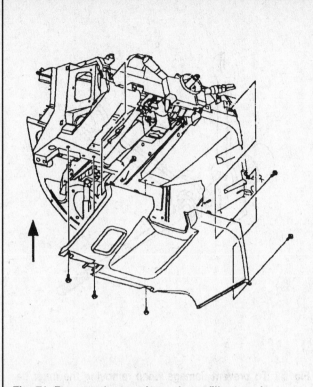

Fig. 71 Remove the steering column filler panel assembly

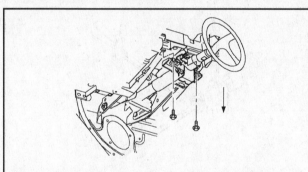

Fig. 72 Remove the 2 upper steering column bolts and carefully lower the column onto the seat

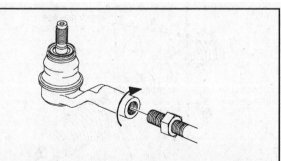

Fig. 75 Mark the rod end position in relation to the threads, then unthread the tie rod end from the inner tie rod

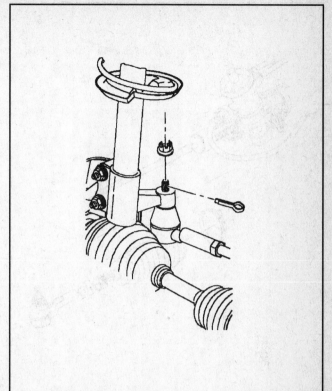

Fig. 73 Remove the cotter pin and castle nut from the tie rod end

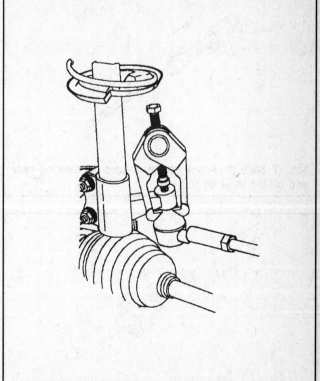

Fig. 74 Use SA91100C or an equivalent jawed separator tool to remove the tie rod end from the steering knuckle

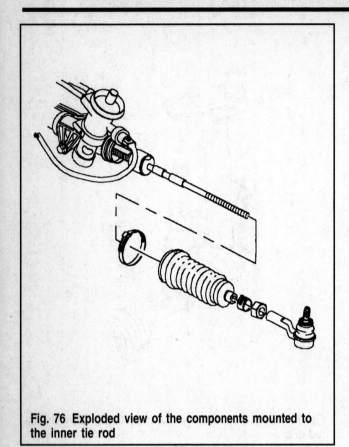

Fig. 76 Exploded view of the components mounted to the inner tie rod

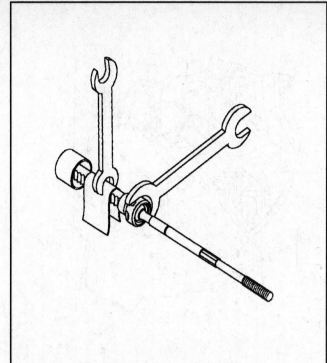

Fig. 78 To prevent damage when removing the inner tie rod, place a shop cloth over the gear teeth and hold the teeth with a suitable open end wrench

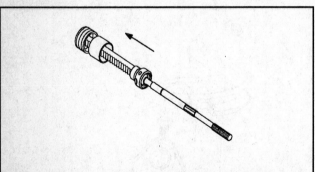

Fig. 77 Slide the shock damper toward the steering gear and off the inner tie rod

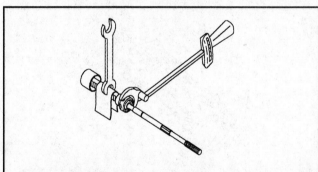

Fig. 80 Use a torque wrench to tighten the inner tie rod to 70 ft. lbs. (95 Nm)

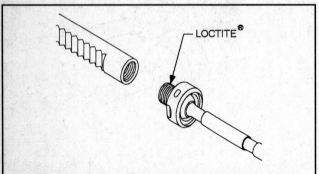

Fig. 79 Apply only enough threadlock to evenly cover the inner tie rod threads

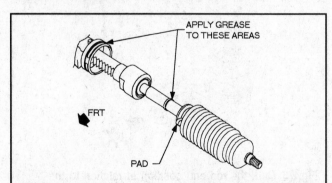

Fig. 81 Apply grease to these locations before installing the boot

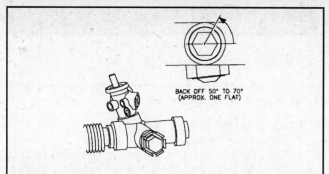

Fig. 82 Adjusting the manual or power steering gear bearing preload

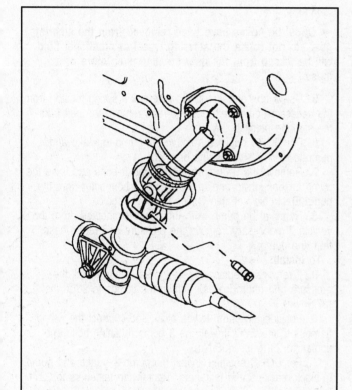

Fig. 83 Move the intermediate shaft cover away from the gear for access to the pinch bolt

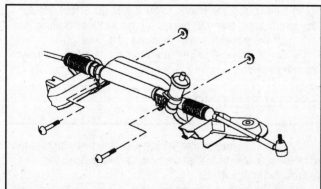

Fig. 84 Remove the steering rack-to-cradle fasteners

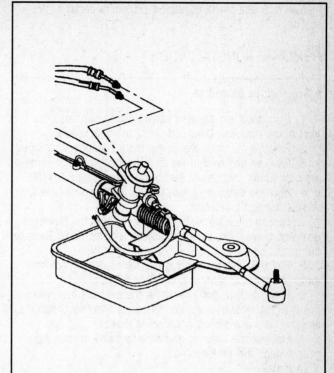

Fig. 85 Disconnect the lines from the steering gear and allow the system to drain

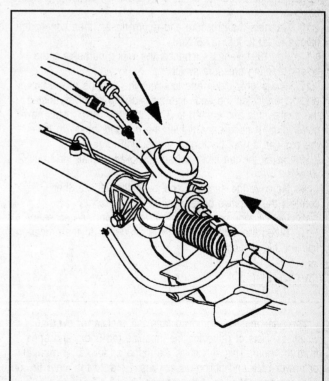

Fig. 86 Connect the pressure and return hoses, then for 1991 vehicles, connect the wiring harness to the power steering pressure switch

manual rack and pinion adjustment procedure earlier in this section.

REMOVAL & INSTALLATION

▶ **See Figures 85 and 86**

1. Disconnect the negative battery cable, then raise the front of the vehicle and support safely using jackstands.
2. Remove the front wheels and the left inner splash shield.
3. Remove and discard the tie rod cotter pins, then remove the castle nuts. Disconnect the tie rod ends using SA91100C or an equivalent separator tool. Do not use a wedge-type tool or seal damage may occur.
4. Loosen the intermediate shaft cover from the steering gear and move it up enough to access the pinch bolt. Remove the pinch bolt.
5. For 1991 vehicles, unplug the power steering pressure switch electrical connector at the steering gear.
6. Place a clean container under the pressure and return hoses at the steering assembly. Disconnect the lines from the steering gear and allow the system to drain.
7. Remove the steering gear fasteners and remove the gear through the left fenderwell.
   To install:
8. Install the steering gear and tighten the steering gear-to-cradle bolts to 52 ft. lbs. (70 Nm).
9. Install the intermediate steering shaft to the gear and tighten the pinch bolt to 35 ft. lbs. (47 Nm). Position the shaft cover.
10. Connect the pressure and return hoses, then tighten the fittings to 20 ft. lbs. (27.5 Nm).
11. For 1991 vehicles, connect the wiring harness to the power steering pressure switch.
12. Thoroughly clean and lubricate the threads of the tie rod ends, then install the ends into the steering knuckles. Install the castle nuts and tighten to 33 ft. lbs. (45 Nm). Install new cotter pins. If necessary, tighten the nut additionally to install the pin, but do not back off the specified torque.
13. Install the left inner splash shield and install the front wheels.
14. Remove the supports and lower the vehicle, then connect the negative battery cable.
15. Check alignment and adjust vehicle toe, as necessary.
16. Bleed the power steering system. Refer to the procedure later in this section.

OVERHAUL

The gear must be removed from the vehicle for overhaul, which consists of removing the inner tie rod boots and ends from the gear. This service is the same on for either manual or power rack and pinion assemblies. Refer to the inner tie rod end procedure earlier in this section.

Power Steering Pump

REMOVAL & INSTALLATION

▶ **See Figures 87, 88, 89 and 90**

1. Disconnect the negative battery cable.
2. Remove the reservoir fill cap.
3. Raise the front of the vehicle and support safely using jackstands. Make sure the vehicle is raised sufficiently to allow both undervehicle and underhood access.
4. Place a clean container under the power steering hoses, then remove the hoses from the steering gear and allow the system to drain.

➡ **Once the hoses have been removed from the steering gear, do not rotate the steering wheel or additional fluid will be forced from the gear creating even more of a mess.**

5. Use a box end wrench to relieve the spring tension from the accessory drive belt tensioner and remove the belt from the steering pump pulley.
6. For DOHC engines, remove the pump-to-intake and pump-to-block fasteners and bracket.
7. Remove the 3 pump bracket-to-block bolts and raise the pump far enough to unplug the electrical connector from the pump Electronic Variable Orifice (EVO) solenoid.
8. Remove the pump, with the hoses connected, from the vehicle. If necessary, remove the pressure and return hoses from the pump.
   To install:
9. If removed, replace the O-ring seals and install the pressure and return hoses. Tighten the fittings to 20 ft. lbs. (27.5 Nm).
10. Position the pump to the block and connect the wiring harness to the EVO. Install the 3 pump retaining bolts and tighten to 28 ft. lbs. (38 Nm).
11. For DOHC engines, install the pump-to-intake and pump-to-block brackets and fasteners. Tighten the fasteners to 22 ft. lbs. (30 Nm).
12. Install the serpentine drive belt to the steering pump pulley.
13. Connect the pressure and return hoses to the steering gear, then tighten the fittings to 20 ft. lbs. (27.5 Nm). Route the return hose, then the pressure hose into the retaining clip.
14. Fill the power steering reservoir with clean fluid.
15. Connect the negative battery cable and bleed the power steering system.

SYSTEM BLEEDING

1. Raise the front of the vehicle just sufficiently so that the drive wheels are off the ground, then safely support the vehicle using jackstands.
2. Fill the reservoir to the full mark.
3. Bleed the system by turning the wheels from side-to-side without hitting the stops. It may take several cycles to bleed the system.
4. Keep the reservoir to the full mark during the procedure.

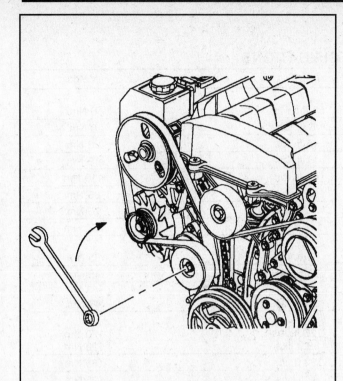

Fig. 87 Use a box wrench to relieve belt tension from the serpentine drive belt

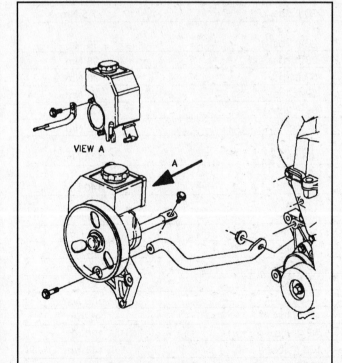

Fig. 88 For DOHC engines, remove the rear pump brackets from the intake manifold and engine brackets

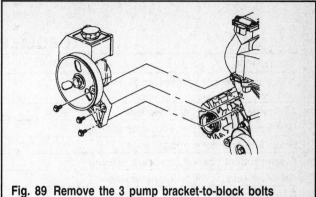

Fig. 89 Remove the 3 pump bracket-to-block bolts

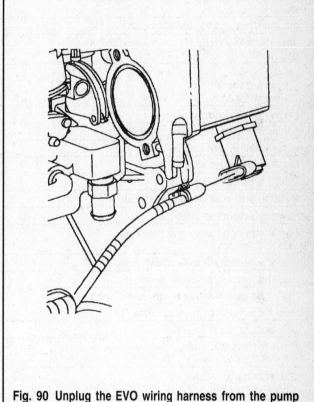

Fig. 90 Unplug the EVO wiring harness from the pump

5. Start the engine and check the fluid level with the engine idling. If necessary, add to bring the level to the full mark.

6. Road test the vehicle and check for proper operation. Recheck the fluid level and make sure it is at or slightly above the full mark after the system has stabilized at normal operating temperature.

TORQUE SPECIFICATIONS

Component	U.S.	Metric
ABS speed sensor harness crossmember bolt	53 inch lbs.	6 Nm
ABS wheel speed sensor fastener	6 ft. lbs.	8 Nm
Brake dust shield (1991/front suspension)	18 ft. lbs.	25 Nm
Brake line and hose (rear) fittings	14 ft. lbs.	19 Nm
Caliper mount bracket (front suspension)	81 ft. lbs.	110 Nm
Caliper mounting bolts (rear suspension)	63 ft. lbs.	85 Nm
Control arm ball joint stud castle nut	55 ft. lbs.	75 Nm
Halfshaft nut	148 ft. lbs.	200 Nm
Hub/bearing assembly bolts (rear suspension)	63 ft. lbs.	85 Nm
Intermediate shaft-to-steering column bolt	33 ft. lbs.	45 Nm
Intermediate steering shaft-to-rack pinch bolt	35 ft. lbs.	47 Nm
Lateral link; Forward most bolt Rear most bolt	126 ft. lbs. 89 ft. lbs.	170 Nm 120 Nm
Lateral link-to-knuckle bolt	122 ft. lbs.	165 Nm
Lower control arm engine cradle bolt	92 ft. lbs.	125 Nm
Lower control arm engine cradle nut	74 ft. lbs.	100 Nm
MacPherson strut knuckle bolts	148 ft. lbs.	200 Nm
MacPherson strut shaft nut	37 ft. lbs.	50 Nm
MacPherson strut upper mount nuts (1)	21 ft. lbs.	29 Nm
Power steering hose fittings	20 ft. lbs.	27.5 Nm
Power steering pump rear brackets; DOHC engine	22 ft. lbs.	30 Nm
Power steering pump retaining bolts	28 ft. lbs.	38 Nm
Rack and pinion adjuster plug locknut	52 ft. lbs.	70 Nm
Rack and pinion assembly-to-cradle bolts	52 ft. lbs.	70 Nm
Rear crossmember-to-body bolts (1)	89 ft. lbs.	120 Nm
SIR module fasteners (1)	106 inch lbs.	12 Nm
Stabilizer bar stud nuts; Front suspension (1)	106 ft. lbs.	144 Nm
Stabilizer bar brackets; Front suspension (2)	103 ft. lbs.	140 Nm
Stabilizer bar-to-rear crossmember brackets	41 ft. lbs.	55 Nm
Stabilizer bar-to-rear link fasteners	30 ft. lbs.	40 Nm
Steering column upper bolts	26 ft. lbs.	35 Nm
Steering wheel nut (1)	30 ft. lbs.	40 Nm
Tie rod (inner)	70 ft. lbs.	95 Nm
Tie rod (outer) jam nut	74 ft. lbs.	100 Nm
Tie rod-to-knuckle castle nut	33 ft. lbs.	45 Nm
Trailing arm-to-body bolts	89 ft. lbs.	120 Nm
Trailing arm-to-knuckle nut	106 ft. lbs.	144 Nm
Wheel assembly lug nuts	130 ft. lbs.	140 Nm

(1)- New fasteners must be used because the torque retention of the old fasteners may not be sufficient
(2)- New fasteners a suitable threadlock must be used

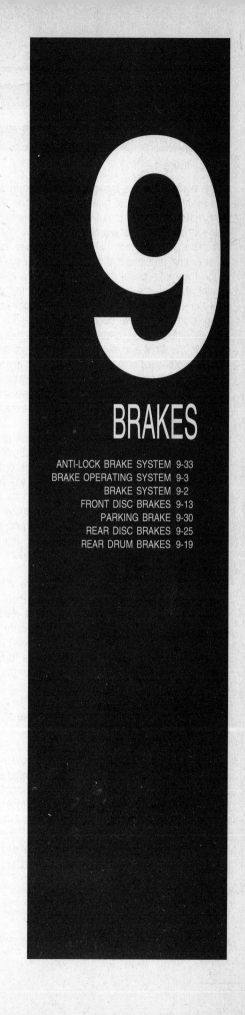

9

BRAKES

BRAKE SYSTEM

Operation

▶ See Figure 1

The hydraulic brake system on your Saturn is a diagonally split system with a dual master cylinder. The left front and right rear are on one brake circuit while the right front and left rear are on another brake circuit.

A set of proportioning valves are threaded into the master cylinder and regulate hydraulic pressure in the brake circuit. When the brake pedal is applied, full brake circuit pressure passes through the proportioning valve to the rear brake circuit until the valves's split point is reached. Above the split point, the proportioning valve begins to reduce hydraulic pressure to the rear brake circuit, creating a balanced braking condition between the front and rear wheels while maintaining balanced hydraulic pressure at each rear wheel. Double walled steel tubing extends from the master cylinder pressure fitting to the system's cylinders or calipers. Flexible hoses make the final connections between the body mounted brake tubes and the suspension mounted brake assemblies.

All Saturn's are equipped with a front disc and rear drum brakes, unless the factory option of an Anti-Lock Braking System (ABS) is chosen. When a Saturn is ordered with ABS, the rear drum brakes are replaced with discs very similar in form and function to front disc's, but the parts are not identical.

When the brake pedal is depressed, it moves a piston mounted in the bottom of the master cylinder. The movement of this piston creates hydraulic pressure in the master cylinder. This pressure is carried to the wheel cylinders or calipers by the brake lines.

When the hydraulic pressure reaches the wheels, after the pedal has been depressed, it enters the wheel cylinders or calipers. Here it comes into contact with a piston or pistons. The hydraulic pressure causes the piston(s) to move, which moves the brake shoes or pads (disc brakes), causing them to come into contact with the drums or rotors (disc brakes). Friction between the brake shoes/pads and the drums/rotors causes the car to slow down. There is a relationship between the amount of pressure that is applied to the brake pedal and the amount of force which moves the brake shoes against the drums. Therefore, the harder the brake pedal is depressed, the quicker the car should stop.

Since a hydraulic system operates on fluids, air is a natural enemy. Air in the system retards the passage of hydraulic pressure from the master cylinder to the wheels. Anytime a hydraulic component below the master cylinder is opened or removed, the system must be bled (of air) to ensure proper operation.

The wheel cylinders used with drum brakes are composed of a cylinder with a polished inside bore, which is mounted on the brake shoe backing plate, two boots, two pistons, two cups, a spring, and a bleeder screw. When hydraulic pressure enters the wheel cylinder, it contacts the two cylinder cups. The cups seal the cylinder and prevent fluid from leaking out. The hydraulic pressure forces the cups outward. The cups in turn force the pistons outward. The pistons contact the brake shoes and the hydraulic pressure in the wheel cylinders overcomes the pressure of the brake springs, causing the shoes to contact the brake drum. When the brake pedal is released, the brake shoe return springs pull the brake shoes away from the drum. This forces the pistons back toward the center of the wheel cylinder. Wheel cylinders can fail in two ways; they can leak or lock up. Leaking wheel cylinders are caused either by defective cups or irregularities in the wheel cylinder bore. Frozen wheel cylinders are caused by foreign matter getting into the cylinders and preventing the pistons from sliding freely.

The calipers used with the disc brakes contain a piston, piston seal, piston dust boot, and bleeder screw. When hydraulic pressure enters the caliper, the piston is forced outward causing the disc brake pad to come into contact with the rotor. When the brakes are applied, the piston seal, mounted on the caliper housing, becomes slightly distorted in the direction of the rotor. When the brakes are released, the piston seal moves back to its normal position and, at the same time, pulls the piston back away from the brake pad. This allows the brake pads to move away from the rotor. Calipers can fail in three ways, two of these being caused by defective piston seals. When a piston seal becomes worn, it can allow brake fluid to leak out to contaminate the pad and rotor. If a piston seal becomes weak, it can fail to pull the piston away from the brake shoe when the brakes are released, allowing the brake pad to drag on the rotor when the car is being driven. If foreign material enters the caliper housing, it can prevent the piston from sliding freely, causing the brakes to stick on the rotor.

Clean, high-quality brake fluid, meeting DOT 3 specs, is essential to the proper operation of the brake system. Always buy the highest quality brake fluid available. If the brake fluid should become contaminated, it should be drained and flushed, and the master cylinder filled with new fluid. NEVER reuse brake fluid. Any brake fluid that is removed from the brake system should be discarded. Remember these are not just your brakes, they're your ability to STOP the vehicle.

Since the hydraulic system is sealed, there must be a leak somewhere in the system if the master cylinder is repeatedly low on fluid.

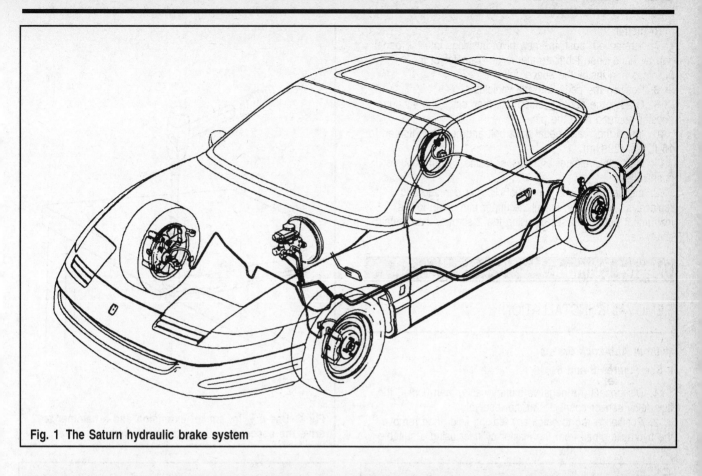

Fig. 1 The Saturn hydraulic brake system

BRAKE OPERATING SYSTEM

Adjustments

DRUM BRAKES

The Saturn features a self-adjuster mechanism that is part of the brake assembly and compensates for normal brake lining wear. No external adjustment is necessary or possible.

When the brake shoes or components of the brake assembly are replaced, the inside diameter of the drum should be measured using a brake shoe clearance gauge. The outer diameter of the brake shoes should then be given the base setting of 0.020 in. (0.5mm) less than the drum's inner diameter. The automatic adjuster will take care of all adjustments from that point.

BRAKE PEDAL HEIGHT

Height of the brake pedal is determined by the geometry of the brake pedal and attached components. If the pedal seems abnormally low, it reaches the carpet before full braking can be achieved, check for bent or damaged components and replace, as necessary.

Brake Light Switch

For removal, installation and adjustment of the brake light switch, refer to Section No. 6 of this manual.

Brake Pedal

REMOVAL & INSTALLATION

▶ See Figures 2, 3 and 4

1. Remove the dashboard 2 upper trim screw caps by carefully prying with a small blunt tool. Remove the upper trim panel screws. Remove the panel by lifting upward to disengage the rear edge clips, then by pulling the panel rearward and from the windshield clips.

2. Remove retainer and washer from the vacuum booster push rod.

3. Remove the brake pedal pivot bolt and nut.

4. Separate the vacuum booster push rod from the brake pedal pushrod pin.

5. Remove the brake pedal from the car.

6. If necessary, replace the pivot bushing. Use a ⅜ in. socket extension and a hammer to drive the spacer tube from the pedal hub. Then use a small prybar to gently pry the bushings from the hub.

To install:

7. If removed, push the new pivot bushings into the pedal hub by hand, then lubricate the inside diameter of the bushings and install the spacer tube.

8. Position the pedal into the vehicle.

9. Grease the pedal pushrod pin, then place the vacuum booster pushrod onto the pin.

10. Install the brake pedal pivot bolt and nut, then tighten to 16 ft. lbs. (22 Nm).

11. Install the retainer and washer to the vacuum booster push rod.

12. Inspect the upper trim panel clips for damage and replace, as necessary. Install the upper trim panel to the instrument panel and secure using the 2 screws, then install screw caps.

Master Cylinder

REMOVAL & INSTALLATION

Without Anti-Lock Brakes

▶ **See Figures 5 and 6**

1. Disconnect the negative battery cable, then unplug the fluid level sensor connector at the reservoir.

2. Position a rag to catch any leaking fluid, then remove the hydraulic pipes from the master cylinder using a suitable

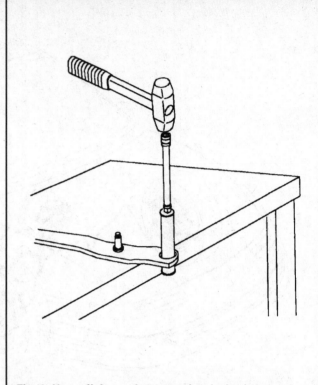

Fig. 3 Use a ⅜ in. socket extension and a hammer to drive the spacer tube from the pedal hub

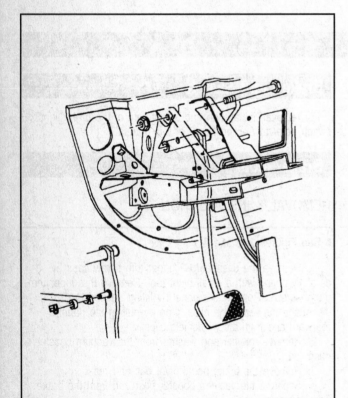

Fig. 2 Remove the booster pushrod retainer and washer, then remove the pedal pivot bolt and nut

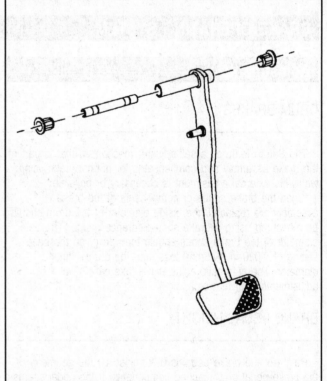

Fig. 4 Exploded view of the pivot spacer tube and bushings

wrench. Plug the pipes and cylinder bores to prevent fluid contamination or loss.

✳✳WARNING

Do not allow brake fluid to spill on or come in contact with the vehicle's finish as it will remove the paint. In case of a spill, immediately flush the area with water.

3. Remove the 2 master cylinder retaining nuts, then remove the master cylinder from the vehicle.

To install:

4. Install the master cylinder onto the brake booster studs, then install the retaining nuts and tighten to 20 ft. lbs. (27 Nm).

5. Remove the protective caps or line plugs, then connect the hydraulic brake pipes to the master cylinder and tighten the fittings to 18 ft. lbs. (24 Nm).

6. Properly bleed the hydraulic brake system. Refer to the procedure later in this section.

7. Install the wiring harness connector to the brake fluid level sensor.

8. Connect the negative battery cable and start the engine. Have a friend depress the brake pedal while you check for leaks.

With Anti-Lock Brakes

The master cylinder for ABS equipped vehicles is part of the ABS control assembly. Refer to the removal and installation procedure located later in this section.

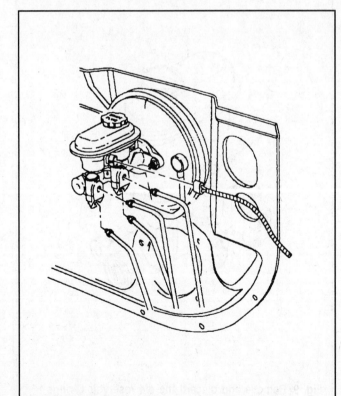

Fig. 5 The hydraulic pipes and level sensor harness are located on the fender side of the master cylinder

OVERHAUL

▶ **See Figures 7, 8, 9, 10, 11, 12 and 13**

Although the removal and installation procedures differ between ABS and non-ABS master cylinders, the same basic component is used on both systems. The overhaul procedure is virtually the same.

1. Remove the master cylinder or the ABS control assembly, as applicable. Refer to the appropriate procedure in this section.

2. Wipe the reservoir cap with a clean cloth. Remove the cap and inspect both the cap and diaphragm for cuts, nicks, cracks or deformation and replace as necessary.

3. Empty reservoir of brake fluid.

✳✳WARNING

Do not allow brake fluid to spill on or come in contact with the vehicle's finish as it will remove the paint. In case of a spill, immediately flush the area with water.

4. For ABS units, remove the master cylinder from the control assembly. Refer to the procedure later in this section.

5. Remove the brake fluid level sensor from the bottom side of the cylinder reservoir.

6. Place the master cylinder in a suitable vise and drive out the reservoir spring pins. Use a ⅛ inch punch to drive the pins, then pull the reservoir from the cylinder body.

7. Remove and discard the old reservoir O-rings from the grooves in the reservoir bayonets or from the master cylinder bores.

8. Insert a wooden dowel into the rear of the cylinder body and depress the primary piston while removing the retainer clip from the end of the cylinder.

9. Use low pressure, non-lubricated compressed air in the forward top brake fluid output port to help release the primary piston assembly and the secondary piston, seals, spring and spring retainer.

To install:

10. Clean all parts in denatured alcohol and dry with low pressure, un-lubricated compressed air.

11. Inspect the pistons and seals for nicks, cuts, cracks, wear or corrosion and replace all worn of damaged parts.

12. Check the master cylinder bore for scoring or corrosion and replace if damage is found. Do not hone the master cylinder bore and allow no abrasives to come into contact with the bore.

13. Lubricate the seals and the master cylinder bore with clean brake fluid.

14. Install the spring into the cylinder bore.

15. Install the secondary piston assembly into the bore.

16. Install the primary piston assembly into the bore.

17. Depress the primary piston assembly with a wooden dowel and install the retainer clip.

18. Lubricate the new reservoir O-rings using clean brake fluid, then install the new O-rings into the reservoir bayonet grooves. Press the reservoir straight onto the cylinder body by hand, then carefully drive in the reservoir retention spring pins.

19. Install the level sensor into the lower side of the reservoir.

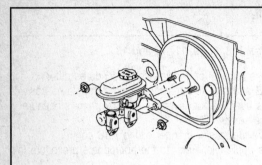

Fig. 6 Remove the retaining nuts and pull the master cylinder from the brake vacuum booster studs

20. For ABS equipped vehicles, install the master cylinder to the ABS control assembly.

21. Install the master cylinder or the ABS control assembly into the vehicle, as applicable.

22. Properly bleed the hydraulic brake system.

Power Brake Booster

REMOVAL & INSTALLATION

▶ See Figures 14 and 15

1. Disconnect the negative battery cable and remove the air cleaner assembly.

2. On ABS equipped vehicles, remove the battery, battery box and tray.

3. Remove the master cylinder to booster nuts, then remove and support the master cylinder aside to allow for booster removal. Be careful not to bend or damage the brake lines.

4. Disconnect the vacuum line at the check valve.

5. From under the dash, remove the retainer and washer from the booster pushrod, then remove the rod from the pedal pin.

6. Remove the 4 retaining nuts, then remove the booster from the vehicle.

To install:

7. Position the booster in the vehicle, but do not install the fasteners at this time.

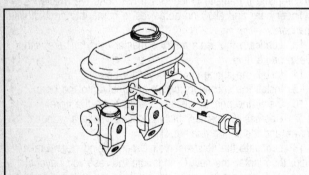

Fig. 7 Remove the level sensor from the lower side of the reservoir

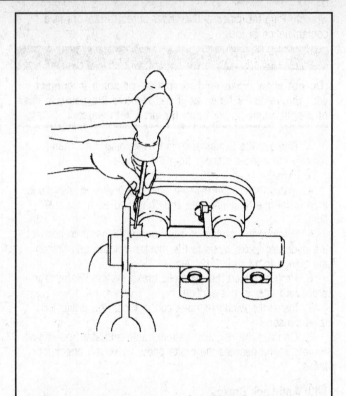

Fig. 8 Mount the assembly in a vise and drive out the reservoir spring pins

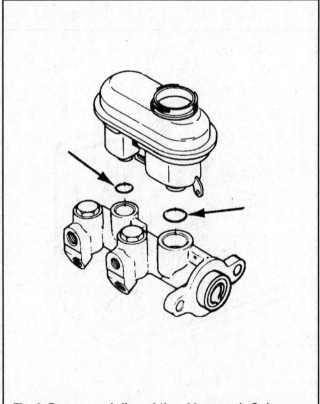

Fig. 9 Remove and discard the old reservoir O-rings

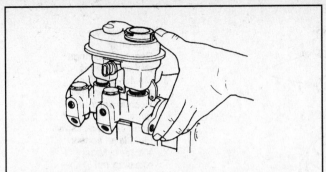

Fig. 10 Remove the reservoir from the top of the master cylinder assembly

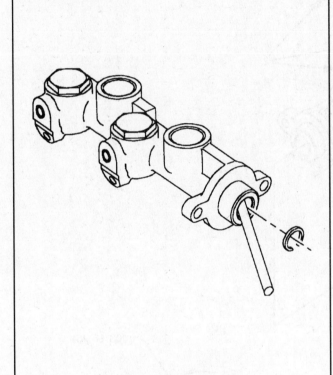

Fig. 11 Use a wooden dowel to depress the primary piston while removing the retainer clip

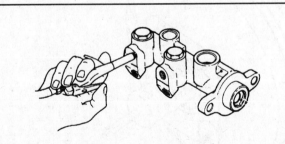

Fig. 12 Non-lubricated compressed air may be blown into the forward top brake fluid port in order to ease removal of the piston assemblies

8. Connect the booster pushrod to the brake pedal pin using the retainer and washer, then tighten the 4 booster retaining nuts to 20 ft. lbs. (27 Nm).

9. Connect the vacuum line to the check valve.

10. Remove the support and reposition the master cylinder to the brake booster studs, then install and tighten the retaining nuts to 20 ft. lbs. (27 Nm).

11. If removed, install the battery tray, battery and cover box.

12. Install the air cleaner assembly and connect the negative battery cable.

Brake Hoses and Pipes

REMOVAL & INSTALLATION

Brake Hose

▶ **See Figures 16, 17 and 18**

1. Raise the end of the vehicle which contains the hose to be repaired, then support the vehicle safely using jackstands.

2. If necessary, remove the wheel for easier access to the hose.

3. Disconnect the hose from the wheel cylinder or caliper and plug the opening to avoid excessive fluid loss or contamination.

4. Disconnect the hose from the brake line and plug the openings to avoid excessive fluid loss or contamination.

To install:

5. Install the brake hose to the brake line and tighten to 14 ft. lbs. (19 Nm) for rear brakes or 18 ft. lbs. (24 Nm) for front brakes.

6. If installing a front brake hose, make sure the hose is routed as shown in Fig. 16; with the loop to the rear of the vehicle.

7. Install the hose to the wheel cylinder or caliper using NEW washers, then tighten the retainer to 36 ft. lbs. (49 Nm).

8. Properly bleed the brake system, then check the connections for leaks.

9. Remove the supports and carefully lower the vehicle.

Brake Line

There are 2 options available when replacing a brake line. The first, and probably most preferable, is to replace the entire line using a line of similar length which is already equipped with machined flared ends. Such lines are usually available from auto parts stores and usually require only a minimum of bending in order to properly fit then to the vehicle. The second option is to bend and flare the entire replacement line (or a repair section of line) using the appropriate tools.

Buying a line with machined flares is usually preferable because of the time and effort saved, not to mention the cost of special tools if they are not readily available. Also, machined flares are usually of a much higher quality than those produced by hand flaring tools or kits.

1. Raise the end of the vehicle which contains the hose to be repaired, then support the vehicle safely using jackstands.

2. Remove the components necessary for access to the brake line which is being replaced.

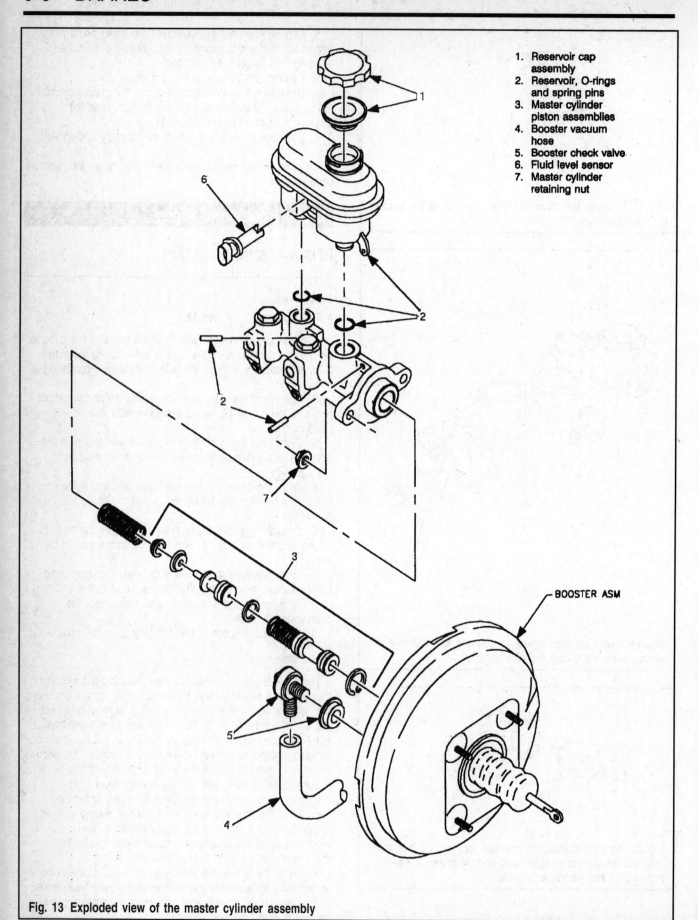

1. Reservoir cap assembly
2. Reservoir, O-rings and spring pins
3. Master cylinder piston assemblies
4. Booster vacuum hose
5. Booster check valve
6. Fluid level sensor
7. Master cylinder retaining nut

BOOSTER ASM

Fig. 13 Exploded view of the master cylinder assembly

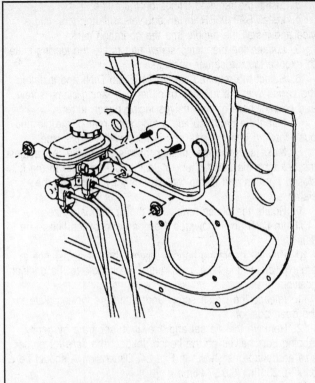

Fig. 14 Position the master cylinder assembly aside to allow for booster removal

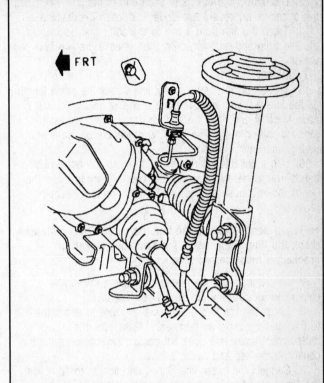

Fig. 16 Forward brake hoses must be positioned with the loop towards the rear of the vehicle

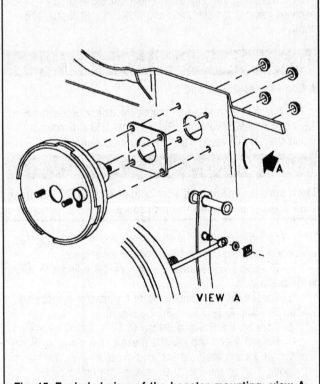

Fig. 15 Exploded view of the booster mounting; view A shows the booster pushrod and retainers

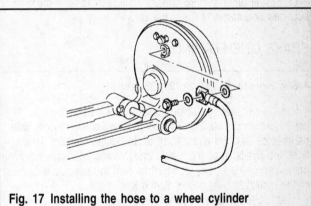

Fig. 17 Installing the hose to a wheel cylinder

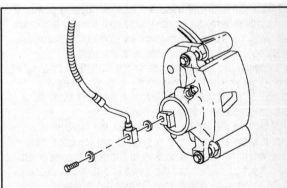

Fig. 18 Installing the hose to a caliper

3. Disconnect the fittings at each end of the line, then plug the openings to prevent excessive fluid loss or contamination.

4. Trace the line from 1 end to the other and disconnect the line from any retaining clips, then remove the line from the vehicle.

To install:

5. Try to obtain a replacement line that is the same length as the line that was removed. If the line is longer, you will have to cut it and flare the end, or if you have decided to repair a portion of the line, see the procedure on brake line flaring, later in this section.

6. Use a suitable tubing bender to make the necessary bends in the line. Work slowly and carefully; try to make the bends look as close as possible to those on the line being replaced.

➡ **When bending the brake line, be careful not to kink or crack the line. If the brake line becomes kinked or cracked, it must be replaced.**

7. Before installing the brake line, flush it with brake cleaner to remove any dirt or foreign material.

8. Install the line into the vehicle. Be sure to attach the line to the retaining clips, as necessary. Make sure the replacement brake line does not contact any components that could rub the line and cause a leak.

9. Connect the brake line fittings and tighten to 18 ft. lbs. (24 Nm), except for the rear line-to-hose fitting which should be tightened to 14 ft. lbs. (19 Nm).

10. Properly bleed the brake system and check for leaks.

11. Install any removed components, then remove the supports and carefully lower the vehicle.

BRAKE LINE FLARING

▸ **See Figures 19, 20, 21, 22, 23 and 24**

Use only brake line tubing approved for automotive use; never use copper tubing. Whenever possible, try to work with brake lines that are already cut to the length needed. These lines are available at most auto parts stores and have machine made flares, the quality of which is hard to duplicate with most of the available inexpensive flaring kits.

When the brakes are applied, there is a great amount of pressure developed in the hydraulic system. An improperly formed flare can leak with resultant loss of stopping power. If you have never formed a double-flare, take time to familiarize yourself with the flaring kit; practice forming double-flares on scrap tubing until you are satisfied with the results.

The following procedure applies to the SA9193BR flaring kit, but should be similar to commercially available brake-line flaring kits. If these instructions differ in any way from those in your kit, follow the instructions in the kit.

1. Determine the length necessary for the replacement or repair and allow an additional $\frac{1}{8}$ in. (3.2mm) for each flare. Select a length of tubing according to the repair/replacement charts in the figure, then cut the brake line to the necessary length using an appropriate saw. Do not use a tubing cutter.

2. Square the end of the tube with a file and chamfer the edges. Remove burrs from the inside and outside diameters of the cut line using a deburring tool.

3. Install the required fittings onto the line.

4. Install SA9193BR, or an equivalent flaring tool, into a vice and install the handle into the operating cam.

5. Loosen the die clamp screw and rotate the locking plate to expose the die carrier opening.

6. Select the required die set (4.75mm DIN) and install in the carrier with the full side of either half facing clamp screw and counter bore of both halves facing punch turret.

7. Insert the prepared line through the rear of the die and push forward until the line end is flush with the die face.

8. Make sure the rear of both halves of the die rest against the hexagon die stops, then rotate the locking plate to the fully closed position and clamp the die firmly by tightening the clamp screw.

9. Rotate the punch turret until the appropriate size (4.75mm DIN) points towards the open end of the line to be flared.

10. Pull the operating handle against the line resistance in order to create the flare, then return the handle to the original position.

11. release the clamp screw and rotate the locking plate to the open position.

12. Remove the die set and line, then separate by gently tapping both halves on the bench. Inspect the flare for proper size and shape as shown in Fig. 24. Dimension A should be 0.272-0.286 in. (6.92-7.28mm).

13. If necessary, repeat Steps 2-12 for the other end of the line or for the end of the line which is being repaired.

14. Bend the replacement line or section using SA91108NE, or an equivalent line bending tool.

15. If repairing the original line, join the old and new sections using a female union and tighten to 14 ft. lbs. (19 Nm).

Non-ABS Brake System Bleeding

▸ **See Figures 25, 26 and 27**

The brake system bleeding procedure differs between the ABS and non-ABS vehicles. Refer to the ABS procedures found later in this section for bleeding procedures.

❋❋WARNING

Make sure the master cylinder contains clean DOT 3 brake fluid at all times during the procedure.

1. The master cylinder must be bled first if it is suspected to contain air. Bleed the master cylinder as follows:

   a. Position a container under the master cylinder to catch the brake fluid.

   b. Loosen the front brake line at the master cylinder and allow the fluid to flow from the front port.

   c. Connect the line and tighten to 18 ft. lbs. (24 Nm).

   d. Have a friend depress the brake pedal slowly one time and hold, loosen the front line and expel air from the master cylinder. Tighten the line, then release the brake pedal. Repeat until all air is removed from the master cylinder.

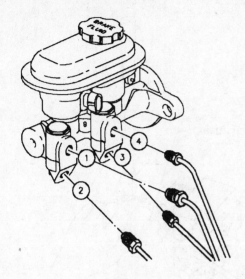

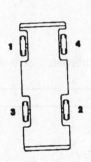

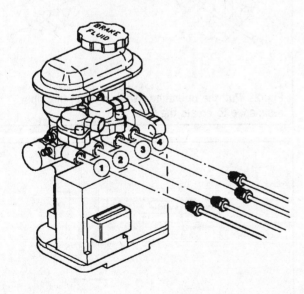

CHART 1				
Brake Pipes to Master Cylinder				
Ref. No.	Circuit	Nut Size		Torque
		Base	ABS	
*1	LF	M12 x 1.0	M10 x 1.0	24 N·m (18 ft–lbs)
2	RR	M10 x 1.0	M11 x 1.5	
3	LR	M13 x 1.5	M10 x 1.0	
4	RF	M11 x 1.5	M11 x 1.5	

CHART 2			
Brake Pipes to Brake Hoses			
Ref. No.	Circuit	Nut Size	Torque
*1	LF	M12 x 1.0	24 N·m (18 ft–lbs)
2	RR	M10 x 1.0	
3	LR		19 N·m (14 ft–lbs)
4	RF		24 N·m (18 ft–lbs)

CHART 3		
Brake Pipes to Union		
Union Size	Nut Size	Torque
M10 x 1.0 Female Connector	M10 x 1.0	19 N·m (14 ft–lbs)

CHART 4	
Nut Color Code	
Size	Color
M10 x 1.0	Olive
M11 x 1.5	Orange
M12 x 1.0	Blue
M13 x 1.5	Green

* On vehicles equipped with ABS, brake pipe No. 1 is serviced with original equipment pipe assembly.

Fig. 19 Brake line repair/replacement information

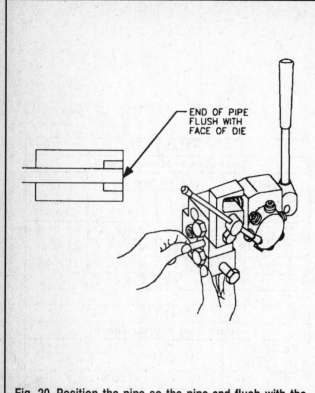

Fig. 20 Position the pipe so the pipe end flush with the die face

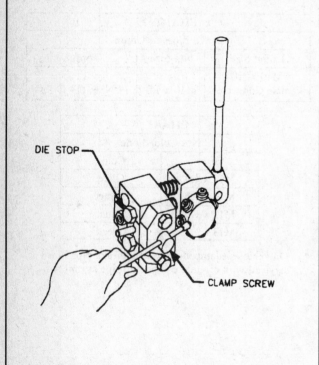

Fig. 21 With the pipe inserted, verify the die halves are against the die stops, then fully close the locking plate by turning the clamp screw.

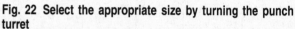
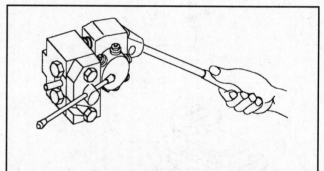

Fig. 22 Select the appropriate size by turning the punch turret

Fig. 23 Pull the operating handle against the pipe resistance to create the flare.

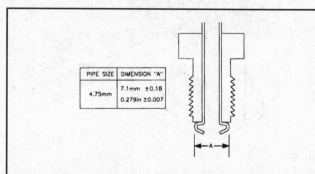

PIPE SIZE	DIMENSION "A"
4.75mm	7.1mm ±0.18
	0.279in ±0.007

Fig. 24 Check dimension A of the flare to assure proper size

e. Tighten the brake line to 18 ft. lbs. (24 Nm) when finished.

✳✳WARNING

Do not allow brake fluid to spill on or come in contact with the vehicle's finish as it will remove the paint. In case of a spill, immediately flush the area with water.

2. If a single line or fitting was the only hydraulic line disconnected, then only the caliper(s) or wheel cylinder(s) affected by that line must be bled. If the master cylinder required bleeding, then all calipers and wheel cylinders must be bled in the proper sequence:

a. Right rear
b. Left front
c. Left rear
d. Right front

3. Bleed the individual calipers or wheel cylinders as follows:

a. Place a suitable wrench over the bleeder screw and attach a clear plastic hose over the screw end.

b. Submerge the other end in a transparent container of brake fluid.

c. Loosen the bleed screw, then have a friend apply the brake pedal slowly and hold. Tighten the bleed screw to 97 inch lbs. (11 Nm) and release the brake pedal. Repeat the sequence until all air is expelled from the caliper or cylinder.

d. Tighten the bleed screw to 97 inch lbs. (11 Nm) when finished.

4. Check the pedal for a hard feeling with the engine not running. If the pedal is soft, repeat the bleeding procedure until a firm pedal is obtained.

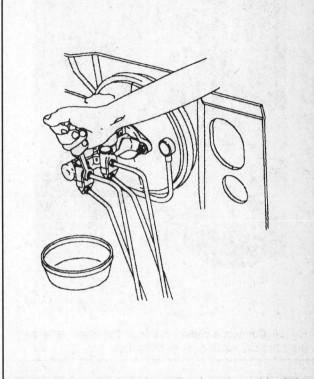

Fig. 25 Loosen the front brake line in order to bleed the master cylinder

FRONT DISC BRAKES

✳✳CAUTION

Brake pads contain asbestos, which has been determined to be a cancer-causing agent. Never clean brake surfaces with compressed air! Avoid inhaling any dust from any brake surface! When cleaning brake surfaces, use a commercially available brake cleaning fluid.

Brake Pads

REMOVAL & INSTALLATION

▶ See Figures 28, 29, 30, 31, 32, 33, 34 and 35

➡ Always replace the brake pads in sets, both front or both rear axle assemblies.

1. Raise the front of the vehicle and support safely using jackstands, then remove the front wheels.

2. Remove the lower caliper lock pin.

➡ The Saturn brake pad replacement procedure states that after removing the lower caliper pin, you may simply pivot the caliper to a vertical position in order to remove the brake pads. This procedure, when attempted on a 1992 SC with ABS, looked as if it would place excessive stress on the brake line. No changes in steering position seemed to alleviate this tension, so a full pivot for pad removal was not attempted. To prevent damage to the brake line you may wish to remove the upper guide pin and support the caliper assembly from the strut using a coat hanger or length of wire.

3. Either pivot the caliper up on the guide pin or remove the upper guide pin and support the caliper from the strut using a coat hanger or length of wire.

4. Remove the 2 brake pads and the pad clips from the caliper support Discard the old pad clips.

5. Check the caliper pins, pin boots and the piston boot for deterioration or damage.

To install:

6. By hand or using a C-clamp, bottom the piston all the way into the caliper bore.

7. Carefully lift the inner edge of the piston boot by hand to release any trapped air.

8. Install new pad clips into the caliper support.

9. Install the inner and outer brake pads into the support. If installed, remove the temporary support wire from the caliper.

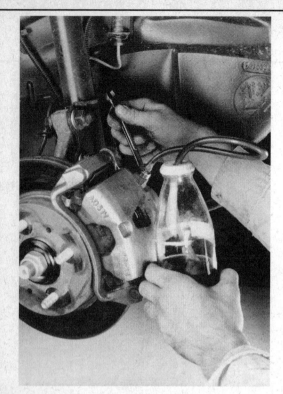

Fig. 26 Connect a bleed hose from the bleed valve on the front caliper to a jar of brake fluid

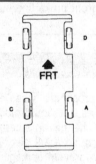

Fig. 27 Always follow the lettered sequence when bleeding the hydraulic brake system

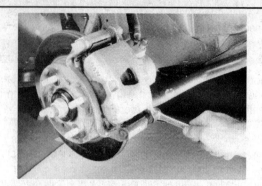

Fig. 28 Loosen the caliper lower lock pin

Fig. 29 Remove the lock pin, being careful not to damage the boot

Fig. 30 Loosen and remove the upper guide pin from the caliper

10. Pivot or position the caliper body on the upper guide pin into position. Compress the boots by hand as the caliper is positioned onto the support.

11. Lubricate the smooth ends of the lock and guide pins with silicone grease, then install the pin and tighten to 27 ft. lbs. (36 Nm). Do not get grease on the pin threads.

12. Repeat the procedure for the opposite side brake pads.

13. Install the front wheels, then remove the supports and carefully lower the vehicle.

14. Prior to operating the vehicle, depress the brake pedal a few times until the brake pads are seated against the rotor and a firm pedal is felt. Do not attempt to move the vehicle until this step is performed. Be careful, it is easy to forget.

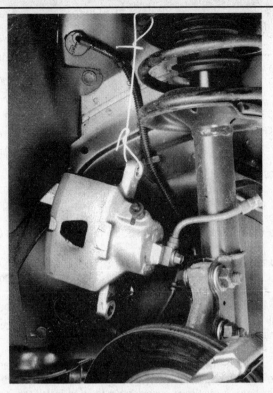

Fig. 31 If removed, support the caliper from the strut using wire or a coat hanger

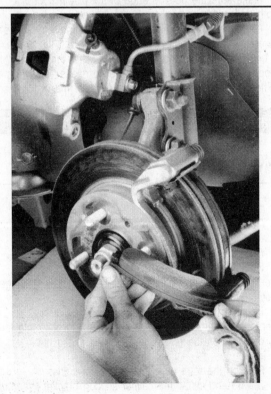

Fig. 32 Remove the brake pads from the caliper support bracket

Fig. 33 Remove and discard the old brake pad retaining clips from the support bracket

Fig. 34 If necessary, use a C-clamp to bottom the caliper piston

Fig. 35 With the new brake pads properly installed, guide the caliper over the pads and onto the support bracket

INSPECTION

When the pads are removed from the caliper, inspect them for oil or grease contamination, abnormal wear or cracking, and for deterioration or damage due to heat. Check the thickness of the pads, the minimum allowable thickness is approximately 3/32 in. (2.4mm).

Most brake pads are equipped with a wear indicator that will make a squealing noise when the pads are worn. This alerts you to the need for brake service before any rotor damage occurs.

Brake Caliper

REMOVAL & INSTALLATION

▶ See Figures 36, 37, 38 and 39

1. Raise the front of the vehicle and support safely using jackstands, then remove the front wheel.
2. Disconnect the brake hose from the caliper. Plug the openings to prevent excessive fluid contamination or loss.
3. Remove the lock pin and guide pin from the caliper and support.
4. Remove the caliper from the support, being careful not to damage the pin boots. Remove the pin boots from the caliper support and inspect for damage.

To install:

5. Make sure the piston is bottomed in the bore. If necessary bottom the piston by hand or using a C-clamp.
6. If removed, install the brake pads to the caliper support.
7. Lubricate the pin boots and guide pins with silicone grease. If removed, install the pin boots into the caliper support.
8. Position the caliper onto the support and over the brake pads, then lubricate the non-threaded portion of the guide and lock pins with silicone grease. Install the pins and tighten to 27 ft. lbs. (36 Nm).
9. Make sure the brake line is properly routed with loop to the rear, then install the brake hose with new washers. Tighten the fitting to 36 ft. lbs. (49 Nm).
10. Properly bleed the hydraulic brake system.
11. Install the wheel, remove the supports and carefully lower the vehicle.

OVERHAUL

▶ See Figures 40, 41, 42 and 43

1. Use a screwdriver or small prybar to carefully remove the piston boot ring. Pry up on one end of the boot ring, then remove it from the caliper.
2. Place the caliper on a bench which is covered with a cloth. Position the caliper so the piston is facing away, then cover the caliper with another cloth.
3. Lift the cloth sufficiently for access to the brake fluid inlet. While wearing proper protection, apply some low

pressure non-lubricated compressed air to the brake fluid inlet and push the piston from the caliper bore.

4. To protect the caliper bore, use a wooden or plastic tool (not metal) to remove the piston seal from the groove in the caliper body.
5. Remove the bleeder valve and cap from the caliper body.
6. Clean all parts in denatured alcohol and dry with non-lubricated, low pressure, compressed air. Make sure all passages of the caliper body and bleeder valve are blown dry.
7. Inspect the piston for scoring, nicks, cracks, wear or corrosion and replace if any piston damage is found.
8. Inspect the caliper piston bore for scoring, nicks, cracks, wear or corrosion. Crocus cloth may be used to remove light corrosion, but the caliper must be replaced if any damage more extensive than that is found. Do not attempt to hone the bore.

To assemble:

9. Install the bleeder valve into the caliper body and tighten to 8 ft. lbs. (11 Nm). Install the bleeder cap.
10. Lubricate a new piston seal with clean brake fluid, then install the seal into the groove in the caliper body. Make sure the seal is properly positioned and not twisted.
11. Lubricate and install the piston boot onto the piston.
12. Lubricate the outside diameter of the piston with clean brake fluid, then push the piston fully into the bottom of the caliper bore. It may take considerable force to install the piston. Be patient and careful so as not to damage the piston boot.
13. Make sure the outside edge of the piston boot is smoothly seated in the caliper body's counterbore.
14. Carefully work the boot ring into the groove near the open end of the bore, making sure not to pinch the piston boot between the ring and caliper body. After the ring is aligned, lift the inner edge of the boot to release any trapped air. The boot must lay flat below the level of the piston face.

Brake Rotor

REMOVAL & INSTALLATION

▶ See Figures 45, 46 and 47

1. Raise the front of the vehicle and support safely using jackstands.
2. Remove the wheel.
3. Remove the 2 caliper support-to-knuckle bolts, then support the bracket from the strut with wire or a coat hanger to protect the brake line from damage.
4. Remove the rotor from the vehicle. If difficulty is encountered, insert two M8 x 1.25 self-tapping bolts into the holes provided on the rotor and drive it from the hub.

To install:

5. Position the rotor over the hub wheel studs.
6. Unwire and install the caliper support bracket assembly. Tighten the bolts to 81 ft. lbs. (110 Nm).
7. Install the wheel.
8. Remove the supports and carefully lower the vehicle.

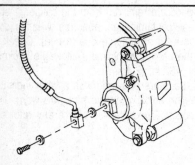

Fig. 36 Remove the retainer and disconnect the brake hose from the caliper

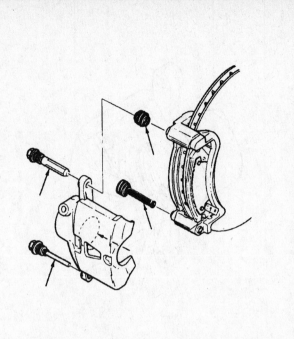

Fig. 37 Remove the guide and lock pins, then remove the caliper from the support. Remove and inspect the pin boots

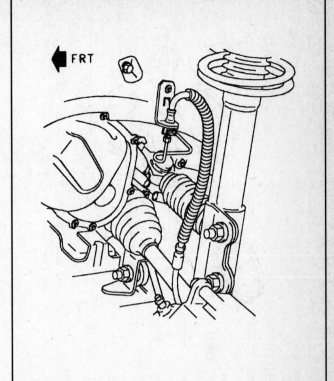

Fig. 39 The brake hose must be properly routed with the loop towards the rear of the vehicle

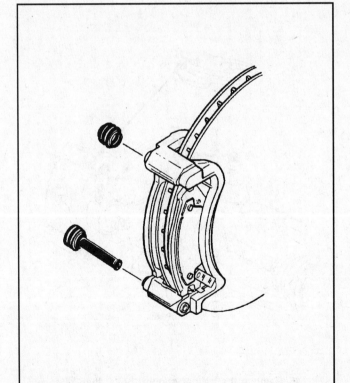

Fig. 38 Lubricate and install the pin boots into the caliper support

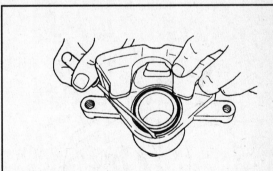

Fig. 40 Pry up on one end of the piston boot ring, then remove it from the caliper

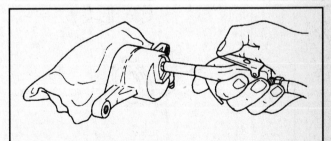

Fig. 41 Apply low pressure non-lubricated compressed air to the brake fluid inlet in order to push the piston from the caliper bore

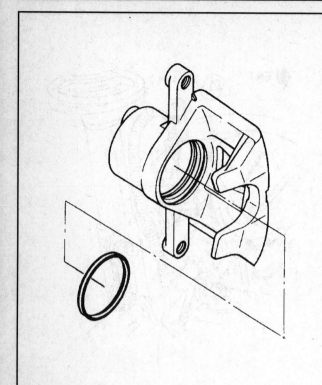

Fig. 42 Remove the piston seal from the groove in the caliper bore

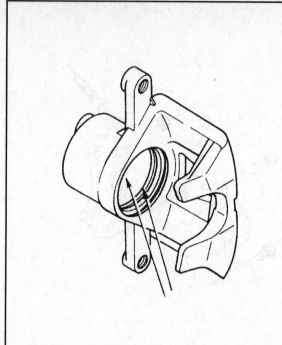

Fig. 44 Inspect the caliper piston bore for damage and replace, if found. The Saturn piston bore cannot be honed

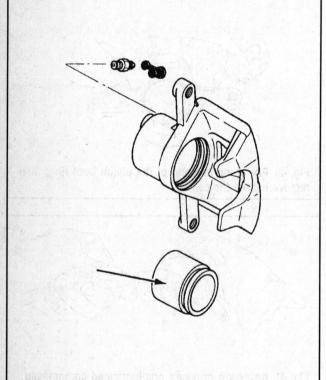

Fig. 43 Remove the bleeder screw and cap from the caliper

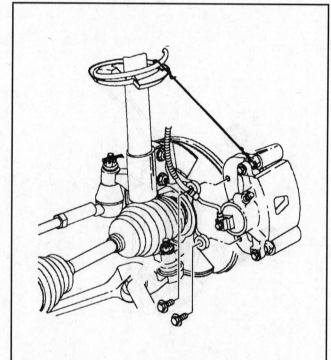

Fig. 45 Remove the caliper support bolts, then remove the caliper and support assembly from the steering knuckle

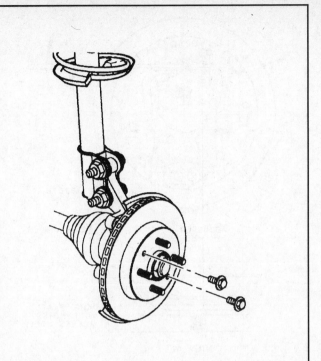

Fig. 46 If necessary use 2 M8 x 1.25 self-tapping bolts, in the holes provided, to apply pressure and loosen the rotor

Check the disc brake rotor thickness using a micrometer or calipers. The brake rotor minimum thickness is 0.625 in. (15.8mm). This is the thickness at which point the rotor becomes unsafe to use and must be discarded. The minimum thickness that the rotor can be machined to is 0.633 in. (16.1mm), as this thickness allows room for rotor wear after it has been machined and returned to service.

Check the rotor for runout using a dial indicator. Install a few lug nuts to hold the rotor against the hub while checking. Mount the dial indicator on the strut and position the indicator foot on the outermost diameter of the contact surface of the disc pads. Make sure there is no wheel bearing free-play. Rotor runout must not exceed 0.005 in. (0.13mm). If the rotor runout exceeds specification, machine the rotor if it is not below the minimum thickness specification for machining. If the rotor runout is still excessive after machining, the rotor must be replaced.

INSPECTION

Check the disc brake rotor for scoring, cracks or other damage. Check the minimum thickness and rotor runout.

REAR DRUM BRAKES

✳✳CAUTION

Brake shoes contain asbestos, which has been determined to be a cancer causing agent. Never clean the brake surfaces with compressed air! Avoid inhaling any dust from any brake surface! When cleaning brake surfaces, use a commercially available cleaning fluid.

Brake Drum

REMOVAL & INSTALLATION

▶ **See Figures 48 and 49**

1. Release the parking brake.
2. Raise the rear of the vehicle and support safely using jackstands.
3. Remove the rear wheel, then remove the brake drum.
4. If difficulty is encountered, turn the star wheel of the brake adjuster assembly through the access hole in the rear of

the brake backing plate using an adjusting tool. This will loosen the brake shoes and allow for drum removal. Do not pry between the drum and plate or the backing plate will be bent and damaged.

INSPECTION

▶ **See Figure 50**

Clean all grease, brake fluid, and other contaminants from the brake drum using brake cleaner. Visually check the drum for scoring, cracks, or other damage and replace, if necessary.

Check the drum inner diameter using a brake shoe clearance gauge. The maximum allowable inner diameter is 7.93 in. (201.4mm). This is the diameter at which point the drum becomes unsafe to use and must be discarded. The maximum diameter that the drum can be machined to is 7.9 in. (200.6mm), as this thickness allows room for drum wear after it has been machined and returned to service.

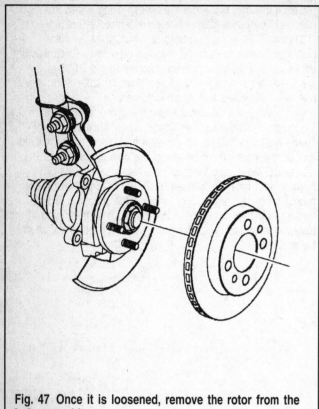

Fig. 47 Once it is loosened, remove the rotor from the hub assembly

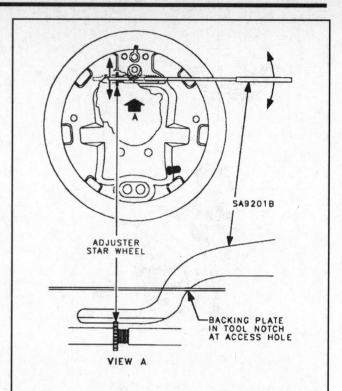

Fig. 49 If necessary, a brake adjusting tool may be used to turn the star wheel and loosen the brake shoes for easier drum removal

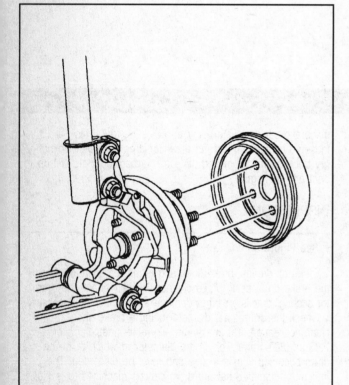

Fig. 48 The rear drums are mounted to the hub and bearing assembly.

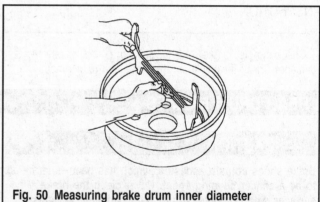

Fig. 50 Measuring brake drum inner diameter

Brake Shoes

INSPECTION

Inspect the brake shoes for peeling, cracking, or extremely uneven wear on the lining. Check the lining thickness using calipers. If the brake lining is less than approximately 3/32 in. (2.4mm), the shoes must be replaced. The shoes must also be replaced if the linings are contaminated with brake fluid or grease.

REMOVAL & INSTALLATION

▶ **See Figures 51, 52, 53, 54, 55, 56, 57 and 58**

➡ **Brake shoes must be replaced as axle sets. Only disassemble 1 side at a time so that a complete assembly is available as a reference. If necessary compare the component positions from the side you are currently installing to the other assembly in order to verify correct positioning; just remember that the other side is a mirror image and is reversed from the side on which you are currently working.**

1. Raise the rear of the vehicle and support using jackstands, then remove the wheels and brake drums.
2. Remove the lower return and adjuster springs using a universal brake spring remover. Do not over extend the springs or they will damaged and will need to be replaced.
3. Compress the leading brake shoe hold-down cup and spring, then from the rear of the backing plate, turn and remove the pin. Release spring compression, then remove the hold-down cup and spring.
4. Pull the leading shoe towards the front of the vehicle and remove the adjuster assembly and lever. It may be necessary to turn the adjuster star wheel to shorten the adjuster's length.
5. Remove the leading shoe by twisting the shoe out of engagement with the upper return spring.
6. Remove the upper return spring from the park brake shoe, then remove the park brake shoe hold-down cup, spring and pin assembly.
7. Push the park brake shoe lever into the cable spring while disengaging the cable from the end lever and remove the parking brake shoe, lever and cable spring from the vehicle.
8. Remove the retainer and wave washer, then remove the park brake lever from the shoe.
9. Disassemble the brake adjuster socket, screw and nut, then clean the components in denatured alcohol. Inspect the assembly, making sure the screw threads smoothly into the adjusting nut over the full threaded length.
10. On the brake backing plate, inspect the wheel cylinder for signs of leakage and for cut or damaged boots. Do not attempt to repair a damaged cylinder, the assembly must be replaced. Refer to the procedure later in this section.

To install:

11. Lubricate the adjuster assembly, the 6 backing plate raised shoe contact pads, the brake lever pin and surfaces which contact brake shoe webs with brake lubricant.
12. Install the park brake lever onto the pin on the brake shoe and secure with the wave washer and retainer clip. Crimp the ends of the retainer to secure the brake lever.
13. Install the cable spring into the cage on the park brake lever, then install the cable through the spring and onto the lever.
14. Install the park brake shoe using the hold-down cup assembly; use a universal spring cup remover/installer tool. Make sure the shoe is correctly engaged into the wheel cylinder (top) and the anchor (bottom).
15. Install the long straight end of the upper return spring into the back hole in the park brake shoe, position the other

brake shoe and install the other end of the spring into the back of the leading shoe.
16. Pull the lead shoe toward the front of the vehicle and install the adjuster between the park and leading brake shoes. Verify that the adjuster notches properly engage the brake shoe notches and that the shoe is properly aligned in the wheel cylinder and anchor.
17. Install the adjuster lever and adjuster spring. Make sure the notch on the lever engages the pin on the park shoe and the notch on the adjusting socket. The lower leg of the lever should engage the teeth of the star wheel adjuster assembly.
18. Secure the leading brake shoe using the hold-down cup assembly.
19. Install the adjuster spring to the upper side of the brake shoes with the short end to the lead shoe and the long end to the park shoe. Then install the lower return spring into the lower holes of the shoes.
20. Verify the correct location of all brake components, if necessary, use the other side brake assembly for comparison.
21. Using a suitable drum clearance gauge, measure the inner diameter of the brake drum and adjust the outside diameter of the brake shoes to 0.02 inch (0.50mm) less than the inner diameter of the drum.
22. Repeat the procedure for the opposite brake shoes and install the brake drums.
23. If the wheel cylinders have been replaced, bleed the hydraulic brake system.
24. Install the rear wheels.
25. Remove the supports and carefully lower the vehicle, then apply and release the brake pedal 20 times to allow the adjuster to properly position the brake shoes.
26. Check and adjust the parking brake cable, as necessary.

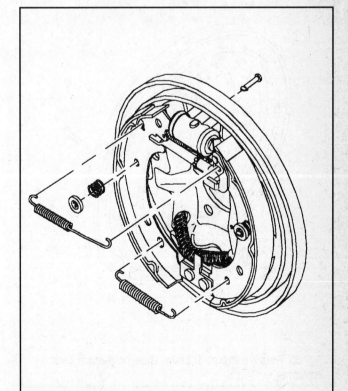

Fig. 51 Remove the lower return and adjuster springs, then remove the leading shoe hold-down cup assembly

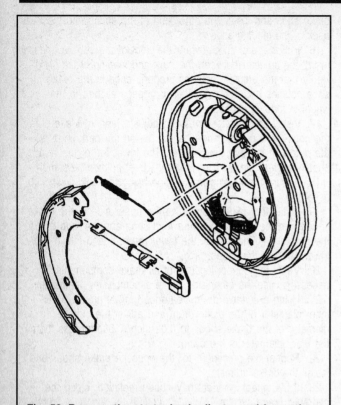

Fig. 52 Remove the start wheel adjuster and lever, then remove the leading shoe and the upper return spring

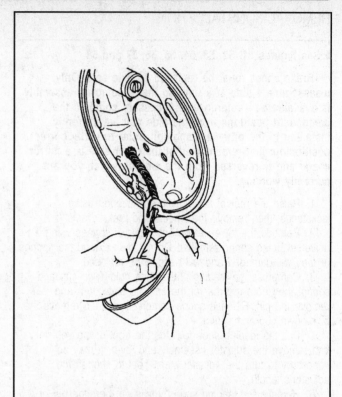

Fig. 54 Disengage the park brake shoe, lever and cable spring from the parking brake cable end

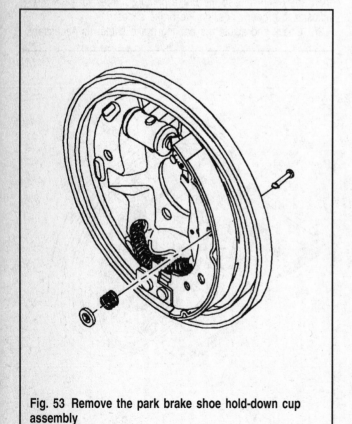

Fig. 53 Remove the park brake shoe hold-down cup assembly

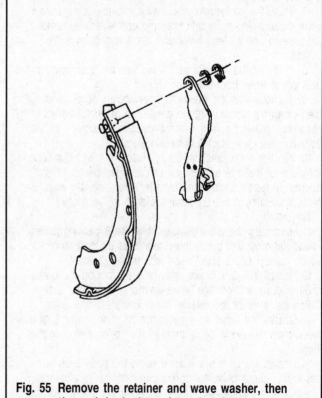

Fig. 55 Remove the retainer and wave washer, then remove the park brake lever from the shoe

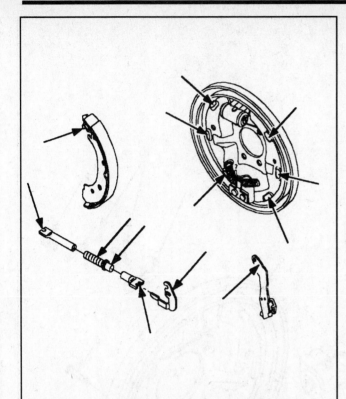

Fig. 56 Lubricate these points with a suitable brake grease prior to assembling the brake components

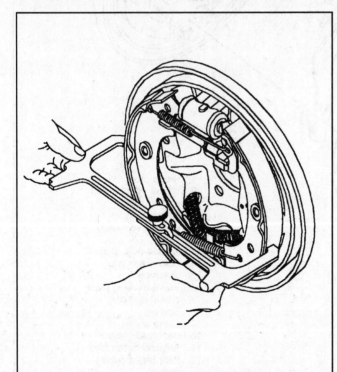

Fig. 57 Adjust the outside diameter of the brake shoes to 0.02 in. (0.50mm) less than the inner diameter of the drum

Wheel Cylinder

REMOVAL & INSTALLATION

▶ See Figures 59 and 60

1. Raise the rear of the vehicle and support safely using jackstands.
2. Remove the wheel and the brake drum.
3. Remove the brake shoes. Refer to the procedure earlier in this section.
4. Remove the retainer, then disconnect the hydraulic brake line and washer from the rear of the wheel cylinder. Plug the openings to prevent excessive fluid loss or contamination.
5. Remove the bleeder valve and cap.
6. Remove the wheel cylinder retaining bolts, then remove the cylinder from the backing plate.

To install:

7. Install the cylinder to the backing plate and tighten the retainers to 89 inch lbs. (10 Nm).
8. Connect the hydraulic brake line using NEW washers and tighten the fastener to 36 ft. lbs. (49 Nm).
9. Install the bleeder valve and tighten the to 66 inch lbs. (7.5 Nm), then install the cap.
10. Install the brake shoes and drum.
11. Properly bleed the hydraulic brake system.
12. Install the wheel assembly, remove the supports and carefully lower the vehicle.
13. Apply a release the brake pedal at least 20 times to make sure the shoes are properly seated in the drum.

Brake Backing Plate

REMOVAL & INSTALLATION

▶ See Figure 61

1. Raise the rear of the vehicle and support safely using jackstands.
2. Remove the wheel and the brake drum.
3. Remove the brake shoes. Refer to the procedure earlier in this section.
4. Remove the wheel cylinder. Refer to the procedure earlier in this section.
5. Remove 4 retaining bolts, then remove the hub and bearing assembly from the knuckle. The backing plate is retained between the hub and the knuckle with these 4 bolts and will be freed upon removal of the hub and bearing assembly. Remove the backing plate from the vehicle.

To install:

6. Position the brake backing plate between the knuckle and the hub/bearing assembly, then install the components with the 4 retaining bolts. Tighten the bolts to 63 ft. lbs. (85 Nm).
7. Install the wheel cylinder assembly. Refer to the procedure earlier in this section.
8. Install the brake shoes. Refer to the procedure earlier in this section.

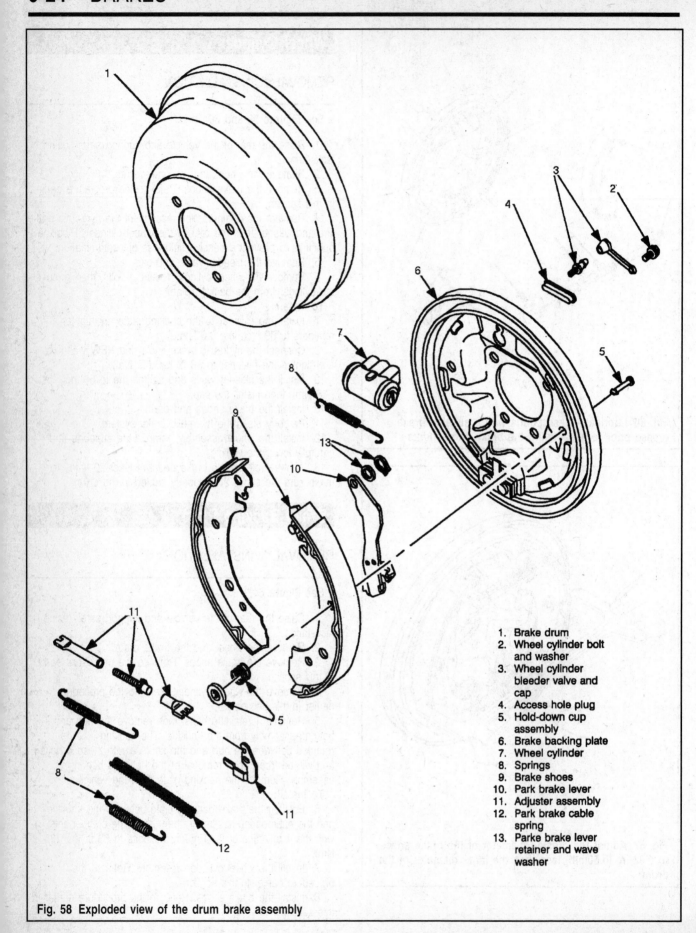

1. Brake drum
2. Wheel cylinder bolt and washer
3. Wheel cylinder bleeder valve and cap
4. Access hole plug
5. Hold-down cup assembly
6. Brake backing plate
7. Wheel cylinder
8. Springs
9. Brake shoes
10. Park brake lever
11. Adjuster assembly
12. Park brake cable spring
13. Parke brake lever retainer and wave washer

Fig. 58 Exploded view of the drum brake assembly

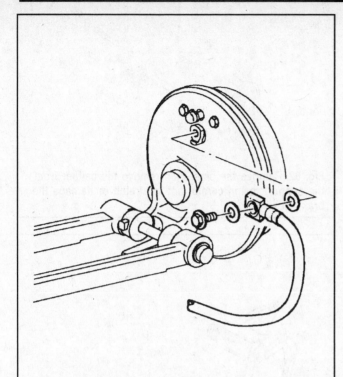

Fig. 59 Disconnect the hydraulic brake line from the rear of the wheel cylinder assembly

9. Install the drum and properly bleed the hydraulic brake system

Rear Disc Brakes

✳✳CAUTION

Brake pads contain asbestos, which has been determined to be a cancer-causing agent. Never clean brake surfaces with compressed air! Avoid inhaling any dust from any brake surface! When cleaning brake surfaces, use a commercially available brake cleaning fluid.

Brake Pads

REMOVAL & INSTALLATION

▶ **See Figures 62, 63, 64 and 65**

➡ **Always replace the brake pads in sets, both front or both rear axle assemblies.**

1. Raise the rear of the vehicle and support safely using jackstands, then remove the rear wheels.
2. Remove the caliper lock and guide pins.
3. Remove the caliper from the support, being careful not to damage the pin boots and suspend the caliper from the strut using wire or a coat hanger.
4. Remove the brake pads, then remove and discard the old brake pad clips from the caliper support.

10. Install the wheel assembly, remove the supports and carefully lower the vehicle.
11. Apply and release the brake pedal at least 20 times to make sure the shoes are properly seated in the drum.

5. Inspect the piston and pin boots for deterioration and the pins for corrosion. Damaged boots must be replaced; if the piston boot is damaged, the caliper must be overhauled. Corroded pins must be replaced; do not attempt to remove the corrosion.

To install:

6. Using SA9158BR or an equivalent piston driver tool, bottom the piston by rotating it clockwise into the caliper bore; do not use a C-clamp to press the piston into the bore or the piston and/or caliper will be damaged.
7. Align the piston slots so the slots run perpendicular to a line drawn through the center of the pin holes in the support as shown in the illustration.
8. Carefully lift the inner edge of the piston boot by hand to release any trapped air. Do not use a sharp tool or damage the piston boot, otherwise caliper overhaul will be necessary.
9. Install new pad clips into the caliper support.
10. Install the inner and outer brake pads into the clips on the support. The pad with the wear sensor should be located outboard. The piston indentation slots should be positioned to correctly accept the brake pads.
11. Position the caliper body onto the support while compressing the pin boots by hand. Lubricate the non-threaded portion of the guide and lock pins using a silicone grease, then install the pins and tighten to 27 ft. lbs. (36 Nm).

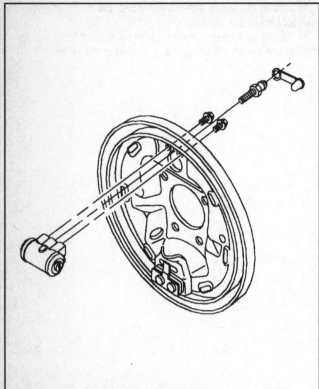

Fig. 60 Remove the retainers, then remove the wheel cylinder from the brake backing plate

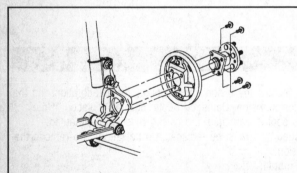

Fig. 61 The brake backing plate is installed between the hub/bearing assembly and the rear suspension knuckle

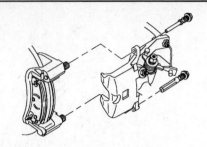

Fig. 62 Remove the pins, then remove the caliper from the support, being careful not to stretch or damage the brake hose

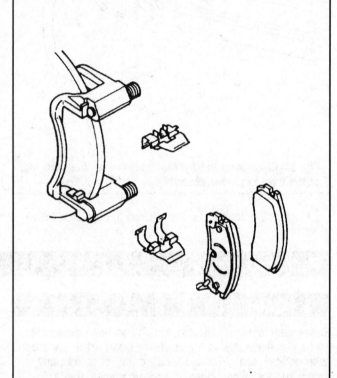

Fig. 63 Remove and discard the old shoes and clips from the caliper support

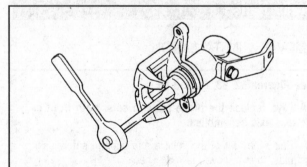

Fig. 64 Use a suitable brake piston driver tool to thread the piston back into the caliper

12. Check the position of the pad clips. If necessary, use a small screwdriver or prybar to re-seat or center the pad clips on the support. Repeat the procedure for the opposite side brake pads.

13. Install the rear wheels, remove the supports and lower the vehicle.

14. Prior to operating the vehicle, depress the brake pedal a few times until the brake pads are seated against the rotor and a firm pedal is felt. Do not attempt to move the vehicle until this step is performed. Be careful, it is easy to forget.

INSPECTION

When the pads are removed from the caliper, inspect them for oil or grease contamination, abnormal wear or cracking,

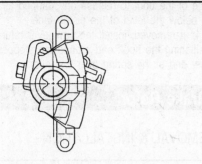

Fig. 65 Once properly threaded, the piston indentation slots will align as shown

and for deterioration or damage due to heat. Check the thickness of the pads, the minimum allowable thickness is approximately 3/32 in. (2.4mm).

Most brake pads are equipped with a wear indicator that will make a squealing noise when the pads are worn. This alerts you to the need for brake service before any rotor damage occurs.

Brake Caliper

REMOVAL & INSTALLATION

▶ See Figures 66, 67 and 68

1. Raise the rear of the vehicle and support safely using jackstands, then remove the rear wheel.
2. Disconnect the brake hose from the caliper. Plug the openings to prevent fluid contamination or loss.
3. Slip the end of the parking cable off the parking brake lever, then remove the cable outer housing from the cable bracket with SA9151BR or an equivalent cable release tool.
4. Remove the lock pin and guide pin.
5. Remove the caliper from the support, being careful not to damage the pin boots. If necessary, remove the pin boots from the caliper support.
6. Inspect the piston and pin boots for deterioration and the pins for corrosion. Damaged boots must be replaced; if the piston boot is damaged, the caliper must be overhauled. Corroded pins must be replaced; do not attempt to remove the corrosion.

To install:

7. Make sure the piston is bottomed in the bore. Do not compress the piston using a C-clamp; instead the piston must be rotated into the caliper on the threads using a piston driver tool.
8. If removed, install the brake pads to the caliper support.
9. Lubricate the pin boots and guide pins with silicone grease. If removed, install the pin boots into the caliper support.
10. Position the caliper, then lubricate the non-threaded portion of the guide and lock pins. Install the pins and tighten to 27 ft. lbs. (36 Nm).
11. Install the brake hose with new washers, then tighten the fitting to 36 ft. lbs. (49 Nm).
12. Connect the parking brake cable.
13. Properly bleed the hydraulic brake system.

14. Install the wheel, then remove the supports and lower the vehicle.
15. Prior to operating the vehicle, depress the brake pedal a few times until the brake pads are seated against the rotor and a firm pedal is felt. Do not attempt to move the vehicle until this step is performed. Be careful, it is easy to forget.

OVERHAUL

▶ See Figures 69, 70, 71 and 72

1. Use a screwdriver or small prybar to carefully remove the piston boot ring. Pry up on one end of the boot ring, then remove it from the caliper.

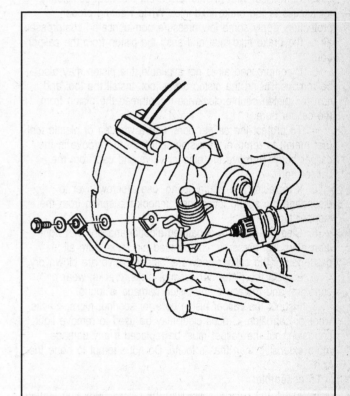

Fig. 66 Remove the retainer, then disconnect the brake line and washers from the caliper

Fig. 67 The parking brake cable attaches to the rear of the caliper/support assembly

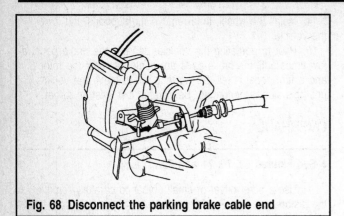

Fig. 68 Disconnect the parking brake cable end

2. Place the caliper on a bench which is covered with a cloth. Position the caliper so the piston is facing away, then cover the caliper with another cloth. Lift the cloth sufficiently for access to the brake fluid inlet. While wearing proper protection, apply some low pressure non-lubricated compressed air to the brake fluid inlet and push the piston from the caliper bore.

3. If compressed air is not available, the piston may also be removed using the piston driver tool. Install the tool and turn the piston counterclockwise to unthread the piston from the caliper bore.

4. To protect the caliper bore, use a wooden or plastic tool (not metal) to remove the piston seal from the groove in the caliper body. Remove the bleeder valve and cap from the caliper body.

5. If replacing the return spring, use a screwdriver to disengage the spring lever, then unhook the spring from the stopper pin.

6. Clean all parts in denatured alcohol and dry with non-lubricated, low pressure, compressed air. Make sure all passages of the caliper body and bleeder valve are blown dry.

7. Inspect the piston for scoring, nicks, cracks, wear or corrosion and replace if any piston damage is found.

8. Inspect the caliper piston bore for scoring, nicks, cracks, wear or corrosion. Crocus cloth may be used to remove light corrosion, but the caliper must be replaced if any damage more extensive than that is found. Do not attempt to hone the bore.

To assemble:

9. Install the bleeder valve into the caliper body and tighten to 8 ft. lbs. (11 Nm). Install the bleeder cap.

10. Lubricate a new piston seal with clean brake fluid, then install the seal into the groove in the caliper body. Make sure the seal is properly positioned and not twisted.

11. Lubricate and install the piston boot onto the piston.

12. Lubricate the outside diameter of the piston with clean brake fluid, then turn the piston fully into the bottom of the caliper bore. Begin installing the piston by hand, then use the piston driver tool to rotate the piston clockwise and into the bore until the slots are properly positioned. Refer to the illustration of the rear brake pad procedure, earlier in this section.

13. Make sure the outside edge of the piston boot is smoothly seated in the caliper body's counterbore. Carefully work the boot ring into the groove near the open end of the bore, making sure not to pinch the piston boot between the ring and caliper body. After the ring is aligned, lift the inner

edge of the boot to release any trapped air. The boot must lay flat below the level of the piston face.

14. If removed, install the new lever return spring by positioning the hook end around the stopper pin and prying the other end of the spring over the lever.

Brake Rotor

REMOVAL & INSTALLATION

▶ See Figures 73 and 74

1. Raise the rear of the vehicle and support safely using jackstands.

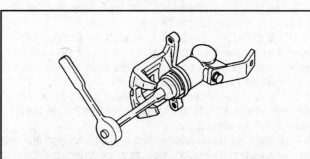

Fig. 69 Remove the piston boot ring from the caliper

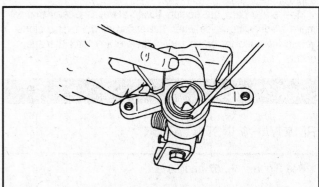

Fig. 70 The piston may be removed using the piston driver tool to turn and unthread the piston from the caliper bore

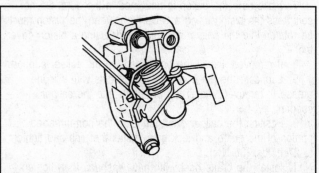

Fig. 71 Remove the return spring only if replacement is necessary

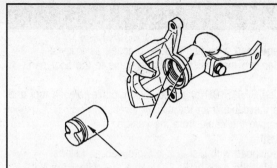

Fig. 72 Inspect the caliper and piston for damage or excessive wear

2. Remove the wheel.

3. Remove the 2 caliper support-to-knuckle bolts, then support the bracket from the strut with wire or a coat hanger to protect the brake line from damage.

4. Remove the rotor from wheels studs on the hub and bearing assembly. If difficulty is encountered, insert two M8 **x** 1.25 self-tapping bolts into the holes provided on the rotor and drive it from the hub.

To install:

5. Position the rotor over the hub wheel studs.

6. Unwire and install the caliper/support bracket assembly. Tighten the bolts to 63 ft. lbs. (85 Nm).

7. Install the wheel.

8. Remove the supports and carefully lower the vehicle.

INSPECTION

Check the disc brake rotor for scoring, cracks or other damage. Check the minimum thickness and rotor runout.

Check the disc brake rotor thickness using a micrometer or calipers. The brake rotor minimum thickness is 0.35 in. (9mm). This is the thickness at which point the rotor becomes unsafe to use and must be discarded. The minimum thickness that the rotor can be machined to is 0.37 in. (9.3mm), as this thickness allows room for rotor wear after it has been machined and returned to service.

Check the rotor for runout using a dial indicator. Install a few lug nuts to hold the rotor against the hub while checking. Mount the dial indicator on the strut and position the indicator foot on the outermost diameter of the contact surface of the disc pads. Make sure there is no wheel bearing free-play. Rotor runout must not exceed 0.005 in. (0.13mm). If the rotor runout exceeds specification, machine the rotor if it is not below the minimum thickness specification for machining. If the rotor runout is still excessive after machining, the rotor must be replaced.

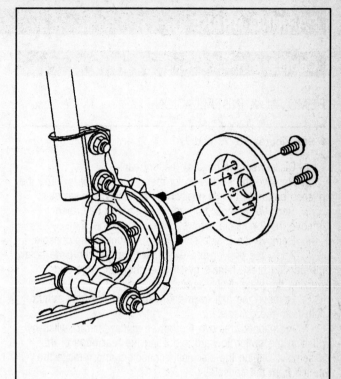

Fig. 74 If necessary, use 2 self-tapping bolts to drive the rotor from the hub and bearing assembly

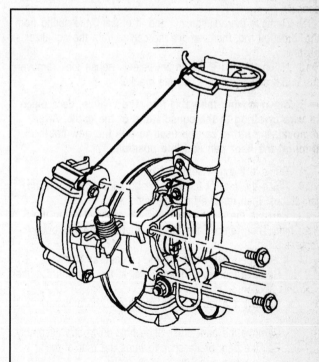

Fig. 73 Remove the 2 caliper support-to-knuckle bolts, then support the bracket from the strut with wire or a coat hanger

PARKING BRAKE

Cables

REMOVAL & INSTALLATION

▶ **See Figures 75, 76 and 77**

1. Disconnect the negative battery cable.
2. Remove the shift knob for manual transaxles or tape the release button to the **IN** position for automatic transaxles.
3. Remove the liner from the rear storage tray, then remove the 2 console screws located under the liner.
4. Remove the 2 side screws at the front of the console.
5. Apply the parking brake and remove the trim plate below the parking brake handle by lifting at the rear edge and working the plate evenly upward.
6. Remove the ash trays and disconnect the front ashtray light from the console.
7. If equipped, remove the power window/mirror switch by pushing the switch forward and lifting the rear edge of the assembly. Unplug the electrical connectors and remove the switch from the console.
8. Remove the instrument panel console lower trim panels by disconnecting the bottom velcro fasteners and pulling the panels from the upper snaps. Lift the rear of the center console and press out the seat belt bezels, then remove the console.
9. Remove the adjuster nut and, if present, the spring from the threaded rod, then remove the cables from the equalizer assembly.
10. Using SA9151BR or an equivalent release tool, remove the brake cable from the console bracket.

➡ **Before removing the cable from the vehicle, tie a piece of wire or string to the console end of the cable. After removal, the string can be used to pull the new cable through the floor pan and into position.**

11. Remove the rear seat cushion.
12. Raise the rear of the vehicle and support safely using jackstands, then remove the rear wheels.
13. Remove the cable grommet/cable assembly from the floor pan. Then remove the trailing arm/park cable to body fasteners.
14. If equipped with drum brakes, proceed as follows:
    a. Remove the brake drum. Refer to the procedure earlier in this section.
    b. Remove the lower return spring and the adjuster spring.
    c. Remove the park brake shoe hold-down cup assembly.
    d. Pull the park brake shoe towards the rear of the vehicle and remove the adjuster assembly.
    e. Disconnect the upper return spring from the park brake shoe.
    f. Remove the park brake cable from the park brake lever and remove the park brake cable spring.
    g. Use SA9151BR or an equivalent cable release tool and remove the cable from the backing plate.

15. If equipped with disc brakes, proceed as follows:
    a. Remove the nut securing the cable to the floor pan stud.
    b. Use SA9151BR or an equivalent cable release tool and remove the cable from the caliper lever.
16. Remove the cable from the vehicle.
To install:
17. If equipped with disc brakes, proceed as follows:
    a. Install the park brake cable into the caliper bracket.
    b. Attach the cable to the caliper park brake lever.
    c. Install the trailing arm/park brake cable to body fasteners, then tighten the fasteners to 89 ft. lbs. (120 Nm).
    d. Install the cable bracket to the floor pan stud. Install the nut and tighten to 25 inch lbs. (2.8 Nm).
18. If equipped with drum brakes, proceed as follows:
    a. Install the cable through the brake backing plate and correctly seat the retaining fingers.
    b. Install the cable spring onto the cable, then install the cable end into the actuator lever.
    c. Connect the short end of the upper return spring to the leading brake shoe, then connect the other end of the spring to the park shoe..
    d. Pull the park brake shoe toward the vehicle's rear and install the adjuster assembly between the shoes, then install the adjuster lever.
    e. Install the adjuster spring with the short end into the leading shoe and the other end into the adjuster lever.
    f. Install the lower return spring, then install the park shoe hold-down cup assembly.
    g. Adjust the brake shoe outer diameter to 0.02 inch (0.50mm) less than the inner diameter of the brake drum and install the brake drum.
    h. Install the trailing arm/park brake cable to body fasteners, then tighten the fasteners to 89 ft. lbs. (120 Nm).
19. Pull the cable into the vehicle with the wire or string positioned during disassembly.
20. Install the grommet into the floor pan.
21. Install the rear wheels.
22. Install the cables into the console bracket, then attach the cables to the equalizer. Refer to the appropriate illustration for equalizers of the first production design, the cable entry holes (rounded side of the equalizer) must face downward. For the seconds design, the cable entry holes may face up or down.
23. Install the cable and equalizer assembly onto the threaded rod, then install the adjusting nut.
24. For rear drum vehicles, apply and release the brake pedal 20 times to allow the drum brake adjuster to position the shown.
25. Adjust the parking brake; refer to the procedure later in this section.
26. Install the center console and the rear seat cushion.
27. Remove the supports and carefully lower the vehicle to the ground.
28. Connect the negative battery cable.

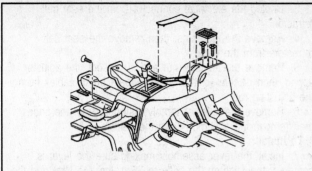

Fig. 75 The center console must be removed to service or adjust the parking brake cable

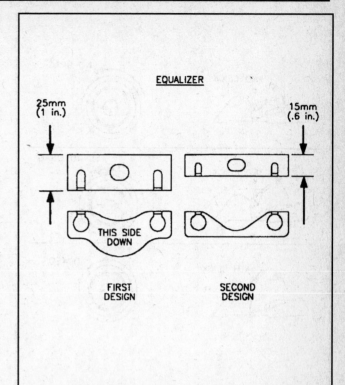

Fig. 77 Two equalizer designs have been used in Saturn production; the first design must be installed with the curved side downward

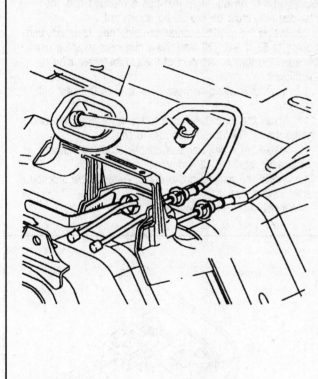

Fig. 76 Remove the brake cable from the console bracket

ADJUSTMENT

▶ See Figures 78 and 79

➡ If equipped with rear drum brakes that have been serviced, before performing parking brake adjustment procedures, apply and release the brake pedal 20 times. This allows the adjuster to position the brake shoes and prevents premature wear of the brake linings due to improper park brake adjustment.

1. Disconnect the negative battery cable and remove the center console assembly. Refer to Section 10 of this manual or to the parking brake cable removal and installation procedure earlier in this section for console procedures.

2. Raise the rear of the vehicle and support safely using jackstands.

3. Pull the park brake lever to the 3rd click from the released position.

4. Tighten the adjuster nut until a slight brake drag is felt at the rear wheels.

5. Apply and release the lever several times.

6. Pull the lever up to the 2nd click. There should be no brake drag at the rear wheels.

7. Pull the lever to the 3rd click and check for a slight drag at the rear wheels.

8. Pull the lever to the 4th click and verify the rear wheels are locked (they cannot be turned by hand).

9. Loosen or tighten the adjuster nut as necessary until these conditions are met.

10. If the proper adjustment cannot be obtained check measurement A, from the center of the pivot pin attachment to the end of the adjuster rod, as shown in the appropriate illustration. If the measurement is 5.78 in. (147mm) or less, replace the brake lever assembly. If the measurement is 6.33 in. or more, check for damage or incorrect installation of the drum brake assembly components, park brake cables and/or park brake lever assembly.

11. Install the center console assembly.

12. Remove the supports, lower the vehicle and connect the negative battery cable.

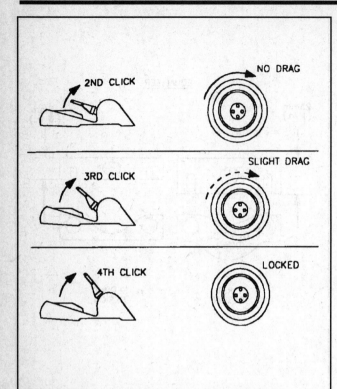

Fig. 78 When properly adjusted, these conditions should be observed while attempting to turn the rear wheel by hand, depending on park brake lever position

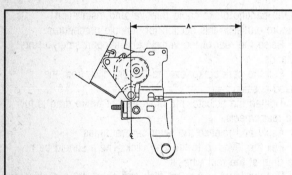

Fig. 79 If correct adjustment cannot be obtained, check dimension A

Brake Lever Assembly

REMOVAL & INSTALLATION

▶ See Figures 80, 81, 82, 83 and 84

1. Disconnect the negative battery cable, then remove the center console assembly. Refer to Section 10 of this manual or to the parking brake cable removal and installation procedure earlier in this section for console procedures.

2. Disconnect the indicator switch by removing the clip and unplugging the switch electrical connector. Remove the fastener from the bracket, then remove the switch from the vehicle.

3. Unplug the electrical connector from the seat belt retractor.

4. Remove the fasteners, then remove the seat belt retractors from the vehicle.

5. Remove the adjuster nut and, if present, the adjuster spring, then disconnect the equalizer/park brake cables from the adjusting rod.

6. Remove the lever assembly fasteners from the floor, then remove the assembly from the vehicle.

To install:

7. Install the lever assembly making sure the lever is centered, then tighten the bolts to 35 ft. lbs. (47 Nm) and the nuts to 23 ft. lbs. (31 Nm).

8. Install the equalizer and cables onto the threaded rod using the adjuster nut and, if applicable, the spring. If equipped with an equalizer that has a rounded half, the rounded side must be positioned downward.

9. Install the seat belt retractor using new fasteners and tighten to 52 ft. lbs. (70 Nm). New fasteners must be used because the torque retention of the old fasteners may be insufficient.

10. Install the wiring harness connector to the seat belt retractor.

11. Install the indicator switch to the lever assembly and tighten the retainer to 53 inch lbs. (6 Nm).

12. Install the wiring harness connector to the indicator switch and install the CPA device.

13. Adjust the parking brake cable. Refer to the procedure earlier in this section.

14. Install the center console.

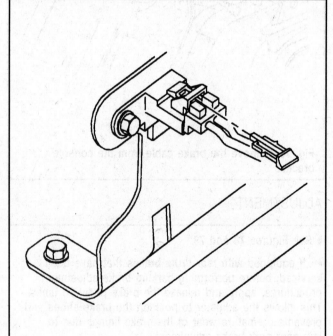

Fig. 80 Remove the Connector Position Assurance (CPA) device from the parking brake indicator electrical connector

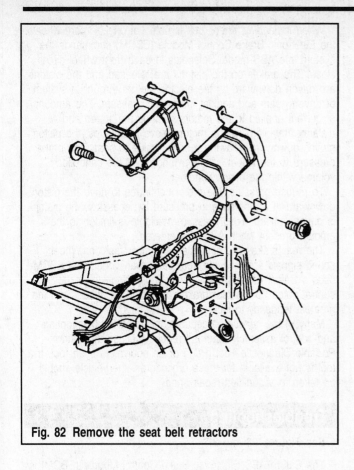

Fig. 82 Remove the seat belt retractors

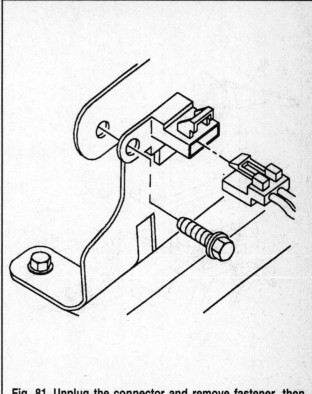

Fig. 81 Unplug the connector and remove fastener, then remove the switch from the vehicle

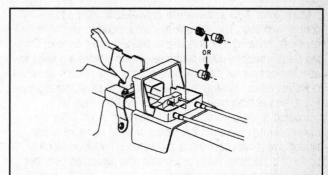

Fig. 83 Disconnect the equalizer/brake cables from the adjuster rod

ANTI-LOCK BRAKE SYSTEM

Description and Operation

▶ See Figure 85

The Saturn Anti-Lock Brake System (ABS) is lightweight, compact and highly efficient at controlling wheel locking. The basic premise of ABS is that in order to slow a vehicle, the brake system needs tire traction (friction). When wheel lock-up occurs during braking (a tire skids rather than rolls), the friction between the tire and road surface decreases enormously. This is extremely undesirable since friction is necessary for both steering and slowing of the vehicle. The Saturn ABS prevents wheel lock-up, increasing braking and steering ability (under certain, otherwise adverse, conditions such as wet pavement) by monitoring wheel speed and activating to relieve brake pressure to the portion of the system which is approaching lock-up. In otherwords, the system monitors how fast each wheel is turning and, if it detects there is an 'odd man out" (a tire is moving much slower than the rest) it will regulate the hydraulic brake pressure to that tire's caliper and prevent wheel lock-up. Absent ABS activation under these conditions, the system acts as a normal hydraulic brake system and does not regulate hydraulic pressure.

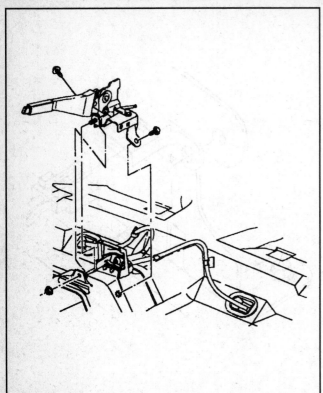

Fig. 84 Remove the parking brake lever assembly from the vehicle

Many other ABS systems use only electric solenoids to control fluid flow. The solenoid is commanded to one of three positions, allowing line pressure to build, release or hold. On the Saturn system, quick-response electric motors are used to alter the position of displacement pistons. The pistons serve as movable valves, altering the line pressure in small increments. Expressed another way, the solenoid systems may be compared to digital circuits, being either on or off while the motor-operated valves in the Saturn system compare to an analog circuit with continuous modulation. This modulation of brake line pressure yields much smoother operation with less pedal vibration during operation.

The system uses input signals from each of 4 wheel sensors. Four output channels (2 front, 2 rear) are controlled by the control module, though only the 2 front channels can be considered independent. Each front channel is provided with a separate piston, solenoid valve and motor so it may be controlled separately, while the rear wheels share a single motor driving 2 pistons and are therefore activated in unison. When locking is detected at one wheel, a solenoid closes the hydraulic path from the master cylinder. The electric motor for that brake circuit cycles the piston up and down to modulate braking force. The system cannot increase the brake pressure above that developed in the master cylinder; the system cannot apply the brakes by itself.

During normal braking, the ABS system is transparent to the operator. Internally, each control piston is in the uppermost or home position allowing brake fluid pressure to pass to the wheels unrestricted. A small internal Expansion Spring Brake (ESB) device is applied to each piston, preventing it from being forced downward by the pressurized fluid passing above it.

When impending wheel lock is noted at one or more wheels, the Electronic Brake Control Module (EBCM) commands the system into ABS mode. Solenoids in each front wheel circuit close. The brakes on the pistons are released and the pistons are driven downward by the electric motors through a system of driven gears and against the spring pressure. The amount of current applied to the motors controls the speed and distance travelled. As the motors move backwards, the piston moves downward, allowing a check valve to seat. The brake pressure to the wheel is now a function of the controlled volume within the piston chamber.

To reduce pressure, the motor continues to drive the piston downward. If an increase in pressure is necessary, the piston is driven upward. Total pressure available is limited to the amount present when ABS was entered.

The rear brakes are controlled in similar fashion. Wheel speed signals are received from each rear wheel. The EBCM uses a Select Low strategy, controlling a single motor to control output to the rear brakes based on the wheel with the greatest tendency to lock.

Many of the service procedures, including troubleshooting and control assembly overhaul require the use the Saturn Portable Diagnostic Tool (PDT) or an equivalent scan tool. If a tool is not available for these procedures, the vehicle should be taken to a qualified repair shop.

Troubleshooting

▶ See Figures 86 and 87

The Saturn ABS Electronic Brake Control Module (EBCM) is similar in many ways to the PCM described in Section No. 4 of this manual. It is an electronic controller of the ABS system which is capable of monitoring system function through the system circuits. It will constantly monitor the output from its various sensors to determine if a sensor or circuit is operating properly.

When the EBCM detects a problem, it will set a trouble code or flag. If the fault is serious enough to affect braking, the EBCM will illuminate the red ANTILOCK warning lamp. Whenever the lamp is lit, the ABS system is disabled and will NOT operate, but normal hydraulic braking will exist. In this way the system is prevented from ever disabling or adversely affecting the vehicle's hydraulic brakes due to a partial or complete ABS failure.

Like with the PCM system, trouble codes and flags are stored in both general information and malfunction history circuits of the control module. General information is cleared each time the ignition switch is turned **OFF**, but codes will reset when the ignition is turned **ON** again and the malfunction is still present. Data will remain in malfunction history for a series of 100 ignition cycles after a fault disappears, unless a scan tool is used to clear the memory earlier. Disconnecting the power will have NO affect on data stored in the EBCM malfunction history circuits.

Unlike the PCM system, on which a jumper wire can activate a flash code readout, a scan tool MUST be used for fault code diagnosis and troubleshooting on the ABS EBCM. The scan tool is connected to the system through the Assembly Line Date Link (ALDL) connector which is under the dash near the driver's door.

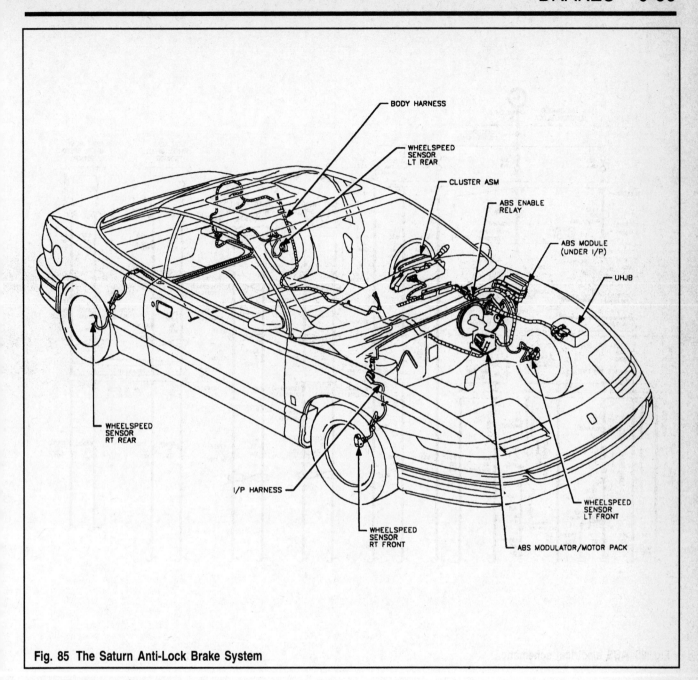

BODY HARNESS

WHEELSPEED SENSOR LT REAR

CLUSTER ASM

ABS ENABLE RELAY

ABS MODULE (UNDER I/P)

UHJB

WHEELSPEED SENSOR RT REAR

WHEELSPEED SENSOR LT FRONT

I/P HARNESS

WHEELSPEED SENSOR RT FRONT

ABS MODULATOR/MOTOR PACK

Fig. 85 The Saturn Anti-Lock Brake System

DIAGNOSTIC CODES

The following diagnostic charts may be used to troubleshoot the ABS system based on scan tool output:

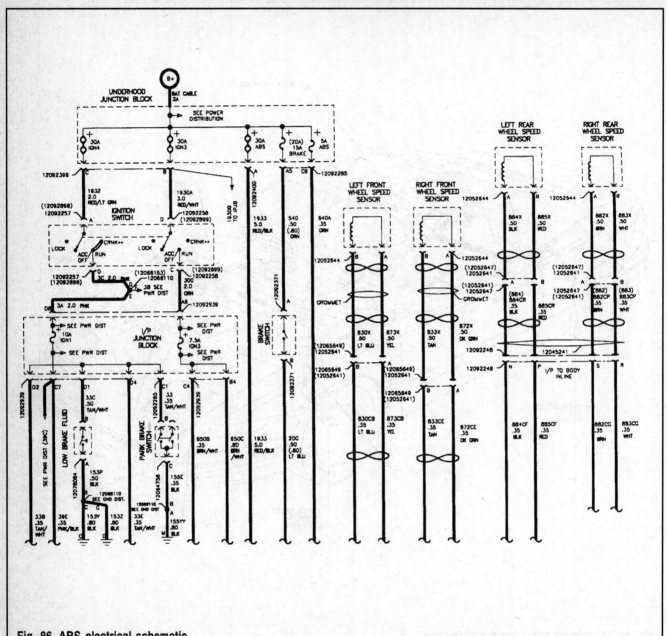

Fig. 86 ABS electrical schematic

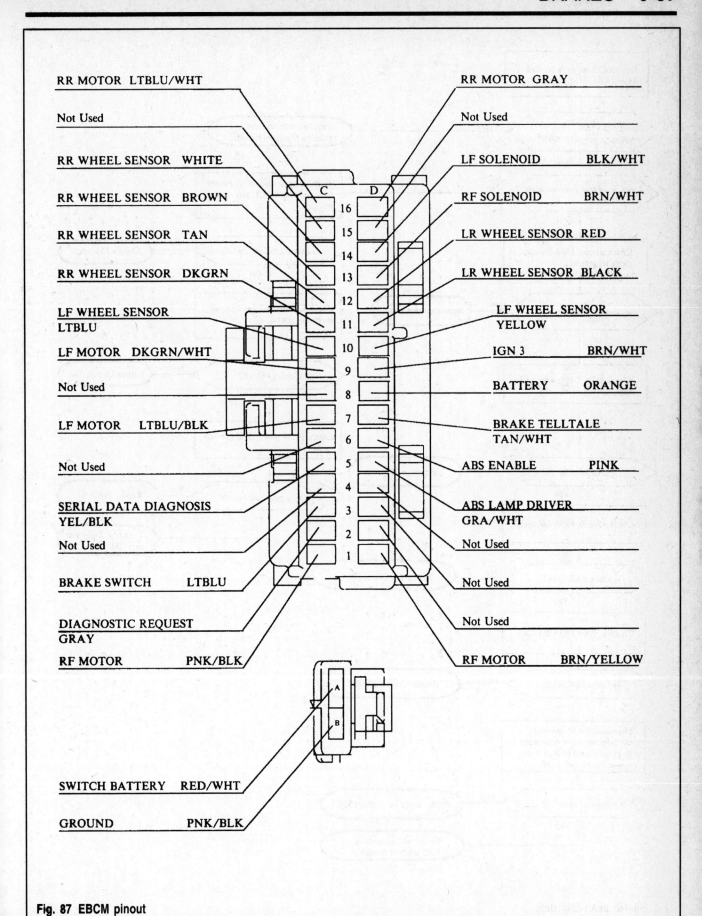

Fig. 87 EBCM pinout

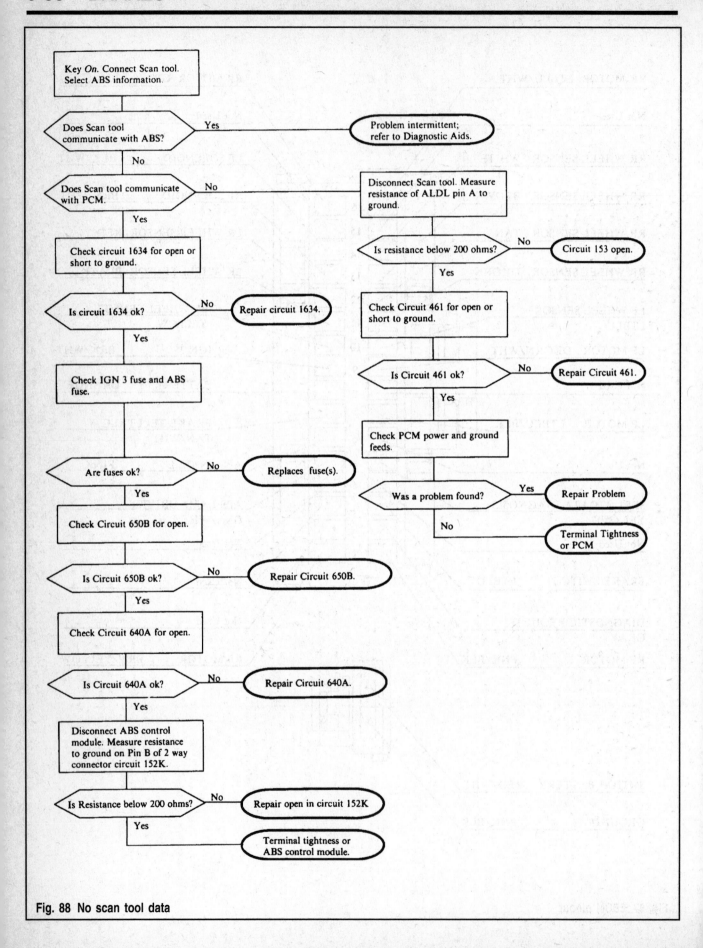

Fig. 88 No scan tool data

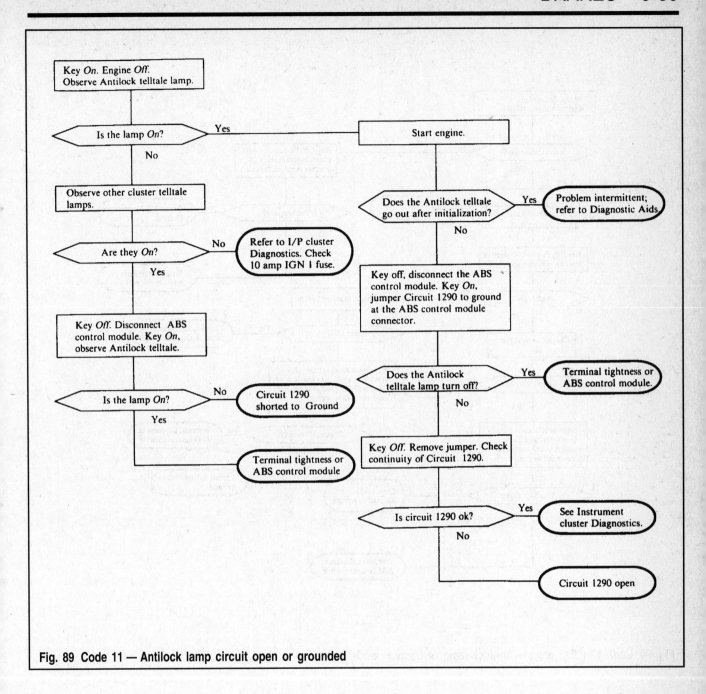

Fig. 89 Code 11 — Antilock lamp circuit open or grounded

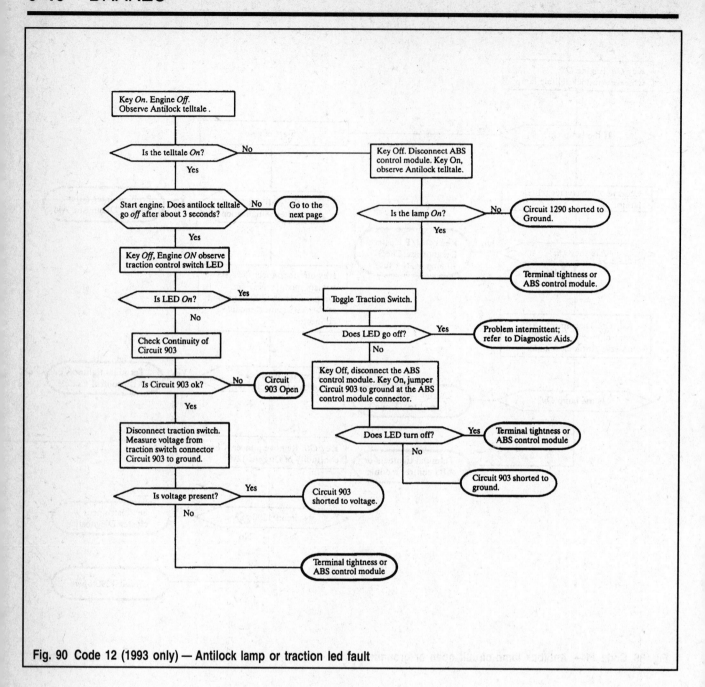

Fig. 90 Code 12 (1993 only) — Antilock lamp or traction led fault

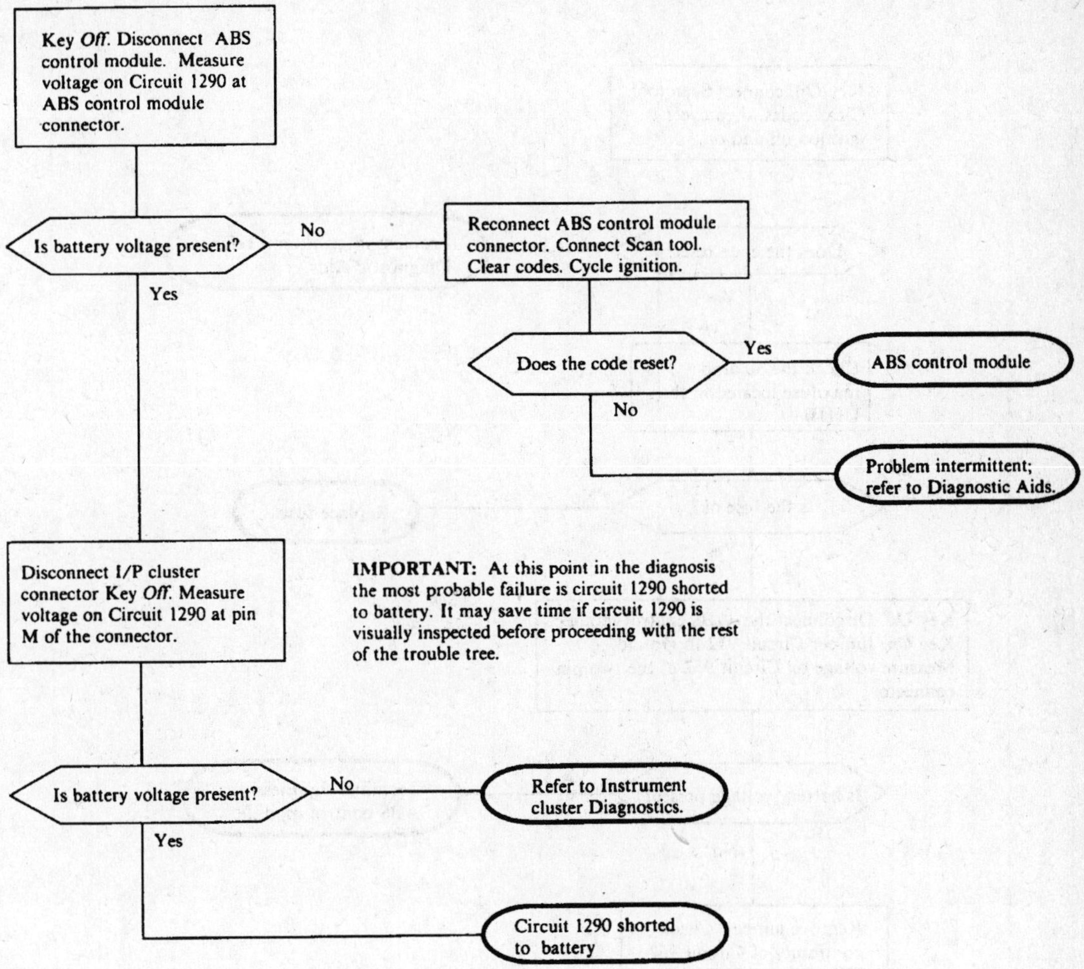
Key *Off*. Disconnect ABS control module. Measure voltage on Circuit 1290 at ABS control module connector.
Is battery voltage present?
No
Reconnect ABS control module connector. Connect Scan tool. Clear codes. Cycle ignition.
Yes
Does the code reset?
Yes
ABS control module
No
Problem intermittent; refer to Diagnostic Aids.
Disconnect I/P cluster connector Key *Off*. Measure voltage on Circuit 1290 at pin M of the connector.
IMPORTANT: At this point in the diagnosis the most probable failure is circuit 1290 shorted to battery. It may save time if circuit 1290 is visually inspected before proceeding with the rest of the trouble tree.
Is battery voltage present?
No
Refer to Instrument cluster Diagnostics.
Yes
Circuit 1290 shorted to battery

Fig. 91 Code 13 — Antilock lamp circuit shorted to B+

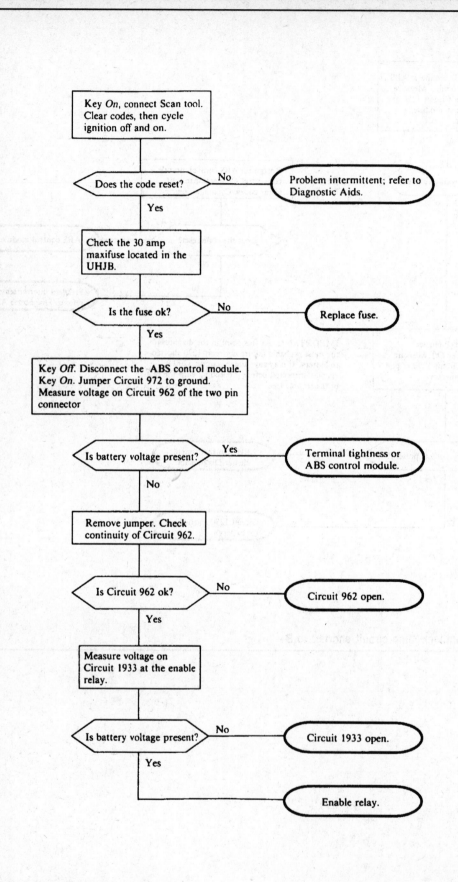

Fig. 92 Code 14 — Switched battery circuit open

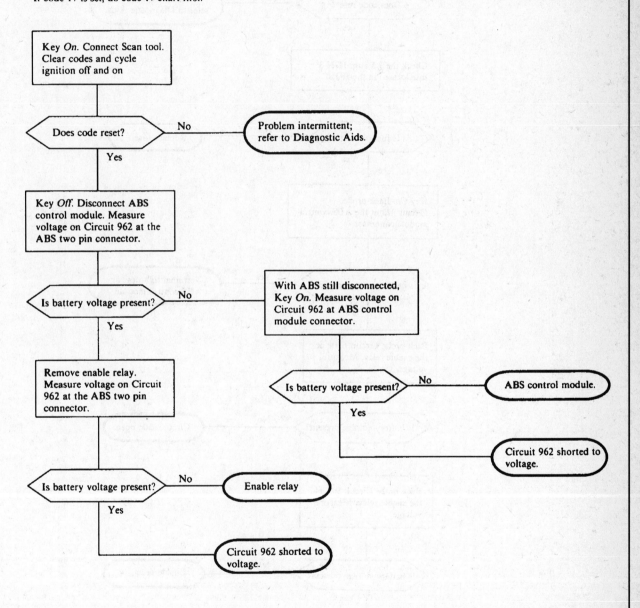

If code 17 is set, do code 17 chart first.

Key *On*. Connect Scan tool. Clear codes and cycle ignition off and on

Does code reset? — No → Problem intermittent; refer to Diagnostic Aids.

Yes

Key *Off*. Disconnect ABS control module. Measure voltage on Circuit 962 at the ABS two pin connector.

Is battery voltage present? — No → With ABS still disconnected, Key *On*. Measure voltage on Circuit 962 at ABS control module connector.

Yes

Remove enable relay. Measure voltage on Circuit 962 at the ABS two pin connector.

Is battery voltage present? — No → ABS control module.

Yes

Circuit 962 shorted to voltage.

Is battery voltage present? — No → Enable relay

Yes

Circuit 962 shorted to voltage.

Fig. 93 Code 15 — Switched battery circuit shorted to B+

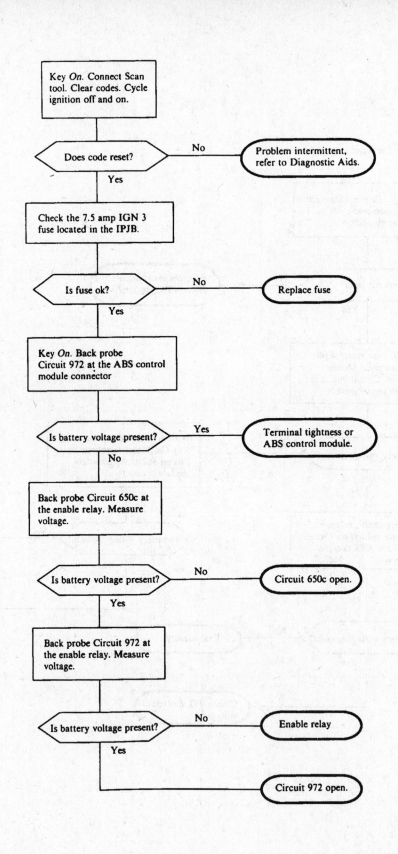

Fig. 94 Code 16 — Enable relay coil circuit open

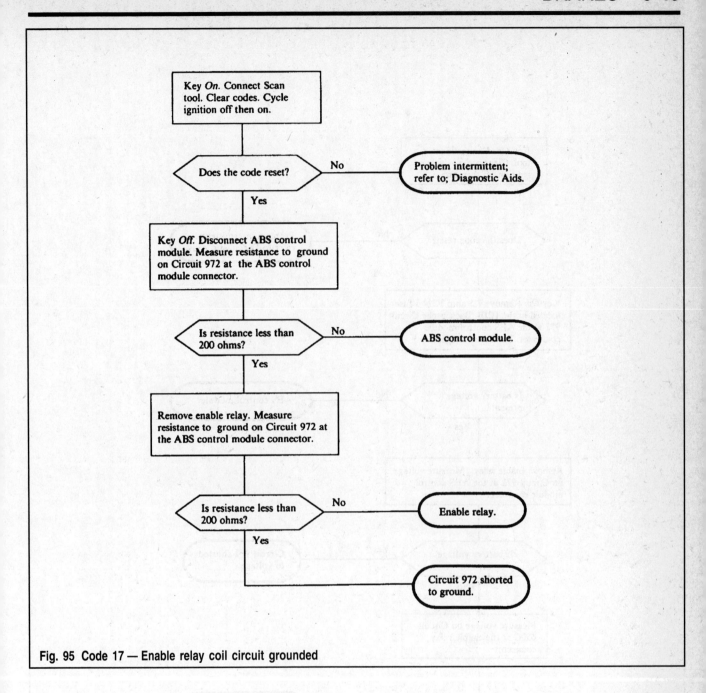

Fig. 95 Code 17 — Enable relay coil circuit grounded

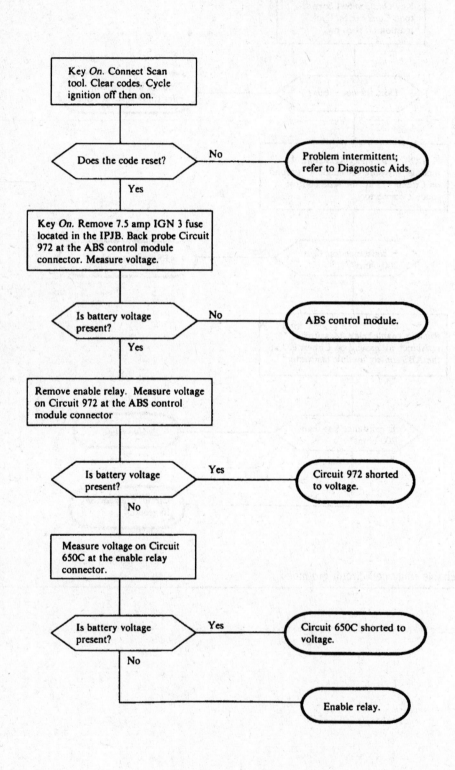

Fig. 96 Code 18 — Enable relay coil circuit shorted to B+

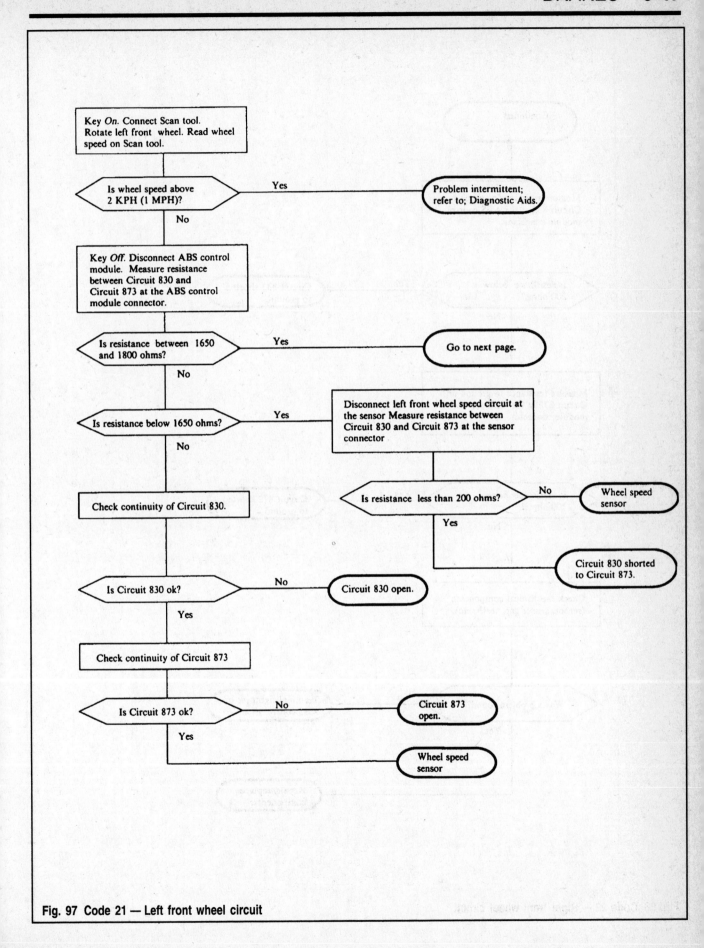

Fig. 97 Code 21 — Left front wheel circuit

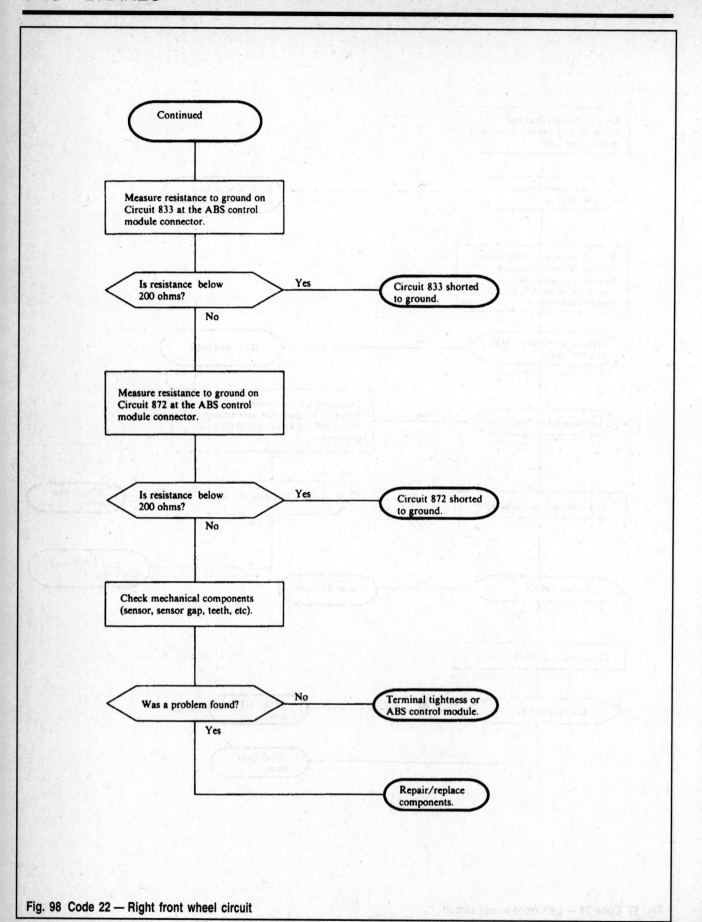

Fig. 98 Code 22 — Right front wheel circuit

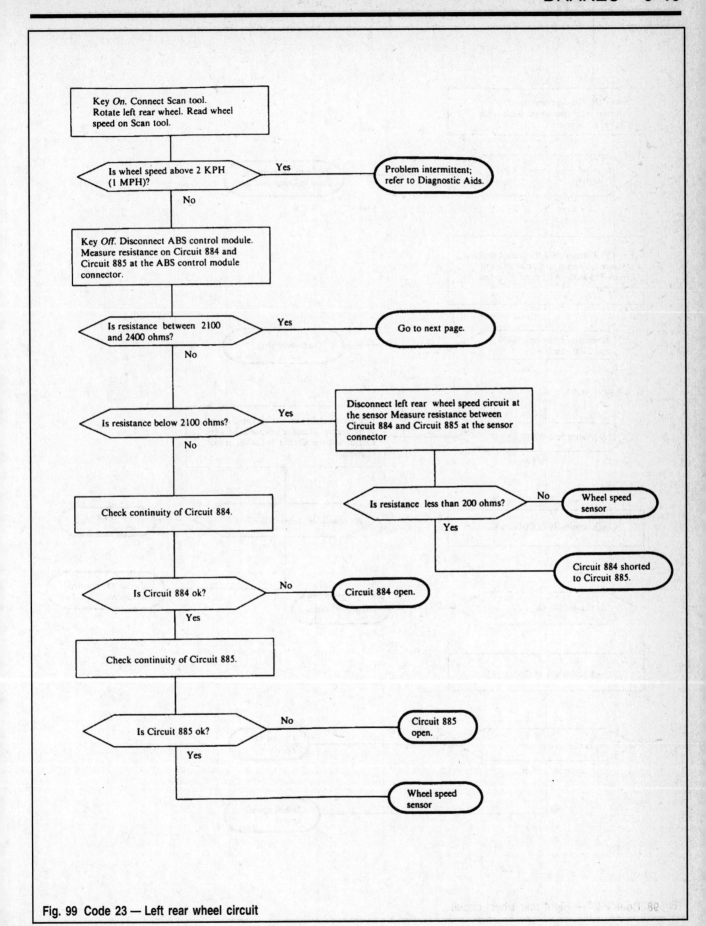

Key *On*. Connect Scan tool. Rotate left rear wheel. Read wheel speed on Scan tool.

Is wheel speed above 2 KPH (1 MPH)? — Yes — Problem intermittent; refer to Diagnostic Aids.

No

Key *Off*. Disconnect ABS control module. Measure resistance on Circuit 884 and Circuit 885 at the ABS control module connector.

Is resistance between 2100 and 2400 ohms? — Yes — Go to next page.

No

Is resistance below 2100 ohms? — Yes — Disconnect left rear wheel speed circuit at the sensor Measure resistance between Circuit 884 and Circuit 885 at the sensor connector

No

Is resistance less than 200 ohms? — No — Wheel speed sensor

Yes

Circuit 884 shorted to Circuit 885.

Check continuity of Circuit 884.

Is Circuit 884 ok? — No — Circuit 884 open.

Yes

Check continuity of Circuit 885.

Is Circuit 885 ok? — No — Circuit 885 open.

Yes

Wheel speed sensor

Fig. 99 Code 23 — Left rear wheel circuit

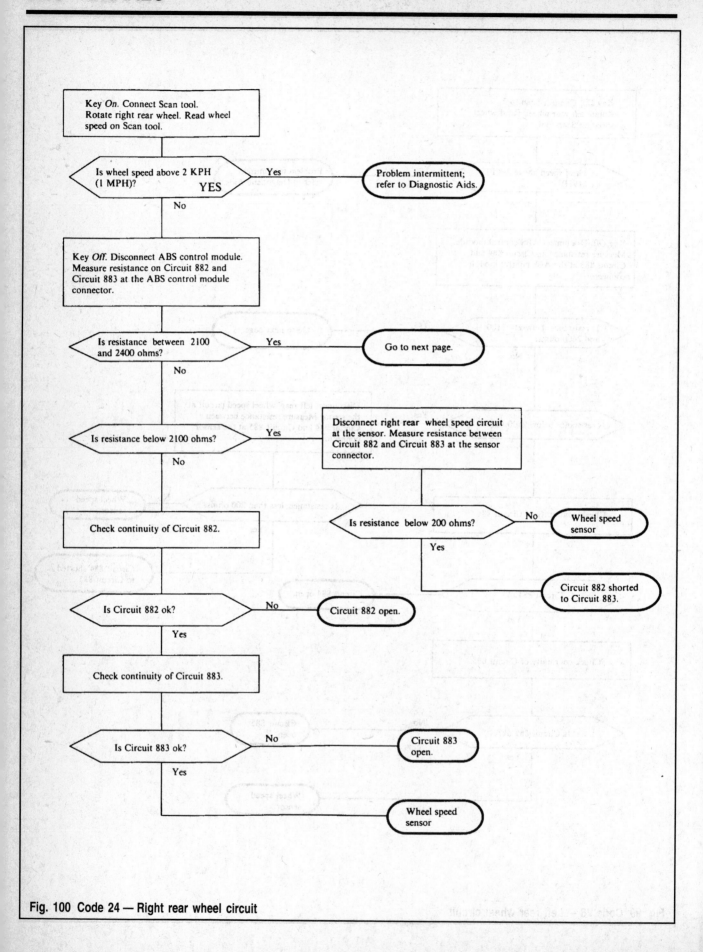

Fig. 100 Code 24 — Right rear wheel circuit

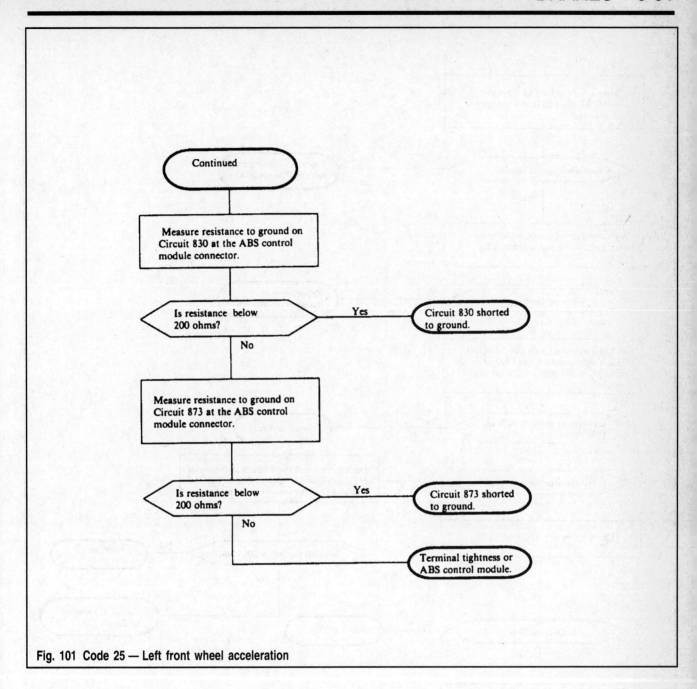

Fig. 101 Code 25 — Left front wheel acceleration

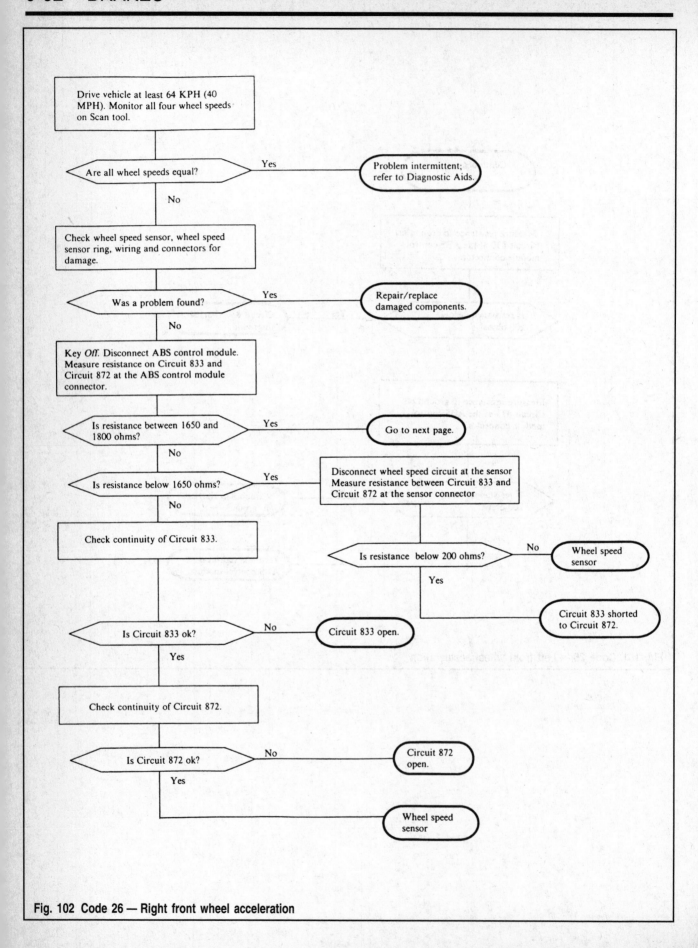

Fig. 102 Code 26 — Right front wheel acceleration

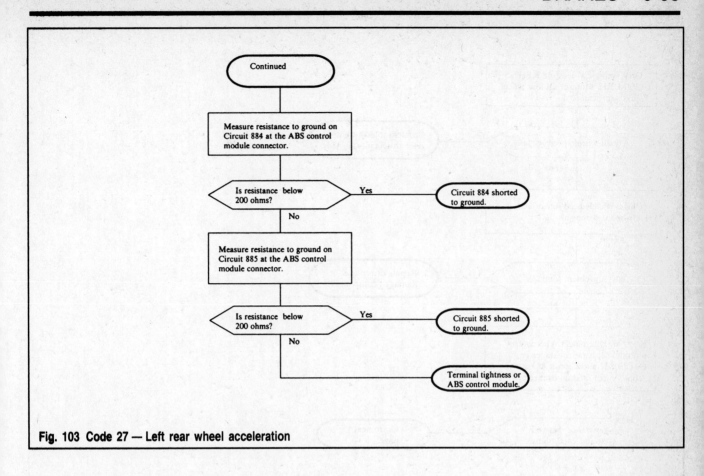

Fig. 103 Code 27 — Left rear wheel acceleration

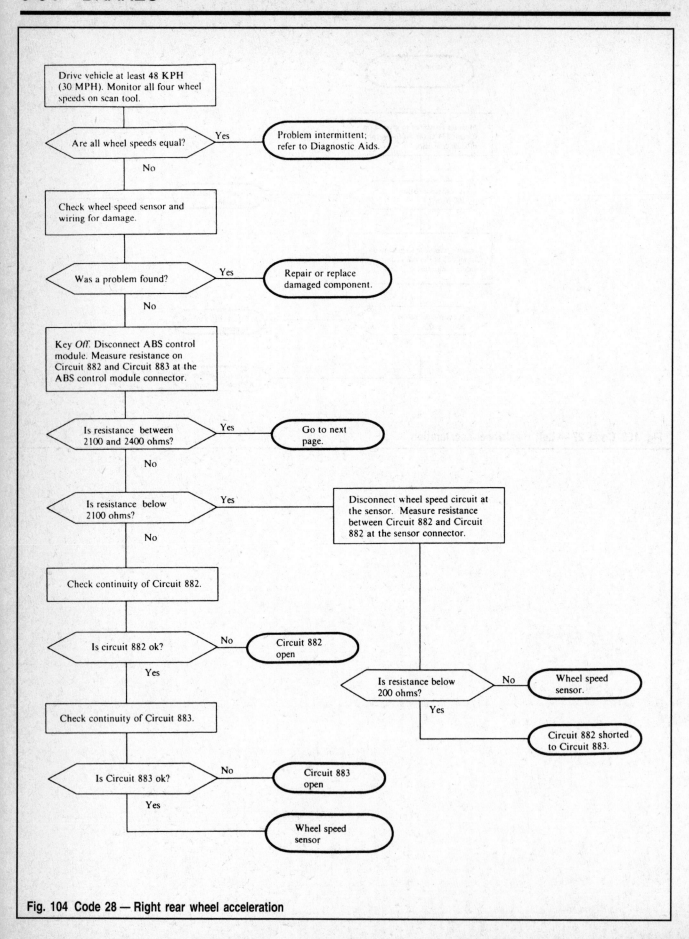

Fig. 104 Code 28 — Right rear wheel acceleration

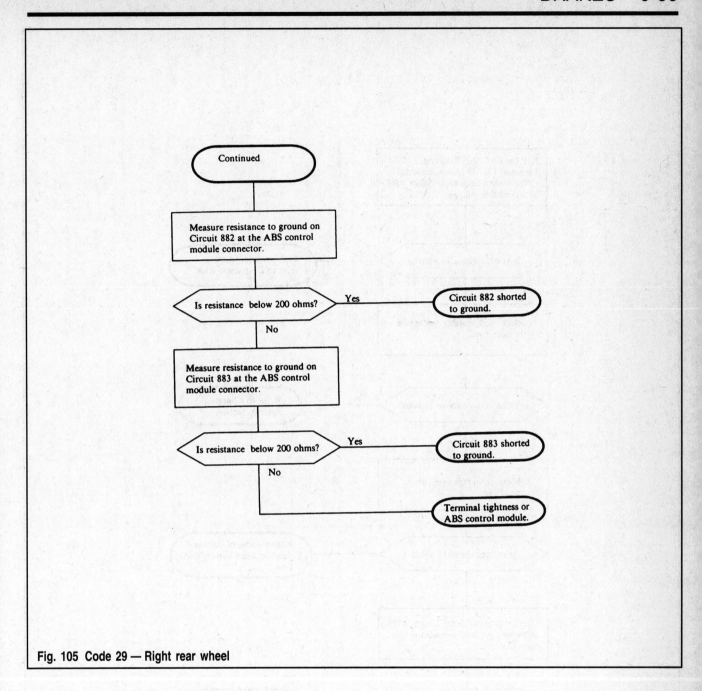

Fig. 105 Code 29 — Right rear wheel

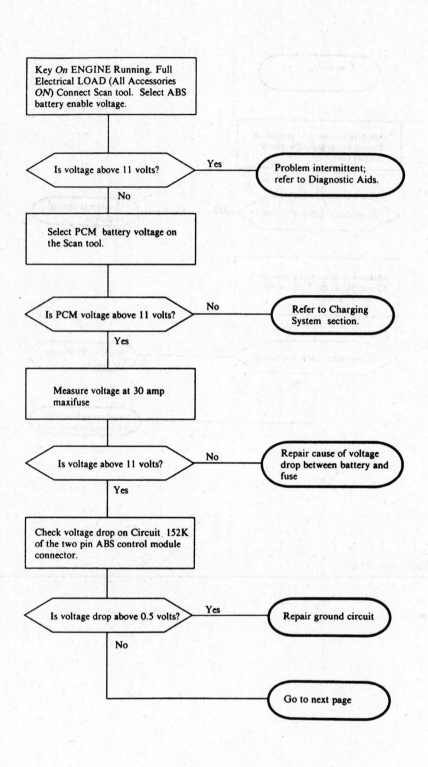

Fig. 106 Code 35 — ABS system voltage low

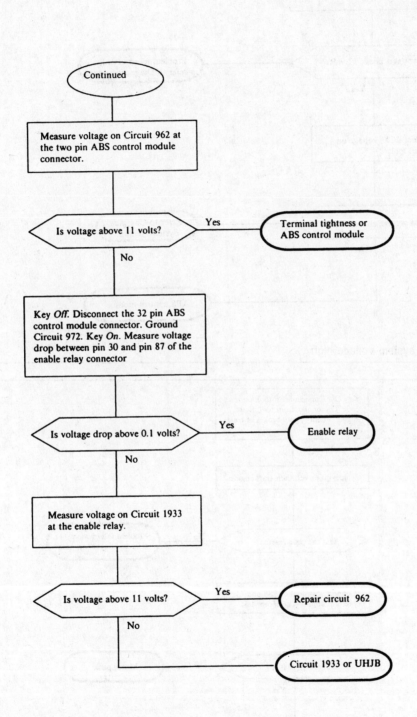

Fig. 107 Code 36 — ABS system voltage low

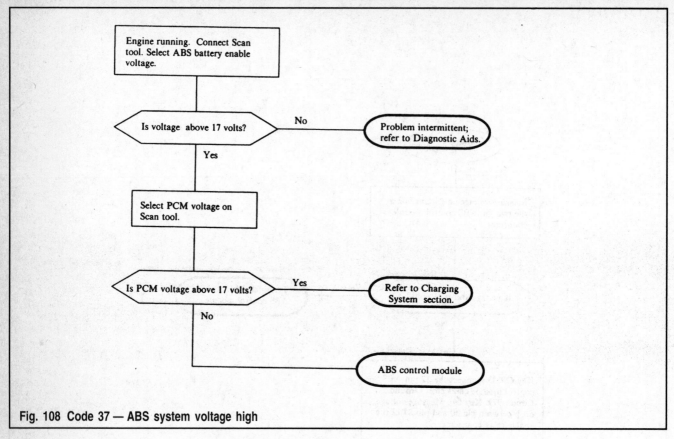

Fig. 108 Code 37 — ABS system voltage high

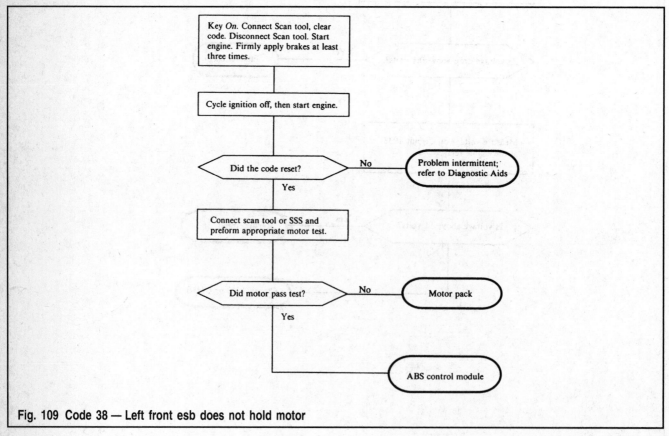

Fig. 109 Code 38 — Left front esb does not hold motor

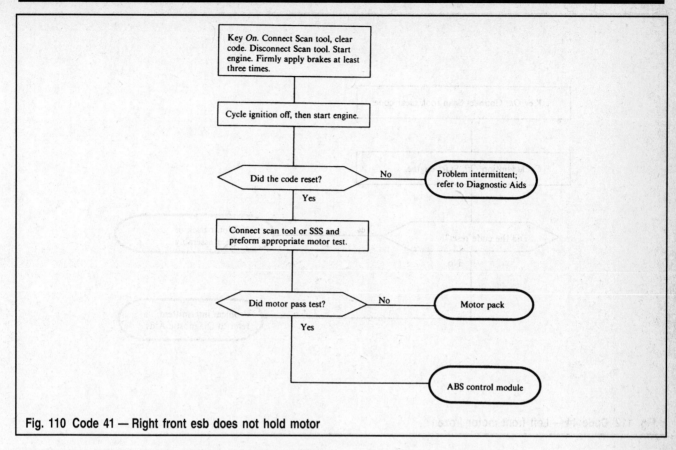

Fig. 110 Code 41 — Right front esb does not hold motor

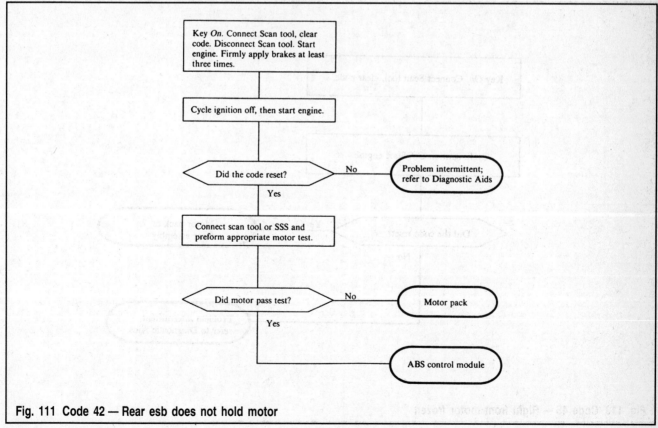

Fig. 111 Code 42 — Rear esb does not hold motor

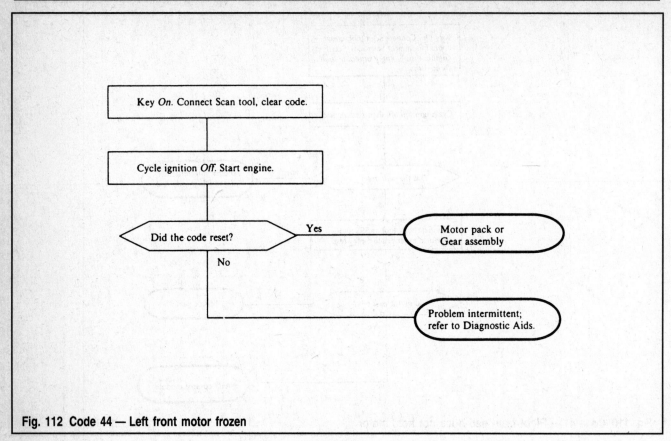

Fig. 112 Code 44 — Left front motor frozen

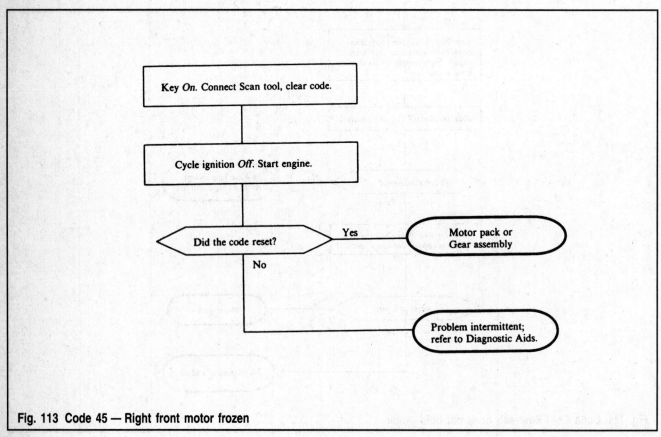

Fig. 113 Code 45 — Right front motor frozen

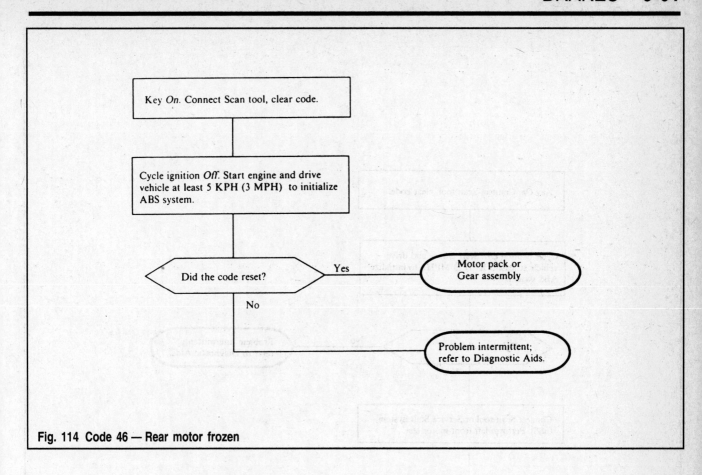

Fig. 114 Code 46 — Rear motor frozen

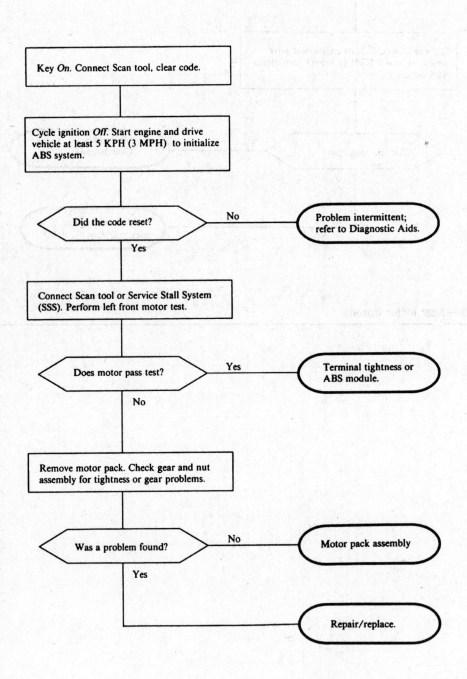

Fig. 115 Code 47 — Left front motor circuit current low

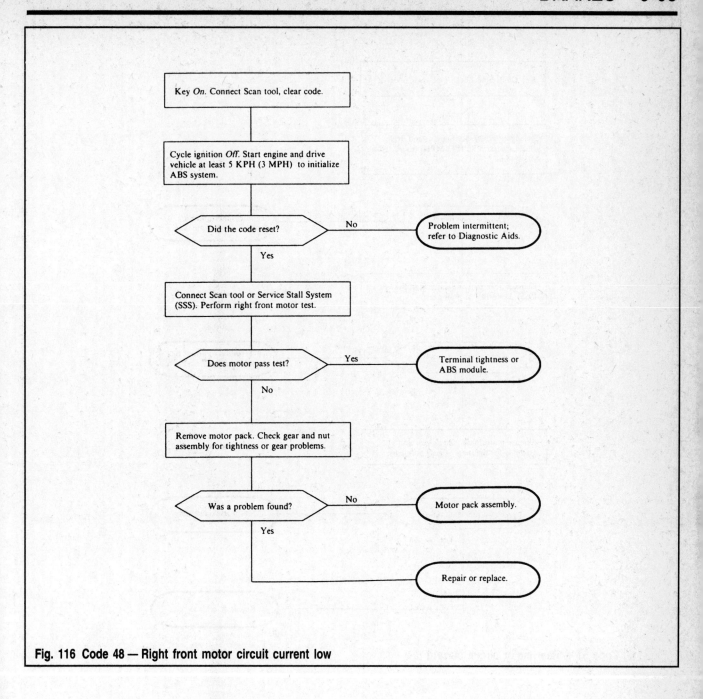

Fig. 116 Code 48 — Right front motor circuit current low

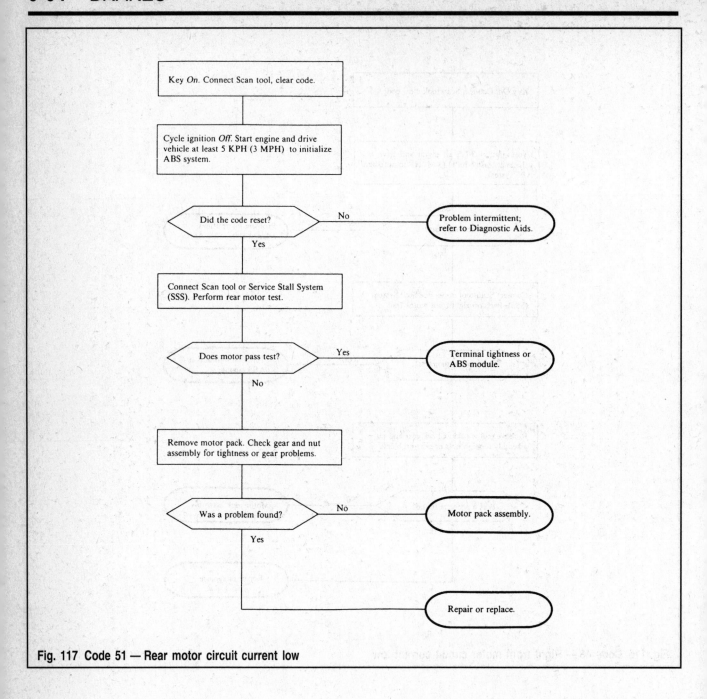

Fig. 117 Code 51 — Rear motor circuit current low

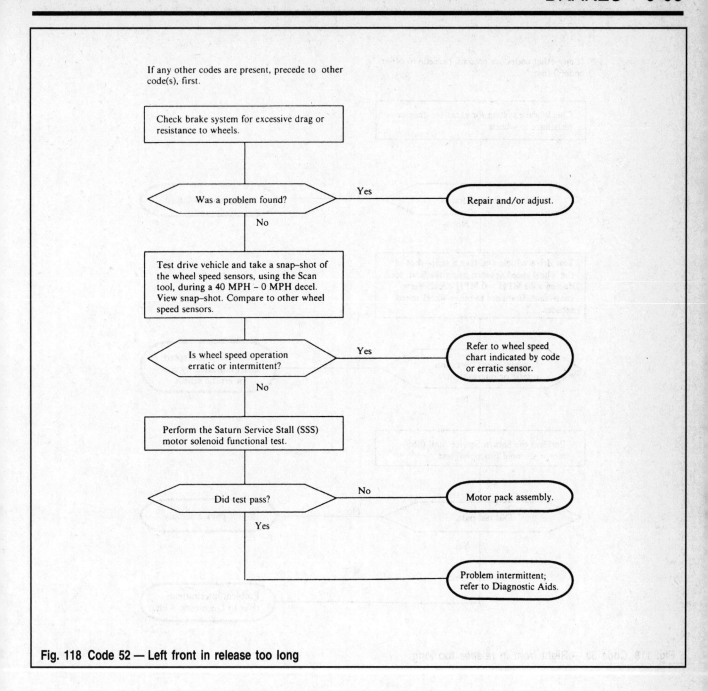

If any other codes are present, precede to other code(s), first.

Check brake system for excessive drag or resistance to wheels.

Was a problem found? — Yes → Repair and/or adjust.

No

Test drive vehicle and take a snap–shot of the wheel speed sensors, using the Scan tool, during a 40 MPH – 0 MPH decel. View snap–shot. Compare to other wheel speed sensors.

Is wheel speed operation erratic or intermittent? — Yes → Refer to wheel speed chart indicated by code or erratic sensor.

No

Perform the Saturn Service Stall (SSS) motor solenoid functional test.

Did test pass? — No → Motor pack assembly.

Yes

Problem intermittent; refer to Diagnostic Aids.

Fig. 118 Code 52 — Left front in release too long

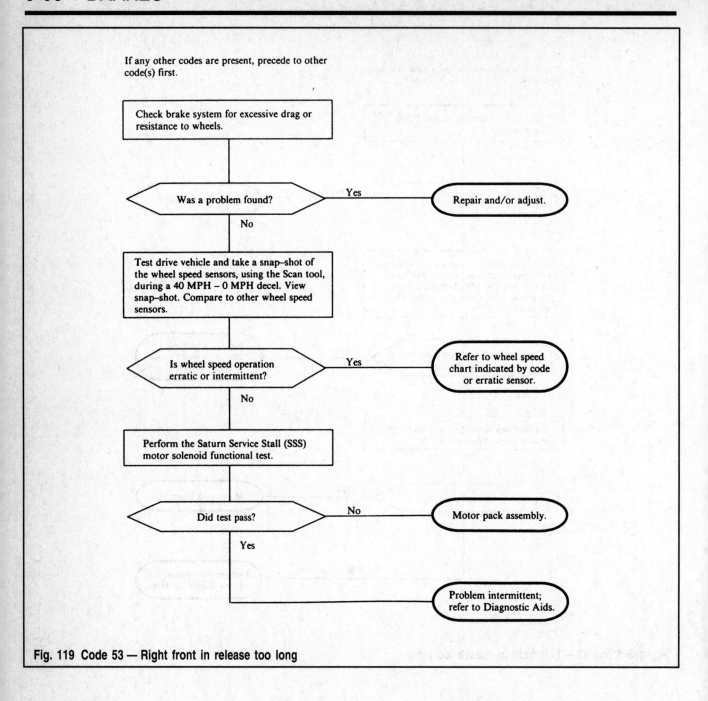

If any other codes are present, precede to other code(s) first.

Check brake system for excessive drag or resistance to wheels.

Was a problem found? — Yes → Repair and/or adjust.

No

Test drive vehicle and take a snap-shot of the wheel speed sensors, using the Scan tool, during a 40 MPH – 0 MPH decel. View snap-shot. Compare to other wheel speed sensors.

Is wheel speed operation erratic or intermittent? — Yes → Refer to wheel speed chart indicated by code or erratic sensor.

No

Perform the Saturn Service Stall (SSS) motor solenoid functional test.

Did test pass? — No → Motor pack assembly.

Yes

Problem intermittent; refer to Diagnostic Aids.

Fig. 119 Code 53 — Right front in release too long

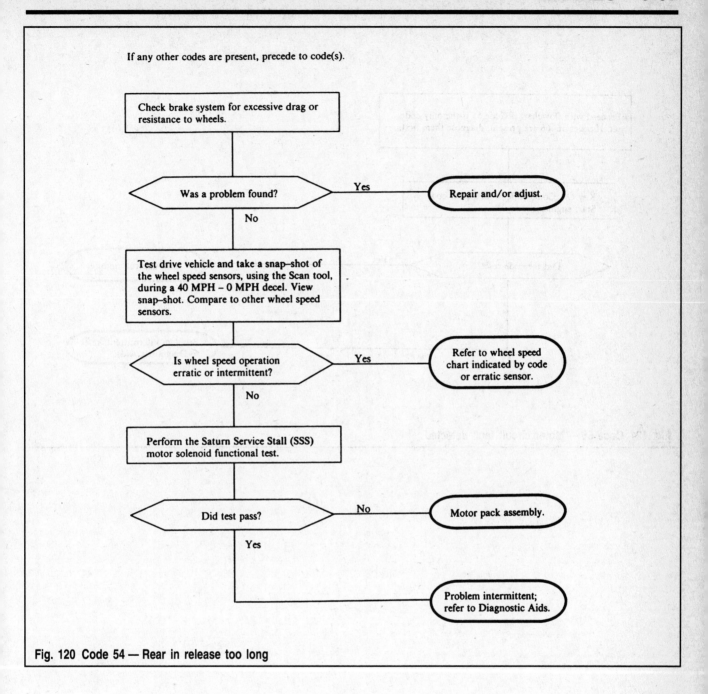

If any other codes are present, precede to code(s).

Check brake system for excessive drag or resistance to wheels.

Was a problem found? — Yes → Repair and/or adjust.

No

Test drive vehicle and take a snap–shot of the wheel speed sensors, using the Scan tool, during a 40 MPH – 0 MPH decel. View snap–shot. Compare to other wheel speed sensors.

Is wheel speed operation erratic or intermittent? — Yes → Refer to wheel speed chart indicated by code or erratic sensor.

No

Perform the Saturn Service Stall (SSS) motor solenoid functional test.

Did test pass? — No → Motor pack assembly.

Yes

Problem intermittent; refer to Diagnostic Aids.

Fig. 120 Code 54 — Rear in release too long

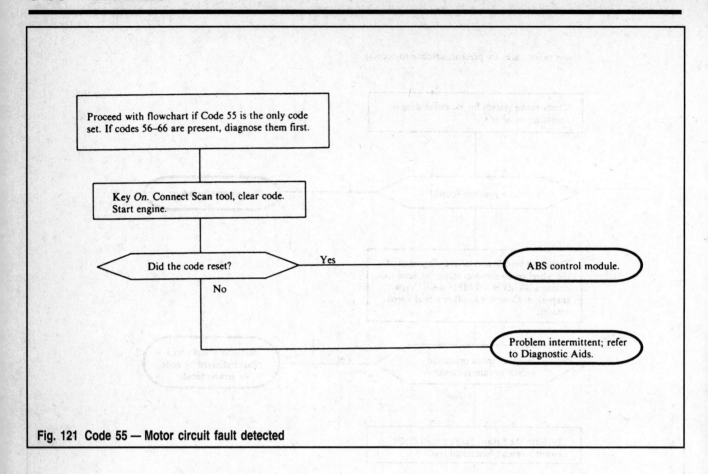

Proceed with flowchart if Code 55 is the only code set. If codes 56–66 are present, diagnose them first.

Key *On*. Connect Scan tool, clear code. Start engine.

Did the code reset? — Yes → ABS control module.

No

Problem intermittent; refer to Diagnostic Aids.

Fig. 121 Code 55 — Motor circuit fault detected

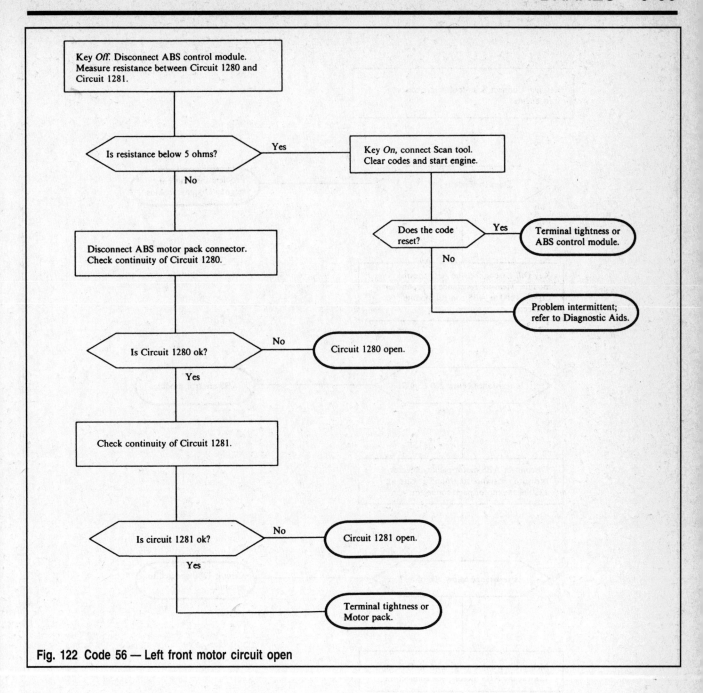

Fig. 122 Code 56 — Left front motor circuit open

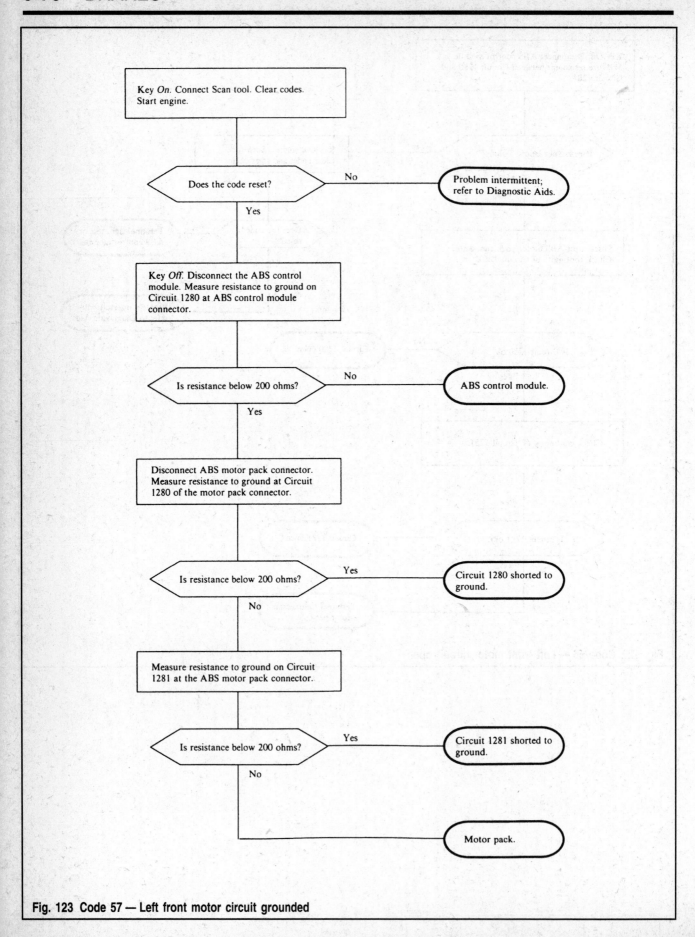

Fig. 123 Code 57 — Left front motor circuit grounded

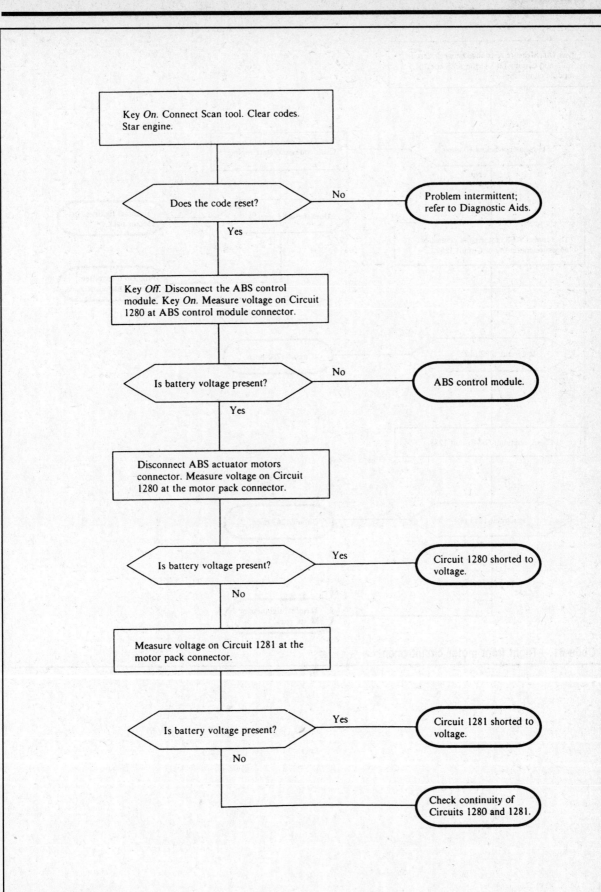

Fig. 124 Code 58 — Left front motor circuit shorted to B+

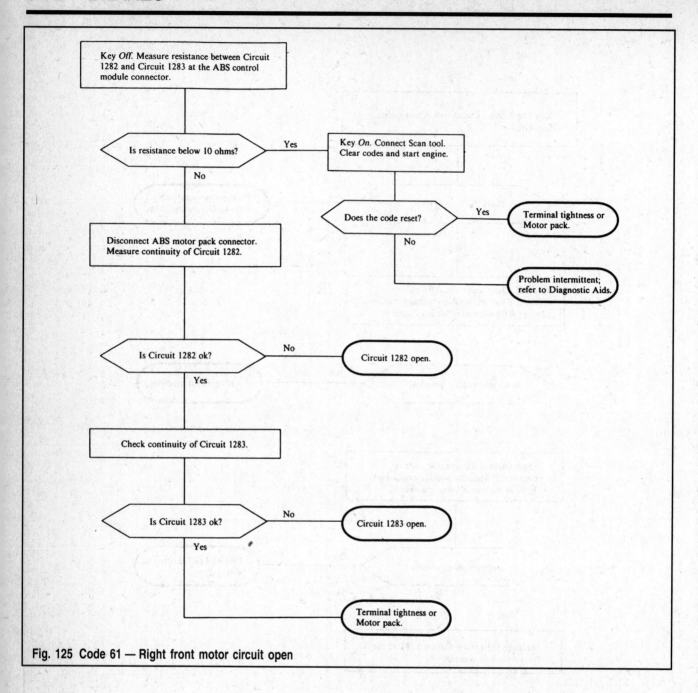

Fig. 125 Code 61 — Right front motor circuit open

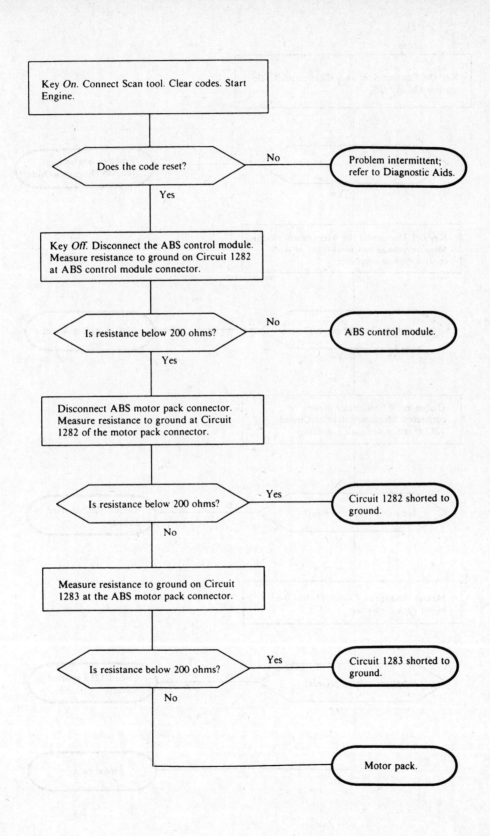

Fig. 126 Code 62 — Right front motor circuit grounded

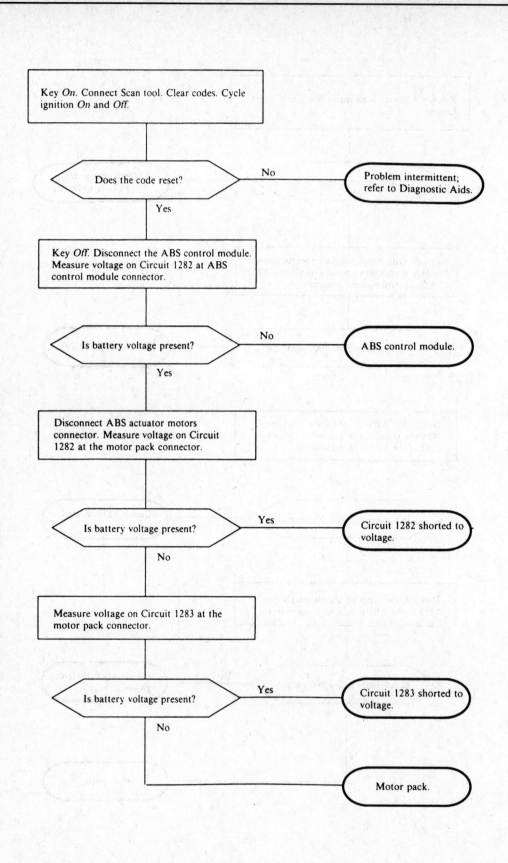

Fig. 127 Code 63 — Right front motor circuit shorted to B+

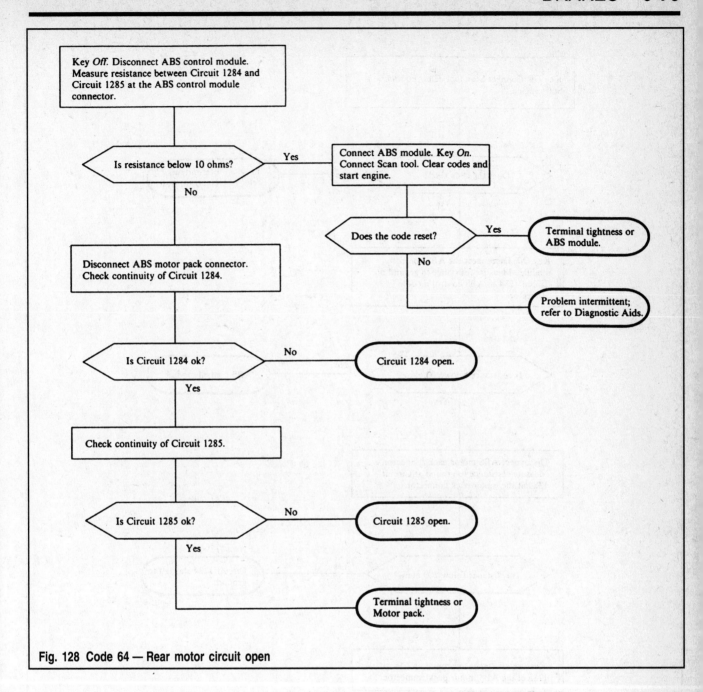

Fig. 128 Code 64 — Rear motor circuit open

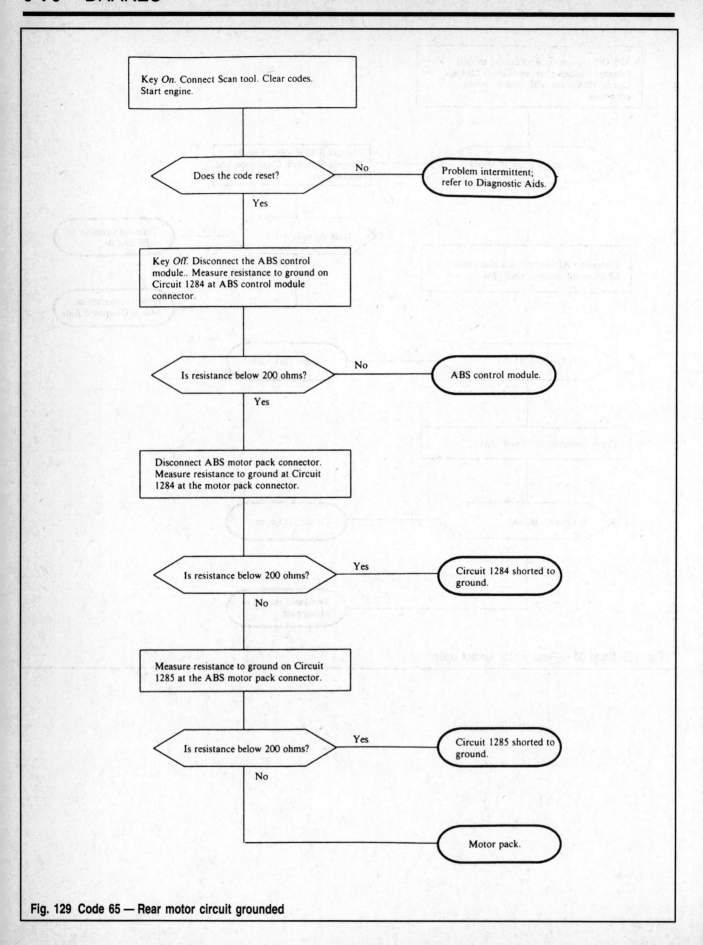

Fig. 129 Code 65 — Rear motor circuit grounded

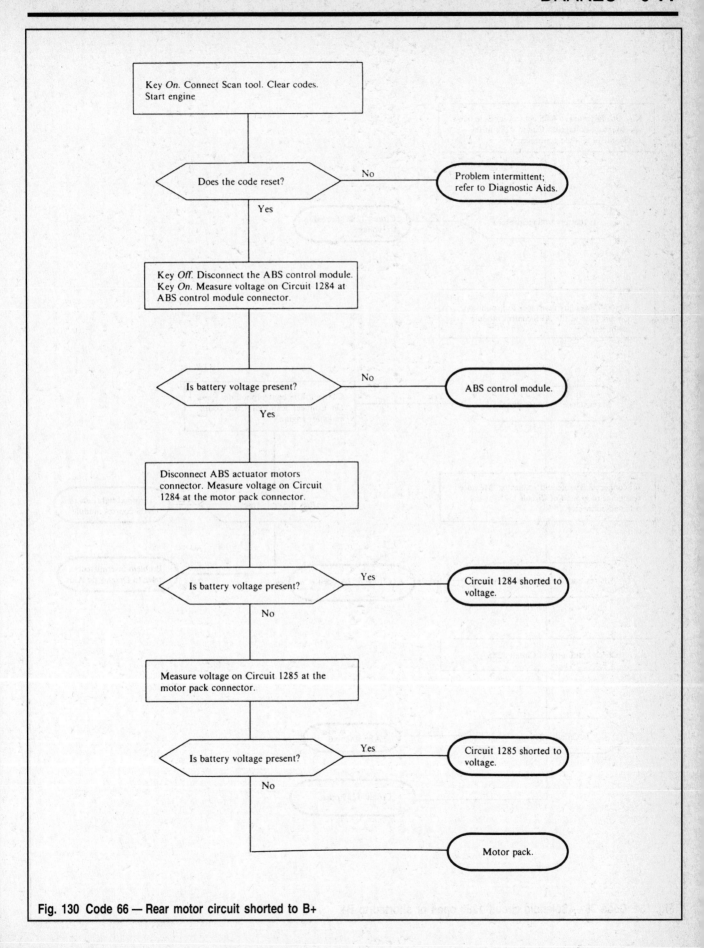

Fig. 130 Code 66 — Rear motor circuit shorted to B+

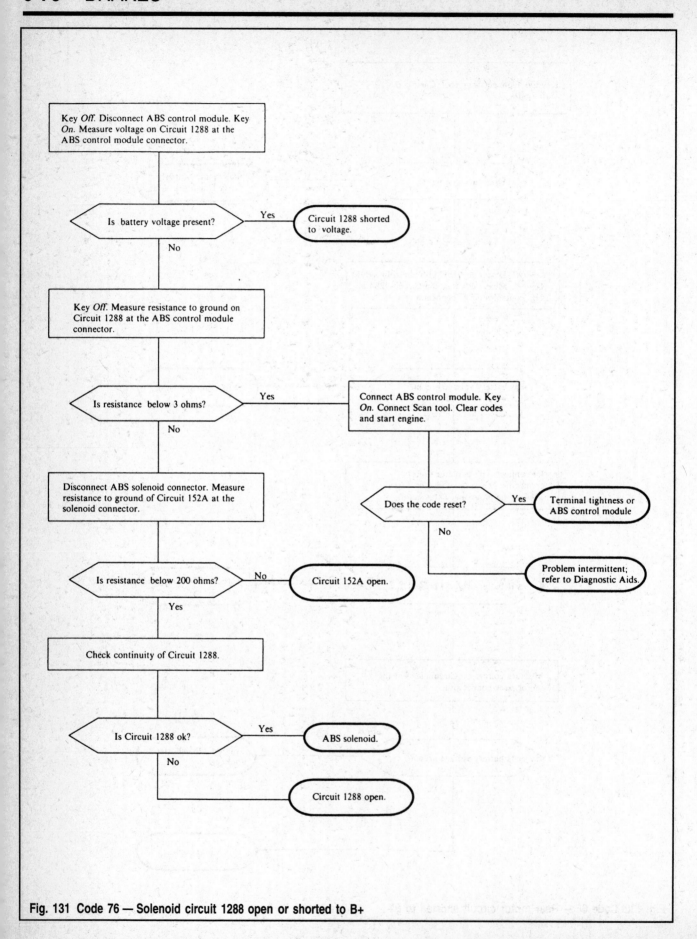

Fig. 131 Code 76 — Solenoid circuit 1288 open or shorted to B+

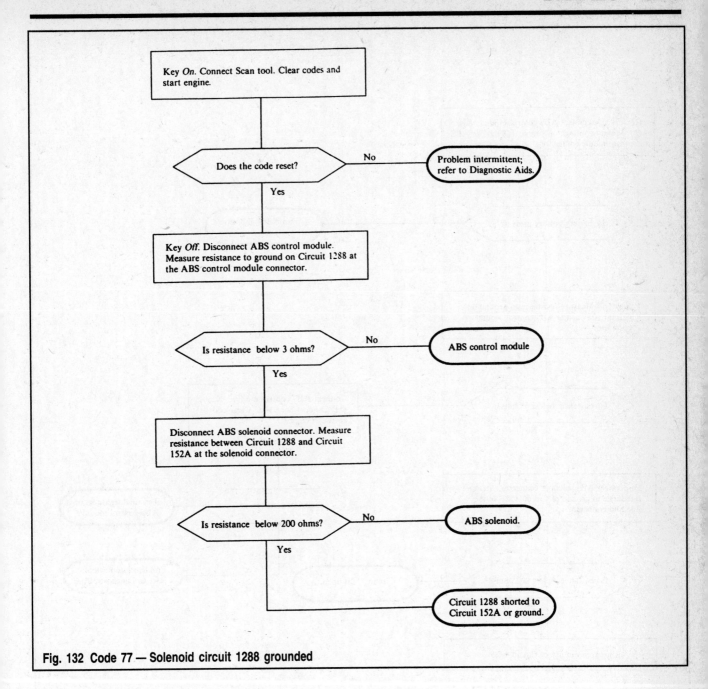

Fig. 132 Code 77 — Solenoid circuit 1288 grounded

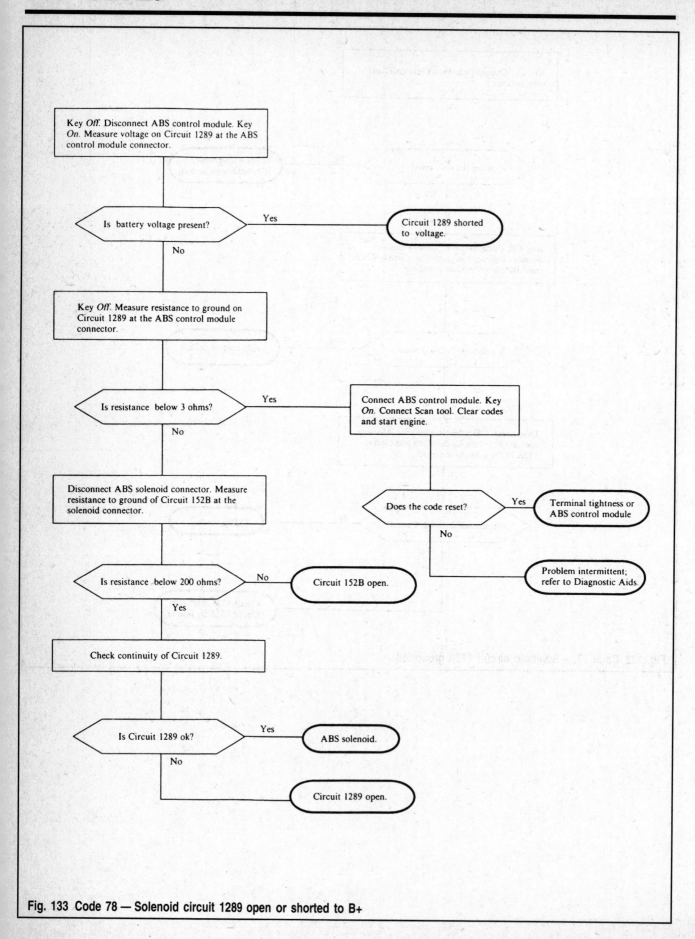

Fig. 133 Code 78 — Solenoid circuit 1289 open or shorted to B+

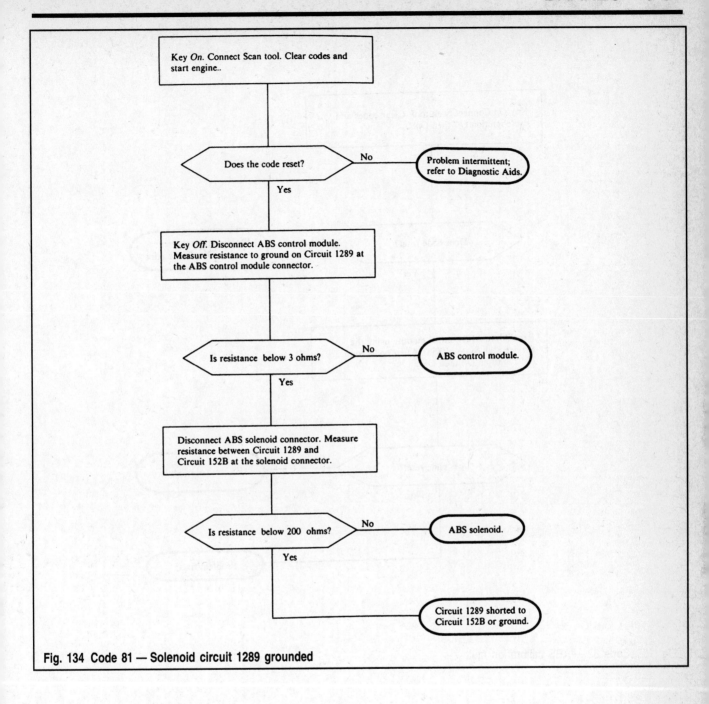

Key *On*. Connect Scan tool. Clear codes and start engine..

Does the code reset? — No — Problem intermittent; refer to Diagnostic Aids.

Yes

Key *Off*. Disconnect ABS control module. Measure resistance to ground on Circuit 1289 at the ABS control module connector.

Is resistance below 3 ohms? — No — ABS control module.

Yes

Disconnect ABS solenoid connector. Measure resistance between Circuit 1289 and Circuit 152B at the solenoid connector.

Is resistance below 200 ohms? — No — ABS solenoid.

Yes

Circuit 1289 shorted to Circuit 152B or ground.

Fig. 134 Code 81 — Solenoid circuit 1289 grounded

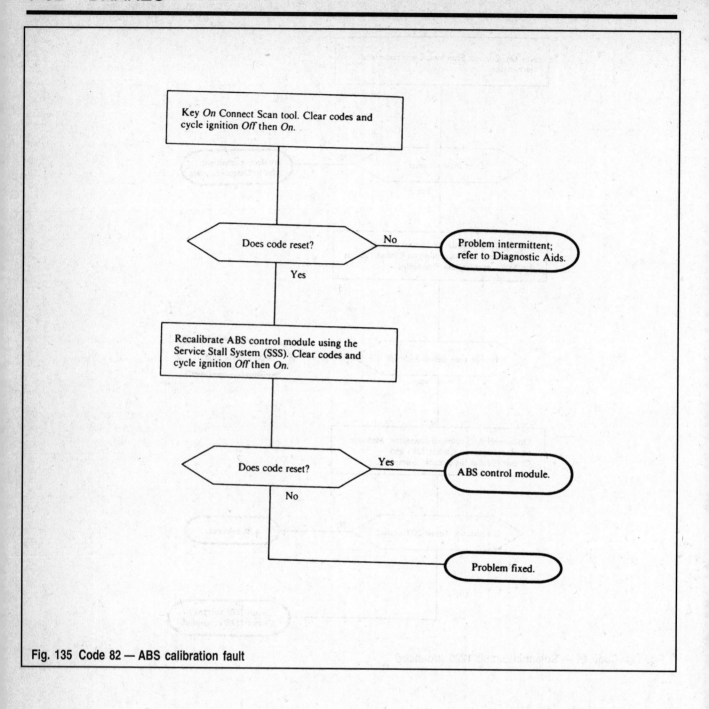

Fig. 135 Code 82 — ABS calibration fault

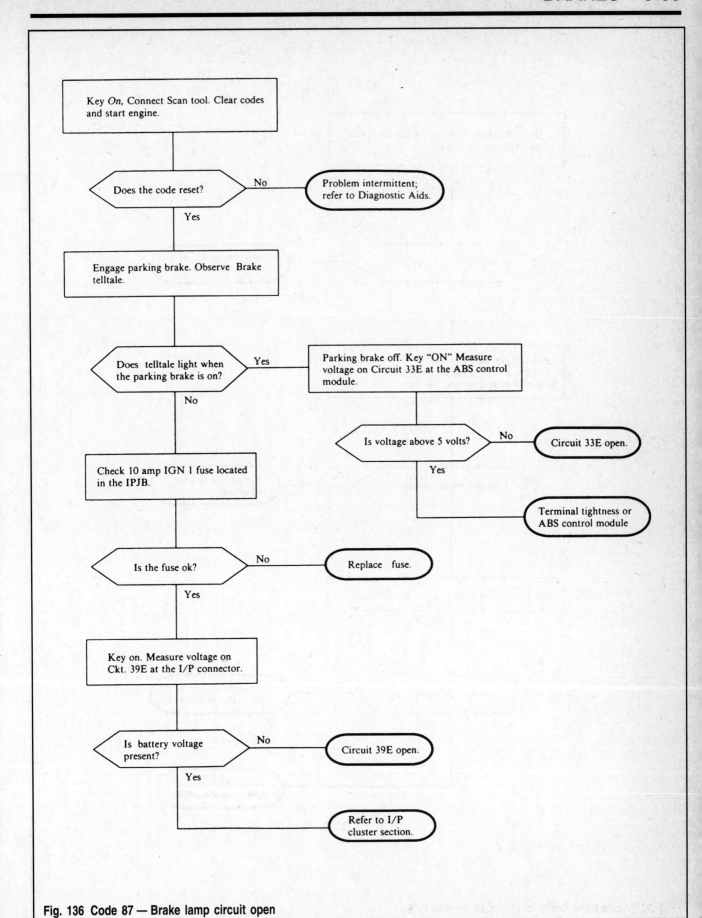

Fig. 136 Code 87 — Brake lamp circuit open

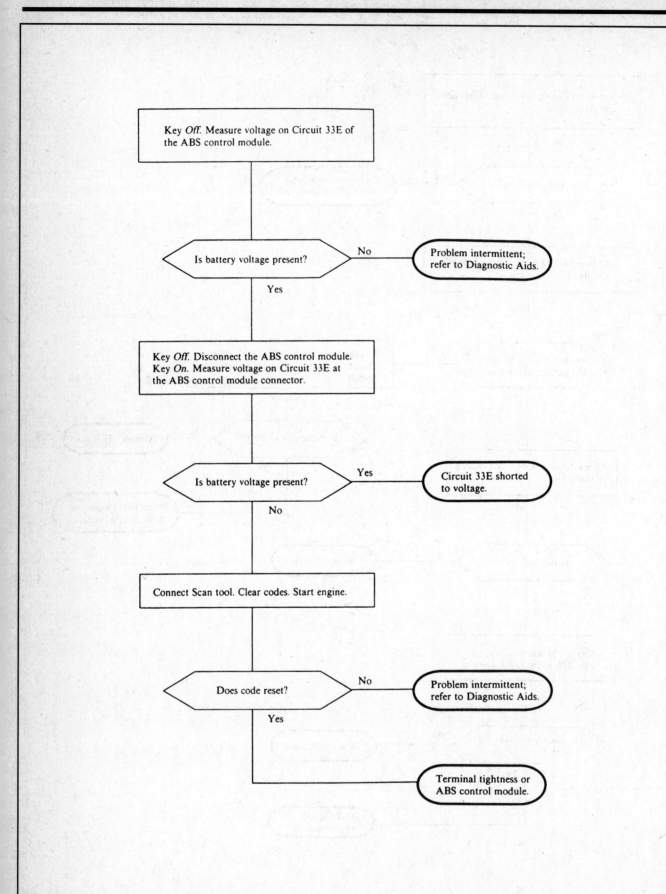

Fig. 137 Code 88 — Brake lamp circuit shorted to B+

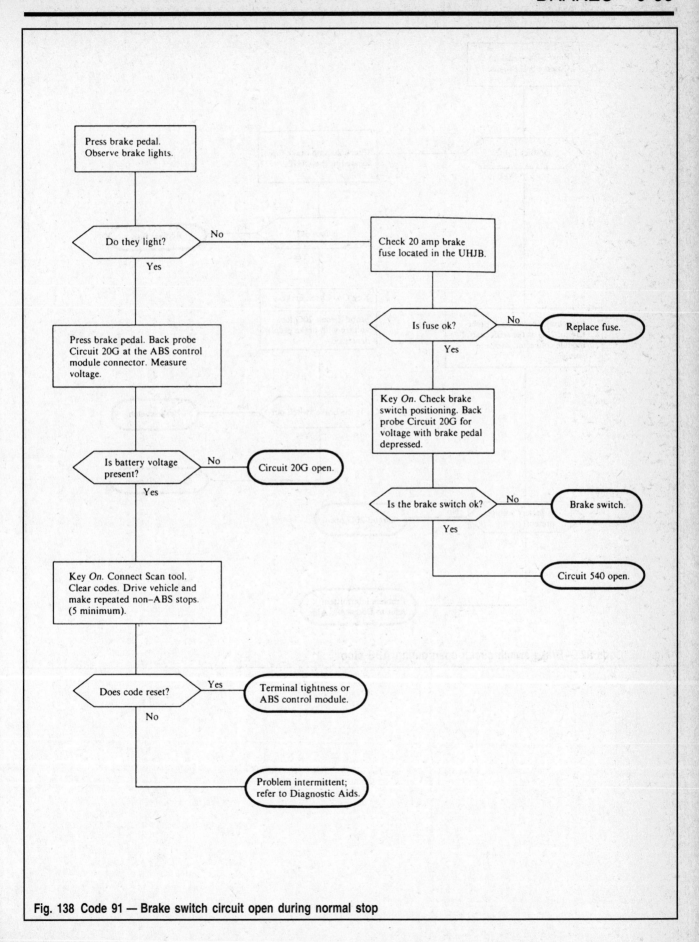

Fig. 138 Code 91 — Brake switch circuit open during normal stop

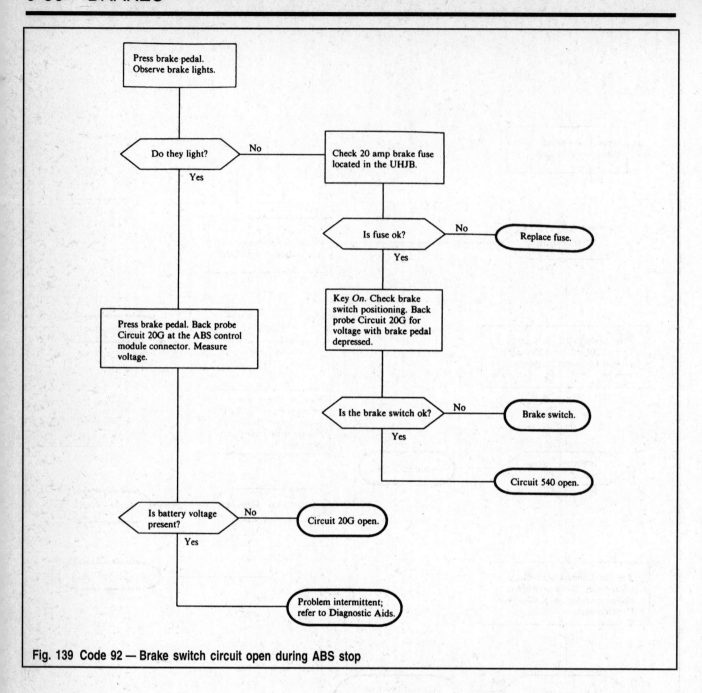

Fig. 139 Code 92 — Brake switch circuit open during ABS stop

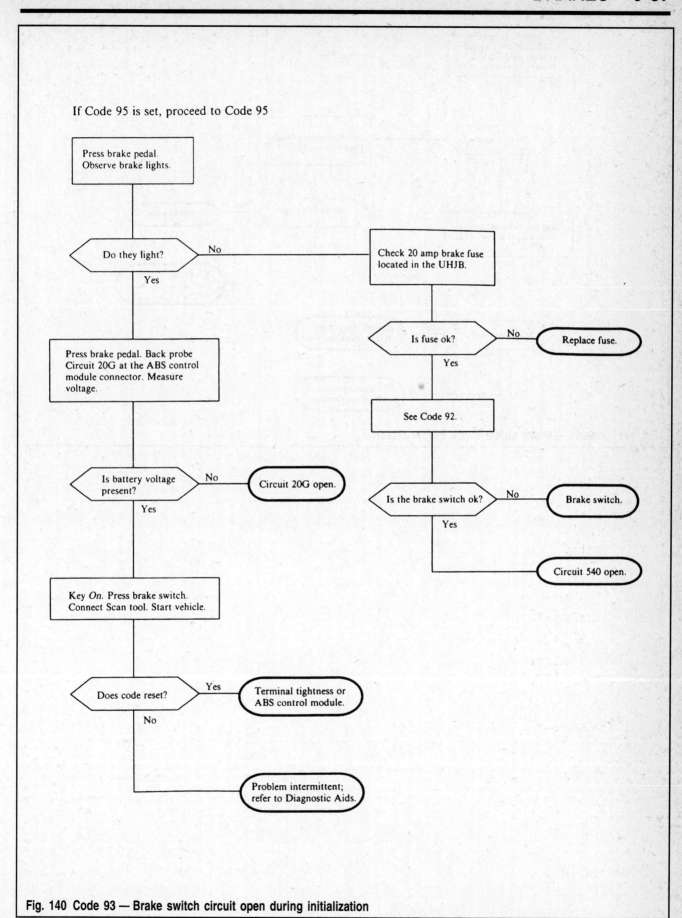

Fig. 140 Code 93 — Brake switch circuit open during initialization

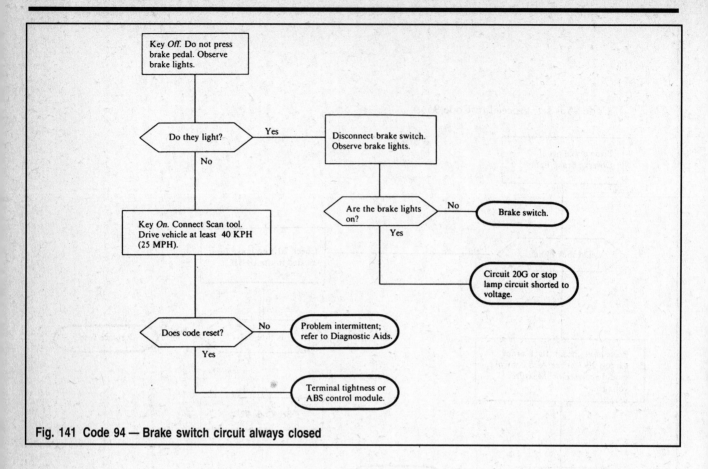

Fig. 141 Code 94 — Brake switch circuit always closed

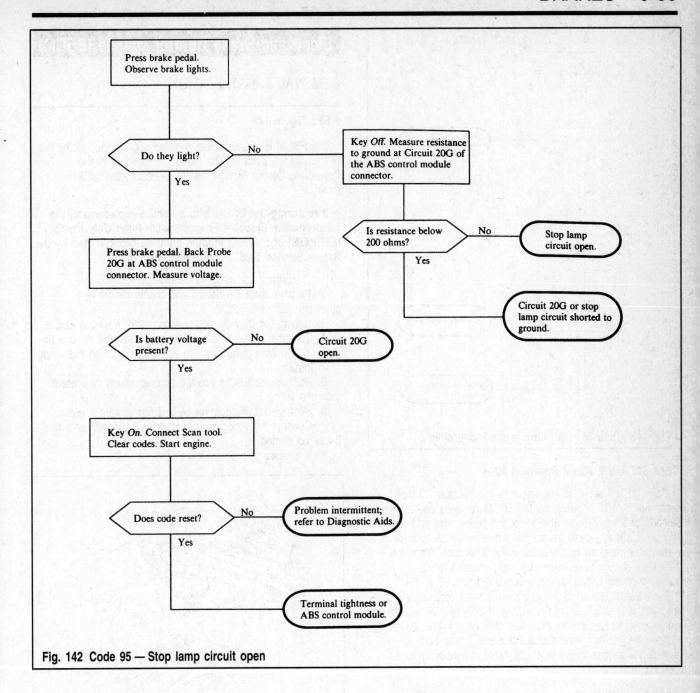

Fig. 142 Code 95 — Stop lamp circuit open

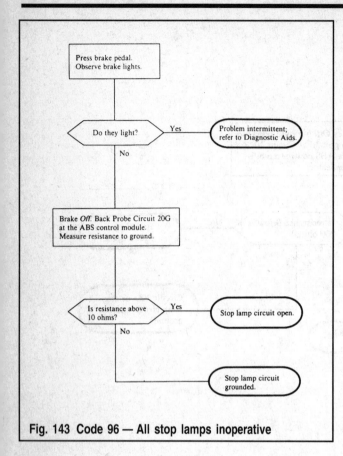

Fig. 143 Code 96 — All stop lamps inoperative

Code 31: Any 2 Wheel Speeds 0 MPH

Code 31 will set if vehicle speed is greater than 10 mph while not in ABS braking and the EBCM receives any 2 wheel speeds of 0 mph. To trouble shoot the code, raise and support the vehicle with jackstands so that wheels may be spun by hand while monitoring output using the scan tool. When the offending circuits have been identified, proceed to the troubleshooting charts for those codes (21, 22, 23 & 25).

Pay close attention to the circuit's electrical connectors since they are a likely cause of this output. If both rear wheels are determined to be causing the code, check the in-line connector located behind the driver's side kick panel or the body extension harness to the rear axle harness connector for a bad connection.

Code 86: Red Brake Lamp Commanded On By ABS Control Module

Code 86 will normally occur with another ABS code. If so, troubleshoot that code first before checking for a normal brake lamp illumination cause (such as low brake fluid). If Code 86 has been set alone (without another ABS code), the ABS EBCM should be replaced. This DOES NOT mean to replace the control module any time the red brake lamp comes on (as this is usually caused by a normal fault condition such as low brake fluid) but only if Code 86 is set without any other faults present.

Electronic Brake Control Module (EBCM)

REMOVAL & INSTALLATION

▶ **See Figure 144**

The EBCM is located under the instrument panel, to the left of the steering column. The module is outboard of the Powertrain Control Module (PCM), closest to the left kick panel.

➡**If replacing the EBCM with a service replacement, the Electronically Erasable Programmable Read Only Memory (EEPROM) of the new module must be programmed by the Saturn Service Stall or equivalent system.**

1. Disconnect the negative battery cable.
2. Remove the CPA device and unplug the 2-way connector form the EBCM.
3. Unplug the 32-way electrical connector from the EBCM.
4. Turn the module retaining screw ¼ turn and remove the module by pulling downward. Be careful not to snag the wiring.

To install:

5. Position the EBCM into the bracket, taking care not to snag the wiring.
6. Seat the retaining screw by pushing upward 2 clicks.
7. Connect the wiring and insert the CPA device onto the 2-way connector.
8. If necessary, program the EEPROM.

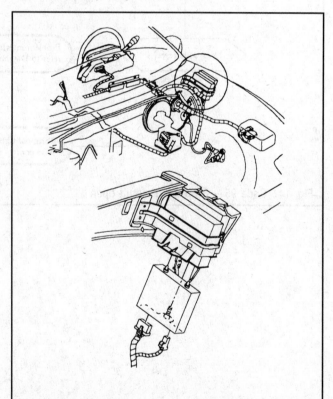

Fig. 144 The EBCM is located under the dash to the left of the steering column and next to the PCM

ABS Solenoid Valve

REMOVAL & INSTALLATION

▶ **See Figure 145**

The valves are located on top of the ABS control assembly which is mounted to the power brake booster. The valves are directly outboard of the master cylinder. There are 2 different valve types which can be identified by an 8 digit number etched on top of the valve and referenced in the Saturn parts catalog. Always be sure to use the correct replacement type.

1. Disconnect the negative battery cable, then clean the dirt from the area surrounding the solenoid valve.
2. Unplug the electrical connector from the valve.
3. Remove the 2 Torx® head retainers, then remove the solenoid.
4. Check to see if the O-ring remained in the valve groove and was lifted up from the modulator bore, as should occur if equipped with the type A solenoids. If using a type B solenoid, or if the type A O-ring remained in the bore, carefully extract the valve lip seal or O-ring from the modulator.

To install:

5. Lubricate the valve O-ring or lip seal with clean brake fluid and install onto the valve. O-rings should be installed into the groove provided on the solenoid. Lip seals should be inserted over the bottom of the valve with the lip or cupped side of the seal facing upward toward the solenoid top.

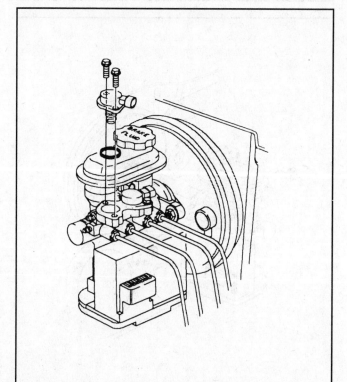

Fig. 145 The ABS solenoid valve is mounted to the top of the control assembly

6. Position the solenoid into the modulator and push downward until the valve flange is fully seated. Install the 2 screws and tighten to 45 inch lbs. (5 Nm).
7. Install the wiring harness electrical connector to the valve, then connect the negative battery cable.
8. Properly bleed the anti-lock brake system. Refer to the procedure later in this section.

ABS Control Assembly

The ABS control assembly consists of the solenoid valves, master cylinder and the hydraulic modulator.

REMOVAL & INSTALLATION

▶ **See Figures 146, 147, 148, 149, 150 and 151**

✳✳CAUTION

The ABS modulator pistons are normally in the HOME or top position. In this position the modulator drive gears are under spring tension and will turn during disassembly if not unloaded. The sudden rotation of gears and release of tension could cause injury if done without extreme care. It is recommended that the pistons be run down and the tension released prior to removing the brake control assembly if the unit is to be disassembled.

1. If removing the unit for disassembly, connect the Saturn Portable Diagnostic Tool (PDT), or an equivalent scan tool, and perform the RUN ABS MOTORS, PISTONS DOWN-REL test to run the modulator pistons down and release spring tension.
2. Disconnect the negative battery cable, then remove the battery box and battery from the vehicle.
3. Tag and unplug the 2 electrical connectors from the solenoids and the connector from the brake fluid level sensor on the lower side of the fluid reservoir.
4. Remove the CPA device from the motor pack 6-way connector and disengage the connector from the bottom of the motor pack.
5. Position a cloth to catch any escaping fluid, then tag and disconnect the brake lines from the control assembly. Plug the openings to prevent excessive fluid contamination or loss.

✳✳WARNING

Once the brake lines are disconnected, do not excessively pull or bend the lines away from the module or the lines may be damaged.

6. Remove the 2 brake control assembly-to-brake booster retaining nuts and remove the assembly.
7. If necessary, disassemble the unit as follows:
   a. Remove the 6 gear cover Torx® screws from the bottom of the assembly and remove the cover. If the entire motor pack assembly is being replaced, skip Step C, and then to the assembly procedure.
   b. Mark the location of the modulator drive gears for reassembly. Insert a small suitable prybar between the holes in the gears to keep them from moving and remove the 3

gear to driveshaft retaining nuts. Remove the gears from the modulator.

   c. Remove the 4 motor pack-to-modulator Torx® screws and separate the motor pack from the modulator.

   d. Remove the 2 modulator-to-master cylinder through-bolts and separate the master cylinder from the assembly.

   e. Remove the 2 transfer tubes and O-rings from the master cylinder and modulator.

   f. Remove the through-bolt O-rings from the master cylinder and modulator.

To install:

8. If necessary, assemble the ABS control unit as follows:

   a. Lubricate the new transfer tube O-rings with clean brake fluid. Press the NEW tubes and O-rings into the modulator by hand until fully bottomed.

   b. Lubricate the new through-bolt O-rings with clean fluid and install the rings into the master cylinder and modulator.

   c. Install the master cylinder onto the modulator, press the transfer tubes into position on the master cylinder.

   d. Install the through-bolts and tighten to 146 inch lbs. (16.5 Nm).

   e. Position the drive gears onto the driveshafts as noted earlier. Hold the gears from turning and tighten the retaining nuts to 75 inch lbs. (8.5 Nm).

   f. Hold the modulator upside down with the gears facing you and carefully rotate each gear counterclockwise until movement stops. This will position the pistons close to the top or HOME position and simplify the bleeding procedure.

   g. Position the motor pack to the modulator aligning the gears and install the 4 motor pack retaining screws. Tighten the screws to 40 inch lbs. (4.5 Nm).

   h. Install the gear cover onto the modulator assembly with the 6 retaining screws, then tighten the screws to 20 inch lbs. (2.25 Nm).

9. Position the control assembly onto the brake booster studs, install the retaining nuts and tighten to 20 ft. lbs. (27 Nm).

10. Position the brake lines into the control assembly as originally noted and tighten the fittings with to 18 ft. lbs. (24 Nm). From the front of the master cylinder moving back the lines are: LF, RR, LR and RF.

11. Install the 6-way wiring harness connector and insert the CPA device. Install the wiring harness connectors to the brake fluid level and 2 solenoid valve electrical connectors.

12. Connect the negative battery cable.

13. If the ABS pistons were run down for unit disassembly, connect the scan tool and perform the RUN ABS MOTORS, PISTONS UP-HOME test to restore tension to the modulator gears before moving the vehicle.

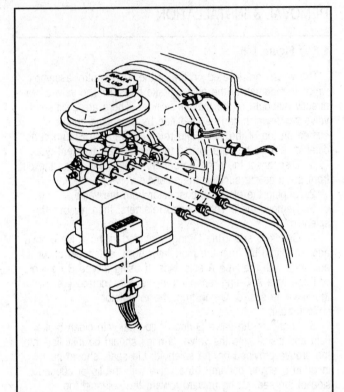

Fig. 146 Label and disconnect the wiring harnesses and brake lines from the control assembly

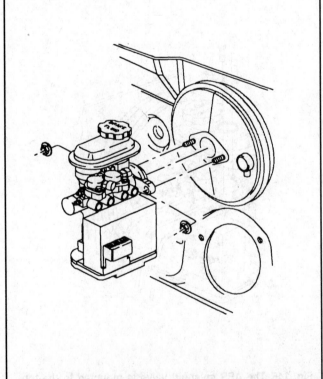

Fig. 147 Remove the control assembly from the brake booster

Fig. 148 View of the control assembly from the driver's side of the vehicle

brake fluid) before affective braking can occur. This will cause excessive brake pedal travel and reduced braking until the system is initialized (at a speed greater than 3 MPH) and the pistons are run back to the HOME position.

14. Fill the reservoir with clean brake fluid and properly bleed the ABS system.

Wheel Speed Sensors

REMOVAL & INSTALLATION

Front

▶ See Figures 152 and 153

1. Disconnect the negative battery cable, then raise the front of the vehicle and support using jackstands.
2. Unplug the electrical connector from the speed sensor.
3. Remove the Torx® head retaining screw from the top of the sensor.
4. Remove the wheel speed sensor from the vehicle.
5. Make sure the sensor locating pin was removed with the sensor. If the pin remained in the knuckle, pull it out with a pair of pliers. A pin which is stuck in the knuckle must be drilled out with an 8mm drill bit. Be very careful not to enlarge the locating hole in the knuckle; incorrect sensor location would result in loss of ABS operation.
6. Use a small wooden dowel with sand paper wrapped around it to clean the locating hole of any corrosion and allow proper sensor seating.
To install:
7. Position the sensor to the steering knuckle, making sure that it is fully seated.
8. Install the fastener and tighten to 89 inch lbs. (10 Nm).
9. Install the wiring harness connector to the sensor.
10. Remove the supports and lower the vehicle, then connect the negative battery cable.

Rear

The rear ABS speed sensor is contained within the hub and bearing assembly and is not serviceable. If the sensor is damaged and in need of replacement, the entire hub and bearing assembly must be replaced. Refer to the rear suspension procedures in Section No. 8 of this manual.

Bleeding the Anti-lock Brake System

▶ See Figures 154, 155 and 156

➡ Prior to bleeding the rear brakes, the rear displacement cylinder pistons must be returned to the top most position or home. To return the pistons to the home position, use a Scan tool to perform special test, RUN ABS PISTONS UP-HOME. This test will run the piston to the top of their travel.

1. Fill the master cylinder with clean brake fluid and keep the reservoir at least ½ full during the bleeding operation.
2. Prime the control assembly as follows:
   a. Attach a clear tube to the rear bleeder valve and submerge the tube to in a transparent container of clean brake fluid.
   b. Slowly open the valve ½-¾ of a turn, then have a friend depress the brake pedal.
   c. Hold the brake pedal until fluid begins to flow from the valve, then close the valve and release the pedal.
   d. Tighten the valve to 62 inch lbs. (7 Nm).
   e. Repeat the procedure at the front bleeder valve.
3. Once fluid flows from both control assembly valves, it may not be completely purged of air. To assure that the unit is free of air, bleed the calipers to remove air from the system's lowest points, then return and bleed the control assembly one last ti
4. Bleed the calipers in the proper order:
   a. Right rear
   b. Left rear
   c. Right front
   d. Left front

➡ If when performing the bleed procedure on the rear calipers, brake fluid does not come out of the bleeder, the rear displacement pistons may not be at the home or top position.

5. Bleed each caliper, in the proper order, as follows:
   a. Attach a clear tube to the caliper bleeder valve and submerge the other end of the tube in a transparent container of clean brake flu
   b. Open the valve ½-¾ of a turn, then have a friend slowly depress the brake pedal and hold.
   c. Watch for air bubbles as the fluid begins to flow from the valve, then close the valve and release the pedal.
   d. Wait 5 seconds and repeat until the pedal feels firm and no air is present in the brake line.
   e. Tighten the valve to 97 inch lbs. (11 Nm).
6. Bleed the control assembly from the 2 valves in the same fashion as the calipers are bled. Tighten the bleeder valves to 62 inch lbs. (7 Nm) when finished.
7. Check the pedal for excessive travel both with the engine **OFF** and with the engine running. If pedal feel is firm go to Step 11.
8. If the pedal feel is not firm, use a Scan tool to run the ABS motor up and down 2 times, make sure the pistons are run up to the home position.
9. Start the engine, let the engine run for 2 seconds after the ABS light goes out then turn the engine **OFF**. Repeat the ignition cycle 9 more times.
10. Re-bleed the entire system.

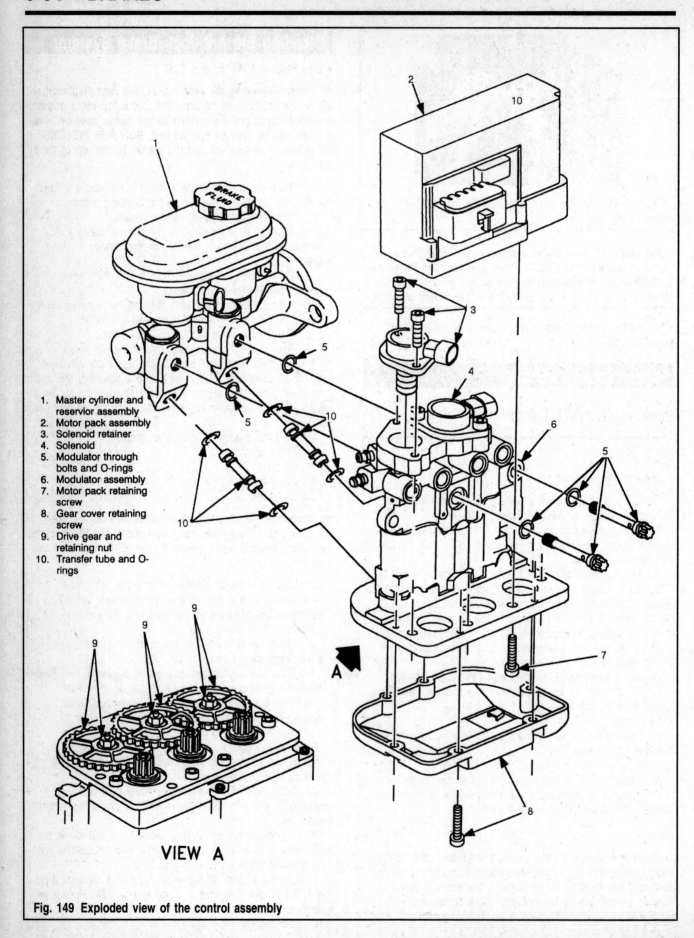

1. Master cylinder and reservoir assembly
2. Motor pack assembly
3. Solenoid retainer
4. Solenoid
5. Modulator through bolts and O-rings
6. Modulator assembly
7. Motor pack retaining screw
8. Gear cover retaining screw
9. Drive gear and retaining nut
10. Transfer tube and O-rings

VIEW A

Fig. 149 Exploded view of the control assembly

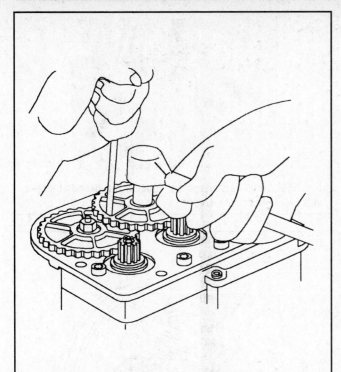

Fig. 150 Use a small prybar in the holes to secure the modulator gears and loosen the drive shaft nuts

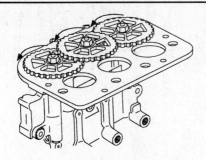

Fig. 151 Gently turn the gears by hand to position the pistons towards the top of the modulator bores

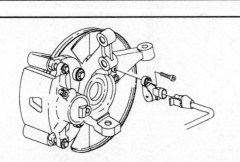

Fig. 152 The front wheel speed sensor in mounted to the steering knuckle and is replaceable separate from other components

Fig. 153 View of the knuckle mounted speed sensor and the sensor ring which is part of the halfshaft/CV-joint assembly — front ABS brakes

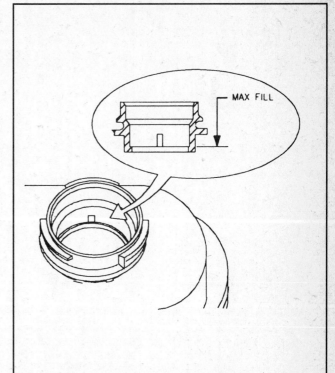

MAX FILL

Fig. 154 On all Saturns, the brake fluid reservoir fill line is equal with the base of the fill neck

11. With the engine running and brake applied, check the system for leaks.

12. Road test the vehicle and make several normal, non-ABS stops. Then make 1-2 ABS stops from a higher speed (about 50 MPH).

13. After road testing the vehicle it is recommended that the entire system be bled and inspected 1 final time.

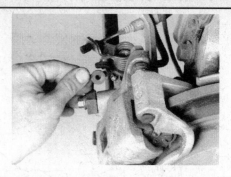

Fig. 156 Attach a transparent tube to the caliper bleeder valve — rear brakes shown

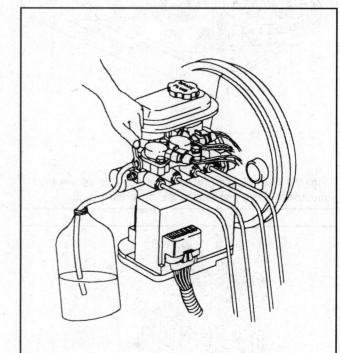

Fig. 155 Attach a transparent tube from the front bleeder screw into a container partially filled with clean brake fluid

BRAKE SPECIFICATIONS

All measurements in inches unless noted.

Year	Model	Master Cylinder Bore	Brake Disc			Brake Drum Diameter			Minimum Lining Thickness	
			Original Thickness	Minimum Thickness	Maximum Runout	Original Inside Diameter	Max. Wear Limit	Maximum Machine Diameter	Front	Rear
1991	All	NA	0.710①	0.633②	0.005	7.87	7.93	7.90	3/32	3/32
1992-93	All	NA	0.710①	0.633②	0.005	7.87	7.93	7.90	3/32	3/32

NA—Not available
① Rear Disc: 0.430
② Rear Disc: 0.370
NOTE: Both front and rear disc specifications are minimums to which the rotors may be machined. The discard wear limit is 0.625 for front discs and 0.350 for rear discs.

TORQUE SPECIFICATIONS

Component	U.S.	Metric
ABS control assembly retaining nuts	20 ft. lbs.	27 Nm
ABS modulator drive gear nuts	75 inch lbs.	8.5 Nm
ABS modulator gear cover screws	20 inch lbs.	2.25 Nm
ABS modulator solenoid screws	45 inch lbs.	5 Nm
ABS modulator through-bolts	146 inch lbs.	16.5 Nm
ABS motor pack screws	40 inch lbs.	4.5 Nm
ABS speed sensor-to-steering knuckle fastener	89 inch lbs.	10 Nm
Bleeder valve screw;		
ABS control assembly	62 inch lbs.	7 Nm
Caliper	97 inch lbs.	11 Nm
Wheel cylinder	62 inch lbs.	7 Nm
Brake booster nuts	20 ft. lbs.	27 Nm
Brake hoses/lines;		
Brake line female repair union	14 ft. lbs.	19 Nm
Front hose-to-line	18 ft. lbs.	24 Nm
Hose-to-wheel cylinder/caliper	36 ft. lbs.	49 Nm
Master cylinder/ABS control assembly	18 ft. lbs.	24 Nm
Rear hose-to-line	14 ft. lbs.	19 Nm
Brake pedal pivot bolt	16 ft. lbs.	22 Nm
Caliper lock/guide pins	27 ft. lbs.	36 Nm
Caliper support bracket assembly bolts;		
Front	81 ft. lbs.	110 Nm
Rear	63 ft. lbs.	85 Nm
Master cylinder retaining nuts	20 ft. lbs.	27 Nm
Park brake cable bracket-to-floor pan nut	25 inch lbs.	2.8 Nm
Park brake lever assembly;		
Bolts	35 ft. lbs.	47 Nm
Nuts	23 ft. lbs.	31 Nm
Park brake lever indicator switch retainer	53 inch lbs.	6 Nm
Rear hub and bearing assembly bolts	63 ft. lbs.	85 Nm
Seat belt retractor fasteners	52 ft. lbs.	70 Nm
Trailing arm/park cable-to-body bolts	89 ft. lbs.	120 Nm
Wheel cylinder-to-backing plate retainers	89 inch lbs.	10 Nm

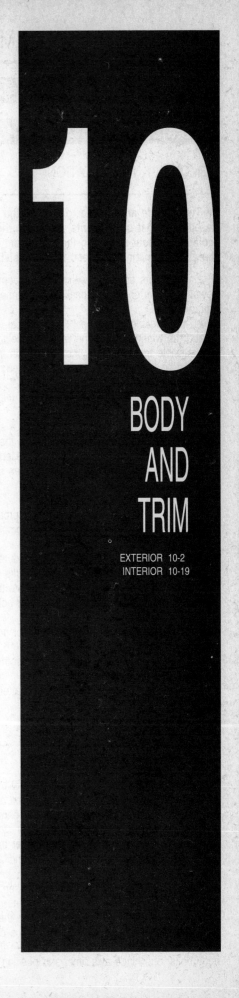

10

BODY AND TRIM

EXTERIOR

Doors

REMOVAL & INSTALLATION

➡ **Two people are needed to replace the entire door assembly. Most components, including the hinges, may be replaced without removing the door from the vehicle and thereby eliminating the need for an assistant.**

1. For Doors equipped with electrical components such as power windows or stereo speakers, disconnect the negative battery cable.

2. If applicable, disconnect the electrical wiring boot and unplug the wiring. Should the wiring connectors be unaccessible from the boot, the interior trim panel(s) must be removed so the wires may be disconnected. Refer to the procedure later in this sections.

3. Remove the check link bolt(s) from the door or the body, whichever is accessible.

4. If the door is to be reinstalled, use a soft marker to outline the hinge positioning in relation to the door assembly.

5. While a friend supports the door assembly, remove the bolts attaching the hinges to the door, then remove the door from the vehicle.

To install:

6. Have a friend support the door assembly to the vehicle and secure using the bolts, but do not completely tighten at this time.

7. Adjust the door. Refer to the procedure later in this section. If reinstalling a door, use the marks made during removal as a starting point and adjust from there, as necessary. Then tighten the hinge-to-door bolts to 26 ft. lbs. (35 Nm).

8. Secure the check link to the door or body using the retaining bolt(s) and tighten to 12 ft. lbs. (16 Nm).

9. Connect the door wiring, then install the trim panel(s) and wiring boot, as applicable.

10. If removed, connect the negative battery cable.

ADJUSTMENT

▶ **See Figures 1, 2 and 3**

1. Determine if adjustment is necessary by opening and closing the door checking for proper fit and alignment. Make sure the door does not bind on adjacent panels.

2. If adjustment is necessary, the door striker must be removed from the body. Use a soft marker to scribe alignment marks, then remove the screws, striker and, if present, shim(s) to allow for proper door adjustment.

3. To adjust the door up or down, loosen the loosen the 4 hinge-to-door bolts and position the door as needed.

4. To adjust the door in or out, loosen the 4 hinge-to-door bolts, one hinge at a time, and position the door as needed.

5. To adjust the door fore or aft, loosen the 4 hinge-to-body bolts, one hinge at a time, and position as needed.

6. When the door has been properly adjusted, tighten the hinge bolts to 26 ft. lbs. (35 Nm).

7. Loosely install the striker, screws and, if present, the shims. Align the striker with the marks made during removal and tighten the retainers to 18 ft. lbs. (25 Nm). Check striker alignment by closing the door.

8. If necessary, adjust the striker alignment. The striker may be adjusted up and down or in and out by loosening the screws and repositioning the striker. Fore and aft adjustments are made by adding or removing shims from the behind the striker. When adjustments are made, tighten the screws to 18 ft. lbs. (25 Nm).

Hood

REMOVAL & INSTALLATION

▶ **See Figure 4**

1. Open the hood and position fender covers to protect the paint. It may also be useful to position rags on top of the firewall, behind the hinges, to protect the vehicle and the hood should is slide back onto the firewall when the bolts are loosened.

2. Using a soft marker, scribe alignment lines of the hood's position on the hinges.

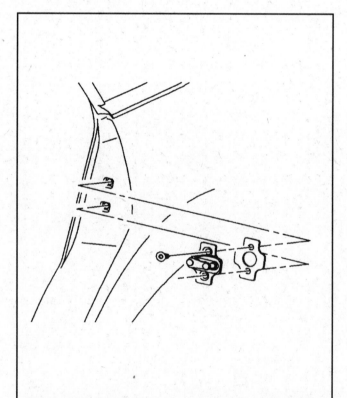

Fig. 1 The striker must be removed when adjusting the door assembly

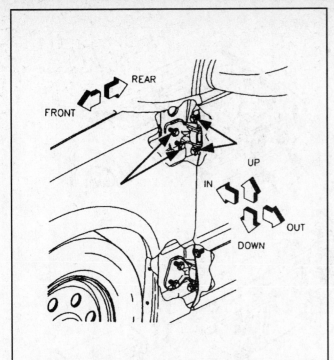

Fig. 2 Body bolts are loosened only to make front and rearward door adjustments, all other adjustments are made by loosening the door bolts

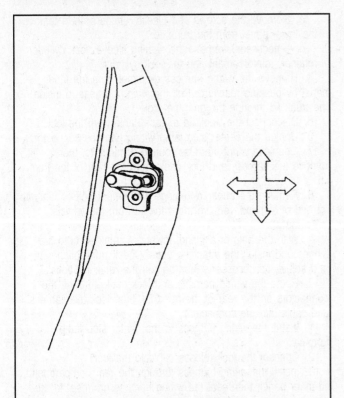

Fig. 3 The striker panel may be adjusted up, down, in or out by loosening the retaining bolts

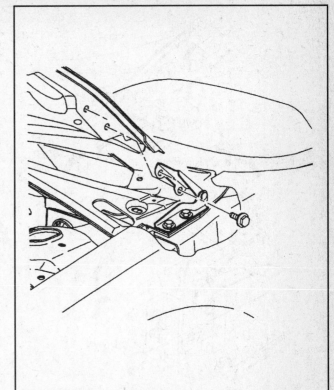

Fig. 4 The hood is attached to the hinges with 2 bolts on each side of the vehicle

3. Have 2 friends hold the hood and remove the 4 retaining bolts. Be careful not to let the hood slip backwards and onto the vehicle when the bolts are removed.

4. Carefully lift the hood from the vehicle. If the hood is to be stored standing, be sure to place rags or protective foam under the hood to protect the paint.

To install:

5. Have your friends lift the hood and position it to the hinges. Make sure the hood aligns with the marks made earlier, then install the retaining bolts.

6. Remove the fender covers, then check and adjust hood alignment, as necessary. Refer to the procedure later in this section. Once the hood is properly adjusted, tighten the retaining bolts to 19 ft. lbs. (25 Nm).

ADJUSTMENT

⏵ **See Figure 5**

1. To adjust the hood fore, aft and cross-car, loosen the hinge-to-body bolts and position the hood, as needed.

2. To adjust the hood up and down at the rear, loosen the hinge-to-hood bolts and position the hood, as needed.

3. To adjust the hood up and down at the front, the hood latch and/or the hood bumpers may be repositioned. The hood latch may be adjusted by loosening the retainers and positioning the latch, as needed. The bumpers are adjusted by turning them to raise or lower their positions, as needed.

4. When all adjustments are completed, tighten the hinge bolts to 19 ft. lbs. (25 Nm) and the hood latch bolts to 89 inch lbs. (10 Nm).

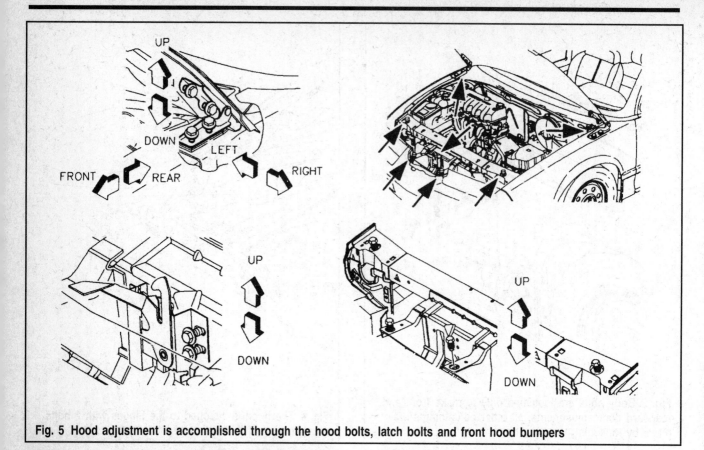

Fig. 5 Hood adjustment is accomplished through the hood bolts, latch bolts and front hood bumpers

Trunk Lid/Liftgate

REMOVAL & INSTALLATION

COUPE AND SEDAN

▶ See Figures 6, 7, 8 and 9

1. Disconnect the negative battery cable.
2. For Sedans, remove the trunk lid center panel and lower outer panel assemblies, as follows:

  a. Remove the trunk center panel assembly bolts, then rotate the panel outboard at the bottom and remove the panel from the vehicle.

  b. Remove the license plate, then disconnect the lock rod from the trunk lock cylinder pawl.

  c. Remove the lower outer panel attachment bolts.

  d. Disengage the panel bottom flange from the inner panel by pulling the top of the panel rearward and the lower panel downward.

  e. Remove the wiring harness retainer clip, then disconnect the license plate bulb sockets from the lamps.

  f. Remove the trunk lid lower outer panel from the vehicle.

3. For Coupes, remove the trunk lid lower panel, as follows:

  a. Remove the retaining screws from the reflex panels located on either side of the trunk lid, then remove the panels from the lid.

  b. Remove the clip and disconnect the lock rod from the lock cylinder.

  c. Remove the screws and plastic retainers, then remove the lower panel from the trunk lid.

  d. If necessary, remove the sealing sleeve, lock cylinder retainer, reinforcement and the lock cylinder.

4. Remove the wiring harness grommet from the inner panel by pushing rearward. Pull the wiring harness to inside the trunk lid through the grommet hole.
5. Disconnect the trunk lid release cable from the lock.
6. Unplug the center stop lamp wiring harness connector.
7. Open the wiring harness routing connectors, then remove the harness and lock cable from the rear of the trunk lid.
8. Remove the trunk lid-to-hinge attachment bolts, then with the aid of a friend, remove the trunk lid from the vehicle.

To install:

9. With the help of a friend, lower the trunk lid onto the hinges and install the attaching bolts. Check trunk alignment and adjust, as necessary, then tighten the retaining bolts.
10. Route the wiring harness and lock cable through the connectors on the rear of the trunk lid, then lock the harness and cable into the connectors.
11. Install the wiring harness to the center stop lamp terminal.
12. Connect the lock release cable to the lock.
13. Install the wiring harness through the rear compartment lid inner panel, then seat the wiring harness grommet to the panel.
14. For Coupes, install the trunk lid lower panel:

  a. If removed, install the lock cylinder into the panel, then install the reinforcement and retainer to the lock cylinder. Install the sealing sleeve to the cylinder.

b. Install the lower panel to the trunk lid and secure using the retaining screws. Tighten the screws slowly and evenly to 53 inch lbs. (6 Nm), using multiple passes.

c. Connect the lock rod to the lock cylinder using the clip.

d. Install the reflex panels using the retaining screws. Make sure the sealing feature of the screws and panels is adequate. If necessary, replace the seals or apply a body caulking compound to make sure no water or moisture will intrude.

15. For the Sedan, install the trunk lid lower outer panel and center panel assemblies, as follows:

a. Position the lower outer panel to the trunk lid and connect the license plate bulb sockets to the license plate lamps.

b. Connect the wiring harness retainer clip to the trunk lid lower outer panel.

c. Install the bottom flange of the lower outer panel over the lower edge of the trunk lid inner panel, then install the attaching bolts and tighten to 53 inch lbs. (6 Nm).

d. Connect the lock rod to the lock cylinder pawl.

e. Position the upper edge of the center panel to the trunk lid, then rotate the bottom of the center panel inboard.

f. Check to see that the sealing feature of the bolts is adequate, and if necessary replace the bolts or seal using a body caulking compound to protect against water intrusion.

g. Loosely install the attaching bolts and check the panel alignment. Adjust the alignment, as necessary and tighten the bolts. Install the license plate.

16. Connect the negative battery cable.

Wagon

▶ See Figure 10

1. Disconnect the negative battery cable.

2. Remove the trim access plate from the inner liftgate trim panel.

3. Unplug the wiring connectors and the window washer hose.

4. Remove the rubber grommet between the liftgate and body, then retrieve the wires and washer hose from the liftgate.

5. Either support the liftgate using a prop or have a friend hold the liftgate, then remove the liftgate struts.

6. Use a soft marker to scribe small alignment marks for installation purposes. With the help of a friend, remove the hinge attachment bolts from the liftgate and remove the liftgate from the vehicle.

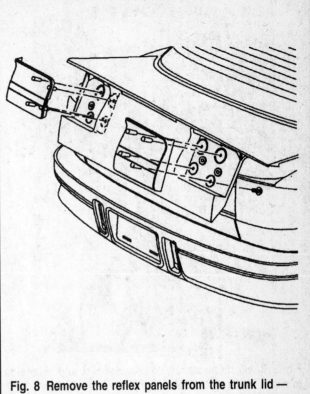

Fig. 8 Remove the reflex panels from the trunk lid — Coupe

To install:

7. Raise the liftgate into position and align the marks made during removal, then install the gate to the hinges and tighten the bolts to 89 inch lbs. (10 Nm).

8. Install the struts.

9. Check and adjust the liftgate alignment, as necessary.

10. Route the wiring harness and washer hose through the liftgate, then connect the harness to the terminals and hose to the window washer.

11. Install the trim panel access plate.

12. Install the rubber grommet between the liftgate and the body.

13. Connect the negative battery cable.

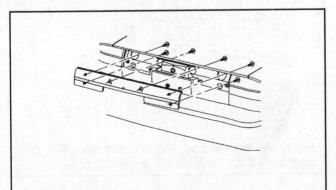

Fig. 6 Trunk lid center panel assembly — Sedan

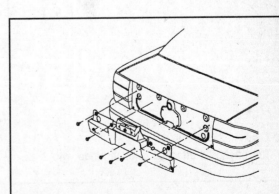

Fig. 7 Trunk lid lower outer panel assembly — Sedan

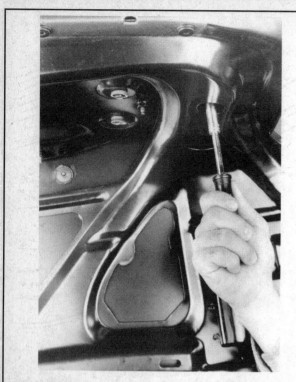

Fig. 9 It will be necessary to use a socket and extension to reach some of the reflex panel screws which are recessed in the trunk lid — Coupe

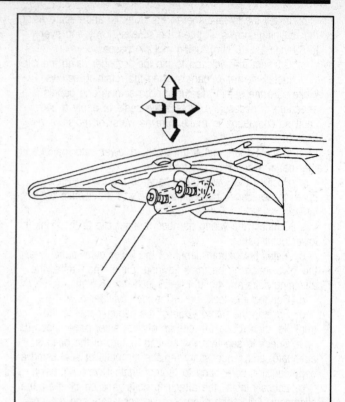

Fig. 11 The front of the trunk lid is adjusted using the hinge bolts

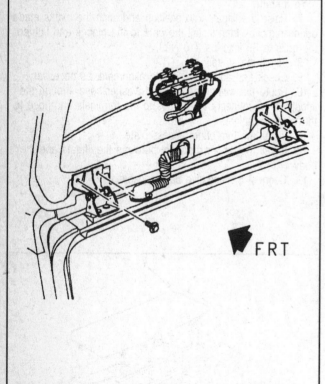

Fig. 10 The liftgate is attached to each hinge with 2 bolts

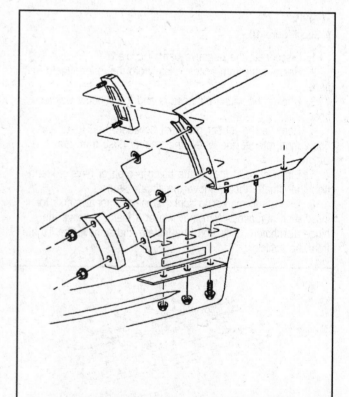

Fig. 12 Remove the stud plate nuts and disconnect the front fascia from the fenders — except SC or SC2

ADJUSTMENT

Coupe and Sedan
▶ See Figure 11

1. To adjust the trunk lid cross-car, loosen the hinge-to-package shelf retainers and position the assembly, as needed.

2. To adjust the front of the trunk lid fore, aft, up or down, loosen the lid-to-hinge arm bolts and position the lid, as needed.

3. To adjust the rear of the trunk lid up and down, loosen the striker retainers and move the striker upward or downward, as needed.

4. When all adjustments are made, tighten the package shelf retainers to 19 ft. lbs. (25 Nm). Tighten the trunk lid bolts and/or striker bolts to 89 inch lbs. (10 Nm).

Wagon

The Wagon liftgate may be adjusted up, down or cross-car by loosening the hinge-to-liftgate bolts. Fore and aft adjustments are usually made using the hinge-to-body bolts.

Bumpers

REMOVAL & INSTALLATION

Front

EXCEPT SC or SC2
▶ See Figures 12, 13 and 14

1. Disconnect the negative battery cable.

2. If equipped with A/C, disconnect the fascia from the air duct by removing the lower retention screws.

3. Remove the rear bolt from the front upper support bracket assembly and loosen the forward attachment nuts. All fasteners are located at the horizontal fender-to-fascia joint.

4. Remove the side marker lamp socket from the marker lamp.

5. Remove the headlamp housing assemblies by removing the housing attachment bolts from the braces-to-radiator support upper and lower locations. Pull the headlamp assembly up and forward, then disconnect the bulb and turn signal sockets from the housing. Remove the housing from the vehicle.

6. Disconnect the front fascia-to-fender attachments by removing the nuts from the stud plates. Remove the vertical stud plates and reinforcements.

7. Remove the fascia center support-to-latch bracket forward bolts, then loosen the rear bolts (slotted holes).

8. Remove the upper and lower fascia assembly from the vehicle.

9. Remove the plastic fasteners, then remove the energy absorber.

10. Remove the air deflector-to-tow pad attachment bolts.

11. Remove the impact bar (bumper)-to-frame rail attachment nuts from the plate bolts.

12. Remove the impact bar and, if necessary, remove the towing pad attachment nuts and bolts.

To install:
13. If removed, install the towing pad attachment nuts and bolts.

14. Check the insulator-to-impact bar at attachment locations. Replace, if missing or damaged.

15. Install the stud plate bolts to the impact bar, then install the impact bar to the frame.

16. Install the energy absorber.

17. Install the air deflector assembly.

18. Position the front fascia assembly over the front bumper energy absorber, then install the fascia ends over the studs extending down from the front fender upper support bracket assembly. Holes in the fascia are slotted to allow for installation without removing the studs. The front fascia support plate should be on the lower side of the fascia.

19. Install the fascia center support-to-latch support bracket forward bolts. Align the fascia center to hood and tighten the rear bolts.

20. Install the front fender stud plates and reinforcements. Align the fascia to the fender and tighten the bolts. Align the fascia to the fender (horizontal side joints), then install the rear bolts in the upper support bracket assembly and tighten the bolts and nuts.

21. Install the headlamp bulb sockets and turn signal sockets into the headlamp assembly.

22. Install the headlamp housing assemblies.

23. Install the side marker lamp sockets to the side marker lamps, then connect the fascia to the air duct.

24. Connect the negative battery cable and adjust the headlamps.

SC or SC2
▶ See Figures 15 and 16

1. Disconnect the negative battery cable.

2. Disconnect the fascia from the air duct, wheel liner and wheelhouse closeout panel by removing the retaining bolts.

3. Lower the front half of the wheelhouse liner by removing the front screws and retainers.

4. Disconnect the fascia from the fender by removing the nuts and plate from the horizontal fender-to-fascia joint.

5. Remove the upper fascia-to-headlamp assembly bolts.

6. Remove the upper fascia support bracket-to-hood latch reinforcement retaining screws.

7. Remove the fascia assembly by raising and moving the forward at the upper fascia support to clear the hood bumpers.

8. Disconnect the tow block from the air dam by removing the fasteners.

9. Drill out the rivets attaching the energy absorber to the bumper bar, then remove the energy absorber.

10. Remove the bumper to frame rail attachment nuts from the plate bolts, then remove the bumper from the vehicle.

11. If replacing the bumper, remove the nuts and bolts, then remove the support blocks.

To install:
12. If replacing the bumper, install the support blocks with nuts and bolts.

13. Check the insulator-to-impact bar at attachment locations. Replace, if missing or damaged.

14. Install the stud plate bolts to the bumper with the retainer clips, then install the bumper to the vehicle with the attaching nuts.

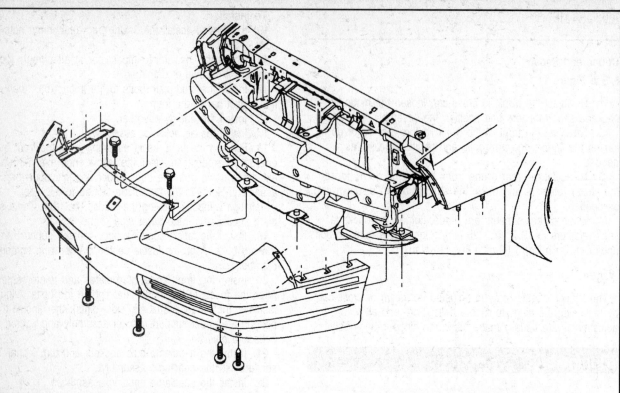

Fig. 13 Remove or loosen the retainers, as necessary, then remove the front upper and lower fascia assembly from the vehicle — except SC or SC2

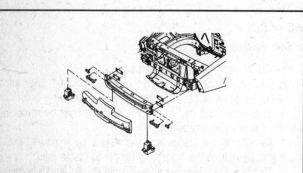

Fig. 14 Exploded view of the front energy absorber and bumper assembly — except SC or SC2

15. Install the energy absorber using rivets.

16. Position the fascia assembly over the energy absorber and lift the upper fascia support bracket to clear the hood bumpers.

17. Install the upper fascia support bracket-to-hood latch reinforcement by loosely installing the retaining bolts. Align the fascia to the fender and tighten the fasteners.

18. Install the fascia ends over the studs extending down from the front fender-to-fascia stud plate, then install the reinforcement plate and nuts. Align the fascia to the fender and tighten the nuts.

19. Install the upper fascia-to-headlamp assembly retaining bolts.

20. Raise the front half of the wheelhouse liner into position, then install the retaining screws and fasteners.

21. Connect the fascia-to-air duct, wheelhouse liner and wheelhouse closeout panel by installing the retaining screws.

22. Connect the negative battery cable.

Rear

EXCEPT SC or SC2

▶ See Figures 17 and 18

1. Raise the trunk lid, then remove the plastic retainers from the bumper filler and remove the filler from the vehicle.

2. Remove the plastic retainers from the rear fascia bottom-to-fascia support brackets.

3. Remove the screws from the wheelhouse liners-to-rear fascia, then slide the fascia assembly rearward and from the vehicle.

4. Using a suitable punch, drive the center pins from the rivets attaching the energy absorber bar. Drill out the rivets, then remove the energy absorber bar.

5. Remove the nuts from the bumper stud plates, then remove the bolts from the lower attachment locations.

6. Remove the bumper assembly from the vehicle. If necessary, remove the push nuts, stud plates and insulators.

To install:

7. If removed, install the insulators over the bumper to prevent bumper-to-body contact. Replace insulators which are torn or damaged.

8. If removed, install the stud plates through the bumper and insulator, then secure using the push nuts.

9. Install the bumper to the vehicle, then secure using the nuts and lower attachment bolts.

10. Install the energy absorber bar to the bumper using rivets.

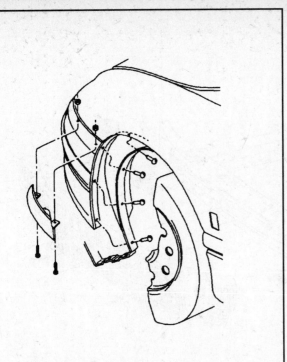

Fig. 15 Remove the front screws and retainers from the wheelhouse liner, then disconnect the horizontal fender-to-fascia joint — SC or SC2

11. Position the fascia assembly over the bumper and energy absorber. Engage the key slot fascia ends over the

studs extending down the from the quarter panel and push the fascia forward to lock onto the quarter panels.

12. Install the screws into the wheelhouse liner and fascia ends.

13. Install the plastic retainers to bottom of the fascia and support brackets.

14. Install the bumper filler, then align and install the plastic retainers.

SC or SC2

▶ **See Figures 19 and 20**

1. Disconnect the negative battery cable.
2. Remove the lower wheelhouse-to-fascia screws.
3. Remove the pushpin fasteners from the fascia. Remove the fascia retainer at the top of the fascia.

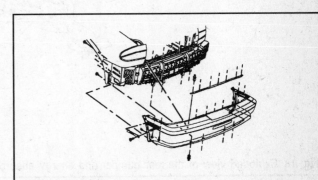

Fig. 17 Exploded view of the rear fascia mounting — Sedan and Wagon

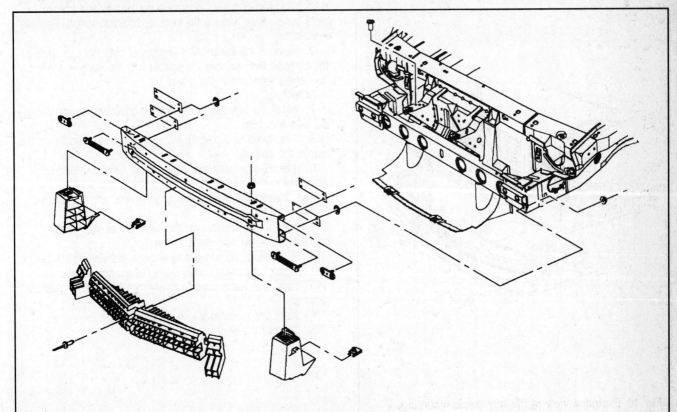

Fig. 16 Exploded view of the front bumper and energy absorber assembly

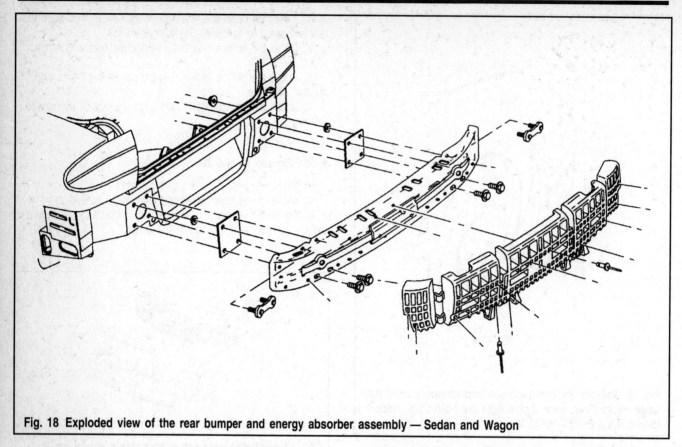

Fig. 18 Exploded view of the rear bumper and energy absorber assembly — Sedan and Wagon

4. Slide the fascia backwards sufficiently, then unplug the backup lamp and license plate lamp electrical connectors.

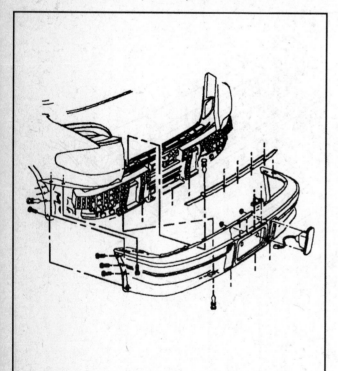

Fig. 19 Exploded view of the rear fascia mounting — Coupe

5. Remove the fascia from the vehicle.

6. If necessary, remove the license plate screws, license plate and push-in screws. Remove the screws and license plate lamps, then remove the nuts and backup lamps. Remove the J-nuts.

7. Remove the lower bolts and upper nuts from the face of the bumper, then remove the spacer and the bumper assembly from the energy absorbing drives.

To install:

8. Install the bumper to the energy absorbing drives using the nuts and bolts.

9. If removed or replaced, install the energy absorber to the rear of the bumper.

10. If removed, install the J-clips, then install the backup lamps using the nuts and the license plate lamps using the screws. Install the license plate push-in nuts and the license plate.

11. Position the fascia over the bumper assembly, then connect the wiring harnesses to the lamps.

12. Slide the fascia forward to engage the slots in the fascia with the studs extending down from the quarter panel.

13. Install the fascia retainer, then install the plastic pushpin fasteners.

14. Install the wheelhouse liner to fascia screws.

15. Connect the negative battery cable.

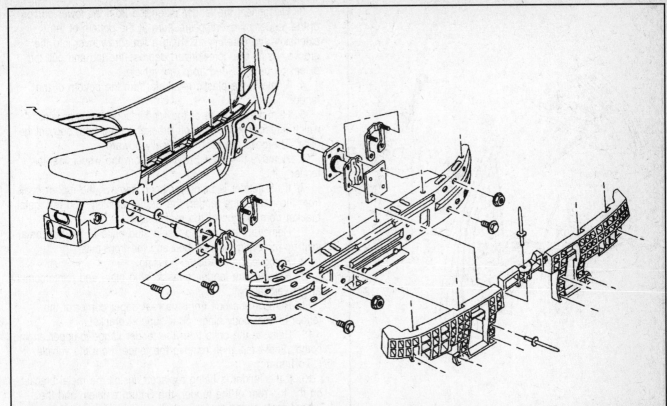

Fig. 20 Exploded view of the rear energy absorbing drives and the bumper/energy absorber assemblies — Coupe

Outside Mirrors

REMOVAL & INSTALLATION

▶ **See Figures 21 and 22**

1. If equipped with a power right side mirror, disconnect the negative battery cable.
2. Remove the screw from the mirror trim panel.
3. Loosen the set screw, then disconnect the cable from the trim panel on the manual mirror.
4. Remove the trim panel from the vehicle.
5. Remove the foam filler from the door frame.
6. If equipped, unplug the wiring harness connector on the power mirror.
7. Remove the nuts from the mirror assembly, then remove the mirror and seal from the vehicle.

To install:

8. Install the seal onto the mirror assembly.
9. If equipped, connect the wiring harness to the right side power mirror.
10. Install the mirror assembly to the door, then tighten the retaining nuts to 53 inch lbs. (6 Nm).
11. Install the foam filler to the door frame.
12. Install the mirror cable into the trim panel and tighten the set screw to 27 inch lbs. (3 Nm), for the manual mirror.
13. Position the trim panel to the door frame, then secure using the screw.
14. If equipped with power right side mirror, connect the negative battery cable.

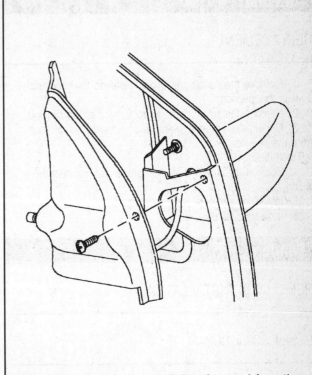

Fig. 21 Remove the screw and the trim panel from the door

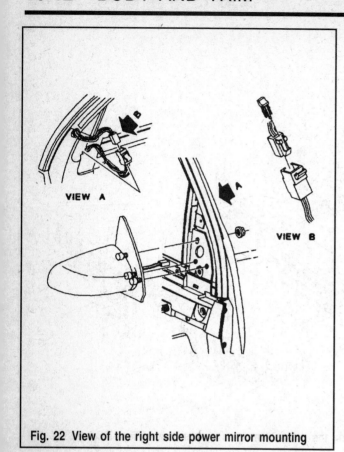

Fig. 22 View of the right side power mirror mounting

Antenna

REPLACEMENT

1. Remove the right front fender. Refer to the procedure later in this section.
2. Remove the retaining bolts from the antenna bracket.
3. Unplug the antenna wiring, then remove the antenna from the vehicle.

To install:

4. Position the antenna to the vehicle and connect the wiring.
5. Install the antenna retaining screws.
6. Install the fender.

Fenders

REMOVAL & INSTALLATION

Except SC or SC2

▶ **See Figures 23, 24 and 25**

1. Remove the plastic retainers from the wheelhouse liner-to-lower fender extension.
2. Remove the plastic retainers from the bottom of the fender extension-to-fender support.

3. Disconnect the fender extension from the lower portion of the fender by exerting pressure at the bottom of the extension and carefully inserting a flat screwdriver into the groove. Using the screwdriver, depress the tab and pull the extension outward and from the vehicle.
4. Remove the plastic retainers from the bottom of the fender.
5. Remove the bolts at the fender upper-to-lower joint which thread into the support bracket on the front body hinge pillar. The bolts are driven vertically upward.
6. Remove the plastic retainers from the wheel liner-to-fender joint.
7. If the fender is being replaced, remove the rubber seals from the rear of the fender, the Saturn emblem and the metal bracket from the top of the rear fender.
8. Remove the fender-to-fascia stud plate at the horizontal joint by removing the rear bolt and the front nuts.
9. Remove the headlamp housing.
10. Remove the fender-to-fascia stud plate and reinforcement at the vertical joint.
11. Remove the bolt from the rear upper corner of the fender-to-front body hinge pillar support bracket.
12. Remove the bolts from the fender flange-to-upper engine compartment rail, then remove the fender from the vehicle.

To install:

13. If the fender is being replaced, install the metal bracket on the top rear of the fender, the Saturn emblem and the rubber seals to the fender rear flange.
14. Position the fender onto the engine compartment side rail.
15. Align the fender to the door and hood, then install the fender flange bolts using the sequence shown in the illustration.
16. Install the fender-to-front body hinge pillar support bracket bolt, then install the fender-to-fascia stud plate and vertical joint reinforcement.
17. Align the fender-to-fascia and tighten the nuts to vertical stud plate. Install the headlamp housing.
18. Install the fender-to-fascia upper support bracket assembly along the horizontal joint using the nuts and bolts.
19. Install the wheelhouse liner to the fender using the plastic retainers.
20. Install the fender-to-body hinge pillar lower bracket bolts.
21. Install the plastic retainers at the bottom of the fender.
22. Align the fender lower extension to the fender and push it rearward to engage the retaining tabs.
23. Install the plastic retainers at the bottom of the fender extension-to-fender support.
24. Install the wheel liner-to-fender extension plastic retainers.
25. Check and adjust headlamp aim, as necessary.

SC or SC2

▶ **See Figures 26 and 27**

1. Remove the plastic retainers from the wheelhouse liner-to-fender extension.
2. Remove the plastic retainers from the bottom of the fender extension-to-fender support.
3. Disconnect the fender extension from the lower portion of the fender by exerting pressure at the bottom of the extension and carefully inserting a flat screwdriver into the

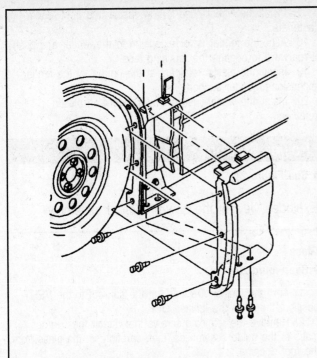

Fig. 23 The fender lower extension must be removed before the fender can be removed from the vehicle — except SC or SC2

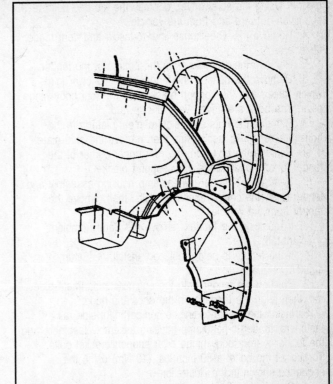

Fig. 25 Install the wheelhouse liner to the fender using the plastic retainers — except SC or SC2

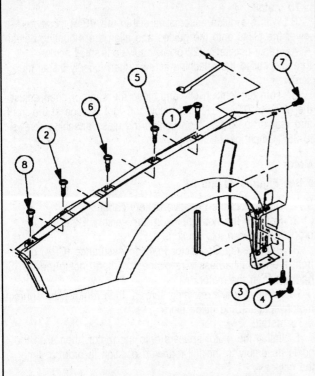

Fig. 24 Install the fender retaining bolts in the proper sequence — except SC or SC2

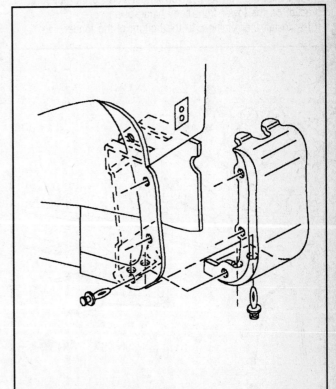

Fig. 26 Remove the lower fender extension from the fender and body — SC or SC2

groove. Using the screwdriver, depress the tab and pull the extension outward and from the vehicle.

4. Remove the wheelhouse liner-to-fascia and front fender fasteners.

5. Remove the retainers from the bottom of the fender.

6. Remove the bolts at the fender upper-to-lower joint which thread into the support bracket on the front body hinge pillar. The bolts are driven vertically upward.

7. Remove the nuts and reinforcement plate from the horizontal fender-to-fascia joint, then remove the stud plate.

8. Remove the bolt from the rear upper corner of the fender-to-front body hinge pillar support bracket.

9. Remove the fender-to-headlamp housing assembly and fender-to-engine compartment rail bolts, then remove the fender from the vehicle.

10. If replacing the fender, remove the Saturn emblem.

To install:

11. If the fender is being replaced, install the Saturn emblem.

12. Position the fender onto the engine compartment side rail, then align the fender with the door and hood.

13. Install the fender-to-engine compartment side rail fasteners, fender-to-headlamp housing assembly fasteners and the fender-to-front body hinge pillar support bracket bolts. Torque all the bolts to 89 inch lbs. (10 Nm) using the sequence shown in the illustration.

14. Connect the fender-to-fascia by lowering the stud plate through the bracket and fender, then install the reinforcement plate and nuts. Align the fender-to-fascia and tighten the nuts.

15. Install the vertically driven fender bolts to the support bracket on the lower front body hinge pillar.

16. Install the retainers to the bottom of the fender.

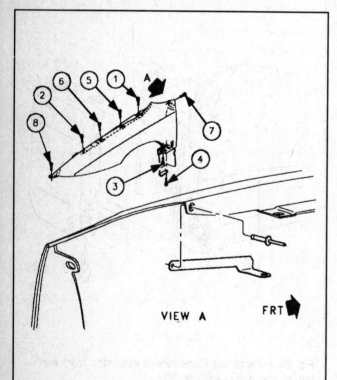

Fig. 27 Tighten the fender bolts in the proper sequence — SC or SC2

17. Install the wheelhouse-to-front fascia and front fender fasteners.

18. Align the fender lower extension to the fender and push it rearward to engage the retaining tabs.

19. Install the plastic retainers at the bottom of the fender extension-to-fender support.

20. Install the wheel liner-to-fender extension plastic retainers.

Power Sunroof

▶ See Figure 28

Exploded view of the power sunroof assembly

Glass

▶ See Figure 29

1. Turn the ignition **ON** and set the sunroof to the VENT position, then turn the ignition **OFF**.

2. Remove the retaining screws that attach the sunroof glass to the guide assemblies, then carefully lift the glass from the roof opening.

✳✳WARNING

Once the glass has been removed from the sunroof, DO NOT cycle the roof to the full closed position or the guide assemblies will be damaged.

To install:

3. With the guide assemblies still in the VENT position, lower the glass onto the guides and align the mounting holes.

4. Apply Loctite® 222 or an equivalent small screw threadlocker to the attaching screws, then loosely install the screws.

5. Turn the ignition **ON** and close the sunroof, then adjust the glass to 0.04 in. (1mm) below the roof surface at the front and rear of the glass, then tighten the glass attaching screws to 35-44 inch lbs. (4-5 Nm).

Motor

▶ See Figures 30 and 31

1. Disconnect the negative battery cable.

2. Remove the headliner from the vehicle. Refer to the procedure later in this section.

3. Remove the Connector Position Assurance (CPA) device from the motor harness wire connector, then unplug the harness from the motor.

4. Remove the 3 retaining screws, then remove the sunroof motor, spacers and guide block.

To install:

5. Install the motor spacers onto the motor, then slide the guide assembly to the full rearward position in order to time the cables.

6. Position the guide block onto the motor, aligning it to the locator pins on the motor housing.

7. Install the sunroof motor using the 3 screws, then tighten the screws to 27-35 inch lbs. (3-4 Nm).

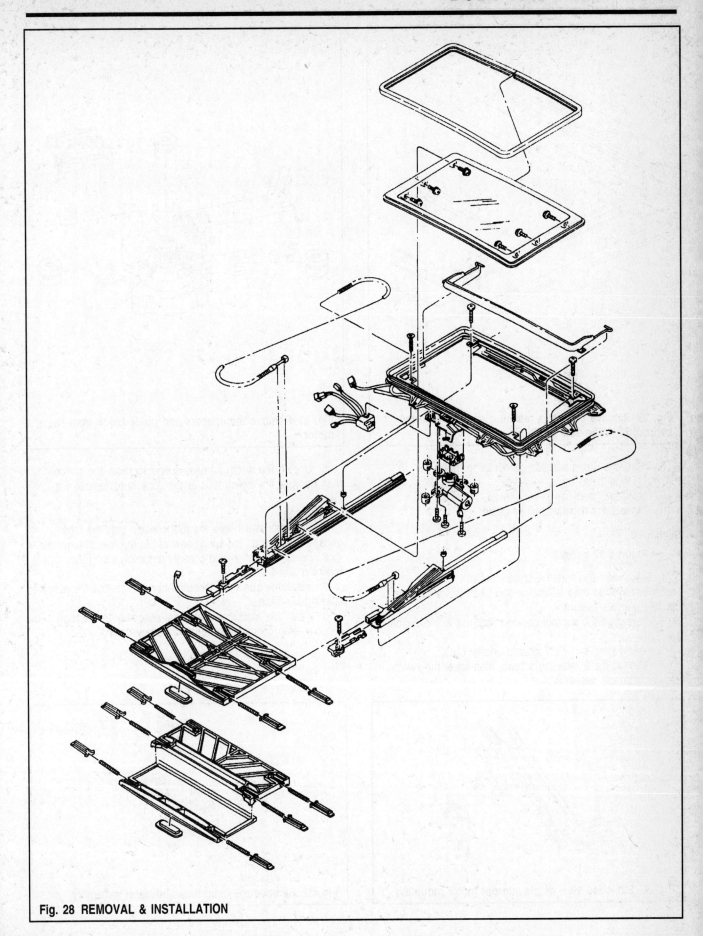

Fig. 28 REMOVAL & INSTALLATION

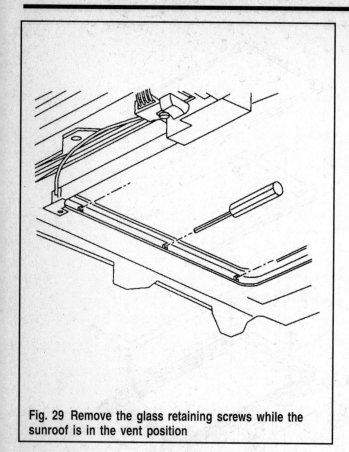

Fig. 29 Remove the glass retaining screws while the sunroof is in the vent position

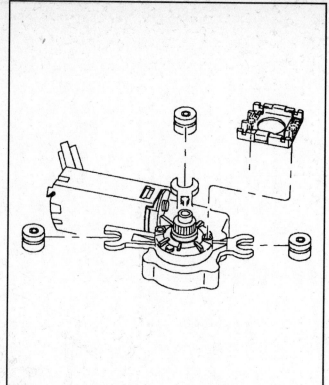

Fig. 31 Remove the spacers and guide block from the motor

8. Install the wiring harness connector to the motor terminals, then install the CPA device.

9. Install the headliner to the vehicle.

10. Connect the negative battery cable.

Switch

▶ See Figures 32 and 33

1. Disconnect the negative battery cable.

2. Remove the map lamp lens and bezel assembly from the roof console assembly.

3. Disengage the sunroof opening windlace at the switch area.

4. Remove the sun visor inboard anchor clips.

5. Remove the 2 retaining screws, then lower the switch and roof console assembly.

6. Unplug the wiring harness connector from the switch, then depress the switch tabs at the console to remove the switch.

To install:

7. Push the switch into the roof console until the tabs engage, then install the wiring harness to the switch terminals.

8. Install the switch and console assembly using the retaining screws.

9. Install the sun visor inboard anchor clips and the sunroof opening windlace.

10. Install the map lens and bezel assembly to the roof console, then connect the negative battery cable.

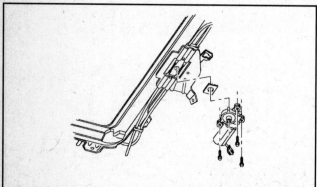

Fig. 30 Exploded view of the sunroof motor mounting

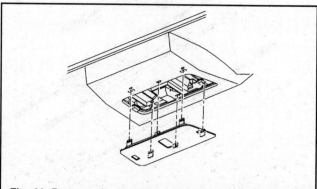

Fig. 32 Remove the lamp lens and bezel assembly

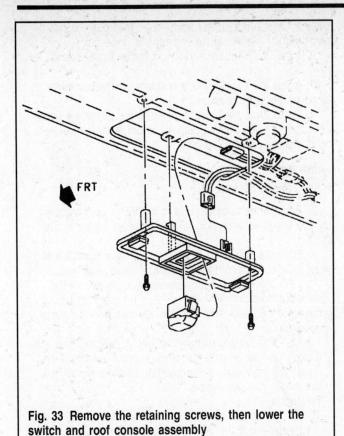

Fig. 33 Remove the retaining screws, then lower the switch and roof console assembly

Guide Assembly
▶ **See Figures 34 and 35**

1. Position the sunroof glass in the VENT position, then remove the glass according to the procedure earlier in this section.

2. If equipped, remove the wind deflector by pushing the spring ends down and forward, then slide the deflector rearward and from the vehicle.

3. Remove the screw from each locator. Remove the locator from the right side, then remove the locator and microswitch from the left side. Each locator may be removed by inserting a screwdriver into the screw hole, tilting the screwdriver toward the center of the vehicle and then sliding it forward.

4. Remove the sunshade from the vehicle. Refer to the procedure later in this section.

5. Lift the drive cable end out of the guide assembly.

6. Remove the guide assembly screws, then remove the rear screw and spacer.

7. Slide the rear of the guide assembly towards the center of the vehicle and remove the guide assembly.

To install:

8. Position the front of the guide assembly at the front mount location with the guide's rear at the opposite corner of the sunroof opening. Slide the rear of the guide under the roof panel and toward the outboard side of the opening to the rear mounting position.

9. Install the guide rear spacer and guide screws, then tighten the screws to 35-44 inch lbs. (4-5 Nrn).

10. Engage the drive cable into the guide assembly.

11. Install the sunshade to the vehicle.

12. Install each locator by positioning the locator into the guide assembly slightly ahead of its installed position. Insert a screwdriver into the locator screw hole, then push rearward and down on the locator to engage it with the guide.

13. Install each locator screw and tighten to 35 inch lbs. (4 Nm).

14. If equipped, install the wind deflector by positioning the deflector front tabs under the roof flange at the front and by engaging the spring ends into the brackets.

15. Install the sunroof glass. Refer to the procedure earlier in this section. Be sure to properly adjust the glass before tightening the retaining screws.

Cables
▶ **See Figure 33**

1. Position the sunroof glass in the VENT position, then remove the glass according to the procedure earlier in this section.

2. Remove the sunroof motor according to the procedure earlier in this section.

3. Remove the screw from each locator. Remove the locator from the right side, then remove the locator and microswitch from the left side. Each locator may be removed by inserting a screwdriver into the screw hole, tilting the screwdriver toward the center of the vehicle and then sliding it forward.

4. Lift the drive cable ends out of the guide assembly, then pull the cables out of the sunroof cable guide tubes.

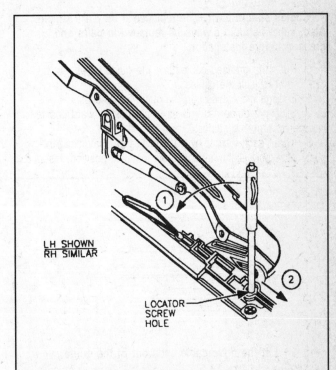

LH SHOWN
RH SIMILAR

LOCATOR
SCREW
HOLE

Fig. 34 After removing the locator screw, insert a screwdriver into the screw hole, tilt the screwdriver toward the vehicle's center and slide it forward to remove the locator

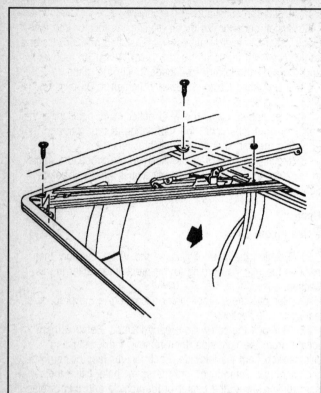

Fig. 35 Remove the retaining screws, then remove the guide assembly from the vehicle

To install:

➡ **Cables should always be replaced if they are kinked. Also, cables should always be replaced in pairs and greased before installation.**

5. Push the greased cables into the guide tubes, but be careful not to kink the cables.
6. Engage the cables into the guide assemblies.
7. Slide the guide assemblies to the full rearward position in order to time the cables.
8. Install each locator by positioning the locator into the guide assembly slightly ahead of its installed position. Insert a

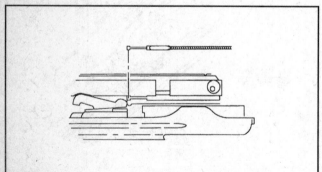

Fig. 36 Lift the drive cable ends out of the guide assembly

screwdriver into the locator screw hole, then push rearward and down on the locator to engage it with the guide.

9. Install each locator screw and tighten to 35 inch lbs. (4 Nm).
10. Install the sunroof motor according to the procedure found earlier in this section.
11. Install the sunroof glass. Refer to the procedure earlier in this section. Be sure to properly adjust the glass before tightening the retaining screws.

Sunshade

▶ **See Figures 37 and 38**

1. Position the sunroof glass in the VENT position, then remove the glass according to the procedure earlier in this section.
2. Push the sunshade slide blocks into the sunshade in order to release them from the sunroof guide assembly:
   a. For the Sedan, both slide blocks on 1 side of the vehicle should be released first, then release both blocks on the other side and remove the shade through the sunroof opening.
   b. For the Coupe, release the rear slide blocks first and remove the rear section out of the sunroof opening, then repeat the procedure at the front slide blocks and remove the shade from the vehicle.

To install:

3. For the Coupe:
   a. Install the front half of the sunshade first by inserting the slide blocks on the right side of the sunshade in the lower slide position of the right guide assembly. Then push the slide blocks on the left side into the sunshade to allow the front half of the shade to drop into position. When positioned, engage the blocks into the lower channel of the left guide.
   b. Push the front half of the sunshade to the full forward position.
   c. Position the rear half of the shade so that the stop tabs are against the bumpers on the guide assembly. Engage the right slide blocks of the shade's upper half into the upper channel on the right guide assembly.
   d. Engage the slide blocks on the left side into the upper channel of the left guide assembly.
   e. Slide the sunshade back and forth to assure proper and smooth operation.
4. For the Sedan:
   a. Insert the slide blocks on the right side of the sunshade into the sunroof guide assembly.
   b. Push the sunshade slide blocks on the left side into the sunshade to allow the sunshade to drop into position. Once the sunshade is positioned, engage the slide blocks into the left guide assembly.
   c. Slide the sunshade back and forth to assure proper and smooth operation.
5. Install the sunroof glass. Refer to the procedure earlier in this section. Be sure to properly adjust the glass before tightening the retaining screws.

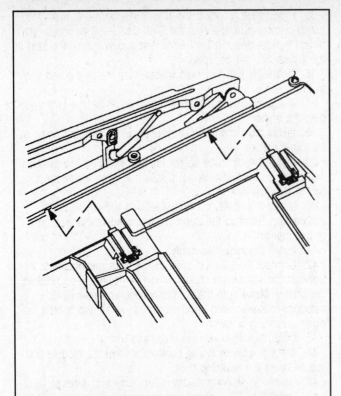

Fig. 38 Two slide blocks are engage into the guide assemblies on either side of the sunshade

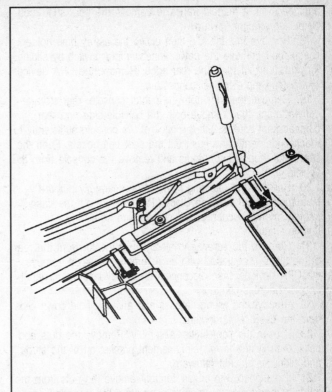

Fig. 37 Push the slide blocks into the sunshade in order to engage or disengage the shade from the guides

INTERIOR

Instrument Panel and Trim Plates

REMOVAL & INSTALLATION

▶ See Figures 39, 40, 41, 42 and 43

1. Disconnect the negative battery cable.
2. Remove the left and right end cap/HVAC air outlet assemblies by removing the attaching screws and pulling each assembly from the retaining clips.
3. For 1991 vehicles, remove the cigarette lighter trim bezel.
4. Carefully remove the center air outlet/trim panel by pulling outward at the clip locations. Begin at the bottom of the panel and work towards the upper clips, being careful not to score or damage the panel.
5. If equipped, remove the trim panel extension strip by pulling outward at the clip locations.
6. Remove the 2 dashboard upper trim panel screw caps (located near the windshield at either end of the dash) by carefully prying with a small flathead tool. Remove the upper trim panel screws.
7. Lift the upper trim panel to disengage the clips at the rear edge, then pull the panel rearward and out of the clips at the base of the windshield. Remove the upper trim panel from the vehicle.

8. Remove the screws from the instrument cluster trim panel, then pull the panel rearward sufficiently to disengage it from the retainers and to reach the electrical wiring behind it.
9. Remove the Connector Position Assurance (CPA) devices, then unplug the electrical connectors from the instrument panel light and the rear window defogger switches. Remove the cluster trim panel from the vehicle.
10. Remove the retaining screws, then pull the instrument cluster outward sufficiently to reach the wiring harness connectors. Unplug the wiring harness connectors by depressing the retainer legs, then remove the cluster from the vehicle.
11. Remove the wiring harness clips from the dash reinforcement.
12. Remove the Assembly Line Data Link (ALDL) screws, then remove the connector from the underside of the dash.
13. Remove the screws and lower the steering column filler panel from under the column. Be careful not to scratch the console with the mounting tabs when removing the panel.
14. Remove the hood release lever screw, located underneath and behind the lever.
15. Remove the radio and HVAC control panel. Refer to the procedures in Section 6 of this manual.
16. Unplug the cigarette lighter connector, then remove the lighter bulb holder by rotating counterclockwise and pulling straight out.
17. Apply the parking brake, then remove the parking brake filler panel by carefully lifting at the rear edge. If the vehicle is

equipped with a manual transaxle, remove the gear shift knob by pulling straight upward.

18. Remove the ashtray, then unclip the astray bulb holder. If equipped, remove the power window/mirror switch by sliding forward, then lifting at the rear edge. Remove the CPA devices and unplug the electrical connectors.

19. Remove the liner from the center console, rear storage compartment, then remove both the console side and rear compartment screws. Lift the back of the console sufficiently to reach underneath and push out the seat belt bezels. Feed the seat belts though the cutouts and remove the console from the vehicle.

20. Remove the retaining screws, then carefully pull the Instrument Panel Junction Block (IPJB) away from the dash reinforcement. Disconnect the ground wire from the reinforcement.

21. Remove the screw and electrical connector from the rear of the IPJB. If equipped with an automatic transaxle, remove the CPA devices, then disconnect the 2-way instrument panel-to-body harness connector.

22. Remove the wiring harness and antenna hold down clips from the dash reinforcement.

23. Loosen the floor shifter assembly. Remove the nuts and bolts, then lift the lower reinforcement bracket off of the studs and slide the bracket rearward.

24. If equipped with cruise control, remove the nuts from the module, then lower the module down from the mounting bracket.

25. Remove the screws and nuts from the dash retainer and the reinforcement bracket.

26. Remove the bolts, then carefully lower steering column assembly onto the driver's seat.

27. Carefully remove the instrument panel/dash assembly from the vehicle.

To install:

28. Install the instrument panel assembly. When positioning the panel, feed the fuse block and wiring harness through the lower reinforcement and into position. Install and tighten the screws and nuts on the dash retainer and reinforcement bracket.

29. Carefully raise the steering column assembly into position, then install the retaining bolts and tighten to 33 ft. lbs. (45 Nm).

30. Install the lower reinforcement bracket and nuts, then tighten the floor shifter assembly.

31. Install the wiring harness and antenna hold down clips onto the dash reinforcement.

32. Install the electrical connector to the rear of the IPJB, then tighten the screw. If equipped with an automatic transaxle, connect the panel-to-body harness connector and install the lock pin. Install the IPJB to the dash reinforcement using the retaining screws, then install the ground wire to the reinforcement.

33. Install the center console while feeding the seat belts and wire harness through the console cut outs. Snap the seat belt bezels into position.

34. Secure the console using the side screws at the front and the compartment screws at the top of the rear. Position the liner into the rear storage compartment and over the screws.

35. If equipped, connect the power window/mirror electrical wiring harnesses and install the CPA devices, then install the switch by inserting the front edge first and snapping the rear of the switch into the console.

36. Install the ash tray bulb holder, then install the ash tray to the console.

37. If equipped with a manual transaxle, push the shift knob onto the shifter.

38. Install the parking brake filler panel by pressing down at the clip locations.

39. Install the cigarette lighter bulb by inserting into position and rotating counterclockwise to lock it in, then install the lighter electrical connector.

40. Install the HVAC control panel and adjust the cables accordingly. Refer to the appropriate procedures in Section 6 of this manual.

41. Install the radio assembly.

42. Connect the harness clips to the dash reinforcement. Connect the instrument cluster wiring harnesses, then position the cluster. Make sure the cluster lighting and rear window defogger harnesses are in position then install and tighten the cluster retaining screws.

43. Install the hood release lever and screw.

44. If equipped with cruise control, position the module and secure using the retaining nuts.

45. Install the steering column filler panel and screws.

46. Install the ALDL connector and screws.

47. Position the instrument cluster trim panel and connect the wiring harness to the instrument light and rear window defogger switches. Install the CPA devices into the electrical connectors, then install the cluster trim panel into the retainers and secure using the screws.

48. Install the upper trim panel by inserting into the clips at the windshield, then snapping the rear of the panel into place. Install the upper trim panel screws, then snap the screw covers into position.

49. Install the center air outlet/trim panel, then install the lower left and right trim panel extensions. For 1991 vehicles, install the cigarette lighter trim bezel. If equipped install the trim panel extension.

50. Install the left and right end cap assemblies, then connect the negative battery cable.

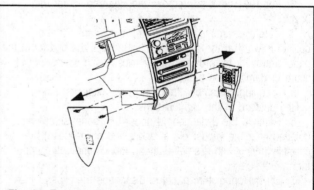

Fig. 39 Remove the lower trim panel extensions

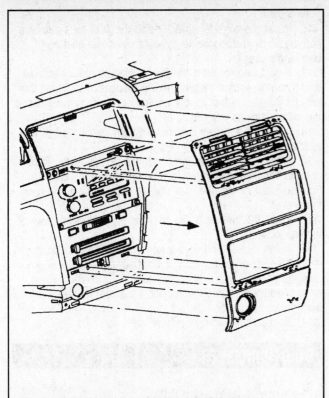

Fig. 40 Remove the center air outlet/trim panel assembly — 1992 and 1993 vehicles shown

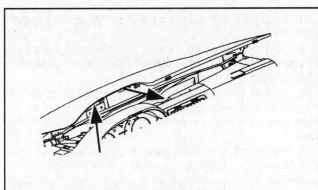

Fig. 41 Remove the upper trim panel from the vehicle

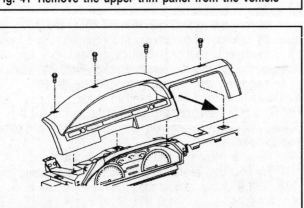

Fig. 42 Remove the instrument cluster trim panel

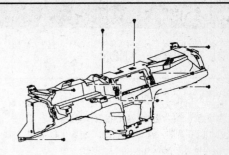

Fig. 43 Remove the screws and nuts from the dash retainer and the reinforcement bracket

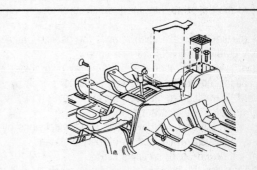

Fig. 44 Remove the rear and side screws, then remove the parking brake filler panel

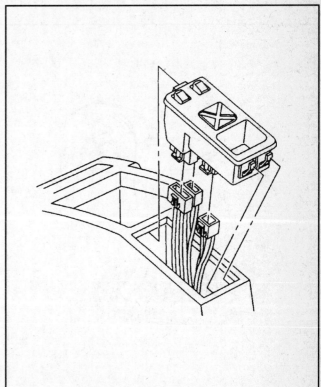

Fig. 45 If equipped remove the power window/mirror switch assembly

Center Console

REMOVAL & INSTALLATION

▶ **See Figures 44, 45 and 46**

1. Disconnect the negative battery cable.
2. If equipped with an automatic transaxle, tape the shift button in on the shifter handle.
3. If the vehicle is equipped with a manual transaxle, remove the gear shift knob by pulling straight upward.
4. Remove the liner from the center console, rear storage compartment, then remove both the rear compartment screws.
5. Remove the 2 screws from the front sides of the console.
6. Apply the parking brake, then remove the parking brake filler panel by carefully lifting at the rear edge.
7. Remove the ashtray, then unclip the astray bulb holder.
8. If equipped, remove the power window/mirror switch by sliding forward, then lifting at the rear edge. Remove the CPA devices and unplug the electrical connectors.
9. Remove the left and right lower trim panel extensions by disconnecting the velcro at the bottom of the panels and pulling them out of the upper retaining clips.
10. Lift the back of the console sufficiently to reach underneath and push out the seat belt bezels. Feed the seat belts though the cutouts and remove the console from the vehicle.

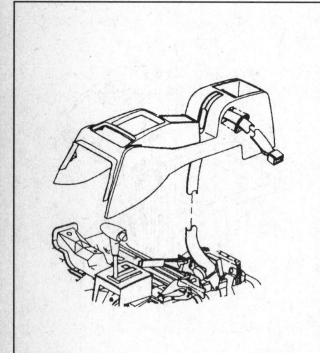

Fig. 46 Install the console while feeding the seat belts through the console cut outs

To install:

11. Install the console while feeding the seat belts and wire harness through the console cut outs. Snap the seat belt bezels into position.
12. If equipped, connect the power window/mirror electrical wiring harnesses and install the CPA devices, then install the switch by inserting the front edge first and snapping the rear of the switch into the console.
13. Install the ash tray bulb holder, then install the ash tray to the console.
14. Secure the console using the side screws at the front, and the compartment screws at the top rear of the console. Position the liner into the rear storage compartment and over the screws.
15. Install the parking brake filler panel by pressing down at the clip locations.
16. Install the left and right lower trim panel extension.
17. If equipped with a manual transaxle, push the shift knob onto the shifter.
18. If equipped with an automatic transaxle, remove the tape from the shifter button.
19. Connect the negative battery cable.

Door Panels

REMOVAL & INSTALLATION

▶ **See Figures 47, 48, 49 and 50**

1. If equipped with power windows, disconnect the negative battery cable.
2. For front door panels, remove the screws and the mirror trim panel. If equipped with a manual remote mirror, allow the panel to hang from the adjustment cable.
3. For rear door panels, remove the inner belt seal from the trim panel. If necessary, use a putty knife which has its blade covered with tape to gently pry the sealing strip from the flange.
4. If equipped, remove the power door lock switch by prying out at the top of the switch with a small, straight screwdriver. Make sure the screwdriver tip is covered with tape to protect the surfaces. Unplug the wiring harness and remove the switch.
5. Remove the screws, then slide the door handle assembly forward and pull the assembly outward. Use a long, thin screwdriver to disengage the lock and latch rods from the retainers, then remove the handle assembly from the vehicle.
6. If equipped with manual windows, disengage the regulator handle clips using a standard handle tool or by working a cloth back and forth between the handle and the bearing plate. Once disengaged, remove the handle and plate from the door.
7. Remove the screws and the door pull cup.
8. For front door panels, remove the inner belt sealing strip.
9. For the Coupe, remove the screw from the rear of the door trim panel.
10. Disengage the door trim panel retainers from the door assembly using a trim panel tool, then remove the panel from the vehicle.

To install:

11. Position the trim panel to the door assembly, then engage the retainers by pressing firmly at the panel retainer locations.

12. Install the door pull cup and screws, then tighten the screws to 22 inch lbs. (2.2 Nm).

13. If equipped, install the manual window regulator handle clip on the handle, then install the bearing plate and handle. The handle should be pointing in a forward and slightly upward position with the window closed.

14. Position the door handle assembly to the trim panel, then tip the handle outward at the top. Using a thin hook shaped tool, lift the latch and lock rods into the retainers and engage the clamps. Push the handle into the trim panel and slide it rearward to engage the tabs. Install and tighten the retaining the screws.

15. If equipped, connect the wiring harness to the power door lock switch and install the switch into the handle assembly.

16. Install the inner belt sealing strip.

17. For front doors, install the mirror trim panel and tighten the retaining screw(s).

18. If applicable, connect the negative battery cable.

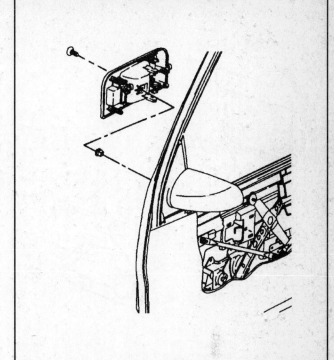

Fig. 48 Remove the screws and disengage the rods from the retainers, then remove the handle assembly from the door

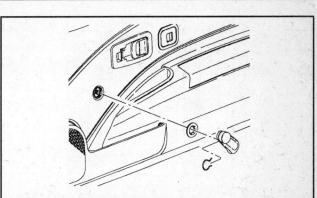

Fig. 49 Remove the handle clip, handle and plate

Interior Trim Panels

REMOVAL & INSTALLATION

Center Pillar Applique

▶ See Figure 51

1. Remove the plastic pins from the applique.

2. Pull the applique outward in the area of the upper fastener, then remove the applique from the vehicle.

To install:

3. Position the applique, then install the upper fastener into the pillar.

4. Secure the applique using the plastic pins.

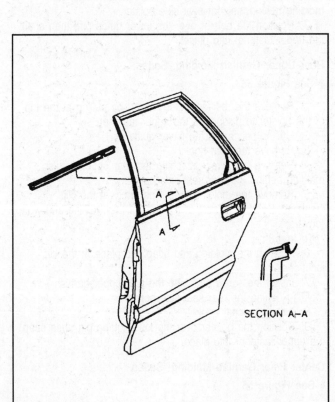

SECTION A–A

Fig. 47 Remove the inner belt seal from the rear door — Sedan and Wagon

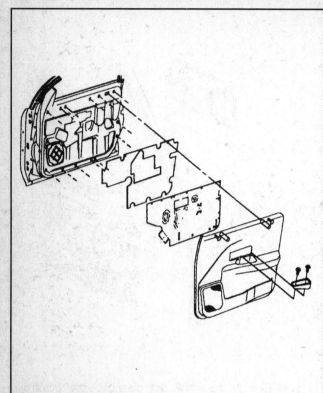

Fig. 50 Exploded view of the front door trim panel assembly — rear door similar

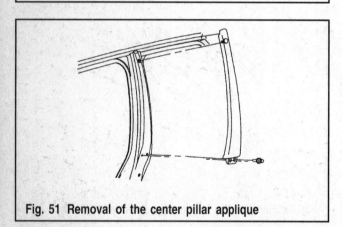

Fig. 51 Removal of the center pillar applique

Front Lower Garnish Sill/Molding: Sedan and Wagon
▶ See Figure 52

1. Remove the 2 retaining screws and the instrument panel end cap/HVAC air outlet.
2. Remove the screw from the top front of the lower garnish molding.
3. Remove the molding by pulling firmly at the clip locations. Be sure to start at the rear of the molding and work forward.

To install:

4. Position the molding and snap into place at the clip locations.
5. Install the screw into the top front of the lower molding.
6. Install the instrument panel end cap assembly.

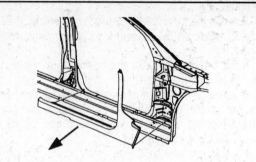

Fig. 52 Front lower garnish/sill molding — Sedan and Wagon

Rear Lower Garnish Sill/Molding: Sedan and Wagon
▶ See Figures 53 and 54

1. Remove the rear seat side bolster by pulling at the top of the bolster to disengage the upper fastener.
2. Lift the bolster off the lower guide pin.
3. Remove the screws attaching the rear lower garnish molding behind the rear seat side bolster.
4. Remove the molding by pulling firmly at the clip locations. Be sure to start at the front of the molding and work rearward.

To install:

5. Position the molding and snap into place at the clip locations.
6. Install the screws attaching the rear lower garnish molding behind the rear seat side bolster.
7. Position the bolster over the lower guide pin, then snap the upper fastener into place.

Rear Upper Garnish Molding: Sedan
▶ See Figure 55

1. Remove the rear seat side bolster by pulling at the top of the bolster to disengage the upper fastener.
2. Lift the bolster off the lower guide pin.
3. Remove the coat hook.
4. Remove the screw attaching the rear upper garnish molding behind the rear seat side bolster.
5. Remove the molding by pulling firmly at the clip locations. Be sure to start at the rear of the molding and work forward.

To install:

6. Position the molding and snap into place at the clip locations.
7. Install the screw attaching the rear upper garnish molding behind the rear seat side bolster.
8. Install the coat hook.
9. Position the bolster over the lower guide pin, then snap the upper fastener into place.

Center Pillar Garnish Molding: Sedan
▶ See Figure 56

1. Pull firmly on the front and rear lower garnish/sill moldings, at the center pillar, to partially remove the moldings for access to the pillar.
2. Starting at the top of the center pillar molding, pull firmly on the bottom of the front upper garnish molding to partially

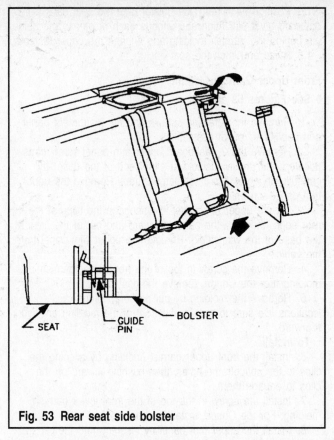

Fig. 53 Rear seat side bolster

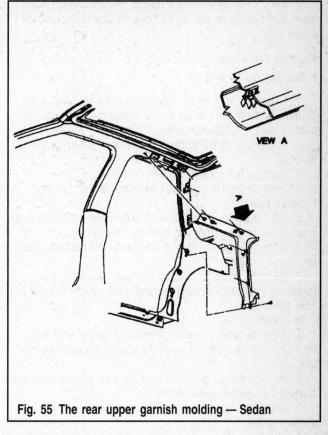

Fig. 55 The rear upper garnish molding — Sedan

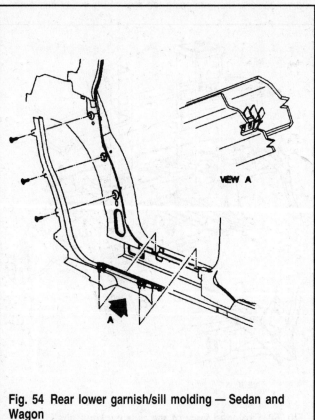

Fig. 54 Rear lower garnish/sill molding — Sedan and Wagon

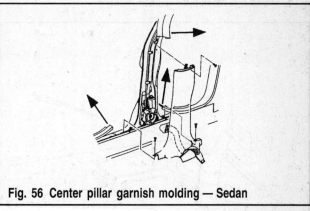

Fig. 56 Center pillar garnish molding — Sedan

remove it and expose the upper screw on the center pillar garnish molding.

3. Remove the screw at the top of the center pillar garnish molding.

4. Starting at the front lower edge of the center pillar garnish molding, guide the edge of the molding in an upward motion, over the body weld flange and remove it from the center pillar.

5. Guide the seat belt through the center pillar garnish molding, then remove the molding from the vehicle.

To install:

6. Position the molding, then guide the seat belt through the opening.

7. Position the molding over the body weld flange and against the center pillar.

8. Install the molding screw at the top of the pillar.

9. Secure the molding by snapping the front upper, front lower and rear lower garnish/sill moldings into position at the center pillar.

Package Shelf Trim: Sedan

▶ **See Figures 57 and 58**

1. Lower the seat backs, then remove the rear seat side bolsters by pulling at the top of the bolster to disengage the upper fastener. Lift each bolster off the lower guide pin.
2. Partially remove the lower half of one rear upper garnish molding.
3. Remove the speaker grilles.
4. Release the rear seat belt restraint bezels from the package shelf.
5. Lift the package shelf simultaneously out from behind the quarter trim in the corner and over the rear seat striker.
6. Slide the seat belt through the slit in the package shelf trim.
7. Slide the package shelf up and out from under the remaining rear upper garnish molding, then remove the shelf from the vehicle.

To install:

8. Slide the shelf under the 1 installed garnish molding, then slide the seat belts through the slits in the package shelf trim.
9. Install the shelf guiding it over the seat back strikers and aligning the speaker grille holes.
10. Install the seat belt restrain bezels, then install the speaker grilles.
11. Install the rear upper garnish molding.

12. Position each rear side bolster onto the seat back outboard pivot pin. Align and engage each bolster to the guide pin behind the garnish molding and engage the upper fastener.
13. Raise and latch the seat backs.

Front Upper Garnish Molding

▶ **See Figures 59 and 60**

1. Remove the retaining screws and the instrument panel end cap/HVAC outlet assemblies.
2. Remove the 2 dashboard upper trim panel screw caps (located near the windshield at either end of the dash) by carefully prying with a small flathead tool. Remove the upper trim panel screws.
3. Lift the upper trim panel to disengage the clips at the rear edge, then pull the panel rearward and out of the clips at the base of the windshield. Remove the upper trim panel from the vehicle.
4. Remove the screw in top of the front lower garnish molding. For the Coupe, remove the coat hook.
5. Remove the molding by pulling firmly at the clip locations. Be sure to start at the front of the molding and work rearward.

To install:

6. Install the front upper garnish molding by aligning the clips to the spaceframe holes, then pushing inward on the clips to engage them.
7. Install the screw in the top of the front lower garnish molding. For the Coupe, install the coat hook.
8. Install the upper trim panel by inserting into the clips at the windshield, then snapping the rear of the panel into place.

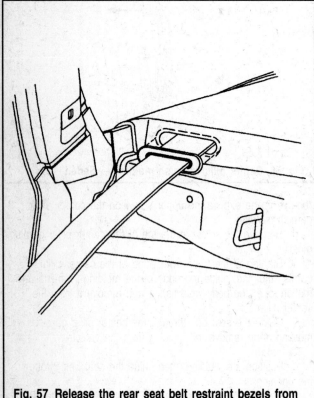

Fig. 57 Release the rear seat belt restraint bezels from the package shelf — Sedan

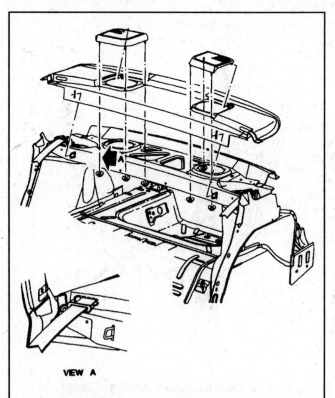

VIEW A

Fig. 58 Exploded view of the rear package shelf assembly — Sedan

Install the upper trim panel screws, then snap the screw covers into position.

9. Install the instrument panel end cap/HVAC outlet assemblies using the retaining screws.

Latch Pillar Upper Trim Molding: Wagon

▶ **See Figure 61**

1. Remove the rear seat bolster.
2. Pull down the top front section of the body rear corner trim panel assembly.
3. Remove the screw at the bottom of the latch pillar upper trim molding assembly.
4. Remove the latch pillar upper trim molding by pulling firmly at the clip locations.

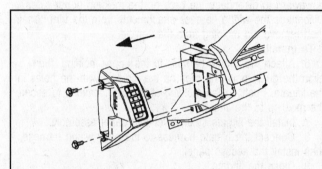

Fig. 59 Remove the instrument panel end cap/HVAC outlet assemblies

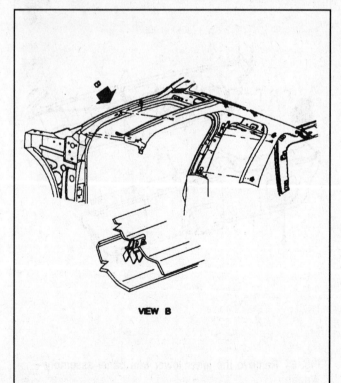

Fig. 60 Remove the front upper garnish molding from the spaceframe

To install:

5. Position the latch pillar molding assembly and secure by pushing at the clip locations.
6. Install the bottom screw to the molding assembly.
7. Secure the body rear corner trim panel assembly by pushing in at the clip locations.
8. Install the rear seat bolster.

Body Rear Corner Trim Panel: Wagon

▶ **See Figure 62**

1. Remove the wheelhouse upper trim panel assembly.
2. Remove the headliner trim panel molding assembly.
3. Remove the body rear corner trim panel by pulling firmly at the clip locations.

To install:

4. Position the body rear corner trim panel assembly and secure by pushing in at the clip locations.
5. Install the headliner trim panel molding assembly.
6. Install the wheelhouse upper trim panel assembly.

Liftgate Inner Lower Trim Panel Assembly: Wagon

▶ **See Figures 63 and 64**

1. Raise the liftgate.
2. Remove the wedge blocks from either end of the liftgate assembly.
3. Remove the lower fasteners from the liftgate lower trim panel, by pushing in the of each center pin approximately $1/8$ inch until it clicks, then remove the fastener.

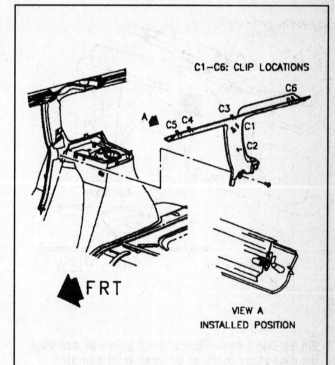

Fig. 61 Latch pillar upper trim molding assembly — Wagon

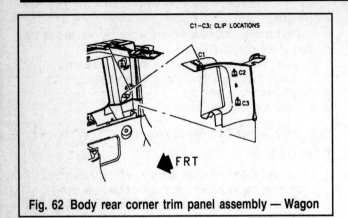

Fig. 62 Body rear corner trim panel assembly — Wagon

4. Insert a screwdriver or small prybar into the hole in the lower trim panel (located near the wiper pivot on the pivot hump) so that the tool sits on top of the pivot as shown. Lift up on the tool handle to disengage the trim panel upper clips, then remove the inner lower trim panel from the vehicle.

To install:

5. Align the upper clips on the lower trim panel to the liftgate slots, then install the panel by pushing at the clip locations.

6. Reset the trim panel push-in fasteners by spreading the center pin tabs and moving the pin so that it sits approximately ¼ in. out of the fastener. Insert the fasteners into the bottom of the trim panel and push the center pin until flush.

7. Install the liftgate wedge blocks.

8. Close the liftgate.

Liftgate Window Upper Garnish Molding: Wagon
▶ **See Figure 65**

1. Raise the liftgate, then remove the access panel from the top of the liftgate molding.

2. Unplug the liftgate harness from the body wiring harness.

3. Remove the liftgate inner lower trim panel assembly. Refer to the procedure earlier in this section.

4. Remove the fasteners from the top and lower end of the liftgate window upper garnish molding. Push the center pin of each fastener approximately ⅛ inch until it clicks, then remove the fastener.

5. Grasp the garnish molding at the lower ends and pull downward to disengage the clips on the molding upper sides. Disengage the wiring harness attachments from the trim panel, then remove the molding from the vehicle.

To install:

6. Attach the liftgate harness to the upper molding, then align the guide pins and clips on the molding with the holes in the liftgate. Push on the molding at the clip locations to secure the molding to the liftgate.

7. Install the liftgate inner lower trim panel assembly.

8. Connect the liftgate harness to the body wiring harness, then install the access panel.

9. Close the liftgate.

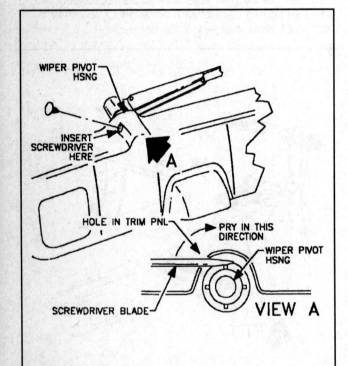

Fig. 63 Use a screwdriver or small prybar to disengage the clips at the center of the inner lower trim panel — Wagon

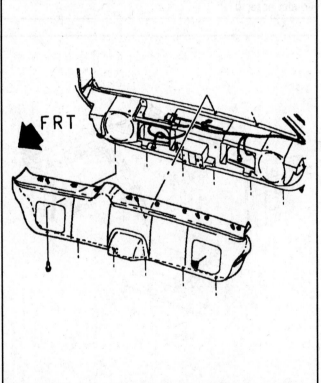

Fig. 64 Remove the inner lower trim panel assembly — Wagon

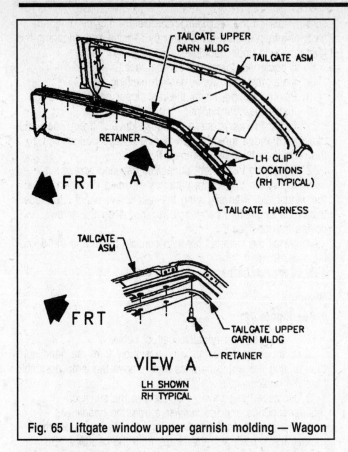

Fig. 65 Liftgate window upper garnish molding — Wagon

Headliner Trim Finish Panel Molding Assembly (Above Liftgate): Wagon

▶ See Figure 66

The trim panel may be removed by pulling downward at the trim locations. When installing, align the molding clips to the liftgate holes, then push on the molding at the clip locations to secure the molding to the liftgate.

Rear End Trim Finish Panel Assembly (Sill Molding): Wagon

▶ See Figure 67

1. Remove the 3 screws from the top of the panel assembly.

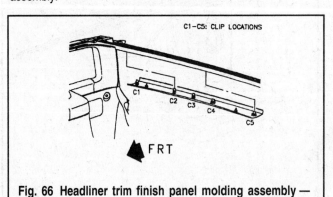

Fig. 66 Headliner trim finish panel molding assembly — Wagon

2. Pull upward on the panel assembly at the clip locations, then remove the assembly from the vehicle.
3. Installation is the reverse of removal.

Rear Wheelhouse Upper Trim Finish Panel Assembly (Shock Tower Cover): Wagon

▶ See Figure 68

1. Remove the 2 barbed fasteners from the front lip.
2. Pull upward and inward on the trim finish panel at the clip locations and remove the panel from the vehicle.
3. Installation is the reverse of removal.

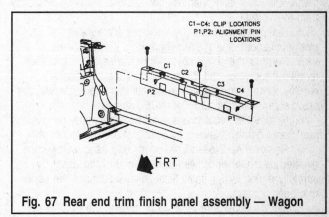

Fig. 67 Rear end trim finish panel assembly — Wagon

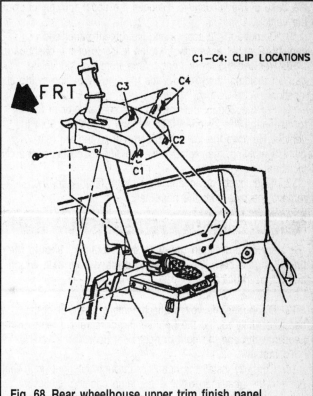

Fig. 68 Rear wheelhouse upper trim finish panel assembly (shock tower cover) — Wagon

Headliner

REMOVAL & INSTALLATION

Coupe and Sedan

▶ See Figures 69, 70 and 71

1. Disconnect the negative battery cable.
2. Remove the bezel from the map lamp or lamp and sunroof switch console by prying at the notch on the outside edge.
3. Disconnect the dome lamp assembly form the headliner, then unplug the wiring harness and remove the lamp assembly from the vehicle.
4. Remove the screws, then remove the sunvisor retainer/supports and the sunvisors from the headliner.
5. Remove the screw covers from the assist straps, then remove the screws and the straps from the headliner. Be careful. If the front assist strap has different color screws, the black screw will have LEFT HANDED threads.
6. Remove the coat hooks, then for the Coupe, remove the rear upper garnish molding by pulling at the clip locations.
7. Remove the 2 dashboard upper trim panel screw caps (located near the windshield at either end of the dash) by carefully prying with a small flathead tool. Remove the upper trim panel screws.
8. Lift the upper trim panel to disengage the clips at the rear edge, then pull the panel rearward and out of the clips at the base of the windshield. Remove the upper trim panel from the vehicle.
9. Remove the 2 screws and instrument panel end cap/HVAC outlet assembly from the left side of the dashboard.
10. Remove the lower front screws from the windshield garnish molding, then remove the molding by pulling at the clip locations.
11. For the Sedan, pull the left rear seat bolster at the top to disengage the fastener, then remove the bolster from the vehicle. Remove the lower rear screw from the left rear garnish molding, then remove the molding by pulling at the clip locations.
12. If equipped, disengage the sunroof finish lace, then remove the lace from the headliner.

✳✳WARNING

Be very careful when handling the headliner. Should the liner become bent it will break and leave a wrinkle which cannot be repaired.

13. Disengage the velcro attachments at the rear of the headliner, fully recline the front seats and carefully remove the headliner through the right or right front door of the vehicle.
    To install:
14. Carefully install the headliner through the right door, then position the headliner to the dome lamp opening, sunvisor attachment points and, if equipped, to the sunroof opening. Engage the velcro attachments at the rear of the headliner.
15. Install the sunvisors.
16. For the Sedan, install the left rear garnish molding by pushing at the clip locations, then install the rear retaining

screw. Position the rear seat side bolster onto the outboard pivot pin, then secure the bolster by aligning and engaging the guide pin and upper fastener.

17. If equipped, install the sunroof lace.
18. Install the front upper garnish molding.
19. For the Coupe, install the rear upper garnish molding.
20. Install the coat hooks.
21. Install the assist strap and strap covers. If equipped, the black left handed thread screw should always be installed in the rearward attachment of the assist strap.
22. Install the instrument panel end cap and screws.
23. Install the upper trim panel by inserting into the clips at the windshield, then snapping the rear of the panel into place. Install the upper trim panel screws, then snap the screw covers into position.
24. Install the map lamp/switch console bezel and the dome lamp assembly.
25. Connect the negative battery cable.

Wagon

▶ See Figure 72

1. Disconnect the negative battery cable.
2. Disconnect the dome lamp assembly form the headliner, then unplug the wiring harness and remove the lamp assembly from the vehicle.
3. Remove the screws, then remove the sunvisor retainer/supports and the sunvisors from the headliner.
4. Remove the screw covers from the assist straps, then remove the screws and the straps from the headliner. Be careful. If the front assist strap has different color screws, the black screw will have LEFT HANDED threads.

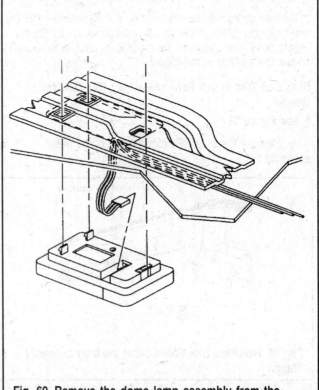

Fig. 69 Remove the dome lamp assembly from the headliner

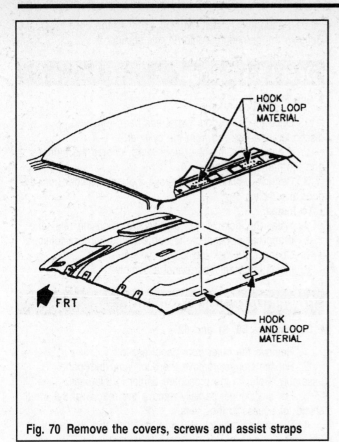

Fig. 70 Remove the covers, screws and assist straps

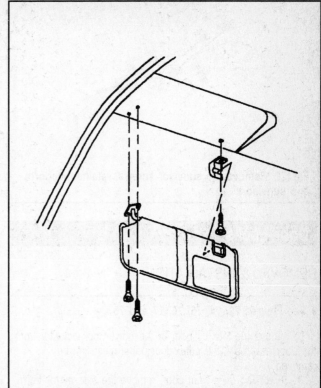

Fig. 71 The headliner is fastened to the rear of the roof using velcro hook and loop material

5. Remove the coat hooks.

6. Remove the 2 dashboard upper trim panel screw caps (located near the windshield at either end of the dash) by carefully prying with a small flathead tool. Remove the upper trim panel screws.

7. Lift the upper trim panel to disengage the clips at the rear edge, then pull the panel rearward and out of the clips at the base of the windshield. Remove the upper trim panel from the vehicle.

8. Remove the 2 screws and instrument panel end cap/HVAC outlet assembly from the left side of the dashboard.

9. Remove the left windshield garnish molding.

10. Pull the left rear seat bolster at the top to disengage the fastener, then remove the bolster from the vehicle.

11. Remove the left rear shock tower cover.

12. Remove the rear headliner trim panel.

13. Remove the left body rear corner trim panel assembly.

14. Remove the left latch pillar upper trim molding assembly.

❄❄WARNING

Be very careful when handling the headliner. Should the liner become bent it will break and leave a wrinkle which cannot be repaired.

15. Disengage the velcro attachments at the rear of the headliner and from the right garnish moldings, fully recline the front seats and carefully remove the headliner through the rear of the vehicle.

To install:

16. With the seats reclined, install the headliner through the rear of the vehicle. Install the right side of the liner into the garnish moldings, then attach the velcro attachments.

17. Install the left latch pillar upper trim molding assembly.

18. Install the left body corner trim panel assembly.

19. Install the rear header trim.

20. Install the left rear shock tower cover.

21. Install the left seat side bolster.

22. Install the left windshield garnish molding.

23. Install the instrument panel end cap and screws.

24. Install the upper trim panel by inserting into the clips at the windshield, then snapping the rear of the panel into place. Install the upper trim panel screws, then snap the screw covers into position.

25. Install the assist strap and strap covers. If equipped, the black left handed thread screw should always be installed in the rearward attachment of the assist strap.

26. Install the coat hooks. Install the sun visor retainer/supports and the sun visors.

27. Install the dome lamp assembly.

28. Connect the negative battery cable.

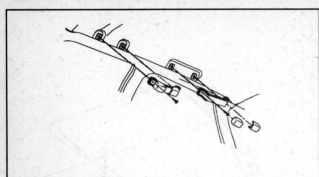

Fig. 72 Remove the sunvisor screws, retainer/supports and sunvisors

Door Locks

REMOVAL & INSTALLATION

▶ **See Figures 73, 74, 75, 76, 77 and 78**

To remove the lock cylinder or the power lock actuator from the door assembly, the outer door panel must first be removed:

1. If working on a front door, remove the side mirror from the door assembly. Refer to the procedure earlier in this section.

2. Disengage the outer seal strip by pulling upward at the rear. If necessary, use a putty knife which has its blade covered with tape to gently pry the sealing strip from the flange.

3. Push the center portion of the handle pushpins through the pins, then pull the pins from the handle. Slide the handle off the pivot assembly and remove the handle from the vehicle.

4. Remove the door panel screws. Remove the door panel by first pulling the front, then the rear outward and finally the entire panel.

5. Inspect the foam tape fillers at the front edge of the door panel and replace, if damaged.

To install:

6. If removed or replacing, install the foam tape panels at the front edge of the outer door panels as shown in Fig. 71. Replacement fillers may be cut to the proper lengths using a suitable foam of the same thickness.

7. If removed, install the foam seal strip to the perimeter of the door structure.

8. Install the outer door panel alignment pins into net hole and slot in the door structure outer reinforcement.

9. For the Sedan or Wagon, install the 10 screws or for the Coupe install the 11 screws, then tighten in the proper sequence to 53 inch lbs. (6 Nm).

10. Install the door handle by lifting the pivot assembly and sliding the handle on the pivot. Insert the pushpins to secure the handle assembly.

11. Install the outer sealing strip by aligning the location tab at the rear of the strip with the slot in the door panel. Fully seat the strip by pushing the strip down on the flange, working from the rear forward.

12. If applicable, install the side mirror to the door assembly. Refer to the procedure earlier in this section.

Door Lock Cylinder

▶ **See Figure 79**

1. Once the outer door panel has been removed, disconnect the lock rod from the cylinder.

2. If equipped with power door locks, unplug the harness and the harness retainer.

3. Remove retainer, then remove the lock cylinder from the door assembly.

To install:

4. Install the lock cylinder and secure using the retainer.

5. If applicable, connect the harness and harness retainer.

6. Connect the lock rod to the cylinder.

7. Install the outer door panel assembly.

Power Door Lock Actuator

▶ **See Figures 80, 81 and 82**

1. Remove the outer door panel assembly.

2. For the Coupe, remove the door inner trim panel assembly. Refer to the procedure earlier in this section.

3. For the Coupe, partially remove the rear ½ of the water shield for access to the rivets.

4. Disconnect the actuator from the lock rod, then unplug the wiring harness.

5. Drive the rivet center pin rearward sufficiently to drill out the head of the rivet. Drill out the rivet(s) and remove the actuator from the door assembly.

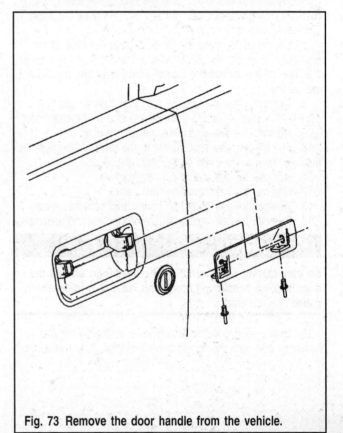

Fig. 73 Remove the door handle from the vehicle.

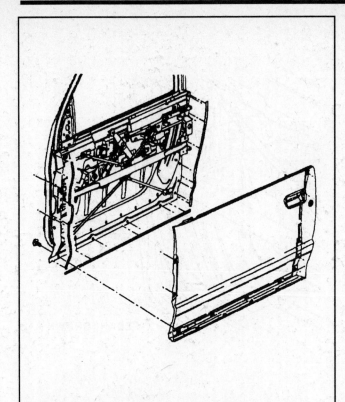

Fig. 74 Remove the retainers, then remove the outer panel from the door assembly

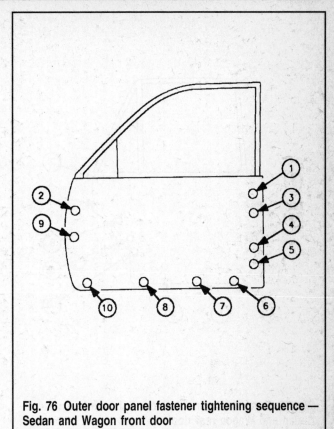

Fig. 76 Outer door panel fastener tightening sequence — Sedan and Wagon front door

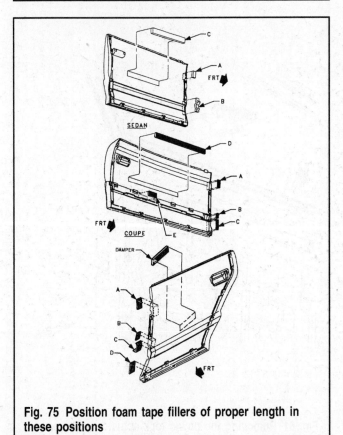

Fig. 75 Position foam tape fillers of proper length in these positions

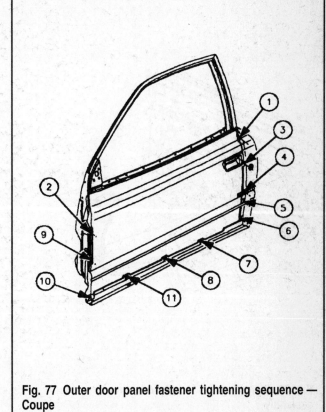

Fig. 77 Outer door panel fastener tightening sequence — Coupe

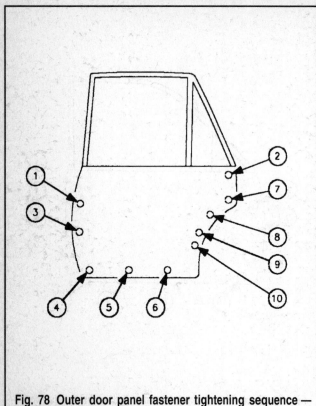

Fig. 78 Outer door panel fastener tightening sequence — Sedan and Wagon rear door

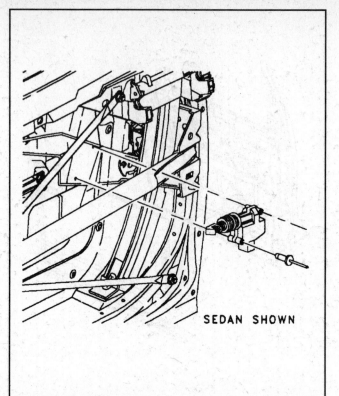

Fig. 80 Removing the power lock actuator — Sedan and Wagon, front door

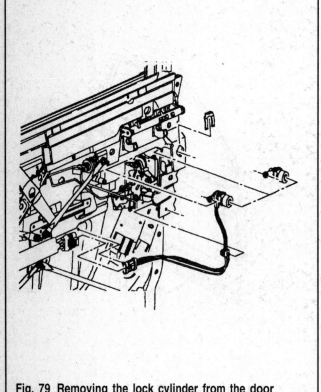

Fig. 79 Removing the lock cylinder from the door assembly

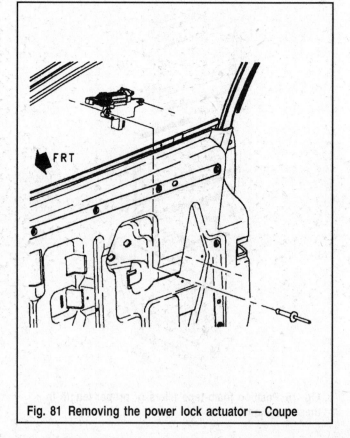

Fig. 81 Removing the power lock actuator — Coupe

6. For the Sedan and Wagon, cut the remaining portion of the rivets short, then push through the hole in the door assembly. Disconnect the inner door trim panel lower fasteners, pry out panel slightly and allow the rivets to fall.

To install:

7. For the Sedan and Wagon rear door, install the foam spacer. Failure to install a spacer will cause rattles.

8. Install the actuator using rivets, then connect the harness and actuator rod. For the Coupe, install the rear ½ of the water shield.

9. Reposition and fasten or install the door assembly trim panel, as applicable.

10. Install the outer door panel assembly.

Trunk Lock

REMOVAL & INSTALLATION

▶ **See Figures 83, 84 and 85**

1. For the Sedan, disconnect the negative battery cable, then remove the trunk lid center panel assembly or reflector.

2. For the Coupe, remove the reflex panels from either side of the trunk lid.

3. Disconnect the lock rod from the cylinder.

4. For the Sedan, remove the license plate, then remove the inner and outer retainers securing the lower outer panel. Pull the panel outward, disconnect the bulb sockets from the lamps and remove the panel from the vehicle.

5. For the Coupe, remove the screws, plastic retainers and the lower panel from the trunk lid.

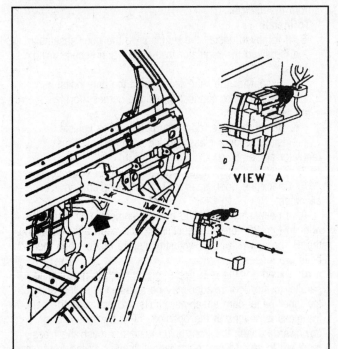

VIEW A

Fig. 82 A foam spacer must be installed on the rear door of the Sedan and Wagon when replacing the power lock actuator

6. Remove the sealing sleeve, lock cylinder retainer, reinforcement and the lock cylinder from the lower panel.

To install:

7. Install the lock cylinder to the panel, then install the reinforcement and the retainer to the cylinder. Install the sealing sleeve.

8. Position the panel to the vehicle. For the Sedan, connect the bulb sockets.

9. Install the lower panel and tighten the retainers. For the Coupe, be sure to follow the proper sequence shown in Fig. 81, then install the plastic retainers.

10. Connect the lock rod to the cylinder using the retaining clip.

11. For the Sedan, install the center panel or reflector using the retaining nuts, then connect the negative battery cable.

12. For the Coupe, install the reflex panels. Make sure the fastener sealing feature is intact. If necessary, apply a body caulking compound to seal against water intrusion.

Liftgate Lock

REMOVAL & INSTALLATION

▶ **See Figure 86**

1. Remove the liftgate lower inner trim panel assembly. Refer to the procedure earlier in this section.

2. Disconnect the cable end from the lock cylinder housing.

3. Remove the lock cylinder retaining clip from inside the liftgate panel, then remove the lock cylinder.

To install:

4. Position the lock cylinder into the into the liftgate outer panel, then install the retaining clip.

5. Connect the latch lock cable to the cylinder housing.

6. Install the liftgate lower inner trim panel.

Door Glass and Regulator

REMOVAL & INSTALLATION

▶ **See Figures 87, 88, 89 and 90**

1. Remove the outer door panel assembly. Refer to the sub-procedure under door locks, earlier in this section.

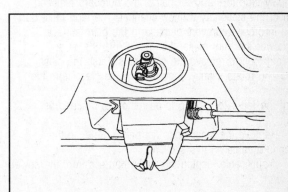

Fig. 83 Disconnect the lock rod from the lock cylinder

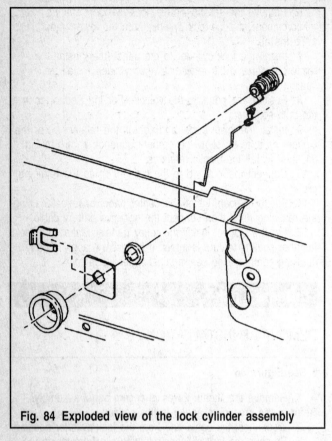

Fig. 84 Exploded view of the lock cylinder assembly

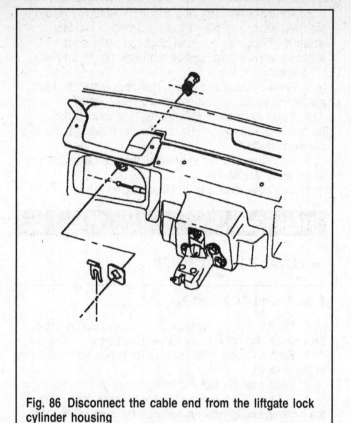

Fig. 86 Disconnect the cable end from the liftgate lock cylinder housing

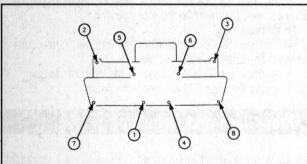

Fig. 85 Tighten the lower panel fasteners in the proper sequence — Coupe

2. For rear doors, loosen the bottom fastener of the rear door stationary window assembly in order to provide clearance, then apply tape to the lower half of the outboard exposed portion of the stationary window channel. The tape must be applied in order to prevent damage to the paint surface.

3. Lower the door glass, then use SA9148B, or an equivalent tool, to remove the glass nuts. Push the glass upward and rotate slightly, then remove the glass from the vehicle.

4. If the regulator is also to be removed, proceed as follows:

   a. Remove the inner door trim panel. Refer to the procedure earlier in this section.

   b. If applicable, unplug the wiring harness from the power regulator.

   c. Except for the rear door, remove the regulator cam bolts.

   d. Drill out the regulator rivets and remove the regulator from the vehicle.

To install:

5. If removed, install the regulator to the door assembly:

   a. Position the regulator to the door and secure using rivets.

   b. Except for the rear door, install the cam bolts.

   c. If applicable, connect the wiring harness to the regulator.

   d. Install the inner door trim panel to the vehicle.

6. Install the door glass into the door and over the regulator studs.

7. Install the glass nuts using SA9148B, or equivalent.

8. Check the door glass for proper operation and alignment.

9. If necessary adjust the glass alignment. For rear doors, refer to Fig. 86; fore/aft adjustments are made after loosening the 'B' bolts, while in/out adjustments are made when the 'A' bolts are loosened.

10. Except for the rear doors, glass which is not running parallel to the door header may be adjusted after loosening the inner panel cam attachment bolts and adjusting the cam. If the glass is floating in the opening, lower the glass ¾ downward, loosen the front guide fasteners, push the glass rearward to seat in the rear channel, then bring the front glass guide back to the front edge of the glass. Apply a light finger pressure on the guide and tighten the attaching fasteners.

11. Once the glass has been properly adjusted and is operating smoothly, install the outer door panel assembly.

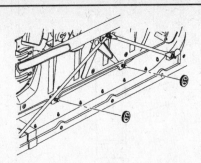

Fig. 87 Remove the glass nuts using a suitable tool —
front door shown

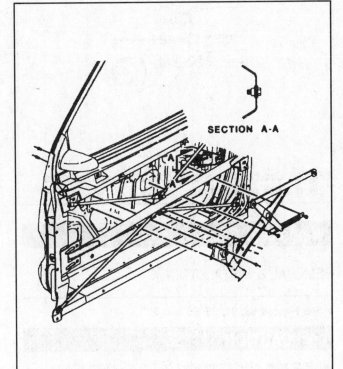

SECTION A-A

Fig. 88 Exploded view of the regulator mounting —
except rear door

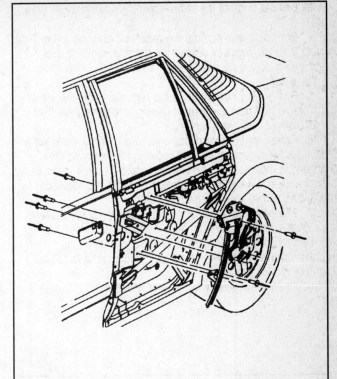

Fig. 89 Exploded view of the rear door regulator
mounting

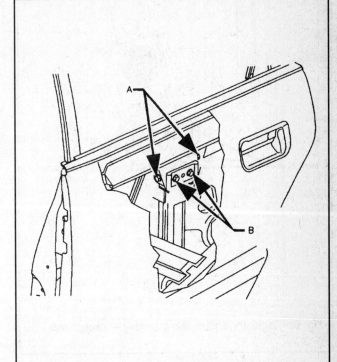

Fig. 90 Adjustments of rear door glass are made after
loosening the 'A'' or 'B'' bolts

Electric Window Motor

REMOVAL & INSTALLATION

▶ See Figures 91 and 92

1. Remove the regulator from the door assembly. Refer to
the procedure earlier in this section.

2. Except for the rear doors, drill a hole through the
regulator sector gear and backplate. Install the bolt and nut to
lock the sector gear in position. Be careful not to drill a hole
closer than 7/16 in. (11mm) from the edge of the sector. Also,
do not drill through the lift arm attaching portion of the sector
or joint integrity will be jeopardized.

3. Drill out ends of the motor attaching rivets using a ¼ in. bit.

4. Remove the motor and the remaining portions of the rivets from the regulator. Except for the rear doors, 1 rivet portion will not be accessible until assembly.

To install:

5. Position the new motor to the regulator. With the aid of a friend, install new rivets by collapsing or crushing the rivet ends using a ball peen hammer.

6. Except for the rear doors, once two of the 3 rivets have been installed, remove the bolt securing the sector to the backplate, then use an appropriate electrical source (such as the vehicle's window motor harness) to rotate the regulator, providing access to the remaining rivet.

7. Except for the rear doors, use a flat nosed rotary file to grind off 1 sector gear tooth from the side which does not contact the driven gear. This is necessary to reach the remaining rivet. Remove the old rivet portion, then install the remaining new rivet.

8. Install the regulator to the door assembly.

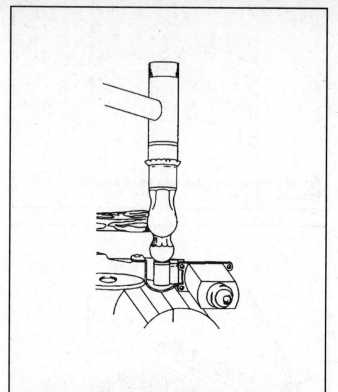

Fig. 92 Secure the rivets by collapsing the rivet ends using a ball peen hammer

Windshield Glass

REMOVAL & INSTALLATION

▶ See Figures 93, 94, 95, 96 and 97

✱✱CAUTION

Always wear safety glasses and heavy gloves when cutting glass from the vehicle. This will help prevent the possibility of glass splinters from entering the eyes or cutting hands.

1. Remove the windshield wiper arm assembly. Refer to Section 6 of this manual.

2. Remove the cowl vent grille and extensions.

3. Remove the rearview mirror.

4. Remove the instrument panel trim cover.

5. Remove the A-pillar garnish moldings.

6. Lower the front half of the headliner, then position lightweight wood or foam to block the headliner away from the roof. Be careful not to bend and break the headliner, if damaged it cannot be repaired, only replaced.

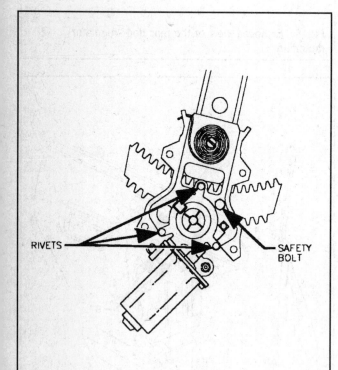

Fig. 91 Regulator and motor assembly — except rear doors

7. Remove the 2 screws from the encapsulated glass retaining tabs at the bottom of the windshield.

✳✳CAUTION

When using tools that might create smoke when cutting urethane sealant, work must be performed in a well ventilated area and/or with NIOSH/MSHA approved air supplied respirator to prevent dangerous exposure. When urethane adhesive is heated enough to give off smoke (by friction during power cutting) Methylene Diisocyanate (MDI) may be present, unprotected exposure to which can cause sever, chronic, debilitating respiratory problems.

8. Using suitable protection and a power glass removal tool, cut the urethane seal along the roof from inside the vehicle, then along the bottom and sides from outside the vehicle. Open the hood to gain access to the bottom.

9. Using a piano wire cutting tool, cut the bottom corners of the urethane seal.

10. With the help of a friend, carefully remove the windshield from the vehicle.

To install:

11. If installing a windshield on an early production Sedan, check to see if 3 spacer blocks are present at the bottom of the windshield areas. If found, remove and discard the spacers.

12. If the replacement windshield has 3 spacer blocks attached, remove and discard the blocks before installing the windshield to the vehicle

13. Using a razor knife, carefully remove the loose urethane and trim any high spots in the remaining material to provide for an even application of the new material.

14. If old glass is to be installed, such as a windshield from the local bone yard, all loose urethane must be removed from the glass.

15. Before installing the new urethane, pre-fit the windshield by centering the glass to the roof and, with upward pressure, seat the glass against the roof. Make sure lip of encapsulated molding laps over roof feature line.

16. With the glass properly positioned, place 2 pieces of masking tape over the edge of the glass, about 16 in. (400mm) on each side of the center line. Slit the tape at the edge of the glass molding. During installation the tape on the glass may be aligned with the tape on the body to guide the glass into the proper position.

17. With the glass pre-fit and the tape markings in place, remove the glass from the vehicle.

18. Clean the window opening and glass bonding surfaces using a clean, lint free, alcohol dampened cloth. Allow the cleaned surfaces to air dry.

19. Cover any exposed metal using a pinch weld primer.

20. If installing an old windshield to a Sedan or Wagon, use double sided foam tape, 3M® 51131-06382 or equivalent. Cut the tape to 3 in. (75mm) pieces and apply as shown, in order to retain encapsulated ears of the windshield in the roof.

21. If installing an old windshield, install $1/4$ in. x $5/32$ in. adhesive back foam tape, or equivalent to the areas specified in the illustration.

22. Apply the primer from a suitable urethane adhesive kit. If using the Saturn kit No. 12345633, 2 primers are provided, of which the clear primer is used on the glass prior to the black primer. Apply the primer around the entire perimeter of the glass in the locations shown, then allow the primer to dry according to the manufacturers instructions.

23. Apply a smooth continuous bead of adhesive around the edge of the glass. The bead dimensions should be A: 0.71 in. (18mm), B: 0.32 in. (8mm) and C: 0.51 in. (13mm).

24. With the help of a friend, use suction cups to lift the glass and position into the window opening. Align the tape on the glass with the tape on the body.

25. Press the glass firmly to wet-out and set adhesive. Use care to avoid excessive squeeze out which would cause an appearance problem. Using duct tape or equivalent, tape the glass to the roof.

26. Install the encapsulated glass retaining screws.

27. Pressure from closing the doors may cause the windshield to move, in order to prevent this open the windows and/or recline the seats and open the trunk/liftgate before slowly closing the doors.

28. Watertest the vehicle using a soft spray. Warm or hot water, if available is preferable, but DO NOT spray hot water on an extremely cold windshield. Also, water applied to the adhesive should accelerate the cure process, but be sure not to spray a strong stream of water directly at the fresh adhesive.

29. Inspect for leaks inside the vehicle. If necessary, paddle in additional adhesive at leak points using a tongue depressor or similar flat flexible tool.

30. Install the A-pillar garnish molding, then install the instrument panel trim cover.

31. Install the rearview mirror.

32. Install the cowl vent grille and extensions.

33. Install the wiper arm assemblies.

34. Allow the vehicle to stand for several hours allowing the adhesive to completely dry.

Stationary Glass

REMOVAL & INSTALLATION

Rear Window (Sedan and Coupe)
▶ **See Figures 98, 99, 100, 101, 102 and 103**

1. Position protective covers on the body to prevent paint damage.

2. Remove the C-pillar garnish.

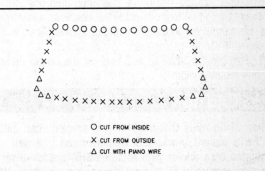

Fig. 93 Cut the urethane seal from the windshield from these locations as noted

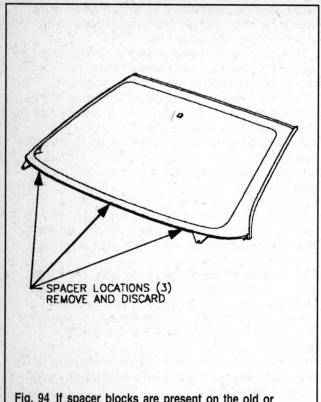

Fig. 94 If spacer blocks are present on the old or replacement windshield, remove and discard the blocks

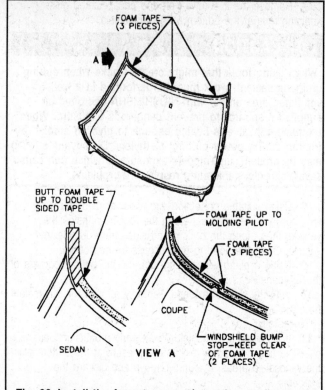

Fig. 96 Install the foam tape as pictured according to the application

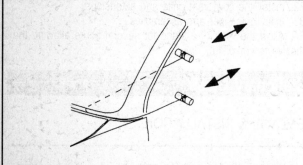

Fig. 95 A piano wire cutting tool is necessary to cut certain portions of the seal

3. Unplug the electrical connector from the buss bars.

4. Remove the package shelf from the vehicle.

5. Lower the rear half of the headliner, then position lightweight wood or foam to block the headliner away from the roof. Be careful not to bend and break the headliner, if damaged it cannot be repaired, only replaced.

6. Remove the trunk lid seal and, for the Sedan, remove the drip molding clips.

✳✳CAUTION

When using tools that might create smoke when cutting urethane sealant, work must be performed in a well ventilated area and/or with NIOSH/MSHA approved air supplied respirator to prevent dangerous exposure. When urethane adhesive is heated enough to give off smoke (by

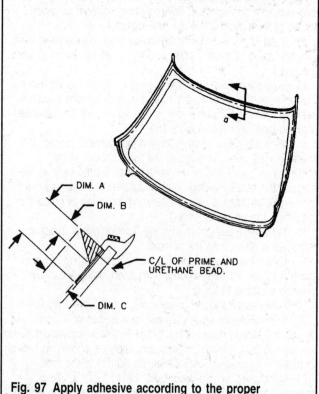

Fig. 97 Apply adhesive according to the proper dimensions

friction during power cutting) Methylene Diisocyanate (MDI) may be present, unprotected exposure to which can cause sever, chronic, debilitating respiratory problems.

7. Using suitable protection and a power glass removal tool, cut the urethane seal along the roof from inside the vehicle, then along the bottom from outside the vehicle.

8. Using a piano wire cutting tool, cut the urethane seal from the sides of the window.

9. With the help of a friend, carefully remove the back glass from the vehicle.

To install:

10. Using a razor knife, carefully remove the loose urethane and trim any high spots in the remaining material to provide for an even application of the new material.

11. If old glass is to be installed, such as a window from the local bone yard, all loose urethane must be removed from the glass.

12. For the Coupe, the encapsulated molding on the quarter glass will need to be tied back with duct tape or equivalent, to provide sufficient clearance to properly load the back glass.

13. Tape the trunk lid in a half opened position in order to provide clearance to install the back glass.

14. Before installing the new urethane, pre-fit the window by centering the glass to the roof and, with upward pressure, seat the glass against the roof. Make sure lip of encapsulated molding laps over roof feature line.

15. With the glass properly positioned, place 2 pieces of masking tape over the edge of the glass, about 16 in. (400mm) on each side of the center line. Slit the tape at the edge of the glass molding. During installation the tape on the glass may be aligned with the tape on the body to guide the glass into the proper position.

16. With the glass pre-fit and the tape markings in place, remove the glass from the vehicle.

17. Clean the window opening and glass bonding surfaces using a clean, lint free, alcohol dampened cloth. Allow the cleaned surfaces to air dry.

18. Cover any exposed metal using a pinch weld primer.

19. If installing an old window in a Coupe, install a 2mm thick spacer 16 in. (400mm) each side of center to area left open in view A of the illustration. Then install $1/4$ in. x $5/32$ in. adhesive back foam tape, or equivalent to the front side of the applied molding to area between spacers and from the spacers to the end of the molding.

20. If installing and old window in a Sedan, apply $1/4$ in. x $5/32$ in. adhesive back foam tape, or equivalent to the areas specified in the appropriate illustration.

21. Apply the primer from a suitable urethane adhesive kit. If using the Saturn kit No. 12345633, 2 primers are provided, of which the clear primer is used on the glass prior to the black primer. Apply the primer around the entire perimeter of the glass in the locations shown, then allow the primer to dry according to the manufacturers instructions. The primer bead dimensions should be A: 0.71 in. (18mm), B: 0.51 in. (13mm) and C: 0.32 in. (8mm) for the Sedan or A: 0.71 in. (18mm) for the Coupe.

22. Apply a smooth continuous bead of adhesive around the edge of the glass. The bead dimensions should be A: 0.71 in. (18mm), B: 0.51 in. (13mm) and C: 0.32 in. (8mm) for the Sedan or B: 0.51 in. (13mm) and C: 0.32 in. (8mm) for the Coupe.

23. With the help of a friend, use suction cups to lift the glass and position into the window opening. Align the tape on the glass with the tape on the body.

24. Press the glass firmly to wet-out and set adhesive. Use care to avoid excessive squeeze out which would cause an appearance problem.

25. Using duct tape or equivalent, tape the glass to the roof.

26. Pressure from closing the doors may cause the window to move, in order to prevent this open the windows and/or recline the seats and open the trunk before slowly closing the doors.

27. Watertest the vehicle using a soft spray. Warm or hot water, if available is preferable, but DO NOT spray hot water on an extremely cold windshield. Also, water applied to the adhesive should accelerate the cure process, but be sure not to spray a strong stream of water directly at the fresh adhesive.

28. Inspect for leaks inside the vehicle. If necessary, paddle in additional adhesive at leak points using a tongue depressor or similar flat flexible tool.

29. For the Sedan, install the drip molding clips.

30. Install the trunk lid seal.

31. Install the headliner, then install the package shelf and associated trim.

32. Install the wiring harness to the electrical connectors.

33. Install the C-pillar garnish.

34. For the Coupe, remove the tape from the quarter glass molding, then apply 2-sided tape to the area show in the illustration.

35. Allow the vehicle to stand for several hours allowing the adhesive to completely dry.

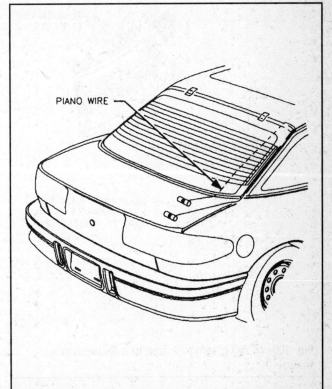

PIANO WIRE

Fig. 98 Cut the urethane seal from the sides of the back window using piano wire

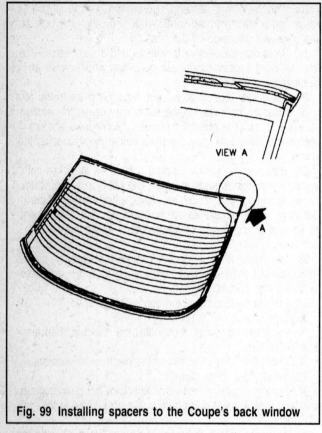

Fig. 99 Installing spacers to the Coupe's back window

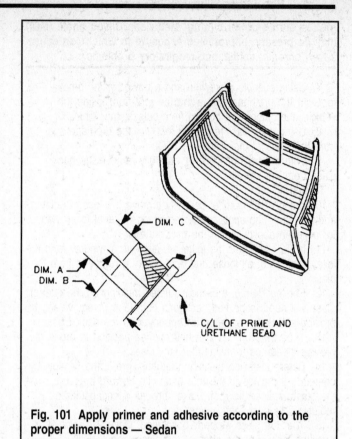

Fig. 101 Apply primer and adhesive according to the proper dimensions — Sedan

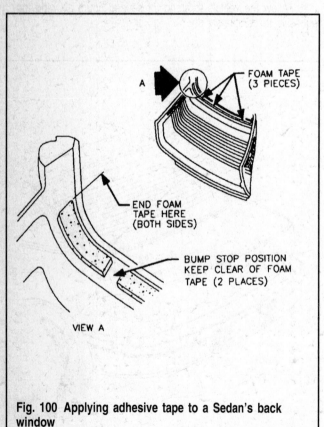

Fig. 100 Applying adhesive tape to a Sedan's back window

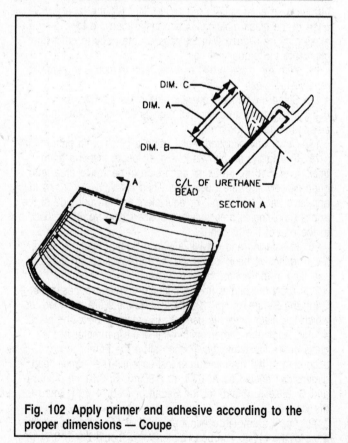

Fig. 102 Apply primer and adhesive according to the proper dimensions — Coupe

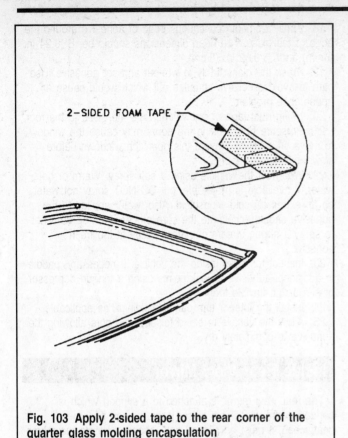

2-SIDED FOAM TAPE

Fig. 103 Apply 2-sided tape to the rear corner of the quarter glass molding encapsulation

Liftgate Back Glass (Wagon)

1. Remove the interior trim from the liftgate. Refer to the procedures earlier in this manual.

2. Remove the wiper module. Refer to the procedure in Section 6 of this manual.

3. Unplug the deicer connections from the left and right sides of the glass.

4. Apply 2 6 in. pieces of duct tape to the top and bottom of the glass to prevent it from falling out when the urethane is cut.

✳✳CAUTION

When using tools that might create smoke when cutting urethane sealant, work must be performed in a well ventilated area and/or with NIOSH/MSHA approved air supplied respirator to prevent dangerous exposure. When urethane adhesive is heated enough to give off smoke (by friction during power cutting) Methylene Diisocyanate (MDI) may be present, unprotected exposure to which can cause sever, chronic, debilitating respiratory problems.

5. Using suitable protection and a power glass removal tool, cut the urethane seal along the sides from outside the vehicle, then cut the urethane from bottom, followed by the top of the glass from inside the vehicle.

6. Using a piano wire cutting tool, carefully cut the urethane seal from the corners of the window.

7. Remove the glass from the liftgate.

To install:

8. Using a razor knife, carefully remove the loose urethane and trim any high spots in the remaining material to provide for an even application of the new material.

9. If old glass is to be installed, such as a window from the local bone yard, all loose urethane must be removed from the glass.

10. Before installing the new urethane, pre-fit the window by aligning the notch at the bottom of the opening with the tab on the backside of the window encapsulation. Verify a proper fit of encapsulation to liftgate along the top and bottom of the glass.

11. With the glass properly positioned, place 2 pieces of masking tape over the edge of the glass, about 16 in. (400mm) on each side of the center line. Slit the tape at the edge of the glass molding. During installation the tape on the glass may be aligned with the tape on the body to guide the glass into the proper position.

12. With the glass pre-fit and the tape markings in place, remove the glass from the vehicle.

13. Clean the window opening and glass bonding surfaces using a clean, lint free, alcohol dampened cloth. Allow the cleaned surfaces to air dry.

14. Cover any exposed metal using a pinch weld primer.

15. Apply the primer from a suitable urethane adhesive kit. If using the Saturn kit No. 12345633, 2 primers are provided, of which the clear primer is used on the glass prior to the black primer. Apply the primer around the entire perimeter of the glass in the locations shown, then allow the primer to dry according to the manufacturers instructions. The primer bead dimensions should be A: 0.71 in. (18mm).

16. Apply a smooth continuous bead of adhesive around the edge of the glass. The bead dimensions should be, B: 0.51 in. (13mm) and C: 0.32 in. (8mm).

17. Press the glass firmly to wet-out and set adhesive. Use care to avoid excessive squeeze out which would cause an appearance problem.

18. Using duct tape or equivalent, tape the glass to the roof.

19. Pressure from closing the doors may cause the window to move, in order to prevent this open the windows before slowly closing the doors.

20. Watertest the vehicle using a soft spray. Warm or hot water, if available is preferable, but DO NOT spray hot water on an extremely cold windshield. Also, water applied to the adhesive should accelerate the cure process, but be sure not to spray a strong stream of water directly at the fresh adhesive.

21. Inspect for leaks inside the vehicle. If necessary, paddle in additional adhesive at leak points using a tongue depressor or similar flat flexible tool.

22. Install the wiper module and interior trim.

23. Connect the wiring harness to the deicer.

24. Allow the vehicle to stand for several hours allowing the adhesive to completely dry.

Quarter Glass

◆ **See Figures 104 and 105**

1. Position protective covers on the body in order to prevent paint damage.

2. Remove the C-pillar garnish.

3. Remove the rear half of A and B-pillar garnish, or any other interfering trim panels.

4. Remove the roof drip molding.

5. Using a heavy gauge tape, secure the quarter panel and roof along the quarter glass in order to protect the paint from damage.

6. Position 2 tongue depressors or small, flat pieces of wood/plastic, under the B-pillar encapsulation, in order to protect the capsulation from the piano wire.

7. Feed the piano wire around the perimeter of the quarter glass, making sure not to damage the quarter panel finish.

8. Tape the quarter glass to the body in order to retain the glass as the seal is cut.

✳✳CAUTION

When using tools that might create smoke when cutting urethane sealant, work must be performed in a well ventilated area and/or with NIOSH/MSHA approved air supplied respirator to prevent dangerous exposure. When urethane adhesive is heated enough to give off smoke (by friction during power cutting) Methylene Diisocyanate (MDI) may be present, unprotected exposure to which can cause sever, chronic, debilitating respiratory problems.

9. Use a sawing motion to careful cut the urethane seal and quarter glass from the body. Work slowly and carefully to prevent vehicle damage and to keep the urethane from heating and smoking. Remove the quarter glass and tape from the vehicle.

To install:

10. Install the roof drip molding. Using a razor knife, carefully remove the loose urethane and trim any high spots in the remaining material to provide for an even application of the new material.

11. If old glass is to be installed, such as a window from the local bone yard, all loose urethane must be removed from the glass.

12. Before installing the new urethane, pre-fit the window by aligning to the roof drip molding, the quarter panel, back glass molding and B-pillar, as applicable.

13. With the glass properly positioned, place 2 pieces of masking tape from the glass over the top and over the back of the glass. Slit the tape at the edge of the glass molding. During installation the tape on the glass may be aligned with the tape on the body to guide the glass into the proper position.

14. With the glass pre-fit and the tape markings in place, remove the glass from the vehicle.

15. Clean the window opening and glass bonding surfaces using a clean, lint free, alcohol dampened cloth. Allow the cleaned surfaces to air dry.

16. Cover any exposed metal using a pinch weld primer.

17. Apply the primer from a suitable urethane adhesive kit. If using the Saturn kit No. 12345633, 2 primers are provided, of which the clear primer is used on the glass prior to the black primer. Apply the primer around the entire perimeter of the glass in the locations shown, then allow the primer to dry according to the manufacturers instructions. The primer bead dimensions should be A: 0.71 in. (18mm). Apply a 2-sided piece of tape to the rear corner of the encapsulation in order to retain the encapsulation to the quarter glass and lower molding.

18. Apply a smooth continuous bead of adhesive around the edge of the glass. The bead dimensions should be, B: 0.24 in. (6mm) and C: 0.32 in. (8mm).

19. Press the glass firmly to wet-out and set adhesive. Use care to avoid excessive squeeze out which would cause an appearance problem.

20. Using duct tape or equivalent, tape the glass to the roof.

21. Pressure from closing the doors may cause the window to move, in order to prevent this open the windows before slowly closing the doors.

22. Watertest the vehicle using a soft spray. Warm or hot water, if available is preferable, but DO NOT spray hot water on an extremely cold windshield. Also, water applied to the adhesive should accelerate the cure process, but be sure not to spray a strong stream of water directly at the fresh adhesive.

23. Inspect for leaks inside the vehicle. If necessary, paddle in additional adhesive at leak points using a tongue depressor or similar flat flexible tool.

24. Install the interior trim panels/moldings, as applicable.

25. Allow the vehicle to stand for several hours allowing the adhesive to completely dry.

Inside Rear View Mirror

The rear view mirror is attached to a support which is bonded to the windshield glass. If the support becomes unattached, it must be aligned and rebonded before the mirror may be mounted.

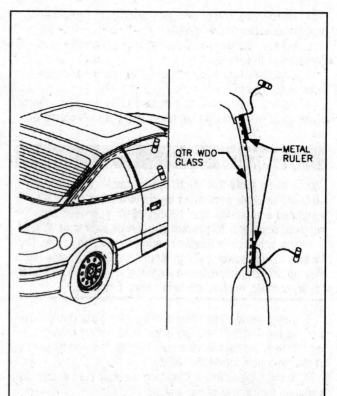

Fig. 104 Carefully cut the urethane seal from the quarter glass using piano wire — Coupe shown

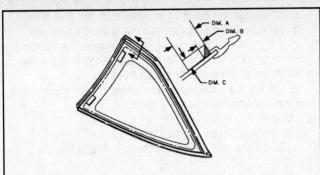

Fig. 105 Apply primer and adhesive according to the proper dimensions — Coupe shown

INSTALLATION

▶ See Figure 106

1. Measure Dimension A, from the bottom of the encapsulated molding roof line to the bottom (flat side) or the mirror support. Dimension A (Fig. 104) is 6.4 in. (162mm) for Sedan and Wagon or 7.9 in. (200mm) for the Coupe.
2. Mark the outside of the windshield glass using a wax pencil or crayon, then make a large diameter circle around the support location mark.
3. Clean the inside glass surface within the large marked circle using a glass cleaning solution or polishing compound. Rub the area until it is completely clean and dry.
4. Once dry, clean the area using an alcohol saturated paper towel to remove any traces of scouring powder or cleaning solution.

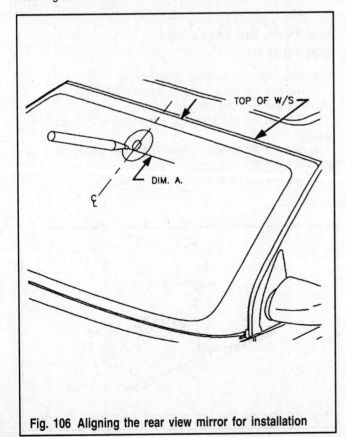

Fig. 106 Aligning the rear view mirror for installation

5. If still attached, use a Torx® bit to separate the mirror from the support, then use a piece of fine grit sandpaper to rough the bonding surface of the mirror support. If the original support is being used, all traces of adhesive must be removed prior to installation.
6. Wipe the sanded mirror support with a clean alcohol saturated paper towel, then allow to dry.
7. Follow the directions on a manufacturer's kit (Loctite® Rearview Mirror adhesive or equivalent) and prepare the support for installation.
8. When ready, position the support to the marked location, making sure the rounded end is pointed upward. Press the support to the glass for 30-60 seconds using steady pressure. After about 5 minutes, any excess adhesive may be removed with an alcohol moistened paper towel or glass cleaning solution.
9. Allow additional time to cure, if necessary, per the adhesive manufacturer's instructions, then install the rear view mirror to the support.

Seats

REMOVAL & INSTALLATION

Front Seats
▶ See Figure 107

1. If removing the driver's seat, disconnect the negative battery cable, then remove the CPA device and unplug the seat buckle wire connector.
2. Push the lap belt through the seat guide loop.
3. Remove the 4 seat adjuster-to-vehicle attaching bolts, then carefully remove the seat assembly from the vehicle. Place the seat on a clean, protected surface.
To install:
4. Position the seat in the vehicle while aligning it to the guide pin on the front inboard attachment point.
5. If installing the driver's seat, connect the wiring harness to the buckle connector, then install the CPA device.
6. Check that the seat adjusters are timed properly by making sure all adjuster mounting tabs are tight against their mounting surfaces and all bolt holes are aligned.
7. Apply a coat of Loctite® 242, or an equivalent threadlock, to the 4 seat adjuster bolts, then install the bolts and tighten to 26 ft. lbs. (35 Nm).
8. Install the lap belt through the seat guide loop.
9. If applicable, connect the negative battery cable.

Rear Seats
▶ See Figures 108, 109 and 110

1. To remove the cushion from the Coupe, remove the inserts and fasteners, then remove the rear seat center console. Disengage the seat cushion front floor clips and guide the cushion out of the rear attachment.
2. To remove the cushion from the Sedan and Wagon, push on the retainer tabs located at the bottom of the seat cushion assembly, then lift the front of the cushion from under the seat backs, guide the seat belt buckles through the cushion and remove the cushion assembly from the vehicle.

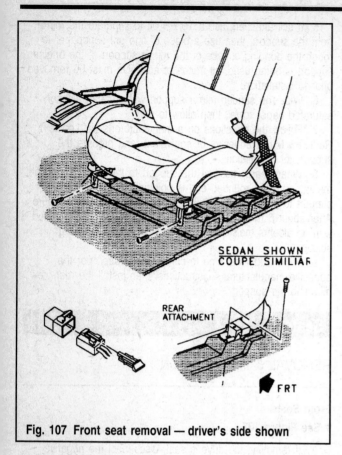

Fig. 107 Front seat removal — driver's side shown

3. To remove the seat backs:
   a. Release the latch and tilt the seat forward.

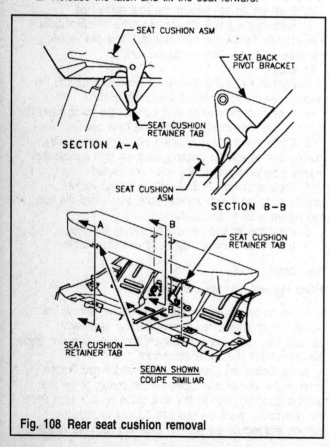

Fig. 108 Rear seat cushion removal

b. disengage the cargo floor carpet from the seat back.
c. Remove the plastic clip from the outboard pivot pin.
d. Slide the seat back toward the outside of the vehicle in order to position the pivot pin relief slot at the floor bracket, then lift the pivot pin out of the floor bracket.
e. Lift the seat back out of the outboard floor bracket and remove the seat back from the vehicle.

To install:
4. If removed, install the seat backs:
   a. Guide the seat back assembly onto the center pivot pin.
   b. Align the outer pivot pin relief with outer bracket, then guide the pin into the bracket.
   c. Slide the seat back inboard to engage the pivot pin into the bracket.
   d. Install the outboard pivot pin clip.
   e. Engage the cargo floor carpet with the seat backs.
5. Install the cushion in the Sedan or Wagon by positioning the cushion (rear edge first). Secure the wire frame correctly at the center buckle and pull the center lap belt through the seat cushion. Guide the seat cushion front floor clips into their floor pan holes, then push firmly on the front of the seat to engage the clips.
6. Install the cushion in the Coupe, by positioning the cushion with the rear edge first, then securing the wire frame at the center buckle. Install the rear center console, fasteners and inserts.

Seat Belt System

REMOVAL & INSTALLATION

Front Passive Seat Belt Retractor
▶ See Figure 111

1. Disconnect the negative battery cable.
2. Remove the center console assembly. Refer to the procedure earlier in this section.
3. Remove the top center fastener holding the 2 retractors together.
4. Remove the retractor anchor bolts, then unplug the wiring harness from the driver's side.
5. Remove the retractors from the vehicle.

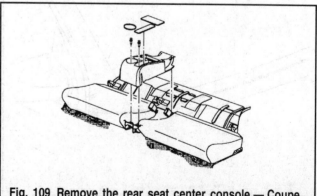

Fig. 109 Remove the rear seat center console — Coupe

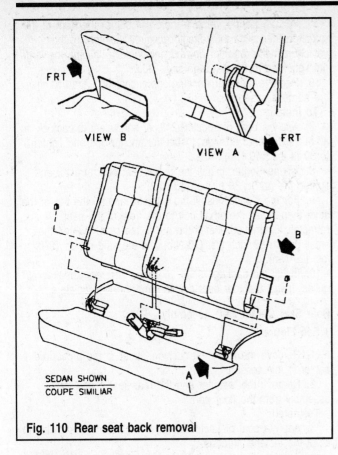

Fig. 110 Rear seat back removal

To install:

6. Position the retractors and connect the wiring harness to the driver's side.

7. Apply a coat of Loctite®242 or equivalent threadlock, to all of the fastener threads.

8. Align the tab on the retractor frame with the hole in the bracket, then install the retractor bolt and tighten to 35 ft. lbs. (47 Nm).

9. Install a new center fastener.

10. Install the center console assembly and connect the negative battery cable.

Front Seat Lap Belt Retractor

▶ See Figure 112

1. Partially remove the front body hinge pillar garnish/sill molding, then partially remove the rear garnish/sill molding.

2. Partially remove the lower end of the upper center pillar garnish molding.

3. Pull the seat belt through the seat trim guide loop and center pillar guide slot, then partially remove the windshield garnish at center pillar lower molding.

4. Remove the center pillar lower molding fasteners, then slide the lap belt through the lower molding and remove the molding from the vehicle.

5. Adjust the front seat to the full forward position for access, then remove the fasteners and the lap belt retractor from the rocker panel.

To install:

6. Install the lap belt retractor to the rocker panel. If the mounting plate was removed from the retractor, make sure it was not installed upside down.

7. Apply a coat of Loctite®242, or equivalent threadlock, to all of the fastener threads, then install the retractor fasteners and tighten to 44 ft. lbs. (60 Nm).

8. Slide the lap belt through the center pillar lower molding and secure the molding to the vehicle. Install the belt to the seat guide loop.

9. Secure the lower end of the center pillar garnish molding, then the rear body lock pillar garnish/sill molding.

10. Secure the front body hinge pillar garnish/sill molding.

Front Seat Lap Belt Buckle

▶ See Figure 113

1. Remove the front seat from the vehicle. Refer to the procedure earlier in this section.

2. Remove the screws and the inboard seat adjuster cover.

3. On the driver's side, unplug the wire lead.

4. Remove the fastener and the seat belt buckle.

To install:

5. Apply a coat of Loctite®242, or equivalent threadlock, to all of the fastener threads.

6. Install the buckle and tighten the fastener to 59 ft. lbs. (80 Nm).

7. Install the inboard seat adjuster cover.

8. Install the front seat to the vehicle.

Front Seat Shoulder Belt Track Assembly

1. Disconnect the negative battery cable.

2. Remove the instrument panel end cap/HVAC outlet assemblies, then remove the instrument panel top cover.

3. Remove the molding/garnish from the door sill. Refer to the trim panel procedures earlier in this section.

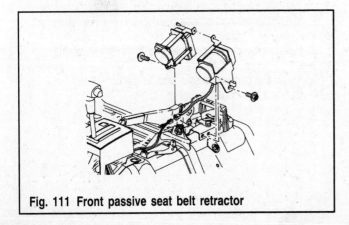

Fig. 111 Front passive seat belt retractor

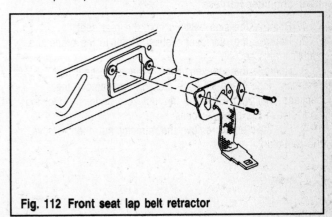

Fig. 112 Front seat lap belt retractor

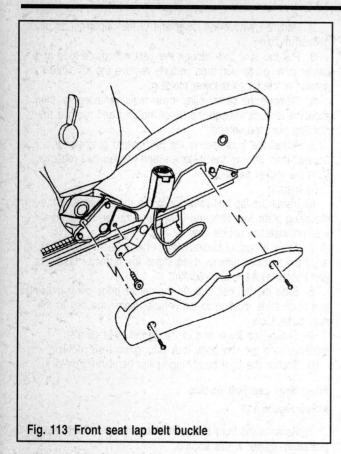

Fig. 113 Front seat lap belt buckle

4. Unplug the wiring harness from the shoulder belt track assembly.

5. Remove the retainers and the track assembly from the vehicle.

To install:

6. Apply a coat of Loctite®242, or equivalent threadlock, to all of the fastener threads, then install the track assembly and tighten the fasteners. Tighten the 2 bottom guide tube clip bolts to 27 inch lbs. (3 Nm) and all other track bolts to 53 inch lbs. (6 Nm). Tighten the upper anchor Torx® head bolt to 30 ft. lbs. (40 Nm).

7. Install the wiring harness to the track assembly.

8. Secure the trim panels.

9. Install the instrument panel top cover and install the end cap assemblies

10. Connect the negative battery cable.

Rear Shoulder Harness

1. Remove the side bolsters from the rear seat.

2. Remove the rear seat cushion. Refer to the procedure earlier in this section.

3. Remove the speaker grilles, release the seat belt restraints, loosen the sill plate molding and remove the package shelf trim. Slide the trim out from under the molding and release the shoulder belts.

4. For the Sedan, remove the retractor nut, then remove the retractor.

5. For the Coupe, remove the small bolt at the front of the retractor, then slide the retractor towards the front of the vehicle. Lift the retractor upward and remove, leaving the large nut tightened to the package shelf stud.

6. Remove the shoulder harness anchor bolt, then remove the harness assembly.

To install:

7. Apply a coat of Loctite®242, or equivalent threadlock, to all of the fastener threads. Install the anchor bolt and tighten to 30 ft. lbs. (40 Nm).

8. for the Sedan, install the upper seat belt retractor and tighten the nut to 30 ft. lbs. (40 Nm).

9. For the Coupe, install the retractor around the top of the stud, then install the small bolt to the front of the seat retractor. If removed, install the nut to the stud. Tighten the small bolt to 89 inch lbs. (10 Nm) and the stud nut to 19 ft. lbs. (25 Nm).

10. Install the package shelf, moldings and rear speaker grilles. Install the rear seat cushion and the side bolsters.

Rear Seat Center Belt Assembly

▶ **See Figure ?**

1. Remove the rear seat cushion. Refer to the procedure earlier in this section.

2. Remove the fastener and the rear seat center belt assembly from the floor pan.

To install:

3. Apply a coat of Loctite®242, or equivalent threadlock, to all of the fastener threads.

4. Position the assembly, then install the fastener and tighten to 30 ft. lbs. (40 Nm).

5. Install the rear seat cushion.

Passive Restrain Control Module (PRCM)

1. Disconnect the negative battery cable.

2. Remove the access panel above the PRCM at the rear of the center console. Remove the 4 screws securing the center console.

3. Raise the parking brake to the fully engaged position.

4. Raise the rear of the console sufficiently to access the PRCM.

5. Gently depress the plastic tab on the rear of the PRCM while lifting upward. Remove the CPA device and remove the PRCM.

To install:

6. Install the PRCM under the console, then snap the rear of the bracket into the metal locking tabs.

7. Install the wiring harness connectors and the CPA device.

8. Position the center console and install the retaining screws.

9. Install the center console access panel.

10. Connect the negative battery cable.

TORQUE SPECIFICATIONS

Component	U.S.	Metric
Door assembly;		
Check link-to-door bolt	12 ft. lbs.	35 Nm
Hinge-to-door bolts	26 ft. lbs.	35 Nm
Outer door panel	53 inch lbs.	6 Nm
Pull cup screws	23 inch lbs.	2.2 Nm
Striker retainers	18 ft. lbs.	25 Nm
Fender fasteners	89 inch lbs.	10 Nm
Hood assembly;		
Hood/hinge retaining bolts	19 ft. lbs.	25 Nm
Latch bolts	89 inch lbs.	10 Nm
Liftgate hinge bolts	89 inch lbs.	10 Nm
Package shelf retainers	19 ft. lbs.	25 Nm
Seat adjuster bolts (1)	26 ft. lbs.	35 Nm
Front seat belt (1);		
Buckle fastener	59 ft. lbs.	80 Nm
Lap belt retractor fasteners	44 ft. lbs.	60 Nm
Passive retractor bolt	35 ft. lbs.	47 Nm
Rear seat belt (1);		
Center seat belt assembly	30 ft. lbs.	40 Nm
Coupe harness small bolt	89 inch lbs.	10 Nm
Coupe harness stud nut	19 ft. lbs.	25 Nm
Sedan retractor nut	30 ft. lbs.	40 Nm
Shoulder harness anchor bolt	30 ft. lbs.	40 Nm
Seat belt track assembly (1);		
Guide tube clip bolts	27 inch lbs.	3 Nm
Track bolts	53 inch lbs.	6 Nm
Upper anchor Torx® head bolt	30 ft. lbs.	40 Nm
Side mirror assembly;		
Retaining nuts	53 inch lbs.	6 Nm
Cable set screw	27 inch lbs.	3 Nm
Steering column assembly bolts;	33 ft. lbs.	45 Nm
Sunroof;		
Glass screws	35–44 inch lbs.	4–5 Nm
Guide screws	35–44 inch lbs.	4–5 Nm
Motor screws	27–35 inch lbs.	3–4 Nm
Trunk lid;		
Lid retainer bolts	89 inch lbs.	10 Nm
Panel screws	53 inch lbs.	6 Nm
Striker bolts	89 inch lbs.	10 Nm

(1)- Coat threads with a suitable threadlocking compound

GLOSSARY

AIR/FUEL RATIO: The ratio of air to gasoline by weight in the fuel mixture drawn into the engine.

AIR INJECTION: One method of reducing harmful exhaust emissions by injecting air into each of the exhaust ports of an engine. The fresh air entering the hot exhaust manifold causes any remaining fuel to be burned before it can exit the tailpipe.

ALTERNATOR: A device used for converting mechanical energy into electrical energy.

AMMETER: An instrument, calibrated in amperes, used to measure the flow of an electrical current in a circuit. Ammeters are always connected in series with the circuit being tested.

AMPERE: The rate of flow of electrical current present when one volt of electrical pressure is applied against one ohm of electrical resistance.

ANALOG COMPUTER: Any microprocessor that uses similar (analogous) electrical signals to make its calculations.

ARMATURE: A laminated, soft iron core wrapped by a wire that converts electrical energy to mechanical energy as in a motor or relay. When rotated in a magnetic field, it changes mechanical energy into electrical energy as in a generator.

ATMOSPHERIC PRESSURE: The pressure on the Earth's surface caused by the weight of the air in the atmosphere. At sea level, this pressure is 14.7 psi at 32{248}F (101 kPa at 0{248}C).

ATOMIZATION: The breaking down of a liquid into a fine mist that can be suspended in air.

AXIAL PLAY: Movement parallel to a shaft or bearing bore.

BACKFIRE: The sudden combustion of gases in the intake or exhaust system that results in a loud explosion.

BACKLASH: The clearance or play between two parts, such as meshed gears.

BACKPRESSURE: Restrictions in the exhaust system that slow the exit of exhaust gases from the combustion chamber.

BAKELITE: A heat resistant, plastic insulator material commonly used in printed circuit boards and transistorized components.

BALL BEARING: A bearing made up of hardened inner and outer races between which hardened steel balls roll.

BALLAST RESISTOR: A resistor in the primary ignition circuit that lowers voltage after the engine is started to reduce wear on ignition components.

BEARING: A friction reducing, supportive device usually located between a stationary part and a moving part.

BIMETAL TEMPERATURE SENSOR: Any sensor or switch made of two dissimilar types of metal that bend when heated or cooled due to the different expansion rates of the alloys. These types of sensors usually function as an on/off switch.

BLOWBY: Combustion gases, composed of water vapor and unburned fuel, that leak past the piston rings into the crankcase during normal engine operation. These gases are removed by the PCV system to prevent the buildup of harmful acids in the crankcase.

BRAKE PAD: A brake shoe and lining assembly used with disc brakes.

BRAKE SHOE: The backing for the brake lining. The term is, however, usually applied to the assembly of the brake backing and lining.

BUSHING: A liner, usually removable, for a bearing; an anti-friction liner used in place of a bearing.

CALIPER: A hydraulically activated device in a disc brake system, which is mounted straddling the brake rotor (disc). The caliper contains at least one piston and two brake pads. Hydraulic pressure on the piston(s) forces the pads against the rotor.

CAMSHAFT: A shaft in the engine on which are the lobes (cams) which operate the valves. The camshaft is driven by the crankshaft, via a belt, chain or gears, at one half the crankshaft speed.

CAPACITOR: A device which stores an electrical charge.

CARBON MONOXIDE (CO): A colorless, odorless gas given off as a normal byproduct of combustion. It is poisonous and extremely dangerous in confined areas, building up slowly to toxic levels without warning if adequate ventilation is not available.

CARBURETOR: A device, usually mounted on the intake manifold of an engine, which mixes the air and fuel in the proper proportion to allow even combustion.

CATALYTIC CONVERTER: A device installed in the exhaust system, like a muffler, that converts harmful byproducts of combustion into carbon dioxide and water vapor by means of a heat-producing chemical reaction.

CENTRIFUGAL ADVANCE: A mechanical method of advancing the spark timing by using flyweights in the distributor that react to centrifugal force generated by the distributor shaft rotation.

CHECK VALVE: Any one-way valve installed to permit the flow of air, fuel or vacuum in one direction only.

CHOKE: A device, usually a moveable valve, placed in the intake path of a carburetor to restrict the flow of air.

CIRCUIT: Any unbroken path through which an electrical current can flow. Also used to describe fuel flow in some instances.

CIRCUIT BREAKER: A switch which protects an electrical circuit from overload by opening the circuit when the current flow exceeds a predetermined level. Some circuit breakers must be reset manually, while most reset automatically

COIL (IGNITION): A transformer in the ignition circuit which steps up the voltage provided to the spark plugs.

COMBINATION MANIFOLD: An assembly which includes both the intake and exhaust manifolds in one casting.

COMBINATION VALVE: A device used in some fuel systems that routes fuel vapors to a charcoal storage canister instead of venting them into the atmosphere. The valve relieves fuel tank pressure and allows fresh air into the tank as the fuel level drops to prevent a vapor lock situation.

COMPRESSION RATIO: The comparison of the total volume of the cylinder and combustion chamber with the piston at BDC and the piston at TDC.

CONDENSER: 1. An electrical device which acts to store an electrical charge, preventing voltage surges.
2. A radiator-like device in the air conditioning system in which refrigerant gas condenses into a liquid, giving off heat.

CONDUCTOR: Any material through which an electrical current can be transmitted easily.

CONTINUITY: Continuous or complete circuit. Can be checked with an ohmmeter.

COUNTERSHAFT: An intermediate shaft which is rotated by a mainshaft and transmits, in turn, that rotation to a working part.

CRANKCASE: The lower part of an engine in which the crankshaft and related parts operate.

CRANKSHAFT: The main driving shaft of an engine which receives reciprocating motion from the pistons and converts it to rotary motion.

CYLINDER: In an engine, the round hole in the engine block in which the piston(s) ride.

CYLINDER BLOCK: The main structural member of an engine in which is found the cylinders, crankshaft and other principal parts.

CYLINDER HEAD: The detachable portion of the engine, fastened, usually, to the top of the cylinder block, containing all or most of the combustion chambers. On overhead valve engines, it contains the valves and their operating parts. On overhead cam engines, it contains the camshaft as well.

DEAD CENTER: The extreme top or bottom of the piston stroke.

DETONATION: An unwanted explosion of the air/fuel mixture in the combustion chamber caused by excess heat and compression, advanced timing, or an overly lean mixture. Also referred to as "ping".

DIAPHRAGM: A thin, flexible wall separating two cavities, such as in a vacuum advance unit.

DIESELING: A condition in which hot spots in the combustion chamber cause the engine to run on after the key is turned off.

DIFFERENTIAL: A geared assembly which allows the transmission of motion between drive axles, giving one axle the ability to turn faster than the other.

DIODE: An electrical device that will allow current to flow in one direction only.

DISC BRAKE: A hydraulic braking assembly consisting of a brake disc, or rotor, mounted on an axle, and a caliper assembly containing, usually two brake pads which are activated by hydraulic pressure. The pads are forced against the sides of the disc, creating friction which slows the vehicle.

DISTRIBUTOR: A mechanically driven device on an engine which is responsible for electrically firing the spark plug at a predetermined point of the piston stroke.

DOWEL PIN: A pin, inserted in mating holes in two different parts allowing those parts to maintain a fixed relationship.

DRUM BRAKE: A braking system which consists of two brake shoes and one or two wheel cylinders, mounted on a fixed backing plate, and a brake drum, mounted on an axle, which revolves around the assembly.

DWELL: The rate, measured in degrees of shaft rotation, at which an electrical circuit cycles on and off.

ELECTRONIC CONTROL UNIT (ECU): Ignition module, module, amplifier or igniter. See Module for definition.

ELECTRONIC IGNITION: A system in which the timing and firing of the spark plugs is controlled by an electronic control unit, usually called a module. These systems have no points or condenser.

ENDPLAY: The measured amount of axial movement in a shaft.

ENGINE: A device that converts heat into mechanical energy.

EXHAUST MANIFOLD: A set of cast passages or pipes which conduct exhaust gases from the engine.

FEELER GAUGE: A blade, usually metal, of precisely predetermined thickness, used to measure the clearance between two parts.

FIRING ORDER: The order in which combustion occurs in the cylinders of an engine. Also the order in which spark is distributed to the plugs by the distributor.

FLOODING: The presence of too much fuel in the intake manifold and combustion chamber which prevents the air/fuel mixture from firing, thereby causing a no-start situation.

FLYWHEEL: A disc shaped part bolted to the rear end of the crankshaft. Around the outer perimeter is affixed the ring gear. The starter drive engages the ring gear, turning the flywheel, which rotates the crankshaft, imparting the initial starting motion to the engine.

FOOT POUND (ft.lb. or sometimes, ft. lbs.): The amount of energy or work needed to raise an item weighing one pound, a distance of one foot.

FUSE: A protective device in a circuit which prevents circuit overload by breaking the circuit when a specific amperage is present. The device is constructed around a strip or wire of a lower amperage rating than the circuit it is designed to protect. When an amperage higher than that stamped on the fuse is present in the circuit, the strip or wire melts, opening the circuit.

GEAR RATIO: The ratio between the number of teeth on meshing gears.

GENERATOR: A device which converts mechanical energy into electrical energy.

HEAT RANGE: The measure of a spark plug's ability to dissipate heat from its firing end. The higher the heat range, the hotter the plug fires.

HUB: The center part of a wheel or gear.

HYDROCARBON (HC): Any chemical compound made up of hydrogen and carbon. A major pollutant formed by the engine as a byproduct of combustion.

HYDROMETER: An instrument used to measure the specific gravity of a solution.

INCH POUND (in.lb. or sometimes, in. lbs.): One twelfth of a foot pound.

INDUCTION: A means of transferring electrical energy in the form of a magnetic field. Principle used in the ignition coil to increase voltage.

INJECTOR: A device which receives metered fuel under relatively low pressure and is activated to inject the fuel into the engine under relatively high pressure at a predetermined time.

INPUT SHAFT: The shaft to which torque is applied, usually carrying the driving gear or gears.

INTAKE MANIFOLD: A casting of passages or pipes used to conduct air or a fuel/air mixture to the cylinders.

JOURNAL: The bearing surface within which a shaft operates.

KEY: A small block usually fitted in a notch between a shaft and a hub to prevent slippage of the two parts.

MANIFOLD: A casting of passages or set of pipes which connect the cylinders to an inlet or outlet source.

MANIFOLD VACUUM: Low pressure in an engine intake manifold formed just below the throttle plates. Manifold vacuum is highest at idle and drops under acceleration.

MASTER CYLINDER: The primary fluid pressurizing device in a hydraulic system. In automotive use, it is found in brake and hydraulic clutch systems and is pedal activated, either directly or, in a power brake system, through the power booster.

MODULE: Electronic control unit, amplifier or igniter of solid state or integrated design which controls the current flow in the ignition primary circuit based on input from the pick-up coil. When the module opens the primary circuit, the high secondary voltage is induced in the coil.

NEEDLE BEARING: A bearing which consists of a number (usually a large number) of long, thin rollers.

OHM:(Ω) The unit used to measure the resistance of conductor to electrical flow. One ohm is the amount of resistance that limits current flow to one ampere in a circuit with one volt of pressure.

OHMMETER: An instrument used for measuring the resistance, in ohms, in an electrical circuit.

OUTPUT SHAFT: The shaft which transmits torque from a device, such as a transmission.

OVERDRIVE: A gear assembly which produces more shaft revolutions than that transmitted to it.

OVERHEAD CAMSHAFT (OHC): An engine configuration in which the camshaft is mounted on top of the cylinder head and operates the valve either directly or by means of rocker arms.

OVERHEAD VALVE (OHV): An engine configuration in which all of the valves are located in the cylinder head and the camshaft is located in the cylinder block. The camshaft operates the valves via lifters and pushrods.

OXIDES OF NITROGEN (NOx): Chemical compounds of nitrogen produced as a byproduct of combustion. They combine with hydrocarbons to produce smog.

OXYGEN SENSOR: Used with the feedback system to sense the presence of oxygen in the exhaust gas and signal the computer which can reference the voltage signal to an air/fuel ratio.

PINION: The smaller of two meshing gears.

PISTON RING: An open ended ring which fits into a groove on the outer diameter of the piston. Its chief function is to form a seal between the piston and cylinder wall. Most automotive pistons have three rings: two for compression sealing; one for oil sealing.

PRELOAD: A predetermined load placed on a bearing during assembly or by adjustment.

PRIMARY CIRCUIT: Is the low voltage side of the ignition system which consists of the ignition switch, ballast resistor or resistance wire, bypass, coil, electronic control unit and pick-up coil as well as the connecting wires and harnesses.

PRESS FIT: The mating of two parts under pressure, due to the inner diameter of one being smaller than the outer diameter of the other, or vice versa; an interference fit.

RACE: The surface on the inner or outer ring of a bearing on which the balls, needles or rollers move.

REGULATOR: A device which maintains the amperage and/or voltage levels of a circuit at predetermined values.

RELAY: A switch which automatically opens and/or closes a circuit.

RESISTANCE: The opposition to the flow of current through a circuit or electrical device, and is measured in ohms. Resistance is equal to the voltage divided by the amperage.

RESISTOR: A device, usually made of wire, which offers a preset amount of resistance in an electrical circuit.

RING GEAR: The name given to a ring-shaped gear attached to a differential case, or affixed to a flywheel or as part a planetary gear set.

ROLLER BEARING: A bearing made up of hardened inner and outer races between which hardened steel rollers move.

ROTOR: 1. The disc-shaped part of a disc brake assembly, upon which the brake pads bear; also called, brake disc.
2. The device mounted atop the distributor shaft, which passes current to the distributor cap tower contacts.

SECONDARY CIRCUIT: The high voltage side of the ignition system, usually above 20,000 volts. The secondary includes the ignition coil, coil wire, distributor cap and rotor, spark plug wires and spark plugs.

SENDING UNIT: A mechanical, electrical, hydraulic or electromagnetic device which transmits information to a gauge.

SENSOR: Any device designed to measure engine operating conditions or ambient pressures and temperatures. Usually electronic in nature and designed to send a voltage signal to an on-board computer, some sensors may operate as a simple on/off switch or they may provide a variable voltage signal (like a potentiometer) as conditions or measured parameters change.

SHIM: Spacers of precise, predetermined thickness used between parts to establish a proper working relationship.

SLAVE CYLINDER: In automotive use, a device in the hydraulic clutch system which is activated by hydraulic force, disengaging the clutch.

SOLENOID: A coil used to produce a magnetic field, the effect of which is produce work.

SPARK PLUG: A device screwed into the combustion chamber of a spark ignition engine. The basic construction is a conductive core inside of a ceramic insulator, mounted in an outer conductive base. An electrical charge from the spark plug wire travels along the conductive core and jumps a preset air gap to a grounding point or points at the end of the conductive base. The resultant spark ignites the fuel/air mixture in the combustion chamber.

SPLINES: Ridges machined or cast onto the outer diameter of a shaft or inner diameter of a bore to enable parts to mate without rotation.

TACHOMETER: A device used to measure the rotary speed of an engine, shaft, gear, etc., usually in rotations per minute.

THERMOSTAT: A valve, located in the cooling system of an engine, which is closed when cold and opens gradually in response to engine heating, controlling the temperature of the coolant and rate of coolant flow.

TOP DEAD CENTER (TDC): The point at which the piston reaches the top of its travel on the compression stroke.

TORQUE: The twisting force applied to an object.

TORQUE CONVERTER: A turbine used to transmit power from a driving member to a driven member via hydraulic action, providing changes in drive ratio and torque. In automotive use, it links the driveplate at the rear of the engine to the automatic transmission.

TRANSDUCER: A device used to change a force into an electrical signal.

TRANSISTOR: A semi-conductor component which can be actuated by a small voltage to perform an electrical switching function.

TUNE-UP: A regular maintenance function, usually associated with the replacement and adjustment of parts and components in the electrical and fuel systems of a vehicle for the purpose of attaining optimum performance.

TURBOCHARGER: An exhaust driven pump which compresses intake air and forces it into the combustion chambers at higher than atmospheric pressures. The increased air pressure allows more fuel to be burned and results in increased horsepower being produced.

VACUUM ADVANCE: A device which advances the ignition timing in response to increased engine vacuum.

VACUUM GAUGE: An instrument used to measure the presence of vacuum in a chamber.

VALVE: A device which control the pressure, direction of flow or rate of flow of a liquid or gas.

VALVE CLEARANCE: The measured gap between the end of the valve stem and the rocker arm, cam lobe or follower that activates the valve.

VISCOSITY: The rating of a liquid's internal resistance to flow.

VOLTMETER: An instrument used for measuring electrical force in units called volts. Voltmeters are always connected parallel with the circuit being tested.

WHEEL CYLINDER: Found in the automotive drum brake assembly, it is a device, actuated by hydraulic pressure, which, through internal pistons, pushes the brake shoes outward against the drums.

MASTER

INDEX